written and researched by

Dilwyn Jenkins

ROUGH
GUIDES

NEW YORK • LONDON • DELHI

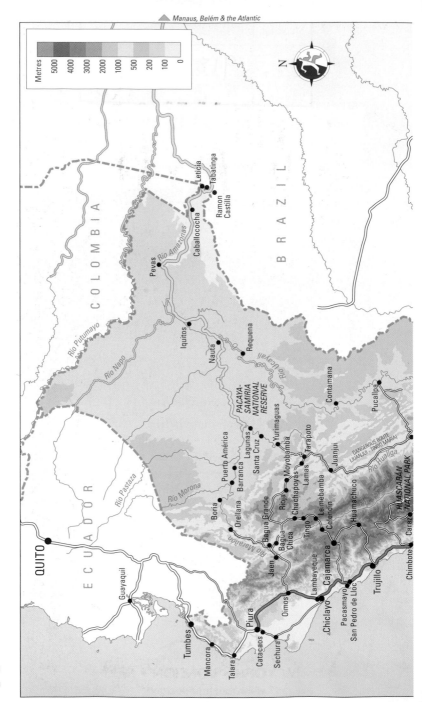

Manaus, Belém & the Atlantic

Metres 5000 4000 3000 2000 1000 500 200 100 0

N

COLOMBIA

BRAZIL

Leticia
Tabatinga
Ramon Castilla
Caballococha
Rio Amazonas
Pevas
Rio Putumayo
Rio Napo
Iquitos
Nauta
Requena
PACAYA-SAMIRIA NATIONAL RESERVE
Rio Ucayali
Contamana
Pucallpa
Lagunas
Yurimaguas
Santa Cruz
Puerto América
Barranca
Moyobamba
Tarapoto
DANGEROUS ROUTE LUANJUI - TINGO MARIA)
Juanjui
Rio Huallaga
Rioja
Chachapoyas
Lamas
Boria
Orellana
Leimebamba
Bagua Grande
Tingo
Celendin
Huamachuco
HUASCARÁN NATIONAL PARK
Rio Morona
Rio Pastaza
ECUADOR
QUITO
Rio Marañón
Bagua Chica
Jaen
Cajamarca
Caraz
Chimbote
Guayaquil
Lambayeque
San Pedro de Lloc
Pacasmayo
Trujillo
Chiclayo
Olmos
Piura
Catacaos
Sechura
Tumbes
Mancora
Talara

ii

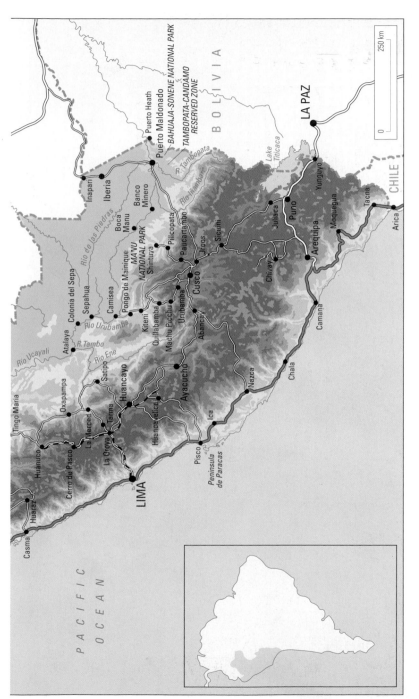

iii

Introduction to

Peru

A fantastic land of gold, Peru was sixteenth-century
Europe's major source of treasure, and also once the home
of the largest empire in the world – the sun-worshipping
Incas. Since then, the riches of the Incas have fired the
European imagination: the country was home to the
world's first stone pyramids, whose genuine antiquity was
only discovered quite recently. Meanwhile the desert coast
is studded with monumental adobe temples and ruins from
several pre-Inca civilizations. These archeological sites
generate more than enough awe and wonder to attract
visitors and pilgrims from all over the globe; however, the
country's real appeal lies in the sheer beauty of its
landscapes, the abundance of its wildlife, and the strong
character of the people – which has withstood a recent,
lengthy period of bloody political upheaval.

The most varied and exciting of all the South
American nations, Peru is often visualized as a
mountainous place, many visitors remaining
unaware of the splendour of the country's
immense **desert coastline** and its vast tracts
of **tropical rainforest**. Dividing these contrasting environments is a range of breath-
taking peaks, **the Andes**, over six thousand metres high and four hundred
kilometres wide in places, rippling the entire length of the nation. So distinct
are these three regions that it is very difficult to generalize about the country, but one thing for sure is that Peru offers a unique opportunity to experience an unusually wide range of spectacular scenery, as well as a wealth of

Fact file

• Ancient Peru developed several very important civilizations, both coastal (Paracas, Nazca, Mochica, Sican and Chimu) and Andean (Tiahuanaco, Chachapoyas, and, of course, the Incas). The Incas were easily and savagely defeated by the Spanish conquistadores in 1533. Peruvian independence was declared in 1821, with the remaining Spanish forces eventually defeated by the end of 1824.

• The population of Peru today is almost 28 million. There are two official languages – Spanish and Quechua – but there are scores of other indigenous languages spoken, including Aymaru in the Southern Andes and many jungle Indian tribal languages.

• The eleventh-highest country in the world, Peru's mountains reach 6768m above sea level in the Cordillera Blanca range. The Andes here are the highest mountain range anywhere in the tropics.

• With 2414km of coastline, and well over half a million square kilometres of Amazon rainforest, Peru is also one of the most ecologically diverse countries in the world. Over 66 percent of Peru has forest or woodland cover, only 3 percent is arable land and around 21 percent permanent pasture. The coast is an unusually dry desert; east of the Andes the Amazon rainforest stretches thousands of miles beyond Peru, all the way to the Atlantic.

human culture. There's a rich diversity of music, dance and fiesta activity from every one of its distinctive regions, and Peruvian cuisine is some of the best in the Americas, partly because of the oceanic and tropical resources from which it draws.

The Incas and their native allies were unable to resist the mounted, fire-armed conquistadores, and following the Spanish Conquest in the sixteenth century the colony developed by exploiting its Inca treasures, vast mineral deposits and the essentially slave labour which the colonists extracted from the indigenous people. After achieving independence from the Spanish in the early nineteenth century, Peru became a republic in traditional South American style, and although

it is still very much dominated by the Spanish and *mestizo* descendants of Pizarro, about half the population are of pure Indian blood. In many rural parts of the country, native life has changed little in the last four centuries. However, "progress" is gradually transforming much of Peru – already most cities wear a distinctly Western aspect, and roads and tracks now connect almost every corner of the republic with the industrial *urbanizaciones* that dominate the few fertile valleys along the coast. Only the Amazon jungle – nearly two-thirds of Peru's landmass but home to a mere fraction of its population – remains beyond the reach of Peru's coastal markets, and even here oil and lumber companies, cocaine producers and settlers often think of themselves as being closer to Brazil and Colombia.

> **The prevailing attitude is that there's always enough time for a chat, a ceviche, or another drink**

Nevertheless, mundane, unaffected pleasures remain in place. The country's prevailing attitude – despite the sometimes hectic pace that permeates the capital, Lima – is that there is always enough time for a chat, a ceviche, or another drink. It's a place where the resourceful and open-minded traveller can break through barriers of class, race, and language far more easily than most of its inhabitants can; and also one in which the limousines and villas of the elite remain little more than a thin veneer on a nation whose roots lie firmly in its ethnic traditions and the earth itself.

Peruvian food

In addition to creating great regional distinctions, Peruvian ecological diversity has helped to produce a proud national **cuisine**, and it would be a shame to spend much time at the many fast-food and westernized places that have popped up across the country rather than in local restaurants. The national dish – **ceviche** – is made from fresh seafood marinated in lime juice and chillies, then served with sweet potato, a cob or corn plus salad. Washed down on Sunday lunchtime with a cool Cusqueña beer, this is an experience not to be missed. Meanwhile, exotic local specialties like *cuy*, or (roast guinea pig), are also worth a try, even if the thought may at first be off-putting. Street snacks are quite tasty and also good value – things like grilled meats and empanadas are available most anywhere, alongside excellent tropical produce.

Where to go

With each region offering so many different attractions, it's hard to generalize about the places you should visit first: the specific attractions of each part of Peru are discussed in greater detail in the chapter highlights and introductions. Apart from the hot and largely unattractive capital, **Lima**, where you are most likely to arrive, **Cusco** is perhaps the most obvious place to start. It's a beautiful and bustling colonial city, the ancient heart of the Inca Empire, surrounded by some of the most spectacular mountain landscapes and palatial ruins in Peru, and by magnificent hiking country. A particularly tough but rewarding journey is the trek along the long and winding **Inca Trail**, which culminates at the high, fog-shrouded Inca citadel of **Machu Picchu**.

Yet along the coast, too, there are fascinating archeological sites – the bizarre **Nazca Lines** south of Lima, the great adobe city of **Chan Chan** in the north – and a rich crop of sea life, most accessible around the **Paracas National Park**. Almost all of the coastal towns come replete with superb beaches, plentiful nightlife and great food. If all that sounds too exhausting, one can always duck away to spend a day lazily sipping wine at the many **Ica Valley bodegas**.

For mountains and long-distance treks there are the stunning glacial lakes, snowy peaks and little-known ruins of the sierra north of Lima, above all around **Huaraz** and **Cajamarca**. If it's wildlife you're interested in, there's plenty to see almost everywhere. But **the jungle** provides startling opportunities for close and exotic encounters. From the comfort of tourist lodges in **Iquitos** to exciting river excursions around **Puerto Maldonado**, the fauna and flora of the world's largest tropical forest can be experienced first-hand perhaps

A particularly tough but rewarding journey is the trek along the long and winding Inca Trail more easily than in any other Amazon-rim country. Not too far from Iquitos there's the **Pacaya Samiria National Reserve**, a remote and stunningly beautiful region which is one of the least-visited parts of the Peruvian rainforest; in the South there's the newly created **Tambopata–Candamo Reserved Zone** which incorporates around 600,000 hectares of the upper Tambopata plus Candamo river and tributaries, containing some of the most exciting jungle and richest flora and fauna in the world.

> The jungle provides startling opportunities for close and exotic encounters

M ROSA CARDENAS

Spiritual tourism

Spending a mosquito-ridden night with other travellers in the lively bars of downtown Iquitos, it's hard to believe that just a few miles away hundreds of tourists are communicating with plant spirits in a hallucinogen- and chant-induced trance. Increasingly, though, this jungle-locked city, reachable only by air or boat, has become a focus for travellers looking for sessions with **traditional local shaman**, who have recently begun to offer their sacred services to groups of tourists – for a fee. Many tourist lodges have their own associate shaman as an added allure to the typical eco-tourist itinerary. In the sessions, shaman and participants imbibe ayahuasca, a bitter-tasting potion that brings on a strong hallucinatory state considered by many to be very therapeutic, physically and emotionally, though the experience is not to be entered into lightly. For more on shamans, see p.555; for details of lodges in Iquitos, see p.479.

When to go

P icking the **best time to visit** Peru's various regions is complicated by the country's physical characteristics. Summer along the **desert coast** more or less fits the expected image of the southern hemisphere – extremely hot and sunny between December and March (especially in the north), cooler and with a frequent hazy mist between April and November – although only in the polluted environs of **Lima** does the coastal winter ever get cold enough to necessitate a sweater. Swimming is possible all year round, though the water itself (thanks to the Humboldt Current) is cool-to-cold at the best of times. To swim or surf for any length of time you'd need to follow local custom and wear a wet suit. Apart from the occasional shower over Lima it hardly ever rains in the desert. The freak exception, every ten years or so, is when the shift in ocean currents of El Niño causes torrential downpours, devastating crops, roads and communities all down the coast. It last broke in 1983.

In **the Andes**, the seasons are more clearly marked, with heavy rains from December to March and a warm, relatively dry period from June to September. Inevitably, though, there are always some sunny weeks in the rainy season and wet ones in the dry. A similar pattern dominates **the jungle**, though rainfall here is heavier and more frequent, and it's hot and humid all year round. Ideally, then, the coast should be visited around January while it's hot, and the mountains and jungle are at their best after the rains, from May until September. Since this is unlikely to be possible on a single trip there's little point in worrying about it – the country's attractions are invariably enough to override the need for guarantees of good weather.

Transportation issues

Generally speaking, public transport has improved significantly over the last decade in Peru. Big modern buses cruise up and down the **Panamerican Highway**, linking all the coastal cities. They also strike up into the main mountain centres, including Cusco and Titicaca, and are cheap and pretty reliable. For some of the Andean journeys, such as from Arequipa to Titicaca and Cusco, the local **train service**, offering spectacular views from their high-altitude routes, can be a more enjoyable way to travel. Air travel around the country is relatively well developed and cheap as a result of distances in Peru being so vast, especially in jungle areas. In the jungle, **riverboats** can offer the most civilized and pleasant form of travel. For more on getting around, see Basics, p.29.

Average daily maximum and minimum temperatures, and annual rainfall

	Oct – April	May – Sept	Temp. range (approx) °C/°F	Annual rainfall mm/In
Coast				
	Sunny season	Some coastal cloud	13–30/ 55–86	0.55/ .02
Andes				
	Rainy season	Dry season	0–18/ 32–64	400–1000/ 16–39
Jungle				
	Rainy season	Dry season	20–35/ 68–95	2000–3900/ 79–154

30

things not to miss

It's not possible to see everything that Peru has to offer in one trip — and we don't suggest you try. What follows is a selective and subjective taste of the country's highlights: colourful neighbourhoods, awe-inspiring ruins, spectacular hikes and interesting wildlife. They're arranged in five colour-coded categories, so you can browse through to find the very best things to see, do, buy and experience. All highlights have a page reference to take you straight into the Guide, where you can find out more.

01 **Lake Llanganuco** Page **318** • The deep blue colour of this lake in the Cordillera Blanca changes with the weather.

03 **Traditional healing** Page 25 • Alternative medicine, using herbs sold in markets and practiced by shamans and other healers, has a long and respected history in Peru.

02 **Andean wildlife** Page **573** • The mild-mannered llamas and alpacas are perhaps the most attractive and approachable creatures that roam the Peruvian Andes.

04 **Huacachina** Page **213** • This sacred healing lagoon, ringed by palm trees and atmospheric hotels, lies hidden among massive sand dunes.

05 **Machu Picchu** Page **169** • Its mysterious temples and palaces nestling among hundreds of terraces, this fabulous Inca citadel never fails to impress.

06 Temple of Fertility
Page 285 • Thought to be an Inca construction, this curious site on the edge of Lake Titicaca contains hundreds of stone phalli.

07 Arequipa
Page 241 • This white stone city, beautiful and intriguing on its own, is watched over by the awesome, ice-capped volcano of El Misti.

08 The Archbishops' Palace
Page 77 • Restored in 1924, the palace is typical of colonial Lima, particularly the elaborate woodwork of the upper storey.

09 Máncora
Page 447 • Peru's most popular surfer hangout features gorgeous beaches and thriving nightlife.

10 Sacsayhuaman Page **136** • The zigzag megalithic defensive walls of this Inca temple-fortess are home to the Inti Raymi annual sun festival.

11 Hiking the Inca Trail Page **165** • Culminating at Machu Picchu, this is one of the most popular and eye-opening trails in the world.

12 Pisac Market Page **155** ● Andean markets serve as true community hubs – not to mention excellent places to sample local goods and produce – and Pisac's thriving morning market is one of the best.

13 Islas Ballestas Page **202** ● You can take a morning boat from Pisco to visit the sea-lion colonies and teeming birdlife of these islands.

14 Nazca Lines Page **215** ● Take a helicopter tour to get the full impact of these intricate symbols, etched into the deserts of southern Peru.

15 **Strolling in San Blas** Page **134** • Cusco's bustling artisan quarter is full of craft shops and quaint museums, and has at its center a lovely plaza around which to relax.

16 **Cordillera Blanca** Page **319** • The glacial scenery of the Cordillera Blanca mountain range is among the finest and most accessible on the planet.

17 Chavín de Huantar
Page **324** • Dating back over 2500 years, this large temple has many striking stone carvings and gargoyles, both externally and within its subterranean chambers.

18 Huanchaco Page **377** • Some of the fishermen in this old village can be hired for exciting rides in their *tortora* reed boats.

19 Ashaninka women Page **584** • Dressed in their traditional cushma robes and fresh achiote-red face paint, these women belong to Peru's largest Amazonian tribe.

20 **Trujillo** Page **366** • Though it doesn't receive the hype of Lima or Cusco, Peru's third city charms with its colonial architecture and surprisingly cosmopolitan atmosphere.

21 **El Valle de Mantaro** Page **339** • Draining a green and beautiful valley in the heart of the Andes between Jauja and Huancayo, the majestic Mantaro river eventually tumbles through cloud-forested slopes to join the headwaters of the mighty Amazon.

22 **Huaca Pucllana** Page **82** • This ancient adobe pyramid rises out of the desert soil in what is today an affluent Lima suburb.

23
Lake Sandoval
Page **503** •
Like many of Peru's jungle lakes, Sandoval offers peace and quiet as well as an opportunity to spot wildlife both underwater and above.

24
Ceviche
Page **39** •
Peru's national dish is a refreshing treat – fresh fish soaked briefly in lime juice and chillies, and best accompanied by a cold *cerveza*.

25 **Pink dolphins** Page **480** • These freshwater mammals are commonly seen playing in the tributaries of the Amazon.

26 **Uros Islands** Page **282** • One of Titicaca's many treasures, these man-and-woman-made floating villages have existed in the lake since Inca times.

27 **Kuelap** Page **406** • The massive, ruined citadel of Kuelap is one of the most overwhelming archeological sites in the Andes.

28 **Terraces** Page **271** • These mountainside terraces in the magnificent Cotahuasi Canyon give evidence of the impressive organization of pre-Conquest native societies.

29 **Ayacucho** Page **344** • Bustling streets, an unusual quantity of churches, highly passionate religious processions and unique artesania make this Andean city a standout.

30 **Puerto Belén** Page **472** • A frenetic, floating jungle port that has been called the Venice of the Peruvian Jungle.

Contents

Using the Rough Guide

We've tried to make this Rough Guide a good read and easy to use. The book is divided into six main sections, and you should be able to find whatever you want in one of them.

Colour section

The front colour section offers a quick tour of Peru. The **introduction** aims to give you a feel for the place, with suggestions about where to go. We also tell you what the weather is like and include a basic fact file. Next, our author rounds up his favourite aspects of Peru in the **things not to miss** section – whether it's great food, amazing sights or a special activity. Right after this comes the Rough Guide's full **contents** list.

Basics

The Basics section covers all the **pre-departure** nitty-gritty to help you plan your trip and the practicalities you'll want to know once there. This is where to find out about money and costs, Internet access, transportation, car rental, local media – in fact just about every piece of **general practical information** you might need.

Guide

This is the heart of the Rough Guide, divided into user-friendly chapters, each of which covers a specific region. Every chapter starts with a list of **highlights** and an **introduction** that helps you to decide where to go, depending on your time and budget. Likewise, introductions to the various towns and smaller regions within each chapter should help you to plan your itinerary. We start most town accounts with information on arrival and accommodation, followed by a tour of the sights, and finally reviews of places to eat and drink, and details of nightlife. Longer accounts also have a directory of practical listings. Each chapter concludes with **public transport** details for that region.

Contexts

Read Contexts to get a deeper understanding of what makes Peru tick. We include a brief history, plus articles about **music, wildlife** and the **environment**, along with detailed reviews of numerous books relating to Peru.

Language

The **language** section gives useful guidance for speaking Spanish, Peruvian-style, and pulls together all the vocabulary you might need on your trip, including a comprehensive menu reader. Here you'll also find a glossary of words and terms peculiar to the country.

Index + small print

Apart from a **full index**, which includes maps as well as places, this section covers publishing information, credits and acknowledgements, and also has our contact details in case you want to send in updates and corrections to the book – or suggestions as to how we might improve it.

Map and chapter list

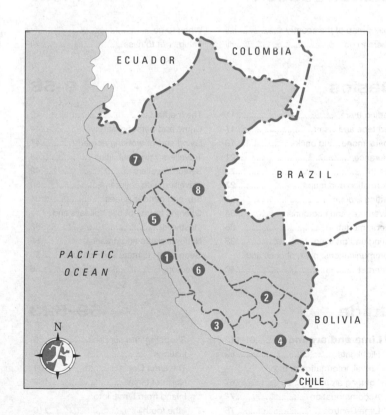

Contents

Contexts 525–602

Language 603–611

Index + small print 613–622

map symbols

maps are listed in the full index using coloured text

▬▬▬	International boundary	◠	Cave
─ ─ ─	Chapter boundary	▲	Mountain peak
▬▬▬	Panamerican Highway	⌂	Mountain range
═══	Major road		Cliffs
═══	Minor road	⌒	Pass
▪ ▪ ▪ ▪	Dirt track	⌂	Hut
▪ ▪ ▪ ▪	4 wheel drive	⌂	Lodge
▬▬▬	Pedestrianized street	◉	Hotel/restaurant
▥▥▥	Steps	⚠	Campsite
─ ─ ─	Path	⋀	Hot spring
▬▬▬	Railway	★	Public transport stop
─ ─ ─	Ferry route	⊞	Hospital
───	Waterway	ℂ	Telephone office
✈	Airport	ⓘ	Information office
◆	Ancient site/point of interest	⊠	Post office
⚱	Church (regional maps)	Ⓢ	Bank
∴	Ruins	■	Building
♟	Museum	⊞	Church
▦	Fort	⬭	Stadium
🏛	Monument	▨	Park
⬥	Viewpoint		

Basics

Basics

Getting there

Unless you're travelling overland through South America – or one of the hardy adventurers taking a freighter – you'll need to fly to reach Peru. Although prices vary depending on the time of year, and the type of ticket, the main airlines seem to hold fares fairly steady. High season is usually mid-December to mid-January and July to mid-August; low season is mid-January to June and mid-August to mid-December.

Barring special offers, the cheapest of the airlines' published fares is usually an **Apex** ticket, although this will carry certain restrictions: you have to book – and pay – at least 21 days before departure, spend at least seven days abroad (maximum stay 3 months), and you tend to get penalized if you change your schedule. Some airlines also issue **Special Apex** tickets to people younger than 24, often extending the maximum stay to a year. Many airlines offer youth or student fares to **under-25s**; a passport or driving licence is sufficient proof of age, though these tickets are subject to availability and can have eccentric booking conditions. It's worth remembering that most cheap return fares involve spending at least one Saturday night away and that many airlines will only give a percentage refund if you need to cancel or alter your journey, so make sure you check the restrictions carefully before buying a ticket.

You can normally cut costs further by going through a **specialist flight agent** – either a **consolidator**, who buys up blocks of tickets from the airlines and sells them at a discount, or a **discount agent**, who in addition to dealing with discounted flights may also offer special student and youth fares and a range of other travel-related services such as insurance, car rental, tours and the like. Bear in mind, though, that penalties for changing your plans can be stiff.

Adventure tours are often good value, though they can be limiting – you'll see only what's in the itinerary – but they do provide a considerable degree of comfort and peace of mind. Always check in advance about what's included – many only provide guides, planning and in-country transport costs, others may have their own vehicles and camping equipment. Other **specialist com-**panies** organize **treks** and **overland travel**, often based around some special interest, such as the rainforest, native culture or Inca sites, offering a far better opportunity to get to know the country. Some of the best of these operators are listed.

Booking flights online

Websites of many airlines now encourage booking online. Good deals can sometimes also be found through discount auction sites.

Online booking agents and general travel sites

ⓦ **www.cheapflights.com** Bookings from the UK and Ireland only. Flight deals to Lima plus links to other travel sites.

ⓦ **www.etn.nl/discount.htm** A hub of consolidator and discount agent web links with some information relevant to Peru flights, maintained by the non-profit European Travel Network.

ⓦ **www.expedia.com** Discount airfares search engine covers most major airlines, and daily deals; some cover on flights to Peru.

ⓦ **www.flyaow.com** Online air travel info and reservations site which includes Peru information.

ⓦ **www.gaytravel.com** Gay online travel agent, concentrating mostly on accommodation; including some details on booking Amazon lodges, visits to Machu Picchu and short tours.

ⓦ **www.geocities.com/thavery2000/** Has an extensive list of airline toll-free numbers and websites, some relevant to Peru.

ⓦ **www.hotwire.com** Bookings from the US only with links to other sites containing flight information for Peru from US and UK.

ⓦ **www.lastminute.com** Offers good last-minute holiday package and flight-only deals (from UK only).

ⓦ **www.priceline.com** Name-your-own-price website that has deals at around 40 percent off standard fares. You cannot specify flight times (although you do specify dates) and the tickets are non-refundable, non-transferable and non-changeable. Only from US.

@ **www.smilinjack.com/airlines.htm** Lists an up-to-date compilation of airline website addresses.
@ **www.travelocity.com** Destination guides, including Peru, with hot web fares and best deals for car rental, accommodation and lodging as well as fares. Provides access to the travel agent system SABRE, the most comprehensive central reservations system in the US.
@ **www.travelshop.com.au** Australian website offering discounted flights, packages, insurance, online bookings.
@ **www.travel.yahoo.com** Incorporates a lot of Rough Guide material in its coverage of destination countries and cities across the world, including Peru, with information about places to eat, sleep, etc.

Flights from the US and Canada

With the exception of Continental's daily non-stop service from Newark to Lima ($580–820), all flights to Peru from the US go **via Miami**. Delta, Continental and American airlines are the main ones serving Peru from the US. Most of the airlines can book connecting flights to Miami from a range of cities throughout the US, and, strangely, fares from New York (via Miami) cost no more than fares from Miami. For example, American's flights **from Miami** to Lima range from $600 to $800, while its twice-daily service **from New York** (via Miami) starts at $600 (low season). Its flights **from Chicago** start at over $700, while flights **from Los Angeles** begin at just under $500. The Peruvian airline Lan Peru offers similar deals, flying daily from Miami to Lima with fares in the range $500–600.

All **flights from Canada** also go **via Miami,** unless you connect with Continental's flight from Newark (see above). Air Canada can book you all the way through, but there are no great deals to be had, except occasionally through discount travel agents. Flying **from Toronto or Montreal** to Miami with Air Canada, then on to Lima with a US or Peruvian airline (see above for details) will cost from CDN$1400.

There are a huge variety of **tours and packages** on offer from the US to Peru, starting from around $500 for a two- to three-day package and ranging up to $3000–4000. Many of the tours involve some sort of **adventure** element, be it trekking the Inca Trail, whitewater rafting or wildlife photo safaris in the Amazonian jungle. You'll also find a number of packages

which include Peru on their itineraries as part of a longer South American tour.

Airlines in North America

Air Canada ☎ 1-800/663-3721 in BC; ☎ 1-800/542-8940 in Alberta, Saskatchewan and Manitoba; ☎ 1-800/268-7240 in eastern Canada; @ www.aircanada.com.
American Airlines ☎ 1-800/433-7300, @ www.aa.com.
Continental Airlines domestic ☎ 1-800/523-3273, international ☎ 1-800/231-0856, @ www.continental.com.
Delta Air Lines domestic ☎ 1-800/221-1212, international ☎ 1-800/241-4141, @ www.delta.com.
Lan Peru ☎ 1-800/735-5590, @ www.lanperu.com.
United Airlines domestic ☎ 1-800/241-6522, international ☎ 1-800/538-2929, @ www.ual.com.

North American discount clubs and travel agents

Air Brokers International ☎ 1-800/883-3273, @ www.airbrokers.com. Consolidator and specialist in round-the-world and Circle Pacific tickets.
Airtech ☎ 212/219-7000, @ www.airtech.com. Standby seat broker; also deals in consolidator fares and courier flights.
Airtreks.com ☎ 1-877/AIRTREKS or 415/912-5600, @ www.airtreks.com. Round-the-world and Circle Pacific tickets. The website features an interactive database that lets you build and price your own round-the-world itinerary.
Council Travel ☎ 1-800/2COUNCIL, @ www.counciltravel.com. Nationwide organization that mostly specializes in student/budget travel. Flights from the US only. Owned by STA Travel.
Educational Travel Center ☎ 1-800/747-5551 or 608/256-5551, @ www.edtrav.com. Student/youth discount agent.
Skylink US ☎ 1-800/247-6659 or 212/573-8980, Canada ☎ 1-800/759-5465, @ www.skylinkus.com. Consolidator.
STA Travel ☎ 1-800/781-4040, @ www .sta-travel.com. Worldwide specialists in independent travel; also student IDs, travel insurance, car rental, rail passes, etc.
Student Flights ☎ 1-800/255-8000 or 480/951-1177, @ www.isecard.com. Student/youth fares, with student IDs.
TFI Tours ☎ 1-800/745-8000 or 212/736-1140, @ www.lowestairprice.com. Consolidator.
Travac ☎ 1-800/TRAV-800, @ www.thetravelsite.com. Consolidator and charter broker with offices in New York City and Orlando.
Travel Avenue ☎ 1-800/333-3335, @ www .travelavenue.com. Full-service travel agent that offers discounts in the form of rebates.
Travel Cuts Canada ☎ 1-800/667-2887, US ☎ 1-

866/246-9762, @www.travelcuts.com. Canadian student-travel organization.
Travelers Advantage ☏1-877/259-2691, @www.travelersadvantage.com. Discount travel club; annual membership fee required (currently $1 for 3 months' trial).
Worldtek Travel ☏1-800/243-1723, @www.worldtek.com. Discount travel agency for worldwide travel.

Specialist operators

Abercrombie & Kent ☏1-800/323-7308 or 630/954-2944, @www.abercrombiekent.com.
Adventure Center ☏1-800/228-8747 or 510/654-1879, @www.adventure-center.com. Hiking and "soft adventure" specialists with some tours in Peru.
Andina Tours and Travel 9805 NE 116th St, Suite 7225, Kirkland, WA 98043-4248 ☏206/820-9966. Customized tours to Peru, including airfare, transfers, accommodation, meals and excursions.
Backroads ☏1-800/GO-ACTIVE or 510/527-1555, @www.backroads.com. Cycling, hiking and multi-sport tour offerings, including Peru.
Brazil Nuts 1150 Post Rd, Fairfield, CT 06430 ☏1-800/553-9959 or 203/259-7900, @www.brazilnuts.com. Specializes in tours to Brazil, but can also do tailor-made add-ons in Peru.
Classic Journeys ☏1-800/200-3887 or 858/454-5004, @www.classicjourneys.com. Offer tours to Machu Picchu from Cusco by train.
Cosmos ☏1-800/276-1241, @www.cosmosvacations.com. Planned holiday packages, including Peru, with an independent focus.
eXito 5699 Miles Ave, Oakland, CA 94618 ☏1-800/655-4053, ℻510/655-4566, ℮exito@wonderlink.com. Latin American specialists in cut-rate fares, student tickets, year-long tickets, land packages and tours, with savings of up to 40 percent off regular fares. Good for travel advice.
Journeys International ☏1-800/255-8735 or 734/665-4407, @www.journeys-intl.com. Worldwide group and individual trips led by experts (some tours to Peru).
Mountain Travel Sobek ☏1-888/MTSOBEK or 510/527-8100, @www.mtsobek.com. Hiking, river rafting and trekking in Peru.
Nature Expeditions International ☏1-800/869-0639, @www.naturexp.com.
Overseas Adventure Travel ☏1-800/955-1925, @www.oattravel.com.
Peru Tourist Centre 130 W 42nd St, Suite 401, New York, NY 10036 ☏212/398-6555. Doesn't sell its own packages, but works with many different tour operators to provide information about a wide range of holidays.
Safaricentre 3201 N Sepuneda Blvd, Manhattan Beach, CA 90266 ☏1-800/223-6046 or 310/546-4411, @www.safaricentre.com. Land-only packages, including a classic Cusco and Machu Picchu trip and a 5-day Inca Trail trek.

University Research Expeditions Program 2223 Fulton St, Desk H22, Berkeley, CA 94720-7050 ☏530/753-0692, @www.urep.ucdavis.edu. Offers research trips to lay travellers, on subjects such as exploring the origins of the Andes, and excavating the prehistoric villages of Lake Titicaca.
Voyagers International PO Box 915, Ithaca, NY 14851 ☏1-800/633-0299. Nature, cultural and photography trips for 12 to 21 days, including visits to Machu Picchu, Cusco, Arequipa, Tambopata and Colca Canyon.
Wilderness Travel 1102 Ninth St, CA 94710 ☏1-800/368-2794 or 510/548-0420, @www.wildernesstravel.com. A variety of programmes in Peru, from 9-day hotel-based holidays to 24-day camping and trekking trips, some of which include Bolivia in the itinerary, plus Inca Trail tours culminating in the Inti Raymi festival in Cusco during the June solstice.

Flights from the UK

As there are no **direct flights** from the UK to Peru, getting there always involves a stopover and, more often than not, a change of planes in either Europe or America. From Heathrow you can expect the journey to take anywhere between 16 and 22 hours, depending on the routing and stopovers. The permutations are endless, but the most common routes are **via Amsterdam** on KLM, **via Madrid** on Iberia, **via Frankfurt** on Lufthansa or **via New York, Miami and Atlanta** on US airlines – most of which involve changing planes in Miami.

Fares vary almost as much as routings, and you'd be well advised to go to a specialist to check out what's on offer – there's also a wide range of **limitations** on the tickets (fixed-date returns within 3 months, yearly returns, Apex, etc), and options such as "open-jaw" flights (flying into Lima and home from Rio, for example). Having established the going rate, you can always check these prices against those on offer at discount flight outlets and other travel agents listed in the press. Flights these days start at around £504 with KLM via Amsterdam. Delta Air Lines also offer a one-year return from £591, via Atlanta. Continental Airlines are usually pretty competitive too, going via New York and Miami.

Some of the best **specialist operators**, like Journey Latin America, are listed here, but it's also worth checking through the classified ads in magazines and newspapers, where the cheapest of flights sometimes crop up. The best deals can usually be found advertised in the London listings magazines like *Time Out* and or in any of the national papers, particularly the Sundays. Children under 12 can sometimes get half fare, while students, school children, and anyone under 26 may be eligible for special fares – contact STA or Campus Travel for details.

It's best to avoid buying international air tickets in Peru, where prices are inflated by a high tax (and are not cheap to begin with). If you're uncertain of your return date, it will probably still work out cheaper to pay the extra for an open-ended return than to buy a single back from Peru.

Airlines in Britain

American Airlines UK ☎0845/7789 789 or 020/8572 5555, Republic of Ireland ☎01/602 0550, ⊛www.aa.com.
Continental Airlines UK ☎0800/776 464, Republic of Ireland ☎1890/925 252, ⊛www.fly-continental.com.
Delta Air Lines UK ☎0800/414 767, Republic of Ireland ☎01/407 3165, ⊛www.delta.com.
Iberia Airlines UK ☎0845/601 2854, Republic of Ireland ☎01/407 3017, ⊛www.iberiaairlines.co.uk.
KLM UK ☎0870/507 4074, ⊛www.klmuk.com.
Lufthansa UK ☎0845/7737 747, ⊛www.lufthansa.co.uk.
United Airlines UK ☎0845/8444 777, ⊛www.unitedairlines.co.uk.

Flight agents in Britain

Bridge the World UK ☎0870/444 7474, ⊛www.bridgetheworld.com. Specializing in round-the-world tickets, with good deals aimed at the backpacker market.
Co-op Travel Care Belfast ☎0870/902 0033, ⊛www.travelcareonline.com. Flights and holidays around the world.
North South Travel UK ☎/℉01245/608 291, ⊛www.northsouthtravel.co.uk. Friendly, competitive travel agency, offering discounted fares worldwide – profits are used to support projects in the developing world, especially the promotion of sustainable tourism.
STA Travel UK ☎0870/1600 599, ⊛www.statravel.co.uk. Worldwide specialists in low-cost flights and tours for students and under-26s, though other customers welcome.
Top Deck UK ☎020/7244 8000, ⊛www.topdecktravel.co.uk. Long-established agent dealing in discount flights.
Trailfinders UK ☎020/7628 7628, ⊛www.trailfinders.co.uk. One of the best-informed and most efficient agents for independent travellers; produce a very useful quarterly magazine worth scrutinizing for round-the-world routes.

Travel Cuts UK ☎020/7255 2082 or 7255 1944, ⊛www.travelcuts.co.uk. Canadian company specializing in budget, student and youth travel and round-the-world tickets.

Specialist tour operators

The Adventure Travel Centre 131–135 Earls Court Rd, London SW5 9RH ☎020/7244 8000. Offer 15- to 105-day tours, most including some time in Peru and Bolivia. They have their own expedition vehicles and tend to choose mid-range hotels.
Discover the World UK ☎01737/218 802, ⊛www.discover-the-world.co.uk. Well-established wildlife holiday specialist, with groups led by naturalists to the cloud forest areas of Peru. Fly-drives available where you buy air-ticket and car rental together in a package.
Dragoman UK ☎01728/861 133, ⊛www.dragoman.com. Extended overland journeys in purpose-built expedition vehicles through the Americas, covering Machu Picchu, Titicaca, Arequipa, Colca, Nazca and other sites in Peru; shorter camping and hotel-based safaris, too.
Exodus UK ☎020/8675 5550, ⊛www.exodus.co.uk. Adventure-tour operators taking small groups on tours to South America, usually incorporating Peru's main destinations; also specialist programmes including walking, biking, overland, adventure, and cultural trips.
Explore Worldwide UK ☎01252/760 000, ⊛www.explore.co.uk. Big range of small-group tours, treks, expeditions and safaris on all continents, including the Cusco and Arequipa areas of Peru.
Guerba Expeditions, Wessex House, 40 Station Rd, Westbury, Wiltshire BA13 3JN ☎01373/826611, ℉858351. Runs 1- to 3-week tours, mainly using local transport and staying in small family-run hotels. Some trips include trekking and camping with Spanish-speaking tour leaders and local guides. Also has an extensive Amazon programme visiting the jungle of Madre de Dios via Puerto Maldonado, as well as treks offering whitewater rafting.
Journey Latin America UK ☎020/8747 3108 or 8747 8315, ⊛www.journeylatinamerica.co.uk. Specialists in flights, packages and tailor-made trips to Latin America. Experienced tour operator using well-informed Spanish-speaking tour guides to accompany small groups, mostly on local transport. Operates a number of tours, some of which include Peru as part of a larger itinerary, and most of which have an option for doing the Inca Trail. Very good value.
Live Limited UK ☎020/8894 6104, ⊛www.live-travel.com. Run by Phil Haines, who styles himself "youngest person to visit every country in the world", they organize tours including Machu Picchu and the Amazon.
Reef and Rainforest Tours 1 The Plains, Totnes, Devon TQ9 5DR ☎01803/866965, ℉865916. Specializes in 14-day tours to the Manu Biosphere Reserve in the Amazon, involving several nights in the rainforest. The tours are well organized and very good for spotting wildlife, but quite expensive.

Thomas Cook UK ☎0870/5666 222,
🌐www.thomascook.co.uk. Long-established one-stop 24-hour travel agency for package holidays or scheduled flights, with bureau de change issuing Thomas Cook travellers' cheques, travel insurance and car rental. These are the most expensive of the tours to Peru, but offer the best-quality travel and accommodation facilities.

Trailfinders 1 Threadneedle St, London EC2R 8JX ☎020/7628 7628, 🌐www.trailfinders.co.uk. One of the best-informed and most efficient agents for independent travellers; they produce a very useful quarterly magazine worth scrutinizing for round-the-world routes (for a free copy call ☎020/7938 3366) as well as offering expert advice on travelling to Peru.

Travelbag Adventures 15 Turk St, Alton, Hampshire GU34 1AG ☎01420/541007, ℱ541022, 🌐www.travelbag-adventures.co.uk. Three-week or longer tours incorporating the Inca Trail and Lake Titicaca; also on offer are shorter tours that don't involve trekking.

World Expeditions UK ☎020/8870 2600, 🌐www.worldexpeditions.co.uk. Australian-owned adventure company offering more than just Antipodean expeditions, with programmes ranging from China to jungle adventures in Peru.

Flights from Australia and New Zealand

Scheduled flights to Peru from this part of the world to Lima are rather limited and tend to involve changing planes somewhere in the Pacific or Los Angeles. High season is December to February; low season is the rest of the year, but prices also vary depending on how long you stay (between a minimum of 21 days and a maximum of a year). There is no Peruvian Tourist Office as such in Australia or New Zealand, but Destination Travel, 34A Main St, Croydon, Victoria (☎03/9725 4655), can provide information about all aspects of travel to South America.

Currently the **cheapest return scheduled fare to Lima** is with Aerolineas Argentinas, who fly twice weekly **from Sydney** in low season and three times a week in high season **via Auckland and Buenos Aires**, with connecting flights to Lima. Fares start at A$1900/NZ$1900 rising to around A$2600/ NZ$2600 in high season. Air New Zealand fly to LA (from A$1450/NZ$1600, depending on length of stay and date of departure) from Australia and New Zealand, but have no connections to Peru. Qantas have four flights a week from Sydney and Auckland (two

code-sharing) to Buenos Aires, with connecting flights to Lima; prices start at A$1900/2500 from Sydney and NZ$1900/2500 from Auckland. Lan Chile offer three flights a week in high season (two in low season) from Sydney via Auckland to Lima; their cheapest tickets are 45-day returns at A$2200/2500, NZ$2150/2350. United Airlines, who fly **daily from Melbourne** via Sydney, Auckland and Los Angeles (stopovers in the US available) have fares that start at A$2320/NZ$2700 for a maximum stay of 45 days and range up to A$3920/NZ$4600 for a six-month return in high season, with connecting flights to Lima.

Round-the-world (RTW) tickets including Peru can work out to be very good value. Aerolineas Argentinas, in combination with other airlines, allow you to stop at up to four places in South America from A$3200/ NZ$3200.

All the Peruvian domestic airlines offering **flight passes** went bust in the late 1990s, and airline companies are in a state of flux in Peru. As new ones arrive and competition for passengers increases, passes are likely to become available again, and it's worth checking with your travel agent or with the major airlines on arrival in Peru.

Airlines in Australia and New Zealand

Aerolineas Argentinas Australia ☎02/9252 5150, New Zealand ☎09/379 3675, 🌐www .aerolineas.com.au.
Air New Zealand Australia ☎13 24 76, New Zealand ☎0800/737 000, 🌐www.airnz.com.
Lan Chile Airlines Australia ☎1300/361 400 or 02/9244 2333, New Zealand ☎09/309 8673, 🌐www.lanchile.com.
Qantas Australia ☎13 13 13, 🌐www .qantas8900.com.au, New Zealand ☎09/357 8900, 🌐www.qantas.co.nz.
United Airlines Australia ☎13 17 77, 🌐www.unitedairlines.com.au, New Zealand ☎09/379 3800 or 0800/508 648, 🌐www.unitedairlines.co.nz.

Travel agents

Budget Travel New Zealand ☎0800/808 480, 🌐www.budgettravel.co.nz.
Destinations Unlimited New Zealand ☎09/373 4033.
Flight Centre Australia ☎13 31 33 or 02/9235 3522, 🌐www.flightcentre.com.au, New Zealand ☎0800/243 544 or 09/358 4310, 🌐www.flight-centre.co.nz.

Northern Gateway Australia ☏1800/174 800,
ⓦwww.northerngateway.com.au.
STA Travel Australia ☏1300/733 035,
ⓦwww.statravel.com.au, New Zealand
☏0508/782 872, ⓦwww.statravel.co.nz.
Student Uni Travel Australia ☏02/9232 8444,
New Zealand ☏09/300 8266, ⓦwww.sut.com.au.
Trailfinders Australia ☏02/9247 7666,
ⓦwww.trailfinders.com.au.

Specialist agents

Adventure World Australia ☏02/8913 0755,
ⓦwww.adventureworld.com.au, New Zealand
☏09/524 5118, ⓦwww.adventureworld.co.nz.
Agents for a vast array of international adventure
travel companies that operate trips to every continent, with several options for Peru.
Austral Tours Australia ☏1800/620 833 or
03/9600 1733, ⓦwww.australtours.com. Central
and South American specialist covering the region
from Ecuador to Easter Island and Tierra del Fuego,
with special tours to Machu Picchu and the Amazon.
Australian Andean Adventures Australia
☏02/9235 1889, ⓦwww.andeanadventures
.com.au. Trekking specialist for Argentina, Peru,
Bolivia and Chile.
South America Travel Centre Australia
☏1800/655 051 or 03/9642 5353, ⓦwww.satc
.com.au. Big selection of tours and city accommodation packages covering most regions of Peru. Short
and long tours available.
The Surf Travel Co Australia ☏02/9527 4722 or
1800/687 873, New Zealand ☏09/473 8388,
ⓦwww.surftravel.com.au. Packages and advice for
catching waves or snow through the whole Pacific
region, including the main sites on the Peruvian
coastline such as Chicama and Mancora.

Tour operators

Adventure Associates Australia ☏02/9389
7466, ⓦwww.adventureassociates.com.au. Tours
and cruises to Central and South America, including
Peru and the Amazon.
Adventure Travel Company New Zealand
☏09/379 9755, ⓦwww.adventuretravel.co.nz.
New Zealand agent for Peregrine (see below).
Peregrine Adventures Australia ☏02/9290
2770, New Zealand see Adventure Travel
Company, ⓦwww.peregrine.net.au. Adventure
tours in South America which aim to explore the Inca
heartlands as well as Amazon rainforest.

Travelling overland from neighbouring countries

Although it's virtually impossible to travel
overland to Peru **from North America**
because of the **Darien Gap** – a section of
Panamanian jungle that's uncrossed by road
or rail – a few hardy souls manage to jeep,

hike, sail or even cycle the swampy route.
Bear in mind, though, that a few would-be
explorers have met bad ends at the hands of
drug smugglers in this area, and the
Peruvian consulate strongly advises against
attempting the journey.

There are ways, however, to avoid the
dangerous Darien Gap, the shortest route
being via **San Andres Island** or **Panama
City** to mainland Colombia. San Andres is a
useful anomaly on international air routes: it's
a bit of Colombian territory in the Caribbean
just east of Nicaragua, and is served by
almost every national airline hereabouts at
least daily. Although San Andres is quite
remote from Colombian cities – 1600km
from Cali, for example – the fact that the
onward flight to Peru is a domestic one
keeps something of a ceiling on fares.
Alternatively, you can take a **ferry** or short
flight directly from Panama to **Barranquilla**
or Cartagena in Colombia. Allow a minimum
of a week to travel the final 1800km overland
from the Colombian Caribbean coast to the
Peruvian frontier.

There are also a number of overland routes
from other South American countries. **From
Brazil**, you can take the boat ride up the
Amazon from Manaus to Iquitos – this is a
ten-day ride which, if you're prepared for a
few discomforts (such as unexciting food
and frequently overcrowded boats), can
prove to be a memorable experience. Take a
hammock and plenty of reading material.
From Brazil's western Amazon department
of Río Acre, there is a relatively simple entry
by bus along jungle roads to Puerto
Maldonado in southeast Peru; from here you
can go by road or fly to Cusco and on to
Lima.

A more commonly followed overland route
arrives in southern Peru **from Bolivia**. The
trip simply requires catching a bus, either
direct or in stages, from La Paz across the
altiplano to Copacabana on Lake Titicaca
and on to Puno or even straight to Cusco
(see Chapter Four, p.285, for details). **From
Chile** it's also an easy bus ride, across the
southern border from Arica to Tacna, which
has good connections with Lima and
Arequipa. **From Ecuador**, there are two
routes, the most popular being a scenic
coastal trip, starting by road from Huaquillas,
crossing the border at Aguas Verdes and
then taking a short bus or taxi ride on to
Tumbes, from where there are daily buses

and flights to Chiclayo, Trujillo and Lima. An alternative crossing, also by a rather scenic road, comes into Peru from Macára in Ecuador over the frontier to La Tina, from where there are daily buses to Sullana on the coast. An almost unused but eminently practical route enters Peru **from Colombia** by river or air at Leticia, at the three-way frontier where Peru, Brazil and Colombia touch. From Leticia there are speedboats up the Río Amazonas more or less daily to Iquitos, and light aircraft which leave from just across the river at the Peruvian port of Santa Rosa, a couple of times a week for Iquitos (see Chapter Eight, p.484, for details).

By sea

There are various options for sea travel, mainly with a handful of freighters which cross the Atlantic. They can be booked through one of a few specialized agencies. The cargo-carrying Polish Ocean Line takes passengers from **Hamburg to Lima**, sometimes via Felixstowe, but it's a long four-week trip costing in the region of £2000. The Panamanian shipping company Promotora de Navegación sails regularly from Vancouver, Seattle and Los Angeles, but you have to book your own flights to the US. Either option is likely to cost considerably more than simply taking a plane. Contact Hamburg-Sud, Hamburg, Germany (ⓕ49/40-37052420) and the Strand Cruise Centre, Charing Cross Shopping Concourse, The Strand, London WC2N 4HZ (ⓣ020/7836 6363, ⓕ7497 0078), for further information on both the above services.

Red tape and visas

EU, US, Canadian, Australian and New Zealand citizens can all currently stay in Peru as tourists for up to ninety days without a visa. However, the situation does change periodically, so always check with your local Peruvian embassy some weeks before departure.

All nationalities, however, need a **tourist or embarkation card** *(tarjeta de embarque)* to enter Peru, issued at the frontiers or on the plane before landing in Lima. Tourist cards are usually valid for between 60 and 90 days – only 60 for US citizens. In theory you have to show an outbound ticket (by air or bus) before you'll be given a card, but this isn't always checked. For your own safety and freedom of movement a copy of the tourist card must be kept on you, with your passport, at all times – particularly when travelling away from the main towns.

Should you want to **extend your visa** (between 30 and 60 additional days), there are two basic options: either cross one of the borders and get a new tourist card when you come back in; or go through the bureaucratic rigmarole at a Migraciones office involving multiple form filling and a visit to the

Banco de la Nación to pay the required fee ($20) to the State, where you get issued an official receipt *(recibo de pago)*. This process is easiest in Lima, but even there expect it to take the best part of a day; best to arrive before 8.30am to be at the front of the queue. As well as the $20 for the *recibo de pago*, a further $7 is needed for the Migraciones forms, and you may also be asked to provide evidence of a valid exit ticket from Peru. Migraciones is also the place to sort out new visas if you've **lost your passport** (having visited your embassy first) and to get passports re-stamped.

Student visas (which last 12 months) are best organized as far in advance as possible through your country's embassy in Lima, your nearest Peruvian embassy and the relevant educational institution. **Business visas** only become necessary if you are to be paid by a Peruvian organization, in which case ask your Peruvian employers to get this for you. Having a business visa means that you are eligible for taxation under Peruvian law and will not be allowed to leave the country until this has been accounted for, which entails obtaining a letter from SUNAT (the Peruvian State Taxation Agency) stating that all outstanding taxes have been settled.

Peruvian embassies and consulates

Australia
40 Brisbane Ave, Barton, Canberra ☏02/6273 8752, ℱ6273 8754.
36 Main St, Croydon, Melbourne ☏03/9725 4908.
Level Three, 30 Clarence St, Sydney ☏02/9262 6464, ℱ9290 2939.

Canada
130 Albert St, Suite 901, Ottawa, ON K1P 5G4 ☏613/238-1777.
10 Mary St, Suite 301, Toronto M4Y 1P9 ☏416/963-9696.

New Zealand
Level Eight, Cigna House, 40 Mercer St, Wellington ☏04/499 8087, ℱ499 8057.
199–209 Great North Rd, Grey Lynn, Auckland ☏09/376 9400.

United Kingdom
52 Sloane St, London SW1X 9SP ☏020/7235 1917.

US
180 N Michigan Ave, Suite 1830, Chicago, IL 6-601 ☏312/853-6170.
5177 Richmond Ave, Suite 695, Houston, TX 77056 ☏713/355-9517.
3460 Wilshire Blvd, Suite 1005, Los Angeles, CA 90010 ☏213/252-5910.
444 Brickell Ave, Suite M135, Miami, FL 33131 ☏305/374-1305.
100 Hamilton Plaza, Twelfth Floor, Paterson, NJ 07505 ☏973/278-3324.
215 Lexington Ave, Twenty-First Floor, New York, NY 10016 ☏212/481-7410.
870 Market St, Suite 579, San Francisco, CA 94102 ☏415/362-5185.
1700 Massachusetts Ave NW, Washington, DC 20036 ☏202/462-1084.

Costs, money and banks

During the late 1980s Peru's rate of inflation was running at thousands of percent, but President Fujimori's economic shock tactics of the early 1990s brought it fairly tightly under control, so that by 2001 it was below the three percent mark. Devaluation is a regular occurrence, however, and in 1986 the whole currency was changed from the sol (Spanish for sun) to the inti (Quechua for sun) and in the process three zeros were removed – one inti was worth 1000 sols. The inti has since been replaced by the nuevo sol, still simply called a "sol" on the streets, and whose symbol is S/. Even with Fujimori off the scene, the sol has remained relatively steady against the US dollar for the first few years of the twenty-first century.

Despite being closely tied to the US dollar, the value of the nuevo sol still varies from day to day, so we have quoted prices throughout this book in US dollars, against which costs have so far remained relatively stable. At time of writing, the exchange rate for the nuevo sol was roughly S/3.49=$1, S/2.27=CDN$1 S/5.61=£1, S/2.06=A$1 and S/1.92=NZ$1.

Costs

Peru is certainly a much cheaper place to visit than Europe or the US, but how much so will depend on where you are and when. As a general rule low-budget travellers should – with care – be able to get by on around $10–20 per person per day, including transport, board and lodging. If you intend on staying in mid-range hotels, eating in reasonable restaurants and taking the odd taxi, $40 a day should be adequate, while $60 a day will allow you to stay in some comfort and sample some of Peru's best cuisine.

In most places in Peru, a good **meal** can still be found for under $3, **transport** is very reasonable, a comfortable double **room** costs $10–35 a night, and **camping** is usually free. Expect to pay a little more than usual in the larger towns and cities, and also in the jungle, as many supplies have to be imported by truck. In the villages and rural towns, on the other hand, things come cheaper – and by roughing it in the countryside, and buying food from local villages or the nearest market, you can live well on next to nothing.

In the more popular parts of Peru, costs vary considerably with the seasons. Cusco, for instance, has its best weather from June to August, when many of its hotel prices go up by around 25–50 percent. The same thing happens at fiesta times – although on such occasions you're unlikely to resent it too much. As always, if you're travelling alone you'll end up spending considerably more than you would in a group of two or more people. It's also worth taking along an international **student card**, if you have one, for the occasional reduction (up to 50 percent in some museums). Once obtained, various official and quasi-official **youth/student ID cards** soon pay for themselves in savings. Full-time students are eligible for the International Student ID Card (ISIC, ⓦwww.isiccard.com), which entitles the bearer to special air, rail and bus fares and discounts at museums, theatres and other attractions. For Americans there's also a health benefit, providing up to $3000 in emergency medical coverage and $100 a day for 60 days in the hospital, plus a 24-hour hotline to call in the event of a medical, legal or financial emergency. The card costs $22 for Americans; CDN$16 for Canadians; A$16.50 for Australians; NZ$21 for New Zealanders; and £6 in the UK.

You only have to be 26 or younger to qualify for the **International Youth Travel Card**, which costs US$22/£7 and carries the same benefits. Teachers qualify for the **International Teacher Card**, offering similar discounts and costing US$22, CDN$16, A$16.50 and NZ$21. All these cards are available in the US from Council Travel, STA, Travel Cuts (see p.12 for contact info) and, in Canada, Hostelling International; in Australia, New Zealand and in the UK from STA.

Several other travel organizations and accommodation groups also sell their own cards, good for various discounts. A university photo ID might open some doors, but is not as easily recognizable as the ISIC card. However, the latter are often not accepted as valid proof of age, for example in bars or liquor stores.

Travellers' cheques, cash and credits cards

For safety's sake the bulk of your money should be carried as **travellers' cheques** – preferably of two different types, as rumoured forgeries make individual brands difficult to exchange from time to time. American Express is probably the best bet since it has its own offices in Lima and Cusco, is widely recognized by casas de cambio (see p.20), hotels and travel agents, and is exchangeable in one of Peru's most efficient banks, the Banco de Credito. American Express also offers an efficient poste restante service. MasterCard travellers' cheques (such as those issued by Thomas Cook and HSBC) are exchangeable for nuevo soles in Interbanc, Banco Wiese and Banco Latino.

US dollars (preferably cash) are by far the best foreign currency to carry in Peru – anything else, apart obviously from soles, will almost certainly prove hard to get rid of outside Lima, and the dollar exchange rate is the one most keenly followed. **Pounds sterling** cash, or even as travellers' cheques, really aren't worth carrying; you often get a very poor exchange rate. **Euros** are easier to exchange than sterling in the larger cities.

Credit cards are accepted in the more expensive restaurants and hotels of large cities throughout Peru, such as Lima, Arequipa, Trujillo and Cusco, and increasingly even in smaller places (especially Visa) such as Puerto Maldonado, Huaraz and Iquitos, as well as for car rental. The better known ones (including MasterCard, Visa, Diners Club and Citicorp) can also be used with larger travel companies, but not to pay for bus or train journeys, or at cheaper hotels or restaurants. American Express cards are not that widely accepted. **Local currency** can be withdrawn from ATMs at a number of banks, including Interbanc (Visa), Banco

Latino (MasterCard and Cirrus), Banco de Wiese (Amex, Citicorp, Diners Club International and MasterCard) and Banco de Credito (Visa), and Unicard (Plus). Be careful using the ATMs, though: they have become a target for muggings. These banks will also advance cash on the cards mentioned for a small fee – the amount varies considerably, so check beforehand.

Getting **change** from your nuevo soles is almost always a problem. Large denominations should be avoided; you'll find them more difficult to change anywhere in South America. It's particularly hard to change the larger notes in jungle towns, and even in Cusco and Lima shopkeepers and waiters are often reluctant to accept them; if they do, they'll end up running around trying to find small change, which is a time-consuming drag for both parties. It's best to break up large notes at every opportunity – in major shops, bars and post offices. If you hang on to the smaller nuevo soles notes you'll have few difficulties in even the remotest villages.

Credit card companies in Peru

American Express Pardo y Aliaga 698, San Isidro, Lima ☎01/4414744 Mon–Fri 9am–5.30pm, Sat 9am–1pm.
Diners Club International, Avenida Canaval y Moreyra 535, San Isidro, Lima ☎ 01/2212050 or 4426572.
MasterCard ☎01/2224242, toll-free 0800/40190.
Visa ☎01/410 581 9754 (collect calling).

Banks, casas de cambio and the black market

Bank opening hours vary enormously from region to region and from bank to bank, but as a general rule most are open weekdays from 9am until 5pm. In Lima, in particular, many banks close for the afternoon at about 1pm from January to March; the Banco de Credito has some branches that open on Saturday mornings, but this isn't the norm. Try to avoid going to the bank on Friday afternoons, and it's generally better to arrive first thing in the morning. Banco de Credito is the most efficient bank, with fast service, a ticket system, and videos to keep you amused should there be queues. The Banco de la Nación is the official bank for dealing with foreign currency, but it's unfortunately the least efficient of them all. Most banks will change dollar travellers' cheques and there are often relatively shorter lines at the Banco Continental and Banco Latin. Interbanc and Citibank usually have air-conditioned offices and shorter waits. As the rate of exchange varies daily, you're better off changing a little money at a time, although there's an enormous amount of time-consuming paperwork involved in even the simplest transactions – some places fill out several copies of each form. You'll always need to show your passport.

Peruvian **hotels** tend to offer the same rate of exchange as the banks, though they may fix their own rate, which is usually slightly worse and averages some five percent below the black market rate. For convenience there's a lot to be said for the **casas de cambio**, which can be found in just about any town on the tourist circuit. They are open all day, are rarely crowded, and the rate of exchange is often better than, or the same as, the banks'. Rates on the streets tend to drop during fiesta and holiday times, so change enough beforehand to see you through.

The very best exchange rates are found on the street in what is loosely called the *mercado negro*, or **black market**. In Peru the difference is never as dramatic as it is in some other South American countries, but it is possible to gain between five and fifteen percent over the official rate. "Black market" is a rather nebulous term, encompassing any buyer from the official **cambistas**, who wear authorization badges from the local municipalities, to hotel clerks and waiters. Official *cambistas* usually offer the best rates of all and can be spotted in the commercial or tourist centre of any large town, generally around the corners by the main city banks, and, rather less official ones, at all border crossings. The *cambistas* in general have become less trustworthy in recent years, so always carefully count your money before completing the transaction and avoid changing money on the street after dark when the official *cambistas* are often replaced by crooks in the larger cities. It is not illegal to buy nuevo soles from street dealers, but if you do exchange on the black market, count your change very carefully and have someone watch your back if you're changing a large amount of money. Theft of signed or unsigned travellers' cheques, sometimes under threat of violence, is always a slight risk, particularly in Lima: when changing money on the street, play it safe – and never hand over your cheques until given the cash. Going into unfamiliar buildings (with hidden back staircases) "to negotiate" is also *not* advisable. Watch out, too, for forgeries, which are generally pretty crude, but frequently good enough to pass to a tourist while street changing. Watch out, too, for the old trick, especially used on $100 bills, where they try to give you back a forgery pretending it's the one you gave them, and pretending that you were trying to give them a damaged bill which is therefore not acceptable.

Wiring money

Having money wired from home using one of the companies listed below is never cheap but can be convenient and particularly useful in emergencies. Western Union are the most ubiquitous of money-wiring companies, with offices in all major cities of Peru (see city listings in relevant chapters of the Guide). It's also possible to have money wired directly from a bank in your home country to a bank in Peru, although this is somewhat less reliable because it involves two separate institutions and usually takes three days. If you go this route, your home bank will need the address of the branch bank where you want to pick up the money and the address and telex number of the Lima head office, which will act as the clearing house; money wired this way normally takes two working days to arrive, and costs around £25/$40 per transaction. The Banco Continental and Interbanc offer a fairly smooth service at the Peru end.

Money-wiring companies

Thomas Cook US ☎1-800/287-7362, Canada ☎1-888/823-4732, UK ☎01733/318 922, Republic of Ireland ☎01/677 1721, ⓦwww.us.thomascook.com.
Travelers Express Moneygram US ☎1-800/926-3947, Canada ☎1-800/933-3278, ⓦwww.moneygram.com.
Western Union US and Canada ☎1-800/325-6000, Australia ☎1800/501 500, New Zealand ☎09/270 0050, UK ☎0800/833 833, Republic of Ireland ☎1800/395395, ⓦwww.westernunion.com.

Emergency cash

If you're in a large city in Peru, probably the quickest method of getting **emergency cash** is to use your credit card to withdraw money from the ATMs of major banks, or get a cash advance on your credit card. Otherwise, you can get a **direct transfer** from an account back home to an affiliated branch of the better Peruvian banks, like Banco de Credito (check with your bank in advance for details). The money is best transferred and picked up in dollars; if you ask for a swiftcode transfer it usually takes five working days. In Lima, Western Union can facilitate more or less immediate money transfers (see p.103).

Insurance

If you fall ill, the bills can mount up rapidly, so some form of insurance – preferably including air evacuation in the event of serious emergency – is essential. Even with insurance most Peruvian clinics will insist on cash up front except in really serious hospital cases, so some emergency cash is a good idea. Keep all receipts and official papers, so that you can make a claim when you get back home.

Before paying for a new policy, however, it's worth checking whether you are already covered: some all-risks home insurance policies may cover your possessions when overseas, and many private medical schemes include cover when abroad. In

Rough Guides travel insurance

Rough Guides offers its own low-cost travel insurance, especially customized for our statistically low-risk readers by a leading British broker, provided by the American International Group (AIG) and registered with the British regulatory body, GISC (the General Insurance Standards Council).

There are five main Rough Guides insurance plans: **No Frills** for the bare minimum for secure travel; **Essential**, which provides decent all-round cover; **Premier** for comprehensive cover with a wide range of benefits; **Extended Stay** for cover lasting two months to a year; and **Annual multi-trip**, a cost-effective way of getting Premier cover if you travel more than once a year. Premier, Annual Multi-Trip and Extended Stay policies can be supplemented by a "Hazardous Pursuits Extension" if you plan to indulge in sports considered dangerous, such as scuba-diving or trekking.

For a policy quote, call the Rough Guide Insurance Line: toll-free in the UK ☎0800/015 09 06 or ☎+44 1392 314 665 from elsewhere. Alternatively, get an online quote at ⊛www.roughguides.com/insurance

Canada, provincial health plans usually provide partial cover for medical mishaps overseas, while holders of official student /teacher/youth cards in Canada and the US are entitled to meagre accident coverage and hospital in-patient benefits.

After exhausting the possibilities above, you might want to contact a specialist travel insurance company, or consider the travel insurance deal we offer (see box). A typical travel insurance policy usually provides cover for the loss of baggage, tickets and – up to a certain limit – cash or cheques, as well as cancellation or curtailment of your journey. Most of them exclude so-called dangerous sports unless an extra premium is paid: in Peru this can mean scuba-diving, white-water rafting, windsurfing and trekking, though probably not kayaking or jeep safaris. Many policies can be chopped and changed to exclude coverage you don't need – for example, sickness and accident benefits can often be excluded or included at will. If you do take medical coverage, ascertain whether benefits will be paid as treatment proceeds or only after return home, and whether there is a 24-hour medical emergency number. When securing baggage cover, make sure that the per-article limit – typically under £500 – will cover your most valuable possession. If you need to make a claim, you should keep receipts for medicines and medical treatment, and in the event you have anything stolen, you must obtain an official statement from the tourist police (*policía de turismo*).

Health

No inoculations are currently required for Peru, but yellow fever is recommended and it's always a good idea to check with the embassy or a reliable travel agent before you go. Your doctor will probably advise you to have some anyway: typhoid, cholera and, again, yellow fever shots are all sensible precautions, and it's well worth ensuring that your polio and tetanus-diphtheria boosters are still effective. Immunization against hepatitis A is also usually recommended.

Yellow fever still breaks out now and again in some of the jungle areas of Peru; it is frequently obligatory to show an inoculation certificate when entering the Amazon region – if you can't show proof of immunization you'll be jabbed on the spot. **Rabies** still exists and people do die from it. If you get bitten by a dog or vampire bat (though bat attack is only likely in some parts of the Amazon region and rabid bats in even fewer areas), you should undergo a series of injections administered to the stomach (available in most Peruvian hospitals) within 24 hours. This is the only cure, unless you have been inoculated in advance with one of the new anti-rabies jabs.

Malaria is quite common in Peru these days, particularly in the Amazon regions to the east of the country. If you intend to go into the jungle regions, malaria tablets should be taken – starting a few weeks before you arrive and continuing for some time after. Make sure you get a supply of these, or whatever is recommended by your doctor, before leaving home. It is very easy to catch malaria without prophylactics. The most commonly recommended against Peruvian malaria tend to be a combination of Paludrin and Chloroquine tablets. Few people who have to spend a lot of time in the rainforest regions use prophylactics, preferring to treat the disease if they contract it, believing that the best prevention is to avoid getting bitten if at all possible, by wearing long sleeves, long trousers, socks, even mosquito-proof net hats, and sleeping under good mosquito netting or well-proofed quarters. Pills are a relatively simple option, but some do have side effects which should be investigated with your doctor ideally more than a month prior to your departure for Peru. There is more information on this issue in Chapter Eight (p.460), or check out Ⓦwww.cdc.gov/travel/regionalmalaria.

Diarrhoea, dysentery and giardia

Diarrhoea is something everybody gets at some stage, and there's little to be done except drink a lot (but not alcohol) and bide your time. You should also replace salts either by taking oral rehydration salts or by mixing a teaspoon of salt and eight of sugar in a litre of purified water. You can minimize the risk by being sensible about what you eat, and by **not drinking tap water anywhere**. There are several portable water filters on the market. Except in trekking-type conditions it isn't difficult to drink clean water, given the extreme cheapness and universal availability of soft drinks and bottled water, while Brazilians are great believers in herbal teas, which often help alleviate cramps.

If your diarrhoea contains blood or mucus, the cause may be dysentery or giardia. Combined with a fever, these symptoms could well be caused by **bacillic dysentery** and may clear up without treatment. If you're sure you need it, a course of antibiotics such as tetracyclin or ampicillin (travel with a supply if you are going off the beaten track for a while) should sort you, but they also destroy "gut flora" which help protect you, so should only be used if properly diagnosed or in a desperate situation. Similar symptoms without fever indicate **amoebic dysentery**, which is much more serious, and can damage your gut if untreated. The usual cure is a course of metronidazole (Flagyl), an antibiotic which may itself make you feel ill, and should not be taken with alcohol. Similar symptoms, plus rotten-egg belches and gas, indicate **giardia**, for which the treatment is again metronidazole. If you suspect you have any of these, seek medical help, and only start on the metronidazole (250mg three times daily for a week for adults) if there is definitely blood in your diarrhoea and it is impossible to see a doctor.

Water and food

Water in Peru is better than it used to be, but it can still trouble non-Peruvian (and even Peruvian) stomachs, so it's a good idea to only drink **bottled water** (*água mineral*), available in various sizes, including litre and two-litre bottles from most corner shops or food stores. Stick with known brands, even if they are more expensive, and always check that the seal on the bottle is intact, since refilling bottles with local water is not uncommon. Carbonated water is generally safer as it is more likely to be the genuine stuff. You should also clean your teeth using bottled water and avoid raw foods washed in local water.

Apart from bottled water, there are various methods of **treating water** whilst you are travelling, whether your source is tap water or natural groundwater such as a river or stream. **Boiling** is the time-honoured method which will be effective in sterilizing water, although it will not remove unpleasant tastes. A minimum boiling time of five minutes (longer at higher altitudes) is sufficient to kill micro-organisms. In remote jungle areas, **sterilizing tablets** are a better idea, although they leave a rather bad taste in the mouth. Pregnant women or people with thyroid problems should consult their doctor before using iodine sterilizing tablets or iodine-based purifiers. In emergencies and remote areas in particular, always check with locals to see whether the tap water is okay (*es potable?*) before drinking it. For more information check out @www.gorge.net/ ham/.

Peruvian **food** has been frequently condemned as a health hazard, particularly during rare but recurrent **cholera outbreaks**. Be careful about anything bought from street stalls, particularly seafood, which may not be that fresh. Salads should be avoided, especially in small settlements where they may have been washed in river water or fertilized by local sewage waters.

The sun

The sun can be deceptively hot, particularly on the coast or when travelling in boats on jungle rivers when the hazy weather or cool breezes can put visitors off their guard; remember, **sunstroke** is a reality and can make you very sick as well as burnt. Wide-brimmed hats, sun screen lotions (factor 15 advisable) and staying in the shade like the locals whenever possible are all good precautions. Note that **suntan lotion** and **sunblock** are more expensive in Peru than they are at home, so take a good supply with you. If you do run out, you can buy Western brands at most *farmacias*, though you won't find a very wide choice, especially in the higher factors. Also make sure that you increase your water intake, in order to prevent dehydration.

Altitude sickness

Altitude sickness – known as *soroche* in Peru – is a common problem for visitors, especially if you are travelling quickly between the coast or jungle regions and the high Andes. The best way to prevent it is to eat light meals, drink lots of coca tea, and spend as long as possible acclimatizing to high altitudes (over 2500m) before carrying out any strenuous activity. Anyone who suffers from headaches or nausea should rest; more seriously, a sudden bad cough could be a sign of pulmonary edema and demands an immediate descent and medical attention – altitude sickness can kill. People often suffer from altitude sickness on trains crossing high passes; if this happens, don't panic, just rest and stay on the train until it descends. Most trains are equipped with oxygen bags or cylinders that are brought around by the conductor for anyone in need. Diamox is used by many from the US to counter the effects of *soroche*. It's best to bring this with you from home since it's rarely available in Peruvian pharmacies.

Insects

Insects are more of an irritation than a serious problem, but on the coast, in the jungle and to a lesser extent in the mountains, the **common fly** is a definite pest. Although it can carry typhoid, there is little one can do; you might spend mealtimes successfully fighting flies from your plate but even in expensive restaurants it's difficult to regulate hygiene in the kitchens. A more obvious problem is the **mosquito**, which in some parts of the lowland jungle carries malaria.

Repellents are of limited value – it's better to cover your arms, legs and feet with a good layer of clothing. Mosquitoes tend to emerge after dark, but the daytime holds even worse biting insects in the jungle regions, among them the **Manta Blanca** (or white blanket), so called because they swarm as a blanket of tiny flying insects. Their bites don't hurt at the time but itch like crazy for a few days after. **Antihistamine creams** or tablets can reduce the sting or itchiness of most insect bites, but try not to scratch them, and if it gets unbearable go to the nearest *farmacia* for advice. To keep hotel rooms relatively clear, buy some of the spirals of incense-like **pyrethrin**, available cheaply everywhere.

HIV and AIDS

HIV and **AIDS** (known as SIDA in Latin America) are a growing problem in South America, and whilst Peru does not have as bad a reputation as neighbouring Brazil, you should still take care. Although all hospitals and clinics in Peru are supposed to use only sterilized equipment, many travellers prefer to take their own sealed hypodermic syringes in case of emergencies. It goes without saying that you should take the same kind of precautions as you would in your country when having sex (see "Contraception", below).

Contraception

Condoms (*profilacticos*) are available from street vendors and some *farmacias*. However, they tend to be expensive and often poor quality (rumour has it that they are US rejects, which have been sold to a less discriminating market), so bring an adequate supply with you. **The pill** is also available from *farmacias*, officially on prescription only, but is frequently sold over the counter. You're unlikely to be able to match your brand, however, so it's far better to bring your own supply. It's worth remembering that if you suffer from moderately severe diarrhoea on your trip the pill (or any other drug) may not be in your system long enough to take effect.

Farmacias

For **minor ailments** you can buy most drugs at a *farmacia* without a prescription. **Antibiotics** and **malaria pills** can be bought over the counter (it is, however, important to know the correct dosage), as can antihistamines (for bite allergies) or medication for an upset stomach (try Lomotil or Streptotriad). You can also buy Western-brand **tampons** at a *farmacia,* though they are expensive, so better to bring a good supply. For any serious illnesses, you should go to a doctor or hospital; these are detailed throughout the Guide in the relevant town Listings, or try the local phone book.

Traditional medicines

Alternative medicines have a popular history going back at least two thousand years in Peru and the traditional practitioners – *herbaleros*, *hueseros* and *curanderos* – are still commonplace. *Herbaleros* sell curative plants, herbs and charms in the streets and markets of most towns. They lay out a selection of ground roots, liquid tree barks, flowers, leaves and creams – all with specific medicinal functions and sold at much lower prices than in the *farmacias*. If told the symptoms, a *herbalero* can select remedies for most minor (and apparently some major) ailments. *Hueseros* are consultants who treat diseases and injuries by bone manipulation, while *curanderos* claim diagnostic, divinatory and healing powers and have existed in Peru since pre-Inca days. For further information on alternative medicine and traditional healing, see p.555.

Medical resources for travellers

Websites

ⓦ **www.fitfortravel.scot.nhs.uk** UK NHS website carrying information about travel-related diseases and how to avoid them.

ⓦ **www.health.yahoo.com** Information on specific diseases and conditions, drugs and herbal remedies, as well as advice from health experts.

ⓦ **www.istm.org** The website of the International Society for Travel Medicine, with a full list of clinics specializing in international travel health.

ⓦ **www.tmvc.com.au** Contains a list of all Travellers Medical and Vaccination Centres throughout Australia, New Zealand and Southeast Asia, plus general information on travel health.

ⓦ **www.tripprep.com** Travel Health Online provides a comprehensive database of necessary vaccinations for most countries, as well as destination and medical service provider information.

In the US and Canada

Canadian Society for International Health 1 Nicholas St, Suite 1105, Ottawa, ON K1N 7B7 ☎613/241-5785, ⓦwww.csih.org. Distributes a free pamphlet, "Health Information for Canadian Travellers", containing an extensive list of travel health centres in Canada.

Centers for Disease Control 1600 Clifton Rd NE, Atlanta, GA 30333 ☎1-800/311-3435 or 404/639-3534, ⓦwww.cdc.gov. Publishes outbreak warnings, suggested inoculations, precautions and other background information for travellers. Useful website plus International Travelers Hotline on ☎1-877/FYI-TRIP.

International Association for Medical Assistance to Travellers (IAMAT) 417 Center St, Lewiston, NY 14092 ☎716/754-4883, ⓦwww.iamat.org, and 40 Regal Rd, Guelph, ON N1K 1B5 ☎519/836-0102. A non-profit organization supported by donations, it can provide a list of English-speaking doctors in Peru, climate charts and leaflets on various diseases and inoculations.

International SOS Assistance Eight Neshaminy Interplex Suite 207, Trevose, PA 19053-6956 ☎1-800/523-8930, ⓦwww.intsos.com. Members receive pre-trip medical referral info, as well as overseas emergency services designed to complement travel insurance coverage.

MEDJET Assistance ☎1-800/863-3538, ⓦwww.medjetassistance.com. Annual membership programme for travellers ($195 for individuals, $295 for families) that, in the event of illness or injury, will fly members home or to the hospital of their choice in a medically equipped and staffed jet.

Travel Medicine ☎1-800/872-8633, Ⓕ413/584-6656, ⓦwww.travmed.com. Sells first-aid kits, mosquito netting, water filters, reference books and other health-related travel products.

Travelers Medical Center 31 Washington Square West, New York, NY 10011 ☎212/982-1600. Consultation service on immunizations and treatment of diseases for people travelling to developing countries.

In the UK and Ireland

British Airways Travel Clinics 156 Regent St, London W1 (Mon–Fri 9.30am–5.15pm, Sat 10am–4pm, no appointment necessary; ☎020/7439 9584); 101 Cheapside, London EC2 (hours as above, appointment required; ☎020/7606 2977); ⓦwww.britishairways.com. Vaccinations, tailored advice from an online database and a complete range of travel healthcare products.

Communicable Diseases Unit Brownlee Centre, Glasgow G12 0YN ☎0141/211 1062. Travel vaccinations including yellow fever.

Dun Laoghaire Medical Centre 5 Northumberland Ave, Dun Laoghaire, Co Dublin ☎01/280 4996, Ⓕ280 5603. Advice on medical matters abroad.

Hospital for Tropical Diseases Travel Clinic 2nd floor, Mortimer Market Centre, off Capper St, London WC1E 6AU (Mon–Fri 9am–5pm by appointment only; ☎020/7388 9600, ⓦwww.thehtd.org). A recorded Health Line (☎09061/337 733; 50p per min) gives hints on hygiene and illness prevention as well as listing appropriate immunizations.

Liverpool School of Tropical Medicine Pembroke Place, Liverpool L3 5QA ☎0151/708 9393. Walk-in clinic Mon–Fri 1–4pm; appointment required for yellow fever, but not for other jabs.

MASTA (Medical Advisory Service for Travellers Abroad) 40 regional clinics (call ☎0870/606 2782 for the nearest). Also operates a pre-recorded 24-hour Travellers' Health Line (UK ☎0906/822 4100, 60p per min; Republic of Ireland ☎01560/147 000, 75p per min), giving written information tailored to your journey by return of post.

Nomad Pharmacy surgeries 40 Bernard St, London WC1; and 3–4 Wellington Terrace, Turnpike Lane, London N8 (Mon–Fri 9.30am–6pm, ☎020/7833 4114 to book vaccination appointment). They give advice free if you go in person, or their telephone helpline is ☎09068/633 414 (60p per min). They can give information tailored to your travel needs.

Trailfinders Immunization clinics (no appointments necessary) at 194 Kensington High St, London (Mon–Fri 9am–5pm except Thurs to 6pm, Sat 9.30am–4pm; ☎020/7938 3999).

Travel Health Centre Mercers Medical Centre, Stephen's St Lower, Dublin ☎01/402 2337. Expert pre-trip advice and inoculations.

Travel Medicine Services PO Box 254, 16 College St, Belfast 1 ☎028/9031 5220. Offers medical advice before a trip and help afterwards in the event of a tropical disease.

Tropical Medical Bureau Grafton Buildings, 34 Grafton St, Dublin 2 ☎01/671 9200, ⓦwww.tmb.ie.

In Australia and New Zealand

Travellers' Medical and Vaccination Centres 27–29 Gilbert Place, Adelaide, SA 5000 ☎08/8212 7522, Ⓔadelaide@traveldoctor.com.au.
1/170 Queen St, Auckland ☎09/373 3531, Ⓔauckland@traveldoctor.co.nz.
5/247 Adelaide St, Brisbane, Qld 4000 ☎07/3221 9066, Ⓔbrisbane@traveldoctor.com.au.
5/8–10 Hobart Place, Canberra, ACT 2600 ☎02/6257 7156, Ⓔcanberra@traveldoctor.com.au.
147 Armagh St, Christchurch ☎03/379 4000, Ⓔchristchurch@traveldoctor.co.nz.
270 Sandy Bay Rd, Sandy Bay, Tas 7005 ☎03/6223 7577, Ⓔhobart@traveldoctor.com.au.
2/393 Little Bourke St, Melbourne, Vic 3000 ☎03/9602 5788, Ⓔmelbourne@traveldoctor.com.au.
Level 7, Dymocks Bldg, 428 George St, Sydney, NSW 2000 ☎02/9221 7133, Ⓔsydney@traveldoctor.com.au.
Shop 15, Grand Arcade, 14–16 Willis St, Wellington ☎04/473 0991, Ⓔwellington@traveldoctor.co.nz.

Information and maps

Peru has no official tourist offices abroad, but you can get a range of information from its embassies in Britain, Europe, North America and Australia and New Zealand. However, you'll probably find that most tour companies can supply better, more up-to-date information.

In Peru you'll find some sort of **tourist office** in most towns of any size, which can help with information and sometimes free local maps. Quite often, though, these are simply fronts for tour operators, and are only really worth bothering with if you have a specific question – about fiesta dates or local bus timetables, for example. The **South American Explorers' Club** is probably your best bet for getting relevant and up-to-date information both before you leave home and when you arrive in Lima. It is a non-profit-making organization founded in 1977 to support scientific and adventure expeditions and to provide services to travellers. In return for membership (from $50 a year) you get four copies of the magazine *South American Explorer* a year, and you can use the club's facilities, which include an excellent library, access to the map collection, trip reports, listings, a postal address, storage space, discounts on maps, guidebooks, information on visas, doctors and dentists and a network of experts with specialist information. They have clubhouses in Lima (see p.103), Cusco (see p.149), and their main office is in the US, at 126 Indian Creek Road, Ithaca, NY 14850 (☎607/277-0488, ℱ277-6122, ⓦwww.samexplo.org), plus there's a clubhouse in Ecuador at Jorge Washington 311, Quito (☎02/225228); postal address, Apartado 21-431, Eloy Alfaro, Quito, Ecuador. A *Peru Guide* booklet is available free from hotels and travel agencies in most major cities; it has a few good city maps and gives recommendations for hotels and restaurants plus other useful information for Lima, Arequipa, Cusco, Huaraz, Chiclayo, Ica/Nazca/Paracas and Iquitos.

Maps

Maps of Peru fall into three basic categories. A standard **road map** should be available from good map sellers just about anywhere in the world (see box overleaf for map outlets in North America, Britain, Australia and New Zealand) or in Peru itself from street vendors or *librerías*; the Touring y Automóvil Club de Peru, Avenida Cesar Vallejo 699, Lince, Lima (☎01/440 3270) is worth visiting for its good route maps. **Departmental maps**, covering each *departmento* (Peruvian state) in greater detail, but often very out of date, are also fairly widely available. **Topographic maps** (usually 1:100,000) cover the entire coastal area and most of the mountainous region. In Lima, they can be bought from the Instituto Geográfico Nacional, Avenida Aramburu 1190, Surquillo (☎01/4759960, ⓔpostmaster@ignperu.gob.pe); Ingemmet, Avenida Canada 1470, San Borja (☎01/2253158); the Touring y Automovil Club del Peru, Avenida Cesar Vallejo 699, Lince (☎01/4403270); and the Sevicio Aerofotografico Nacional, Base Fap, Las Palmas Mon–Fri 9am–5pm (☎01/4671341). Maps are also available at the South American Explorers' Club (see above), along with a wide variety of hiking maps and guidebooks for all the most popular hiking zones and quite a few others.

Map outlets

In the US and Canada
Adventurous Traveler.com US ☎1-800/282-3963, ⓦwww.adventuroustraveler.com.
Book Passage 51 Tamal Vista Blvd, Corte Madera, CA 94925 ☎1-800/999-7909, ⓦwww.bookpassage.com.
Distant Lands 56 S Raymond Ave, Pasadena, CA 91105 ☎1-800/310-3220, ⓦwww.distantlands.com.
Elliot Bay Book Company 101 S Main St, Seattle, WA 98104 ☎1-800/962-5311, ⓦwww.elliotbaybook.com.
Globe Corner Bookstore 28 Church St,

Cambridge, MA 02138 ℡1-800/358-6013,
ⓦwww.globercorner.com.
Map Link 30 S La Patera Lane, Unit 5, Santa
Barbara, CA 93117 ℡1-800/962-1394,
ⓦwww.maplink.com.
Rand McNally US ℡1-800/333-0136,
ⓦwww.randmcnally.com. Around thirty stores
across the US; dial ext 2111 or check the website
for the nearest location.
The Travel Bug Bookstore 2667 W Broadway,
Vancouver V6K 2G2 ℡604/737-1122,
ⓦwww.swifty.com/tbug.
World of Maps 1235 Wellington St, Ottawa, ON
K1Y 3A3 ℡1-800/214-8524, ⓦwww.world-
ofmaps.com.

In the UK and Ireland

Blackwell's Map and Travel Shop 50 Broad St,
Oxford OX1 3BQ ℡01865/793 550,
ⓦwww.maps.blackwell.co.uk.
Easons Bookshop 40 O'Connell St, Dublin 1
℡01/858 3881, ⓦwww.eason.ie.
Heffers Map and Travel 20 Trinity St, Cambridge
CB2 1TJ ℡01865/333 536, ⓦwww.heffers.co.uk.
Hodges Figgis Bookshop 56–58 Dawson St,
Dublin 2 ℡01/677 4754,
ⓦwww.hodgesfiggis.com.
The Map Shop 30a Belvoir St, Leicester LE1 6QH
℡0116/247 1400,
ⓦwww.mapshopleicester.co.uk.
National Map Centre 22–24 Caxton St, London
SW1H 0QU ℡020/7222 2466,
ⓦwww.mapsnmc.co.uk.
Newcastle Map Centre 55 Grey St, Newcastle-
upon-Tyne NE1 6EF ℡0191/261 5622.
Ordnance Survey Ireland Phoenix Park, Dublin 8
℡01/802 5300, ⓦwww.osi.ie.
Ordnance Survey of Northern Ireland Colby
House, Stranmillis Ct, Belfast BT9 5BJ ℡028/9025
5755, ⓦwww.osni.gov.uk.
Stanfords 12–14 Long Acre, London WC2E 9LP
℡020/7836 1321, ⓦwww.stanfords.co.uk.
The Travel Bookshop 13–15 Blenheim Crescent,
London W11 2EE ℡020/7229 5260,
ⓦwww.thetravelbookshop.co.uk.

In Australia and New Zealand

Mapland 372 Little Bourke St, Melbourne, Victoria
3000 ℡03/9670 4383, ⓦwww.mapland.com.au.
The Map Shop 6–10 Peel St, Adelaide, SA 5000

℡08/8231 2033, ⓦwww.mapshop.net.au.
MapWorld 173 Gloucester St, Christchurch
℡0800/627 967 or 03/374 5399, ⓦwww
.mapworld.co.nz.
Perth Map Centre 1/884 Hay St, Perth, WA 6000
℡08/9322 5733, ⓦwww.perthmap.com.au.
Specialty Maps 46 Albert St, Auckland 1001
℡09/307 2217, ⓦwww.ubdonline.co.nz/maps.

Websites

Peru is surprisingly switched on to electronic communications, with **Internet cafés** in all
towns of any size and in many small, out-of-
the-way places. There's a vast list of sites for
the armchair enthusiast, potential visitor, or
traveller in the field, and we've listed a few of
the more useful ones below.
Andean Travel Web ⓦwww.andeantravelweb
.com/peru. An excellent site for linking to a whole
range of travel-related features and listings,
including sites, towns, accommodation and adventure activities.
Enjoy Peru ⓦwww.enjoyperu.com. Information
and pictures of travel, restaurants, accommodation, local events, fiestas and ceremonies.
Machu Picchu ⓦwww.machupicchuperu.com.
Facts, reports and listings for this popular trekking
destination at the end of the Inca Trail as well as
other sites in the region.
Peru Links ⓦwww.perulinks.com. Has English
pages on a range of Peruvian topics: art, Internet,
business, education, entertainment, travel, society
etc.
Peru Traveller Guide ⓦwww.geocities.com
/perutraveller/. Highly informative online guide for
independent travellers to Peru.
PromPeru ⓦwww.peruonline.net. Great source of
general background information, including history,
culture and activities, in English and Spanish.
Rumbos ⓦwww.rumbosperu.com. Environmental
and travel magazine, loaded with practical tips on
tours and background information on all the sites.
South American Explorers' Club ⓦwww
.samexplo.org. The latest travel reports on Latin
America.
Virtual Peru ⓦwww.virtualperu.net. Covers
Peruvian geography, history and people with satellite photos, maps and other information.

Getting around

With the distances in Peru being so vast, many Peruvians and travellers are increasingly flying to their destinations, as all Peruvian cities are within a two-hour flight of Lima. Most Peruvians get around the country by bus, as these go just about everywhere and are extremely good value. However, wherever possible, visitors tend to use one of the country's trains – an experience in itself – despite being considerably slower than the equivalent bus journey. Approximate journey times and frequencies of all services can be found in "Travel Details" at the end of each chapter, and local peculiarities are detailed in the text of the Guide.

Driving around Peru is generally not a problem outside of Lima, and allows you to see some out-of-the-way places that you might otherwise miss. However, the traffic in Lima is abominable, both in terms of its recklessness and the sheer volume. Traffic jams are ubiquitous between 8 and 10am and again between 4 and 6pm every weekday, while the pollution from too many old and poorly maintained vehicles is a real health risk, particularly in Lima Centro and to a lesser extent in Arequipa.

By bus

Peru's **buses** are run by a variety of private companies, all of which offer remarkably low **fares**, making it possible to travel from one end of the country to the other (over 2000km) for under $30. Long-distance bus journeys cost from around $1.50 per hour on the fast coastal highway, and are even cheaper on the slower mountain and jungle routes. The condition of the buses ranges from the efficient and relatively luxurious Cruz del Sur fleet that runs along the coast, to the scruffy old ex-US schoolbuses used on local runs throughout the country. Some of the better bus companies, such as Cruz del Sur, Ormeño, Linea and Movil, offer excellent onboard facilities including sandwich bars and video entertainment. The major companies generally offer two or three levels of service anyway, and many companies run the longer journeys by night. If you don't want to miss the scenery, you can hop relatively easily between the smaller towns, which usually works out at not much more. Cruz del Sur (Ⓦwww.cruzdelsur.com.pe)

now operates an excellent website with timetables and ticket purchase option (credit cards accepted).

As the only means of transport available to most of the population, buses run with surprising regularity, and the coastal Panamerican Highway and many of the main routes into the mountains have now been paved (one of President Fujimori's most successful construction programmes), so on such routes services are generally punctual. On some of the rougher mountainous routes, punctures, arguments over rights of way and, in the rainy season, landslides may mean you arrive several hours late.

At least one **bus depot** or **stopping area** can be found in the centre of any town. Peru is investing in a series of **terminal terrestres**, or **terrapuertos**, centralizing the departure and arrival of the manifold operators, but it's always a good idea to double-check where the bus is leaving from, since in some cities, notably Arequipa, bus offices are in different locations to the bus terminal. Lima has so many buses that the major companies are in the middle of rationalizing their own private terminals and departure points (presently incredibly complex) while the rest still cling to depots mostly in the traffic-congested heart of Lima Centro. If you can't get to a bus depot or terminal terrestre, you can try to catch a bus from the police *control* point found on the outskirts of most Peruvian cities, though there's no guarantee of getting a ride or a seat. For intercity rides, it's best to buy **tickets** in advance direct from the bus company offices; for local trips, you can buy tickets on the bus itself. On long-distance journeys, try to avoid getting seats right over the jarring wheels, especially if the bus is tackling mountain or jungle roads.

Taxis, mototaxis and colectivos

Taxis can be found anywhere at any time in almost every town. Any car can become a taxi simply by sticking a taxi sign up in the front window; a lot of people, especially in Lima, take advantage of this to supplement their income. Whenever you get into a taxi, always fix the **price** in advance since few of them have meters, even the really professional firms. Relatively short journeys in Lima generally cost around $1.50, but it's cheaper elsewhere. Radio taxis, minicabs and airport taxis tend to cost more. Even relatively long taxi rides in Lima are likely to cost less than $10, except perhaps to and from the airport, which ranges from $9 to $20, depending on how far across the city you're going, how bad the traffic is and how much you're prepared to pay for a stylish vehicle. Taxi drivers in Peru do not expect tips.

In many rural towns, you'll find small cars – mainly Korean Ticos and motorcycle rickshaws, known variously as **mototaxis** or **motokars** – all competing for customers. The latter are always cheaper if slightly more dangerous and not that comfortable, especially if there's more than two of you or if you've got a lot of luggage.

Colectivos (shared taxis) are a very useful way of getting around that's peculiar to Peru. They connect all the coastal towns, and many of the larger centres in the mountains. Like the buses, many are ageing imports from the US – huge old Dodge Coronets with a picture of the Virgin Mary dangling from the rear-view mirror – though, increasingly, fast new Japanese and Korean minibuses are running between the cities. Colectivos tend to be faster than the bus, though often as much as twice the price. Most colectivo **cars** manage to squeeze in about six people plus the driver (3 in the front and 4 in the back), and can be found in the centre of a town or at major stopping places along the main roads. If more than one is ready to leave it's worth bargaining a little, as the price is often negotiable. Colectivo **minibuses**, also known as **combis**, can squeeze in twice as many people, or often more.

In the cities, particularly in Lima, colectivos (especially combis) have an appalling reputation for **safety**. There are crashes reported in the Lima press every week, mostly caused by the highly competitive nature of the business. There are so many combis covering the same major arterial routes in Lima that they literally race each other to be the first to the next street corner. They frequently crash, turn over and knock down pedestrians. Equally dangerous is the fact that the driver is in such a hurry that he does not always wait for you to get in. If you're not careful he'll pull away while you've still got a foot on the pavement, putting you in serious danger of breaking a leg.

By train

Peru's spectacular **train** journeys are in themselves a major attraction, and you should aim to take at least one long-distance train during your trip, especially as the trains connect some of Peru's major tourist sights. At the time of writing, the **Central Railway**, which climbs and switchbacks its way up from Lima into the Andes as far as Huancayo on the world's highest standard-gauge tracks, is closed for passengers.

The **Southern Railway** runs passenger services inland from Puno on Lake Titicaca north to Cusco, from where another line heads out down the magnificent Urubamba Valley as far as Machu Picchu. The trains move slowly, and are much bumpier than buses, depending both on the level of track maintenance (presently poor between Cusco and Puno, for instance) and, of course, the state of the comparative road the bus is taking. Trains, however, generally allow ample time to observe what's going on outside, but you do have to keep one eye on events inside, where the carriages – often extremely crowded – are notorious for **petty thefts**. Wherever possible **tickets** should be bought in advance by at least a day. Trains in Peru offer three tourist classes of carriage from Cusco to Machu Picchu: Vistadome ($86), Backpacker ($58), Backpacker Shuttle (only operates in high season and departs from Urubamba via Ollantaytambo to Machu Picchu). There is a slower local train, but this is meant for Peruvians and local people living and working in the valley and it's difficult to buy the much cheaper tickets as a gringo. Trains departing from Huanchac station in Cusco for Puno on Lake Titicaca offer both a Tourist Class and a First

Class service, the latter only operating when there's sufficient demand (20-passenger minimum) and running on the same timetable but it costs $81 and offers quality waiter service with meals included. For all train journeys, it's advisable to buy tickets at least one day before travelling and further in advance during high season.

By plane

Some places in the jungle can only sensibly be reached by **plane** and Peru is so vast that the odd flight can save a lot of time. There are three major companies: Aero Continente, who fly to all of the main cities and many smaller destinations; TANS, the commercial arm of the Peruvian Air Force; and Lan Chile, which has strong links with Lan Chile. A couple of smaller companies – Aero Condor and ATSA (for Cajamarca) – are offering expanded or new domestic services. **Tickets** can be bought from travel agents or airline offices in all major towns. The most popular routes, such as Lima–Cusco cost upwards of $50 and usually need to be booked at least a few days in advance (more during the run-up to and including major fiestas). Other, less busy routes tend to be less expensive.

On all flights it's important to **confirm your booking** two days before departure. Flights are often cancelled or delayed, and sometimes they leave earlier than scheduled – especially in the jungle where the weather can be a problem. If a passenger hasn't shown up twenty minutes before the flight, the company can give the seat to someone on the waiting list, so it's best to be on time whether you're booked or are merely hopeful. The luggage allowance on all internal flights is 16kg, not including hand luggage.

There are also **small planes** (6- and 10-seaters) serving the jungle and certain parts of the coast. A number of small companies fly out of Jorge Chavez Airport in Lima most days (their counters are between the international check-in counters and the domestic departure area), but they have no fixed schedules and a reputation for being dangerous and poorly maintained. The jungle towns, such as Pucallpa, Tarapoto, Satipo and San Ramon, also tend to have small **air colectivo** companies operating scheduled services between larger settlements in the region, at quite reasonable rates. For an

expresso **air taxi**, which will take you to any landing strip in the country whenever you want, you'll pay over $200 an hour; this price includes the return journey, even if you just want to be dropped off.

All the Peruvian domestic airlines offering **flight passes** went bust in the late 1990s, and airline companies are still consequently in a state of flux in Peru. As new ones arrive and competition for passengers increases, passes are likely to become available again, and it's worth checking with your travel agent or with the major airlines on arrival in Peru.

Airlines in Peru

Aero Condor Juan de Arona 781, San Isidro, Lima ℡01/4425663.
Aero Continente Avenida José Pardo 605, Miraflores, Lima ℡01/2424260, Ⓦwww .aerocontinente.com.pe.
Aero Santander 2 de Mayo 294, Cusco ℡084/571754.
Lan Peru Avenida Los Incas 172, Eighth Floor, San Isidro, Lima ℡01/2138200 or 2138300, Ⓦwww.lanperu.com.
TANS Calle Belen 1015, Lima Centro and Av Arequipa 5200, Miraflores ℡01/2418510 or Avenida Inca Garcilaso de la Vega 981 ℡01/4249438 or Calle San Martin 550, Miraflores ℡01/4441919, for reservations call ℡01/2136000.

By car

Cars can be very handy for reaching remote rural destinations or sites, though, as stated before, not for exploring Lima.

If you bring a car into Peru that is not registered there, you will need to show (and keep with you at all times) a *libreta de pago por la aduana* (proof of customs payment) normally provided by the relevant automobile association of the country you are coming from. **Spare parts**, particularly tyres, will have to be carried as will a tent, emergency water and food. The chance of **theft** is quite high – the vehicle, your baggage and accessories are all vulnerable when parked.

What few **traffic signals** exist are either completely ignored or used at the drivers' "discretion". The pace is fast and roads everywhere are in bad shape: only the Panamerican Highway, running down the coast, and a few short stretches inland, are paved. **Mechanics** are generally good and always ingenious – they have to be, due to a lack of spare parts! Also, the 95-octane **petrol** is much cleaner than the 84, though both are cheap by European, North American or Australian and New Zealand standards. **International driving licences** are generally valid for thirty days in Peru, after which a permit is required from the Touring y Automóvil Club del Peru, Cesar Vallejo 699, Lince, Lima (Mon–Fri 9am–4.45pm; ☎01/4403270, ⓕ4225947, ⓦwww.hys.com.pe/tacp).

Renting a car costs much the same as in Europe and North America. The major rental firms all have offices in Lima, but outside the capital you'll generally find only local companies are represented; see the relevant Listings for details. You may find it more convenient to rent a car in advance from your own country (see below for details) – expect to pay around US$35/£21 a day, or US$200/£130 a week for the smallest car. In the jungle it's usually possible to **hire motorbikes** or **mopeds** by the hour or by the day: this is a good way of getting to know a town or to be able to shoot off into the jungle for a day.

Car rental agencies

Australia
Avis   ☎1800/225533
Budget   ☎1300/362848
Hertz   ☎1800/550067

New Zealand
Avis   ☎09/5262847
Budget   ☎09/3752222
Hertz   ☎09/3090989

North America
Avis   ☎1-800/331-1084
Budget   ☎1-800/527-0700
Dollar   ☎1-800/800-6000
Hertz   ☎1-800/654-3001(US)
              ☎1-800/263-0600 (Canada)

UK
Avis   ☎0990/900500
Budget   ☎0800/181181
Hertz   ☎0990/996699

By boat

There are no coastal **boat** services in Peru, but in many areas – on **Lake Titicaca** and

especially in the **jungle regions** – water is the obvious means of getting around. From Puno, on Lake Titicaca, there are currently no regular services to Bolivia by ship or hydrofoil (though check with the tour agencies in Puno), but there are plenty of smaller boats that will take visitors out to the various islands in the lake. These aren't expensive and a price can usually be negotiated down at the port.

In the jungle areas **motorized canoes** come in two basic forms: those with a large outboard motor and those with a Briggs and Stratton *peque-peque* engine. The outboard is faster and more manoeuvrable, but it costs a lot more to run. Occasionally you can hitch a ride in one of these canoes for nothing, but this may involve waiting around for days or even weeks and, in the end, most people expect some form of payment. More practical is to **hire a canoe** along with its guide/driver for a few days. This means searching around in the port and negotiating, but you can often get a *peque-peque* canoe from around $40–50 per day, which will invariably work out cheaper than taking an organized tour, as well as giving you the choice of guide and companions. Obviously, the more people you can get together, the cheaper it will be per person.

On foot

Even if you've no intention of doing any serious hiking, there's a good deal of walking involved in checking out many of the most enjoyable Peruvian attractions. Climbing from Cusco up to the fortress of Sacsayhuaman, for example, or wandering around at Machu Picchu, involves more than an average Sunday afternoon stroll. Bearing in mind the rugged terrain throughout Peru, the absolute minimum footwear is a strong pair of running shoes. Much better is a pair of hiking boots with good ankle support.

Hiking – whether in the desert, mountains or jungle – can be an enormously rewarding experience, but you should go properly equipped and bear in mind a few of the **potential hazards**. Never stray too far without food and water, something warm and something waterproof to wear. The weather is renowned for its dramatic changeability, especially in **the mountains**, where there is always the additional danger of *soroche* (altitude sickness – see p.24). In **the jungle** the biggest danger is getting lost. If this happens, the best thing to do is follow a water course down to the main stream, and stick to this until you reach a settlement or get picked up by a passing canoe. If you get caught out in the forest at night, build a leafy shelter and make a fire or try sleeping in a tree.

In the mountains it's often a good idea to hire a **pack animal** to carry your gear. **Llamas** can only carry about 25–30kg and move slowly, a **burro** (donkey) carries around 80kg, and a **mule** – the most common and best pack animal – will shift 150kg with relative ease. Mules can be hired from upwards of $5 a day, and they normally come with an *arriero*, a muleteer who'll double as a guide. It is also possible to hire mules or horses for **riding** but this costs a little more. With a guide and beast of burden it's quite simple to reach even the most remote valleys, ruins and mountain passes, travelling in much the same way as Pizarro and his men over four hundred years ago.

Hitching

Hitching in Peru usually means catching a ride with a truck driver, who will almost always expect payment. Always agree a sum before getting in as there are stories of drivers stopping in the middle of nowhere and demanding unreasonably high amounts (from foreigners and Peruvians alike) before going any further. Hitching isn't considered dangerous in Peru, but having said that, few people, even Peruvians, actually hitch. Trucks can be flagged down anywhere but there is greater choice around markets, and at police *controls* or petrol stations on the outskirts of towns. Trucks tend to be the only form of public transport in some less accessible regions, travelling the roads that buses won't touch and serving remote communities, so you may end up having to sit on top of a pile of potatoes or bananas.

Hitchhiking in **private cars** is not recommended, and, in any case, it's very rare that one will stop to pick you up.

Organized tours

There are hundreds of **travel agents** and **tour operators** in Peru, and reps hunt out customers at bus terminals, train stations and in city centres. While they can be expensive, **organized excursions** can be a quick and relatively effortless way to see some of the popular attractions and the more remote sites, while a prearranged trek of something like the Inca Trail can take much of the worry out of camping preparations and ensure that you get decent campsites, a sound meal and help with carrying your equipment in what can be difficult walking conditions.

Many **adventure tour companies** offer excellent and increasingly exciting packages and itineraries – ranging from mountain biking, whitewater rafting, jungle photo-safaris, mountain trekking and climbing, to more comfortable and gentler city and countryside tours. Tours cost $35–200 a day and, in Cusco and Huaraz in particular, there's an enormous selection of operators to choose from. **Cusco** is a pretty good base for hiking, whitewater rafting, canoeing, horse-riding or going on an expedition into the Amazonian jungle with an adventure tour company (see p.151); **Arequipa** and the **Colca Canyon** offer superb hiking and the surrounding area boasts two of the deepest canyons on the planet, all serviced by tour companies (see p.256); **Huaraz** is a good base for trekking and mountaineering; **Iquitos**, on the Amazon river, is one of the best places for adventure trips into the jungle and has a reasonable range of tour operators (see p.479). Several of these companies have branches in Lima, if you want to book a tour in advance; see Lima Listings on p.103. For up-to-the-minute information and recommendations, contact the Asociación Peruana de Operadores de Turismo, Bajada Balta 169, Dpto 203, Miraflores (℡01/4460422, ℂapotur@amauta.rcp.net .pe), or the Asociación Peruana de Tursimo de Aventura y Ecoturismo, Santander 170, Miraflores (℡01/2214283).

Adventure- and ecotourism

Few of the world's countries can offer anything remotely as varied, rugged, remote and stunningly beautiful as Peru when it comes to ecotourism and trekking. Ecotourism is most developed in the Amazon rainforest region of Peru, particularly around Iquitos, Manu and the Tambopata region around Puerto Maldonado. In these areas there's a wide choice of operators leading tours up rivers, to jungle lodges as bases from which to explore the forest on foot and in smaller, quieter canoes. The focus is on wildlife and flora. There are often cultural elements to tours, including short visits to riverside communities, and, sometimes, indigenous Indian villages. Prices vary and so does the level of service and accommodation quality as well as the degree of sustainability of the operation. One or two operators pride themselves on their enlightened approach to wildlife and promote the fact that they don't have pets or caged animals at their lodges.

Ecotourism is also very much alive in the Peruvian Andes, too, with several tour operators offering expeditions on foot or on horseback into some of the more exotic high Andes and cloud forest regions. The most popular areas for these are the same as the **trekking zones**: north and south of Cusco; the Colca Canyon; and the Cordillera Blanca. But there are many other equally biodiverse and culturally rich trekking routes in other departmentos. Cajamarca and Chachapoyas possess challenging but rewarding mountain trekking. The desert coast, too, has exceptional and unique econiches which are most easily explored from Lima, Trujillo, Chiclayo, Nazca, Pisco, Ica and Arequipa where there is some tourism infrastructure to support visits.

The main tours and treks have been listed throughout the Guide in their appropriate geographical context. Chapter Five, which includes Huaraz and the Cordillera Blanca, contains further information on trekking in the Andes, or Andinismo (see p.305). The Cusco and Arequipa chapters also contain extensive listings of tour and trek operators as well as camping and climbing equipment rental.

Mountaineering and winter sports information

Casa de Guías Parque Ginebra 28-G, Huaraz (Mon–Fri 9am–1pm & 4–8pm, Sat 9am–1pm; ☎044/721811, ℱ722306, ⊛www.clientes .telematic.com.pe/agmp.

Club Andino Peruano Avenida Dos de Mayo 1545, Oficina 216, Lima 27.
Club de Andinismo de la Universidad de Lima Avenida Javier Prado Este, Lima 33 ☎01/4376767, extension 30775.
Club de Montañismo Américo Tordoya Tarapacá 384, Lima ☎01/4606101 or 4311305.
Federación Peruana de Andinismo y Desportes de Invierno block 3 of Jose Diaz, Lima Centro ☎01/4240063.
South American Explorers' Club (see p.27).

Canoeing and whitewater rafting

Again, Peru is hard to beat for these adventurous activities. The rivers around Cusco and the Colca Canyon, as well as Huaraz and, nearer to Lima, at Lunahuana, can be exciting and demanding, though there are always sections also ideal for beginners.

Cusco is one of the top **whitewater rafting and canoeing** centres in South America, with easy access to a whole range of river grades, from 2, 3, 4 and 5 on the Río Urubamba (shifting up grades in the rainy season) to the most dangerous whitewater on the Río Apurimac. On the Vilcanota, some 90km south of Cusco, at Chukikahuana there's a 5km section of river which, between December and April, offers a constant level 5 (see Chapter Two for more information). One of the most amazing trips from Cusco goes right down into the **Amazon Basin** (see Chapter Eight). It should be noted that these rivers can be very wild and the best canoeing spots are often very remote, so you should only attempt running rivers with reputable companies and knowledgeable local guides.

The main companies operating in this field are listed in the relevant chapters. Trips range from half-day to several days of river adventure, sometimes encompassing both mountain and jungle terrain. Transport, food and accommodation are generally included in the price where relevant; but the costs also depend on levels of service and overnight accommodation required.

Cycling

In Peru, **cycling** is a major national sport, as well as one of the most ubiquitous forms of transport available to all classes in towns and rural areas virtually everywhere. Consequently, there are bike shops and bicycle repairs workshops in all major cities and larger towns. Perhaps more importantly, a number of tour companies offer **guided cycling tours** which can be an excellent way to the best of Peru. Huaraz and Cusco are both popular destinations for bikers.

In Lima, **Cycling equipment** is available from: Biclas, Av. Conquistadores 641, San Isidro (℡01/4400890); Bike Mavil, Av. Aviación 4011 (℡01/4498435, ℮bikemavil @correo.dnet.com.pe); Cicloroni, Calle de Las Casas, block 32, Av. Petit Thouars, San Isidro (℡01/2217643); and Will-Pro, Av. 2 de Mayo 430, San Isidro (℡01/2220289). And excellent tours in a number of Peru's regions are run by the very professional outfit Peru Expeditions, Av. Arequipa 5241 – 504, Miraflores (℡01/4472057, ℻4459683, ℗www.peru-expeditions.com), who specialise in mountain biking, but also offer tours on the coast to Pisco, Ica, Nazca as well as up to Arequipa, Cusco and sometimes the Huaraz area (with 4WD support vehicle). In Cusco, **bicycle hire** is available from Bicycle Centro Atoq, Calle Saphi 674 (℡084/236324), which apparently has a high standard of bike maintenance (expect to pay around $5 an hour and $30 for a day and try and book in advance if possible). For **mountain biking tours** there is Ecomontana, Calle Garcilaso 265, Of. 3, a professionally run company operating 30 different circuits; and Vision Trek, at Portal de Harinas 181 (℡084/243039, ℗www .quia.happy.com), can organize mountain biking.

In Arequipa, **mountain bike hire** is available from the reputable Campamento Base, Jerusalen 401b (℡054/424223 or 202768). Around Huaraz, **Mountain Bike Adventures**, Jiron Lucre y Torre 530, second floor, or by post Casilla Postal 111, Huaraz (℡044/724259, ℗www.andeanexplorer.com /chakinaniperu), have a wonderful website with a wide range of information and offer guided bike tours and rent mountain bikes (TREK USA 850 with front suspension) and helmets; they also have English-speaking guides and run three spectacular routes that cross the Cordillera over mountain passes around 5000m on circuits lasting from 4 to 7 days (for cyclists with particular interests they offer a variety of alternative routes – such as Ulta–Chacas–Chavin loop).

For further information check the relevant chapter sections or contact the Federación Peruana de Ciclismo, Estadio Nacional, Lima Centro (℡01/4336646, ℮fpciclo @infomodem.com.pe; Mon–Fri 9am–1pm & 2–5pm).

Surfing

People have been **surfing** the waves off the coast of Peru for thousands of years and the traditional *caballitos de tortora* from the Huanchaco (p.377) and Chiclayo (p.418) beach areas of Peru are still used by fishermen who ride the surf daily. Every year around 12,000 surfers come to Peru whose best beaches – Chicama, Cabo Blanco, Punta Rocas – rival those of Hawaii and Brazil. Good websites to find out more about the scene include: ℗www.perutravels.net and ℗www .enjoyperu.com/deporteavent/tab.

The environment and ethical tourism

Tourism's growth in Peru over the past decade has been spectacular. It has been a boon for the economy, but with serious and potentially disruptive effects environmentally, socially, culturally, and economically. Machu Picchu and the Inca Trail are Peru's most significant honey-pots as far as tourism goes and there are already serious problems of degradation which are demanding new management measures.

Local issues have been covered throughout this book. If you are at all concerned about the impact of tourism or environmental matters, get in touch with the organizations mentioned in the text, or the ones listed below. Read also "Wildlife and ecology" (p.572) and "Indigenous rights and the destruction of the rainforest" (p.584), both in the Contexts section of this book.

Contacts

Campaign for Environmentally Responsible Tourism (CERT) ⓦ www.c-e-r-t.org. Lobbies to educate tour operators and tourists in a sensitive approach to travel, focusing on immediate practical ways in which the environment can be protected.

Partners in Responsible Tourism (PIRT) ⓦ www.pirt.org, ⓔ info@pirt.org. An organization of individuals and travel companies promoting responsible tourism to minimize harm to the environment and local cultures. Their website features a "Traveler's Code for Traveling Responsibly".

Tourism Concern ☎ 020/7753 3330, ⓦ www.tourismconcern.org.uk. Campaigns for the rights of local people to be consulted in tourism developments affecting their lives, and produces a quarterly magazine of news and articles. Also publishes the *Good Alternative Travel Guide*. Their website lists tour operators that run trips to Peru which are sensitive to the concerns of local peoples.

Accommodation

Peru has the typical range of Latin American accommodation, from top-class international hotels at prices to compare with any Western capital down to basic rooms or shared dorms in hostals, which are unaffiliated to Hostelling International. The biggest development over the last ten years has been the rise of the mid-range option, reflecting the growth of both domestic and international tourism. Camping is frequently possible, sometimes free and perfectly acceptable in most rural parts of Peru, though there are very few formal campsites.

Accommodation denominations of *hotel*, *hostal*, *residencial*, *pensión* or *hospedaje* are almost meaningless in terms of what you'll find inside. Virtually all upmarket accommodation will call itself a **hotel** or, in the countryside regions, a **posada**. In the jungle, *tambo* **lodges** can be anything from quite luxurious to an open-sided, palm-thatched hut with space for slinging a hammock. Technically speaking, somewhere that calls itself a *pensión* or *residencial* ought to specialize in longer-term accommodation, and while they may well offer discounts for stays of a week or more, they are just as geared up for short stays.

There's no standard or widely used rating system, so, apart from the information given in this book, the only way to tell whether a place is suitable or not is to walk in and take a look around – the proprietors won't mind this, and you'll soon get used to spotting places with promise. A handy phrase is "*quisiera ver un cuarto (con cama matrimonial)*" ("I'd like to see a (double) room").

Hotels

The **cheaper hotels** are generally old – sometimes beautifully so, converted from colonial mansions with rooms grouped

---

Accommodation price codes

Unless otherwise indicated, **accommodation** in this book is coded according to the categories below, based on the average price of a double room in high season.

❶ under $5	❹ $15-25	❼ $50–70
❷ $5–10	❺ $25-40	❽ over $70
❸ $10-15	❻ $40–50	

around a courtyard – and tend to be within a few blocks of a town's central plaza, general market, or bus or train station. At the low end of the scale, which can be fairly basic with shared rooms and a communal bathroom, you can usually find a bed for between $5 and $10, and occasionally even less. For a few dollars more you can find a good, clean single or double room with private bath in a **mid-range hotel**, generally for somewhere between $15 and $45. A little haggling is often worth a try, and if you find one room too pricey, another, perhaps identical, can often be found for less: the phrase "*Tiene un cuarto más barato?*" ("Do you have a cheaper room?") is useful. Savings can invariably be made, too, by sharing rooms – many have two, three, even four or five beds. A double-bedded room (*con cama matrimonial*) is usually cheaper than one with two beds (*con dos camas*).

The privatized chain of formerly state-run hotels – *Hotels de Turistas* – has been carved up and the hotels sold off to a number of entrepreneurs. The hotels can be found in all the larger Peruvian resorts as well as some surprisingly offbeat ones, often being the only place around with a swimming pool and generally among the flashiest places in town. Since privatization they have lost their corporate-chain image and are increasingly being known by new names, though taxi drivers will still recognize them as *Hotels de Turistas*. They still tend to be among the best **upmarket accommodation** options in all towns outside of Lima. Out of season some of these can be relatively inexpensive (from around $15–20 per person), and if you like the look of a place it's often worth asking. Note that all luxury hotels in Peru charge eighteen percent **tax** and often ten percent **service** on top of this again; always check beforehand whether the quoted price includes these extras. There are few five-star hotels in Peru and they are nearly all in Lima. Arequipa, Cusco, Trujillo and Iquitos all have top-quality accommodation, mainly in spacious traditional or modern purpose-built properties. Five- and four-star accommodation offers excellent service, some fine restaurants and very comfortable rooms with well-stocked minibars. In the mid-range options, generally three-star, the service on offer is often still good, but the food and luxury levels, particularly in the bathrooms, are significantly lower (though you can still expect towels, hot water etc).

One point of caution – it's not advisable to pay tour or travel agents in one city for accommodation required in the next town. By all means ask agents to make reservations but do not ask them to send payments; it is always simpler and safer to do that yourself.

Youth hostels

There are currently 28 **youth hostels** (*hostals*) spread throughout Peru. They are not the standardized institution found in Europe, but are relatively cheap and reliable; expect to pay $4–10 for a bed, perhaps slightly more in Lima. All hostels are theoretically open 24 hours a day and most have cheap cafeterias attached. Many of the hostels don't check that you are a member, but if you want to be on the safe side, you can join up at the Asociación Peruana de Albergues Turísticos Juveniles, Casimiro Ulloa 328, Miraflores (☎01/4465488 or 2423068, ℉4448187, ⓦwww.limahostell .com.pe). You can get a full list of all the country's hostels here, and they can also make advance bookings for you.

Camping

Camping is possible almost everywhere in Peru, and it's rarely difficult to find space for a tent. Camping is free since there are only one or two organized campsites in the whole country. It's also the most satisfactory way of seeing Peru, as some of the country's most fantastic places are well off the beaten track: with a tent – or a hammock – it's possible to go all over without worrying if you'll make it to a hostel.

It's usually okay to set up camp in fields or forest beyond the outskirts of settlements, but ask **permission** and advice from the nearest farm or house first. Apart from a few restricted areas, Peru's enormous sandy coastline is open territory, the real problem not being so much where to camp as how to get there; some of the most stunning areas are very remote. The same can be said of both the mountains and the jungle – camp anywhere, but ask first, if you can find anyone to ask.

There have been reports of tourists being attacked and robbed while camping in fairly **remote areas**. Reports of robberies, particularly along such popular routes as the Inca Trail, are not uncommon; so travelling with someone else or in groups is always a good idea. But even on your own there are a few basic **precautions** that you can take: let someone know where you intend to go; be respectful, and try to communicate with any locals you may meet or be camping near; and be careful who you make friends with en route.

Camping equipment is difficult to find in Peru and relatively expensive. One or two places sell, rent or buy secondhand gear, mainly in Cusco, Arequipa and Huaraz, and there are some reasonably good, if quite

expensive, shops in Lima. It's also worth checking the noticeboards in the popular traveller's hotels and bars for equipment that is no longer needed or for people wanting trekking companions – something you might find useful to do yourself to cut down on baggage, or by hawking it around the rental shops. Camping Gaz butane canisters are available from most of the above places and from some *ferreterías* (hardware stores) in the major resorts. A couple of essential things you'll need when camping in Peru are a mosquito net and repellent, and some sort of water treatment system (see p.24).

Eating and drinking

As with almost every activity, the style and pattern of eating and drinking varies considerably between the three main regions of Peru. The food in each area, though it varies depending on availability of different regional ingredients, is essentially a *mestizo* creation, combining indigenous Indian cooking with four hundred years of European – mostly Spanish – influence.

Guinea pig (*cuy*) is the traditional dish most associated with Peru, and you can find it in many parts of the country, especially in the mountain regions, where it is likely to be roasted in an oven and served with chips. It's possible, however, that hamburgers and pizza are more readily available than guinea pig – given that fast food has spread so quickly in Peru over the past two decades.

Snacks and light meals

All over Peru, but particularly in the large towns and cities, you'll find a good variety of traditional fast foods and snacks such as *salchipapas* (fries with sliced sausage covered in various sauces), *anticuchos* (a shish kebab made from marinated lamb or beef heart) and *empanadas* (meat- or cheese-filled pies). These are all sold on street corners until late at night. Even in the villages you'll find cafés and restaurants which double as bars, staying open all day and serving anything from coffee with bread to steak and fries or lobster. The most popular sweets in Peru are made from either

manjar blanco (sweetened condensed milk) or fresh fruits.

In general, the **market** is always a good place to head for – you can buy food ready to eat on the spot or to take away and prepare, and the range and prices are better than in any shop. Most food prices are fixed, but the vendor may throw in an orange, a bit of garlic, or some coriander leaves for good measure. Markets are the best places to stock up for a trek, for a picnic, or if you just want to eat cheaply. Smoked meat, which can be sliced up and used like salami, is normally a good buy.

Restaurants

All larger towns in Peru have a fair choice of **restaurants**, most of which offer a varied menu. Among them there's usually a few *chifa* (**Chinese**) places, and nowadays a fair number of **vegetarian** restaurants too. Most restaurants in the larger towns stay open seven days a week from around 11am until 11pm, though in smaller settlements they may close one day a week, usually Sunday.

Often they will offer a *cena*, or **set menu**, from morning through to lunchtime and another in the evening. Ranging in price from $1 to $3, these most commonly consist of three courses: soup, a main dish, and a cup of tea or coffee (which appears to count as a course) to follow. Every town, too, seems now to have at least one restaurant that specializes in *pollos a la brasa* – spit-roasted chickens. **Tipping** in budget or average restaurants is normal, though not obligatory and you should rarely expect to give more than about 50¢. In fancier places you may well find a **service charge** of ten percent as well as a **tax** of eighteen percent added to the bill, and in restaurants and peñas where there's live music or performances the **cover charge** can go up to $5. Even without a performance, cover charges of around $1 are sometimes levied in the flashier restaurants in major town centres.

Along the coast, not surprisingly, **seafood** is the speciality. The Humboldt Current keeps the Pacific Ocean off Peru extremely rich in plankton and other microscopic life forms, which attract a wide variety of fish. Ceviche is the classic Peruvian seafood dish and has been eaten by locals for over two thousand years. It consists of fish, shrimp, scallops or squid, or a mixture of all four, marinated in lime juice and chilli peppers, then served "raw" with corn and sweet potato and onions. *Ceviche de lenguado* (soul fish) and *ceviche de corvina* (sea bass) are among the most common, but there are plenty of other fish and a wide range of seafoods utilized and on most menus. You can find it, along with fried fish and fish soups, in most restaurants along the coast for around $2. *Escabeche* is another tasty fish-based appetizer, this time incorporating peppers and finely chopped onions. The coast is also an excellent place for eating scallops – known here as *conchitas* – which grow particularly well close to the Peruvian shoreline. *Conchitas negras* (black scallops) are a delicacy in the northern tip of Peru. Excellent **salads** are also widely available, such as *huevos a la rusa* (egg salad), *palta rellena* (stuffed avocado), or a straight tomato salad, while *papas a la Huancaina* (a cold appetizer of potatoes covered in a spicy light cheese sauce) is great too.

Mountain food is more basic – a staple of potatoes and rice with the meat stretched as far as it will go. *Lomo saltado*, or diced prime beef sautéed with onions and peppers, is served anywhere at any time, accompanied by rice and a few French fries. A delicious snack from street vendors and cafés is *papa rellena*, a potato stuffed with vegetables and fried. **Trout** is also widely available, as are cheese, ham and egg sandwiches. *Chicha*, a **corn beer** drunk throughout the *sierra* region and on the coast in rural areas, is very cheap with a pleasantly tangy taste. Another Peruvian speciality is the *Pachamanca*, a roast prepared mainly in the mountains but also on the coast by digging a large hole, filling it with stones and lighting a fire over them, then using the hot stones to cook a wide variety of tasty meats and vegetables.

In the **jungle**, the food is different. **Bananas** and **plantains** figure highly, along with *yuca* (a manioc rather like a yam), rice and plenty of fish. There is **meat** as well, mostly chicken supplemented occasionally by **game** – deer, wild pig, or even monkey. Every settlement big enough to get on the map has its own bar or café, but in remote areas it's a matter of eating what's available and drinking coffee or bottled drinks if you don't relish the homemade *masato* (cassava beer).

Drinking

Beers, wines and spirits are served in almost every bar, café or restaurant at any time, but there is a deposit on taking beer bottles out (canned beer is one of the worst inventions to hit Peru this century – some of the finest beaches are littered with empty cans).

Most **Peruvian beer** – except for *cerveza malta* (black malt beer) – is bottled lager almost exclusively brewed to five percent alcohol content, and extremely good. In Lima the two main beers are Cristal and Pilsen. Cusqueña (from Cusco) is one of the best and by far the most popular at the moment, but not universally available; you won't find it on the coast in Trujillo, for example, where they drink Trujillana, nor are you likely to encounter it in every bar in Arequipa where, not surprisingly perhaps, they prefer to drink Arequipeña beer. You can usually buy Cuzqueña in Lima, though. **Soft drinks** range from mineral water, through the ubiquitous Coca Cola and Fanta, to home-produced novelties like the gold-coloured Inka Cola, with rather a homemade taste, and the red, extremely sweet Cola Inglesa. **Fruit juices** (*jugos*), most commonly papaya or orange, are prepared fresh in most places, and you can get **coffee** and a wide variety of herb and leaf **teas** almost anywhere. Surprisingly, for a good coffee-growing country, the coffee in cafés and restaurants leaves much to be desired, commonly prepared from either *café pasado* (previously passed or percolated coffee mixed with hot water to serve) or simple powdered Nescafé. You have to search out the odd café in larger towns that prepares good fresh espresso, cappuccino or filtered coffee.

Peru has been producing **wine** (*vino*) for over four hundred years, but with one or two exceptions it is not that good. Among the better ones are Vista Alegre (the Tipo Familiar label is generally OK) – not entirely reliable but only around $1 a bottle – and Tacama Gran Vino Blanco Reserva Especial, about $7 or $8 a bottle. A good Argentinian or Chilean wine will cost from $10 upwards.

As for **spirits,** Peru's main claim to fame is pisco. This is a white-grape brandy with a unique, powerful and very palatable flavour – the closest equivalent elsewhere is probably tequila. Almost anything else is available as an import – Scotch whisky is cheaper here than in the UK – but beware of the really cheap whisky imitations or blends bottled outside of Scotland which can remove the roof of your mouth with ease. The jungle regions produce *cashassa*, a sugar-cane rum also called *aguardiente*, which has a distinctive taste and is occasionally mixed with different herbs, some medicinal. Whilst it goes down easily, it's incredibly strong stuff and leaves you with a very sore head the next morning.

Communications: post, phones and Internet

Communictions in Peru have improved dramatically with the widespread availability of Internet cafés. The phone service, too, has improved in the last seven years since taken over by a Spanish company. Postal services are slow but quite acceptable for normal letters and postcards.

The postal service

The Peruvian postal service – branded as Serpost – is reasonably efficient, if slightly irregular. Letters from Europe and the US generally take around one or two weeks – occasionally less – while outbound letters to Europe or the US seem to take between ten days and three weeks. Stamps for airmail letters to the UK, the US, and to Australia and New Zealand all cost around $1.

Be aware that **parcels** are particularly vulnerable to being opened en route – in either direction – and expensive souvenirs can't be sure of leaving the building where you mail them. Likewise, Peruvian postal workers are liable to "check" incoming parcels which contain cassettes or interesting foods.

Poste restante

You can have mail sent to you **poste restante** care of any main post office (Correo Central), and, on the whole, the system tends to work quite smoothly. Have letters addressed: full name (last name in capitals), Poste Restante, Lista de Correos, Correo Central, city or town, Peru. To pick up mail you'll need your passport, and you may have to get the files for the initials of all your names (including Ms, Mr, etc) checked. Rather quirkily, letters are sometimes filed separately by sex, too – in which case it's worth getting both piles checked. Some post offices let you look through the pile, others won't let you anywhere near the letters until they've found one that fits your name exactly.

An alternative to the poste restante is to use the **American Express** mail collection service. Their main offices in Peru are in Lima at Pardo y Aliaga 698, San Isidro ☎4414744, ✆4414660. Officially, American Express charges for this service unless you have one of their cards or use their travellers' cheques, though they rarely seem to. The **South American Explorers'**

Club (see p.27) offers members a postal address service.

Telephones

With a little patience you can make **international calls** from just about any town in the country. In recent years the telephone system has dramatically improved, partly due to being taken over by a Spanish telephone company and partly because of modernization and an increasing use of satellites.

All Peruvian towns have a **Telefónica del Peru** or **Locutorio Telefónico** office, which offers an operator service; give the recep-

tionist your destination number and they will allocate you to a numbered phone booth when your call is put through (you pay afterwards); or, just dial direct from the booth. These offices also have phones taking cards (see below). In Lima, the central Telefónica del Peru office (see p.103) is often crowded, so a better option is to phone from your hotel or from the street **telephone kiosks**.

All phone kiosks are operated by coins or *tarjetas telefónicas* – **phone cards** – which are available in a variety of denominations, and nuevo sol coins. You can buy phone cards from corner shops, *farmacias* or on the street from cigarette stalls in the centres

Dialling codes and useful numbers

Useful telephone numbers
Directory enquiries ☎103
Emergency services ☎105
Operator ☎100
International operator ☎108

To phone abroad from Peru
Dial the country code (given below) + area code (minus initial zero) + number
Australia ☎0061
Canada ☎001
Ireland ☎00353
New Zealand ☎0064
UK ☎0044
USA ☎001

To phone Peru from abroad
Dial the international access code (see below) + 51 (country code for Peru) + area code in Peru (minus intitial zero; see below) + number.
International access code
Australia ☎0011
Canada ☎001
Ireland ☎00
New Zealand ☎00
UK ☎00
USA ☎001

Peruvian town and city codes
Please note that as this book went to press, Peru was undergoing massive changes with its phone code system; these changes are not reflected throughout the guide, but are listed below. Those entries that begin with an * denote locations

with new codes; the current code comes first, followed by the oudated number (in parentheses).

Arequipa ☎054
*Ayacucho ☎066 (064)
*Cajamarca ☎076 (044)
Cusco ☎084
Chiclayo ☎074
Chincha ☎034
*Huancavelica ☎067 (064)
Huancayo ☎064
*Huánuco ☎062 (064)
* Huaraz ☎043 (044)
*Ica ☎056 (034)
*Iquitos ☎065 (094)
Jauja ☎064
Juliaca ☎054
La Oroya ☎064
Lambayeque ☎074
Lima ☎01
*Moquegua ☎053 (054)
* Moyobamba ☎042 (094)
* Nazca ☎056 (034)
Pisac ☎084
* Pisco ☎056 (034)
*Piura ☎073 (074)
*Puerto Maldonado ☎082 (084)
*Pucallpa ☎061 (064)
*Puno T051 (054)
Quillabamba T084
*Tacna T052 (054)
* Tarapoto T042 (094)
Tarma T064
Trujillo T044
*Tumbes T072 (074)

of most towns and cities. There are currently two main phone outfits, Telefónica del Peru and Telepoint, both of which produce their own cards for use in their phones only.

Other companies, such as Nortek, offer cards with greater discounts, particularly on international calls from most types of street phone kiosks.

If you need to contact the **international operator**, dial ☎108. **Collect calls** are known either simply as *collect* or *al cobro revertido* and are fairly straightforward. Calls are cheaper at night. Most shops, restaurants or corner shops in Peru have a phone available for public use, which you can use for calls within Peru only.

Mobile phones

If you want to use your **mobile phone** abroad, you'll need to check with your phone provider whether it is will work abroad, and what the call charges are.

The Internet

Peru has good **Internet** connections, with cyber cafés and Internet cabins in the most unlikely of small towns, breaking down barriers of distance more effectively than the telephone ever did. Lima and Cusco have abundant Internet facilities, closely followed by Arequipa, Huaraz, Puno, Iquitos and Trujillo; beyond that it gets a little patchy, but the odd public access office or café does exist and many hotels now offer access too. Most seem to have reasonably fast DSL or ADSL connections with Explorer, Netscape and Hotmail readily available. The general rate is 50¢ to $1 an hour, though thirty- and fifteen-minutes options are often available. One of the most widespread and professional **service providers** in Peru is RCP (Red Científica Peruana) ⓔwebmaster@rcp.net.pe.

The media

There are many poor-quality newspapers and magazines available on the streets of Lima and throughout the rest of Peru. Many of the newspapers stick mainly to sex and sport, while magazines tend to focus on terror and violence and the frequent deaths caused by major traffic accidents. Meanwhile, many get their news and information from television and radio, where you also have to wade through the panoply of entertainment-oriented options.

Newspapers and magazines

The two most established (and establishment) **daily newspapers** are *El Comercio* and *Expreso* the latter devoting vast amounts of space to anti-Communist propaganda. *El Comercio* (ⓦwww.elcomercio.com.pe) is much more balanced but still tends to toe the political party of the day's line. *El Comercio*'s daily *Seccion C* also has the most comprehensive cultural listings of any paper – good for just about everything going on in Lima. In addition, there's the sensationalist tabloid *La Republica* (ⓦwww.larepublica.com.pe),

which takes a middle-of-the-road to liberal approach to politics; and *Cambio*, which provides interesting tabloid reading. One of the better weekly **magazines** is the fairly liberal *Caretas*, generally offering mildly critical support to whichever government happens to be in power. There's one environmental and travel magazine – *Rumbos* – which publishes articles in both Spanish and English and has excellent photographic features.

Cusco Weekly (ⓦwww.cuscoweekly.com) is an excellent **English-language newspaper**, available in the major cities. It reports on issues relevant to tourism plus news around South America and world issues. The business weekly *Lima Herald*, also in English, can be bought in Lima Centro and sporadically in Cusco. For more serious, in-depth coverage, the *Lima Post* is available online (ⓦ www.limapost.com) with good coverage of Peruvian and Latin American news, politics and business.

International newspapers are fairly hard to come by; your best bet for **English papers** is to go to the Embassy in Lima, which has a selection of one- to two-week-old papers, such as *The Times* and *Independent*, for reference only. **US papers** are easier to find; the bookstalls around Plaza San Martin in Lima Centro and those along Avenida Larco and Diagonal in Miraflores sell the *Miami Herald*, the *Herald Tribune*, and *Newsweek* and *Time* magazines, but even these are likely to be four or five days old. If you're not moving around too much, consider having *The Guardian Weekly*, which has comprehensive international coverage, sent to you poste restante.

Television and radio

Peruvians watch a lot of **television** – mostly soccer and soap operas, though TV is also a main source of news. Many programmes come from Mexico, Brazil and the US (*The Flintstones* and *Bewitched* are perennial favourites), with occasional eccentric selections from elsewhere and a growing presence of manga-style cartoons. There are nine main terrestrial channels, of which channels 7 and 13 show marginally better-quality programmes.

Cable and **satellite channels** are increasingly forming an important part of Peru's media. Partly due to the fact that it can be received in even the remotest of settlements and partly because it is beyond the control of any government or other censorship, satellite TV appears set to dominate the media scene and the worldview of the nation's youth.

If you have a **radio** you can pick up the BBC World Service at most hours of the day – frequencies shift around on the 19m, 25m and 49m short-wave bands; for a schedule of programmes, contact the British Council in Lima (see p.101). The Voice of America is also constantly available on short wave. The radio station Sol Armonia is dedicated to classical music on FM89. Also, the RPP (Radio Programmes del Peru) on FM 89.7 has 24-hour news bulletins.

Alternatively, you can tune in to an incredible mess of **Peruvian stations**, nearly all of which play music and are crammed with adverts. International pop, salsa and other Latin pop can be picked up most times of the day and night all along the FM wave band, while traditional Peruvian and Andean folk music can usually be found all over the AM dial. Radio Miraflores (96FM) is one of the best, playing mainly disco and new US/British rock, though also with a good jazz programme on Sunday evenings and an excellent news summary every morning from 7 to 9am. Radio Cien (100FM) has the occasional programme in English (on Sunday mornings, for example).

Crime and personal safety

The biggest problem for travellers in Peru is, without a doubt, thieves, for which the country has one of the worst reputations in South America. Whilst pickpockets are remarkably ingenious in Peru, this country no longer deserves such a poor reputation when compared to Venezuela, Colombia and even Ecuador or Brazil. As far as violent attacks go, you're probably safer in Peru than in New York, Sydney or London; nevertheless muggings do happen in certain parts of Lima (eg in the Centro main shopping areas and also in the parks of Miraflores), Cusco, Arequipa and to a lesser extent Trujillo. And as for terrorism – as the South American Explorers' Club once described it – "the visitor, when considering his safety, would be better off concentrating on how to avoid being run over in the crazed Lima traffic".

Theft

The dangers of **pickpockets and robberies** cannot be over emphasized, though the situation does seem to have improved since the dark days of the late 1980s. Although you don't need to be in a perpetual state of paranoia and constant watchfulness in busy public situations, common sense and general alertness are still recommended. The South American Explorers' Club (see p.27) can give you the low-down on the latest thieving practices, some of which have developed over the years into quite elaborate and skilful techniques.

Generally speaking, **thieves** (*ladrones*) work in teams of often smartly dressed young men and women, in crowded markets, bus depots and train stations, targeting anyone who looks like they've got money. One of them will distract your attention (an old woman falling over in front of you or someone splattering an ice cream down your jacket) while another picks your pocket, cuts open your bag with a razor, or simply runs off with it. Peruvians and tourists alike have even had earrings ripped out on the street. Bank **ATMs** are a target for muggers in cities, particularly after dark, so visit them with a friend or two during daylight hours or make sure there's a policeman within visual contact. **Armed mugging** does happen in Lima, and it's best not to resist. The horrific practice of "strangle mugging" has been a bit of a problem in Cusco and Arequipa, usually involving night attacks when the perpetrator tries to strangle the victim into unconsciousness. Again, be careful not to walk down badly lit streets alone in the early hours. **Theft from cars** and even more so, theft of car parts, is rife, particularly in Lima. Also, in some of the more popular hotels in the large cities, especially Lima, bandits masquerading as policemen break into rooms and steal the guests' most valuable possessions while holding the hotel staff at gunpoint. Objects left on restaurant floors in busy parts of town, or in unlocked hotel rooms, are obviously liable to take a walk.

You'd need to spend the whole time visibly guarding your luggage to be sure of keeping hold of it; even then, though, a determined team of thieves will stand a chance. However, a few simple **precautions** can make life a lot easier. The most important is to keep your ticket, passport (and tourist card), money and travellers' cheques on your person at all times (under your pillow while sleeping and on your person when washing in communal hotel bathrooms). **Money belts** are a good idea for travellers' cheques and tickets, or a holder for your passport and money can be hung either under a shirt, or from a belt under trousers or skirts. A **false pocket**, secured by safety pins to the inside of trousers, skirts or shirts also makes it harder for thieves or muggers to find your cash reserve (and is easy to transfer between items of clothing). Some people go as far as lining their bags with chicken wire (called *maya* in Peru) to make them knife-proof, and wrapping wire around camera straps for the same reason (putting their necks in danger to save their cameras).

The only certain course is to **insure** your gear and cash before you go (see p.21). Take refundable travellers' cheques, register your passport at your embassy in Lima on arrival (this doesn't take long and can save days should you lose yours), and keep your eyes open at all times. If you do get ripped off, report it to the **tourist police** in larger towns (see p.46), or the local police in more remote places, and ask them for a certified *denuncia* – this can take a couple of days. Many insurance companies will require a copy of the police *denuncia* in order to reimburse you, though some only require proof of your whereabouts at the time of the incident (for example a hotel bill or a tour company letter or report). Check with your insurance company before leaving for Peru as to what their requirements are.

Cities are most dangerous in the early hours of the morning and at bus or train stations where there's lots of anonymous activity. In rural areas robberies tend to be linked to the most popular towns (again, be most careful at the bus depot) and treks (the Inca Trail for instance). Beyond that, rural areas generally are and normally feel safe. If you're camping near a remote community, though, it's a good idea to ask permission and make friendly contact with some of the locals; and letting them know what you are up to will usually dissolve any local paranoia about tomb-robbers or kidnappers.

Terrorism

Terrorism is much less of a problem in Peru these days than it was in the 1980s and 1990s. You can get up-to-date information on the situation in each region from the South American Explorers' Club (see p.27), Peruvian embassies abroad (see p.18) or your embassy in Lima (see p.102). There are two main **terrorist groups** active in Peru – the Sendero Luminoso (the Shining Path) and Tupac Amaru (MRTA).

The **Sendero Luminoso** sprang from rural Quechua and educated middle-class dissidents originally operating mainly in the central highlands and Lima. They had a reputation in the past for ruthless and violent tactics, sweeping away all left-wing and popular resistance to their aims and methods by the rule of the gun. When their leader Guzman was captured in 1992, the movement began to fade fast, and with the cap-

ture of their number two, Feliciano, in 1999, it appears for now that their activities are limited almost exclusively to narco-terrorism (cocaine producing and smuggling) in the **Alto Huallaga** valley. This area – basically the region and road between Tingo Maria and Tarapoto – should still be avoided at all costs. It's often difficult to distinguish between drug trafficking and terrorism in certain places, and much of the coca-growing area of the eastern Andes and western Amazon is beyond the law.

The **Tupac Amaru**, on the other hand, have a slightly more populist image, focusing on military or political targets. They rose to prominence at Christmas 1996 when they took hostages at the Japanese Embassy in Lima, but this ended fatally for the terrorists and took the wind out of their sails quite severely. Incidents these days are very rare; they might still stop the odd bus in remote jungle areas, but they're more likely to ask for a "voluntary" contribution than execute the passengers on political grounds.

So far, neither group has resorted to taking foreigners hostage and tourists are not considered political targets. Keep to the beaten track, keep yourself well informed, travel in the daytime, and you should be safe. For more background on this subject, see Contexts, p.542.

The police

Most of your contact with the **police** will, with any luck, be at frontiers and *controls*. Depending on your personal appearance and the prevailing political climate the police at these posts (*Guardia Nacional* and *Aduanas*) may want to search your luggage. This happens rarely, but when it does it can be very thorough. Occasionally, you may have to get off buses and register documents at the police *controls* which regulate the traffic of goods and people from one *departmento* of Peru to another. The *controls* are usually situated on the outskirts of large towns on the main roads, but you sometimes come across a *control* in the middle of nowhere. Always stop, and be scrupulously polite – even if it seems that they're trying to make things difficult for you.

In general the police rarely bother travellers but there are certain sore points. The possession of (let alone trafficking in) either soft or hard **drugs** (basically grass or cocaine) is

Ⓑ

considered an extremely serious offence in Peru – usually leading to at least a ten-year jail sentence. There are many foreigners languishing in Peruvian jails after being charged with possession, some of whom have been waiting two years for a trial – there is no bail for serious charges. If you want to visit one of them you can get details from your embassy.

Drugs apart, the police tend to follow the media in suspecting all foreigners of being **political subversives** and even gun-runners or terrorists; it's more than a little unwise to carry any Maoist or radical literature. If you find yourself in a tight spot, don't make a statement before seeing someone from your embassy, and don't say anything without the services of a reliable translator. It's not unusual to be given the opportunity to pay a **bribe** to the police (or any other official for that matter), even if you've done nothing wrong. You'll have to weigh up this situation as it arises – but remember, in South America bribery is seen as an age-old custom, very much part of the culture rather than a nasty form of corruption, and it can work to the advantage of both parties, however irritating it might seem. It's also worth noting that all police are armed with either a revolver or a submachine gun and will shoot at anyone who runs.

The tourist police

It's often quite hard to spot the difference between tourist police and the normal police. Both are wings of the *Guardia Civil*, though the tourist police sometimes wear white hats rather than the standard green. Increasingly, the tourist police have taken on the functions of informing and assisting tourists (eg in preparing a robbery report or *denuncia*) in city centres. The best way to find them is through the relevant city listings.

If you're unlucky enough to have anything stolen, your first port of call should be the **tourist police** (*policía de turismo*), from whom you should get a written report. Bear in mind that the police in popular tourist spots, such as Cusco, have become much stricter about investigating reported thefts, after a spate of false claims by dishonest tourists. This means that genuine victims may be grilled more severely than expected, and the police may even come and search your hotel room for the "stolen" items. Peru's **headquarters** for the tourist police is the Centro Policial de Servicio al Turista in Lima at Jr Tambo Belen, Cercado Lima ☎01/4242053, Ⓔdirpolture@hotmail.com.

If you feel you've been ripped off or are unhappy about your treatment by a tour agent, hotel, restaurant, transport company, customs, immigration or even the police, you can call the 24-hour **Tourist Protection Service** hotline (Servicio de Protección al Turista, also known as i-peru, an arm of INDECOPI and PromPeru); see below for numbers to call. Staff are trained to handle complaints in English and Spanish. If an immediate solution is not possible, the service claims to follow up disputes by filing a formal complaint with the relevant authorities.

Tourist Protection Service

Main offices
Cusco INDECOPI, Portal de Carrizos 250, Plaza de Armas.
Lima Airport, Sala Principal
Ⓔiperu@promperu.gob.pe.

Hotline numbers
National toll-free 24hr ☎01/5748000
Arequipa ☎054/444564
Ayacucho ☎064/818305
Cusco ☎/Ⓔ084/252974
Iquitos ☎094/233409
Lima ☎01/5748000
Piura ☎074/332609
Puno ☎054/366138
Trujillo ☎044/294561

Living and/or working abroad

Your only real chance of earning money in Peru is teaching English in Lima, or, with luck, in Arequipa or Cusco. Given the state of the economy there's little prospect in other fields, though in the more remote parts of the country it may sometimes be possible to find board and lodging in return for a little building work or general labour.

There is an enormous amount of bureaucracy involved if you want to work (or live) officially in Peru. For biology, geography or environmental science graduates there's a chance of free board and lodging and maybe a small salary if you're willing to work very hard for at least three months as a tour guide in a jungle lodge, under the Resident Naturalist schemes. Several lodges along the Río Tambopata offer such schemes and other research opportunities. For more details, write to the lodges directly; for independent advice contact the Tambopata Reserve Society, PO Box 33153, London, NW3 4DR, UK. Arrangements need to be made at least six months in advance. Mosoq Ayllu Pasaje, San Antonio 113–115, San Carlos, Huancayo (☏064/223956, ✉mosoq_ayllu@yahoo.com), is a new organization with a volunteer programme; their aim is to help people in economically depressed communities in the Peruvian highlands through education, mainly teaching English, computing and artistic activities.

Teaching English

There are two options: find or prepare for finding work before you go, or just wing it and see what you come up with while you're out there, particularly if you already have a degree and/or teaching experience. **Teaching English** – often abbreviated as ELT (English Language Teaching) or TEFL (Teaching English as a Foreign Language) – is the way many people finance their way around the greater part of the world; you can get a CELTA (Certificate in English Language Teaching to Adults) qualification before you leave home or even while you're abroad. Strictly speaking, you don't need a degree to do the course, but you'll certainly find it easier to get a job with the degree/certificate combination. Certified by the RSA, the

course is very demanding and costs about £900 for the month's full-time tuition; you'll be thrown in at the deep end and expected to teach right away. The British Council's website (Ⓦwww.britishcouncil.org/work /jobs.htm) has a list of English-teaching vacancies.

Useful publications and websites

Another pre-planning strategy for working abroad, whether teaching English or otherwise, is to get hold of *Overseas Jobs Express* (☏01273/699611, Ⓦwww.overseasjobs .com), a fortnightly publication with a range of job vacancies, available by subscription only. Vacation Work also publishes books on summer jobs abroad and how to work your way around the world; call ☏01865/241978 or visit Ⓦwww.vacationwork.co.uk for their catalogue. The reliable travel magazine *Wanderlust* (Ⓦwww.wanderlust.co.uk) have a Job Shop section which often advertises job opportunities with tour companies, while Ⓦwww.studyabroad.com is a useful website with listings and links to study and work programmes worldwide.

Study and work programmes

Note: most universities have semester- or year-abroad programmes to certain countries; the following are independent organizations that run programmes in lots of countries.

From the US

Earthwatch Institute ☏1-800/776-0188 or 978/461-0081, Ⓦwww.earthwatch.org. International non-profit organization with offices in Boston, Oxford, Melbourne and Tokyo. Around 50,000 members and supporters are spread across the US, Europe, Africa, Asia and Australia and volunteer their time and skills to work with 120 research scientists each year on Earthwatch field research projects. In Peru they have university links and projects on archeology, macaws in the Amazon as well as river exploration.

Harper Collins Perseus Division ℡1-800/242-7737. Publishes *International Jobs: Where They Are, How to Get Them.*

Peace Corps ℡1-800/424-8580, ⓦwww.peacecorps.gov. Places people with specialist qualifications or skills in two-year postings in many developing countries. On December 12, 2001, Peru's president, Alejandro Toledo, officially invited the Peace Corps to return to Peru. Peace Corps Volunteers now serve in Peru by providing critical support to communities in two primary areas: small business development and community health promotion. In 2002, an estimated 27 Peace Corps Volunteers and Volunteer Trainees served in Peru.

Volunteers for Peace ℡802/259-2759, ⓦwww.vfp.org. Non-profit organization with links to a huge international network of "workcamps", two- to four-week programmes that bring volunteers together from many countries to carry out needed community projects. Most workcamps are in summer, with registration in April–May. Annual membership including directory costs $20. In Peru

most projects are located in remote Andean communities.

From the UK and Ireland

British Council ℡020/7930 8466. Produces a free leaflet which details study opportunities abroad. The Council's Central Management Direct Teaching (℡020/7389 4931) recruits TEFL teachers for posts worldwide (check ⓦwww.britishcouncil.org/work /jobs.htm for a current list of vacancies), and its Central Bureau for International Education and Training (℡020/7389 4004, ⓦwww.centralbureau .org.uk) enables those who already work as educators to find out about teacher development programmes abroad. It also publishes a book, *Year Between*, aimed principally at gap-year students detailing volunteer programmes, and schemes abroad.

Earthwatch Institute ℡01865/318838, ⓦwww.uk.earthwatch.org. Long-established international charity with environmental and archeological research projects worldwide (130 projects in around 55 countries). Participation mainly as a paying volunteer (pricey) but fellowships for teachers and students available. See under "From the US", above for more information on Peru programmes.

Travellers with disabilities

Peru is not well set up in terms of access infrastructure for welcoming travellers with disabilities, but nevertheless, in the moment many Peruvians will support and help. Even the best buses have mostly ordinary steps. Airlines have facilities and will assist in most of Peru's airports. Further information may be obtained from the South American Explorers' Club (see p.27). Lima is the only city where disabled access has been thought about for some of the upmarket hotels and restaurants; elsewhere it's really a free-for-all.

Contacts for travellers with disabilities

In the US and Canada

Access-Able ⓦwww.access-able.com. Online resource for travellers with disabilities.

Directions Unlimited 123 Green Lane, Bedford Hills, NY 10507 ℡1-800/533-5343 or 914/241-1700. Travel agency specializing in bookings for people with disabilities.

Mobility International USA 451 Broadway, Eugene, OR 97401 ℡541/343-1284, ℻343-6812, ⓦwww.miusa.org. Information and referral services,

access guides, tours and exchange programmes. Annual membership $35 (includes quarterly newsletter).

Society for the Advancement of Travelers with Handicaps (SATH) 347 5th Ave, New York, NY 10016 ℡212/447-7284, ⓦwww.sath.org. Non-profit educational organization that has actively represented travellers with disabilities since 1976.

Wheels Up! ℡1-888/389-4335, ⓦwww .wheelsup.com. Provides discounted airfare, tour and cruise prices for disabled travellers; also publishes a free monthly newsletter and has a comprehensive website.

In the UK and Ireland

Access Travel 6 The Hillock, Astley, Lancashire M29 7GW ☎ 01942/888844, ⓦ www.access-travel .co.uk. Tour operator that can arrange flights, transfers and accommodation. This is a small business, personally checking out places before recommendation.

Irish Wheelchair Association Blackheath Drive, Clontarf, Dublin 3 ☎ 01/818 6400, Ⓕ 833 3873, ⓦ www.iwa.ie. Useful information provided about travelling abroad with a wheelchair.

Tripscope Alexandra House, Albany Rd, Brentford, Middlesex TW8 0NE ☎ 0845/758 5641, Ⓕ 020/8580 7021, ⓦ www.justmobility.co.uk/trip-scope. This registered charity offers a national telephone information service offering free advice on UK and international transport for those with a mobility problem.

In Australia and New Zealand

ACROD (Australian Council for Rehabilitation of the Disabled) PO Box 60, Curtin, ACT 2605; Suite 103, 1st Floor, 1–5 Commercial Rd, Kings Grove 2208; ☎ 02/6282 4333, TTY 02/6282 4333, Ⓕ 6281 3488, ⓦ www.acrod.org.au,. Provides lists of travel agencies and tour operators for people with disabilities.

Disabled Persons Assembly 4/173–175 Victoria St, Wellington, New Zealand ☎ 04/801 9100 (also TTY), Ⓕ 801 9565, ⓦ www.dpa.org.nz. Resource centre with lists of travel agencies and tour operators for people with disabilities.

Senior travellers

Senior travellers in reasonable health should have no problem in Peru. Anyone taking medication should obviously bring enough supplies for the duration of the trip, though most drugs are available over the counter in Lima and other cities. The altitude is likely to be the most serious issue, so careful reading of the section on altitude sickness (p.24) becomes even more crucial. So does taking great care with what food you eat (see p.24).

As far as accommodation for seniors goes, most middle- to top-range hotels are clean and comfortable; it's mostly a matter of clearly asking for what you need when booking or on arrival at the hotel. This is particularly true if you have special requirements such as a ground-floor room.

Contacts for senior travellers

In the US

American Association of Retired Persons ☎ 1-800/424-3410 or 202/434-2277, ⓦ www.aarp.org. Can provide discounts on accommodation and vehicle rental. Membership open to US and Canadian residents aged 50 or over for an annual fee of US$12.50.

Elderhostel ☎ 1-877/426-8056, ⓦ www .elderhostel.org. Runs an extensive worldwide network of educational and activity programmes, cruises and homestays for people over 60 (companions may be younger). Programmes generally last a week or more and costs are in line with those of commercial tours.

Saga Holidays ☎ 1-800/343-0273, ⓦ www.sagaholidays.com. Specializes in worldwide group travel for seniors. Saga's Road Scholar coach tours and their Smithsonian Odyssey Tours have a more educational slant.

Vantage Deluxe World Travel ☎ 1-800/322-6677, ⓦ www.vantagetravel.com. Specializes in worldwide group travel for seniors.

In the UK

Saga Holidays ☎ 0130/377 1111, ⓦ holidays.saga.co.uk. The country's biggest and most established specialist in tours and holidays aimed at older people.

Travelling with children

South Americans hold the family unit in high regard and children are central to this, but outlined below are some pointers to help prepare for a family visit to Peru.

Consult your doctor before leaving home regarding **health issues**. Sunscreen is an important consideration, as are sun-hats (cheap and readily available in Peru) and even a parasol for the really small. Conversely, it can get cold at night in the Andes, so take plenty of warm clothing. In the mountains, the altitude doesn't seem to cause children as many problems as it does their elders, but they shouldn't walk too strenuously above 2000m without full acclimatization. In Lima, where the water is just about good enough to clean your teeth but not to drink, the issues for local children are mainly bronchial or asthmatic, with humid weather and high pollution levels causing many long-lasting chest ailments. This shouldn't be a problem for any visiting children unless they already have difficulties. The major risk around the regions is a bad stomach and **diarrhoea** from water or food. The best way to avoid and treat this is outlined on p.23; the only difference where children are concerned, particularly those under 10, is that you should be more ready to act sooner, particularly with rehydration salts. In the jungle, the same precautions for adults apply to children (see p.460).

The **food and drink** in Peru is varied enough to appeal to most kids. Pizzas are available almost everywhere, as are good fish, red meats, fried chicken, French fries, corn-on-the-cob and nutritious soups, and vitamin supplements are always a good idea. There's also a wide range of **soft drinks**, from the ubiquitous Coca Cola and Sprite to Inka Cola. Some recognizable commercial **baby food** (and nappy brands)

is available in all large supermarkets. **Restaurants** in Peru cater well to children and some offer smaller, cheaper portions; if they don't publicize it, it's worth asking.

Like restaurants, **hotels** are used to handling kids. They will sometimes offer discounts, especially if children share rooms or beds. The lower- to mid-range options are the most flexible in this regard, but even the expensive ones can be helpful. Many, hostels included, have collective rooms, large enough for families to share, at reasonable rates.

Prices can often be cheaper for children. Tours to attractions can occasionally be negotiated on a family-rate basis and entry to sites is often half-price or less (and always free for infants). Children under 10 generally get half-fare on local (but not inter-regional) buses, while trains and boats generally charge full fare if a seat is required. Infants who don't need a seat often travel free on all transport except planes, when you pay around ten percent of the fare.

Travelling around the country is perhaps the most difficult activity. Bus and train journeys are generally long (12 hours or more). Crossing international borders is a potential hassle; although Peru officially accepts children under 16 on their parents' **passports**, it is a good idea for them to have their own to minimize problems. For more information, contact Travel with Your Children (☎1-888/822-4388 or 212/477-5524), which publishes a regular newsletter, *Family Travel Times* (ⓦwww.familytraveltimes.com), as well as a series of books on travel with children.

Sex and gender issues

So many limitations are imposed on women's freedom to travel together or alone that any advice or warning seems merely to reinforce the situation. However, machismo is well ingrained in the Peruvian male mentality, particularly in the towns, and female foreigners are almost universally seen as liberated and therefore sexually available. Having said that, in most public places, women travelling on their own tend to get the "pobrecita" ("poor little thing") treatment because they are alone, without family or a man. In Cusco it's noticeable that gangs of trendy young Peruvian men make a living out of attaching themselves to gringas; they are collectively known locally as *bridgeros*, a term which hints at both sexual activity and being a bridge between two cultures.

Harassment and safety

On the whole, the situations female travellers will encounter are more annoying than dangerous, with frequent comments such as *que guapa* ("how pretty"), intrusive and prolonged stares, plus whistling and hissing in the **cities**. Worse still are the occasional rude comments and groping, particularly in crowded situations such as on buses or trains. Blonde and fair-skinned women are likely to suffer much more of this behaviour than darker, Latin-looking women. Mostly these are situations you'd deal with routinely at home – as Limeña women do here in the capital – but they can, understandably and rightly, seem threatening without a clear understanding of Peruvian Spanish and slang. To avoid getting caught up in something you can't control, any provocation is best ignored. In a public situation, however, any real harassment is often best dealt with by loudly drawing attention to the miscreant.

In the predominantly Indian, **remote areas** there is less of an overt problem, though surprisingly this is where physical assaults are more likely to take place. They are not common, however – you're probably safer hiking in the Andes than walking at night in most British or North American inner cities. Two obvious, but enduring, pieces of advice are to travel with friends (being on your own makes you most vulnerable), and if you're camping, to be quite open about it. As ever, making yourself known to locals gives a kind of acceptance and insurance, and it may even lead to the offer of a room – Peruvians, particularly those in rural areas, can be incredibly kind and hospitable. It's also sensible to check with the South American Explorers' Club (p 27), particularly in Cusco, for information on the latest trouble spots.

The feminist movement

Though a growing force, **feminism** is still relatively new to Peru, and essentially urban. However, there are two major feminist groups: Flora Tristan, which is primarily a political organization running courses and campaigns, but a good point of contact for feminist networks. The other is the less radical Peru Mujer, though neither of these is likely to be of enormous interest to travellers.

Women's organizations in Peru

CHIRAPAQ Centre of Indian Cultures
Horacio Urteaga 534, Oficina 203, Lima 11
℡01/4232757, ℉4232757. The centre is a platform for indigenous women of the Andes and Amazon, has a programme for elementary food relief for the extreme poor and organizes discussions on and exhibitions of indigenous people's culture.
Flora Tristan Parque Hernan Velarde 42, Lima 1
℡01/4332765, ℮diana@flora.org.pe.
Latin American Committee for Defence of National Women's Council of Peru Francia 706, Miraflores, Lima 6.
Peru Mujer Apartado 11-02-06, Lima 11.
Women's Documentation Centre.
Women's Rights (CLADEM) PO Box 11-0470, Lima.

Peru's one **feminist magazine**, *Mujeres y Sociedad* (*Women and Society*), is published quarterly. For other literature and advice, try Flora Tristan, the Librería de la Mujer bookshop in Avenida Arenales, Lima; or the

Women's Centre, Quilca, Lima, which is run by nuns. The **Peruvian Women's Association** (Association Peru Mujer) can be contacted at Leon Velarde 1275, Lima ☎01/4223655, 4415187 or 4711524.

Gay and lesbian travellers

Homosexuality is pretty much kept underground in what is still a very macho society, though in recent years Lima has seen a liberating advance and transvestites can walk the streets in relative freedom from abuse. However, there is little or no organized gay life. The Peruvian Homosexual and Lesbian Movement can be contacted at C Mariscal Miller 828, in Jesus Maria ☎01/4335519. There are few specialist gay organizations, hotel facilities, restaurants or even clubs. Where they exist they are listed in the relevant sections of the Guide. Further information can be accessed on ⓦgaylimape.tripod.com, which advises gay and lesbian travellers in Peru and lists some of the gay-friendly clubs, restaurants and accommodation. It also has a useful links page.

Contacts for gay and lesbian travellers

In Peru
Gay Peru ⓦ www.gayperu.com. A lively website with links, news and contact messengering.

In the US and Canada
Damron ☎1-800/462-6654 or 415/255-0404, ⓦwww.damron.com. Publisher of the *Men's Travel Guide*, a pocket-sized yearbook full of listings of hotels, bars, clubs and resources for gay men; the *Women's Traveler*, which provides similar listings for lesbians; the *Road Atlas*, which shows lodging and entertainment in major US cities; and *Damron Accommodations*, which provides detailed listings of over 1000 accommodations for gays and lesbians worldwide. All of these titles are offered at a discount on the website. No specific city guides – everything is incorporated in the yearbooks.
gaytravel.com ☎1-800/429-8728, ⓦwww .gaytravel.com. The premier site for trip planning, bookings, and general information about international gay and lesbian travel.
International Gay & Lesbian Travel Association ☎1-800/448-8550 or 954/776-2626, ⓦwww.iglta.org. Trade group that can provide a list of gay- and lesbian-owned or -friendly travel agents, accommodation and other travel businesses.

In the UK
ⓦwww.gaytravel.co.uk Online gay and lesbian travel agent, offering good deals on all types of holiday. Also lists gay- and lesbian-friendly hotels around the world.

In Australia and New Zealand
Gay and Lesbian Tourism Australia
ⓦwww.galta.com.au. Directory and links for gay and lesbian travel in Australia and worldwide.
Parkside Travel ☎08/8274 1222, ⒺΡ parkside@herveyworld.com.au. Gay travel agent associated with local branch of Hervey World Travel; all aspects of gay and lesbian travel worldwide.
Silke's Travel ☎1800/807 860 or 02/8347 2000, ⓦwww.silkes.com.au. Long-established gay and lesbian specialist, with the emphasis on women's travel.
Tearaway Travel ☎03/9510 6644, ⓦwww .tearaway.com. Gay-specific business dealing with international and domestic travel.

Opening hours, public holidays and festivals

Public holidays, Carnival and local fiestas are all big events in Peru, celebrated with an openness and a great gusto that gives them enormous appeal for visitors. The main national holidays take place over Easter, Christmas and during the month of October, in that order of importance. Be aware, though, that during public holidays, Carnival and even the many local fiestas everything shuts down: banks, post offices, information offices, tourist sites and museums. It is worth planning a little in advance to make sure that you don't get caught out.

Opening hours

Most **shops** and **services** in Peru open Monday to Saturday 9am–5pm or 6pm. Many are open on Sunday as well, if for more limited hours. Peru's more important **ancient sites** and ruins usually have opening hours that coincide with daylight – from around 7am until 5pm or 6pm daily. Smaller sites are rarely fenced off, and are nearly always accessible 24 hours a day for moonlit strolls. For larger sites, you normally pay a small admission fee to the local guardian – who may then walk round with you, pointing out features of interest. Only Machu Picchu charges more than a few dollars' entrance fee – this is one site where you may find it worth presenting an ISIC or FIYTO student card (which generally gets you in for half-price).

Of Peru's **museums**, some belong to the state, others to institutions, and a few to individuals. Most charge a small admission fee and open Monday to Saturday 9am–noon and 3–6pm.

Churches open in the mornings for mass (usually around 6am), after which the smaller ones close. Those which are most interesting to tourists, however, tend to stay open all day, while others open again in the afternoon from 3 to 6pm. Very occasionally there's an admission charge to churches, and more regularly to monasteries (*monasterios*). Try to be aware of the strength of **religious belief** in Peru, particularly in the Andes, where churches have a rather heavy, sad atmosphere. You can enter and quietly look around all churches, but in the Andes especially you should refrain from taking photographs.

Fiestas, festivals and public holidays

Peruvians love any excuse for a celebration and the country enjoys a huge number of **religious ceremonies, festivals** and **local events**. Cusco, in particular, is a great place for both Christian celebrations and for Inca festivals like Inti Raymi in June. In October, Lima, and especially its suburb of La Victoria, takes centre stage, with processions dedicated to Our Lord of Miracles, in memory of the ever-present earthquake danger. **Carnival** time (generally late Feb) is lively almost everywhere in the country, with fiestas held every Sunday – a wholesale licence to throw water at everyone and generally go crazy. It's worth noting that most hotel prices go up significantly at fiesta times and bus and air transport should be booked well in advance.

In addition to the major regional and national celebrations, nearly every community has its own saint or patron figure to worship at town or **village fiestas**. These celebrations often mean a great deal to local people, and can be much more fun to visit than the larger countrywide activities. Processions, music, dancing in costumes, and eating and drinking form the core activities of these parties. In some cases the villagers will enact symbolic dramas with Indians dressed up as Spanish colonists, wearing hideous blue-eyed masks with long hairy beards. In the hills around towns like Huaraz and Cusco, especially, it's quite common to stumble into a village fiesta, with its explosion of human energy and noise, bright colours, and a mixture of pagan and Catholic symbolism.

However, such celebrations are very much local affairs, and while the occasional traveller will almost certainly be welcomed with great warmth, none of these remote communities would want to be invaded by tourists waving cameras and expecting to be feasted for free. The dates given below are therefore only for established events which are already on the tourist map, and for those that take place all over the country. For full details of celebrations in the Cusco region – one of the best places to catch a fiesta – see p.116.

In many coastal and mountain haciendas (estates), **bullfights** are often held at fiesta times. In a less organized way they happen at many of the village fiestas, too – often with the bull being left to run through the village until it's eventually caught and mutilated by one of the men. This is not just a sad sight, it can also be dangerous for you, as an unsuspecting tourist, if you happen to wander into an apparently evacuated village. The Lima bullfights in October, in contrast, are a very serious business; even Hemingway was impressed.

Major festivals and public holidays

January
1 New Year's Day.

February
2 Candlemas.
Folklore music and dancing throughout Peru, but especially lively in Puno at the Fiesta de la Virgen de la Candelaria, and in the mountain regions.

Carnival
Wildly celebrated immediately prior to Lent, throughout the whole country.

March/April
Easter Semana Santa (Holy Week).
Superb processions all over Peru (the best are in Cusco and Ayacucho), with the biggest being on Good Friday and in the evening on Easter Saturday, which is a public holiday.

May
1 Labour Day.
2–3 Fiesta de la Cruz (Festival of the Cross). Celebrated all over Peru in commemoration of ancient Peruvian agro-astronomical rituals and the Catholic annual cycle.

June
Beginning of the month Corpus Christi. This takes places exactly nine weeks after Maundy Thursday, and usually falls in the first half of June. It's much celebrated, with fascinating processions and feasting all over Peru, but is particularly lively in Cusco.
24 Inti Raymi. Cusco's main Inca festival (see p.117 for details).
29 St Peter's Day. A public holiday all over Peru, but mainly celebrated with fiestas in all the fishing villages along the coast.

July
15–17 Virgen de Carmen. Dance and music festivals at Pisac and Paucartambo (see p.117 for details).
28–29 National Independence Day. Public holiday with military and school processions.

August
13–19 Arequipa Week. Processions, firework displays, plenty of folklore dancing and craft markets take place throughout Peru's second city.
30 Santa Rosa de Lima. Public holiday.

September
End of the month Festival of Spring. Trujillo festival involving dancing, especially the local Marinera dance and popular Peruvian waltzes (see p.374 for details).

October
8 Public holiday to commemorate the Battle of Angamos.
18–28 Lord of Miracles. Festival featuring large and solemn processions (the main ones take place on October 18, 19 and 28); many women wear purple for the whole month, particularly in Lima, where bullfights and other celebrations continue throughout the month.

November
1–30 International Bullfighting Competitions. These take place throughout the month, and are particularly spectacular at the Plaza de Acho in Lima.
1–7 Puno Festival. One of the mainstays of Andean culture, celebrating the founding of the Puno by the Spanish conquistadores and also the founding of the Inca Empire by the legendary Manco Capac and his sister Mama Ocllo who are said to have emerged from Lake Titicaca. The fifth is marked by vigorous colourful community dancing.
1 Fiesta de Todos los Santos (All Saints Day). Public holiday.
2 Día de los Muertos (All Souls Day). A festive remembrance of dead friends and relatives taken very seriously by most Peruvians and a popular time for baptisms and roast pork meals.

12–28 Pacific Fair. One of the largest international trade fairs in South America – a huge, biannual event, which takes place on a permanent site on Avenida La Marina between Callao and Lima Centro.

December
8 Feast of the Immaculate Conception. Public holiday.
25 Christmas Day.

National parks and preserves

Almost ten percent of Peru is incorporated into some form of protected area, including seven national parks, eight national reserves, seven national sanctuaries, three historical sanctuaries, five reserved zones, six buffer forests, two hunting reserves, and an assortment of communal reserves and national forests.

The largest of these protected areas is the **National Reserve of Pacaya-Samiria**, an incredible tropical forest region in northern Peru covering over two million hectares. This is closely followed in size by the **Manu National Park and Biosphere Reserve**, another vast and stunning jungle area of about 1.5 million hectares, and the **Tambopata-Candamo Reserved Zone and Bahuaja-Sonone National Park**, again an Amazon area, over 1,400,000 hectares in extent, with possibly the richest flora and fauna of any region on the planet. Smaller but just as fascinating to visit are the **Huascarán National Park** in the high Andes near Huaraz, a popular, 340,000-hectare trekking and climbing region, and the lesser-visited **National Reserve of Pampa Galeras**, close to Nazca, which was established mainly to protect the dwindling but precious herds of *vicuña*, the smallest and most beautiful member of the South American cameloid family.

Bear in mind that the parks and reserves are enormous zones, within which there is hardly any attempt to control or organize nature. The term "park" probably conveys the wrong impression about these huge, virtually untouched areas, which were designated by the National System for Conservation Units (SNCU), with the aim of combining conservation, research and, in some cases (such as the Inca Trail; see p.149), recreational tourism.

In December 1992, the Peruvian National Trust Fund for Parks and Protected Areas (PROFONANPE) was established as a trust fund managed by the private sector to provide funding for Peru's main protected areas. It has assistance from the Peruvian government, national and international non-governmental organizations, the World Bank Global Environment facility and the United Nations Environment Program.

Visiting the parks

There's usually a small charge **to visit** the national parks or nature reserves. Sometimes, as at the Huascarán National Park, this is a daily rate; at others, like the Paracas Reserve on the coast south of Pisco, you pay a fixed sum to enter. If the park is in a particularly remote area, which most of them are, permission may also be needed – either from the National Institute of Culture, by the Museo de la Nación at Avenida Javier Prado Este 2465, San Borja (☎01/4769873), who are responsible for all matters of cultural heritage, and/or the Instituto Nacional de Recursos Naturales, Calle 17, 355 Urb. El Palomar, San Isidro (☎01/2251053, ✉inrena_dganpfs@eletrodata .com.pe), who are responsible for Peru's protected areas; you need permission from them to enter some of Peru's Natural Park areas. For more details check with the South American Explorers' Club in Lima (see p.27) or at the local tourist office.

Geography, climate and seasons

Peru is one of the larger South American countries – some ten times the size of England – covering an area of 1,285,000 square kilometres and with a population of over 26 million. Around 70 percent of its inhabitants live in cities, which are mainly located along the coast and half a dozen thin but relatively fertile river valleys running into the Pacific.

Peru is unique in possessing such a wide variety of **ecosystems** ranging from the driest hot desert in the Americas, to the high Andean peaks (over 7600m above sea level); from a 2000-kilometre-long belt of cloud forest, rich in flora and fauna, to a vast area of lowland Amazon jungle, covering about half the country. The three main zones of Peru are known as **La Costa** (the coast), **La Sierra** (the mountains) and **La Selva** (the jungle). Within a matter of hours, you can leave the scorching desert coastline with some of the Pacific Ocean's best fishing, cross the world's highest tropical mountain range – the Andes – and plunge down into our planet's biggest tropical rainforest.

The unusual **weather conditions** in Peru are created mainly by the offshore ocean currents – the cold Humbolt and the warm, tropical **El Niño** (see Introduction for more details).

Directory

Addresses These are frequently written with just the street name and number: for example, Pizarro 135. Officially, though, they're usually prefixed by Calle, Jirón (street) or Avenida. The first digit of any street number (or sometimes the first two digits) represents the block number within the street as a whole. Note too that many of the major streets in Lima and also in Cusco have two names – in Lima this is a relic of the military governments of the 1970s, in Cusco it's more to do with a revival of the Inca past.

Artesania Traditional craft goods from most regions of Peru can be found in markets and shops in Lima. Woollen and alpaca products, though, are usually cheaper and often better quality in the sierra – particularly in Cusco, Juliaca and Puno; carved gourds are imported from around Huancayo, while the best places to buy ceramic replicas are Trujillo, Huaraz, Ica and Nazca. The best jungle crafts are from Pucallpa and Iquitos.

Bargaining You are generally expected to bargain in markets and with taxi drivers (before getting in). Nevertheless, it's worth bearing in mind that travellers from Europe, North America and Australasia are generally much wealthier than Peruvians, so for every penny or cent you knock them down they stand to loose plenty of nuevo soles. It's also sometimes possible to haggle over the price of hotel rooms, especially if you're travelling in a group. Food and shop prices, however, tend to be fixed.

Customs Regulations stipulate that no items of archeological or historical value or interest may be removed from the country. Many of the jungle crafts which incorporate feathers, skins or shells of rare Amazonian animals are also banned for export – it's best not to buy these if you are in any doubt about their scarcity. If you do try to export anything of archeological or biological value, and get caught, you'll have the goods confiscated at the very least, and may find yourself in a Peruvian court.

Diving and fishing For information on this contact the Federación Peruana de Caza Submarina y Actividades Acuaticas, Estadio Nacional, Lima Centro ☎01/4336626, ⓔdidimar@mail.cosapidata.com.pe.

Electric current 220 volt/60 cycles AC is the standard all over Peru, except in Arequipa where it is 220 volt/50 cycles. In some of Lima's better hotels you may also find 110 volt sockets to use with standard electric shavers. Don't count on any Peruvian power supply being 100 percent reliable and, particularly in cheap hostels and hotels, be very wary of the wiring, especially in electric shower fittings.

Football Peru's major sport is football and you'll find men and boys playing it in the streets of every city, town and settlement in the country down to the remotest of jungle outposts. The big teams are Cristal, Alianza and El U (for Universitario) in Lima and Ciencianco from Cusco. The "Classic" game is between Alianza, the poor man's team from the La Victoria suburb of Lima, and El U, generally supported by the middle class. In recent years the sport has taken a European turn in the unruly and violent nature of its fans. This is particularly true of Lima where, in late 1995, the "Classic" had to be stopped because of stones thrown at the players by supporters. Known as *choligans* (a mixture of the English "hooligan" and the Peruvian *cholo*, which means dark-skinned Quechua-blooded Peruvian), these unruly supporters have taken to painting their faces, attacking the opposing fans and causing major riots outside the football grounds. To get a flavour for just how popular football is in Peru try a visit to the *Estadio Restaurant* in Lima (p.90) which has great murals, classic team shirts and lifesize models of the world's top players – well worth a visit for anyone even vaguely interested in football.

Insults Travellers sometimes suffer insults from Peruvians who begrudge the apparent relative wealth and freedom of tourists. Remember, however, that the terms "gringo" or "mister" are not generally meant in an offensive way in Peru.

Language lessons You can learn Peruvian Spanish all over Peru, but the best range of schools are in Lima, Cusco, Arequipa and Huancayo. Check the relevant Listings sections in the Guide.

Laundry Most basic hotels have communal washrooms where you can do your washing; failing this, labour is so cheap that it's no real expense to get your clothes washed by the hotel or in a *lavandería* (laundry). Things tend to disappear from public washing lines so be careful where you leave clothes drying.

Natural disasters Peru has more than its fair share of avalanches, landslides and earthquakes – and there's not a lot you can do about any of them. If you're naturally cautious you might want to register on arrival with your embassy; they like this, and it does help them in the event of a major quake (or an escalation of terrorist activity). Landslides – *huaycos* – devastate the roads and rail lines every rainy season, though alternative routes are usually found surprisingly quickly.

Photography The light in Peru is very bright, with a strong contrast between shade and sun. This can produce a nice effect and generally speaking it's easy to take good pictures. One of the more complex problems is how to take photos of people without upsetting them. You should always talk to a prospective subject first, and ask if s/he minds if you take a quick photo (*una fotito, por favor* – "a little photo please"); most people react favourably to this approach even if all the communication is in sign language. Slide film is expensive to buy, and not readily available outside of the main cities; colour Kodak and Fuji films are easy to find, but black and white film is rare. If you can bear the suspense it's best to save getting films developed until you're home – you'll probably get better results. Pre-paid slide films can't be developed in Peru.

Punctuality Whilst buses, trains or planes won't wait a minute beyond their scheduled departure time, people almost expect friends to be an hour or more late for an appointment (don't arrange to meet a Peruvian on the street – make it a bar or café). Peruvians stipulate that an engagement is *a la hora inglesa* ("by English time") if they genuinely want people to arrive on time, or, more realistically, within half an hour of the time they fix.

Time Peru keeps the same hours as Eastern Standard Time, which is (generally) five hours behind GMT.

Guide

Guide

Lima and around

CHAPTER 1 Highlights

✷ **Huaca Pucllana** A vast pre-Inca adobe pyramid mound in the middle of suburban Miraflores, this is a good place to get a taste of ancient Lima. See p.82

✷ **A colectivo ride** Head along the Avenida Arequipa between the old Centro and downtown Miraflores, by far the most authentic experience of Lima life. See p.70

✷ **Cevicheria El Peñon** Spend a hot, lazy Sunday afternoon sitting in the shade sipping cool Cuzqueña beer while waiting for sumptuous ceviche to arrive. See p.90

✷ **Museo Larco Hererra** One of the city's most unusual museums, it contains more than 400,000 excellently preserved ancient ceramics. See p.86

✷ **Larco Mar** During the 1990s these sandy clifftops in Miraflores were transformed into an ambitious shopping and dining centre, with tremendous views over the Pacific Ocean. See p.82

✷ **Museo de la Inquisición** Headquarters of the Inquisition for Spanish America from 1570 until 1820, with requisite creepy dungeons and torture chambers. See p.78

✷ **El Cordano** One of Lima's last surviving traditional bar/restaurants, bustling with locals. See p.88

Lima and around

O nce reputed to be the most beautiful city in Spanish America, and long established as Peru's seat of government, **Lima** still retains a certain elegance, though it is far from exotic. That said, however, the central areas have been cleaned up in recent years – streets swarm with orange-uniformed sweepers – and are packed with colonial relics and twenty-first-century features. The city is now home to more than eight million people, over half of whom live in relative poverty without decent water supplies, sewage or electricity. This is not to say you can't enjoy the place. Limeños are generally very open, and their way of life is distinctive and compelling – but it's important not to come here with false expectations. The pollution and the ever-increasing traffic are problematic, though environmental awareness is rising almost as fast as Lima's *pueblos jovenes* (shantytowns) and neon-lit middle-class suburban neighbourhoods spread farther and farther across the desert, extremely poor and ultra-rich families each clinging to the sides of the small foothills beyond which lies the blossoming modern "valley" of La Molina.

With its numerous facilities and firm footing as a transport and communications hub, Lima makes a good base from which to explore the surrounding area and beyond. That area offers plenty of reasons to delay your progress on towards Arequipa or Cusco. Within an hour or so's bus ride south is the coastline, often deserted, lined by a series of attractive beaches. Above them the imposing fortress-temple complex of **Pachacamac** sits on a sandstone cliff, near the edge of the ocean. In the neighbouring Rimac Valley you can visit the pre-Inca sites of **Puruchuco** and **Cajamarquilla**, and, in the foothills above Lima, intriguingly eroded rock outcrops and megalithic monuments surround the natural amphitheatre of Marcahuasi.

Lima

Crowded into the mouth of a river valley with low sandy mountains closing in around its outer fringes, **LIMA** is a boisterous, macho city, that's somehow

63

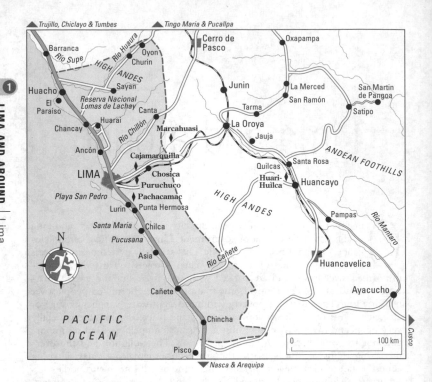

still relaxed and laid-back, boasting an irresistible, underlying energy, with money and expensive cars ruling the roost – you can buy anything here if you have the cash, particularly in **Lima Centro**, the colonial zone of the city. The city's population has increased dramatically in the last thirty years, swollen with people arriving from the high Andes to make camp in the shantytowns that line the highways. The main plazas, once attractive meeting places, are now thick with pickpockets, exhaust fumes and, not infrequently, riot police. The **climate** seems to set the mood: in the height of summer (Dec–March) Lima buzzes with energy and excitement, though during the winter months (June–Sept) a low mist descends over the arid valley in which the city sits, forming a solid grey blanket from the beaches almost up to Chosica in the foothills of the Andes – a phenomenon undoubtedly made worse by traffic-related air pollution – which dampens the buzz of this normally lively city.

Lima is brimming with culture and heritage, though it's not obvious at first. On a strictly guidebook level, there are the **museums** (the best of which are excellent and should definitely be visited before setting off for Machu Picchu or any of Peru's other great Inca ruins), the Spanish **churches** in the centre, and some distinguished **mansions** in the wealthy suburbs of Barranco and Miraflores. But there's a powerful atmosphere of unity and striving in the *pueblos jovenes*, where Peru's landless peasants have made their homes. In addition, Lima's noisy, frenetic craziness is mellowed by the presence of the sea and beaches. The mix of lifestyles, peoples and overlapping cultures is a fascinating world of its own: from the snappy, sassy, cocaine-influenced criolla style – all big, fast American cars, cruising the broad main streets – to the easy-going, happy-go-lucky attitude of the poorer citizens (which can seem a godsend when you're trying to get through some bureaucratic hassle). Even if you choose not to spend much time seeking out the delights and agonies of Lima, it's possible to get a good sense of it all in a few days. As anyone who stays more than a week or so finds, Limeño hospitality and kindness are almost boundless once you've established an initial rapport.

Some history

Out at Ancón, now a popular beach resort just north of Lima, an important **pre-Inca** burial site shows signs of occupation – including pottery, textiles, and the oldest-known archer's bow in the entire Americas – from at least three thousand years ago. Although certainly one of the most populous valleys in the area, the Rimac area first showed indications of true urbanization around 1200 AD with the appearance of a strong, independent culture – the **Cuismancu State** – in many ways parallel to, though not as large as, the contemporary Chimu Empire which bordered it to the north. Cajamarquilla, a huge, somewhat crowded, adobe city-complex associated with the Cuismancu, now rests peacefully under the desert sun only a few kilometres beyond Lima's outer suburbs. Dating from the same era, but some 30km south of the modern city, is the Temple of Pachacamac. For hundreds of years, until ransacked by the conquistadores, this shrine attracted thousands of pilgrims from all over Peru, the Incas being the last in a series of groups to adopt Pachacamac as one of their own major *huacas*.

When the Spanish first arrived here in 1533 the valley was dominated by three important **Inca**-controlled urban complexes: Carabayllo, to the north near Chillón; Maranga, now partly destroyed, by the Avenida La Marina, between the modern city and the Port of Callao; and Surco, now a suburb within the confines of greater Lima but where, until the mid-seventeenth century, the adobe houses of ancient chiefs lay empty yet painted in a variety of colourful images; now they've faded back into the sandy desert terrain, only the larger pyramids remain sticking up here and there among the modern concrete constructions. Francisco Pizarro founded **Spanish Lima**, "City of the Kings", in 1535, within three years of the invasion. The name is thought to have been derived from the Río Rimac, while others suggest that the name "Lima" is an ancient word which described the lands of Taulichusco, the chief who dominated this area when the Spanish arrived. Evidently recommended by mountain Indians as a site for a potential capital, it proved essentially a good choice, apart perhaps from the winter coastal fog, offering a natural harbour nearby, a large well-watered river valley, and relatively easy access up into the Andes. By the 1550s the town had grown up around a large plaza with wide streets leading through a fine collection of elegant mansions and well-stocked shops run by wealthy merchants. Since the very beginning, Spanish Lima has been different from the more popular image of Peru in which generally Andean peasants are pictured toiling on Inca-built mountain terraces. Lima is a cosmopolitan city that looks out, away from the Andes and the past, towards the Pacific for contact with and inspiration from the world beyond, but in particular the culture of North America.

Lima rapidly developed into the capital of a Spanish viceroyalty which encompassed not only Peru but also Ecuador, Bolivia and Chile. The University of San Marcos, founded in 1551, is the oldest on the continent, and Lima housed the Western hemisphere's headquarters of the Spanish Inquisition from 1570 until 1820. It remained the most important, the richest, and – hardly credible today – the most alluring city in South America, until the early nineteenth century.

1

Perhaps the most prosperous era for Lima was the **seventeenth century**. By 1610 its population had reached a manageable 26,000, made up of 40 percent blacks (mostly slaves), 38 percent Spanish, no more than 8 percent pure Indian, another 8 percent (of unspecified ethnic origin) living under religious orders, and less than 6 percent of mixed blood – now probably the largest proportion of inhabitants. The centre of Lima was crowded with shops and stalls selling silks and fancy furniture from as far afield as China. Even these days it's not hard to imagine what Lima must have been like, as a substantial section of the colonial city is still preserved – many of its streets, set in large regular blocks, are overhung by ornate wooden balconies, and elaborate Baroque facades bring some of the older churches to life, regardless of the din and hassle of modern city living. Rimac, a suburb just over the river from the Plaza Mayor, and the port area of Callao, both grew up as satellite settlements – initially catering to the very rich, though they are now predominantly slum sectors.

The **eighteenth century**, a period of relative stagnation for Lima, was dramatically punctuated by the tremendous earthquake of 1746, which left only twenty houses standing in the whole city and killed some five thousand residents – nearly ten percent of the population. From 1761 to 1776 Lima and Peru were governed by Viceroy Amat, who, although more renowned for his relationship with the famous Peruvian actress La Perricholi, is also remembered as the instigator of Lima's rebirth. Under him the city lost its cloistered atmosphere, and opened out with broad avenues, striking gardens, Rococo mansions and palatial salons. Influenced by the Bourbons, Amat's designs for the city's architecture arrived hand in hand with other transatlantic reverberations of the Enlightenment, such as the new anti-imperialist vision of an independent Peru.

In the **nineteenth century** Lima expanded still further to the east and south. The suburbs of Barrios Altos and La Victoria were poor from the start; above the beaches at Magdalena, Miraflores and Barranco, the wealthy developed new enclaves of their own. These were originally separated from the city's centre by several kilometres of farmland, at that time still studded with fabulous pre-Inca *huacas* and other adobe ruins, many still just about surviving among the suburbs, some (like Huaca Pucllana) open to the public or being renovated. It was President Leguia who, in **1919–30**, revitalized Lima by renovating the central areas. Plaza San Martín 's attractive colonnades and the *Gran Hotel Bolívar* were erected, the Palacio de Gobierno was rebuilt, and the city was supplied with its first drinking-water and sewage systems. This was the signal for Lima's explosion into the modern era of ridiculously rapid growth. The 300,000 inhabitants of 1930 had become over three and a half million by the **mid-1970s**, and the population has more than doubled again in the last thirty years or so. Standing at more than eight million today, most of Lima's recent growth is accounted for by massive immigration of peasants from the provinces into the *barriadas* or *pueblos jovenes* (young towns) now pressing in on the city on all sides. Many of these migrants escaped from the theatre of civil war that raked many highland regions between the early 1980s and 1993.

Today the city is as cosmopolitan as any other in the developing world, with a thriving middle class enjoying living standards comparable to those of the West or better, and an elite riding around in chauffeur-driven Cadillac's and flying to Miami for their monthly shopping. The vast majority of Lima's inhabitants, however, barely scrape together meagre incomes to provide for their families.

Arrival, information and getting around

You will either arrive in Lima **by plane**, landing at the Jorge Chavez airport, 7km northwest of the city centre, **by bus**, most of which arrive in the older, more central areas of town, or perhaps **by train** from the Andes right into the city centre, if and when the service ever reopens. **Driving** into the city is really only for the adventurous, as the roads are highly congested with sometimes frustrating traffic levels plus the general madness of fellow drivers, which will either send you insane or turn you into an equally skilful but unpredictable road hog. Wherever you arrive, it can be a disorienting experience, as there are few landmarks to register the direction of the centre of town.

By air

After landing at the modern, bustling **Jorge Chavez airport** (flight inquiries on ☎5751712 for international and ☎5745529 for domestic), named after an early Peruvian pilot, the quickest way to get into the city is by **taxi**, which will take around 45 minutes to Lima Centro or downtown Miraflores. Simplest is to go to the taxi kiosk inside the terminal where you can book an official taxi to most parts of Lima for $9. If you don't use this service, remember to fix the price with the driver before getting in. An unofficial taxi to Lima Centro or Miraflores can usually be found for between $5 and $8 if you're prepared to haggle and shop around during daylight hours, particularly if you're prepared to carry your bags outside the airport gates and search for a taxi there. Unofficial taxis abound in the streets of Lima; they're basically ordinary cars with temporary plastic "taxi" stickers on their front windows. They are cheaper than the official taxis which are based at taxi ranks and licensed by the city authorities (most but not all their cars have taxi signs on the roof; some of the larger taxi companies are radio-controlled). Take extra care looking for a taxi around the perimeter and on the road into Lima, as there have been thefts in these areas. A cheaper and very efficient alternative is to take the **airport express** bus that usually leaves from outside domestic arrivals doors, some heading for Miraflores, others for Lima Centro via Tacna; tickets are around $5–6 per person.

If you need to **change money** at the airport, there are counters (daily 9am–6pm) located between the international and domestic flight departure areas, but you'll get better rates in the centre of Lima or Miraflores.

By bus

If you arrive in Lima by **bus**, you'll probably come in at one of the **bus terminals** or offices between the *Hotel Sheraton* and Parque Universitario, or in the district of La Victoria along Avenida 28 de Julio and Prolongación Huánuco. However, many operators have depots out in the suburbs, in an attempt to avoid the Lima Centro traffic jams. One of the most reliable operators, Cruz del Sur, has its busy depot at Javier Prado Este 1109 (☎4249772, Ⓦwww.cruzdelsur.com.pe) on the edge of La Victoria and San Isidro. For full details of Lima bus companies and their terminals, see Listings, p.101. Whichever terminal you arrive at, your best bet is to hail the first decent-looking **taxi** you see and fix a price – about $3 to anywhere in the central area, or $5 for anywhere else in Lima.

The phone code for Lima and its surrounding regions is ☎01.

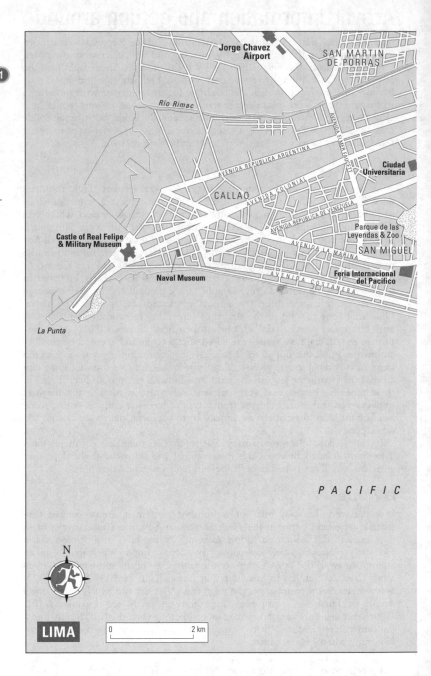

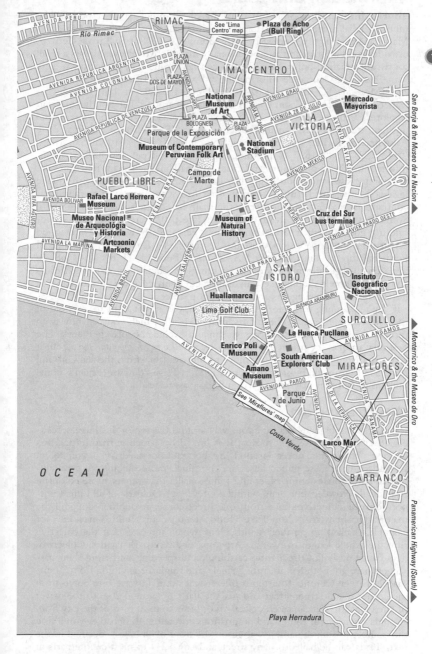

RIMAC

AVENIDA PERU

Río Rimac

See 'Lima Centro' map

● Plaza de Acho (Bull Ring)

PLAZA UNION

AVENIDA REPUBLICA ARGENTINA

AVENIDA COLONIAL

PLAZA DOS DE MAYO

LIMA CENTRO

AVENIDA GRAU

AVENIDA REPUBLICA DE VENEZUELA

National Museum of Art

AVENIDA 28 DE JULIO

■ Mercado Mayorista

PLAZA BOLOGNESI

PLAZA GRAU

LA VICTORIA

AVENIDA AVIACION

Parque de la Exposición

Museum of Contemporary Peruvian Folk Art

● **National Stadium**

AVENIDA MEXICO

PUEBLO LIBRE

AVENIDA BRAZIL

Campo de Marte

LINCE

PASEO DE LA REPUBLICA

AVENIDA BOLIVAR

Rafael Larco Herrera Museum

Museum of Natural History

Cruz del Sur bus terminal

AVENIDA JAVIER PRADO OESTE

AVENIDA RIVA AGUERO

Museo Nacional de Arqueológia y Historia

AVENIDA LA MARINA

Artesania Markets

AVENIDA SALAVERRY

AVENIDA JAVIER PRADO ESTE

SAN ISIDRO

AVENIDA AREQUIPA

Insituto Geografico Nacional

AVENIDA BRAZIL

Huallamarca

Lima Golf Club

COMANDANTE ESPINAR

AVENIDA ARAMBURU

SURQUILLO

AVENIDA ANGAMOS

La Huaca Pucllana

AVENIDA EJERCITO

Enrico Poli Museum

Amano Museum

South American Explorers' Club

MIRAFLORES

AVENIDA LARCO

PASEO DE LA REPUBLICA

AVENIDA PANAMA

AVENIDA J. PARDO

Parque 7 de Junio

See 'Miraflores' map

Costa Verde

Larco Mar

O C E A N

BARRANCO

Playa Herradura

Information and tours

Tourist information offices in Lima are plentiful but rather dispersed. The municipalidad office of Información Turística, Calle Los Escribanos 145, Plaza Mayor (Mon–Fri 9am–6pm, Sat 10am–5pm; ☎4276080), in **Lima Centro**, provides good information and occasionally maps. In **Miraflores** there's a small tourist information point, based in the central Parque 7 de Junio (open daily 9am–9pm); the Central de Informacion y Promoción Turística, Avenida Larco 770 (Mon–Fri 8.30am–5pm; ☎4462649 or 4463959 ext 114), usually has leaflets, information and some maps of Lima and around. The South American Explorers' Club (see Basics, p.27) has good information, including maps, listings and travel reports, available to its members. The office of Información y Asistencia al Turista, run by i-peru from Jorge Basadre 610 in San Isidro (☎4211227 or 4211627, ✉iperulima@promperu.gob.pe), also has a range of information sheets on regions and cities of Peru, but their main function is in providing assistance for tourists if they have serious complaints or wish to take legal actions against Peruvian tourism operators who have failed to fulfil their contracts; they also have an office in the main hall at the airport (☎5748000). Some of the commercial tour companies (see p.103) are also geared up for offering good tourist information, notably Fertur Peru, who also offer good **city tours**, and Lima Vision, who also do tours. The *Peru Guide*, published in Peru monthly by Lima Editora S.A., Avenida Benavides 1180 (☎4443849), gives up-to-date information on most things in Lima, from scheduled tours and treks to hotels, shopping, events and practical advice; it's readily available in hotels, tour and travel agents and information offices.

If you're planning to explore Lima in depth, you might want to get hold of the *Guía de Transportes*, a cheap **bus map** ($1.50), which you can buy from most of the stalls around Plaza San Martín and Avenida Nicolas de Pierola. The best **city map** is the pricey *Lima Guía "Inca" de Lima Metropolitan* ($13), but it is increasingly difficult to obtain; more readily available, from the stalls around Plaza San Martín and most bookshops, the *Lima Plano 2000* street map is comprehensive, but you may need a magnifying glass to read it.

City transport

It's a fairly simple matter to find your way around the rest of this huge, spread-eagled city. Almost every corner of it is linked by a regular **municipal bus service**, with flat-rate tickets (around 15¢) bought from the driver as you board. In tandem with these public buses are the much more ubiquitous, privately-owned **microbuses**, some older and some smaller than others, more colourful and equally crowded, but again with flat rates (25¢). Quickest of all Lima transport, **combi colectivos** race from one street corner to another along all the major arterial city roads. You'll see "Todo Arequipa" or "Todo Benavides", for example, chalked up on their windscreens, which indicates that the colectivo runs the whole length of Avenida Arequipa or Avenida Benavides. Colectivos dash dangerously fast (frequently crashing), and speeding off before their passengers have got both feet into the vehicle, and might be anything from a ramshackle Dodge Coronet to a plush fifteen-seat minibus; wave one down from the corner of any major street and pay the flat fare (around 20¢) to the driver or fare collector. You can catch colectivos or buses to most parts of the city from Avenida Abancay; for routes and destinations covered in this chapter you'll find the number or suburb name (written on the front of all buses) specified in the text. **Taxis** can be hailed on any street, and cost $2–4 to most central parts of the city. It's worth reiterating that **driving in Lima** is incredibly anarchic – it's not that fast, but it is assertive, with drivers, especially *taxistas*, often finding gaps in traffic that don't appear to exist (one reason why there are so many damaged cars). You can find recommended reliable taxi firms on p.103. If you want to **rent a car** to take out of the city, see p.101.

Accommodation

There are three main areas of Lima in which to stay – **Lima Centro**, which boasts hotels in just about every category imaginable, **Miraflores** and **Barranco**. Even more than most Peruvian cities, modern hotels in Lima tend to be very exclusive and expensive. There are no **campsites**, official or otherwise.

Lima Centro

Most travellers on a tight budget end up in one of the traditional gringo dives around the **Plaza Mayor** or the **San Francisco** church. These are mainly old buildings and tend to be full of backpackers, but they aren't necessarily the best choices in the old centre, even in their price range. If you can spend a little bit more and opt for the mid-range hotels, you'll find some interesting old buildings bursting with bygone atmosphere and style.

Budget

Hostal de los Artes Chota 1460 ☎4330031, ✉artes@terra.com.pe. At the southern end of Lima Centro, one block from Plaza Bolognesi, this clean, gay-friendly place is popular with travellers; has a book exchange, good English and Dutch is spoken and there's a nice patio with mosaics. Most rooms have private bath, but there's also a dormitory which costs much less. Downstairs rooms are a little gloomy. ❶–❸

Hostal España Jr Azángaro 105 ☎/℉4285546, ✉hotel_espana@hotmail.com. This popular, centrally located, very secure hostel has a dormitory, plus rooms with or without private bath, Internet connection, book exchange and its own tour operator service, all based around a nice courtyard and rooftop patio. ❷–❸

Hostal Roma Ica 326 ☎4277576, ⊛www .hostalroma.8m.com. A pleasant, safe and gay-friendly place, if a bit shabby. It's also quite central and offers a choice of private or communal bathrooms (but only one shower for women) and a reliable luggage storage service. ❸

Hostal Samaniego Emancipación 184 (no phone). Small with shared rooms only, but welcoming, very clean and with access to cooking facilities. ❷

Hotel Europa Jr Ancash 376 ☎4273351. One of the best-value budget pads, centrally located opposite the San Francisco church, with a lovely courtyard. Be aware, though, that it is very popular and fills up quickly. Shared and private rooms. ❷

Hotel Richmond Emancipación 123 ☎4279270. An interesting place for its rambling, if grimy, corridors and rooms, it's set in an impressive old mansion with plenty of space; friendly and central, overlooking the seventh block of the main shopping drag Jirón de la Unión. ❸

Pensión Rodriguez Av Nicolas de Pierola 730 ☎4236465. Excellent value but often crowded, with shared rooms and baths. ❷

Plaza Francia Inn Jr Rufino Torrico 1117 ☎3306080, ⊛www.incacountry.com. Parallel with block 9 of Avenida Garcilaso de la Vega, but on the Plaza San Martín side of the Plaza Francia, this popular and very central hostel offers dormitories and private rooms and will organize airport pick-ups if advised well in advance. ❷–❸

Moderate

El Balcon Dorado Jr Ucayali 199 ☎4276028, ℉4276029 or ☎04/4367176, ✉balcondorado@hotmail.com. Very well located, close to the Plaza Mayor, this colonial-style hotel is a reasonable option for this category. All rooms with private bath. Price includes breakfast. ❺

Hostal La Estrella de Belen Belen 1051 ☎4286462. Very clean and pleasant rooms with private baths in a friendly hostel in the middle of Lima's busiest zone, just two blocks from the Plaza San Martín. ❹

Hostal Granada Huancavelica 323 ☎4279033. A welcoming place with small but tidy rooms, private baths and a genial atmosphere; breakfast available. ❹

Hostal Residencial Don Luis Av Breña 331 ☎4239293, ⓕ4231379. Relatively close to the city centre, by the Plaza Bolognesi, it can be noisy early in the morning, but it is comfortable and has a colonial feel to it. ❺

Hotel Ritual Jirón Ucayali 199 ☎4276028, ⓕ4276029. Right in the heart of Lima and just a block from the Plaza Mayor, this place offers comfort and safety at a reasonable price. ❹

La Posada del Parque Parque Hernan Velarde 60 ☎4332412, ⓕ3326927, ⓦwww.incacountry.com. Situated in a quiet cul-de-sac in the pleasant Santa Beatrice suburb and within walking distance of Lima Centro. Friendly and comfortable, and good English is spoken. ❹

Expensive

Gran Hotel Bolivar Jirón de la Unión 958 ☎4277672, ⓕ4287674. This old, very luxurious hotel dominating the northwest corner of the Plaza San Martín has certainly seen better times and usually has more staff than guests. It's probably not worth the money to stay, but check out the cocktail lounge and restaurant, which often have live music on Sat nights. ❽

Hotel Kamana Jr Camana, Lima Centro ☎4277106, ⓕ4260790, ⓦwww.hotelkamana.com. A very homely and adequate if small hotel in the heart of Lima Centro; the rooms are nicely furnished and the service is friendly. ❻

Hotel El Plaza Av Nicolas de Pierola 850 ☎4247242. Good value for a comfortable, central hotel, with reasonable service and OK facilities, but definitely at the bottom end of the expensive offerings. ❺–❻

Lima Sheraton Hotel Paseo de la República 170 ☎3155022, ⓕ3155024, ⓔreservas@sheraton.com.pe. A standard top-class modern international hotel – concrete, tall and blandly elegant. ❽

Miraflores and other suburbs

Many people opt to stay further out of the city in **Miraflores**, which is still close to most of Lima's nightlife, culture and commercial activity. However, most hostels here start at around $20 per person and quite a few hotels go above $200. As a trendy ocean–clifftop suburb **Barranco** is more and more the *in* place for the younger traveller. Apart from the artist's quarter vibe and the clubs and restaurants, though, the suburb actually has little to offer the visitor. Other suburban options include **San Isidro**, **San Antonio**, and **Callao**.

Miraflores

Budget

Casa del Mochilero Jirón Cesareo Chacallana 130a, second floor ☎4449089, ⓔpilaryv@hotmail.com. Located close to block 10 of José Pardo, this safe place is remarkably good value, with hot water, cable TV and kitchen facilities. It's not right at the centre of Miraflores action but it's close enough. ❷

Friends House Jirón Manco Capac 368 ☎4466248. A small, popular hostel in a superb Miraflores location; comfortable and clean rooms, hot water, cable TV and open kitchen. ❸

Hospedaje Turistico Flying Dog Jr Diez Canseco 117 ☎4450940, ⓕ4452376, ⓔFlyingdog@mixmail.com. A basic but clean and homely backpackers bed-and-breakfast-style hostel smack bang in the middle of Miraflores; rooms are shared but the maximum size is 4 beds. There's an open kitchen facility and cable TV lounge. Price includes breakfast. ❸–❹

Hostal Carlos Tenaud Carlos Tenaud 119 ☎4219091. Excellent-value hostel, just off block 42 of Avenida Arequipa, within 15 minutes' walk of central Miraflores. ❸

Lex Luthor's House Jr Porta 550 ☎2427059, Eluthorshouse@hotmail.com. Located within easy stroll of the ocean, between the first and second blocks of 28 de Julio and the ninth and nineteenth blocks of Larco, this hostel (named after the owner's adolescent nickname) offers excellent value with hot water, access to kitchen, breakfasts, cable TV and table games; rooms are basic but clean and comfortable. ❸

Moderate

B&B Hostal Tradiciones Av Ricardo Palma 995 ☎4456742, ⓕ4462177, ⓦwww.taxis.com.pe/tradiciones. Centrally located in a safe environment, this reasonably-priced, family-run place offers cable TV, private bath, and fax and laundry services. ❺

Hikers Hostal Doña Catalina 358, Los Rosales,

Surco ☎2717970, ✉a-mauriz@us.nety. Located in the *segunda etapa* (second part) of Surco, level with block 38 of the Avenida Tomás Marsano, this is both comfortable and good value. Very clean and with all the services you'd expect from a mid-range hostel. **④**

Hospedaje Yolanda Domingo Elias 230 ☎4457565, ✉pensionyolanda@com.pe. Very well situated just off block 47 of the Avenida Arequipa, it's close to Surquillo market and the Alliance Francaise. Comfortable and clean. **④**

Hostal El Carmelo Bolognesi 749 ☎4460575, ✉camelo@amauta.rcp.net.pe. Friendly, safe and popular, located close to the heart of Miraflores, one block from the seafront. Clean, modern rooms with private bath; there's a small bar, cafetería and parking spaces. **⑥**

Hostal Mami Panchita Av Federico Gallesi 198 ☎2637203, ☎2630749, ✉raymi_travels@perusat.net.pe. Very pleasant but small hostel with a shared dining room and TV lounge. They also offer an airport pickup ($15 for a group, maximum of four). Price includes breakfast. **④**

Hostal Martinika Av Arequipa 3701, close to the boundary of Miraflores and San Isidro ☎4223094. Comfortable and friendly, offering rooms with private bath. Very reasonably priced and in an excellent location, if a little noisy in the mornings. **④**

Hostal El Ovalo Av Jose Pardo 1110 ☎4465549. Reasonably clean and cosy; also good value with adequate service, a rarity in this part of Miraflores. **④**

Hotel Bellavista 215 Jirón Bellavista 215 ☎/℗ 4442938. A good hotel in central Miraflores, offering double rooms with bath and TV. Breakfast included. **④**

Hotel El Patio Diez Canseco 341 ☎4442107, ℗4441663, ⊛www.andix.com/hostalelpatio. A very agreeable and secure little place right in the heart of Miraflores; gay-friendly. Often fully booked, so reserve in advance; more expensive mini-suites and suites also available. **⑤–⑦**

Marieta Bed & Breakfast Inn Malecon Cisneros 840 ☎4469028, ℗4466485, ✉gato@amauta.rcp.net.pe. A spotless and friendly small bed and breakfast set in a lovely house in one of Lima's more exclusive locations overlooking the ocean; private bath and terrace. The family that runs the B&B also operate a number of tours in and around Lima and will pick guests up from the airport for a reasonable fee. **⑥**

Suites Eucaliptus San Martín 511 ☎4458594. A variety of accommodation from basic rooms up to luxurious presidential suites at a corresponding

range of prices; good location and good security. **⑤–⑦**

El Zanguan Lodging Av Diez Canseco 736 ☎4469356, ⊛www.elzanguanlodging.com. A relatively new hostel, located very close to the action but in a relatively tranquil street near the Parque Tradiciones; the rooms are very pleasant, the service good and the breakfasts generous. **④**

Expensive

Boulevard Av José Pardo 771 ☎4446564, ℗ 4446602, ✉boulevard@amauta.rcp.net.pe. A full-on luxury hotel, one of the finest in the entire city. Quite well located in the hubbub of Miraflores. **⑧**

Cesar's Hotel Av La Paz 463 ☎4441212, ℗ 4444444. Incredibly swish pad with excellent service, a penthouse cocktail lounge and restaurant giving spectacular views across the city; the height of luxury. **⑧**

Colonial Inn Comandante Espinar 310 ☎2417471, ℗4466662, ✉coloinn@telematic.edu.pe. Great value, good service and exceptionally clean, slightly away from the fray of Miraflores. Has a lunchtime restaurant whose Belgian owner produces surprisingly good Peruvian and European cuisine. **⑥**

Embajadores Hotel Juan Fanning 320 ☎2429127, ℗ 2429131, ✉htelembajadores@mixmail. Part of the Best Western chain, this is located in a quiet Miraflores area, just a few blocks from Larco Mar and the seafront. Extremely comfortable, with a gym, small rooftop pool, conference rooms, individual safes and a restaurant. **⑧**

Faraoña Calle Manuel Bonilla 185 ☎4468218, ℗4469403, ⊛www.faraonagrandhotel.com. A plush, secure, quite modern hotel in a central part of this busy suburb; the lobby is cool and there's a pretty good restaurant. **⑧**

Grand Hotel Miraflores Av 28 de Julio 151 ☎4479641. Very well priced, with friendly staff and in a reasonably central Miraflores location. Has a lively disco some weekends. **⑦**

Hostal Aleman Av Arequipa 4704 ☎4464045, ℗4473950, ✉haleman@correo.dnet.com.pe. Very good value, most rooms being spacious and well furnished; tight on security and staff are sometimes a bit unfriendly. Within walking distance of downtown Miraflores. **⑥**

Hostal Miraflores Av Petit Thouars 5444 ☎4458745. Popular and close to most of Miraflores' shops and nightlife; good service and hard to beat for value. **⑥**

Hostal Polonia Av Republica de Panama 6599 ☎4464138, ℗4460760. A comfortable, quiet and attractive little hotel, but a bit on the expensive side for what you get and not in a brilliant spot, though within a short taxi ride of both Miraflores and Barranco. ⑥

Hotel Antigua Miraflores Av Grau 350 ☎2416116, ℻2416115, ℮hantiqua@amauta.rcp.nt.pe. Pretty central to Miraflores but in a relatively quiet spot, it has all modern conveniences but is still very old-fashioned and elegant with gardens and balconies. Luxury suites and standard rooms available. ⑧

Hotel Ariosto Av La Paz 769 ☎4441414. All modern comforts, good security and excellent service; good, central location in Miraflores. ⑧

Miraflores Park Plaza Avenida Malecon de la Reserva 1035 ☎2423000, ℻2423393, ℮mirapph@ibm.net. Very modern place that belongs to the exclusive Small Luxury Hotels of the World commercial chain; it has great views over Miraflores, the city and the Pacific. ⑧

Sonesta Posada del Inca – Miraflores Alcanfores 329 ☎2417688, ℻4471164, ℮reservas@sonestaperu.com. A very plush, excellently run and modern downtown hotel (part of the Sonesta Posadas del Inca chain). There's a 10 percent discount and complimentary breakfast for guests who have a copy of this book. ⑦

Barranco

Hospedaje Domeyer Domeyer 296 ☎2471413, ⓦwww.page.to/domeyerhostel. Not far from the action and nightlife of Barranco, all the rooms here are carpeted, with private baths, hot water and cable TV; price includes breakfast. ⑤

Mochileros Backpackers Pedro de Osma 135 ☎4774506, ⓦwww.backpackersperu.com. One of the more popular travellers' dives, based in the lively and trendy suburb of Barranco. Good facilities, including laundry, kitchen, bar, cable TV, luggage storage and lounge. It's clean, safe and pretty close to the beach; rooms are shared but have secure lockers. They also offer bicycle rental. Discounts available to South American Explorers' Club members. ❸

The Point Malecon Junin 300 ☎2477997, ℮the_point@hotmail.com. A bed and breakfast backpacker hostel created by two *mochilleros* ("backpackers") in a colonial house with relaxing gardens; there's also a shared kitchen and useful tourist information. ❷–❸

Other suburbs

Hotel Libertador Los Eucaliptos 550, San Isidro ☎4216666, ℻4423011, ⓦwww.libertador.com.pe. A top-class hotel well located in a well-to-do Lima suburb. The service and room standards are excellent. ⑧

Hotel El Marqués Chinchon 461, San Isidro ☎4420046, ℻4420043, ⓦwww.elmarques.com. This is a very comfortable business hotel with colonial-style rooms close to San Isidro's commercial centre. Has meeting rooms and is overall pretty good value. ⑦

Lima Youth Hostel Casimiro Ulloa 328, San Antonio ☎4465488 or 2423068, ℻4448187, ⓦwww.limahostell.com.pe. Unbeatable value. It's located just over the Paseo de la Republica highway from Miraflores in the relatively peaceful suburb of San Antonio, in a big house with a pool. ❷–❸

Malka Youth Hostal Los Lirios 165, San Isidro ☎4420165. Well located, cheerful and has an initimate atmosphere as well as being good value for this part of the city. ❷

Pension Jose Luis Francisco de Paula de Ugarriza 727, San Antonio ☎4441015, ℻4467177, ⓦwww.hoteljoluis.com. Comfortable, modern and in a good location close to Miraflores and the ocean, based in a private house with private baths and hot water; phone, fax and Internet access available. It's popular with English-speaking travellers. ❹

La Punta Jr. Saenz Pena 486–490, La Punta, Callao ☎4291553, ℮info@bed-and-breakfast-la -punta.com. Some 25 minutes by car from Lima Centro, this fine bed and breakfast is located on the seafront in elegant La Punta. Not all rooms in this newly renovated 1930s mansion have bath; breakfast included. ❹–⑥

Sonesta Posada del Inca - El Olivar Pancho Fierro 194, San Isidro ☎2212121 ℻4224345, ⓦwww.sonesta.com. Modern but pleasant luxury retreat by the olive grove park of San Isidro. There's a 10 percent discount and complimentary breakfast for guests who have a copy of this book. ⑧

Swissotel Lima Via Central 150, Centro Empresarial Real, San Isidro ☎4219888, ℻4214360, ℮peovl@ibm.net. Luxurious with all the modern conveniences you'd expect; good for business travellers and well located for banks and cross-city communications. ⑧

The City

Laid out across a wide, flat, alluvial plain, Lima fans out in long, straight streets from its heart, **Lima Centro**. The old town focuses on the colonial **Plaza Mayor** (often still called the Plaza de Armas) and the more modern **Plaza San Martín**, which are separated by some five blocks of the **Jirón de la Unión**, Lima Centro's main shopping street. At its river end, the Plaza Mayor is fronted by the Cathedral and Palacio de Gobierno, while there's greater commercial activity around Plaza San Martín – money-changing facilities, large hotels and airline offices are all based here. The key to finding your way around the old part of town is to acquaint yourself with these two squares and the streets between.

From Lima Centro, the city's main avenues stretch out into the sprawling suburbs. The two principal routes are **Avenida Colonial**, heading out to the harbour area around the suburb of **Callao** and the airport, and perpendicular to this, the broad, tree-lined **Avenida Arequipa** reaching out to the old beach resort of **Barranco**. Some 7 or 8km down Avenida Arequipa, the suburb of **Miraflores** is the modern, commercial heart of Lima, where most of the city's businesses have moved during the last thirty years. Lima's other main suburban sectors – **San Isidro, Barranco and Callao** – all have their own specific characteristics and points of interest.

Lima Centro

Since its foundation, Lima has spread steadily out from the **Plaza Mayor** – virtually all of the Río Rimac's alluvial soil has now been built on and even the sand dunes beyond are rapidly filling up with migrant settlers. When Pizarro arrived here he found a valley dominated by some 400 temples and palaces, most of them pre-Inca, well spread out to either side of the river. As usual, Pizarro's choice for the site of this new Spanish town was influenced as much by politics as it was by geography: he founded Lima on the site of an existing palace belonging to Tauri Chusko, the local chief who had little choice but to give up his residence and move away.

The Plaza Mayor

Today the heart of the old town is around the **Plaza Mayor** – until a few years ago known as the Plaza de Armas, or "armed plaza" (Plaza Armada) as the early conquistadores called it. There are no remains of any Indian heritage in or around the square; standing on the site of Tauri Chusko's palace is the relatively modern Palacio de Gobierno, while the Cathedral occupies the site of an Inca temple once dedicated to the Puma deity, and the Municipal Building lies on what was originally an Inca envoy's mansion. The **Palacio de Gobierno** – also known as the Presidential Palace – was Pizarro's house long before the present building was conceived. It was here that he spent the last few years of his life, until his assassination in 1541. Its grounds might even be considered "sacred" since as he died, his jugular severed by an assassin's rapier, Pizarro fell to the floor, drew a cross, then kissed it. The clean, sufficiently pretentious facade of the building you can see today, however, is modern, having been completed in 1938. The **changing of the guard** takes place outside the palace (Mon–Sat starting at 11.45am) – it's not a particularly spectacular sight, though the soldiers look splendid in their scarlet and blue uniforms. There are free **guided visits** (daily 10am-12.30pm) in English and Spanish, which include seeing the changing of the guard; to get on one you have to register with the Departamento de Actividades, office 201, Jr de la Unión, Plaza Pizarro

Convento de los Descalzos & Plaza de Acho

LIMA CENTRO

0   200 m

RIMAC

JULIAN PIÑEYRO

Puente de
Piedra

Río Rima

JIRÓN AYACUCHO

Casa
Aliaga

Train
Station

San
Francisco

JIRÓN ANCASH

Casa Pilatos

Santo
Domingo

Palacio
de
Gobierno

Ⓐ
②

Ⓑ ①

③

Ⓒ

Casa de Osamblea

JIRÓN LIMA (CONDE DE SUPERUNDA)

JIRÓN JUNIN

④

Museo de la
Inquisición

Chinatown & Central Market

Sancturio de
Santa Rosa
de Lima

Municipal
Building

PLAZA
MAYOR

Cathedral

JIRÓN HUALLAGA

JIRÓN CALLAO

Torre Tagle
Palace

JIRÓN CAYLLOMA

JIRÓN CAMANÁ

JIRÓN DE LA UNIÓN

JIRÓN CARABAYA

⑤
⑥

JIRÓN LAMPA

JIRÓN UCAYALI

AVENIDA ABANCAY

AVENIDA TACNA

JIRÓN ICA

Ⓓ

San
Pedro

Municipal
Theatre

San
Augustin

Casa de
Riva-
Aguero

JIRÓN MIRO QUESADA

HUANCAVELICA

⑧

JIRÓN RUFINO TORRICO

⑨

La Merced

Las
Nazarenas

⑩

AVENIDA EMANCIPACIÓN

AVENIDA CUSCO

JIRÓN AZANGARO

⑪

Ⓔ

MOQUEGUA

JIRÓN PUNO

Jesus Maria

JIRÓN OCOÑA

Ⓢ

⑫

PLAZA
SAN
MARTIN

Buses to Pachachamac & Lurin

AVENIDA NICOLAS DE PIEROLA (LA COLMENA)

Ⓢ

⑬

AVENIDA NICOLAS DE PIEROLA

Ⓒ

Parque
Universitario

AVENIDA GARCILASO DE LA VEGA

⑭

Ⓕ

MONZON

Lima Tours ⓘ

⑮

JR. RUFINO TORRICO

⑯

BELEN

PACHITEA

AVENIDA ABANCAY

Buses &
Colectivos
to Miraflores

PLAZA
FRANCIA

COTABAMBAS

Omeño & Mariscal Caceres buses

JIRÓN QUILCA

★ Cruz del Sur

AVENIDA ROOSEVELT

N

★ Tepsa

PASEO DE LA REPUBLICA

ACCOMMODATION

El Balcon Dorado	6	Hotel Samaniego	10
Gran Hotel Bolivar	12	Lima Sheraton Hotel	17
Hostal España	3	Pension Rodriguez	13
Hostal La Estrella de Belen	15	Plaza Francia Inn	16
Hostal Granada	8		
Hostal Lima	2	**RESTAURANTS & BARS**	
Hostal Roma	7	Cordano Café	A
Hostal Wiracocha	4	De Cesar / Machu Picchu	B
Hotel Europa	1	El Estadio	F
Hotel El Kamana	9	L'Eau Vive	D
Hotel El Plaza	14	Natur	E
Hotel Richmond	11	Las Trece Monedas	C
Hotel Ritual	5		

⑰

PASEO ESPAÑA

Parque
Neptuno

Museum of
Italian Art

PLAZA
GRAU

National
Museum of Art

PASEO COLÓN

▼ Avenida Arequipa

(☎ 3113908), at least 48 hours prior to when you want the tour. You'll also get to see the imitation Baroque interior of the palace and its rather dull collection of colonial and reproduction furniture.

Less than 50m away is the squat and austere **Cathedral** (Mon–Sat 10am–4.30pm; $1.50). Designed by Francisco Becerra, it was modelled on that in the Spanish town of Jaén and, like Jaén, it has three aisles in a Renaissance style. When Becerra died in 1605, however, the cathedral was far from completion. The towers alone took another 40 years to finish and, in 1746, further frustration arrived in the guise of a devastating earthquake, which destroyed much of the building; the current cathedral, which is essentially a reconstruction of Becerra's design, was rebuilt throughout the eighteenth and nineteenth centuries, then again after another quake in 1940. It is primarily of interest for its **Museum of Religious Art and Treasures** (daily 10am–4.30pm; $1.50), which contains seventeenth- and eighteenth-century paintings and some choir stalls with fine wooden carvings by Catalan artist Pedro Noguero. Its other highlight is a collection of human remains thought to be Pizarro's body (quite fitting since he placed the first stone shortly before his death), which lie in the first chapel on the right. Although gloomy, the interior retains some of its appealing Churrigueresque (highly elaborate Baroque) decor. The stalls are superb and, even more impressive, the choir stalls were exquisitely carved in the early seventeenth century by a Catalan artist. The **Archbishop's Palace** next door was rebuilt as recently as 1924.

Directly across the square, the **Municipal Building** (Mon–Fri 9am–1pm; free) is a typical example of a half-hearted twentieth-century attempt at something neocolonial. Brilliant white on the outside, its most memorable features are permanent groups of heavily armed guards and the odd armoured car waiting conspicuously for some kind of action. Actual civil unrest is generally little more than single-issue street protesting maybe once or twice a year.

Inside, the **Pinacoteca Museum** (same hours) houses a selection of Peruvian paintings, notably those of Ignacio Merino from the nineteenth century. For those with significant interest, the library has the city's Act of Foundation and Declaration of Independence on display; probably not of much interest to most visitors.

Set back from one corner of the main square is the church and monastery of **Santo Domingo** (Mon–Sat 9am–1pm & 3–6pm, Sun & holidays 9am–1pm; $2). Completed in 1549, Santo Domingo was presented by the pope, a century or so later, with an alabaster statue of Santa Rosa de Lima. Rosa's tomb, and that of San Martín de Porres, are the building's great attractions, and much revered. Otherwise it's not of huge interest or architectural merit, although it is one of the oldest religious structures in Lima, built on a site granted to the Dominicans by Pizarro in 1535. There's a growing concentration of **artesania shops** around Santo Domingo itself, the largest being Santo Domingo, right opposite the monastery. Nearby at Jirón Conde de Superunda 298, you'll find the recently restored early nineteenth-century **Casa de Osambela**, which has five balconies on its facade and a lookout point from which boats arriving at the port of Callao could be spotted.

East of the Plaza Mayor

Jirón Ancash leads away from the Palacio de Gobierno towards one of Lima's most attractive churches, **San Francisco** (daily 9.30am–5.30pm; $1.80). A large seventeenth-century construction with an engaging stone facade and towers, San Francisco's vaults and columns are elaborately decorated with Mudéjar (Moorish-style) plaster relief. It's a majestic building that has withstood the passage of time and the devastation of successive earth tremors. The San Francisco Monastery, part of the same architectural complex, also contains a superb library and a room of paintings by (or finished by) Pieter Paul Rubens, Jordaens and Van Dyck. You can take a 40-minute guided tour of the monastery and its **Catacombs Museum** (daily 9.30am–5pm; $1.80), both of which are worth a visit. The museum is inside the church's vast crypts, which were only discovered in 1951 and contain the skulls and bones of some seventy thousand people.

Opposite San Francisco, at Jirón Ancash 390, is **La Casa Pilatos** (Mon–Fri 11am–1.30pm; free), now the home of the Instituto Nacional de Cultura. Quite a simple building, and no competition for Torre Tagle (see below), it nevertheless has an attractive courtyard with an unusual stone staircase leading up from the middle of the patio. The fine wooden carving of the patio's balustrades adds to the general picture of opulent colonialism.

A couple of blocks away, the **Museo de la Inquisición**, Jirón Junin 548 (daily 9am–5pm; free but by guided tour only), faces out onto Plaza Bolivar near the Congress building. Behind a facade of Greek-style classical columns, the museum contains the original tribunal room with its beautifully carved mahogany ceiling. This was the headquarters of the Inquisition for the whole of Spanish-dominated America from 1570 until 1820, and, beneath the building, you can look round the dungeons and torture chambers, which contain a few gory, life-sized human models. The few blocks behind the museum and Avenida Abancay are taken over by the **central market** and **Chinatown**. Perhaps one of the most fascinating sectors of Lima Centro, Chinatown is now swamped by the large and colourful (if also smelly and rife with pickpockets) daily market. An ornate Chinese gateway, crossing over Jirón Huallaya, marks the site of Lima's best and cheapest *chifa* (Chinese) restaurants (see p.89).

Heading from Chinatown back towards the Plaza Mayor along Ucayali, you'll pass **San Pedro** (Mon–Sat 10am–noon & 5–6pm; free) on the corner of Jirón Azángaro. Built by the Jesuits and occupied by them until their expulsion in 1767, this richly decorated colonial church dripping with art treasures is worth a brief look around. However, just over the road, you'll find the far more spectacular **Torre Tagle Palace**, at Ucayali 358 (Mon–Fri 9am–5pm; free), pride and joy of the old city. Now the home of Peru's Ministry for Foreign Affairs and recognizable by the security forces with machine guns on the roof and top veranda, Torre Tagle is a superb, beautifully maintained mansion built in the 1730s. It is embellished with a decorative facade and two wooden balconies, which are typical of Lima architecture in that one is larger than the other. The porch and patio are distinctly Andalucian, with their strong Spanish colonial style, although some of the intricate wood carvings on pillars and across ceilings display a native influence; the *azulejos*, or tiles, also show a strong fusion of styles – this time a combination of Moorish and Limeño tastes. In the left-hand corner of the patio you can see a set of scales like those used to weigh merchandise during colonial times, and the house also contains a magnificent sixteenth-century carriage (complete with mobile toilet). Originally, mansions such as Torre Tagle served as refuges for outlaws, the authorities being unable to enter without written and stamped permission – now anyone can go in (afternoons are the quietest times to visit).

North of the Plaza Mayor: Rimac

Heading north from the Plaza Mayor along Jirón de la Unión, you pass the **Casa Aliaga**, at no. 224, an unusual mansion, reputed to be the oldest in South America, and occupied by the same family since 1535. It's also one of the most elaborate mansions in the country, with sumptuous reception rooms full of

Louis XIV mirrors, furniture, and doors. You need to call Lima Tours in advance to arrange a visit ($3; ☎4245110 or 2417751). Continuing up Jirón de la Unión, it's a short walk to the **Puente de Piedra**, the stone bridge which arches over the Río Rimac – usually no more than a miserable trickle – behind the Palacio de Gobierno. Initially a wooden construction, today's bridge was built in the seventeenth century, using egg whites to improve the consistency of its mortar. Its function was to provide a permanent link between the centre of town and the district of San Lazaro, known these days as **Rimac**, or, more popularly, as Bajo El Puente ("below the bridge"). This zone was first populated in the sixteenth century by African slaves, newly imported and awaiting purchase by big plantation owners; a few years later Rimac was beleaguered by outbreaks of leprosy. Although these days its status is much improved, Rimac is still one of the most run-down areas of Lima and can be quite an aggressive place at night – unfortunate, since some of the best "*peñas*" (Peruvian nightclubs, especially ones with folkloric music) are located down here. However, a one-hour guided **tour** (Sat & Sun 10am–9pm, departing every 15min) through old Rimac and up to the top of San Cristobal departs from outside Santo Domingo monastery (see p.77) and is a good and safe way to see many of Rimac's rather run-down sites. Take one in the afternoon, when the visibility is generally better.

Rimac is also home to the **Plaza de Acho**, at Hualgayoc 332, Lima's most important bullring, which also houses the **Museo Taurino de Acho**, or Bullfight Museum (Mon–Sat 9am–6pm, Sun 10am-6pm; $1.80; ☎4823360), containing some original Goya engravings, several interesting paintings, and a few relics of bullfighting contests. A few blocks to the right of the bridge, you can stroll up the **Alameda de los Descalzos**, a fine tree-lined walk designed for courtship, and an afternoon meeting place for the early seventeenth-century elite. It leads past the foot of a distinctive hill, the Cerro San Cristobal, and, although in desperate need of renovation, it still possesses twelve appealing marble statues brought from Italy in 1856, each one representing a different sign of the zodiac. At the far end of the Alameda a fine, low Franciscan monastery, **Convento de los Descalzos** (Mon–Sat 9.30am–1pm & 3–6pm; $1.80, usually including a 40-minute guided tour; ☎4810441), houses a collection of colonial and Republican paintings from Peru and Ecuador, and its Chapel of El Carmen possesses a beautiful Baroque gold-leaf altar. Founded in 1592, the monastery was situated in what was then a secluded spot beyond the town, originally situated here as a retreat from the busy city heart at the base of Cerro San Cristobal. Now, of course, the city runs all around it and way beyond.

West of the Plaza Mayor

Two interesting sanctuaries can be found on the western edge of old Lima, along Avenida Tacna. The **Sanctuario de Santa Rosa de Lima** (daily 9.30am–12.30pm & 3.30–6.30pm; free), on the first block of Tacna, is a fairly plain church named in honour of the first saint canonized in the Americas. The construction of Avenida Tacna destroyed a section of the already small seventeenth-century church, but in the patio next door you can visit the saint's **hermitage**, a small adobe cell, and a fascinating **Museo Etnografico**, containing crafts, tools, jewellery and weapons from jungle tribes, plus some photographs of early missionaries.

At the junction of Avenida Tacna and Huancavelica, the church of **Las Nazarenas** (daily 6am–noon & 5–8pm; free) is again small and outwardly undistinguished but it has an interesting history. After the severe 1655 earthquake, a mural of the crucifixion, painted by an Angolan slave on the wall of his hut, was apparently the only object left standing in the district. Its survival was deemed a miracle – the cause of popular processions ever since – and it was on this site that the church was founded. The widespread and popular processions for the Lord of Miracles, to save Lima from another earthquake, take place every autumn (Oct 18, 19, 28 & Nov 1), based around a silver litter which carries the original mural. Purple is the colour of the procession and many women in Lima wear it for the entire month.

LIMA AND AROUND | The City

South of the Plaza Mayor

The stretch between the Plaza Mayor and Plaza San Martín is the largest area of old Lima. Worth a quick look here is the church of **San Augustin** (daily 8.30am–noon & 3.30–5.30pm; free), founded in 1592 and located on the corner of Ica and Camana. Although severely damaged by earthquakes (only the small side chapel can be visited nowadays), the church retains a glorious facade, one of the most complicated examples of Churrigueresque architecture in Peru. Just across the road at Camana 459, the **Casa de Riva-Aguero** (daily 10am–1pm & 2–8pm; free) is a typical colonial house, built in the early nineteenth century and donated to the Catholic University. Its patio has been laid out as a **Museo de Arte Popular**, displaying crafts and contemporary paintings from all over Peru. The building also functions as the Riva-Aguero Institute, which looks after a library and historic archives.

Perhaps the most noted of all religious buildings in Lima is the **Iglesia de la Merced** (daily 8am–1pm & 4–8pm; free), just two blocks from the Plaza Mayor on the corner of Jirón de la Unión and Jirón Miro Quesada. Built on the site where the first Latin mass in Lima was celebrated, the original church was demolished in 1628 to make way for the present building. Its most elegant feature, a beautiful colonial facade, has been adapted and rebuilt several times – as have the broad columns of the nave – to protect the church against tremors. But by far the most lasting impression is made by the **Cross of the Venerable Padre Urraca**, whose silver staff is smothered by hundreds of kisses every hour and witness to the fervent prayers of a constantly shifting congregation. If you've just arrived in Lima, a few minutes by this cross will give you an insight into the depth of Peruvian belief in miraculous power. The attached **cloisters** (daily 8am–noon & 3–6pm; free) are less spectacular though they do have a historical curiosity: it was here that the Patriots of Independence declared the Virgin of La Merced their military marshal. A couple of minutes' walk further towards the Plaza San Martín, at the corner of Camana and Jirón Moquegua, stands the church of **Jesus María** (daily 7am–1pm & 3–7pm; free), home of Capuchin nuns from Madrid in the early eighteenth century. Take a look inside at its outstanding, sparkling Baroque gilt altars and pulpits.

The **Museo del Banco Central de Reserva del Peru**, at the corner of Lampa and Ucayali (Tues–Fri 10am–4.30pm, weekends 10am–1pm), has many antique and modern paintings, as well as a good collection of pre-Inca artefacts, mainly from grave robberies and only recently returned to Peru.

Plaza San Martín and around

The **Plaza San Martín** is a grand, large square with fountains at its centre. It's virtually always busy by day, with traffic tooting its way around the square, and buskers, mime artists, clowns and soapbox politicos attracting small circles of interested faces, while shoeshine boys and old men with box cameras on wooden tripods try to win your attention. The Plaza San Martín has seen most of Lima's political rallies over the past hundred years and the sight of rioting office workers and attendant police with water cannons and tear gas is still a possibility. Ideologically, the Plaza San Martín represents the sophisticated, egalitarian and European spirit of intellectual liberators like San Martín himself, while remaining well and truly within the commercial world.

The wide Avenida Nicolas de Pierola (also known as La Colmena) leads off the plaza, west towards the **Plaza Dos de Mayo**, which sits on the site of an old gate dividing Lima from the road to Callao and hosts a great street market where some fascinating bargains can be found. Built to commemorate the repulse of the Spanish fleet in 1866 (Spain's last attempt to regain a foothold in South America), the plaza is probably one of the most polluted spots in Lima and is markedly busier, dirtier and less friendly than Plaza San Martín. East of Plaza San Martín, Avenida Nicolas de Pierola runs towards the **Parque Universitario**, site of South America's first university, San Marcos. Nowadays, the park itself is a base for colectivo companies and street hawkers, and is almost permanently engulfed in crowds of cars and rushing pedestrians. The amphitheatre in the park is sometimes used for free public performance by a range of musicians and artists.

South of Plaza San Martín, Jirón Belén leads down to the Paseo de la República and the shady **Parque Neptuno**, home to the pleasant **Museo de Arte Italiano**, Paseo de la República 250 (Mon–Fri 10am–5pm; $1; ☎4239932). Located inside an unusual Renaissance building, the museum exhibits contemporary Peruvian art as well as reproductions of the Italian masters and offers a very welcome respite from the hectic modern Lima outside. Just south of here at Paseo Colón 125 is the **Museo de Arte** (closed Wed 10am–5pm; $2; ☎4235149), housed in the former International Exhibition Palace built in 1868. It contains interesting, small collections of colonial art and many fine crafts from pre-Columbian times, and also hosts frequent temporary exhibitions of modern photography and other art forms. Film shows and lectures are offered on some weekday evenings (for details check posters at the museum lobby). Walk 50m or so west from the museum along Paseo Colón and you'll come to the large **Parque de la Exposición**, which stretches down to Avenida 28 de Julio. Created for the International Exhibition of 1868, the park has been revamped around the Millennium but still seems mainly to attract courting couples who have nowhere else to go, particularly on Sundays. Not far away, at Jirón Washington 1946 (Mon–Fri 9am–1pm & 2.30–5.30pm; free; ☎3306074), the **Casa Museo de Jose Carlos Mariategui**, an impressive early twentieth-century house which has been restored by the Instituto Nacional de Cultura; it was the home of the famous Peruvian political figure and writer Mariategui during some of his most intensely creative periods.

The suburbs

The old centre of Lima is surrounded by a number of sprawling **suburbs**, or *distritos*, which spread across the desert between the foothills of the Andes and the coast. Just south of Lima Centro lies the lively suburb of **Miraflores**, a slick, fast-moving and very ostentatious mini-metropolis, which has become Lima's business and shopping zone and doubles up as a popular meeting place for the wealthier sector of Lima society; a relatively modern clifftop development, Larco Mar, has been built at the bottom of Miraflores' main street, adding to the appeal. Sandwiched between Lima Centro and Miraflores is the plush suburb of **San Isidro**, boasting a golf course surrounded by sky-scraping apartment buildings and ultramodern shopping complexes, as well as many square kilometres of simple houses looking almost pre-Inca in style – with rectangular, often flat-roofed structures gilded with subtle geometric features and symbols, lurking even within the form of metal grill gates mainly there to keep out robbers.

South of Miraflores begins the oceanside suburb of **Barranco**, one of the oldest and most attractive parts of Lima, located above the steep sandy cliffs of the **Costa Verde**, and hosting a small but active nightlife. Southwest of Lima Centro lies the city's port area, the suburb of **Callao**, an interesting, if rather old and insalubrious zone, and the peninsula of **La Punta**, with its air of slightly decayed grandeur. Other than these neighbourhoods, the main reason for venturing into Lima's suburbs is to visit some of its select museums scattered about the city's sprawl, namely the comprehensive **Museo Nacional de Arqueología, Antropología y Historia del Peru** and the modern **Museo de la Nación**.

Miraflores

As far as Lima's inhabitants are concerned, **MIRAFLORES** is the major focus of the city's action and nightlife, its streets lined with cafés and the capital's flashiest shops. Although still connected to Lima Centro by the long-established Avenida Arequipa, another road – Paseo de la República (also known as the Via Expressa) – now provides the suburb with an alternative approach. The fastest way to get here is to take the yellow bus marked "Via Expressa" from Avenida Abancay and get off, after about 25 minutes, at the Benavides bridge. Alternatively, take a yellow bus (#2) or colectivo from the first few blocks of Avenida Garcilaso de la Vega (a continuation of Avenida Tacna) and get off at *El Haiti* café/bar, the stop just before Miraflores central park.

A good place to make for first is the **Huaca Pucllana** in General Borgoño block 8 (Mon & Wed–Sun 9am–1pm & 1.30–5pm; $1; ☏4458695), a vast pre-Inca adobe mound which continues to dwarf most of the houses around and has a small site museum, craft shop and restaurant. It's just a two-minute walk from Avenida Arequipa, on the right as you come from Lima Centro at block 44. One of a large number of *huacas* – sacred places – and palaces that formerly stretched across this part of the valley, little is known about the Pucllana, though it seems likely that it was originally named after a pre-Inca chief of the area. It has a hollow core running through its cross-section and is thought to have been constructed in the shape of an enormous frog, symbol of the rain god, who evidently spoke to priests through a tube connected to the cavern at its heart. This site may well have been the mysteriously unknown oracle after which the Rimac (meaning "he who speaks") Valley was named; a curious document from 1560 affirms that the "devil" spoke at this mound.

From the top of the *huaca* you can see over the office buildings and across the flat roofs of multicoloured houses in the heart of Miraflores. The suburb's central area focuses on the attractive, almost triangular **Parque 7 de Junio** (Miraflores Park) at the end of the Avenida Arequipa. The park divides into four areas of activity: at the top end is the pedestrian junction where the shoeshiners hang out; further down there's a small amphitheatre, which often has mime acts or music; next you come to a raised circular area, which has a good craft and antiques market set up on stalls every evening (6–10pm); and just down from here is a small section of gardens and a children's play area. The streets around the park are lined with flashy cafés and bars and crowded with shoppers, flower-sellers and young men washing cars. In the park, particularly on Sundays, there are artists selling their canvases – some quite good, though aimed at making money from tourists. **Larco Mar**, the flash new development at the bottom of Avenida Larco, has done an excellent job of integrating the park end of Miraflores with what was previously a rather desolate point. Essentially a shopping zone with patios and walkways open to the sky, sea and

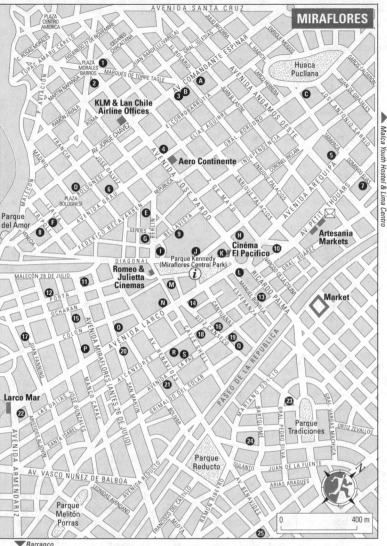

MIRAFLORES

Huaca Pucllana

KLM & Lan Chile Airline Offices

Aero Continente

Parque del Amor

Artesania Markets

Cinéma El Pacifico

Parque Kennedy (Miraflores Central Park)

Romeo & Julietta Cinemas

Market

Larco Mar

Parque Tradiciones

Parque Reducto

Parque Melitón Porras

Barranco

▶ Malca Youth Hostel & Lima Centro

0   400 m

ACCOMMODATION			
Boulevard	4	Hostal El Ovalo	2
Casa del Muchillero	1	Hostal Miraflores	10
Cesar's Hotel	19	Hotel Antigua Miraflores	6
Colonial Inn	3	Hotel Ariosto	21
Embajadores Hotel	17	Hotel Bellavista	9
Faraoña	13	Hotel El Patio	16
Friends House	15	Lex Luthor's House	12
Grand Hotel Miraflores	11	Lima Youth Hostel	24
Hospedaje Turistico		Marriott Hotel	22
Flying Dog	14	Pension Jose Luis	25
Hospedaje Yolanda	7	Sonesta Posada del Inca	18
Hostal Aleman	5	Suites Eucaliptus	20
Hostal El Carmelo	8	El Zanguan Lodging	23

RESTAURANTS AND NIGHTLIFE			
Brenchley Arms	H	Lacto-Ovo Vegetariano	Q
Las Brujas de Cachiche	D	Muelle Viejo	E
Café Café	J	Naturisto El Paraiso	R
Café Haiti	K	O'Murphy's Irish Pub	N
Cevicheria El Oro Algarrobo	O	La Pergola/The Old Pub	I
Chifa Long	P	Piccolo Café	M
Colina	G	La Tasca	B
Curich	F	La Tiendecita Blanca	L
Dinnos Pizza	A		
El Farolito	O		
Huaca Pucllana	C		
Jazz Zone	S		

cliffs, Larco Mar is also home to several decent bars, ice-cream parlours, restaurants, cinemas and nightclubs.

From the end of Avenida Arequipa, **Avenida Larco** and **Diagonal** both fan out along the park en route to the ocean less than 2km away. Near to where Avenida Larco reaches the shore, the attractive **Parque del Amor** sits on the clifftops above the Costa Verde and celebrates the fact that for decades this area has been a favourite haunt of young lovers, particularly the poorer Limeños who have no privacy at their often-overcrowded homes. A huge sculpture of a loving Andean couple clasping each other rapturously is usually surrounded by pairs of real-life lovers walking hand in hand or cuddling on the clifftops above the ocean, especially on Sunday afternoons. Take note that there have been recent reports of muggings in and around here.

Miraflores' only important mansion open to the public is the **Casa de Ricardo Palma**, at General Suarez 189 (Mon–Fri 10am–12.30pm & 4–7pm, Sat 10am–noon; free), where Palma, probably Peru's greatest historian, lived for most of his life. There are two museums worth visiting, one of which, the **Enrico Poli Museum**, Lord Cochrane 466 (hours by appointment; $10 per person for a minimum of five; ☎4222437), contains some of the finest pre-Inca archeological treasures in Lima, including ceramics, gold and silver. The highlight of this private collection is the treasure found at Sepan in northern Peru, in particular four golden trumpets, each over a metre long and over a thousand years old. The private **Amano Museum**, on Calle Retiro 160, off block 11 of Angamos Oeste (Mon–Fri, hours by appointment; entry by donation; ☎4412909), also merits a visit for its fabulous exhibition of Chancay weavings (among the best of pre-Columbian textiles), as well as beautiful ceramics.

Barranco and the Costa Verde

BARRANCO, a quieter place than Miraflores, about 5km or 10-15 minutes away, is easily reached by picking up many of the buses or colectivos (those marked Barranco in their front window, or with the conductor shouting out Barranco) travelling along Diagonal (which is one-way, from the central park towards Larco Mar and the ocean). Overlooking the ocean, and scattered with old mansions as well as fascinating smaller homes, this was the capital's seaside resort during the nineteenth century and is now a kind of Limeño Left Bank, with young artists, writers, musicians and intellectuals taking over many of the older properties. Only covering three square kilometres, Barranco is quite densely populated, with some 40,000 inhabitants living in its delicately coloured houses. The primary attraction of Barranco is its bars, clubs and cafés clustered around the small but attractive **Plaza Municipal de Barranco**, which buzz with frenetic energy after dark whilst retaining much of the area's original charm and character. There's little else to see, specifically, though you may want to take a look at the clifftop remains of a funicular rail-line, which used to carry aristocratic families from the summer resort down to the beach.

One block inland of the funicular, the impressive **Church of the Hermit** sits on the cliff, with gardens to its front. Local legend says that the church was built here following a miraculous vision of a glowing Christ figure on this very spot. Beside the church there's the Puente de Suspiros, an attractive wooden bridge crossing a gully – the Bajada de Banos – which leads steeply down the gully to the ocean, passing exotic dwellings lining the crumbling gully sides. A path leads beside the church along the top edge of the gully to the **Mirador Catalina Recavarra**, located at the point where the top of the gully more or less meets the sea cliff; here there's a two-storey pub, *La Posada del Mirador*, and some other pleasant cafés and bars, buzzing during weekend evenings. Also worth a browse is the **Museum of Electricity**, Pedro de Osma 105 (daily 9am–5pm; free), very close to the main plaza in Barranco, which displays a wide range of early electrical appliances and generating techniques. Just down the road, at Pedro de Osma 421, the **Museo de Arte Colonial Pedro de Osma** (Tues–Sun 10am–1pm & 2.30–6pm; $3; ☎4670063) holds a number of treasures and antiques in the form of oil paintings, colonial sculptures and silverware.

Down beside the pounding rollers stands the **COSTA VERDE**, so named because of vegetation clinging to the steep sandy cliffs. A bumpy road follows the shore from an exclusive yacht club and the Chorrillos fishermen's wharf, at the southern end, northwest past both Barranco and Miraflores, almost to the suburb of Magdalena. The sea is cold and not too clean – and there's nothing here really, other than sand, pebbles, a couple of beach clubs, a few restaurants (good for their seaside atmosphere rather than their reputation for high cuisine) and a resident surfing crowd. But Lima would seem sparse without it, and swimming in the surf is as good a way as any to extend a day mooching about Barranco and Miraflores. As everywhere else, keep a sharp eye on your clothes and valuables.

San Isidro

Unless you're shopping, banking, living there or simply looking for a sauna or disco, there are few other reasons to stop off in **SAN ISIDRO**. One, though, is to take a stroll through the **Bosque El Olivar**, just 150m west from block 34 of Avenida Arequipa. A charming grove first planted in 1560, it's now rather depleted in olive trees but you can still see the old press and millstone as well as a stage where concerts and cultural events are often held; mostly, though, El Olivar is simply one of Lima's relatively few large open, green spaces. A few blocks northwest, just off Avenida El Rosario, is an impressive reconstructed adobe *huaca*, **Huallamarca**, Nicolas de Rivera 201 (Tues–Sun 9am–5pm; $1), now surrounded by wealthy suburbs. Like Pucllana, this dates from pre-Inca days and has a small museum displaying the archeological remains of ancient Lima culture, such as funerary masks and artwork found in the *huaca* – including textiles oddly reminiscent of Scottish tartans. San Isidro has just one colonial mansion worth checking out, the **Casa de la Tradición**, at Avenida Salaverry 3032 (Mon–Fri 2.30–5pm; $1.50). A rather elegant old house, it contains an interesting private collection of artefacts and pictures covering the history of Lima.

Jesus Maria

The workaday suburb of **JESUS MARIA**, just west of San Isidro and south of Lima Centro, only has one real attraction: the little-visited, but quite fascinating, **Museum of Natural History**, Avenida Arenales 1250 (Mon–Fri 8am–1.30pm, Sat 9am–noon; $1.50; ☎4710117). The museum presents a comprehensive overview of Peruvian wildlife and botany, with its highlight, a "sun fish", being one of only three known examples in the world of this colourful fish that can be found in the American coastal waters. To get there take microbus #13 (red and cream) from Avenida Tacna.

Pueblo Libre

The suburb of **PUEBLO LIBRE**, which lies between San Isidro and Callao, is home to a trio of Lima's major museums. Primary among them is the **Museo Nacional de Arqueología, Antropología y Historia del Peru,** on Plaza

Bolivar at the corner of San Martín and Antonio Pola (Tues–Sun 9am–5pm; $3; ☏4635070), which possesses a varied exhibition of pre-Inca artefacts and a number of historical exhibits relating mainly to the Republican period of Peru's history (1821 until the late nineteenth century). Although there's plenty to see, much of the museum's immense collection is in storage and has been for decades, though some has shifted to the Museo de la Nación on the other side of town (see p.88). Recently renovated displays give a detailed and accurate perspective on Peru's prehistory, a vision that comes as a surprise if you'd previously thought of Peru simply in terms of Incas and conquistadores. The galleries are set around two colonial-style courtyards, the exhibits including stone tools some eight thousand years old, famous carved **Chavin stones** such as the magnificent Estela Raymondi, a diorite block intricately engraved with feline, serpent and falcon features, and the Tello Obelisk, a masterpiece in granite. The Manos Cruzados, or Crossed Hands stone from **Kotosh**, is also on display, evidence of a mysterious cult from some five thousand years ago. From **Paracas** there are sumptuous weavings and many excellent examples of deformed heads and trepanned skulls: one shows post-operative growth, and a male mummy, "frozen" at the age of 30 to 35, has fingernails still visible and a creepy, sideways glance fixed on his misshapen head. From **Nazca** there are incredible ceramics representing marine life, agriculture, flora, sexuality, wildlife, trophy-heads, and scenes from mythology and everyday life. The **Mochica** and **Chimu cultures** are represented, too, and there are also exhibits devoted to the **Incas**. To get to the museum take microbus #41 (white and blue) from Avenida Tacna in Lima Centro.

The **National Museum of History**, adjacent to the Archeological and Anthropological Museum (same hours and ticket) and entered by the same door, is housed in a nineteenth-century mansion. It displays dazzling antique clothing, extravagant furnishings, and other period pieces, complemented by early Republican paintings. The liberators San Martín and Bolivar both lived here for a while.

A fifteen-minute walk from here – you can literally just follow a blue line which has been painted on the pavement north up Avenida Sucre then west along Avenida Bolivar for ten blocks – brings you to one of the city's most unusual museums, the **Rafael Larco Herrera Museum**, Avenida Bolivar 1515 (daily 9am–6pm; $6; ☏4611835, ⓦwww.museolarco.perucultural .org.pe), which contains hundreds of thousands of excellently preserved ceramics, many of them Chiclin or Mochica pottery from around Trujillo. The museum is divided into three sections: the main museum; the warehouse museum; and, most intriguingly, the erotic art museum, which contains a selection of pre-Inca exhibits, the museum's highlight. From Lima Centro, you can get to the museum either by bus #23 from Avenida Abancay, by green microbus #37 from Avenida Nicolas de Pierola, or on bus #41 from Avenida Emancipación or Plaza Dos de Mayo; however, it's much easier and quicker to take a taxi (about $3).

Parque de las Leyendas and the Zoo

Head west from the Larco Herrera museum to the end of Avenida Bolivar, then skirt round to the southwest of the Catholic university campus in the suburb of San Miguel, and you'll come to the **Zoo** and **Parque de las Leyendas** (daily 9am–5pm; $2, $1 for students). Located in a relatively deserted spot on the sacred site of the ancient Maranga culture, the park is laid out according to the three regions of Peru – *costa*, *sierra* and *selva*. The park and zoo has been much improved in recent years, though there's little attempt to create the appropriate habitats and the animals are caged. Nevertheless, it's a good place to get a glimpse of many of Peru's animal and bird species – condors, jaguars, sea lions, snakes and pumas, king vultures, elephants, bears, and other exotica. It's a fine spot for a picnic, too, and there are good artesania stalls just outside, selling cases of magnificent dead insects, including colourful Amazonian butterflies and tarantulas. Yellow bus #48 goes directly there from the Plaza Mayor or you can take almost any of the colectivos along Avenida La Marina or west along Avenida Javier Prado; a taxi, though easier, may cost $2 or $3.

Callao and La Punta

Stuck out on a narrow, boot-shaped peninsula, Callao and La Punta (The Point) form a natural annex to Lima, looking out towards the ocean. Originally quite separate, they were both founded in 1537, and were destined to become Peru's principal treasure-fleet port before eventually being engulfed by Lima's other suburbs during the course of the twentieth century, and these days it's a crumbling but attractive area.

Still the country's main commercial harbour, and one of the most modern ports in South America, **CALLAO** lies about 14km west of Lima Centro. It's easily reached on bus #25 from Plaza San Martín, which runs all the way there – and beyond to La Punta – or by taking buses (marked "La Punta") from Avenida Arequipa west along either Avenida Angamos or Avenida Javier Prado. The suburb is none-too-alluring a place – its slum zones, infamous for prostitution and gangland assassins, are considered virtually no-go areas for the city's middle classes – but if you're unworried by such associations, you will find some of the best ceviche restaurants anywhere on the continent.

Further along, away from the rougher quarters and dominating the entire peninsula, you can see the great **Castle of Real Felipe** (Mon–Fri 9am–2.30pm; $1.30; ☏4658394), located on the Plaza Independencia. Built after the devastating earthquake of 1764, which washed ships ashore and killed nearly the entire population of Callao, this is a superb example of the military architecture of its age, designed in the shape of a pentagon. Although built too late to protect the Spanish treasure fleets from European pirates like Francis Drake, it was to play a critical role in the battles for independence. Its firepower repulsed both Admiral Brown (1816) and Lord Cochrane (1818), though many Royalists (Peruvians loyal to the Spanish Crown) starved to death here when it was besieged by the Patriots (those patriotic to Peru but keen to disengage from the Spanish colonial authorities) in 1821, just prior to its surrender. The fort's grandeur is marred only by a number of storehouses, built during the late nineteenth century when it was used as a customs house. Inside, the **Military Museum** (Mon–Fri 9.30am–4pm; free) houses a fairly complete collection of eighteenth- and nineteenth-century arms and has various rooms dedicated to Peruvian war heroes. Also in Callao is the **Naval Museum**, Avenida Jorge Chavez 121, off Plaza Grau (Mon–Fri 9am–4pm; free; ☏4297278), displaying the usual military paraphernalia, uniforms, paintings, photographs and replica ships.

Out at the end of the peninsula, what was once the fashionable beach resort of **LA PUNTA** is now overshadowed by the Naval College and Yacht Club. Many of its old mansions, although slowly crumbling, still remain, some of them very elegant, others extravagant monstrosities. Right at the peninsula's tip, an attractive promenade offers glorious views and sunsets over the Pacific, while at the back of the strand there are some excellent restaurants serving traditional local food (many of these are difficult to find – it's best to ask locally for directions).

The Museo de la Nación and the Museo de Oro

In the east of the city lie two of Lima's most compelling museums. The **Museo de la Nación**, Javier Prado Este 2465 in the suburb of San Borja (Tues–Sun 9am–5pm; $1, $3 extra for exhibitions; ☎4769878), is Lima's largest modern museum and contains permanent exhibitions covering most of the important aspects of Peruvian archeology, art and culture. Exhibits are displayed mainly in vast salons and include a range of traditional, regional peasant costumes from around the country and life-sized and miniature models depicting life in pre-Conquest times. The museum can be visited by taking a colectivo along Avenida Javier Prado east from Avenida Arequipa; after ten to fifteen minutes, you'll see the vast, concrete building on the left.

After the Museum of the Nation, take any bus or colectivo from the junction of Avenida Javier Prado and Avenida Aviación south to Avenida Angamos where you can catch the #72 microbus (yellow and red) or a Monterrico colectivo to the Centro Comercial shopping. From here, Lima's **Museo de Oro**, Avenida Alonso de Molina 1100 (daily 11.30am–7pm; $8; ☎3451292), is a three-block walk up Avenida Primavera, then two to the right along Santa Elena. Housed in a small fortress-like building set back in the shade of tall trees and owned by the high-society Mujica family, this museum is a must-see. Upstairs there are some excellent tapestry displays, while the ground level boasts a vast display of **arms and uniforms**, which bring to life some of Peru's bloodier historical episodes. The real gem, however, is the basement, crammed with original and replica pieces from **pre-Columbian** times. The pre-Inca weapons and wooden staffs and the astounding Nazca yellow-feathered poncho designed for a noble's child or child high-priest are especially fine pieces. One object which usually causes a stir is a skull enclosing a full set of pink quartz teeth.

The **Casa Ecologica**, affiliated with the Universidad Catolica's Group for Assistance to the Rural Sector, has an interesting exhibit of an ecologically-friendly house with wind, solar electric, solar thermal and solar cooking facilities set in an organic garden. You need to contact Miguel Hazdich in advance to visit (☎4602870, ⓦwww.pucp.edu.pe/~grupo).

Eating

Among South American capitals, Lima ranks alongside Rio and Buenos Aires for its selection of **places to eat and drink**, with restaurants, bars and cafés of every type and size crowding every corner of the city, from expensive hotel dining rooms to tiny set-meal street stalls. Regardless of class or status, virtually all Limeños eat out regularly, and having a meal out usually ends up as an evening's entertainment in itself.

Cafés and snackbars

Lima Centro

Bar/Restaurant Machu Picchu Ancash 312. A busy place opposite San Francisco church in Lima Centro, serving inexpensive snacks; a good spot for meeting up with other travellers. Daily 8am–11pm.
Cordano Ancash 202 ☎4270181. Beside the Palacio de Gobierno in Lima Centro, this is one of the city's last surviving traditional bar/restaurants – very good value, with old-fashioned service.

Worth visiting if only to see the decaying late nineteenth- and early twentieth-century decor. Mon–Sat 8am–11pm.
Natur Moquegua 132. A surprisingly good vegetarian restaurant, catering to vegans as well as, and, perhaps because of the generous portions, a very popular Lima Centro lunchtime meeting place, just a couple of blocks from the Plaza San Martín. Mon–Fri 10am–5pm.

Miraflores

Café Café Matir Olaya 250. A groovy and gay-friendly coffee shop playing good rock music just off Diagonal in downtown Miraflores. Daily 10am–midnight.

Café Haiti Diagonal 160 ☎4463816. The most popular meeting place for middle-class Limeños, based by the Cinema El Pacifico in the heart of Miraflores; excellent snacks and drinks but expensive. Daily 8am–midnight.

Oro Verde Calle Colon 569. A pleasant, traditional coffee shop attached to the Zona de Arte photographic gallery. Mon–Sat 10am–7pm.

La Tiendecita Blanca Av Larco 111. Another popular meeting place, with a superb range of cakes and pastries, though they are all a bit pricey; located right on the busiest junction in Miraflores. Daily 8am–8pm.

Barranco

Las Mesitas Av Grau 341 ☎4774199. Not cheap, and not as stylish or quaint as it used to be in its old location, but still a tasteful and tasty Lima café serving quality snacks, meals and delicious sweets.

Restaurants

Predictably, Lima boasts some of the best **restaurants** in the country, serving not only traditional Peruvian dishes, but cuisines from all parts of the world. Seafood is particularly good here, with **ceviche** – raw fish or seafood marinated in lime juice and served with onions, chillis, sweet corn and sweet potatoes – being the speciality. Many of the more upmarket restaurants fill up very quickly, so it is advisable to reserve in advance; where this is the case we have included the phone number. All the restaurants listed below are open roughly 10.30am–11pm daily unless otherwise indicated.

Budget

Cevicheria El Oro Algarrobo San Martín 445, Miraflores. A good place for seafood at very reasonable prices; it's not slick or haute cuisine, but the food is quite satisfactory and the place is located on one of those rare, quiet Miraflores streets.

Chifa Chun Yion Calle Unión 126, Barranco ☎4770550. An excellent and very busy Chinese restaurant, quite traditional with some private booths in the back room; again, not high quality, but very reasonable.

Chifa Kun San Martín 459, Miraflores. A small, relatively quiet Chinese restaurant, just half a block from Avenida Larco between the Park and Larco Mar; plentiful dishes.

Colina Jirón Berlin 317, Miraflores. Relatively low-key but has good service, cold beers and serves passable meals and snacks; conveniently located just beyond the hustle and bustle of Miraflores' crowded main streets. Mon–Sat 11am–11pm.

De Cesar Ancash 300, Lima Centro ☎4288740. Great little café-cum-restaurant and bar right in the heart of old Lima; food is fine and cheap, service friendly, the surroundings pleasant and the range of breakfasts quite endless.

El Farolito San Martín 435, Miraflores ☎4453568. Best at lunchtimes for its full and delicious set menus, it's an inexpensive place very popular with locals, located in a quiet part of Miraflores; a family-run restaurant virtually hidden in the suburbs.

Piccolo Café Diez Canseco 126, Miraflores. A cosy little café near the Parque 7 de Junio, serving inexpensive sandwiches, snacks and ice creams; vaguely Italian in style, this is another good place for a respite from the often crowded streets.

Restaurant Lacto-Ovo Vegetariano Diez Canseco 487, Miraflores. Excellent natural yogurt available by the litre; great veggie lunches. Very central.

Restaurant Naturista El Paraiso Alcanfores 416–453, Miraflores. An inexpensive but very tasty vegetarian restaurant; a cheerful place to shelter from the hustle and bustle of the Miraflores streets.

La Tasca Av Comandante Espinar 300, Miraflores. A very fine restaurant for a lunchtime set menu ($3–5 with a choice of main course) in terms of quality and value for money; not to be missed if you're in this part of Miraflores.

Vegetariano Restaurant Naturista Av Petit Thouars 4747, Miraflores. An excellent vegetarian restaurant, a little out of the heart of Miraflores; targeted at office workers, it nevertheless has a pleasant atmosphere and set lunches for under $2.

Vista Alegre Bonilla 178b. Another tasteful vegetarian restaurant run with a lot of good heart and experience; cheap set lunch menu and great fruit salads. There may not be a sign, so it can be hard to locate.

Moderate

Bircher Benner Diez Canseco 487 ☎ 4444250. A mainly vegetarian restaurant and health-food shop in downtown Miraflores; relatively expensive, except for the very affordable set lunches; tasty meals and a large choice of tropical fruit juices. Tues–Sat 8.30am–10.30pm.

El Catamaran Av Republica de Panama 225, Barranco. Good reputation for seafood (try the *ceviche de mariscos*); elegant but relaxed surroundings. Expensive but accepts all major credit cards.

El Ceviche de Arturo Berlin 192, Miraflores. A centrally located lunchtime seafood restaurant; the food is decent although by no means the best in town.

Cevicheria El Peñon Honorio Delgado 106, La Victoria ☎ 2260614. Located between blocks 13 and 14 of Av Canada, this restaurant is another brilliant and unpretentious cevichería; very friendly and the owner speaks English. Call to book in advance.

El Cevillano Av Aviación 3333. A relatively inexpensive cevichería serving excellent seafood dishes; rather far out, though, in the suburb of San Borja. Tues–Sun noon–5pm.

Chifa Capon Ucayali 774. An excellent and traditional Limeño Chinese restaurant, the best of many in this block of Chinatown, close to the centre. It offers a range of authentic *chifa* dishes, but doesn't stay open very late.

Curich Bolognesi 753, Miraflores ☎ 4445005. A few blocks from the Parque del Amor, this is a quality restaurant, piano-bar and snack bar serving great tamales, among other things.

Dinnos Pizza Comandante Espinar 408, Miraflores ☎ 2420606. Some of the best pizza in Lima, this restaurant offers relatively fast and glitzy service.

El Estadio Restaurant Bar Nicolas de Pierola 926, Plaza San Martín ☎ 4288866, ⓦ www.Estadio.com.pe. The theme is strongly football and the walls on several floors are covered in murals and paraphernalia fascinating even for those only remotely interested in the sport; plus you can have your picture taken next to a lifesize bust of Pele while you're here. Both the food and bar are decent and there are sometimes disco evenings in the basement.

Govinda Vegetarian Restaurant Shell 634, Miraflores. Offers good, simple fare at very reasonable prices, particularly if you go for the set menus. Run by the International Association for Krishna Consciousness, it has a pleasant, relaxed atmosphere and an attached health-food shop.

L'Eau Vive Ucayali 370 ☎ 4275612. Opposite the Torre Tagle Palace, this very reasonably priced and interesting restaurant serves superb French food cooked by nuns; it has a set menu for lunches and evening meals and closes after a chorus of *Ave Maria* most evenings; Mon–Sat noon–2.45pm & 8.15–10.30pm.

Manolo Malecon Pardo, block 1, La Punta, Callao. A fine seafood restaurant and bar on the seafront in La Punta; over on the western edge of Lima (best when sunny rather than windy).

Meulle Viejo Berlin 505–507. An inexpensive and pretty good seafood restaurant specializing in lunchtime ceviches for shop and office workers in Miraflores – try the ceviche *mixto*. Slightly off the beaten track but worth the trip.

Naylamp Av 2 de Mayo 239, Barranco ☎ 4675011. Another excellent if trendy restaurant in a superb setting; specialities are traditional Peruvian dishes, mainly comida criolla like *aji de gallina, carapulcra* etc.

Oro Verde Colon 571. A quiet little café that specializes in coffees and set lunch menus at reasonable prices; located on the premises of a dance school, it has pleasant garden tables out the back.

El Otro Sitio Calle Sucre 317, Barranco. An excellent evening restaurant serving criolla dishes, often accompanied by criolla music, in a romantic setting close to the Puente de Suspiros. Wed–Sun 8pm–midnight.

El Peñon Av Nicolas de Arriola 787, Santa Catalina ☎ 4720229. Just north of San Isidro, this is one of the best cevicherias in Lima, yet it remains little known; traditional if basic setting and quality seafood dishes created by a small, proud family business. Wed–Mon 11am–6pm.

La Pergola Boulevard San Ramon 225. Probably the best of the Italian restaurants in the "Little Italy" complex off Diagonal in Miraflores; very busy at weekends, this interesting place shares a building with the *Chemnitz* video pub and *La Glorietta Pizzeria*.

Sin Thai Restaurant Av Caminos del Inca 467, Chacarilla. Superb Thai food in a delightful environment; very reasonable service and prices. Best to take a taxi.

Las Trece Monedas Jirón Ancash 536 ☎ 4276547. A popular and centrally located restaurant based in one of Lima's old colonial mansions, with a very good atmosphere but relatively expensive.

La Vieja Taberna Av Grau 268, Barranco ☎ 2473741. A historic place built in 1903 and the venue where the political party APRA was created. It's very stylish, with vintage photos lining the walls, and it has fine views over the Barranco plaza as well as, sometimes, live music at weekends. Particularly good for tasty traditional Limeño cuisine.

Expensive

Las Brujas de Cachiche Av Bolognesi 460 ☎4471883. An interestingly conceived, top-class restaurant and bar which serves mainstream Peruvian dishes as well as a range of pre-Columbian meals using only ingredients available more than 1000 years ago. Very trendy and expensive.

Carlin Av La Paz 646 ☎4444134. Located in the flashy El Suche commercial complex in the back streets of Miraflores, this pricey restaurant serves gourmet Peruvian and international cuisine.

La Carreta Av Rivera Navarrete 740, San Isidro ☎4422690. One of the best *churrascarias* (Brazilian-style steakhouse) in Lima, based close to San Isidro's Centro Comercial; open late.

Chifa Lung Fung Av Republica de Panama 3165, San Isidro ☎4418817. One of Lima's best Chinese restaurants, with wonderful gardens inside.

Club Suizo Genaro Iglesias 550, Aurora-Miraflores ☎4459230. Exquisite Swiss cuisine, from extravagant fondues to lavish *Zürcher Eintopf* (meat and vegetable hotpot) in a very pleasant environment.

Restaurant Costa Verde Playa Barranquito ☎4775228. An exclusive restaurant serving good-quality Peruvian and international cuisine at exceptionally high prices; don't forget your credit card.

Restaurant Fuji Av Paseo de la República 4090 ☎4408531. A superb, expensive Japanese restaurant conveniently located in Miraflores.

Restaurant Huaca Pucllana Gral. Borgoño, block 8, Miraflores ☎4454042. Tasty, modern Peruvian cuisine in elegant surroundings with excellent service. Mon–Sat 12.30pm–midnight, Sun 12.30–4pm.

Restaurante Abdala Av Grau 340, Lima Centro ☎4775577. Serves excellent Arabic, Peruvian and German dishes. Mon, Thurs & Sun 8am–midnight, Fri & Sat 8am–3am.

La Rosa Nautica Espigon 4, Costa Verde ☎4470057. One of Lima's more expensive seafood restaurants, based on a pier by the ocean in Miraflores, with excellent views. All major cards accepted.

El Señorio de Sulco Malecon Cisneros 1470 ☎4410183. Specializes in Peruvian cuisine, using the finest ingredients and preparing mainly traditional dishes in the traditional way, many cooked only In earthen pots, this place serves meals that can be found on street stalls all over Peru, only in this case you pay extra because the chef is top quality. Mon–Sat noon to midnight.

Sushi Ito Jirón Miguel Dasso 110, San Isidro. An exclusive, excellent sushi restaurant that serves sashimi and *maki-temaki*, among other dishes.

Drinking and nightlife

The daily *El Comercio* provides the best **information** about music events, and its Friday edition carries a comprehensive supplement guide to Lima's nightlife, which is easy to understand even if your Spanish is limited. The suburb of Barranco is now the trendiest and liveliest place to hang out.

Live music and dance

All forms of **Peruvian music** can be found in Lima, some of them, like salsa and Afro-Peruvian (see Contexts p.566) better here than anywhere else in the country. Even Andean folk music is close to its best here (though Puno, Cusco and Arequipa are all contenders). As far as the **live music scene** goes, the great variety of traditional and hybrid sounds is one of the most enduring reasons for visiting the capital. Things are at their liveliest on Friday and Saturday nights, particularly among the folk group *peñas* and the burgeoning *salsadromos* (nightclubs more or less exclusively dedicated to salsa music, though in recent years they have tended to broaden out to include other modern Latin dance music). Most places charge around $5–10 entrance which often includes a drink and/or a meal.

Behind the Palacio de Gobierno, on the Paseo Santo (the former Polvos Azules) there are three **open-air amphitheatres** where, every evening, live traditional music is played (usually 6–9pm, earlier at weekends). Sometimes, too, some of the bigger restaurants like the *Costa Verde* and large hotels such as the *Maria Angola* stage live events with top bands.

Bullfighting

Bullfighting has been a popular pastime among a relatively small, wealthy elite from the Spanish Conquest to the present day, despite some 160 years of independence from Spain. Pizarro himself brought out the first *lidia* bull for fighting in Lima, and there is a great tradition between the controlling families of Peru – the same families who breed bulls on their haciendas – to hold fights in Lima during October and November. They invite some of the world's best bullfighters from Spain, Mexico and Venezuela, offering them up to $25,000 for an afternoon's sport at the prestigious **Plaza de Acho** in Rimac. **Tickets** can be bought in advance from the ticket office (block 2 of Huancavelica), or on the door an hour or so before the fights, which take place most Saturday and Sunday afternoons throughout the year. The best time, however, to catch a fight is in October or November, when the international bullfighters come to Lima.

Peñas

The *peñas* – some of which only open at weekends – are the surest bet for listening to authentic **Andean folk**, although some of them also specialize in Peruvian **criolla,** which brings together a unique and very vigorous blend of Afro-Peruvian, Spanish, and, to a lesser extent, Andean music. These days it's not uncommon for some of Lima's best *peñas* to feature a fusion of criolla and Latin jazz. Generally speaking, *peñas* don't get going until after 10pm and usually the bands play through to 3 or 4am, if not until first light.

Las Brisas del Titicaca Jirón Wakulski 168. One of the busiest and most popular venues for tourists in the know and local city people alike; excellent bands and yet one of the cheapest of the city's *peñas*, located in Lima Centro.

Del Carajo Jr. San Ambrosio 328, Barranco ☎2477977. This is a lively and popular *peña* playing a range of criolla, Andean and coastal traditional and modern music. Thurs–Sat 10pm–3am.

La Estacion de Barranco Av Pedro de Osma 112 ☎2470344. In Barranco, just across the road from the suburb's main plaza, this established *peña* regularly varies its flavour between folklore, criolla and even Latin jazz at times; it has a very good atmosphere most Fridays and Saturdays.

Manos Morenas Av Pedro de Osma 409 ☎4670421. A few blocks south of the small plaza in Barranco, this club usually hosts criolla gigs, often with big names like Eva Ayllon and internationally renowned dance groups such as Peru Negro; excellent food and shows, though the

atmosphere can be a little constrained.

Peña La Palizada Av del Ejercito 800, Miraflores. A large restaurant-cum-club, which specializes in criolla; very popular with Lima's middle classes.

La Peña Poggi Luna Pizarro 587, Barranco ☎4770878. A pleasant, intimate club, hosting most forms of live music.

Peña Sachún Av del Ejercito 657, Miraflores ☎4414465. Very lively and popular tourist restaurant with a good reputation for live folklore music and criolla dancing at weekends, usually until at least 2am.

Peña Wifala Cailloma 633, Lima Centro. Smaller and more tourist-oriented than most of the other *peñas*, but still quite good.

Taberna 1900 Av Grau 268. Another popular Barranco *peña* which can get pretty hectic at weekends and rarely finishes much before dawn; hosts both Andean folk and Peruvian black music.

Salsadromos

Lima is an excellent place to experience the Latin American **salsa** scene, and there are *salsadromos* scattered around many of the suburbs. They play a mix of tropical music, salsa, merengue and technocumbia (see Contexts p.559 for details on the various musical forms). Most open Friday and Saturday 10pm–3am.

Bertoloto Av Malecon Bertoloto 770, San Miguel. Has spicy salsa most Friday and Saturday nights.

Fiesta Latina Federico Villareal 259, Miraflores. A

lively place to get a feel for popular salsa music. Thurs–Sat 10pm–2am.

Kimbala, Av Republica de Panama 1401, La

Victoria. A very unpretentious nightspot, with vibrant salsa music.

Latin Brothers José Leal 1281 ☎ 4700150. A traditional seafood restaurant with background salsa music constantly blaring out; also presents salsa

shows some weekends.

Tropical Plaza Av Manco Capac 618, La Victoria. An inexpensive, no-frills place with great music at weekends.

Jazz, rock and Latin jazz

Lima is pretty hot on **jazz** and **rock** music and has several excellent **Latin jazz** bands of its own.

10 Sesenta Los Nardos 1060, San Isidro ☎ 4410744. Club-cum-pub which serves good food and puts on live Latin jazz and criolla shows.

Bar La Parada San Martín 587, Miraflores ☎ 9431211, ✉ febril@telematic.edu.pe. Live rock music every night, with open jam sessions on Wednesdays.

La Casona de Barranco Av Grau 329, Barranco. Very popular club with Lima's trendy under-40s and has particularly good live jazz most weekends.

El Ekeko Av Grau 266, by the municipal plaza in

Barranco ☎ 4775823. Often has Latin jazz at weekends, though also hosts Peruvian Andean and coastal music, mainly criolla.

Jazz Zone La Paz 656, Pasaje El Suche, Miraflores ☎ 2427090. Open evenings from Tuesday to Saturday for piped and frequently good live jazz.

Media Cuadra San Martín, half a block from Av Larco. An excellent live music venue with an ever-changing variety of sounds; best from Thursday to Saturday.

La Posada del Angel Pedro de Osma, Barranco. Good Troba music.

Cultural centres

Centro Cultural Av Nicolas de Pierola 1222. Often presents folk music and dance, though this is more of a performance and less participatory. The centre is run by the Universitario de San Marcos, on the Parque Universitario and performances are publicized on the noticeboard at the entrance.

Centro Cultural Parra del Riego Av Pedro de

Osma 135. Presents Andean and criolla music concerts, usually Thursday to Saturday.

Centro Cultural Ricardo Palma Av Larco 770, Miraflores. Often hosts excellent concerts of Andean music, but doesn't really have the same engaging, informal and participatory atmosphere of the *peñas* listed above.

Bars and clubs

Lima boasts a wide range of exciting **clubs**, with the vast majority of its popular **bars** and discos located out in the suburbs of **San Isidro** and **Miraflores**. Most open Thursday to Saturday 10pm–2am or 3am. Many clubs have a members-only policy, though if you can provide proof of tourist status, such as a passport, you usually have no problem getting in.

Bars

Brenchley Arms Atahualpa 174, Miraflores. A bar trying hard to replicate a typical English pub, with a pleasant atmosphere, good beer and music; also dart board and English taped music.

La Castañuela Tasca Pub Av Comandante Espinar 349. A bar aimed at the over-30s; pleasant atmosphere, good cocktails, but quite expensive.

Dirty Nelly's Irish Pub Pedro de Osma 135, Barranco. A lively young bar just off the plaza in Barranco.

Irish Pub Calle Shell 627, Miraflores ☎ 2421212. Open Mon–Sat all day and until late, it's a spacious, modern-looking joint and a good meeting place in the heart of Miraflores.

Juanito's Av Grau 687. Probably the most traditional of Barranco's bars; facing onto the Parque Municipal, it is small and basic and offers an excellent taste of Peru as it used to be. There is no pop music and the front bar is designated for couples only during weekend evenings.

Ludwig Bar Beethoven Av Grau 687. In the midst of the hectic and trendy area of Barranco this unusual bar specializes in fine classical music with a late-night, cultured ambience.

O'Murphy's Calle Shell 627, Miraflores. An Irish pub in downtown Miraflores; it's a large bar open day and evenings and has ritzy metallic furniture, plus it's very convenient for popping in while in central Miraflores.

The Old Pub San Ramon 295, Miraflores ☎2428155, ⓦwww.theoldpub.eb.com. The most authentic of the English-style pubs in Lima; it's actually run by an Englishman, and also plays good music. Easy to find just a block or two from the park in Miraflores, at the far end of Little Italy (San Ramon).

La Posada del Mirador Barranco. Located on the clifftop point behind the Puente de Suspiros and church in Barranco, this is a popular evening bar with great views and a lively atmosphere.

Clubs

Bar Kitsch Bolognesi 243, Barranco. A mixed straight and gay crowd come here for the floral wallpaper, sequined mermaids and generally kitsch decor. Plays disco and is pretty crowded at weekends. No entry fee.

Bar Quispe Parque Raimondi, one block from Bolognesi, Barranco. Interesting photos on the walls and plays a wide range of music; peach brandy from a large vat is free to punters.

Discoteca Gotica Larco Mar, Miraflores. Music is excellent and the service, too; a popular, even famous, Lima club.

La Esquina del Parque on the corner of Grau and the Boulevard, Barranco. Right by the plaza in Barranco, this is very popular with the younger Lima set; but as much of a music café as a club.

El Grill Barranquito Beach, Barranco. A small place with a good traditional bar and disco; not particularly busy even at weekends, possibly because it's a little expensive.

Heaven Av Larco 481, Miraflores ⓦwww.heaven-nentraffic.com. A clever club that plays Latin, US and European music; sometimes live sets. Very popular and easy to find in Miraflores. Entrance generally $10.

La Noche Av Bolognesi 307, El Boulevard, Barranco. Right at the top end of the Boulevard, this gets really packed at weekends. Small entry fee when there's live music and free jazz sessions on Monday evening. Fine decor, arguably the top night spot in Barranco and one of the best places for meeting people.

Strokers Av Benavides 325, Miraflores. Low-key, traditional disco, with pool tables and bars as well as dance spaces.

Teatrix Larco Mar, Miraflores. A very trendy and popular club which plays loads of trance.

Gay and lesbian Lima

There are few gay meeting places in Lima, though the Parque Kennedy and Larco Mar centre in Miraflores are a bit cruisy in the evenings. The gay community is relatively small and more on a par with a city like Santiago, Chile, than it is with, say, Rio de Janeiro. The male culture is primarily macho, so as a visitor keeping a relatively low profile makes for an easier time. Check out ⓦwww.gaylimape.tripod.com for further details.

Bars and clubs

Avenida 13 Manuel Segura 270, Lince (a suburb encircled by San Isidro, La Victoria and Jesus Maria) ☎2653694. Located off block 15 of the Avenida Arequipa, this gay-friendly disco is popular at weekends and is the only club to have a ladies-only night (Fridays).

Divas Gonzalez Prada 458, Surquillo ☎4460078. Generally busy at weekends with lesbian and gay clientele; pretty basic venue but good live shows

at weekends and reasonably priced booze.

Downtown Vale Todo Pasaje Los Pinos 160, Miraflores ☎4446433. Arguably the best gay club in Lima, there are frequently caged go-go dancing boys and a cruise bar as well as dance floors.

Queens Camano 993, Lima Centro. Only gays allowed in this one; it's large, has a busy dance floor, but it's in a part of the centre that gets relatively dodgy after midnight (so make sure you arrive and depart in a radio taxi).

Arts and entertainment

Lima is a cultured city in at least two primary ways: its intellectual and better-educated citizens have the Latin passion for music and the fine arts on the one hand, and the generally less educated Indian population produces a treasure trove of textiles, carvings, crafts, paintings and other art forms. All of these forms are accessible through Lima's markets, shops, galleries and theatres. Cinema, too, is still a popular feature of Lima life. Again, the best source of **information** about film, theatre, sporting events and exhibitions is the daily *El Comercio*, especially its Friday supplement. Going to the **cinema**, **theatre** and **exhibitions** is an important part of life in Lima.

Cinema

Cinema-going is an especially popular pastime for all Limeños, while the theatre attracts a small, select and highly cultured audience. There are clusters of **cinemas** all around the Plaza San Martín, Jirón de la Unión and Avenida Nicolas de Pierola in Lima Centro, and on the fringes of the park in Miraflores. For any film that might attract relatively large crowds, it's advisable to buy tickets in advance; alternatively, be prepared to purchase them on the black market at inflated prices – queues are often long and large blocks of seats are regularly bought up by touts. The British Council often shows **English-language films**, though other cinemas show films in their original language with subtitles.

ABC San Borja 1–2 Ucello 176, San Borja ☎4753120.

Alcazar 1–4 Santa Cruz 814, Miraflores ☎4226345.

Benavides Av Benavides 4981, Surco ☎2754323.

British Council Cinema Jirón Camana 787 ☎4277927.

El Cine PUCP Av Camino Real 1075, San Isidro ☎2226899.

Cinemark Peru Jockey Plaza 12, Av Javier Prado 4200 ☎4340034.

El Conquistador Av España 241 ☎9846837.

Julieta Porta 115, Miraflores ☎4440135.

Larco Mar 1–12 Centro Comercial Parque Salazar, Larco Mar ☎4467336.

Lido Jirón Moquegua 568, Lima Centro ☎4423394.

Orrantia Av Arequipa 2701, San Isidro.

El Pacifico 1–12 Av Jose Pardo 121, Miraflores ☎4456990.

Roma 1–3 Emilio Fernandez 242, at the Lima Centro end of Avenida Arequipa ☎2412956.

Romeo Porta 115, Miraflores ☎2143524.

Theatre, ballet and classical music

Lima possesses a prolific and extremely talented **theatre** circuit, with many of its best venues based in Miraflores. In addition to the major theatres, short performances sometimes take place in the bars of the capital's top theatres. The country's major prestige companies, however, are the **National Ballet Company** and the **National Symphony**, both based seasonally at the Teatro Municipal in downtown Lima at block 3 of Jirón Ica (☎4282302). There are frequent performances, too, by international musicians and companies, often sponsored by the foreign cultural organizations, such as the Alianza Francesa, Avenida Arequipa 4595, Miraflores, the Anglo-Peruvian Cultural Association Theatre, Avenida Benavides 620, Miraflores (☎4454326) and Instituto Cultural Peruano Norte Americano, Avenida Angamos 120, Miraflores. The British Council (see p.101) is quite active in sponsoring such events, and surprisingly imaginative, while the Teatro Britanico, Bellavista 527, Miraflores (☎4454326), puts on amateur plays in English.

Art and photographic galleries

Lima's progressive culture of **art** and **photography** is deeply rooted in the Latin American tradition, combining indigenous ethnic realism with a political edge. The city boasts a few permanent galleries, with temporary exhibitions on display in many of the main museums.

Artco Calle Rouad y Paz Soldan 325, San Isidro ☎ 2213579, ⓦ www.artcogaleria.com. One of the happening painters' galleries in Lima, usually well worth checking out; Mon–Fri 11am–8pm, Sat 10.30am–1.30pm & 3.30–7.30pm.

Arte y Cultura El Allyu Av San Martín 537 ☎ 2417587. Mostly indigenous ceramic artists. Mon–Sat 9am–6pm; free.

Centro Cultural de la Municipalidad de Miraflores corner of Avenida Larco and Diez Canseco. Hosts a series of interesting photographic exhibitions. Daily 10am–10pm; free.

Centro Cultural de la Universidad Catolica Av Camino Real 1075, San Isidro. Art gallery hosting visiting exhibitions by foreign artists. Daily 10am–10pm; free.

Centro Cultural Ricardo Palma Larco 770, Miraflores. In the same building as Miraflores Tourist Information (daily 9am–10pm), houses fixed and changing exhibitions of paintings, photographs and sculpture.

Corriente Alterna Las Dalias 381, Miraflores. Often presents shows by non-Peruvian painters. Mon–Fri 10am–8pm; free.

Extramuros Paseo de la República 6045. Not exclusively photographic, but frequently exhibits works by major Latin American photographers. Mon–Sat 4–9pm; free.

Forum Av Larco 1150. A small but important gallery dedicated mainly to modern Peruvian art. Mon–Fri 10am–1.30pm & 5–8pm, Sat 5–9pm; free.

Galeria L'Imaginaire Av Arequipa 4595, Miraflores. Usually exhibits Latin American painters and sculptors. Mon–Sat 5–9pm; free.

Parafernalia Gonzales Prada 419, Surquillo. Specializes mainly in Peruvian artists, primarily fine art and sculpture. Mon–Fri 10am–1pm & 2–7pm, Sat 10am–2pm & 3.30–7.30pm; free.

Sala Cultural del Banco Wiese Av Larco 1101. A contemporary, international art gallery in the Banco Weise in the heart of downtown Miraflores. Mon–Sat 10am–2pm & 5–9pm; free.

Trapecio Av Larco 743, Miraflores. Specializes in oils and sculpture. Mon–Sat 5–9pm; free.

Shopping and supplies

When it comes to **shopping** in Peru's towns and cities, Lima is the most likely to have what you're looking for. It is certainly your best bet for shoes and clothing, particularly if you want a large selection to choose from. The same is true of electronic goods, stationery and recorded music, though bear in mind that most Limeños who can afford it do their main shopping in Miami. Lima also has a good selection of reasonably priced arts and crafts markets and shops, which means you don't have to carry a sack full of souvenirs back from Cusco or Puno. The flashiest indoor **shopping centre** is the Centro Comercial on Camino Real, near the Lima Golf Club in the heart of San Isidro. For **supermarkets** try Wongs, which you'll find across the city, notably at the San Isidro Comercial Centre, at the Ovalo Gutierrez and on Avenida Benavides in San Antonio; in downtown Miraflores, the Santa Isabela supermarket, Avenida Benavides 487, is open 24 hours.

The usual **shopping hours** are Monday to Saturday 9am–6pm, though in Miraflores, the main commercial area, many shops and artesania markets stay open until 7 or 8pm. Some shops, but by no means all, shut for a two-hour lunch break, usually from 1 to 3pm, and most shops shut on Sundays, though the artesania markets on Avenida La Marina and Petit Thouars tend to stay open all week until 7pm.

Arts and crafts

All types of Peruvian **artesania** are available in Lima, including woollen goods, crafts and gem stones. Some of the best in Peru are on Avenida Petit Thouars, which is home to a handful of markets between Avenida Ricardo Palma and Avenida Angamos, all well within walking distance of Miraflores centre. Artesania Gran Chimu, Avenida Petit Thouars 5495, has a wide range of jewellery and carved wooden items, as does Mercado Artesanal, also on Avenida Petit Thouars, at no. 5321. More places selling artesania are listed below.

Artesania

Agua y Tierra Diez Canseco 298 ☎ 4446980. An interesting range of ethnic and traditional healing or *curanderos'* artefacts.

Antisuyo Av Tacna 460, Miraflores ☎ 2416451. This store sells crafts from Peru's Amazon tribes.

La Casa de Alpaca La Paz 679, Miraflores. Good-quality but expensive alpaca clothing.

Collacocha Colon 534, parallel to block 11 of Avenida Larco ☎ 4474422. A very nice, if small, collection of Andean arts and crafts.

Las Pallas Cajamarca 212, Barranco ☎ 4774629. A fascinating, veritable museum of artesania, run by a British woman who has spent most of her life collecting fine works and who may be able to show you the rest of her collection (ring for an appointment).

Silvana Prints Conquistadores 915, San Isidro. This shop produces and sells a colourful range of mainly cotton fabrics and items like cushion covers, incorporating ancient pre-Inca motifs in the design.

Slightly cheaper are the artesania markets on blocks 9 and 10 of Avenida La Marina in Pueblo Libre and the good crafts and antiques market, which takes place every evening (6–9pm) in the Miraflores Park between Diagonal and Avenida Larco. The Hatun Raymi Artesania Festival (late July/early August) is a great gathering of Lima-based artesania producers; it's located on the massive esplanade of the Museo de la Nación and entry is free. In Lima Centro the Artesania Santo Domingo, at Jr. Conde de Superunda 221–223 (a little square pavement area just a stone's throw from the Correo Central), is good for beads, threads and other artesania items.

For **jewellery**, Casa Wako, Jirón de la Unión 841, is probably the best place in Lima Centro, specializing in reasonably priced Peruvian designs in gold and silver, while Platería Pereda, Jirón Venecia 186a, Miraflores, stocks fine silver jewellery to suit most tastes. Nazca, Avenida La Paz 522, has a nice range of offerings, much of it in silver. For good-quality **antiques** there's Rafo, Martinez de Pinillos 1055, Barranco (☎ 2470679), who have a good lunchtime restaurant too, and also Collacocha, Calle Colon 534, parallel to block 11 of Avenida Larco in Miraflores.

Books, stationery and maps

A few shops on Avenida Nicolas de Pierola stock **English-language books** (try the store at no. 689), and The Book Exchange, just around the corner at Ocoña 211, sells or swaps second-hand paperbacks. Epoca, Avenida José Pardo 399, Miraflores, has a good range of titles including many in English. The ABC Bookstores at Colmena 689, Lima Centro, and in the Todos shopping complex, San Isidro, are well supplied with all kinds of works in English, including books on Peru. On the Jirón de la Unión, the Librería Ayza usually has some interesting publications and maps, while in Miraflores the Librería Ibero, Diagonal 500 and Larco 199, generally have a wide range of books and magazines in English. **Stationery** is available from Librería Minerva, Larco 299, Miraflores.

Map stores

Ingemmet Av Canada 1470, San Borja ☎ 2253158. This store stocks a wide range of plans.

Instituto Geográfico Nacional Av Aramburu 1190, Surquillo ☎ 4759960, ☺ postmaster@ignperu .qob.pe. They offer charts covering most of Peru in detail.

Servicio Aerofotografico Nacional at Las Palmas Airforce Base in Barranco ☎ 4773682. Also carries many highly detailed charts of Peru.

South American Explorers Club See p.27.

Touring y Automóvil Club de Peru Av Cesar Vallejo 699, Lince ☎ 4403270. Good for road maps. Mon–Fri 9am–5pm.

△ Lima

Food

The best place to buy **food** for a picnic is Surquillo Market (daily 6.30am–5.30pm, roughly), a couple of blocks from Miraflores over the Avenida Angamos road bridge, on the eastern side of the Paseo de la República freeway. This colourful place is fully stocked with a wonderful variety of breads, fruits, cheeses, and meats, though it can be a bit dodgy in terms of petty thieving, so keep your wallet and passport close. Alternatively, you could try one of the Wong supermarkets, in San Antonio, on the corner of Avenida Republica de Panama and Avenida Benavides, or the smaller branch at Ovalo Gutierrez on the corner of Avenida Comandante Espinar and Avenida Santa Cruz; all the branches also change cash dollars. In the centre of Lima you can buy most basic foodstuffs – bread, fruit and so on – either from stalls on Avenida Emancipación or in the central market to the east of Avenida Abancay (see p.78). The best things to buy for a tasty picnic are the delicious *queso fresco* (white cheese), avocados and pecans. For **health food**, try Naturalix, Jirón Diez Canseco 440, Miraflores, or Octavios, Los Jazmines 219, Lince, which stocks a wide range of healing herbs from the Amazon and the Andes. Other good options are the Natural Co-op on Moquegua, near the corner with Torrico, and El Girasol, Camana 327, not far from the Plaza Mayor; Eco Natura, Jirón Schell 634; or Botiquin Naturista, Centro Comercial Camino del Inca, Surco, Tienda 157, upstairs.

Photographic equipment

Photographic equipment, accessories and film developing are all a little expensive in Lima. Try Kodak Express, Avenida Larco 1005, or Lab Color Professional, Avenida Benavides 1171 (☎4467421), both in Miraflores, for films and developing. Agfafoto, Diez Canseco 172, Miraflores, has films and peripherals, while Renato Service, 28 Julio 442, Miraflores, has excellent camera and video equipment. Foto Digital, Avenida Larco 1005 (☎4479398) is good for fast developing. Kodak's laboratories on Avenida Arriola, just off Javier Prado Este in La Victoria, will develop Ektachrome but not Kodachrome. For **camera repairs**, try the Camera House, Larco 1150, Oficina 39 (☎9617590) in Miraflores towards the bottom (sea) end of Larco.

Outdoor activities

For **trekking** advice and trail maps, visit the Trekking and Backpacking Club, Jirón Huascar 1152, Jesus Maria (☎4232515), or the South American Explorers' Club (see p.27). Of the **trekking companies**, most run trips to the Cordillera Blanca, around the Cusco area and along the Inca Trail; some of the best are listed below.

For **whitewater rafting**, contact Explorandes (listed below); **cruise boats** to the Islas Palomino to see the marine mammals, quite a nice trip if the weather is clear, can be joined through Ecocruceros, Avenida Arequipa 4960, Of. 202, Miraflores (☎2426655, ⓔecocruceros@infonegocio.com.pe). For advice on **mountain-climbing**, try the Club Andino, Avenida Paseo de la República 932 (☎2637319) or the Asociación de Andinismo de la Universidad de Lima, based at the university on Javier Prado Este (☎4376767; meet Wed evenings). Rainforest Expeditions, which offers **jungle expeditions**, have an office at Aramburu 166 #48, Miraflores (☎4218183, ⓦwww.perunature.com).

Trekking companies

Expediciones Mayuc Conquistadores 199, San Isidro ☎4225988.

Explorandes San Fernando 320, Miraflores ☎4450532 or 4458683, ⓕ4454686, ⓔpostmast@explorandes.com.pe.

Incatrek ☎2427843, ⓔincatrek@hotmail.com. This outfit sometimes run tours to Tarma, Oxapampa, Pozuzo and Satipo.

Peru Expeditions Av Arequipa 5241 (Of.504), Miraflores ☎4472057, ⓕ4459683, ⓦwww .peru-expeditions.com. A professional, helpful company specializing in environmentally sound adventure travel in the Cusco region, they offer trekking, mountain biking and 4WD tours, and their leaders are experts in all kinds of adventure activities. Also worth checking are their associated web sites: ⓦwww.perumountainbike.com, ⓦwww .peru4WD.net, ⓦwww.incatreks.com, and ⓦwww.andesperu.com.

Tarpuy Av Faucett 421, Oficina 201, San Miguel ☎4511114.

Trek Andes Av Benavides 212, Oficina 1203, Miraflores ☎4478078.

Camping and sports equipment

Alpamayo, Av Larco 345 Miraflores (☎4451671) is great for a range of camping equipment and help to locate other sources; Altamira, Arica 800, a block from the Ovalo Gutierrez roundabout, sells a good range of quality **camping equipment**. Best, Avenida Espinar 320, Miraflores, sells rucksacks, cycling equipment and surfing gear, while Todo Camping, Avenida Angamos Oeste 350, has a range of tents and other equipment. There's also the Camping Centre, Avenida Benavides 1620 (☎2421779) in Miraflores or Sisperu, Caminos del Inca 257 (☎3720428) in Chacarilla, and the South American Explorers' Club (see p.27) is worth trying too.

For **surfing gear** go to Best (see above), Billa Bong, Ignacio Merino 711, O'Niells, Avenida Santa Cruz 851, or Waves, Bolivar 149, all of which are in Miraflores; in Barranco there's Wayo Whilar, Avenida 28 de Julio 287. **Cycling equipment** is available from Biclas, Avenida Conquistadores 641, San Isidro (☎4400890); Bike Mavil, Avenida Aviación 4011 (☎4498435); Cicloroni, Calle de Las Casas, block 32, Avenida Petit Thouars, San Isidro (☎2217643); and Will-Pro, Avenida 2 de Mayo 430, San Isidro (☎2220289).

Listings

Airlines Aero Condor, Juan de Arona 781, San Isidro ☎4425663; Aero Continente, Avenida José Pardo 605, Miraflores ☎2424260, ⓕ2423453, ⓔaerocont@aerocontinente.com; Aeroparacas, ☎2716941, ⓔaeroparacas@wayna.rcp.net.pe; American Airlines, Jirón Juan de Arona 830, fourteenth floor, San Isidro ☎4428610; Avianca, Avenida Paz Soldan 225, Oficina C-5, Los Olivos, San Isidro ☎2217822; British Airways, represented in Lima by Air Latin at Andalucia 174, Miraflores ☎4426600, 4220889 or 4452888; Continental Airlines, Victor Andrés Belaúnde 147, Oficina 101, Edificio Real, San Isidro ☎2214340 or 2227080; Iberia, Avenida Camino Real 390, Office 902, San Isidro ☎4417801; KLM, Avenida José Pardo 805, Miraflores ☎2421240; Lan Chile, Avenida José Pardo 269, Miraflores ☎2138200 or 2138300; Lan Peru, Avenida Los Incas 172, eighth floor, San Isidro or Avenida José Pardo 269, Miraflores ☎2138200 or 2138300; Lloyd Aero Boliviano, Avenida José Pardo 231, first and seventh floors, Miraflores ☎2415210; TACA Peru, Avenida Comandante Espinar 331, Miraflores ☎2137000, ⓕ4453277, ⓦwww.taca.com; TANS, Calle Belen 1015, Lima Centro and Av Arequipa 5200, Miraflores ☎2418510, or Avenida Inca Garcilaso de la Vega 981 ☎4249438, or Calle San Martín 550, Miraflores ☎4441919, for reservations call 2136000; Varig, Avenida Camino Real 456, Central Tower, office 803/804, San Isidro ☎4424163.

Airport Lima airport applies a flat $25 departure tax on international flights, paid on departure at the airport. For domestic flights the departure tax is around $4. The airport boasts lots of shops, cafés, Internet facilities, a post office and a rather expensive left luggage deposit in the international departure area.

American Express Based at Lima Tours, Belen 1040, near Plaza San Martín (Mon–Fri 9.15am–4.45pm; ☎276624, 4261765 or 4240831). Offers a poste restante service and has a subsidiary office in Miraflores at Avenida Santa Crus 621 ☎6900900, ℮info@travex.com.pe.
Anti-Rabies Centre Centro Antirabico ☎4256313. For emergency treatment.
Banks Banco de la Nación, Avenida Nicolas de Pierola 1065 and Avenida Abancay 491; Banco Latino, Paseo de la República 3505, San Isidro, which has a MasterCard ATM; Banco de Credito, Jirón Lampa 499, Avenida Larco 1099, Miraflores (well run and with small queues), and on the corner of Rivera Navarrete and Juan de Arona, San Isidro, both of which offer good rates on travellers' cheques; Banco Continental, Avenida Larco, Miraflores; Citibank, Las Begonias 441, San Isidro; Interbank, in the Metro Supermarket, corner of Alfonso Ugarte and Venezuela, Lima Centro; and Banco Wiese, Jirón Cusco 245, Lima Centro, and Alfonso Ugarte 1292, Diagonal 176, Miraflores.
British Council Calle Alberto Lynch 110, near the Ovalo Gutierrez roundabout, San Isidro ☎4704350; postal address PO Box 14-0114, Santa Beatriz, Lima, Peru.
Bus companies Always check which terminal your bus is departing from when you buy your ticket. El Aguilla, Jirón Galvez, La Victoria (☎4240836), for Trujillo and Huaraz. Carhuamayo, Jirón Montevideo 855 (☎2260785), for Arequipa and Cusco. Chanchamayo, Manco Capac 1052, La Victoria (☎4701189), for Tarma, La Oroya, San Ramon and La Merced. Cial, Av Abancay 947 and Terminal Paseo de la República 646 (☎3304225), for the North coast including Mancora, Cajamarca and Huaraz. Condor de Chavin, Montevideo 1039 (☎4288122), for Callejón de Huaylas, Huaraz and Chavín. Cruz del Sur, the best choice if not the cheapest for most destinations, have several terminals: in Lima Centro it's Jirón Quilca 531 (☎4271311 or 4235594 or 3175566) and the corner of Zavala with Montevideo (☎4282570), for the coast, Huaraz, Huancayo, Cusco, Arequipa and Puno; for international services it's at Avenida Javier Prado at the corner with Nicolas Arriola (☎2256200 or 2256163, tickets can be booked and paid for on their website ⓦwww.cruzdelsur.com.pe); for their Ideal service, which includes the coast, Cusco, Arequipa, Puno, Cajamarca, Huancayo and Huaraz it's Paseo de la República 809, La Victoria ☎3324000. El Condor, Avenida Carlos Zavala 101, Lima Centro (☎4270286), for Trujillo or Huancayo. Enlaces, Avenida Paseo de la República 749 (☎4333311), for Arequipa. Empresa Huaral, 131 Avenida

Abancay, Lima Centro (☎4282254), for Huaral, Ancon and Chancay. Empresa Rosario, Jirón Ayacucho 942 (☎5342685), for Huánuco and La Unión. Emtrafasa, Jr. Humbolt 109 (☎423 0046) for the whole North coast and also Cajamarca. Flores Buses, Montevideo 529, Lima Centro (☎4310485). Hidalgo, Bolivar 1535 (☎4240522). Leon de Huánuco, Avenida 28 de Julio, La Victoria 1520 (☎43290880), for Cerro de Pasco, Huánuco, Tarma and La Merced. Huamanga, Jr Montevideo 619 and Luna Pizarro 455 (☎3302206), the latter address is for departures to Ayacucho, Chiclayo, Moyobamba, Tarapoto and Yurimaguas. Libertadores, Avenida Grau 491, Lima Centro (☎4268067), for Ayacucho, Satipo, and Huanta. Linea, Avenida Jose Galvez 999 (☎4240836), for Huaraz, Trujillo, Chiclayo, Piura and Cajamarca. Lobato Buses, 28 de Julio 2101–2107, La Victoria (☎4749411), for Tarma, La Merced and Satipo. Mariscal Caceres, Avenida 28 de Julio 2195, La Victoria (☎4747850). Morales Moralitos, Avenida Grau 141 (☎4286252). Movil Tours, Avenida Paseo de la República 646 (☎3320024), for Huaraz, Caraz and Trujillo; head office at Jr. Montevideo 581 (☎4275309). Oltursa, Avenida Aramburu 1160 (☎4758559), for most coastal destinations. Ormeño, Avenida Javier Prado Este 1059 (☎4721710, ⓦwww.grupo-ormeno.com), for main national and international services, though they also pass through the central depot at Carlos Zavala 177, Lima Centro (☎4275679): Chinchano, a subsidiary of Ormeño, serves the coast as far as Cañete, Chincha and Pisco. Palomino, Av 28 de Julio 1750, La Victoria, for Cusco via Nazca and Abancay. Soyuz/Peru Bus, Avenida Carlos Zavala y Loyaza 221 (☎4276310) and Avenida Mexico 333, La Victoria, for the best buses to Ica. Señor de Luren, Manco Capac 611, for Nazca. Transportes Rodriguez, Avenida Roosevelt 354 (☎4280506), for Huaraz, Caraz and Chimbote. Tepsa, Avenida Paseo de la República 129 (☎4275642 or 4271233); ticket office at Jirón Lampa 1237, Lima Centro (☎4275642). Turismo Apostolo San Pedro, Avenida Grau 711, Paruro 1457 (☎4287810), for Huancayo and Tarma. Wari, Montevideo 809 (☎4286356 or 4288591), for Puno, Abancay, Nazca and Cusco.
Car rental Budget, at Avenida La Paz 522 (☎4444546 in Miraflores, at the airport ☎5751674; 24hr) and at Avenida Canaval y Moreyra 569, San Isidro (☎4419458, ⓦwww.budget.tci.net.pe); Dollar, La Paz 438, Miraflores (☎4444920; at the airport 4526741); Inka's, Av Cantuarias 160, Miraflores (☎4472129); National, Avenida España 453, Lima Centro (☎4333750) or in San Isidro at Los Eucaliptos 555

(☎2221010, ✉national@terra.com.pe).

Courier services DHL, Los Castaños 225, San Isidro (☎5172500), Las Begonias 429, San Isidro, and in Lima Tours, Belen 1040, Lima Centro and Avenida Pardo 392, Miraflores (all branches Mon–Fri 8.30am–7.30pm & Sat 9am–noon); Federal Express, Pasaje Olaya 260, Miraflores (Mon–Fri 8.30am–6pm; ☎2423399).

Dentists Dr Yolanda Montoro, Mercedes G. de Parks 314, Urbino Pando, in the *segunda etapa* (second part) of San Miguel, close to block 22 of the Avenida La Marina ☎5660915; or Clinica Dental Flores, Calle Centauro 177, Monterrico ☎4352153. Your embassy can supply a list of English-speaking dentists.

Doctors Dr Bazan is recommended and works as a "backpackers medic" in Lima ☎7352668, ✉backpackers@yahoo.com; Dr Aste, Antero Aspillaga 415, Oficina 101, San Isidro ☎4417502, speaks English; Dr Alicia Garcia, Instituto de Ginecología, Avenida Monterrico 1045, Surco ☎4342650; Dr Raul Morales, Clinica Padre Luis Tezza, Avenida del Polo 570, Monterrico ☎4346990, speaks good English; and Dr Roberto Luna Victoria, Clinica Adventista de Miraflores, Malecon Balta 956, Miraflores ☎4435395.

Embassies and consulates Australia, Avenida Victor Belaúnde 147, Via Principal 155, building 3 of 1301 San Isidro ☎2228281; Bolivia, Los Castaños 235, San Isidro ☎4428231; Brazil, Avenida José Pardo 850, Miraflores ☎4215650; Canada, Calle Libertad 130, Miraflores ☎4444015; Chile, Javier Prado Oeste 790, San Isidro ☎2212818 or 2212817; Ecuador, Las Palmeras 356, San Isidro ☎2212880; Ireland, Angamos Este 340, Miraflores ☎4463878; Jamaica, Avenida Jorge Basadre 255, Of 501, San Isidro ☎4428828; New Zealand, see the UK; UK, Torre Parque Mar, Avenida Larco 1301, twenty-third floor Miraflores ☎6173050, ☏6173055; US, La Encalada, block 17, Monterrico ☎4343000, ☏4343037.

Exchange *Cambistas* gather on the corner of Ocoña, at the back of the Gran Hotel Bolivar. Alternatively, you can change cash and travellers' cheques in the smaller hostels and the many casas de cambio around Ocoña: Tuscon Express, Ocoña 211a; LAC Dollar, on Camana 779, second floor; and two unnamed offices at Camana 814 and Camana 758, both near the corner with Ocoña; and El Trueque at Camana 846. Universal Money Exchange, Avenida José Pardo 629, Oficina 16, Miraflores or Koko's Dollar, Avenida Ricardo Palma 437, Stand 21, Comercial Las Estaciones, in Miraflores, are both OK. Also in Miraflores there are several *cambistas* working Larco, particularly

on the corners of the first 5 or 6 blocks down from the Ovalo. The Wong supermarkets (see "Shopping and supplies", p.96) take dollars and will give change in dollars or nuevo soles. You can also change money at the airport, but rates are poorer than in the city centre.

Farmacias Boticas Fasa, Avenida Benavides 847 (☎6190000), 24hr delivery, accept major credit cards; Inka Farma (☎6198000) delivery service.

Fax services Bunkers, Avenida Ricardo Palma 280 ☎9539721, ☏ 2411090; and Innova, Avenida Larco 1158, Miraflores ☎4459267.

Hospitals The following are all well equipped: Clinica Anglo Americana, Avenida Salazar, San Isidro ☎2213656; Clinica Internacional, Washington 1475, Lima Centro ☎4288060; Clinica Ricardo Palma, Av Javier Prado Este 1066, San Isidro ☎2248027 or 2222224; and Clinica San Borja, Avenida Guardia Civil 337, San Borja ☎4754000. All have emergency departments which you can use as an outpatient, or you can phone for a house-call. For an ambulance call ☎4400200 or 4413141, but if you can, take a taxi – it'll be much quicker.

INRENA Calle 17, 355 Urb. El Palomar, San Isidro ☎2251053, ✉inrena_dganpfs@eletrodata.com.pe. Responsible for Peru's protected areas; you need permission from them to enter some of Peru's Natural Park areas.

Internet services CyberSandeg, Jirón de la Unión 853, Oficina 210, in Galerias Boza-Costado, by the Plaza Martin in Lima Centro; El Allyu Cyber Café, Avenida San Martín 537, Miraflores ☎4460385, ⊛www.allyu-peru.org; Dragon Fans, Calle Tarata 230, Miraflores, open 24 hours ☎4466814; Inter Palace, Diez Canseco 180, Miraflores ☎2422070, fast, private cabins, coffee; Phantom Internet Café Bar, Avenida Diagonal 344, Miraflores ☎2427949, ⊛www.phantom.com.pe; Mondonet, Avenida Ancash 412 ☎4279196, Internet and telephone service; Plazanet, Avenida 28 de Julio 451, Miraflores ⊛www.plazanet.com.pe, which is open 24hr and has a café and TV; Red Cientifica Peruana, Augusto Tamayo 125, San Isidro ☎4224848, ✉webmaster@rcp.net.pe; Web-On-Line, Avenida Wilson 1160, Lima Centro ☎4250390; Web Land, Avenida Diez Canseco 380–392.

Laundry Many hotels will do this cheaply, but there are numerous *lavanderías* in most areas; the Lavandería Saori, Grimaldi del Solar 175, Miraflores (Mon–Sat 8am–7pm; ☎4443830), is fast; LavaQueen, Avenida Larco 1158, Miraflores, does washing by the kilo at reasonable prices.

Optician Avenida José Pardo 495, Miraflores.

Police Peru's **headquarters** for the tourist police is the Centro Policial de Servicio al Turista in Lima at Jr. Tambo Belen, Cercado Lima ☏ 4242053, ℮ dirpolture@hotmail.com; and there are secondary offices at Jirón More 268, Magdalena (by block 38 of Avenida Brasil), ☏ 4600844 or ☏ 4601006.

Postal services The main post office is at Pasaje Piura, Jirón Lima, block 1 near the Plaza Mayor (Mon–Sat 8am–8pm & Sun 8am–2pm), with other branches on Avenida Nicolas de Pierola, opposite the *Hotel Crillon* (Mon–Sat 8am–8pm, Sun 8am–noon), and in Miraflores, at Petit Thouars 5201, a block from the corner of Angamos (Mon–Fri 8am–8pm). The best bet for sending large parcels is to use KLM (see "Airlines", above) who charge about $12 a kilo to Europe. Concas Travel, Alcanfores 345, Oficina 101, Miraflores (☏ 2417516), can arrange larger shipments. Poste restante letters are kept for up to 3 months in the main post office (see above); address mail to Poste Restante, Correo Central, Jirón Conde de Superunda, Lima Centro, Peru. American Express (see p.101) also offer poste restante.

South American Explorers' Club The clubhouse is at Calle Piura 135, Miraflores (Mon–Sat 9.30am–5pm; ☏ 4453306 ⓦ www.saexplorers .org); the postal address is Casilla 3714, Lima 100.

Spanish Language Courses Lima School of Languages, Av Grimaldo del Solar 469, Miraflores (☏ 2427763, ⓦ www.idiomasperu.com), where you can start any Monday for small-group or private tuition, full- or part-time.

Taxis and transfers Good 24hr taxi companies include: Taxi Seguro ☏ 2752020; San Borja Taxis ☏ 4768945, 4755630 or 2258600; and P&P Transport Turistico ☏ 4249556. For transfers, call the airport shuttle, Ricardo Palma 280 in Miraflores ☏ 4469872; Calderon ☏ 9407603; De Primera ☏ 4754631; or Transporte Turistico La Inmaculada ☏ 9172142, 9758342 or 3302195. Always agree on a price beforehand.

Telephones Phone kiosks are found all around the city. In Lima Centro the main Teléfonica del Peru office is near the corner of Wiese and Carabaya 933 (daily 8am–9pm), on Plaza San Martín.

Tourist Protection Service Basadre 610, San Isidro (☏ 4211227 or 5748000, 24hr), particularly for help with claims against tourism operators who have failed to fulfil their contracts in one way or another. Their symbol is *i-peru* and they also have an office in Lima airport, Aeropuerto Internacional Jorge Chavez.

Translation services Ibanez Traducciones, Miguel Dasso 126, Oficina 301, San Isidro ☏ 4216526 or 4216511, ℱ 4414122.

Travel agents and tour operators For specialist outdoor activities in and around Lima, see p.100. Otherwise, the best are: Aguamarina, Avenida Sergio Bernales 465, Urbino Aurora, Miraflores (☏ 2412562 or 2419685); Fertur Peru, Jirón Junin 211, Lima Centro (☏ 4271958, ℱ 4283347, ℮ fertur@terra.com.pe); HIRCA, Bellavista 518, Miraflores (☏ 2412317 or 2420275); Kinjyp Travel, Plaza San Martín 971 (☏ 4276760); Lima Tours, Belén 1040, near Plaza San Martín (☏ 4247560 or 4245110, ℱ 3304488, ⓦ www.limatours.com.pe); Lima Vision Jr. Chiclayo 444, Miraflores (☏ 4470482 or 4475323, ℱ 4469969, ⓦ www.limavision.com), who do a variety of city tours, Pachacamac, Nazca and Cusco; Marili Tours, Diez Canseco 392, Miraflores (☏ 4440889, 2410142 or 2410384, ℮ marili@amauta .rcp.net.pe), who have guides and go to most of Peru, including Cusco, Madre de Dios, Puno and the northern desert region; Overland Expeditions, Jirón Emilio Fernandez 640, Santa Beatrice (☏ 4247762), who specialize in the Lachay Reserve; Panamericana de Turismo, Avenida Benavides 560–564 (☏ 4441377 or 4443250, ℱ 4444665); Paracas Tours, Avenida Rivera Navarette 723, San Isidro (☏ 2222621, ℮ paracas @paracastours.com.pe), small office but very professional air ticketing service; Peruvian Life, Calle Diez Canseco 337 (☏ 4448825, ℱ 4463246, ℮ peruvian@peru.itete.com.pe); Peruvian Safaris, Avenida Inca Garcilaso de la Vega 1334 (☏ 4316330); Rainforest Expeditions, Aramburu 166-4b, Miraflores (☏ 2214182 or 9638759, ℱ 4218183, ⓦ www.perunature.com); Raymi Travels, Avenida Federico Gallesi 198 (☏ 2637203, ℱ 2630749); TEBAC, Jirón Huascar 1152, Jesus Maria (☏ 4232515), who specialize in trips to Marcahuasi; and Viajes Lazer, Avenida Comandante Espinar 331, Miraflores (☏ 4479499, ℱ 4478717).

Visas Migraciones, corner of Prolongacion Avenida España and Jirón Huaraz.

Western Union Avenida Javier Prado Este 307, San Isidro ☏ 4219089; Jirón Carabaya 675, Lima Centro; Avenida Petit Thouars 3595, San Isidro ☏ 4220036 or 4229723, ℱ 4407625; and Avenida Larco 826, Miraflores.

Around Lima

Stretching out along the coast in both directions, the **Panamerican Highway** runs the entire 2600-kilometre length of Peru, with Lima more or less at its centre. Towns along the sometimes arid coastline immediately north and south of the capital are of minor interest to most travellers, though there are some **glorious beaches** – with next to no restrictions on beach camping – and a very impressive ruin at **Pachacamac**.

The foothills above Lima contain several places of interest, not least the animistic rock outcrops of **Marcahuasi**, a weekend trip from the city. A more ambitious trip would be to the high sierra of the Andes, still only a matter of hours away by comfortable bus or slightly faster colectivo. The attractive mountain towns of **Huancay**, **Huancavelica** and **Tarma**, all interesting destinations in their own right, are within a day's easy travelling of the capital (see Chapter Six).

The Lima Coast

Most of the better **beaches** within easy reach of Lima are to the south, beginning about 30km out at the hulking pre-Inca ruins of **Pachacamac**, a sacred citadel which still dominates this stretch of coastline. The site can easily be combined with a day at one or other of the beaches and it's little problem to get out there from the capital. A good stopover en route to Pisco is the former plantation town and oasis of **Chincha**, a fertile coastal zone in ancient times as exemplified by the substantial number of pre-Inca sites in the region. To the north of Lima, the desert stretches up between the Pacific Ocean and the foothills of the Andes. There's not a huge amount of interest to the visitor here and very little in the way of tourist facilities, but it has a scattering of archeological sites, all of which are difficult to reach, plus – with easier access – some interesting eco-niches known as *lomas*, shrub-covered hills with their own unique climatic conditions and flora and fauna, of which the **Reserva Nacional Lomas de Lachay** is the best.

Pachacamac

PACHACAMAC (daily 9am–5pm; $2; ☎4300168) is by far the most interesting of the Rimac Valley's ancient sites, and well worth making time for even if you're about to head out to Cusco and Machu Picchu. The entry fee for the citadel includes admission to the site museum, which merits a quick browse around on the way in; allow a good two hours to wander around the full extent of the ruins. **Buses** leave every two hours for Pachacamac from Avenida Abancay and around the Parque Universitario on calles Montevideo and Inambari in Lima Centro. Alternatively, many of the tour agencies in Lima offer half-day tours to the site (see p.103).

Pachacamac means (more or less) "the Earth's Creator", and the site was certainly occupied by 500 AD and probably for a long time before that. When other *huacas* were being constructed in the lower Rimac Valley, Pachacamac was already a temple-citadel and centre for mass pilgrimages. The god-image of Pachacamac evidently expressed his/her anger through tremors and earth-

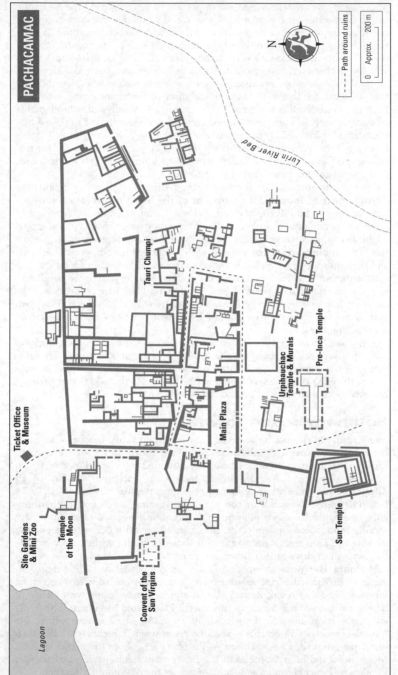

PACHACAMAC

Site Gardens
& Mini Zoo

Ticket Office
& Museum

Temple
of the Moon

Convent of the
Sun Virgins

Lagoon

Tauri Chumpi

Main Plaza

Urpihauchac
Temple & Murals

Pre-Inca Temple

Sun Temple

Lurín River Bed

N

- - - - Path around ruins

0   Approx.   200 m

quakes, and was an oracle used for important matters affecting the State: the health of the ruler, the outcome of a war, and so on. Later it became one of the most famous shrines in the Inca Empire, with Pachacamac himself worshipped along with the sun. The Incas built their Sun Temple on the crest of the hill above Pachacamac's own sacred precinct. In 1533, Francisco Pizarro sent his brother Hernando to seize Pachacamac's treasure, but was disappointed by the spoils, which consisted of just a wooden idol, now shown today in the site museum. This wooden representation of Pachacamac may well have been the oracle itself: it was kept hidden inside a labyrinth and behind guarded doors – only the high priests could communicate with it face to face. When Hernando Pizarro and his troops arrived they had to pass through many doors to arrive at the main idol site, which was raised up on a "snail-shaped" (or spiralling) platform, with the wooden carving stuck into the earth inside a dark room, separated from the world by a jewelled curtain.

Entering **the ruins** today, after passing the restored sectors which include the **Temple of the Moon** and the **Convent of the Sun Virgins** (or *Mamaconas*), you can see the **Sun Temple** directly ahead. Constructed on the top level of a series of pyramidical platforms, it was built tightly onto the hill with plastered adobe bricks, its walls originally painted in gloriously bright colours. Below this is the **main plaza**, once covered with a thatched roof supported on stilts, and thought to have been the area where pilgrims assembled in adoration. The rest of the ruins, visible though barely distinguishable, were once dwellings, storehouses and palaces. From the very top of the Sun Temple there's a magnificent view west beyond the Panamerican Highway to the beach (Playa San Pedro) and across the sea to a sizeable island which appears like a huge whale approaching the shore.

Going away from the Pachacamac site via the pueblo of the same name you pick up a hard road heading for the Quebrada Verde area. Within a few kilometres you come across the **Lomas de Lucumo**, a beautiful natural ecosystem at the edge of the desert replete with shrubs and the odd flower thriving on little more than seasonal coastal fog.

Southern beach towns

South from Pachacamac lie some of Lima's most attractive beaches. Closest to the ruins, just a couple of kilometres outside, is **Playa San Pedro**, a vast and usually deserted strip of sand. Constantly pounded by rollers, however, it can be quite dangerous for swimming. Much more sheltered, the bay of **El Silencio**, 6km to the south, was one of the most popular beaches in the 1980s but, suffering at the hands of bad regional planning, it has lost its charming edge due to the low-level pollution that occasionally appears here from new local beachside developments. You might be better off heading to one of the excellent seafood restaurants on the cliff above, or to the smaller, more secluded bays a short drive further down the coast.

At **Punta Hermosa**, about ten minutes on the bus beyond El Silencio, you come to an attractive clifftop settlement and, down below, what's becoming Lima's leading surf resort, **Santa Maria**, a great family haunt, with plenty of hotels and a reasonable beach. Finally there's **Pucusana**, a southern fishing village, gathered on the side of a small hilly peninsula, which is now perhaps the most fashionable of the beaches – a holiday resort where Limeños stay rather than just driving out for a swim. **Buses** to Pucusana leave from the corner of Jirón Montevideo and Jirón Ayacucho in Lima every two hours, passing Pachacamac, El Silencio, Punta Hermosa and Santa Maria on the 65-kilometre journey.

Continuing south, the road cruises along the coast, passing the long beach and salt-pools of **Chilca** after 5km, and the curious lion-shaped rock of **León Dormido** (Sleeping Lion) after another 15km or so. About 20km on from Chilca on the highway, where it bypasses the town of Malfa, is the **cafetería** *Dona Paulina*, a great place to sample the best *chicharones* (chunks of deep-fried pork) in the region. **Asia**, 10km down the road and spread out along it from Km 95 to 103, is essentially a small agricultural town, producing cotton, bananas and corn; the long beach here is ideal for **camping**, particularly its southern end. Some interesting archeological finds in local graveyards reveal that this site was occupied from around 2500 BC by a pre-ceramic agricultural community associated also with the earliest examples of a trophy-head cult (many of the mummies were decapitated). About 20km on from Asia is the growing surfers' resort of **CERRO AZUL**, located where the dual carriageway from Lima ends and becomes a single two-way road. The **hostels** *La Casita* (❷) and *Cerro Azul* (❷) offer reasonable accommodation, but fill up quickly and charge more in main holiday periods. Another 8km and you come to the larger settlement of **Cañete**, an attractive town with a colonial flavour, surrounded by marigolds and cotton fields, though probably not a place you'll want to stop in, unless you happen to arrive during its annual **festival** (late August), which consists of ten days of wild dancing to black Peruvian music. Chilca, Asia, Cañete and Chincha (see below) are all served from Lima by Cruz del Sur **buses** from Jirón Quilca 531, and Ormeño buses from Carlos Zavala 177, most of which continue on to Pisco, Nazca and Arequipa.

Chincha

If you feel like breaking the journey before Pisco, the best candidate is **CHINCHA**, a relatively rich oasis town that appears after a stretch of almost Saharan landscape – and a mightily impressive sand dune – at the top of the cliff. A busy little coastal centre renowned for its cheap wines and variety of **piscos**, Chincha is a strong cultural hub for Afro-Peruvian culture, having grown up around the early colonial cotton plantations worked by slaves who were mainly from Guinea in Africa. This is clearly evidenced by the high percentage of black faces in the streets, descendants of the slaves, some of whom were brought over to make rich hacienda owners even wealthier as early as the sixteenth century. Of all the South American countries, racial repression was among the harshest in Peru, with prohibitions on mixed race (criollos) from holding public office. Afro-Peruvians were even banned from playing drums (that's how the Peruvian percussive instrument – the cajón – was invented, see Contexts p.566). It wasn't until 1854 that slavery was abolished in Peru and Afro-Peruvians became technically free.

One of the best places for pisco and local wine (*vino dulce*) is at the 100-year-old **Bodega Naldo Navarro** in Sunampe, 1km north of Chincha, offering free guided tours and samples. Several other local bodegas offer similar tours. For **festivals**, the third Saturday in September is National Pisco Day, when things really get lively along this section of the coast. The area is also well known for its traditionally rhythmic music and annual, athletic dance festival, Verano Negro, which takes place at the end of February, while in November the Festival de Danzas Negras is an excellent event; in both cases the celebrations are liveliest in El Carmen, 10km southeast of Chincha.

This town is also renowned for its **ruins**, with numerous *huacas* lying scattered about the oasis. Dominated in pre-Inca days by the Cuismancu (or Chincha) state, activity focused around what were probably ceremonial pyramids. One of these, the majestic **Huaca Centinela**, also known as the little city of Chinchacamac, sits in the valley below the Chincha tableland and the ocean, around thirty minutes' walk from the *Hotel El Sausal* turning (see below), some 8km off the Panamerican. Not far from Chincha, 40km up the Castrovireyna road which leaves the Panamerican Highway at Km 230, is another impressive Cuismancu ruin, Tambo Colorado (see p.205).

Don't miss the **Hacienda San José**, Pueblo San José (daily 9am–6pm; free), 9km southeast of Chincha, in an extensive plantation, where you can see impressive Churrigueresque domed towers built in the 1680s. Its colourful history includes the tale of an owner murdered on the house's main steps by his slaves. Now a semi-luxurious **hotel** (℡034/221458; ❻), the hacienda is also bookable in Lima through Juan Fanning 328, Oficina 202, Miraflores (℡4445524, ✉hsanjose@bellnet.com.pe). It's open to visitors to use the pool, watch local folklore shows and there are 45-minute **tours** ($3) around the labyrinthine catacombs containing prison cells still showing clearly the poor conditions in which slaves were once shackled.

As well as the *Hacienda San José*, **accommodation** options include the flashy *Hotel El Sausal* (❺), Km 197 Panamerican Highway, with its own pool, on the right as you come into town; the *Hostal El Sotelo* (❷), one block from the plaza; the *Hotel El Valle* (❹) on the main road in the centre of town; or one of the cheaper hotels along the main street (left at the fork in the road) beyond the Ormeño bus depot; the *Hotel Imperio* (❹), on the Panamerican Highway, two blocks south of the central plaza, offers good rooms at reasonable prices. For **eating**, the *Palacio de Mariscos* at the *Hotel El Valle* is excellent and the restaurants *El Fogon* and *Café El Atrio* are reasonable alternatives, both on the main plaza.

North of Lima

There are a couple of shortish trips becoming increasingly popular as long weekend breaks from Lima. One of these heads up the Huara Valley from Huacho; although the road can be traced all the way to Huánuco, most people only get as far up into the Andes as Churin where their efforts are pleasantly rewarded with a visit to the hot springs. Another interesting route at this location is a horseshoe loop nearer to Lima connecting the Chillón and Chancay valleys via the beautiful town and region of Canta in the foothills of the Andes.

Sayan and Churin

Just beyond Huacho a side road turns east into the **Huara Valley** and the foothills of the Andes to reach **SAYAN**, a small farming town where little has changed for decades – the church here has a very attractive colonial interior. An acceptable but fairly basic **place to stay** is *Hostal Tolentino*, Balta 541 (℡371018; ❷), above a bakery. The **restaurant** *Jalisco*, Balta 342, serves large portions of good food – river shrimp and wine are local specialities. **Colectivos** run between Sayan and Huacho every thirty minutes.

Further up the valley lies **CHURIN**, a small thermal spa town that's very popular with Limeños during holidays. Most of the farmland on the valley floor and the Sayan to Churin road was washed away in the 1998 El Niño, and a new, rough road has been carved out between the boulders littering the valley floor. There are two **spas** in town, both fairly cool, with private and communal baths, but the El Fierro spa, ten minutes by colectivo from town, is the hottest and is reputed to be the most curative; all cost about 50¢.

There are several **buses** to and from Lima daily (a 6–7hr journey), the best being run by Transportes Estrella Polar; expect to pay around $5. There are many **places to stay**, but they all get packed out in the main holiday periods, when prices double. All the hotels are within a couple of blocks of each other in the town centre; try the *Santa Rosa* (☎373014; ❺ and *Internacional* (☎373015; ❺, both modern and with a range of facilities, or the *Hotel Las Termas* (☎373005; ❹, which has nicer rooms and a pool. The hostels *Beatriz* (❸) and *Danubio* (❸) are modern, clean and friendly. Churin has many good **restaurants** and cafés, mostly around the main plaza, and local specialities include honey, *alfajores*, *manjar blanca* and cheeses.

An excellent day-trip from Churin can be made to more thermal baths at **Huancahuasi**. Colectivos leave from Churin church at around 8am ($3 return), returning mid-afternoon. There are two sets of hot baths at Huancahuasi (both 50¢), and snacks such as *pachamanca* are prepared outside them. En route to Huancahuasi you'll spot a remarkable early colonial carved facade on the tiny church at Picoy.

North to Chillón and Chancay valleys

Leaving Lima and heading north, the Panamerican Highway passes through the **Chillón valley**, dotted with ancient ruins, of which the most important are on the south side of the Río Chillón within 3 or 4km of the Ventanilla road. The most impressive is the 2000–3000-year-old **Temple El Paraiso**, which was built by a sedentary farming community of probably no more than 1500 inhabitants and consists of three main pyramids built of rustic stones.

From here, the Panamerican Highway passes the yacht and tennis clubs that make up the fashionable beach resort of **Ancón**, about 30km from Lima, then crosses a high, often foggy, plateau from the Chillón to the **Chancay valley**. This foggy zone, still covered by sparse vegetation, was a relatively fertile *lomas* area (where plants grow from moisture in the air rather than rainwater or irrigation) in pre-Inca days, and evidence of winter camps from five thousand years ago has been found. The highway bypasses the market town of Huaral and runs through **Chancay**, some 65km north of Lima, worth a visit only for its excellent clifftop seafood restaurants, as the sea is too dangerous to swim in at this location. Nearby the Ecotruly Ashram, Km 63 on the Panamerican Highway, by Chacra y Mar beach (☎4444747 or 4708804, ⓦwww.vrindavan .org/trulys) is set at the foot of desert cliffs and close to the pounding ocean. They offer guided tours of their adobe huts and organic gardens, plus yoga and meditation, hikes and workshops on ecology. Always book visits in advance.

Continuing north from Chancay, the road passes through stark desert for 20km until you reach the **Reserva Nacional Lomas de Lachay**, a protected area of unique *lomas* habitat some 5000 hectares in extent and around 600m above sea-level. The easiest way to get there is with an organized tour from Lima (Overland Expeditions are experts in the area; see p.103), but if you are doing it alone continue up the Panamerican Highway for about 6km beyond the turning for Sayan and Churin. The turn-off to the reserve is signposted at the top of a hill, but from the road it's still an hour's walk along a sandy track to the interpretive centre (daily 7am–7pm) at the entrance to the reserve. Run by the Ministry of Agriculture, the centre maintains the footpaths that thread through the reserve's beautiful scenery. Formed by granite and diorite rocky intrusions some seventy million years ago, the *lomas* – at its best between June and December when it is in full bloom – is home to more than forty types of birds including hummingbirds, parrots, partridges, peregrines and even condors; you also may spot various species of reptile and native deer.

A little further north of the reserve, at Km 133, a track turns off onto a small peninsula and leads to the secluded bay of **El Paraiso** – a magical beach perfect for camping, swimming and scuba-diving. Crossing more bleak sands, the Panamerican Highway next passes through **Huacho**, an unusual place with some interesting colonial architecture and a ruined church in the upper part of town, but most of the settlement made up of recent concrete constructions; being so close to Lima, it's been one of the first to be hit by expanding and migratory populations as well as wealthy Lima families taking on a second home or farmstead. Other than turning off the Panamerican Highway to Sayan and Churin, only the town and port of Supe breaks the monotonous beauty of desert and ocean, until you reach Barranco and the labyrinthine ruins of the Fortress of Paramonga (see p.293).

Caral – the world's oldest stone-built pyramids

Inland from Puerto Supe, along the desert coast in a landscape which looks more lunar than agricultural, archeologists have recently uncovered one of the most important archeological finds of the past century. Thought to be the oldest city in the Americas, the **ancient pyramids of Caral** have overturned many longstanding assumptions. It's not yet officially open to the general public since much excavation work is yet to be done, but it is possible to see the site with permission from INRENA (see Listings p.102) on visits organized by some of the better tour companies. Difficult to reach without a 4WD car, it's connected to the Panamerican Highway by a badly rutted dirt-track road.

This site represents human achievements that took place four thousand years earlier than the Incas. The stone ceremonial structures at Caral were flourishing 100 years before the Great Pyramid at Giza was built. The heart of the site covers about 150 acres. There are two sunken circular plazas at the base of the largest mound which itself measures 154m by 138m at the bottom, evidently making it the largest pyramid yet found in Peru. Excavations have revealed that this Pirimide Mayor (main pyramid) was terraced with a staircase leading up to an atrium-like platform, culminating in a flattened top housing enclosed rooms and a ceremonial fire pit. Some of the best artefacts discovered here include 32 flutes made from pelican and animal bones and engraved with the figures of birds and even monkeys, demonstrating a connection with the Amazon region.

Inland from Lima: into the foothills

There are several destinations in the **foothills of the Andes** which are within relatively easy reach of Lima. The most spectacular is the mystical plateau of Marcahuasi (see p.335), but much closer to Lima are the impressive sites of **Puruchuco** and **Cajamarquilla**, which are typical of ruins all over Peru and make a good introduction to the country's archeology. Both Puruchuco and Cajamarquilla lie near the beginning of the Central Highway, the road that climbs up behind Lima towards Chosica, La Oroya and the Andes. The two sites are only 6km apart and are most easily visited on a half-day guided tour from Lima (see Listings, p.103). Alternatively, you could take a colectivo from Calle

Montevideo (daily from 7am; $2) and return by waving down virtually any of the passing buses on the main Carretera Central, though the Chosica to Lima bus will be the most likely to have spare seats.

Puruchuco

An 800-year-old, pre-Inca settlement, **PURUCHUCO** (daily 9am–5pm; $1.50) comprises a labyrinthine villa and a small but interesting museum containing a complete collection of artefacts and attire found at the site (all of which bears a remarkable similarity to what Amazon Indian communities still use today). The name itself means "feathered hat or helmet" and recent building work in the locality discovered that the Puruchuco site was also a massive graveyard, revealing greater quantities of buried pre-Incas than most other sites in Peru. The original adobe structure was apparently rebuilt and adapted by the Incas shortly before the Spanish arrival: it's a fascinating ruin, superbly restored in a way which vividly captures what life was like before the Conquest. Very close by, in the Parque Fernando Carozi (ask the site guard for directions), two other ruins – **Huaquerones** and **Catalina Huaca** – are being restored, and at **Chivateros** there's a quarry apparently dating back some twelve thousand years.

Cajamarquilla

For **CAJAMARQUILLA**, the colectivo will drop you off at the refinery turn-off before Km 10 of the Carretera Central, then it's about 4km, or an hour's walk, to the **ruins** (daily 9am–5pm; $1.50), which are well hidden next to an old hacienda. First occupied in the Huari era (600–1000 AD), Cajamarquilla flourished under the **Cuismancu culture**, a city-building state contemporary with the better-known Chimu in northern Peru. It was an enclosed city containing thousands of small complex dwellings clustered around a higher section, probably nobles' quarters, and numerous small plazas. The site was apparently abandoned before the Incas arrived in 1470, possibly after being devastated by an earthquake. Pottery found here in the 1960s by a group of Italian archeologists suggests habitation over 1300 years ago. The **Centro Ecologico Recreacional Huachipa** (daily 9am–4.30pm; ☎3563141, ✉cerh@sedapal .com.pe), a fun theme park and zoo located at Km 9.5 of the Carretera Central (close to the Cajamarquilla turn-off), is somewhere kids might enjoy; there's a large space with walk-on pirate boat, a water world area, imaginative play area and a zone full of exotic plants and wildlife. A few kilometres east of here, around Km 12.5 of the Carretera Central, there's another archeological site on the right bank of the Río Rimac: the Inca administrative centre now known as **San Juan de Pariachi**, dating from at least a thousand years ago.

A further 20km into the foothills through sprawling developments, the road comes to the town of **Chosica**, a narrow settlement squeezed in between the steepening dry and rocky foothills and the turbulent river below. Just 35km from Lima itself, Chosica has long been a traditional weekend escape from the city. It's unique attraction is as a winter escape from the Lima mist and smog. There's not really that much to visit in Chosica, just some recreation centres, mostly private, in the valley below, but if you want to stay, the *Hospedaje Chosica* at Avenida 28 de Julio 134 (☎3610841; ❷) is very pleasant and exceptionally good value; a family-run place, they have six rooms without baths and four with. For **eating** it's difficult to do better than the *Restaurant Liluzca*, Jirón Chiclayo 250, in a small side street off the main road by the plaza; it has outside seating and serves decent food, though it usually closes before 7pm. Above Chosica the road starts to climb fast, winding its way past some impressive-looking hydro power stations into the Andes towards Ticlio and way beyond the beautiful Mantaro Valley (see p.339). There are plenty of minibus colectivos connecting Lima with Chosica for around $1, but catching a bus on from Chosica to Huancayo, Tarma or Huánuco can be trickier since, although they pass through here, they may well be full already. Colectivos or shared taxis may be an easier solution.

Travel details

Buses and colectivos

Lima to: Arequipa (12 daily; 13–16hr); Chincha (8 daily; 3hr); Cusco (8 daily, some change in Arequipa; 30–40hr); Huacho (12 daily; 2–3hr); Huancayo (10 daily; 6–8hr); Huaraz (10 daily; 9–10hr); Ica (16 daily; 3–4hr); La Merced (6 daily; 7–8hr); Nazca (6 daily; 6hr); Satipo (2 daily; 12–16hr); Pisco (6 daily; 3hr–3hr 30min); Tacna (6 daily; 20–22hr); Tarma (8 daily; 6–7hr); Trujillo (10 daily; 8–9hr).

Flights

Lima to: Arequipa (3 daily; 1hr 20min); Chiclayo (3 daily; 1hr 40min); Cusco (6 daily; 1hr); Huánuco (1 daily; 1hr); Iquitos (2 daily; 1hr 45min); Juliaca for Puno (2 daily; 2hr); Piura (2 daily; 1hr 30min); Pucallpa (2 daily; 1hr); Rioja/Moyabamba (5 weekly; 1hr 30min); Tacna (2 daily; 2hr 30min); Tarapoto (4 weekly; 1hr); Trujillo (3 daily; 45min); Tumbes (2 daily; 2hr 30min); Yurimaguas (4 weekly; 2hr).

Cusco and around

CHAPTER 2 # Highlights

✱ **Pisac** Standing at this Inca citadel offers one of Peru's most amazing panoramas. **See p.155**

✱ **The Inca Trail** In danger of being damaged because of its own success, the Inca Trail connects the Sacred Valley to Machu Picchu, but is quite breathtaking all on its own. **See p.165**

✱ **Machu Picchu** This most stunning and awe-inspiring of Inca citadels is set against spiky, forested mountains and distant glacial summits dwarfed only by the sky. **See p.169**

✱ **San Blas** Take in the scene of Cusco's vibrant artists' quarter at a table outside the *Muse Bar* overlooking the Plazoleta San Blas. **See p.134**

✱ **Paucartambo Festival** During the Fiesta Virgen del Carmen this quiet town changes into a colourful, haunting display of music and surreal outfits. **See p.183**

✱ **Solar light show** Sunrises at Tres Cruces, particularly during the June winter solstice, are spectacular and brightly coloured, with multiple suns. **See p.184**

✱ **Whitewater rafting** Four days on the Vilcanota or Apurimac is one of the most exciting rafting experiences in the world. **See p.150**

Cusco and around

K nown to the Incas as the "navel of the world", **CUSCO** is still an exciting and colourful city, built by the Spanish on the remains of Inca temples and palaces, and as rich in human activity today as it must have been
at the height of the empire. Enclosed between high hills and dominated in equal degree by the imposing ceremonial centre and fortress of
Sacsayhuaman and the white Christ figure, it's one of South America's
biggest tourist destinations, with its thriving culture, substantial Inca ruins and
architectural treasures from the colonial era attracting visitors from every corner of the world. Yet despite its massive pull, this welcoming city of 300,000
(mostly native **Quechua Indians)** remains relatively unspoiled, its white-

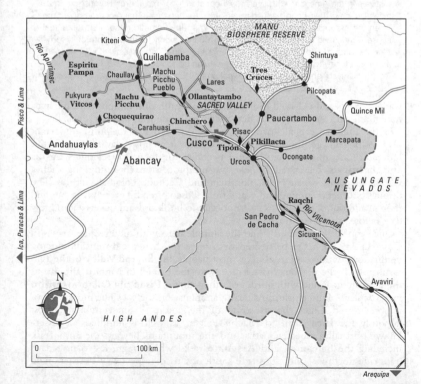

Fiestas in the Cusco region

Around Jan 20 Adoración de los Reyes (Adoration of the Kings). Ornate and elaborate processions leave from San Blas church and parade through Cusco.

Last week of Jan Pera Chapch'y (Festival of the Pear). A harvest festival in San Sebastian, 4km southeast of Cusco, with lively street stalls and processions.

February Festividad Carnavales. Folk dancing and traditional food in the streets of Coya, Pisac and Calca; each village celebrates in a different week of the month (check with the tourist office).

First week of March Festival de Durasno (Festival of the Peach). Food stalls and folk dancing in Yanahuara and Urubamba.

Easter Week Semana Santa. On Easter Monday there's a particularly splendid procession through Cusco, with a rich and evocative mix of Indian and Catholic iconography. The following Thursday a second procession celebrates the city's patron saint, El Señor de los Temblores (Lord of Earthquakes), and on Easter Friday, street stalls sell many different traditional dishes.

May 2–3 Cruz Velacuy, or Fiesta de las Cruces (Festival of the Cross). All church and sanctuary crosses in Cusco and the provinces are veiled for a day, followed by traditional festivities with dancing and feasting in most communities. Particularly splendid in Ollantaytambo.

Weekend before Corpus Christi Qoyllur Riti (Snow Star, or ice festival). Held on the full-moon weekend prior to Corpus Christi in an isolated valley above the road from Cusco via Urcos and Ocungate to the Amazon town of Puerto Maldonado. The festival site lies at the foot of a glacier, opposite the sacred mountain of Ausangate, but below another mountain considered an *apu*, or god. This is one of the most exciting festivals in the Americas with live music constantly for days, processions, communities bringing their bands and dancers for an annual spiritual recharge at a time when the mountain is said to be blossoming in an energetic rather than botanical sense. You'll need to camp, and at around 4600m it's only for the adventurous; some tour operators do go there, but it's primarily a Quechua Indian festival, with villagers arriving in their thousands in the weeks running up to it.

Corpus Christi (annually, exactly 9 weeks after Easter) In this festival, imposed by

washed streets and red-tiled roofs home to a wealth of traditional culture, lively nightlife and a seemingly endless variety of museums, walks and tours.

As the imperial capital during Inca times, Cusco was the most important place of pilgrimage in South America, a status it retains today. During Easter, June and Christmas, the city centre becomes the focus for relentless **fiestas and carnivals** celebrated by extravagant processions bringing together a vibrant blend of pagan pre-Columbian and Catholic colonial cultures. The throngs of tourists coming and going from Cusco often fill every plane, bus and train in and out of the city, so it's important to book onward tickets a good few days before you intend travelling.

Once you've acclimatized – and the altitude here, with the Plaza de Armas in Cusco at 3399m, has to be treated with respect – there are dozens of enticing destinations within easy reach. For most people, the **Sacred Valley** of the Río Urubamba is the obvious first choice, with the citadel of **Machu Picchu** as the ultimate goal, and with hordes of other ruins – **Pisac** and **Ollantaytambo** in particular – amid glorious Andean panoramas on the way. The mountainous region around Cusco boasts some of the country's finest trekking, most famously the **Inca Trail** to Machu Picchu, as well as hundreds of lesser-known, virtually unbeaten paths into the mountains beyond the Inca Trail, including the **Salcantay** and **Arsenate** treks, which begin less than a day's train ride northwest and a bus ride south of Cusco, respectively. Further afield the Spanish to replace the Inca tradition of parading ancestral mummies, a procession of saints' effigies are carried through the streets of Cusco, even as the local *mayordomos* (ritual community leaders) throw parties and feasts combining elements of religiosity with outright hedonism. The effigies are then left inside the Cathedral for eight days, after which they are taken back to their respective churches, accompanied by musicians, dancers and exploding firecrackers.

Second week of June Cusqueña International Beer and Music Festival. Lively, week-long festival in Cusco, hosting fairly big Latin pop and jazz names, at its best from Thursday to Sunday.

June 16–22 Traditional folk festivals in Raqchi and Sicuani.

June 20–30 Fiesta de Huancaro. An agricultural show packed with locals and good fun, based in Huancaro sector of Cusco ($1 taxi ride from Plaza de Armas, or go down Avenida Sol and turn right at the roundabout before the airport).

Last week in June Cusco Carnival, or Cusco Week. Daily processions in the Plaza de Armas by army, school and civil defence groups and folk dancers, plus lively music on the streets throughout the day and night, peaking with Inti Raymi.

June 24 Inti Raymi. Popular, commercial fiesta re-enacting the Inca Festival of the Sun in the grounds of Sacsayhuaman.

July 15–17 Virgen de Carmen. Dance and music festival celebrated all over the high lands, but at its best in Paucartambo.

July 28 Peruvian Independence Day. Festivities nationwide, not least in Cusco.

Sept 14–18 Señor de Huanca. Music, dancing, pilgrimages and processions take place all over the region but especially lively in Calca, with a fair in the Sacred Valley.

Sept 25 to early Oct Semana Turistica (Tourist Week). Conferences and street processions in Cusco, but all rather fake and touristy.

First week of Dec Yawar Fiesta. A vibrant, uncommercial *corrida de toros* (bullfight) at the end of the week in Paruro, Cotabambas and Chumbivilcas. A condor, captured by hand, is tied to the back of a bull that battles to the death.

Dec 24 Santuranticuy. Traditional fair of artesania, including hand-made, wooden toys in Cusco.

you can explore the lowland **Amazon rainforest** in Madre de Dios, such as the Tambopata and Candamo Reserved Zone, or the slightly nearer Manu Reserved Zone (all covered in Chapter Eight), among the most accessible and bio-diverse wildernesses on Earth.

Southeast of Cusco lie more Inca and pre-Inca sites at **Tipón** and **Pikillacta**, nearly as spectacular as those in the Sacred Valley yet far less visited, not least because of the lack of local infrastructure for food and travel. Travelling south from these, the highly scenic **train journey** to Puno and Lake Titicaca passes through scenery as dramatic as any in the country. To the west of Cusco is the traditional Andean region around Ayacucho (see p.344).

The **best time to visit** the area around Cusco is during the dry season (May–Sept), when it's warm with clear skies during the day but relatively cold at night. During the wet season (Oct–April) it rarely rains every day or all week, but when it does, downpours are heavy.

Cusco

The **Cusco Valley** and the **Incas** are synonymous in most people's minds, but the area was populated well before the Incas arrived on the scene and built their empire on the toil and ingenuity of previous cultures. The **Killki** culture, which dominated the scene around 700–800 AD, although primarily agriculturists, built structures from the hard local diorite and andesite stones. Some of these structures still survive, while others were incorporated into later Inca constructions – the sun temple of Koricancha, for example, seems to have been built on the foundations of a Killki sun temple. Early Inca pots, too, are stylistically close to Killki-produced items, while classical Inca pots demonstrate

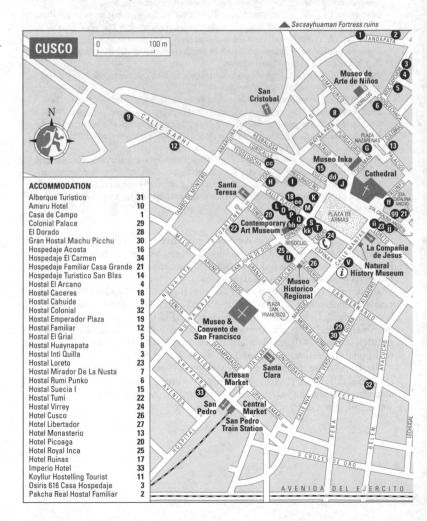

▲ *Sacsayhuaman Fortress ruins*

CUSCO

0   100 m

ACCOMMODATION

Alberque Turistico	31
Amaru Hotel	10
Casa de Campo	1
Colonial Palace	29
El Dorado	28
Gran Hostal Machu Picchu	30
Hospedaje Acosta	16
Hospedaje El Carmen	34
Hospedaje Familiar Casa Grande	21
Hospedaje Turistico San Blas	14
Hostal El Arcano	4
Hostal Caceres	18
Hostal Cahuide	9
Hostal Colonial	32
Hostal Emperador Plaza	19
Hostal Familiar	12
Hostal El Grial	5
Hostal Huaynapata	8
Hostal Inti Quilla	3
Hostal Loreto	23
Hostal Mirador De La Nusta	7
Hostal Rumi Punko	6
Hostal Suecia I	15
Hostal Tumi	22
Hostal Virrey	24
Hotel Cusco	26
Hotel Libertador	27
Hotel Monasterio	13
Hotel Picoaga	20
Hotel Royal Inca	25
Hotel Ruinas	17
Imperio Hotel	33
Koyllur Hostelling Tourist	11
Osiris 616 Casa Hospedaje	3
Pakcha Real Hostal Familiar	2

strong similarities to ceramics produced around 1000 AD by the **Lucre** culture, which was centred around Choquepugio, 35km from modern Cusco. The Lucre also used significant amounts of diorite stone in their constructions and, like the Incas later, utilized boulders in multi-angular, earthquake-proof formations. Later Inca pottery shows a strong **Wari** influence (see Contexts, p.527 for more on pre-Inca cultures).

According to Inca legend, Cusco was founded by **Manco Capac** and his sister Mama Occlo around 1200 AD. There is evidence that the early Inca founders of Cusco claimed to have found only "savagery and barbarism" and there may have been "holy wars" with other groups in the area around this time. Over the next two hundred years the valley was home to the Inca tribe, one of many localized warlike groups then dominating the Peruvian sierra. It wasn't until **Pachacuti** assumed leadership of the Incas in 1438 that Cusco

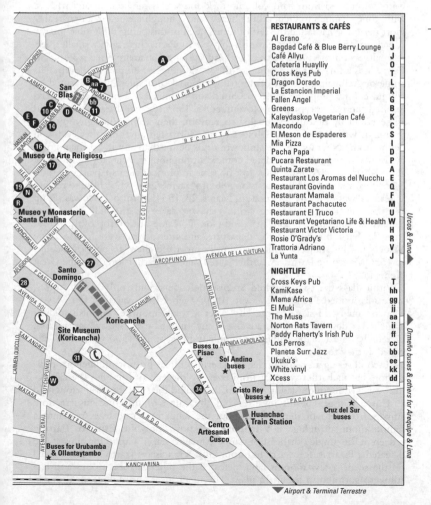

RESTAURANTS & CAFÉS

Al Grano	N
Bagdad Café & Blue Berry Lounge	J
Café Allyu	O
Cafetería Huaylliy	T
Cross Keys Pub	L
Dragon Dorado	K
La Estancion Imperial	G
Fallen Angel	B
Greens	K
Kaleydaskop Vegetarian Café	C
Macondo	S
El Meson de Espaderes	I
Mia Pizza	D
Pacha Papa	P
Pucara Restaurant	A
Quinta Zarate	E
Restaurant Los Aromas del Nucchu	Q
Restaurant Govinda	F
Restaurant Mamala	M
Restaurant Pachacutec	U
Restaurant El Truco	W
Restaurant Vegetariano Life & Health	H
Restaurant Victor Victoria	R
Rosie O'Grady's	V
Trattoria Adriano	J
La Yunta	

NIGHTLIFE

Cross Keys Pub	T
KamiKase	hh
Mama Africa	gg
El Muki	jj
The Muse	aa
Norton Rats Tavern	ii
Paddy Flaherty's Irish Pub	ff
Los Perros	cc
Planeta Surr Jazz	bb
Ukuku's	ee
White.vinyl	kk
Xcess	dd

Urcos & Puno ▶

Ormeño buses & others for Arequipa & Lima ▶

▼ *Airport & Terminal Terrestre*

became the centre of an expanding empire and the surrounding "barbarism" was subdued and incorporated, through "holy wars" where necessary. As Pachacuti pushed the frontier of Inca territory outwards, so he also master-minded the design of imperial Cusco, canalizing the Saphi and the Tullumayo, two rivers that ran down the valley, and building the centre of the city between them. Cusco's city plan was conceived in the form of a puma, a sacred animal: **Sacsayhuaman**, an important ritual centre and citadel, is the jagged, tooth-packed head; **Pumacchupan**, the sacred cat's tail, lies at the junction of the city's two rivers; between these two sites lies **Koricancha**, the Temple of the Sun, reproductive centre of the Inca universe, the loins of this sacred beast; the heart of the puma was **Huacapata**, a ceremonial square approximating in both size and position to the present-day Plaza de Armas. Four main roads radiated from the square, one to each corner of the empire. The overall achievement was remarkable, a planned city without rival at the centre of a huge empire, and in building their capital the Incas endowed Cusco with some of its finest structures. All important buildings were constructed from hard volcanic rock and streets ran straight and narrow, with stone channels to drain off the heavy rains. Though created in a remarkably short period, it has lasted the test of time, much of this being still visible today.

Back in 1532, when the Spanish arrived in Peru, they saw a smaller, less refined version of Cusco in the northern sierra at Cajamarca (see p.390). But Cusco was a thriving city, capital of the world's biggest empire at the time. Its emperor, Atahualpa, the last of the truly imperial Inca rulers, was captured by conquistadores while en route to Cusco and in his place **Francisco Pizarro** reached the native capital on November 15, 1533 after stealing as much gold as he could by holding Atahualpa to ransom, then killing him anyway. The Spaniards were astonished: the city's beauty surpassed anything they had seen before in the New World, the stonework was better than any in Spain and precious metals were used in a sacred context throughout the city, though most of all in Koricancha. As usual, they lost no time in plundering its fantastic wealth.

The Spanish city, divided up among 88 of Pizarro's men who chose to remain as settlers, was officially founded on March 23, 1534. **Manco Inca** was set up as a puppet ruler, governing from a new palace on the hill just below Sacsayhuaman. Pizarro's sons Juan and Gonzalo came out on top of the power struggle that followed Pizarro's departure, and after a year were free to abuse Manco and his subjects, which eventually provoked them to open resistance. In 1536 Manco fled to Yucay, in the Sacred Valley, to gather forces for the Great Rebellion.

Within days the two hundred Spanish defenders, with only eighty horses, were surrounded in Cusco by over 100,000 rebel Inca warriors. On May 6, Manco's men laid siege to the city. After a week, mounted Spanish soldiers launched a desperate counterattack on the Inca base in Sacsayhuaman and, incredibly, defeated the native stronghold, putting some 1500 warriors to the sword as they took it.

Cusco never again came under such serious threat from its indigenous population, but its battles were far from over. By the end of the rains the following year, a rival conquistador, Almagro, threatened the small Spanish stronghold at Cusco. Unsure of his loyalties and the cause of the Inca insurrection, Almagro tried to befriend Manco but the emperor chose to retreat into a remote mountain refuge at **Vilcabamba** – now known as **Espiritu Pampa** – deep in the jungle northeast of Cusco. Almagro seized Cusco for himself and defeated a Pizarrist force arriving from Lima. Francisco Pizarro himself arrived on the scene a few months later, defeated the rebel Spanish troops and had Almagro garroted in the main plaza. The rebel Incas, meanwhile, held out in

Vilcabamba until 1572, when the Spanish colonial viceroy, Toledo, captured Tupac Aymaru – one of Manco's sons who had succeeded as emperor – and beheaded him in the Plaza de Armas.

From then on the city was left in relative peace, ravaged only by the great earthquake of 1650. After this dramatic tremor, remarkably illustrated on a huge canvas in the Cathedral, **Bishop Mollinedo** was largely responsible for the reconstruction of the city, and his influence is also closely associated with Cusco's most creative years of art. The **Cusqueña school**, which emerged from his patronage, flourished for the next two hundred years, and much of its finer work, produced by native Quechua and *mestizo* artists such as Diego Quispe Tito, Juan Espinosa de los Monteros, Fabian Ruiz and Antonio Sinchi Roca, is exhibited in museums and churches around the city.

Today, Cusco possesses an identity above and beyond the legacy left in the andesite stones carved by the Incas. Like its renowned art, Cusco is dark, yet vibrant with colour; one minute you're walking down a high, narrow, stone-walled alley listening to the soft moans of a blind old busker, then suddenly you burst onto a plaza full of brightly dressed dancers from the countryside, joining in what, at times, seems like the endless carnival and religious festival celebrations which Cusco is famous for. It's a politically active, left-of-centre city where street demonstrations organized by teachers, lecturers, miners or some other beleaguered profession are commonplace. The leading light of Cusco's left, ex-mayor **Daniel Estrada**, left the city in 1996 to become a member of Congress in Lima, taking with him much of Cusco's political vigour. However, with the help of local architect **Guido Gallegos**, he left behind a visual legacy for the city, in its elegant Inca-like modern fountains and statues, such as the Condor and Pachacutec monuments and the new plaza in San Blas, mostly built in the early 1990s under his auspices. Since then a huge, largely concrete and circular sundisc monument has been erected on the lower part of Avenida Sol, near Huanchac station and Cusco's largest artesania market. The community spirit remains strong, if diverse, and street demonstrations protesting against council policies are a regular occurrence. Teachers and bankers regularly strike, taking to the streets in noisy processions numbering in the hundreds, shouting their complaints in unison as they pass strategic buildings and following a similar route to the more colourful festival processions.

Arrival, information and city transport

Cusco **airport** (☎222611 or 222601) is 4km south of the city centre. You can either take a taxi from outside the arrivals hall ($2–3 to the city centre) or a colectivo combi from outside the airport car park (frequent departures 50¢), which goes to Plaza San Francisco via Avenida Sol and Plaza de Armas. Note that the airport is full of tour touts, who should be avoided. If you're coming in by train from Juliaca, Puno or Arequipa, you'll arrive at the Huanchac **train station** in the southeast of the city; you can hail a taxi on the street outside (around $1 to the centre), or turn left out of the station and walk about a hundred metres to Avenida Sol, from where you can either catch the airport colectivo detailed above, or walk the eight or nine blocks up a gentle hill to the Plaza de Armas, essentially the city centre.

The phone code for Cusco and the surrounding region is ☎084.

Mountain sickness

Soroche, or mountain sickness, is a reality for most people arriving in Cusco by plane from sea level and needs to be treated with respect. It's vital to take it easy, not eating or drinking much on arrival, even sleeping a whole day just to assist acclimatization (coca tea is a good local remedy). After three days at this height most people have adjusted sufficiently to tackle moderate hikes at similar or lesser altitudes. Anyone considering tackling the major mountains around Cusco will need time to adjust again to their higher base camps. For more information on *soroche* see Basics p.24.

Something maybe worth trying in the first day or two – in order to get up to Sacsayhuaman without the breathtaking experience of walking up there before you've really acclimatized to the altitude - is the **Tranvia Cusco** woodenbus (T224377 or 740640; $2 or less, small children free) which takes a scenic ride through the historic centre up to Sacsayhuaman and back most days; it's usually found parked outside the *Hostal Familiar* on Calle Saphi.

Apart from Cruz del Sur, who have their own independent depot at Avenida Pachacutec, a few blocks east of Huanchac railway station and Avenida Sol, **inter-regional and international buses** (see Listings, p.147, for details) arrive and depart from the rather scruffy Terminal Terrestre, southeast of the centre, close to the Pachacutec monument and roundabout (*ovalo*) and roughly halfway between the Plaza de Armas and the airport. Taxis from here to the city centre cost $1–2, or you can walk to the Pachacutec *ovalo* and catch a colectivo uphill to either the Plaza San Francisco or the Plaza de Armas; otherwise, it's about a half-hour walk. **Regional buses** from the Sicuani, Urcos and Paucartambo areas stop around blocks 15 and 16 of Avenida de la Cultura, from where it's a bit of a hike, so you'll almost certainly want to take a taxi ($1–2) or bus or combi colectivo (30¢) to the centre. Almost all Sacred Valley buses come and go from Avenida Grau 525 (for Pisac, Urubamba, Chincheros, Ollantaytambo), near Puente Grau, or Tullumayu 207 (for Pisac).

Information

The main **tourist office**, operated by the Direccion Regional de Industria y Turismo (DRIT) at Mantas 117-A (Mon–Fri 8am–7pm, Sat 8am–2.30pm; T263176), is a short block from the Plaza de Armas, with information kiosks at the airport and the Terminal Terrestre. The downtown office is well staffed, spacious and offers a friendly service with sound advice on where to go and how to get there, as well as maps and brochures. Some tourist information is also provided by i-Peru Tourist Assistance from Portal Carrizos 250, Plaza de Armas (daily 8.30am–7.30pm; T252974 or 234498, Eiperucusco@pro.peru .gob.pe), as well as from a booth at the airport (daily 6am–1.30pm, sometimes later; T237364). There's also an information kiosk with very limited information (irregular hours between 8am and 6pm) at the Terminal Terrestre bus terminal. Other sources are **tour agents** around the Plaza de Armas or along calles Plateros and Procuradores, running uphill from the plaza. They provide leaflets promoting their own tours, but many also offer customized generic plans of the city and simple maps of the Sacred Valley and nearby regions. The weekly English-language newspaper *Cusco Weekly*, located at Choquechaca 188 (Wwww.cuscoweekly.com), is available for free all over Cusco from bookshops and on the streets; it's a professional publication with local information and interesting up-to-the-minute articles on cultural and news events among many

Crime in Cusco

Cusco police have made a real effort to clean up the city's poor reputation for pick-pocketing, bag snatching and street muggings. However, in recent years there have been reports of "strangle muggings", wherein tourists are jumped and strangled to the point of fainting before being robbed. Although crimes in general are rare, it's still best to avoid walking along empty streets late at night, especially if alone. The police claim that robberies are virtually non-existent around the Plaza de Armas or Avenida Sol, but admit that incidents are still possible in the Central Market area. The train stations tend to be well policed by private security, and inside the railway compounds problems are almost unknown. If you are unlucky enough to have anything stolen, report it to the **Tourist Police**. On the other hand, if you need help or advice to make a claim against a local tourism operator or service provider who has seriously failed to deliver what they promised (it's always a good idea to get this written down and signed as agreed by the operator before paying) you'll get better results by going to the i-peru Tourist Assistance office (see opposite), or contact your consulate.

other things. These websites are also good sources of information about Cusco: Ⓦ www.minicusco.gob.pe (Spanish only) and Ⓦ www.cuscoperu.com (good historical and cultural information).

City transport

Cusco's centre is small enough to **walk** around. **Taxis** can be waved down on any street, particularly on the Plaza de Armas, Avenida Sol and around the market end of Plaza San Francisco; rides within Cusco cost under $1 and are $2–3 for trips to the suburbs or up to Sacsayhuaman and Quenko (some *taxistas* may prefer to do a round-trip, charging $5 and waiting for you there, in which case give them half in advance and the remainder at the end of the journey). The city **bus** network is incredibly difficult to fathom, though it's cheap enough and fast, but it's also largely unregulated, with minibuses chalking up their destinations in the front windscreens. More useful are the **colectivos** that run up and down Avenida Sol every couple of minutes during daylight hours, stopping at street corners if they have any seats left; these charge a flat fare (about 20¢) and can be hailed on virtually any corner along the route.

Accommodation

Much of the city's budget **accommodation** is in the zone to the north of the Plaza de Armas along calles Plateros, Procuradores and Saphi – calles Procura-

Cusco Tourist Ticket

The **Cusco Tourist Ticket** ($10 for 10 days, students $5; a one-day ticket costs $6, no discounts) is a vital purchase for most visitors. It's the only way to get into 16 of the city and region's main attractions and comes with useful maps and other information, including opening times. It's theoretically available from all of the sites on the ticket, but in practice only from two main offices in Cusco and at the entrances to Sacsayhuaman or the Cathedral. The Cusco offices are: in the Casa Garcilaso on the corner of Garcilaso and Heladeros (Mon–Fri 7.45am–6pm, Sat 8.30am–4pm, Sun 8am–noon); Avenida Sol 103, office 106 (Mon–Fri 8am–6pm, Sat 8.30am–1pm).

dores and Plateros are particularly noisy at night – but there are relatively inexpensive and reasonable mid-range hostels and hotels in most corners of the city. You can find slightly pricier and more luxurious locations further up Calle Saphi, around Plaza Regocijo, towards San Blas and, if you are prepared to walk a little, along Choquechaca and Tandapata, further up the hill from the centre. The San Pedro region around the Central Market is cheap but pretty down-at-heel, rife with pickpockets and quite dangerous at night. As well as a wide range in prices and comfort levels, Cusco also offers a variety of architectural environments to choose from, ranging mainly between Inca- and colonial-style constructions, or combinations of the two.

Budget

Albergue Turistico Av Sol, block 5, Pasaje Grace, Edificio Sanjorge ☎235617. Linked to Hostelling International, this place is located in a basement in the alley on the other side of Avenida Sol from Koricancha. Rooms are basic, shared or private; breakfast for $1. ❶–❷

Gran Hostal Machu Picchu Calle Quera 282 ☎231111. About two blocks from the Plaza de Armas, this hostel is hard to beat for friendly atmosphere and value in one package. Rooms (with or without bath) are set around a colonial courtyard. ❸–❹

Hospedaje Acosta Calle Choquechaca 124 ☎249995. Only small rooms in this tucked-away but quite central place; very plain but friendly and with a communal gas cooker. ❷–❸

Hospedaje El Arcano Carmen Alto 288 ☎244037, ☏232703. A pleasant family-run hostel on the edge of the attractive San Blas area which has a good hot-water system, laundry, family-sized rooms and a comfortable lounge. Rooms come with or without private bath. ❷

Hospedaje Familiar Casa Grande Santa Catalina Ancha 353 ☎264156, ☏243784. A large and very central place with an open courtyard, some newly furbished rooms as well as more basic ones, with or without bathrooms. ❷–❸

Hostal Caceres Calle Plateros 368 ☎232616 or 228012. A popular travellers' hangout, half a block from the Plaza de Armas. It's got a courtyard and is within a stone's throw of most of Cusco's best bars and cafés. Rooms are simple and unpretentious, many being shared dorms; you may have to ask for hot water. ❷

Hospedaje El Carmen Tullumayu 860 ☎231363. A bed and breakfast in a spacious house; good value but not very central, though the slightly seedy neighbourhood is actually quite quiet and very handy for buses to Pisac, the Huanchac station and the Centro Artesenal Cusco. ❶

Hostal Colonial Matará 288 ☎231811 or 247046. Pretty basic, but clean and with pleasant service. Many of its rooms are based around an airy courtyard in an old colonial building.

Bathrooms are communal. ❶

Hostal Familiar Calle Saphi 661 ☎239353. Quiet, safe and one of Cusco's best budget options (it's wise to reserve in advance). Rooms are spartan but cool, clean and nicely furnished, with or without private bath (in which case showers are communal), and there's usually hot water in the mornings. Good breakfasts are served in the café, plus there's a free safety deposit box, a cheap left-luggage system and a laundry service. ❷–❸

Hostal El Grial Atoqsayk'uchi 594 ☎223012, ☏grial_celta@yahoo.com. A pretty central place with a nice energy, clay-oven fireplace and pleasant furnishings. Their rooms are modernized, spotless and pleasant, with or without private bathroom; Spanish lessons are available and there's a comfortable lounge as well as a TV room. Hot water is solar with an electric backup, and there's a balcony with views over the city.

Hostal Inti Quilla Atoqsayk'uchi 281 ☎252659. Small and cheerful hostel, quite a few steps up from the main square, but great value with cosy but by no means luxurious rooms with or without bathrooms set around a pretty little courtyard dominated by a massive Andean pine tree. ❷–❹

Hostal Suecia I Calle Suecia 132 ☎233282, ☏hsuecia1@hotmail.com. A popular backpacker place set around a lovely covered courtyard, this is comfortable, stylish, safe and very good value. Rooms are with or without private bath. ❸

Hostal Tumi Siete Cuartones 245 ☎244413. Just off Plateros and a little way up from Iglesia Santa Teresa, this place is popular with young travellers, quite central, has a spacious courtyard, plain bedrooms, shared bathrooms, access to a kitchen and a notice board. ❷

Imperio Hotel Calle Chaparro ☎228981. A pleasant and surprisingly homely hostel in an ugly building and a rather dodgy part of town near the Central Market and right by San Pedro station, but has water all day, is exceptionally clean and is undoubtedly good value. ❷

IPakcha Real Hostal Familiar Tandapata 300, San Blas ☎237484. An excellent family-run hostel in the attractive San Blas suburb, four steep blocks from Plaza de Armas. This pleasant, good-value modern home has a shared kitchen, a TV room and patio, constant hot water and reasonable security. Rooms are with or without bath. High above the city centre, it's a bit of a hike, which can be testing on arrival from sea level. ❸–❹

Koyllur Hostelling Tourist Carmen Bajo 186, San Blas ☎241122 or 225354, ⓔ koyllur@peru.com. A quiet hostel literally just around the corner from the Plazoleta San Blas, heart of Cusco's trendy artesan barrio. Rooms are on two floors around a pleasant courtyard garden; all with private bath. The lobby has an interesting altar and mural dedicated to the wild Qoyllur Riti Festival (see Festivals box p.116). ❸

Osiris 616 Casa Hospedaje Atoqsayk'uchi 616 ☎234572. Ramshackle and rustic but pretty little place with occasional hot water. English, French and Spanish are spoken, plus they have a fax service, notice board and use of a kitchen and patio. They also run tours. ❷

Moderate

Amaru Hostal Cuesta San Blas 541 ☎/ⓕ225933, ⓔ amaru@telser.com.pe. There's a pleasant colonial feel here, with a lovely garden patio at its centre and another out back with views over town. There are laundry, safety deposit and left-luggage facilities, plus bottled oxygen for those in need. Service is very good, some rooms are old and stylish, while those out the back are newer but less interesting, most with and a few without private bath. ❹

Casa de Campo Tandapata 296b ☎244404, ⓕ243069, ⓔ info@hotelcasadecampo.com. Attractive rooms and cabins (best booked in advance) with great views over the city and a large patio. Its quiet, pleasant location on the upper edge of Cusco is dauntingly high for your first couple of days, so take a taxi to avoid exhaustion or altitude sickness. They offer combined accommodation and language-school courses with the AMAUTA language school. Ten percent discount to holders of the *Rough Guide Peru* and members of the South American Explorers' Club. ❺

Colonial Palace Hostal Calle Quera 270 ☎232151, ⓕ232329, ⓔ cuzco@colonialpalace.com. An attractive colonial building with pleasant courtyards and clean, comfortable rooms, but still rather pricey in that it's all slightly down-at-heel. Hot water guaranteed 5am–1pm and 5.30–10pm; other facilities include a restaurant, grocery and artesania. All rooms have private bath. ❺

Hospedaje Turistico San Blas Cuesta San Blas 326 ☎225781, ⓔ sanblascusco@yahoo.com.

Located in the quiet and attractive artesan suburb of San Blas, this friendly place features a glass-covered courtyard. Most rooms have private bath and a safe deposit is available. The owners also organize tours to the Inca Trail and do river rafting on the Vilcanota. A good lower mid-range option. ❸

Hostal Emperador Plaza Santa Catalina Ancha 377 ☎227412 or 261733, ⓕ263581, ⓔ emperador@blockbuster.com.pe or emperador@nexoperu.com. Comfortable and central, though modernized and rather faceless, with 24hr hot water, bath and cable TV in all rooms. Rates include breakfast. ❻

Hostal Huaynapata Huaynapata 369 ☎228034, ⓔ hostalhuaynapata@terra.com. Modernized 1970s-style, safe and friendly. It's not that far from the main plaza, and the covered roof terrace has splendid views across the Cathedral and down the valley to Ausangate. Price includes breakfast. ❺

Hostal Loreto Calle Loreto 115 ☎226352. An interesting old place on the corner of an Inca stone-lined alleyway connecting Plaza de Armas with Koricancha. The best rooms incorporate the original Inca masonry of the Temple of the Virgins of the Sun, and all have private bath and hot water. Prices vary according to the room you choose and the number of people in it. ❺

Hostal Mirador de la Nusta Tandapata 682 ☎248039, ⓔ elmiradordelanusta@hotmail.com. An intimate, cosy and superbly located place directly overlooking the Plazoleta San Blas in the artists' quarter. It has ten nice rooms, an attractive little yard, breakfast, laundry service and reliable hot water. ❹

Hostal Rumi Punku Choquechaca 339 ☎221102, ⓦ www.rumipunku.com. A friendly establishment built on an old Inca temple site in one of Cusco's nicest streets. The rooms have private hot showers, are stylish for the price, plus there's access to kitchens, a patio, a *comedor* and a small sitting room with a fireplace. Best booked in advance in high season. Price includes breakfast. ❺

Hostal Virrey Portal Comercio 165, Plaza de Armas ☎221771, ⓕ235349, ⓔ hvirrey@amauta .rep.net.pe. As central as possible, but unfortunately it only has two rooms with views over the plaza. Rooms feature private bathrooms and cable TV. Price includes breakfast. ❺

Expensive

El Dorado Av Sol 395 ☎231235 or 233112, ⓕ240993, ⓔ reservasdorado@terra.com.pe. A classic four-star pseudo-colonial, relatively modern hotel. Rooms are spotless and the service is good, but the location – less than two blocks from the Plaza de Armas – can be a bit noisy. ⑥–⑧

Hacienda Hotel Incatambo San Cristobal, 2km along the *carretera* to Sacsayhuaman ☎221918 or 222045. A beautiful hacienda converted into a hotel, close to Sacsayhuaman and sharing some of the same magnificent views over the Cusco Valley and down to the city. Rooms are luxurious and many are set around a stunning colonial courtyard. Horse-riding is offered on their ample estate. ⑦

Hostal Cahuide Calle Saphi 845 ☎222771, ⑤222361, ⑥hotelcahuide@mixmail.com. A few blocks uphill from the Plaza de Armas. A bit pricey but better value in low season, it's pleasant with clean, modern rooms and a useful message board. ⑦

Hotel Cusco Heladeros 150 ☎224821, 221811 or 222961, ⑤222832. Well established and central, with a popular restaurant and bar, plus conference rooms. It's slightly down-at-heel these days but still has comfortable rooms with bath, TV and telephone. ⑦

Hotel Libertador Plazoleta Santo Domingo 259 ☎231961, ⑤233152, ⑩www.libertador.com.pe. One of the most luxurious hotels in Peru, set in a thoroughly modernized old mansion close to Koricancha, just a few blocks from the Plaza de Armas. ⑧

Hotel Monasterio Calle Palacio 136, Plazoleta Nazarenas ☎241777, ⑤237111, ⑥reserlima@ peruhotel.com. Cusco's newest luxury establishment, costing over $200 for a double. It's a fantastic place, set around massive sixteenth-century monastery cloisters. There are tables in the courtyard where you can sip drinks and eat delicious food from the plush bar and restaurants. ⑧

Hotel Picoaga Santa Teresa 334 ☎221269 or 227691, ⑤221246, ⑥picoaga@correo.dnet.compe; in Lima ☎01/465 0689, ⑤429 1134. A first-class hotel in one of Cusco's finest colonial mansions, close to the heart of the city. Service is excellent, and there's a large bar and restaurant. ⑧

Hotel Royal Inca I Plaza Regocijo 299 ☎231067 or 222284, ⑤234221. A fairly luxurious hotel (which has a more expensive sister hotel – *Royal Inca II* – more or less next door) with a sauna and massage rooms. Very popular with upmarket package travellers. ⑧

Hotel Ruinas Ruinas 472 ☎260644 or 245920, ⑤236291, ⑥ruinas@terra.com.pe. A very well-appointed option with superb rooms, many with views from private balconies down to Ausangate. Exceptionally clean, with minibars and safes in each room; there's also a fine lobby, restaurant and bar, and there's email and fax facilities. ⑧

The City

Despite the seemingly complex street structure, it doesn't take long to come to grips with Cusco. The city divides roughly into at least five main zones based around various squares, temples and churches, with the **Plaza de Armas** at the heart of it all.

Zone one starts along the broad **Avenida Sol** running downhill and southeast from the corner of the plaza by the university and Iglesia de la Compañía towards the Inca sun temple at **Koricancha**, Huanchac train station and on to the airport in the south. You don't really need to explore beyond Huanchacwhere you'll also find Cusco's biggest artisan market.

Running uphill and southwest from the top of Avenida Sol, zone two follows Calle Mantas uphill past **Plaza San Francisco** and the Iglesia de Santa Clara, and then continues towards the Central Market and San Pedro train station.

A third distinct zone begins just one block west of the central plaza, where you'll find the smaller, leafier, neighbouring **Plaza Regocijo**, which has Inca origins and is home to some of the city's finest mansions as well as the modest municipal palace.

From the northeast corner of Plaza de Armas, Calle Triunfo leads along into zone four, steeply uphill through a classic Inca stone-walled alley before rising steeply through cobbled streets towards the artisan barrio of **San Blas**. En route it's possible to visit the tiny but elegant **Plaza Nazarenas**, northeast of the centre.

A fifth and final zone worth visiting in Cusco follows Calle Plateros heading northwest, again uphill from Plaza de Armas, leading to Calle Saphi and Calle

Suecia, both of which run uphill through quaint streets and on towards the fortress of Sacsayhuaman above the city.

Each of these zones is within easy walking distance of the Plaza de Armas and their main features can be covered easily in half a day, allowing a little extra time for hanging out in the bars and shops en route. It's probably better to split your time into two or three half-day sessions in order to get the best out of the city and allow time for exploring some of the museums and archeological complexes in some depth. Zones one, four and five are probably the most interesting to tackle. But in any of these areas of the city, as you wander around, you'll notice how many of the important Spanish buildings were constructed on top of Inca palaces and temples, often incorporating their exquisitely constructed walls and doorways into the lower parts of churches and colonial structures. The closer you are to the Plaza de Armas, the more obvious this becomes.

Around the Plaza de Armas

Cusco's modern and ancient centre, the **Plaza de Armas** – whose location corresponds roughly to that of the ceremonial *Huacapata*, the Incas' ancient central plaza – is the most obvious place to get your bearings. With the unmistakable ruined fortress of **Sacsayhuaman** towering above, you can always find your way back to the plaza simply by locating Sacsayhuaman or, at night, the illuminated white figure of Christ that stands beside the fortress on the horizon. The plaza is always busy, its northern and western sides filled with shops and restaurants. The **Portal de Panes** is a covered cloister pavement, like those frequently found around Spanish colonial squares, where the buildings tend to have an upper-storey overhang, supported by stone pillars or arches, creating rain-free and sun-shaded walking space virtually all the way around. Usually the *portales* host processions of boys trying hard to sell postcards, and waiters and waitresses attempting to drag passing tourists into their particular dive. Recent restrictions have relegated stalls and shoeshine boys to the hinterland of backstreets emanating from the plaza, particularly the zone facing onto the Plaza Regocijo, behind the Plaza de Armas. The Portal de Panes used to be part of the palace of Pachacuti, the ancient walls of which can still be seen from inside the *Roma Restaurant* close to the corner of the plaza and Calle Plateros. The plaza's exposed northeastern edge is dominated by the squat **Cathedral**, while the smaller **Iglesia de la Compañía de Jesus**, with its impressive pair of belfries, sits at the southeastern end. To the north of the Cathedral is the relatively new **Balcon de Cusco**, a small square outside the Museo Inka with great views over the plaza and where dances and firework celebrations tend to happen at festival times. There's also a panoramic walkway leading off it, following the rootops up to the cobbled backstreets of upper Cusco, directly beneath the ruins of Sacsayhuaman.

The Cathedral

The **Cathedral** (Mon–Sat 10am–noon & 2–5pm, Sun 2–5pm; entry by Cusco Tourist Ticket, see p.123) sits solidly on the foundations of the Inca Viracocha's palace, its massive lines looking fortress-like in comparison with the delicate form of the nearby La Compañía. Construction began in 1560, with the Cathedral being built in the shape of a Latin cross and its three-aisled nave supported by just fourteen massive pillars. There are two entrances, one via the main central Cathedral doors; the other, more usual, way is through the **Triunfo Chapel**, the first Spanish church to be built in Cusco. Check out its finely carved granite altar and the huge canvas depicting the terrible 1650 earthquake, before moving into the main Cathedral to see the intricately carved Plateresque pulpit and beautiful, cedar-wood seats, as well as a Neoclassical high altar, made entirely of finely beaten embossed silver, and some of the finest paintings of the Cusqueña school. In the **Sacristy**, on the right of the nave, there's a painting of the crucifixion attributed to Van Dyck. Ten smaller chapels surround the nave, including the **Chapel of the Immaculate Conception**, and the **Chapel of El Señor de los Temblores** (The Lord of Earthquakes), the latter housing a 26-kilo crucifix made of solid gold and encrusted with precious stones. To the left of the Cathedral is the adjoining **Iglesia de Jesus Maria**, built in the early eighteenth century.

The Cathedral's appeal lies as much in its mingling of history and legend, as in any tangible sights. Local myth claims that an Indian chief is still imprisoned in the right-hand tower, awaiting the day when he can restore the glory of the Inca Empire. The Cathedral also houses the huge, miraculous gold and bronze bell of Maria Angola, named after a freed African slave girl and reputed to be one of the largest church bells in the world. And on the massive main doors of the Cathedral, native craftsmen have left their own pagan adornment – a carved puma's head.

The Museo Inka

North of the Cathedral, slightly uphill beside the Balcon de Cusco, you'll find one of the city's most beautiful colonial mansions, **El Palacio del Almirante** (The Admiral's Palace). This palace now houses the **Museo Inka** (Mon–Sat 8am–5pm; $1.70). The museum has been recently renovated and features excellent exhibits of mummies, trepanned skulls, Inca textiles and a range of Inca wooden *quero* vases (a specific style of slightly tapering drinking vessels). There are also displays of ceramics, early silver metalwork and a few gold figurines, but it's the spacious but organized layout and imaginative and well-interpreted presentation that make this one of the best museums in Cusco to gain a quick understanding of the development of civilization in the Andes. Again constructed on Inca foundations – this time the Waypar stronghold, where the Spanish were besieged by Manco's forces in 1536 – the building itself is noteworthy for its simple but well-executed Plateresque facade, surmounted by two imposing Spanish coats of arms.

The Iglesia de la Compañía de Jesus

Looking downhill from the centre of the plaza, the **Iglesia de la Compañía de Jesus** dominates the Cusco skyline. First built over the foundations of Amara Cancha – originally Huayna Capac's Palace of the Serpents – in the late 1570s, it was resurrected over fifteen years after the earthquake of 1650, which largely destroyed the first version, which was in a Latin cross shape. The interior is cool and dark, with a grand gold-leaf altarpiece, a fine wooden pulpit displaying a relief of Christ, high vaulting and numerous paintings of the Cusqueña school, its transept ending in a stylish Baroque cupola. The guilded altarpieces are made of fine cedar wood and the church contains interesting oil paintings of the Peruvian Princess Isabel Ñusta. Its most impressive features are the two majestic towers of the main facade, a superb example of Spanish colonial Baroque design which has often been described in more glowing terms than the Cathedral itself. On the right-hand side of the church, the **Lourdes Chapel**, restored in 1894, is used mostly as an exhibition centre for local crafts.

The Natural History Museum

Alongside La Compañía, an early Jesuit university building houses the **Natural History Museum** (Mon–Fri 9am–noon & 3–6pm; 30¢). The entrance is off an inner courtyard, up a small flight of stairs to the left. The exhibits cover Peru's coast, the Andes and the Amazon jungle, with a particularly good selection of stuffed mammals, reptiles and birds. For a small tip, the doorman outside the university building sometimes allows visitors up the stairs to the top of the cupola to admire the view across the plaza.

South to Koricancha

Leading away from the Plaza de Armas, Callejón Loreto separates La Compañía Church from the tall, stone walls of the ancient Acclahuasi, or **Temple of the Sun Virgins**, where the Sun Virgins used to make *chicha* beer for the Lord Inca. Today the Acclahuasi building is occupied by the **Convent of Santa Catalina**, built in 1610, with its small but grand side entrance half a short block down Calle Arequipa; just under thirty sisters still live and worship here. Inside the convent is the **Museo de Arte y Monasterio de Santa Catalina** (Mon–Thurs & Sat 9am–5.30pm, Fri 9am–3pm; entry by Cusco Tourist Ticket, see p.123), with a splendid collection of paintings from the Cusqueña school, as well as an impressive Renaissance altarpiece and several gigantic seventeenth-century tapestries depicting the union of Indian and Spanish cultures. The theme of inter-racial mixing runs throughout much of the museum's fascinating artwork and is particularly evident in the Cusqueña paintings. A common feature of much of the Cusqueña art here is the downward-looking, blood-covered disproportionate head, body and limbs of the seventeenth-century depictions of Christ, which represent the suffering of the Andean Indians and originate from early colonial days when Indians were not permitted to look Spaniards in the eyes.

Another highlight of the museum, on the first floor at the top of the stairs, is a large fold-up box containing miniature three-dimensional religious and mythological images depicting everything from the Garden of Eden to Mary and Joseph's flight to Egypt, to an image of God with a red flowing cape and dark beard, a white dove and angels playing drums, Andean flutes and pianos.

On the corner of Maruri and Q'aphchik'ijllu, on the way from Santa Catalina towards Koricancha, there's the **Museo y Sala Cultural** (Mon–Fri 9am–1pm & 4–6pm; free) at the Banco Wiese, where displays include

The Cusqueña school

The **Cusqueña art** movement, which worked mainly in oils and blended indigenous and Spanish iconography, was limited to the Cusco region in the sixteenth century, but during the seventeenth century it spread to Titicaca and Bolivia, after which much of its technique was developed and elaborated. By the eighteenth century the style had been disseminated as far afield as Quito in Ecuador, Santiago in Chile, and even into Argentina, making it a truly South American art form and one of the most distinctive indigenous to the Americas. The most famous Cusqueña artists were **Bernardo Bitti** (sixteenth century), **Diego Quispe Tito Inca** (seventeenth century), an artist of mixed blood who was influenced by the Spanish Flamenco school – and whose paintings were vital tools of communication used by priests attempting to convert Indians to Catholicism – and **Mauricio Garcia** (eighteenth century), who helped to move the form into a fuller *mestizo* synthesis, mixing Spanish and Indian artistic forms. Many of the eighteenth- and nineteenth-century Cusqueña-*mestizo* works display bold composition and use of colour. The Cusqueña school is best known for portraits or religious scenes, with dark backgrounds, serious-looking, even tortured characters and plenty of gold-leaf decoration.

historical documents and archeological and architectural features; exhibitions vary throughout the year. The focus is often on the restoration work of the Banco Wiese's own premises, an attractive mansion that was once part of the Tupac Inca Yupangui's Pucamarca palace.

Koricancha

The supreme example of Inca stonework underlying colonial buildings is just a short walk from the Plaza de Armas, through the Inca walls of Callejón Loreto, then along the busy Pampa del Castillo. The **Koricancha** complex, located at the intersection of Avenida Sol and Calle Santo Domingo (Mon–Sat 8am–5pm; $1), can't be missed, with the Convento de Santo Domingo rising imposingly but rudely from its impressive walls, which the conquistadores laid low to make way for their uninspiring seventeenth-century Baroque church – a poor contrast to the still-imposing Inca masonry evident in the foundations and chambers of the Sun Temple. Before the conquistadores set their gold-hungry eyes on it, Koricancha must have been even more breathtaking, consisting as it did of four small sanctuaries and a larger temple set around a central courtyard. This whole complex was encircled on the inside walls by a cornice of gold, which probably explains the meaning of the temple name (Koricancha means "golden enclosure"). Some of the inner walls, too, were hung with beaten sheets of gold, and in a large, slightly trapezoidal niche on the inside of the curved section of the retaining wall, close to the chamber identified as the Temple of the Sun, there stood a huge, gold disc in the shape of the sun, **Punchau**, which was worshipped by the Incas. Punchau had two companions in the temple: a golden image of **Viracocha**, on the right; and another, representing **Illapa**, god of thunder, to the left. Below the temple was an artificial garden in which everything was made of gold or silver and encrusted with precious jewels, from llamas and shepherds to the tiniest details of clumps of earth and weeds, including snails and butterflies. Not surprisingly, none of this survived the arrival of the Spanish.

Koricancha's position in the Cusco Valley was carefully planned. Dozens of *ceques* (power lines, in many ways similar to ley lines, though in Cusco they appear to have been related to imperial genealogy) radiate from the temple towards more than 350 sacred *huacas*, special stones, springs, tombs and ancient quarries. In addition, during every summer solstice, the sun's rays shine directly into a niche – the **tabernacle** – in which only the Inca emperor (often referred to as *the* Inca) was permitted to sit. Mummies of dead Inca rulers were seated in niches at eye level along the walls of the actual temple, the principal idols from every conquered province were held "hostage" here, and every emperor married his wives in the temple before assuming the throne. The niches no longer exist, though there are some in the walls of the nearby Temple of the Moon, where mummies of the emperor's concubines were kept in a foetal position.

The **Chapel of Santo Domingo** (Mon–Fri 9.30–11.30am & 3–5pm) is accessed via the complex reception desk, or by walking past the Temple of the Moon and the Catholic Sacristy to a tiny section of the inner edge of the vast curved wall which, from the outside, seems to support the chapel. Trapped between the Inca retaining wall and the western end of the chapel, it is hard not to feel a sense of loss over the destruction of the Sun Temple itself, though as slight compensation you can see the large niche which once held Punchau, the golden sun disc. Returning from here via the sacristy, it is possible to see the Catholic priest's vestments, some boasting gold thread and jewels.

To reach the **Koricancha Site Museum** (daily 9.30am–6pm; entry by Cusco Tourist Ticket, see p.123), or Museo Arqueológico de Qorikancha, it's a

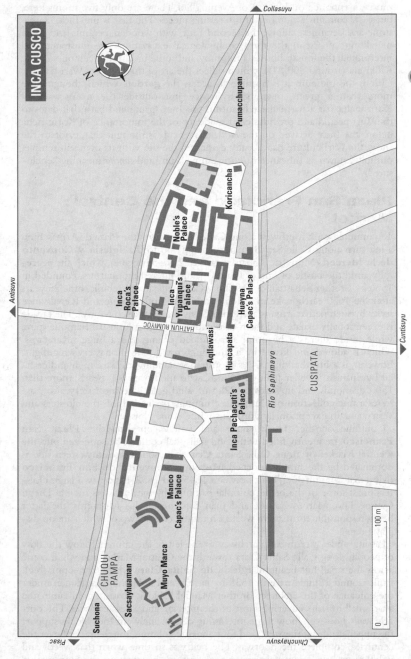

INCA CUSCO

N

Collasuyu ▲

Antisuyu ▲

Pumacchupan

Koricancha

Noble's Palace

Inca Yupanqui's Palace

Inca Roca's Palace

HATHUN RUMIYOC

Huayna Capac's Palace

Aqllawasi

Huacapata

Cuntisuyu ▼

Inca Pachacuti's Palace

Río Saphimayo

CUSIPATA

Manco Capac's Palace

CHUQUI PAMPA

Sacsayhuaman

Muyo Marca

Suchona

Pisac ▲

Chinchaysuyu ▼

100 m

0

three-minute walk downhill from the Complex reception to the underground museum entrance on block 3 of Avenida Sol. There are only five rooms here, but each contains a number of interesting pieces. The first is pre-Inca, mainly stone and ceramic exhibits; the second Inca, with wooden, ceramic and some metallurgic crafts; in the third, archeological excavations are illustrated and interpreted; the fourth houses a mummy and some bi-chrome ceramics of the Killki era (around 800 AD), which reflect the art of the pre-Inca Wari culture.

From the museum it is possible to access the **garden**, which, though little more than a green, open, grassy space just outside the main walls of Koricancha, has a particularly beautiful pre-Inca spring and bath that dates to the Wari period and provides clear evidence of the importance of Koricancha before the Incas arrived on the Andean scene. It is thought that, prior to the Incas, the Wari culture had already dedicated the site with its own sun temple, possibly known as Inticancha (*inti* meaning "sun" and *cancha* meaning "enclosure").

Plaza San Francisco and the Central Market

Ten minutes' walk southwest along Calle Mantas from the Plaza de Armas, then a left turn along Calle San Bernardo, brings you to the **Iglesia y Convento de la Merced** (Mon–Sat 8.30am–noon & 2.30–5pm; 50¢), which sits peacefully amid the bustle of one of Cusco's more interesting quarters. Founded in 1536 by Brother Sebastian de Trujillo y Castañeda, it was rebuilt some 25 years after the 1650 earthquake in a rich combination of Baroque and Renaissance styles by such native artisans as Alonso Casay and Francisco Monya. The facade is exceptionally ornate and the roof is endowed with an unusual Baroque spire, while inside there's a beautiful star-studded ceiling and a huge silver cross, which is adored and kissed by a shuffling crowd. The monastery's highlight, however, is a breathtaking 1720s monstrance standing a metre high and crafted by Spanish jeweller Juan de Olmos, who used over 600 pearls, more than 1500 diamonds and upwards of 22kg of solid gold. The monastery also possesses a fine collection of Cusqueña paintings, particularly in the cloisters and vestry, and an exceptionally gorgeous white-stone cloister.

Continue another block south and you'll come to the **Plaza San Francisco**, frequently filled with food stalls that couldn't be squeezed into the Central Market or along Calle Santa Clara. The square's southwestern side is dominated by the simply adorned **Museo y Convento de San Francisco** (Mon–Sat 2–5pm; 30¢), built between 1645 and 1652. Inside, two large cloisters boast some of the better colonial paintings by local masters such as Diego Quispe Tito, Marcos Zapata, and Juan Espinosa de los Monteros, the latter being responsible for massive works on canvas, one or two of which are on display here.

Passing under a crumbling archway to the left of the church, follow the flow of people along Calle Santa Clara towards the Central Market and you'll come across the small but beautiful **Iglesia de Santa Clara** (daily 6am–6pm; free). Built around a single nave in 1558 by *mestizo* and indigenous craftsmen under the guidance of the architect Brother Manuel Pablo, it boasts a gold-laminated altar, small mirrors covering most of the interior, and a few canvases. The outside walls, however, show more interesting details: finely cut Inca blocks support the upper, cruder stonework, and four andesite columns, much cracked over the centuries, complete the doorway. The belfry is so time-worn that weeds and wildflowers have taken permanent root. Just up the street, in the busy market area next to San Pedro train station, stands another sixteenth-century colonial church, the **Iglesia de San Pedro** (10am–noon & 2–5pm, not Sun), whose steps are normally crowded with Quechua market traders. The interior is decorated with paintings, sculptures, gold-leaf and some wooden carvings, and an elaborate, carved pulpit. Relatively austere, with only a single nave, the church's main claim to fame is that somewhere among the stones of its twin towers are ancient blocks dragged here from the small Inca fort of Picchu.

In the area around the **Central Market** (daily 8am–5pm), street stalls sell excellent-value alpaca goods, while the shops around the indoor market building sell antique textiles. At its top end, the Central Market itself is full of stalls selling colourful Andean foods, with a few interesting herb stalls, and magic kiosks displaying everything from lucky charms to jungle medicines. At the bottom end are fruit and vegetable stalls plus some of the best and cheapest street meals in Peru.

Around Plaza Regocijo

The **Plaza Regocijo**, today a pleasant garden square sheltering a statue of Bolognesi, was originally the Inca *cusipata*, an area cleared for dancing and festivities beside the Inca's ancient central plaza. Only a block southwest of the Plaza de Armas, Regocijo is dominated on its northwestern side by an attractively arched municipal building housing the Contemporary Art Museum, with a traditional Inca rainbow flag flying from its roof. Opposite this is the *Hotel Cusco*, formerly the grand, state-run *Hotel de Turistas*, while on the southwest corner of the plaza lies an impressive mansion where more Inca stones mingle with colonial construction, home to the Museo Histórico Regional y Casa Garcilaso. Leading off from the top of Regocijo, **Calle Santa Teresa** is home to the House of the Pumas and leads to the Iglesia de Santa Teresa.

Museo Histórico Regional y Casa Garcilaso

Once the residence of Garcilaso de la Vega, a prolific half-Inca (his mother may have been an Inca princess), half-Spanish poet and author, the mansion now known as the **Museo Histórico Regional y Casa Garcilaso** (Mon–Sat 8am–5.30pm; entry by Cusco Tourist Ticket, see p.123) is currently home to significant regional archeological finds and much of Cusco's historic art. Fascinating **pre-Inca** ceramics from all over Peru are displayed, plus a Nazca mummy in a foetal position and with typically long (1.5m) hair, embalming herbs and unctures, black ceramics with incised designs from the early Cusco culture (1000–200 BC), and a number of **Inca** artefacts such as *bolas*, maces, architects' plumb-lines and square water-dishes for finding horizontal levels on buildings. The museum also displays gold bracelets discovered at Machu Picchu in 1995, some gold and silver llamas found in 1996 in the Plaza de Armas when reconstructing the central fountain, and golden pumas and figurines from Sacsayhuaman. From the **colonial** era there are some weavings, wooden *quero* drinking vessels and dancing masks.

The main exhibition rooms upstairs house mainly period furniture and a multitude of Cusqueña paintings, which cross the range from the rather dull (religious adorations) to the more spectacular (like the famous eighteenth-century *Jacob's Ladder*). As you progress through the works you'll notice the rapid intrusion of cannons, gunpowder and violence throughout the 1700s, something which was reflected in Cusco art as a microcosm of what happened across the colonial world – emanating from Europe as part of the general march of technological "progress".

The Contemporary Art Museum

The **Contemporary Art Museum** (Mon–Sat 9am–5pm; free) is a welcome and relatively new feature in Cusco, an outlet for the many talented local artists. **Sala 1** shows images of Cusco, mainly paintings but sometimes photos of subjects like Inca dancers as well as abstract features, plus some sculpture. **Sala 2** is dedicated to non-Cusco-inspired contemporary art, some of it very abstract but with exhibits changing quite regularly; the sala leads off into a large courtyard with a typically attractive colonial fountain; here you'll find glass cases with dolls in traditional costumes, some regional variations of dance masks (from Paucartambo dance groups, for example) and models of buildings in different Cusco styles. The upstairs **Sala 3** houses more images of Cusco, both ancient and modern.

Calle Santa Teresa

On **Calle Santa Teresa** you'll find the **House of the Pumas** (no. 385), though this isn't as grand as it sounds and is now a small café: the six pumas above its entrance were carved during the Spanish rebuilding of Cusco. Turn right at the end of this street and you pass the **Iglesia de Santa Teresa** (daily 6am–6pm; free), an attractive but neglected church with stone walls, the upper half of which have paintings featuring St Teresa. Inside, the small brick ceiling is finely domed and there's a gold-leaf altar inset with paintings. There's a small **chapel** next door with intricately painted walls (featuring yet more images of St Teresa), usually beautifully candle-lit.

Around Plaza Nazarenas and San Blas

Calle Cordoba del Tucman runs northeast from Plaza de Armas along the northern edge of the Cathedral, past the Museo Inka (see p.128) and up to the small, quiet **Plaza Nazarenas**. The unmistakable **Casa Cabrera** (Mon–Fri 8am–5.30pm, Sat 10am–noon & 3–5pm; free), at the top, uphill end of this small square has a few exhibition rooms displaying interesting nineteenth- and twentieth-century photography, some of it by indigenous artists, plus unusual period artefacts.

On the northeastern side of Plaza Nazarenas, the ancient, subtly ornate **Chapel of San Antonio Abad** was originally connected to a religious school before becoming part of the university in the seventeenth century. It's not open to the public, but you can usually look around the courtyard of the **Nazarenas Convent**, virtually next door and now home to the plush *Hotel Monasterio* (see p.126); ask permission at the reception desk. Nuns lived here until the 1950 earthquake damaged the building so badly that they had to leave; the central courtyard has since been sensitively rebuilt and has an attractive garden where good (but pricey) meals and drinks are served. Beside the convent, the Inca passage of Siete Culebras (Seven Snakes) leads onto Choquechaca; just up here on the left, at block 3 of Choquechaca, the **Museo de Arte de Niños "Irq'i Yachay"**, Ladrillos 491 (Wed–Sun 10am–1pm & 3-6pm; free), shows paintings by children of the region, including by those from remote villages who are taught by a mobile school.

San Blas

From Choquechaca, turn left into Cuesta de San Blas and after one and a half blocks you'll come to the tiny **Chapel of San Blas** (Mon–Wed, Fri & Sat 10–11am & 2–5.30pm; entry by Cusco Tourist Ticket, see p.123). The highlight here is an incredibly intricate pulpit, carved from a block of cedar wood in a complicated Churrigueresque style; its detail includes a cherub, a sun-disc,

A short history of San Blas

Originally known as T'oqokachi ("salty hole"), the **San Blas** barrio was one of twelve administrative sectors in Inca Cusco. After the Conquest it became a colonial parish of some importance and the residence for many defeated Inca leaders. It rapidly grew into one of the more attractive districts in the city, reflecting strong *mestizo* and colonial influences in its architecture and high-quality artesania – even today it's known as the barrio *de los artesanos* (artisans' quarter). Hit hard by the 1950 earthquake, it has been substantially restored, and in 1993 was given a major face-lift that returned it to its former glory. At the barrio's centre, on the southeast side of the Chapel of San Blas, lies the **San Blas Plazoleta**, with 49 gargoyles set on a fountain that's laid out in the form of a *chakana*, or Inca cross, with four corners and a hole at its centre.

faces and bunches of grapes, all believed to have been carved by native craftsman Tomas Tuyro Tupa in the seventeenth century. Outside, along Calle Plazoleta (also called Suytuccato), there are a few art workshops and galleries, the most notable of which is Galería Olave, at no. 651. The **Museo de Cerámica**, Carmen Alto 133, is worth checking out for its pottery, while on the plazoleta is the **Museo Taller Hilario Mendivil**, containing a number of Cusqueña paintings, some interesting murals and religious icons; both operate the standard local shop hours of 10am–6pm.

Hathun Rumiyoq and the Museo de Arte Religioso del Arzobispado

Backtracking down the Cuesta de San Blas and continuing over the intersection with Choquechaca, head straight on until you come to the narrow alley of **Hathun Rumiyoq**. One of the classic examples of superb Inca stonework, the large cut boulders on the museum side, about halfway along, boast one that has twelve angles in its jointing with the stones around it. Not just earthquake resistant, it is both a highly photographed work of ancient architectural value and a work of art in its own right. At the end of this passageway, and just one block from the Plaza de Armas, along Calle Triunfo, you'll find the broad doors of the **Museo de Arte Religioso del Arzobispado** (Mon–Sat 8–11am & 3–5.30pm; entry by Cusco Tourist Ticket, see p.123), housed in a superb Arabesque-style mansion built on the impressive foundations of Hathun Rumiyoq palace. Once home to Brother Vicente de Valarde and the Marquises of Rocafuert, and later the archbishop's residence, the museum now contains a significant collection of paintings, mostly of the Cusqueña school. There are stunning mosaics in some of the period rooms, and other significant features include the elaborate gateway and the gold-leaf craftsmanship on the chapel's altar.

Inca sites near Cusco

The megalithic fortress of **Sacsayhuaman**, which looks down onto the red-tiled roofs of Cusco from high above the city, is the closest and most impressive of several historic sites scattered around the Cusco hills. However, there are four other major Inca sites in the area. Not much more than a stone's throw beyond Sacsayhuaman lie the great *huaca* of **Qenko** and the less-visited **Salumpuncu**, thought by some to be a moon temple. A few kilometres further on, at what almost certainly formed the outer limits of the Inca's home estate, you come to the small, fortified hunting lodge of **Puca Pucara** and the stunning imperial baths of **Tambo Machay**.

All these places are an energetic day's **walk** from Cusco, but you'll probably want to devote a whole day to Sacsayhuaman and leave the others until you're more adjusted to the rarefied air. If you'd rather start from the top and work your way downhill, it's possible to take one of the regular **buses** to Pisac and Urubamba run by Empresa Caminos del Inca (from Calle Huascar 128) and Empresa Urubamba (from Inti Cahuarina 305, 200m from Koricancha, just off Tullumayo). Ask to be dropped off at the highest of the sites, Tambo Machay, from where it's a relatively easy two-hour walk back into the centre of Cusco, or at Qenko, which is closer to Sacsayhuaman and the city. Alternatively, you can take a **horseback tour** incorporating most of these sites, though you will have to get to Sacsayhuaman or Qenko first (a $1–2 taxi ride from the centre of Cusco).

Sacsayhuaman

Although it looks relatively close to central Cusco, it's quite a steep forty-minute, two-kilometre climb up to the ruins of Sacsayhuaman from the Plaza de Armas. The simplest route is up Calle Suecia, then right along the narrow cobbled street of Huaynapata to Pumacurco, which heads steeply up to a small café-bar with a balcony that commands superb views over the city. It's only another ten minutes from the café, following the signposted steps all the way up to the ruins. By now you're beyond the built-up sectors of Cusco and walking in countryside, and there's a well-worn path and crude stairway that takes you right up to the heart of the fortress.

SACSAYHUAMAN (daily 7am–5.30pm; entry by Cusco Tourist Ticket, see p.123) forms the head of Cusco's ethereal puma, whose fierce-looking teeth point away from the city. The name Sacsayhuaman is of disputed origin, with different groups holding that it means either "satiated falcon", "speckled head" or "city of stone". Protected by such a steep approach from the town, the fortress only needed defensive walls on one side. Nevertheless, this "wall" is one of South America's archeological treasures, actually formed by three massive, parallel stone ramparts zigzagging together for some 600m across the plateau just over the other side of the mountain top from Cusco city and the valley below. These zigzag walls, incorporating the most monumental and megalithic stones used in ancient Peru, form the boundary of what was originally designed as a "spiritual distillation" of the ancient city below, with many sectors named after areas of imperial Cusco. Little of the inner structures remains, yet these enormous ramparts stand 20m high, quite unperturbed by past battles, earthquakes and the passage of time. The strength of the mortarless stonework – one block weighs more than 300 tonnes – is matched by the brilliance of its design: the zigzags, casting shadows in the afternoon sun, not only look like jagged cat's teeth, but also seem to have been cleverly designed to expose the flanks of any attacking force to the defensive retaliation of Inca bowmen and stone-wielding soldiers using catapults and slings. Recently, however, many sacred and ritual objects excavated here have caused archeologists to consider Sacsayhuaman as more of a ceremonial centre than a fortress, with the zigzag form of these outer walls possibly symbolizing the important deity of lightning.

It was the Emperor Pachacuti who began work on Sacsayhuaman in the 1440s, although it took nearly a century of creative work to finish it. The chronicler Cieza de León, writing in the 1550s, estimated that some twenty thousand men had been involved in Sacsayhuaman's construction: four thou-

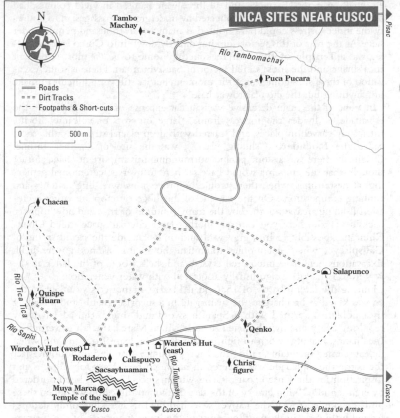

INCA SITES NEAR CUSCO

N

Roads
Dirt Tracks
Footpaths & Short-cuts

0   500 m

Pisac

Tambo
Machay

Río Tambomachay

Puca Pucara

Chacan

Salapunco

Río Tica Tica

Quispe
Huara

Río Saphi

Qenko

Warden's Hut (west)

Warden's Hut
(east)

Rodadero   Calispucyo

Río Tullumayo

Christ
figure

Sacsayhuaman

Muya Marca
Temple of the Sun

Cusco

Cusco   Cusco   San Blas & Plaza de Armas

sand cutting blocks from quarries; six thousand dragging them on rollers to the
site; and another ten thousand working on finishing and fitting the blocks into
position. According to legend, some three thousand lives were lost while dragging just one huge stone. Various types of rock were used, including massive
diorite blocks from nearby for the outer walls, Yucay limestone from more than
15km away for the foundations, and dark andesite, some of it from over 30km
away at Rumicolca, for the inner buildings and towers. First, boulders were
split by boring holes with stone or cane rods and wet sand; next, wooden
wedges were inserted into these holes and saturated to crack the rocks into
more manageable sizes; finally the blocks were shifted into place with levers.
With only natural fibre ropes, stone hammers and bronze chisels, it must have
been an enormous task.

Originally, the inner "fort" was covered in buildings, a maze of tiny streets
dominated by three major towers. The tower of **Muyu Marca**, whose foundations can still be clearly seen, was round, over 30m tall and with three concentric circles of wall, the outer one roughly 24m in diameter. An imperial residence, it apparently had lavish inner chambers and a constant supply of fresh
water, carried up through subterranean channels. The other two towers – **Salla
Marca** and **Paunca Marca** – had rectangular bases about 20m long and were

137

essentially warriors' barracks, and all three were painted in vivid colours, had thatched roofs, and were interconnected by underground passages: in its entirety, the inner fortress could have housed as many as ten thousand people under siege. At the rear of this sector, looking directly down into Cusco and the valley, was a **Temple of the Sun**, reckoned by some to be *the* most important Inca shrine and the most sacred sector of Sacsayhuaman. There is some excavation of these sites going on at the moment, but it's still very difficult to make out anything but the circular tower base.

In front of the main defensive walls, a flat expanse of grassy ground – the esplanade – divides the fortress from a large outcrop of volcanic diorite. Intricately carved in places, and scarred with deep glacial striations, this rock, called the **Rodadero** ("sliding place"), was the site of an Inca throne. Originally there was a stone parapet surrounding this important *huaca*, and it's thought that the emperor would have sat here to oversee ceremonial gatherings at fiesta times, when there would be processions, wrestling matches and running competitions. On the far side of this huge outcrop are larger recreational sliding areas, smoothed by the many centuries of Inca and now tourists' backsides. From here you can see another large circular space called Qocha Chincanas, possibly an Inca graveyard, and on its far side the sacred spring of **Calispucyo**, where ceremonies to initiate boys into manhood were held. Excavations here have uncovered crystals and shells (some of the latter all the way from Ecuador), a sign usually associated with water veneration.

During the fateful battle of 1536, Juan Pizarro, Francisco's younger brother, was killed as he charged the main gate in a surprise assault, and a leading Inca nobleman, armed with a Spanish sword and shield, caused havoc by repulsing every enemy who tried to scale Muyu Marca, the last tower left in Inca hands. Having sworn to fight to the death, he leapt from the top when defeat seemed inevitable, rather than accept humiliation and dishonour. After the battle the esplanade was covered in native corpses, food for vultures and inspiration for the Cusco coat of arms which, since 1540, has been bordered by eight condors "in memory of the fact that when the castle was taken these birds descended to eat the natives who had died in it". The conquistadores wasted little time in dismantling most of the inner structures of the fortress, using the stones to build Spanish Cusco. Today the most dramatic event to take place at Sacsayhuaman is the colourful – if overly commercial – **Inti Raymi festival** in June (see p.117). However, throughout the year, you may stumble across various **sun ceremonies** being performed here by mystics from the region.

Qenko

An easy twenty-minute walk from Sacsayhuaman, the large limestone outcrop of **QENKO** (daily 7am–5.30pm; entry by Cusco Tourist Ticket, see p.123) was another important Inca *huaca*. Head towards the Cusco–Pisac road along a track from the warden's hut on the northeastern edge of Sacsayhuaman, and Qenko is just over the other side of the main road; the route is straightforward but poorly signposted.

This great stone, carved with a complex pattern of steps, seats, geometric reliefs and puma designs, illustrates the critical role of the Rock Cult in the realm of Inca cosmological beliefs (the surrounding foothills are dotted with carved rocks and elaborate stone terraces). The name of this *huaca* derives from the Quechua word *quenqo*, meaning "labyrinth" or "zigzag", and refers to the patterns laboriously carved into the upper, western edge of the stone. At an annual festival priests would pour sacrificial llama blood into a bowl at the serpent-like top of the main zigzag channel; if it flowed out through the left-hand bifurcation, this was a bad omen for the fertility of the year to come. If, on the other hand, it continued the full length of the channel and poured onto the rocks below, this was a good omen.

The stone may also be associated with solstice and equinox ceremonies, fertility rites and even marriage rituals (there's a twin seat close to the top of Qenko which looks very much like a lovers' kissing bench). Right on top of the stone two prominent round nodules are carved onto a plinth. These appear to be mini versions of *intihuatanas* ("hitching posts" of the sun), found at many Inca sacred sites – local guides claim that on the summer solstice, at around 8am, the nodules' shadow looks like a puma's face and a condor with wings outstretched at the same time. Along with the serpent-like divinatory channels, this would complete the three main layers of the Inca cosmos: sky (condor), earth (puma) and the underworld (snake). Beneath Qenko are several **tunnels and caves**, replete with impressive carved niches and steps, which may have been places for spiritual contemplation and communication with the forces of life and earth. It's been suggested that some of the niches may have been where the mummies of lesser nobles were kept.

At the top end of the *huaca*, behind the channelled section, the Incas constructed an impressive, if relatively small, semicircular **amphitheatre** with nineteen vaulted niches (probably seats for priests or nobles) facing in towards the impressive limestone. At the heart of the amphitheatre rises a natural standing stone, which looks like a frog (representative of the life-giving and cleansing power of rain) from some angles and like a puma from others, both creatures of great importance to pre-Conquest Peru.

Salapunco

A twenty-minute stroll uphill and through the trees above Qenko, to the right of the small hill, along the path (keeping the houses to your right), then emerging onto the fields and turning right, leads to **SALAPUNCO**. Yet another sacred *huaca*, though off the beaten track – also known as the Temple of the Moon and locally called Laqo – this large rock outcrop contains a number of small caves where the rock has been painstakingly carved. There's worn relief work with puma and snake motifs on the external rock faces, while in the caves there are altar-like platforms and niches that were probably for holding mummies. The largest of the caves was probably then (and sometimes is now) used for ceremonies celebrating the full moon, when an eerie silver light filters into the usually dark interior. Close to Salapunco there's another site, called K'usilluchayoq, which has some more rock carvings. It's possible to walk down from here to Plaza de Armas via interconnecting trails that go initially through some new barrios above the main Cusco–Pisac road, then down to San Blas.

Chacan and Quispe Huara

An important but little-visited Inca site, **CHACAN** lies about 5km from Sacsayhuaman on the opposite side of the fortress from Qenko and the road to Tambo Machay. It can be safely, though not easily, reached in the dry season (May–Sept) by following the rather indistinct footpaths directly north from the Rodadero at Sacsayhuaman. When you hit the gully coming from the west, follow this up to the site; if you've been walking for ninety minutes or more and haven't found it, the chances are you've already passed it. Chacan itself was a revered spring, and you can see a fair amount of terracing, some carved rocks and a few buildings in the immediate vicinity; like Tambo Machay, it demonstrates the importance of water as an ever-changing, life-giving force in Inca religion. A pleasant but more difficult walk leads down the Tica Tica stream (keep to the right-hand side of the stream and stay well above it), until you come to **Quispe Huara** ("crystal loincloth"), where a two- to three-metre-high pyramid shape has been cut into the rock. Close by are some Inca stone walls, probably once part of a ritual bathing location. You really need a local map to find your way with any certainty.

Puca Pucara

Although a relatively small ruin, **PUCA PUCARA** (daily 7am–5.30pm; entry by Cusco Tourist Ticket, see p.123), meaning "Red Fort", is around 11km from the city, impressively situated overlooking the Cusco valley, right beside the main Cusco–Pisac road, and well worth the trip. Between one and two hours' cross-country walk, uphill from Sacsayhuaman and Qenko (longer if you keep to the sinuous main road), this area is dotted with cut rocks. The zone was well populated in Inca days, and many of those people may have been worked to obtain stones for building.

Although in many ways reminiscent of a small European castle, Puca Pucara is more likely to have been a hunting lodge or out-of-town lodgings for the emperor than simply a defensive position. Thought to have been built by the Emperor Pachacutec, it commands views towards glaciers to the south of the Cusco valley. Easily defended on three sides, it could have contained only a relatively small garrison and may have been a guard post between Cusco and the Sacred Valley, which lies to the northeast; it could also have had a sacred function, as it has excellent views towards the Apu of Ausangate – a good example of how the Incas tended to combine comfort and recreation for the elite with social control and military defence. Its semicircle of protective wall is topped by a commanding esplanade.

Tambo Machay

TAMBO MACHAY (daily 7am–5.30pm; entry by Cusco Tourist Ticket, see p.123), less than fifteen minutes' walk along a signposted track that leads off the main road just north of Puca Pucara, is one of the more impressive Inca baths, or Temple of the Waters, evidently a place for ritual as well as physical cleaning and purification. Situated at a spring near the Inca's hunting lodge, its main construction lies in a sheltered gully where some superb Inca masonry again emphasizes the Inca fascination with, and adoration of, water.

The ruins basically consist of three tiered platforms. The top one holds four trapezoidal niches that may have been used as seats; on the next level, underground water emerges directly from a hole at the base of the stonework, and from here cascades down to the bottom platform, creating a cold shower just about high enough for an Inca to stand under. On this platform the spring water splits into two channels, both pouring the last metre down to ground level. Clearly a site for ritual bathing, the quality of the stonework suggests that its use was restricted to the higher nobility, who perhaps used the baths only on ceremonial occasions.

About 1km further up the gully, you'll come to a small **grotto** where there's a pool large enough for bathing, even in the dry season. Whilst it shows no sign of Inca stonework, the hills on either side of the stream are dotted with stone terraces and caves, one or two of which still have remnants of walls at their entrance. In Inca, *machay* means "cave", suggesting that these were an important local feature, perhaps as sources of water for Tambo Machay and Puca Pucara.

Eating and drinking

Generally speaking, although **eating out** in Cusco is enjoyable, the food itself is not quite as interesting or as varied as on the coast or in Lima, with a couple of exceptions. The city prides itself on its traditional foods, and while you'll find it easier to get pizza than roast guinea pig, the more central **cafés and restaurants** accommodate most tastes, serving anything from a toasted cheese sandwich to authentic Andean or criolla dishes (a Peruvian form of Creole). The most popular area for restaurants and bars is around the **Plaza de Armas** and along calles **Plateros** and **Procuradores**, home to several decent, cheap cafés and a few good restaurants. The trendy San Blas barrio has two excellent restaurants – *Pacha Papa* and *Greens* – offering an alternative to the more conventional cuisine found in most places.

If you're **self-catering**, the Central Market by San Pedro train station sells a wonderful variety of meats, tropical and imported fruits, local vegetables, Andean cheeses and other basics. The market also has a wide range of daytime hot-food stalls where you can get **takeaway** food (if you have a container to put it in) or eat on the spot.

Cafés and snack bars

Bagdad Café Portal de Carnes 216, Plaza de Armas. Next to and above *La Yunta* (another more easily found café – see below), a popular location not least because it has tables on a colonial balcony overlooking the plaza. Serves good pizzas, breakfasts, sandwiches, some pasta dishes and cool drinks.

El Buen Pastor Cuesta San Blas 579. An exceptional bakery and fine cake shop.

Café Ayllu Portal de Carnes 208, Plaza de Armas. Has one of the best breakfasts in Peru, including fruit, yogurt and toasted sandwiches, and very fast service, though it's not cheap. Centrally located with downstairs views across the plaza, it's Cusco's most traditional meeting place.

Café Cultural Ritual Choquechaca 140. This quiet and pleasant little café serves great breakfasts and also has a good vegetarian menu as well as dishes like *quinoa andina*, a pancake of *quinoa* with fried manioc. Mon–Sat 8.30am–11pm.

El Pie Shop Carmen Alto 254a, San Blas. Has arguably the best espresso in Cusco and serves a daily selection of freshly baked sweet and savoury pies; also very friendly people who are sometimes up for a game of cards or backgammon.

La Tertulia Café Cultural Calle Procuradores 50. A travellers' hangout in Cusco's heartland passage with a good book exchange, great snacks and some board games; sometimes hosts live music or theatre.

Trotamundos Portal de Comercio 177, Plaza de Armas. An Internet café that's better known for serving food and drinks. The Internet section is partitioned off from the café itself, which has views over the plaza, a notice board, a stove-fire and games.

Varayoc Calle Espaderos 142 ☏232404. A welcoming *café literario* with a strong Andean intellectual as well as Swiss atmosphere. It's okay for breakfasts, snacks or even fondue, and has a magazine rack and several tables where students, tourists and locals mingle, generally sipping hot chocolate, pisco or *mate de coca* (coca-leaf tea – highly recommended for altitude sickness).

La Yunta Portal de Carnes 214, Plaza de Armas. A groovy establishment right on the plaza, specializing in pizza but also offering large, good-value salads, soups, omelettes, fish, French fries and excellent juices and jugs of *limonada*. Perfect for lunch or supper and a popular meeting place for adventure tour guides in the early evening.

Restaurants

Cusco **restaurants** range from the cheap and cheerful to expensive gourmet establishments. Many serve international cuisine but the *quintas*, basic local eating houses, serve mostly traditional **Peruvian food**, full of spice and character, in typical Cusco ambience, which is at times rough-and-ready with live guinea pigs running around in the kitchens and old tables strewn about the covered garden patio. *Pacha Papa*, though, offers a more refined approach with tablecloths and tourist-oriented service. Generally speaking, trout is plentiful, reasonably priced and often excellent, and roast guinea pig (*cuy*) can usually be ordered, but **pizza** seems to lead in the popularity stakes. This isn't a region particularly noted for its **beef**, but there are a few places serving steaks, and **British** and **Asian** cooking can be found, the latter in some fairly average *chifas*, and one very good **curry** house – *Al Grano*. Unless otherwise stated, most restaurants open daily at around 11am and serve until 10.30pm–midnight.

Budget

Blueberry Lounge Portal de Carnes 235 ☎740053. A restaurant and relaxing lounge bar; the music is good and the food, largely Thai-inspired, is delicious. Good breakfasts and outdoor seating (weather permitting).

Cafetería Huaylliy Plateros 363. Uninspiring decor but some of the best-value breakfasts in Cusco, plus pizzas, *chifa* meals and cakes.

Kaleydaskop Vegetarian Café Portal de Panes 167 and Triunfo 393 ☎221187. Good vegetarian meals and snacks, with esoteric books on sale, mainly promoting the mystic side of Cusco. The Triunfo branch is the nicer of the two.

Mia Pizza Procuradores 379. One of the better places for pizzas and other Italian dishes in this busy alley.

Moni Café Restaurant San Agustin 311 ☎231029. A superb, brightly decorated vegetarian restaurant with comfy sitting area and magazines to read in English and Spanish. Everything is cooked fresh to order. Calm, relaxed and welcoming.

Restaurant Los Aromas del Nucchu Choquechaca 130. Possibly the best-value set menus in central Cusco; tends to be busy at lunch times. Pleasant enough space but no frills.

Restaurant Govinda Calle Espaderos 128. The original vegetarian eating house in Cusco, serving simple healthy food: the fruit-and-yogurt breakfasts are generally very good and the set lunches excellent value. If you get the chance, eat upstairs where there's more atmosphere and more room. Daily 8.30am–7pm.

Restaurant Mamala Choquechaca 509 ☎246090. Exceptionally good and very cheap set lunches amid pleasant ambience, conveniently located between San Blas and the Plaza de Armas. Also serves decent pizzas and burgers.

Restaurant Vegetariano "La Waki de Cristal" Choquechaca 132. A small place with good, wholesome vegetarian snacks and set meals, plus a friendly atmosphere with rainbows and crystals over the doorway.

Restaurant Vegetariano Life and Health Kuychipunku 353. Just two blocks from Avenida Sol on the road towards Puente Grau, this is a very basic health-food café with cheap set lunch menus.

Restaurant Victor Victoria corner of Tigre and Teqsecocha. A basic eating house with good, inexpensive set menus, very popular with budget travellers at both lunch and supper. Daily 8am–8pm.

Sambois Sandwiches Calle Medio at the corner with the Plaza de Armas. Small, speedy burger joint which also happens to do great fried egg sandwiches, French fries and juices.

Moderate

Bagdad Café Portal de Carnes 216 ☎239949. Fine views over plaza if you can get a table on the small balcony; failing that, console yourself with a large, relatively inexpensive pizza, or an expensive plate of *cuy* for two.

Dragon Dorado Calle Plateros 373 ☎245192. A small Chinese restaurant near the Plaza de Armas with good food, ample portions and quick service; try the delicious *kamlu wantan*, crispy meatballs in a tamarind sauce.

Al Grano Santa Catalina Ancha 398 ☎228032. A friendly place serving delicious Asian lunches and suppers, including superb curries, in a civilized atmosphere. They have particularly good deals on set lunch menus (for example, soup and main course for $2). Closes around 9pm.

Macondo Cuesta San Blas 571 ☎229415. A cosy and homely gay-friendly restaurant with wacky decor and serving some of the best nouveau

Andean and Amazonian cuisine you'll find any-where; try the *yuquitas* stuffed with chimbivalcano cheese, the vegetarian curry or the *alpaca mignon a la parmesana*. Best in evenings (book in advance), but serves a full menu during the day.

Pacha Papa Plaza San Blas 120 ☎241318. A great, inexpensive restaurant set around an attrac-tive courtyard, serving a range of hard-to-find Andean dishes, from a *gulash de alpaca* to the highly nutritious *sopa de quinoa*. Reservations rec-ommended.

Pucara Restaurant Calle Plateros 309 ☎222027. Popular with tourists, this pleasant restaurant offers inexpensive set menus, fine salads and well-prepared Peruvian cuisine. There's occasional music in the evenings.

The Quinta Eulalia Calle Choquechaca 384 ☎241380. One of the very best and most tradi-tional local eating houses, in a backstreet a few blocks above the Plaza de Armas. Plays fine criolla music and is good for *cuy chactado* (guinea pig fried with potatoes, tamales and *rocoto*).

The Quinta Zarate Totora Paccha 763 ☎245114. Excellent traditional food and atmosphere, close to the San Blas plazoleta, though it's difficult to find without a taxi.

Rosie O'Grady's Santa Catalina 360 ☎247935. Find good beer and even better full meals at this swish Irish pub and restaurant. The beefsteak is among the best in Peru.

Expensive

La Estancia Imperial second floor, Portal de Panes 177 ☎224621. Situated on the Plaza de Armas and specializing in pizzas and chickens, it's definitely worth trying, especially if you can get a table with a view.

Fallen Angel Plazoleta Nazarenas 221 ☎258184. A gay-friendly restaurant with games suspended on stools from the ceiling and fake leopard-skin trunks. There's also a resident DJ who often plays decent trip hop and dance. The decor is arty, inspired and definitely worth a visit in its own right; but the food and cocktails are equally exquisite. Try the Andean steak with cheese topping. Best to book in advance.

Greens Tandapata 700 ☎243820. A Peruvian-British partnership, this brilliantly run restaurant has a very good reputation for Sunday roasts among other dishes like fettuccini or curries. Plays nice music, has cool decor and is well situated in San Blas. Reservations are advised.

El Meson de Espaderos second floor, Calle Espaderos 105 ☎235307. Overlooking the Plaza de Armas and specializing in steaks, grills and *cuy*.

Pachacutec Restaurant Portal de Panes 105 ☎245041. A grill-based restaurant on a busy cor-ner of Plaza de Armas, with Inca stones from the Inca Pachacuti's palace lining the walls. *Comida tipica* and *internacional*. With folklore shows at weekends and evenings from 8pm, it's worth the extra few soles.

Restaurant El Truco Plaza Regocijo 261 ☎235295. Delicious and pricey traditional Cusco food in one of the city's flashiest restaurants, with fine beef and fish dishes. Music and Andean folk dancing is usually performed during the evenings.

La Trattoria Adriano Calle Mantas 105, corner of Av Sol ☎233965. Of all the Italians in Cusco this serves the best-quality cuisine, especially the pasta dishes, and has a fine selection of good South American and European wines.

Nightlife and entertainment

Apart from Lima, no Peruvian town has as varied a **nightlife** as Cusco. The corner of Plaza de Armas, where Calle Plateros begins, is a hive of activity until the early hours, even during the week. Most nightspots in the city are simply **bars** with a dance floor and sometimes a stage, but their styles vary enor-mously, from Andean folk joints with panpipe music to reggae or jazz joints and more conventional **clubs**. Most places are within staggering distance of each other, and sampling them is an important part of any stay in Cusco. Many open around 9pm and keep going until 2 or 3am.

During any of the major **fiestas** (see pp.116–117) you will encounter colour-fully costumed dance groups in the streets, but there are few other opportuni-ties to see **folk dancing** beyond the occasional show at a few of the large hotels and more expensive restaurants. Only two groups offer regular per-formances: Dance Performances, at the Centro Qosqo de Arte Nativo, Avenida Sol 612 (daily 6–10pm; around $5; ☎227901).

Pubs and bars

The Cross Keys Pub first floor, Portal Confituras 233. One of the hubs of Cusco's nightlife, this classic drinking dive has the feel of a London pub, with good music, soccer scarves adorning the walls and pool tables. Food is available and there are often English-language newspapers and magazines.

The Muse Bar Café Art Gallery Tandapata 682. Located on the terrace above the Plazoleta San Blas. It has a cozy atmosphere, good drinks and food all day, with tables outside; also plays live music from roughly 10pm most weekends and sometimes during the week.

Norton Rats Tavern second floor, Calle Loreto 115. Just off the Plaza de Armas, with great views over the square, by Iglesia La Compañía. Best known as a bar, it has a wonderful, spacious atmosphere, serves special jungle cocktails (including herbs and medicinal plants, each with its own special effect), plays rock, blues, jazz and Latin music and has a pool table and dartboard, plus cable TV for sports. There's also a café serving grills.

Paddy Flaherty's Irish Pub Calle Triunfo 124 ☎246903. Looking much like a British pub, though its wood-panelled walls are spattered with Irish artefacts. The atmosphere is pleasant and gets particularly lively at weekends, when they often have live Irish music. Serves Guinness.

Los Perros Teqsecocha 436. Billing itself as "the original couch bar", *Los Perros* is a trendy hangout where travellers snack, drink and play board games or read from the wide-ranging library and magazines (books can be exchanged – give two, take one). There's often jazz music at weekends.

Planeta Sur Jazz Café Plazoleta San Blas 630. Small but very nice jazz bar with books and magazines to browse as well as music, including Afro-Peruvian rhythms, dance, jazz and karaoke from 10pm.

Rosie O'Grady's Santa Catalina 360 ☎247935. A spacious, tasteful Irish pub and restaurant (see above) with a range of beers, Guinness included. There's great live music on Thursdays and Fridays, plus a popular Friday evening "boat race" drinking competition; cable TV for sports.

Clubs and dance bars

Café Ta Cuba Portal de Panes 109, third floor, Plaza de Armas. A bar and disco playing mainly Latin music; colourful lights, large dance space; friendly and lively at weekends.

KamiKase Bar Portal Cabildo 274, Plaza Regocijo ☎233865. One of Cusco's best-established nightspots, with modern Andean rock-art decor and basic furnishings. Drinks are quite cheap, though when it hosts live music (most weekends), there's usually a small entrance fee, but it's worthwhile if you're into rock and Andean folk. Happy hour 8.30–9.30pm; live music usually starts around 10pm.

Mama Africa Portal Belen 115, Plaza de Armas, upstairs. A good, buzzing dance bar with a small entrance fee, popular with an under-thirties crowd of locals and gringos. Drinks are a bit pricey, and they also do food. Daily 9pm–2am or later. Often shows videos in the afternoons and sometimes offers dance classes in salsa and samba.

El Muki Disco Santa Catalina Angosta 114 ☎227797. Near the Plaza de Armas, *El Muki* has been pumping out pop every night for over twenty years. With its atmospheric catacomb-like dance floors, it's a safe space for late-night bopping, charging $2 entrance.

Ukuku's Bar Calle Plateros 316, down the alley and upstairs ☎242951. A highly popular venue with one of the best atmospheres in Cusco, thronging with energetic revellers most nights by around 11pm, when the music gets going. There's a small dance floor and a long bar, with music ranging from live Andean folk with panpipes, drums and *charangos* (small Andean stringed instruments) to taped rock. There's often an entrance charge – usually less than $1.50 – and happy hour lasts from 8pm to 9.35pm and thirty seconds. Daily 7.30pm–2am, plus large-screen movies most afternoons.

White.vinyl Espaderos 135, second floor ✉ viniloblanco@yahoo.com. Aiming to change the face of nightlife in Cusco, trendy *White.vinyl* plays mainly the latest groovy, non-pop music releases from across the world and lays on special events at any excuse. It has two main spaces, the main bar approached by a long black catwalk amid white vinyl lounge furniture and chill-out areas – very *Clockwork Orange*, but definitely fun; the main dance floor has another bar. There are periodic performances of dance, acrobatics and creative body art as well as fashion shows.

Xcess Portal de Carnes 298 ☎229839. One of Cusco's most popular dance bars, playing a wide range of music, from Latin pop to reggae. Free drinks 10–11.30pm with the pass handed out on the street outside.

Shopping

Most of the touristy artesania and jewellery **shops** are concentrated in the streets around the Plaza de Armas and up Triunfo, though Calle San Agustin (first right off Triunfo as you head towards San Blas) has slightly cheaper but decent shops with leather and alpaca work. It's worth heading off the beaten track, particularly around the upper end of Tullumayo or up around the Central Market, to find outlets hidden in the backstreets. In the markets and at street stalls you can often get up to twenty percent off, and even in the smarter shops it's quite acceptable to bargain a little.

Cusco **opening hours** are generally Monday to Saturday 10am to 6pm, though some of the central gift stores open on Sundays and don't close until well into the evening. If you're worried about being robbed while making a substantial purchase, it's fine to ask the shopkeeper to bring the goods to your hotel so that the transaction can take place in relative safety.

Camera equipment and film

Agfa Foto Heladeros 172. A small range of films.
Foto Nishiyama Mantas 109 and Triunfo 346. Both branches stock a wide range of Kodak films as well as other brands and offer good-quality film developing and processing, plus some camera equipment.

Kodak Express Av Sol 180. Sells and develops film.
Quantu Colours Av Sol 761 B. Opposite the post office, this is a laboratory and photo studio offering one-hour developing, a range of films and batteries for cameras.

Camping equipment

Rental or purchase of **camping equipment** is easy in Cusco, but if renting you may be asked to leave your passport as a deposit on more expensive items; always get a proper receipt. For basics such as such as pots, pans, plates and so on, try the stalls in Monjaspata, less than half a block from the bottom end of San Pedro market, while others such as buckets, bowls and sheets are sold in various shops along Calle Concebidayoq, close to the San Pedro market area.

Andean Life Calle Plateros 341, Plaza de Armas ☎221491. An adventure tour operator with a whole range of camping equipment for rent or sale.
Eric Adventures Plateros 324, ☎228475. Have a small selection of camping equipment, new and old.
Expediciones Vilca see p.151.
Gregory's Tours Portal Comercio 177. Tents, sleeping bags, bed mats, stoves and gas to rent. Equipment also for sale and rent at Portal

Comercio 121–129.
Inkas Trek Calle Medio 114. All the gear you'll need, and all available to rent.
Killak Sur Calle Medio 120. A good choice of equipment, plus they change dollars.
Tattoo Outdoors & Travel Plazoleta Las Nazarenas 211. Outdoor pursuits shop with quality clothing and accessories.
X-Treme Tourbulencia Expeditions Plateros 358 ☎245527 or 222405. Quite a range of used equipment.

Crafts, artesania and jewellery

Crafts and **artesania** are Cusco's stock in trade, with the best alpaca clothing outside Lima. It's an ideal place to pick up woollen sweaters, ponchos, jackets, weavings or antique cloths, while inexpensive and traditional musical instruments like panpipes, and colourful bags and leather crafts are also common. The unnamed artisans' market in the road running parallel with Santa Clara in the San Pedro district is particularly good value, especially if you bargain (watch out for pickpockets, though). There's also a more central and safer artesania market on the right-hand side going up block 1 of Plateros from the Plaza de

Armas, and higher up in Calle Saphi there's an artesanía market area more or less opposite the *Hostal Familiar*. The new *Centro Artesanal Cusco* at the corner of Huanchac and Tullumayu, close to the huge sun-disc fountain on Avenida Sol, has probably the largest and best-value collection of artesanía under one roof in Peru; it's a nice, clean and relatively hassle-free shopping environment very close to the train ticket office at Huanchac station. The barrio of San Blas is the traditional quality artisan area of Cusco, home to a number of **jewellers**, art and antique shops. The Cuesta San Blas itself contains some of the finest artesanía, new and old oil paintings, and craft shops, while Hathun Rumiyoq has more good artesanía shops at its bottom end. Around the San Blas plazoleta there are some funky shops and bars, and the main street market day there is Saturday, 10am–6pm. Out of town there are good markets at Pisac and Chinchero, main days being Sunday and Thursday respectively (see p.155 and p.182 for more details).

Agua y Tierra Cuesta San Blas 595. Some excellent jungle textiles, ceramics, jewellery and cushma robes.

Alpaca 3 Ruinas 472. Good alpaca fabrics, yarns, sweaters and scarves.

Alpaca Golden Portal de Panes 151, Plaza de Armas. Alpaca sweaters and a range of other well-made items.

Andean Music Museum Hathun Rumiyoq 487. An interesting range of traditional instruments – *charangos, quenas*, panpipes and drums – plus sheet music and a good selection of books; they also have traditional music workshops on Fridays at around 7pm.

Arte Inkari Choquechaca 138. A good range of traditional Andean costumes, hats and weavings from the Cusco area, plus some antiques.

Artesanías Yamelin Procuradores 342. A superb bead shop.

Feria Artisanal El Inka corner of San Andreas and Quera 218. A small but bursting artesanía market within a stone's throw of Avenida Sol and only a few blocks from the main plaza. Good bargains available, particularly for textiles and ponchos.

Galeria Olave Calle Plazoleta 651. A superb craft workshop which produces replica religious art and traditional Cusco cabinets and furniture.

Hecho en Cusco T-Shirts Carmen Alto 105, San Blas ☎221948. Superb hand-crafted T-shirts, some with Inca and pre-Inca designs fabulously reproduced, badges and other paraphernalia.

Joyeria Oropesa Portal de Carrizos, corner of Calle Loreto. Jewellery for the seriously wealthy, specializing in silverwork.

La Mamita Portal de Carnes 244. This excellent shop is an outlet for the Cusco region's more progressive and stylish artesanía, such as the ceramics of Pablo Seminario (see p.158), basketry, batiks, jewellery and cotton clothing.

Manos Magicos San Blas Plazoleta. Traditional pre-Conquest silverworking techniques combined with local and imported gem stones, inspired by dream world imager. Pricey but of phenomenal quality.

Pedazo Arte Plateros 334b. Stocks new handicrafts: all handmade and of good quality.

Taller de Instrumentos Hathun Rumiyoq 451 (head through the back to the second patio). Rustic workshop (no entry charge) producing *charangos, quenas* and panpipes, often to professional standards.

Tienda Museo Portal Comercio 173 on the Plaza de Armas and Santa Clara 501, up towards the San Pedro market. Alpaca and sheep's wool textiles. Their *mantas*, ponchos and other items are of excellent quality.

Food

Central Market San Pedro. The best place for generally excellent and very cheap food – including all the main typical Peruvian dishes like *cau cau* (tripe), rice with meats and veggies, *papas a la huancaina* – provided you feel comfortable with a street-stall standard of hygiene.

El Chinito Grande Matará 271, a large Chinese-run supermarket with good prices and selection.

El Croissant Plaza San Francisco 134. Good French baking, so ideal for croissants, French sticks and, best of all, delicious cream pastries.

The Delicatessen Calle Medio 110. Just off the Plaza de Armas, with a great selection of cheeses, wines and dried fruits.

Gato's Market Santa Catalina Angosta, corner of Plaza de Armas and close to the Cathedral. A good range of typical Peruvian foods.

Granja Heidi in the lobby of the *Hostal Colonial*, Matará 288. Delicious organic yogurt and muesli.

El Pepito's Plaza San Francisco 158. Sweets and chocolates.

The Supermarket Calle Plateros 346. Small and

packed to the gills with food for trekking expeditions – cheese, biscuits, tins of tuna, nuts, chocolate, raisins and dried bananas. **Tierra Atlas** Plaza Nazarenas 211. Natural food

products grown at the Hacienda Yaravilca in the Urubamba Valley, as part of an effort to cultivate crops and foodstuffs that have disappeared from Peruvian kitchens over the centuries.

Newspapers, books, music and videos

New World News, an excellent weekly **English-language newspaper** costing under $1, is available from bookstores and street sellers around Cusco. If you've finished with any books and want to try something new, **book exchange** is available at a number of places, including the *La Tertulia Café Cultural* (see p.141), the South American Explorers' Club (see p.149) and *Los Perros* (see p.144).

Librería Los Andes Portal Comercio 125, Plaza de Armas. A good bookshop on Plaza de Armas, with a fair selection of English- and Spanish-language books on Peru and the Cusco region.
Librería SBD Av Sol 781-A. Good selection of literature and tourism books mostly aimed at the English-speaking market; opposite the post office.

El Mini Shop Portal Confiturias 217, Plaza de Armas. Friendly, central and well stocked with interesting guides and history books about Cusco, the Incas and Peru, including ones in English. It also sells educational videos and the cheapest postcards in town.
Music Centre Av Sol 230. The best range of Andean and Peruvian cassettes and CDs in Cusco.

Listings

Airlines Aero Condor, Avenida Sol 789a ☎225000, 252774 or 624005, ℻223393; Aero Continente, Portal de Carnes 245, Plaza de Armas ☎235666, 243031 or 263978, ℻235660, ⓦwww.aerocontinente.com.pe; Helicusco, Calle Triunfo 379 ☎243555, ℻227283, ⓔdfhi @amauta.rcp.net.pe, ⓦwww.rcp.net.pe /HELICUSCO; Imperial Air, corner of Garcilaso and Plaza San Francisco ☎238000, ℻238877; Lan Peru (and Lan Chile), Avenida Sol 627b ☎255551 or 255553 and at the airport ☎255550, for Lima, Puerto Maldonado, Juliaca, Tacana and Arequipa; Lloyd Aero Boliviano, Avenida Pardo 675b ☎229220; TACA Peru, Avenida Sol 226 ☎249921, ℻249926, ⓔgtacuz@grupotaca.com.pe, for Lima (from about $70 standard, including tax); TANS, Calle San Agustin 315 ☎242727 or 251000. Departure tax is $10 for international departures, $4 for domestic flights.
Airport Aeropuerto Internacional Velasco Astete ☎222611.
American Express Lima Tours, Avenida Machu Picchu D-6, Urbina. Manuel Prado ☎228431 or 235241.
Banks and exchange Interbanc, Avenida Sol 380 (also has ATM at airport), is good for travellers' cheques, cash exchange and credit card extraction and has an ATM compatible with MasterCard, Visa, Cirrus and Amex Mon-Fri 9am-6pm, Sat 9am-12.30pm; Banco de la Nación, corner of Avenida

Sol and Almagro; Banco de Credito, Avenida Sol 189; Banco Continental, Avenida Sol 366, change cash and most travellers' cheques; Banco del Sur, Avenida Sol 457, has an external 24hr ATM accepting Visa and MasterCard; Banco Wiese, Jirón Maruri 315–341. There's a MasterCard machine outside the *El Dorado Inn*. For faster service and better rates than banks, try Cambio Cusco, Portal Comercio 177, Oficina B (☎238861; daily 9am–10pm), one of the better and more central money-changing offices; the *tienda* next door at #181 is also OK for exchange; Casa de Cambio, Oficina 1, Avenida Sol 345, is also good. Lastly, street *cambistas* can be found on blocks 2 and 3 of Avenida Sol, around the main banks, but as usual take great care here.
Bus companies Inter-regional and international buses depart from Terminal Terrestre, Sector Molino Pampa, right side of Río Huatanay, in the district of Santiago ☎224471; except for those run by Cruz del Sur, which leave from Avenida Pachacutec 510 (5.30am–8pm for tickets); ☎221909, Imperial or Economico services to Arequipa ($15 or $8) and Puno ($15 or $5), daily. At the Terminal Terrestre there is an embarkation tax of 30¢, which you pay before alighting. Recommended operators include: CIVA for Puno and Arequipa; El Chasqui (☎252994) for Arequipa, Tacna and Lima; Cruz del Sur (☎221909 or 233383) for Arequipa and Desaguadero; Espresso

147

Wari (☎261703) for Lima via Abancay and Nazca; Libertad (☎247174) for Juliaca, Puno and Copacabana/La Paz; Ormeño (☎233469) for Espinar, Tintaya, Arequipa, Lima, Copacabana and La Paz; Power (☎246515) for Juliaca and Puno; San Jeronimo (☎261142) for Andahuaylas and Ayacucho; Tours Wari (☎229717) for Puno, Abancay, Nazca and Lima; Trans International Litoral for La Paz; Trans Turismo Colca, for Sicuani and Arequipa; Transportes Pardo for Arequipa and Lima; Tranzela (☎238223) for Puno, Copacabana and La Paz; Turismo Abancay for Abancay; Turismo Ampay (☎227541) for Abancay and Quillabamba; and Urkupiña (☎229962) for Juliaca and Puno.

Car rental Aventurismo Cusco, San Borja K-1 Wanxhaq Cusco (☎227730, ⓦwww.4x4cusco .com), have 4WD cars for rent; as do Inka Planet, Belen C-25 ☎240507; and AVIS, Avenida Sol 808 ☎248800, ⓔavis-cuscol@terra.com.pe.

Chemist Botica San Judas, Procuradores 398

Cinemas Amauta, Avenida de la Cultura 764 ☎226431; Garcilaso, Unión 117 ☎232461; Ollanta, Meloc 417 ☎22052; and Vicoria, Huayruropata 931 ☎223271.

Consulates Bolivia, Avenida Pardo, Pasaje Espinar ☎231412; Dutch, Avenida Pardo 584 ☎264103; UK, Avenida Pardo 895 ☎239974 (Mon–Fri 9am–1pm); for the USA contact the Instituto de Cultura Peruana Norte Americana, Avenida Tullumayo 125 ☎224112.

Courier services DHL, Avenida Sol 393 ☎244167.

Cultural centre The Alliance Française, Avenida de la Cultura 804 (☎223755), runs a full programme of events including music, films, exhibitions, theatre and music; phone for details.

Customs office Calle Teatro 344 ☎228181.

Dentists Dr Virginia Valcarcel Velarde, upstairs at Portal de Panes 123, Plaza de Armas ☎231558; and Dr Pintur, Centro Comercial Santa Cecilia, by the Sandy Colour Fotografia, Avenida Sol ☎233721 or 651211.

Diners Club Avenida Sol 615 ☎234051 or 236890.

Doctors Dr Oscar Tejada ☎233836 (24hr) is a member of International Assistance for Medical Assistance to Travellers; Dr Dante Valdivia (☎231390, 620588 or 252166) speaks English and German; and Dr Maria Helena (☎650122 or 227385) will visit.

Films Good contemporary films are frequently shown in the afternoon and evenings by a number of popular establishments; for most places entrance free but you're expected to consume at the bar or restaurant concerned: Xcess nightclub, Portal de Carnes 298, have a large video screen operating most afternoons; Sunset Video Café, Calle Teqsecocha 2, second floor, offer sandwiches, cakes and drinks to their 3 daily movies.

Hospitals and clinics Hospital Regional, Avenida de la Cultura (☎223691); Clinica Pardo, Avenida de la Cultura 710 ☎240387 or 620126, which runs a 24hr service, with some English spoken; Hospital Antonio Lorena, Plaza de Belen ☎226511; and Clinica Laboratorio Louis Pasteur, Tullumayo 768 ☎234727 which has a gynaecologist. For 24hr emergency treatment, try Tourist Medical Assistance, or TMA ☎621838, or Medic Fast ☎688154, 252854 or 273155.

Immigration Migraciones, Avenida Sol, block 6 ☎222741.

Instituto Nacional de Cultura Calle San Bernado ☎236061.

Internet facilities Ukukos Internet, first floor, Calle Plateros 316, is a large space with good food and bar service; Kafe Internet, Plateros 361 (ⓔkfe@latinmail.com); Cybercafé, Procuradores 320; all have 12 computer terminals. Internet at Procuradores 340 also offers scanning, printing and netphoning; Internet Station Speed X, Teqsecocha 400, is central, cheap and has a rapid connection; Los Togas Internet Café-Bar, Portal de Carnes 258, is more of a shop really but is very central; Ink@net Cybercafé, Carmen Alto 113, San Blas, is small but OK; Intinet Choquechaca 115c, small but also does international phone calls; Telesur, Calle Medio 117, also has a good link; Internet, with several computers next to the lobby of the *Gran Hotel Machu Picchu* at Quera 284. La Cabina de Estudiantes Intej, upstairs at Portal Comercio 141, also do ISIS Travel insurance and student cards; open 8am–10pm daily. Expect to pay around $1 an hour for logging on at all places.

Language schools Amigos Spanish School at Zaguan del Cielo B-23 ☎242292, ⓦwww .spanishcusco.com, a not-for-profit institution which funds education and food for local young people through its teaching of Spanish; family stays can also be organized if required. Staff speak English, Dutch, German, French and Japanese; extra-curricular activities include salsa and merengue dance lessons, cooking classes and aerobics at 3400m. Also, Academia Latinamericana de Español, Avenida Sol 580 (☎243364, ⓔlatinocusco@goalsnet.com.pe), which offers group or individual classes, afternoon activities and, if required, homestay (volunteer work sometimes available).

Laundry Ña P'asña, Saphi 578a. Fairly cheap and efficient, with self-service also available; T'Aqsana Wasi, Santa Catalina Ancha 345; Lavamachine in both Santa Teresa 383 and Procuradores 50; and Laundry, Teqsecocha 428.

Motorbike hire Loreto Tours, Calle Medio 111
ⓣ226331 or 228264, ⓔloretotour@planet
.com.pe. Rent out bicycles (from $15 a day with
suspension) and motorbikes (from $40 a day).
Park Office, Manu Parque Nacional del Manu, Av
Micaela Bastidas 310 ⓣ240898.
Post office The main office, at Avenida Sol 800
(ⓣ225232), operates a quick and reliable poste
restante system. Mon–Sat 7.30am–8pm, Sun
7.30am–2.30pm.
South American Explorers' Club Choquechaca
188 #4 (ⓣ245484), Apartado 500, Cusco, Peru
(ⓦwww.saexplorers.com). Good information
sheets, trip reports and files on virtually everything
about Cusco and Peru, including transport,
trekking, hotels, Internet cafés and tour companies. The excellent clubhouse has a luggage
deposit, notice board, library and book exchange.
Membership fees would be covered by the discount SE Club members get with some companies
on just one tour to Manu. Mon–Fri 9.30am–5pm.
Taxis Alo Cusco ⓣ222222; Llama taxi ⓣ222000;
Reynaldo Gamarra ⓣ621854.
Telephones Telesur, Calle Medio 117 (ⓣ242222),
is right by the Plaza de Armas and has pretty fast
service with Internet facilities too; Telefonica, Av
Sol 608 (Mon–Sat 8am–9pm Sun 10am–6pm),
good for international calls with private cabins,
also has fax service.
Tourist police Calle Saphi 581 ⓣ249654 and

also Monumento Pachacutec ⓣ211961.
Tourist protection service Servicio de
Protección al Turista, Portal de Carrizos 250, Plaza
de Armas (Mon–Fri 8am–8pm; ⓣ/ⓕ252974).
Train tickets The Estación Huanchac ticket office
(Mon–Fri 7am–noon & 2–5pm, Sat 7am–noon, Sun
8–10am; ⓣ238722 or for reservations 221992,
ⓕ221114, ⓦwww.perurail.com) sells Puno and
Machu Picchu tickets. For Machu Picchu it's best
to buy in advance from here, though, if available,
the remainder can be bought on the day by queu-
ing at San Pedro station (5–7am & 3–4pm;
ⓣ238722 for reservations and sales).
Travel agents America Tour, Portal de Harinas 175
(ⓣ227208), mostly book and sell air tickets;
Orellana Tours, Calle Garcilaso 206 (ⓣ263455,
ⓕ236083, ⓔorellanotours@terra.com.pe), air tickets and some tours; Milla Turismo, Avenida Pardo
689 (ⓣ231710, ⓕ231388,
ⓦwww.millaturismo.com), will organize travel
arrangements, tours, study tours and cultural
tourist-related activities.
Vaccinations Cusco Regional Hospital offers free
yellow fever inoculations on Sat from 11am to
1pm.
Visas Migraciones, Avenida Sol 620 ⓣ222741;
Mon–Fri 9am–5pm.
Western Union Santa Catalina Ancha 311
ⓣ248028; and at Calle Medio 117 ⓣ242222.

Tours in and around Cusco

Tours in and around Cusco range from a half-day city tour to an expedition
by light aircraft or a full-on adventure down to the Amazon. **Prices** range from
$20 to over $100 a day, and service and facilities vary considerably, so check
exactly what's provided, whether insurance is included and whether the guide
speaks English. The main agents are strung along three sides of the Plaza de
Armas, along Portal de Panes, Portal de Confiturias and Portal Comercio, up
Procuradores and along the calles Plateros and Saphi and, although prices vary,
many are selling places on the same tours and treks, so always hunt around.
Avoid the **tour touts** at the airport or in the plaza at Cusco, and check out
the operators in advance at the South American Explorers' Club (see above) if
you're able to (members also receive a discount with some outfits). There are
also a few Lima-based operators in this area (see p.151).

Standard tours around the city, Sacred Valley and to Machu Picchu range
from a basic bus service with fixed stops and little in the way of a guide, to luxury packages including guide, food and hotel transfers. The three- to six-day
Inca Trail is the most popular of the **mountain treks**, with thousands of people hiking it every year. Many agencies offer trips with guides, equipment and
fixed itineraries; but it's important to remember (see p.166) that entry to the
Inca Trail is restricted and requires tourists to travel with a guide or tour as well
as to be registered with the Unidad de Gestión (your tour company does this)

at least two days before departure. In selecting the right Inca Trail tour option it's a good idea to make comparisons before deciding; prices vary considerably between $60 and $300 and don't always reflect genuine added value. Check exactly what's provided: train tickets (which class), quality of tent, roll mat, sleeping bag, porter to carry rucksack and sleeping bag, bus down from ruins, exactly which meals and transport to start.

Adventure tourism

In reality of course, the Inca Trail isn't so popular because it's the most wonderful of all hikes in the Peruvian Andes; it's because of where you end up, the fine trail name and the hype that it gets in the media and by word of mouth. The mountains to the south and the north of Cusco are full of amazing trekking trails, some of them little touched, most of them still rarely walked. Other popular hikes are around the snow-capped mountains of Salcantay (6264m) to the north and Ausangate (6372m) to the south, a more remote trek which needs at least a week plus guides and mules. Less adventurous **walks** or **horse rides** are possible to Qenko, Tambo Machay, Puca Pucara and Chacan, in the hills above Cusco and in the nearby Sacred Valley (as described above). You can also rent out **mountain bikes** for trips to the Sacred Valley and around, and some outfits arrange guided tours (or contact Renny Gamarra Loaiza, a good biking guide; ☎231300). Many **jungle trip** operators are based in Cusco, and those that also cover the immediate Cusco area are listed below as well as in Chapter Eight, where their jungle-specific trips are detailed.

Cusco is also a great **whitewater rafting** centre, with easy access to classes 2 to 5 (rivers are generally rated from class 1 - very easy – to class 5 – very difficult/borderline dangerous) around Ollantaytambo on the Río Urubamba and classes 1 to 3 between Huambutio and Pisac, on the Río Vilcanota. From Calca to Urubamba the river runs classes 2 to 3, but this rises to 5 in the rainy season. Calca to Pisac (Huaran) and Ollantaytambo to Chilca are among the most popular routes, while the most dangerous are further afield on the Río Apurimac. The easiest stretch is from Echarate to San Baray, which passes by Quillabamba. Remember that most travel insurances exclude this kind of adventure activity and always ensure that you are fully equipped with a safety kayak, helmets, and lifejackets.

Bungee jumping is the latest craze in Cusco. The tallest **bungee jump facility** in the Americas (122m) is offered by Action Valley Cusco (ⓦwww .actionvalley.com), just a fifteen-minute walk from the Plaza in Poroy (buses here from block 8 of Avenida Sol). Equally breathtaking but slightly less scary is the option of a **hot air balloon** adventure in the Cusco or Sacred Valley areas; contact Globos de los Andes, Calle Arequipa (Q'aphchik'ijllu) 271 ☎232352, ⓦwww.globosperu.com.

Psychedelic tourism

Psychedelic tourism is popular in Cusco these days, though not as developed as in Iquitos (see p.483). This doesn't mean that a lot of people take "drugs" and wander around the Andes. Essentially, psychedelic tourism is based on traditional healing techniques that tend to focus on inner consciousness and well-being through often highly ritualized ceremonies. San Pedro or Ayahuasca, the two principal indigenous psychedelic plants that have been used ceremonially in Peru for over 3500 years (see Contexts, p.555) can be experienced in the Sacred Valley at the San Pedro International Meditation and Retreat Centre in

Urubamba (☎201428, ⓦwww.geocities.com/Athens/Agora/6972/).
Ayahuasca Therapy, whose slogan is "ecology of the spirit", can be contacted in
Cusco on ☎680780, ⓔecologiadelespiritu@yahoo.com. Another Planet, Calle
Triunfo 120 (☎241168), offers organized spiritual tours, Ayahuasca and San
Pedro ceremonies and day-trips. And there's also the Casa de la Serenidad,
Tandapata 296a (☎222851), which, besides assisting with altitude problems,
offers coca-leaf readings, Reiki, flower and herb baths, and Ayahuasca or San
Pedro ceremonies.

Cusco tour operators

Andean Life Calle Plateros 341, Plaza de Armas, Cusco ☎235970, ⓦwww.andeanlife.com. Strong on the Inca Trail but generally specialists in small-group treks including Salcantay, Lares, Ausangate as well as whitewater rafting and jungle trips.

Apumayo Calle Garcilaso 265, Oficina 3, Cusco ☎246018 ⓔapumayo@terra.com.pe. Expert operators offering trekking in the Sacred Valley region, mountain biking around Cusco and the Sacred Valley, historic and archeological tours, tours for disabled people (with wheelchair support for visiting major sites), horse-riding, and rafting on the ríos Urubamba and Apurimac. They can customize their trips to suit your agenda, though note that they usually only work with pre-booked groups.

Chaparral Ranch Urbino Balconcillo Altok-10 ☎241474 6–9am & 7–10pm for reservations. Very reasonably priced specialists in horse-riding tours to Qenko, Salampunco, Puca Pucara and Tambo Machay.

Colibri Travel Portal Mantas 132, Plaza de Armas, Cusco ☎247849, ⓔcoliobritravel@terra.com.pe. Specialists on the Inca Trail and will arrange transport and collection from hotel. Also offer treks to Salcantay, Ausangate, Choquequirao and Vilcabamba.

Ecomontana Calle Garcilaso 265, Oficina 3, Cusco ☎223216, ⓔecomontana@hotmail.com. A professional company with good guides and thirty different mountain-bike tours.

Eric Adventures Plateros 324, Cusco ☎228475, ⓔcusco@ericadventures.com, ⓦwww.ericadventures.com. A good selection of tours, from the Inca Trail to trekking, and with a good reputation for rafting.

Expediciones Vilca Plateros 363, Cusco ☎/ⓕ251872 ⓕ244751, ⓦwww.cbc.org.pe/manuvilca; or Calle Saphi 456 ☎681002. A well-established trekking company with a variety of treks but they specialize in expeditions to Manu (see p.510). They can rent you any camping gear you need.

Explorandes Av Garcilaso 316-A, Wanchaq, Cusco ☎238380, ⓕ233784, ⓦwww.explorandes.com; or San Fernando 320, Miraflores, Lima ☎01/4450532 or 4458683, ⓕ4454686). A long-established company with a range of tours and treks that include the Inca Trail and Cordillera Vilcanota. For their jungle rafting expeditions, see p.508.

Inca Explorers Calle Suecia 339, Cusco ☎239669, ⓕ243736, ⓦwww.incaexplorers.com. A mid-range trekking agency with a good reputation for the Inca Trail. They have fixed departures on Monday, Tuesday and Thursday and offer a discount to South American Explorers' Club Members.

INSTINCT Calle Procuradores 50, Cusco ☎233451, ⓦwww.instinct-travel.com. A well-organized company offering rugged river-rafting. They also do treks, particularly around the Ollantaytambo area.

Jenly Adventures Calle Medio 127, Plaza de Armas, Cusco ☎257258, ⓔjenlyadventures @yahoo.es. Operate conventional tours, trekking (including Inca Trail and Choquequirao), biking, rafting, climbing, horse-riding and rafting; they also rent out motorbikes from $30–40 a day.

Kantu Portal Carrizos 258, Plaza de Armas, Cusco ☎243673. Good for budget rafting, and prices include food and somewhere to sleep overnight (usually a tent).

Loreto Tours Calle Medio 111, Cusco ☎228264. Particularly recommended for their one-day rafting outings which range as far afield as Apurimac and Tambopata. Also offer mountain-biking tours.

Manu Aventuras Ecologicas Portal Carnes 236, Cusco ☎/ⓕ233498 or 225562. Jungle specialists but also offering mountain biking and whitewater rafting in the Sacred Valley and "personal healing" trips involving shamanism.

Manu Expeditions Av Pardo 895, Cusco ☎226671, ⓕ236706, ⓦwww.ManuExpeditions .com. Although specializing in trips to Manu (see p.517), they organize other adventure tours, including to Espirito Pampa, the Inca site of Choquequirao through the Vilcabamba mountains, to Machu Picchu from Ollantaytambo via Anacachcocha and the Huyaanay peaks, and more traditional treks like the Inca Trail.

Manu Nature Tours Av Sol 582, Cusco
⊕224384, ⓕ234793, ⓔpostmaster@mnt
.com.pe. Good, nature-based adventure travel in
the jungle (see p.517), plus longer tours, mountain
biking, birdwatching and rafting.

MAYUC Portal Confiturias 211, Cusco ⊕232666,
ⓦwww.mayuc.com. Highly reliable outfit with the
experience to organize any tour or trek of your
choice, from an extended Inca Trail to visiting the
Tambopata-Candamo area. Whitewater rafting is
their speciality with standard scheduled 4-day/3-
night excursions involving grade 2 to 5 rapids from
about $230.

Mountain Bike & Trekking Calle Plateros 364,
Cusco ⊕635259. Bike tours and treks to a variety
of locations, including Laras, ruins around Cusco,
Manu cloud-forest run, the Pongo de Mainique, the
Cordillera Urubamba and Choquequirao.

Peru Expeditions Av Arequipa 5241–504,
Miraflores, Lima ⊕01/4472057, ⓕ4459683,
ⓦwww.peru-expeditions.com. Professional, helpful company specializing in environmentally sound
adventure travel in the Cusco region; their leaders
are experts in all kinds of adventure activities.

Peruvian Andean Treks Av Pardo 705, Cusco
⊕225701, ⓕ238911, ⓔpostmaster
@patcusco.com.pe. Expensive, top-quality options
for the Inca Trail, plus treks in Cusco and the
Peruvian Andes. Worth contacting in advance for
their brochure.

Pony's Expeditions Santa Catalina Ancha 353,
office in *Hotel Casa Grande* ⊕791642,
ⓔponyexp@terra.com.pe. This highly professional
outfit have been running excellent trekking trips
for many years in the Cordillera Blanca. Offer most
of the usual treks, plus mountain-bike tours.

SAS Travel Portal de Panes, Plaza de Armas,
Cusco ⊕237292, ⓔinfo@sastravelperu.com; with
a second office at Calle Medio 123 ⊕243050.
Reliable and professional tour and trek operators,
specialists in the Inca Trail but also do Salcantay,
Choquequirao, Ausangate and Vilcabamba as well
as the main jungle destinations. Usually good
value.

United Mice Calle Plateros 351, Cusco and a second office at Calle Triunfo 392, # 218
⊕/ⓕ221139, ⓔunitedmi@terra.com.pe. The top
specialists in guided tours of the Inca Trail and
reasonably priced (4 days, 3 nights for $220
including tax, discounts for students), with good
guides, many speak of whom speak English. Food
is of a high standard and their camping equipment
is fine. If anything, their popularity is a drawback,
since groups are largish in high season. Tours
which avoid the Inca Trail tax include: an excellent
option is the 5-day trek approaching Machu Picchu
via Mollepata and Salcantay, crossing the river at
the hydroelectric station down river from the ruins
for access to Machu Picchu; another interesting 5-
day trek heads for Choquequirao with a minimum
group size of 8 costing around $195 per person; a
6-day trek to Ausangate which, also for around
$195 per person, has a minimum group size of 10.

Welcome South America Travel Calle Qera 235,
office 35, Cusco ⊕236927, ⓔwelsat@terra.com
.pe. Run by the friendly Wilbert Salas, WSAT offer tailored visitor services with professional English-
speaking guides, all-terrain vehicles and good camping equipment. The Inca Trail and other treks are
also covered. Cultural tours including the opportunity
to meet and consult Quechua shamans.

The Sacred Valley and Machu Picchu

The **Sacred Valley**, known as Vilcamayo to the Incas, traces its winding, astonishingly beautiful course to the northwest of Cusco. It's a steep-sided river valley that opens out into a still narrow but very fertile alluvial plain which was
well exploited agriculturally by the Incas. Even within 30km or so of valley,
there are several microclimates allowing specializations in different fruits,

maizes and other important local plants. The river itself starts in the high Andes south of Cusco and is called the Vilcanota until the Sacred Valley; from here on down river it's known as the Río Urubamba, a magnificent and energetic river which flows on right down into the jungle to merge with other major headwaters of the Amazon.

Standing guard over the two extremes of the Sacred Valley, the ancient **Inca citadels** of Pisac and Ollantaytambo perch high above the stunning Río Vilcanota-Urubamba and are among the most evocative ruins in Peru. **Pisac** itself is a small, pretty town just 30km northeast of Cusco, close to the end of the Río Vilcanota's wild run from Urcos. Further downstream are the ancient villages of **Calca**, **Yucay** and **Urubamba**, the last of which has the most visitors' facilities plus a developing reputation as a spiritual and meditative centre, yet somehow still retains its traditional Andean charm. At the far northern end of the Sacred Valley, even the magnificent ancient town of **Ollantaytambo** is overwhelmed by the astounding temple-fortress clinging to the sheer cliffs beside it. The town is a very pleasant place to spend some time, perhaps taking a tent and trekking above one of the Urubamba's minor tributaries, or following the **Inca Trail** up to Machu Picchu.

Beyond Ollantaytambo the route becomes too tortuous for any road to follow. Here, the valley closes in around the rail tracks, the Río Urubamba begins to race and twist below **Machu Picchu** itself, the most famous ruin in South America and a place that – no matter how jaded you are or how commercial it seems – is never a disappointment. If you're tempted to explore further afield, the bus journey from Ollantaytambo to Chaullay is exciting, following a precipitous but newly laid road. From Chaullay you can set out for the remote ruins of **Vilcabamba**, the legendary refuge of the last rebel Incas, set in superb hiking country. The main road from Chaullay, however, continues to descend towards the jungle, following the presently defunct rail line to the tropical town of Quillabamba, springboard to the Amazon rainforest.

Getting to the Sacred Valley and Machu Picchu

The classic way to see the Sacred Valley – and Machu Picchu as well – is to take the three- to five-day **hike** along the stirring Inca Trail, which you can do with an official guide or by taking one of the guided treks offered by the many operators in Cusco (see p.151). By road, you can follow the Sacred Valley only as far as Ollantaytambo: the Inca Trail starts just a few kilometres further on.

By bus

Buses for Ollantaytambo leave from the Terminal Terrestre and in the afternoons from a depot at Avenida Grau 525 at 4pm, 5pm and 5.30pm ($1.80); apart from here, near the Puente Grau you'll sometimes find colectivos taking people in minibuses to Ollantaytambo for $3 (1hr 10min). Once in the valley, there are plenty of pickup points in Pisac, Calca and Urubamba. **Buses** depart Cusco from the depot at Avenida Grau 525 (℡805639) for Urubamba ($1) via Chincheros (50¢) – you only pay according to where you're going to – every fifteen minutes from about 5am daily. Some buses from here that are marked for Puputi pass by Tambo Machay and Pisac. Smaller buses leave every thirty minutes for Pisac and Calca (via Tambo Machay) from Tullumayu 207 most mornings, less frequently in afternoons. (**Taxis** to Pisac cost more – about $10 one way.) You can also hail one of the many cheap buses or colectivos that con-

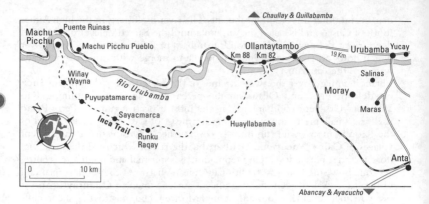

stantly drive up and down the main road. From Ollantaytambo, afternoon buses to Cusco ($2) leave regularly from the small yard just outside the train station, often coinciding with the train timetable. In the mornings they mostly depart from Ollantaytambo's main plaza.

By train

The **train** connects Cusco with Ollantaytambo as well as Machu Picchu, in addition to a recently reopened line to Urubamba (only used in high season, see Backpacker Shuttle below). The train trip from Cusco all the way to Machu Picchu is almost as spectacular as walking the Inca Trail, but buy your tickets well in advance (see Listings, p.149) as carriages are often fully booked in high season. There are three tourist classes: **Vistadome** ($86 return/$50 one way all the way from Cusco, departing 6am, arriving 9.15am and starting return journey at 3pm; or $67 return/$40 one way from Ollantaytambo to Machu Picchu, departing at 7.05am, 10.30am and 2.50pm, returning at 8.55am, 1.20pm and 4.45pm), **Backpacker** ($58 return/$34 one way from Cusco); **Backpacker Shuttle**, which only operates in high season (departs from Urubamba via Ollantaytambo to Machu Picchu, leaving 9.25am, arriving 11am, return departure at 5pm from Machu Picchu). All Cusco departures for Machu Picchu leave from San Pedro station; it's sometimes possible to queue from 5am to buy tickets for the same day but it's less stressful if you book in advance from the PeruRail office at Huanchac station, Avenida Pachacutec ℡238722 or 221992, Ⓦwww.perurail.com. The Backpacker train (not the shuttle) takes about ninety minutes to reach Ollantaytambo, then another ninety on to Machu Picchu. There is a slower local train, but this is meant for Peruvians and local people living and working in the valley and it's difficult to buy the much cheaper tickets as a gringo.

By air

A much more expensive alternative (though even more dramatic) means of transport direct to Machu Picchu is to fly into the valley **by helicopter**; Helicusco, Calle Triunfo 379 (℡243635, Ⓕ227283, Ⓦwww.rcp.net.pe /HELICUSCO), offer the 25-minute flight there from Cusco for $85 ($150 return). Fears have been voiced about detrimental effects large helicopters might have on both the stone fabric of ancient Machu Picchu and its reputed mystical energies. However, they never venture nearer than a couple of kilometres from the most important Inca ruins.

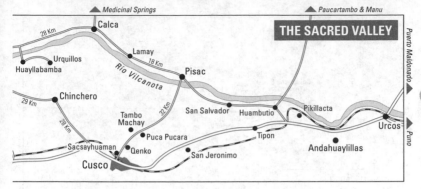

Pisac

A vital Inca road once snaked its way up the canyon that enters the Sacred Valley at **PISAC**, and the ruined **citadel** which sits at the entrance to the gorge controlled a strategic route connecting the Inca Empire with Paucartambo, on the borders of the eastern jungle. Nowadays, less than an hour by bus from Cusco, Pisac is best known for its thriving Tuesday, Thursday and Sunday morning **market**, held in the town's main square, the Plaza Constitución, where you can buy hand-painted ceramic beads and pick up the occasional bargain. When the market's not on, there are still a number of excellent artesania shops, particularly along Calle Bolognesi, which connects the Sacred Valley road and river bridge with the plaza. The **Iglesia San Pedro Apóstol**, on the plaza, is an unusually narrow concrete church, rather overshadowed by the lovely nearby trees and the bustle of commerce going on in front of it. The main local **fiesta** – Virgen del Carmen (July 16–18) – is a good alternative to the simultaneous but more remote Paucartambo festival of the same name, with processions, music, dance groups, the usual firecracker celebrations, and food stalls around the plaza.

The citadel

It takes a good ninety minutes to climb directly to the **citadel** (daily 7am–5.30pm; entry by Cusco Tourist Ticket, see p.123), heading up through the agricultural terraces still in use at the back of Plaza Constitución, but the astounding views and ancient ruins on display are more than worth it. Alternatively, you can catch a bus (20¢) from the end of Calle Mariscal Castilla (the road that runs along the eastern edge of the plaza), or take a taxi, colectivo or pickup ($3–5) from the main road, on the corner of Calle Bolognesi and close to the Urubamba bridge; it's usually possible to share the cost on market days, when the town is busier. Set high above a valley floor patchworked by patterned fields and rimmed by centuries of terracing amid giant landslides, the stonework (water ducts and steps have been cut out of solid rock) and panoramas at the citadel are magnificent. A semicircle of buildings is gracefully positioned on a large natural balcony under row upon row of fine stone terraces thought to represent a partridge's wing (*pisac* meaning "partridge").

In the upper sector of the ruins, the citadel's **Temple of the Sun** is the equal of anything at Machu Picchu and more than repays the exertions of the steep

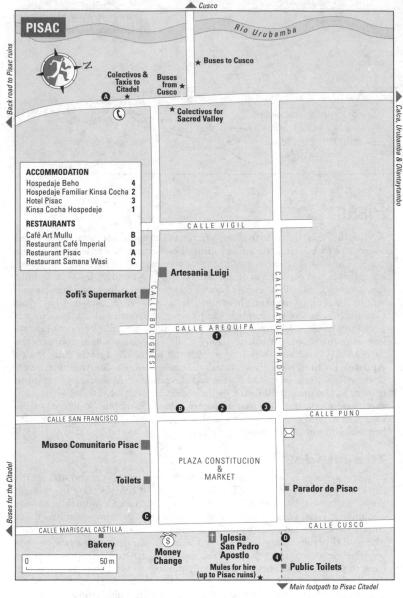

climb. Reached by many of the dozens of paths that criss-cross their way up through the citadel, it's poised in a flattish saddle on a great spur protruding north–south into the Sacred Valley. The temple was built around an outcrop of volcanic rock, its peak carved into a "hitching post" for the sun. The "hitching post" alone is intriguing: the angles of its base suggest that it may have been used for keeping track of important stars, or for calculating the changing seasons with the accuracy so critical to the smooth running of the Inca Empire. Above the temple lie still more ruins, largely unexcavated, and among the higher crevices and rocky overhangs several ancient burial sites are hidden.

Practicalities

The only time when **accommodation** in Pisac may be hard to find is in September, when the village fills up with pilgrims heading to the nearby sanctuary of Huanca, home of a small shrine which is very sacred to local inhabitants. The most luxurious place to stay is the *Hotel Royal Inca* (☎203064, ⓕ203067, ⓦwww.royalinkahotel.com; ➌), which has a pool and all mod cons, though it's 2km out of the village on the long road that winds up towards the ruins. About 1km down the valley from Pisac on the main road towards Urubamba there's also the pleasant *Inti Wasi* (☎203047, ⓕ203170, ⓔintiwasi@latinmail.com; ➎), which has a restaurant and offers bungalow-style accommodation. In Pisac itself there's a good selection of places to stay. By far the most agreeable is the *Hotel Pisac*, Plaza Constitución 333 (☎203058; ➌), with lavishly decorated bedrooms (with or without private bath) and a rock-heated sauna, plus good breakfasts and lunches, including vegetarian food (restaurant open to non-residents). They also rent out mountain bikes and can book tours to nearby ruins and change money. Just off the plaza, the *Hospedaje Beho* (☎/ⓕ203001; ➋) has a large patio with rooms set around it, with or without private bath, plus a few more rooms upstairs, and occasional hot water. Close to the plaza, the friendly *Kinsa Cocha Hospedaje*, Calle Arequipa 307 (☎203101; ➊), offers simple rooms. Alternatively, you can usually **rent rooms** at low prices from villagers (ask for details at the *Restaurant Samana Wasi*; see below), or there is a **campsite** (ask at the *Kinsa Cocha Hospedaje* for details).

There are a few decent **restaurants** in Pisac, but it's hard to beat the excellent *Restaurant Samana Wasi*, on the corner of Plaza Constitución at no. 509, with a pleasant little courtyard out the back and very tasty trout, salad and fried potatoes. The *Honey Café*, at the corner of Bolognesi and the plaza, is okay for cheap set lunches, but cheaper and better is the *Restaurant Pisac*, a dingy yet friendly place back down on the main road by the taxis at no. 147, which also serves generous portions of other standard basic Peruvian fare. The *Restaurant Café Imperial,* on the opposite side of the plaza from the *Restaurant Samana Wasi*, serves reasonable lunches of local dishes for around $5, while *Café Art Mullu* also on the the plaza, by the corner with Calle Bolognesi, is a groovy little place offering meals, snacks – particularly fine pizzas - and drinks. There's a good **shop**, Doña Clorinda, at Bolognesi 592, on the corner of the plaza, selling great cakes, and a traditional **bakery** with an adobe oven just over the plaza at the corner of Puno with Manuel Prado. Among the best shops for buying locally crafted beads and artesania are the unnamed *tienda* at Bolognesi 569 and also the unnumbered Artesania Luigi in the second block of Bolognesi, just down from Sofi's Supermarket. **Money changing** can be had in the jeweller's shop on the corner of the plaza close to *Samana Wasi*, and there's a **post office** selling postcards and artesania, on the corner of the plaza where Intihuatana meets Calle Comercio.

From Pisac to Urubamba

The first significant village between Pisac and Urubamba is **Lamay**, known for its medicinal springs, just 3km away. High above this village, on the other side of the Río Vilcanota and just out of sight, are the beautiful Inca terraces of Huchiq'osqo. A little further down the road you come to the larger village of **CALCA**, with the popular thermal baths of Machacanca within ninety minutes' walk of the modern settlement, signposted from the town and to which combi colectivos (30¢; a 15min trip) run quite frequently, particularly on Sunday. Situated under the hanging glaciers of Mount Sahuasiray, this place was favoured by the Incas for the fertility of its soil, and you can still see plenty of maize cultivation. Moving down the valley from here the climate improves and you see pears, peaches and cherries growing in abundance, and in July and August vast piles of maize sit beside the road waiting to be used as cattle feed.

YUCAY, the next major settlement before you get to Urubamba, had its moment in Peruvian history when, under the Incas, Huayna Capac, father of Huascar and Atahualpa, had his palace here, and you can observe the ruined but finely dressed stone walls of another Inca palace (probably the country home of Sayri Tupac though also associated with an Inca princess) located on the Plaza Manco II. If you fancy a hike, you can also follow the stream up behind the town to the village of San Juan. There are a couple of good **hostels** in Yucay; the *Hostal Y'llary*, Plaza Manco II 107 (☎226607 or 201112; ❺), is very friendly, comfortable and excellent value with private bathrooms, a lovely garden and large rooms in an attractive old building. More luxurious, the *Sonesta Posada del Inca*, Plaza Manco II (☎201107, ℉201345, ⓦwww.sonesta.com; ❽), is based in a beautifully converted eighteenth-century monastery that houses a small museum (open to non-residents) of fine precious metal objects and ceramics. The nearby *Posada del Libertador* (☎201115, ℉201116; ❻) is another fine colonial mansion noted for accommodating Simon Bolivar when he was in the region with leaders of Peru's patriot army for the public declaration and royal oath of independence sworn in Cusco in 1825. The *Casa Luna* **restaurant**, Plaza Manco II 107, right next to the *Libertador*, offers great pizzas, sandwiches and drinks in a pleasant environment with Internet and fax services, bike rental, 4WD tours and also house and bungalow accommodation (❸).

Urubamba and around

URUBAMBA, about 80km from Cusco via Pisac or around 60km via Chinchero, is only a short way down the main road from Yucay's Plaza Manco II, and here the Río Vilcanota becomes the Río Urubamba (though many people still refer to this stretch as the Vilcanota). Although it has little in the way of obvious historic interest, the town is well endowed with tourist facilities and is situated in the shadow of the beautiful Chicon and Pumahuanca glaciers.

The Plaza de Armas is laid-back and attractive, with palm trees and a couple of pines surrounded by interesting topiary. At the heart of the plaza is a small fountain topped by a maize plant sculpture, but it is dominated by the red sandstone **Iglesia San Pedro** with its stacked columns below two small belfries. The church's cool interior has a vast three-tier gold-leaf altar, and at midday, light streams through the glass-topped cupola. At weekends there's a large **market** on Jirón Palacio; and at the large **ceramic workshops** set around a lovely garden at Avenida Berriozabal 111 (☎201002, ℉201177), new and ancient techniques are used to produce colourful, Amerindian-inspired items for sale.

Because of its convenient location and plentiful facilities, Urubamba makes an ideal base from which to **explore** the mountains and lower hills around the

Sacred Valley, which are filled with sites of jaw-dropping splendour. The eastern side of the valley is formed by the Cordillera Urubamba, a range of snow-capped peaks dominated by the summits of Chicon and Veronica. Many of the ravines can be hiked, alone or with local guides (found only through the main hotels and hospedajes), and on the trek up from the town you'll have stupendous views of Chicon. **Moray**, a stunning Inca site, part agricultural centre and part ceremonial, lies about 6km north of Maras village on the Chinchero side of the river, within a two- to three-hour walk from Urubamba. The ruins are deep, bowl-like depressions in the earth, the largest comprising seven concentric circular stone terraces, facing inward and diminishing in radius like a multi-layered roulette wheel.

Also within walking distance, the salt pans of **Salinas**, still in use after more than four hundred years, are situated only a short distance from the village of Tarabamba, 6km along the road from Urubamba to Ollantaytambo. Cross the river by the footbridge in the village, turn right, then after a little over 100m downstream along the riverbank, turn left past the cemetery and up the canyon along the salty creek. After this you cross the stream and follow the path cut into the cliffside to reach the salt pans, which are soon visible but still a considerable uphill hike away. The trail offers spectacular views of the valley and mountains. The Inca salt pans are set gracefully against an imposing mountain backdrop.

Practicalities

Regular **buses** connect Urubamba with Cusco, Pisac, Calca and Ollantaytambo. Buses for Ollantaytambo, Cusco and Chinchero leave regularly from Terminal Terrestre, on the main road more or less opposite the *Hotel Incaland*. The *Neuvo Mundo Café* (see below) has some local **tourist information**.

The two most upmarket **accommodation** options in town are *Hotel San Augustin*, Km 69, Panamerican Highway (℗201025; ❼), twenty minutes' walk down the main road towards Cusco, just beyond the bridge over the Río Urubamba, which boasts a small pool and a popular restaurant (delicious buffet

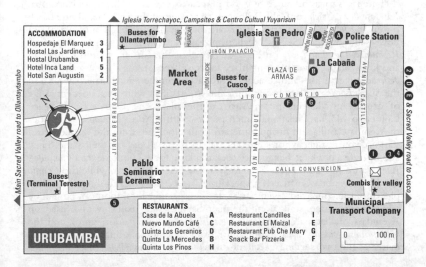

lunches served Tues, Thurs & Sun); and the *Hotel Incaland*, on Avenida Ferrocarril (☎201071 or 201126, ℱ201071, ⓦwww.enperu.com; ❽), a large Best Western hotel and conference centre with Internet access, a pool and tennis courts, which has plans to develop as a spa centre and has its own rail link to Machu Picchu on which it sometimes operates the Backpacker Shuttle (see p.154). The basic but friendly and cheaper *Hostal Urubamba*, Jirón Bolognesi 665 (no phone; ❶), is behind the police station, one and a half blocks from the Plaza de Armas. The *Hospedaje El Marquez*, Convención 429 (☎201304; ❶), is a clean, family-run hostel, but at no. 459 the *Hostal Las Jardines* (no phone; ❷) has better rooms based around a lovely garden. The *Posada Las 3 Marias*, Jirón Zavala 307 (☎201006 or in Cusco at ☎225252), has new, very clean and intimate accommodation, large enough for up to sixteen people over several rooms (❸).

In recent years the highly rural valley areas in the hills behind Urubamba and under the glaciated peaks have begun to develop smaller rural accommodation units, some of them offering specialist workshops. The *Yuyarisun Workshops*, Apartado Postal 112, Correo Central, Cusco (☎683438; ❶–❷), offer both rooms and camping in a tranquil rural spot about 2km from Urubamba on the Pumahuanca road, by the Q'erokancha canal. *Yuyarisun* features comfortable rooms, a large garden, and a wooden guesthouse (accessed by ladder) built atop a vast boulder; the cooking is vegetarian and the workshops employ local people to make beautiful hand-made wooden toys, textiles and clothes (generally on sale in Pisac market). About another 2km up the valley from *Yuyarisun* is the *Guest House Las Chullpas* (☎685713 or 695030, ⓦwww.chullpas.com; ❶–❸), a rustic vegetarian hostel with hot water, gardens, hammocks and free use of kitchen. *Las Chullpas* also runs natural medicine lessons, sweat lodges, mountain-bike tours, hikes in Pumahuanca valley and treks around the Lares area (a remote Andean valley located to the east of the glacial peaks of the Sacred Valley). **Camping** is available at *Camping Los Cedros* ($3 per tent) and *Los Girasoles* ($2.50 per person), which also has private bungalows (❸) and shower facilities. Both sites are on the Pumahuanca road, a few blocks beyond Iglesia Torrechayoc, a medium-sized church on the northern edge of town, and are signposted just as the road leaves the built-up area of Urubamba.

There is a surprising range of good **places to eat** in and around Urubamba. *La Casa de la Abuela*, in Calle Bolognesi to the left of the church and one block up on the left, is a very friendly restaurant that has a lovely courtyard full of flowers and trees, and serves excellent pizzas and very good lasagna. Or try the *Restaurant Pub Che Mary* on Plaza de Armas at the corner of Jirón Comercio and Jirón Grau, a good meeting place for travellers, serving alpaca steaks, *ponche de leche*, juices, drinks and ceviche. More or less on the same corner, there's also the *Snack Bar Pizzeria*, at Jirón Comercio (☎201554), which has a decent range of drinks and delivers pizza. Also on the plaza, the *Quinta La Mercedes*, Comercio 445, has cheap, set-lunch menus. At the *Nuevo Mundo Café*, corner of Avenida Castilla and Jirón Comercio (four blocks up from the Texaco petrol station), you can get wholesome vegetarian meals all day on their patio. They also operate a book exchange and stock trekking food. The *Restaurant Candilles*, Avenida Castilla 207, serves good, reasonably priced chicken, while the *Quinta Los Pinos,* Avenida Castilla 812, specializes in excellent local dishes, served in a pleasant little courtyard. Even better (though pricier) local food can be had by taking a ten-minute walk along the main Sacred Valley road towards Cusco, on Avenida Conchatupa at the *Restaurant El Maizal* (daily noon–6pm), and the *Quinta Los Geranios* (daily noon–7pm). Both are enjoyable, but *Los Geranios* the better of the two, serving excellent dishes such as *rocoto relleno, chupe de quinoa* and *asado a la olla* in a splendid, but usually busy, garden environment. There's also a reasonably good **mini-market**, La Cabana, on the Plaza de Armas.

Urubamba is home to one of Peru's premier **horse-riding** centres, the Perol Chico, Jirón Grau 203 (☎201694, ✆info@perolchico.com), which offers one-to twelve-day luxury horseback riding tours on pure-bred, quality Peruvian *caballos de paso*.

Ollantaytambo and around

On the approach to **OLLANTAYTAMBO** from Urubamba, the river runs smoothly between a series of impressive Inca terraces that gradually diminish in size as the slopes get steeper and rockier. Just before the town, the rail tracks reappear and the road climbs a small hill to an ancient plaza. The backstreets radiating up from the plaza are littered with well built stone water channels, which still come in very handy during the rainy season, carrying the gushing streams tidily away from the town and down to the Urubamba river. Ollantaytambo was built as an Inca administrative centre rather than a town and is laid out in the form of a maize corn cob: it's one of the few surviving examples of an Inca grid system, with a plan that can be seen from vantage points high above it, especially from the hill opposite the fortress. An incredibly fertile sector of the Urubamba valley, at 2800m above sea level and with temperatures of 11–23°C, with good alluvial soils and water resources, this area was also the gateway to the Antisuyo (the Amazon corner of the Inca Empire) and a centre for tribute-gathering from the surrounding valleys. Beyond Ollantaytambo, the Sacred Valley becomes a subtropical, raging river course, surrounded by towering mountains and dominated by the snowcapped peak of Salcantay.

A very traditional little place, it's worth stopping over for a few days and is particularly colourful during its **fiestas** (the Festival of the Cross, Corpus Christi and Ollantaytambo Raymi fiesta – generally on the Sunday after Cusco's Inti Raymi), or at Christmas, when locals wear flowers and decorative grasses in their hats. On the Fiesta de Reyes, around January 6, there's a solemn procession around town of the three *Niños Reyes* (Child Kings), sacred effigies, one of which is brought down from the sacred site of Marcaquocha, about 10km away in the Patacancha valley, the day before. Many local women still wear traditional clothing and it's common to see them in the main plaza with their intricately woven *manta* shawls, black and red skirts with colourful zigzag patterns, and inverted red and black hats.

Some history

The valley here was occupied by a number of pre-Inca cultures, notably the Chanapata (800–300 BC), the Qotacalla (500–900 AD) and the Killki (900–1420 AD), after which the Incas dominated only until the 1530s, when the Spanish arrived. Legend has it that **Ollantay** was a rebel Inca general who took arms against Pachacutec over the affections of the Lord Inca's daughter, the Nusta Cusi Collyu. What is definite is that a fourteen-kilometre canal, that still feeds the town today, was built to bring water here from the Laguna de Yanacocha, which was probably Pachacutec's private estate. The later Inca Huayna Capac is thought to have been responsible for the trapezoidal Plaza Maynyaraqui and the largely unfinished but impressive and megalithic temples. As strategic protection for the entrance to the lower Urubamba Valley and an alternative gateway into the Amazon via the Pantiacalla pass, this was the only Inca stronghold to have resisted persistent Spanish attacks. After the unsuccessful siege of Cusco in 1536–37 (as described on p.120), the rebel Inca **Manco** and his die-hard force withdrew here, with Hernando Pizarro, some seventy horsemen, thirty foot soldiers and a large contingent of native forces in hot pursuit. But as they approached, they found that not only had the Incas diverted the Río Patacancha to make the valley below the fortress impassable, but that they had also joined forces with neighbouring jungle tribes to form an army so great in numbers that they supposedly overflowed the valley sides. After several desperate attempts to storm the stronghold, Pizarro and his men uncharacteristically slunk away under cover of darkness, leaving much of their equipment behind. However, the Spanish came back with reinforcements, and in 1537 Manco retreated further down the valley to Vitcos and Vilcabamba. In 1540, Ollantaytambo was entrusted to Hernán Pizarro, brother of the conquistador leader.

During the next 400 years, Ollantaytambo remained a large agricultural town, little more than a quiet market place and nodal point for a wide-ranging peasant population. Since the agrarian reform of 1968, Ollantaytambo has been divided into five rural communities, each with an elected president and a committee of *reidores* who represent peasant interests within local government. Outside of bus and train connection times for Machu Picchu, it's still a quiet town today, though the peace was shattered once or twice by terrorist raids on the police station in the plaza during the late 1980s and early 1990s. Generally a very friendly town, well served with hostels and cafés, it is also a popular base for rafting groups.

The Town

The main focuses of activity in town are the main **plaza** – the heart of civic life and the scene of traditional folk dancing during festive occasions – the Inca fortress and the train station. The useful **Ollantaytambo Heritage Trail** helps you find most of the important sites with a series of blue plaques around town. Close to the central plaza there's the recently refurbished **CATCCO Museum** (Tues–Sun 10am–1pm & 2–4pm; $1.75), a small but very interesting museum containing interpretative exhibits in Spanish and English about local history, culture, archeology and natural history. It also has a ceramic workshop where you can buy some good pottery.

Downhill from the plaza, just across the Río Patacancha, is the old Inca **Plaza Mañya Raquy**, dominated by the fortress. There are a few artesania shops and stalls in here, plus the town's attractive church, the Templo de Santiago Apóstol, built in 1620 with its almost Inca-style stone belfry containing two great bells supported on an ancient timber. The church's front entrance is surrounded by simple yet attractive *mestizo* floral relief painted in red and cream. Climbing up through the **fortress** (daily 7am–5.30pm; $4.50, or by Cusco Tourist Ticket, see p.123), the solid stone terraces, jammed against the natural contours of the cliff, remain frighteningly impressive. Above them, huge red granite blocks mark the unfinished sun temple near the top, where, according to legend, the internal organs of mummified Incas were buried. A dangerous path leads from this upper level around the cliff towards a large sector of agricultural terracing which follows the Río Patacancha uphill, while at the bottom you can still make out the shape of a large Inca plaza, through which stone aqueducts carried the water supply. Below the ruins are Andenes de Mollequasa **terraces** which, when viewed

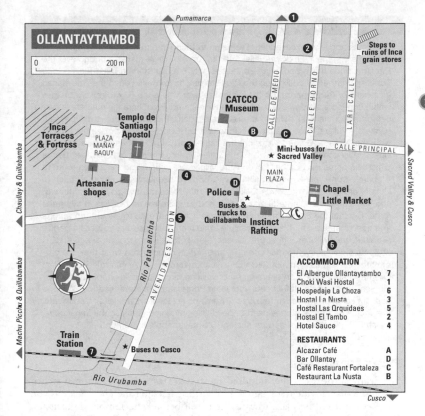

OLLANTAYTAMBO

0   200 m

Pumamarca

Steps to
ruins of Inca
grain stores

CALLE DE MEDIO

CALLE HORNO

LARI CALLE

CATCCO
Museum

Templo de
Santiago
Apostol

Inca
Terraces
& Fortress

PLAZA
MAÑAY
RAQUY

CALLE PRINCIPAL

Mini-buses for
★ Sacred Valley

MAIN
PLAZA

Artesania
shops

Police

Chapel
Little Market

Buses &
trucks to
Quillabamba

★

Instinct
Rafting

Río Patacancha

AVENIDA ESTACION

N

Train
Station

★ Buses to Cusco

Río Urubamba

Chaullay & Quillabamba

Machu Picchu & Quillabamba

Sacred Valley & Cusco

Cusco

ACCOMMODATION	
El Albergue Ollantaytambo	7
Choki Wasi Hostal	1
Hospedaje La Choza	6
Hostal La Nusta	3
Hostal Las Orquidaes	5
Hostal El Tambo	2
Hotel Sauce	4

RESTAURANTS	
Alcazar Café	A
Bar Ollantay	D
Café Restaurant Fortaleza	C
Restaurant La Nusta	B

from the other side of the Urubamba valley (a 20min walk up the track from
the train station), look like a pyramid.

High up over the other side of the Río Patacancha, behind the town, are
rows of **ruined buildings** originally thought to have been prisons but now
considered likely to have been granaries. In front of these, it's quite easy to
make out a gigantic, rather grumpy-looking profile of a face carved out of the
rock, possibly an **Inca sculpture** of Wiraccochan, the mythical messenger
from Wiraccocha, the major creator god of Peru. According to sixteenth- and
seventeenth-century histories, such an image was indeed once carved, representing him as a man of great authority; this particular image's frown certainly implies presence, and this part of the mountain was also known as
Wiraccochan Orcco ("peak of Wiraccocha's messenger"). From here, looking
back towards the main Ollantaytambo fortress, it's possible to see the mountain, rocks and terracing forming the image of a mother llama with a young
llama, apparently representing the myth of Catachillay, which relates to the
water cycle and the Milky Way. *The Sacred Valley of the Incas – Myths and
Symbols* (available in most Cusco bookshops), written by a couple of Cusco
archeologists, is good for its useful identification and interesting interpretations of sites in this part of the valley.

Trekking around Ollantaytambo

Ollantaytambo is an excellent spot to begin **trekking** into the hills. One possibility is to head along the main down-valley road to Km 82, where there's a bridge over the Río Urubamba that's becoming an increasingly popular starting point for the **Inca Trail**. Alternatively, travelling up the Río Patacancha will take you to the little-visited Inca ruins of **Pumamarca**, on the left of the river where the Río Yurumayu merges with it under the shadows of the Nevada Helancoma. From here the main track carries on along the right bank of the Río Patacancha through various small peasant hamlets – Pullata, Colqueracay, Maracocha and Huilloc – before crossing the pass, with the Nevada Colque Cruz on the right-hand side. It then follows the ríos Huacahuasi and Tropoche down to the valley and community of Lares, just before which are some Inca baths. Beyond the village are several more ruins en route to Ampares, from where you can either walk back to Urubamba, go by road back to Cusco, or head down towards Quillabamba. It's at least a two-day walk one way, and you'll need camping equipment and food as there are no facilities at all on the route. Contact the South American Explorers' Club in Cusco for recent trip reports and good maps to use. It's also possible to do it on horseback, or you can organize a guided trek with an agency in Cusco (see p.151). The local Museo CATCCO (☎204024, ©otikary@hotmail.com)   also has information on what they are promoting as Rutas Ancestrales de Ollantaytambo – Ancestral Routes of Ollantaytambo. This is an entire menu of walking circuits that link important archeological sites and beautiful spots, including Pumamarca, the pre-Inca fort; Wiloc, a peasant community descended directly from ancient local *ayllus* (clans); Cachiccata, the source of the fine stones used to build Ollantaytambo; and Laguna Yanacocha, which is where the canal serving ancient Ollantaytambo started from.

Practicalities

The **train station** is a few hundred metres down Avenida Estación which is little more than a wide track entered by turning left after the *Hotel Sauce* as you come down from the plaza towards (but well before) the Templo de Santiago Apóstol; by **road**, you'll arrive at the main plaza. **Tourist information** can be obtained from the CATCCO Museum, or call ☎204024. The **telephone** and **post offices** are on the main plaza. Ollantaytambo is something of a centre for **river rafting**, with a Rafting Adventure office on the main plaza; contact INSTINCT in Cusco (see p.151), for information in advance. The river around Ollantaytambo is class 2–3 in dry season and 3–4 during the rainy period (Nov–March).

There are several **hotels**, but the best option is the attractive *El Albergue Ollantaytambo*, Casilla 784 (☎204014; ❸, discounts to families), which is located right next to the river and the train station at the bottom end of town (the entrance is on the station platform) – contact them well in advance during the high season. Its spacious rooms are stylishly rustic, plus there's a sauna, and they serve tasty breakfasts. For full meals (available to non-guests) you need to book in advance. Further up the track from the station towards the town, the *Hostal Las Orquídeas* (☎204032; ❸) offers small rooms set around a courtyard, with breakfasts available. The hospitable and good-value *Hostal La Ñusta*, on Carretera Ocobamba (☎204035 or 204077; ❷), has simple rooms, a *comedor* (dining room), and a patio offering excellent views across to the mountains and the Wiraccochan face (see p.163). The owner also hires out horses at $10 a day (Pumamarca is reachable in about two hours). Similar, but slightly more comfortable for the same price, there's the *Choki Wasi*, Calle Medio some two blocks from the plaza (no phone; ❷); breakfast is available and it's nicely furnished. Nearby is the modern and rather plush *Hotel Sauce*, Ventideiro 248 (☎204044, ⓕ204048, ⓔhostalsauce@tsi.com.pe; ⓻), which has elegant rooms with fine views. Southeast of the main plaza, the *Hospedaje La Choza*, in Zona Pilquahuasi (no phone; ⓷), is modern but charmless and a little chaotic. The basic, family-run *Hostal El Tambo* (no phone; ⓶), on Calle Horno, just off the main plaza behind some classical Inca stone walls, is the cheapest accommodation in town; it's very rustic and homely, but extremely basic.

For a decent **meal**, it's hard to beat *El Albergue* (see above), though there are a couple of good-value cafés in the main plaza, notably the *Bar Ollantay*, often serving superb *quinoa* soup (made from *quinoa* grains which grow around here in the high Andes) as part of its set-lunch menus. The plaza is home to a few gringo-oriented cafés, all with similar menus and most with vegetarian options. These include the *Café Restaurant Fortaleza* (☎204047), which serves good pancakes and inexpensive pizzas, and the *Restaurant La Ñusta* (☎204035 or 204077), a very friendly café/shop with excellent breakfast, snacks and soups made from fresh vegetables (unusual for this region). The *Alcazar Café*, on Calle Medio (☎204034), just a couple of short blocks off the plaza, serves full meals and snacks but doesn't stay open very late. If you want to try the local *chicha* maize beer, pop into any of the private houses displaying a red plastic bag on a pole outside the door – the beer is cheap and the hosts usually very friendly and great fun. In the old days, red flowers were used rather than plastic bags to indicate which family in the village had enough *chicha* beer to share with friends and neighbours.

The Inca Trail

Although just one of a multitude of paths across remote areas of the Andes, what makes the world-famous **Inca Trail** so popular is the fabulous treasure of **Machu Picchu** at the end. That's not to say you won't see plenty of wonders along the way. The Inca Trail is set in the **Santuario Histórico de Machu Picchu** (National Sanctuary of Machu Picchu), an area of more than 32,000 hectares set apart by the Peruvian state to protect its range of ecological niches from 6271m at the high Andean glacial peak of Nevado Salcantay down to Amazon cloud forest at less than 2000m in Aguas Calientes at the foot of Machu Picchu. Acting as a bio-corridor between the Cusco Andes, the Sacred Valley and the lowland Amazon forest, the sanctuary possesses over 370 species of birds, 47 mammal species, and over 700 butterfly species. Some of the more notable residents include the cock-of-the-rock (*Rupicola Peruviana*, known as tunkis here), spectacled bear (*Tremarctos ornatus*) and condor (*Vultur gryphus*). Not to mention around 300 different species of orchids hidden up in the trees of the cloud forest.

It's important to choose your **season** for hiking the Inca Trail. Local tradition states that the perfect time is around the full moon, though May is the best month, with clear views, fine weather and verdant surroundings. Between June and September it's usually a pretty cosmopolitan stretch of mountainside, with travellers from all over the globe converging on Machu Picchu the hard way, but from mid-June to early August the trail is too busy (and the campsites are noisy), especially on the last stretch. From October until April, in the rainy season, it's far less crowded but also, naturally, very wet.

The sanctuary authorities (the Unidad de Gestión del Santuario Histórico de Machu Picchu) have imposed a limit of up to 500 trekkers a day on the Inca

Trail. In addition, they have made it mandatory for trekkers to go with a **tour or licensed guide**. Most people select a tour to suit them from among the 88 agencies registered for the Inca Trail (for a selection see p.151); the company will take care of everything including your registration, but they will need your details and probably an advance booking deposit. For a basic Inca Trail tour (note: some agency prices do and others do not include things like transport or entry to the Inca Trail and Machu Picchu in their price offers) you can expect to pay $60–$250 for a three- or four- day trek, though competition between the agencies has seen the price drop below $50 at times, a reduction that manifests itself in a lower level of service and, not least, the wages of the porters. Frequently, those around the $200 mark offer good value in their guiding service, food, camping equipment quality and the all-inclusiveness of their price offers. It's a good idea to check the precise details of exactly what you are paying for and what, if anything, is not included in the price. Additionally, names and passport or identity numbers of everyone going on the trek now need to be **registered** in Cusco at least 36 hours before departure by your tour company; in effect this means at least a three-day wait, and some of the better companies recommend a minimum of five days' advance booking. This provides some time to acclimatize to the altitude before engaging in any serious physical activity, which you should be doing anyway, especially if you've flown straight up from sea level.

If you decide to do it independently with a guide, you will still benefit from a map, and you should be aware that within the Sanctuario Histórico de Machu Picchu, which incorporates the entire trail, you must only **camp** at a designated site. So many people walk this route every year that toilets have now been built, and hikers are strongly urged to take all their rubbish away with them – there's no room left for burying any more tin cans. It is still possible to hire **pack horses** ($5–10) – if they're available you'll spot them by the ticket office (or ask in Huayllabamba) close to the start of the trail – to help carry your rucksacks and equipment up to the first pass, but beyond this pack animals are not allowed. **Porters** charge $8–12 a day but clearly deserve more, and can be arranged through trekking agencies in Cusco (see p.151) or in the plaza at Ollantaytambo, distinguished by their colourful dress. If you can only spare three days for the walk, you'll be pushing it the whole way – it *can* be done but it's gruelling. It's far more pleasant to spend five or six days, taking in everything as you go along. Those trekkers who aim to do it in two and a half days should at least give themselves a head start by catching the afternoon train and heading up the Cusichaca Valley as far as possible the evening before.

Setting off

There are two **trailheads** for the Inca Trail. Organized tours usually approach the trail by road via Ollantaytambo and then take a dirt track from there to **Chilca**, which adds a few hours to the overall trek but forms the **road trailhead**. Minibuses from Ollantaytambo to Chilca cost $1. For independents and groups arriving by train, however, the **rail trailhead** is at Km 88 along the tracks from Cusco, at a barely noticeable stop announced by the train guard. Have your gear ready to throw off the steps, since the train pulls up only for a few brief seconds and you'll have to fight your way past sacks of grain, flapping chickens, men in ponchos, and women in voluminous skirts.

The recent hike in entrance fees to the trail ($50, or $25 for students, including Machu Picchu) caused an outcry by Peruvians since it effectively banned all but the very wealthy. Proponents of the new scheme say, however, that higher fees and greater restrictions are necessary to halt deterioration and overuse of the trail.

The Camino Sagrado de los Incas

The **Camino Sagrado de los Incas**, a truncated Inca Trail, starts at Km 104 of the Panamerican Highway, 8km from Machu Picchu. The footbridge here ($25 entry, free to under-12s, includes Machu Picchu) leads to a steep climb (3–4hr) past Chachabamba to reach Wiñay Wayna (see p.169), where you join the reminder of the Inca Trail.

From the station, a footbridge sees you across the Río Urubamba. Once over the bridge the main path leads to the left, through a small eucalyptus wood, then around the base of the Inca ruins of Llactapata (worth a visit for archeology enthusiasts, though most people save their energy for the trail and other archeological remains ahead) before crossing and then following the Río Cusichaca upstream along its left bank. It's a good two hours' steep climb to **Huayllabamba**, the only inhabited village on the route and the best place to hire horses or mules for the most difficult climb on the whole trail, the nearby **Dead Woman's Pass**. This section of the valley is rich in Inca terracing, from which rises an occasional ancient stone building. To reach Huayllabamba you have to cross a well-marked bridge onto the right bank of the Cusichaca. Many groups spend their first night at Huayllabamba **campsite**.

The first and second passes

The next five hours or so from Huayllabamba to the Abra de Huarmihuañusca, **the first pass** (4200m) and the highest point on the trail, is the hardest part of the walk – leave this (or at least some of it) for the second day, especially if you're feeling the effects of the altitude. There are three possible places to camp between Huayllabamba and Huarmihuañusca. The first and most popular, known as **Three White Stones**, is at the point where the trail crosses the Río Huayruro, just half a kilometre above its confluence with the Llullucha stream. The next camp, just below the **Pampa Llullucha**, has toilets and space for several tents. Another twenty minutes further up, there's plenty more camping space on the pampa within sight of the pass – a good spot for seeing rabbit-like *viscachas* playing among the rocks.

The views from the pass itself are stupendous, but if you're tempted to hang around savouring them, it's a good idea to sit well out of the cutting wind (many a trekker has caught a bad chill here). From here the trail drops steeply down, sticking to the left of the stream into the Pacamayo Valley where, by the river, there's an attractive spot to **camp**, and where you can see playful **spectacled bears** if you're very lucky, or take a break before continuing up a winding, tiring track towards the **second pass** – Abra de Runkuracay – just above the interesting circular ruins of the same name. About an hour beyond the second pass, a flight of stone steps leads up to the Inca ruins of **Sayacmarca**. This is an impressive spot to **camp**, near the remains of a stone aqueduct that supplied water to the ancient settlement (the best spots are by the stream just below the ruins).

From the third pass to Machu Picchu

From Sayacmarca, make your way gently down into increasingly dense cloud forest where delicate orchids and other exotic flora begin to appear among the trees. By the time you get to the **third pass** (which, compared to the previous two, has very little incline) you're following a fine, smoothly worn flagstone path where at one point an astonishing tunnel, carved through solid rock by

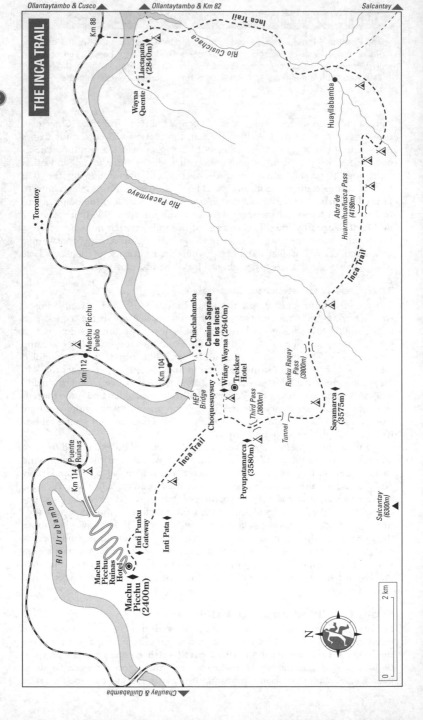

THE INCA TRAIL

Ollantaytambo & Cusco • Ollantaytambo & Km 82 • Salcantay

Km 88

Llactapata (2840m)

Wayna Quente

Inca Trail

Río Cusichaca

Huayllabamba

Torontoy

Río Pacaymayo

Abra de Huarmihuañusca Pass (4198m)

Inca Trail

Machu Picchu Pueblo

Km 112

Km 104

Chachabamba

Camino Sagrada de los Incas (2640m)

Choquesuysuy

Wiñay Wayna

HEP Bridge

Trekker Hotel

Third Pass (3600m)

Runku Raqay Pass (3800m)

Tunnel

Sayamarca (3575m)

Puente Ruinas

Km 114

Puyupatamarca (3580m)

Inca Trail

Machu Picchu Ruinas Hotel

Inti Punku Gateway

Inti Pata

Machu Picchu (2400m)

Río Urubamba

Salcantay (6300m)

2 km

N

0

Chaullay & Quillabamba

the Incas, lets you sidetrack an otherwise impossible climb. The trail winds down to the impressive ruin of **Puyupatamarca** – "Town Above the Clouds" – where there are five small stone baths and in the wet season constant fresh running water. There are places to **camp** actually on the pass (ie above the ruins), commanding stunning views across the Urubamba valley and, in the other direction, towards the snowcaps of Salcantay (Wild Mountain): this is probably one of the most magical camps on the trail (given good weather), and it's not unusual to see deer feeding here.

It's a very rough, two- or three-hour descent along a non-Inca track to the next ruin, a citadel almost as impressive as Machu Picchu, **Wiñay Wayna** – "Forever Young" – another place with fresh water. These days there's an official *Trekker Hotel* here (no phone; $8 a bed; $3 floor space; $1 for a hot shower) and restaurant too – nothing splendid, but with a welcome supply of cool drinks.

Wiñay Wayna was a companion site for Machu Picchu, just two hours' walk away. Comsisting of only two major groups of architectural structures – a lower and an upper sector – its most visible features are stone baths with apparently as many as nineteen springs feeding them, all set amidst several layers of fine Inca terracing. Nearby there's also a small waterfall created by streams coming down from the heights of Puyupatamarca. As it's used today, Wiñay Wayna was probably used as a washing, cleansing and resting point for travellers before their arrival at the grand Machu Picchu citadel.

This is usually the spot for the last night of camping, and, especially in high season, the crowds mean that it's a good idea to pitch your tent soon after lunch, but don't be surprised if someone pitches their tent right across your doorway. To reach Machu Picchu for sunrise the next day you'll have to get up very early with a flashlight to avoid the rush.

A well-marked track from Wiñay Wayna takes a right fork for about two more hours through sumptuous vegetated slopes to **Intipunku**, for your first sight of Machu Picchu – a stupendous moment, however exhausted you might be. Aim to get to Machu Picchu well before 9.30am, when the first train hordes from Cusco arrive, if possible making it to the "hitching post" of the sun before dawn, for an unforgettable sunrise that will quickly make you forget the long hike through the pre-dawn gloom – bring a torch if you plan to try it.

Machu Picchu

The most dramatic and enchanting of Inca citadels lies suspended on an extravagantly terraced saddle between two prominent peaks. The beautiful stone architecture is enhanced by the Incas' exploitation of local 250-million-year-old rocks of grey-white granite with a high content of quartz, silica and feldspar among other minerals. **MACHU PICCHU** (daily 6.30am–5pm; $10) is one of the greatest of all South American tourist attractions, set against a vast, scenic backdrop of dark-green forested mountains that spike up from the deep valleys of the Urubamba and its tributaries. The distant glacial summits are dwarfed only by the huge sky.

With many legends and theories surrounding the position of Machu Picchu, most archeologists agree that the sacred geography and astronomy of the site were auspicious factors in helping the Inca Pachacuti decide where to build this citadel here at 2492m. The name Machu Picchu apparently means simply Old or Ancient Mountain. It's thought that agricultural influences as well as geo-sacred indicators prevailed and that the site secured a decent supply of sacred coca and maize for the Inca nobles and priests in Cusco. However, it is quite possible to enjoy a visit to Machu Picchu without knowing too much about the history or archeology of the site or the specifics of each feature; for many it is enough just to absorb the atmosphere. Virtual travellers should check out Ⓦ www.machupicchu.com.

Some history

Never discovered by the Spanish conquerors, for many centuries the site of Machu Picchu lay forgotten, except by local Indians and settlers, until it was rediscovered by the US explorer **Hiram Bingham**, who, on July 24, 1911, accompanied by a local settler who knew of some ruins, came upon a previously unheard-of Inca citadel. It was a fantastic find, not least because it was still relatively intact, without the usual ravages of either Spanish Conquistadores or tomb robbers. Accompanied only by two locals, Bingham left his base camp around 10am and crossed a bridge so dodgy that he crawled over it on his hands and knees before climbing a precipitous slope until they reached the ridge at around midday. After resting at a small hut, he received hospitality from some local peasant who described an extensive system of terraces where they had found good fertile soil for their own crops. Bingham was led to the site by an 11-year-old local boy, Pablito Alvarez. It didn't take Bingham long to see that he had come across some important ancient Inca terraces – over a hundred of which had recently been cleared of forest for subsistence crops. After a little more exploration Bingham found the fine white stonework and began to realize that this might be the place he was looking for. Bingham's theory was that Machu Picchu was the lost city of Vilcabamba, the site of the Incas' last refuge from the Spanish conquistadores. Not until another American expedition surveyed the ruins around Machu Picchu in the 1940s did serious doubts begin to arise over this assertion, and more recently the site of the Incas' final stronghold has been shown to be Espiritu Pampa in the Amazon jungle (see p.179).

Meanwhile, Machu Picchu began to be reconsidered as the best-preserved of a series of agricultural centres which served Cusco in its prime. The city was conceived and built in the mid-fifteenth century by Emperor Pachacuti, the first to expand the empire beyond the Sacred Valley towards the forested gold-lands. With crop fertility, mountains and nature so sacred to the Incas, an agricultural centre as important as Machu Picchu would easily have merited the site's fine stonework and temple precincts. It was clearly a ritual centre, given the layout and quantity of temples; but for the Incas it was usual not to separate out things we consider economic tasks from more conventional religious activities. So, Machu Picchu represents to many archaeologists the most classical and best-preserved remains of a citadel which the Incas used as both a religious temple site and an agricultural (perhaps experimental) growing centre.

Arrival and accommodation

If you arrive **by train**, you'll get off at **Machu Picchu Pueblo station**, at the nearest town to the ruins, which has experienced explosive growth over the last decade or so and is occasionally still referred to by its older name, Aguas Calientes. You walk down the steps from the station and over the bridge, where you can catch one of the **buses** to the ruins (the first buses leave at 6.30am and continue until 7.30, after that they leave hourly 9.30am–12.30pm, returning continuously 12.30–5.30pm; $9 return, $4.50 oneway, children under 4

△ Ollantaytambo ruins

Train journey to Machu Picchu

The new improved service offered by PeruRail between Cusco and Machu Picchu – one of the finest mountain train journeys in the world – enhances the thrill of riding tracks through such fantastic scenery even further by offering very good service and comfortable, well-kept carriages. Rumbling out of Cusco around 6am the wagons zigzag their way through the backstreets, where little houses cling to the steep valley slopes. It takes a while to rise out of the teacup-like valley, but once it reaches the high plateau above, the train rolls through fields and past highland villages before eventually dropping rapidly down into the Urubamba valley utilizing several major track switchbacks, which means you get to see some of the same scenery twice. It reaches the Sacred Valley floor just before getting into Ollantaytambo, where from the windows you can already see scores of impressively terraced fields and, in the distance, more Inca temple and storehouse constructions. Ollantaytambo's pretty railway station is right next to the river, and here you can expect to be greeted by a handful of Quechua women selling their mainly woollen craft goods. The train continues down the valley, stopping briefly at Km 88, where the Inca Trail starts, then follows the Urubamba river as the valley gets tighter (that's why there's no road!) and the mountain more and more forested as well as steeper and seemingly taller. The end of the line these days is usually the new station at Machu Picchu Peublo (also known as Aguas Calientes), a busy little town crowded into the valley just a short bus ride from the ruins themselves.

half-price). The ticket office is to the right of the bridge, andbuses leave from the street lined with artesania stalls that leads down to the left of the bridge towards the river. Tickets are stamped with the date, so you have to return the same day. It's possible to walk from Machu Picchu Pueblo to the ruins, but it'll take one and a half to three hours, depending on how fit you are and whether you take the very steep direct path or follow the more roundabout paved road. **Helicopters** land at the small helipad on the opposite side of Machu Picchu Pueblo from the ruins, from where it's a short walk to catch a bus up to the site.

A **cable car** planned to carry visitors straight to the ruins from Machu Picchu Pueblo has caused considerable debate, not least because engineers would have to blast away a section of the Incas' sacred mountain of Putukusi to site a supporting tower, and while the views from the cable car will no doubt be spectacular, the increased volume of visitors could well prove damaging to the site. So far the project has been kept at bay.

The local *consejo*-run **campsite** ($2, collected every morning) is just over the Río Urubamba on the railway side of the bridge, from where the buses start their climb up to the ruins of Machu Picchu. The *Machu Picchu Sanctuary Lodge* hotel (☎241777, ⓕ247111, ⓦwww.monasterio.orient-express.com; ❽), located right at the entrance to the ruins, is something of a concrete block, but it's comfortable and has a restaurant, and staying here allows you to explore the site early in the morning or in the afternoons and evenings when most other people have left. Also, it's the only hotel in the immediate area. In the main, however, travellers tend to stay at Machu Picchu Pueblo (see p.176).

Next to the entrance to the ruins there's a **left-luggage office** (no backpacks or camping equipment are allowed inside; price per item $1.20), toilets, a shop and the **ticket office** (daily 6am–5.30pm; $20, $10 students or $5 at night), where you can also hire a guide ($3.50 per person, for a minimum of 6) and buy a **map**.

The ruins

Though it would take a lot to detract from Machu Picchu's incredible beauty and unsurpassed location, it is a zealously supervised place, with the site guards frequently blowing whistles at visitors who have deviated from one of the main pathways. The best way to enjoy the ruins – and avoiding the guards' ire – is to hire a guide, or buy the map and stick to its routes.

Though more than 1000m lower than Cusco, Machu Picchu seems much higher, constructed as it is on dizzying slopes overlooking a U-curve in the Río Urubamba. More than a hundred flights of steep stone steps interconnect its palaces, temples, storehouses and terraces, and the outstanding views command not only the valley below in both directions but also extend to the snowy peaks around Salcantay. Wherever you stand in the ruins, spectacular terraces (some of which are once again being cultivated) can be seen slicing across ridiculously steep cliffs, transforming mountains into suspended gardens.

Entering the main ruins, you cross over a dry moat. The first site of major interest is the **Temple of the Sun**, also known as the *Torreon*, a wonderful, semicircular, walled, tower-like temple displaying some of Machu Picchu's finest stonework, its carved steps and smoothly joined stone blocks fitting neatly into the existing relief of a natural boulder that served as some kind of altar and also marks the entrance to a small cave. A window off this temple provides views of both the June solstice sunrise and the constellation of the Pleiades, which rises from here over the nearby peak of Huayna Picchu. The Pleiades are still a very important astronomical Andean symbol relating to crop fertility: locals use the constellation as a kind of annual signpost in the agricultural calendar, giving information about when to plant crops and when the rains will come. Below the Temple of the Sun is a cave known as the **Royal Tomb**, despite the fact that no graves or human remains have ever been found there. In fact, it probably represented access to the spiritual heart of the mountains, like the cave at the Temple of the Moon (see overleaf).

Retracing your steps 20m or so back from the Temple of the Sun and following a flight of stone stairs directly uphill, then left along the track towards Intipunku (see p.176), brings you to a path on the right, which climbs up to the thatched **guardian's hut**. This hut is associated with a modestly carved rock known as the **funerary rock** and a nearby graveyard where Hiram Bingham found evidence of many burials, some of which were obviously royal.

Back down in the centre of the site, the next major Inca construction after the Temple of the Sun is the **Three-Windowed Temple**, part of the complex based around the **Sacred Plaza**, and arguably the most enthralling sector of the ruins. Dominating the southeastern edge of the plaza, the attractive Three-Windowed Temple has unusually large windows looking east towards the mountains beyond the Urubamba river valley. From here it's a short stroll to the **Principal Temple**, so called because of the fine stonework of its three high main walls, the most easterly of which looks onto the Sacred Plaza. Unusually (as most ancient temples in the Americas face east), the main opening of this temple faces south, and white sand, often thought to represent the ocean, has been found on the temple floor, suggesting that it may have been allied symbolically to the Río Urubamba: water and the sea.

A minute or so uphill from here along an elaborately carved stone stairway brings you to one of the jewels of the site, the **Intihuatana**, also known as the "hitching post of the sun". This fascinating carved rock, built on a rise above the Sacred Plaza, is similar to those created by the Incas in all their important ritual centres, but is one of the very few not to have been discovered and

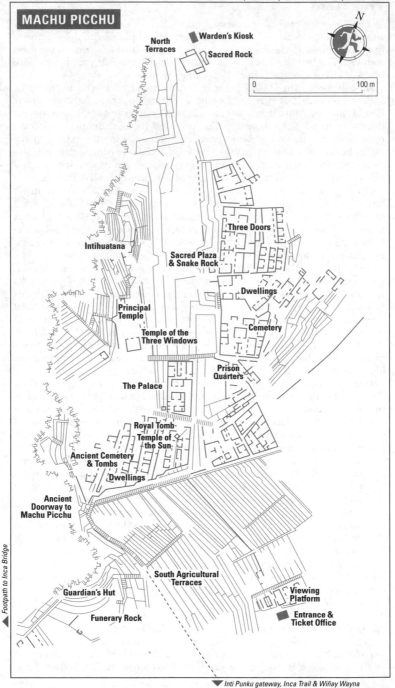

Footpath to Huayna Picchu & the Temple of the Moon

MACHU PICCHU

North Terraces

Warden's Kiosk

Sacred Rock

0   100 m

N

Three Doors

Intihuatana

Sacred Plaza & Snake Rock

Dwellings

Principal Temple

Cemetery

Temple of the Three Windows

Prison Quarters

The Palace

Royal Tomb-Temple of the Sun

Ancient Cemetery & Tombs

Dwellings

Ancient Doorway to Machu Picchu

Footpath to Inca Bridge

Guardian's Hut

South Agricultural Terraces

Viewing Platform

Entrance & Ticket Office

Funerary Rock

Inti Punku gateway, Inca Trail & Wiñay Wayna

destroyed by the conquistadores. This unique and very beautiful survivor, set in a tower-like position, overlooks the Sacred Plaza, the Río Urubamba and the sacred peak of Huayna Picchu. Intihuatana's base is said to have been carved in the shape of a map of the Inca Empire, though few archeologists agree with this. Its main purpose was as an astro-agricultural clock for viewing the complex interrelationships between the movements of the stars and constellations. It is also thought by some to be a symbolic representation of the spirit of the mountain on which Machu Picchu was built – by all accounts a very powerful spot both in terms of sacred geography and its astrological function. The Intihuatana appears to be aligned with four important mountains: the snow-capped mountain range of La Veronica lies directly to the east, with the sun rising behind its main summit during the equinoxes; directly south, though not actually visible from here, sits the father of all mountains in this part of Peru, Salcantay, only a few days' walk away; to the west, the sun sets behind the important peak of Pumasillo during the December solstice; and due north stands the majestic peak of Huayna Picchu.

Following the steps down from the Intihuatana and passing through the Sacred Plaza towards the northern terraces brings you in a few minutes to the **Sacred Rock**, below the access point to Huayna Picchu. A great lozenge of granite sticking out of the earth like a sculptured wall, little is known for sure about the Sacred Rock, but its outline is strikingly similar to the Incas' sacred mountain of Putukusi, which towers to the east.

The prominent peak of **Huayna Picchu** juts out over the Urubamba Valley at the northern end of the Machu Picchu site, and is easily scaled by anyone reasonably energetic. The record for this vigorous and rewarding climb is 22 minutes, but most people take about an hour. Access to this sacred mountain (daily 7am–1pm; last exit by 3pm) is generally controlled by a guardian from his kiosk just behind the Sacred Rock. From the summit, there's an awe-inspiring panorama, and it's a great place from which to get an overview of the ruins suspended between the mountains among stupendous forested Andean scenery.

About two-thirds of the way back down, another little track leads to the right and down to the stunning **Temple of the Moon**, hidden in a grotto hanging magically above the Río Urubamba, some 400m beneath the pinnacle of Huayna Picchu. Not many visitors make it this far and it's probably wise to have a guide (and if you've already walked up Huayna Picchu, you might want to save this for another day because it's another 45min each way at least). The guardian by the Sacred Rock will often take people for a small fee (around $1 per person, provided there are 2 or more). Once you do get there, you'll be rewarded by some of the best stonework in the entire site, the level of craftsmanship hinting at the site's importance to the Inca. Its name comes from the fact that it is often lit up by the moonlight, but some archeologists believe the temple was most likely dedicated to the spirit of the mountain. The main sector of the temple is in the mouth of a natural cave, where there are five niches set into an elaborate white granite stone wall. There's usually evidence – small piles of maize, coca leaves and tobacco – that people are still making offerings at these niches. In the centre of the cave there's a rock carved like a throne, beside which are five cut steps leading into the darker recesses, where you can see more carved rocks and stone walls, nowadays at least inaccessible to humans. Immediately to the front of the cave is a small plaza with another cut stone throne and an altar. Outside, steps either side of the massive boulder lead above the cave, from where you can see a broad, stone-walled room running along one side of the cave boulder. There are more buildings and beautiful little stone sanctuaries just down a flight of steps from this part of the complex.

If you don't have the time or energy to climb Huayna Picchu or visit the Temple of the Moon, simply head back to the guardian's hut on the other side of the site and take the path below it, which climbs gently for thirty minutes or so, up to **Intipunku**, the main entrance to Machu Picchu from the Inca Trail. This offers an incredible view over the entire site with the unmistakable shape of Huayna Picchu in the background.

Machu Picchu Pueblo (Aguas Calientes)

Many people who want to spend more than just a day at Machu Picchu base themselves at the settlement of **MACHU PICCHU PUEBLO** (previously known as Aguas Calientes), which is connected to the ruins by bus and has good accommodation, restaurants and shops. Its warm, humid climate and surrounding landscape of towering mountains covered in cloud forest make it a welcome change to Cusco, but the main attraction (apart from Machu Picchu itself) is the natural **thermal bath** (daily 6am–8.30pm; $2), which is particularly welcome after a few days on the Inca Trail or a hot afternoon up at Machu Picchu. You can find several communal baths of varying temperatures right at the end of the main drag of Pachacutec, around 750m uphill from the town's small plaza.

There is also a recently restored **trail** (90min each way) up the sacred mountain of Putukusi, starting just outside of the town, a couple of hundred yards down on the left if you follow the rail track towards the ruins. The walk offers stupendous views of the town and across to Machu Picchu, but watch out for the small poisonous snakes reported to live on this mountain.

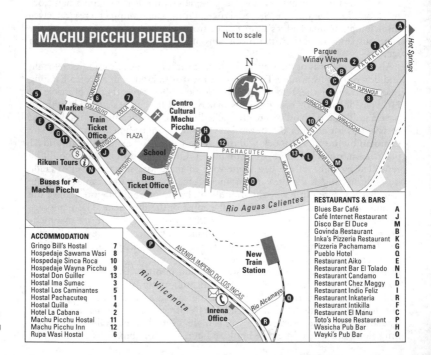

By now, Machu Picchu Pueblo's explosive growth has reached the limits of the valley; there's very little flat land that hasn't been built on or covered in concrete. Not surprisingly, this boom town has a lively, bustling feel and enough restaurants and bars to satisfy a small army. For **tourist information**, maps of local walks, money exchange, or credit card cash, go to Avenida Imperio de los Inca 119, the shop front with the telephones on the old station platform, which is the office for Rikuni Sacred Experience Tours (☎211036). It's also worth checking out a couple of dedicated websites: Ⓦwww.machupicchu .com and Ⓦwww.machupicchuhostals.com. INRENA, responsible for the Sanctuario Histórico de Machu Picchu administration, has two offices in town, one in the Centro Cultural Machu Picchu, near the school, just above the plaza; their other, more useful, location can be found back along the rail tracks towards Cusco, only 100m or so, on the right just beyond the post office. The train ticket office on Avenida Imperio de los Incas is open 5–6am and again from 8.30am to 5.30pm.

Accommodation

Although there is an overwhelming choice of **places to stay** in Machu Picchu Pueblo, there can be a lot of competition for lodgings during the high season (June–Sept), when large groups of travellers often turn up and take over entire hotels. Coming to town on an early train will give you some increased choice in where to stay, but for the better places try and book at least a week or two, if not months, in advance. **Camping** is also possible at a safe and secure site with evening campfires, just ten minutes' walk from Machu Picchu Pueblo at Campamento Intiwasi, M-23 ($5 per tent); contact via Rikuni Tours, Imperio de los Incas 119 (☎/🖶211036 or ☎211151, Ⓔhanan65@latinmail.com, or ask in the *Café Internet Restaurant* for details). The other camping option is the *consejo*-run site (see p.172).

Gringo Bill's Colla Raymi 104 ☎211046, Ⓔgringobills@yahoo.com, Ⓦwww .machupicchugringobills.com. Also known as the *Hostal Q'oni Unu*, this is the best mid-range choice in town, offering money change, laundry, lunch packs, ample hot water, a relaxed environment, breakfasts included, grilled meats in the evening, rooms with interesting decor, and a book exchange. ❸–❹

Hospedaje Rupa Wasi Calle Huanacaure 110 ☎211101, Ⓦwww.rupawasi.com. This very homely place is something of an eco-spiritual centre as well as a hostel. It has small pleasant rooms, some with balconies, with or without baths. The staff can organize tours, massage and Ayahuasca sessions. All in all, a very nice place but the music can get pretty loud at night – which may not go down well if you've got to get up at the crack of dawn and hike up to Machu Picchu.

Hospedaje Samana Wasi on Inca Yupanqui, turn right off Pachacutec ☎211170. This is a pleasant, reasonably priced place that has hot water and some rooms with private bath. ❸

Hospedaje Wayna Picchu Pachacutec 127 ☎211089. A plain-looking hostel, it nevertheless has clean rooms and decent service. ❸

Hostal la Cabaña Pachacutec M20–Lot 3 ☎/🖶211048, Ⓔlacabana_mapi@latinmail.com. Price unusually includes breakfast in this safe and friendly hostel. Other features include comfy, stylish rooms with fresh flowers, open lounge areas, a laundry and library (one of the owners is also a local guide). ❹

Hostal Los Caminantes Av Imperio de los Incas 138 ☎211007. An older, rambling building over on the other side of the tracks that has rooms with or without bath and hot water, but not much else. ❷–❸

Hostal Don Guiller Pachacutec 136 ☎211128. Located in the same building as the *Restaurant Candamo*, this is a well-run hostel with clean, comfortable rooms, hot water in private bathrooms and breakfast included. ❸

Hostal Inca Av Imperio de los Incas 135 ☎211034, 🖶231288. This is a clean and smart place, almost next door and with the same owner as the *Hostal Machu Picchu*, but much more upmarket with all private bathrooms, some rooms with views over the Río Urubamba. ❼

Hostal Machu Picchu Av Imperio de los Incas 127 ☎211034, 🖶231288. Located right beside the old station platform on the river side of the tracks; some bathrooms are shared in this reputable but not very special hostel. ❺

Hostal Pachacuteq at the top end of Pachacutec ☎211061, ✉pachacuteq@hotmail.com. It has plain but nice enough rooms, a cafetería, laundry service and will help with train or bus tickets if required. ❹

Hostal Quilla ☎211009, ✉quillalex@hotmail .com. A very friendly hostel offering breakfasts and good tourist information. Rooms have private bath. ❸

El Indio Feliz Lloque Yupanqui Lote 4m-12 ☎211090. This is a relatively new and very comfortable place, attached to the excellent restaurant

of the same name (see below); rooms have TV and Internet access. ❻

Machu Picchu Inn Av Pachacutec 109 ☎211011, ⒲www.peruhotel.com. A comfortable but plain-looking hotel, it has a nice geranium garden, pool room, and fine restaurant. ❼

Pueblo Hotel Km 110 on the rail line ☎211122, 🖷221124, ⒲www.inkaterra.com; Lima sales office: Andalucia 174, Miraflores ☎01/4226574. The most elegant and interesting hotel around, its almost hidden entrance is on the left just beyond the edge of town as you walk up the rail track towards Cusco. The *Pueblo* has its own swimming pool, extensive gardens and five hectares of cloud forest. ❼–❽

Eating and drinking

As well as the **food stalls** specializing in excellent herb teas and fruit juices, which can be found near the little market by the police station, just over the tracks, there are plenty of full-fledged **restaurants** in Machu Picchu Pueblo. *Restaurant Aiko*, Imperio de los Incas 153 (☎211001), is one of the closest restaurants to the Machu Picchu end of the tracks in the pueblo; it features good service in a cool interior and dishes out reasonably priced meals including trout, soups, pastas, burgers and delicious falafels (unfortunately not always on the menu). *Restaurant Inti Killa*, Imperio de los Incas 147 (☎211012), serves very good pizzas and trout, with tables outside and local new-age paintings inside along with Inca relief murals; nearby the *Restaurant Pizzeria Pachamama*, at Imperio de los Incas 143 (☎212231), opposite the small market, specializes in pizzas, pancakes, breakfasts and lomo steak in mushroom sauce. On the other side of the rail tracks you'll find the *Café Internet Restaurant*, which has fast access and good friendly service for coffees, omelettes, pizzas, trout, spaghetti; this place is also a contact for the campsite Inti Wasi, less than ten minutes' walk from here.

On the plaza, the *Inka's Pizzeria Restaurant* is very popular, with a large space and fine murals; as well as the obvious it serves soups, trout, chicken and juices. For a proper **vegetarian** meal, there's the ubiquitous *Govinda* up the top end of Pachacutec, on the left. *Donofrio's* ice-cream shop, Pachacutec 120, does reasonable lunch menus. *El Indio Feliz*, Lloque Yupanqui Lote 4m-12 (☎211090), serves exceptional three- or four-course meals of French and local cuisines at remarkably inexpensive prices; try to reserve a table as far in advance as possible. *Restaurant El Manu*, on Pachacutec, has a nice open dining area (sometimes doubling up as a dance space, quite lively at night), and specializes in trout and pizzas. *Totos House Restaurant*, Imperio de los Incas (☎211020), is a vast restaurant with great views and some tables out front by the rail tracks; they offer buffet lunch daily for $10, expensive but quite good. For something a little livelier, *Chez Maggy's*, Pachacutec 156 (☎211006), serves OK meals (their speciality being pizzas) and sometimes plays rock music. On its own really, at least in terms of location, there's the *Restaurant Inkaterra*, overlooking the Río Urubamba and rail line by the entrance to the splendid *Pueblo Hotel*; it's not cheap, but the quality international and local cuisine justifies the price tag.

The *Blues Jazz Bar*, at the top end of Pachacutec towards the entrance to the Thermal Springs, is a sexy little café with a dark interior, good drinks, groovy music, decent food, money exchange and occasionally shows movies. *Wasicha*

Pub, Calle Lloque Yupanqui, Lote 2, M-12 (☎211157), is the town's loudest, hottest nightspot, with a vibrant dance floor, a good bar and a spacious restaurant attached as well. *Waki's Pub Bar* on Capac Yupanqui 2 (☎227699) is a jungle-themed pizzeria with a dance floor that sometimes has live bands on Saturdays and shows movies most days.

Listings

Drug store In small market by rail tracks.

Exchange Available in the pool room and café next to *Hostal Los Caminantes*.

INRENA Instituto Nacional de Cultura offices, responsible for management of the national sanctuary of Machu Picchu, are on the rail line, just past the post office, towards the *Pueblo Hotel* end.

Internet services *Café Internet Restaurant*, corner of Avenida Imperio de los Incas next to the old train station, has decent service plus cakes, snacks and drinks 6.30am–10pm; Bar El Toldo Internet, Avenida Imperio de los Incas 115, six computer connections and great views from back over river; Café Internet World Net, Avenida Pachacutec 147-b, seems to have a good link; Inkanet, Avenida Contisuyo 101.

Laundry Two-hour laundry service available in *Hostal Machu Picchu*, Imperio de los Incas 127.

Photography There's a Kodak shop with films, including Fuji, on Avenida Imperio de los Incas, the same block as the *Café Internet*.

Police Avenida Imperio de los Incas, next to the small market just down from the old train station (☎211178).

Post office On the rail tracks, right-hand side, towards *Pueblo Hotel*.

Telephones Centro Telefonica, Avenida Imperio de los Incas 132 (☎211091, ℻211174). The post office (see above) also has a public phone.

Tour operators Rikuni Tours, Imperio de los Incas 119 (☎/℻211036 or ☎211151, ℮rikuni@mixmail.com or rikunis@yahoo.com.ai, or ask in the *Café Internet Restaurant* for details). They offer a wide range of local outings, including Machu Picchu by night, the Temple of the Moon, Chaskapata ruins, Wiñay Wayna, and Chacabamba ruins.

Beyond Machu Picchu: into the jungle

The area along the Río Urubamba from Machu Picchu onwards is a quiet, relatively accessible corner of the Peruvian wilderness. As you descend by road from Ollantaytambo, over a pass and then down to Chaullay and the jungle beyond, the vegetation along the valley turns gradually into jungle, thickening and getting greener by the kilometre and the air gets steadily warmer and more humid. Most people going down here get as far as the town of Quillabamba, but the road continues deeper into the rainforest where it meets the navigable jungle rivers at Kiteni (see p.521). Some people come to the region to explore the mountains, cloud forest and rainforest areas of this zone either to check out known Inca ruins or to search out more new ones.

It is relatively easy to visit the hilltop ruins of the palace at **Vitcos**, a site of Inca blood sacrifices, and possible, though an expedition of six days or more, to explore the more remote ruins at **Espiritu Pampa**, now thought to be the site of the legendary lost city of Vilcabamba. The easiest way to see the ruins is on a guided tour with one of the adventure tour companies listed on p.151. If you'd rather travel independently, at least book a local guide through one of the companies in Cusco before setting off.

Major Inca sites are still being discovered in this region. In April 2002 Hugh Thomson (author of *The White Rock*, see p.601) and Gary Zeigler, following rumours of a lost city, led an expedition which discovered an Inca city in the virtually inaccessible valley bottom at the confluence of the ríos Yanama and Blanco in the Vilcabamba region. Apparently seen briefly by Hiram Bingham nearly 100 years ago, the coordinates were never recorded and this settlement of forty main buildings set around a central plaza hadn't been spotted since. Although very difficult to access – due to river erosion – there appears to have been an Inca road running through the valley, probably connecting this site to the great Inca citadel of Choquequirao (see p.185). This settlement is believed to have been Manco Inca's hideout during his rebellion against the conquistadores, which lasted until his execution in Cusco in 1572.

Pukyura

If you want to visit the ruins at Vitcos or Espiritu Pampa independently, it's best to go via the villages of **PUKYURA** and **Huancacalle**, in the Vilcabamba river valley. They are reached in six hours by trucks which are usually easily picked up (small fee charged) at Chaullay on the Ollantaytambo–Quillabamba road. Pukyura has a long history of guerrilla fighting and a tradition of wilful anti-authoritarian independence. Chosen by Manco Inca as the base for his rebel state in the sixteenth century, this area was also the political base for land reformer and Trotskyist revolutionary Hugo Blanco in the early 1960s. When the economy was in dire straits, domestic prices soaring and in 1952 alone there were some two hundred strikes and several serious riots in Peru, a much more radical feeling was aroused in the provinces by **Hugo Blanco**, a charismatic *mestizo* from Cusco who had joined a Trotskyist group – the Workers Revolutionary Party. Blanco created nearly 150 syndicates, mainly in the Cusco region, whose peasant members began to work their own individual plots while refusing to work for the hacienda owners. Many landowners went bankrupt or opted to bribe workers back with offers of cash wages. The second phase of Blanco's "reform" was to take physical control of the haciendas, mostly in areas so isolated that the authorities were powerless to intervene. Blanco was finally arrested in 1963 but the effects of his peasant revolt outlived him: in future, Peruvian governments were to take agrarian reform far more seriously. In 2002 Hugo Blanco was hospitalized, victim of a brain hemorrhage while visiting the peasant communities of this region. He managed to get to Mexico City, where he was being treated in hospital during 2003.

Camping at Pukyura is possible and you can usually arrange independently for an *arriero* here to take you over the two- or three-day trail to Espiritu Pampa. Narciso Huaman is recommended ($10 per day, including 2 horses), contactable through Genaro, the Instituto Nacional de Cultura representative in Huancacalle. The hour-long walk uphill to Vitcos from Pukyura is easy to do independently, however. If you're seriously interested in exploring this region, you should also check on the prevailing **political and access rights** situation with the Instituto Nacional de Cultura (see Cusco Listings, p.148) before attempting what is a very ambitious journey.

Vitcos and Espiritu Pampa

In 1911, after discovering Machu Picchu, Hiram Bingham set out down the Urubamba Valley to Chaullay, then up the Vilcabamba valley to the village of Pukyura, where he expected to find more Inca ruins. What he found – **VITCOS** (known locally as Rosapata*)* – was a relatively small but clearly palatial ruin, based around a trapezoidal plaza spread across a flat-topped spur. Down below the ruins, Bingham was shown by local guides a spring flowing from beneath a vast, white granite boulder intricately carved in typical Inca style and surrounded by the remains of an impressive Inca temple. This fifteen-metre-long and eight-metre-high sacred white rock – called Chuquipalta by the Incas – was a great oracle where blood sacrifices and other religious rituals took place. According to early historical chronicles, these rituals had so infuriated two Spanish priests who witnessed them, that they exorcized the rock and set its temple sanctuary on fire.

Within two weeks Bingham had followed a path from Pukyura into the jungle as far as the Condevidayoc plantation, where he found some more "undiscovered" ruins at **ESPIRITU PAMPA** – "Plain of the Spirits". After briefly exploring some of the outer ruins at Espiritu Pampa, Bingham decided they must have been built by Manco Inca's followers and deduced that they were post-Conquest Inca constructions since many of the roofs were Spanish-tiled. Believing that he had already found the lost city of Vilcabamba in Machu Picchu, Bingham paid little attention to these newer discoveries. Consequently, and in view of its being accessible only by mule, Espiritu Pampa remained covered in thick jungle vegetation until 1964, when serious exploration was undertaken by US archeological explorer Gene Savoy. He found a massive ruined complex with over sixty main buildings and some three hundred houses, along with temples, plazas, wells and a main street. Clearly this was the largest Inca refuge in the Vilcabamba area, and Savoy rapidly became convinced of its identity as the true site of the last Inca stronghold. More conclusive evidence has since been provided by the English geographer and historian John Hemming who, using the chronicles as evidence, was able to match descriptions of Vilcabamba, its climate and altitude, precisely with those of Espiritu Pampa. Getting to these sites really requires expedition-type preparation, the hire of local guides (best done through Cusco tour agents) and possibly even mules. You'll need a week or more even to cover the nearer sites. There are no services or facilities as such at any of the sites, none of which is staffed by permanent on-site guardians, so they are free and open as long as you have permission from the Instituto Nacional de Cultura (see Cusco Listings, p.148).

The Cusco region

Cusco is easily the most exciting region in Peru, but all too many visitors overlook the area's lesser-known attractions. Many people choose to spend at least three days in the immediate vicinity of the city, and nearly everyone takes at least another two or three days to visit Machu Picchu and the other sites in the Sacred Valley, but there's a huge number of other villages and sites to stimulate the energetic traveller with more than a week to spend. The Instituto Nacional de Cultura, for example, has identified no fewer than 36,000 known archeological sites in this region. **Chinchero**, an old colonial settlement resting on Inca foundations overlooking the Sacred Valley and boasting a spectacular market, is only forty minutes' drive northwest of the city of Cusco. To the northeast, towards the jungle, the attractive village of **Paucartambo**, built in colonial style and famous for its annual festival, nestles among breathtakingly high Andean panoramas close to **Tres Cruces**, a remote mountain spot where locals and globetrotters alike go to experience a uniquely spectacular sun rising from the depths of lowland Amazonia. To the south are the superb **ruins** of Tipón, Pikillacta, Raqchi and Rumicolca, the rustic and legendary village of

Urcos, as well as superb trekking country around the sacred **Nevado Ausangate** glaciers (6384m) between the small settlement of **Ocongate** and the larger town of **Sicuani**. And even if you aren't planning to spend time around Lake Titicaca, the rail journey south to Puno (see p.273), which starts off through the Cusco region, is one of the most soul-stirring train rides imaginable, though the track is a little bumpy compared to the new road to Puno. One last trip, the highland route between Cusco and Lima, passes through Abancay, Andahuaylas and **Ayacucho**, the latter a beautiful and highly traditional city famous for its churches and artesania.

Chinchero

CHINCHERO ("Village of the Rainbow") lies 3762m above sea level, 28km northwest from Cusco and off the main road, overlooking the Sacred Valley, with the Vilcabamba range and the snowcapped peak of Salcantay dominating the horizon to the west. The bus ride here takes you up to the Pampa de Anta, which used to be a huge lake but is now relatively dry pasture, surrounded by snowcapped *nevadas*. The town itself is a small, rustic place, where the local women, who crowd the main plaza during the market, still wear traditional dress. Largely built of stone and abobe, the town blends perfectly with the magnificent display of Inca architecture, ruins and megalithic carved rocks, relics of the Inca veneration of nature deities. The best time to visit is on September 8 for the lively traditional **fiesta**. Failing that, the market, smaller but less touristy than Pisac's, has good local craftwork.

The **market** (Sunday morning) is in the lower part of town, reached along Calle Manco II. Uphill from here, along the cobbled steps and streets, you'll find a vast **plaza**, which may have been the original Inca marketplace. It's bounded on one side by an impressive wall somewhat reminiscent of Sacsayhuaman's ramparts, though not as massive – it too was constructed on three levels, and some ten classical Inca trapezoidal niches can be seen along its surface. On the western perimeter of the plaza, the raised Inca stonework is dominated by a carved **stone throne**, near which are puma and monkey formations. The plaza is also home to a superb colonial adobe **church** (daily 7am–5.30pm; entry by Cusco Tourist Ticket, available here or in Cusco – see p.123). Dating from the early seventeenth century, it was built on top of an Inca temple or palace, perhaps belonging to the Inca emperor Tupac Yupanqui, who particularly favoured Chinchero as an out-of-town resort – most of the area's aqueducts and terraces, many of which are still in use today, were built at his command. The church itself boasts frescoes, murals and paintings (though decaying, still very beautiful and evocative), many pertaining to the Cusqueña school and celebrated local artist Mateo Cuihuanito. The most interesting depict the forces led by local chief Pumacahua against the rebel Tupac Amaru II in the late eighteenth century (for more detail see Contexts, p.537).

Buses leave Cusco from Avenida Grau 525 (☎805639) for Urubamba ($1) via Chincheros (50¢) every fifteen minutes from about 5am daily until early afternoon usually; you'll need to keep an eye out for the town or ask the driver to let you know when to get off because the road only passes the outskirts of Chinchero. There are just two **places to stay** in town, of which the *Hotel Los Incas* (❷) is the better value, with a pleasant, rustic restaurant. It's also possible to **camp** below the terraces in the open fields beyond the village, but, as always, ask someone local for permission or advice on this. There are several restaurants, all cheap and cheerful, though *Camucha*, Avenida Mateo Pumacahua 168, at the junction of Calle Manco Capac II and the main road to Cusco, has a particularly good set lunch.

Northeast of Cusco

The two major places to visit northeast of Cusco are **Paucartambo**, 112km from Cusco, and **Tres Cruces**, another 50km beyond Paucartambo. The road between the two follows the **Kosnipata Valley**, whose name means "Valley of Smoke", then continues through cloudy tropical mountain scenery to the mission of Shintuya on the edge of the Manu National Park (see p.516). Legend has it that the Kosnipata enchants anyone who drinks from its waters at Paucartambo, drawing them to return again and again.

Paucartambo

Eternally spring-like because of the combination of altitude and its proximity to tropical forest, and guarding a major entrance to the jungle zone of Manu, the pretty village of **PAUCARTAMBO** ("The Village of the Flowers") is located some 110km from Cusco **in a wild and remote Andean region**. A slave-driven silver-mining colony in the seventeeth and eighteenth centuries, it's now a popular destination that's at its best in the dry season between May and September, particularly in mid-July when the annual **Fiesta de la Virgen de Carmen** (see box below) takes place; visitors arrive in their thousands

---

The Fiesta de la Virgen de Carmen

Paucartambo spends the first six months of every year gearing up for the **Fiesta de la Virgen de Carmen**. It's an essentially female festival: tradition has it that a wealthy young woman, who had been on her way to Paucartambo to trade a silver dish, found a beautiful (if torso-less) head that spoke to her once she'd placed it on the dish, Arriving in the town, people gathered around her and witnessed rays of light shining from the head, and henceforth it was honoured with prayer, incense and a wooden body for it to sit on.

The energetic, hypnotic **festival** lasts three or four days (usually July 16–19, but check with the tourist office in Cusco – see p.122), and features throngs of locals in distinctive traditional costumes, dancers and musicians, with market stalls and a small fair springing up near the church. Clamouring down the streets are throngs of intricately costumed and masked dancers and musicians, the best-known of whom are the black-masked Capaq Negro, recalling the African slaves who once worked the nearby silver mines. Also memorable are those in grotesque blue-eyed masks and outlandish costumes acting out a parody of the white man's powers – malaria, a post-Conquest problem, tends to be a central theme – in which an old man suffers terrible agonies until a Western medic appears on the scene, with the inevitable hypodermic in his hand. If he manages to save the old man (a rare occurrence) it's usually due to a dramatic muddling of prescriptions by his dancing assistants – and thus does Andean fate triumph over science. On Saturday afternoon there's a procession of the Virgen del Carmen itself, with a brass band playing mournful melodies as petals and emotion are showered on the icon of the Virgin – which symbolizes worship of Pachamama as much as devotion to Christianity. The whole event culminates on Sunday afternoon with the dances of the *guerreros* (warriors), during which good triumphs over evil for another year.

and the village is transformed from a peaceful habitation into a huge mass of frenzied, costumed dancers.

The beautiful main **plaza**, with its white buildings and traditional blue balconies, has concrete monuments depicting the characters who perform at the fiesta – demon-masked dancers, malaria victims, lawyers, tourists and just about anything that grabs the imagination of the local communities. Also on the plaza is the rather austere **church**, restored in 1998 and splendid in its own way, simple yet full of large Cusqueña paintings. It's also the residence of the sacred image of the Virgen del Carmen, unusual in its Indian (rather than European) appearance: when the pope visited Peru in the mid-1980s, it was loaded onto a truck and driven to within 30km of Cusco, then paraded on foot to the city centre so that the pope could bless the image. Even if you don't make it to Paucartambo for the festival, you can still see the ruined *chullpa* burial towers at Machu Cruz, an hour's walk from Paucartambo; ask in the village for directions. Travellers rarely make it here outside of festival time, unless on route to the rainforest by road.

Transportes Gallinos de las Rocas **buses** leave from an office at Avenida Diagonal 1952 (T226895) daily to Paucartambo ($2; a 4–5hr journey) and three times a week to Pilcopata. **Trucks**, which leave from the end of Avenida Garcilaso, beyond the Ormeño office, are slightly cheaper but slower and far less comfortable. Buses generally stop off in Paucartambo at the market place, from where you cross the stone bridge into the main part of town up to the plaza, where, during festival times only, there's a **tourist information** office. Whenever you go, it's best to take a tent, because **accommodation** is difficult to find: the only options are the *Albergue Municipal* (no phone; ❷) and, by the lower bridge, the *Hotel Quinta Rosa Marina* (no phone; ❷), both central and very basic. When the festival is on, they're fully booked, but it's possible to rent out spaces in some local residents' homes.

Tres Cruces

The natural special effects during **sunrise** at **TRES CRUCES** are in their own way as magnificent a spectacle as the Fiesta de la Virgen de Carmen. At 3739m above sea level, on the last mountain ridge before the eastern edge of the Amazon forest, the view is a marvel at any time: by day a vast view over the start of a massive cloud forest with all its weird vegetation; by night an enormous star-studded jewel. Seen from the highest edge of the Manu Biosphere Reserve, the sunrise is spectacular, particularly around the southern hemisphere's winter solstice in June: multi-coloured, with multiple suns, an incredible light show that lasts for hours. **Transport** to Tres Cruces can be a problem, except during the fiesta; however, on Monday, Wednesday and Friday, Transportes Gallinos de las Rocas buses (see above) to Paucartambo continue on to Pilcopata or Salvación; beyond Paucartambo, you can disembark at the Tres Cruces turn-off ($2.50; about 8hr from Cusco), but be prepared to walk the remaining 14km into Tres Cruces itself, though you may get a lift with a passing vehicle (especially early in the day from late June to mid-July). Cusco tour operators (see p.151) can organize a trip, or you can check the notice boards in the main cafés and backpacker joints in Cusco for people trying to gather together groups to share the cost of a colectivo and driver for the two- to three-day trip – usually $30–50 a day, plus food and drink for the driver – or even post a notice yourself. The only **accommodation** in Tres Cruces is an empty house that's used as a visitors' shelter, which fills up very fast at festival times, when camping is the only real option, so take a warm sleeping bag, a tent and enough food.

Northwest from Cusco

It takes about thirty hours or so to travel **from Cusco to Lima** via Abancay, Andahuaylas and Ayacucho, then down to the Pisco valley on the coast, which is just a few hours from Lima. A more direct route, though only knocking off around four hours from the trip, goes to Abancay, then crosses the Andes to join the coast at Nazca (5–6hr from Lima). If you do go on to Ayacucho, it's at least another eight hours by bus to Lima.

Whichever route you choose, you'll pass through the village of **Carahuasi**. Within its district are a couple of diverting sights: by the community of Concacha, and some 3500m above sea level, is the archeological complex of Sahuite, comprising three massive, beautifully worked granite boulders, the best of which graphically depict an Inca village (though the boulders have been partially defaced in recent years). And some 7km from Carahuasi there are the crystal-clear **thermal baths of Conoc**; the healing properties of the water are said to be particularly good for rheumatism, arthritis and muscular pain.

Choquequirao

An increasingly popular alternative to the Inca Trail is the hike to **Choquequirao**, an archeological site located in the district of Vilcabamba on the slopes of the glaciated peak of Yanacocha. Unlike Machu Picchu this is still in the early years of being visited. The most direct route up is by road to Cachora in Apurimac, over 100km from Cusco and some 93km south of Abancay; from here it's a further 30km (15–20hr) of heavy but stunningly beautiful trekking to the remains of the Choquequirao citadel. You can go in and come out the same way in four to five days. Consisting of nine main sectors, the site was a political and religious centre well served by a complex system of aqueducts, canals and springs. Most of the buildings are set around the main ceremonial courtyard or plaza and are surrounded by well-preserved and stylish Inca agricultural terracing. The long and scenic route to Choquequirao involves taking a twelve-day hike from Huancacalle and Pukyura and then over the Pumasillo range, through Yanama, Minas Victoria, Choquequirao, and across the Apurimac ending in Cachora.

On to Abancay

About 50km on from Carahuasi and some six or seven hours' drive from Cusco you'll find **ABANCAY**, 2378m up above sea level and capital of the Andean *departmento* (province) of Apurimac. It's a large market centre in a beautiful area, but has little to offer the casual traveller save a roof for the night and transport out the next day by bus or truck. **Buses** arrive and leave from near the market at the terminal on Avenida Arenas 200 (☎321288). For **accommodation**, the most comfortable place is the *Hotel de Turismo*, Avenida Diaz Barcenas 500 (☎/⊕321017; ❹), or the more basic *Hostal Sahuite* on Calle Nunez. The Banco de Credito, Libertad 218, and the Banco de la Nación at Lima 816 both provide money **exchange**. The **post office** is at Jirón Arequipa 213.

Apart from using it for visiting Choquequirao, the Apurimac canyon – which is formed by the Río Apurimac as it tumbles down into the Amazon – itself repays the trials of getting the 73km northeast (2–3hr in a car) with its magnificence and depth. There is also the Sanctuario Nacional de Ampay, about 5km north from Abancay (20min by car), where orchids and bromeliads, foxes, deer, spectacled bears, *viscachas*, falcons and owls are often spotted. The forest here is almost 4000 hectares of protected land mostly covered in endangered

Intimpa trees. It is open with no entrance fee or staff/guards at entrance.

From Abancay you can take the (relatively) direct road to Lima, which goes via the coast and the Nazca valley (allow two to three days in the wet season), or you can carry on to **ANDAHUAYLAS**, set against the backdrop of a splendid Andean valley. The **airport** here has flights to Arequipa, Cusco and Lima (Aero Continente at Avenida Peru 137 ☎751515). The bus terminal is at Avenida Lazaro Carillo, in the first block and the **buses** travel to Lima and Cusco (several daily). Of the **hotels**, *El Encanto de Oro Hotel*, Pedro Casafranca 424 (☎723066; ❸), is pleasant enough; cheaper still, the *Hotel Los Libertadores Wari*, Juan Ramos 425 (☎721434; ❶), is fairly basic, though the *Hotel Residencial San Juan*, Juan Ramos 126 (☎721119; ❷), is slightly better. As for **banks**, the Banco de Credito can be found at Juan Antonio Trelles 255, and the Banco de la Nación at Ramon Castilla 545. The **post office** is at Avenida Peru 243 (Mon–Sat 8am–8pm & Sun 8am–3pm; no phone).

Only 21km from Andahuaylas the archeological remains of **Sondor** can be found in the mountains about 2km beyond Laguna Pacucha at 3200m (45min in bus from town). This region, notably in the province of Cotabamba at the village of Ccoyllurqui, is home to the Yawar Fiesta that takes place every July, usually near the end of the month. The festival involves capturing a live condor and tying it to the back of a bull; the latter represents the conquistadores and the condor indigenous Peru. Usually the condor kills the bull.

South from Cusco

The first 150km of the road (and rail) south from Cusco towards Lake Titicaca passes through the beautiful valleys of Huatanay and Vilcanota, from where the legendary founders of the Inca Empire are said to have emerged. A region outstanding for its natural beauty and rich in magnificent archeological sites, it's easily accessible from Cusco and offers endless possibilities for exploration or random wandering. The whole area is ideal for **camping** and **trekking**, and in any case, only the towns of **Urcos** and **Sicuani** are large enough to provide reasonable accommodation.

Between Cusco and Urcos lie some 40km of road and a string of small villages. The Inca remains of **Tipón** lie high above the road, little visited but extensive and evocative. Closer to the road, the Huarai city of **Pikillacta** is easier to find and worthy of an hour or two. Beyond Urcos but before **Sicuani**, a rather boring transport node of a town, the great **Temple of Raqchi** still stands unusually high as a monument to Inca architectural abilities.

By train and bus

Trains depart from Huanchac station in Cusco; buy tickets at least one day before travelling and further in advance during high season. The tourist class train to Puno leaves at 8am Monday, Wednesday and Saturday, arriving 6pm (includes a scenic stop at the La Raya Pass). A first class train runs when there's sufficient demand (20-passenger minimum); it has the same timetable but costs $81 and offers very good waiter service with meals included. Trains return from Puno to Cusco with exactly the same timetable, crossing at the halfway point. As the trains are slow, it makes more sense instead to take one of the frequent **buses** or **minibuses**; El Zorro and Oriental run daily services (from 3.40am every 20min until early afternoon ☎240406) from Avenida de la Cultura 1624 as far as Urcos and Sicuani, passing all the sites covered below except La Raya.

Other buses for Sicuani and Urcos leave with Empresa Vilcanota, and others to Urcos (80¢), from a depot behind the Churascaria at the end of block 13 of Avenida de la Cultura (opposite the Hospital Regional). The inter-regional buses for Puno and Arequipa are included in the Cusco Listings (see p.147).

Heading south from Cusco by road, after about 5km you pass through the little pueblo of **San Sebastián**. Originally a small, separate village, it's now become a suburb of the city. Nevertheless, it has a tidy little church, ornamented with Baroque stonework and apparently built on the site of a chapel erected by the Pizarros in memory of their victory over Almagro. The next place of any interest is picturesque **Oropesa**, some 25km on, traditionally a town of bakers, whose adobe church, boasting a uniquely attractive three-tiered belfry with cacti growing out of it, is notable for its intricately carved pulpit and the beautiful, Cusqueña-esque interior murals which look to have been painted between 1580 and 1630. However, the town's main attraction is the ruined Inca citadel of **Tipón**, a walk of 5–6km uphill.

The Tipón temples and aqueducts

Both in setting and architectural design, **Tipón ruins** (daily 7am–5.30pm; entry by Cusco Tourist Ticket, see p.123) are one of the most impressive Inca sites. Rarely visited, and with a guard who seems to be permanently on holiday, it's essentially open all the time and free. From Oropesa, the simplest way to reach the ruins is by backtracking down the main Cusco road some 2km to a signposted track. Follow this up through a small village, once based around the now crumbling and deserted hacienda Quispicanchi, and continue along the gully straight ahead. Once on the path above the village, it's about an hour's climb to the first ruins.

Well hidden in a natural shelf high above the Huatanay valley, the **lower sector** of the ruins is a stunning sight: a series of neat agricultural terraces, watered by stone-lined channels, all astonishingly preserved and many still in use. The impressive stone terracing reeks of the Incas' domination over an obviously massive and subservient labour pool; yet at the same time it's clearly little more than an elaborate attempt to increase crop yield. At the back of the lower ruins water flows from a stone-faced "mouth" around a spring – probably an aqueduct subterraneously diverted from above. The entire complex is designed around this spring, reached by a path from the last terrace. Another sector of the ruins contains a **reservoir** and **temple block** centred around a large exploded volcanic rock – presumably some kind of *huaca*. Although the stonework in the temple seems cruder than that of the agricultural terracing, its location is still very good. By contrast the construction of the reservoir is very fine, as it was originally built to hold nine hundred cubic metres of water which gradually dispersed along stone channels to the Inca "farm" directly below.

Coming off the back of the reservoir, a large tapering stone aqueduct crosses a small gully before continuing uphill, about thirty minutes' walk, to a vast zone of **unexcavated terraces** and dwellings. Beyond these, over the lip of the hill, you come to another level of the upper valley literally covered in Inca terracing, dwellings and large stone storehouses. Equivalent in size to the lower ruins, these are still used by locals who've built their own houses among the ruins. So impressive is the terracing at Tipón that some archeologists believe it was an Inca experimental agricultural centre, much like Moray (see p.159), as well as a citadel.

With no village or habitation in sight, and fresh running water, it's a breathtaking place to **camp**. There's a splendid stroll back down to the main road –

△ Machu Picchu

take the path through the locals' huts in the upper sector over to the other side of the stream, and follow it down the hillside opposite Tipón. This route offers an excellent perspective on the ruins, as well as vistas towards Cusco in the north and over the Huatanay/Vilcanota valleys to the south.

Pikillacta and Rumicolca

About 7km south of Oropesa, the neighbouring pre-Inca ruins of Pikillacta and Rumicolca can be seen alongside the road. After passing the Paucartambo turn-off, near the ruins of an ancient storehouse and the small red-roofed pueblo of Huacarpay, the road climbs to a ledge overlooking a wide alluvial plain and Lucre Lake (now a weekend resort for Cusco's workers). At this point the road traces the margin of a stone wall defending the pre-Inca settlement of Pikillacta.

Spread over an area of at least fifty hectares, **Pikillacta**, or "The Place of the Flea" (daily 7am–5.30pm; entry by Cusco Tourist Ticket, see p.123), was built by the Huari culture around 800 AD, before the rise of the Incas. Its unique, geometrically designed terraces surround a group of bulky two-storey con-structions: apparently these were entered by ladders reaching up to doorways set well off the ground in the first storey – very unusual in ancient Peru. Many of the walls are built of small cut stones joined with mud mortar, and among the most interesting finds here were several round turquoise statuettes. These days the city is in ruins but it seems evident still that much of the site was taken up by barrack-like quarters. When the Incas arrived early in the fifteenth cen-tury they modified the site to suit their own purposes, possibly even building the aqueduct that once connected Pikillacta with the ruined gateway of Rumicolca, which straddles a narrow pass by the road, just fifteen minutes' walk further south.

This massive defensive passage, **Rumicolca** (open all day; free), was also ini-tially constructed by the Huari people and served as a southern entrance to and frontier of their empire. Later it became an Inca checkpoint, regulating the flow of people and goods into the Cusco Valley: no one was permitted to enter or leave the valley via Rumicolca between sunset and sunrise. The Incas improved on the rather crude Huari stonework of the original gateway, using regular blocks of polished andesite from a local quarry. The gateway still stands, rearing up to twelve solid metres above the ground, and is one of the most impressive of all Inca constructions.

Andahuaylillas and Huaro

About halfway between Rumicolca and Urcos, the otherwise insignificant vil-lages of Andahuaylillas and Huaro hide deceptively interesting colonial church-es. In the tranquil and well-preserved village of **Andahuaylillas**, the adobe-towered church sits above an attractive plaza, fronted by colonial houses, just ten minutes' walk from the roadside restaurant where buses and minibuses drop off and pick up passengers. Built in the early seventeenth century on the site of an Inca temple, the church has an exterior balcony from which the priests would preach. While it's a fairly small church with only one nave, it is never-theless a magnificent example of provincial colonial art. Huge Cusqueña can-vases decorate the upper walls, while below are some unusual murals, slightly faded over the centuries; the ceiling, painted with Spanish flower designs, con-trasts strikingly with a great Baroque altar.

To the south, the road leaves the Río Huatanay and enters the Vilcanota Valley. **Huaro**, crouched at the foot of a steep bend in the road 3km from

Andahuaylillas, has a much smaller **church** whose interior is completely covered with colourful murals of religious iconography, angels and saints; the massive gold-leaf altarpiece dominates the entire place as you enter. Out in the fields beyond the village, as you climb towards Urcos, you can see boulders which have been gathered together in mounds, to clear the ground for the simple ox-pulled ploughs which are still used here.

Urcos

Climbing over the hill from Huaro, the road descends to cruise past **Lake Urcos** before reaching the town which shares the lake's name. According to legend, the Inca Huascar threw his heavy gold chain into these waters after learning that strange bearded aliens – Pizarro and his crew – had arrived in Peru. Between lake and town, a simple chapel now stands poised at the top of a small hillock: if you find it open, go inside to see several excellent Cusqueña paintings.

The town of **URCOS** rests on the valley floor surrounded by weirdly sculpted hills and is centred around the Plaza de Armas, where a number of huge old trees give shade to Indians selling bread, soup, oranges and vegetables. On one side of the plaza, which is particularly busy during the town's excellent, traditional **Sunday market**, there's a large, crumbling old church; on the other, low adobe buildings.

Practicalities

You can usually find a **room** around the Plaza de Armas. Try *Hostal Luvic*, Belaunde 196 (no phone; ❶), just to the right of the church; *Alojamiento Municipal*, Jirón Vallejo 137 (no phone; ❶), next to the telephones; the *Alojamiento El Amigo*, half a block up from the left of the church (no phone; ❶); or an unnamed place, Calle Arica 316 (no phone; ❶), on the street coming from Cusco. All are very basic, crumbling old buildings with communal bathrooms.

There are a couple of reasonable **restaurants** on the Plaza de Armas, notably *El Cisne Azul* and the *Comedor Municipal*, both serving the Andean speciality *quinoa* soup, made of a highly nutritious grain grown at high altitudes and reputed to be good for skin problems. Although Urcos is not really a tourist town, the occasional traveller is made welcome; in the backstreets you can stop off at one of the *tiendas* (advertised by a pole with a blob of red plastic on the end) for a glass of *chicha* beer and some friendly conversation. Note that **electricity** only lasts until midnight, so take some candles or a torch if you plan to be out late. You can get a truck from Urcos all the way to **Puerto Maldonado** in the jungle (see p.498), a journey that takes anything from three days to two

---

Viracocha's huaca

One of the unusually shaped hills surrounding Urcos is named after the creator-god **Viracocha**, as he is said to have stood on its summit and ordered beings to emerge from the hill, thus creating the town's first inhabitants. In tribute, an ornate *huaca*, with a gold bench, was constructed to house a statue to the god, and it was here that the eighth Inca emperor received a divinatory vision in which Viracocha appeared to him to announce that "great good fortune awaited him and his descendants". In this way the emperor obtained his imperial name, Viracocha Inca, and also supposedly his first inspiration to conquer non-Inca territory, though it was his son, Pachacuti, who carried the empire to its greatest heights.

weeks depending on how much it rains (at its worst between December and March).

The Ausangate Circuit

You'll see very few people, apart from the occasional animal herder, once you leave the start and end point for this trail – one of the most challenging and exciting treks in Southern Peru – at the village of Tinqui at 3800m. Tinqui is reached by a hardgoing six- to eight-hour drive in a combi or truck from Urcos. The management at the *Hostal Ausangate* (❶) in Tinqui can get guides and an *arriero* for trekkers. There are no shops to speak of in Tinqui, so all supplies should be brought in. A good map is essential and a local guide strongly recommended. The Ausangate Circuit explores the **Cordillera Vilcanota**, weaving around many peaks over 6000m. Ausangate, the highest peak at 6372m, remains at the hub of the standard trail. Many of the camps are over 4600m and there are two passes over 5000m to be tackled.

The first day's walking uphill from Tinqui brings you to a natural campsite on a valley floor almost 4500m above sea level close to the hot springs near Upis. Day two requires about six hours of walking, following the valley up and over into the next valley heading for the camping area at Laguna Jatun Pucacocha; from here you can see the Nevado Ausangate's western ice-fall. Day three tackles a high pass early on. From here there are views over Laguna Ausangatecocha, and the walking continues up and down, passing the Ausangate climb base camp, for another three or four hours but offers some of the best scenery, particularly the Ausangate peak itself. Day four continues downhill towards the Pitumarca valley, which you follow left uphill to a campsite beyond Jampa but just this side of the pass. Day five takes you uphill again through the cairn-filled Campa pass (5050m); from here it's a three- or four-hour descent to the campsite at Pacchanta. After that, it's another three-hour walk back to Tinqui.

The Temple of Raqchi, the Puente Colgante and Sicuani

Between Urcos and Sicuani the road passes through **San Pedro de Cacha**, the nearest village (4km) to the imposing ruins of the **Temple of Raqchi** (daily 9am–5.30pm; $1.75). Buses pass within a few hundred metres of the temple entrance. The temple was evidently built to appease the god Viracocha after he had caused the nearby volcano of Quimsa Chata to spew out fiery boulders in a rage of anger, and even now massive volcanic boulders and ancient lava flows scar the landscape in constant reminder. With its adobe walls still standing over 12m high on top of polished stone foundations, and the site scattered with numerous other buildings and plazas, such as barracks, cylindrical warehouses, a palace, baths and aqueducts, Raqchi was clearly an important religious centre. Today the only ritual left is the annual **Raqchi Festival** (usually June 16–22), a dramatic, untouristy fiesta comprising three to four days of folkloric music and dance – performed by groups congregating here from as far away as Bolivia to compete on the central stage. The performances are well stage-managed but the site, in a boggy field, can be mayhem, with hundreds of food stalls, a funfair, Quechua women selling *chicha* maize beer and their drunken customers staggering through the tightly knit crowds.

Also accessed from the Urcos to Sicuani road, there's the **Puente Colgante**, a hanging or suspension rope bridge which has evidently been rebuilt almost ceremonially every year since before the Spanish conquest. Annually, up to a thousand locals gather on the second Sunday in June to rebuild the bridge using traditional techniques and materials, including *ichu* grasses, to make ropes for the 33-metre span. The building and celebrations generally take three or four days and conclude with ceremony and dancing between the area's principal *ayllus*, or clans. To get to the Puente Colgante you have to get off a bus or combi at Combapata, about 30km before Sicuani and 10km further south than Checacupe. From Combapata it's another 31km (45min more by car) to the suspension bridge.

SICUANI, about 20km from Raqchi, is capital of the province of Canchis and quite a thriving agricultural and market town, not entirely typical of the settlements in the Vilcanota Valley. Its busy **Sunday market** is renowned for cheap and excellent woollen artefacts, which you may also be offered on the train if you pass through Sicuani between Puno and Cusco. Although not a particularly exciting place in itself – with too many tin roofs and an austere atmosphere – the people are friendly and it makes an excellent base for trekking into snowcapped mountain terrain, being close to the vast Nevada Vilcanota mountain range which separates the Titicaca Basin from the Cusco Valley. **Camping** is the best way to see this part of Peru, but if you haven't got a tent there are several **hotels** in town, including the reasonably comfortable *Hostal Tairo*, Calle Mejia 120 (☎351297; ❷), and the more basic *Hostal Manzanal*, Avenida 28 de Julio 416 (❶). The train journey south continues towards Puno and Lake Titicaca (see pp.273, 281), with the Vilcanota valley beginning to close in around the line as the tracks climb **La Raya Pass** (4300m), before dropping down into the desolate pampa that covers much of inland southern Peru.

Travel details

Buses

Cusco to: Abancay (2 daily; 10hr); Arequipa (3 daily; 9hr); Argentina (3–4 weekly; 3 days); Ayacucho (1 daily; 18hr); Juliaca (3 daily; 7hr); La Paz (5 weekly; 20hr); Lima via Nazca (1 daily; 30–50hr), via Pisco and Ayacucho (2 weekly; 36–60hr); Puno (3 daily; 8hr); Santiago, Chile (2 weekly; 2 days 6hr).

Trucks

Cusco to: Atalaya (2 weekly; 20hr); Puerto Maldonado (1 or 2 daily; 2–3 days in dry season, up to 7 days in wet season); Atalaya/Shintuya (3–4 weekly; 8–10hr).

Trains

Cusco to: Juliaca/Puno (June–Sept daily, Oct–May 4 weekly; 10–11hr); Machu Picchu (4 daily; 3–5hr).

Flights

Cusco to: Arequipa (2 daily; 90min); Ayacucho (2 weekly; 30min); Juliaca (2 daily; 50min); La Paz (2 weekly; 90min); Lima (4 daily; 1hr); Puerto Maldonado (2 daily; 40min).

Nazca and the South Coast

CHAPTER 3   # Highlights

* **Paracas National Reserve** A beautiful desert peninsula and haven for coastal wildlife, with a museum dedicated to the ancient Paracas culture. See p.202

* **Ballestas Islands** Accessible in a morning by boat from the town of Pisco, these are guano islands covered in bird and mammalian marine life. See p.202

* **Huacachina** A magical oasis surrounded by some of the most arid sand-dune desert landscapes in the Americas, Huacachina is both a leisure resort and a healing spa. See p.213

* **Ica's bodegas** The Ica Valley grows the best wine grapes in Peru, which can be amply enjoyed either in the bodegas of Ica town or at one of the local vineyards. See p.211

* **Nazca** The world-famous Nazca Lines dazzle with geometric figures and complex animal designs etched, seemingly impossibly, into a massive desert pampa. See p.215

* **Puerto Inca** Once the Incas' main port, now one of Peru's finest and more secluded beaches, offering fine diving and fishing. See p.227

Nazca and the South Coast

The coastal area south of Lima all the way to Chile contains over 1330km of desert road which offers access to enough ancient remains and unusual landscapes – including some of the best assortments of wildlife in South America – to tempt almost any traveller off the Panamerican Highway, the two-lane road that runs the entire length of Peru. The south has been populated as long as anywhere in Peru – for at least nine thousand years in some places – but until last century no one guessed the existence of this arid region's unique cultures, whose enigmatic remains, particularly along the coast, show signs of a particularly sophisticated civilization. With the discovery and subsequent study, beginning in 1901, of ancient sites throughout the coastal zone, it now seems clear that this was home to at least three major cultures: the **Paracas** (500 BC–400 AD), the influential **Nazca** (500–800 AD) and finally, contemporaneous with the Chimu of northern Peru and the Cuismancu around Lima, the **Ica Culture**, or **Chincha Empire**, overrun by and absorbed into Pachacutec's mushrooming Inca Empire around the beginning of the fifteenth century.

South of Lima there are three significant towns along the coastal desert region, **Pisco**, **Ica** and **Nazca**, but of these, only Pisco is close to the ocean. Close to Pisco the adobe Inca remains of **Tambo Colorado** make an interesting trip, perhaps rounded off by a great seafood dinner at the fisherman's wharf in **San Andres**. All three of these energetic and quite welcoming towns preserve important and intriguing sites from the three cultures. Around Pisco, 200km south of Lima, the unspoiled coastline is superb for bird-watching, while the desert plains around **Nazca** are indelibly marked by gigantic, geometric animal and alien-looking figures scratched into the brown earth over a thousand years ago. In the cooler hills above the desert coastal strip you can search out herds of the soft-woolled *vicuña* or see pink flamingos in their natural Andean habitat at the stunning **Lake Parinacochas**. The **Nazca Lines**, a perplexing network of perfectly straight lines and giant figures etched over almost 500 square kilometres of bleak pampa, are southern Peru's most enduring and mysterious archeological features. And for those interested in wildlife, Pisco and Nazca offer three of the most outstanding reserves in the country – the **Ballestas Islands** and **Paracas National Reserve** (outside Pisco), and the rare *vicuña* reserve of **Pampa Galeras** (in the Andes above Nazca). One hour by car south of Nazca,

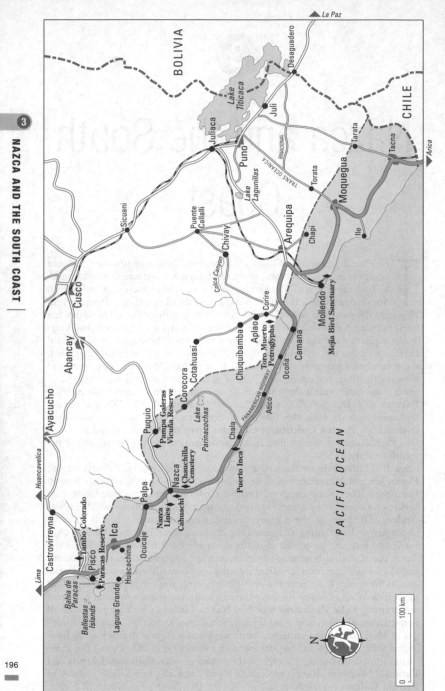

in the middle of the desert, there's an amazing little museum at **Sacaco**, built over the fossilized carcass of an ancient whale. Further south, just before the town of Chala, **Puerto Inca** is a stunning but still relatively undeveloped beach resort, which was also the key coastal port for the nobles of Inca Cusco.

Once past the town of Camana, south of Chala, the Panamericana Sur highway runs inland to within almost 40km of Arequipa (see Chapter Four), where there's a fast road connection into that city. From this junction the highway cuts south across undulating desert to the calm and essentially attractive colonial town of Moquegua, increasingly visited as a springboard for the region's archeological heritage, before heading south another 150km to **Tacna**, the last pit stop before the **frontier with Chile**.

Transport is not usually a problem along the South Coast, with local buses connecting all the towns with each other and with Lima, and express buses ploughing along the coastal road between Lima and Arequipa day and night. All the major towns have a decent range of accommodation and restaurants, and **camping** in the wild is possible in many places, though there are formal campsites only around Nazca and Puerto Inca.

Pisco and around

Less than three hours by bus from Lima, **PISCO** is a rewarding stop en route to Nazca, Arequipa or the frontier with Chile. Although of little interest in itself, it makes a pleasant base, boasts several excellent hotels and hostels – and, importantly, provides access to the **Paracas National Reserve**, the wildlife of the **Ballestas Islands**, and the well-preserved Inca coastal outpost of **Tambo Colorado**. Just off the Panamerican Highway, it is also a crossroads for going up into the Andes: you can take roads from here to Huancavelica and Huancayo, as well as to Ayacucho and Cusco.

Arrival and getting around

If you come into Pisco on one of the frequent **buses** run by Ormeño or Cruz del Sur, you'll arrive respectively at San Francisco 259 (☎034/532764) or San Francisco 255, one block east of the Plaza de Armas. The Soyuz (Peru Bus) terminal for Lima and Ica services has a drop-off point 8km east at the Pisco turn-off on the Panamericana (the company organizes free taxis from here to their offices on the corner of San Juan de Dios and Perez de Figuerola in the Plaza de Armas), and if you arrive from Ica by Saki bus you end up on Calle Dos de Mayo, just one block west of the Plaza. Coming from Huancavelica or Ayacucho on an Oropesa bus, you'll arrive at Comercio.

Tourist information is available from the regional tourism directorate (DRITINCI, Mon–Fri 8am–7pm) in the Subprefectura's office next to the police station on the Plaza de Armas; they will also show visitors a list of official guides in the area and they sometimes have maps and photocopied information on the town, islands and local beaches. A somewhat better information service is offered by the staff at the *Posada Hispana Hostal*, Bolognesi 236 (☎034/536363), who will respond with objective details to most enquiries about local sites of interest and good places to eat. Getting around Pisco is easy – it's small enough to **walk** around the main places of interest, and a **taxi** anywhere in the central area should cost less than $1. The Avenida San Martín, which stretches from the Plaza de Armas out to the seafront, is safe enough to stroll by day, but should be avoided on foot at night. If you're heading for the **Paracas National Reserve** or the **Ballestas Islands**, the cheapest way is to catch a bus from Pisco market, on the corner of calles Beatita de Humay and Fermin Tanguis. Most of the buses from here only go as far as the waterfront at **San Andres**, which can also be reached for $2 in a taxi from town. From here, there are usually at least two buses an hour on to the Playa El Chaco wharf in El Balneario, where boats leave for the Ballestas Islands. If you only want to go as far as the San Andres waterfront, you can also take a bus from Calle Pedemonte, two blocks from Plaza de Armas. Pretty well all travellers, however, use one of the many tour companies (see p.201) in town to get the most out of their time in and around Pisco. Most of the tour companies have competing offices in and around the

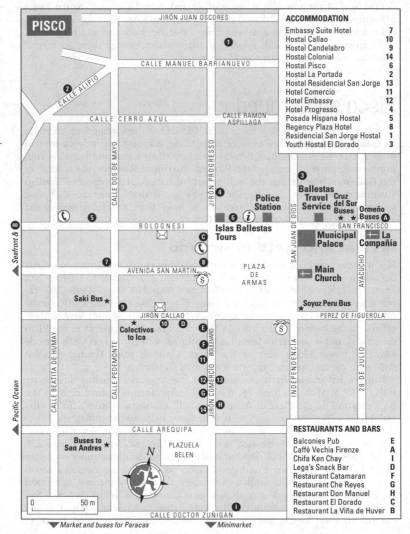

PISCO

JIRÓN JUAN OSCORES

CALLE MANUEL BARRIANUEVO

CALLE ALIPIO

CALLE CERRO AZUL

CALLE RAMON ASPILLAGA

CALLE DOS DE MAYO

JIRÓN PROGRESSO

◀ Seafront & B

BOLOGNESI

SAN JUAN DE DIOS

Police Station

Ballestas Travel Service

Cruz del Sur Buses ★ ★

Ormeño Buses Ⓐ

Islas Ballestas Tours

SAN FRANCISCO

Municipal Palace

La Compañía

AVENIDA SAN MARTIN

PLAZA DE ARMAS

AYACUCHO

Main Church

◀ Pacific Ocean

Saki Bus ★

JIRÓN CALLAO

Soyuz Peru Bus ★

Colectivos to Ica ★

PEREZ DE FIGUEROLA

CALLE BEATITA DE HUMAY

CALLE PEDEMONTE

BOULEVARD

JIRÓN COMERCIO

INDEPENDENCIA

28 DE JULIO

CALLE AREQUIPA

Buses to San Andres ★

PLAZUELA BELEN

N

CALLE DOCTOR ZUÑIGAN

0   50 m

▼ Market and buses for Paracas   ▼ Minimarket

ACCOMMODATION

Embassy Suite Hotel	7
Hostal Callao	10
Hostal Candelabro	9
Hostal Colonial	14
Hostal Pisco	6
Hostal La Portada	2
Hostal Residencial San Jorge	13
Hotel Comercio	11
Hotel Embassy	12
Hotel Progresso	4
Posada Hispana Hostal	5
Regency Plaza Hotel	8
Residencial San Jorge Hostal	1
Youth Hostal El Dorado	3

RESTAURANTS AND BARS

Balconies Pub	E
Caffé Vechia Firenze	A
Chifa Ken Chay	I
Lega's Snack Bar	D
Restaurant Catamaran	F
Restaurant Che Reyes	G
Restaurant Don Manuel	H
Restaurant El Dorado	C
Restaurant La Viña de Huver	B

Plaza de Armas and along Calle San Francisco. It's hard to cross the plaza as a traveller without attracting the attention of at least one tour company sales representative, and these days, with most tour companies offering the same deals at the same price, there really isn't that much to choose between them. Nevertheless, it's advisable to take your time on arrival and check out two or three of the companies to see which one offers you the best and most professional service at the time.

Accommodation
In Pisco

La Casona San Martín 1148. A well-maintained and well-furnished small mansion with 10 rooms. As much a museum as a hotel, this place is elegant and beautiful. ❹

Embassy Beach Hotel San Martín 1119 ☎034/532568, ℱ532256. Easily the flashiest hotel in town, just two blocks from a rather sorry seafront. All modern conveniences and a relatively large pool with bar area and restaurant. ❼

Hostal Callao Jr Callao 163 ☎034/532991. One of the cheapest hostels in the town centre, very rudimentary, but some rooms have private bath. ❷

Hostal El Candelabro Jr Callao 190–198 ☎034/532620. Quite luxurious, with excellent service; all rooms boast a minibar, TV and bath. ❹

Hostal Colonial C Comercio 194 ☎034/532035. The old and quite attractive building located in the busy but pedestrianized boulevard doesn't necessarily make up for the very basic facilities and shared bathrooms; at least hot water is usually available. ❷

Hostal Pisco San Francisco 115 ☎034/532018. A friendly hostel with its own evening music bar – *La Vela* – in a pleasant position on Plaza de Armas, but quite basic for the price; rooms mostly have private bath. ❷–❸

Hostal La Portada Alipio Ponce 250 ☎034/532098. Located a few blocks from the plaza, this is quite good value, featuring pleasant rooms with private bath, hot water and TV. ❸

Hostal Residencial San Jorge Jr Juan Oscores 267 ☎034/532885, ℯhotel_san_jorge_residencial @hotmail.com. A good-value, modern hotel, three short blocks north of the town centre. Rooms are clean and well furnished with own bathrooms; and there's a pleasant garden and ample parking. There are now two entrances, the new main one being on the Barrio Nuevo road, one block nearer the plaza than Jr Juan Oscores. ❹

Hostal Suite San Jorge Comercio 187 ☎034/534200, ℯhotel_san_jorge@hotmail.com. Not as pleasant as its sister hotel a few blocks out, but this is comfortable enough and very central in the pedestrian Boulevar. Rooms are clean and service is OK. ❹

Hotel Comercio Jr Comercio, El Boulevar 168 ☎034/533547. Airy and pleasant; some rooms have hot water. ❷

Hotel Embassy Jr Comercio 180 ☎034/532809. Reasonable value but a little run-down, with private bathrooms and a rooftop breakfast bar. ❸

Hotel Progreso Jr Progreso 254 ☎034/532303. A large and stylish, old-fashioned building. Quite clean and with 60 rooms, but few have windows or bath and the staff are not particularly helpful. ❷

Posada Hispana Hostal Av Bolognesi 236 ☎034/536363, ℱ536363, ℯposadahispana @terra.com.pe. One of the best choices in Pisco, very safe, friendly, and helpful with all sorts of enquiries. The place is attractively decorated, rooms are clean with TV and telephones. Clothes-washing facilities are available and all rooms have private bath and constant hot water. There's also a rooftop patio for breakfasts. ❹

Youth Hostal El Dorado San Juan de Dios 228 ☎034/533610. This 28-bed hostel conveniently close to the Plaza is in a quaint and small family-run house where it's possible to use a kitchen and Internet facilities. ISIC student card holders can get really good deals. ❷–❸

Out of town

Hostal El Mirador El Chaco ☎01/4458496. A popular place which serves meals and will help organize tours; best to make advance reservation. ❸

Hostal Los Zarcillos Av Paracas Lote 106, Urb. El Golf ☎034/545082, ℱ545082. Modern and comfortable, this hostel is fairly close to the beach area for what it's worth. ❹

Hostería Paracas Av Los Libertadores, El Balneario. A cheaper alternative to the *Hotel Paracas*, in a good position close to the entrance to Paracas Reserve. ❺

Hotel Paracas Av 173, Ribera del Mar ☎034/227022, ℱ227023, ℯwww.hotelparacas .com. A luxurious place with pool, excellent bar and restaurant (open to non-residents) right on the ocean and the edge of Paracas Reserve, close to Playa El Chaco wharf. Very popular as a weekend retreat for wealthy Limeños and worth the money. Quite good for surfing. ❻

The Town

Perhaps because of its ease of access, the Spanish considered making **Pisco** their coastal capital before eventually deciding on Lima. Today the town's old port has been superseded by the smelly fish-meal factories south along the bay towards Paracas, and even more so by modern Puerto San Martin north of the Paracas Reserve.

Pisco's focus of activity is the **Plaza de Armas** and adjoining **Jirón Comercio**; every evening the plaza is crowded with people walking and talking, buying *tejas* (small sweets made from pecan nuts) from street sellers, or chatting in one of several laid-back cafés and bars around the square. Clustered about the plaza, with its statue of liberator San Martín poised in the shade of ancient ficus trees, are a few fine colonial showpieces, including the mansion where San Martín stayed on his arrival in Peru; half a block west of the plaza, it's now the **Club Social de Pisco**, but you can still wander in and look around. Another impressive building, inaugurated in 1932 and unusual in its Moorish style, is the **Municipal Palace** (or Consejo Provincial), just to the left if you're facing the church on the Plaza de Armas, painted in striking blue and white in memory of the liberator San Martín's own colours. One block further away from the plaza down Calle San Francisco, the heavy Baroque **Iglesia de la Compañía**, built in 1689, boasts a superb carved pulpit and gold-leaf altarpiece, plus some crypts with subterranean galleries; however, its state of disrepair means it's likely to be closed off to the public.

On a more banal note, the swimming pool at the *As de Oro's* leisure complex, San Martín 472 (☎034/532010), can be used on hot days for under $1 a person.

Avenida San Martín and the ACOREMA Centre

If you have an hour or so to spare, it's worth exploring Avenída San Martín from the plaza west to the sea. Here you can see the decaying remains of the old pier, second in size only to the Muelle de Pacasmayo in the north of Peru, and notice just how much further out the sea edge is today than it clearly was a hundred years or so ago. The Avenida San Martín is also home to many of Pisco's finest mansions, one of which has now been converted into the **ACOREMA Centre**, Av San Martín 1471 (daily 10am–1pm & 2–6pm; Ⓦwww.acorema.org; $1), a small maritime ecology museum with collections of shells, interpretative displays, bones of a five-metre humpback whale and the skeleton of a Gray's beaked whale. The ACOREMA Centre is home to the campaign against the local tradition (now illegal) of putting sea turtles on the lunch menu.

Restaurants and nightlife

You don't have to look far for good food in Pisco, with most **restaurants** specializing in a wide range of locally caught fish and seafood. Sea turtles are in danger of extinction along the coast here, so it's actually illegal to serve or eat turtle as a food (though it is still on offer in some restaurants). **Nightlife** is restricted to the lively *Balconies* pub and the occasional party at the *Hostal Pisco*, both more or less on the Plaza de Armas; or, alternatively, the *As de Oro's* leisure complex at San Martín 472 (☎034/532010), which has a disco, pool and karaoke evenings,.

Balconies Pub Jr Comercio 108. One of the few regular music bars with OK sounds and decent drinks.

Caffe Vecchia Firenze San Francisco 327, ☎034/536613. A great little snack bar with the best coffee in town.

Chifa Ken Chay C Doctor Zunigan 131, ☎034/534557. Just two blocks south of the plaza, this Chinese restaurant serves surprisingly good-quality *chifa* dishes for a relatively small town; good food at great value.

La Estrada San Francisco 247. A small, pleasant coffee shop next to the Ballestas Travel Service office.

Lega's Snack Bar C Callao 131. Nothing flash, but a good place for juices, cakes and hot sandwiches.

Restaurant Acapulco Av Genaro Medrano 620, ☎034/542304. Located just 50 yards or so from the main fisherman's wharf at San Andres, this is one of the more traditional and popular seafood restaurants in the region. Massive fish dishes at reasonable prices.

Restaurant Catamaran Jr Comercio 166. Less than half a block from Plaza de Armas, this is the best place in town for vegetarian bites as well as large and tasty pizzas, but it isn't cheap.

Restaurant Che Reyes Jr Comercio 158. Inexpensive and quite large portions of the usual meals, plus some vegetarian options.

Restaurant El Chorrito ☎034/545045. A pretty tasty seafood restaurant out at El Balneario, en route to Paracas.

Restaurant Don Manuel Jr Comercio 179, ☎034/532035. Just off the Plaza de Armas, serving typical local food, including very fresh fish and shrimps, it's popular with locals and tourists despite being relatively expensive. Open from 6am for breakfasts.

Restaurant El Dorado C Progreso 171. Fairly cheap but offering extensive lunch menus, juices, sandwiches, breakfasts and a range of fish as well as criolla dishes.

Restaurant La Viña de Huver Prolongación Cerro Azul, next to the Parque Zonal ☎034/533199. Just a little way from the centre of town, this is easily the busiest lunch spot in Pisco serving excellent, huge and relatively inexpensive ceviche and other seafood dishes in a bustling and appealing environment.

Listings

Banks and exchange Banco de Credito, Perez Figuerola 162, and Banco Continental, next door on the corner of the Plaza and Independencia. Interbanc, Calle Progreso, Plaza de Armas, is the best place in town for changing travellers' cheques. Most hotels and the tour companies will change dollars cash, but the best rates are from the *cambistas* on the corner of the pedestrian Boulevar between Comercio and Progreso and Plaza de Armas.

Bus companies Cruz del Sur, San Francisco 255; Ormeño (☎034/532764), on the corner of Ayacucho and San Francisco; Oropesa, Calle Commercio; Soyuz Peru Bus has an office on the Plaza de Armas (☎034/535526), corner with Independencia and Perez de Figuerola, but they organize free taxis for passengers from here to the pickup point (☎034/531014) at the *cruce* – bus stops and offices at the major road intersection where the Pisco turn-off meets the Panamerican Highway – some 8km from the plaza in Pisco; the cheaper Saki buses connecting Pisco and Ica leave from Calle Pedemonte, just a block and a half from the Plaza; Empresa Willy Lily, C Callao 172.

Hospital C San Juan de Dios 350.

Internet access Computer 2000, Av San Martín 143 (fast; 8.30am–midnight, daily). Embassy Café Internet, Jr Comercio 178 (fast; 10am–2am, daily). EC-C@B, Jr Comercio 150 (fairly fast; 8am–1am, daily). J&M Sistems Internet Cabins, San Martín 106.

Pharmacy Antigua Botica, San Francisco 197, Plaza de Armas. Botica El Sol, Boulevar/Comercio 120.

Photography Perfect Color, Jr Comercio 196, for a limited range of films and film developing.

Police Plaza de Armas, C San Francisco (☎034/532165).

Post office C Callao, half a block from plaza. Mon–Sat 8am–6pm.

Telephone office Locutorio Telefónico, C Progreso 123A, Plaza de Armas. Daily 7am–11pm.

Tour operators Reservas Tours Pisco, C San Francisco 257 (☎034/534993), Zarcillo Connections, C San Francisco 111, Plaza de Armas (☎034/536543, ✉zarcillo@terra.com.pe), Ballestas Travel, San Franscisco 249 (☎034/533095, Ejpachecot@terra.com.pe), Ballestas Expeditions, San Francisco 219 (☎034/532373), Ballestas Full Tours, San Francisco 219 (☎034/533843), operate package excursions to the Islas Ballestas and Paracas with good guides and a reliable service. The standard arrangement is for hotel pickup around 7am for a bus to pickup the speedboat for the Ballestas Islands; after this most people continue on the tour from the Playa El Chaco Wharf to the main sites in the Paracas National Reserve. It's a standard package costing $10 for the islands morning trip and a further $10 for the afternoon tour of the reserve.

Most of these companies also organize tours to Tambo Colorado and offer a discount for ten or more people; some of them, such as Reservas Tours Pisco, can arrange for flights over the Nazca Lines.

San Andres, El Balneario and the Ballestas Islands

One of the best trips out from Pisco takes in San Andres, El Balneario and the stunning Ballestas Islands. Local tour operators (see Listings, above) run combined bus and boat tours leaving Pisco early in the morning and returning towards midday. Tickets ($10) are best bought the day before: you'll be picked up around 7am, from the plaza in front of the *Hotel Pisco*, your hotel or the tour company office.

The tour buses – and local buses which leave from Pisco market – run south along the shore past the old port of San Andres, where you can watch the fishermen bringing in their catch. The tour buses usually stop here on the way back. San Andres is still famous for its sea turtle dishes, even though it is now illegal to serve them due to the danger of extinction. Warm turtle blood is occasionally drunk in the region, reputedly as a cure for bronchial problems. These days, to save these rare turtles from extinction, it's recommended that visitors avoid turtle dishes and perhaps even consider the merits of reporting any restaurant which offers it to them (☏034/532046, ✉acorema@mail.cosapidata.com.pe). The seas around here are traditionally rich in fish life, and dolphins are often spotted; the abundant plankton in the ocean around Pisco and Paracas attracts five species of whales, and in 1988 a new, small species – the *Mesoplodon Peruvianus*, which can be up to 4m long – was discovered after being caught accidentally in fishermen's nets.

At the far end of San Andres the road passes the big Pisco Air Force Base before reaching **EL BALNEARIO**, a resort for wealthy Limeños, whose large bungalows line the beach. You can **camp** on the sand, though the Paracas Reserve (see below) is a much nicer place to pitch a tent; there are many private beach bungalows and also a few seaside restaurants and hotels here (see p.199). However, most travellers just pass through, using El Balneario as a jumping-off point to visit the Ballestas Islands. Tour buses will drop you here at **Playa El Chaco Wharf**, surrounded by pelicans, where you board speedboats, and zip across the sea, circling one or two of the islands and passing close to the famous Paracas Trident – a huge cactus-shaped figure drawn in the sandstone cliffs (see overleaf).

The **Ballestas Islands** (often called the Guano Islands, as every inch is covered in bird droppings), which lie off the coast due west from Pisco, seem to be alive and moving with a mass of flapping, noisy pelicans, penguins, terns, boobies and Guanay cormorants. The name *Ballesta* is Spanish for crossbow, and may derive from times when marine mammals and larger fish were hunted with mechanical crossbow-style harpoons. The waters around the islands are equally full of life, sometimes sparkling black with the shiny dark bodies of sea lions and the occasional killer whale. The female sea lions have one baby each every year and live in harems of up to fifteen or more per adult male.

Paracas National Reserve

Of greater wildlife interest than the Ballestas Islands, the **Paracas National Reserve**, a few kilometres south of El Balneario, was established in 1975, mainly to protect the marine wildlife – including marine cats and hundreds of sea lions – and amazing birdlife. Its bleak 117,000 hectares of pampa are frequently lashed by strong winds and sandstorms (*paracas* means "raining sand" in Quechua). Home to some of the world's richest seas (a couple of hundred hectares of ocean is included within the reserve's borders), an abundance of marine plankton gives nourishment to a vast array of fish and marine species, who in turn have their attendant predators. This unique desert is also a staging point for a host of migratory birds and acts as a sanctuary for many endangered species. Schools of dolphins play in the waves offshore, condors scour the peninsula for food, small desert foxes come down to the beaches looking for birds and dead sea lions, and lizards scrabble across the hot sands. Humankind has also been active here – predecessors of the pre-Inca **Paracas** culture arrived here some 9000 years ago, reaching their peak between 2000 and 500 BC.

Plan to stay for a few days, and take food, water and a sun-hat – facilities are almost non-existent. The reserve's natural attractions include plenty of superb, deserted beaches where you can **camp** for days without seeing anything except the lizards and birdlife, and maybe a couple of fishing boats. **Cycling** is encouraged in the reserve, though there are no rental facilities and, if you do enter on a bike, keep on the main tracks because the tyre marks will damage the surface of the desert. It's a 21-kilometre bus journey from Pisco (local buses leave Pisco market every 20min; 80¢ each way), or take an organized tour from one of the operators listed on p.201).

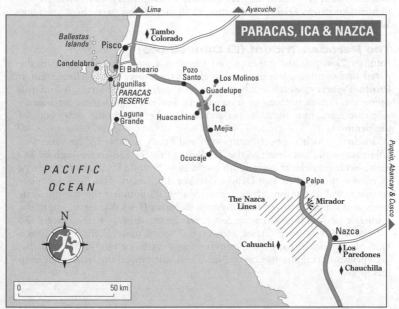

On the way from Pisco to the reserve, the road passes some unpleasant-smelling fish-processing factories, which are causing environmental concern due to spillages of fish oil that pollute the bay, endangering bird and sea-mammal life. Just before the entrance to the reserve, you'll pass a bleak but unmistakable concrete obelisk in the vague shape of a nineteenth-century sailing boat, built in 1970 to commemorate the landing of San Martín here on September 8, 1820, on his mission to liberate Peru from the Spanish stranglehold.

The **entrance** to the reserve is marked by a barrier-gate and guard post (24hr), just off the Panamerican Highway, where you pay the $1.50 entrance fee, which permits you to stay in the park for up to a week. From here most of the roads are sand tracks, though one surfaced *carretera* continues along the shore line towards the new port and connects with the park office, museum and track for Lagunillas and the beaches beyond. Not far from the barrier is a **park office**, where maps are sometimes available, and a little further on, at Km 27, the **Museo de Sitio Julio Tello** (Tues–Sun 9am–5pm; $1) is located right between the two major Paracas archeological sites – Cerro Colorado and Cabeza Largas. The museum depicts human life here over the last 9000 years and contains interpretative exhibits relating to the National Park and a wide range of Paracas artefacts – mummies, ceramics, funerary cloths and a reconstructed dwelling.

Right next to the museum is the oldest discovered site in the region, the **Necropolis of Cabeza Largas**, dating from over five thousand years ago and once containing up to sixty mummies in one grave. Most were wrapped in *vicuña* skins or rush matting, and buried along with personal objects like shell beads, bone necklaces, lances, net bags and cactus-spine needles. A little further on, near the beach where dozens of pink flamingos hang out between July and November (they return to the high Andean lakes for breeding from December to May), are the remains of a Chavin-related settlement, known as **Disco Verde**, though all there is left to see now are a few adobe walls.

The Paracas Trident (El Candelabro)

Another 2km past the museum you come to a fork in the main road: the paved part continues straight on, parallel to the shore, ending after 20km at **Punta Pejerrey**, which holds the modern port of San Martin, full of fish canneries. There's nothing of interest here, but just before the port a sandy side road leads away from the sea and around the hills on the outer edge of the peninsula.

This trail, which is poorly signposted and barely passable by car, takes you 13km across the hot desert to **the Trident**, a massive 128-metre-high by 74-metre-wide candelabra carved into the hillside. No one knows its function or its creator, though Eric Von Daniken, author of *Chariots of the Gods*, speculated that it was a sign for extraterrestrial spacecraft, pointing the way (inaccurately as it happens) towards the mysterious Nazca Lines that are inland to the southeast (see p.215); others suggest it was constructed as a navigational aid for eighteenth-century pirates. However, it seems more likely that it was a kind of pre-Inca ritual object, representing a cactus or tree of life, and that high priests during the Paracas or Nazca eras worshipped the setting sun from this spot.

Lagunillas and around

Unless you want to see the Trident figure, instead of heading on toward Punta Pejerrey, it's a better idea to take the dusty sand track which cuts off to the left of the main road, towards the tiny and likeable port of **Lagunillas**, some 6km from the entrance to the park. A fishing hamlet with no accommodation but a few huts serving *conchitas* (scallops) and other seafood, Lagunillas is really the point on Paracas to make for – a strange, very beautiful part of the peninsula, so flat that if the sea rose just another metre the whole place would be submerged. Pelicans and sea lions hang around the bobbing boats waiting for a fisherman to drop a fish, and little trucks regularly arrive to carry the catch back into Pisco.

From Lagunillas the rest of the Paracas Reserve is at your feet. Nearby are the glorious **beaches** of **La Mina** and **Yimaque**, where you can **camp** for days, often without seeing anyone. A track goes off 5km north from Lagunillas to a longer sandy beach, **Arquillo**; on the cliffs a few hundred metres beyond there's a **viewing platform** (Mirador de los Lobos) looking out over a large colony of sea lions (though they were depleted in number by the 1998 El Niño). Another path leads north from here, straight across the peninsula to the Trident and on to Punta Pejerrey. There have been reports of stingrays on some of the beaches, so take care, particularly if you're without transport or company; check first with the fishermen at Lagunillas which beaches are the safest.

South around the bay from Lagunillas, drive or walk along the track turning right across the sandy hills and heading away from the museum. While it used to be only an hour's walk to the spectacular **cathedral cave** (La Catedral), a landslide had barred access in 2002. Assuming a new trail is created, it will soon be possible once again to see first-hand La Catedral's high vaulted ceilings lined by bats. A family of sea otters (known in Peru as *gatos marinos*, or "sea cats") lives under the cave's floor of sea-worn boulders; they can sometimes been seen sleekly avoiding the huge waves which pound the rocky inner cave walls. The cave lies at the end of a vast, curved, gravelly beach whose waves are so strong that local fishermen call it **Playa Supay** (or "Devil's Beach"), so don't be tempted to swim – it's far too dangerous. This track continues to the fishing village of **Laguna Grande**, from where it's possible to track back inland to Ocucaje on the Panamerican Highway between Ica and Nazca. Even in a good 4WD this will take the best part of a day and isn't really recommended without a local guide.

Tambo Colorado

Some 48km northeast of Pisco, and 327km south of Lima, the ruins at **TAMBO COLORADO** were originally a fortified administrative centre, probably built by the Chincha before being adapted and used as an Inca coastal outpost. Its position at the base of steep foothills in the Pisco river valley was perfect for controlling the flow of people and produce along the ancient road down from the Andes. You can still see dwellings, offices, storehouses and row upon row of barracks and outer walls, some of them even retaining traces of coloured paints. The rains have taken their toll, but even so this is considered one of the best-preserved adobe ruins in Peru – roofless, but otherwise virtually intact. Though in an odd way reminiscent of a fort from some low-budget Western, it is an adobe complex with everything noticeably in its place – autocratic by intention, oppressive in function, and rather stiff in style.

The easiest way to get to Tambo Colorado is on a **guided tour** from Pisco (see Listings, p.201, for details), which costs less than $15 per person, provided there are at least ten people. You can also travel there independently from Pisco: take the Ormeño **bus** from Jirón San Francisco or the Oropesa bus from Calle Comercio (both leave most mornings, but check first with the bus company as departure times and frequencies vary from day to day; approximately $3.50 each way). The bus takes the surfaced Ayacucho road, which runs straight through the site, and the ruins are around twenty minutes beyond the village of Humay.

③ South from Pisco

South from Pisco, the Panamerican Highway sweeps some 70km inland to reach the fertile wine-producing Ica Valley, a virtual oasis in this stretch of bleak desert. **Pozo Santo**, the only real landmark en route, is distinguished by a small, towered and whitewashed chapel, built on the site of an underground well. Legend has it that when Padre Guatemala, the friar Ramon Rojas, died on this spot, water miraculously began to flow from the sands. Now there's a restaurant here where colectivo drivers sometimes stop for a snack, but little else.

Beyond Pozo Santo, the Panamerican Highway crosses the Pampa de Villacuri. At the Km 280 marker, there's a track leading north; after about an hour's hike, you'll reach the ruins of an unnamed adobe **fortress** complex, where you can see dwellings, a plaza, a forty-metre-long outer wall, and ancient man-made wells, which are still used by local peasants to irrigate their cornfields. Seashells and brightly coloured plumes from the tropical forest which have been found in the graves here suggest that there was an important trade link between the inhabitants of the southern coast and the tribes from the eastern jungles on the other side of the formidable Andean mountain range.

Farther down the Panamerican Highway, the pretty roadside village of **Guadalupe** (at Km 293) signals the beginning of the Ica oasis. To the right there's a large, dark, conical hill, Cerro Prieto, behind which, in amongst the shifting sand dunes, there are even more **ruins**, dating from 500 BC. Just a few kilometres on, beyond a string of wine bodegas and shantytown suburbs, you reach Ica itself.

Ica and around

An attractive, old but busy city with around 170,000 inhabitants, **ICA** is famous throughout Peru for its wine and pisco production. Its very foundation (in 1563) went hand in hand with the introduction of grapevines to South America, and for most Peruvian visitors it is the bodegas, or **wineries**, that are the town's biggest draw. A further attraction is the **Museo Regional**, whose superb collections of pre-Columbian ceramics and Paracas, Ica and Nazca cultural artefacts would alone make the city worth an excursion. Ica's streets and plazas are crowded with hundreds of little *tico* taxis, all beeping their horns to catch potential passengers' attention and making crossing the streets a dangerous affair. Aside from the traffic and the occasional pickpocket – particularly round the market area – Ica is a pleasant but busy place with a friendly and curious population. After a day or less, though, most visitors are ready to head for the relaxing desert oasis resort of **Huacachina**, a few kilometres to the southwest, a much more exotic and restful place to pass the hot sunny afternoons. On the edge of town is the rather ramshackle suburb of **Cachiche**, known throughout Peru as a traditional sanctuary for white witches.

The witches of Cachiche

In the down-at-heel suburb of Cachiche, history and mythology have merged into a legend of a local group of **witches**. The story dates back to the seventeenth century, when, hounded for their pagan beliefs by the Inquisition, Spanish witches apparently emigrated to Peru. However, the persecution in Lima equalled that in their homeland, and they fled to the countryside and, in particular, the Ica Valley, though even then they were forced into outlying villages; the white witches apparently moved to Cachiche, the black ones to Huamangia, the east of the city. Cachiche resurfaced in the Peruvian consciousness in the 1980s, when a powerful congressman was dramatically cured on TV of a terminal illness by one of the last Cachiche witches. Even now, Cachiche is synonymous with witchcraft and healing magic in the Peruvian consciousness, so much so that a very trendy restaurant opened up in Lima called *Las Brujas de Cachiche* (see p.91).

Arrival, information and city transport

If you arrive in Ica with Ormeño, Jr Lambayeque 180 (℡034/215600) or Cruz del Sur **buses**, or with Saki bus from Pisco, you'll come in along Prolongación Lambayeque, a few blocks west of Plaza de Armas. Soyuz Peru Bus fast services from Lima arrive close by on Av Matías Manzanilla 130 (℡034/224138), Expresso Sudamericano arrive at Av Municipalidad 336, and Flores come in at Salaverry 396, on the corner with Lambayeque.

To get around the town itself, most people take **taxis**, mostly small, flimsy and dangerous *tico* cars (try to use one of the rarer, but larger and more solid vehicles), with journeys within town rarely costing more than $2. Cheaper still – around $1 for anywhere in town and under $3 to Huacachina – are the **bicycle rickshaw taxis**, which can be hailed anywhere in town. For longer journeys to the outlying parts of town, you can take one of the **microbuses**, which leave from Jirón Lima or Prolongación Lambayeque and have their destinations chalked up on their windscreens. **Tourist information** is available from some of the bodegas and tour offices on the Jirón Lima side of the Plaza de Armas or at the Automóvil Club at Manzanilla 523.

Accommodation

Colibri Inn Av Grau 387 ℡034/231764, ⓔcolibrigo@hotmail.com. A popular little, backpacker-friendly hostel, it has kitchen and laundry facilities; but most rooms have communal baths and it's a bit noisy (being over an amusement arcade). ❷

Hospedaje Salaverry Salaverry 146 ℡034/214019. Clean but noisy and basic, with communal bathrooms. ❷

Hostal La Arboleda C Independencia 165 ℡034/234597. Surprisingly good value, very cheap yet set in a stylish old building, with reasonable service but very basic rooms and cold water only. ❶

Hostal Aries C Independencia 181 ℡034/235367. The best of Ica's budget hostels, with clean rooms, though bathrooms are communal; there's a pleasant patio with room for bikes or motorbikes and service is OK. ❶

Hostal Belle Sand Av Casuarines B1-3, Residencial La Angostura ℡034/256039, ⓕ256814. Not central, but in a tranquil, attractive, natural setting and offering friendly family service as well as good value with a pool, colour TVs and private bathrooms. ❹

Hostal Callao Jr Callao 128 ℡034/235976. Very central – just a few metres from the Plaza de Armas – basic, clean and quite friendly. Some rooms have private shower. ❷

Hostal Europa C Independencia 258 ℡034/232111. Would be good value if it weren't so noisy. Located very close to the market area, it's friendly and clean, with sinks in some rooms but communal toilets. ❷

Hostal Loma Blanca Urb La Angostura, La Salcedo 135 ℡01/4375532 or 034/256670, ⓔrenzo_campos_castro@latinmail.com. Although located out of the town centre, this is a safe, friendly and good-value hostel offering room service and TVs. ❹

Hostal Oasis C Tacna 216 ☎034/234767. Hot water and some private bathrooms available in this rather basic pad. ❷

Hostal Palace Jr Tacna 185 ☎034/211655. Modern building with its own café next door; private bathrooms but no single rooms. ❸

Hostal San Isidro Los Jasminez 127, San Isidro ☎034/235474. Although not particularly central, this pleasant hostel offers economy and comfort in large rooms. Affiliated with Hostelling International. ❷

Hostal Sol de Ica Jr Lima 265 ☎034/236168, ✉soldeica_hotel@peru.com. Located between the town centre, Huacachina and the Regional Museum, it's quite modern and clean, with a nice swimming pool, though the building has suffered some earthquake damage and no longer looks its best. ❺

Hotel Arameli C Tacna 239 ☎034/239107. A new hotel where all rooms have private bath and hot water; it's clean, central amd very friendly. ❸

Hotel Las Dunas Av la Angostura 400, Km 300, Panamerican Highway ☎034/231031, ✉invertur@invertur.com.pe. Very swish, out-of-town luxury hotel with a pool and plenty of amenities. ❼

Hotel Real de Ica Av Los Maestros ☎034/233330 or 233320. Located on the outskirts of town near the hospital and en route to Huacachina. One of a luxury chain of ex-government-run *turistas* hotels, with a nice pool open to non-residents for a fee of around $2. Fantastic buffet lunches are served during the main fiesta periods. Taxi drivers may still know it as *El Hotel de Turistas*. ❼

Sol y Luna Salaverry 292 ☎034/227241. A modern, very clean hotel. Service and facilities are superior to others of a similar price. ❸

The Town

Founded in 1563, and originally called Villa de Valverde de Ica, after only five years the settlement was moved, due to earthquake activity in the region, and renamed San Jerónimo de Ica. It was moved several times again until finding itself in its present position in a relatively sheltered river valley protected slightly from the coastal weather (especially the mists) by large sand dunes, but still quite a way from the foothills of the Andes to the east. Ica is one of the first places south of Lima where you can virtually guarantee nice sunny weather most of the year. Ica's quite a sprawl these days, and although prone to earthquakes, the flooding caused by El Niño in 1998 resulted in the most recent damage, when the Plaza de Armas and most of the main streets were submerged under more than a metre of water.

Ica's colonial heart – the inevitable **Plaza de Armas**, site of an early declaration of independence from Spain – remains its modern centre, smart and friendly, with the inclusion of an obelisk and fountains. Running east from here, the modern commercial spine is the busy Avenida Grau with the market area parallel a couple of blocks to the north. It's not recommended walking alone east of this area as a visitor, as muggings are not unknown. Most of the important **churches** can be found within a few blocks of the plaza, none of them of great architectural merit but considerably revered within the region. The church of **La Merced**, southwest of the plaza, contains Padre Guatemala's tomb – said to give immense good fortune if touched on New Year's Day. Around the corner on Avenida Municipalidad is the more recent, grander **San Francisco** church, whose stained-glass windows dazzle against the strong Ican sunlight. To the south of the plaza, down Jirón Lima, then left along Prolongación Ayabaca, is a third major church, **El Sanctuario de Luren**. Built on the site of a hermitage founded in 1556, the present construction, Neoclassical in style and with three brick-built *portales*, houses the Imagen del Señor de Lurin, a statue of the patron saint of the town, something of a national shrine and centre for pilgrimage on the third Sundays of March and October.

There are a few **mansions** of note in Ica, including the Casona del Marqués de Torre Hermosa, in Calle Libertad and near the plaza. Now belonging to the Banco Continental, it is one of the few examples of colonial architecture to

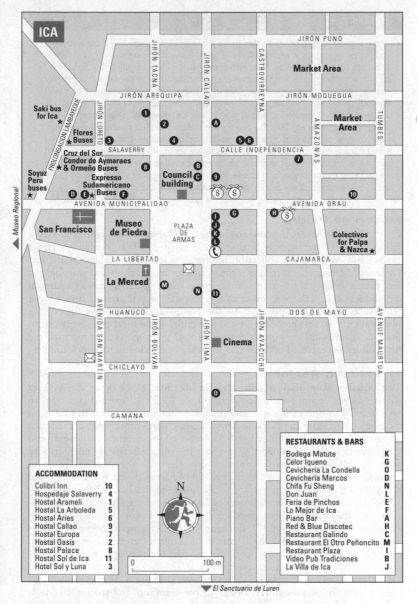

ICA

JIRÓN PUNO

Market Area

JIRÓN TACNA

JIRÓN CALLAO

CASTROVIRREYNA

JIRÓN AREQUIPA   JIRÓN MOQUEGUA

Saki bus
for Ica ★

Flores
★ Buses

Cruz del Sur,
Condor de Aymaraes ★
& Ormeño Buses

Soyuz
Peru
buses ★

Market
Area

AMAZONAS

TUMBES

JIRÓN LORETO

PROLONGACIÓN LAMBAYEQUE

SALAVERRY

CALLE INDEPENDENCIA

Expresso
Sudamericano
Buses

Council
building

AVENIDA MUNICIPALIDAD

AVENIDA GRAU

Museo Regional ◄

San Francisco

Museo
de Piedra

PLAZA
DE
ARMAS

Colectivos
for Palpa
& Nazca ★

LA LIBERTAD

CAJAMARCA

La Merced

AVENIDA SAN MARTÍN

HUANUCO

JIRÓN BOLÍVAR

JIRÓN LIMA

JIRÓN AYACUCHO

DOS DE MAYO

AVENUE MAURTUA

CHICLAYO

Cinema

CAMANA

N

0   100 m

RESTAURANTS & BARS

Bodega Matute	K
Celor Iqueno	G
Cevicheria La Condella	O
Cevicheria Marcos	D
Chifa Fu Sheng	N
Don Juan	L
Feria de Pinchos	E
Lo Mejor de Ica	F
Piano Bar	A
Red & Blue Discotec	H
Restaurant Galindo	C
Restaurant El Otro Peñoncito	M
Restaurant Plaza	
Video Pub Tradiciones	B
La Villa de Ica	J

ACCOMMODATION

Colibri Inn	10
Hospedaje Salaverry	4
Hostal Arameli	1
Hostal La Arboleda	5
Hostal Aries	6
Hostal Callao	9
Hostal Europa	7
Hostal Oasis	2
Hostal Palace	8
Hostal Sol de Ica	11
Hotel Sol y Luna	3

▼ El Sanctuario de Luren

survive in the earthquake-stricken city. In the first block of Calle 2 de Mayo, you can find the Casona de José de la Torre Ugarte, once home to the composer of the Peruvian National Anthem. The Casona Alvorado, now belonging to the Banco Latino, at Cajamarca 178, is the region's only example of a copy of the *greco-romana* architectural style, while the Casona Colonial El Porton, C Loreto 233, conserves some fine colonial architecture and houses a restaurant-peña – *Almuerzos Criollos* – (see "Bars and nightlife", p.212).

Fiestas in Ica

There are several important **fiestas** in Ica throughout the year. The most enjoyable time to be in town is in **March** after the grape harvest has been brought in, when there are open-air concerts, fairs, handicraft markets, cockfighting and *caballo de paso* (horse dressage – where horses are trained by riders to dance and prance for events or competitions) meetings. Over the **Semana de Ica** (June 12–19), based around the colonial founding of Ica, there are more festivities, including religious processions and fireworks, and again in the last week of September for the **Semana Turística**. On July 25, there's the nationwide **Día Nacional de Pisco**, essentially a big celebration for the national brandy (rather than the town of the same name), mostly celebrated in the bodegas south of Lima, particularly around Ica. As in Lima, **October** is the main month for religious celebrations, with the focus being the ceremony and procession at the church of El Sanctuario de Luren (main processions on the third Sunday and following Monday of October).

Museo de Piedra

On the Plaza de Armas, the **Museo de Piedra**, Bolivar 178b (daily from 10am; guided tours by arrangement; ☎034/213026 or 231933), contains a rather bizarre and controversial collection of engraved stones, assembled by the late Dr Javier Cabrera. He claimed that the stones are several thousand years old but few people believe this – some of the stones depict patently modern surgical techniques and, perhaps more critically, you can watch artisans turning out remarkably similar designs over on the pampa at Nazca. Nevertheless, the stones are remarkable pieces of art and one enthusiastic local guidebook claims that "dinosaur hunts are portrayed, suggesting that Ica may have supported the first culture on earth". The museum doors are often closed, so knock loudly.

The Museo Regional

The **Museo Regional Maria Reiche de Ica**, block 8 of Av Ayabaca (Mon–Sat 9am–6pm, Sun & fiestas 9am–1pm; $1.50, $2 extra if you want to take photos), is one of the best archeological museums in Peru. To find it on foot, head west from the Plaza de Armas along Calle Municipalidad, then turn left onto Callia Elias; continue south for half a kilometre, then turn right onto Calle Ayabaca and the museum is just over the road. Alternately take bus #17 from the Plaza de Armas. Either way you can't miss the concrete museum building stuck out on its own in the middle of barren desert parkland. Behind the Museo there's an excellent large-scale model of the Nazca Lines.

The most striking of the museum's collections is its display of **Paracas textiles**, the majority of them discovered at Cerro Colorado on the Paracas Peninsula by Julio Tello in 1927. Enigmatic in their apparent coding of colours and patterns, these funeral cloths consist of blank rectangles alternating with elaborately woven ones – repetitious and identical except in their multi-directional shifts of colour and position.

The first room to the right off the main foyer contains a fairly gruesome display of **mummies**, **trepanned skulls**, **grave artefacts** and **trophy heads**. It seems very likely that the taking of trophy heads in this region was related to specific religious beliefs – as it was until quite recently among the head-hunting Jivaro of the Amazon Basin. The earliest of these skulls, presumably hunted and collected by the victor in battle, come from the Asia Valley (north of Ica) and date from around 2000 BC.

The museum's main room is almost entirely devoted to pre-Columbian **ceramics and textiles**, possibly the finest collection outside Lima. On the left as you enter are spectacular Paracas urns; one is particularly outstanding, with an owl and serpent design painted on one side, and a human face with arms, legs and a navel on the other. There is some exquisite Nazca pottery, too, undoubtedly the most colourful and abstractly imaginative designs found on any ancient Peruvian ceramics. The last wall consists mainly of artefacts from the Ica-Chincha culture. A highlight is the beautiful **feather cape**, with multicoloured plumes in almost perfect condition. Displayed also in the main room are several **quipus**, ancient calculators using bundles of knotted strings as mnemonic aids that were also used for the recitation of ancient legends, genealogies and ballads. They have survived better here on the coast than in the mountains and the Ica collection is one of the best in the country.

Bodegas

The best way to escape Ica's hot desert afternoons is to wander around the cool chambers and vaults and sample the wines at one of the town's **bodegas** or wineries. One of Peru's best is **Vista Allegre** (daily 9am–2pm), easily reached by walking down Avenida Grau from the main plaza, crossing over the Río Ica bridge, then turning left (or take the orange microbus #8 from Avenida Grau or the market). Follow this road for about twenty minutes until you come to a huge yellow colonial gateway on your right; the arch leads via an avenue of tall eucalyptus trees to the bodega itself, an old hacienda still chugging happily along in a forgotten world of its own. There's usually a guide who'll show you around free of charge, then arrange for a wine and pisco tasting session at the shop. You don't have to buy anything, but you're expected to tip (say 10 percent at most).

If you follow the road beyond Vista Allegre for another 6km you'll come to **Bodega Tacama** (daily 9am–1pm), a larger, better and more well-known wine producer about 3km from the centre of Ica, which also offers guided tours and tastings. The vineyards here are still irrigated by the Achirana canal, which was built by the Inca Pachacutec (or his brother Capac Yupanqui) as a gift to Princess Tate, daughter of a local chieftain. According to legend, it took 40,000 men just ten days to complete this astonishing canal, which brings cold, pure water down 4000m from the Andes to transform what was once an arid desert into a startlingly fertile oasis. Clearly a romantic at heart, Pachacutec named it Achirana – "that which flows cleanly towards that which is beautiful". About 35km further south, the tourist oasis of **Bodega Ocucaje** is another of Peru's finest vineyards. You can stay here at the *Hotel Ocucaje* (④) and explore the surrounding desert, particularly the Cerro Blanco site where whalebone remains have been found.

Restaurants

Most of the restaurants in Ica can be found on or within a block or two of the Plaza de Armas. Their quality in terms of food and general ambience varies enormously, but there is ample choice from breakfast through to evening meal.

Calor Iqueno Av Grau 103. Small and fairly quiet, this snack bar/coffee shop has great hot drinks, yogurts and local *empanadas* (pasties filled with meat, onions and olives).
Cevichería La Candella block 4 of Jr Lima. Decent food and affordable prices, plus a lively atmosphere and a bar that's open evenings.
Cevichería Marcos Av Municipalidad 350. Good seafood lunches at very reasonable prices.
Chifa Fu Sheng Jr Lima 243. Very affordable Chinese restaurant, packed with locals in the evenings.
Don Juan Tejas y Chocotejas Lima 171. Some of the best local *dulces* to be tasted in town.
El Eden C Andaguayllas 204. A popular vegetarian restaurant making good use of local ingredients.
Gran Pollería las Nieves C Piura 400, Plaza Bolognesi. A well-liked place that serves good chicken and chips.
El Otro Peñoncito Bolivar 255 ☏034/233921.

Less than a block from the plaza, this stylish restaurant has walls tastefully adorned with artwork from Andean cosmology by an Iqueño artist; their speciality is *pollo iqueño* - chicken stuffed with spinach and pecan nuts topped with a pisco sauce. Open daily until midnight.
Restaurant Galindo C Callao 145, just off the Plaza de Armas. A popular locals' dive serving big portions and sometimes the Ica speciality *carapulchra* (pork, chicken and potato casserole). A busy atmosphere, with a loud TV.
Restaurant Plaza Jr Lima 125, Plaza de Armas. This is Ica's slightly upmarket downtown eating and meeting place serving pretty fine traditional cuisine, including lots of fresh seafood. Has a relatively inexpensive set-lunch menu.

Bars and nightlife

Not surprisingly, Ica wines are very much a part of the town's life, and locals pop into a **bodega** for a quick glass of pisco at just about any time of the day; most are open 9am–9pm. The best places to do likewise are *La Villa de Ica*, Jr Lima 139, or the *Bodega Matute*, Jr Lima 143, close to each other on the Plaza de Armas with good ranges of piscos, wines, *tejas* and juices which can be sampled over the counter. Another shop for this is the *Casa de Artesania* on Calle Cajamarca, just a few yards from the plaza, which serves drinks and sells bottles as well as artesania, including local leather craft.

More of a café-cum-bar, the rather unusual *Quimeras Piano Bar*, C Callao 224 (℡034/213186) opens from 8pm until late most evenings and performs criollo, Mexican, Cuban and other international numbers. The only **nightclub** in town is the *Red & Blue Discotheque*, in block three of Jirón Grau. There's also the *Video Pub Tradiciones Peruanos*, Callao 179, which has cold beers and also serves some food but is a bit spit-and-sawdust. *Almuerzos Criollos* restaurant-*peña* in the Casona Colonial El Porton, C Loreto 233, often has shows at weekends.

Listings

Banks and exchange Travellers' cheques and cash can be changed at Banco de Credito, Av Grau 109 (Mon–Fri 8am–5pm); Caja Municipa, Av Municipalidad 148 (Mon–Fri 8.30am–6pm); and the Banco de la Nación, Av Matías Manzanilla (Mon–Fri 9am–6pm). For dollars cash try any of the *cambistas* on the corners of the Plaza de Armas.
Bus companies Peru Bus, Av Matías Manzanilla 150 ℡034/224138, have the fastest and most frequent connections for Pisco and Ica; Condor de Aymaraes, Prolongación Lambayeque 152a; Cruz del Sur, Prolongación Lambayeque 148 ℡034/233333; Expresso Sudamericano, Municipalidad 336; Flores, Salaverry 396; Ormeño, Prolongación Lambayeque 180 ℡034/23262.
Internet access Space Net, Huánuco 177, one block from plaza (slow; 9am–10pm daily, ℡034/217033), De Cajon.com, Huánuco 201, large (fast, daily 9am–midnight, ℡034/237396); Cabinas Internet, first block of Av Grau, small (slow).
Pharmacy and photography Kodak Express, Jr Lima 252, films and developing.
Police The Tourist Police are on block 1 of Prolongación Lambayeque ℡034/233632.

Post office San Martín 398, 3 blocks south of Plaza de Armas. Mon–Sat 8am–6.30pm.
Sweet shops Helena, Cajamarca 139, just around the corner from the plaza, sells the fanciest *tejas* and chocolates; Farmacia Lima, C Lima 538, sells equally good, but much cheaper hand-made *tejas* (try the lemon *tejas*).
Taxi Juan Caico ℡034/218313 is a safe and reliable local taxi driver.
Telephones Telefonica Locutorio, Lima 149, Plaza de Armas, 8am–8pm, daily.
Tour operators There are several tour operators in town offering similar excursions such as Ica City Tour (including Huacachina, wine bodegas, the Museo Regional and the barrio of Cachiche) and also trips to the Palpa Valley, various Nazca archeological attractions, the Ballestas Islands and Paracas; most have shop fronts on the Plaza de Armas and all can arrange for flights over the Nazca Lines: Colibri Tours, Lima 121 ℡034/214406; Desert Travel and Service, Lima 171 (in Tejas Don Juan shop) ℡034/234127; Diplomatic Travel, Av Municipalidad 132, Of 13 ℡034/237187; Edwards Travel Service, Lima 139 ℡034/312799, ©marleni34@hotmail.com. For 4WD desert adventure tours try Solo Ica 4WD, Brunias 17, San Isidro, Ica ℡634/682682.

Around Ica: Huacachina

According to myth, the lagoon at **HUACACHINA**, about 5km southwest of Ica, was created when a princess stripped off to bathe, but, on looking into a mirror, saw that a male hunter was watching her; startled, she dropped the mirror, which turned into the lagoon. More prosaically, during the late 1940s, the lagoon became one of Peru's most elegant and exclusive resorts, surrounded by palm trees, sand dunes and waters famed for their curative powers, and with a delightfully old-world atmosphere. Since then the lagoon's subterranean source has grown erratic and it is supplemented by water pumped up from artesian wells, making it less of a red-coloured thick, viscous syrup and more like a green salty swimable lagoon; it retains considerable mystique, making it a quiet, secluded spot to relax. The **curative powers** of the lagoon attract people from all over: mud from the lake is reputed to cure arthritis and rheumatism if you plaster yourself all over with it; and the sand around the lagoon is also supposed to benefit people with chest problems such as asthma or bronchitis, so it's not uncommon to see locals buried up to the neck in the dunes. **Sand dune surfing** on the higher slopes is all the rage and you can rent wooden boards or foot-skis for around $2 an hour from the cafés along the shoreline. Boats can be rented for rowing or peddling on the lagoon. The settlement, still little more than twenty houses or so, is growing very slowly, but one end of the lagoon has been left fairly clear of constructions.

Practicalities

To get to Huacachina from Ica, take one of the orange **buses** from outside the Sanctuario de Luren, or from Jirón Lima; buses leave at least once every fifteen minutes and the journey itself takes fifteen to twenty minutes. On arrival, you'll find a small wooden kiosk, frequently staffed by the local tourist police; they have information sheets and rather poor maps, and will also direct you to accommodation or other services.

The most stylish accommodation around is the luxurious and exceptionally elegant *Hotel Mossone* (☎034/213630, ℱ213630, ℮hmossone@derramajal .org.pe; ❼), once the haunt of politicians and diplomats, who listened to concerts while sitting on the colonial-style veranda overlooking the lagoon. Outside high season it is sometimes possible to get very reasonable deals, but if your budget won't stretch to this, the *Hotel Salvatierra*, Malecón de Huacachina (☎034/232352 or 236132, ℮javosalvati@hotmail.com; ❸), alongside, is excellent value, and has an enormous amount of character; its splendid dining room holds a number of important murals by the Ica artist Servulo Gutierrez (1914–61), who evidently drank his way through a massive number of pisco bottles in his time here. Most rooms have private facilities, and the owner's family offer transport to and from Ica whenever possible. The *Hostería Suiza*, Balconario de Huacachina 264 (☎034/238762, ℮hostesuiza @yahoo.com; ❺), is very comfortable, cozy, quiet and located at the far end of the lake. There are a couple of hostels with new swimming pools including the *Hospedaje Titanic* (❸) above the left end of the *malecón*. It's possible to camp in the sand dunes around the lagoon – rarely is it cold enough to need more than a blanket. The restaurant *Curasi*, next to the *Mossone*, has a wide range of reasonably priced Peruvian dishes on offer. The *Mossone* itself has a wonderful restaurant, too, but it's very pricey. There are a couple of other decent options: the *Restaurant Moron* for lunches under the bandstand beside the lake, and *Restaurant Mayo* (☎034/229003), on Cassino Mossone just around the corner, for snacks and evening meals. *Mayo* also organizes 4WD desert fun rides

△ Paracas peninsular and bay

exploring the more remote dune areas ($10 for 2 hours), rents sand boards and offers campers a room for bag storage and a shower.

The Nazca Lines

One of the great mysteries of South America, the **Nazca Lines** are a series of animal figures and geometric shapes, none of them repeated and some up to 200m in length, drawn across some five hundred square kilometres of the bleak, stony Pampa de San José. Each one, even such sophisticated motifs as a spider monkey or a hummingbird, is executed in a single continuous line, most created by clearing away the brush and hard stones of the plain to reveal the

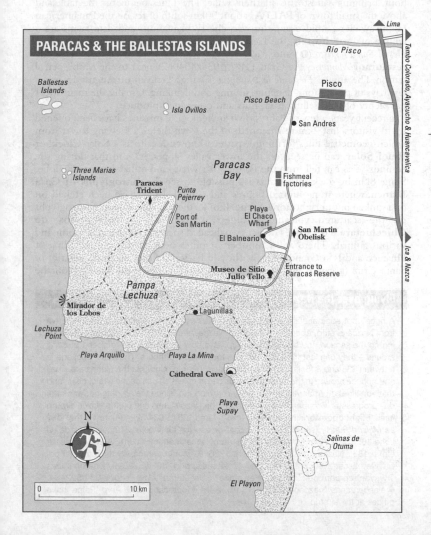

PARACAS & THE BALLESTAS ISLANDS

Lima

Río Pisco

Ballestas
Islands

Pisco

Isla Ovillos

Pisco Beach

San Andres

Three Marias
Islands

Paracas
Bay

Paracas
Trident

Punta
Pejerrey

Fishmeal
factories

Port of
San Martin

Playa
El Chaco
Wharf

San Martin
Obelisk

El Balneario

Museo de Sitio
Julio Tello

Entrance to
Paracas Reserve

Pampa
Lechuza

Mirador de
los Lobos

Lagunillas

Lechuza
Point

Playa Arquillo

Playa La Mina

Cathedral Cave

Playa
Supay

Salinas de
Otuma

N

El Playon

0   10 km

Tambo Colorado, Ayacucho & Huancavelica

Ica & Nazca

215

fine dust beneath. They were possibly a kind of agricultural calendar to help regulate the planting and harvesting of crops, while perhaps at the same time some of the straight lines served as ancient sacred paths connecting *huacas*, or power spots. One theory proposes that the Lines were used as running tracks in some sort of sporting competition; whichever theory you favour, they are among the strangest and most unforgettable sights in the country.

Getting to the Lines

The road to Nazca from Ica crosses the large strip of desert called the **Pampa de Gamonal** after the unfortunate man who, as the local story goes, found a vast amount of treasure here, buried it, and then promptly developed amnesia as to its whereabouts. Winds here frequently achieve speeds of up to 45km per hour, bringing sandstorms in their wake. The Lines begin on the tableland above the small town of **PALPA**, about 90km south of Ica on the Panamerican Highway. Here, amid orange groves, cherry plantations and date farms are a couple of small **hostels**, the basic *Hostal Palpa* (❶) and the simple but clean *Hostal San Francisco* (❷) and, for great *chupe* or *tortilla de camarones*, there's the **restaurant** *Monterrey*, Av Grau 118 (☎034/404062), next to the Mobil petrol station. The annual *Fiesta de la Narancja* (Orange Festival) on August 15 sees a few days of processions, dancing, singing and drinking. Usually, the main street has plenty of stalls selling fruit, nuts and other local produce.

In recent years, a few of Palpa's own archeological treasures have been opened up to visitors. Just 2km to the north of the town there's a viewing tower from which geometric lines forming a pattern known locally as a Solar Clock, or **Reloj Solar**, can be seen on the lower valley slopes. It's said that during the equinox seers can tell from the Reloj Solar what kind of harvest there will be. Some 8km by track from Palpa it's possible to see the **petroglyphs of Casa Blanca**, where stone human figures and cuboid shapes have been etched on one sunken but upright stone. Some 4km further on are a series of petroglyphs on the scattered volcanic boulders, known as the **petroglyfos de Chicchictara**. The images depict two-headed snakes, a sun burst, a moon and various animals. There are a number of other petroglyph sites, including at Huaraco and Río Grande, and, at the old hacienda Huayuri, in the district of Santa Cruz (accessed by the San Francisco village: turn off Km 384 on the

---

Flying over the Nazca Lines

A pricey but spectacular way of seeing the Lines is to **fly** over them. Flights leave from Nazca airstrip, about 3km south of Nazca, and cost $30–50 a person depending on the season, the size of the group, and how long you want to spend buzzing around – they can last from ten minutes to a couple of hours. The usual package is between $35 and $45, lasting 30–45 minutes. Bear in mind that the planes are small and bounce around in the changeable air currents, which can cause airsickness, and that you'll get a better view on an early morning trip, since the air gets hazier as the day progresses. Companies are located in the Nazca Lines and on the Nazca airstrip itself. **Flight operators** include Aero Ica, C Lima 103 (☎034/522434), or via the hotel *La Maison Suisse* (see p.222) in Nazca, or see Ica Listings, p.212; Aero Nazca, C Lima 165, Nazca (☎/℮034/522297, ✉aeroNazca@Latinmail.com); Aeroparacas, Jr Lima 185, Nazca (☎034/521027, ℻522688, ✉aeroparacas@wayna.rcp.net.pe, 🌐www.nascatravel.com); or at Km 447 Nazca airport ☎034/522699, ✉aeroparacas @wayna.rcp.com.pe); Alas Peruanas, Jr Lima 168 (☎/℻034/522444, ✉alasperuanas@nazcaperu.com). Both Aero Montecarlo and Aero Palpa have offices at the airstrip.

Panamericana Sur highway), the **lost city of Huayuri**, dating from 1200–1400 AD.

It's still another 30km until you're on the plateau where some of the best Nazca Lines can be seen. At Km 420 of the Panamerican Highway, a tall metal **viewing tower** (or *mirador*, 30¢) has been built above the plain. Unless you've got the time to climb up onto one of the hills behind, or take a **flight** over the Lines (see box), this is the best view you'll get. The rather underdeveloped **Casa Museo y Mausoleo Maria Reiche** (Mon–Sat 9am–5pm; $1), about 1km beyond the *mirador*, based in her old adobe home in the shadow of the pampa, consists of three main rooms containing displays of photos, drawings and ceramics relating to the Nazca Lines and the studies of Maria Reiche (a premier Nazca Lines researcher). One room just contains Reiche's personal possessions and shows the spartan reality of her daily life here, right down to her flipflops (for more on Maria Reiche, see below). The vast majority of people base themselves in Nazca and take a **guided tour** (see p. 225) or a flight from there. However, you can visit independently, by taking a **local bus** from Nazca (70¢), a **taxi** from Nazca, which will wait and bring you back again for around $10, or one of the **intercity buses** for Ica and Lima, which leave every couple of hours from the corner of the Panamerican Highway and Jirón Lima on the outskirts of Nazca and let you off at the *mirador*. The return bus to Nazca passes Km 420 of the Panamerican Highway every couple of hours and can be waved down.

The lines are actually a combination of straight lines continuing for many kilometres in some cases across the sandy, stone-strewn plateau; others look like trapezoidal plazas, perfectly formed by clearing the stones from the surface to create the required pattern. Other "lines" are actually stylized line drawings of real birds and animals, possibly symbolizing both astrological phases and possible ancient Nazca clan divisions – with each symbol representing, perhaps, the totem of a particular sub-group of this pre-Inca society.

Theories about the Nazca Lines

The greatest expert on the Lines was undoubtedly **Maria Reiche**, who worked at Nazca almost continuously from 1946 until her death in 1998, and who believed that the Lines were an astronomical calendar linked to the rising and setting points of celestial bodies on the east and west horizons. The whole complex, according to her theories, was designed to help organize planting and harvesting around seasonal changes rather than the fickle shifts of weather. In most developed Central and South American cultures there was a strong emphasis on knowledge of the heavens, and in a desert area like Nazca, where the coastal fog never reaches up to obscure the night sky over the pampa, this must have been highly advanced.

In many cases the Lines connect with low hills on the plain or the foothills of the Andes along its edge. Fragments of Nazca pottery found around these hills suggest that they may have been sacred sites, perhaps as important in terms of ritual as the celestial movements. Recent theories regarding the Lines take this as evidence that at least some of them were *ceques*, or sacred pathways, between *huacas*. In Inca Cusco, *ceques* radiated from the Sun Temple, Koricancha, to surrounding *huacas*, many of these being hills on the distant horizon. Each of the *ceques* was under the protection of a particular *allyu* or kinship group. This theory is all the more feasible since, if the Lines were purely for astronomical observations, they wouldn't need to be so long.

Tony Morrisson, one of the proponents of this idea, discovered many similar *ceques* in the mountains between Cusco and La Paz. They were related to *huacas* and still "owned" by specific local kinship groups. Morrisson concludes that the various stone piles often found at the end of lines at Nazca were ancient *huacas*, and the lines were paths between these sacred places. They were in a straight line, he says, simply because this is the shortest distance between any two *huacas*. It follows that the cleared areas were ceremonial sites for larger *allyu* gatherings. The animal figures might be explained by taking them to pre-date the straight lines; this would fit into the early and late pottery phases (the former being most closely associated with animalistic motifs).

Maria Reiche's theory isn't necessarily contradictory of most of the other major theories. Many other alignments were confirmed by Hawkins's computer (particularly those for the solar solstices) and even if the Lines and animal designs were made at different times, there's still a connection: designs like the spider and the monkey might be representations of the constellations of Orion and Ursa Major. It's difficult for a Western mind to visualize the constellations except through the stereotyped images we've grown accustomed to. The Nazca people, on the other hand, were free to impose their own ideas and there are remarkable similarities between the motifs they drew on the pampa and some of the major constellations.

The latest theory, which both builds on previous work, but also may well make a significant leap forward, is that suggested in 2000 by **Dr Anthony Aveni**, one of the world's leading archeoastronomers (a respected academic who specializes in both archeology and astronomy), who believes that at least some of the Nazca Lines were pathways meant to be walked in rituals relating to the acquisition of water. A statistically significant number of these lines point towards a section of the horizon where the sun used to rise at the beginning of the rainy season, suggesting that perhaps the lines were created in relation to some offering to the rain gods. This wouldn't be surprising given that similar theories have arisen about the orientation of the early U-shaped temples in the northern deserts of Peru (see Contexts, p.530). Interestingly, in 2002 a water dowser from the US, **David Johnson**, took Dr Aveni's theory further by putting forward evidence that the ancient Nazcas mapped the desert to mark the surface where aquifers appeared.

Other theories for why and how the lines and figures were drawn by the ancient Nazca include the concept of shamanic flight or out-of-the-body experience, with the symbolic "flight path", as it were, already mapped out across the region. Such an experience is known to be induced by some of the "teacher plants", such as the mescaline cactus San Pedro, which are still used by traditional healers on the coast of Peru as they have been for at least 3000 years. Some of the psychedelic-induced chants of Peruvian forest Indian tribes sing about flying over the forests and rivers of their known territory, honouring their local and tutelary spirits. Perhaps the Nazca shaman utilized the figures and lines to guide them around their sacred space during ritual sessions.

On a slightly less esoteric level many have noted how many of the extended lines are uncannily straight. One theory is that they were made using three cane poles and a rope, in much the same manner as a surveyor uses ranging sticks and a theodolite; when the late Maria Reiche first came to Nazca some of the locals could indeed remember wooden poles at the end of certain lines – perhaps sighting posts for the stars. How long it took to construct them is a last, inevitable question – and since the Lines can't be properly seen from the ground it is tempting to believe they must have been the skilled product of numerous generations. In strictly physical terms this isn't necessarily so – a local school once tried building its own line and from its efforts calculated that a thousand patient and inspired workers could have made them all in less than a month.

Nazca and around

Some 20km south of the viewing tower, the colonial town of **NAZCA** spreads along the margin of a small coastal valley. Although the river is invariably dry, Nazca's valley remains green and fertile through the continued use of an Inca subterranean aqueduct. It's a small town – slightly at odds with its appearance on maps – but an interesting and enjoyable place to stay. Indeed, these days it has become a major attraction, boasting, in addition to the Lines, the excellent **Museo Didattico Antonini**, the adobe Inca ruins of **Paredones** only a couple of kilometres to the south, and the **Casa Museo y Mausoleo Maria Reiche** (see p.217), with access to several of the Nazca desert's animal figures, and two or three important **archeological sites** within an easy day's range.

The face of Nazca changed after the 1996 earthquake, which necessitated the rebuilding of about half the town. Beyond the airport there's ample evidence of the town's rapid development in the form of new squatter settlements parcelled off into 200-square-metre plots. After about six months the squatters receive their legal right to the land, and water and electricity usually follow a few years later.

September is one of the **best times to visit** if you want to participate in one of its fiestas, when the locals venerate the Virgen de Guadalupe (Sept 8) with great enthusiasm. In May, the religious and secular festivities of the Fiesta de las Cruces, go on for days.

Arrival, information and getting around

Roughly halfway between Lima and Arequipa, Nazca is easily reached by bus, colectivo, or even by small **plane** from Lima with Aero Condor (see p.100 for details); colectivos link the airstrip with *jiróns* Bolognesi and Grau in town. Cruz del Sur buses drop off opposite the Alegria Tours office Lima–Arequipa service; Ormeño buses arrive at Av de los Incas 112 several times weekly; most others stop around the start of Jirón Lima, by the *ovalo* on Avenida Los Incas. Señor de Luren, from Lima and Ica, and Civa both have terminals on the same *ovalo* which is at the main intersection of the Panamerican Highway with Jirón Lima.

Colectivos from Ica arrive at the (presently closed) *Hotel Montecarlo*, Jr Callao 123, on the corner of Avenida Los Incas and Micaelo Bastidas; those from Vista Alegre leave from the corner of Bolognesi and Grau. Wherever you arrive you're likely to be besieged by tour touts, who should be ignored (or told firmly that you've already booked a hotel and tour). Most people use the noisy, beeping little *tico* **taxis** or **motorcycle-rickshaws**, which can be hailed anywhere and compete to take you in or around town cheaply – you shouldn't pay more than $2 for any destination in town. Buses leave every hour for the Nazca airstrip, from the corner of Grau with Jirón Bolognesi, and are normally marked "B-Vista Alegre".

For **tourist information** the best places are Nasca Trails, Bolognesi 550, on the Plaza de Armas (☎034/522858, ☎523710, ☻www.nascalinesperu.com) or Alegria Tours, C Lima 168 (☎034/522444, ☻info@nazcaperu.com).

Accommodation

Finding a **hotel** in Nazca is simple enough, with an enormous choice for such a small town; most places are along Jirón Lima or within a few blocks of the Plaza de Armas. There is no official campsite in or around Nazca, but **camping** is sometimes permitted at the *Hostal Alegria* in town, the *Hostal Wasipunko*

NAZCA

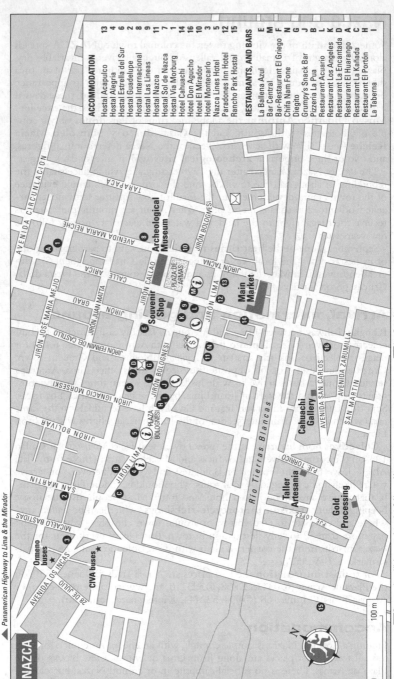

◀ Panamerican Highway to Lima & the Mirador

▼ Panamerican Highway to Arequipa & Nazca Airport

▼ Los Paredones

ACCOMMODATION	
Hostal Acapulco	13
Hostal Alegria	4
Hostal Estrella del Sur	6
Hostal Guadelupe	2
Hostal Internacional	8
Hostal Las Lineas	9
Hostal Nazca	11
Hostal Sol de Nazca	7
Hostal Via Morburg	1
Hotel Cahuachi	14
Hotel Don Agucho	16
Hotel El Mirador	10
Hotel Montecarlo	3
Nazca Lines Hotel	5
Paradones Inn Hotel	12
Rancho Park Hostal	15

RESTAURANTS, AND BARS	
La Ballena Azul	E
Bar Central	M
Bar-Restaurant El Griego	F
Chifa Nam Fone	N
Diegito	G
Grumpy's Snack Bar	J
Pizzeria La Pua	B
Restaurant Acuario	L
Restaurant Los Angeles	K
Restaurant La Encantada	D
Restaurant El Huarango	A
Restaurant La Kañada	C
Restaurant El Portón	H
La Taberna	I

Ormeno buses

CIVA buses

Archeological Museum

PLAZA DE ARMAS

Souvenir Shop

Main Market

PLAZA BOLOGNESI

Cahuachi Gallery

Taller Artesania

Gold Processing

Rio Tierras Blancas

(see below) and the *Nido del Condor*, the closest hotel to the airstrip at Km 447 of the Panamerican Highway, which for $2 per person allows you to pitch a tent in its grounds.

Hostal Acapulco Jr Lima 668 ⊕/ⓕ 034/522277. A fairly basic place more accustomed to Peruvian guests, where the service can be erratic, but it is friendly. With or without private bath. ❷

Hostal Alegria Jr Lima 166 ⊕ 034/522702, ⓕ 522444, ⓦ www.nazcaperu.com. Popular with travellers, it has rooms with or without private bath set around an attractive garden, as well as a number of newer, plusher, chalet-style rooms with fans and bath. It also has a café that serves good, affordable set lunches, and their travel agency can arrange tours and bus connections to Lima or Arequipa. Camping is sometimes allowed. ❷–❺

Hostal Estrella del Sur Callao 568 ⊕ 034/522764, ⓔ estrelladelsurhotel@yahoo.com.mx. Good value, though only some of the compact rooms have windows. ❸

Hostal Guadelupe San Martín 225 ⊕ 034/522249. A laid-back place with a pleasant little garden. Good value and most rooms have private bath. ❷–❸

Hostal Internacional Av Maria Reiche 112 ⊕ 034/522744. Good value and with its own cafetería; most rooms have private bathrooms, some have TVs; it's got hot water all day and some bungalows out the back. ❷

Hostal Las Lineas Jr Arica 299 ⊕/ⓕ 034/522488, ⓔ lineas@terra.com.pe. This modern, good-value hotel overlooks the Plaza de Armas and has its own decent restaurant; rooms have private bath and hot water. ❹

Hostal Nazca Jr Lima 438 ⊕ 034/522085. Friendly, basic place with shared bathrooms, very clean, airy and popular. It also has a pleasant restaurant and they can exchange dollars and organize taxis, tours and good-value flights over the Lines. ❷

Hostal Oropesa Jr Bolognesi 728. Nazca's cheapest accommodation, though not particularly clean or friendly. ❷

Hostal Sol de Nazca C Callao 586 ⊕/ⓕ 034/522730, ⓔ dsalasm@Latinmail.com. Modern, clean hostel with TVs, private bathrooms and a rooftop breakfast space. Excellent value with constant hot water and the very friendly service. ❷

Hostal Via Morburg Jr Jose Maria Mejia 108 ⊕ 034/522566. A modern, secure place offering comfortable rooms with private bath, constant hot water, and a small pool. Very good value and in a quiet part of town. ❸

Hotel Cahuachi Jr Arica 115 ⊕ 034/523786, ⓔ cahuachi@terra.com.pe. This spotless, modern hotel overlooks the market area near the bridge and has a rooftop patio with views to the mountains. Rooms are with or without bath. ❸

Hotel Don Agucho Av Paredones, at corner with Av San Carlos 100 ⊕/ⓕ 034/522048. One of the nicest options in and around Nazca, this hacienda-style place has comfortable rooms, with bath and TV, entered via cactus-filled passages. There's also a pool and a bar-restaurant; breakfast included in price. ❺

Hotel El Mirador Jr Tacna 436 ⊕/ⓕ 034/523741 or 523121. A pleasant new hotel looking straight onto the Plaza de Armas; rooms are mostly rather dark (except those on the top floor) and it has a rooftop patio. Rooms are with or without bath and breakfast is included. ❸

Hotel Montecarlo Callao, first block ⊕ 034/523373 or 521051. Has seen better days, but is an interesting and rambling hotel with swimming pool and drab but OK rooms with private baths. The hotel also runs their own air company and offer reasonable deals, including transfer to airstrip. ❹

Nazca Lines Hotel Jr Bolognesi ⊕ 034/522293, ⓕ 522112. Luxurious, with its own well-kept pool and an excellent restaurant. Non-residents can also use the pool for approximately $5 a day. ❼

Paradones Inn Hotel C Lima 600 ⊕/ⓕ 034/522181, ⓔ paredoneshotel @terra.com.pe. A brand-new hotel in the heart of Nazca's small commercial area; smart, clean and good value with TVs, private bathrooms, hot water. ❹

Out of town

Hostal Wasipunko Km 457, Panamerican Highway, Pajonal ⊕ 034/522330, ⓔ wasipunko@hotmail.com. A delightful, rustic country hostel, with its own small ecological and archeological museum. It has no electricity, but it's very clean and some rooms have private bath. Rooms are set around a lovely courtyard and the restaurant specializes in tasty pre-Inca dishes. It is signposted on the right of the highway some 15km south of Nazca; a taxi from Nazca will cost around $5, or take one of the Marcona colectivos. ❸–❹

Hotel de la Borda Km 447, Panamerican Highway ⊕ 034/522750. A luxurious hacienda hotel set in an oasis just 2km off the highway close to the Nazca airstrip, it's not quite as well kept as it once

was, but is still an attractive and comfortable place to stay. The hotel also runs tours, including some to wildlife havens on the nearby coast. **❻**
La Maison Suisse Km 447, Panamerican Highway ☎034/522434. A plush joint, with its own swimming pool. **❼**
Nido del Condor Km 447, Panamerican Highway ☎034/522424, ⓦwww.aerocondor.com.pe. A modern hotel with pools and a camping area; good-value deals sometimes offered to include flight over the Lines with Aero Condor. **❸**
Rancho Park Hostal Turístico Km 444, Panamericana Sur ☎034/521153 or 3814946. Somewhat isolated on the outskirts of town, this rather odd hostel doesn't have much apart from the pool to appeal to travellers; located by the road, it's like a big motel. **❹**

NAZCA AND THE SOUTH COAST | Nazca and around

The Town

As you come into town, Jirón **Bolognesi**, the main street, leads straight into the **Plaza de Armas** where there are a few restaurants, bars and a couple of hotels. If you continue straight across the plaza and head along Avendia de la Cultura you soon come to the new town museum - the fascinating **Museo Didattico Antonini**, an Italian pre-Columbian archeological research and study centre, Av de la Cultura 600 (daily 9am–7pm; ☎034/523444, ⓕ523100, ⓦwww.digilander.iol.it/MDAntonini). Opened in 1999, the museum stretches for six long blocks from the Plaza de Armas along Bolognesi and presents excellent interpretative exhibits covering the evolution of Nazca culture, a good audio-visual show and scale model reconstructions of local remains such as the Templo del Escalonado at Cahuachi. The museum complex extends to almost a hectare and includes an archeological park that contains the *Bisambra* aqueduct (fed by the reservoir higher up the valley) and some burial reconstructions.

South along Calle Arica from the Plaza de Armas, the town's **main market**, offering the usual food and electronic goods, is based in a ramshackle collection of huts and stalls, on the left just before the river bridge on Calle Arica. The **Taller Artesania**, Pasaje Torrico 240, in Barrio San Carlos, a short walk south of the plaza over the bridge, is worth a visit for its wonderful ceramics; if a few people turn up at the same time, they'll demonstrate the process of ceramic-making from moulding to polishing. San Carlos suburb also boasts the **Taller de Cerámica Juan Jose**, at Pasaje Lopez 400, and a **gold processing** operation, both located on the right-hand side about 500m down the Avenida San Carlos from the market bridge. Don't be put off by the fact that they're in someone's back garden – it's fascinating to watch them grind rocks into powder and then extract gold dust from it.

After visiting all that lot in the dusty hot sun of Nazca it's possible to take a swim in the enticing **swimming pool** at the *Nazca Lines Hotel* (see above for review; $5 includes swim, snack and cold drink).

Los Paredones, the graveyard and the Inca canal

The most impressive archeological sites around Nazca are some distance out (see p.224), but if you have an afternoon to spare, there are a few interesting spots you could walk to. The route covered below will take a leisurely three to four hours on foot.

To walk to **Los Paredones**, an Inca trade centre where wool from the mountains was exchanged for cotton grown along the coast, follow Calle Arica from the Plaza de Armas, cross the bridge, and keep going straight (off the main road which curves to the right). The modern road follows the same route as the ancient one from Nazca to Cusco, and passes just below the ruins about

1km ahead, at the foot of the sandy valley mouth, underneath a political slogan – APRA – etched into the hillside.

The adobe buildings are in a bad state of repair and the site is dotted with *huaqueros'* pits, but if you follow the path to the prominent central sector you can get a good idea of what the town must have been like. Overlooking the valley and roads, it's in a commanding position – a fact recognized and taken advantage of by local cultures long before the Incas arrived. At the foot of the ruins, you can usually look round a collection of funeral pieces collected and displayed by the Pomez family in their adobe home adjacent to the site.

Another 2km up the Puquio road from Los Paradones (with Nazca in front of you, turn right leaving Paradones) there's a **Nazca graveyard**, its pits open and burial remains spread around. Though much less extensive than the cemetery at Chauchilla (see p.224), it is still of interest – full of (rather hard to find) subterranean galleries. A half-hour walk up the valley from the graveyard through the cotton fields and along a track will bring you to the former hacienda of **Cantay**, now a model agricultural co-operative; its central plaza houses a **swimming pool** (50¢) and a small cafetería. Just a little further above the co-operative settlement, you can make out a series of inverted conical dips, like swallow-holes in the fields. These are the air vents for a vast underground canal system that siphons desperately needed water from the Bisambra reservoir; designed and constructed by the Incas, it is even more essential today. You can get right down into the openings and poke your head or feet into the canals – they usually give off a pleasant warm breeze and you can see small fish swimming in the flowing water.

Eating and drinking

Eating in Nazca offers more variety than you might imagine given the town's small size. Most places are in or around Bolognesi and Lima, where, for vegetarians, there are a number of pizza, pasta and snack places worth trying out. What little **nightlife** exists is mainly based around **restaurants** and **bars**, particularly on Jirón Lima, Plaza de Armas and Jirón Bolognesi.

La Ballena Azul corner of Grau with Callao 698. Considering there's no ocean in sight, this is a surprisingly good cevichería, serving up very tasty seafood; popular for lunches with local business people.

Bar-Restaurant El Griego Bolognesi 287 ☏034/521480. A friendly local eating house with fine food and decent drinks at reasonable prices. Good breakfasts and can be fun in the evening.

Chifa Nam Fone on the corner of Lima with Grau. The best in town for a spicy Chinese meal; also offers a range of OK veggie options.

Diegito Jr Castillo 375. Aimed at locals rather than tourists, this pleasant restaurant serves mainly criolla dishes, plus pastas and soups; very reasonable set lunches.

Grumpy's Snack Bar Jr Bolognesi 282. Small with earthen floor and bamboo walls; it serves cool drinks and good breakfast in a friendly atmosphere.

Pizzeria La Pua Lima 169 ☏034/522990. A very popular trattoria and snack bar, located out of the town centre opposite the *Hostal Alegria*.

Restaurant Acuario Arica 211. Very good value, particularly the set-menu lunches.

Restaurant Los Angeles C Bolognesi 493 ☏034/522294. A reasonably nice restaurant and soda fountain, close to the centre of Nazca.

Restaurant La Encantada Jr Callao 592 ☏034/522930. Excellent criolla food in a nice atmosphere, though pricey.

Restaurant El Huarango C Arica 602 ☏034/521287. The finest restaurant in Nazca, it has a rooftop patio and a great ambience. The delicious food, mostly traditional coastal Peruvian dishes but also including some more international cuisine, is very well priced.

Restaurant La Kañada Jr Lima 160 ☏034/522917. Nice decor and a pleasant atmosphere, often full of gringos eating the delicious seafood dishes; also offers Internet access.

Restaurant Pizzeria-Heladeria Jambouy II C Bolognesi 226. Small and inexpensive, with decent food.

Restaurant El Portón C Ignacio Moresky 120 ℡034/523490. A lively restaurant at night, especially at weekends. Pastas, meat and seafood dishes in a good atmosphere, plus there's a dance floor and a bar. Frequently presents folk music. Restaurant Turístico Las Lineas C Arica 299.

Central place with an unassuming choice of breakfasts and juices.
La Taberna Jr Lima 321. Serves a good selection of local and international dishes, plus a variety of drinks; its walls are covered with graffiti scrawled over the years by passing groups of travellers. Lively most evenings until midnight.

Listings

Banks and exchange Banco de Credito, Jr Lima 495; Interbanc, C Arica 363; and Banco de la Nación, Jr Lima 463. The best rates for dollars cash are with the *cambistas* in the small park outside the *Hotel Nazca*, where Jr Bolognesi and Jr Lima merge, or outside the Banco de Credito.
Buses companies Cruz del Sur, Lima 103 ℡034/522495 and 523500; Civa, block 1 of Av Guardia Civil ℡034/523019, though note that there's a restaurant out front; Cueva, Av Los Incas 106 ℡034/523061; Ormeño, Av Los Incas ℡ 034/522058; Señor de Luren, at the roundabout near *Restaurant La Kañada*.
Internet facilities Available at *Mundo Virtual*, Bolognesi 395 ℡034/522361, smallish (slow);

Restaurant La Kañada (see "Eating and drinking", above).
Pharmacy Botica Central, Bolognesi 355 at corner with Fermin del Castillo; Botica Alejandra, Arica 407.
Police Block 5, Jr Lima ℡034/522442.
Post office Fermin del Castillo 379. Mon–Sat 8am–8pm.
Shopping For food and drink, try the small market, on Jr Lima, the Panificadora La Esperanza bakery at Jr Bolognesi 389, and the Licoria liquor store at Arica 401. Camera films can be bought at Comercial Charito, Arica 296, and the unnamed shop at Jr Bolognesi 600, which also develops. Oscar, Jr Bolognesi 465, sells local artesania.
Telephones Jr Lima 525. Daily 7am–11pm.

Archeological sites around Nazca

Chauchilla Cemetery and **Cahuachi**, after the Lines the most important sites associated with the Nazca culture, are both difficult to reach by public transport, and unless your energy and interest are pretty unlimited you'll want to take an organized tour or at least a local guide-cum-taxi driver (see box).

Chauchilla Cemetery

Some 27km southeast of Nazca along the Panamerican Highway to Km 464.20, then out along a dirt road beside the Poroma riverbed, **Chauchilla Cemetery** certainly rewards the effort it takes to visit. Once you reach the atmospheric site you realize how considerable a civilization the riverbanks must have maintained in the time of the Nazca culture. Scattered about the dusty ground are literally thousands of graves, most of which have been opened by grave robbers, leaving the skulls and skeletons exposed to the elements, along with broken pieces of pottery, bits of shroud fabric and lengths of braided hair, as yet unbleached by the desert sun. Further up the track, near Trancas, there's a small ceremonial **temple** – Huaca del Loro – and beyond this at Los Incas you can find Quemazon **petroglyphs**. These last two are not usually included in the standard tour, but if you hire your own guide, you can negotiate with him to take you there – expect to pay $5 extra.

Cahuachi

The ancient centre of Nazca culture, **Cahuachi** lies to the west of the Nazca Lines, about 30km from Nazca and some 20km from the Pacific. All of the landscape between Nazca town and the distant coastline is a massive, very barren desert-scape – almost always hot, dry and sunny. In many ways it's hard to imagine how ancient peoples managed to build such a high culture here; but,

Tours around Nazca

Some well-established companies arrange **tours** to the major sites around Nazca, all offering similar trips to Los Paredones, Cantalloc, Cahuachi, Chauchilla and the Lines. Tours around Chauchilla Cemetery last two and a half hours for about $10 a person; a trip to the viewing tower and the Casa Museo Maria Reiche also takes two and a half hours and costs around $10. Tours out to the ruined temple complex in the desert at Cahuachi (see above) last four hours and cost in the region of $50 for a party of four or five; these need to be arranged in advance. The best **tour operators** are Nazca Trails, Bolognesi 550, Plaza de Armas (☎/℗034/522858, ℮Nazca@correo.dnet.com.pe); Alegria Tours, C Lima 168 (☎034/522444, ℮info@nazcaperu.com). Otherwise try Tour Peru, C Arica 285, Of 1 (☎034/522481) an established agency specializing in Nazca flights and local tours; NaNazca Tours, and Souvenirs, C Lima 160 (☎/℗034/522917, ℮naNazcatours@yahoo.com); Huarango Travel Agency, C Lima 165 (☎034/522297); and Viajes Nazca, Jr Lima 185 (☎034/521027). Alternatively you might want to organize a trip with a guide-cum-driver for your own group; **recommended guides** include Juan Tohalino Vera and Orlando Etchebarne, contactable through Nazca Trails; Alex Frank Severino (contact through the *Hostal Sol de Nazca*); Miguel Angel Llaja Chavez, block 3 of Av Circunvalación (☎034/522097); and Joao Bologner, contactable through Oscar's Shop, Jr Bolognesi 465. For **flights** over the Nazca Lines, see the box on p.216.

as in northern Peru, it had much to do with a close religious and technical relationship with natural water sources, all the more important because of their scarcity. The site consists of a religious citadel split in half by the river, with its main temple (one of a set of six) constructed around a small natural hillock. Adobe platforms step the sides of this twenty-metre mound and although they're badly weathered today, you can still make out the general form. Separate courtyards attached to each of the six pyramids can be distinguished, but their exact use is unknown.

Quite close to the main complex is a construction known as **El Estaqueria**, The Place of the Stakes, retaining a dozen rows of *huarango* log pillars. *Huarango* trees (known in the north of Peru as *algarrobo*) are the most common form of desert vegetation. Their wood, baked by the sun, is very hard, though their numbers are much reduced nowadays by locals who use them for fuel. The Estaqueria is estimated to be 2000 years old, but its original function is unclear, though other such constructions are usually found above tombs. The bodies here were buried with ceramics, food, textiles, jewellery and chaquira beads. Italian archeologist Giuseppe Orefici has worked on Cahuachi for nearly twenty years and has uncovered over 300 graves, one of which contained a tattooed and dreadlocked warrior. Also around 2000 years old, he's a mere whippersnapper compared to other evidence Orefici has unearthed relating to 4000-year-old pre-ceramic cultures.

Cahuachi is typical of a Nazca ceremonial centre in its use of natural features to form an integral part of the structure. The places the Nazcans lived their everyday lives in showed no such architectural aspirations – indeed there are no major towns associated with the Nazcans, who tended to live in small clusters of adobe huts, villages at best. One of the largest of these, the walled village of **Tambo de Perro**, can be found in Acari, the next dry valley to the south of modern-day Nazca. Stretching for over a mile, and situated next to an extensive Nazca graveyard, it was apparently one of the Nazcans' most important dwelling sites.

Until 1901, when Max Uhle "discovered" the Nazca culture, a group of beautiful **ceramics** in Peru's museums had remained unidentified and unclassifiable. With Uhle's work all that changed rapidly (though not quickly enough to prevent most of the sites being ransacked by grave robbers before proper excavations could be undertaken – a problem that continues today) and the importance of Nazca pottery came to be understood. Many of the best pieces were found here in Cahuachi.

Unlike contemporaneous Mochica ware, Nazca ceramics rarely attempt any realistic reproduction of images. The majority – painted in three or four earthy colours and given a resinous surface glaze – are relatively stylized or even completely abstract. Nevertheless, two main categories of subject matter recur: naturalistic designs of bird, animal and plant life, and motifs of mythological monsters and bizarre deities. In later works it became common to mould effigies onto the pots, and in Nazca's declining phases, under Huari-Tiahuanaco cultural influence (see p.530), workmanship and design became less inspired.

The style and content of the early pottery, however, show remarkable similarities to the symbols depicted in the Nazca Lines, and although not enough is known about the Nazca culture to be certain, it seems reasonable to assume that the early Nazca people were also responsible for those drawings on the Pampa de San José. With most of the evidence coming from their graveyards, though, and that so dependent upon conjecture, there is little to characterize the Nazca and little known of them beyond the fact that they collected heads as trophies, that they built a ceremonial complex here in the desert at Cahuachi, and that they scraped a living from the Nazca, Ica and Pisco valleys from around 200 to 600 AD.

The only section of Cahuachi to have been properly excavated so far is the **Templo Escalonado**, a multilevel temple on which you can see wide adobe walls and, on the temple site, some round, sunken chambers. A hundred metres away, from the top of what is known as the main pyramid structure, you can look down over what was once the main ceremonial plaza, though it's difficult to make out these days because of the sands.

East of Nazca

Some 90km inland from Nazca, the Pampa Galeras is one of the best places in Peru to see the *vicuña*, a llama-like animal with very fine wool. The *vicuña* have lived for centuries in the **Pampa Galeras Vicuña Reserve**, which is now maintained as their natural habitat and contains more than five thousand of the creatures. Well signposted at Km 89 of the Nazca to Cusco road, the reserve is easily reached by hopping off one of the many daily Nazca to Cusco buses (Tour Huari runs to Puquio at around 4pm; ask the driver to tell you where to get off). The reserve has some shelter, but it's a very basic concrete shack with no beds, and you need written permission from the Ministry of Agriculture and Fauna in Lima; it's best to take an **organized tour** with one of the Nazca companies (see p.225). However, you can **camp** here without a permit. You can also take a taxi or arrange for a car through one of the tour companies in Nazca (around $50 for the day for two).

The *vicuña* themselves are not easy to spot. When you do notice a herd, you'll see it move as if it were a single organism. They flock together and move swiftly in a tight wave, bounding gracefully across the hills. The males are strictly territorial, protecting their patches of scrubby grass by day, then returning to the rockier heights as darkness falls.

Puquio, Coracora, Chumpi and Lago Parinacochas

Head east of the Pampa Galeras Vicuña Reserve along the Cusco road and you reach **PUQUIO**. As soon as you cross over the metal bridge at the entrance to the town, you'll sense that it's very different from the hot desert town of Nazca. In fact, Puquio was an isolated community until 1926, when the townspeople built their own road link between the coast and the sierra. If you have to break your journey here, you have a choice of three hostels, though none of them is particularly enticing. The road divides here, with the main route continuing over the Andes to Cusco via Abancay.

A side road goes south for about 140km along the mountains to Lago Parinacochas (see below); although frequently destroyed by mudslides in the rainy season, the road always seems full of passing trucks which will usually take passengers for a small price. After about 100km, the road passes the small provincial capital, **Coracora**, a remote town with only one hotel. Around the main plaza there are some reasonable restaurants but there's little here to interest most travellers. Far better to continue the 16km to **Chumpi**, an ideal place to camp amid stunning sierra scenery. Within a few hours' walk of the town is the amazingly beautiful lake, **Lago Parinacochas**, named after the many flamingos that live there and probably one of the best unofficial nature reserves in Peru. If you're not up to the walk, you could take a day-trip from Nazca for about $40; try Alegria Tours (see p.225 for details). From Chumpi you can either backtrack to Puquio, or continue down the road past the lake, before curving another 130km back down to the coast at Chala.

South from Nazca: the Panamerican Highway

There's relatively little of great interest in the 170km of desert between Nazca and Chala. **Sacaco**, a fossil site with a small museum, can be reached by Cueva bus from Nazca to Las Lomas – ask the driver where to disembark – after which it's a thirty-minute walk. **LAS LOMAS** itself is an attractive fishing village with a **beach** that's especially good for spotting pelicans, about 90km to the south of Nazca and off the Panamerican Highway. If you're based in Nazca you can take a tour here (see p.225), often taking in Sacaco, or catch the Cueva bus here (a one-hour journey). The **hotel** *Capricho de Verano* (contact through the *Hotel Don Agucho*, see p.221; ➍) has a lovely location looking right down onto the beach, and you can also **camp** in the area.

Avoid **Puerto San Juan**, it's the one place of any real size on this stretch of coast, but actually just a modern industrial port for local iron-ore and copper mines. Continue on until you find the first break in the area's starkness, at the olive groves in the Yauca Valley. Just beyond this, at Km 595 of the Panamerican Highway, is a strange-looking and slightly eerie geologically uplifted zone, a natural oasis with its own microclimate stretching for about 20km. It's an unusual but interesting enough place to spend some time **camping** and exploring; there are Inca and pre-Inca ruins hidden in the *lomas*, but today the area is virtually uninhabited.

Just 10km before Chala stand the ruins of **PUERTO INCA**, the Incas' main port for Cusco, where there's an excellent **beach** and fine diving and fishing to be had. There's a small **hotel** on the beach, the *Coste Hotel*, Km 603, Panamericana Sur (➋034/210224; ➍). To get to the ruins, take a taxi from

Chala (about $10), or catch an Arequipa-bound bus along the Panamerican Highway and ask to be dropped off at Km 603. You can walk the 3–4km from here – a rustic but passable road follows a narrow gully to the coast.

CHALA itself, the main port for Cusco until the construction of the Cusco–Arequipa rail line, is now an agreeable little fishing town, where you can overindulge in fresh seafood. If you want **to stay** in Chala, try the *Hotel de Turistas* (☎014/501110; ❹) for a little comfort, or the much more basic *Hotel Grau* (❷), close to the pleasant, sandy beach.

Camana

About 200km south from Chala, **CAMANA** is a popular Arequipeño beach resort from December to March, when the weather is hot, dry and relatively windless, but outside this period it has little to offer. The most popular **beach** here is at **La Punta**, around 5km along the Arequipa road. If you do end up here, there are a few decent **places to stay**. The *Hostal Montecarlo*, Av Lima 514 (☎054/571101; ❸), opposite the hospital, is modern and has reasonable rooms with or without private bath, while the *Gran Hostal Premier*, Garci Carabajal 117 (❸), is also fine, if not as good value. The *Hotel de Turistas*, Av Lima 138 (☎054/571113 or 571608; ❸), is slightly neglected but retains a certain charm. The *Hostal Señor Hans*, on the beach at La Punta (☎054/572288; ❸), has great views. For **eating**, the best seafood joints are *Cevichería Los Faroles*, Sebastian Barrianca 254a, hard to beat for its set lunches; *Cevichería Rosa Nautica*, right on the seafront at La Punta, which catches its own fish; and *Restaurant Lider*, Av Grau 266. The *Restaurant Turístico Señor Hans*, Km 827, at El Puente, is good for lunch. The *La Noche Disco*, Mariscal Castilla 668, and the nearby *La Miel* are the only worthy **clubs**.

The **Banco de la Nación** is at Av Mariscal Castilla 102, and there's a **telephone** office at Av Lima 149 and another at Av Lima 300. **Buses** stop right in the centre of town, around the Grifo El Niño petrol station. **Colectivos** for La Punta (30¢; a 15min journey) are on block 1 of Prolongación Quilca, not far from the *Hotel de Turistas*.

Continuing toward Arequipa (see Chaper Four), the tarmac keeps close to the coast wherever possible, passing through a few small fishing villages and over monotonous arid plains before eventually turning inland for the final uphill stretch into the land of volcanos and Peru's second largest city. At Km 916 of the Panamerican Highway, a road leads off into the Maches Canyon towards the Toro Muerto petroglyphs, the Valley of the Volcanos and the increasingly popular destination of **Cotahuasi Canyon** (see p.271). At Rapartición, the road splits: east to Arequipa and south towards Mollendo, Moquegua, Tacna and Chile.

Mollendo, Moquegua, Ilo and Tacna

There are three major destinations south of Camana: Mollendo, Moquegua and Tacna. **Mollendo** serves as a coastal resort for Arequipa and home of the **Mejia National Reserve**, a marvellous lagoon-based bird sanctuary. Most people, actually, choose to go on to the old colonial town of **Moquegua**, now an important nodal point on the fast-developing Peruvian road infrastructure, but also an attractive and peaceful place. The important port of **Ilo**, which serves both Arequipa and the south coast towns, is little visited by tourists. Going South from Moquegua, the Panamerican continues on through the desert to

Tacna, whose only attraction is that it's the jumping-off point for **crossing the border into Chile**.

Mollendo and the Mejia bird sanctuary

MOLLENDO is a pleasant old port with a decent beach and a laid-back atmosphere. It's a relaxed spot to spend a couple of days chilling out on the beach and makes a good base from which to visit the nearby nature reserve lagoons at Mejia, also known as the **Mejia bird sanctuary**, just south of town. These can be easily reached by colectivos from the top end of Calle Castilla (every 10min).

Several **buses** daily arrive from Arequipa, Moquegua and Tacna, including Empresa Aragon, Calle Comercio, four blocks north of Plaza de Armas; Tepsa, Alfonso Ugarte 320 (℡054/532872); and Cruz del Sur, on Alfonso Ugarte. Mollendo has a reasonable choice of **accommodation**: *Hostal Cabaña*, Comercio 240 (℡054/533833; ❸), with private bathrooms and good hot water, is the best value in town, the *Hostal Brisas del Mar*, Tupac Amaru (℡054/533544; ❹), is a popular place close to the beach, *Hostal El Muelle*, Arica 144 (℡054/533680; ❸), is clean, friendly and good value, and *Hostal Paraiso*, Areqipa 209 (℡054/533215; ❸), fills up very quickly in January but has nice rooms and a pleasant view.

As befits a coastal holiday town, Mollendo has a good selection of **restaurants**. First choice is the superb seafood restaurant *Cevichería Alejo*, Panamerican Highway South, Miramar – it's a little out of town, but worth the twenty-minute walk for its excellent, reasonably priced dishes. At the lower end of the budget, there's a decent pizzeria on the Plaza de Armas, or try the excellent *Chifa Restaurant*, Comercio 412, serving tasty Chinese meals for under $3.

If you need to change **money**, you'll get the best rates for dollars cash from the *cambistas* on Plaza Bolognesi; for travellers' cheques, try the Banco de la Nación, Areqipa 243; the Banco de Credito, Comercio 323; or the Banco del Sur, Plaza Bolognesi 131.

The National Sanctuary and Lakes of Mejia

The **National Sanctuary and Lakes of Mejia**, 7km south of Mollendo, is an unusual ecological niche consisting of almost 700 hectares of lakes separated from the Pacific Ocean by just a sand bar, and providing an important habitat for many thousands of migratory birds. Of the 157 species sighted at Mejia, around 72 are permanent residents; the best time for sightings is early in the morning. To get there, take an Empresa Aragon **bus** from Arequipa (see above); you'll see the lagoons just before you get to Tambo Valley.

Moquegua

Situated on the northern edge of the Atacama desert, most of which lies over the border in Chile, the **MOQUEGUA** region is traditionally and culturally linked to the Andean region around Lake Titicaca, and many ethnic Colla and Lupaca from the mountains live here. The local economy today is based on copper mining, fruit plantations and wine. More interestingly, for those partial to spirits, Moquegua has a reputation for producing Peru's best pisco. Historically, this area is an annex of the altiplano which was used as a major thoroughfare first by the Tiahuanacu and later the Huari peoples. In the future it might well be the main route for the gas pipeline out of Peru's eastern rainforest regions to the coast. Right now, though, located in a relatively narrow valley, the colonial town of Moquegua has winding streets, an attractive plaza and a lot of adobe houses roofed in thatch and clay.

There's little in town, but the Plaza de Armas is picturesque with its ornate metal fountain designed in 1877 by Gustave Eiffel, and the grand ficus trees that fill the space. Close to the plaza, at the corner of calles Tacna and Ayacucho, the Iglesia de Santo Domingo has a large single nave, two finely worked *retablos*, and, in one of its towers, the first clock to arrive in Moquegua from London. To the south of the plaza lies the **Regional Museum** (Mon–Fri 8am–3.30pm; 50¢), located in an old stone building originally constructed in 1778 to house the town prison; it's now home to a modest collection of archeological and colonial exhibits. On the western side is the **Museo Contisuyo**, C Tacna 294 (Mon–Sat 8am–1pm & 3–8pm; free), a new archeological museum that exhibits relics from the region including specimens from the coastal Chiribaya culture.

Around Moquegua

About 24km away, **Torata** is a picturesque district of country homes made with traditional *mojinete* roofs. There's also an imposing church and old stone mill, both from the colonial period. You can get there by bus from the Carretera Binacional ($1, a 30min journey), and there are a few decent restaurants. The **petroglyphs of Torata**, which depict llamas, geometric shapes and what look like maps and water symbols, are within relatively easy reach of Moquegua by following the small *quebrada*, a dry canyon which runs east 200m from the bridge at Km 120.45 of the Carretera Binacional.

For most visitors, it's **Moquegua's bodegas** that are probably the greatest attraction here. Initially established during the colonial era, Moquegua's bodegas have various lines in piscos (including *italia* and *mosto verde*), cognacs, aniseed liqueurs and wines. One of the best for visiting is the Bodega Villegas, e Hijos, C Ayacucho 1370 (Mon–Sat 8am–noon & 2–5pm; ℡054/761229), run these days by the welcoming Alberto Villegas Vargas, grandson of the original founder Norberto Villegas Talavera, one of the town's benefactors. The Bodega Zapata, at Km 1142 of the Panamericana Sur (℡054/761164), also produces fine piscos from *quebranta* and *italia* grapes.

Before you hit the bodegas, it might be advisable to check out some of the ancient sites in the region; that way you'll have the opportunity to work up a justifiable thirst. One of the bigger sites around is the archeological remnant of a Huari (600-1100 AD) citadel which is easily visited by taxi from Moquegua. Sitting atop a truncated hill – **Cerro Baúl**, after which the ruins are named – some 17km northeast of the town, this commanding site once offered its ancient inhabitants a wide view around the Moquegua valley, allowing them to control the flow of goods and people at this strategic point. Also within striking distance of Moquegua are the majestic Ubinas (5673m, with a 350m crater) and Huaynaputina (4800m) **volcanos**. Visiting these is an adventurous operation which demands 4WD support from one of the local travel agencies. Also in the sierra is the remote town of **Omate**, 130km (3hr) from Moquegua and famous for its crayfish, on the back mountain road to Arequipa, and surrounded by unique and impressive terrain formed by rock, volcanic ash and sands. Just 10km from Omate, the natural **thermal baths** of Ulucan (3100m) can be enjoyed.

Into the hills southeast of Moquegua, the town and mysterious **caves of Toquepala** (2500m), relating to a group of hunter-gatherers from the archaic era around 9000 years ago, are fascinating but rarely visited. Close to the mine of the same name, these caves contain roughly drawn pictures of cameloid animals, hunting scenes and Andean religious symbols. Again, the best way to find this site is by taking a short tour with a local travel agency. The little-seen **geoglyphs of**

△ Monkey Figure, Nazca lines

Chen Chen can be accessed by car from Moquegua, by taking the track towards Toquepala which leaves the Panamericana Sur between Km 98 and 97; the track passes along the base of some hills where the geoglyphs, mainly large Nazca-like representations of llamas, are scattered around, some hidden from the road.

Practicalities

Moquegua is the starting point for two important roads into the Andes: Carretera Binacional to Desaguadero and the Carretera Trans-oceanica connecting Ilo on the coast to Puno and Juliaca. For buses serving Lima, Tacna, Arequipa and Desaguadero, there's Cruz del Sur, Av La Paz 296 (℡054/762005), Tepsa, at Av del Ejercito 33b (℡054/761171), and also Flores, Av del Ejercito, corner with Calle Andres A. Caceres (℡054/762181, ⓔflorbus@terra.com.pe). For buses to and from Arequipa, Mollendo and Tacna, Empresa Aragon have offices on Calle Balta, four blocks southwest of the Plaza de Armas; and Civa, who go to most destinations in Peru, are at Av del Ejercito 32b. Altiplano, Av Ejercito 444 (℡054/726672), runs direct services to Puno (9hr). Tourist information is available from the Camara de Turismo, Jr Ayacucho 625 (℡054/762008 or 762342), the Regional Tourism Directorate at Jr Ayacucho 1060 (℡054/762236), and from Ledelca Tours, Jr Ayacucho 625 (℡/ⓕ054/762342, ⓔledelca@viabcp.com); also some historical information is available from the Museo Contisuyo, in the Plaza de Armas. Fast Internet access is available at a few places: Sybernet, Jr Moquegua 434, half a block from the plaza (daily 8am–11pm); Café Internet, Jr Moquegua 418, which serves drinks (daily 8am–10pm); Niv@net, C Tacna 323, Plaza de Armas (Mon–Fri 8am–10.30pm, Sat 5.30–10.30pm). The telephone office is the Locutorio Publico, C Moquegua 617 (Mon–Sat 7am–10pm, Sun 7am–1pm & 4–10pm). The post office can be found at C Moquegua 560, on the Plaza de Armas.

Car rental for the Moquegua area can be found at Mili Tour, Av del Ejercito 32 (℡054/764000; from around $25 a day). Mili Tours also offer a **colectivo car** service to Desaguadero on the Bolivian frontier, several cars daily doing this four-hour trip; they also run two or three cars a day to Arequipa. **Colectivos for Tacna** are run by Comite 1, Comite 11 and El Buen Samaritano, each taking four or five passengers, every day (6am–1pm, journey time 1hr 45min, $3). El Buen Samaritano, Av del Ejercito s/n, runs **colectivos to Desaguadero** ($10) and offers *expresso* services to take passengers anywhere they like. Transportes Korimayo, Av del Ejercito s/n, also run **buses to Desaguadero** (5hr; $5) and Puno (7hr; $6). Similarly, Expreso Turismo San Martin, Av del Ejercito 19, runs buses all the way to Desaguadero, Puno and Juliaca.

If you want to stay over here, there are a few reasonable **hotels** to select from. *Alameda Hotel*, Jr Junin 322 (℡054/762008, ⓕ763971, ⓔalamedahotel@terra-mail.com.pe; ❺), is friendly, well run, and has a great little café. *Hostal Arequipa*, C Arequipa 360 (℡054/761338; ❸–❹), is reasonable value and fairly comfortable. *Hostal Adrianela*, Miguel Grau 239 (℡054/763469; ❸), comes with private baths, colour TVs and good hot water, but is located in the busy and sometimes noisy commercial sector of town close to the market. *Hostal Carrera*, Jr Lima 320 (℡054/762113; ❷), is basic but clean, one block parallel to Plaza de Armas. *Hostal Limoñeros*, Jr Lima 441 (℡054/761649; ❸), one and a half blocks northwest of the plaza, has 24-hour hot water, cable TV, attractive gardens, semi-rustic atmosphere and a swimming pool of sorts. The smartest in town is the *Hotel El Mirador* in Alto de Villa (℡054/761765, ⓕ761895, ⓔmirador@invertur.com.pe; ❻), with swimming pool and all mod cons.

Some of the better **restaurants** can be found on the **outskirts of town**, such as the *Restaurante Recreo Turístico Las Glorietas*, in the Calle Antigua de

Samegua, serving very good local food in a traditional atmosphere and, on the same street, the equally savoury *Restaurante El Totoral*. **In town** choices include *Restaurant Moraly*, corner of calles Lima and Libertad, for great breakfasts, *Restaurante Palmero*, C Moquegua 644 (6.30am–10pm daily), just half a block from the plaza, which serves mouthwatering comida criolla and some local specialities in an open and friendly space. There are two reasonably good Italian restaurants: the *Trattoria La Toscana*, C Tacna 505 (☎054/761043) and the *Pizzeria-Bar Casa Vieja*, C Moquegua 326 (6.15am–11pm daily; ☎054/761647), the former serving the better pizzas and pastas. There's really only one **bar** to speak of and that's the *Bandido Pub*, C Moquegua 333 (Mon–Sat 6pm–midnight; ☎054/761676), where they play good music and serve pizzas cooked in wood-fired earth ovens, and reasonably priced drinks.

Money can be changed at the Banco de la Nación, Jr Lima 616, the Banco de Credito on the corner of Moquegua 861, or with the *cambistas* outside Plaza Bolívar. The one local **tour company,** Ledelca Tours, Jr Ayacucho 625 (☎/℮054/762342, ⓦwww.apavitperu.com/ledelca/), sell airline tickets and are the local representatives for **DHL** and **Western Union**. They offer city tours (3hr) and the usual countryside tour (3hr) which generally includes a visit to a bodega, or a longer tour to the Chen Chen geoglyphs and the archeological site of Cerro Baúl (4hr).

Ilo

About 95km southeast of Moquegua, **Ilo** is a busy port on the Peruvian Atacama desert coastline, with a population of over 65,000 inhabitants and an economy based around fishing and mining. The most strategically, and economically, important port in Peru, in itself Ilo doesn't offer visitors very much, but it does have one or two interesting **attractions**. As you'd expect, the Plaza de Armas is the civic heart of the city, dominated by the **Templo de San Geronimo**, built originally in 1871, and located just two blocks from the *malecón costero* and the seafront developments. The *malecón* boasts *La Glorieta*, an iron bandstand structure built onto a huge boulder overlooking the sea as well as the very modern architecture of the Municipalidad. Nearby, in the *Capitano del Puerto*'s offices, there's a small **Museo Naval** with documents and artefacts relating to the maritime past. Next to the nineteenth-century iron pier, *el Muelle Fiscal*, today you can find a busy wharf utilized by artisan fishermen – fishermen who use small boats and simple nets – and a seafood market.

Ilo is also quite popular for its fifteen or so **beaches** spreading out both north and south of the town. The nearest and most popular is the **Playa Pozo de Lisas**, near the airport. At the other end of town, to the north, the **Playa Boca del Rio** has fine sand and good views back to the city. About 20km further north, the Playa Pocoma is ideal for camping; the nicer Playa Waikiki is another 4km further north.

Arguably the most interesting local attraction, however, is the **Museo de Sitio El Algarrobal**, about 15km east of town. The museum presents exhibits from the pre-Hispanic cultures of the Ilo region, including textiles from the local Chiribaya culture and mummies, and offers views over the valley of Algarrobal and the old hacienda Chiribaya (1000-1350 AD).

Practicalities

Buses for Bolivia leave from the corner of Matara and Junin, **buses for Chile** and Arica leave daily with Flores Hnos., on the corner of Jirón Ilo with Matara, and there are also **colectivos** leaving for Arica regularly from the same corner. For **buses to Lima and Arequipa** the best company is probably Cruz del Sur, at the corner of Matara with Jirón Moquegua (☎054/782206). There are **flights from Ilo** to Cusco, Juliaca, Arequipa and Lima with Aero Continente, TANS Peru and Lan Peru. **Tour agencies** include Mar y Mar Tours, 28 de Julio 605 (☎/℻054/783318, ✉marymar@sistemasilo.co.pe), and Romes Tours, Abtao 528 (☎054/781121). **Money change** can be found at the casa de cambio Dolares Vilca, 28 de Julio 331 (☎054/782728).

As far as **accommodation** goes, one of the most comfortable in town is the *Gran Hotel Ilo*, A.A. Caceres (☎054/782412; ❺); more modest in style and comfort, the *Hostal Torrelio*, Callao 531 (☎054/785349; ❸), is central, clean and friendly. Among the better **restaurants**, *Calienta Negros*, Costanera Sur Km 02 (☎054/782839 or 785184), is popular for most types of Peruvian and standard international dishes and can also cater to vegetarians, while the less expensive *Los Cangrejos*, 28 de Julio 362 (☎054/784324), offers seafood and comida criolla in a pleasing environment. The *Chifa Choy Yin*, Jr 2 de Mayo 430 (☎054/782760), is the obvious place to head for Chinese cuisine.

Tacna

Over three hours south of Moquegua and five times larger, **TACNA,** at 552m above sea level, is the last stop in Peru. The only real reason to stop here is if you're coming from or going over the border into **Chile** (see box opposite) and the border crossing timing demands you stop, or if you feel like a break in your overland journey. Created as San Pedro de Tacna in 1535, just three years after the Spanish first arrived in Peru, it was established by Viceroy Toledo as a *reducción de indígenas*, a forced concentration of normally scattered coastal communities, making them easier to tax and use as labour. Almost 300 years later, in 1811, Francisco Antonio de Zela began the first struggle for independence from Spanish colonialism here. The people of Tacna suffered Chilean occupation from May 1880 until the Treaty of Ancón was signed in August 1929, after a local referendum. Tacna, in fact, has long been noted for its loyalty to Peru and was also highly active in Peruvian emancipation from Spain, though nowadays it's better known as an expensive city that's infamous for both its contraband and pickpockets. Realistically, though, the reputation is worse than the reality; the usual precautions (see p.44) are generally adequate and it's not a violent city. Tacna is designated a Zona Franca (a tax- or duty-free zone) where visitors can spend up to $1000 in any one trip (with a limit of $3000 in a year) on a range of tax-free electronic, sports and other luxury items. Tacna is also a centre for cyclists, particularly in August when there's usually a bicycle festival attracting competitors and enthusiasts from Bolivia and Chile as well as Peru.

The main focus of activity in this sprawling city is around the **Plaza de Armas** and along the Avenida Bolognesi. At the centre of the plaza, the ornamental *pileta*, designed by Gustave Eiffel, has a Neoclassical base depicting the four seasons while on top of the main fountain are four children holding hands. The nearby Arco Parabólico was erected in honour of the Peruvian dead from the War of the Pacific. Fronting the plaza is the **Cathedral**, designed by Eiffel in 1870 (though not completed until 1955) and built from *cantera* stones quarried from the hills of Intiorko and Arunta. Around the corner there's the **Museo Histórico** (Mon–Sat 9am–6pm; free) where, if you have an hour to spare, you can browse around the pre-Conquest artefacts and exhibitions related to the nineteenth-century wars with Chile. The **Alameda Bolognesi**, near the *Hotel de Turistas*, is an attractive palm-lined avenue constructed in 1840; it's dotted with busts of local dignitaries and also one in fine marble of

Christopher Columbus. The **Casa de Zela**, C Zela 542, houses a small archeological museum exhibiting ceramics largely discovered in the region.

For rail enthusiasts there's the **Museo Ferroviario** (Mon–Fri 9am–5.30pm, Sat 9am–1pm; 30¢), on the corner of Calle Albarracin and Avenida Dos de Mayo, just five minutes' walk from the plaza, containing locomotives, machinery and documents mainly relating to the Tacna–Arica line, but also a collection of train-related stamps from around the world. There's also a **Parque de la Locomotora**, built on Avenida Grau in 1977, dedicated exclusively to housing the antique Locomotive No. 3, which carried troops to the historic battle of Morro de Arica in 1879. Some 8km north of Tacna, on Cerro Intiorko, the eight steel sculptures of **Campo de Alianza** stand in memory of the war heroes; there's also a small Museo de Sitio which houses some old uniforms, arms and missiles left over from the historic battles.

Practicalities

Buses leave three times a week from outside the train station, on Avenida 2 de Mayo, or from the Terminal Terrestre (℡054/727007) on Hipolito Unanue, for Lake Titicaca, though this route is often impassable between January and March. For **Lima** (18hr) **Arequipa** (5hr) and **Cusco** (18hr), daily Cruz del Sur (℡054/726692) and Ormeño (℡054/723292) buses leave from the Terminal Terrestre (bus station), Avenida Manuel Odría, from bays 16–17 and 21–22, respectively; both Civa (℡054/741543) and Flores (℡054/726691) depart for

---

Crossing the Chilean border

The **border with Chile** (daily 9am–10pm) is about 40km south of Tacna. Regular buses and colectivos to Arica (25km beyond the border) leave from the modern bus terminal, on Hipolito Unanue in Tacna, and three trains a day depart from the station, on Calle Coronel Albarracin (at 7am, 8.30am and 3pm). At around $3.50, the **train** is the cheapest option, but it's slow and you have to visit the Passport and Immigration Police, on Plaza de Armas, and the Chilean Consulate, Presbitero Andia, just off Coronel Albarracin, beforehand. You will already have cleared Peruvian customs control on your way into Tacna, along the Panamerican Highway. Tepsa (Leguis 981) and Ormeño (Araguex 698) **buses** leave the bus terminal every couple of hours or so for the one- to two-hour journey to Arica ($4). **Colectivos** (normally $6) are quicker and slightly more expensive than the bus, but well worth it given the hassle saved, since they'll wait at the border controls while you get your Peruvian exit stamp and Chilean tourist card.

Arica, the first town in Chile, is a fun place to get acquainted with the excellent Chilean wines. Bus and air services from here to the rest of Chile are excellent. The *Hotel Casa Blanca* (❷–❸), General Lagos 557, is cheap and very pleasant, and the moderately priced *Hostal Muñoz*, C Lynch 565 (❸), is excellent value. Good restaurants abound.

Coming back into Peru from Arica is as simple as getting there. Colectivos run throughout the day and the train leaves at the same times as the one from Tacna. Night travellers, however, might be required to have a *salvoconducto militar* (safe-conduct card), particularly in times of tension between the two countries. If you intend to travel at night, check first with the tourist office in Arica, C Prat 305, on the second floor.

    Consulado de Bolivia Av Bolognesi 1721 (℡054/711960).

    Consulado de Chile Presbitero Andia, block 1 (Mon–Sat 8am–5.30pm; ℡054/721846 or 715792).

    Oficina de Migraciones (Peru) Av Circunvalación (Mon–Fri 8am–4pm; ℡054/743231).

Puno, Cusco, and the coast, from bays 8-9 and 10-12, respectively. For Desaguadero and La Paz, the company San Martin, Avenida Circunvalación Norte 1048 (℡054/840499) run several times a week. The best taxi service is offered by Radiotaxi, Gral. Valera 397 (℡054/726532). There are three airline offices in town: Aero Continente, Apurimac 256 (℡054/747300); Lan Peru, Apurimac 107 (℡054/743252); and TANS Peru, San Martin 617 (℡054/747002). The airport itself, Aeropuerto Carlos Ciriani Santa Rosa, is out on the Panamericana Sur at Km 5 (℡054/844503).

If you do need a place to stay, the cheap and reasonable Hotel Alcazar, Bolivar 295 (℡054/724991; ❷), is good value. Alternatively, the Hotel Las Lido, C San Martin 876 (❷), is comfortable and centrally located just off the Plaza de Armas; the Gran Hotel Central, Av San Martin 561 (℡054/712281; ❸), close by the Plaza de Armas, is a modern building and has many rooms with private baths and hot water; and the Hostal Hogar, 28 de Julio 146 (℡054/726811; ❹), is good value, secure and has nice rooms with private baths and TV. The best place for a cheap meal is the Comedor in the market, but the Genova, Av San Martin 649 (℡054/744809), serves good grills and a wide range of the usual international dishes (like spaghetti, steaks, burgers etc). El Caquique, C Jose Rosa Ara 1903 (℡054/714582), is the local picantería, and as such probably the best place to try guinea pig. The Gerolamo Ristorante Di Mare, San Martin 981 (℡054/721212), has fine seafood, while the popular La Olla de Barro, Billinghurst 951 (℡054/727572), prides itself on Peruvian dishes typical of the region, such as the delicious choclo con queso (sweet corn and cheese) or the spicy picante de Tacnena (duck in a chili and oregano sauce).

Tourist information is sometimes available from the tourist office at San Martin 405 (Mon–Fri 9am–6pm & Sat 9am–1pm; ℡054/715352), or the Plaza de Armas offices at Av Bolognesi 2088 (Mon–Sat 8am–3pm; ℡054/713501 or 713778), or the Regional Tourism Directorate, Blondell 50 (℡054/722784). Failing that, try the Dirección Regional de Industria y Turismo, Jr Blondell 506. For money matters, cash and travellers' cheques can be changed at the Banco de la Nación, San Martin 320, on the Plaza de Armas; Banco del Sur, Apurimac 245; Banco Continental, San Martin 665; Banco de Wiese, at Av San Martin 476; Banco de Credito, San Martin 574; and the Banco Latino, San Martin 507. Cambistas hang around in avenidas Bolognesi and Mendoza. It's a good idea to get rid of your extra nuevo soles before going into Chile (exchange them for US dollars or, if not, Chilean pesos), and the cambistas in Tacna usually offer better rates than those in Santiago or Arica anyway.

Travel details

Buses and colectivos

Ica to: Arequipa (6 daily; 12hr); Lima (20 daily; 4hr); Nazca (6 daily; 2hr).

Nazca to: Arequipa (2 nightly, several daily; 12hr); Cusco, via Arequipa (daily; 35hr); Cusco via Ayacucho (daily; 30hr); Lima (2–3 daily; 5hr).

Moquegua to: Lima (6 daily, 20hr); Arequipa (10 daily, 2hr); Puno (3–4 daily; 6hr); Desaguadero (2 daily; 5hr); Tacna (6 daily; 2hr).

Pisco to: Ayacucho (3 weekly; 12hr); Lima (20 daily; 3hr); Ica (10 daily; 1hr); Nazca (2 daily; 3hr).

Tacna to: Arequipa (5 daily; 6–7hr); Arica (10 daily; 1–2 hr); Lima (4 daily; 22hr); Puno (3 weekly; 8hr); Moquegua (6 daily, 2hr).

Flights

Tacna to: Lima (4 weekly, 1hr 30min).

Arequipa, Puno and Lake Titicaca

CHAPTER 4

Highlights

✳ **Cruz del Condor** A breathtaking viewing point in Colca Canyon, offering sightings of up to a dozen condors sailing below, around and above. See p.265

✳ **Mirador of Yanahuara** The most popular viewing point in Peru, this *mirador* frames the perfect snow-capped cone of volcano El Misti. See p.251

✳ **Tradición Arequipeña** This massive restaurant bustles with people enjoying delicious *cuy* or *rocoto relleno*. See p.253

✳ **Santa Catalina** Just exploring the labyrinthine sunlit streets of this nunnery is a calming, even spiritual experience in its own right. See p.247

✳ **Cotahuasi Canyon** Not only the deepest canyon in the world, this is also one of the most remote places that the adventurous traveller can easily reach in Peru. See p.271

✳ **Taquile and Amantani** Spending time on either of these beautiful islands is like being transported back in time at least 500 years. See p.283

✳ **Temple of Fertility** One of the weirdest archeological sites in the whole of Peru: a hundred stone phalluses jammed within the temple space like spectators' seats in a theatre. See p.285

Arequipa, Puno and Lake Titicaca

While the southern coast of Peru boasts all manner of intriguing cultural sites, the interior of the south is much better known for its geographical features. The Andes take hold again here, punctuated by spectacular lakes, towering volcanos and deep, stark canyons – a landscape well suited for adventurous explorations and hitting some fairly remote locales. The region can be more or less broken down into two distinct areas, one centring on Arequipa, itself not terribly far removed from the coast though high above sea level, and the other on storied Lake Titicaca, up on a plateau in the Andes at the northern end of the Bolivian altiplano. Both feel quite detached from the rest of the country – something played out to great effect in Arequipa's political leanings – and the whole of the southern interior is not particularly quick or easy to get around.

Arequipa, second city of Peru and a day's journey from Lima, sits poised at the edge of the Andes against an extraordinary backdrop of volcanic peaks. The white stone architecture of Arequipa - particularly the Monastery of Santa Catalina, a complex enclosing a complete world within its thick walls - constitutes perhaps the city's main appeal to travellers, but the startlingly varied countryside that is within reach, from the gorges of both the Colca Canyon, massive but dwarfed by the glaciers and volcanos on either side of the valley, and the more distant Cotahuasi Canyon, to the unsettling isolation of the Valley of the Volcanos, is worth your time as well. If you're coming from the north, it's one of the last places to really merit a stop before continuing on south to the Chilean border.

Further inland from Arequipa, you'll probably want to spend time in the **Lake Titicaca** area, getting to know its main town and port – **Puno**, a high, quite austere city with a cold climate and incredibly rarefied air. **Juliaca**, to its north, makes an alternative base for exploring the lake, or the countryside of this poor, largely peasant area. Alternatively you might fancy some time on one of the huge lake's islands where life has changed little in the last five hundred years. The Titicaca region is renowned for its folk dances and Andean music and, along with Puno, makes an interesting place to break your journey from Arequipa to Cusco or into Bolivia.

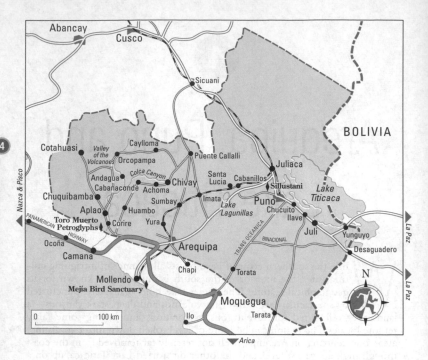

Arequipa and around

The name Arequipa is probably derived from the Quechua phrase "*ari quepay*", meaning "OK, let's stop here", which, according to local legend, is exactly what the fourth Inca emperor, Mayta Capac, said to his generals on the way back from Cusco after one of his conquest trips. Situated well above the coastal fog bank, at the foot of an ice-capped volcano – **El Misti** – and close to four other prominent volcanos (Chachani, Ampato, Coropuna and Pichupichu), the place has long been renowned for having one of the most beautiful settings and pleasant climates of all Peru's cities. The Ampato volcano is presently active, the source of those wisps of smoke appearing on the horizon. Chachani itself has four main craters: Coronada (5400m), Fatima (5900m), Angel (6005m) and Chachani (6075m), while Pichupichu – which means peak to peak – has thirteen different craters, one known as the Indio Dormido (Sleeping Indian), whose face can be made out if you study the volcano's form carefully from the city.

The Incas were not alone in finding Arequipa to their liking. When Pizarro officially "founded" the city in 1540, he was moved enough to call it Villa Hermosa, or Beautiful Town, and *Don Quixote* author Miguel de Cervantes extolled the city's virtues, saying that it enjoyed an eternal springtime. Today, despite a disastrous earthquake in 1687, it's still endowed with some of the country's finest colonial **churches** and **mansions**, many of which were constructed from white volcanic *sillar*, cut from the surrounding mountains and often flecked with black ash. The last major earthquake to hit the city was on June 23, 2001 when 110 people died, several schools were razed to the ground and one of the Cathedral towers was tumbled. Fortunately, however, the quake happened at 3pm on a Saturday, so many children were spared.

Apart from its splendid colonial city, the Arequipa region posseses some of the finest scenery and pre-Inca terracing in the Andes as well as the two deepest canyons in the world. Furthermore, the outlying towns and villages, particularly around **Chivay** and the **Colca Canyon**, are relatively accessible yet still surprisingly traditional and stunningly beautiful.

Arequipa

An active city, some 2400m above sea level, and with a relatively wealthy population of over 750,000, **AREQUIPA** maintains a rather aloof attitude towards the rest of Peru. Most Arequipans feel themselves distinct, if not culturally superior, and resent the idea of the nation revolving around Lima. With **El Misti**, the dormant, 5821-metre volcano poised dramatically above, it must be admitted that the place does have a rather mythic and unique appearance. Arguably the oldest and most traditional of Arequipa's restaurants – *La Tradición Arequipeña* – goes so far as to issue Arequipa passports to its clients, only partly in jest. But besides being the country's second biggest and arguably, after Cusco, most attractive city, Arequipa has some very specific historical connotations for Peruvians. Developing late as a provincial capital, and until 1870 connected with the rest of Peru only by mule track, it has acquired a reputation as *the* centre of **right-wing political power**: while populist movements have tended to emerge around Trujillo in the north, Arequipa has traditionally represented the solid interests of the oligarchy. Sanchez Cerro and Odria both began their coups here, in 1930 and 1948 respectively, and Belaunde, one of the most important presidents in pre- and post-military coup years, sprang into politics from one of the wealthy Arequipa families. The social extremes are quite clear today; despite the tastefully ostentatious architecture and generally well-heeled appearance of most townsfolk, there is much poverty in the region and there's been a huge increase in the number of street beggars in Arequipa. Things came to a head in 2002, when the city's streets were ripped up in political protest against President Toledo's plans to sell off the local electric utility on the cheap, with the fear that the new private company would charge much more for power. Asserting its independence, once again Arequipa triumphed, if perhaps only temporarily, over Lima's dominance, as the president was forced to back off.

One of the best times to visit is around mid-August, when there's a **festival** celebrating Arequipa's foundation with processions, music and poetry. There's also a folklore festival in the first week of July.

Arrival, information and city transport

Generally, Arequipa is an almost unavoidable stopping-off point between Lima and the Titicaca, Cusco and Tacna regions, and is a hub for most journeys in the southern half of Peru. From Arequipa you can continue to Cusco by bus or train or plane, to Titicaca by bus (trains have been suspended because buses can do it in half the time) and over the border to Chile by international bus. Tacna and the Chilean frontier are even nearer and highly accessible from Arequipa by road.

Crime in Arequipa

The worst reports from Arequipa in recent years have concerned a spate of **"strangle-muggings"** wherein tourists are jumped and strangled to the point of fainting before being robbed. Although such attacks are still relatively rare, it's best to avoid walking along empty streets late at night, especially if alone. Much more common is **pickpocketing**, which is most likely in the Central Market area and on Jerusalen or San Juan de Dios. If you have anything stolen, report it to the **Tourist Police** (see below) and also ask for assistance and advice at the **i-Peru Tourist Office** (see below), or contact your consulate.

Flights land at Arequipa airport, 7km northwest of town. A red shuttle bus meets most planes and will take you to any hotel in the town centre for $1; alternatively, a taxi will cost $3–4. Most long-distance **buses** arrive at the modern, concrete Terminal Terreste bus station about 4km south from the centre of town or at the newer Terrapuerto, next door; a taxi to the Plaza de Armas should cost no more than $2. It's worth noting, too, that when leaving these terminals by bus, there's a 30¢ charge per head. For full details of operators, contact details and where they connect to, see Listings, p.288.

Information

Tourist information is available from the official **i-Peru Promperu office of tourist information and assistance** at Portal de la Municipalidad 112, Plaza de Armas (daily 8.30am–7.30pm; ℡054/221228, ℮iperuarequipa @promperu.gob.pe); the **Tourist Police**, Jerusalen 315 (℡054/201258), are also particularly helpful with maps, information and safety precautions, plus they have a small exhibition of photos and postcards of major local attractions. The **Terminal Terrestre** also has a kiosk with details of hotels and tour companies, and sometimes maps. For information on **guided tours** of the city and the surrounding area, see the box on p.256. There's an **i-Peru information office at the airport** (daily 6.30am–6.30pm; ℡054/444564), where they have maps of the city, information on sights and cultural events, and can recommend guides, tour companies and hotels.

City transport

It's easy enough to **walk** around the city centre, but we've listed relevant **bus** services where you might want to avoid a longish walk (see p.255). If you want a **taxi** it's easy to hail one anywhere in the city; rides within the centre cost about 80¢. For a highly recommended service call Taxi Seguro, Pasaje 7 de Junio 200, Mariano Melgar (℡054/450250) or, second best, Taxi Sur (℡054/465656); other useful contacts include the taxi drivers Pablo Roman (℡054/934328) and Abel Cuba; both of these can usually be found outside the *Casa de mi Abuela* hostel (see p.244), and offer reasonable deals for trips to the immediate suburbs and countryside.

Accommodation

Arequipa has a good selection of **accommodation** in all price ranges, with most of the better options mainly within a few blocks of the Plaza de Armas or along Calle Jerusalen.

Budget

Albergue Juvenil Ronda Recoleta 104
℡054/257085. Arequipa's youth hostel, out near

the Recoleta Monastery. Simple, but it suffices. ❷
Colonial House Inn Puente Grau 114
℡054/223533, ℮colonialhouseinn@hotmail.com.

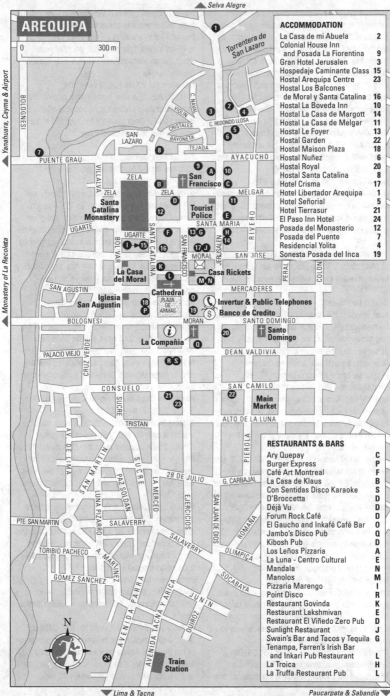

Pleasant place with a pretty covered courtyard, electric heated showers, private bathrooms and access to TV and Internet facilities. Well worth it, not least for the nice rooftop breakfast option. ❸

Hospedaje Caminante Class Santa Catalina 207a ☎054/203444, ✆caminanteaqp@terra.com. Very clean and pleasant, six-room family-run pad; safe and well managed, some rooms with and some without private bathrooms. There's a rooftop terrace with views and a laundry facility. ❷–❹

Hostal Arequipa Centre Alvarez Thomas 305 ☎054/496169. Central, simple but spotlessly clean, with a range of rooms from basic to suites with jacuzzis and cable TV. ❷–❹

Hostal La Boveda Inn Jerusalen 402 ☎054/202562. Cheap and rough but conveniently located on the second floor of an old building, with a vegetarian restaurant beneath. Bathrooms are mostly communal and have fairly constant hot water. ❷

Hostal La Casa de Melgar Melgar 108-B ☎054/222459. A nice place, old and stylish; the best rooms are those with views over the street. ❸

Hostal Le Foyer The name outside says La Villa Real, which is the name of the mansion this popular backpackers' hostel is located in. You'll need to ring the bell to get in. It's clean and friendly, right at the heart of the action and has a spacious first-floor patio as well as a small, useful book exchange. Some rooms with bath. ❷–❸

Hostal Garden San Camilo 116 ☎/✆ 054/237440. A misleading name but still excellent value, with solar-heated communal showers and lovely, old-fashioned, clean rooms with or without private bath. Located very close to the central market. ❷–❸

Hostal Latino Carlos Llosa 135 ☎054/244770. Has excellent hot showers and a very trustworthy luggage deposit if you want to make a trek out of town. Family-operated, homely and rarely overcrowded. ❷

Hostal Nuñez Jerusalen 528 ☎054/218648, ✆hostal_nunez@terr.com.pe. A friendly, family-run place with attractive patios, constant hot water, laundry service and secure luggage deposit; a few rooms have private bath. You can have breakfast on the terrace. ❷–❸

Hostal Santa Catalina Santa Catalina 600 ☎054/243705. Pleasant but elementary, it has a spacious and cool café; only a few rooms have their own toilets and showers, but there are great views to El Misti from the roof terrace, where you can also dry your clothing. ❷

Hotel Premier Av Quiroz 100 ☎054/241091, ⓦwww.barrioperu.terra.com.pe/hotelpremier. Associated with Youth Hostelling International, this

hostel is clean, safe and friendly; also runs cultural trips, which you can check out on their website. ❸

Posada La Fiorentina Puente Grau 110 ☎054/242668. This place has 24hr hot water, small but comfortable rooms and a nice courtyard. Good value. ❷

Residencial Yolita Pasaje Velez 204 ☎054/226505. A new, comfortable lodging, close to *La Casa de mi Abuela*, so a possible alternative if you find *La Casa* full. Very friendly, and some upstairs rooms have good views. ❷

Moderate

La Casa de mi Abuela Jerusalen 606 ☎054/241206, ✆242761, ✆lperezwi@ucsm.edu.pe. Innovative family-run hostel, whose name translates as "My Grandma's House", combining elegance, comfort and great value. Rooms are set in a variety of environments around lovely gardens; there are spacious colonial quarters, chalets, family apartments and a fine swimming pool. It's very secure, has a good library and an excellent cafetería. Reserve well in advance during high season. ❹–❺

Hostal Los Balcones de Moral y Santa Catalina C Moral 217 ☎/✆054/201292, ⓦwww.losbalconeshotel.com. All rooms are on the second floor and have private bathrooms, 24hr hot water (solar by day) and a sun terrace but no street views. Also has cafetería, laundry and luggage deposit. Breakfast included in the price. ❺

Hostal La Casa del Margott C Jerusalen 304 ☎054/229517, ✆283022, ✆lacasademargotthostal@hotmail.com. Based around a colonial courtyard which is slightly crowded by a massive palm tree, this hostel has a tiny bar, good new mattresses and cable TV in rooms. Some of the downstairs rooms have *sillar* walls and ceilings. Rooms with or without private bath. ❹–❺

Hostal Terrapuerto in the centre of Terrapuerto bus station ☎054/422277, ext 232. Surprisingly clean and bearable for a bus station, though rooms are windowless. There's hot water, while rooms have TV and are with or without private bath. Has a casino in the same complex. ❸–❹

Hotel Señorial Carlos Llosa 106 ☎/✆ 054/288061. Modern and comfortable, though with little character. All rooms have private bath. ❹

El Paso Inn Hotel Av Parra 119 ☎054/229523, ✆243649. A new hotel, several blocks southwest of the Plaza de Armas on a continuation of La Merced; has private bathrooms, its own restaurant and the occasional disco at weekends. ❸

Posada del Puente Bolognesi 101
ⓣ054/253132, ⓕ253576. Very comfortable and
relatively well situated. ⑤

Expensive

Gran Hotel Jerusalen Jerusalen 601
ⓣ054/244441 or for reservation 287421,
ⓔjerusalen@terra.com.pe. Fairly luxurious and
reasonably good value, with TVs and minibars in
the carpeted rooms, all of which have private bath.
Also has a pleasant dining room and bar. ⑤

Hostal Maison Plaza Portal San Agustin 143
ⓣ054/218929, ⓕ218931,
ⓔarequipa@lanet.com.pe. Fairly plush with a
lovely *sillar*-domed reception area, and well located on the Plaza de Armas; unusually for Peru the
price includes a decent breakfast. ⑤

Hotel Crisma Moral 107 ⓣ054/215290. A relatively smart place with a laundry service, restaurant, and TV in all rooms. Price includes American
breakfasts. ⑤

Hotel Libertador Arequipa Plaza Bolivar, Selva
Alegre ⓣ054/215110, ⓕ241933, ⓦwww
.libertador.com.pe. Formerly the state-run *Hotel de
Turistas*, this luxurious, spacious hotel has a pool
and sports facilities and serves excellent breakfasts (not included). Quite a few blocks from
downtown in a beautiful setting on the spur above
the Barrio San Lazaro, surrounded by the eucalyptus trees of Selva Alegre Park. ⑥

La Posada del Monasterio ⓣ054/206565,
ⓔlaposadadelmonasterio@star.com.pe. An early
eighteenth-century building where families of the
nuns once stayed when visiting their relatives; it
has a fine *sillar* courtyard but much of the hotel
has been modernized, creating a labrynthian but
plush and pretty pleasant environment with a view
from many rooms and an inner garden area as
well as a bar. ⑦

Sonesta Posada del Inca Portal de Flores 116
ⓣ054/215530, ⓕ234374, ⓔposada@sonestaperu
.com. Very smart and central, with a top-class
restaurant, conference rooms and, more importantly, a rooftop pool and patio with superb views
across the city to the southeastern mountains. This
is the only hotel in Arequipa with dehumidifiers in all
rooms, which also boast cable TV, a minibar and an
Internet connection. ⑧

Tierrasur Hotel Consuelo 210 ⓣ054/227132,
ⓕ286564, ⓦwww.tieraasur.com. A pleasant modern hotel, just two blocks south of the Plaza de
Armas; the rooms are smart and clean with cable
TV; service is friendly and good English is spoken.
⑤–⑥

The City

Arequipa's deeply ingrained architectural beauty comes mainly from the colonial period, characterized here by white *sillar* stone and arched interior ceilings. In general, the style is stark and almost clinical, except where Baroque and
mestizo influences combine, as seen on many of the fine sixteenth- to eighteenth-century facades. Of the huge number of religious buildings spread
about the old colonial centre, the **Monastery of Santa Catalina** is the most
outstanding and beautiful. Also, within a few blocks of the colonial **Plaza de
Armas** are half a dozen churches well deserving of a brief visit, and a couple
of superb old mansions. Further out, but still within walking distance, you can
visit the attractive suburbs of **San Lazaro**, **Cayma** and **Yanahuara**, the latter
being particularly renowned for its dramatic views of the valley, with the volcanos, notably El Misti, patiently watching the city from high above. Another
amazing vantage point for views over the city to El Misti is the very impressive black iron viaduct, or Puente de Fierro; although spanning half a kilometre, it was designed so well by Gustave Eiffel and built to such high standards
by the railway baron Henry May, that it has successfully withstood the test of
Arequipa's severe earthquakes and tremors for over a hundred years.

The Plaza de Armas and around

The **Plaza de Armas**, one of South America's grandest, and the focus of the
town's social activity in the early evenings, comprises a particularly striking array
of colonial architecture, dotted with palms, flowers and gardens. At its heart sits a
newly renovated bronze fountain, topped by an angel fondly known as *turututu*
because of the trumpet it carries, but it's the arcades and elegant white facade of

the seventeenth-century **Cathedral** (daily 6–11am & 5–7pm; free) that demand your attention, even drawing your sight away from El Misti towering behind. There are two bronze medallions in the facade symbolizing the Peruvian–Bolivian confederation, and the whole thing looks particularly beautiful when lit up in the evenings. Gutted by fire in 1844 and restored in 1868 by Lucas Poblete, it displays some French influence in its neo-Renaissance style. However, apart from the massive Belgian-built organ, said to be one of the largest in South America, and a marble altar created by Felippo Moratillo, the admittedly vast interior is rather disappointing in its generally austere and bland design.

Also on the plaza is the **Casona Flores del Campo**, Portal de Flores 136 (daily 10am–5pm; 50¢), older than most houses in Arequipa, dating back to the sixteenth century (it was apparently once used by Fernando Pizarro), but not completed until 1779 by one Coronel Manuel Flores del Campo. It's quite easy to distinguish different stages in the construction of this *casona* (colonial mansion), most notably the double arch and balcony from the late eighteenth century. These days it's home to a reasonably wide-ranging exhibition of artesania.

On the southeast corner of the plaza, opposite from the Cathedral, and rather more exciting architecturally, is the elaborate **Iglesia La Compañía** (Mon–Fri 9–11.30am & 3–5.30pm; 30¢), with its extraordinary zigzagging *sillar* stone doorway. Built over the last decades of the seventeenth century, the magnificently sculpted doorway, with a locally inspired *mestizo*-baroque relief, is curiously two-dimensional, using shadow only to outline the figures of the frieze. Inside, by the main altar hangs a *Virgin and Child* by Bernardo Bitto, which arrived from Italy in 1575. In what used to be the sacristy (now the Chapel of San Ignacio), the polychrome cupola depicts jungle imagery alongside warriors, angels and the Evangelists. Next door to the church are the **Jesuit Cloisters** (Mon–Sat 8am–10pm, Sun noon–8pm; 50¢), superbly carved back in the early eighteenth century. In the first cloister, squared pillars support white stone arches and are covered with intricate reliefs showing more angels, local fruits and vegetables, seashells and stylized puma heads. The second cloister is, in contrast, rather austere.

Santo Domingo (daily 7–11am & 3–6pm; free), two blocks east of La Compañía, was originally built in 1553 by Gaspar Vaez, the first master architect to arrive in Arequipa, though most of what you see today started in 1650 and was finished in 1698. Although badly damaged by earthquakes in 1958 and 1960, it has been well restored, and on the main door you can make out an interesting example of Arequipa's *mestizo* craftsmanship – an Indian face amid a bunch of grapes, leaves and even cacti.

Opposite the northeast corner of the Cathedral, at C San Francisco 108, stands a particularly impressive colonial mansion, **La Casa de Tristan del Pozo**, also known as La Casa Rickets (Mon–Sat 9am–12.30pm & 5–8pm; free). Built in 1737 as a *seminario*, it later became the splendid residence of the Rickets family, who made their fortune from the wool trade in the late nineteenth century, and boasts an extremely attractive facade. The stonework above the main door depicts Christ's geneaology, with highly stylized plants supporting five discs, or Jesuit medallions, with JHS (the abbreviation for Jesus) at the centre, Maria and Jose to the side of this, and Joaquin and Ana on the extremes. Now owned and lavishly restored by the Banco Continental, the mansion houses a small museum and art gallery.

North of the plaza, at Santa Catalina 101, the **Casa Arróspide** (also known as the Casa Iriberry) is home to the Complejo Cultural Chavez de la Rosa (Mon–Sat 10am–6pm; free). This attractive colonial house, built in 1743, belongs to the Law Faculty of the University of San Augustin and hosts changing selections of modern works by mostly Peruvian artists. It possesses three main galleries as well as an art store with local art and crafts for sale (Mon–Sat 10am–1pm & 4–8pm). Around the corner is the eighteenth-century **La Casa del Moral**, C Moral 318 (Mon–Sat 9am–5pm, Sun 9am–1pm; $1.80), restored and refurbished with period pieces. Its most engaging feature is a superb stone gateway, carved with motifs that are similar to those on Nazca ceramics – puma heads with snakes growing from their mouths – surrounding a Spanish coat of arms. The mansion's name – nothing to do with ethics – comes from an old *mora* tree, still thriving in the central patio. One block down Calle Sucre from the Casa del Moral, the elegant **Iglesia San Agustín**, on the corner with Calle San Agustín (daily 4–9pm; free), boasts one of the city's finest Baroque facades; its old convent cloisters are now attached to the university, while inside only the unique octagonal sacristy survived the 1868 earthquake.

Two blocks down from the Plaza de Armas, on the corner of La Merced with Consuelo, is the **Casa Arango**, owned by the Standard Chartered company. Built in the late seventeenth century in what was then the city's most important street, it brings together a number of architectural styles, including both *mestizo*-Baroque and nineteenth-century Neoclassical.

Santa Catalina Monastery

Just two blocks north of the Plaza de Armas, the vast protective walls of **Santa Catalina Monastery** (daily 9am–4pm; $7.50, guides are optional at around $3) housed almost two hundred secluded nuns and three hundred servants until it opened some of its outer doors to the public in 1970. The most important and prestigious religious building in Peru, its enormous complex of rooms, cloisters and tiny plazas takes a good hour or two to explore. Some thirty nuns still live here today, but they're restricted to the quarter bordered by calles Bolivar and Zela, worshipping in the main chapel only outside of opening hours.

Originally the concept of Gaspar Vae in 1570, though only granted official licence five years later, it was funded by the Viceroy Toledo and the wealthy Maria de Guzmán, who later entered the convent with one of her sisters and donated all her riches to the community. The most striking feature of the architecture is its predominantly Mudéjar style, adapted by the Spanish from the Moors, but which rarely found its way into their colonial buildings. The quality of the design is emphasized and harmonized by a superb interplay between the strong sunlight, white stone and brilliant colours in the ceilings and the deep-blue sky above the maze of narrow interior streets. You notice this at once as you enter, filing left along the first corridor to a high vaulted room with a ceiling of opaque *huamanga* stone imported from the Ayacucho valley. Beside here are the **locutorios** – little cells where on holy days the nuns could talk, unseen, to visitors.

The **Novices Cloisters**, beyond, are built in solid *sillar*-block columns, their antique wall paintings depicting the various qualities to which the devotees were expected to aspire and the Litanies of the Rosary. Off to the right, the **Orange Tree Cloister**, painted a beautiful blue with birds and flowers over the vaulted arches, is surrounded by a series of paintings showing the soul evolving from a state of sin to the achievement of God's grace. In one of the side rooms, dead nuns were mourned, before being interred within the monastic confines.

A new convent, where the nuns now live, is on the right off Calle Cordoba. **Calle Toledo**, a long, very narrow street that's the oldest part of the monastery and connects the main dwelling areas with the *lavandería*, or communal

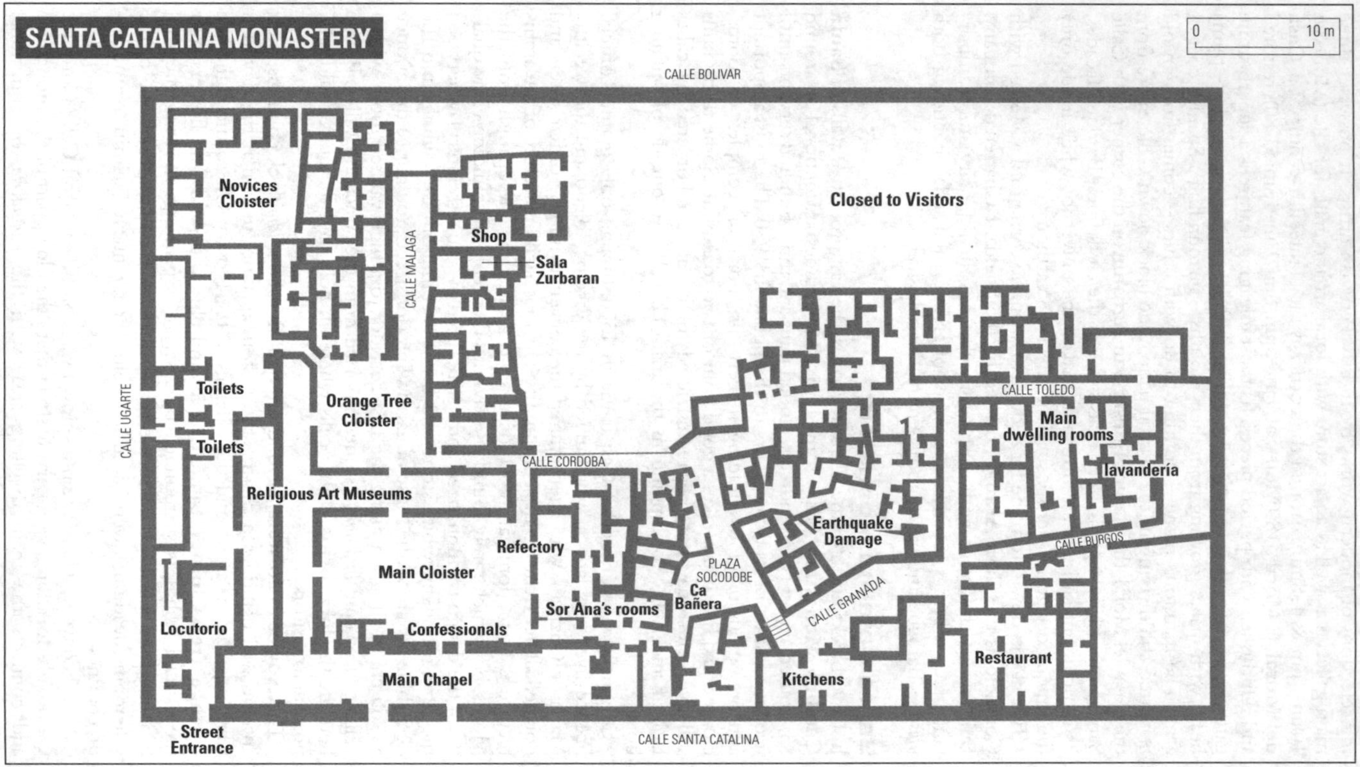

SANTA CATALINA MONASTERY

0   10 m

CALLE BOLIVAR

Closed to Visitors

CALLE TOLEDO

Lavandería

Main
dwelling rooms

CALLE BURGOS

Earthquake
Damage

CALLE GRANADA

Restaurant

Kitchens

PLAZA
SOCODOBE

Ca
Bañera

CALLE CORDOBA

Refectory

Sor Ana's rooms

CALLE SANTA CATALINA

Shop

Sala
Zurbarán

CALLE MALAGA

Orange Tree
Cloister

Religious Art Museums

Main Cloister

Confessionals

Main Chapel

Novices
Cloister

CALLE UGARTE

Toilets

Toilets

Locutorio

Street
Entrance

washing sector, is brought to life with permanently flowering geraniums. There are several rooms off here worth exploring, including small chapels, prayer rooms and a kitchen. The **lavandería** itself, perhaps more than any other area, offers a captivating insight into what life must have been like for the closeted nuns; open to the skies and city sounds yet bounded by high walls, there are twenty halved earthenware jars alongside a water channel. It also has a swimming pool with sunken steps and a papaya tree in the lovely garden.

There's a **restaurant**, serving reasonably priced snacks and drinks, just off to the left along the broad Calle Granada, while heading straight on brings you to the **Plaza Socodobe**, a fountain courtyard to the side of which is the **bañera** where the nuns used to bathe. Around the corner, down the next little street, are **Sor Ana's rooms**. By the time of her death in 1686, the 90-year-old Sor Ana was something of a phenomenon, leaving behind her a trail of prophecies and cures. Her own destiny in Santa Catalina, like that of many of her sisters, was to castigate herself in order to offer up her torments for the salvation of other souls – mostly wealthy Arequipan patrons who paid handsomely for the privilege. Sor Ana was beatified by Pope John Paul II in the 1990s.

The **refectory**, immediately before the main cloisters, is deceptively plain – its exceptional star-shaped stained-glass windows shedding dapples of sunlight through the empty space. Nearby, confessional windows look into the **main chapel**, but the best view of its majestic cupola is from the top of the staircase beside the cloisters. A small room underneath these stairs has an intricately painted wall niche with a centrepiece of a heart being pierced by a sword. The ceiling is also curious, painted with three dice, a crown of thorns, and some other less recognizable items. The **cloisters** themselves are covered with murals following the life of Jesus and the Virgin Mary; although they were originally a communal dormitory, their superb acoustics now make them popular venues for classical concerts and weddings.

Leaving this area and entering through the **lower choir room** you come to the **tomb of Sor Ana** within the quite grand and lavishly decorated **main chapel**. Beyond the last sector of the monastery is a rather dark museum full of obscure seventeenth-, eighteenth- and nineteenth-century paintings. The best of these are in the final outer chamber, lined mainly with works from the Cusqueña school. One eye-catching canvas, the first on the left as you enter this room, is of Mary Magdalene. Painted by a nineteenth-century Arequipan, it's remarkably modern in its treatment of the flesh of Mary and the near-cubism of its rocky background.

Around Santa Catalina

The **Museo Santuarios Andinos** (Mon–Sat 9am–5.45pm; $5), located at Santa Catalina 210 around a pleasant colonial courtyard, has displays of Inca mummies and a range of archeological remains; guides are obligatory but their fee, which is additional, negotiable. The main exhibit is *Juanita*, the sacrificed "princess" uncovered in her icy ritual grave in 1995 by an expedition from the Catholic University of Santa Maria de Arequipa. The gravesite, located at the incredible altitude of 6380m on Ampato volcano, is estimated to be about 500 years old. The girl, or "ice-maiden", Juanita was somewhere around 12–14 years old when sacrified after some time of fasting and herbal sedation. Note that the museum is slated to move to La Merced 310 in late 2003. Just above Santa Catalina, on the Plazuela de San Francisco, is Arequipa's city museum, the **Museo de la Ciudad** (Mon–Fri 8.30am–1pm & 4–6.30pm; $1), which devotes itself principally to local heroes – army chiefs, revolutionary leaders, presidents and poets (including the renowned Mariano Melgar). It's rather a dull collection of memorabilia, though some rooms have interesting photographs of the city. The university museums, located on the outskirts of the city, are of greater interest (see below).

Also on the Plazuela de San Francisco, off Calle Melgar, just one block east of Santa Catalina, you can find a striking Franciscan complex, dominated by the church of **San Francisco** (daily 6–11am & 3.30–7pm; $1.50). Yet another of Gaspar Vaez's projects, this one dating back to 1569, it shows an interesting mix of brick and *sillar* work both inside and on the facade. The central nave was originally covered with paintings by Baltazar de Prado, but these were destroyed by the earthquake of 1604; however, it retains its most impressive feature – a pure-silver **altar**. Adjoining the church are rather austere cloisters and the very simple **Chapel of the Third Order** (daily 8–11am & 3–5pm; free), its entrance decorated with modest *mestizo* carvings of St Francis and St Clare, founders of the first and second orders. The San Francisco complex also houses a small **Regional History Museum**, containing artefacts from the colonial period and the war with Chile.

Monastery of La Recoleta

The **monastery** (Mon–Sat 9am–noon & 3–5pm; $1.80; ☎054/270996) is located on the western side of the Río Chili which runs its generally torrential course through Arequipa from Selva Alegre directly south, dividing the old heart of the city from what has become a more modern downtown sector including Yanahuara and Cayma. This is a large Franciscan monastery standing conspicuously on its own on Callejón de la Recoleta, Ronda Recoleta 117, just ten to fifteen minutes' walk east of the Plaza de Armas. Founded in 1648 by the venerable Father Pedro de Mendoza and designed by Father Pedro de Peñaloza, the stunning major and minor cloisters were built in 1651; in 1869 it was converted to an Apostolic Mission school administered by the Barefoot Franciscans. A public museum since 1978, the monastery houses two rooms of pre-Columbian artefacts including textiles and ceramics, a religious and modern art gallery plus a renowned historic **library** with some 25,000 sixteenth- and seventeenth-century volumes.

Near the cloisters the fascinating **Museo Amazonico**, dedicated to the Franciscans' long-running missionary activity in the Peruvian tropical rainforest regions, displays artefacts collected over the years from jungle Indian tribes and examples of forest flora and fauna. There's also a religious-art museum, with a picture from the Van Dyck school representing the descent of Christ from the cross. The picture gallery is home to the most precious paintings owned by the convent, which also has a showcase of pre-Columbian exhibits located in front of the chapel.

The university museums

San Agustin (Mon–Sat 8.30am–12.30pm & 3–5pm; $1.50; call first for an appointment on ☎054/29719) is the largest of Arequipa's museums, with good collections of everything from mummies and replicas of Chavin artwork to colonial paintings and furniture. Stuck out in the university campus along Avenida Independencia (by the corner with Victor Morales), it's not very far from the road to Paucarpata and the exit route across the mountains to Puno and Cusco. The **Museo de la Universidad de Santa Maria** (Mon–Fri 8am–noon; $1.75, includes a video and guided tour) belongs to the Catholic University and concentrates on items from pre-Conquest cultures such as the Huari, Tiahuanuco, Chancay and Inca.

The suburbs: San Lazaro, Yanahuara and Cayma

The oldest quarter of Arequipa – the first place the Spaniards settled in this valley – is the barrio **San Lazaro**, an uncharacteristic zone of tiny, curving streets stretching around the hillside at the top end of Calle Jerusalen, all an easy stroll north from the plaza. If you feel like a walk, and some good views of El Misti, you can follow the streambed from here to Puente Grau – a superb vantage point. From here, a longer stroll takes you across to the west bank of the Chili, along Avenida Ejercito and out to the suburbs of Yanahuara (1–2km) and Cayma (3–4km), once quite distinct villages until the railway boom of the late nineteenth century, which brought peasant-migrants to Arequipa from as far away as Cusco. Both are built-up now, though they still command stunning views across the valley, above all from their **churches**. There are also one or two fine restaurants in these sectors, particularly Yanahuara. Buses and colectivos to these areas leave from avenidas Ayacucho and Puente Grau.

The municipal plaza at **Yanahuara** possesses a beautiful **viewing point** (*mirador*) which has been made famous by postcards. Buses and colectivos to Yanahuara's *mirador* can be caught from the corner of Grau with Santa Catalina (near the *Hostal Santa Catalina*), or it's a fifteen-minute walk from Puente Grau, between blocks 2 and 3 of Av Ejercito. The small **Iglesia Yanahuara** on the tranquil main plaza dates to the middle of the eighteenth century, and its Baroque facade, with a stone relief of the tree of life incorporating angels, flowers, saints, lions and hidden Indian faces, is particularly fine.

Another kilometre or so further out, **Cayma**, once a small suburb with some views over the city, now also reflects the modern commercial, even flashy side of Arequipa with large shops and even one or two nightclubs. Views of the Chachani volcano can be taken in from here. The **Iglesia de San Miguel** (daily 9am–4pm), built in the early eighteenth century, houses the image of the Virgen de la Candelaria, donated to the city by King Carlos V. It's possible to climb up to the roof of the church which offers great views across Yanahuara and towards the volcanos to the north.

Eating and drinking

Arequipa boasts all sorts of **restaurants** dotted about the town serving a wide variety of foods. It's particularly famous for a dish called *ocopa*, a cold appetizer made with potatoes, eggs, olives and a fairly spicy yellow chilli sauce; other delicacies include *rocoto relleno* (a spicy meat-stuffed Andean pepper), *cuy chactado* (the name comes from the round and flat stone – or *chaqueria* – which is placed on top of the guinea pig while frying it), *chupe de camarones* (river shrimp casserole) and *adobo* (pork soaked and cooked in vinegar with maize-beer sediment, onions and chillis). As it's not too far from the Pacific, the town's better restaurants are also renowned for their excellent fresh seafood. Unless otherwise indicated, all the places below open daily from 11am to 11pm. **Picanterías** – traditional Peruvian eating houses serving spicy seafood – are particularly well established here. Easier to find than picanterías, there are a number of restaurants on both the western – and to a lesser extent the eastern – side of the plaza, many of them having interconnecting first-floor terraces with fine views to the Cathedral and square below. Some also offer live music, especially on weekend evenings.

Cafés and bars

Burger Express Portal San Agustin 123. An Italian-style café serving sandwiches, burgers and other fast foods, and full meals. Has some of the best and strongest coffee in Arequipa, but is otherwise a fairly standard café set-up at street level. **Helados Artika** General Moral 110. Within a block of the Plaza de Armas, this is probably the best ice cream parlour in Arequipa, though it's not cheap.

Inkafe Café Bar Portal de Flores, Plaza de Armas. Upstairs to the right of Cinesur and linked to the luxurious *Sonesta Posada del Inca*, it's located on one of only two sunny terraces on the east side of the plaza; it serves fine sandwiches, pastas and main dishes. It's expensive but the service is high-quality.

Inkari Pub Restaurant Pasaje Catedral 113. Half-bar, half-restaurant, this serves good pizzas as well as other food (beef, chicken, pasta) in an often lively environment; there's a dartboard dangerously close to the front entrance, tables outside and just about enough room for musicians at weekends.

Los Leños Pizzaria Jerusalen 407. Just below the corner of Jerusalen and Puente Grau, this café serves a large range of tasty pizzas, pastas and some main dishes, all very good value. The walls are covered with graffiti from travellers from every continent.

Manolos Mercaderes 113. One of Arequipa's longest-established snack bars, offering good service and a tasty selection of meals, cakes and sweets, as well as excellent coffee. Portions are big and prices similar. There's another *Manolos*, newer but almost identical, on the same street at 117.

Restaurant El Cafe San Francisco 125. Breakfasts, good juices and fine snacks, but a little on the expensive side. Daily 7am–1am.

Restaurant Lakshmivan Jerusalen 402. A very popular lunchtime vegetarian cafetería at the back of a small patio, which also sells a range of health-food products, yogurts and wholemeal bread; it plays classical music and has a pleasant ambience.

Tacos y Tequila Ugarte 112. Very popular little place playing Mexican music and serving Pancho Villa's favourite food – *bolas de la revolución* – as well as the usual enchiladas, tacos and burritos. Daily 7.30am till late.

Tenampa Pasaje Catedral 108. A small vegetarian snack bar in the lane behind the Cathedral; has good set menus, great yogurt and tasty Mexican tacos. Prices are very reasonable but portions not overly generous.

Restaurants

Ary Quepay Jerusalen 502. A large restaurant serving local food, such as alpaca steaks, as well as international dishes, vegetarian options and fine pisco sours; frequently busy at night, service is good and there's sometimes live folk music.

Café Istanbul and El Turko I C San Francisco 216. Between them serving Turkish sweets and doner kebabs. Small but very popular and open till late.

El Camaroncito Over 30 years old but recently renamed, this fine lunchtime restaurant is located in the suburb of Cayma a couple of kilometres from the town centre, but it's well worth the trip especially if you like exquisite seafood dishes. There's also a good bar and sometimes folklore shows on Sunday afternoons.

La Cantarilla C Tahuaycani. A notable, modern *picantería* located in a suburban district to the south of Yanahuara, best at lunchtime where you can enjoy the shaded spacious patios; everything is cooked over wood fires.

Complejo Turístico Bob Gourmet Alameda Pardo 123 ☎054/270528. Combining two of the finest restaurants in the city, this complex is based in the old Club Aleman, overlooking the city from the western banks of the Río Chili, with shady pagodas and a kids' play area. *El Montonero* is its excellent lunchtime restaurant which is attempting to rescue some traditional regional dishes such as *senca* meat balls and *pesque*, which is made from *quinoa* with a cheese and steak topping. *Che Carlitos* is an Argentinian grill and bar which is quite fancy, serving excellent beef and alpaca cuts, but catering to vegatarians as well.

El Gaucho Portal de Flores 112. On the plaza but below ground level, this is one of the best meat restaurants in town at quite reasonable prices; try the grills or the *lomo gaucho*.

Mandala Jerusalen 207. A quiet little vegetarian restaurant with Hindu influence on decor and dishes. Has daily set lunch menus and also offers speciality local cuisine such as *ocopa* and *rocoto relleno*.

Picantería Cau Cau II C Tronchadero 404 ☎054/254496. One of Arequipa's best value *picantería* restaurants with fine views towards El Misti and the city from its patio garden.

Restaurant El Cerrojo Portal San Augustin, 111-A. Serves good food on an attractive patio overlooking the Plaza de Armas; excellent value and at its best in the evenings.

Restaurant Govinda Santa Catalina 120a ☎054/285540. Excellent breakfasts, natural yogurt, juices and mueslis plus very good and inexpensive vegetarian set meals. A highly recommended veggie restaurant with a distinctive atmosphere. Also linked to the Centro Cultural Bhakti Yoga, which offers daily classes (Mon–Sat 6am–8pm).

Restaurant and Peña Tuturutu Portal San Agustin ☎054/201842. One of the most agreeable restaurants on the western side of the Plaza de Armas, this place serves ostrich from its own farm as well as relatively inexpensive drinks. There are several rooms to the back, with a bar and small dance floor and rustic ambience. Sometimes presents good live music on weekend evenings. Daily 6.30am–11pm.

Restaurant Sol de May Jerusalen 207. Tables set around attractive gardens, live music and superbly prepared, traditional Peruvian dishes in a good atmosphere. It's quite expensive but worth it, including the $2 taxi ride out to Yanahuara; alternatively it's a 15min walk over Puente Grau, then a few blocks up Av Ejercito. Daily 10am–7pm.

Restaurant El Viñedo San Francisco 319 ☎054/205053. Quite a large, posh place offering quality service. Pricey but worth it for arguably the best Argentinian-style steaks and grills in southern Peru.

Sunlight Restaurante Moral 205. A very small but excellent and inexpensive Asian vegetarian restaurant with set lunch menus at giveaway prices.

Tradición Arequipeña Av Dolores 111 ☎054/426467. Opened in 1991 and located several blocks east of the city centre, this is probably the best *picantería* in town. It has a pleasant garden, covered and indoor spaces and is usually bustling with locals enjoying the extremely fresh and tasty food. This is *the* place to try your first *cuy chactado* or *rocoto relleno*.

Nightlife and entertainment

It's often hard to distinguish between **bars**, restaurants and **nightclubs** (or **discos**, as most are referred to), as many restaurants have a bar and live music while many bars and clubs also serve food. The welcoming **peña** restaurants, for example, concentrated along and in the streets between Santa Catalina and Jerusalen, often have better, more traditional music than either the bars or clubs. Arequipa has a very strong tradition of folk singing and poetry, and folk musicians will wander from *peña* to *peña*, often performing the region's most authentic music: *Yaraví* singing, usually lamenting vocalists accompanied by a guitar. Most *peñas* are open Thursday to Saturday from 8.30pm to midnight, while discos and nightclubs, many just a couple of blocks from the Plaza de Armas on Palacio Viejo, are open nightly until the early hours and usually charge a small entrance fee (around $2.50). In recent years the youth of Arequipa have developed a preference for Latin and Cuban-style ballads accompanied by electric guitars, drums and sometimes keyboards, so the choice at weekends can be quite extensive.

Arequipa's **cinema** scene is based around the Cinesur, on the plaza at Portal de Flores 112, and the Cine Fenix, General Moran 104. Otherwise the **cultural institutes** put on occasional programmes, especially the Instituto Cultural Peruano-Aleman, Ugarte 207, which has a cultural events notice board, shows good films in Spanish and German and sometimes has children's theatre. Also worth a try are the Alianza Francesa, at Santa Catalina 208, where there's also a gallery displaying local artists' work, and the Instituto Cultural Peruano Norte Americano, Melgar 109.

Bars

Blue's Bar San Francisco 319-A. Serves food and drink, accompanied most nights by a variety of music, ranging from classical to rock.

D' Broccetta Pub-Pizzaria San Francisco 317 ☎054/221904. A popular video bar with good table service, it also happens to serve pretty good pizzas and *broccettas*; it's usually very busy.

La Casa de Claus Zela 207. A German drinking house, very popular in the evenings and quite stylish with good music and German food.

Déja Vu San Francisco 319. Small and popular, this place serves seafood, spaghetti and meat dishes, plus, of course, drinks. Has a big video screen and a nice rooftop patio which can get crowded at weekends.

Farrens' Irish Bar Pasaje Catedral 107. Unfortunately, there's rarely any real Irish ale served here, but it's a tidy bar with a wide range of cocktails and whiskies which can be drunk to good rock music, or you can sit at the outside tables. Food also served.

Forum Rock Café San Francisco 317. The liveliest and funkiest scene in the city, with live music on Friday and Saturday. Also has a café, a decent bar and serves snacks.

Siwara Santa Catalina 210 ☎054/206051. A trendy evening bar usually packed with the town's arty students, the drinks are reasonably priced and the food is good. Usually it's just a video bar, but some weekends there's live music.

Swain's Bar Ugarte 106a ☎054/454462 or 602337. Run by a friendly young Englishman and his Peruvian wife, this bar offers a decent range of drinks, some snacks, frequent fun and games as well as a dartboard and cable TV to access European sports events. Soccer is a dominant theme, with Liverpool paraphernalia being particularly prevalent.

Zero Pub San Francisco 317. Popular with young locals and known as a "temple to rock'n'roll", this bar has a couple of decent pool tables and is decorated with rock iconographic posters.

Clubs

Con Sentidos Disco Karaoke Palacio Viejo 204b. Another fairly ordinary disco, though quite plush, with loud music, a semicircular dance floor and attendant disco lights. Busy at weekends.

Jambos Disco Pub Palacio Viejo 125. Rather dark, with a huge video screen and a sunken central dance floor; usually plays pop.

Karaoke Disco Zoom Santa Catlina 111b. Has two big rooms, a bar and a lounge, a loud sound system and a reasonably large dance floor; slightly seedy, but it plays decent Latin pop and rap.

Kibbosh A lively new disco located just off San Francisco; pretty popular with young locals.

Papus Disco Pub Palacio Viejo 111. Located up an alley, this has the usual video screen but is divided into four different ambiences in balcony, bar, dance and lounge areas. Music is mostly Latino and it gets hectic at weekends.

POINT Disco Palacio Viejo 204. A disco pub with lots of tables, a video screen and a smallish dance floor.

Peñas

Café Art Montreal Ugarte 210. Although open for breakfasts and lunches, this attractive place set around a fine stone courtyard really comes to life at night when excellent foods are served up to live local rock and Latino ballad bands. This is a *peña* but certainly isn't folkloric. The cocktails here are very interesting. Wed–Sat 10am–2am

La Luna – Centro Cultural Jerusalen 400b ☎054/203118. Quite tricky to categorize, this is a bar and something of a restaurant but only gets exciting at night when live rock and Latin ballad bands play on the backroom stage, surrounded by New Age-y murals and other paintings. Usually open at weekends. Thurs–Sat 10pm–3am.

Marengo Pizzeria Santa Catalina 221 ☎054/284883. A small and cosy place serving really good pizzas and inexpensive pasta dishes, it's best known for good Andean folk music most Saturday evenings.

Restaurant Peña Las Quenas Santa Catalina 302 ☎054/206440. One of the better and larger venues in town, it dishes out authentic Andean music, food and good pisco sours; music most weekends and also during the week from June to Sept. Closed on Sundays, but open all other days from 10am for breakfast.

La Troica Jerusalen 522a. A reasonably OK folklore venue with music almost every night in high season; well frequented by tour groups.

El Tuturutu Portal San Agustin 105. Right on the Plaza de Armas and overlooking the angel fountain of the same name, this restaurant and *peña* has a great atmosphere when busy at weekends.

Shopping

Arequipa's **central market** is one of the biggest and liveliest in Peru, though it's also a prime spot for pickpockets. Located a couple of blocks down from Santo Domingo, it sells all sorts of food, leather work, musical instruments, inexpensive artesania and even llama and alpaca meat, as well as offering an excellent range of hats, herbs and even cheap shoe repairs. You can also get a selection of fruit juices, including some combined with eggs and dark, sweet, stout beer. Other places for top-quality **artesania, alpaca** goods and **silver** jewellery or wares include Aqlla, Pasaje Catedral 112; El Zanguan, Santa Catalina 105; Millma's, Pasaje Catedral 117; the stalls and shops around the courtyard at Centro Artesanal Fundo El Fierro, on the second block of Grau; and in the very new and plush Patio del Ekeko, Mercaderes 141, near the corner with Jerusalen. This last place is a shopping mall with a difference: quite upmarket in appearance, the products – silverware, artesania, clothing, quality food - are surprisingly inexpensive. On the second floor there's a very good Internet service (not so cheap), cafetería and bar where live shows are presented now and again (every 30min in high season); on the third floor there's a museum of textiles from southern Peru; and on the fourth you'll find an audio-visual exhibition.

For a good selection of colonial and older **antiques**, the antiques and art shops at Puente Grau 314b and along blocks 1 to 4 of Santa Catalina are excellent. Of the latter, the best is Arte Colonial, where there are several jam-packed rooms to explore.

The best bakers in town is La Cañasta, Jerusalen 120, at the back of the patio where you can also eat breakfasts or snacks at their tables; it also has a small **delicatessen** counter. The best **bookshops** are the Librería San Francisco, San Francisco 221, where they stock a wide range of English-language books, including many on the history and wildlife of Peru, and nearby the Librería El Lecto, at San Francisco 133, which sells a number of books in English, has the best book exchange service in Arequipa and a cultural events notice board.

Camera film and development is available centrally from Fotos J. Cano, San Juan de Dios 103; Casa Glave, Portal de la Municipalidad 122, Plaza de Armas; Foto Jerusalen, Jerusalen 503; and Foto Alvis, Portal de Flores 140, Plaza de Armas. For reliable **camera repairs**, go to Fernando Delange, 303 Zela, near the north side of Santa Catalina. **Camping equipment** and maps are best from Campamento Base, Jerusalen 401b, where they stock a good range of tents, sleeping bags and all other essentials, plus maps. They're also a good contact for expert guides. Similarly, Zarate Adventures, Santa Catalina 204, has a significant range of camping and climbing equipment. There are other tour companies which rent out equipment, but not all are of the same quality; some of these are listed in the box on p.256. Regional maps are also sold at the Instituto de Cultura (see p.253).

Listings

Airlines Aero Continente, airport ☎054/444468, Santa Catalina 118a, and Lan Peru, Santa Catalina 118c, are main offices, but you can also buy air tickets for Lan Peru flights from Portal San Agustin 135 ☎054/203637. Aero Continente tickets can also be bought on the plaza at Portal San Agustin 113 ☎054/204020 or 212989, ☎219914. TANS airline is represented at Portal San Agustin 143a ☎054/203637, ☎203517. The Trotomundo office at Portal San Augustin 121 sells tickets for all three airlines. There's a $5 departure tax on all flights except those to Colca Canyon.

Banks and exchange Banco de Credito, San Juan de Dios 125 (accepts Visa and has an ATM); Banco Continental, block 1 of San Francisco; Banco Latino, San Juan de Dios 112 (MasterCard and American Express); Banco Wiese, Av Mercaderes 410; Interbanc, Mercaderes 217; or Banco de la Nación, Mercaderes 127. It's usually quicker and the rates generally as good or almost as good in the casas de cambio such as at San Juan de Dios 120, opposite Banco de Credito; in the Kodak Express shop at San Juan de Dios 103; just by the plaza at San Francisco 103 and 109; and at the Portal de la Municipalidad 124, near the tourist information office. There are also several casas de cambio on the first block of San Jose, 3 blocks from the plaza.

Bus operators Angelitos Negros, San Juan de Dios 510 (☎054/213094), for Chapi, Moquegua, Ilo and Tacna; Aragon, Terminal Terrestre (☎054/693040), for Lima, Moquegua, Tacna, Ilo, Mollendo, Mejia, La Punta and Cusco; Carhuamayo, Terminal Terrestre (☎054/426835), for Cusco and Lima; CIVA, Terminal Terrestre or Av Salaverry (☎054/426563), for Cusco, Puno, Lima and Tacna; Cristo Rey, San Juan de Dios 510 (☎054/213094 or 259848) for Chivay and Cabanaconde; Cromotex, Terminal Terrestre (☎054/421555), for Lima, Cusco, Camana, Puno, Chuquibamba, Cotahuasi and Alcha; Cruz del Sur, Terrapuerto (☎054/427728, ⊛www.crusdelsur.com.pe); Del Carpio, Terminal Terrapuerto (☎054/427049 or 430941), for the Majes Valley, Aplao and Pampacolca; El Chasqui, Terminal Terrestre (☎054/218142), for Cusco; Flores Hermanos, Terminal Terrestre (☎054/244988), for Lima and Tacna; Imaculada Concepción, Av Olimpia 109 (☎054/670071), for Juliaca, Puno, Chuquibamba and Salamanca; Ispacas, Av Olimpica 100b (☎054/284936), for Chuquibamba, Andaray, Yanaquilca; Jacantay,

Tours, trekking and climbing in Arequipa and around

Taking a guided tour is the easiest way to get around this otherwise quite difficult region. It's difficult in a number of ways – the sheer terrain is inhospitable, massive and wild; the altitude changes between Arequipa city and, say, Chivay can affect you for a couple of days (mountain sickness with headaches), which makes driving your own rented car tricky until you're properly adjusted. All operators tend to offer similar packages. **City tours** last around three hours, cost $10–20 and usually include the Santa Catalina monastery, La Compañía, the Cathedral, the church of San Augustín and the Yanahuara *mirador*. **Countryside tours** (*tur de campiña*) usually consist of a roughly three-hour trip to the rural churches of Cayma and Sachaca, the old mill at Sabandia, Tingo lagoon and local *miradors* for $10–30. Most companies offer one- to three-day trips out to the **Colca Canyon** for $20–80 (sometimes with *very* early morning starts) or to the petroglyphs at **Toro Muerto** for $20–40. Trips to the **Valley of the Volcanos** and the **Cotahuasi Canyon** are only offered by a few companies. Specialist adventure activities, such as rafting in the Colca Canyon, mountaineering or serious trekking can cost anything from $55 to $350 for a three- to six-day outing. Of course, all prices vary according to the season, the quality you demand (in terms of food, transport to start point and whether you have *arrieros* with mules to carry your gear) and the size of the group. Mountain-bike rental ranges from $10 to $35 a day depending on the type of bike required, size of group, whether or not a guide is needed and which route is selected.

Competition between companies is high, so check out all the options and determine exactly what you're getting – from the quality of your guide (ask to see written reports by travellers who've been with the company and used the same guides – most tour agents keep a record book of happy customers) to the standard of transport and accommodation, to the quality of equipment used for adventure activities, and whether there may be any supplementary charges (for entry to museums and so on). Because of the dangers of mountain sickness, also check whether oxygen is provided – even a bus trip to Chivay can bring on *soroche* if you've only recently arrived from sea level.

Campamento Base and Colca Trek Jerusalen 401b ☎054/206217, 224378 (24hr) or 600170, ⑩www.colcatrek.com. An excellent tour, trek, climbing, mountain-biking and canoeing company which also specializes in customized tours permitting a mix of the above (trekking and mountain biking mix particularly well in this region); the owner, Vlado Soto, also operates a well-stocked camping shop and employs excellent guides for the Colca Canyon and more adventurous treks, including Cabanaconde, Tapay and especially Cotahuasi areas. The office is a good source of information on the wider region and they will organize transport (eg to Cotahuasi, for a $1 fee).

EcoAventur Santa Catalina 114 ☎/⑦054/231648, ©ecoadventure@latinmail .com.pe. Good guides (English spoken) and excellent treks and canoeing trips to the Colca Canyon, the Río Chili, as well as to the Toro Muerto petroglyphs and the Laguna Salinas area. Will take oxygen on treks if requested to.

Terminal Terrestre, for Juliaca, Puno, Desaguadero and La Paz; Oltursur, Terminal Terrestre (☎054/235110), for bus camas along the coast to Lima and Trujillo; Ormeño, Terminal Terrestre (☎054/218885 or 424187), for the north coast, Lima, Mollendo, Huaraz and Tacna (departures from Terrapuerto and Terrestre); San Cristoval, Terminal Terrestre (☎054/422068), for Lima, Cusco, Puno and Juliaca; San Roman, Terminal Terrestre (☎054/425919), for Puno and Juliaca; Señor de los Milagros, Terminal Terrestre or Av Olimpica 109a, for Chuquibamba and Salamanca; Sur Express, San Juan de Dios 537 (☎054/213335), for Chapi, Chivay and Cabanaconde; Tepsa, Terminal Terrestre and Terrapuerto (☎054/212451), for Lima, Mollendo, Tacna, Santiago, Buenos Aires, Rio de Janeiro, Quito and Bogotá; Reyna, Terminal Terrestre

Giardino Agencia de Viajes Jerusalen 606a ☎054/241206 or 226416, ⓕ242761, ⓦwww.giardinotours.com. A well-organized outfit with excellent two-day tours to Colca, trekking and climbing trips, plus the usual city and countryside trips as well as very reliable air and bus ticket buying service.

Gold Tours Jerusalen 206-B ☎054/238270. City and countryside tours and one-day trips to Colca, some with English-speaking guides.

Hilton Travel and Tours Santa Catalina 217 ☎054/225948 ⓔhiltontravel@wayna .rcp.net.pe. Air tickets, city tours and treks to Colca, plus a 24-hour trip up El Misti and frequent rides to Toro Muerto. Also offer a five-day adventure tour to Cotahuasi Canyon.

Illary Tour Santa Catalina 205 ☎054/220844, ⓔillarytour@hotmail.com. A friendly and professional outfit with English-speaking guides who take enjoyable trips of two days and more in the Colca Canyon. They provide oxygen, accommodation, folk music and transport.

Invertur San Juan de Dios 113 ☎054/213585, ⓕ219526. City and countryside tours, but its speciality is an all-inclusive two-day trip to Colca. Good English-speaking guides are available.

Naturaleza Activa Santa Catalina 221 ☎054/695793, ⓦwww.axb.it/naturaleza. This company specializes in trekking and mountain-bike tours and equipment rental.

Pablo Tour Jerusalen 400a ☎054/203737, ⓔpablotour98@mixmail.com. Specialists in adventure tourism, with links to hostels in Cabanaconde and the Oasis *tambo* in the Colca Canyon.

Peru Colca Bike Jerusalen 500 ☎054/224517, ⓦwww.geocities.com/aventuras _colca/. Offers bike tours in and around the city (Chilina, Yura, Tiabaya and Yumina) as well as in the Colca Canyon.

Peru Expeditions Av Arequipa 5241-504, Miraflores, Lima ☎01/4472057, ⓦwww.peru-expeditions.com. Highly professional and helpful Lima-based company, offering environmentally sound adventure travel in the Arequipa region, including the Colca Canyon and Majes Valley.

Santa Catalina Tours Santa Catalina 223 ☎054/284883 or 216994, ⓕ216994, ⓔsantacatalina@rh.com.pe. City tours, local and Colca Canyon trips, plus ascents up El Misti and occasional rafting on the Río Chili, all at reasonable prices. Good, reliable guides.

Zarate Adventures Santa Catalina 204, Of 3 ☎054/202461, ⓕ054 /263107, ⓦwww.rh.com.pe /zarate. A good expedition outfitter as well as a leading trekking and climbing company with over 25 years' experience, this option usues only professional and qualified guides, such as Carlos Zarate, the internationally renowned founder. Treks include rock climbing and canoeing in the usual places such as Colca, El Misti and Cotahuasi, but they also offer more adventurous routes such as from Colca to the Valley of the Volcanos and another to the Mismi Nevado, official source of the Amazon which overlooks the Colca Canyon from the north.

(☎054/430612), the best for Cotahuasi, Colca, Chivay, Cabanaconde, Andagua in the Valley of the Volcanos and Cusco; Transportes Romaliza, Terrapuerto, for Lima and Cusco; Tranzela, Terrapuerto, for Juliaca, Puno, Cusco and Lima; Tulsa Angeles Tours, Terminal Terrestre (☎054/430843), for Puno; Turismo Alex, Av Olimpico 203 (☎054/202863), for Andaray, Chuquibamba, Cotahuasi (all departing from Terminal Terrestre);

Turismo Expreso Pluma, Terrapuerto, for Lima; TZ Turismo, Terminal Terrestre (☎054/421949), for Corire and Aplao; Ultra Tours, San Juan de Dios 510, for Chapi; Valdivia, Av Olimpica (☎054/224801), for Juliaca, Puno, Chuquibamba and Salamanca; Zeballos, Av Salaverry 107 (☎054/201013), for Lima, Corire, Aplao and Ilo.

Car rental Aerotur and B&G, Santa Catalina 213 (☎054/219291, ⓕ219224, ⓔbusgom@terra

.com.pe), are a reliable company which rents out 4WD vehicles with or without driver and/or guide; they also hire out satellite phones. Servitours, Jerusalen 400 (☎054/202856, ⓔservitours @hotmail.com), also rent 4WD vehicles. Standard cars and sometimes pickups are available from AKAL, Av Ejercito 311, Oficina 301 (☎054/272663); ALKILA/Localiza, Av Villa Hermosa 803, Cerro Colorado (☎054/252499); or AVIS, Palacio Viejo 214 (☎054/282519, ⓕ212123), and at the airport (☎054/443576).

Consulates Bolivia, Piérola 209, Oficina 311 ☎054/213391; United Kingdom, Arica 145 ☎054/241340; Chile, Mercaderes 212, Oficina 401 ☎054/226787.

Courier services DHL, La Merced 106 ☎054/220045 or 234288; and J.L. Bustamante y Rivero, Urbino Monterey A-17 ☎054/422896.

Dentist Dr Morales, Santa Catalina 115; or Clinica dental de Sur, Oficina 1, Av Ejercito 803 ☎054/271371.

DHL and Western Union Their combined offices are at Santa Catalina 115 ☎054/234288. Mon–Fri 8.30am–7.30pm, Sat 9am–noon.

Doctor Dr Jaraffe (Mon–Fri 3–7pm; ☎054/215115).

Hospitals Clinica Arequipa, Av Bolognesi ☎054/253416; and the General Hospital, on the corner of Peral and Dom Bosco ☎054/231818.

Internet facilities La Red are probably the best in town; CHIPS Internet, San Francisco 202a are pretty good; ONLINE, Jerusalen 412a are OK and also offer international calling through their server; there's a cybercafé on the plaza at Portal San Agustin 105; and, close to the plaza there's Catedral Internet, Pasaje Catedral 101

(8am–11pm). All stay open 7 days a week, some until 8pm or later.

Language courses Centro de Idiomas Europeos, José Santos Chocano 249, Umacollo, in front of the Parque Libertad de Expresión (☎054/252619). Courses in Spanish and Portuguese.

Laundry Lavandería Rapida, Jerusalen 404b and Magic Laundry, Jerusalen 404b.

Pharmacies The most central and elegant is the Farmacia Americana on the plaza at Portal San Agustin 103; but there's also the Botica Popular, Mercaderes 128; and Farmacia Sudamerica, San Francisco 131.

Photographic film Fotodigital, Mercaderes 111, has a reasonable stock of Kodak films as well as cameras and binoculars; it offers 1hr film developing service. Foto Peru, Mercaderes 118, sell and develop most standard Kodak films; Casa Clave, Portal Municipalidad 122, sell Kodak films and develop; Foto Alvis, Portal de Flores, 126, have a wider range of films, including Kodak and Fuji.

Police The Tourist Police are at Jerusalen 315 ☎054/251270, 239888 or 254000.

Post office C Moral 118. Mon–Sat 8am–7pm.

Telephone Locutorio Publico, San Juan de Dios 10. One of the best options is Perutsat, Santa Catalina 105 (Mon–Fri 9am–8pm, Sat 9am–6pm), which offers the best prices and good service especially on international calls.

Trains Although no trains are presently running, it may be worth checking on arrival with Perurail, Av Tacna y Arica 200 (☎054/205540, ⓦwww.peru-rail.com).

Visas Migraciones, Urbino Quinta Tristán, Bustamante y Rivero ☎054/421759.

Around Arequipa

The spectacular countryside around Arequipa rewards a few days' exploration, with some exciting and adventurous possibilities for trips from the city. Climbing **El Misti** is a demanding but rewarding trek, while the Inca ruins of **Paucarpata** at the foot of the volcano offer excellent scenery, great views and a fine place for a picnic. The attractive village of **Chapi** makes a good day-trip, while the **Sumbay caves**, just a few hours' drive from Arequipa on the road towards Caylloma, contain hundreds of unique pre-historic cave paintings.

The **Colca Canyon**, some 200km to the north of Arequipa, is second only to Machu Picchu as a major attraction, and developing fast as a trekking and canoeing destination (best in the dry season, May–Sept). Called the "Valley of Marvels" by the Peruvian novelist Mario Vargas Llosa, it is nearly twice the size of Arizona's Grand Canyon and one of the country's most extraordinary natural sights. Around 120km west of Arequipa, you can see the amazing petroglyphs of **Toro Muerto,** and perhaps go on to hike amid the craters and cones of the **Valley of the Volcanos**. A little further north is the **Cotahuasi Canyon**, which some people believe could usurp Colca's claim to being the deepest canyon in the world.

Getting there

Most people visit these sites on an **organized trip** with one of the tour companies in Arequipa (see box on p.256). If you are prepared to put up with the extra hassle, you can visit many of the sites by much cheaper **public transport**. Reyna (☎054/430612; probably the best option) and El Cristo Rey run buses from the Terminal Terrestre in Arequipa daily via Chivay ($2.50, a 3–4hr trip) and down along the Colca Canyon to Cabanaconde ($3.50, a 6hr trip); these return from Cabanaconde two or three times a day (morning and night); check the times on or before arrival. Transportes Colca run similar itineraries, as do Turismo Milagros and Andalucia. Angelitos Negros buses leave from San Juan de Dios for Chapi at 6am and 7am (3hr; $3). Transportes Mendoza runs two or three buses a week to Toro Muerto, Valley of the Volcanos and the Cotahuasi Canyon from La Merced 301.

The most popular trip is without doubt to Chivay and the Colca Canyon. **The road to Chivay and Colca** is itself always a fascinating experience, especially the first hour or so climbing high to the Reserva Nacional de Aguada Blanca, where it's usually possible to spot groups of wild *vicuñas* roaming the pampa. The next landmark is the crossroads where the trails split between the Chivay or Cusco routes and the old road to Juliaca and Puno. From this junction it's possible to make out the unusual volcanic ash strata sandwiched into the impressive cliffs on the northwestern horizon. The road goes uphill from the junction, bearing north and away from the more westerly Cusco road, soon passing the access track down to the caves of Sumbay (70¢). To stay at Sumbay you'll have to **camp**, but if you have a vehicle it's easy enough to take an hour en route, following the signpost (at Km 103 from Arequipa) down a bad track to the village of Sumbay (4532m), about 1.5km. At this point you'll need to find the guardian of the cave, frequently a young lad, who can open the gate for your car to continue another kilometre to a parking area. From the gate it's a ten-minute walk to the caves, down into a small canyon just before the bridge. The guardian will have to unlock another gate to give you access to the site. Although small, the main Sumbay cave contains a series of 8000-year-old rock paintings representing shamans, llamas, deer, pumas and *vicuñas*. The surrounding countryside is amazing in itself: herds of alpacas roam gracefully around the plain looking for *ichu* grass to munch, and vast sculpted rock strata of varying colours mix smoothly together with crudely-hewn gullies.

Back on the main road for Chivay, the route continues past circular corals used as breeding stations for *vicuñas* and alpacas. The next major landmark is the region's highest pass at 4800m. The occasional *viscacha* is often seen around this point, darting between the many rocks and boulders which litter the scene. Another rare species, the yapat plant, can also be spotted at this altitude. Green, semi-spherical and looking like a cross between a brain and a broccoli flower, the yapat plant is traditionally used as a cooking fuel, though it is in danger of extinction and so only local peasants are allowed to utilize them. The road then descends via a winding route towards the Colca Canyon. About forty minutes before arriving at the valley floor, the first of the area's fantastic pre-Inca agricultural terraces can be seen, with the town of Chivay nestled among them.

Paucarpata and around

For an afternoon's escape into the countryside, **PAUCARPATA** is a good target. About 7km out of central Arequipa (a good 2hr walk or a quick ride on a local bus, leaving every 30min from the corner of Salverry and San Juan de Dios), it's a large village surrounded by farmland based on perfectly regular pre-Inca terraces, or *paucarpata* – the Quechua word from which it takes its name. Set against the backdrop of El Misti, this is a fine place to while away an afternoon with some wine and a picnic lunch. There's a small colonial church on the southwestern edge of the suburb that contains a few Cusqueña school paintings. Colectivos travel to Paucarpata from the market area or San Juan de Dios in Arequipa for around 50¢.

Another 2–3km beyond Paucarpata is **SABANDIA**, where there's a reconstructed colonial **mill** (daily 9am–5pm; $1) with attractive lawns and a few alpacas and llamas hanging around. The nearby riverbank is another ideal place for a picnic (no food allowed in the mill itself). Built in 1661 to supply the city, along with three others in the region, the mill operated continuously for some three hundred years and was capable of milling 800kg of grain in one eight-hour shift with a single operator. It was only abandoned when industrial milling took root. The surrounding scenery, characterized by Inca terracing and broad vistas of surrounding mountains, is also home to a restored seventeenth-century **windmill**. There's a nearby restaurant, which is expensive but has a swimming pool. The return trip by **taxi** from Arequipa is about $10, or you can take the Arequipa–Paucarpata colectivo (see p.259), which goes on to Sabandia for the same fare from Arequipa.

If you have your own transport, or take a taxi from Arequipa ($15 return), you can travel the ten kilometres beyond here, in the fertile Socabaya Valley, to the **Casa del Fundador** (daily 10am–5pm), which houses a colonial museum with period furnishings and attractive gardens. Once owned by Garcia Manuel de Carbajal, the original founder of Arequipa, it became the property of the Jesuits, who built a small chapel within the mansion, which was restored in 1821 by the Archbishop José Sebastian de Goyeneche y Barreda, one of Arequipa's greatest nineteenth-century benefactors. After the Jesuits were expelled from Peru, the building was bought at auction, then resold to the Goyeneche family, who kept it until 1947 when the estate was sold off; it was restored in the late 1980s by some local architectural enthusiasts.

Chapi

CHAPI, 45km southeast of Arequipa, just a few hours away by bus, is easily manageable as a day's excursion (see p.256 for details). Though less dramatic than the Colca Canyon, the landscape here is still magnificent, surrounded as it is by mining territory but few peaks much over 5000m. Chapi itself is famous for its white church, the **Sanctuary of the Virgin**, set high above the village at the foot of a valley which itself is the source of a natural spring. Thousands of pilgrims come here annually on May 1 to revere the image of the Virgin, a marvellous burst of processions and fiesta fever. There's no hotel, so if you intend to stay overnight you'll need a tent, but there are several basic places to eat.

El Misti

If you feel compelled to climb **EL MISTI**, 20km northeast of Arequipa, bear in mind that it's considerably further away and higher (5821m) than it looks

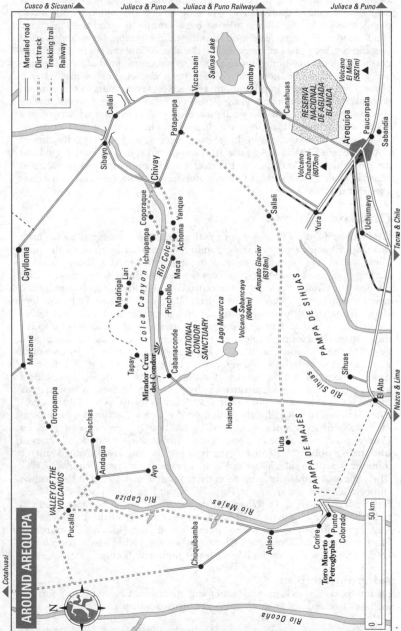

AROUND AREQUIPA

Cusco & Sicuani ▲   Juliaca & Puno ▲   Juliaca & Puno Railway ▲   Juliaca & Puno ▲

Metalled road
Dirt track
Trekking trail
Railway

Salinas Lake

Vizcachani

Sumbay

Callali

Patapampa

Canahuas

Volcano El Misti (5821m)

Paucarpata

Sibayo

Chivay

RESERVA NACIONAL DE AGUADA BLANCA

Volcano Chachani (6075m)

Arequipa

Sabandia

Coporaque

Ichupampa   Yanque

Achoma

Sallali

Uchumayo

Madrigal   Lari

Maca

Río Colca

Colca Canyon

Pinchollo

Ampato Glacier (6318m)

Yura

Tacna & Chile ▼

Caylloma

Tapay

Mirador Cruz del Condor

Cabanaconde

NATIONAL CONDOR SANCTUARY

Lago Mucurca

Volcano Sabancaya (6040m)

PAMPA DE SIHUAS

Marcane

Huambo

Río Sihuas

Sihuas

Orcopampa

Lluta

El Alto

Nazca & Lima ▼

Chachas

Andagua   Ayo

VALLEY OF THE VOLCANOS

Río Capiza

PAMPA DE MAJES

Pucalla

Río Majes

Chuquibamba

Aplao

Corire   Punto Colorado

Toro Muerto Petroglyphs

Cotahuasi ▲

Río Ocoña

N

50 km

0

4

from Arequipa. It is a perfectly feasible hike, allowing just two days for the ascent with another day to get back down. Buses (marked "Chiguata"; a 1hr trip) leave Avenida Sepulveda and will drop you at the trailhead, from where there's a seven- to eight-hour hike to **base camp**. To spend the night here you'll need at the very least food, drink, warm clothing, boots and a good sleeping bag. Your main enemies will be the altitude and the cold night air, and during the day strong sunlight requires you to wear some kind of hat, sunglasses and a good sunscreen; note that the climate is changeable and that water is scarce. From the base camp it's another breathless seven hours to the summit, with its excellent panoramic views across the whole range of accompanying volcanos. Any of the tour companies listed on p.256 can drop walkers off at a higher starting point than Chiguata, cutting off a few hours of the first day.

The largest protected area in this region, covering some 300,000 hectares of plateau behind El Misti is **Aguada Blanca**, 4000m above sea level. A cold and dry *puna* (highland Andes, above the treeline), it's home to *vicuña*, *guanacos* and *viscachas*, while its reservoirs of El Farile and Aguada Blanca are known for their excellent trout fishing.

Chivay

CHIVAY, 150km north of Arequipa and just three to four hours by bus from there, lies amongst fantastic hiking country, surrounded by some of the most impressive and intensive ancient terracing in South America. Today, Chivay is notable as a market town that dominates the head of the Colca Canyon. It's not the best place from which to see the canyon, though there is an impressive fast river running through a deep narrow chasm clearly visible from the Puente Inca along the exit road towards Cororaque and the other northern bank settlements. But these days, Chivay is ever more bustling with gringos eager to use the town as a base for exploring the Colca Canyon either in the traditional way, by bus to the Mirador Cruz del Condor, or, more adventurously, by mountain bike, kayak, raft or serious trekking. Chivay has a growing range of accommodation, restaurants and bus services for these visitors, making it a reasonable place to stay while you acclimatize to the high altitude. Serious trekkers will soon want to move on to one of the other canyon towns, likely Cabanaconde.

Just 5km east of town, slightly further up the Colca Canyon, the road passes mainly through cultivated fields until it reaches the tiny settlement of **La Calera**, which boasts one of Chivay's main attractions – a wonderful series of **hot spring pools** ($1.50), fed by the bubbling, boiling brooks which emerge from the mountain sides all around at an average natural temperature of 85°C. These thermal baths have been recently renovated, making them the cleanest and best-serviced hot springs in Peru. There are four main pools. Open from 5am until around 7pm, La Calera baths are a delight not to be missed. You can walk there from Chivay in under an hour or take one of the colectivos that leave approximately every twenty minutes from the church-side corner of Plaza de Armas in Chivay (25¢). Chivay also makes a good base if you want to go whitewater rafting on the Río Colca or mountain biking.

Accommodation

Despite periodic problems with water and electricity, Chivay boasts a surprising choice of reasonably comfortable **accommodation**.

In town
Estancia Pozo del Cielo ☎ 054/531144 or 531041, ⓦ www.pozodelcielo.com.pe, or in

Arequipa ☎ 054/205838, ⓕ 202606. This very nice hotel just over the Puente Inca from Chivay and next to the terraces topped by pre-Inca towers

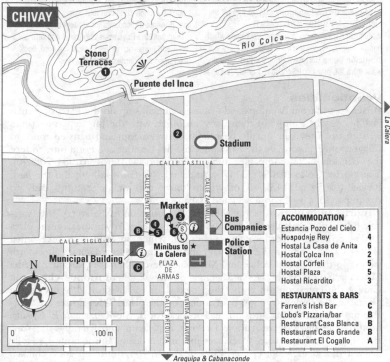

Corporaque, Lari, Madrigal & Colca Lodge ▲ Caylloma, Puente Callalli & Sicuani

Río Colca

Stone Terraces ❶

Puente del Inca

❷ Stadium

La Calera

CALLE CASTILLA

CALLE PUENTE INCA

CALLE ZARUMILLA

Market
Ⓐ ❸
Ⓑ ❺ ❻
ⓢ
ⓘ

CALLE SIGLO XX

Bus Companies

Minibus to La Calera ★

Police Station

ⓘ
Municipal Building
Ⓒ
PLAZA DE ARMAS

CALLE AREQUIPA

AVENIDA SALAVERRY

N

0   100 m

Arequipa & Cabanaconde

ACCOMMODATION

Estancia Pozo del Cielo	1
Hospedaje Rey	4
Hostal La Casa de Anita	6
Hostal Colca Inn	2
Hostal Corfeli	5
Hostal Plaza	5
Hostal Ricardito	3

RESTAURANTS & BARS

Farren's Irish Bar	C
Lobo's Pizzaria/bar	B
Restaurant Casa Blanca	B
Restaurant Casa Grande	B
Restaurant El Cogallo	A

offers the most luxurious option in town, though in rustic style with open fire in the reception area. The rooms are warm and very comfortable and the service is homely. ❻

Hostal La Casa de Anita Plaza de Armas 606 ☎054/531114. Inexpensive but not so basic and offers rooms with or without private baths. ❷–❸

Hostal Colca Inn Salaverry 307 ☎054/631088, ⓕ531111, ⓦwww.planet.com.pe/hotelcolcainn. Probably the best mid-range hotel in Chivay; it's clean and modern with private bath, hot water and a decent restaurant. ❺

Hostal Corfeli Plaza de Armas 702 ☎054/531017. Offers standard accommodations, but has a decent solar water-heating system for the showers. ❷

Hostal Los Leños Francisco Bolognesi 906 ☎054/521028 or 286828. Simple, dependably excellent value and very clean. ❷

Hostal Municipal on the plaza ☎054/531093. With private baths in a modern building with plain rooms and, though quaint in its own way, little or no style. ❷

Hostal Plaza Plaza de Armas 705. Basic but clean

and set round a small courtyard adorned with beautiful flowers. ❷

Hostal Ricardito Av Salaverry 121 ☎054/531051. Has reasonably decent rooms and fairly permanent hot water. ❷

Outside Chivay

Colca Lodge ☎054/212813, ⓔcolcalodge@grupoinca.com.pe. A few kilometres beyond Cororaque, just before the river bridge back south to the village of Yanque, there's this grand hotel, which has its own thermal-spring swimming pool and offers horse-riding as well as mountain biking and short treks or tours to local sites of interest. ❻–❼

Mamma Yacchi Hotel ☎054/241206 ⓕ242761, ⓦwww.lacasademamayacchi.com. Out in the countryside on the north side of the canyon, just 20min by car or combi colectivo, *Mamma Yacchi* offers that little bit extra compared to most accommodation in the region, with great food, lovely architecture, very comfortable rooms, excellent service (including hot-water bottles at bedtime) and a touch of local culture with music and

dancing with local staff after supper. ❻
El Mirador de los Collaguas C Piura just off the plaza ☎054/521015, ℱ01/2644981, ℮ellago@terra.com.pe. A pleasant *pousada* which has fine views across the valley. ❺
Tradición Colca Carretera Principal just a 10min walk from the plaza ☎054/280454 or in Arequipa 205336, ℱ424926, ⓦwww.tradicioncolca.8m .com. A French-run hotel that caters to backpackers (5 percent discounts for students, visitors who arrive with the Reyna bus company) and offers bike and horse-riding tours, excellent food, book exchange and games room. ❶–❷

Practicalities

Buses to and from Arequipa and Cabanaconde all stop on the Plaza de Armas in Chivay, where most of them have an office with the bus departure times written up. They can usually be caught between 5am and 6am en route to Cabanaconde, passing by the Mirador Cruz del Condor at a good time to spot the condors. The companies include Turismo Milagros (☎054/708090), Transportes Colca (☎054/531173), Andalucia (☎054/445089), and the best, Reyna (☎054/531143), all of whom travel two or three times daily to Arequipa ($3, a 3–4hr journey) and Cabanaconde.

Tourist information is available from an office on Av Salaverry 106 (variable hours, but generally 2–8pm) and also from Colca Adventures, on the plaza (☎054/531081, ℮rcordova@terra.com.pe), which specializes in bike rental ($10–15 a day), rafting ($25 half-day) and kayaking ($40 a day); it's also worth talking to the Tourism Police and Mountain Rescue Service (Salvamento Alta Montana Colca) by the *Hostal Municipal* on the plaza. For **money change** in Chivay, the fastest option is the shop next door to Turismo Milagros on the plaza; the Banco de la Nación is, of course, on the plaza. **Telephones** are available in the Turismo Milagros office. For local **food**, the *Restaurante El Cogallo*, fronting the plaza, serves simple fare but is pleasant and friendly; the *Casa Blanca*, also on the square, specializes in chicken dishes and is quite tastefully decorated; and the *Casa Grande*, Plaza de Armas 705, dishes up good chicken and chips as well as pizzas, alpaca and vegetarian options.

For **nightlife**, there's *Laikgana Bar*, just off the plaza on Calle Puente Inca, which serves a mean pisco sour; *Restaurante Los Sismos*, by the petrol station on the road in from Arequipa, which frequently stages folklore *peñas* as well as serving good alpaca steaks, tasty *quinoa* and carrot juice, and sometimes even the local cactus drink, *sancayo*; *Farrens Irish Pub*, opposite the church on the plaza, which is popular for its rock music and decent range of cocktails; and *Lobos Pizzaria and Bar* on the plaza (☎054/531081, ℮lobosbar_colca @mixmail.com), which has a pool table, Internet service and a happy hour between 6 and 8pm and is also a contact point for tourist information, though not the official office. The **Internet** is available in the *Lobos Restaurant and Bar* on the plaza, as well as *Restaurant Albicsa*, under the radio station, just a block downhill from the plaza, beside *Lobos Pizzeria*. For shopping, there's a large market along Avenida Salaverry and also some artesania shops in the same street.

The Colca Canyon

Still claiming to be the deepest canyon in the world at more than 1km from cliff-edge to river bottom, the **Colca Canyon** may be an impressive sight but is actually some 170m less deep than its more remote rival the Cotahuasi Canyon (see p.271). Despite its status as one of Peru's most popular tourist attractions, the Colca Canyon's sharp terraces are still home to more-or-less traditional Indian villages. The Río Colca forms part of a gigantic watershed that empties into the Pacific near Camana. It was formed by a massive geological fault situated between the two enormous volcanos of Coropuna (6425m) and Ampato (6318m). To the north of Colca sits the majestic Nevado Mismi, a snow-capped peak which belongs to the Chila mountain range, and, according to *National Geographic*, is the official source of the Amazon river.

The valley is highly scenic because of what are arguably the finest examples of pre-Inca terracing in Peru, attributed in the main to the Huari cultural era. Massive mountains, huge herds of llamas, and traditionally dressed Andean peasants complete the picture. The indigenous communities of this valley form two distinct ethnic groups: the Aymaru speaking Collaguas, and the Quechua-speaking Cabanas. Traditionally, both groups used different techniques for deforming the heads of their children. The Collaguas elongated them and the Cabanas flattened them – each trying to emulate the shape of their respective principal *apu* (mountain god). Today it is the shape of their hats (taller for the Collaguas and round flat ones for the Cabanas), rather than heads, which mainly distinguishes between the two groups.

Francisco Pizarro's brother, Gonzalo, was given this region in the 1530s as his own private *encomienda* (official colonial Spanish landholding) to exploit for tribute. But in the seventeenth century, the Viceroy Toledo split the area into *corregimientos* that concentrated the previously quite dispersed local populations into villages. The effect of this was to begin the declining use of the valley's agricultural terracing, as the locals switched to farming the land nearer their new homes. The *corregimientos* created the fourteen main settlements that still exist in the valley today, including Chivay, Yanque, Maca, Cabanaconde, Corporaque, Lari and Madrigal. Most of the towns still boast unusually grand and Baroque-fronted churches, underlining the importance of this region's silver mines during the seventeenth and eighteenth centuries. During the Republican era, Colca's importance dwindled substantially and interest in the zone was only rekindled in 1931 when aerial photography revealed the astonishing natural and man-made landscape of this valley – especially its exceptionally elaborate terracing on the northern sides of the mountains which border the Colca Canyon – to the outside world.

The road to the Mirador Cruz del Condor and Cabanaconde

In the mountains to the southwest, dominated by the glaciers of Ampato and Hualca, the volcano Sabancaya can often be seen smoking away in the distance as you travel the 50km or so to the **Mirador Cruz del Condor** and **Cabanaconde**. From Chivay, the first village the road winds through is **Yanque**, where there's a fine white church, a small archeology museum, thermal baths down by the river, horse-riding facilities, mountain-bike rental and some of the area's best-preserved pre-Inca ruins; then comes **Achoma**, followed by the more interesting **Maca**. This town lies right on the fault line and is an extremely high tremor zone whose visible effects can be seen in various land movements, abandoned houses, deep fissures running here and there across fields or through settlements, and road re-routings as the route continues on through a very dark tunnel just beyond Maca. Immediately after this tunnel, a number of hanging pre-Inca tombs – *las chulpas colgantes* – are high up in seemingly impossible locations, facing perhaps the best example of agricultural terracing in Peru across the valley.

The next port of call is close to the settlement of **Pinchollo**, where there's a **small museum** and **tourist information** point with photos and a model representing the canyon; this is also the gateway to Mirador Cruz del Condor, where all visitors are charged $4 for the Colca area **tourist ticket**

△ Achoma, in the Colca Canyon

which covers access to the Mirador Cruz del Condor as well as all the churches in the valley (which in practice don't actually charge). Just a little further down the road, the *mirador* is the most popular point for looking into the depths of the canyon – it's around 1200m deep here – and where you can almost guarantee seeing several condors circling up from the depths against breathtaking scenery (best spotted 7–9am, the earlier you get there the more likely you are to have fewer other spectators around). For safety's sake, however, stand well back from the edge. These days it's a popular spot and most mornings there will actually be more tourists here than in the Plaza de Armas in Arequipa.

The bus terminal at the small but growing town of **Cabanaconde** (3300m), 10km on, is a good base from which to descend into the canyon. An impressive high wall and painted gateway mark the town's eighteenth-century cemetery. The town is also home to several semi-destroyed stone buildings and doorways left over from the late colonial (or Viceregal) era. The road becomes a little-used dirt track continuing down the valley via Huambo and Sihuas to the coastal Panamerican Highway, where you can catch buses back to Arequipa to complete the circuit. Few trucks use this route and it's only recommended in the dry season (June–Sept) for those well prepared with food and camping equipment.

You'll need a couple of days to begin exploring the area and three or four to do it any justice, but several tour companies offer one-day tours as well as extended trips with overnight stops in either Chivay, a *pousada* en route, in Cabanaconde itself, or even at *Oasis* or one of the other campsites and small villages dotted around the edges of the canyon (maps can be obtained in Arequipa, see p.255). Although it's possible to travel along the northern edge of the Colca Canyon by local transport from Chivay, to Corporaque, Lari and Madrigal, most people only have time to take one of the Arequipa buses passing through Chivay along the southern rim of the valley as described above. If you get to Corporaque, though, there's a rewarding two-hour walk to the pre-Inca Huari tombs and ruined village (see box, p.268).

There's a surprising range of **accommodation** in Cabanaconde itself. There are only a few streets in this small settlement, but on the main street as you enter there's the *Hostal Virgen del Carmen* (❷–❸), which is basic but has hot water much of the time, and *La Posada del Conde* (☎054/036809 or 947707, ✉pdelconde@yahoo.com; ❹–❺), which is certainly one of the better options, noted for well-sprung mattresses and an excellent restaurant; it's advisable to book in advance because it's often full. Next door, there's the *Hostal Canyon del Colca* (❷), much cheaper and more basic. The *Hotel Kuntur Wassi* (☎054/252989, ✉kunturwassi@terra.com.pe; ❺–❻) is a new place built on the hill, some 80m above the plaza; it has fine views right across the canyon to the Huaro waterfall, and the attractive rooms are laid out in an unusual way, clinging to the hill and incorporating some natural rock features and unusual domed roofs; it also has a restaurant and bar as well as solar water heating. The *Hostal Valle del Fuego* (☎054/280367; ❷) is a good backpackers' pad and is complemented by the attractive Inca-style restaurant *Rancho del Sol*, close to the plaza. They are both run by the same family that operates the *Oasis* (❷), a rustic lodge and campsite right down in the bottom of the canyon, below Cabanaconde. Closer to the cliff-edge, but only a hundred yards or so from the plaza, the *Casa de Pablo* (❷), with quaint rooms, also run by the same family, and the *Restaurant Rancho del Colca*, offer similarly inexpensive lodging for backpackers. They also rent mountain bikes for around $15 a day. The **tourist information** office (☎054/280212) is on the main plaza, but although it has

There are dozens of **treks** in the Colca Canyon, but if you're planning on descending to the **canyon floor**, even if just for the day, it's best to be fit and prepared for the altitude – it's tough going and becomes quite dangerous in sections. Guides are recommended, and several tour operators offer this service (see p.256), for which you'll pay $35–70 a day per person. For decent **maps**, contact the South American Explorers' Club in Cusco (see p.149).

The top of the Colca Canyon is just ten minutes' walk along a fairly clear track beyond the *Casa de Pablo* hostel. The descent follows an incredibly steep path, quite dangerous in parts, down to the *Oasis* below; it takes one and a half to two hours to descend and four or five to get back up. It's possible to walk from here to Andagua in the Valley of the Volcanos, with a guide, if you've got five or six days.

Alternative routes include a popular seven-hour hike from Cabanaconde to Lake Mucara, some eight hours' walk, where the beautiful Ampato volcano is reflected in its crystalline waters. From here you can walk on along a trail to Ampato. A quieter, seven-hour route goes from Huambo down to the hacienda at Canco, where the Río Huambo meets the Río Colca. It's another day's hike up to Ayo, a winemaking settlement, from where the road and buses go to Andagua. There's also a well-used trekking route connecting Cabanaconde with the small settlement of Tapay, a four-day hike through fine scenery and the tiny villages of Cosnihua and Malata as well as various Inca and pre-Inca ruins. There are no facilities at all in the area.

A relatively easy two-hour walk from the village of Corporaque takes in some Huari (pre-Inca) tombs that were constructed at the foot of the cliffs on Cerro Yurac Ccacca (also known as Cerro San Antonio). A path leads out from a block or two just below the plaza, crossing the stream as you leave the settlement behind, and climbing steadily towards a prominent, pink rocky outcrop. The tombs are just below the 4000-metre contour line. To the southwest, the partly tumbled but still impressive Huari village can be clearly seen stretching from the tombs down to a major *tambo*-style building on the bottom corner, which commands views around the valley. Because it's little visited, the path for entry, even to the main, partly-fortified *tambo* section, isn't marked and more or less leaves you to find your own route; given this, it's important to take care not to damage the stone walls and agricultural plots you have to find your way through. To get back to Corporaque, you can either drop down to the road and trace this back up to the settlement, or go along the small aqueduct which follows the contour of the hill from the *tambo* back to where you started to climb towards the tombs.

very little in the way of printed information to give out, the staff are very friendly and willing to tell all they know. It's also a good contact point for finding local trekking guides and *arrieros* (men with mules), such as Hugo Barrio Jimenez. Guides for the region generally cost $10-20 a day (one guide for two people) plus $20 for two mules and *arriero*, if required (15-20 percent more if going over 4000m). The plaza is also where you can find the offices of the four main bus companies connecting this settlement with Arequipa and Chivay: Andalucia, Reyna, Turismo Milagros and Transportes Colca.

Toro Muerto and the Valley of the Volcanos

It's difficult not to be overwhelmed by the sheer size and isolation of **Toro Muerto** and the **Valley of the Volcanos**. These two locations, though over 100km apart, are linked by the fact that the rocks on which the Toro Muerto petroglyphs are carved were spewed out by volcanos, possibly from as far away as Coropuna or Chachani during the Tertiary period, about fifty million years ago. Both Toro Muerto and the valley can be visited on guided tours from Arequipa (see p.256 for details of tour companies), but many people choose to do one of the most exciting – albeit long and exhausting – trips in southern Peru independently. To combine these two sights by public transport you'll need at least four or five days. Wandering around the petroglyphs takes a day or two; catching the next bus on to the valley will give you another couple of days' camping and hiking. After, you can return to Arequipa by the same route, or by continuing up the valley and circling back via Caylloma and Chivay, or meeting up with the Arequipa–Cusco/Puno roads high up on the altiplano.

Getting to Toro Muerto

Leaving Arequipa the bus follows the Lima road to **Sihuas**, a small oasis town where you can see drainage channels cut into the hillside waiting for water to irrigate the desert pampa north of the town. At present, the fertile strip of Sihuas is very narrow – little more than 200m in width in 1983 – but recently sprinklers have begun to water the sandy plain above and small patches of alfalfa have been planted. This is the first stage of the vast $650 million **Majes Project**, which plans to irrigate 150,000 acres of the dry pampa, build two hydroelectric power plants, and develop a number of new towns to house some two hundred thousand people. With costs escalating to more than $10,000 an acre, many people consider the project a complete waste of time and money, despite the fact that the plans are very similar in theory to successful Inca irrigation projects, like the Achirana aqueduct, which still maintains the Ica oasis after five hundred years.

Just beyond the sprinklers, a few kilometres north of Sihuas, the bus turns off the Panamerican Highway, at a junction marked by an archway over the road and a few restaurants, to head east across stony desert. After around 20km you find yourself driving along the top of a cliff, a sheer drop of almost 1000m separating the road from the Majes Valley below. This striking contortion was created by a fault line running down the earthquake belt that stretches all the way from Ayacucho. Descending along winding asphalt, you can soon see right across the well-irrigated valley floor, the cultivated fields creating a green patchwork against the stark, dusty yellow moonscape. At the bottom, a steel-webbed bridge takes the road across the river to the small village of **Punto Colorado**, dwarfed below a towering and colourful cliff – an ancient river bluff. At the *Condesuyos* **restaurant** here, on the left just after the bridge, they serve fresh river crayfish caught locally. It's just 3km from here to the turn-off to the petroglyphs, which is marked by a large sign on the left – "Petroglifos de Torro Muerto", close to the chapel and before the petrol station. From here a track runs almost another 2km to a T-junction by some sandy cliffs; turn right here and continue to the hamlet, keeping left at the electricity pylon. The **entrance to Toro Muerto** is slightly uphill, on the left, where there's a gate-barrier and ticket hut ($1). The petroglyphs are still a stiff kilometre or so uphill along a desert track from here – ask for directions at the entrance.

The best **place to stay** locally is **CORIRE**, about 2km further down the main road from the signposted turn-off to Toro Muerto – just keep going past past the petrol station. There are a few good **hostels** at Corire and one or two restaurants. The *Hostal El Molino*, Progreso 121 (☎054/472056 or 472002, or in Arequipa 449298; ❷), is very pleasant and is a good contact for canoeing or 4WD tours in the valley, or less adventurous visits to the local pisco-producing hacienda. The *Hostal Solar*, on the corner of the plaza (❷), is good value with solar-heated hot water and rooms with bath and TV; and *Hostal Willy*, on

Avenida Progreso (☎054/472180 or in Arequipa 251711, ⓕ257157; ❷), is a very reasonable hostel, most rooms having private bath and a few TV. There's a *chifa* **restaurant** under *Hostal Willy* and the *Snack-Bar Pollería El Molino* on the plaza is great, with fresh chicken and chips on Sundays. This small town is well endowed, with a **Banco de Credito**, block 1 of 28 de Julio and a **casa de cambio,** Don Rufo, nearby. There are public **telephones** at Av Progreso 121.

There are fairly regular daily **buses** to Corire from Arequipa. Operating from early morning to early evening, the most regular are with Transportes Zeballos, with others run by TZ Turismo and Del Carpio (see Listings, p.255). Returning buses depart from the Plaza de Armas in Corire and, unless full, can be flagged down on the main road at the Toro Muerto turn-off.

The Toro Muerto petroglyphs

The **Toro Muerto petroglyphs** consist of carved boulders strewn over a kilometre or two of hot desert. More than a thousand rocks of all sizes and shapes have been crudely, yet strikingly, engraved with a wide variety of distinct representations. No archeological remains have been directly associated with these pictures but it is thought that they date from between 1000 and 1500 years ago; they are largely attributed to the Wari culture, though with probable additions during subsequent Chuquibamba and Inca periods of domination in the region. The engravings include images of humans, snakes, llamas, deer, parrots, sun discs and simple geometric motifs. Some of the figures appear to be dancing, others with large round helmets look like spacemen – obvious material for the author Eric Von Daniken's extraterrestrial musings, particularly in view of the high incidence of UFO sightings in this region.

Some of the more abstract geometric designs are very similar to those of the Huari culture, who may well have sent an expeditionary force in this direction, across the Andes from their home in the Ayacucho basin, around 800 AD. There's no very clear route to the **petroglyphs**, which are a good hour's walk from the road, and at least 500m above it. What you're looking for is a vast row of **white rocks**, believed to have been scattered across the sandy desert slopes by a prehistoric volcanic eruption. After crossing through corn, bean and alfalfa fields on the valley floor, you'll see a sandy track running parallel to the road along the foot of the hills. Follow this to the right until you find another track heading up into a large gully towards the mountains. After about 1km – always bearing right on the numerous crisscrossing paths and trying to follow the most well-worn route – you should be able to see the line of white boulders: over three thousand of them in all. The natural setting is almost as magnificent as the petroglyphs themselves, and even if you were to camp here for a couple of weeks it would be difficult to examine every engraved boulder. Unfortunately many have been smashed to make portable souvenirs for the tourist market, and this highly illegal, "entrepreneurial" behaviour continues to destroy the boulders.

Getting to the Valley of the Volcanos

Going on to the **Valley of the Volcanos**, the bus winds uphill for at least another ten hours. After tracing around Mount Coropuna, the second highest Peruvian peak at 6450m, the little town of **Andagua**, at a mere 3450m, appears at the foot of the valley. Buses continue to Orcopampa, from where you can walk the whole 60km or so down the valley - only for serious hikers wishing to explore the Valley of the Volcanos and who can stand the heat. Most passengers get off and base themselves at Andagua. The mayor of Andagua offers a roof and meals to travellers when he's in town, but there are no hotels or restaurants as such. However, the local people are generally very hospitable, often inviting strangers they find camping in the fields to sleep in their houses. Because this is a rarely visited region, where most of the locals are pretty well self-sufficient, there are only the most basic of shops – usually set up in people's houses.

From Andagua, you can get a bus two or three times a week for the six-hour journey to Cotahausi, or, from Orcopampa, there are infrequent buses and occasional slow trucks that climb up the rough track to **Caylloma**, from where there's a bus service to Chivay and Arequipa; however, it is actually quicker to backtrack to Arequipa via Toro Muerto, on the bus, due to the appalling state of the roads and transport connections. Returning via Caylloma and Chivay, however, rewards with exceptional scenery and an opportunity to see the colonial churches of Caylloma.

The Valley of the Volcanos

At first sight just a pleasant Andean valley, the **Valley of the Volcanos** (Valle de los Volcanos) is in fact one of the strangest geological formations you're ever likely to see, its surface scored with extinct craters varying in size and height from 200 to 300m, yet perfectly merged with the environment. The main section of the valley is about 65km long; to explore it in any detail you'll need to get **maps** (two adjacent ones are required) from the South American Explorers' Club or the Instituto Geográfico in Lima (see p.103), or from the Instituto de Cultura in Arequipa (see p.253). You won't need a tent to **camp** here – a sheet of plastic and a good sleeping bag will do – but you will need good supplies and a sun-hat; the sun beating down on the black ash can get unbelievably hot at midday.

The best overall view of the valley can be had from Anaro Mountain (4800m), looking southeast towards the Chipchane and Puca Maura cones. The highest of the volcanos, known as Los Gemelos (The Twins), are about 10km from Andagua. To the south, the Andomarca volcano has a pre-Inca ruined settlement around its base.

Cotahuasi Canyon

First navigated by a Polish expedition in 1981 and declared a Zona de Reserva Turística Nacional in 1988, the magnificent **COTAHUASI CANYON** (Cañon de Cotahuasi), 378km from Arequipa, has since opened up to visits that don't necessarily involve major rafting trips. However, getting to this wild and remote place is even more adventurous and less frequently attempted than the trip to the Valley of the Volcanos. Another claimant to the title of world's deepest canyon, along with nearby Colca and the Grand Canyon in the US, it runs more or less parallel to the Cordillera de Chila, official source of the Amazon river, and is in possession of some pretty impressive statistics: around 3400m deep and over 100km long.

Arriving from the south along the difficult road from Arequipa (some 375km long) the route passes along the bottom part of the canyon, where the main settlement, **Cotahuasi pueblo**, can be found. It has a variable climate but isn't particularly cold and is rapidly developing a name as an adventure-travel destination. Continuing north to the village of **Alcha** (near to the hot springs of Luicho), the road forks. To the right, it heads into the deeper part of the canyon where you'll find the village of **Pucya** and, further up the valley, heading pretty well northwest you end up at the astonishingly beautiful plateau of

Lauripampa, from where you can walk down into the canyon or explore the large natural spread of the massive Puya Raimondi catci. The left fork continues to the pueblo of **Pampamarca**, where the locals weave lovely woollen blankets. Above the pueblo it's possible to walk to the Uscuni waterfalls on one side of the valley and the natural rock formations of the Bosque de Piedras on the other. A little further on you'll find the thermal springs of Josla.

About 40km from Cotahuasi, the Wari ruins of **Marpa** can be seen straddling both sides of the river, but another hour away is the larger and better-preserved Wari city of **Maucallacta**.

Practicalities

The remote and attractive pueblo of **Cotahuasi** (2684m above sea level), with its quaint narrow streets and a small seventeenth-century church, makes a good base for exploring the canyon. If you want to stay at Pampamarca, the main alternative, you'll need to take a cooking stove, since there are no cafés or restaurants here, though the six-bedroom *Municipality* (❷) offers very basic accommodation. The village of Alcha has a couple of hotels and a restaurant, but the pueblo of Cotahuasi itself offers by far the best facilities, or at least has an additional hostel and restaurant.

The easiest way to get to Cotahuasi is by taking a **guided tour** from Arequipa (see p.256); the tour specialist is Canyon Tours, San Pedro 139, Arequipa (☎054/288081), or for an independent guide, try Marcio Ruiz Sánchez (☎054/581050). Reyna and Turismo Alex **buses** run the twelve-hour route from Arequipa (see Listings, p.255 for details); Reyna (the best option) has an office on the plaza in Cotahuasi, at Av Arequipa 201 (☎054/581017). The main plaza has a few places to stay, most of which also provide **information** about visiting the canyon. The **Banco de la Nación** is at Plaza de Armas 104.

Puno and Lake Titicaca

An immense region both in terms of its history and the breadth of its magical landscape, the **Titicaca Basin** makes most people feel like they are on top of the world. The skies are vast and the horizons appear to bend away below you. The high altitude means that recent arrivals from the coast have to take it easy for a day or two, though those coming from Cusco will already have acclimatized. The scattered population of the region is descended from two very ancient Andean ethnic groups or tribes – the Aymara and the Quechua. The Aymara's Tiahuanaco culture pre-dates the Quechua's Inca civilization by over three hundred years.

The first Spanish settlement at **Puno** sprang up around a silver mine discovered by the infamous Salcedo brothers in 1657, a camp that forged such a wild and violent reputation that the Lima viceroy moved in with soldiers to crush and finally execute the Salcedos before things got too out of hand. At the same time – in 1668 – the viceroy created Puno as the capital of the region, and from then on it became the main port of Lake Titicaca and an important town on the silver trail from Potosi. The arrival of the railway, late in the nineteenth century, brought another boost, but today it's a relatively poor, rather grubby sort of town, even by Peruvian standards, and a place that has suffered badly from recent drought and an inability to manage its water resources.

On the edge of the town spreads the vast **Lake Titicaca** – enclosed by white peaks and dotted with unusual **floating islands**, basically huge rafts built out of reeds and home to a dwindling and much-abused Indian population. More spectacular by far are two of the populated, fixed islands, **Amantani and Taquile**, whose still-traditional lifestyle gives visitors a genuine taste of pre-Conquest Andean Peru. Densely populated since well before the arrival of the Incas, the lakeside Titicaca region is also home to the curious and ancient tower tombs known locally as **chullpas**, which are rings of tall, cylindrical stone burial chambers, often standing in battlement-like formations.

Puno

With a dry, chilly climate – temperatures frequently fall below freezing in the winter nights of July and August – **PUNO** is just a crossroads to most travellers, en route between Cusco and Bolivia or Arequipa and maybe Chile. In some ways this is fair, for it's a breathless place (at 3870m above sea level), with a burning daytime sun in stark contrast to icy evenings, and a reputation for pickpockets, particularly at the bus and train terminals. Yet the town is immensely rich in tradition and has a fascinating ancient history. Puno's port is a vital staging point for exploring the northern end of Lake Titicaca, with its floating islands and beautiful island communities just a few hours away by boat. Perhaps more importantly, though, Puno is famed as the folklore capital of Peru, particularly relevant if you can visit in the first two weeks of February for the **Fiesta de la Candelaria**, a great folklore dance spectacle, boasting incredible dancers wearing devil-masks; the festival climaxes on the second Sunday of February. If you're in Puno at this time, it's a good idea to reserve hotels in advance (hotel prices can double). The **Tinajani Festival of Dance**, based around June 27, is set in the bleak altiplano against the backdrop of a huge wind-eroded rock in the Canyon of Tinajani. Off the beaten trail, it's well worth checking out for its raw Andean music and dance, plus its large sound systems; ask at the tourist offices in Puno or Cusco for details. Just as spectacular is the **Semana Jubilar** (Jubilee Festival) in the first week of November, which takes place partly on the Isla Esteves and celebrates the Spanish founding of the city and the Incas' origins, which legend says are from Lake Titicaca itself. Even if you miss the festivals, you can find a group of musicians playing brilliant and highly evocative music somewhere in the labyrinthine town centre on most nights of the year.

Arrival and information

However you arrive in Puno, you'll be immediately affected by the altitude and should take it easy for at least the first day, preferably for the first two, although if you arrive from Cusco or Bolivia, the chances are you will already be accustomed to the altitude. Arriving **by bus** you are most likely to end up somewhere central on Jirón Tacna or a few blocks east towards the lake along Avenida Titicaca or Jirón Melgar; see Listings (p.279) for details of the different companies and their terminals. Colectivos to and from Juliaca and **Juliaca Airport** (Aeropuerto Manco Capac) also use Jirón Tacna. If you're coming in from Cusco by train, you'll arrive at the **train station** (information on ☎054/351041) on Avenida la Torre. Taxis and motorcycle rickshaws leave from immediately outside the station and will cost less than $2 to anywhere in the centre of town. The main **port**, used by boats from Bolivia (contact Capitan del Puerto, Av El Sol 725, for information), as well as the Uros Islands, Taquile and Amantani, is a fifteen- to twenty-minute walk from the Plaza de Armas, straight up Avenida El Puerto, crossing over Jirón Tacna, then up Jirón Puno.

The helpful and friendly **tourist information office** is at Jr Lima 585 (Mon–Fri 7.30am–7pm, Sat 8am–1pm) and can provide photocopied town plans, leaflets and other information. The **tourist police**, Jr Deustua 538, are very helpful and also give out free maps. The Dirección Regional de Industria and Turismo has an office on Jirón Ayacucho (☎054/356097, ⓕ353104). Only the tourist information office regularly has English-speakers available.

Accommodation

There is no shortage of **accommodation** in Puno for any budget, but the town's busy and narrow streets make places hard to locate, so you may want to make use of a taxi or motorcycle rickshaw.

Budget

Hostal Europa Jr Alfonso Ugarte 112 ☎054/353023. Good rates, friendly, secure (with safe luggage store) and very popular with travellers, with 24hr hot water but few private bathrooms. ❷

Hostal Monterrey Lima 447 ☎054/351691. Quiet, central and pretty basic but nevertheless pleasant; has rooms with or without bath. ❷

Hostal Nesther Deustua 268 ☎054/363308. All rooms have private bath and hot water, but it hasn't got much style and has seen better days. Nevertheless it's a reasonably priced and central option. ❷

Hostal Presidente Tacna 248 ☎054/351421. Excellent value with a lot of character; hot water most evenings, all rooms with private baths. Has a nice, small café on the first floor for breakfast. ❷

Hostal Q'oña Wasi Av la Torre 119 ☎054/353912. An inexpensive hostel close to the station, with or without private bath in the rooms, with its own breakfast room. Friendly but a bit run-down and dingy. ❷

Hotel Extra Moquegua 124. An old building set around a small colonial courtyard, but very run-down and with basic facilities. ❷

Hotel Torina Libertad 126 ☎054/351061. Very basic, but incredibly cheap. ❶

Moderate

Hostal Imperial Jr Teodoro Valcarcel 145 ☎054/352386. Has private baths and usually plenty of hot water 6–10am and 6–10pm; modernish and quite comfortable, friendly and very helpful. ❹

Hostal Internacional Libertad 161 ☎054/352109. A modern building, with clean and well-kept rooms; cheaper accommodation available without private baths. ❸

Hostal Residencial El Buho Lambayeque 142 ☎/ⓕ054/366122, Ⓔzuluqv@mix.mail.com. A pleasant and comfortable place with private baths in all rooms and hot water much of the time; also has its own tour company. ❸–❹

Hostal Vylena Jr Ayacucho 505 ☎ /ⓕ054/351292. Very clean and quite smart, this friendly family-run hotel offers excellent value; has its own small restaurant and lounge areas. ❸–❹

Hotel Allyu Av Laykakota 299 ☎054/351555, ⓕ354372, Ⓦwww.unap.edu.pe/allyu. A well-run, modern hotel frequented by several European tour companies. Many rooms have superb views, and it offers good, friendly service. ❹

Hotel Balsa Inn Jr Cajamarca 555 ☎054/363144, ⓕ365652, Ⓦwww.hotelbalsainn .com. A pleasant, modern hotel conveniently located about one block from the plaza; it has some 20 comfortable rooms, most with cable TV, all with private baths and heating. ❺

Hotel Embajador Av Los Incas 289 ☎054/352072, ⓕ352562. Plenty of nice modern rooms, carpeted and warm, with hot water in the mornings. ❹

Expensive

Hacienda Hostal Jr Deustua 297 ☎/ⓕ054/356109. Very comfortable and stylish, with hot water, TV and private bath in the rooms, and luggage storage facilities. ❻

Hostal Italia Teodoro Valcarcel 122 ☎054/352521, ⓕ352131. A tastefully furnished, warm and comfortable haven, if slightly overpriced and not particularly friendly. All rooms have private baths and 24hr hot water. ❻

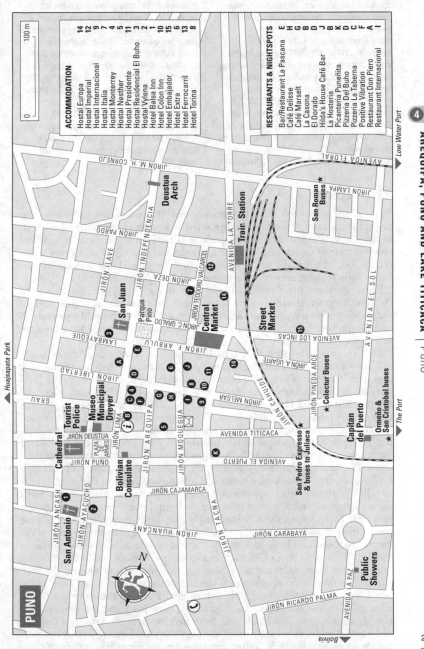

PUNO

ACCOMMODATION

Hostal Europa	14
Hostal Imperial	12
Hostal Internacional	9
Hostal Italia	7
Hostal Monterrey	4
Hostal Nesther	5
Hostal Presidente	11
Hostal Residencial El Buho	3
Hostal Vylena	2
Hotel Balsa Inn	1
Hotel Colon Inn	10
Hotel Embajador	15
Hotel Extra	6
Hotel Ferrocarril	13
Hotel Torina	8

RESTAURANTS & NIGHTSPOTS

Bar/Restaurant La Pascana	E
Café Delisse	H
Café Marselt	G
La Casona	B
El Dorado	D
Hilda's House Café Bar	J
La Hosteria	B
Picanteria Puneñita	K
Pizzeria Del Buho	D
Pizzeria La Taberna	C
Positive Vibration	F
Restaurant Don Piero	A
Restaurant Internacional	I

Huajsapata Park ▲

▼ Low Water Port

▼ The Port

Bolivia ▶

Hotel Colon Inn Tacna 290 ☏054/351432. Newly converted and very plush, with carpets, private baths and constant hot water; excellent value overall. ⑤

Hotel Ferrocarril Av la Torre 185 ☏/℉054/351752 or 352011. Very close to the station and reasonably priced with good, old-fashioned service and an excellent restaurant. Rooms have private bath but can get cold at night. ⑥

Hotel Libertador Isla Esteves ☏054/353870, ⓦwww.libertador.com.pe. Flashy former *Hotel de Turistas* on an island out to the north of town, with a top-notch restaurant; far from the fray of Puno's daily life. ⑦

Hotel Qelqatani Jr Tarapaca 355 ☏054/366172, ℉351053, ⓦwww.punonet.com/qelqatani. Modern and very smart, the rooms in this attractive new hotel have TV and private baths, and there's a bar and restaurant. Security is excellent, plus there are fax and Internet facilities. ⑦

Hotel Sillustani Lambayeque 195 ☏054/351881 or 352641, Ⓔhtl-sill@unap.edu.pe. A bright, airy place that's excellent value, with private bath, TV, fridge-bar and telephone in all rooms. There's also a pleasant dining room. ⑦

Hotel Taypikala Chucuito ☏054/356042, ℉355887. A new, rather fantastic and stylish New Age-style hotel, built next to the Templo de la Fertilidad. Superb rooms, pool and meditation suites. ⑥

The Town

Puno is one of the few Peruvian towns where the motorized traffic seems to respect pedestrians. Busy as it is, there is less of a sense of manic rush here than in most coastal or mountain cities, perhaps because of the altitude. It lacks the colonial style of Cusco or the bright glamoumr of Arequipa's *sillar* stone architecture, but it's a friendly town, whose sloping corrugated iron roofs reflect the heavy rains that fall between November and February.

There are three main points of reference in Puno: the spacious **Plaza de Armas**, the **train station** several blocks north, and the vast, strung-out area of old, semi-abandoned docks at the ever-shifting **Titicaca lakeside port**. It all looks impressive from a distance but, in fact, the real town-based attractions are few and quickly visited.

The seventeenth-century **Cathedral** on the Plaza de Armas (daily 7.30am–6pm; free) is surprisingly large with an exquisite Baroque facade, and, unusually for Peru, a very simple and humble interior, in line with the local Aymara Indians' austere attitude to religion. Opposite its north face, the **Museo Municipal Dreyer**, Conde de Lemos 289 (Mon–Sat 8am–2pm; $1), contains an interesting collection of archeological pieces, including ceramics, textiles and stone sculptures, mainly removed from some of the region's *chull-pas*. The nearby **Church of San Antonio**, on Jirón Ayacucho, one block to the south, is smaller and colourfully lit inside by ten stained-glass circular windows. The church's complex iconography, set into six wooden wall niches, is highly evocative of the region's mix of Catholic and Indian beliefs.

High up, overlooking the town and Plaza de Armas, the **Huajsapata Park** sits on a prominent hill, a short but steep climb up Jirón Deustua, turning right into Jirón Llave, left up Jirón Bolognesi, then left again up the Pasaje Contique steps. Often crowded with cuddling couples and young children playing on the natural rock-slides, Huajsapata offers stupendous views across the bustle of Puno to the serene blue of Titicaca and its unique skyline, while the pointing finger on the large white statue of Manco Capac reaches out towards the lake.

In the northern section of town, at the end of the pedestrianized Jirón Lima, you'll find an attractive, busy little plaza called **Parque Pino**, dominated in equal parts by the startlingly blue **Church of San Juan** and the scruffy, insistent shoeshine boys. Two blocks east from here, towards the lake, you find the **old central market**, which is small and very dirty, with rats and dogs competing for scraps, and beaming Indian women selling an incredible variety of fruits and vegetables. Head from here down Avenida Los Incas, initially between

Tours around Puno

The streets of Puno are full of touts selling guided tours and trips, but don't be swayed, always go to a respected, established **tour company**, such as one of those listed below. There are four main local tours on offer in Puno, all of which will reward you with views of abundant bird and animal life, immense landscapes and genuine living traditions. The trip to **Sillustani** normally involves a three- or four-hour tour by minibus and costs $5–8 depending on whether or not entrance and guide costs are included. Most other tours involve a combination of visits to the nearby **Uros Floating Islands** (half-day tour; $5–10), **Taquile and the Uros Islands** (full day from $7, or from $12 overnight), and **Amantani** (2–5 days from $7 a day, including transport and food). Of the independent tour **guides** operating in Puno, Andres Puelino Arucutipa Inta (☎054/353847 or 689775) is reliable and knowledgeable about the sites around Puno and Titicaca, while Andres Lopez is good and can be contacted through any of the town's hotels.

All Ways Travel Jr Tacna 234 ☎/℻054/355552, ℮awtperu@tera .com.pe. The most progressive, friendly and helpful of all the tour companies in Puno and the Titicaca region, running most of the usual tours but also offering trips to the wildlife haven of Anapia, close to the Bolivian border, where they work with locals on a sustainable tourism project.

Cusi Travel Teodoro Valcarcel 103 ☎054/369072. The office front doesn't look much, but this reliable company offers all the usual tours at reasonable prices.

Edgar Adventures Jr Lima 328 ☎054/353444, ℻354811, ℮edgaradventures@viaexpresa.com.pe. Islands tours at average prices, but more interestingly they also go to Chucuito and the Templo de Fertilidad for about $10 a person, as long as there are four or more in the group.

Feiser Jr Teodoro Valcarcel 153 ☎054/353112 or 355933, ℮feiser @puno.perured.net. Offers the standard tours at pretty reasonable prices; can also arrange

short trips onto the lake in faster boats, or pleasure rides on reed boats from Isla Esteves.

Kontiki Tours Jr Melgar 188 ☎054/355887, ℻353473. A bit out of the ordinary, this company offers mystic tours focusing on the ancient power centres of the region. They are reliable, very professional and work in other regions too, such as Cusco and Nazca.

Lake Country Treks Lima 458 ☎054/355785 or 352259. Standard tours plus a range of more outward-bound options and alternative trips to Taquile or even to *chullpas* at Cutimbo and the Templo de Falos near Chucuito.

Transturin Libertad 176 ☎054/352771. Travel agent offering catamaran trips to Bolivia.

Tur Puno Lambayeque 175 ☎054/352001, ℮turpuno@via_expresa.com. The normal tours and, for groups, very good deals on the one-day Taquile trip. Also free transport to Juliaca if you buy your air travel with them.

the old rail tracks, to a much more substantial **street market**, whose liveliest day is Saturday.

Moored either down in the port or sometimes out at the Isla Esteves by the *Hotel Libertador*, the nineteenth-century British-built steamship, the **Yavari** (usually Wed–Sun 8am–5pm; for guided tours call ☎054/622215; free), provides a fascinating insight into maritime life on Lake Titicaca over a hundred years ago and the military and entrepreneurial mindset of Peru in those days. Delivered by mule from the coast of Peru in over 1300 different pieces, it started life as a Peruvian navy gunship complete with bullet-proof windows, but ended up delivering the mail around Lake Titicaca.

Eating, drinking and nightlife

Puno's **restaurant** and **nightlife** scene is fairly busy and revolves mainly around Jirón Lima, but bear in mind that places here shut relatively early – not much happens after 11pm on a weekday. The city's strong tradition as one of the major Andean folklore centres in South America means that you're almost certain to be exposed to at least one live band an evening. Musicians tend to visit the main restaurants in town most evenings from around 9pm, playing a few folk numbers in each, usually featuring music from the altiplano – drums, panpipes, flutes and occasional dancers. The food in Puno is generally nothing to write home about, but the local delicacies of trout and kingfish (*pejerey*) are worth trying and are available in most restaurants.

Nightlife centres around Jirón Lima, a pedestrian precinct where the locals, young and old alike, hang out, parading up and down past the hawkers selling woollen sweaters, craft goods, cigarettes and sweets. Most **bars** are open Monday to Friday 8 to 11pm or midnight, but keep going until 2am at the weekends. Also fun at weekends are a couple of **salsa and mixto music clubs** (*mixto* generally means a mix of techno and *cumbia*) based on Calle Libertad, namely *Dominos* and *Tojoros*.

Restaurants and cafés

Bar Delta Café Jr Lima 284. Excellent for snacks and early morning breakfasts; located on the Parque Pino.

Bar/Restaurant La Pascana Jr Lima 339–341. Particularly good for evening meals, with a fine selection for vegetarians and interesting murals on the walls.

Café Delisse Moquegua 200. A small, pleasant vegetarian restaurant that serves great, healthy breakfasts, though service here is not quite what it used to be.

Café Marselt Libertad 215. Small and a bit dingy, but serves very good breakfasts.

La Casona Jr Lima 517. The best restaurant in town, particularly for evening meals, serving excellent criolla dishes in an attractive traditional environment. It is also something of a museum, with antique exhibits everywhere, and is very popular with locals.

El Dorado Jr Lima 371. Very friendly place with good service dishing up tasty international and Chinese food, including trout.

Hilda's House Café Bar Moquegua 189. Open for breakfast; serves good pancakes and fish, and has taped music in the evenings.

Picantería Puneñita Tacna 429. Serves very cheap lunchtime set menus and good-value breakfasts; service is fast and it can get pretty busy between noon and 1pm.

Pizzeria La Taberna Jr Lima 453. A lively evening spot serving warming alcoholic drinks and scrumptious pizzas; the garlic bread baked in a real-fire oven is particularly good.

Quinta Bolivar Av Simon Bolivar 405, Barrio Bellavista. Quite far from the centre, but worth the trip for its wide range of quality local foods in a traditional setting.

Restaurant Don Piero Jr Lima 364. A favourite with travellers, it's relatively inexpensive, has good breakfasts, a fine selection of cakes and a magazine rack for customer use.

Restaurant Internacional corner of Libertad and Moquegua. Popular with locals for lunch and supper, who come for its good range of reasonably priced meals; upstairs has the best atmosphere.

Restaurante La Pyramide Jr Teodoro Valcarcel 158. A very small, simple vegetarian restaurant that's open odd hours, usually for lunch, serving pretty good food, including their natural yogurts.

Bars and nightlife

Apu Salcantay Jr Lima 425. Good drinks and food at this bar, and the disco is accompanied by the latest Latin and European pop videos.

Casa del Abuelo on the corner of Tarapaca and Libertad. A folklore *peña* at its most lively on Sat nights.

Discoteca Monaco Jr Monaco 108. A popular, modern, dance music dive, packed with young locals at the weekend.

La Hostería Jr Lima 501. A smart pizzeria and bar, busy in the evenings and a good meeting place.

Pizzeria Del Buho Libertad 386 and Jr Lima 347. Probably the best pizzas in Puno and a warm, pleasant environment to boot; crowded and popular with travellers on Puno's cold dark evenings; serves delicious mulled wines and often has good music.

Positive Vibration Jr Grau 148. A decent bar environment, trendy and popular with young locals and travellers alike; also serves decent breakfasts and plays hot rock and reggae music.

Listings

Airline Faucett, Libertad 265 ☎054/355860 or 351301.

Banks and exchange Banco Continental, Lima 400; Banco de la Nación, on the corner of Grau and Ayacucho 269; Banco de Credito, on the corner of Lima with Grau; and Banco del Sur, Arequipa 459. *Cambistas* hang out at the corner of Jr Tacna near the central market. There are casas de cambio at Tacna 232, Lima 440, and at Vilca Marilin, Tacna 255.

Bus companies Jr Tacna, Jr Melgar and Av Titicaca are the main areas for buses. Companies and their terminals include: Altiplano, Av Titicaca 270 (☎054/369592), for Moquegua and Ilo; Cruz del Sur, Av El Sol 668 (☎054/352451), for Cusco, Arequipa, the coast, Desaguadero and La Paz; Dur Oriente, Av Titicaca 254 (☎054/368133), for Moquegua and Tacna; Expreso San Ramon, Jr Lampa 301 (☎054/352121), for Arequipa; Huanca, Melgar 250 (☎054/364335), for Cusco and Arequipa; Latino Tours, Av Titicaca 238 (☎054/364260), for Desaguadero, Moquegua, Tacna and Ilo; Ormeño, Melgar 338 (☎054/352321), for Lima and Arequipa; Porvenir, Av Titicaca 258 (☎054/363627), for Moquegua and Tacna; Rodriguez, Melgar 328 (☎054/363741), for Lima and Arequipa; San Cristoval, Melgar 338 (☎054/352321). for Lima and Arequipa; San Martin, Av Titicaca 210 (☎054/363326), for Juliaca, Moquegua and Puno; Señor de los Milagros, Melgar 308 (☎054/351481), for Lima; and Tranzela, Melgar 300 (☎054/364192), for Cusco and Arequipa.

Cinemas Ciné Puno, Arequipa 135; and Cine Teatro Municipal, Arequipa 101.

Consulate Bolivia, Jr Arequipa 120 ☎054/351251.

Couriers DHL services are available from Tur Puno, Lambayeque 175.

Dentist Dental Valencia, Jr Tarapaca 179 ☎054/363379.

Hospital For emergencies call ☎054/352931. Otherwise, try Clinica Los Pinos (☎054/351071) or the Hospital Regional, Av El Sol (☎054/351020).

Internet facilities *The Café Internet*, Jr Lima 425 ☎054/363955, has the best speed and prices; also try *TM* at corner of Jr Puno with Jr Arequipa ☎054/352900; or *J. M. Data*, Pasaje Grau 140 ☎054/356437.

Migraciones Libertad 403 ☎054/357103 or 352801.

Police The Tourist Police are at Jr Deustua 538 ☎054/357100

Post office Moquegua 269.

Shopping The unnamed shop at Jr Arbulu 231 sells most traditional Andean musical instruments; instruments can be bought extremely cheaply in the street market, on Av Los Incas. Laboratorio Fotografico, Jr Lima 120, Foto Prisma, Lima 389, and Full Color, Lima 525, sell and develop film.

Taxis ☎054/351616 or 332020.

Telephones and faxes Telefónica del Peru, corner of Federico More and Moquegua (daily 7am–11pm); and Mabel Telecommunications, Jr Lima 224 (Mon–Fri 7am–noon & 2–7pm).

Theatre The Teatro Municipal, block 1 of Arequipa, has folklore music, dance and other cultural events; for details of what's on, check at the box office.

By train to Arequipa and Cusco

Trains from **Puno to Arequipa** depart Monday and Friday at 7.45pm, arriving at 6am ($19 Pullman, $10 Económico); **Puno to Cusco** trains leave Monday, Wednesday, Thursday and Saturday at 8am and pull in at 6pm ($23 Turismo Inka, $19 Pullman, $7 Económico). However, the railway has recently been privatized, so always check with the ticket office at the station (Mon & Wed 6.30–10.30am & 4–8pm, Tues 6.30–10.30am & 2–6pm, Thurs 7am–3pm, Sat 6.30–8.30am & 6–8pm, Sun 4–6pm; not open Fri). It's best to buy your seats a day in advance and, as with all train journeys in Peru, keep your valuables well hidden and a good eye on your gear as you board the carriage and find your seat.

It's worth noting, however obvious, that if you book train (or for that matter, bus) tickets through an agent you will inevitably pay more for them than if you buy them directly yourself.

The first town out of Puno towards Cusco is **Juliaca** (see below), an hour away across a grassy pampa, where it's easy to imagine a straggling column of

Spanish cavalry and foot soldiers followed by a thousand Inca warriors – Almagro's fated expedition to Chile in the 1530s. Today, much as it always was, the plain is scattered with tiny isolated communities, many of them with conical kilns, self-sufficient even down to kitchenware.

Passing beyond here through a magnificent glacial landscape, the train pulls up outside **Ayavari** station (3903m). Once a great Inca centre with a palace, sun temple and well-stocked storehouses, it's now a market town, notable for the local women's weird and wonderful hats. You can see an interesting old church from the train – low but with two stone towers and a cupola – and it's a perfect place for trekking to if the urge grabs you.

Next stop is **La Raya**, a scenic pass between the Vilcanota Valley in the Amazon watershed and the Titicaca Basin which flows down into the Pacific. Enclosed by towering mountains, some of them snowcapped, it's the sort of spot that makes you feel like leaving the train and heading for the horizon. See Chapter Two for accounts of the villages north of La Raya pass.

Juliaca

There's no particular reason to stop in **JULIACA**, in many ways an uninspiring and very flat settlement, but at the same time it's hard to avoid. If you come by air to Titicaca, it's Juliaca airport you'll arrive at, even if Puno is your destination. If you're going by road or rail to Cusco from Puno, or anywhere along Lake Titicaca, you have to pass through Juliaca en route. It's less than half an hour by colectivo or taxi from Puno, inland from the lakeside. It certainly isn't an inviting town, looking like a large but down-at-heel and desert-bound work camp. However, there are some good **artesania** stalls and shops on the Plaza Bolognesi, and excellent woollen goods can be purchased extremely cheaply, especially at the **Monday market**. The daily market around the station is worth a browse and sells just about everything – from stuffed iguanas to second-hand bikes.

If you get stranded here and need to sample one of Juliaca's several bland **hotels**, the first choice is the comfortable and safe *Hostal Peru*, San Ramon 409 (❷) on the station plaza. If it's full, try the immaculate *Hostal Royal,* San Ramon 158 (❸), or the more upmarket *Hotel Santa Maria*, one block from the plaza along Avenida Noriega (❸). Frequent **colectivos** to Puno (45min; $2) and Lake Titicaca leave from Plaza Bolognesi and from the service station Grifo Los Tres Marias, off Avenida Noriega, two blocks from the plaza. Cruz del Sur **buses** leave from Huancane 443 (☎054/322011) twice a day for Arequipa and Lima; Empresa San Martin operate from Jr Tumbes 920 to Puno and Moquegua; San Ramon, for Arequipa, are next door at no. 918 (☎054/324583). Local buses and colectivos to Puno leave every thirty minutes ($1.50, a 1hr trip) from Plaza Bolognesi, outside the station, and from the airport, or you can take a taxi for around $10 or a colectivo for $2. **Flights** leave daily from the Aeropuerto Manco Capac, 2km north of Juliaca, for Cusco, Arequipa and Lima. The following all have reliable and regular flights (departure tax is $9): Aero Peru, Ramon 160 (☎054/322490); Americana, Jr Noriega 325 (☎054/321844) and at the airport (☎054/325005); and Faucett, Loretto 113–140 (☎054/321966). You can **change money** with the street dealers on Plaza Bolognesi, with the casa de cambio J.J. Peru on Mariano Nuñez or with the money-changing shops on block 1 of San Martin; alternatively, banks include the Banco de la Nación, Lima 147; Banco Continental, San Ramon 441; Banco del Sur, San Ramon 301, at the corner of San Ramon with San Martin; the Banco Wiese, Jr San Martin 510; the Banco de Credito, Mariano

Nuñez 136; and the Banco Latino, Av Mariano Nuñez 570. However, rates are much better in Puno.

Lake Titicaca

Lake Titicaca is an undeniably impressive sight. Titicaca skies are vast, almost infinite, and deep, deep hues of blue; below this sits a usually placid mirror-like lake reflecting the big sky back on itself. All along the horizon, too, the green Andean mountains can be seen raising their ancient backs and heads towards the sun; over on the Bolivian side it's sometimes possible to make out the ice-caps of the Cordillera Real mountain chain. A National Reserve since 1978, the lake has over sixty varieties of birds, fourteen species of native fish and eighteen types of amphibians. It's also the world's largest high-altitude body of water, at 284m deep and more than 8500 square kilometres in area, fifteen times the size of Lake Geneva in Switzerland and higher and slightly bigger than Lake Tahoe in the US. It's often seen as three separate regions: Lago Mayor, the main, deep part of the lake; Wiñaymarka, the area incorporating various archipelagos that include both Peruvian and Bolivian Titicaca; and the Golfi de Puno, essentially the bay encompassed by the peninsulas of Capachica and Chucuito. The villages that line its shores depend mainly on grazing live-stock for their livelihood, since the altitude limits the growth potential of most crops. Titicaca is where the Quechua Indian language and people merge with the more southerly Aymaras. Curious Inca-built **Chullpa burial tombs** circle

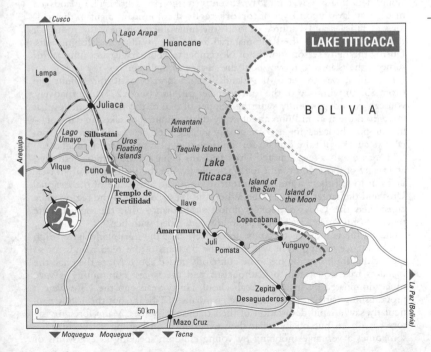

the lake and its man-made **Uros Floating Islands**. These islands have been inhabited since their construction centuries ago by Uros Indians who were retreating from more powerful neighbours like the Incas. Floating platform islands, weird to walk over and even stranger to live on, they are now a major tourist attraction. More powerful and self-determined are the communities who live on the fixed islands of **Taquile** and **Amantani**, often described as the closest one can get to heaven by the few travellers who make it out this far into the lake. There are, in fact, more than seventy islands in the lake, the largest and most sacred being the **Island of the Sun**, an ancient Inca temple site on the Bolivian side of the border which divides the lake's southern shore. Titicaca is an Aymara word meaning "Puma's Rock", which refers to an unusual boulder on the Island of the Sun. The island is best visited from Copacabana in Bolivia, or through trips arranged by one of the tour companies in Puno (see p.277).

Not surprisingly, fish is an important part of the diet of the Titicaca inhabitants, for both the islanders and the ibis and flamingos which can be seen along the pre-Inca terraced shorelines. The most common fish is a small piranha-like specimen called *carachi*. Trout arrived in the lake, after swimming up the rivers, during the first or second decade of the twentieth century. *Pejerey* (kingfish) established themselves only thirty years ago but have been so successful that there are relatively few trout left. *Pejerey* fishing is an option for tourists.

The Uros Floating Islands

Although there are more than forty of these islands, most guided tours limit themselves to the largest, **Huacavacani**, where several Indian families live alongside a floating Seventh Day Adventist missionary school. The islands are made from layer upon layer of **tortora reeds**, the dominant plant in the shallows of Titicaca and a source of food (the inner juicy bits near the roots) for the people, as well as the basic material for roofing, walling and fishing rafts. During the rainy season months of November to February it's not unusual for some of the islands to move about the surface of the lake.

The easiest way to get to the islands is on a short two- to three-hour trip (from $3.50) with one of the tour agencies in Puno (see p.277). Alternatively, you can go independently with the skipper of one of the many launches that leave from the port in Puno about every thirty minutes, or take the daily public transport boat leaving at 9am, usually getting back between noon and 1pm (always check with the captain for the time they plan to depart the islands).

There are only a few hundred **Uros Indians** living on the islands these days, and many of those you might meet actually live on the mainland, only travelling out to sell their wares to the tourists; most are a mixture of the original Uros and the larger Aymara tribe. When the Incas controlled the region, they considered the Uros so poor – almost subhuman – that the only tribute required of them was a section of hollow cane filled with lice.

Life on the islands has certainly never been easy: the inhabitants have to go some distance to find fresh water, and the bottoms of the reed islands rot so rapidly that fresh matting has to be constantly added above. More than half the islanders have converted to Catholicism, and the largest community is very much dominated by its evangelical school. Thirty years ago the Uros were a proud fishing tribe, in many ways the guardians of Titicaca, but the 1980s, particularly, saw a rapid devastation of their traditional values. Many foreign visitors have been put off by what they experience on landing at the island – sometimes a veritable mobbing by young children speaking a few words of

English ("sweets", "money", "what's your name?" and "give it to me") and fighting each other for your gifts. However, things have improved over recent years and you do still get a glimpse of a very unusual way of life and the opportunity to ride on a *tortora* reed raft.

Taquile and Amantani

Two genuine – non-floating – islands in Titicaca can also be visited. **Taquile** and **Amantani**, peaceful places that see fewer tourists, are both around 25–30km across the water from Puno, just beyond the outer edge of the Gulf of Chucuito. Amantani is the least visited of the two and, consequently, has fewer facilities and costs slightly more to reach by boat.

Daily **boats** for Taquile leave Puno at 8am, returning by around 5.30 or 6pm, while they usually leave for Amantani at 9am, returning at 4–4.30pm; as usual, check with the captain for the time they plan to depart the islands. You can go on an organized trip with one of the tour companies listed on p.277, but the agencies use the same boats and charge at least twice the going rate. The sun's rays reflected off the lake can burn even well-tanned skins so it's a good idea to protect your head and shoulders during this voyage. The launches tend to be ageing wooden boats with engines from old North American cars, like the 1962 Dodge which belongs to one of the island captains. Most boats return after lunch the same day, but since this doesn't give you enough time to look around, many visitors prefer to stay a night or two in bed and breakfast **accommodation** (from around $3). The only way to guarantee a place to stay is to book in advance through one of Puno's tour agencies (see p.277); if you arrive on spec, you could ask the relevant island authorities or talk to the boat's captain and you may be lucky, but don't bank on it. Sleeping bags and toilet paper are recommended, and fresh fruit and vegetables are appreciated by the host islanders.

Taquile

The island of **TAQUILE** has been inhabited for over ten thousand years, with agriculture being introduced about 4000 BC. It was dominated by the Aymara-speaking Tiahuanaco culture until the thirteenth century, when the Incas conquered it and introduced the Quechua language. In 1580, the island was "bought" by Pedro Gonzalez de Taquile and so came under Spanish influence. During the 1930s it was used as a safe exile/prison for troublesome characters like former president Sanchez Cerro, and it wasn't until 1937 that the residents – the local descendants of the original Indians – regained legal ownership by buying it back.

Approaching Taquile, the most attractive of the islands and measuring some 1km by 7km, it looks like a huge ribbed whale, large and bulbous to the east, tapering to its western tail end. The horizontal striations of the island are produced by significant amounts of ancient terracing along Taquile's steep-sided shores. Such terraces are at an even greater premium here in the middle of the lake where soil erosion would otherwise slowly kill the island's largely self-sufficient agricultural economy, of which potatoes, corn, broad beans and the hardy *quinoa* are the main crops. Without good soil Taquile could become like the main floating islands, depending almost exclusively on tourism for its income.

The main heart of the island is reached by some 525 gruelling steps up a steep hill from the small stone harbour. The view from the top is spectacular – looking towards the southeast of the island you can see the hilltop ruins of Uray K'ari, built of stone in the Tiahuanaco era around 800 AD; looking to the west you may glimpse the larger, slightly higher ruins of Hanan K'ari. On arrival you'll be met by a committee of locals who delegate various native families to look after particular travellers – be aware that your family may live in basic conditions and speak no Spanish, let alone English (Quechua being the first language). There is no electricity on the island, apart from a solar-powered community loudspeaker and one or two individual houses with solar lighting, so take a torch and candles. There are no medical facilities or hotels either, though there is a small store and a few **places to eat** around the small plaza, where fish and chips and honey pancakes are the specialities.

Most of Taquile's population of 1200 people are weavers and knitters of fine alpaca wool – renowned for their excellent cloth. You can still watch the locals drop-spin, a common form of hand-spinning that produces incredibly fine thread for their special cloth. The men sport black woollen trousers fastened with elaborate waistbands woven in pinks, reds and greens, while the women wear beautiful black headscarves, sweaters, dark shawls and skirts trimmed usually with shocking-pink or bright-red tassels and fringes.

Amantani

Like nearby Taquile, **AMANTANI**, a basket-weavers' island and the largest on the lake, has managed to retain some degree of cultural isolation and autonomous control over the tourist trade. Of course, tourism has had its effect on the local population, so it's not uncommon to be offered drinks, then charged later, or for the children to sing you songs without being asked, expecting to be paid. The ancient agricultural terraces are excellently maintained, and traditional stone masonry is still practised, as are the old Inca systems of agriculture, labour and ritual trade. The islanders eat mainly vegetables, with meat and fruit being rare commodities, and the women dress in colourful clothes, very distinctly woven. The island is dominated by two small hills: one is the **Temple of Pachamama** (Mother Earth) and the other the **Temple of Pachatata** (Father Earth). Around February 20, the islanders celebrate their main festival with half the 5000-strong population going to one hill, the other half gathering at the other. Following ancient ceremonies, the two halves then gather together to celebrate their origins with traditional and colourful music and dance.

Currently the only available **accommodation** is staying in an islander's house (see above) though there are plans to build a hostel. There are no restaurants, but you can buy basic supplies at the artesania trading post in the heart of the island. If you're lucky, the mayor of Amantani may be available to act as a guide for a few dollars a day; unsurprisingly, he is very knowledgeable about the island and its history.

The Chullpa Tombs of Sillustani

Scattered all around Lake Titicaca you'll find *chullpas*, gargantuan white stone towers up to 10m in height in which the Colla tribe, who dominated the region before the Incas, buried their dead. Some of the most spectacular are at **SILLUSTANI**, set on a little peninsula in Lake Umayo overlooking Titicaca, 30km northwest of Puno. This ancient temple-cum-cemetery consists of a ring of stones more than five hundred years old – some of which have been tumbled by earthquakes or, more recently, by tomb-robbers intent on stealing the rich goods (ceramics, jewellery and a few weapons) buried with important mummies. Two styles predominate at this site: the honeycomb *chullpas* and those whose superb stonework was influenced by the advance of the Inca

Empire. The former are set aside from the rest and characterized by large stone slabs around a central core; some of them are carved, but most are simply plastered with white mud and small stones. The later, Inca-type stonework is more complicated and in some cases you can see the elaborate corner jointing more typical of Cusco masonry.

The easiest way to get here is on a **guided tour** from Puno (see p.277); alternatively, you can take a **colectivo** from Avenida Tacna most afternoons at around 2–2.30pm, for under $5. If you want to **camp** overnight at Sillustani (remembering how cold it can be), the site guard will show you where to pitch your tent. It's a magnificent place to wake up, with the morning sun rising over the snowcapped Cordillera Real on the Bolivian side of Titicaca.

South to Bolivia

The most popular routes to Bolivia involve overland road travel, crossing the frontier either at **Yunguyo** or at the river border of **Desaguadero** (this latter route is little frequented these days due to the poor condition of the road). En route to either you'll pass by some of Titicaca's more interesting colonial settlements, each with its own individual style of architecture. Several **bus companies** run services from Puno over these routes: Empresa Los Angeles has twice-weekly buses to Desaguadero ($1.50, a 3hr trip); Tour Peru runs daily to Copacabana ($1.50, also 3hr) and La Paz ($6, a 7hr trip); Altiplano buses go most days to La Paz ($6); Colectur runs to Copacabana and La Paz daily for around $5; and San Pedro Express runs daily to Yunguyo, Desaguadero and Copacabana ($8). From Yunguyo some buses connect with a minibus service to Copacabana, then a Bolivian bus on to La Paz, see Puno Listings, p.279, for addresses and phone numbers of bus companies.

Chucuito to Juli

CHUCUITO, 20km south of Puno, is dwarfed by its intensive hillside terracing and the huge igneous boulders poised behind the brick and adobe houses. Chucuito was once a colonial town and its main plaza retains the **pillory** (*picota*) where the severed heads of executed criminals were displayed. Close to this there's a **sundial**, erected in 1831 to help the local Aymara people regulate their working day according to European hours. The base is made from stones taken from the Inca **Templo de Fertilidad** – itself located behind the *Hotel Taypikala* (see p.276) – which remains Chucuito's greatest treasure. Inside the temple's main stone walls are around a hundred stone phalluses, row upon row

---

By ferry into Bolivia

Until recently, the best way into Bolivia was undoubtedly on the **steamship** across Lake Titicaca from Puno to Guaqui. The steamer is currently not running, but it's worth checking with the tourist office or at the jetty in Puno's main port for up-to-date information. Expensive, irregular **hydrofoils** from Puno to La Paz are run by Crillon Tours in the US (1450 S Bayshore Dr, Suite 85, Miami, FL 33131; ☎305/358-5353), also bookable through the tourist office or tour operators in Puno, but you need to book well in advance in all cases. A similarly upmarket **catamaran** service runs on demand; contact Transturin (see p.277) for details.

jammed within the temple space, ranged like seats in a theatre. Some of the larger ones may have had particular ritual significance, and locals say that women who have difficulty getting pregnant still come here to pray for help on the bold giant phalluses. Also on the plaza is the **Iglesia Santo Domingo**, constructed in 1780 and displaying a very poor image of a puma. For **accommodation**, try the *Hotel Las Cabañas*, Jr Bolognesi 334 (☎054/351276; ❷), affiliated to Hostelling International and where you stay in small huts with constant hot water and a fire for the cool nights.

Crossing the Bolivian border

Yunguyo–Copacabana

The **Yunguyo–Copacabana** crossing is by far the most enjoyable route into Bolivia, though unless you intend staying overnight in Copacabana (or taking the 3hr Puno–Copacabana minibus) you'll need to set out quite early from Puno; the actual **border** (8am–6pm) is a two-kilometre walk from Yunguyo. The Bolivian passport control, where there's usually a bus for the 10km or so to Copacabana, is a few hundred metres on from the Peruvian border post. The best **hotel** in Yunguyo is the *Hostal Residencial Isabel*, San Francisco 110 (☎054/856084; ❷), which has hot water but only communal bathrooms. You can change money at the Banco de la Nación at Triunfo 219 and 28 de Julio, but there are several **casas de cambio** and street *cambistas* nearby, usually offering better rates and dealing in a greater variety of currencies, though even then you should change only enough to get you to La Paz, as the rate is poor. The cheap afternoon bus service from Copacabana takes you through some of the basin's most exciting scenery. At Tiquina you leave the bus briefly to take a passenger ferry across the narrowest point of the lake, the bus rejoining you on the other side from its own individual ferry. Once across the lake it's a four- to five-hour haul on to La Paz.

The Desaguadero Crossing

Very little traffic now uses the **Desaguadero Crossing** over the Peru–Bolivia border; it's less interesting than going via Yunguyo, but has the advantage of passing the ruined temple complex of Tiahuanaco in Bolivia. If you do want to travel this route, take one of the early morning colectivos (6–9am) from Jr Tacna in Puno to **Desaguadero** ($2, a 3–4hr trip); you'll need to get a stamp in your passport from the Peruvian control by the market and the Bolivian one just across the bridge. If you arrive here by bus, it's a short walk across the border and you can pick up an Ingravi bus on to La Paz more or less hourly (4–5hr), which goes via Tiahuanaco. Money can be changed on the bridge approach but the rates are poor, so again buy only as much as you'll need to get you to La Paz. It's not a very friendly town, but there are a few hotels, all basic and not particularly clean; the *Hostal San Carlos* is probably the best, with a hot shower option (❶–❷). Similarly, none of the restaurants can really be recommended, but the *Pollería El Rico Riko*, close to the border crossing, is not too bad.

From Bolivia to Peru

For anyone **coming into Peru from Bolivia** by either route, the procedure is just as straightforward. One difference worth noting is that when leaving Copacabana, a customs and passport check takes place in two little huts on the left just before the exit barrier. Now and again Bolivian customs officials take a heavy line and thoroughly search all items of luggage. In some cases bribery has to be resorted to, simply to avoid undue hassle or delay (see Basics, p.46). If you get stranded crossing the border and need a basic **hostel**, try the *Hotel Amazonas*, on the main plaza in Yunguyo (❷); the only option in Desaguadero is the rather sordid *Alojamiento Internacional* on the central plaza (❶).

Some 8km beyond Chucuito you pass through the **Aymara** settlement of Plateria, so named for the coins manufactured here in colonial days, but there's little to stop here for. Similarly, the next village, **Acora**, has a busy Sunday market and is renowned for its fish, but little else. Off the main road, however, about 6km southeast of Acora there are vestiges of the Tiahuanaco culture and the Chullpas of Molloq'o.

About halfway between Puno and Juli you pass through the village of **ILAVE**, where a major side road heads off directly down to the coast for Tacna (320km) and Moquegua via Trata (231km). Situated at an arterial road intersection, Ilave is quite an important market town and has a large **Sunday market** selling colourful clothing and coca leaves, and also hosts a few shamanic fortune-tellers. Ilave also has a surprisingly large and modern Terminal Terrestre, where all the **buses** from Puno stop and from where it's possible to catch services to Tacna and Moquegua on the coast. The town has a large Plaza de Armas, where there's a statue to Coronel Francisco Bolognesi, hero of the Arica battles between Peru and Chile. Half a block to the south, the ancient and crumbling **Iglesia de San Miguel** has an impressive cupola and belfry. If you want a **place to stay**, the very basic *Hostal Grau*, on the plaza at Jr Dos de Mayo 337 (❶), is just about bearable. For **food**, try the *Pollería Ricos Pollo*, Jr Andino 307, towards the market from the plaza.

After crossing the bridge over the Río Ilave, the road cuts 60km across the plain towards Juli, passing by some unusual rock formations scattered across the altiplano of the Titicaca basin, many of which have ritual significance for the local Aymara population. The most important of these is the rock that's been worked to represent the face of **Amarumuru**, said by indigenous mystics to have been transformed by a race of giants and to act as a doorway into another dimension.

A few kilometres on from the Amarumuru rock is the relatively large town of **JULI**, now bypassed by the new road, but nestling attractively between gigantic round-topped and terraced hills. Juli is also known as Pequeña Roma (Little Rome) because of the seven prominent mountains immediately surrounding it, each one of them of spiritual significance to the indigenous inhabitants in terms of earth-magic, healing and fertility. Perhaps because of this, the Jesuits chose Juli as the site for a major mission training centre, which prepared missionaries for trips to the remoter regions of Bolivia and Paraguay. The concept they developed, a form of community evangelization, was at least partly inspired by the Inca organizational system and was extremely influential throughout the seventeenth and eighteenth centuries. The Jesuits' political and religious power is reflected in the almost surreal extravagance of the church architecture.

Fronting the large open plaza is the stone-built parish church of **San Pedro**, known for its intricately carved Plateresque side altars. Constructed in 1560, it has an impressive cupola, and the cool, serene interior, awash with gold-leaf, is home to many superb examples of Cusqueña school artwork. Behind the altar there's a wealth of silver and gold, the woodwork dripping with seashells, fruits and angels. In front of this church you'll often see local shamanic fortune-tellers. Across the plaza from here is the amazing-looking **Casa Zavala** (House of the Inquisition), with its thatched roof and fantastically carved double doors, which is also known as *el carcel* ("the Prison"). Juli's numerous other churches display superb examples of the Indian influence, particularly the huge brick and adobe **Iglesia San Juan** (Mon–Sat 9am–5pm; $1.20), with its *mestizo* stonework on some of the doors and windows. Cold and musty but with a rather surreal interior, due in part to the play of light through its few high windows, this church was founded in 1775 but is now an excellent museum of religious art and architecture, which handsomely rewards the inquisitive visitor. Of the few **hostels** here, try the basic *Hostal Treboles* (❷) on the main plaza, or the *Hostal Municipal* (❷) on the left as you enter the town from the Puno road.

Twenty kilometres on lies the historic town of **POMATA**, with its pink granite church of **Santiago Apóstol**, built in 1763. Outside the church, in a prominent location overlooking the lake, is a circular stone construction known as the **glorieta**; crumbling today, it's still the site where local authorities meet for ceremonial purposes. Pomata's name is derived from the Aymara word for "puma", and you'll see the puma symbol all over the fountain in the Plaza de Armas and outside the church. If you happen to be around the area in October, try to get to Pomata for the **Fiesta de la Virgen de Rosaria** on the first Sunday of the month, a splendid celebration with processions, music and folk dancing, as well the usual drinking and feasting.

Travel details

Buses and colectivos

Arequipa to: Chivay (6 daily; 3–4hr); Colca (3 daily; 5–6hr); Cusco (several daily; 9–12hr); Desaguadero (3 daily; 7–9hr); Lima (8–10 daily; 14–18hr); Moquegua (4 daily; 3–4hr); Paucarpata (every 30min; 15min); Puno (6 daily; 5–6hr);Tacna (2–3 daily; 5hr).

Ica to: Arequipa (6 daily; 14hr); Lima (12 daily; 4hr); Nazca (6 daily; 2hr).

Nazca to: Arequipa (1 nightly, several daily; 12hr); Cusco, via Arequipa (daily; 35hr); Lima (2–3 daily; 5hr).

Pisco to: Ayacucho (7 weekly; 14hr); Ica (20 daily; 1hr); Lima (3 daily; 3hr); Nazca (2 daily; 3hr).

Puno to: Cusco (8 daily; 6–9hr); Juliaca (3–4 hourly; 30–40min); La Paz via Desaguadero (2 daily; 7–9hr), via Yunguyo (6–8 daily; 7–8hr); Moquegua (daily; 10–12hr); Tacna (3 weekly; 17hr).

Tacna to: Arequipa (5 daily; 6–7hr); Arica (10 daily; 1–2 hr); Lima (4 daily; 22hr); Puno (3 weekly; 17hr).

Trains

Puno to: Cusco (4 weekly; 10hr), via Juliaca (1hr 30min) and Sicuani (6hr 30min).

Flights

Arequipa to: Cusco (2 daily; 1hr); Juliaca, for Puno (4 weekly; 40min); Lima (3 daily; 1hr).

Juliaca (Puno) to: Arequipa (daily; 40min); Cusco (daily; 40min); Lima (daily; 2hr).

Huaraz and the
Cordillera Blanca

CHAPTER 5

Highlights

* **Huascarán** Dividing the Amazon Basin from the Pacific watershed, this mountain is the highest peak in Peru. See p.319

* **Chavín de Huantar** One of the most important ancient temple sites in the Andes – associated with a cult dedicated to a terrifying feline god. See p.324

* **Monterrey/Chancos** Relaxing in either of these two natural thermal baths is both a healthy and a hedonistic experience to remember. See p.312 & 316

* **Cordillera Blanca** Hiking or climbing in this region is one of the highlights of any Peru trip and is as scenic a journey as you could hope to find anywhere outside of the Himalayas. See p.319

* **Lago Llanganuco** This calm, turquoise-coloured, glacial lake sits 3850m above sea level, dramatically surrounded by Peru's highest peaks. See p.318

* **Caraz** A quaint, attractive town known for its honey and milk products, quietly settled below the enormous Huandoy Glacier, close to the little-visited ruins of Tunshucayco. See p.320

* **Sechin** A unique warrior temple site whose outer wall is clad with some of the most gruesome ancient artwork to be found anywhere in South America. See p.294

5

Huaraz and the Cordillera Blanca

S liced north to south by parallel ranges of high Andean peaks, the *departmento* of **Ancash** is home to a stunning mountain region some 200–300km north of Lima. This area, whose heartland is the Huaraz Valley between the Cordillera Negra and the Cordillera Blanca, offers more in terms of trekking and climbing, beautiful snowcapped scenery, flora and fauna, glaciated valleys, history and traditional cultures than anywhere else in the country. Ancash unfurls along an immense desert coastline, where pyramids and ancient fortresses are scattered within easy reach of several small resorts linked by vast, empty beaches. Behind are the barren heights of the dark, dry Cordillera Negra, and beyond that the spectacular backdrop of the snowcapped Cordillera Blanca; between the two the Huaraz Valley, known locally as the **Callejón de Huaylas**, around 3000m above sea level, is an ideal base from which to explore some of the best hiking and mountaineering in the Americas located in the Cordillera Blanca, a mountain range which contains Peru's highest peaks, including Huascarán, the dominant glacier.

Nestling in the valley, the *departmento's* capital, **Huaraz** – six or seven hours by car from Lima – makes an ideal base for exploring the region. It's the place to stock up, hire guides and mules, and relax after a breathtaking expedition. Besides being close to scores of exhilarating mountain trails, the city is also near the ancient Andean treasure, **Chavín de Huantar**, an impressive stone temple complex which was at the centre of a culturally significant puma-worshipping religious movement just over 2500 years ago.

The Ancash Coast

Most people travelling along the **Ancash Coast** from Lima to Huaraz or Trujillo (or vice versa) do the whole trip in a single six-or eight-hour bus ride.

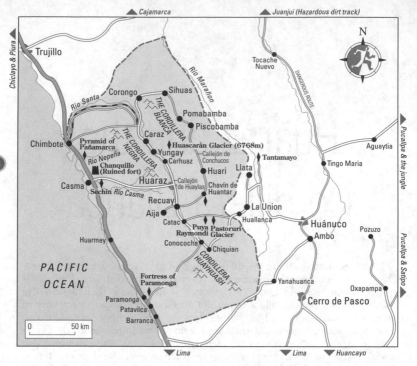

For Trujillo this means sticking to the stunning desert scenery of the Panamerican Highway. En route to Huaraz, a well-maintained road climbs furiously from sea level to the breathless heights of the Callejón de Huaylas. Whichever route you take, it's well worth at least considering a stop at the small beach resort of **Barranca** or the farming and fishing villages of **Casma** and **Chimbote** – all three of which have some intriguing archeological sites nearby, as well as offering alternative routes up to Huaraz. Facilities for tourists in these coastal parts are hardly overwhelming, but there are enough services that you won't go wanting.

Barranca, Patavilca and the Fortress of Paramonga

North of Lima, the **Fortress of Paramonga** is the first site of real interest, the best-preserved of all Peru's coastal outposts, built originally to guard the southern limit of the powerful Chimu Empire. To explore the ruins, it's best to base yourself at **BARRANCA**, 7km south of the fortress, where there are a few simple **hotels** and two or three places to eat. The *Hotel Jefferson*, at Jr Lima 946 (**2**), is cheap and quite comfortable, or there's the basic *Hostal Colón*, Jr Galvez 407 (**1**). The best place to eat is the excellent Chinese **restaurant** on the main street. Nearly all buses and colectivos on their way between Lima and Trujillo or Huaraz stop at Barranca. To get from Barranca to Paramonga, take the efficient local bus service, which leaves from the garage at the northern end of town, every hour or so.

Five kilometres north of Barranca is the smaller town of **PATAVILCA**, where Bolivar planned his campaign to liberate Peru. The main paved road to

Huaraz and the Cordillera Blanca leaves the Panamerican Highway here and heads up into the Andes, but the only facilities in the village are a basic **café**, the *Restaurant Conejo*, and a small **museum** (Mon–Sat 9am–5pm; 50¢), containing local archeological finds, including ceramics.

The Fortress of Paramonga

The **Fortress of Paramonga** (daily 8am–5.30pm; $1.50) sits less than 1km from the ocean and looks in many ways like a feudal castle. Constructed entirely from adobe, its walls within walls run around the contours of a natural hillock and are similar in style and situation to the Sun Temple of Pachacamac (see p.104). As you climb up from the road, you'll see the main entrance to the fortress on the right by the site's small **museum** (daily 8am–5pm) and ticket office. Heading into the maze-like **ruins**, you'll find the rooms and sections get smaller and narrower the closer you get to the top – where sits the original palace-temple. From here there were once commanding views across the desert coast in either direction; looking south today, you see vast sugar-cane fields, formerly belonging to the US-owned Grace Corporation, once owners of nearly a third of Peru's sugar production. In contrast to the verdant green of these fields, irrigated by the Río Fortaleza, the fortress stands out in the landscape like a huge, dusty yellow pyramid.

There are differences of opinion as to whether the fort had a military function or was purely a ritual centre, but as most pre-Conquest cultures built their places of worship around the natural personality of the landscape (rocks, water, geomorphic features and so on), it seems likely that the Chimu built it on an older *huaca*, both as a fortified ritual shrine and to mark the southern boundary of their empire. It was conquered by the Incas in the late fifteenth century, who built a road down from the Callejón de Huaylas. Hernando Pizarro was the first Spaniard to see Paramonga, arriving in 1533 en route from Cajamarca to Pachacamac. He described it as "a strong fort with seven encircling walls painted with many forms both inside and outside, with portals well built like those of Spain and two tigers painted at the principal doorways". There are still red- and yellow-based geometric murals visible on some of the walls in the upper sector, as well as some chessboard-style patterns.

Huarmey and around

North of Paramonga, sand dunes encroach on the main coastal road as it continues the 75km to **HUARMEY**, where you'll find the exhilarating and usually deserted beaches of La Honda, El Balneario and Tuquillo. If you want **accommodation**, there's the basic *Hotel Venus* (❷), plus there's a 24-hour **restaurant**, *El Piloto*, geared towards truck-drivers. Leaving Huarmey, the road closely follows the shoreline, passing the magnificent **Playa Grande**, a seemingly endless beach with powerful rolling surf – often a luminous green at night due to phosphorescent plankton being tossed around in the whitewater crests – and a perfect spot for **camping**. Some of the desert you pass through has no plant life at all, beyond the burned-out tumbleweeds that grow around the humps and undulations fringed with curvy lines of rock strata – intrusions of volcanic power from the ancestral age. In places, huge hills crouch like sand-covered jellyfish squatting on some vast beach.

Casma and around

The town of **CASMA**, 70km north of Huarmey, marks the mouth of the well-irrigated Sechin river valley. Surrounded by corn and cotton fields, this small settlement is peculiar in that most of its buildings are just one storey high and all are modern. Formerly the port for the Callejón de Huaylas, the town was razed by the 1970 earthquake, whose epicentre was just offshore. There's not a lot of interest here and little reason to break your journey, other than to explore the nearby ruins, such as the temple complex of **Sechin**, the ancient fort of **Chanquillo**, or the **Pañamarca Pyramid**, 20km north.

The town boasts several roadside cafés and a small selection of **hotels**: the new *Hostal Celene*, Luis Ormeño 595 (❶), has nine excellent-value and very clean rooms; close by the *Hostal Gregori*, C Ormeño 579 (☎044/711073; ❸), is also very clean and almost as comfortable; and the *Hotel El Farol*, Tupac Amaru 350 (☎044/711064; ❸), two blocks from the Plaza de Armas, is tidy, friendly and comfortable with a decent restaurant. En route to the Sechin ruins there's the well-run *Hospedaje Las Dunas* (no tel; ❷), which also has a good **restaurant** and is only ten minutes from town by car; more central and arguably a better restaurant, *Tio Sam*, Huarmey 138, serves comida criolla as well as decent *chifa* food. Turismo Chimbote **buses** run at least three times a day to Lima (5hr) and Chimbote (40min); Huandoy, Av Luis Ormeño 158 (☎044/712336), connect with Huaraz and Caraz; while Empresa Moreno buses take the scenic but dusty track three times a week over the Cordillera Negra via the Callan Pass to Huaraz (5-7hr).

The Sechin ruins

Just over an hour's walk from Casma – head south along the Panamerican Highway for 3km, then up the signposted side road to Huaraz for about the same distance – lies the ruined temple complex of **SECHIN** (daily 9am–6pm; $2). The site's main section, unusually stuck at the bottom of a hill, consists of an outer wall clad with around ninety monolithic slabs engraved with some-times monstrous representations of bellicose warriors and mutilated sacrificial victims or prisoners of war. Some of these stones, dating from about 750 BC, stand 4m high. Hidden behind the standing stones is an interesting inner sanctuary – a rectangular building consisting of a series of superimposed platforms with a central stairway on either side – but it is currently closed to the public. The site also has a small museum, the **Museo Max Uhle**, which displays photographs of the complex plus some of the artefacts uncovered here.

It is rare for granite stone to be used so extensively in coastal construction, which generally favoured adobe. Some of the ceremonial centres at Sechin were built before 1400 BC, including the massive U-shaped **Sechin Alto** complex, at the time the largest construction in the entire Americas. Around 300m long by 250m wide, the massive stone-faced platform pre-dates the similar ceremonial centre at Chavín de Huantar (see p.324) possibly by as much as four hundred years. This means that Chavín could not have been the original source of temple architectural style, and that much of the iconography and legends associated with what has until recently been called the Chavín cultural phase of Peruvian prehistory actually began 3500 years ago down here on the desert coast.

If you're not up to the walk here, your best option is to take a **motorcycle taxi** from Casma, for $1–2. There are no buses, but some local **colectivos** come here in the mornings from the market area of Casma; alternatively, there are **taxis** from the Plaza de Armas, for around $10, including an hour's wait.

Chanquillo and Mojeque

Several other, lesser-known sites dot the **Sechin Valley**, whose maze of ancient sandy roadways constituted an important pre-Inca junction. The remains of a huge complex of dwellings can be found on the **Pampa de Llamas**, though all you will see nowadays are the walls of adobe huts, deserted more than a thousand years ago. At **Mojeque**, you can see a terraced pyramid with stone stairs and feline and snake designs. Both these sites are best visited from Casma by taxi; expect to pay around $5–10.

Some 12km southeast of Casma lies the ruined, possibly pre-Mochica fort of **Chanquillo**, around which you can wander freely. Trucks leave for here every morning at around 9am from the Petro Peru filling station in Casma – ask the driver to drop you off at "El Castillo", from where it's a thirty-minute walk uphill to the fort. It's an amazing ruin set in a commanding position on a barren hill, with four walls in concentric rings and watchtowers in the middle, keeping an eye over the desert below.

The pyramid of Pañamarca

Heading north from Casma, the first major landmark is the Nepeña river valley. At Km 395 of the Panamerican Highway there is a turn-off on the right that leads 11km to the ruined adobe pyramid of **Pañamarca**. Three large painted panels can be seen here, and on a nearby wall a long procession of warriors has been painted – but all this artwork has been badly damaged by rain. Although an impressive monument to the Mochica culture, dating from around 500 AD, it's not an easy site to visit; the best way is to get a **taxi** from the Plaza de Armas in Casma for around $5.

Chimbote

Until the early part of the twentieth century, **CHIMBOTE** – another 25km beyond the turn-off to Pañamarca – was a quiet fishing port and popular honeymoon spot. Now, it's a busy, rather ugly, modern city characterized by the stench of fish, and with little of interest for tourists. Its sprawling development, which constitutes the country's most spectacular urban growth outside Lima, was stimulated by the Chimbote–Huallanca rail line (built in 1922), a nearby hydroelectric plant, and government planning for an anticipated boom in the anchovy and tuna fishing industry. The population grew rapidly from 5000 in 1940 to 60,000 in 1961 (swollen by squatter settlers from the mountains), and nearly tripling in the next decade to an incredible 159,000 – making it Peru's fifth-largest city, despite the destruction of nearly every building during the 1970 earthquake.

Chimbote has more than thirty fish-packing factories, which explains the rather hard to handle stench of stale fish, a cloud of which the town seems to permanently live under. Even with the crisis in the fishing industry since the early 1970s – overfishing and El Niño have led to bans and strict catch limits for the fishermen – Chimbote accounts for more than 75 percent of Peru's fishing-related activity, and its canning equipment is among the world's most modern.

Practicalities

Most travellers remain in Chimbote overnight at most. The *Hotel Venus*, on Avenida Prado (℡044/321339; ❸), is bearable and not too expensive. The Hostal *El Ruedo*, Lote 15, Urbino Los Pinos (℡044/335560; ❷), a little way from the noisy town centre, is fine and relatively free of the smell. The *Gran Hotel Chimú*, Jr José Galvez 109, on the Plaza 28 de Julio (℡044/321741; ❻), is reasonably priced, offering comfortable rooms and mod cons, and its restaurant, though not cheap, serves some of the best food found along this part of the coast. Another option for eating out is the *Chifa Pekin*, Av Pardo 600 (℡044/346273), just one block from the main plaza, which combines fish and Chinese cuisine in a tasty fashion.

Most important is knowing how to get out of town. Almost all the coastal **buses** travelling north to Trujillo and south to Lima along the Panamerican Highway stop along Bolognesi, just off the Plaza 28 de Julio; Movil Tours, Turismo Chimbote, Expresso Huandoy and Trans Moreno all run daily buses to Huaraz via Patavilca and Casma and mostly nightly services to Caraz via Huallanca (Cañon del Pato) from Jirón Pardo, between Jirón José Galvez and Manuel Ruiz. Turismo Huaraz run the only direct Chimbote–Huaraz bus, twice daily (one daytime, one at night) from Av Pardo 1713 (℡044/321235); buses usually leave from the Terminal Terrestre (stand 42), but also occasionally from the company office, and travel via the rough and adventurous route up the Cañon del Pato (8–9hr to Caraz). **Colectivos** to Trujillo (2–3hr away) leave regularly from opposite the *Hostal Los Angeles*, while colectivos to Lima hang around on Manuel Ruiz, one block towards the sea off Avenida Prado. The **tourist office**, Bolognesi 421 (Mon–Sat 9am–5pm), can advise on transport to sites nearby and sometimes stocks town and regional maps.

The Great Wall of Peru

The desert area around Chimbote, though rarely visited, is littered with archeological remains, including an enormous defensive wall known as the **Great Wall of Peru**, thought to be over a thousand years old. Twenty kilometres north of Chimbote, the Panamerican Highway crosses a rocky outcrop into the Santa Valley, where the wall – a stone and adobe structure more than 50km long – rises from the sands of the desert. The enormous structure was first noticed in 1931 by the Shippee-Johnson Aerial Photographic Expedition, and there are many theories about its construction and purpose. Archeologist Julio Tello thought it was pre-Chimu, since it seems unlikely that the Chimu would have built such a lengthy defensive wall so far inside the limits of their empire. It may also, as the historian Garcilaso de la Vega believed, have been built by the Spaniards as a defence against the threat of Inca invasion from the coast or from the Callejón de Huaylas.

The wall stretches from Tambo Real near the Río Santa estuary in the west up to Chuquicara in the east, where there are scattered remains of pyramids, fortresses, temples and stone houses. To see the wall, take any Trujillo bus north from Chimbote (see above) along the Panamerican Highway, and get off when you see a bridge over the Río Santa. From here, head upstream for three to four hours and you'll arrive at the best surviving section of the wall, just to the west of the Hacienda Tanguche, where the piled stone is cemented with mud to more than 4m high in places.

Further up the valley lies a double-walled construction with outer turrets, discovered by Gene Savoy's aerial expedition in the late 1950s. Savoy reported finding 42 stone-built **strongholds** in the higher Santa Valley in only two days' flying, evidence that supports historians' claims that this was the most populated valley on the coast prior to the Spanish conquest. Hard to believe today, it seems more probable if you bear in mind that this desert region, still alive with wildlife such as desert foxes and condors, is fed by the largest and most reliable of the coastal rivers. In 1962 Savoy led an expedition into the area on foot, finding that most of the parapeted defensive structures he had seen from the air were well hidden from the valley floor. Once you climb up to them, however, you can see (on a clear day) the towering peaks of the Cordillera Blanca to the east and the Pacific Ocean in the west. The climate here is hot but ideal for **camping**, and the only things you'll need to carry are a sun-hat, sunblock, food, ample drinking water and a sleeping roll (blanket and mat); detailed **maps** of the region are available from the Instituto Geografico Nacional in Lima (see p.97). Remember, though, that this is off the beaten track and there is no tourism infrastructure whatsoever, so make sure someone knows where you're going and your expected return date.

The Viru Valley

Continuing north towards Trujillo, the Panamerican Highway cuts up the usually dry riverbed of Chau, a straggling, scrubby green trail through the absolutely barren desert of the **Viru Valley**. In the Gallinazo period, around 300 AD, the Viru Valley saw great changes: simple dwelling sites became full-fledged villages with stone pyramids; improved irrigation produced a great population increase; and a society with complex labour patterns and distribution systems began to develop. The Gallinazo started to build defensive walls, just prior to being invaded by the Mochicas (around 500 AD) in their military conquests south as far as the Santa and Nepeña valleys. Later on, during the Chimu era, the population was dramatically reduced again, perhaps through migration north to Chan Chan, capital of this highly centralized pre-Inca state.

Viru and around

The valley's main town is **VIRU**, a small place at Km 515 of the Panamerican Highway, with a bridge over the riverbed that, in the dry season, looks as though it has never seen rain. An impressive cultural centre around 300 AD, when it was occupied by the Gallinazo or Viru people, today the town offers very little to the tourist. The only reason to consider staying here is to visit the abundant **archeological remains** in the vicinity, though you're probably better off taking a guided tour from Trujillo with one of the companies listed on p.375.

The most interesting ruin in the area is the **Grupo Gallinazo** near Tomabal, 24km east of Viru up a side road just north of the town's bridge. Here in the valley you can see the dwellings, murals and pyramids of a significant religious and administrative centre, its internal layout derived from kinship networks. The site covers an area of four square kilometres and archeologists estimate that it once held over 30,000 rooms. All the buildings at the site are built entirely of adobe, with separate cultivation plots irrigated by an intricate canal system. You can also make out the adobe walls and ceremonial platform of a Gallinazo temple, on one of the hilltops at Tomabal.

From Viru, the Panamerican Highway cuts north across a desert plain, close to the sea. Before reaching Trujillo, the road runs down into the expansive plains of the Moche Valley, with its great Mochica temples of the Sun and Moon (see p.384).

Huaraz and the Cordillera Blanca

Situated in the steeply walled valley of the **Callejón de Huaylas, Huaraz** is the focal point of inland Ancash. Although not one of Peru's most interesting towns, Huaraz has a lively atmosphere and makes an ideal springboard for exploring the surrounding mountains. It is dominated by the **Cordillera Blanca**, the highest tropical mountain range in the world, and **Huascarán**, Peru's highest peak. Only a day's bus ride from Lima or Trujillo, it's one of the best places to base yourself if you have any interest in hiking, mountaineering or just sightseeing. The region's best weather comes between May and September when the skies are nearly always blue and it rains very little. Between October and April, however, the skies are often cloudy and most afternoons you can expect some pretty heavy rains.

Besides the mountain scenery, the region boasts spectacular ruins such as **Chavín de Huantar**, at the bottom end of the **Callejón de Conchucos**, the natural thermal baths at **Monterrey** and **Chancos**, and immense glacial lakes, like **Lago Parón**, surrounded by snowcapped peaks, and the beautiful **Llanganuco**. Throughout the whole area, too, you come upon unusual and exotic flora like the enormous, tropical *Puya Raymondi* plants, and traditional mountain villages where unwritten legends are encapsulated only in ancient carved stones and the memories of the local peasant population.

Huaraz

Less than a century ago, **HUARAZ** – some 400km from Lima – was still a fairly isolated community, barricaded to the east by the dazzling snowcapped peaks of the Cordillera Blanca and separated from the coast by the dry, dark Cordillera Negra. Between these two mountain chains the powerful Río Santa has formed a valley, the **Callejón de Huaylas**, a region with strong traditions of local independence. In 1885 the people of the Callejón waged a guerrilla war against the Lima authorities, which led to the whole valley being in rebel hands for several months. The revolt was sparked by a native leader, the charismatic Pedro Pablo Atusparia, and thirteen other village mayors protesting against excessive taxation and labour abuses. They were sent straight to prison and humiliated by having their braided hair (a traditional sign of status) cut off, so the local peasants reacted by overrunning Huaraz, freeing their chieftains, and expelling all officials before looting the mansions of wealthy landlords and merchants (many of them expatriate Englishmen who had been here since the Wars of Independence). The rebellion was eventually quashed by an army battalion from the coast, which recaptured Huaraz while the Indians were celebrating their annual fiesta. But even today, Atusparia's memory survives close to local hearts, and inhabitants of the area's remote villages remain unimpressed by the central government's attempts to control the region.

Arrival and information

Most people arrive by **bus** from Lima, which takes eight or nine hours; the road is pretty good and so are the buses. You can expect to pay $8–12 for the journey, depending on the level of comfort; Cruz del Sur are, as usual, the safest and most comfortable option, closely followed by Movil Tours. Both offer day and night buses and a range of services from standard to deluxe, which includes a packed lunch and video. Some cheaper bus companies, as well as Colectivos Comité 14, also run daily services here from Jirón Leticia in Lima Centro. Companies coming from and going to Trujillo (8–10hr; around $8) include Cruz del Sur, Turismo Chimbote and Colectivos Comité 14. Coming from or going to Chimbote (5–7hr; $7) or Caraz (6–8hr; $7), you'll probably travel with Turismo Chimbote, Rodriguez or Empresa Huandoy; arriving direct from Casma (4–5hr; $6) you'll almost certainly travel on Empresa Moreno. All the above buses come in at and leave from or close to their companies' offices (see p.310 for details).

Few people arrive **by air** since there is no regular service, though Aero Condor flies from Lima around once a week between June and August. This drops you off at a small airstrip close to the village of Anta, some 23km north of Huaraz; from here it's thirty minutes into the city by colectivo or bus, both of which leave from the main road outside the airstrip.

Tourist information is available from the Oficina de Promoción Turística, Pasaje Alfonso Martel Oficina 1, just off Avenida Luzuriaga by the Plaza de Armas (Mon–Fri 9am–1pm & 5–8pm, Sat 9am–1pm). Staff are very helpful and offer free photocopies of trekking maps but often do not have any city maps; these can usually be obtained, though, from good hotels or tour companies.

Getting around

Much of Huaraz town can be easily negotiated on foot once you've acclimatized to the altitude (3091m); however, some of the more remote sectors should not be walked alone at night since mugging and even rape are rare but not unknown in recent years. The **Avenida Luzuriaga** is the town centre's north–south axis, where most of the restaurants, nightlife and tour agencies are based. The **Parque Ginebra**, set just behind Luzuriaga and the Plaza de Armas, is a pleasant little plaza but something of an afterthought in terms of city planning and not yet fully integrated into the network of roads. A city centre **taxi** ride costs less than $1, while motorbike rental can be arranged through the *Restaurant Monte Rosa* (see p.307) any afternoon or evening.

Colectivos and **local buses** connect Huaraz with all the main towns and villages north – Anta, Marcara, Carhuaz, Yungay and Caraz – at very reasonable rates (50¢–$2 for up to 2hr); these can be caught from just over the river bridge from the town centre, on either side of the main road, beside the Río Quillcay. Just before the bridge in Huaraz colectivos heading south to Catac (80¢) and Olleros ($1) can be caught daily every thirty minutes from the end of Jirón Caceres, just below the market area. Buses to Chiquián are run by Chiquián Tours from block 1 of Calle Huascarán, near the market, and leave every hour or so. For short journeys **within the city**, the best option is one of the regular colectivos, which run on fixed routes along avenidas Luzuriaga and Centenario (40–60¢).

Accommodation

Even in the high season, around August, it's rarely difficult to find **accommodation** at a reasonable price. Within the centre of town, from the Plaza de Armas

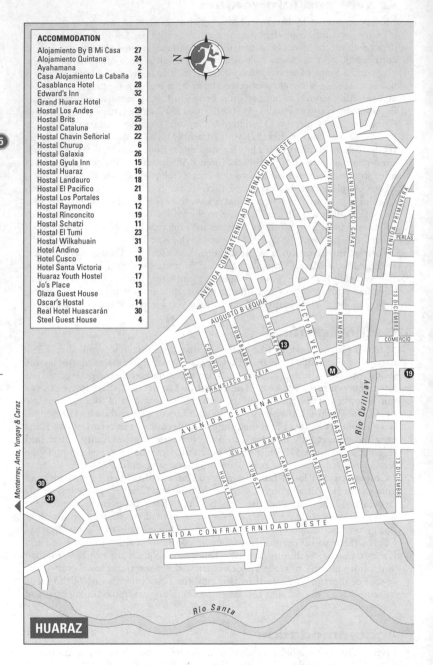

ACCOMMODATION

Alojamiento By B Mi Casa	27
Alojamiento Quintana	24
Ayahamana	2
Casa Alojamiento La Cabaña	5
Casablanca Hotel	28
Edward's Inn	32
Grand Huaraz Hotel	9
Hostal Los Andes	29
Hostal Brits	25
Hostal Cataluna	20
Hostal Chavin Señorial	22
Hostal Churup	6
Hostal Galaxia	26
Hostal Gyula Inn	15
Hostal Huaraz	16
Hostal Landauro	18
Hostal El Pacifico	21
Hostal Los Portales	8
Hostal Raymondi	12
Hostal Rinconcito	19
Hostal Schatzi	11
Hostal El Tumi	23
Hostal Wilkahuain	31
Hotel Andino	3
Hotel Cusco	10
Hotel Santa Victoria	7
Huaraz Youth Hostel	17
Jo's Place	13
Olaza Guest House	1
Oscar's Hostal	14
Real Hotel Huascarán	30
Steel Guest House	4

Monterrey, Anta, Yungay & Caraz

HUARAZ

Río Santa

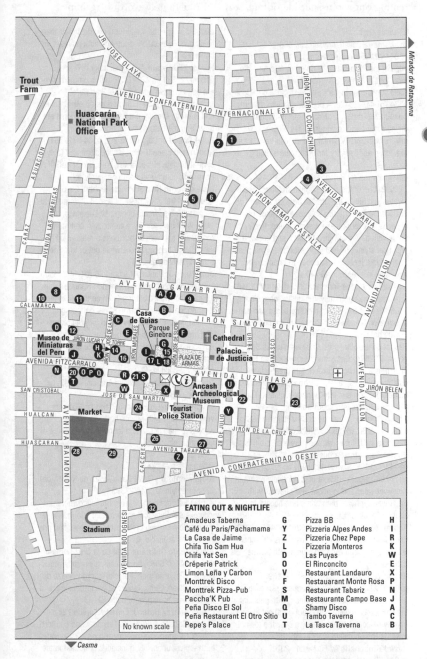

Trout Farm

Huascarán National Park Office

Mirador de Rataquena

Casa de Guias

Parque Ginebra

Cathedral

Palacio de Justicia

PLAZA DE ARMAS

Ancash Archeological Museum

Tourist Police Station

Market

Museo de Miniaturas del Peru

Stadium

Casma

EATING OUT & NIGHTLIFE

Amadeus Taberna	**G**	Pizza BB	**H**
Café du Paris/Pachamama	**Y**	Pizzeria Alpes Andes	**I**
La Casa de Jaime	**Z**	Pizzeria Chez Pepe	**R**
Chifa Tio Sam Hua	**L**	Pizzeria Monteros	**K**
Chifa Yat Sen	**D**	Las Puyas	**W**
Créperie Patrick	**O**	El Rinconcito	**E**
Limon Leña y Carbon	**V**	Restaurant Landauro	**X**
Monttrek Disco	**F**	Restauarant Monte Rosa	**P**
Monttrek Pizza-Pub	**S**	Restaurant Tabariz	**N**
Paccha'K Pub	**M**	Restaurante Campo Base	**J**
Peña Disco El Sol	**Q**	Shamy Disco	**A**
Peña Restaurant El Otro Sitio	**U**	Tambo Taverna	**C**
Pepe's Palace	**T**	La Tasca Taverna	**B**

No known scale

along Avenida Luzuriaga, there are countless **hostels** and many smaller places renting out rooms; outside of high season it is definitely worth bargaining.

Budget

Ayahamana Pasaje Agustin Loli 463 ⊤044/721266. A pleasant place on the eastern edge of the Plazuela de la Soledad, it is also the base for Llamatrek (see p.306). ❸

Casa Alojamiento La Cabaña Jr José de Sucre 1224 ⊤044/723428. A popular and very friendly *pensión* with safe, comfortable accommodation, a dining room and hot water all day. Rooms have private bath and TV, while guests also have access to kitchen and laundry facilities, plus a dining room. ❷

Edward's Inn Av Bolognesi 121 ⊤/Ⓕ044/722692. One of the most popular trekkers' hostels, located just below the market area (at the end of Jr Caceres) and offering an excellent range of services in a very pleasant atmosphere. Rooms come with or without private bath, and hot water is almost always available. The owner, who speaks English, is a highly experienced trekker, climber and mountain rescuer. ❷–❸

Hostal Los Andes Tarapaca 316 ⊤044/721346. A pleasant enough family-run hostel, on a slightly noisy street, it has a useful notice board and some information on trekking; rooms are with or without private bath. ❷

Hostal Churup Jr Pedro Campos 735, La Soledad ⊤044/722584. Just 5 minutes' walk from Plaza de Armas and with a garden, this great-value establishment has a family atmosphere and offers laundry, kitchen and left-luggage facilities. They also have lots of info about trekking. ❷–❸

Hostal Galaxia Jr Juan de la Cruz Romero 638 ⊤044/722230, Ⓕ726535. Quite central, with an amicable staff, hot water and private bathrooms. ❸

Hostal Gyula Inn Parque Ginebra 632 ⊤044/721567, Ⓦwww.hostalgy.on.to. Located above an Internet office, this is relatively plain but excellent value and is bright and cheerful with great views, private bathrooms and access to kitchen facilities. ❷

Hostal Huaraz Av Luzuriaga 529 ⊤044/721982. Centrally located, basic, this place has little character but is cheap even for rooms with private bath. ❷

Hostal Landauro Jr José de Sucre 109 ⊤044/721212. One of the cheapest places in town, right on the Plaza de Armas, with pleasant but small rooms (with or without bath) set along narrow balconies boasting views over the town towards the Cordillera Blanca. ❷

Hostal Rinconcito Av Fitzcarrald 236 ⊤044/727591. A bit too close to the bus terminals, but very good value for a slightly better than basic pad. Reasonably clean and with private baths. ❷

Hostal Wilkawain Av Centenario 1167 ⊤044/727331 or 722211. Situated on the northern edge of town opposite the *Gran Hotel Huascarán* (see p.304), this offers excellent value and is pretty friendly if a bit rough; the rooms are basic and the bathrooms shared. ❷

Hotel Cusco Jr Cajamarca 204 ⊤044/722561. A modernized place that's friendly, clean and fairly central, though hidden away up a side street off Av Raimondi; communal bathrooms only. ❷

Huaraz Youth Hostel Parque Ginebra 28-G ⊤044/721811, Ⓕ722306. Located on a quaint little plaza in the streets behind Av Luzuriaga, this place is modern and very clean, with communal rooms and showers at reasonable rates. You can safely leave baggage here while out of town on trekking expeditions. ❷

Jo's Place Jr Daniel Villarzan 276 ⊤044/725505. Located north of the main street in Huaraz, some 10 minutes' walk from the town centre, over the river bridge, then the fourth street on the right. Its relaxed, secure atmosphere, comfortable rooms and great value make it popular with backpackers. It also has a large garden and terrace and views across to the Cordillera Blanca. English newspapers are available. ❷

Olaza Guest House Jr Julio Arguedas 1242, La Soledad ⊤044/722529, Ⓦwww.andeanexplorer.com. Nice large rooms, very clean and with private baths as well as access to the kitchen and laundry; good source of local information. ❸

Moderate

Alojamiento B y B Mi Casa Av 27 de Noviembre 773, Tarapaca ⊤044/723375, Ⓔbmark@ddm.com.pe. Very friendly owners provide excellent service; some tourist information, a dining room serving breakfasts, hot water and private baths available. ❷–❹

Alojamiento Quintana Juan de la Cruz Romero 411 ⊤044/726060. An increasingly popular backpacker joint, less than 3 blocks from the Plaza de Armas. Clean, comfortable and well managed, and most rooms have private bath. ❸–❹

Grand Huaraz Hotel Jr Larrea y Loredo 721 ⊤044/722227, Ⓕ726536. This new and comfortable hotel offers the usual mod cons – TV, private bath – plus, unusually, it includes breakfast in the price. ❺

Hostal Los Portales Av Raimondi 903
044/728184. A spacious, often dimly-lit hotel;
the beds are large and comfortable and it's well
situated for most bus terminals and with a large,
safe luggage store for trekkers. Rooms are clean
and comfortable with private baths, and there's a
restaurant. ⑤
Hostal Raymondi Av Raimondi 820
044/721082. Large, clean with a spacious, old-
fashioned lobby. Full of character, it has plenty of
rooms with private bath. ④
Hostal Schatzi Jr Simón Bolivar 419
044/723074, schatzihs@yahoo.com. A lovely
little place set around a lush garden patio; very
friendly. ③–④
Hotel Santa Victoria Av Gamarra 690
044/722422, 724870. Pretty good value,
offering fairly modern rooms with TV and private
shower (which usually have hot water); ask for a
room with a view towards the Cordillera Blanca. ⑤
Oscar's Hostal Jr José de la Mar 624 /
044/722720, marciocoronel@hotmail.com.
Pretty central but a bit dark and uninspiring,
though the rooms are clean and many have private
bath. ③–④
Steel Guest House C Alejandro Maguina 1467, in
front of the *Hotel Andino* 044/729709,
steelguesthouse@yahoo.com. A five-storey
building with a pleasant communal area on the
second floor offering TV, small library and a billiard
table. Rooms have private baths, 24hr hot water
and there's a laundry available. ③–④

Expensive

Casablanca Hotel Av Tarapaca 138
044/722602, 724801. A quite comfortable
and upmarket hotel that seems quite out of place
on this downmarket street; used by a lot of tour
groups. ⑥
Hostal Brits Jr Mariscal Caceres 399
/044/722771. A smart new place, rooms have
private bath and colour TV. Other comforts include
a restaurant and bar. ⑥
Hostal El Tumi Jr José de San Martin 1121
044/721784 or 721913, hottumi@net
.cosapidata.com.pe. Reasonable value, featuring
clean, comfortable rooms with private bath and TV.
There's also a large restaurant and a travel agent.
⑥
Hotel Andino Jr Pedro Cochachín 357 044/
721662, 722830, andino@mail.cosapidata
.com.pe. An uphill hike away from the centre of
town, with beautiful views over the Cordillera Blanca
and plush rooms in the best hotel in town. A variety
of rooms to choose from, with or without terraces
and fireplaces. The food is also excellent. ⑦–⑧

Real Hotel Huascarán block 10 of Av Centenario
/ 044/721640, 722821 or 721709,
jezquerra@infotex.com.pe. The biggest hotel in
Huaraz. It's quite plush, with cabins and suites,
carpeting, good service, a games room and pleasant bedrooms. ⑦

Out of town

Centro Turístico Las Cordilleras Yungar
044/614530, 721111, cordilleras@rocket-
mail.com. Excellent value in a beautiful setting,
most rooms are cabins with fine views. Horse-
riding is offered around the Cordillera Negra, but
even if you don't intend to stay here, it's worth visiting for the views from its restaurant *El Herraje*,
which serves excellent local cuisine under the
shade of avocado trees. You can also camp here
($2 per person). ④
Hostal Nogal Jr Los Libertadores 106, Monterrey
044/725929. Just a couple of hundred yards from
the thermal baths at Monterrey, this is a very affordable place with hot water; rooms or slightly more
expensive suites (these with TV) are available. ④–⑤
Hostal El Patio de Monterrey Av Monterrey,
Monterrey 044/724965, 726967,
elpatio@terra.com.pe; reservations
01/4496295, 4480254. Located in the village
of Monterrey and just a couple of hundred yards
from the thermal baths. A luxurious complex of
clean, attractive rooms and more expensive bungalows based around an attractive patio and lovely
mock-colonial gardens. ⑥–⑧
Hostal Las Retamas Cascapampa 250
044/721722, 722191. Located just before the
turn-off to Wilkawain, over the bridge beyond the
Gran Hotel Huascarán, this is a pleasant place with
rooms and bungalows based around a grassy garden. It also has a games room, a nice lounge and
a cafetería. Discounts for mountaineers. ⑤
Hostal Sterling Tarica 044/790299. A kilometre
or so beyond Paltay, just off the road to Carhuaz,
this is a rather quaint, quiet, friendly place not too
far out of Huaraz, with a rustic restaurant
attached. The village of Tarica itself doesn't have
much to offer, besides decent views. ③
Hotel Eccame Km 18 from Huaraz towards
Carhuaz 044/721933. A full-on Peruvian holiday
resort offering stylish accommodation, a restaurant, sports facilities and horse-riding. ⑤
Real Hotel Baños Termales Monterrey Av
Monterrey, Monterrey 044/727690. An old hotel
full of character and style and attached to thermal
baths (residents have free access). The fine rooms
have hot showers, and there's a splendid restaurant overlooking the heated pool. They also have
bungalows, which cost a bit more. ④–⑥

The City

Although well over 3000m above sea level, Huaraz has a somewhat cosmopolitan, and very busy, city centre. It has developed rapidly in terms of tourism and commerce since the completion of the highway through the river basin from Paramonga, and the opening of mainly US- and Canadian-owned zinc, silver and gold mines both in the Cordillera Negra and the Callejón de Conchucos. The town itself has a distinct lack of cultural emphasis within the tourism industry, though this is made up in part, of course, by the conventional tours to major rural sites like Chavín de Huantar.

Virtually the entire city was levelled by the 1970 earthquake, and the old houses have been replaced with single-storey modern structures topped with gleaming tin roofs. Surrounded by eucalyptus groves and fields, it's still not quite the vision it once was, but it's a decent enough place in which to recuperate from the rigours of hard travel. There are many easy walks just outside of town, and if you fancy an afternoon's stroll you can simply go out to the eastern edge and follow one of the paths or streams uphill.

With glaciated peaks and significant trekking country close to the city, Huaraz is dominated by the prospect of mountaineering, and the city's only real tourist attraction is the **Ancash Archeological Museum**, at Av Luzuriaga 762, facing the modern Plaza de Armas (Mon–Sat 8.30am–6.30pm, Sun 9am–noon; $1.50). Fronting attractive, landscaped gardens, this small but interesting place contains a superb collection of Chavín, Chimu, Wari, Mochica and Recuay ceramics, as well as some expertly trepanned skulls. It also displays an abundance of the finely chiselled stone monoliths typical of this mountain region, most of them products of the Recuay and Chavín cultures. One of its most curious exhibits is a *goniometro*, an early version of the surveyor's theodolite, probably over a thousand years old and used for finding alignments and exact 90-degree angles in building construction. On the other side of the Plaza de Armas from the museum is the **Cathedral** (daily 7am–7pm; free). Completely rebuilt after being destroyed in the earthquake, it has nothing special to see inside, but its vast blue-tiled roof makes a good landmark and, if you look closely, appears to mirror one of the glaciated mountain peaks, the Nevado Huanstán (6395m), behind. Also close to the Plaza de Armas, the Banco Wiese has a **Sala Cultural** where they rotate exhibitions of photos or artwork, mainly relevant to the city or region (Mon–Fri 9am–1pm & 4.30–6.30pm; free). The only other museum to merit a brief visit is the **Museo de Miniaturas del Peru** (Mon–Fri 9am–5.30pm; 85¢), in the gardens of the *Gran Hotel Huascarán*, which contains an interesting collection of pre-Hispanic art from the Huaraz region and a range of local folk art and crafts, including the fine red Callejón de Huaylas ceramics. It also displays a small model of Yungay (see p.317) prior to the entire town being buried under a mudslide, also the result of the 1970 earthquake.

A fifteen-minute walk up Avenida Raimondi from the centre of Huaraz, then across the Río Quillcay bridge and down Avenida Confraternidad Internacional Oeste brings you to the regional **Trout Farm** (daily 7am–6pm; 20¢, includes guided tour), or *Estación Pesqueria*, run by the Ministero de Pesqueria. It breeds thousands of rainbow trout every year and you can observe the process from beginning to end (more interesting than you might think); much of the excellent trout available in the restaurants of Huaraz comes from here.

There are one or two vantage points on the hills around the city of Huaraz, but the best and most accessible is the **Mirador de Rataquenua**, about a two-hour walk each way, though not advisable for single tourists since there have been muggings reported on this route. Notwithstanding this, it commands a splendid location, high above the town to the southeast, and looks out over the Callejón de Huaylas. To get there, follow Avenida Villón out beyond the cemetery and up through the woods to the cross. Most taxi drivers will take you there and back for less than $8, which is certainly safer than walking if you're on your own.

Hiking in the Huaraz region

In 1932 a German expedition became the first group to successfully scale Huascarán and the concept of *Andinismo* – Andean mountaineering – was born. However, you don't have to be a mountaineer to enjoy the high Andes of Ancash, and there is plenty of scope for trekking as well in the two major mountain chains accessible from Huaraz. The closest is the **Cordillera Blanca**, detailed on p.319. The **Cordillerra Huayhuash**, about 50km south of the Cordillera Blanca, is still relatively off the beaten tourist trail. About 31km long, it is dominated by the Yerupajá glacier, and *Andinistas* claim it to be one of the most spectacular trekking routes in the world. Wherever you end up, be sure to pay heed to the rules of **responsible trekking**: carry away your waste, particularly above the snow line, where even organic waste does not decompose (if you can pack it in the first place, you can pack it back out). Note too that you should always use a camping stove – campfires are strictly prohibited in Huascarán National Park, and wood is scarce anyway. Just as important, though, is to realize that the solar irradiation in this part of the Andes is stronger than that found in the North American Rockies, European Alps or even the Himalayas. This creates unique glacier conditions, making the ice here less stable and consequently the addition of an experienced local guide essential for the safety of any serious climbing or ice-walking expedition. It's also vital to be fit, particularly if you are going it alone.

If you intend to hike at all, it's essential to spend at least a couple of days **acclimatizing** to the altitude beforehand; for high mountain climbing, this should be extended to at least five days. Although Huaraz itself is 3060m above sea level, most of the Cordilleras' more impressive peaks are over 6000m. If you're going to trek in Huascarán National Park, register beforehand with the **park office**, at the top end of Avenida Raimondi (☎044/722086), and at the **Casa de Guías**, Parque Ginebra 28-G (Mon–Fri 9am–1pm & 4–8pm, Sat 9am–1pm; ☎044/721811, ⓕ722306, ⓦclientes.telematic.com.pe/agmp), where there's also a helpful notice board, worth checking to see if there are any groups about to leave on treks that you might want to join. The National Police (☎044/793327, ⓕ793292, ⓔusam@pnp.gob.pe) have a mountain rescue team.

Ideally you should have detailed maps and one or other of the excellent **guidebooks**, *Backpacking and Trekking in Peru and Bolivia*, *Trails of the Cordillera Blanca and Huayhuash*, or *The High Andes: A Guide for Climbers* (all detailed on p.602). These aren't always available in Huaraz, though you should be able to get them at the South American Explorers' Club in Lima (see p.103). **Maps**, too, are available there, or from the Casa de Guías, where there's also a list of official local mountain guides, as well as lots of local expertise and the Andean Mountain Rescue Corp on hand. Both the Casa de Guías and the park office can give you up-to-the-minute advice on the best and safest areas for trekking, since this region is not without its political danger zones. For additional information on trekking in the region, try the tourist information office (see p.299), one of the tour and travel companies listed on p.310, or the guides listed opposite. Also offering very useful assistance to climbers, AOTUM (the Asociación Peruana de Operadores de Turismo de Montaña ⓦ www.andean-explorer.com/apotum) is based at the *Hotel Andino*. Other Peruvian **mountaineering associations** are all based in Lima (see p.99).

There are three levels of **guides** available: certified mountain guides, who cost from $60 a day; mountain guides undergoing the one-year trial period after training, from $40 a day; and trekking guides, who cost from $30 a day. Note that these costs don't include transport or accommodation. Recommended guides include Alberto Cafferata, a trekking guide contactable through Pony Expeditions (see p.311); David Gonzales Castromonte, Pasaje Coral Vega 354, Huarupampa, Huaraz (ⓣ044/722213); Oscar Ciccomi, who is based in Lima and is contactable through Viajes Vivencial, Los Cerezos 480, Chaclacayo, Lima (ⓣ/ⓕ01/4972394); or Eduardo Figueroa, at *Edward's Inn* (see p.302). All speak English and Spanish. For local **tour operators** offering guided treks, see the box on p.310). High Mountain Guides (members of UIAGM - Unión Internacional de Asociaciones de Guías de Montaña), contactable through the Casa de Guias, include: Selio Billón, with 22 years' experience and one of the founders of La Asociación de Guías and the Casa de Guías; Arista Monasterio, who provides integrated and customised services; Michel Burger (owner of the restaurant *Bistro de los Andes* in Huaraz), who offers trekking and fishing (see ⓦ www.perouvoyage.com).

Porters cost between $15 and $20 a day, depending on whether they are leaders or assistants, and are not supposed to climb over 6000m, while **mule drivers** (*arrieros*) charge from $5 to $8 a day, plus around $4 a day per animal. Expedition **cooks** usually charge the same as *arrieros*. **Llama-packing**, whereby llamas carry the baggage, is a new initiative designed to promote ecotourism in the region; for Llamatrek, contact Jorge Martel Alva, C Agustin Loli 463, Plazuela de la Soledad, Huaraz (ⓣ044/721266, ⓦ www.geocities.com /perullamatrek) or ask for details in the Casa de Guías, Parque Ginebra, Huaraz (ⓣ044/721811).

Eating, drinking and entertainment

There's no shortage of **restaurants** in Huaraz, though they do vary considerably in value and quality. There's also a lively nightlife scene, with several **peñas** hosting traditional Andean music, as well as a few **clubs** where locals and tourists can relax, keep warm and unwind during the evenings or at weekends. Nightlife joints start to open from 7pm and can go on until 3am. There's a **cinema** next to Banco de Wiese, on Jirón José de Sucre. A new **folklore centre** opened in 2002, Centro Folklorico Cultural – Waracushun (Jr Bolivar 1101, Belen, Huaraz) with the aim of making the local and regional music and dance culture more accessible; open daily 11am–11pm, it generally has live music and dance shows at weekends, and most days serves reasonable meals and snacks.

Restaurants

Café de Paris Jr San Martin 687. Open 24hr for breakfast, snacks, kebabs and French pastries.
La Casa de Jaime A Gridilla 267, four blocks west of the Plaza de Armas. An inexpensive and very friendly place where they serve a mix of Peruvian meals and tasty snacks. You're also likely to meet other travellers, trekkers and climbers.
Chifa Tio Sam Hua in the passage at block 8 of Av Luzuriaga. The most traditional and arguably

the best *chifa* in Huaraz, they offer a broad selection of Chinese and Peruvian meals in a friendly environment.
Chifa Yat Sen on the corner of Av Raimondi and Comercio. A pleasant little Chinese restaurant, offering amazing-value ($1.50) three-course set lunches with a Peruvian twist; it also has a range of standard Chinese dishes available most evenings from around 6pm.

Fiestas in Huaraz

Throughout the year various **fiestas** take place in the city and its surrounding villages and hamlets. They are always bright, energetic occasions, with *chicha* (beer) and *aguardiente* flowing freely, as well as roast pigs, bullfights, and vigorous communal dancing with the town folk dressed in outrageous masks and costumes. The main festival in the city of Huaraz is usually in the first week of **February** and celebrates Carnival. In **June** (check with the tourist office for exact dates each year), Huaraz hosts the Semana del Andinismo (the Andean Mountaineering and Skiing Week), which includes trekking, climbing and national and international ski competitions, on the Pastoruri Glacier. Note that during this period prices of hotels and restaurants increase considerably. Other festivals include the folklore celebrations in the first week of **August** for Coyllur-Huaraz, plus the Virgen de la Asunción, in Huata and Chancas during mid-August. Late **September** sees the festival of the Virgen de Las Mercedes, celebrated in Carhuaz, and other rural get-togethers that you'll often come across en route to sites and ruins in the Callejón de Huaylas.

Crêperie Patrick Av Luzuriaga 422 ☎044/692474. Centrally located close to the corner with Av Raimondi, serving excellent crêpes at bearable prices; they also serve guinea pig, *rabbit al vino*, fondue and nice sweets.

La Estación Av Luzuriaga 1045, Plaza Belen ☎044/723190. A decent grill and steak restaurant with a range of meats and other dishes, plus a video bar that's fun at weekends.

Limón Leña y Carbón Luzuriaga 1002 ☎044/693360. A really good seafood restaurant which has fresh fish delivered from Chimbote; open daily 9am until midnight, they also serve local trout, meat dishes and pizzas in the evening.

Monttrek Pizza-pub Luzuriaga 646 ☎044/721124, ©monttrek@terra.com.pe. A spacious place, very popular with trekkers and a great meeting place with a useful notice board for contacting like-minded backpackers. Serves delicious food and plays good music. Has a climbing wall, maps and aerial photos of the region.

Pachamama San Martin 687 ☎044/721834, ⓦwww.huaraz.net/pachamama. A fine café-bar, with a spacious and attractive environment, good music, games and itinerant exhibitions and silver craft work; serves good wines, a range of other drinks, fish, chicken, meats and pastas.

Pepe's Palace Av Raimondi 622. Dishes up decent international food, including pizzas, and is a good place to meet fellow trekkers, though it's only open June–Sept.

Pizza BB José de la Mar 674. Cheap pizzas at this hole-in-the-wall.

Pizzeria Chez Pepe Av Luzuriaga 570. Run by the same Pepe who runs *Pepe's Palace*; again, the food is good, but more importantly this is the place to make contact with other trekkers and local trek leaders. Pepe will also change dollars cash.

Pizzeria Monteros Jr José de la Mar 661. An upmarket pizzeria with good beer and delectable meat dishes. Like many restaurants and pizzerias in Peru, it tries to cover all bases as far as popular dishes go.

Las Puyas Jr Morales 535. An old-fashioned restaurant popular with visitors and locals, serving cheap breakfasts, snacks and lunches of all kinds.

Restaurant Alpes Andes Parque Ginebra 28 ☎044/721811. Commonly thought of as the *Casa de Guías* restaurant because of its location in the same building, this place dishes up superb pizzas and pastas for very good prices, and great mulled wine.

Restaurant Bistro de los Andes Jr Morales 823 ☎044/726249, ©michel@hotmail.com. A great place for breakfast (though not open Sunday mornings), with seats outside, good yogurts, coffee and pancakes; also popular during the evening. Features a book exchange as well.

Restaurant Landauro Jr José de Sucre 109. Well worth visiting for its cheap pizzas, though gets very busy on weekend nights.

Restaurant Monte Rosa Av Luzuriaga 496. Excellent pizzas and one or two other Italian dishes, plus a wide range of snacks and cold drinks; popular with travellers but not that cheap.

Restaurant Tabariz corner of avs Raimondi and Fitzcarrald. A popular local eating house, it has a wide range of snacks, soups and meals at reasonable prices in a hectic environment, with old-fashioned decor. Good set menus.

Restaurant Vegeteriano Nuevo Horizonte Jr José de Sucre 476. An inexpensive café that serves mainly (but not exclusively) vegetarian meals and snacks. Specialities include muesli and yogurt breakfasts, pizzas and special vitamin-enhanced juices.

Vegetarian Café Av Luzuriaga 672, second floor. Specializing in decent vegetarian fare and Italian dishes; a worthwhile place for breakfasts, fruit salads, yogurt, omelettes, soups, pancakes etc. Excellent set menus at lunchtime.

Restaurante Campo Base Av Luzuriaga 407 ☎044/725772, @andeway@terra.com.pe. A good pizzeria which also serves local and international dishes well aimed at the trekking and climbing crowd. Excellent food and drinks, and often hosting live folk music at weekends. It's the best place in the city for *cuy à la Huaracina* (guinea pig, Huaraz-style); daily 4.30–11pm

Pubs, music bars and clubs

Amadeus Taberna Parque Ginebra. Situated at the back of the Interbanc, in an alley between the Plaza de Armas and Parque Ginebra, this is Huaraz's most established nightclub. It serves meals and plays popular dance music, as well as hosting Andean folk groups. Entry $1.

Monttrek Disco by the Plaza de Armas on Jr José de Sucre. One of the better discos in town; large with quite exciting music, especially at weekends.

Paccha'K Pub Centenario 290. A good trekkers' joint with a notice board for messages, it hosts lively Andean folk music shows most weekends.

Peña Disco El Sol Av Luzuriaga. The liveliest disco in the city, particularly during October and November, when high school kids visit the region en masse. Entry $1.

Peña Restaurant El Otro Sitio 28 de Julio 570. More of a restaurant than a nightclub, though there's good live folk and criolla music at weekends.

Peña Tio Tiburcio 28 de Julio 560. Just one block up from the Plaza de Armas, this popular spot with locals and travellers hosts Andean folk and pop most weekends.

El Refugio Jr Teófilo Castillo 556 ☎044/724604. A video pub with a decent range of Latin and European sounds; food is fine, mainly meats, pastas and trout, but some Chinese dishes, too.

El Rinconcito Julián de Morales 757. A video pub with quite a few movies, good food and snacks.

Shamy Disco Av Gamara 678. A popular disco and video bar, playing mostly international and Latin pop. Entry $1.

Tambo Taverna Jr José de la Mar 776. A restaurant-cum-*peña* serving good drinks, with occasional live music after 10pm – one of Huaraz's best nightspots.

La Tasca Taberna Simon Bolivar 653. A small, friendly video bar with some decent Latin music and international pop and rock.

Shopping

Huaraz is a noted **crafts** centre, producing, in particular, very reasonably priced hand-made leather goods (custom-made if you've got a few days to wait around). Other bargains include woollen hats, scarves and jumpers, embroidered blankets, and interesting replicas of the Chavín stone carvings. Most of these items can be bought from the stalls in the small **artesanía market** in covered walkways set back off Avenida Luzuriaga (daily 2pm–dusk), or, for more choice, in the Mercado Model. For individual shops, try Tierras Andinas, Parque Ginebra, which has some fine handicrafts and local artwork, or the Centro Artesanal, next to the Post Office on the plaza, which sells textiles, ceramics, jewellery, stone and leather work.

Huaraz is also renowned for its **food**, in particular its excellent local cheese, honey and *manjar blanco* (a traditional sweet made out of condensed milk). These can all be bought in the **food market**, in the backstreets around Avenida José de San Martin (daily 6am–6pm). Market Ortiz, Av Luzuriaga 401, is one of the best **supermarkets** in town, while Centro Naturista, Fitzcarrald 356, is good for natural medicines, yogurt, herbs and cosmetics.

Photographic equipment can be bought from Shala, Firzcarrald 369; Photo Blas, Av Luzuriaga 547; Video River, Av Luzuriaga 641; Kodak Shop, Av Luzuriaga 625; and Foto Shop, Av Luzuriaga 419, which also does one-hour developing. **Camping equipment** is available to rent from most of the adventure-tour companies (see overleaf) plus Mount Climb, Jr Mariscal Caceres 421, which also sells trekking foods, has a contact notice board and stocks a range

△ Huascarán, at 6768m, Peru's highest peak

of tents, boots, sleeping bags, crampons, ice axes and other essentials for rent. Galaxia Expeditions, Leonisa y Lescanao 603, also has mountaineering equipment for sale and rental. Other places to try include Pizzeria Monteros, Jr José de la Mar 661; Lobo Adventure, Av Luzuriaga 557; Andean Sports Tours, Av Luzuriaga 571; and *Edward's Inn*, Av Bolognesi 121.

Listings

Banks and exchange All banks open Mon–Fri 9am–6pm. Try Banco Wiese, Jr José de Sucre 766; Interbanc, on Plaza de Armas; Banco de Credito, Av Luzuriaga 691; and Banco de la Nación, Av Luzuriaga. *Cambistas* gather where Morales and Luzuriaga meet, or try the casa de cambio at Luzuriaga 614, and Oh Na Nay, on the Plaza de Armas, for good rates on dollars.

Buses For local colectivos and buses to Anta, Marcara, Carhuaz, Yungay and Caraz, see "Getting around", p.299. Other companies include: Chavín Express, Jr Mariscal Caceres 338 (☎044/724652), for Sihuas, Chavín, Huari and other destinations; Colectivos Comité 14, Av Fitzcarrald 216

(☎044/721202 or 721739), for Lima and Trujillo; Cruz del Sur, Jr Lucar y Torré 585 (☎044/722491), for Lima and Trujillo; El Aguila, Raimondi 901 (☎044/726666), for Trujillo and Lima; Empresa Sandoval, Tarapaca 582 (☎044/726930), for Catac, Chavín, Pomacha, Huari; Empresa Condor de Chavín, Jr Tarapaca 312 (☎044/722039), for Chavín and Lima; Empresa Huandoy, Av Fitzcarral 261 (☎044/722502); Empresa Huascarán, Jr Tarapaca 133 (☎044/722208), for Chavín; Empresa Rapido, Jr Huascarán 117 for Chiquián; Empresa Rosario, Jr Caraz 605, for Pomabamba, La Unión and Huánuco; Expresso Ancash/Ormeño, Av Raimondi

---

Tours and activities in and around Huaraz

Most of the tour agencies in Huaraz are located along Avenida Luzuriaga and offer guided **city tours**, including stopping at all the major panoramic viewpoints (4hr, $8). For the surrounding area the most popular outings are to the **Llanganuco Lakes** (8hr, $10–15 per person), **Chavín de Huantar** (9–11hr, $10–15 per person), including lunch in Chavín before exploring the ruins, and to the edge of the **Pastoruri Glacier** at 5240m (8hr, $10 per person), where you can walk on the ice and explore naturally formed ice caverns beneath the glacier's surface. This last tour, which usually includes a visit to see the *Puya Raymondi* plants (see p.315), is rather commercialized and there is often a lot of rubbish lying around the most commonly visited parts of the glacier; it's also worth remembering that Pastoruri is very high and can be bitterly cold, so make sure you're well acclimatized to the altitude, and take warm clothing with you. Most agents also can arrange trips to the thermal baths at **Chancos** (4hr, $8) and **Caraz** (6hr, $10), and some offer **adventure activities** in the area. Always check if the guide leading your tour speaks English. These are the standard basic tour prices; some companies might charge more if they consider their service superior. There's greater price variation in the more adventurous tours, treks and river-rafting type trips.

Guides and operators

Andean Kingdom Av Luzuriaga 522 (upstairs), Huaraz ☎044/725353, ⊛www .andeankingdom.com. Friendly guides with some good English spoken, offering ice climbing, rock climbing, mountaineering, trekking, canoeing and the conventional tours; also rent out equipment. Their office is a good place to meet fellow travellers over evening videos.

Andean Sport Luzuriaga 571, Huaraz ☎044/721612. Pretty energetic and adventurous, this company offers rafting, climbing and mountain-biking tours.

Baloo Tours Av Julián de Morales 605, Huaraz ☎044/723928, ℗725994, ℮nilocamp@hotmail.com. Expeditions throughout the Cordillera Blanca and Huayhuash, with mountaineering equipment for rent, including tents.

Chavín Tours Av Luzuriaga 502, Huaraz ☎044/721578, ℗724801, ℮Chavín

527 (☎044/721102 or 724915), for Lima and Caraz; Movil Tours, Av Raimondi 730 (☎044/722555), for Lima, Chimbote and Trujillo; Rodriguez, Tarapaca 629 (☎044/722631 or 721353), for Lima; Turismo Atusparia, Tarapaca 574 (☎044/726745), for Lima; Turismo Chimbote, Av Raimondi 815 (☎044/721984), for Chimbote and Lima; Turismo Huaraz, Jr Caraz 605, for Caraz, Piscobamba, Pomabamba and Chimbote; and Yungay Express, Av Fitzcarrald 261 (☎044/727507), for Chimbote and Patavilca.

Doctors and dentists Dr Simon Komori, Jr 28 de Julio 602 (☎044/613100; 24hr); or try the surgery at Av Luzuriaga 618 (Mon–Fri 9am–5pm).

Hospital Av Luzuriaga ☎044/721861.

Internet facilities Portal Net, Av Luzuriaga 999 (☎044/725936), has 9 computers and fast access via satellite (7 days, 9am–midnight); Digi Net Alpamayo, Parque Ginebra 630 (☎044/729129),

has 12 cabins and also offers local, national and international phone calling at reasonable prices; Andes on Line, Jr Morales 759, upstairs; and the basic public cabins (*cabinas de Internet*) at Av Centenario 577.

Laundry Lavandería BB, Jr la Mar 674, is the best; otherwise, try Lavandería Huaraz, on Av Fitzcarral, close to the bridge; and Lavandería El Amigo, on the corner of Jr Bolivar and Jr José de Sucre.

Police The Tourist Police are at Jr Larrea y Loredo 716 ☎044/721341 ext 315.

Post office Plaza de Armas, on the corner of Jr José de Sucre and Av Luzuriaga. Mon–Sat 8am–8pm & Sun 9am–1pm.

Telephones Locutorio Emtelser, Jr José de Sucre 797, open 7 days a week, 7am–11pm.

Tourist Protection Service ☎044/613542.

Western Union Av Luzuriaga 556 ☎044/726410.

@telematic.edu.pe. Runs most of the standard tours, including around the city, Wilcahuain and Monterrey, plus day-trips to Llanganuco, Pastoruri (and *Puya Raymondi*) and to Chavín de Huantar. Can also organize canoeing and rafting on the Río Santa.

J.M. Expeditions Av Luzuriaga 465, Oficina 4, Huaraz ☎/℻044/728017, ℮mmazuelos@hotmail.com; main shopfront and store in the Centro Comercial, Manzana Unica, Lote 35, between the Casa de Guías and Luzuriaga. Lots of mountaineering equipment to rent and some professional high-mountain guides on call.

Monttrek Av Luzuriaga 646, Huaraz ☎044/721124, ℻726976, ﹫www.monttrek .com. Professional climbing, guides, treks, horse-riding, river rafting and snowboarding in the region, and stocks new and used camping and climbing equipment. The office is a great place to meet other trekkers.

Mountain Bike Adventures Castilla Postal 111, Jr Lucre y Torre 530, Huaraz ☎044/724259, ℮julio.olaza@terra.com.pe. Customizable guided bike tours with mountain bikes to rent. They also have English-speaking guides and offer a book exchange in their office. For cyclists with particular interests they offer a variety of alternative routes.

Pablo Tours Av Luzuriaga 501, Huaraz ☎/℻044/721145, ℮pablot@net.telematic .com.pe. One of the best agencies for standard tours and good for organized treks, though they get booked up very quickly.

Peru Trek Expeditions Av Luzuriaga 502, Huaraz ☎044/721578 or 722602. Adventure trips, such as rafting on the Río Santa, as well as reasonably priced tours to Llanganuco, Pastoruri, Chavín and around the city.

Pony Expeditions Sucre 1266, Caraz ☎/℻044/791642, ℮ponyexp@terra.com.pe. A very professional organization that fits out and guides expeditions in the area. An excellent source of local trekking and climbing information, they also run treks in other regions, such as the Cordillera Huayhuash, the Inca Trail and Ausungate.

Wilkawain Tours Av Luzuriaga 534, Oficina 202, Huaraz ☎044/723186. Offers most of the standard tours, plus one that finishes with a visit to the Fountain of Youth thermal baths and natural cave saunas at Chancos.

Around Huaraz

There are a number of worthy sights within easy reach of Huaraz. Only 7km north are the natural thermal baths of **Monterrey**; a similar distance, but higher into the hills, is the dramatic **Wilkawain temple**, its inner labyrinths open for exploration. On the other side of the valley, just half an hour by bus, **Punta Callan** is an ideal spot for magnificent views over the Cordillera Blanca, while to the south of the city you can see the intriguing cactus-like *Puya Raymondi* in the **Huascarán National Park**.

Monterrey

Just fifteen minutes by colectivo from the centre of Huaraz (every 10min or so from the corner of avenidas Fitzcarral and Raimondi; 40¢), the vast **thermal baths of Monterrey** (daily 7am–6pm; 85¢) include two natural swimming pools and a number of individual and family bathing rooms. Luxuriating in these slightly sulphurous hot springs can be the ideal way to recover from an arduous mountain trekking expedition, but make sure you are fully acclimatized, otherwise the effect on your blood pressure can worsen any altitude sickness. If you're staying at the wonderful old *Real Hotel Baños Termales Monterrey* (p.303), the baths are free. There's also an impressive **waterfall** just

ten minutes' walk behind the hotel and baths. There's no town here as such, just a street of a few properties, some of which have been converted or purpose-built as hostels or restaurants. At the top end of this street is the hotel and thermal baths, the reason that there's any settlement here at all. As far as eating goes, the best **restaurant** is *El Monte Rey*, opposite Artesania Johao (the ceramic workshop on the main access lane to the baths), which serves great local food at excellent prices. A close second is the *Hotel Monterrey* itself, which serves very reasonable dishes in some style in their elegant, old-fashioned restaurant.

The temple at Wilkawain

Wilkawain, 8km from Huaraz, can be reached from the centre of the city by colectivo from the corner of Jirón Comercio and 13 de Diciembre (parallel with the second block of Avenida Fitzcarrald); or by following Avenida Centenario downhill from Avenida Fitzcarral, then turning right up a track (just about suitable for cars) a few hundred metres beyond the *Real Hotel Huascarán*. From here, it's about an hour's stroll, winding slowly up past several small hamlets, to the signposted ruins. If there are four or five of you, a taxi there and back shouldn't come to more than about $3 each.

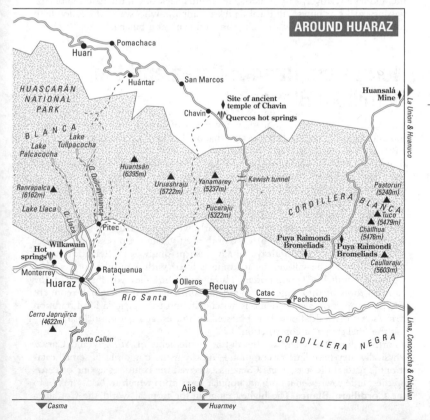

The **temple** is an unusual two-storey construction, with a few small houses around it, set against the edge of a great bluff. With a torch you can check out some of its inner chambers, where you'll see ramps, ventilation shafts, and the stone nails that hold it all together. Most of the rooms, however, are still inaccessible, filled with the rubble and debris of at least a thousand years. The temple base is only about 11m by 16m, sloping up to large slanted roof slabs, long since covered with earth and rocks to form an irregular domed top. The construction is a small replica of the Castillo at Chavín de Huantar (see p.326), with four superimposed platforms and stairways, and a projecting course of stones near the apex, with a recessed one below it. There was once a row of cats' heads beneath this, which is a typical design of the Huari-Tiahuanaco culture that spread up here from the coast sometime between 600 and 1000 AD.

Punta Callan

Some 24km west of Huaraz, **Punta Callan** is reached in about two hours on the Casma bus from Av Raimondi 336. Ask the driver to drop you off at Callan, shortly before the village of Pira along the road to Casma; from here it's a twenty-minute walk up the path to the promontory. No other spot can quite match the scintillating views of the Cordillera Blanca, so save it for a really clear afternoon, when you can best see Huascarán's towering ice-cap. Callan and Pira are surrounded by grazing land as pleasant as you could find for a picnic, and it's a relatively easy walk of a few hours back down the road to Huaraz. Passing trucks or buses will usually pick up anyone who waves them down en route. Go early in the day, to make sure you can get a bus back.

North from Huaraz: Caraz and the Cordillera Blanca

The Cordillera Blanca extend their icy chain of summits for 140 to 160km north of Huaraz. Under their western shadow lie the Callejón towns, all small, rustic with generally attractive accommodation and busy little markets. No one should come to the **Callejón de Huaylas** without visiting these northern valley towns, and many travellers will want to use them as bases from which to explore one or more of the ten snow-free passes in the Cordillera Blanca. Simply combining any two of these passes makes for a superb week's trekking. Travelling north along the valley from Huaraz you'll immediately notice the huge number of **avocado** trees, particularly when their fruit is ripening during the rainy season (Nov–Feb). One of the first villages you pass through after leaving Huaraz is called **Paltay**, which, unsurprisingly, is Peruvian for avocado. Just outside the village, the roadside is lined with a number of ceramics workshops, which sell good pottery. Throughout the valley, you'll notice on the pantiled roofs of the houses an abundance of ornate crosses, which represent Christ's protection against demons, witchcraft and bad spirits, a local tradition that also involves the house being blessed by a priest at a communal party during the final stages of construction.

Further along the valley are the distinct settlements of **Yungay** and **Caraz**. Physically they have little in common – Yungay is the tragic site of several catastrophic natural disasters, while Caraz has survived the centuries as one of Peru's prettiest little towns – but both are popular bases from which to begin treks into the **Cordillera Blanca**. The highest range in the tropical world, the Cordillera

Blanca consists of around 35 peaks poking their snowy heads over the 6000-metre mark, and until early this century, when the glaciers began to recede, this white crest could be seen from the Pacific. Of the many mountain lakes in the range, **Lake Parón**, above Caraz, is renowned as the most beautiful. Above Yungay, and against the sensational backdrop of Peru's highest peak, **Huascarán** (6768m), are the equally magnificent **Llanganuco Lakes**, whose waters change colour according to the time of year and the sun's daily movements, and are among the most accessible of the Cordillera Blanca's three hundred or so glacial lakes.

Fortunately, most of the Cordillera Blanca falls under the protective auspices of the **Huascarán National Park**, and as such the habitat has been left relatively unspoiled. Among the more exotic **wildlife** that hikers can hope to come across are the *viscacha* (Andean rabbit-like creatures), *vicuña*, grey deer, pumas, foxes, the rare spectacled bear, and several species of hummingbirds. All of these animals are shy, so you'll need a good pair of binoculars and a lot of patience to get close to any of them.

The number of possible **hikes** into the Cordillera depends mostly on your own initiative and resourcefulness. There are several common routes, some of which are outlined below; anything more adventurous requires a local guide or a tour with one of the local operators. **Maps** of the area, published by the Instituto Geográfico Militar, are good enough to allow you to plot your own routes, or you can follow one of the standard paths outlined in books such as *Backpacking and Trekking in Peru and Bolivia* by Hilary Bradt or *Trails of the Cordillera Blanca and Huayhuash of Peru* by Jim Bartle (see p.602 for details). The most popular hike is the **Llanganuco to Santa Cruz Loop** (outlined on p.319), which begins at Yungay and ends at Caraz.

The Puya Raymondi

The gigantic **Puya Raymondi** plant, up to 12m high and with a lifespan of around forty years, is found in the **Huascarán National Park**. Most people assume the *Puya Raymondi* is a type of cactus, but it is, in fact, the world's largest bromeliad, or member of the pineapple family. Known as *cuncush* or *cunco* to locals (and *Pourretia gigantea* to botanists), it only grows between altitudes of 3700m and 4200m, and is unique to this region; May is the best month to see them, when they are in full bloom and average 8000 flowers and six million seeds per plant. Dotted about the Quebrada Pachacoto slopes like candles on an altar, the plants look rather like upside-down trees, with the bushy part as a base and a phallic flowering stem pointing to the sky. Outside of late April, May, and early June, the plants can prove disappointing, often becoming burned-out stumps after dropping their flowers and seeds, but the surrounding scenery remains sensational, boasting grasses, rocks, lakes, llamas and the odd hummingbird.

By far the easiest way to see the *Puya Raymondi* is on an **organized tour** with one of the companies listed on p.310; most of the Pastoruri Glacier tours include a stop here. Alternatively, you could take a **combi colectivo** to Catac, leaving daily every thirty minutes from the end of Jirón Caceres in Huaraz (80¢). From Catac, 45km south of Huaraz, there are a few buses and trucks each day down the La Unión road, which passes right by the plants. Alternatively, get off the combi colectivo 5km beyond Catac at Pachacoto (where there are a couple of cafés often used as pit stops by truck drivers) and hitch from here along the dirt track which leads off the main road across barren grasslands. This track is well travelled by trucks on their way to the mining settlement of Huansala, and after about 15–20km – roughly an hour's drive – into this isolated region, you'll be surrounded by the giant bromeliads. From here, you can either continue on to La Unión (see p.357), via the Pastoruri Glacier, or return to Huaraz by hitching back to the main road.

Chancos

Known traditionally as the Fountain of Youth, the **thermal baths of Chancos**, 30km north of Huaraz, consist of a series of natural saunas inside caves, with great pools gushing hot water in a beautiful stream (daily 8am–6pm; 50¢–$1 depending on treatment). It is claimed that the thermal waters are excellent for respiratory problems, but you don't have to be ill to enjoy them, and they make an ideal end to a day's strenuous trekking.

To get there take any of the frequent **buses** or **colectivos** from the first block of Avenida Fitzcarral or the market area in Huaraz, along the valley towards Yungay or Caraz. Get off at the attractive little village of **Marcara** and follow the rough road uphill for about 4km, passing several small peasant settlements en route, until you reach the baths. There's no accommodation in Chancos, but the valley bus service is good enough to get you back to Huaraz within an hour or so, or you could **camp** (ask permission to camp on one of the grassy patches up or down hill from the baths). There are a couple of basic **restaurants** on hand which are famous for their strong *chicha*, and are particularly popular with locals on Sunday afternooons.

From Chancos a small track leads off to the hamlet of **Ullmey**, following the contours of the Legiamayo stream to the upper limit of cultivation and beyond into the barren zone directly below the glaciers. Keeping about 500m to the right of the stream, it takes ninety minutes to two hours to reach **Laguna Legia Cocha**, at 4706m above sea level. Hung between two vast glaciers and fed by their icy melted water, the lake is an exhilarating spot, with the added bonus of amazing views across the Santa Valley to Carhuaz in the north, Huaraz in the south, and Chancos directly below. If you leave Huaraz early in the morning, you can do a fine day-trip, stopping here for lunch, then heading down to Chancos for a stimulating bath before catching the bus back into town from Marcara.

Carhuaz and Mancos

One of the major towns along the valley, **CARHUAZ**, some 30km from both Huaraz and Yungay, has an attractive, central Plaza de Armas, adorned with palm trees, roses and labyrinths of low-cut hedges and dominated by the solid, concrete **Church of San Pedro** on its south side. On Sundays the streets to the north and west of the plaza are home to a thriving traditional **market**, where Andean and tropical foodstuffs, herbs and crafts, in particular gourd bowls, can be bought very cheaply. The colourfully dressed women here often sell live guinea pigs from small nets at their feet, and wear a variety of wide-brimmed hats – ones with blue bands indicate that they are married, ones with red bands show that they are single. Many also wear glass beads, on their hats or around their necks, as a sign of wealth.

Combi **colectivos** to Huaraz (50¢), Chancos (30¢) and Caraz (40¢) leave from one block west beyond the market side of the plaza, while the **buses** to Lima, Huaraz and Caraz leave from a terminal on block 2 of Avenida La Merced, which is a continuation of the road from the market side of the plaza to the main highway. In the unlikely event that you'll need them, **the local police** can be called at ☎044/794197.

There are a few basic **hostels** in Carhuaz: the *Hostal La Merced*, Jr Ucayali 724 (☎044/794241; ❸), has comfortable rooms with or without private bath; the *Hostal Residencial Huaraz*, Av Progreso 586 (☎044/794139; ❷), is relatively comfortable and attractive, with hot water and good-value laundry facilities; while the *Hostal Las Delicias*, Av Progreso 117 (☎044/794132; ❷), is slightly cheaper but not as nice. About 1.5km above Carhuaz, a lovely eco-ranch, the *Casa de Pocha* (☎044/613058, ✉lacasadepocha@yahoo.com; ❾), at the foot of Hualcan mountain, offers accommodation in a traditional adobe lodge with eight spacious rooms under red-tiled roofs; hot water is available 24 hours, there's a sauna, twelve metre swimming pool, horse-back riding and nearby hot springs of La Merced. As well as Spanish, the owner speaks English, French and Italian.

On the east side of the plaza, *Restaurant Heladería Huascarán*, Av Progreso 757, has good local **food**, including trout and ice cream; *Café Heladería El Abuelo* also serves ice creams, snacks and meals (ask for the local delicacy of beanshoots); *Restaurant y Peña La Punta Olimpica*, Av La Merced 500, which specializes in fish dishes and *comida criolla*, is good and cheap, with music at weekends.

In the 1980s a **cave** was discovered a few kilometres north of Carhuaz, on the other side of the Río Santa in the Cordillera Negra. It can be accessed in just over an hour's walk, beyond the sports stadium and up the stream past the unusual church, which sits beside the road from Carhuaz to Yungay. The cave contained bones of mastodons and llamas and suggested human occupation dating from as far back as 12,000 BC. Situated close to a natural rock formation that looks vaguely like a guitar, the site is now known as the cave of Hombre Guitarrera (Guitar Man).

A little further on from Carhuaz, over a river, the road comes to the village of **MANCOS**, where there's an unusually attractive plaza, with palm trees and a quaint, modern church with twin belfries sitting under the glistening glacier of Huascarán. On the plaza there's **accommodation** at the *Casa Alojamiento* (❷), which offers clean, comfortable rooms and shared bathrooms, and there are several restaurants around, none ecpially good. The village's main **fiesta**, August 12–16, is in honour of its patron, San Royal de Mancos, and the plaza becomes the focus of highly colourful religious processions and dancing and, later, bullfighting.

Yungay

YUNGAY, 58km up the valley from Huaraz, and just past Mancos, was an attractive, traditional small town until it was obliterated in seconds on May 31, 1970, during a massive **earthquake**. Long before its final destruction this so-called "Pearl of the Huaylas Corridor" had shown itself to be unwisely situated: in 1872 it was almost completely wiped out by an avalanche, and on a fiesta day in 1962 another avalanche buried some five thousand people in the neighbouring village of Ranrahirca. The 1970 quake also arrived in the midst of a festival and caused a landslide, and although casualties proved impossible to calculate with any real accuracy, it's thought that over 70,000 people died. Almost the entire population of Yungay, around 26,000, disappeared virtually instantaneously, though a few of the town's children survived because they were at a circus located just above the town, which fortuitously escaped the landslide. Almost eighty percent of the buildings in neighbouring Huaraz and much of Carhuaz were also razed to the ground by the earthquake.

The **new town**, an uninviting conglomeration of modern buildings – including some ninety prefabricated cabins sent as relief aid from the former Soviet Union – has been built around a concrete Plaza de Armas. Yungay still cowers beneath the peak of Huascarán, but is hopefully more sheltered than its predecessor from further dangers. On the way into town from Carhuaz, a car park and memorial monument mark the entrance to the site of the buried **old town** of Yungay (daily 8am–6pm; 50¢), which has developed into one of the region's major tourist attractions. The site, entered through a large, blue concrete archway, is covered with a grey flow of mud and moraine, now dry and solid, with a few stunted palm trees to mark where the old Plaza de Armas once stood. Thousands of rose bushes have been planted over the site – a gift from the Japanese government. Local guidebooks show before and after photos of the scene, but it doesn't take a lot of imagination to reconstruct the horror. You can still see a few things like an upside-down, partially destroyed school bus, stuck in the mud. The **graveyard** of Campo Santo, above the site, which predates the 1970 quake, gives the best vantage point over the devastation. A tall statue of Christ holds out its arms from the graveyard towards the deadly peak of Huascarán itself, as if pleading for no further horrors.

Practicalities

The best reason for staying here is to make the trip up to the Llanganuco Lakes and Huascarán (trucks leave most mornings from the Plaza de Armas) or simply to use the town as a base for exploring from the heart of the Callejón de Huaylas. Despite its looks, modern Yungay is a reasonable place to stay, and there are a number of acceptable **hostels**. The best value, and thus the most popular is the *Hostal Gledel* on Avenida Aries Graziani (℡044/793048; **●**), at the northern end of town; the upstairs rooms are best, and though all rooms share toilet facilities, the hostel is spotlessly clean and a good place to meet trekkers and climbers. For those on a very tight budget, there's the very basic *Hostal Sol de Oro* (**●**), or you can **camp** in a eucalyptus wood at *Hostal Blanco*, next to the hospital, which also has doubles (**❸**). The *Hostal Yungay*, on the Plaza de Armas (**❷**), gives out free **maps** and information on the area. Nearby there's the *Alojamiento La Suiza Peruana*, Av Aries Graziani, Lote 7 (℡044/793003; **❷**), which has shared bathrooms and a bar set around a patio. In terms of **restaurants**, on the northeast corner of the plaza there's the *Restaurant El Sabroso*, which is good for breakfast and lunches including trout; and the friendlier *Bar/Restaurant El Rosario*, close by, open for lunches, evening meals as well as drinking. The plaza is also the place to catch combi colectivos for the road up to Llanganuco ($2, 1hr); and it's also where you'll find the Banco de la Nación (Mon–Fri 8.30am–1.30pm & 2.15–4pm) for **money change**.

Llanganuco Lakes

The **Llanganuco Lakes**, at 3850m above sea level, are only 26km northeast of Yungay (83km from Huaraz), but take a good ninety minutes to reach by bus or truck, on a road that crawls up beside a canyon that is the result of thousands of years of Huascarán's meltwater. On the way you get a dramatic view across the valley and can clearly make out the path of the 1970 devastation. The last part of the drive – starkly beautiful but no fun for vertigo sufferers – slices through rocky crevices, and snakes around breathtaking precipices surrounded by small, wind-bent *quenual* trees and orchid bromeliads known locally as *weclla*. Well before reaching the lakes, at Km 19 you pass through the entrance to the **Huascarán National Park** (daily 6am–6pm; $1.50 for day visitors, or $20 for trekkers or mountaineers), located over 600m below the level of the lake; from here it's another thirty minutes or so by bus or truck to the lakes.

The first lake you come to after the park entrance is **Chinan Cocha**, named after a legendary princess. You can rent rowing boats by the car park here to venture onto the blue waters (80¢ for 15min), and, if you're hungry, take a picnic from the food stalls at the lakeside nearby. The road continues around Chinan Cocha's left bank and for a couple of kilometres on to the second lake, **Orcon Cocha**, named after a prince who fell in love with Chinan. The road

According to local legend, a goblin called **Ichic Ollco**, a little man with pointed ears, a grotesque face, small legs, massive arms and a penchant for stealing small children and pretty young women, once lived around the Llanganuco Lakes. One day, the legend says, a child went up on a mountain near Llanganuco and met Ichic Ollco, and the two played together, but when the child wanted to go home the goblin persuaded him to stay another hour – then another, and then another. After several hours, Ichic Ollco gave the child permission to go home on the condition that he returned again one day. When the child arrived home, a stranger answered the door and told him that his parents had died many years before. In tears, the young boy started back up the mountain; as he went up he got older and older with every step, eventually turning into a pile of dust as he reached the Llanganuco Lakes.

ends here and a **loop trail** begins (see below). A third, much smaller, lake was created between the two big ones, as a result of an avalanche caused by the 1970 earthquake, which also killed a group of hikers who were camped between the two lakes.

Immediately to the south of the lakes is the unmistakable sight of the massive **Huascarán ice-cap**, whose imposing peak tempts many people to make the difficult climb of 3km to the top. Surrounding Huascarán are scores of lesser, glaciated mountains that stretch for almost 200km and divide the Amazon Basin from the Pacific watershed.

Hiking in and around the Cordillera Blanca

There are many excellent hikes in the Cordillera Blanca, almost all of which require acclimatization to the rarefied mountain air, a certain degree of fitness, good camping equipment, plenty of food and good maps. Bear in mind that for some of the hikes you may need guides and mules to help carry the equipment at this altitude. One of the most popular routes, the **Llanganuco to Santa Cruz Loop** (see below), is a well-trodden trail offering spectacular scenery, some fine places to camp and a relatively easy walk that can be done in under a week, even by inexperienced hikers. There are shorter walks, such as the trails around the **Pitec Quebrada**, within easy distance of Huaraz, and a number of other loops like the **Llanganuco to Chancos** trek. Experienced hikers could also tackle the circular **Cordillera Huayhuash** route. Detailed information on all these walks is available from the South American Explorers' Club in Lima (see p.103), the Casa de Guías (see p.305), the tourist office (see p.299), or tour companies in Huaraz (see p.310). Below are outlines of two popular treks of differing grades.

The Llanganuco to Santa Cruz Loop

The **Llanganuco to Santa Cruz Loop** starts at the clearly marked track leading off from the end of the road along the left bank of Orcon Cocha. The entire trek shouldn't take more than about five days for a healthy (and acclimatized) backpacker, but it's a perfect hike to take at your own pace. It's essential to carry all your food, camping equipment and, ideally, a medical kit and emergency survival bag. Along the route there are hundreds of potential **campsites**. The best time to attempt this trek is in the dry season, between April and October, unless you enjoy getting stuck in mud and being soaked to the skin.

From Orcon Cocha the main path climbs the **Portachuelo de Llanganuco pass** (4767m), before dropping to the enchanting beauty of the **Quebrada**

Morococha (a *quebrada* is a river gully) through the tiny settlement of **Vaqueria**. From here you can go on to Colcabamba and Pomabamba, in the Callejón de Conchucos (though not in the rainy season, when you may well find yourself stranded), or continue back to the Callejón de Huaylas via Santa Cruz. The loop trail then heads north from Vaqueria up the **Quebrada Huaripampa** and around the ice-cap of **Chacraraju** (6000m) – a stupendous rocky canyon with a marshy bottom, snowy mountain peaks to the west, and Cerro Mellairca to the east. Following the stream uphill, with the lakes of Morococha and Huiscash on your left, you pass down into the Pacific watershed along the **Quebrada Santa Cruz**. Emerging eventually beside the calm waters of **Lake Grande**, you go around the left bank and continue down this perfect glacial valley for about another eight hours to the village of **CASHAPAMPA**, which has very basic accommodation. From here it's just a short step (about 2km) to the inviting and very hot (but temperature-controllable) thermal baths of **Huancarhuaz** (daily 8am–5pm; 75¢), and there's a road or a more direct three-hour path across the low hills south to Caraz.

Hualcayan to Pomabamba

This is one of the longest treks in the Cordillera Blanca and requires good acclimatization as well as fitness. It takes about a week to cover the route's total distance of around 78km – altitudes vary between 3100m and 4850m. You can get to Hualcayan (3100m) from Caraz by bus (1.5hr). Camp sites along the way include: Jamacuna (4050m), Osoruri (4550m), at Jancanrurish (4200m); two nights recommended here, Huillca (4000m), Yanacollpa (3850m). The trail terminates at the village of Pomabamba, where there are thermal baths, basic hotel and buses back to Yungay.

Caraz and around

The attractive town of **CARAZ**, known as a fantastic hiking area as well as for its honey and milk products, is a little less than 20km down the Santa Valley from Yungay, and sits quietly at an altitude of 2285m well below the enormous Huandoy Glacier. Palm trees and flowers adorn a classic colonial **Plaza de Armas**, while the small daily **market**, three blocks north of the plaza, is normally vibrant with activity, good for fresh food, colourful basketry, traditional gourd bowls, religious candles and hats. A couple of kilometres northeast of town along 28 de Julio, close to the Lago Parón turn-off, are the interesting ruins of **Tunshucayco**, probably the largest ruins in the Callejón de Hualyas. A possible ceremonial centre, it may well also have had a defensive function given its dominating position overlooking the valley.

One of the best **places to stay** is the modern *Hostal Perla de los Andes,* Plaza de Armas (☎044/792007; ❸) – its marbled lobby completely out of character with the laid-back, quite rustic flavour of the rest of Caraz – offering comfortable rooms with hot water, private bath and TV; it also has a very nice restaurant. Across the plaza, the attractive old *Hotel La Suiza Peruana,* at Jr San Martin 1133, close to the Plaza de Armas (☎044/722166; ❷), is cheap, basic, and has its own restaurant. Also near the plaza, the better-organized and cleaner *Hostal Chavín,* Jr San Martin 1135 (☎044/791171; ❷), is good value and some rooms have private bath. The cheapest places in town are the **youth hostel**, *Los Pinos* at Parque San Martin 103 (☎044/7791130, ✉lospinos@terra.com.pe; ❶) which also offers camping spaces for $2 a person and has reasonable Internet facilities; or the *Alojamiento Ramirez,* Daniel Villar 407 (no tel; ❶). One other rather unusual hostel is the *Hostal Chamanna,* a little out of town down 28 de

Mountain climbing in the Cordillera Blanca

To give a flavour of what you might expect from mountain climbing in the Cordillera Blanca, the expeditions below are some of the most popular among serious mountaineers. Remember to take a local guide if you do any of these.

Pisco
One of the easier climbs, up to 5752m, this is a good way to cut your teeth in the Cordillera Blanca. Little more than a hard trek, really, access is via the Llanganuco Valley (3800m) and it takes only three days. Rated easy to moderate.

Urus
A two-day climb reaching heights of around 5500m; access is via Collon to Quebrada de Ishinca and it takes only two days. Rated easy to moderate for the peaks Ishinca and Urus; or moderate to difficult if you tackle Tocllaraju mountain (6034m).

Alpamayo
A serious and quite technical mountain rising to 5947m, it requires good acclimatization on an easier climb. Access is from Cashapampa (get here by bus from Caraz), and it usually takes a week. It's rated as difficult.

Huascarán
The south summit at 6768m is the classic route and really requires excellent acclimatization. Access is via Mancos, 1hr by bus to the village Musho; and it normally needs a good week to tackle effectively. Rated, not surprisingly, as difficult.

Julio, at Av Nueva Victoria 185 (℡044/682802, ℻791642, ⓦwww.welcome.to /chamanna; ❹), which is set in a lovely labyrinth of gardens, streams and patios; not all rooms have private bath but they are very stylish and have distinctive ethnic murals.

For **places to eat**, the *Café Oasis*, Jr Raimondi 425 (℡044/791785), just a small stone's throw from the plaza, is good for snacks and also has four pretty cheap rooms (❶). The *Café de Rat*, just down at the bottom southwestern edge of the Plaza de Armas, serves decent pasta and pizzas, pancakes and vegetarian food, as well as having darts, maps, guidebooks, music and Internet access. Fronting the plaza, *Polleria El Mirador* serves reasonably priced lunches and evening meals of Peruvian and international food. The *Restaurant Esmeralda*, Jr Alfonso Ugarte 404, does good, simple breakfasts. Just up above the plaza, on block 10 of Jirón San Martin, *La Boca del Lobo* serves tasty local dishes in a vibrant atmosphere, often accompanied by loud music. The helpful **tourist information** office (Mon–Sat 7.45am–1pm & 2.30–5.30pm), with maps and brochures covering the attractions and some of the hikes (including the relatively demanding 6-8hr Patapata walk) in the immediate area, is on the Plaza de Armas, while the **telephone office** is at Raimondi 410. There's only one **Internet café** – Cabinas Internet Caraz – at Av 1 de Mayo 189. For **money exchange** there's a Banco de Credito at Jr Daniel Villar 217 or there's the Banco de la Nación on Jirón Raimondi, half a block from the Plaza de Armas. For trekking **guides**, local information or help organizing and fitting out an expedition, the excellent Pony Expeditions (see p.311) can't be beaten.

Most of the **bus** offices are along calles Daniel Villar and Cordova, within a block or two of the Plaza de Armas: Chinachasuyo serve Trujillo; Empresa Turismo go to Lima and Chimbote; Ancash to Lima; Movil Tours to Huraz and

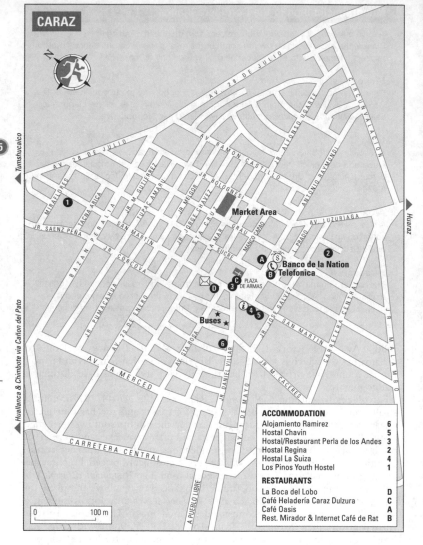

CARAZ

Tumshucaico

Huallanca & Chimbote via Cañon del Pato

Huaraz

Market Area

Banco de la Nation
Telefonica

PLAZA
DE ARMAS

Buses

ACCOMMODATION
Alojamiento Ramirez   6
Hostal Chavin   5
Hostal/Restaurant Perla de los Andes   3
Hostal Regina   2
Hostal La Suiza   4
Los Pinos Youth Hostel   1

RESTAURANTS
La Boca del Lobo   D
Café Heladería Caraz Dulzura   C
Café Oasis   A
Rest. Mirador & Internet Café de Rat   B

0   100 m

Lima; Region Norte runs buses to Yungay, Huaraz and Recuay; and Transporte
Moreno to Chimbote. **Colectivos** for Huaraz leave from just behind the market every thirty minutes, more or less.

Huata

Nine kilometres across the Río Santa from Caraz, set on the lower slopes of
the Cordillera Negra, is the small settlement of **HUATA**, a typical rural village
with regular truck connections from the market area in Caraz. The village is a
good starting point for a number of easy **walks**, such as the eight-kilometre

stroll up to the unassuming lakes of **Yanacocha** and **Huaytacocha** or, perhaps more interesting, north about 5km along a path up Cerro Muchanacoc to the small Inca **ruins of Cantu**. It's possible to **camp** around Huata if you ask permission from a local family, but Caraz is pretty close by with facilities for sleeping and eating, so it's rare anyone will camp here.

Lake Parón

Some 30km, more or less, east of Caraz, the deep-blue **Lake Parón** (4185m) is sunk resplendently into a gigantic glacial cirque, hemmed in on three sides by some of the Cordillera Blanca's highest ice-caps. There's a mountain **refuge** (a basic hut open to anyone to shelter from the night or bad weather) at the lake, run by the private company which operates the electricity plant at Huallanca; but there are only basic facilities available (toilet and hot water). It's always open for access, however, since two guards (one a radio operator) live there. **Camping** is possible at the refuge or on the east side of the lake, to which there's a clear path on the north bank. **Buses** and **colectivos** (4.50am & 1pm; $1) from Caraz market travel up to Pueblo Parón, from where it's a hike of 9km (3hr) up to the lake. The last transport back from Pueblo Parón to Caraz is usually at 2.30pm. **Taxis** to the lake (about $10 per person) leave most days from the Plaza de Armas in Caraz.

The Cañon del Pato

One of Peru's most exciting roads runs north from Caraz to Huallanca, squeezing through the spectacular **Cañon del Pato** (Duck's Canyon). An enormous rocky gorge cut from solid rock, its impressive path curves around the Cordillera Negra for most of the 50km between Caraz and Huallanca. Sheer cliff faces rise thousands of metres on either side while the road passes through some 39 tunnels – an average of one every kilometre. Situated within the canyon is one of Peru's most important hydroelectric power plants; the heart of these works, invisible from the road, is buried 600m deep in the cliff wall. Unfortunately, the road is often closed for a number of reasons – causes include terrorists, bandits, landslides in the rainy season, or just the sheer poor quality of the road surface. Much of the first section has been improved in recent years, but from Huallanca to Chimbote it's more like a dry riverbed than a dirt track. Check with the tourist office in Huaraz and local bus companies (see p.299) about the physical and political condition of the road before attempting this journey.

At the end of the canyon the first village you come to is **Huallanca**, reached by daily buses from Huaraz (9am–6.30pm). From here, it's 8km on to Yuramarca where you can either branch off west along an alternative road to Chimbote (another 140km) on the coast, or continue along the valley to Corongo and the Callejón de Conchucos.

The Callejón de Conchucos and Chavín de Huantar

To the east of the Cordillera Blanca, roughly parallel to the Callejón de Huaylas, runs another long natural corridor, the **Callejón de Conchucos**. Virtually inaccessible in the wet season, and off the beaten track even for the most hardened of backpackers, the valley makes a challenging target, with the town of **Pomabamba** in the north and the spectacular ruins at **Chavín de Huantar** just beyond its southern limit. There's little of interest between the two; the villages of **Piscobamba** (Valley or Plain of the Birds) and **Huari** are likely to appeal only as food stops on the long haul (141km) through barren mountains between Pomabamba and Chavín. This is one of the few regions of Peru where bus drivers sometimes allow passengers to lounge around on the roof as they career along precipitous mountain roads, plummeting into each steep drop of the dusty road – an electrifying experience with the added bonus of a 360-degree, ever-changing view.

The Callejón de Conchucos was out of bounds to travellers between 1988 and 1993, when it was under almost complete Sendero Luminoso terrorist control; many of the locals were forced to flee the valley after actual or threatened violence from the terrorists. The region's more distant history was equally turbulent and cut-off from the rest of Peru, particularly from the seat of colonial and Republican power on the coast. Until the Conquest, this region was home to one of the fiercest ancient tribes – the Conchucos – who surged down the Santa Valley and besieged the Spanish city of Trujillo in 1536. By the end of the sixteenth century, however, even the fearless Conchuco warriors had been reduced to virtual slavery by the colonial *encomendero* system.

Pomabamba

The small town of **POMABAMBA**, 3000m up in dauntingly hilly countryside, is surrounded by little-known archeological remains that show common roots with Chavín de Huantar (see below). Today the town makes an excellent trekking base; from here you can connect with the **Llanganuco to Santa Cruz Loop** (see p.319) by following tracks southwest to either Colcabamba or Punta Unión. Or, a hard day's hike above Pomabamba, you can walk up to the stone remains of **Yaino**, an immense fortress of megalithic rock. On a clear day you can just about make out this site from the Plaza de Armas in Pomabamba; it appears as a tiny rocky outcrop high on the distant horizon. The climb takes longer than you might imagine, but locals will point out shortcuts along the way. The area also abounds in little-explored **ruins**; try Pony Expeditions in Caraz (see p.311) for further information on these, as well as maps, equipment and advice on trekking in this region.

Practicalities

Direct Empresa Los Andes **buses** leaves from the Plaza de Armas in Yungay at 8.30–9am, while Turismo Huaraz in Huaraz (see Listings, p.311) go to Piscobamba and Pomabamba. Alternatively, you can get here from Huaraz via Chavín, on a bus from Lima that comes north up the Callejón de Conchucos more or less every other day. Pomabamba has a few small **places to stay**, the best being the *Hotel Estrada* (no phone; ❷) one block from the plaza on Calle Lima; the others are more basic, simple and slightly cheaper: the *Hostal Pomabamba* (no phone; ❶) is just off the Plaza de Armas, and the *Hotel San Martin* (no phone; ❷) is on the edge of town. Ultimately, though, you'll be better off asking the locals for good **camping** spots.

Chavín de Huantar

Only 30km southeast of Huari, or a three- to four-hour journey from Huaraz, the magnificent temple complex of **CHAVÍN DE HUANTAR** is the most important site associated with the Chavín cult (see box on p.326), and although partially destroyed by earthquakes, floods and erosion from the Río Mosna, enough of the ruins survive to make them a fascinating sight for anyone even vaguely interested in Peruvian archeology. The religious cult that inspired Chavín's construction also influenced subsequent cultural development throughout Peru, right up until the Spanish Conquest some 2500 years later, and the temple complex of Chavín de Huantar is equal in importance, if not grandeur, to most of the sites around Cusco.

Getting there

The vast majority of people approach the temple complex from Huaraz. Empresa Condor de Chavín, Empresa Huascarán, Chavín Express and Empresa Sandoval **buses** leave Huaraz daily around 10am ($4, a 3–4hr trip) for Chavín (see p.310 for bus company details), while all the tour companies in Huaraz (see p.310) offer a slightly faster, though more expensive, service ($10–15, a 3hr trip). The buses turn off the main Huaraz to Lima road at the town of **Catac**, and take a poorly maintained road which crosses over the small Río Yana Yacu (Black Water River). It then starts climbing to the beautiful **Lake of Querococha** (*quero* is Quechua for "teeth", and relates to the teeth-like rock formation visible nearby), which looks towards two prominent mountain peaks – **Yanamarey** and **Pucaraju** ("Red Glacier" in Quechua). From here the road, little more than a track now, climbs further before passing through the **Tunel de Cahuish**, which cuts through the solid rock of a mountain to emerge in the **Callejón de Conchucos**, to some spectacular but quite terrifying views. A couple of the more dangerous and precipitous curves in the road are known as the **Curva del Diablo** and **Salvate Si Puedes** ("Save Yourself If You Can"), from which you can deduce that this journey isn't for the squeamish or for vertigo sufferers.

An even more adventurous way to reach Chavín is by following the two- to four-day **trail** over the hills from **Olleros**. Colectivos leave daily every thirty minutes from the end of Jirón Caceres in Huaraz, for Olleros ($1), from where the hike is fairly simple and clearly marked all the way. It follows the Río Negro up to Punta Yanashallash (4700m), cuts down into the Marañón watershed along the Quebrada Shongopampa, and where this meets the Jato stream coming from north, the route follows the combined waters (from here known as the Río Huachesecsa) straight down, southwest to the Chavín ruins another 1500m below. It's quite a hike, so take maps and ideally a guide and pack-llamas (see p.306). A good account of this walk is given in Hilary Bradt's *Backpacking and Trekking in Peru and Bolivia* (see Contexts, p.602), and the South American Explorers' Club in Lima (see p.103) can give advice and information about it.

The temple complex

The magnificent temple complex of **Chavín de Huantar** (daily 8am–5pm; $1) evolved and elaborated its own brand of religious cultism during the first millennium BC. The original temple was built here by at least 800 BC, though it was not until around 400 BC that the complex was substantially enlarged and its cultural style fixed. Some archeologists claim that the specific layout of the temple, a U-shaped ceremonial courtyard facing east and based around a raised stone platform, was directly influenced by what was, in 1200 BC, the largest architectural monument in the New World, at Sechin Alto (see p.294). By 300 BC, Sechin Alto had been abandoned and Chavín was at the height of its power and one of the world's largest religious centres, with about three thousand resident priests and temple attendants. The U-shaped temples were probably dedicated to powerful mountain spirits or deities, who controlled

The **Chavín cult** had a strong impact on the Paracas culture, and later on the Nazca and Mochica civilizations. Theories as to the origin of its religious inspiration range from extraterrestrial intervention to the more likely infiltration of ideas and individuals or entire tribes from Central America. There is an affinity between the ceramics found at Chavín and those of a similar date from Tlatilco in Mexico, yet there are no comparable Mexican stone constructions as ancient as these Peruvian wonders. More probable, and the theory expounded by Julio Tello, is that the cult initially came up into the Andes (then down to the coast) from the Amazon Basin via the Marañón Valley. The inspiration for the beliefs themselves, which appear to be in the power of totemic or animistic gods and demons, may well have come from visionary experiences sparked by the ingestion of **hallucinogens**: one of the stone reliefs at Chavín portrays a feline deity or fanged warrior holding a section of the psychotropic mescalin cactus San Pedro, still used by *curanderos* today for the invocation of the spirit world, thus providing an Amazonian link.

Chavín itself may not have been the centre of the movement, but it was obviously an outstanding ceremonial focus: the name of Chavín comes from the Quechua *chaupin*, meaning navel or focal point. As such, it might have been a sacred shrine where natives flocked in pilgrimage during festivals, much as they do today, visiting important *huacas* in the sierra at specific times in the annual agricultural cycle. The appearance of the Orion constellation on Chavín carvings fits with this theory since it appears on the skyline just prior to the traditional harvest period in the Peruvian mountains.

meterological phenomena, in particular rainfall that was vital to the survival and wealth of the people.

The complex's main building consists of a central rectangular block with two wings projecting out to the east. The large, southern wing, known as the **Castillo**, is the most conspicuous feature of the site: massive, almost pyramid-shaped, the platform was built of dressed stone with gargoyles attached, though few remain now.

Some way in front of the Castillo, down three main flights of steps, is the **Plaza Hundida**, or sunken plaza, covering about 250 square metres with a rectangular, stepped platform to either side. Here, the thousands of pilgrims thought to have worshipped at Chavín would gather during the appropriate fiestas. And it was here that the famous Tello Obelisk (now in the Archeological and Anthropological Museum in Lima; see p.86) was found, next to an altar in the shape of a jaguar and bedecked with seven cavities forming a pattern similar to that of the Orion constellation.

Standing in the Plaza Hundida, facing towards the Castillo, you'll see on your right the **original temple**, now just a palatial ruin dwarfed by the neighbouring Castillo. It was first examined by Julio Tello in 1919 when it was still buried under cultivated fields; during 1945 a vast flood reburied most of it and the place was damaged again by the 1970 earthquake and the rains of 1983. Among the fascinating recent finds from the area are bone snuff tubes, beads, pendants, needles, ceremonial shells (imported from Ecuador) and some quartz crystals associated with ritual sites. One quartz crystal covered in red pigment was found in a grave, placed after death in the mouth of the deceased.

Behind the original temple, there are two entrances leading to underground passages. The one on the right leads down to an underground chamber, containing the awe-inspiring **Lanzon**, a prism-shaped block of carved white granite that tapers nearly 4m down from a broad feline head to a point stuck in the ground. The entrance on the left takes you into the labyrinthine inner chambers, which run underneath the Castillo on several levels connected by ramps and steps. In the seven major subterranean rooms you'll need a torch to get a decent look at the carvings and the granite sculptures (even when the electric lighting is switched on), while all around you can hear the sound of water dripping. Another large stone slab discovered at Chavín in 1873 – the Estela Raymondi, also now in the Archeological and Anthropological Museum – was the first of all the impressive carved stones to be found. The most vivid of the carvings remaining at the site are the gargoyles (known as Cabeza Clavos), guardians of the temple that again display feline and birdlike characteristics.

Most theories about the **iconography** of these stone slabs, all of which are very intricate, distinctive in style and highly abstract, agree that the Chavín people worshipped three major gods: the Moon (represented by a fish), the Sun (depicted as an eagle or a hawk), and an overlord, or creator divinity, normally shown as a fanged cat, possibly a jaguar. It seems very likely that each god was linked with a distinct level of the Chavín cosmos: the fish with the underworld, the eagle with the celestial forces, and the feline with earthly power. This is only a calculated guess, and ethnographic evidence from the Amazon Basin suggests that each of these main gods may have also been associated with a different subgroup within the Chavín tribe or priesthood as a whole.

Practicalities

The pretty village of **Chavín de Huantar**, with its whitewashed walls and traditional tiled roofs, is just a couple of hundred metres from the ruins and has a reasonable supply of basic amenities. The best **accommodation** is at the *Hotel La Casona de JB*, Wiracocha 130 (☎044/754020; ❸), just next door to the town hall on the plaza; it's relatively new and very good value, with hot showers. There's also friendly family lodging at the *Casa del Señor Chapaco* (❷), while *Hotel Inca*, at Wiracocha 160 (❷), has hot water most evenings but shared bathrooms, and there are basic but clean rooms at *Hotel Monte Carlo*, at C 17 de Enero 1015 (❷), on the plaza. Alternatively, you can **camp** by the Baños Quercos thermal springs (daily 7am–6pm; 50¢) some twenty minutes' stroll from the village, 2km up the valley. For **places to eat** the best bets are the *Restaurant Chavín Turístico*, 17 de Enero Sur 439, or the *Restaurant La Ramada*, a few doors further up the same road at no 577. Getting back to Huaraz or Catac, there are buses daily from Chavín, more or less on the hour from 3pm to 6pm. There's a **post and telephone office** at C 17 de Enero 365 (6.30am–10pm), plus a small **tourist information** office on the corner of the Plaza de Armas, next to the market, though it doesn't have regular hours.

North from Chavín

Some 8km north of Chavín is the lovely village of **SAN MARCOS**, a good base for mountain hiking. There are **buses** every hour from Chavín, or you can walk there in well under two hours. **Accommodation** is available at the *Casa del Señor Luis Alfaro* (❷), though it's a good idea to take a tent just in case all rooms are full. From San Marcos you can climb up another 300m in altitude to the smaller community of **Carhuayoc**, a 100-year-old village whose population specialize in the production of fine textiles, mainly blankets and rugs (it's a 9hr round-trip). About 35km from San Marcos, the town of **Huari** is a good base for a short trek to the scenic Lago Purhuay; it's only 8km from the town and a climb of some 400m, but it usually takes between five and six hours to get there and back. To continue on to Pomabamba from Huari, there are **buses** every other day, usually leaving at 9pm ($5, a 7hr journey).

Covering a distance of 164–186km and, comfortably, taking 14 days (give or take a couple, depending on your fitness, walking ability and desire), this trail lies at altitudes between 2750m and 5000m. Rated as Class IV (difficult), as the name suggests, the Chiquián Loop starts and finishes in Chiquián.

Route description

Day 1: Chiquián - Llamac

This is an easy first-day walk. The wide and clearly marked path takes hikers to the far end of the valley. After crossing three times from one valley to the other, a short way up will lead walkers to Llamac, a typical highland village.

Day 2: Llamac - Matacancha

A two-hour descent leads hikers to another little Andean village called Pocpa, from where walkers must take the left bank of the river and start climbing to the campsite. The first mountain that appears on the way is the Ninashanca at 5607m (18,391ft). The camping spot is found almost at the far end of this dry and treeless valley.

Day 3: Matacancha - Janca

The first ascent to the Cacananpunta Pass at 4880m (16,006ft) is difficult and must be reached before midday. At the end of the ascent and the arrival at the highest point culminates the first part of this trek, considered by many to be the most difficult one in the world. The descent to the camp does not need a major effort.

Day 4: Janca - Carhuacocha Lake

Ascents and descents, as well as the beautiful peaks, are characteristic of the day's walk. Looking back, one can see almost the entire scenery of the Cordillera Huayhuash. Down by the lake and from the camp, one can see peaks that make up the majestic Cordillera Huayhuash.

Day 5: Carhuacocha Lake - Carnicero

The next pass opens out to Carnicero Valley. A not very steep and beautiful climb takes the hiker to the Rinconada, where the pass forms visually spectacular rocky scenery approximately 300m (984ft) long.

The Cordillera Huayhuash

To the south of Huaraz, the **Cordillera Huayhuash** offers much less frequented but just as stunning trekking trails as those in the Cordillera Blanca. Most treks start in the small town of **Chiquián**, 2400m above sea level. The most popular trekking route has two options: one for fourteen days, and the second for sixteen days, both of them leaving Chiquián heading for Llamac and the entire cordillera loop (see box above). There are, of course, easier routes, one of which is briefly described below. The mountains here, although slightly lower than the Cordillera Blanca and covering a much smaller area, nevertheless rise breathtakingly to 6634m at the Nevada Yerupajá, some 50km southeast of Chiquián as the crow flies. Yerupajá actually forms the watershed between the Cordillera Huayhuash to the north and the lower-altitude Cordillera Raura to the south. Large and stunning lakes, flocks of alpaca, herds of cattle and some sheep can be seen along the way. High levels of fitness and some experience are required for hiking or climbing in this region and it's always best to tackle it as part of a team, or at least to have a local guide along. The guide will help to avoid the rather irritating dogs that help to look after the animals in these remote hills and his presence will also provide protection against the possible, but unlikely, threat of robbery. After the town of Chiquián, it's virtually impossible to buy

Day 6: Carnicero - Huayhuash - Altuspata
The descent continues to the next valley. One can see several small lakes and rivers along the way.
Day 7: Altuspata - Viconga Lake
The ascent continues towards the pass, which leads the way to Viconga. Walking around the lake through the narrow valley one can reach the next camping spot.
Day 8: Viconga Lake - Huanacpatay
A very long way and one of toughest hikes, this is where one crosses the Cuyoc Pass at 5100m (16,728ft) next to Mount Cuyoc and close to Puscanturpa at 5442m (17,854ft). Descending from the pass, a small, steep, and difficult corridor leads to the Huanacpatay valley.
Day 9 and 10: Two days must be set aside for climbing two of the peaks around the Diablo Mudo Pass.
Day 11: Huanacpatay - Huatiac
Another long trekking day. Descending deeply to the endless valley of Huallapa river one starts seeing trees and plants. The trail passes close by Huallapa village.
Day 12 : Huatiac - Jahuacocha Lake
The climb continues up to Diablo Mudo Pass at 5000m (16,400ft), an area bare of plant life. Everything is downhill from the pass until Lake Jahuacocha and past it to the beautiful Cordillera Huayhuash campsite beside this lake.
Day 13: Jahuacocha Lake - Llamac
After almost two weeks the path crosses again into Llamac village. There are two paths from Jahuacocha which lead back to Llamac's campsite, one is direct and very steep and is done in a shorter time, while the second one is longer but with no major or sudden descents.
Day 14: Llamac - Chiquián - Huaraz
A repeat of this stretch, which was the first day's hike: a tough, but marvellous trek through the Cordillera Huayhuash, one of the least-visited such trails worldwide.

food, so it's a good idea to get most of this in Huaraz or in Lima before arriving, just supplementing with extras such as bread, dry biscuits, dairy products (including good local cheeses), rice and pasta when you arrive here.

One popular Huayhuash **trek** from Chiquián follows a route to Llamac-Pampa de Llamac (a very difficult pass), then on to Jahuacocha Lake, where troutfishing is possible. Taking about five days, the scenery on the trek can only be described as breathtaking, the hiking itself as quite hard. The only downside is that you have to walk Chiquián–Llamac twice, and between Rondoy and Llamac a mining company destroys much of the beautiful countryside, apparently also polluting the river as well as building a rather ugly road. Most people who come this far prefer to do the Chiquián Loop (see box above), which entails a tough couple of weeks, though the really fit might manage it in ten days at a push.

Practicalities
Chiquián is easily reached by **bus** with Empresa El Rapido, Mariscal Caceres 312 (☎044/726437) from Huaraz (3hr) who run about six buses daily. For **accommodation** there are a few basic hostels in Chiquián, one of the best being *San Miguel,* Jr Comercio 233 (☎044/747001; ❶), which has reasonably clean and comfortable beds as well as a pleasant little garden; but the *Hotel Los Nogales*, Jr Comercio 1301 (☎044/747121, ✉hotel_nogales_chiquian@yahoo

.com.pe; ❷–❸) offers good value with or without private bathrooms. Only simple food is available in two or three **restaurants**, with *El Refugio de Bolognesi*, on the fourth block of Tarapaca, offering perhaps the best set-lunch menus. In late August and early September there are some colourful **fiestas** in the town, for the Virgen de Santa Rosa, during the last day of which there is always a "bullfight" and the local football stadium is transformed into an arena. The aim of the game is, as with most rural Peruvian "bullfights", just to play with the bull (without hurting him) and this is done not only by the toreador, but by anyone who feels the urge to become a toreador (local youth, drunk men); they can challenge the bull with their poncho, which guarantees a lot of excitement and fun, with the public scattering when the irritated bull comes too close.

Travel details

Buses and colectivos

Barranca to: Casma (6 daily; 2hr); Chimbote (12 daily; 3hr); Huaraz (10–12 daily; 5hr); Lima (16 daily; 3hr).
Chimbote to: Caraz (2 daily; 6–7hr); Huaraz (6–8 daily; 8hr); Lima (12 daily; 6–8hr); Trujillo (12 daily; 3hr).
Huaraz to: Casma (5 daily; 6hr); Chavín (4 daily; 3–4hr); Chimbote (6–8 daily; 7–8hr); Chiquián (5–6 daily; 3–4hr); Lima (6–8 daily; 8hr); Trujillo (3–4 daily; 8–10hr).

Flights

Chimbote to: Lima (1 daily; 1hr); Trujillo (1 daily; 1hr).
Huánuco to: Lima (daily; 1hr); Tarapota (1 daily; 2hr); Tingo Maria (1 daily; 1hr).
Huaraz to: Lima (occasionally in high season; 1hr).

The Central Sierra

CHAPTER 6 # Highlights

✳ **Marcahuasi** This high plateau makes for out-of-this-world weekend camping. See p.335

✳ **Tarma** A very attractive colonial town particularly famous for its fantastic Easter Sunday procession. See p.351

✳ **Huancayo – Huancavelica train** A breathtaking high-altitude railway journey that is arguably one of the finest in the world. See p.344

✳ **San Pedro de Cajas** This scenic and remote village is home to some of the craftspeople who produce much of Peru's superb modern weavings. See p.352

✳ **Temple of Kotosh** Over 4000 years old, this impressive site's massive stone constructions suggest that complicated stonework began here centuries before anywhere else in the Americas. See p.355

✳ **Ayacucho** One of the most traditional and architecturally fascinating cities in the Peruvian Andes – renowned for its thirty-odd churches and boisterous fiestas. See p.344

6

The Central Sierra

Once one of the first stops on the itinerary of any visit to Peru, the **Central Sierra** was hit hard by the rise of terrorism during the 1980s, and the closing of the very scenic high mountain railway connecting Lima with Huancayo led to a severe decline in tourists. Happily, though, the region has been free of violence for several years now and is again very much open to visitors. Tourism infrastructure has been redeveloped and the region boasts some of Peru's finest cultural heritage – both pre-Columbian and colonial – in the series of very traditional towns and cities that punctuate the remote valleys and cordilleras.

Travelling from Lima into the Central Sierra is, thanks to the much-improved Carretera Central, faster and safer than ever before. Given this, visitors are less likely to suffer the *soroche* (mountain sickness) often produced by the train's slow climb through the high Ticlio Pass (over 4800m). Cars can just whiz through here now, with passengers hardly noticing the altitude. It's still advisable, however, to take the first few days over 3000m pretty easy to avoid breathlessness and headaches.

Huancayo is the obvious place to start exploring the region, particularly if you're coming from Lima. It's the largest urban centre in the area and is easily reached in a day's travel. If you're approaching from Cusco or the south coast, you are more likely to enter the region via **Ayacucho**, one of the cultural jewels of the Andes with all its colonial churches and fine artesania.

En route up through the Cordillera Occidental – the massive mountain range which separates Huancayo and the beautiful Mantaro Valley from the coast – you may want to stop off for a day or two at the enigmatic rock formations of **Marcahuasi**, though this can also be accessed directly from Lima. The region divides naturally into three sectors pivoting around Huancayo. To the north there's **Huánuco**, a very pleasant town and a good base for exploring some of Peru's most interesting archeological remains, and **Tingo Maria**, gateway to the jungle port of Pucallpa. To the northeast you'll find the beautiful and fairly laid-back town of **Tarma**, which has a relatively pleasant climate influenced by the cloud forest to the east, and is a major nodal point for tourists and traders alike. South of Huancayo are the two most traditional of all the Central Sierra's towns: Ayacucho and **Huancavelica**.

Getting to the Central Sierra

The **road journey** from Lima to Huancayo is almost as spectacular as the world-famous *Tren de la Sierra* trip used to be, offering many travellers their first sight of llamas and of Peru's indigenous Indian mountain culture. It

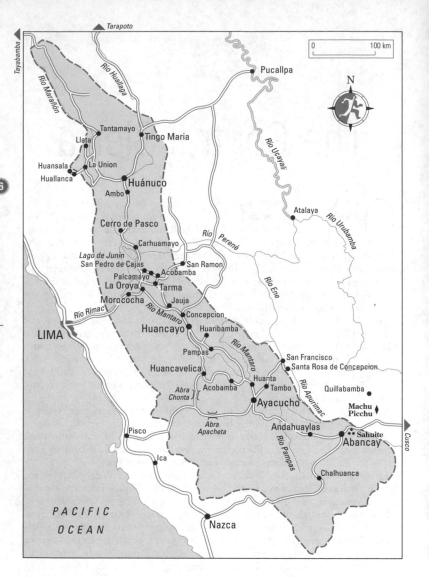

usually takes around four to five hours to get to **La Oroya** by road; nearly all of this time is spent high in the Andes as the factories and cloudy skies of Lima are swiftly left behind. **Marcahuasi** and **San Pedro de Casta**, reached via a northern spur road off the Carretera Central en route to La Oroya, are worth spending a couple of days on if you've got the time and inclination. From La Oroya you have the choice of turning north and winding through 130km or so of rather desolate landscape to **Cerro de Pasco**, a bleak mining town and a possible approach to Huánuco, Tingo Maria and Pucallpa in the Amazon jungle. However, most travellers head east from La Oroya to Tarma and on to the jungle region of Chanchamayo, or 100km or so south to Huancayo, through the astonishing **Jauja Valley**, which boasts beautiful scenery, striped by fabulous coloured furls of mountain.

Marcahuasi and San Pedro de Casta

MARCAHUASI is a high plateau frequently visited by hikers and campers wanting to see its many unusual rock formations; standing at just over 4000m above sea level, it's one of Peru's lesser-known marvels and something of a mystical enigma. It also makes a fantastic weekend camping jaunt and is one of the more adventurous but popular weekend excursions from Lima. Its main attractions are the incredible **rock formations** themselves which, particularly by moonlight, take on weird shapes – llamas, human faces, turtles, even a hippopotamus. There's also a large clearing known as the amphitheatre, which hosts an incredible annual village **festival** involving three days of ceremony, music, dance and festivities on July 28–30. The easiest way to visit the site, 90km east of Lima and easily reachable as a day-trip from the city, is with TEBAC, a Lima-based tour company (see Listings, p.103), who can also organize trips to the annual **Festival de Aventura** which takes place in Marcahuasi in early November and incorporates live music with outward-bound activities such as mountain biking, marathon running and motocross. For further Marcahuasi information contact the Oficina de Información San Pedro de Casta, Av Guzman Blanco 240, office 403, Lima (☎064/4337591).

Unless you're camping, you'll have to stay in the village of **SAN PEDRO DE CASTA**, two or three hours' hard walking back down the mountain path that you will necessarily have arrived on. There are no direct buses from Lima to San Pedro, but if you take a bus (marked "Chosica"), from block 15 of Nicolas de Pierola, one block beyond the Parque Universitario, or a colectivo from Calle Montevideo, just off Avenida Abancay, in Lima Centro to Chosica, you can pick up buses and trucks to San Pedro from Parque Echinique. Empresa Santa Maria **buses** usually have signs reading "San Pedro" or "Marcahuasi", but for **trucks** it's a matter of asking all drivers where they're bound. If your bus or truck terminates at Las Cruces, you'll have half an hour's walk further to San Pedro.

In San Pedro almost everything is centred around the Plaza de Armas. It's a small and simple Andean village, quaint but without much choice in its small range of facilities. The **tourist office**, Plaza de Armas (Mon–Fri 9am–6pm, Sat 9am–1pm), can arrange accommodation and even mules for the uphill climb, though note that to visit the mountain you have to register next to the *albergue municipal* (municipality-run hostel) and pay a small entrance fee. For **places to stay**, there's the *albergue municipal* with sixteen beds (no phone; ❷), the *Hostal Communal* (no phone; ❶–❷), which only has communal rooms, and the *Hotel Huayrona* (no phone; ❷), which is actually the schoolteacher's house but also lets out rooms. *Tienda Natches* (no phone; ❶), which doubles up as a tourist information centre when the official tourist office is closed, also offers cheap floor space to travellers. There are two **cafés**, but they are not always open, so make sure to bring your own food.

La Oroya

LA OROYA is not a particularly inviting place, a bleak little mining town which gets fiercely cold at night. Located in a desolate spot above the treeline, some four hours or so by steeply uphill road from Lima, La Oroya is some 50km beyond the highest point, the pass or *abra* of Ticlio (4758m). It's also where the road splits: south to Huancayo or northeast to Tarma or Huánuco. If you have

The Andes rail line

The **rail line** into the Andes has had a huge impact on the region and was a major feat of engineering. For President Balta of Peru and many of his contemporaries in 1868, the iron fingers of a railway, "if attached to the hand of Lima would instantly squeeze out all the wealth of the Andes, and the whistle of the locomotives would awaken the Indian race from its centuries-old lethargy". Consequently, when the American rail entrepreneur **Henry Meiggs** (aptly called the "Yankee Pizarro") arrived on the scene it was decided that coastal guano deposits would be sold off to finance a new rail line, one which faced technical problems (ie. the Andes) never previously encountered by engineers. With timber from Oregon and the labour of thousands of Chinese workers (the basis of Peru's present Chinese communities), Meiggs' railway finally reached La Oroya via 61 bridges, 65 tunnels and the startling pass at 4800m. An extraordinary accomplishment, it nevertheless produced a mountain of debt that bound Peru more closely to the New York and London banking worlds than to its own hinterland and peasant population.

Departures these days are limited to occasional special trips and the odd short run during high season. Check this out with the tourist information office in Lima or at Desamparados train Station behind the Palacio de Gobierno.

to **stay** overnight, try the very basic *Hostal Inti*, Arequipa 117 (☏064/391098; ❶–❷), with lukewarm water and shared bathrooms; the *Hostal Chavín*, around the corner on Calle Tarma, is even worse; for a bit more comfort there's the *Hostal Arenales*, Arenales 162 (☏064/723088; ❹), close to the bus terminal. For **food**, try the *Restaurant Punta Arenas*, Zeballos 323, which is very good for seafood and Chinese dishes, or *Restaurant Los Angeles*, Jr Libertad, block 2 by the Plaza de Armas, with an excellent, inexpensive set-lunch menu. **Buses** to all destinations leave from the terminal five blocks from the Plaza de Armas on Arenales.

Huancayo

HUANCAYO, resting at 3249m and only six hours by car from Lima, is a large commercial city and capital of the Junín *departmento*. An important market centre thriving on agricultural produce and dealing in vast quantities of wheat, it makes a good base for exploring the Mantaro Valley and experiencing the region's distinct culture.

The settlement itself is very old and the cereal and textile potential of the region has long been exploited. Back in the 1460s the native Huanca tribe was conquered by the Inca Pachacuti's forces during his period of imperial expansion. Occupied by the Spanish from 1537, Huancayo remained little more than a staging point until the rail line arrived in 1909, transforming it into a city. Huancayo was paralysed in the years of terror during the 1980s and 1990s, more than every other city – except perhaps Ayacucho. With a major army base here, it became the heart of operations in what was then a military emergency zone. At times, whole villages and groups of journalists were found murdered, and to this day, some of these incidents remain a mystery as to whether they were acts of terrorism or the handiwork of the army. In 1999, an extensive army operation captured the leader of **Sendero Luminoso**, Oscar Ramirez Durand, who had taken over from Guzman in 1992. This essentially cleaned up the area (coincidentally at the start of the presidential electoral campaigns). Consequently, Huancayo is considered a safe destination (though there are still reports of petty street crime, so the usual precautions should be adhered to) and one where tourists can easily find good accommodation and all the usual facilities offered by large Peruvian towns.

Relatively modern, Huancayo has little of architectural or historical merit, though it's a lively enough place and has the extremely active weekend **Feria Dominical market** on blocks 2–12 of Avenida Huancavelica (best on Sun). Established in 1572 to assist the commerce of the local Indian population, it still sells fruit and vegetables, as well as a good selection of woollen and alpaca clothes and blankets, superb weavings, and some silver jewellery. It's also worth trying to coincide with the splendid **Fiesta de las Cruces** each May, when Huancayo erupts into a succession of boisterous processions, parties and festivities.

Arrival and information

There are more than ten daily direct **bus** services from Lima to Huancayo via Jauja; the journey costs around $10 and takes six to seven hours. Cruz del Sur (℡064/235650) offer the best and most expensive service, operating out of their office on block 2 of Ayacucho. All buses arrive at their respective company offices (see Listings, p.339), but many can be found on Avenida Mariategui blocks 10–12 in the Tambo district. For a quicker journey between Lima and Huancayo (5–6hr), you can take **colectivos** which can usually be found on Calle Loreto daily from 7am until 6pm and charge $12–15.

Trains to Huancavelica (℡064/235011) leave from the Avenida Ferrocarril in Chilca district: the cheaper Tren Ordinario (5hr; $3) on Mondays to Saturdays at 6.30am, 12.30pm and 2pm, or the faster and better Autovagon (3hr; $4) only on Fridays at 6.20am and 6pm. The **tourist office** (Mon–Fri 9am–2pm & 4–8pm) is inside the Casa de Artesano, just on the Plaza de la Constitución where Calle Real and Paseo La Breña meet.

Accommodation

The best Huancayo offers in accommodation is its choice between rambling old or modern **traditional city centre hotels** and a more familial setting in smaller outlying **hostels**. It doesn't offer anything spectacular in terms of rooms with views; for that you need to get out of town.

Casa Alojamiento de Aldo y Soledad Bonilla Huánuco 332 ℡064/232103. A friendly, family-run hostel with constant hot water and where good English is spoken, though it's some 8 blocks from the main plaza. ❷–❸

La Casa de la Abuela Av Giraldez 693. Basic and no rooms with private baths, but otherwise good facilities including private rooms and a shared dormitory, table tennis, a dartboard, and showers. ❶–❷

Hostal Alpeca Av Giraldez 494 ℡064/223136. New, friendly and carpeted, with TVs in most rooms. ❸

Hostal Plaza Ancash 171 ℡064/210509. Good-value rooms with private baths; go for the rooms at the front as they have most light and best views. ❸

Hostal San Martin Ferrocarril 362. A charming little hostel, but no hot water; located close to the train station. ❶

Hostal Santa Felicita Giraldez 145 ℡064/235285. Located on the Plaza de la Constitución. A very nice, affordable place; clean pleasant rooms, private showers. ❸–❹

Hotel Baldeon Amazonas 543 ℡064/321634. Very cheap, hot showers available on request,

friendly, family-run and offers use of kitchen facilities; close to the colectivos for Jauja and only a few blocks from the Plaza Constitución. **①**
Hotel Confort Ancash 231 ☏064/233601. Big rooms, most with private baths, but not all have hot showers; also has car park. **②**–**③**
Hotel Kiya Giraldez 107 ☏064/214955. A reasonably pleasant, centrally located hotel with private bathrooms, hot water and accommodating staff. **④**

Hotel Presidente C Real 1138 ☏064/231275, ✉hotelhyo@correo.dnet.com.pe. Quite luxurious for Huancayo, clean rooms and with good, friendly service; close to buses and only a few blocks from the heart of the city. **⑤**
Turismo Hotel Ancash 729 ☏064/231072, ℻235211, ✉hotelhyo@correodnet.com.pe. Another of the town's best hotels, with comfortable rooms, though its elegance has faded somewhat; restaurant generally fine, though its pisco sour drinks aren't what they should be. **⑤**

The town and around

There are two main squares in Huancayo. **Plaza de la Constitución** is named in honour of the 1812 Liberal Constitution of Cadiz and is where you'll find monuments in honour of Mariscal Ramon Castilla, who abolished slavery in Huancayo in 1854. The **Plaza Huamanga**, closer to the heart of the city, is the site where Huancayo was founded in 1572. Surrounded by the **cathedral** (daily 7.30–9.30am & 5–7.30pm; free), and some of the town's major public buildings and offices, it was once home to the Feria Dominical market, which shifted in the mid-1990s to alleviate traffic problems. Calle Real is the main drag running on the western edge of the plaza; it's here you'll find the **Capilla La Merced** (daily 9am–noon & 3–6.30pm), a colonial church, and the site for the preparation and signing of the 1839 Peruvian Constitution, which is now designated a historic monument. Another significant sight within the city centre is the **Museo del Colegio Salesiano**, at Prolongación Arequipa 105 (Mon–Fri 9am–1pm & 3–5pm; 60¢; ☏064/247763), an excellent natural history museum which has exhibits of local flora and fauna as well a selection of interesting rocks and minerals.

About 1km to the east of Huancayo, only five minutes by bus at the end of Avenida Giraldez, the hill **Cerrito de la Libertad** offers great views across the city and partial views over the Mantaro Valley. Another kilometre further on, about fifteen minutes' walk, you'll find the geological formation known as **Torre Torre**, naturally eroded stone towers offering much better views across the valley. Just 5km from the city centre in the Barrio de San Antonio, the **Parque de la Humanidad** covers nearly 6000 hectares, much of it pleasant green spaces open for public enjoyment; the main entrance is in the form of a giant gourd, one of the typical regional artesania products, and inside there's a *mirador* (viewing platform), some shady pergolas, cacti and the Laguna de Amalu.

Restaurants and nightlife

There's a number of worthwhile **restaurants** dotted around the Plaza de la Constitución: *El Parque*, on the southwest corner of Avenida Giraldez, is especially recommended for its regional dishes; and the excellent *Restaurant El Padrino*, Av Giraldez 133, also serves local dishes, including *papas a la Huancaina*, a delicious local speciality of potatoes in a mildly spicy cheese sauce, topped with sliced egg, a black olive and some green salad. A small, nameless café at Puno 209 serves cheap but tasty sandwiches and breakfasts. There are three reasonably good **chifas**, all offering some vegetarian options: *Chifa Rapido* at Arequipa 511 (☏064/214466) serves authentic, good-quality and inexpensive Chinese dishes; *Chifa Centro*, near the main plaza at Giraldez 238; and, quite a bit further out, *La Chifa*, Huánuco 286.

Huancayo boasts plenty of traditional dance as well as more participatory **nightlife**: local music and dance is performed most Sundays at 3pm in the *Coliseo* on Calle Real; there are some good criolla and folklore *peñas* – *Taka Wasi*, on Calle Huancavelica is the best, but only really gets going on Fridays and Saturdays; for Latin and European dance music try *A1A* on the second block of Bolognesi, open most evenings, including Sundays.

Listings

Banks and exhange For travellers' cheques, the Banco de Credito, C Real 1039, is best. To change dollars cash, try the street *cambistas* along C Real.

Bicycle rental A good way to explore the local countryside; try Huancayo Tours, C Real 543.

Buses Antezama, Arequipa 1301, for Ayacucho and Andahuaylas; Buenaventura, Lima 180, for Lima; Central, Av Ferrocarril, for Chanchamayo and Tarma; Cruz del Sur, Ayacucho 287, for Lima; Etusca, Puno 220, for Lima; Express Molina, Angaraes 334, for Ayacucho and Andahuaylas; Hidalgo, Loreto 350, for Lima and Huancavelica; Hualtapallana, Calixto 450, for Lima; Oriental, Ferrocarril 146, for Cerro de Pasco, Huánuco and Pucallpa; Ormeño, Paseo la Breña 218, for Lima; San Juan, Quito 136, for Chanchamayo and Tarma; San Pablo, Ancash 1248, for Huancavelica; Transel, Av Giraldez 247, for Ayacucho and Andahuaylas; Transfano, opposite Molina, for Ayacucho and Andahuaylas; Transportes Salazar, Giraldez 245, for Cerro de Pasco, Huánuco and Pucallpa; Turismo

Mariscal Caceres, C Real, between Angaraes and Tarapaca, for Lima.

Hospital C Independencia.

Post office Plaza Huamaumarca Mon–Sat 8am–7pm.

Spanish lessons Taught by Katia Cerna (☎064/201959, ✉katiacerna@hotmail.com) from her family home, her Spanish lessons are offered at all levels and, if required, can include accommodation; Karia can also arrange for city tours, rural outings and cultural or music events. Prices start at around $200 a week.

Telephones The Telefónica Peru office is on Plaza Huamanga.

Tour operators and guides Turismo Huancayo, C Real 517 (☎064/233351) offers tours throughout the region. Lucho Hurtado, operating out of the *Casa de la Abuela* hostel in Huancayo (☎/℻064/222395, ⊛www.incasdelperu.org), is a well-recommended local tour guide.

Around Huancayo

Using Huancayo as a base you can make a number of excursions around the stunningly scenic Mantaro Valley. The **Convento de Santa Rosa de Ocopa** (Mon & Wed–Sun 9am–noon & 3–6pm; $1.20), about forty minutes or 30km out of town, is easily reached by taking a microbus from outside the Church of Immaculate Conception in Huancayo's Plaza de la Constitución to the village of **Concepción**, where another bus covers the last 6km (a comfortable and very pleasant walk) to the monastery. Founded in 1724, and taking some twenty years to build, the church was the centre of the Franciscan mission into the Amazon, until their work was halted by the Wars of Independence, after which the mission villages in the jungle disintegrated and most of the natives returned to the forest. The cloisters are more interesting than the church, though both are set in a pleasant and peaceful environment, and there's an excellent library with chronicles from the sixteenth century onwards, plus a **Museum of Natural History and Ethnology** containing lots of stuffed animals and native artefacts from the jungle. You can also stay at the convent **guesthouse (❶)**.

A trip to the *convento* can be conveniently combined with a visit to the nearby village of **San Jerónimo**, about 12km west, well known for its Wednesday market of fine silver jewellery.

Another good day-trip from Huancayo (30min by frequent bus from the Church of Immaculate Conception) is to the local villages of **Cochas Chicas** and **Cochas Grandes**, whose speciality is crafted, carved gourds. Strangely,

Travelling through the Andes **at night** doesn't seem to be a problem these days. However, general advice is to travel by day if possible, and although it is possible to hitch rides on trucks, these are more at risk of being stopped and robbed during night journeys.

Cochas Grandes is the smaller of the two villages, and you have to ask around if you want to buy gourds here. You can buy straight from co-operatives or from individual artisans; expect to pay anything from $3 up to $150 for the finer gourds, and if you are ordering some to be made, you'll have to pay half the money in advance. The etchings and craftsmanship on the more detailed gourds is incredible in its microscopic depth, creativity and artistic skill. On some, whole rural scenes, like harvest, marriage and shamanic healing are represented in tiny storyboard format. The less expensive, more simple worked gourds have fairly common geometric designs, or bird, animal and flower forms etched boldly acoss the curvaceous surface of the gourds.

Some 7km west of Huancayo ($4 by taxi) near the present-day pueblo of **Huari**, stand the **Huari–Huilca Archeological Remains** (800–1200 AD), the sacred complex of the Huanca tribe who dominated this region for over two hundred years before the arrival of the Incas. At the site is a small museum (daily 8am–6pm; $1) showing collections of ceramic fragments, bones and stone weapons.

Further afield, the **Reserva Nacional de Junin** is located 165km northwest of Huancayo, but an excellent trip if you can afford the time and car rental or tour. Located at around 4100m above sea level on the Pampa de Junin, it abounds with aquatic birds around the lakes as well as being home to plenty of *viscachas* in its 5300 hectares. It's possible to camp here, but there are no facilities at all.

Jauja

Forty kilometres from Huancayo, on the road to La Oroya, is **JAUJA**, a little colonial town that was the capital of Peru before the founding of Lima. Surrounded by some gorgeous countryside, Jauja is a pleasant place, whose past is reflected in its unspoiled architecture, with many buildings painted light blue. A much smaller and more languid town than Huancayo, its streets are narrow and picturesque and the people friendly. Selected as a temporary capital of colonial Peru prior to the founding of Lima, Jauja today is more renowned for its traditional and well-stocked Sunday and Wednesday markets. Among the town's cultural assets, the **Capilla de Cristo Pobre** (daily 7–9am & 3–6pm), located between San Martin and Colina, shares some similarities with Notre Dame in Paris and, perhaps a tenuous claim to fame, it was also the first concrete religious construction in the Central Sierra. You can rent boats ($2 for an hour) on the nearby **Laguna de Paca** (10–15min in colectivos from Jauja; 30¢), and row out to the Isla de Amor; although romantic, this lake is rumoured to be home to a mermaid who lures men to their deaths. The lake is surrounded by *tortora* reeds and brimming with birdlife. The shoreline is lined with cafés where decent trout meals can be bought, and, at weekends, *pachamanca* are served.

Buses and **combis** for Jauja leave every hour from the market in Huancayo – the combi marked "izquierda" goes via the small towns in the valley, while the "derecha" combi is more direct, but both take around an hour. Empresa San Juan buses to Jauja leave from C Quito 136 in Huancayo, and Turismo

Central buses leave from Avenida Ferrocarril. For the return journey to Huancayo, both buses and combis leave from Jauja's Puente Ricardo Palma, or you can catch a through bus from Lima to Huancayo, which stops two or three times daily in Jauja's Plaza de Armas. Local transport is mostly by **motorcycle rickshaw**.

If you fancy **staying** in Jauja, the best bottom-end option is the hotel/restaurant *Ganso de Oro*, at Ricardo Palma 249 (❶); and there are three other hostels, less good value, including *Cabezon's Hostal*, Ayacucho 1027 (☎064/362206; ❷), with shared bathrooms; and the *Hostal Francisco Pizarro*, Bolognesi (❶), the cheapest place in town, opposite the market. Beside the lake there's the recently privatized *Hotel de Turistas* (❻), which is clean and very comfortable. As far as **food** goes, the *Ganso de Oro* restaurant is fine, and the *Marychris*, Jr Bolivar 1166, serves excellent traditional criolla lunches, but there aren't many other choices unless you love chicken and chips.

South of Huancayo

The mountainous and remote region south of Huancayo, largely out of bounds for much of the 1980s and 1990s, is now attracting visitors by the thousands every year. Not only does this bring in welcome income for many local people but it also ensures that the very Andean towns of Huancavelica and Ayacucho are open to the eyes of the world once again. **Ayacucho** is a must for anyone interested in colonial architecture, particularly fine churches; **Huancavelica** offers a slightly darker history lesson as an area which has suffered both in colonial times as well as more recently in the days of terrorism. At least the trip out here is appealing, by train some 130km from Huancayo. Ayacucho is further afield, some nine hours by bus (see p.344).

Huancavelica

Not a bad base for a little hiking, the remote town of **HUANCAVELICA**, at 3676m, is surprisingly almost purely Indian in its ethnic makeup in spite of a long colonial history and a fairly impressive array of Spanish-style architecture. Originally occupied by hunter-gatherers from about 5000 years ago, it then turned to sedentary cultivation, the local population being first taken over by the Huari tribe around 1100 AD, before being conquered by the Incas a few centuries later. The weight of its past, however, lies heavily on its shoulders. After mercury deposits were discovered here in 1563, the town began producing ore for the silver mines of Peru – replacing expensive imports previously used in the mining process. In just over a hundred years so many Indian labourers had died of mercury poisoning that the pits could hardly keep going: after the generations of locals bound to serve by the *mitayo* system of virtual slavery had been literally used up and thrown away, the salaries required to attract new workers made many of the mines unprofitable. Today the mines are working again and the ore is taken by truck to Pisco on the coast. The Mina de la Muerte, as the **Santa**

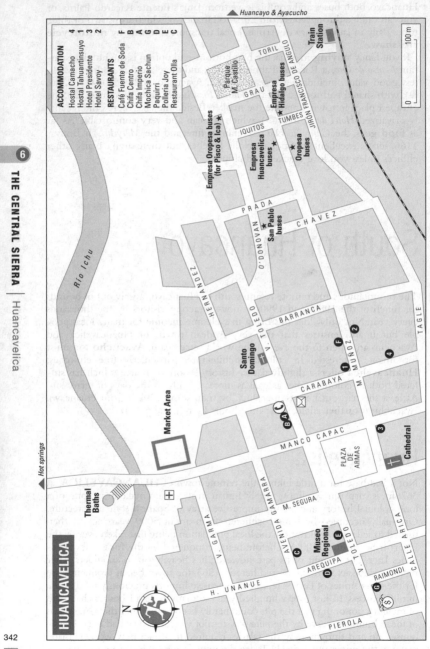

▲ Huancayo & Ayacucho

▲ Hot springs

HUANCAVELICA

N

Río Ichu

Thermal Baths

Market Area

Santo Domingo

Empresa Oropesa buses (for Pisco & Ica) ★

Empresa Huancavelica buses ★

San Pablo buses ★

Oropesa buses ★

Empresa Hidalgo buses ★

Parque M. Castillo

Train Station

Museo Regional

PLAZA DE ARMAS

Cathedral

ACCOMMODATION
Hostal Camacho	4
Hostal Tahuantinsuyo	1
Hotel Presidente	3
Hotel Savoy	2

RESTAURANTS
Café Fuente de Soda	F
Chifa Centro	B
Chifa Imperio	A
Mochica Sachun	G
Paquirri	D
Pollería Joy	E
Restaurant Olla	C

TORIL

GRAU

TUMBES

IQUITOS

JIRÓN FRANCISCO DE ANGULO

PRADA

O'DONOVAN

CHAVEZ

HERNANDEZ

BARRANCA

V. TOLEDO

MUÑOZ

M. RAMOS

TAGLE

CARABAYA

MANCO CAPAC

M. SEGURA

V. GARMA

AVENIDA GAMARRA

H. UNANUE

AREQUIPA

V. TOLEDO

CALLE ARICA

RAIMONDI

PIEROLA

0   100 m

Barbara mines tend to be called around Huancavelica, are also an attraction in their own right, located only 4 or 5km southeast of town (about 1.5hr by foot); the shield of the Spanish Crown sits unashamedly engraved in stone over the main entrance to this ghostly settlement. There's plenty of scope for exploring, but like all mines, some sections are dangerous and not visitor-friendly.

The Town

Huancavelica's main sights are around the main **Plaza de Armas**, and include the **Cathedral**, with its fine altar. Work on construction started here in 1673, but it took a hundred years to complete. These days it's home to the sacred image of the city's patron – Nuestra Señora de las Mercedes. Inside there is a distinct Baroque style in the volcanic stone craftsmanship. Religious paintings that decorate the interior represent the sky, purgatory, hell, the Last Supper and the Crucifixion. There are a handful of other notable churches, two of which – **San Francisco** and **Santo Domingo** – are connected to the Cathedral by an underground passage. San Francisco, built in 1774 by the Franciscan Order has just about survived several major earthquakes; it has a single nave and some fancy Baroque and Churrigueresque *retablos* of wood and gold-leaf. During the nineteenth-century war with Chile, this church was commandeered by the Peruvian army who sold its fine collection of musical instruments to finance the war effort. Today, the steps of San Francisco are the site of the awe-inspiring traditional scissor-dancing performances *(danza tijera)* generally done by men wielding two long machete-like swords apiece, but only on December 24 and 25.

Santo Domingo is a church and convent complex, founded in 1601, just thirty years after the city was established. Inside there are fine paintings, brought from Rome, of the Virgen del Rosario and the patron St Dominic as well as a fine Baroque altar with some gold-leaf adornment; in the sacristy you can find a painting dating from 1666 repesenting El Señor de la Sentencia y Resurrección. The church is said to be connected to others via underground tunnels and it's claimed that an entrance was once found in the lateral nave. The entrance is made from red stone brought from the Pucarumi quarry. The **Iglesia de San Antonio** on the Plaza de Armas (Mon–Sat 7–8.30am & 5.30–7.30pm, Sun 5.30–11.30am) is a fine, stone Baroque temple dating from the seventeenth century; its elaborate gold-leaf altar was carved from wood, and the silver sheets on display beside it were created by the Cusqueña and Huamanguina schools.

The town also boasts a small **Regional Museum**, on the Plaza San Juan de Dios at Jirón Arica (Mon–Fri 9am–1pm & 4–6pm; 80¢), containing archeological exhibits, fossils from the Tertiary period, petrified marine species and dispays on pre-Inca Andean cultures. There's also a **Museo de Arte Popular** located within the Museo Daniel Hernandez, one block from the Plaza de Armas in the Instituto Nacional de Cultura building (free), showing paintings and objects depicting local culture. In the same building there's the small **Museo de Antropología y Arqueología** with displays of remains going back 10,000 years. These apart, there's little else of interest here, except the Sunday **market**, which sells local food, jungle fruits, and carved gourds. A couple of pleasant **walks** from town are to the natural **hot springs** on the hill north of the river, and to visit the **weaving co-operative**, 4km away at Totoral.

Practicalities

There's not a wide choice of **accommodation** available in town – the best is the comfortable *Hotel Presidente*, Plaza de Armas (☏064/952760; ❸–❹), which has both private and communal bathrooms. Otherwise, *Hostal Camacho*, Carabaya 481 (❶), is excellent value, with communal bathrooms and hot water most mornings; *Hotel Savoy*, Muñoz 296 (❶), is basic with small rooms and cold communal showers and toilets; and *Hostal Táhuantinsuyo*, on the corner of Muñoz and Carabaya (❷), is dingy but at least has hot water most mornings. Reasonable **food** is available from the *Café Fuente de Soda*, on the second block of Manchego Muñoz, which serves great juices, sandwiches and other snacks; the restaurant *Chifa Centro*, Jr Virrey Toledo 275, serves okay but not brilliant Chinese food; the *Mochica Sachun,* Toledo 303, does a great set lunch for around $1; *Paquirri* on Arequipa serves good local dishes and the *Restaurant Olla* on Avenida Gamarra dishes up reasonably priced international and Peruvian meals in a pleasant atmosphere. The best place for chicken and chips is *Pollería Joy*, on Calle M. Segura. The **Banco de Credito** and **telephone office** are along Toledo; but the **post office** can be found at Manchego Muñoz 759 (Mon–Fri 8am–6pm). For reasonably priced **artesanía**, including the locally typical ceramics and weavings, the **Mercado Central** on Jirón Victor Garma is your best bet.

Two types of **trains** travel from Huancavelica through beautiful countryside to Huancayo. The Train Ordinario, a slow, local train (5hr), leaves Monday to Saturday at 6.30am and 2.30pm and Sundays only at 6.30am; the faster (3hr) Autovagon departs on Fridays at 5.30am and Mondays at 6.30pm only. All trains leave from the station on Avenida Agusto Leguia (☏064/752898). By far the easiest way to get to Lima is **by bus** via Huancayo. There's also a daily bus to Ayacucho, leaving at 5am with Empresa Ticllas from Av Cáceres 235. For Pisco and Ica (6-10hr depending on condition of road) on the coast, Empresa Oropesa buses leave around 5.30pm from their office on the Plaza Santa Ana.

Ayacucho

Roughly halfway between Cusco and Lima, the city of **AYACUCHO** ("Purple Soul", from its Quechua origins) sits in the Andes around 2800m high in one of Peru's most archeologically important valleys, with evidence from nearby caves at Pikimachay suggesting that the region has been occupied for over 20,000 years. Ayacucho was the centre of the Huari culture which emerged in the region around 700 AD and spread its powerful and evocative religious symbolism throughout most of Peru over the next three or four hundred years. The city later became a major Inca administrative centre. The original Spanish site for the city at Huamanguilla was abandoned in 1540 in favour of the present location. Ayacucho's strategic location, vitally important to both the Incas and the Spanish colonials, meant that the city grew very wealthy as miners and administrators decided to put down roots here, eventually sponsoring the exquisite and unique wealth of the city's churches.

The bloody **Battle of Ayacucho**, which took place near here on the Pampa de Quinoa in 1824, finally released Peru from the shackles of Spain. The armies met early in December, when Viceroy José de la Serna attacked Sucre's Republican force in three columns. The pro-Spanish soldiers were, however, unable to hold off the Republican forces, who captured the viceroy with relative ease. Ayacucho was the last part of Peru to be liberated from colonial power.

Ayacucho is renowned for having over thirty fine **churches**, which demonstrate the clearly high level of masonic and woodworking skills held by the

AYACUCHO

Museum of
Archeology &
Anthropology

INDEPENDENCIA

JIRÓN LIBERTAD

JIRÓN GARCILAZO DE LA VEGA

JIRÓN 9 DE DICIEMBRE

JIRÓN ASAMBLEA

(A)

**Transportes Chankas
& Ayacucho**

JIRÓN MARISCAL CACERES

**Iglesia
Santo
Domingo**

(B)

JIRÓN SOL

(C)

JIRÓN M P BELLIDO

**Money
Change**

(1)

(D)

(3)

JIRÓN CUSCO

JIRÓN FCO PIZARRO

(2)

(4)

JIRÓN CALLAO

(5)

**PLAZA
DE
ARMAS**

(i)

(E)

Cathedral

JIRÓN LIMA

JIRÓN AREQUIPA

**Templo de
la Compañia**

(F)

(6)

**Casona
Jauregui**

**Tourist
Police**

JIRÓN TRES MASCARAS

JIRÓN SAN MARTIN

(G)

**Market
Area**

JIRÓN C F VIVANCEO

Río Alameda

**Ormeño
buses for Lima**

★

JIRÓN GRAU

JIRÓN 28 DE JULIO

**Iglesia
San Francisco
de Asis**

(H)

JR LONDRES

S J DE DIOS

CORCOBADO

ITANA

RAYMONDI

CHORRO

**Casona
Vivanco**

JIRÓN 2 DE MAYO

(7)

**Barrio
Santa Ana**

0   200 m

◄ Pisco

► Huari & buses

► Airport, Abancay & Cusco

6

THE CENTRAL SIERRA | Ayacucho

345

ACCOMMODATION

Ayacucho Hotel Plaza	1
La Colmena	3
Hostal San Blas	7
Hostal Santa Rosa	5
Hotel Crillonesa	6
Hotel Samari	4
Hotel San Francisco	2

RESTAURANTS

Alamo	E
Arco Blanco	B
Los Portales	D
Restaurant La Casona	C
Restaurant La Pileta	F
Restaurant Traditional	G
Restaurant Turistico	A
Restaurant Typic	H

local crafts people. The city's main plaza is surrounded on all four sides by stone arches, each facing towards the central monument to Mariscal Antonio José. Its **climate**, despite the altitude, is pleasant all year round – dry and temperate with blue skies nearly every day – and temperatures average 16°C. The surrounding hills are covered with cacti, broom bushes and agave plants, adding a distinctive atmosphere to the city. Despite the political problems of the last few years (see box opposite), most people on the streets of Ayacucho, although quiet and reserved (seemingly saving their energy for the city's boisterous **fiestas**), are helpful, friendly and kind. You'll find few people speak any English; Quechua is the city's first language, though most of the town's inhabitants can also speak some Spanish.

Arrival, information and tours

Most visitors arrive in Ayacucho from Lima or Cusco, either on the thirty-minute **flight**, which lands at the airport 4km from town – a taxi into town costs $2–3, buses cost 30¢ and leave from just outside the terminal – or overland by **bus**. If you're arriving overland from Huancayo, Huancavelica, Cusco or Lima the bus companies mostly have their depots along Jirón 3 Mascaras or Avenida Mariscal Caceres, both within a few blocks of the Plaza de Armas (see Listings, p.349 for details). **Tourist information** is available from the municipalidad building on the Plaza Mayor (Mon–Sat 9am–8pm; ☎064/818308), which has helpful staff who can arrange trips in the area; there's also a tourist information kiosk at the airport (Mon–Sat 8am–8pm).

Accommodation

Finding a room in Ayacucho is easy enough outside of the Easter period when, because of the colourful religious festivals, the town is bursting at the seams with visitors from Lima and elsewhere. Most of the **hotels** are located in interesting old properties, but service is generally good and many places have been tastefully modernized.

Ayacucho Hotel Plaza Jr 9 de Diciembre 184 ☎064/812202, ⑤812314. Easily the most luxurious hotel in town, with a reasonable restaurant, though food service can be slow. Centrally located on the Plaza de Armas. ❼
La Colmena Jr Cusco 140 ☎064/812146. Clean and good value with the added luxury of a beautiful, flowered courtyard. ❷
Hostal San Blas Jr Chorro 167 ☎064/810552. Good value with friendly service, reasonably comfortable rooms, private bathrooms and a reliable hot-water system. ❷
Hostal Santa Rosa Jr Lima 166 ☎064/812083, ⑤812083. Only half a block from the Plaza de

Armas, with a decent restaurant and friendly service. ❹
Hotel Crillonesa C Zazareo ☎064/812350. Hostel with great views of the city and valley from its rooftop terrace; there's hot water and a laundry service, and rooms are clean and very good value. ❶
Hotel Samari Jr Callao 329 ☎064/812442. A fine, welcoming place to relax for a few days, just two blocks east of the Plaza de Armas. ❷
Hotel San Francisco Jr Callao 290 ☎064/812959. High standards and good value, with a nice café on the roof overlooking town. Rooms have TV and shower; breakfast included. ❸

The Town

Ayacucho is an attractive colonial city, with splendid churches and mansions packed together in dense blocks around the central **Plaza de Armas** (also known as the **Plaza Mayor**) at whose centre rests a monument to Mariscal José Sucre. The **Templo de San Cristóbal**, on block 7 of Jr 28 de Julio, dates

A radical university town with a long left-wing tradition, Ayacucho is known around the world for the outbreaks of **violence** between terrorists and the Peruvian armed forces during the 1980s. Most non-militaristic people in the region remember this era as one where they were trapped between two evils. A large proportion of villagers from remote settlements in the region were forced to leave the area, often moving to the shantytowns around Lima. The exact figure isn't known but something like ten thousand people disappeared (presumed dead) in this region over a twelve-year period. Entire villages were massacred and hundreds of young students evidently liquidated while the army, the media and the Sendero Luminoso argued over who was responsible. Even today there's little evidence to prove anything either way, but most people believe that some of the atrocities were committed by Sendero while others were plainly perpetrated by the military.

Since the mid-1990s, travellers have returned in force to Ayacucho, and many of the refugees who fled their homes in the surrounding area have also come back and begun rebuilding their communities. After more than ten years of terror the city and region regained their previous stability and are now safe again for tourists, both Peruvians and foreigners, whom it actively welcomes. Nevertheless, it will take a long time for the scars to heal. You shouldn't have any problems in the area, provided you stick to a few basic ground rules: always stop at any army checkpoints; treat soldiers with respect and never try to photograph them. For further details of the Sendero Luminoso and the history and politics of the area, see Contexts (p.542).

from 1540 and was the first church built in Ayacucho; it has a single nave and only one altar, plus an interesting stone and adobe roof. But the **Cathedral** (Mon–Sat 11am–3pm; free), just off the Plaza Mayor, is of more interest. Built of red and grey stone between 1612 and 1671, it has a fine, three-aisled nave culminating in a stunning Baroque gold-leaf altarpiece. The **Iglesia de Santo Domingo**, block 2 of Jr 9 de Diciembre, was founded in 1548 and posseses one of the most beautiful exteriors in the city; it contains three arches of brick and lime, said to be where heretics were hung and tortured during the Spanish Inquisition. It has a Baroque and Churrigueresque gold-leaf altar and houses two images – El Señor del Santo Sepulcro and the Virgen Dolorosa - only brought out for the Easter processions. In block 1 of 28 de Julio is the **Jesuit Templo de la Compañía**, built in 1605 and renowned for its distinctive Churrigueresque-styled main altar. The **Casona Jauregui**, on block 2 of Jr 2 de Mayo (Mon–Fri 8.30am–4pm; free), is a lovely seventeenth-century mansion built by Don Cayetano Ruiz de Ochon; it has a superb patio and balcony with two lions statues and a stone shield of Indian influence displaying a two-headed eagle. The **Museo Pinacoteca de San Francisco de Asís**, in block 3 of 28 de Julio, is known for its library of unique historical works, and there are a couple of **art galleries** in town: the Casona Vivanco, Jr 28 de Julio 518 (Mon–Sat 10am–1pm & 3–6pm; 50¢), with a particularly good collection of colonial art, and the Popular Art Gallery, Jr Asamblea 138 (Mon–Sat 9am–6.30pm; free), specializing in regional art.

Further out, the **Museum of Archeology and Anthropology** (or **Museo INC**), on Avenida Independencia (Mon–Sat 9am–noon & 2–6pm; 80¢; ☎064/912056), about a thirty-minute walk (taxi, 5min) from the old centre, is full of local archeological finds, mainly ceramics, dating from several millennia ago, plus exhibits from the Chavín, Huarpa, Nazca and Inca eras.

If you can be in Ayacucho for **Semana Santa**, the Holy Week beginning the Friday before Easter, you'll see fabulous daily processions and pageants and nightly candlelit processions centred on the Cathedral. But beware of the beautiful procession of the **Virgen Dolores** (Our Lady of Sorrows), which takes place the Friday before Palm Sunday: pebbles are fired at the crowd (particularly at children and foreigners) by expert slingers so that onlookers take on the pain of La Madre de Dios, and so supposedly reduce her suffering. This is a bit of an Andean Catholic phenomenon, whereby pain is suffered to obtain forgiveness of sins; in this particular instance, the Virgin and the Mother of God are one and the same. Around May 23, there is the elaborate religious procession of the **Fiesta de las Cruces**, when festivities often involve the local "scissors" folkdance performed by two men, each wielding a rather dangerous pair of cutlasses.

Arts and crafts in Ayacucho

Many visitors come for Ayacucho's thriving **craft industry**, mainly woven rugs and *retablos* (finely worked little wooden boxes containing intricate three-dimensional religious scenes made mainly from papier-mâché). Among the best shops for a wide variety of arts and crafts are artesanias Helme, Portal Unión 49, and Pokra, Jr 2 de Mayo 128.

If you've got the time to spare, however, it's more interesting and less expensive to visit some of the actual craft workshops and buy from the artisans themselves. Most of these workshops are found in the barrio of **Santa Ana**, just uphill from the Plaza de Armas. Some of the best-quality *retablos* are made by the Jimenez family: their simpler works are not all that expensive, but if you want one of their more complicated modern pieces it could cost as much as $300, and take up to three months to complete. For rugs, check out Edwin Sulca – probably the most famous weaver here – who lives opposite the church on the Plaza Santa Ana. His work sells from around $100 (almost double this in Lima's shops), and many of his designs graphically depict the horrors of the political situation around Ayacucho in the recent past. Gerado Fernandez Palomino, another excellent weaver, lives at Jr Paris 600, also in Santa Ana. The best artesania markets can be found around the Plazoleta Maria Pardo de Bellido, and at Jr Libertad, blocks 7–9, the first block of Jirón Paris, second block of Pasaje Bolognesi and the first two of Jirón Asamblea.

Alabaster carvings – known in Peru as **Huamanga stone carvings** – are another speciality of Ayacucho artisans (Huamanga being the old name for the city). Señor Pizarro, Jr San Cristoval 215, has a reputation as one of the best carvers in town, and the craft co-operative Ahuacllacta, Huanca Solar 130, is also worth checking out. The tourist office can also make a few recommendations.

Restaurants and nightlife

Food and **nightlife** are both surprisingly good in Ayacucho, which has a distinctive cuisine. Be sure to try *puca picante*, made from pork and potatoes seasoned with yellow chilli peppers and ground toasted peanuts, and the local *chorizo*, which is prepared with ground pork soaked with yellow chilli and vinegar, then fried in butter and served with diced fried potatoes. One of the better **restaurants** is *Alamo,* Jr Cusco 215, where you can savour the local dishes. *Restaurant La Pileta,* Jr Lima 166, is excellent for dinner, while the good-value *Restaurant Tradicional,* San Martin 406, offers a wide range of Peruvian and international dishes in a sophisticated atmosphere, and *Restaurant La Casona*, Jr Bellido, like *Alamo*, serves excellent Andean criolla dishes. *Restaurant Typic,* Jr Londres 196, and *Turístico*, Jr 9 de Diciembre 396, are both recommended for set-lunch menus at reasonable prices.

If you're after **live music** in the evenings, check out some of Ayacucho's excellent *peñas*: *Arco Blanco*, Jr Asamblea 280, plays Andean folk music most Friday and Saturday nights from 9pm to midnight, while *Machi*, on Jirón Grau, specializes in criolla and *huayno*. *Los Balcones*, block 1 of Jr Asamblea, plays rock and salsa, while *Los Portales*, Portal Unión 33, has mainly disco music at weekends. *La Casona*, Jr Bellido 463, is a stylish place combining good food with a pleasant atmosphere and live music. The hippest places these days are *Calle 8*, on Avenida Mariscal Caceres, and *Amor Serrano*, on Garcilaso de la Vega.

Listings

Airline Aero Continente, Jr 9 de Diciembre ☏064/912816.

Airport Av del Ejercito 950 ☏064/812088.

Banks and exchange Travellers' cheques can be changed at the Banco de Credito, on the Plaza Mayor (Mon–Fri 9.15am–6pm) or sometimes in the larger hotels. Black market *cambistas* gather on Jr 9 de Diciembre, near the corner of the Plaza Mayor, giving good rates, but will only accept dollars and euros cash.

Bus companies The best company is Cruz del Sur, Jr 9 de Diciembre, for Lima; next up is Ormeño, Jr Libertad 257 (☏064/812495), also for Lima. Others include: Empresa Libertadores, Jr 3

Mascaras 496, for Lima, Abancay and Cusco; Empresa Molina, Jr 3 Mascaras 551, for Huancayo; Transmar, Av Mariscal Caceres 896, for Lima, Abancay and Cusco; and Transportes Chankas, 3 blocks north of the Plaza Mayor on Jr Mariscal Caceres, for Andahuaylas. Other bus companies can be found along blocks 7–17 of Av Mariscal Caceres or blocks 2–4 of Av Manco Capac.

Post office Asamblea 295, 2 blocks from the plaza. Mon–Sat 8am–6pm.

Telephone office Jr Asamblea 293. Daily 8am–10pm.

Tourist police Corner of 2 de Mayo with Jr Lima, right on the plaza and close to the Cathedral.

Around Ayacucho

Although the city itself is certainly the main pull, there are some quite fascinating places near Ayacucho that are possible to visit. Having said that, it's always a good idea to check with the tourist office beforehand. The political situation is always changing and certain villages are more sensitive than others. The cave of **Pikimachay**, 24km west of Ayacucho, on the road to Huanta, where archeologists have found human (dated to 15,000 BC) and gigantic animal remains, is best visited on a guided tour with one of the tour companies listed in the box below. This is also true of the ancient city of **Huari** (sometimes written "Wari"), about 20km north of Ayacucho on the road to Huancayo. Covering an area of about 2000 hectares, historians claim that this site used to

Tours around Ayacucho

One of the easiest ways to visit the sites around Ayacucho is to take a **guided tour**, and the tourist information office in Ayacucho can arrange trips in the area. Alternatively, all the following companies offer half-day tours to Pikimachay for around $15 and half-day tours to Huari for a similar price. Full-day trips to Huari and Quinua will set you back around $25. Companies to try in Ayacucho include: Quinua Tours, Jr Asamblea 195 (☏064/912191); Urpillay Tours, Portal Independencia 62 and Jr Asamblea 145; and Wari Tours, Portal Independencia 91.

house some 50,000 people just over a thousand years ago. You can still make out the ancient streets, plazas, some reservoirs, canals and large structures. The small site museum displays skulls and stone weapons found here in the 1960s.

About 37km northeast of Ayacucho, the charming and sleepy village of **Quinua** is just a short bus ride away through acres of tuna cactus, which is abundantly farmed here for both its delicious fruit (prickly pear) and the red dye (cochineal) extracted from the *cochamilla* – larvae that thrive at the base of the cactus leaves. The site of the historic nineteenth-century **Battle of Ayacucho** is marked by a striking obelisk (the village's most unique feature). There are still some artisans working in Quinua: at San Pedro Ceramics (at the foot of the hill leading to the obelisk) it's often possible to look round the workshops, or try Mamerto Sanchez's workshop on Jirón Sucre. About 120km away, some four hours by road, you can also find **Vilcasayhuaman**, a pre-Conquest construction with a Temple of the Sun, Temple of the Moon and a ceremonial pyramid. Another 25km on from Vilcasayhuaman, at a site called **Intihuatana**, there's another archeological complex, with a palace, artificial lake and a stone bath.

East to Cusco

With much improved roads – one of Fujimori's better legacies - it now only takes about 20–28 hours to travel **from Ayacucho to Cusco** via Andahuaylas and Abancay, a distance of almost 600km.

It's a long, ten-hour, 270-kilometre haul from Ayacucho across mountains passes and through several valleys to **ANDAHUAYLAS**, a lovely region, but with little to see or do in the town, despite its setting against the backdrop of splendid highland scenery. The **airport** here has flights to Arequipa, Cusco and Lima (Aero Continente are at Av Peru 137; ☎084/751515), plus there are **buses** to Lima and Cusco (several daily). Of the **hotels**, *El Encanto de Oro Hotel*, Pedro Casafranca 424 (☎/☎084/723066; ❸), is pleasant enough. At the budget end of things is the fairly basic *Hotel Los Libertadores Wari*, Juan Ramos 425 (☎084/721434; ❶), though the *Hotel Residencial San Juan*, Juan Ramos 126 (☎084/721119; ❷), is slightly better. As for **banks**, the Banco de Credito can be found at Juan Antonio Trelles 255, and the Banco de la Nación at Ramon Castilla 545.

It's only another 136km to **ABANCAY**, usually covered in five to seven hours, depending on condition and type of vehicle. Abancay is a larger town, at 2378m above sea level, in the Andean *departmento* of Apurimac. It's a bustling market centre in a beautiful area, but with little tourist infrastructure and with the best places being hard to reach and little known, it has little to offer the traveller apart from a roof for the night and transport out by truck or bus. For **accommodation**, the most comfortable place is the *Hotel de Turistas*, Av Diaz Barcenas 500 (☎/☎084/321017; ❹). For money **exchange**, the Banco de Credito is at Libertad 218 and the Banco de la Nación at Lima 816. Within the locality, overlooking the Apurimac canyon, are the superb Inca ruins of **Choquequirau**, currently accessible only with a planned expedition through one of the Cusco tour operators (see p.151), but with the potential to become a major attraction.

The rest of the journey is a little less than 200km, usually taking five or six hours and passing en route through archeologically interesting terrain. Shortly before crossing into the *departmento* of Cusco (see Chapter Two), for instance, the road goes through the village of **Carahuasi** where the community of

Concacha (3500m) is home to the archeological complex of Sahuite, comprising three massive, beautifully worked granite boulders, the best of which graphically depict an Inca village (though they have been partially defaced in recent years); while nearby at Conoc there are hot medicinal springs.

North of Huancayo

The area north of Huancayo divides into two main routes. The nearest takes you to **Tarma**, a gentle mountain area which stands at the top of one of Peru's steepest roads down from the Andes into the Central Selva of Chanchamayo and beyond to Satipo, which encompasses the fascinating Germanic settlement of Pozuzo. Further north, some 280km from Huancayo, lies **Huánuco**, interesting for its nearby archeological remains, and another important gateway to the Central Selva, in particular the large jungle port town of Pucallpa. Huánuco is around 200km north of La Oroya, which is the main connection point to and from Lima for this corner of the Andes.

Tarma and around

The region around **Tarma**, some 60km east of La Oroya, is one of Peru's most beautiful Andean regions, with green rather than snow-capped mountains stretching down from high, craggy limestone outcrops into steep canyons forged by Amazon tributaries powering their way down to the Atlantic. By far the nicest mountain town in this part of Peru, Tarma sits on the edge of the Andes almost within spitting distance of the Amazon forest. It's always a good idea to check with your embassy in Lima for up-to-the-minute intelligence on this area since the occasional terrorist column has been known to be active in its remoter sectors. The nearby towns of **Palcamayo**, **San Pedro de Cajas** and **Acobamba** make for pleasant day-trips from Tarma. The well-established settler towns of San Ramon and La Merced, both on the Río Tulumayo, San Ramon and La Merced are separated by only 10km of road, some 2500m below Tarma, and are surrounded by exciting hiking country (see Chapter Eight).

The Town

TARMA itself is a pretty colonial town, making a good living from its traditional textile and leather industries, and from growing flowers for export as well as for its own use. The town's greatest claim to fame is its connection with Juan Santos Atahualpa's rebellion in the 1740s and 1750s: taking refuge in the surrounding mountains he defied Spanish troops for more than a decade, though peace returned to the region in 1756 when he and his allies mysteriously disappeared. Today Tarma is a quiet place, disturbed only by the flow of trucks climbing up towards the jungle foothills, and the town's famous Easter Sunday procession from the main plaza, when the streets are covered by carpets of dazzling flowers.

Practicalities

Tourist information is available from Turismo Tarama, Huaraz 537 (Mon–Sat 9am–6pm; ☎064/321286); the **post office** is on Callao, within two blocks of the plaza; and the **telephone office** is on the Plaza de Armas. **Money** can be changed at the Banco de Credito, Lima 407. Most of the **bus** and **colectivo** offices are clustered on Callao and Castilla near the petrol station, with Transportes Chanchapoyo's office, for services to Lima, at Callao 1002 and Empresa San Juan, whose buses run to Chanchamayo hourly, at 2 de Mayo 316. Expresso Satipo and Hidalgo buses to Huancayo and Lima have offices on Avenida Tarma, while the Lobato office, for buses to Lima, La Merced and Satipo, is on the corner of Calle Arica and Avenida 2 de Mayo.

The best **accommodation** in town is at the *Hotel Los Portales,* Av Castilla 512 (☎064/321411; ❺); slightly cheaper are the *Hotel Internacional,* 2 de Mayo 307 (☎064/321830; ❹), which has hot water between 6pm and 8am, and the *Hotel Galaxia,* Plaza de Armas (❸), with private bathrooms and a car park. Cheaper still are the *Hospedaje El Dorado,* Jr Huánuco 488 (☎064/321598; ❶), which is good value and better than the *Hostal Central,* Huánuco 614 (❷), which has its own observatory that non-guests can use on clear Friday nights, and the *Hostal Bolivar,* Huaraz 389 (☎064/321060; ❷), with hot water and some rooms with private bathrooms. The best place **to eat** is the *Señorial,* Huánuco 138, which serves good standard Peruvian fare; there's *Lo Mejorcito* in the same block at no. 190, or for local fish try *La Cabaña de Bryan* at Paucartambo 450 or one of the many *chifa* restaurants or *pollerías* located within a couple of blocks' radius of the Plaza de Armas.

Staying out of town in *La Hacienda Santa Maria* (contact in Lima ☎01/4451214 or 4467440, ⓦwww.geocities.com/haciendasantamaria; ❺) is a special treat; this very comfortable old hacienda, owned by the Santa Maria family for two centuries, is just 1.2km from Tarma in the barrio of Sacsamarca. First-floor rooms have private baths and there's a great restaurant. The *Hacienda* also runs excellent tours, to the Gruta de Huagapo caves and the Sanctuary of Muruhuay.

Around Tarma

An interesting day-trip from Tarma – though better appreciated if you camp overnight – is to the rural village of **PALCAMAYO** (90min by bus). From here it's an hour's climb to the caves known as **La Gruta de Huagapo**, which are the country's deepest explored caves; if dry they are generally accessible, taking great care, for about 180m without specialized equipment, or up to 1.8km with a guide and full speleological kit. If you've got your own transport, continue 20km along the same road (the only road in the valley) west to the beautiful village of **SAN PEDRO DE CAJAS**, where crafts-people produce superb-quality weavings. Coincidentally (or not) the village lies in a valley neatly divided into patchwork field-systems – an exact model of the local textile style.

Also within easy day-tripping distance from Tarma (12km) – just a short colectivo ride (about 40¢) – is the small settlement of **ACOBAMBA**, home of the **Sanctuary of the Lord of Muruhuay** (daily 7am–7pm; free), a small church built in 1972 around a rock painting where a vision of Christ on the cross led to this site becoming a major centre of pilgrimage. The chapel has an altar with weavings representing the Resurrection and the Last Supper. Some of the **restaurants** by the church serve excellent *cuy* (guinea pig) and *pachamanca.*

Huánuco and around

The *departmento* of **Huánuco** offers the possibility of several fascinating excursions – the 4000-year-old **Temple of Kotosh** and the impressive ruins at **Tantamayo**, to name but two – as well as the option of penetrating the wilder parts of the Amazon Basin. Its capital, also called **Huánuco**, is a modern market town and an ideal stopping point on the way to the jungle town of **Tingo Maria** and the coca-growing slopes at the upper end of the Río Huallaga. The region is usually reached via the Central Highway, which snakes along the spine of the Central Sierra, and La Oroya, then north through Cerro de Pasco. However, for anyone already in or around Huaraz, or those willing to risk possible hardship and delays in return for magnificent scenery, there is a direct route over the Cordillera Blanca which takes you to **La Unión** and the preserved Inca ruins of **Huánuco Viejo**, before continuing to the city of Huánuco.

Huánuco

The charming modern city of **HUÁNUCO**, more than 100km east of the deserted Inca town of the same name, and around 412km from Lima, sits nestled in a beautiful Andean valley some 1900m above sea level. It's a relatively peaceful place, located on the left bank of the sparkling Río Huallaga, that depends for its livelihood on forestry, tea and coca, along with a little low-key tourism. Its old, narrow streets ramble across a handful of small plazas, making a pleasant environment to spend a day or two preparing for a trip down into the jungle beyond Tingo Maria or exploring some of the nearby archeological sites, such as the Temple of Kotosh and the ruins at Tantamayo.

The city itself boasts no real sights, save a handful of fine old churches and a small natural history museum. The sixteenth-century cathedral church of **San Francisco** (daily 6am–9pm; free) on the Plaza de Armas houses the tomb of the town's original founder and shows a strong indigenous influence, its altars featuring richly carved native fruits – avocados, papayas and pomegranates. It also boasts a small collection of sixteenth-century paintings. The church of **La Merced** (daily 6am–9pm; free), three blocks south and west from the Plaza de Armas on Calle Hermilio Valdizan, is worth a brief look around for its spectacular gold-leaf altarpiece. The **San Cristobal** church (daily 7am–9pm; free), three blocks west of the plaza on Calle Damaso Beraun, also has some fine gold-leaf altarpieces, and is said to be built on the site where the chief of the Chupacos tribe once lived and where Portuguese priest Pablo Coimbra celebrated the first mass in the region. The natural history museum, **Museo de Ciencias**, Jr General Prado 495 (Mon–Fri 9am–6pm, Sat 9am–1pm; 75¢),

---

Fiestas in Huánuco

If you can, you should aim to be in Huánuco around August 15, when **carnival week** begins and the city's normal tranquillity explodes into a wild fiesta binge. **Peruvian Independence Day** (July 28) is also a good time to be here, when traditional dances like the *chunco* take place throughout the streets. At Christmas time, children put on their own dance performances. On January 1, 6 and 18, you can witness the **Dance of the Blacks** (El Baile de los Negritos) in which various local dance groups, dressed in colourful costumes with black masks, representing the slaves brought to work in the mines here run and dance throughout the main streets of the city; food stalls stay open and drinking continues all day and most of the night.

△ A shepherd and flock, near Tarma

houses archeological finds, mainly pottery, from the region and a small display of Andean flora and fauna.

Practicalities

The best of the budget **accommodation** options is the downmarket *Hotel Astoria,* Jr General Prado 988 (☏064/512310; ❷), a couple of blocks from the Plaza de Armas, with shared bathrooms but clean and comfortably furnished rooms, or the well-run but basic *Hostal Residencial Huánuco* on Calle Huánuco (☏064/512050; ❸), an attractive colonial building that's also close to the plaza. Pricier options include the *Hotel Cusco,* C Huánuco 616 (☏064/512244; ❹), just one and a half blocks from the plaza, which has private bathrooms, and the much more upmarket and very comfortable *Gran Hotel Huánuco* (☏064/512410; ❻), which sits right on the Plaza de Armas in the shade of some beautiful old trees. Alternatively, you can **camp** down by the Río Huallaga near the stadium, but watch out for the active insect life.

El Café, on the Plaza de Armas, is the best **restaurant** for international cuisine, as well as a variety of criolla dishes, though the *Restaurant Vegetariano,* Dos de Mayo 751, three blocks from the plaza, has nicer food if you're looking for something lighter or simply different. For a better atmosphere in the evenings and the local speciality, *picante de queso* – a spicy sauce made from yellow chillis and onions, poured over cold cheese and potatoes – try *La Casona de Gladys* at General Prado 908.

Tourist information is available from ICTA-Huánuco, Jr General Prado 722, right by the Plaza de Armas (Mon–Fri 9am–1pm & 4–6pm). The **post office** is on the Plaza de Armas (Mon–Sat 8am–7pm), and the **telephone office** is two blocks away along 28 de Julio (daily 8am–9pm). You can change **money** with the *cambistas* on the corner of Dos de Mayo and the Plaza de Armas, or at the Banco de Credito, on Dos de Mayo, less than a block up from the plaza. **Guided tours** to places of interest in the locality, such as Kotosh, are available from Ecotur Tour and Travel Agent, 28 de Julio 1033 (☏064/512410).

Buses to La Unión (8–9hr) leave daily at 8am from the market, while buses, colectivos and trucks to Tingo Maria (4–5hr) and Pucallpa leave daily from Jr General Prado, just three blocks east of the Plaza de Armas, over the Río Huallaga bridge. Direct Leon de Huánuco buses to Lima ($12, a 10–12hr trip), via the Central Highway and La Oroya, leave daily from the terminal on Jirón Ayacucho, close to the river. Trucks and buses for Tantamayo ($8, a 14hr trip) leave most days at around 6pm from the market area, close to the corner of Jirón Aguilar with Calle San Martin. There are no direct buses from Huánuco to Junin and Huancayo; the best you can do is try to catch one of the Lima buses that passes through La Oroya, where you should disembark and catch a bus or colectivo to the Huancayo area.

The Temple of Kotosh

Only 6km from Huánuco along the La Unión road, the fascinating, though poorly maintained, **Temple of Kotosh** lies in ruins on the banks of the Río Tingo. At more than 4000 years old, this site pre-dates the Chavín era by more than a thousand years. More or less permanent settlement continued here throughout the Chavín era (though without the monumental masonry and sculpture of that period) and Inca occupation, right up to the Conquest. The most remarkable feature of the Kotosh complex is the **crossed-hands symbol** carved prominently onto a stone – the gracefully executed insignia of a very early culture about which archeologists know next to nothing – which now lies in the Archeology Museum in Pueblo Libre, Lima. The site today consists of three sacred stone-built enclosures in generally poor condition; but with a little imagination and/or a good local guide, it is both atmospheric and fascinating to explore one of the most ancient temple sites in the Americas.

To get to the site, you can either walk along the La Unión road, or take the La Unión bus (see above) from Huánuco and ask the driver to drop you off at the path to Kotosh. Alternatively, a **guided tour** from Huánuco will cost around $10 per person (see above), or a **taxi** from the Plaza de Armas will cost around $8.

Tantamayo

About 150km north of Huánuco, poised in the mountainous region above the higher reaches of the Río Marañón, lies the small village of **TANTAMAYO**, with its nearby extensive ruins. In the village you can hire local **guides** (from $5 a day) to take you on the two- to three-hour hike to the scattered sites, and excellent **accommodation** is offered at the Swiss-style tourist lodge known as the *Hotel Turística* (no tel; ❹), where English is spoken. There are also a couple of other more basic hostels in town.

The ruins of Tantamayo

The precise age of the remote pre-Columbian **ruins of Tantamayo** is unknown. Its buildings appear to fit into the Tiahuanaco-Huari phase, which would make them some 1200 years old, but physically they form no part of this widespread cultural movement, and the site is considered to have developed separately, probably originating from tribes migrating to the Andes from the jungle and adapting to a new environment over a long period of time.

At Tantamayo the architectural development of some four centuries can be clearly seen – growing from the simplest of structures to complex edifices. Tall buildings dot the entire area – some clearly **watchtowers** looking over the Marañón, one of Peru's most important rivers and a major headwater of the Amazon, others with less obvious functions, built for religious reasons as temple-palaces, perhaps, or as storehouses and fortresses. One of the major constructions, just across the Tantamayo stream on a hill facing the village, was named **Pirira** by the Incas who conquered the area in the fifteenth century. At its heart there are concentric circles of carved stone, while the walls and houses around are all grouped in a circular formation – clearly this was once an important centre for religious ritual. The **main building** rises some 10m on three levels, its bluff facade broken only by large window niches and by centuries of weathering.

A detailed archeological survey of the ruins may well reveal links with Chavín de Huantar (see p.324) and Kotosh (see previous page). In the meantime, the thirty separate, massive constructions make an impressive scene, offset by the cloud forest and jungle flourishing along the banks of the Marañón just a little further to the north.

West of Huánuco: La Unión to Huánuco Viejo

A dusty minor road to **La Unión** turns east off the main Huaraz to Lima road 7km south of Catac, cutting through the Huascarán National Park past the *Puya Raymondi* and Pastoruri Glacier. From **Catac**, it's possible to hitch a ride in a truck to the rather cold, bleak and miserable mining settlement of **Huansala** (an hour or two up the road), but try not to get stuck here overnight, as there are no facilities for travellers. From Huansala, you can either get one of the daily buses, or walk the 10km to Huallanca, where there are frequent trucks all the way to La Unión; with luck you can do the whole trip in a day. However, most people will take the much easier route via Conococha and Chiquián (9hr). Empresa Rapido run buses from Huaraz daily ($3, a 4–5hr journey), from where they continue directly to La Unión. If snow makes the pass difficult, the bus arrives at 8–10pm, making a stopover in La Unión pretty inevitable.

La Unión

LA UNIÓN, a small market town high up on a cold and bleak pampa, is a base for visiting the Inca ruins of Huánuco Viejo, a two- or three-hour hike away. If you do need a **place to stay**, there's the very basic, dirty *Hostal Dos de Mayo* (no phone; ❶), or *Hostal Turista* (no phone; ❷), which is slightly more salubrious but still has shared bathrooms. There are a few **restaurants** around the market area, including the *Restaurant El Danubo*, for simple meals such as rice, chicken and stews.

There are usually two or three **buses** a day to Huánuco from the market area in La Unión, with the last one leaving around 11pm for the nine-hour ($5) journey. Alternatively, you can ride on top of one of the **trucks** that leave La Unión market for Huánuco most mornings. There are no buses or public transport to Huánuco Viejo and the only way to get there is to walk, or take a **taxi** from the Plaza de Armas ($4–5).

Huánuco Viejo

From La Unión a dusty track continues along precipitous and winding mountain roads, sections of which are frequently washed away during the rainy season. It takes at least half a day (sometimes longer) to reach the superb Inca stonework of **HUÁNUCO VIEJO** (daily 8am–6pm; free), lying on the edge of a desolate pampa, virtually untouched by the Spanish conquistadores. Although abandoned by the Spanish shortly after their arrival in 1539, the city became a centre of native dissent – Illa Tupac, a relative of the rebel Inca Manco and one of the unsung heroes of the Indian resistance, maintained clandestine Inca rule around Huánuco Viejo until at least 1545. As late as 1777 the royal officials were thrown out of the area in a major – albeit short-lived – insurrection.

One of the most complete existing examples of an Inca provincial capital and administrative centre, Huánuco Viejo gives a powerful impression of a once-thriving city – even though it's been a ghost town for four hundred years. The grey stone houses and **platform temples** are set out in a roughly circular pattern radiating from a gigantic *unsu* (Inca throne) in the middle of a plaza. To the north are the **military barracks** and beyond that the remains of suburban dwellings. Directly east of the plaza is the palace and temple known as Incahuasi, and next to this is the Acllahuasi, a separate enclosure devoted to the Chosen Women, or Virgins of the Sun. Behind this, and running straight through the Incahuasi, is a man-made water channel diverted from the small Río Huachac. On the opposite side of the plaza you can make out the extensive administrative quarters.

Poised on the southern hillside above the main complex are over five hundred **storehouses** where all sorts of produce and treasure were kept as tribute for the emperor and sacrifices to the sun. Well away from the damp of the valley floor, and separated from each other by a few metres to minimize the risk of fire, they also command impressive views across the plain.

Arriving here in 1539, the Spanish very soon abandoned the site of Huánuco Viejo to build their own colonial administrative centre at a much lower altitude, more suitable for their unacclimatized lungs and with slightly easier access to Cusco and Lima. The modern city of Huánuco, built along the standard city plans specified by royal decree, grew thoroughly rich, but was still regarded by the colonists as one of those remote outposts (like Chile) where criminals, or anyone unpopular with officialdom, would be sent into lengthy exile.

From Huánuco to the jungle

The Amazon is the obvious place to move on to from Huánuco unless you're heading back to Lima and the coast. The spiralling descent north is stunning, with views across the jungle, as thrilling as if from a small plane. By the time the bus reaches **Tingo Maria**, the Río Huallaga has become a broad tropical river, navigable downstream in shallow canoes or by balsa raft. And the tropical atmosphere, in the shadow of the forested ridges and limestone crags of the **Bella Durmiente** (Sleeping Beauty) mountain, is delightful. From Tingo Maria you can continue the 260km directly northeast through virgin forest, going through the **Pass of Padre Abad**, with its glorious waterfalls, along the way, to Pucallpa, jumping-off point for expeditions deep into the seemingly limitless wilderness of tropical jungle (see Chapter Eight).

Tingo Maria

Once known as the "Garden City", because for people from the Andes or coast it is hard to believe the ease with which gardens, tropical fruit, vegetables and wild flora grow in such abundance. The ramshackle settlement of **TINGO MARIA**, 130km north of Huánuco, lies at the foot of the Bella Durmiente mountain, where, according to legend, the lovesick Princess Nunash awaits the waking kiss of Kunyaq, the sorcerer. These days the town welcomes more travellers than ever due to the decreased local activity in the region's cocaine trade. (This is still probably the area's main industry but things aren't quite as wild as they were at times during the 1980s and 1990s; currently the hot spots are deeper into the jungle along the road to Tarapoto.) Despite its striking setting – 670m above sea level on the forested eastern slopes of the Andes, amid the fecund tropical climate of the *ceja de selva* – Tingo Maria, today, is a tatty, ugly town, on which the ravages of Western civilization have left their mark. Dominated by sawmills and plywood factories financed by multinational corporations, with its forest of TV aerials the town displays symbols of relative affluence, but the tin roofs and crumbling walls across the township betray the poverty of the majority of its inhabitants. There's little for visitors to see, beyond the rather sorry **zoo and botanical gardens** (Mon–Fri 9am–5pm; free) attached to the university on the edge of town, or – about 14km out of town – the **Cueva de las Lechuzas** (Owls' Cave), the vast, picturesque home to a flock of rare nocturnal parrots (you'll need a torch). Tingo Maria's major **fiesta** period is the last week of July – a lively and fun time to be in town, but on no account leave your baggage unattended then.

Practicalities

Accommodation is available at the *Hotel Viena*, Tulumayo 245 (☎064/562194; ❷), which is surprisingly comfortable as well as reasonably priced; the simple but excellent-value *Hostal La Cabaña* at Av Raymondi 342

(☎064/562146; ❶), where the rooms are small and all bathrooms shared; and the clean and friendly *Hotel Royal* on Av Benavides 206 (☎064/562166; ❸). However, the best option is the upmarket *Madera Verde Hotel* (☎064/562047, ⓕ561608; ❺–❻), 2km south of town, with its own pool (open to non-residents for around $1), and clean, comfortable rooms, most with private bath. For **food** it's hard to beat the *Café Rex* at Av Raymondi 500, while *La Cabaña*, Av Raymondi 644, serves up tasty Peruvian evening meals and lunches.

Into the jungle

The **bus** from Tingo Maria to Pucallpa ($9) leaves three times a day from Avenida Raymondi; the journey takes eight to ten hours, depending on whether it's the dry (May–Oct) or rainy (Nov–April) season. Leon de Huánuco travel this road from Lima via Tingo to Pucallpa more or less daily and can be picked up in town, or Transtel Buses leave from Avenida Raymondi. However, you should always book in advance – nearly all the buses arrive full on their way from Lima and Huánuco. Colectivos leave at all times for both Pucallpa and Huánuco from the corner of Callao with Raymondi, about five blocks from the Plaza de Armas. If you get stuck you can always **fly** to Pucallpa ($40–60), with Aero Condor or Aero Continente, bookable through Tingo Maria Travel, Avenida Raymondi (☎064/562501). There are also colectivo combis which leave Tingo Maria most mornings. The road is largely unpaved and the journey can get really hot; to make matters worse, a number of military checkpoints are in operation along the way, mainly to counter the drug trafficking problem (apparently the road is sometimes used as an airstrip by unmarked light aircraft).

Buses and **trucks** leave from Avenida Raymondi just about every day to **Tarapoto** (24hr), along the road that follows the Huallaga Valley north via Juanjui (18hr), but this route is not recommended for travellers due to the high level of cocaine smuggling, terrorist activity and army presence in this remote region.

Travel details

Buses, trucks and colectivos

Ayacucho to: Cusco (8 daily; 20–28hr); Lima (5 daily; 8–10hr); Huancayo (3 daily; 9–10hr); Pisco (6 daily; 6–8hr).

Huancavelica to: Ayacucho (2 daily; 7–9hr); Huancayo (6 daily; 2–3hr); Lima (2 daily; 9hr).

Huancayo to: Ayacucho (3 daily; 9–10hr); Cerro de Pasco (2 daily; 4hr); Huánuco (2 daily; 5–6hr); Huancavelica (6 daily; 2–3hr); Tarma (8–10 daily; 3hr); Lima (over 10 daily; 5–7hr).

Huánuco to: La Unión (1 daily; 8hr); Lima (2 daily; 10hr); Pucallpa (4 daily; 8–12hr); Tantamayo (1 daily; 12–14hr); Tingo Maria (3 daily; 4–5hr).

Trains

Huancavelica to: Huancayo (12 weekly; 5hr & 2 weekly; 3hr).

Huancayo to: Huancavelica (12 weekly; 5hr & 2 weekly; 3hr).

Flights

Ayacucho to: Lima (1 daily; 1hr); Cusco (1 daily; 1hr 30mins).

Huancayo to: Lima (1 daily; 40mins).

Huánuco to: Lima (1 daily; 1hr 30mins).

Trujillo and the North

CHAPTER 7

Highlights

✳ **Valley of the Pyramids** Standing in the hot dry desert of northern Peru is this magnificent collection of adobe pyramids with views of the forested valley around. See p.426

✳ **Kuelap** Less than 1500 visitors make it annually to this remote but majestic fortified town built by the ancient Chachapoyas people. See p.408

✳ **Chan Chan** A massive urban and religious complex built by the Chimu civilization in the thirteenth century, located by the ocean near the city of Trujillo. See p.380

✳ **Huanchaco Beach Restaurant** Eat some of the best and freshest

seafood in the world from a balcony with a dreamlike view of the Pacific Ocean. See p.379

✳ **Batán Grande** Sitting next to the beautiful Río de la Leche, it's not hard to see why ancient people made this complex of over twenty adobe pyramids their major ceremonial centre. See p.423

✳ **Museo de las Tumbas** An excellent museum whose exhibits include precious objects from the royal tomb of the Lord of Sipán. See p.426

✳ **Usha Usha** This atmospheric bar high up in the Andes mesmerizes locals and tourists. See p.397

7

Trujillo and the North

hough very remote and little visited, the northern reaches of Peru possess unique treasures in culture, archeology and natural environments; this fascinating region definitely rewards anyone who has the time to explore it. It's an immensely varied corner of the country, ranging from the cities that stand out as welcoming oases of cultural vitality along the desert coast, up to secluded villages in the Andes where you may well be the first foreigner to pass through for years. On top of this, the entire area is brimming with imposing and important pre-Inca sites, some of them only discovered in the last decade or two.

Trujillo is one of the country's undiscovered jewels, located on the seaward edge of the vast desert plain at the mouth of the Moche Valley. Its attraction lies partly in its nearby ruins – notably **Chan Chan** and the huge sacred pyramids of the **Huaca del Sol** and **Huaca de la Luna** – partly in the city itself, and partly in its excellent beach communities. **Huanchaco**, only 12km from Trujillo, is a good case in point, essentially a fishing village and a likeable resort within walking distance of sandy beaches and massive ancient ruins.

The northern desert coast beyond Trujillo offers a wide variety of other towns and equally amazing sites. Known as the **Circuito Nororiental**, this whole region, including Trujillo, the vivid archeological sites around Chiclayo, the beaches between Piura and Tumbes, plus the big loop east to Kuelap, Chachapoyas and also Cajamarca high up in the Andes, is almost a country in its own right and is being heavily promoted as a fresh destination.

There are established touring routes through the Andean region above Trujillo, all of which take the beautifully situated mountain town of **Cajamarca** as their main focus. It was here that Pizarro first encountered and captured the Inca Emperor Atahualpa to begin the Spanish conquest of Peru, and around the modern city are a number of fascinating Inca ruins – many linked with water and ritualized baths. Cajamarca is also one of the springboards for visiting the smaller town of **Chachapoyas** and the ruined citadel complex of **Kuelap**, arguably the single most overwhelming pre-Columbian site in Peru. Beyond, there are two possible routes down Amazon headwaters to the jungle town of **Iquitos** – both long and arduous, but well worth it if you have the time, enthusiasm and necessary equipment. You can also head to Trujillo from Cajamarca (or vice versa) via the old colonial outpost of **Huamachuco** and, for the really adventurous, visit the remote ruins of **Gran Pajaten**.

The coastal strip north of Trujillo, up to **Tumbes** by the Ecuadorian border, is for the most part a seemingly endless desert plain, interrupted by many small, isolated villages, but only two substantial towns, **Chiclayo** and **Piura**. Just

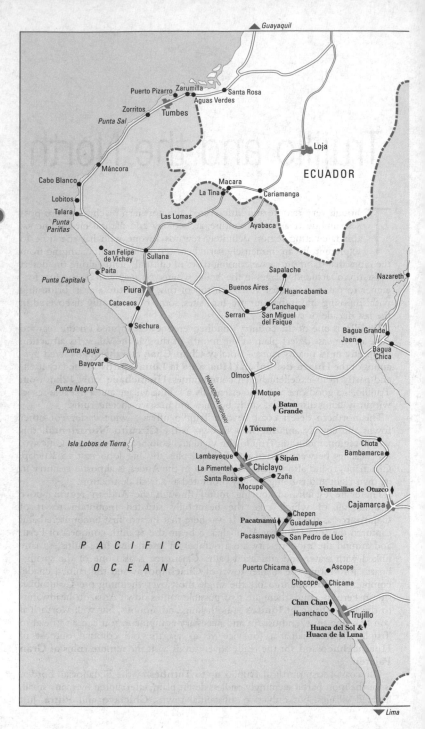

▲ *Guayaquil*

Puerto Pizarro Zarumilla
Santa Rosa
Aguas Verdes
Zorritos Tumbes
Punta Sal

Loja

ECUADOR

Máncora
Macara
Cabo Blanco
La Tina Cariamanga
Lobitos
Talara
Punta Pariñas Las Lomas
Ayabaca

San Felipe
de Vichay Sullana
Nazareth
Paita
Punta Capitala Sapalache
Buenos Aires Huancabamba
Piura Canchaque
Catacaos Serran San Miguel
del Faique
Sechura

Bagua Grande
Jaen
Bagua
Punta Aguja Chica
Bayovar Olmos

Punta Negra Motupe

Isla Lobos de Tierra **Batan
Grande**

Túcume
Chota
Bambamarca
Lambayeque **Sipán**
La Pimentel **Chiclayo**
Santa Rosa Zaña
Mocupe **Ventanillas de Otuzco**

Cajamarca
Chepen
Pacatnamú Guadalupe
Pacasmayo San Pedro de Lloc

P A C I F I C

O C E A N Puerto Chicama Ascope
Chocope Chicama

Chan Chan
Huanchaco **Trujillo**
**Huaca del Sol &
Huaca de la Luna**

PANAMERICAN HIGHWAY

▼ *Lima*

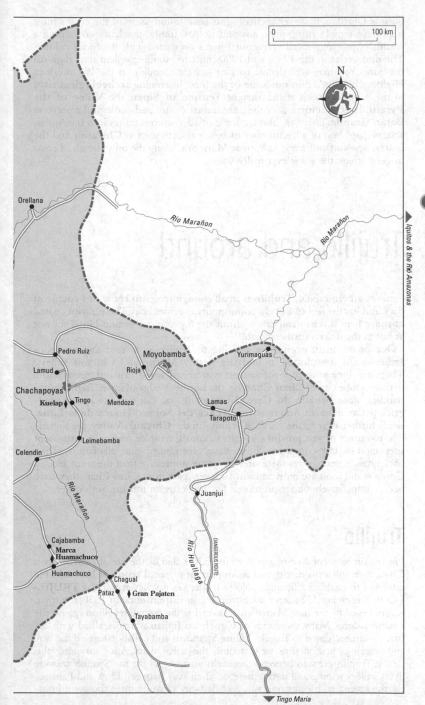

Orellana

Río Marañón

Río Marañón

Pedro Ruiz

Moyobamba

Yurimaguas

Lamud

Rioja

Chachapoyas

Kuelap ◆ Tingo   Mendoza

Lamas

Tarapoto

Leimebamba

Celendín

Río Marañón

Juanjuí

Río Huallaga

DANGEROUS ROUTE

Cajabamba

Marca
Huamachuco ◆

Huamachuco

Chagual

Pataz ◆ Gran Pajaten

Tayabamba

0   100 km

N

▼ Tingo María

outside Chiclayo, however, archeologists have found some of the coast's most important temple ruins, pyramids and nobles' tombs, the latter containing a wealth of precious-metal ceremonial items associated with the Sicán culture. The discoveries in the 1980s and 1990s initiated some excellent new regional museums. You may well decide to pass straight through on the Panamerican Highway, but you'd miss out some of the most interesting **archeological sites** in the Americas, such as the ancient **Temple of Sipán**, the **Valley of the Pyramids** at **Túcume**, and the ceremonial centre and ecological reserve at **Batán Grande**. There are also a couple of adventurous routes into the Andes, and, perhaps best of all, a number of beach resorts, such as **Chicama** and the hottest new surf and scene in Peru at **Máncora**, along the only stretch of coast in Peru where the sea is ever really warm.

Trujillo and around

Peru's northern capital, **Trujillo** is small enough to get to know in a couple of days, and has the feel of a lively, cosmopolitan regional city. The pleasant coastal **climate** here is warm and dry, without the fog you get around Lima, but not as hot as the deserts further north.

One of the main reasons for coming to Trujillo is to visit the numerous archeological sites dotted around the nearby Moche and Chicama valleys. There are three main zones of interest within easy reach, first and foremost the massive adobe city of **Chan Chan** on the northern edge of town. To the south, standing alone beneath the Cerro Blanco hill, you can find the largest mud-brick pyramids in the Americas, the **Huaca del Sol** and **Huaca de la Luna**, while further away to the north of Trujillo, in the **Chicama Valley**, the incredible remnants of vast pre-Inca irrigation canals, temples, and early settlement sites stand in stark contrast to the massive, green, sugar-cane plantations of the haciendas. In many ways these sites are more impressive than the ruins around Cusco – and most are more ancient too; yet apart from Chan Chan, they have been comparatively under-promoted by the Peruvian tourism authorities.

Trujillo

Pizarro, on his second voyage to Peru in 1528, sailed by the site of ancient Chan Chan, then still a major city and an important regional centre of Inca rule. He returned to establish a Spanish colony in the same valley, naming it **TRUJILLO** in December 1534 after his birthplace in Estremadura. In 1536, the town was besieged by the Inca Manco's forces during the second rebellion against the conquistadores. Many thousands of Conchuco Indian warriors, allied with the Incas, swarmed down to Trujillo, killing Spaniards and collaborators on the way and offering their victims to Catequil, the tribal deity. After surviving this attack, Trujillo grew to become the main port of call for the Spanish treasure fleets, sailors wining and dining here on their way between Lima and Panama. By the seventeenth century it was a walled city of some three thousand houses covering three square miles. The only sections of those walls that remain are the Herrera rampart and a small piece of the facade on Avenida España.

Trujillo continued to be a centre of popular rebellion, declaring its independence from Spain in the Plaza de Armas in 1820, long before the Liberators arrived. The enigmatic APRA (American Popular Revolutionary Alliance) leader, Haya de la Torre, was born here in 1895, running for president, after years of struggle, in the elections of 1931. The dictator, Sanchez Cerro, however, counted the votes and declared himself the winner. APRA was outlawed and Haya de la Torre imprisoned, provoking Trujillo's middle classes to stage an uprising. Over one thousand deaths resulted, many of them APRA supporters, who were taken out to the fields of Chan Chan by the truckload and shot. Even now, the 1932 massacre resonates amongst the people of Trujillo, particularly the old APRA members and the army, and you can still see each neighbourhood declaring its allegiance in graffiti to one side or the other.

It was the Revolutionary Military government in 1969 that eventually unshackled this region from the stranglehold of a few sugar barons, who owned the enormous haciendas in the Chicama Valley. The haciendas were then divided up among the worker co-operatives – the Casa Grande, a showcase example, is now one of the most profitable and well-organized agricultural ventures in Peru. The mid-1980s and early 1990s, however, were dominated by the violence of Sendero Luminoso and the corruption of the first, and probably the last ever, APRA president of Peru – the young, charismatic but disappointing Alan Garcia (see Contexts, p.543).

Nowadays the city, just eight hours north of Lima along the Panamerican Highway, looks every bit the oasis it is, standing in a relatively green, irrigated valley bounded by arid desert at the foot of the brown Andes mountains.

Arrival, information and city transport

You're most likely to arrive in the city by bus or colectivo from Lima. Most of the **buses** have terminals close to the centre of town near the Mansiche Stadium, on avenidas Daniel Carrion or España to the southwest, or east of it along avenidas America Norte or Ejercito (see Listings, p.375, for details). **Colectivos** also mostly leave from and end up on Avenida España. If you're arriving by day it's fine to walk to the city centre, though at night it's best to take a taxi ($2–3).

If you **fly** into the city, you'll arrive at the airport, about 10km away, near Huanchaco. Taxis into the city will cost around $5, or you can get a bus, which leaves every twenty minutes from the roundabout just outside the airport gates, for about 30¢.

Information

For **tourist information** and photocopied city maps, go to the very helpful i-Peru office at Jr Pizarro 402 (Mon–Fri 9am–5pm; ☎044/294561, Ⓔiperutrujillo@promperu.gob.pe) on the Plaza Mayor. The **tourist police**, at POLTUR, Jr Independencia 630 (daily 9am–1pm & 4–7pm; ☎044/291705 or 200200), are very helpful, too. The official **Camara Regional de Turismo** (Mon–Fri 9am–1pm & 4–8pm, Sat 9am–1pm), is next door to the Tourist Police at Independencia 628 (☎044/203718), where further information and maps are available.

City transport

The colonial heart of the city consists of about fifty relatively small bocks, all encircled by the Avenida España. More or less at the centre of the circle is the

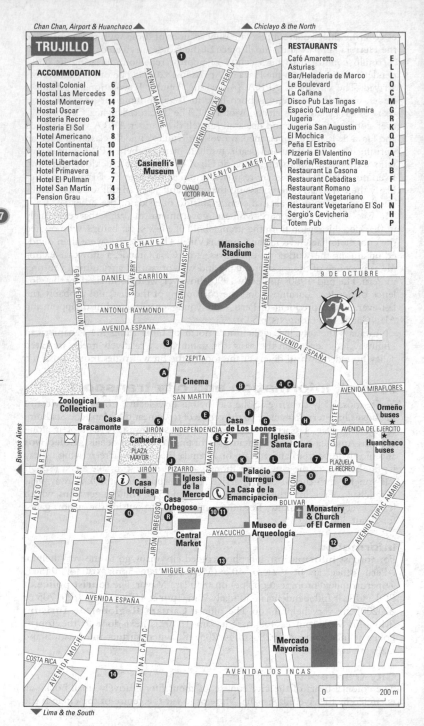

ubiquitous main plaza, known as the Plaza Mayor or the Plaza de Armas. The main streets of Pizarro and Independencia originate at the plaza; the only other streets you really need to know are San Martín and Bolivar, parallel to Pizarro and Independencia, and Gamarra, where many of the banks are to be found.

Getting around the city and its environs is cheap and easy, using the numerous **local buses** and **colectivos** (flat rates around 30¢) and **minibuses**. **Taxis** cost less than $1 for rides within Trujillo and can be hailed anywhere, but if you need to call one, Taxi Seguro (☎044/253473) is best. **Car rental** is available at Jr Ayacucho 414, Oficina 11 (☎/⒡044/234985). **Hitchhiking** is possible though not particularly easy; going north towards Huanchaco and Chan Chan, the best places to start from are beside the stalls near the Mansiche Stadium, or from the Petro Peru filling station at the start of the Panamerican Highway. Going south, your best bet is the big service station at the junction where the Panamerican Highway heads towards Moche and Chimbote.

Accommodation

The majority of Trujillo's **hotels** are within a few blocks of the central Plaza Mayor: most of them are to the south, but a number of reasonable ones are to be found along Jirón Pizarro, Independencia and San Martín. However, many people prefer to stay out of the city centre, at the nearby beach resort of Huanchaco (see p.376).

Budget

Clara Bravo's Hospedaje Cahuide 495
☎044/243347, ⒡255043,
ⓦwww.xanga.com/CasadeClara. Very nice bargain accommodation, with private bathrooms and food available. They also organize reliable and affordable tours in the region. ②

Hostal Monterrey Av Los Incas 256
☎044/241673. One of Trujillo's more basic hostels, located in a slightly dodgy part of town, with simple small rooms and shared bathrooms, all a bit run-down; nevertheless, the staff are helpful. ②

Hostal Oscar Jr Orbegoso 172 ☎044/257033. Cheap, with small, very simple rooms that have private bath. Reasonably clean and central but security might be an issue. ②

Hostal Trujillo Jr Grau 581 ☎044/243921,
⒡244241. Highly recommended hostel that has a helpful sliding price scale. ②

Hotel Americano Jr Pizarro 764 ☎044/241361. Plenty of character but a bit shabby; the rooms, like everything else in this grand old hotel, are spacious but not spotless. This is a favourite with budget travellers, not least for its friendly service and great prices. ②

Hotel Internacional Bolivar 646 ☎044/245392. Located in a fairly central, grand old building, with clean, if very basic rooms. It's good value but not that comfortable; some rooms have toilets but no showers, while a few have full private bathrooms. ②

Pensión Grau Calle Grau 631. Good central location, basic but clean and some rooms with private bathrooms. ②

Moderate

Hostal Las Mercedes Jr Colón 525
☎044/222179. Pretty central, with a full range of facilities like hot water, private baths, cable TV and even a sauna. ④

Hostería Recreo C Estete 647 ☎044/246991. A very comfortable hotel with its own restaurant and friendly service. ④

Hostería El Sol Los Brillantes 224, off block 12 of Av Mansiche ☎044/231933. Built in the shape of a Bavarian castle, it's slightly out of the way but has good rooms with private bath. ③

Hotel San Martín San Martín 743–749
☎044/235700, ⒡252311. Lots of decent rooms in a large, relatively modern, though tired-looking, building. Good service, and all rooms have private bath. ④

Expensive

Hostal Colonial Jr Independencia 618
☎044/268261, ⒡223410,
ⓔhostalcolonialtruji@hotmail.com. An attractive, central place, where some English is spoken. Rooms are fine and have TV, plus there's a patio and cafetería. ⑤

Hostal Portada del Sol Av 28 de Julio 140
☎044/245346. Some 5 or 6 blocks from the main plaza, it has laundry, restaurant, and modern

rooms with TVs and private baths. **❼**

Hotel Continental Gamarra 663 ☎044/241607, ℱ249881. Plain but centrally located and popular with Peruvian business types. Rooms are clean with private bath, TV and reliable hot water. Breakfast is included. **❺**

Hotel Libertador Jr Independencia 485 ☎044/232741, ℱ235641, ⓦwww.libertador.com.pe. Formerly the *Hotel de Turistas*, this place is particularly grand, with excellent service and a superb restaurant

renowned for its criolla dishes. The large, plush rooms have all mod cons. **❼**

Hotel Primavera Av Nicolas de Pierola 872 ☎044/231915. Located close to the Panamerican Highway, this concrete building lacks style but offers air-conditioned comfort, large clean rooms and good service. **❺**

Hotel El Pullman Pizarro 833 ☎/ℱ044/203624, ⓔpullmanhotel@ots.com.pe. One of the city centre's newest and nicest hotels, it is cool and plush with solar water heating, good restaurant and bar plus all mod cons. **❻**

The City

From the graceful colonial mansions and Baroque churches at its heart, Trujillo's grid system gives way to commercial buildings, light industry and shantytown suburbs, before thinning out into rich sugar-cane fields that stretch far into the neighbouring Chicama Valley. At the city's centre is its dominating force – the university **La Libertad**. Founded by Bolivar in 1824, the picturesque university is surrounded by elegant, Spanish-style streets, lined with ancient green ficus trees and overhung by long, wooden-railed balconies. **Gamarra** is the main commercial street, dominated by ugly, modern, brick and glass buildings, shops, hotels and restaurants. The other main avenue, older and more attractive, is **Jirón Pizarro**, where much of the city's nightlife is centred and which has been pedestrianized from block 8 to the pleasant **Plazuela El Recreo**. Life for most Trujillanos still revolves around the old town, centred on **Plaza Mayor** and bounded roughly by San Martín, Ayacucho, Almagro and Colón.

In addition to the city's many **churches**, Trujillo is renowned for its **colonial houses**, most of which are in good repair and are still in use today. These should generally be visited in the mornings (Mon–Fri), since many of them have other uses at other times of day; some are commercial banks and some are simply closed in the afternoons.

Around Plaza Mayor

Trujillo's **Plaza Mayor** (also known as the **Plaza de Armas**) is packed with sharp-witted shoeshine boys around the central statue – the *Heroes of the Wars of Independence*. Although the plaza is sinking noticeably year by year, subsidence doesn't seem to have affected the two colonial mansions that front it, both of which have been tastefully restored. The **Casa Bracamonte**, Jr Independencia 441, is closed to visitors but has some interesting cast ironwork around its patio windows, while the **Casa Urquiaga** (also known as Casa Calonge and owned by the Banco de la Nación), Jr Pizarro 446 (Mon–Fri 9am–1pm; free 30min guided tours often available), said to be the house where Bolivar stayed when visiting Trujillo, is home to some first-class Rococo-style furniture and a fine collection of ancient ceramics.

Plaza Mayor is also home to the city's **Cathedral** (daily 6–9am & 5–9pm; free), built in the mid-seventeenth century, then rebuilt the following century after earthquake damage. Known locally as the Basilica Menor, it's plain by Peruvian standards but houses some colourful Baroque sculptures and a handful of paintings by the Quiteña school (a style of painting that originated in eighteenth-century Quito). Inside the Cathedral, a **museum** (daily 8am–2pm;

$2) exhibits a range of mainly eighteenth- and nineteenth-century religious paintings and sculptures.

Just behind the plaza at San Martín 368, is a **zoological collection** (Mon–Fri 7am–7pm; 70¢), full of dozens of bizarre stuffed animals from the coastal desert and Andean regions, as well as a large bird display and lots of amazing sea creatures (including a now extinct crab some 70cm across) and a number of reptiles.

From Plaza Mayor to the Central Market

Just off the plaza, the **Iglesia de La Merced**, Jr Pizarro 550 (daily 8am–7pm; free), built in 1636, is worth a look for its unique, priceless Rococo organ, plus its attractive gardens. Around the corner from here, between the Plaza de Armas and the Central Market, stands the most impressive of Trujillo's colonial houses – the **Casa Orbegoso**, at Jr Orbegoso 553 (Mon–Sat 9am–4pm; free). This old mansion was the home of Luís José Orbegoso, former president of Peru, and houses displays of period furniture, glass and silverware amid very refined decor. Born into one of Trujillo's wealthiest founding families, Orbegoso fought for independence and became president of the republic in 1833 with the support of the liberal faction. However, he proved to be the most ineffective of all Peruvian leaders, resented for his aristocratic bearing by the *mestizo* generals, and from 1833 to 1839, although still officially president, he lost control of the country – first in civil war, then to the Bolivian army, and finally to a combined rebel and Chilean force. Orbegoso's rule marked a low point in his country's history, and he disappeared from the political scene to return here to his mansion in disgrace. Today even his family home has been invaded – although it's still in perfect condition and outstandingly elegant, the main rooms around the courtyard have been converted into offices.

Trujillo's main market, the **Central Market**, is only 100m from here, on the corner of Ayacucho and Gamarra. As well as selling most essentials, such as juices, food and clothing, it has an interesting line in herbal stalls and healing or magical items – known locally as the Mercado de los Brujos (the Witches' Market) – not to mention unionized shoe-cleaners. There's a second, much busier market, the Mercado Mayorista, further out, on Avenida Costa Rica in the southeast corner of town.

From the market, head east along Ayacucho until you reach the corner of Junín, where you'll find the University's **Museo de Arqueología y Antropología**, Jr Junín 602 (Mon 9.30am–2pm, Tues–Fri 9.15am–1pm & 3–7pm, Sat & Sun 9.30am–4pm; $1.50, including optional 30min guided tour in Spanish; ☎044/249322, ⓦwww.unitru.edu.pe/arq/indice.html), which is a pretty interesting place, specializing in ceramics, early metallurgy, textiles and feather work.

East of Plaza Mayor

East of the plaza, on the corner of Jirón Pizarro and Gamarra, stands another of Trujillo's impressive mansions, **La Casa de la Emancipación**, at Jr Pizarro 610 (Mon–Sat 10am–8pm; free). The building was remodelled in the mid-nineteenth century by the priest Pedro Madalengoitia (why it is also sometimes known as the Casa Madalengoitia), and is now head office of the Banco Continental. The main courtyard and entrance demonstrate a symmetrical and austere design, while the wide gallery has some impressive marble flooring. Inside are a couple of interesting late eighteenth-century murals depicting peasant life, and paintings or historical photographs are usually exhibited in at least one of its rooms.

Further down the same road, two blocks east of the Plaza Mayor, is the **Palacio Iturregui**, Jr Pizarro 688 (Mon–Fri 8.30–10.30am; free), a striking mid-nineteenth-century mansion. Built by the army general Don Juan Manuel de Iturregui y Aguilarte, the house is used today by the city's Central Club, who allow visitors to look round some of the rooms. The courtyard can be seen at any time of the day, just by popping your head inside. The highlight of the building is its pseudo-classical courtyard, encircled by superb galleries, with tall columns and an open roof which gives a wonderful view of the blue desert sky.

At the eastern end of Jirón Pizarro, five blocks from the Plaza Mayor, there's a small, attractive square known as the restored **Plazuela El Recreo** where, under the shade of some vast 130-year-old ficus trees, a number of bars and food stalls act like a magnet for young couples in the evenings. This little plaza was, and still is, an *estanque de agua* – a water distribution point – built during colonial days, but tapping into even more ancient irrigation works.

A couple of minutes' walk south from the Plazuela, on the corner of Colón and Bolívar, stands the most stunning of the city's religious buildings, the **Monastery and Church of El Carmen** (Mon–Sat 9am–1pm; $1). Built in 1759 but damaged by earthquake in the same year, its two brick towers were then rebuilt using bamboo for safety in case they toppled again. The church was also built above ground level to save it from El Niño's periodic flooding. Inside you can see the single domed nave, with exquisite altars and a fine gold-leaf pulpit. The processional and recreational cloisters, both boasting fine vaulted arches and painted wooden columns, give access to the **Pinacoteca** (picture gallery), where you can see Flemish works including a *Last Supper* (1625) by Otto van Veen, one of Rubens' teachers. There are also some interesting figures carved from *huamanga* stone and a room showing the process of restoring oil paintings.

Northeast of Plaza Mayor

Jirón Independencia runs northeast from the Plaza Mayor and boasts a couple of minor attractions. Just one block from the plaza, at Independencia 628, stands the **Casa de los Leones** (Mon–Fri 9am–6pm; free), a colonial mansion that's larger and more labyrinthine than it looks from the outside and which holds exhibitions of photos, art, culture, crafts and wildlife, mostly of local historical or environmental interest. A few minutes further along Jirón Independencia, on the corner of Junín, you'll find the **Iglesia Santa Clara** (daily 8am–9pm; free), which contains fine religious paintings and examples of Baroque architecture. If you go in, be sure to check inside its chapel to see the altar covered with gold-leaf and the pulpit with high-relief carvings.

Casinelli's Museum

The most curious museum in Trujillo is set in the middle of the road, in the basement of the Mobil filling station at Nicolas de Pierola 601, on the Ovalo Victor Raul, just north of the large Mansiche Stadium. **Casinelli's Museum** (Mon–Sat 9am–1pm & 3–7pm, Sun 9.30am–1pm & 3.30–6.30pm; $1.80) is stuffed with pottery and artefacts spanning thousands of years, collected from local *huaqueros*. The Salinar, Viru, Mochica, Chimu, Nazca, Huari, Recuay and Inca cultures are all represented, with highlights including **Mochica pots** with graphic images of daily life, people, animals and anthropomorphic deities. Señor Casinelli sometimes shows his visitors around personally and will point out his exquisite range of **Chimu silver artefacts**, including a tiny set of panpipes. Also of note are the small pottery owl figures, symbols for magic and witchcraft, and the perfectly represented miniature ceramic **Salinar houses**, which give you an idea of the ancient culture much more successfully than any site restoration.

Eating and drinking

There's no shortage of **bars** or **restaurants** in Trujillo. Some of the liveliest are along Jirón Independencia, Pizarro, Bolivar and Ayacucho, to the east of Plaza Mayor. A speciality of the city is good, reasonably priced **seafood**, particularly ceviche, which is probably best appreciated on the beach at the nearby resorts of Buenos Aires or Huanchaco (see p.376).

Asturias Jr Pizarro 739. Tasty fruit juices plus alcoholic drinks, meals and snacks at this busy coffee bar.

Le Boulevard Pizarro 844. A pleasant lunchtime spot in the pedestrianized section of Pizarro, with a nice little patio and very good, inexpensive, set-lunches.

Café Amaretto Gamarra 368. Great coffee and good cakes, breakfast and snacks.

Chifa Vegetariano "La Nueva Eden" Pizarro 687. Chinese health-food and vegetarian restaurant serving dishes with yogurts, *quinoa* with *maca*; it has cheap set lunches.

Espacio Cultural Angelmira on the corner of Independencia with Junin ☎044/297200. A plush, fascinating little café and bar with the associated Museo del Juguette (Toy Museum) in the same building as well as an art gallery and library.

Jugeria Pasaje San Agustin 126. A small place near the central market, opposite the west side, it's cheap for breakfasts, including fruit salads and juices.

Jugeria San Augustin Jr Pizarro 691 ☎044/259591. An excellent juice bar offering an enormous choice of tropical drinks, beers, sandwiches and snacks in a plastic but friendly environment that's very popular with Trujillo's youth. Will take phone orders and delivers to your door.

El Mochica Bolivar 462. A superb, smart restaurant serving exquisite criolla dishes.

Oveido Café Jr Pizarro 737. Stuck between *Restaurant Romano* and *Restaurant/Bar Heladeria Demarco*, this is a quality café which serves very nice breakfasts; bit pricey, though.

Pizzeria El Valentino Jr Orbegoso 224 ☎044/246643. Opposite the Ciné Primavera, this flashy place serves decent Italian food of all kinds; the ambience and service are pleasant, but it gets very busy at weekends.

Pollería/Restaurant Plaza Jr Pizarro 501. A very popular roast chicken joint on the corner of the Plaza Mayor; the fried potatoes aren't bad either.

Restaurant La Casona San Martín 677. A modest, quiet restaurant serving local dishes; excellent lunches at fantastically cheap prices.

Restaurant Cebaditas Junin 336. A simple little place, perfect for snacks, sandwiches and breakfasts.

Restaurant Romano Jr Pizarro 747 ☎044/252251. Small, friendly restaurant specializing in good Peruvian and Italian dishes. Good-sized portions, and exceptional value with its *económico familia* or *turístico* set menus, but it gets very crowded in the evenings, so reservations are advised.

Restaurant Vegetariano Plazuela El Recreo. Located on the small plaza, this is relatively cheap and prepares soya-based meals as well as fine omelettes.

Restaurant Vegetariano El Sol Jr Pizarro 660. Open for lunches and evening meals, *El Sol* serves simple vegetarian fare (the best in town), mostly based on rice, alfalfa, soya, maize and fresh vegetables, at reasonable prices. It's particularly popular with locals at lunchtime.

Restaurant/Bar Heladeria Demarco Jr Pizarro 725 ☎044/234251. A flashy, Italian-style ice-cream parlour-cum-bar and restaurant serving international and Peruvian dishes.

Sergio's Cevichería Independencia 925. A small and surprisingly cheap seafood restaurant that serves very fresh food and is excellent value for lunch.

Totem Pub Jr Pizarro 922. A pleasant restaurant-cum-bar on the Plazuela El Recreo, with a romantic atmosphere in the evenings. It serves good drinks and freshly grilled kebabs, accompanied by taped music from the likes of Frank Sinatra.

Nightlife and entertainment

Trujillo boasts a fairly active **nightlife**, with several **peñas** and **nightclubs** celebrating local culture, dance and music, as well as Latin rhythms and the latest global popular sounds (see below). One feature of Trujillo nightlife is **drive-in**

disco pubs, mostly associated with motels, pickup joints or other places for illicit affairs. They tend to be located around the outskirts of the city; try *Pussy Cat*, Av Nicolas de Pierola 716, or *La Herradura*, Av Teodoro Valcarcel 1268, both in Urbino Primavera. On a more cultural level, the city is famous for its January *Marinera* **dance fiesta** and occasional international dance jamborees. Occasional exhibitions, performances and **films** are presented at some of the **cultural centres**: the Instituto Nacional de Cultura at Independencia 572, half a block from the plaza, behind the cathedral; the Instituto Cultural Peruano-Norte Americano at Av Venezuela 125, Urbano El Recreo (☎044/245832); and the Alliance Française at San Martín 862. The Cine Primavera has six screens and often shows good films in English with Spanish subtitles.

Clubs and peñas

Burbujas Night Club Av Tupac Amaru 340, Urbino H. Grande. A classic nightclub, popular with most age groups.

La Canana San Martín 791 ☎044/232503. A highly popular restaurant-*peña* (as well as a discotheque), serving excellent meals; has a great atmosphere and good danceable shows that generally start after 10pm and carry on into the early hours.

Disco Pub Las Tinajas corner of Pizarro and Almagro. Very central and lively at weekends; plays rock and pop.

Peña El Estribo San Martín 810. A large, newly restored and very popular dance and music venue with great weekend shows of coastal folklore and *musica negra*.

Cinema

In the 1950s, the writer George Woodcock noted that the uninhibited and infectious response of Trujillo's movie-going audiences "made one realize how much the use of sound in films had turned audiences into silent spectators instead of vociferous participants". Trujillo's audiences are still undaunted by the technology of the screen: however boring the film, you always leave with the feeling that you've shared a performance instead off passively viewing a spectacle. The cinema scene may not be as strong now as in the 1950s, with videos and satellite TV having taken their toll, but Trujillo still offers a better range of films than in most Peruvian towns.

The vast majority of cinemas show **original language films**, with Spanish subtitles, so you should be able to watch any mainstream US movie. There are several **cinemas** clustered within a few blocks of the Plaza Mayor, showing anything from old classics to Hollywood's latest. The most popular downtown establishment is the Ciné Primavera, on Jirón Orbegoso, one and a half blocks northwest of the Plaza Mayor.

Fiestas

Trujillo's main **fiestas** turn the town into even more of a relaxed playground than it is normally, with the **marinera** dance featuring prominently in most celebrations. This regional dance originated in Trujillo and is accompanied by a combination of Andalucian, African and Aboriginal music played on the *cajón* (rhythm box) and guitar. Energetic and very sexual – traditionally seen as the seduction by a servant man of an elegant, upper-class woman – the *marinera* involves dancers holding handkerchiefs above their heads and skillfully prancing around each other. You'll see it performed in *peñas* all over the country but rarely with the same spirit and conviction as here in Trujillo. The last week in January is the main **Festival de la Marinera**, with a National Marinera Competition taking place during the entire month.

The main **religious fiestas** are in October and December, with October 17 seeing the procession of El Señor de los Milagros, and the first two weeks of

December being devoted to the patron saint of Huanchaco – another good excuse for wild parties in this beach resort. February, as everywhere, is **Carnival** time, with even more *marinera* dancing evenings taking place throughout Trujillo.

Listings

Airlines Aero Condor, Bolivar 613 ☎044/256794 or 232865; Aero Continente, Av España 307 ☎044/244592; Air Lider ☎044/204470; TANS, Av España 106 ☎044/255722; VARIG, Independencia 533 (☎044/254763). All flights out of Trujillo airport are liable to $4 airport tax.

Banks and exchange Banco de Credito, Jr Gamarra 562; Banco Wiese, Jr Pizarro 314; Banco Latino, Jr Gamarra 574; Banco de la Nación, Jr Almagro 297. America Tours, Jr Pizarro 470, Casa de Cambio, Jr Pizarro 336, or the Casa de Cambios Martelli, Jr Bolivar 665, give the best rates in town for dollars cash, or try the *cambistas* (though be very careful, especially after dark, because they are known to be particularly shady here, see Basics p.20) on the corner of Jr Pizarro and Gamarra, or on the Plaza Mayor. A safer bet are the numerous casas de cambio found on block 6 of Pizarro.

Buses Alto Chicama, José Sabogal 305, Urbino Palermo (☎044/203659), for Chicama; Cruz del Sur, Amazonas 437 (☎044/261801), for all coastal destinations, Cajamarca and Huancayo; El Aguila, Nicaragua 220 (☎044/243211), for Lima, Chimbote and Huaraz; El Dorado, Av America Norte 2400 (☎044/291778), for Chiclayo, Tumbes and Lima; Emtrafesa, Av Tupac Amaru 165 (☎044/208348), for Cajamarca, Chiclayo, Piura, Tumbes or Lima; Linea, Av Carrion 140 for Chiclayo and Piura or from Av America Sur 2857 for Cajamarca, Huaraz or Lima; Leon del Norte, Av Mansiche 413 (☎044/260906), for Piura; Mercurio, Av Mansiche 413 (☎044/250906), for Cajamarca; Movil, Av America Sur 3959 (☎044/286538), for Huaraz and Lima; Ormeño, Av Ejercito 233 (☎044/259782), for the coast and international destinations; Palacios, Av España 1005 (☎044/233902), for Huamachuco; San Pedro Express, Av Mansiche 375, for Chepen; San Pedro Express, Av Mansiche 335 (☎044/528039) for the north coast; Trans Negreiros, Zarumilla 199, Prolongación C. Vallejo (☎044/210725), for Huamachuco; Trans Sanchez Lopez, 1 block from Negreiros, for Huamachuco; Tepsa, Diego de Almagro 849 (☎044/205017), for Lima or the north coast; Transportes Chiclayo, Av America Norte 2404 (☎044/243341), for Chiclayo, Piura and Tumbes; Transportes Guadalupe, Av Mansiche 331 (☎044/246019), for Tarapoto, Yurimaguas and

Juanjui; Turismo Chimbote, Jr Nicaragua 194–198 (☎044/245546), for Chimbote, Casma, Huaraz and Caraz; Turismo Expreso Chan Chan, Orbegoso 308 (☎044/234111), for Chimbote, Lima and Huaraz; Vulcano, Av Daniel Carrion 140 (☎044/235847), for Chiclayo, Cajamarca and Piura.

Consulates UK, Av Jr Nazareth 312 ☎044/235548, 📠 255818.

Courier service DHL, Jr Pizarro 356 ☎044/220916, 📠 203689.

Hospital Bolivar 350 ☎044/245281.

Imigraciones Av Larco 1220, Urbanización Los Pinos for visa renewals.

Internet facilities There are several Internet cafés along Pizarro (Macrochips at 183a, Masterdata at 197, Megaltel at 510, Net@House at 551) between the Plaza Mayor and Gamarra. 24hr service is available at Interc@ll, Zepita 728 (☎044/246465); otherwise, there's also Vizzio Internet at Ayacucho 496.

Laundry Two of the best places in town are Luxor, Jr Grau 637, and Lavandería El Carmen, Pizarro 759.

Photography Foto Express, Jr Pizarro 582, is centrally located and has a reasonably good range of film, plus offering developing.

Post office Serpost (Mon–Sat 8am–7.45pm) is based at Independencia 286, a block and a half southwest of the plaza.

Shopping For traditional musical instruments, try the shop at Jr Pizarro 721; for artesania go to Los Tallanes, San Martín 455; for films and photographic equipment, try Foto Para Ti, Jr Pizarro 645 or Foto Expres Trujillo, Pizarro 582. There's a good supermarket for general provisions at Junin 372.

Telephones Telefónica del Peru, Bolivar 658 (daily 7am–11pm). There's also a telephone and fax office at Bolivar 611.

Tour operators and guides Most companies offer tours to Chan Chan for $15–20 (including the site museum, Huaca Arco Iris and Huaca Esmeralda), and to *huacas* del Sol and Luna from $8. For Chicama sites, expect to pay $20 plus. Recommended operators include Clara Brava's Tours, Cahuide 495 (☎044/243347, 📠 255043, 🌐 www.xanga.com/CasadeClara); Condor Travel, Jr Independencia 533 ☎044/254763; Guía Tours, Independencia 580 ☎044/234856, 📠 246353; Trujillo Tours, Diego de Almagro 301

☎044/257518, ✉ttours@pol.com.pe; and
America Tours, Jr Pizarro 476 ☎044/235182.
Good, English-speaking guides for Trujillo and
around include Clara Brava ☎044/243347;
Takanga López Edith ☎044/222705; Soto Ríos
José ☎044/251489; and Fajardo Linares Luis
☎044/248917.

Tourist complaints ☎/℻044/204146.
Tourist Police ☎044/200200.
Western Union Pizarro 203 ☎044/257501,
℻243913.

Around Trujillo

The closest of the coastal resorts to Trujillo is the beachfront barrio of **Buenos Aires**, a five-kilometre stretch of sand southwest of Trujillo – very popular with locals and constantly pounded by surf. Like other coastal resorts, its seafood restaurants are an attraction, though it doesn't have as much style or life as **Huanchaco** or Las Delicias.

Two kilometres south of Trujillo, after crossing the Río Moche's estuary, you come to the settlements of **Moche** and **Las Delicias**, both within an easy bus ride of the Huaca del Sol and Huaca de la Luna (see p.384). Moche is a small village some 4km south of the city, slightly inland from the ocean, blessed with several **restaurants** serving freshly prepared seafood, including one of the best in the whole Trujillo region, the *Restaurant Mochica* (try their *shamba*, a very substantial soup). Close by, Las Delicias, 5km south of Trujillo, boasts a beautiful, long beach and a handful of restaurants. To reach Las Delicias from Trujillo, catch the direct **bus** marked "Delicias" from the corner of Avenida Moche and Avenida Los Incas. For **accommodation**, the clean and pleasant *Hostal Janita*, C Montero 340 (☎044/485286; ❸), overlooking the sea in Las Delicias, is the only choice at the moment. Las Delicias' main claim to fame is that the *curandero* El Tuno once lived at Lambayeque 18, right on the beach. By arrangement with his family there you can witness the fascinating diagnostic healing sessions that are now practised by El Tuno's apprentices, often involving rubbing a live guinea pig over the patient's body, then splitting the animal open and removing its innards for inspection while the heart is still pumping. It might not do much for your appetite, but apparently reveals the patient's problems, after which he or she is sent away with a mix of healing herbs. It's possible to participate as a patient in these sessions if you make prior arrangements with the *curandero* (almost always involving a dollar price tag).

Another option for getting a taste of *curanderismo* (see Contexts, p.555, and the section on Salas, p.430, for more details of this esoteric and psychedelic healing art) is through the relatively newly developed Escuela y Museo de Chamanes de Alto Poder (School and Museum of High Power Shamans), which is based out in Huanchaquito, in front of the ocean at Mz 24, Lote 15 (☎044/461624); this school offers ceremonial sessions with San Pedro, luck-raising, cures for alcoholism and drug addiction as well as tours to the enchanted lakes of Huancabamba (see p.439), which are said to be the source of most San Pedro healers' powers.

Huanchaco

Although no longer exactly a tropical paradise, **HUANCHACO,** 12km west, or twenty minutes by bus, from Trujillo, is still a beautiful and relatively peaceful resort. Until the 1970s, Huanchaco was a tiny fishing village, quiet and little known to tourists. Today it is one of the fastest-growing settlements in Peru, its half-finished adobe houses, concrete hotels and streets slowly spreading back towards Trujillo. However, it still makes an excellent base for visiting many of the sites around the region, in particular the nearby ruins of Chan Chan, and the development hasn't entirely diminished its intrinsic fishing village appeal. There is a long jetty (18¢) which has been recently renovated, where you can jostle with fishermen for the best fishing positions. Just at the entry to the pier is a small artesania market.

Stacked along the back of the beach, you'll see rows of *caballitos del mar* – the ancient seagoing rafts designed by the Mochicas and still used by locals today. They are constructed out of four cigar-shaped bundles of *tortora* reeds, tied together into an arc tapering at each end. The fishermen kneel or sit at the stern and paddle, using the surf for occasional bursts of motion. The local boat-builders here are the last who know the craft of making *caballitos* to the origi-

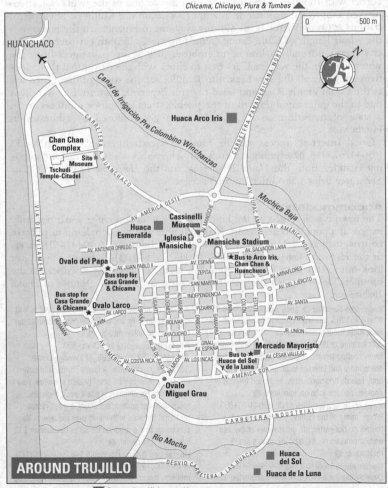

nal design of the Mochicas. Some of the fishermen offer ten- to fifteen-minute trips ($1.50) on the back of their *caballitos*.

The town's only historical sight is the old, square **Iglesia Soroco**, perched high on the coastal cliffs – a fifteen-minute walk uphill from the seafront. Claiming to be the second church in Peru to be built by the Spanish, it sprang up in 1540 on top of a pre-Inca temple dedicated to the idol of the Golden Fish and was rebuilt after being being destroyed by the earthquakes of 1619–1670.

The best time to visit Huanchaco is during its June **fiesta** week, at the end of the month, when a large *tortora* raft comes ashore accompanied by a smaller flotilla of *caballitos*. But even out of season the town is always lively, with people on the beach, others fishing, and a few travellers hanging around the restaurants. To get to Huanchaco from Trujillo, taxis cost around $4-5, or it's easy enough to take the frequent orange and yellow **microbus** from Avenida España block 13 (on the far side of the road from the town centre), by the corner with Independencia, or pick up a bus or one of the white colectivos marked Empresa Caballitos de Tortora (30¢) from the Mobil or Shell petrol stations at Ovalo Victor Raul. On the way out to Huanchaco the bus travels the whole length of Calle Estete (returning via Colón); to get back into the city there's normally a line of microbuses picking up passengers from the waterfront. On the way back, it's best to check with the driver that the colectivos are going all the way back into Trujillo, because some of them turn left at the Ovalo Victor Raul and head towards Esperanza instead. Be aware that due to the quite rapid growth of the pueblo, street and block numbers are in a state of transition, so it's quite easy to get confused by addresses in Huanchaco.

Good **Internet access** can be found at Beach Internet, Los Pinos 533 (☎044/673016, ✉sefyamo@tsi.com.pe), where they also offer fax and copying facilities. Both the *Hostal Bracamonte* and the *Hospedaje Familiar La Casa Suiza* (see below) also offer Internet access.

Accommodation

The town is well served by the kind of accommodation range you'd normally expect at a popular beach resort. Many families also put people up in **private rooms**, such as the *Hospedaje Las Gaviotas*, Los Pinos 535 (☎044/461858; ❷) or the *Hospedaje Jimenez*, Colón 378 (☎044/461844; ❷). To locate others, just look out for the signs reading "Alquila Cuarto" on houses, particularly in the summer (Dec–Feb). It's also possible to **camp** here, on the grounds of *Hostal Bracamonte*.

Hospedaje Familiar La Casa Suiza Los Pinos 451 ☎044/461285, ✇www.casasuiza.com. One of the best, most friendly budget places in Huanchaco, with a range of different rooms (some with bath), a lovely rooftop terrace and book exchange. There are laundry and Internet facilities, they rent out body boards and surfboards, and good English is spoken; popular with backpackers. ❷

Hospedaje Sunset Ribera 600 ☎044/461863. Where many of the visiting surfers hang out; there's no hot water, but great views of the sea and hammocks on the balcony, plus a small restaurant. ❶

Hostal Ancla La Rivera 101 ☎044/461030. Overlooking the beach, this well-established lodg-

ing has an interesting collection of old photos and memorabilia in its bar and cafetería. Rooms at the front can be noisy, though. ❸

Hostal Bracamonte Los Olivos 503 ☎044/461162, ✆461266, ✇www.welcome .to/hostal_bracamonte. A lovely complex of different-sized chalets with solar-heated showers. Very welcoming for children, it has a pool, a games room, Internet access, a laundry, a good restaurant, and terraces with views over the ocean. You can camp in the grounds for $3 per person or $12 including tent rental. ❹

Hostal Las Brisas Raymondi 146 ☎044/461186, ✆244605, ✉lasbrisas@hotmail.com. Clean and modern, though somewhat lacking in character. ❸

Hostal Caballito de Tortora La Ribera 219
℡/℻044/461154, @www.caballitodetortora
.tripod.com. Right on the seafront, this place offers
rooms with ocean views plus cheaper, less
panoramic options. There's also a small pool, garden, cafetería and sun terraces; pretty good
English, French and Italian are spoken by some of
the staff. Price includes breakfast. It's quite a lot
cheaper in low season. ❹–❺

Hostal Los Esteros Larco 618 ℡044/461272. An
attractive place with sea views. The tidy rooms all
come with private bath and hot water. ❸

Hostal El Malecón Av La Ribera 225
℡044/461275, @hostal_emalecon@yahoo.com.
A converted house right on the seafront, rooms
with own baths, TV. ❸

Hostal OK Jr Atahualpa 147 ℡044/461457. Fairly
recently converted place, though simple and family-run, located three blocks back from the
seafront; it's friendly, has hot water and 5 rooms,
each with private baths, as well as a laundry area.
Will also rent rooms for the month (from around
$70). Try to avoid the rooms without external win-
dows. ❷

Hostal Solange Los Ficus 484 (no phone). This is
a small, very nice, family-run hostel where you can
do your own cooking if you wish; just 2 blocks
from the beach. ❷

Huanchaco Hostal Larco 287 ℡044/461272,
℻461688, @www.solui.com
/HUANCHACOHOSTAL. Good-value, comfortable hostel with pleasant gardens, a cafetería and a small
pool. The service is excellent and all rooms have TV
and private bath. There's a pool room and parking.
One of the entrances faces the sea, and the other
opens onto the tiny but attractive Plaza de Armas. ❹

Eating and nightlife

There are seafood **restaurants** all along the front in Huanchaco, one or two
of them with verandas extending to the beach. Not surprisingly, seafood is the
local speciality, including excellent crab, and you can often see women and
children up to their waists in the sea collecting shellfish. The fishermen can also
usually be seen returning around 3–4pm on their *caballitos*. A kilo of fresh fish
can be bought for just $1–2, but the catches these days aren't huge.

Anyone looking for **nightlife** should check out *Sun Kella Bar*, at the southern end of the beach. Alternatively there's the *Sunset Pub*, on La Ribera, just
one block from the pier, with a balcony overlooking the sea. Both are popular
hangouts with young locals and visiting surfers.

La Barca at Jr Unión 209/Pasaje Raymondi 111
℡044/461052. Based close to the seafront, close
to the bus drop-off point and the Estadio
Municipal, it's a pleasant enough place that serves
mainly seafood and prides itself on its bar.

Club Colonial Grau 272 ℡044/461015. A beautifully restored colonial house adorned with paintings, old photos and fine stained-glass work. The
food is sumptuous, with an extensive menu of traditional dishes, but it's not cheap. The garden is
the residence of some penguins and a couple of
rare Tumbes crocodiles.

Huanchaco Beach Restaurant Malecón Larco
602. Very tasty fish dishes, and excellent views
across the ocean and up to the clifftop Iglesia
Soroco.

El Pescadito C Grau 482 ℡044/461484. Located
one block from the ocean, this is one of the smaller, less expensive restaurants in the backstreets of
Huanchaco; the views are not so good as those
from places along the seafront, but the seafood is
just as fresh and well prepared.

Restaurant AH Gusto Los Pinos 135. A small and
fairly simple café which serves mainly pizzas and
some seafood dishes; slightly less expensive than
most places in town.

Restaurant El Caribe Atahualpa 100. Really close
to, but just around the corner from, the seafront to
the north of the pier, this restaurant has great
ceviche and is very popular with locals.

Restaurant El Chino La Rivera 822. No real
views, but more importantly, the food is excellent
and it's very popular at lunchtimes with locals.

Restaurant Don Pepe Malecón Larco 502
@donpepe@huanchaco.zzn.com. Among the best-
positioned seafront restaurants, with a balcony
overlooking the *caballitos del mar* and the fishermen mending their nets; it's not cheap, but the
food, especially their selection of seafood dishes,
is quite good.

Restaurant El Erizo Av La Rivera 735. Virtually on
the beach, next to the small municipal building and
within a stone's throw of the pier, *El Erizo* ("the sea
urchin"– a local delicacy and reputedly a strong
aphrodisiac) serves good seafood dishes, including
excellent crab and sea urchin if you're lucky.

Restaurant Estrella Marina Malecón Larco 594.
Very good, fresh ceviche served in a seafront

location, which often plays loud salsa music and is popular with locals.

Restaurant Marimar Av Victor Larco 525. Just north of the pier, this is another good spot for

seafood and great views of the pier and ocean; try the *sudado de pescado* or the *langostino al ajo* for full-flavour dishes.

The Chan Chan complex

The ruined city of **CHAN CHAN** stretches across a large sector of the Moche Valley, beginning almost as soon as you leave Trujillo on the Huanchaco road, and ending just a couple of kilometres from Huanchaco. A huge complex even today, it needs only a little imagination to raise the weathered mud walls to their original grandeur, and picture the highly civilized, rule-bound society, where slaves carried produce back and forth while artisans and courtiers walked the streets slowly, stopping only to give orders or chat with people of similar status.

Chan Chan was the capital city of the **Chimu Empire**, an urban civilization which appeared on the Peruvian coast around 1100 AD. The Chimu-built cities and towns throughout the region stretch from Tumbes in the north to as far south as Paramonga. Their cities were always elaborately planned, with large, flat-topped buildings for the nobility and intricately decorated adobe pyramids serving as temples. Chimu artwork, particularly ceramics, was mass-produced, with quantity being much more important than quality. Recognized as fine goldsmiths by the Incas, the Chimu panelled their temples with gold and cultivated palace gardens where even the plants and animals were made from precious metals. The city walls were brightly painted, and the style of architecture and relief decoration is sometimes ascribed to the fact that the Mochica migrated from Central America into this area, bringing with them knowledge and ideas from a more advanced civilization, like the Maya. The Chimu inherited ideas and techniques from a host of previous cultures along the coast, and, most importantly, adapted the techniques from many generations of trial and experiment in irrigating the Moche Valley. In the desert, access to a regular water supply was critical in the development of an urban civilization like that of Chan Chan, whose very existence depended on extracting water not only from the Río Moche but also, via a complicated system of canals and aqueducts, from the neighbouring Chicama Valley.

With no written records, the **origins of Chan Chan** are mere conjecture, but there are two local legends. According to one, the city was founded by **Taycanamu**, who arrived by boat with his royal fleet; after establishing an empire, he left his son, Si-Um, in command and then disappeared into the western horizon. The other legend has it that Chan Chan's construction was inspired by an original creator deity of the same name, a dragon who made the sun and the moon and whose earthly manifestation is a rainbow. Whatever the impulse behind Chan Chan, it remains one of the world's marvels and, in its heyday, was one of the largest pre-Columbian cities in the Americas. By 1450, when the Chimu Empire stretched from the Río Zarumilla in the north to the Río Chancay in the south and covered around 40,000 square kilometres, Chan Chan was the centre of a chain of provincial capitals. These were gradually incorporated into the Inca Empire between 1460 and 1480.

The events leading to the city's demise are better documented than those pertaining to its birth: in the 1470s Tupac Yupanqui led the Inca armies down from the mountains in the east and cut off the aqueducts supplying Chan Chan with its vital water supply. After lengthy discussions, the Chimu council managed to persuade its leader against going out to fight the Incas, knowing full

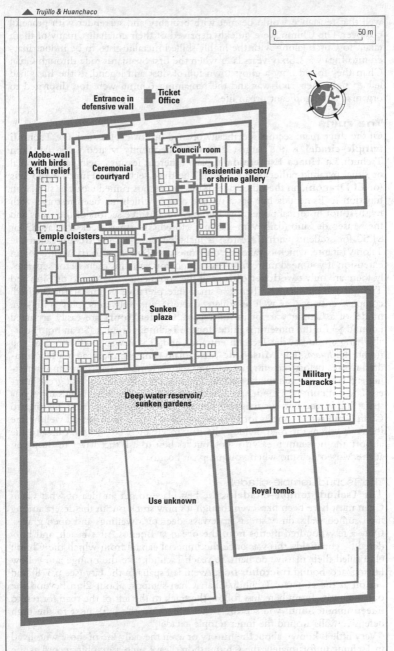

Ticket
Office

Entrance in
defensive wall

N

Adobe-wall
with birds
& fish relief

Ceremonial
courtyard

'Council' room

Residential sector/
or shrine gallery

Temple cloisters

Sunken
plaza

Military
barracks

Deep water reservoir/
sunken gardens

Use unknown

Royal tombs

0   50 m

7

TRUJILLO AND THE NORTH | Around Trujillo

CHAN CHAN TSCHUDI TEMPLE-CITADEL

well that resistance would be met with brutality, and surrender with peaceful takeover. The Chimu were quickly deprived of their chieftains, many of them taken to Cusco (along with the highly skilled metallurgists) to be indoctrinated into Inca ways. Sixty years later when the first Spaniards rode through Chan Chan they found only a ghost town full of dust and legend, as the Incas had left to fight their civil war and the remaining Chimu were too dispirited to organize any significant urban life.

The ruins

Of the three main sectors specifically opened up for exploration, the **Tschudi temple-citadel** is the largest and most frequently visited. Not far from Tschudi, **La Huaca Esmeralda** displays different features, being a ceremonial or ritual pyramid rather than a citadel. The third sector, the **Huaca Arco Iris** (or **El Dragon**), on the other side of this enormous ruined city, was similar in function to Esmeralda but has a unique design which has been restored with relish, if not historical perfection. Entrance to all three sectors of the ruins and the Museo de Sitio (daily 9am–4.30pm, closed Christmas week & May; $3, or $1.50 for students with ID cards) is included on the same **ticket**, called the Talon Visitante, which is valid for only one day (but you can try asking for an extension if you need more time). Although you can visit each sector separately, there are only two **ticket offices**, at the entrance to the Museo de Sitio and Tschudi temple-citadel. There's a small interpretative centre at the Tschudi complex entrance, as well as toilets, cafetería and souvenirs, plus a full-size model of a Chimu warrior in full regalia. **Guided tours** are easily arranged (around $3 for the museum); guides for the Tschudi complex ($6 an hour) usually hang around at the Tschudi entrance, and, if you want, will also take you round the *huacas*. The **Museo de Sitio** (daily 9am–4pm), located a few hundred metres before the entrance to the Tschudi temple-citadel, has an interesting eight-minute multimedia show in Spanish, but not much else of great interest. The museum uses models, ceramics and other archeological finds to reconstruct life in the hot but irrigated desert before Trujillo was built. Getting to Chan Chan is the same as for Huanchaco, only you have to get off well before the *ovalo* where the road divides, one way to Huanchaco and the other to the airport; the museum is easy to spot, but it's best to ask the driver to drop you at the Museo de Sitio when you jump on board.

The Tschudi temple-citadel

The Tschudi temple-citadel is the best place to get an idea of what Chan Chan must have been like, even though it's now stuck out in the desert among high ruined walls, dusty streets, gateways, decrepit dwellings and open graves. Only a few hundred metres from the ocean at Buenos Aires beach, and bordered by cornfields, this was once the imperial capital from which the Chimu elite ruled their massive domain. To reach Tschudi take the orange and yellow Huanchaco-bound **microbus** from Avenida España in the city (see p.378) and get off at the concrete Tschudi/Chan Chan signpost about 2km beyond the outer suburbs. From here, just follow the track to the left of the road for ten to fifteen minutes until you see the ticket office (on the left), next to the high defensive walls around the inner temple-citadel.

Very little is known about the history or even the daily life of those who lived in Tschudi; unfortunately, the Chimu didn't leave such a graphic record as the earlier Mochica culture, whose temples were built on the other side of the Moche Valley. But following the marked route around the citadel through a maze of corridors, chambers, and amazingly large plazas, you will begin to form your own picture of this highly organized ancient civilization. In a courtyard just past the entrance gateway, some 24 seats are set into niches at regular intervals along the walls, and you can experience an unusual acoustic effect. By sitting in one niche and whispering to someone in another, you can witness how this simply designed **council room** amplifies all sounds, the niches sounding like they're connected by adobe intercoms.

Fishing net motifs are repeated throughout the citadel's design, but particularly in the **sunken ceremonial patio**, an antechamber to the entrance to the *audiencias*, or little temples area, and show how important the sea was for the Chimu people, both mythologically and as a major resource. The *audiencias* lead to the **principal plaza** and also to the corridor of fish and bird designs. The **audiencias** themselves were dedicated to divinities and designed to hold the offerings and tributes. The westernmost open point of the site is the burial area, known as the **Recinto Funerario**, and was the most sacred part of Tschudi, where the tomb of El Señor Chimo and his wives was located. Beyond the citadel extend acres of untended ruins that are dangerous for foreigners – some certainly have been robbed after wandering off alone.

La Huaca Esmeralda

One of the most beautiful, and possibly the most venerated of Chimu temples, **La Huaca Esmeralda** lies in ruins a couple of kilometres before Tschudi, just off the main Trujillo to Huanchaco road. Unlike Tschudi, the *huaca*, or sacred temple, is on the very edge of town, stuck between the outer suburbs and the first cornfields. To get here, catch a colectivo (see p.378) or the orange and yellow Huanchaco-bound **microbus** from Avenida España and get off at the colonial church of **San Salvador de Mansiche**, at blocks 14 and 15 of Avenida Mansiche, then follow the path along the right-hand side of the church for three blocks (through the modern barrio of Mansiche), until you reach the *huaca*.

La Huaca Esmeralda (Emerald Temple) was built in the twelfth or early thirteenth century – at about the same time as the Tschudi temple-citadel – and is one of the most important of the *huacas* scattered around Trujillo. It was uncovered only in 1923, but its adobe walls and decorations were severely damaged in the freak rains of 1925 and 1983. Today, because of the rains, you can only just make out what must have been an impressive multicoloured **facade**. All the relief work on the adobe walls is original, and shows marine-related motifs including friezes of fishing nets containing swimming fishes, waves, a flying pelican, a sea otter and frequent repetitive patterns of geometrical arabesques. The *huaca* has an unusually complex structure, with two main platforms, a number of surrounding walls, and several sloping pathways giving access to each section. From the top platform, which was obviously a place of worship and possibly also the cover to a royal tomb, you can see west across the valley to the graveyards of Chan Chan, out to sea, over the cultivated fields around the site, and into the primitive brick factory next door. Only some shells and *chaquiras* (stone and coral necklaces) were found when the *huaca* was officially dug out some years ago, long after centuries of *huaqueros* (treasure hunters) had exhausted its more valuable goods. These grave robbers nearly always precede the archeologists. In fact, archeologists are often drawn to the sites they eventually excavate by the trail of treasures that flow from the grave robbers through dealers' hands into the market in Lima and beyond.

You may still be offered *chaquiras* to buy, by the people of **Mansiche**, a small settlement next to the *huaca*. Apparently direct descendants of the Chan Chan people, the Mansiche locals claim that the stone and coral necklaces came from remote graves in the Chan Chan complex, though this is highly unlikely.

La Huaca Arco Iris

La Huaca Arco Iris – the Rainbow Temple – is the most fully restored ruin of the Chan Chan complex. Its site is just to the left of the Panamerican Highway, about 4km north of Trujillo in the middle of the urban district of La Esperanza. To get there, take the regular Comité 19 red and blue **microbus** from the centre of Trujillo, or any of the other colectivos heading north from Trujillo to Esperanza (they are usually clearly marked in the windscreens). Get off the bus at the blue concrete sign on the side of the main road; the *huaca* is to the west of the highway, surrounded by a tall wall and set back a hundred metres or so, but largely hidden by urban sprawl.

The *huaca* of Arco Iris, which flourished under the Chimu between the twelfth and fourteenth centuries, consists of two tiers. The **first tier** is made up of fourteen rectangular chambers, possibly used for storing corn and precious metals for ritual purposes. A path slopes up to the **second tier**, a flat-topped platform used as a ceremonial area where sacrifices were held and the gods apparently spoke. From here there is a wide view over the valley, towards the ocean, Trujillo, and the city of Chan Chan.

Several interpretations have been made of the **central motif**, which is repeated throughout the *huaca* – some consider it a dragon, some a centipede, and some a rainbow. The dragon and the rainbow need not exclude one another, as both can represent the creator divinity, though local legend has it that the rainbow is the protector of creation and, in particular, fertility and fecundity. The centipede, however, is a fairly widespread motif (notably on the Nazca ceramics), though its original meaning seems to have been lost. Most of the main **temple inner walls** have been restored, and they are covered with the re-created central motif. The outer walls are decorated in the same way, with identical friezes cut into the adobe, in a design that looks like a multi-legged serpent arching over two lizard-type beings. Each of the serpents' heads, one at either end of the arc, seems to be biting the cap (or tip of the head) off a humanoid figure.

Huaca del Sol and Huaca de la Luna

Five kilometres south of Trujillo beside the Río Moche, in a barren desert landscape, are two temples that really bring ancient Peru to life. The stunning **Huaca del Sol** (Temple of the Sun) is the largest adobe structure in the Americas, and easily the most impressive of the many pyramids on the Peruvian coast. Its twin, **La Huaca de la Luna** (Temple of the Moon), is smaller, but more complex and brilliantly frescoed. This complex is believed to have been the capital, or most important ceremonial and urban centre, for the Moche culture, at its peak between 400 and 600 AD.

Although very much associated with the Moche culture and nation (100–600 AD), there is evidence of earlier occupation at these sites, dating back two thousand years to the Salinar and Gallinazo cultures, indicated by constructions underlying the *huacas*. The area continued to be held in high regard after the collapse of the Moche culture, with signs of Wari, Chimu and Inca offerings here demonstrating a continued importance. The latest theory suggests that these *huacas* were mainly ceremonial centres, separated physically by a large graveyard and an associated urban settlement. Finds in this intermediate zone have so far revealed some fine structures, plus pottery workshops and storehouses.

Collectively known as the **Huacas del Moche**, these sites make a fine day's outing and shouldn't be missed. To get there from Trujillo take one of the golden-coloured **colectivos**, marked "Campina de Moche", which run every thirty minutes from the corner of Suarez with Los Incas, near the market, to the base of Huaca del Sol (30¢); or, pick up one of the blue colectivos with gold stripe that leave from the south side of Ovalo Grau (every 10–15 mins). Some colectivos go all the way to the Huaca de la Luna, but many prefer to drop you off on the road, a ten- to fifteen-minute walk away.

Huaca del Sol

The **Huaca del Sol** itself is presently off limits to visitors, but it's an amazing sight from the grounds below or even in the distance from the Huaca de La Luna which is very much open. Built by the Mochica around 500 AD, and very weathered, its pyramid edges still slope at a sharp 77 degrees to the horizon. Although still massive, what you see today is about thirty percent of the original construction. On top of the base platform is the demolished stump of a four-sided, stepped pyramid, surmounted about 50m above the desert by a ceremonial platform. From the top of this platform you can clearly see how the Río Moche was diverted by the Spanish in 1602, in order to erode the *huaca* and find treasure. They were quite successful at washing away a large section of the site but found precious little, except adobe bricks. The first scientific, archeological work here was done by Max Uhle in the early 1900s; he discovered more than 3400 objects and ceramics, most of which were taken to the University of California at Berkeley museum. New excavations are under way.

Estimates of the pyramid's **brickwork** vary, but it is reckoned to contain somewhere between 50 million and 140 million adobe blocks, each of which was marked in any one of a hundred different ways – probably with the maker's distinguishing signs. It must have required a massively well-organized labour supply to put together – Calancha, a Spanish historian, wrote that 200,000 Indian workers were required. How the Mochica priests and architects decided on the shape of the *huaca* is unknown, but if you look from the main road at its form against the silhouette of Cerro Blanco, there is a remarkable similarity between the two, and if you look at the *huaca* sideways from the vantage point of the Huaca de la Luna, it has the same general outline as the hills behind.

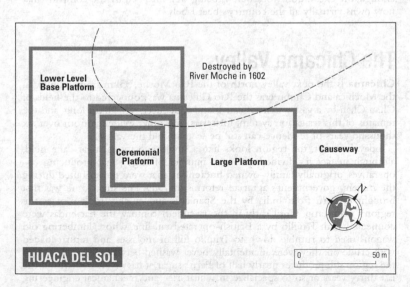

Clinging to the bottom of Cerro Blanco, just 500m from the Sun Temple, is another Mochica edifice, the **Huaca de la Luna** (9am–4pm; $3, includes a 45min guided tour; ☎044/291894 for information from the university museum in town), a ritual and ceremonial centre that was built around the same time as the Huaca del Sol. What you see today is only part of an older complex of interior rooms built over six centuries that included a maze of interconnected patios, some covered and adorned lavishly with painted friezes. The friezes are still the most striking feature of the site, rhomboid in shape and dominated by an anthropomorphic face surrounded by symbols representing nature spirits, such as the ray fish (symbol of water), pelicans (symbol of air), and serpent (symbol of earth). Its feline fangs and boggle-eyes are stylizations dating back to the early Chavín cult, and it's similar to an image known to the Moche as **Ai-Apaec**, master of life and death. The god that kept the human world in order, he has been frequently linked with human sacrifice, and in 1995, archeologists found 42 skeletons of sacrificial victims here. Sediment found in their graves indicates that these sacrifices took place during an El Niño weather phenomenon, something that would have threatened the economic and political stability of the nation. Ceramics dug up from the vast graveyard that extends between the two *huacas* and around the base of Cerro Blanco suggest that this might have also been a site for a cult of the dead, while the fact that it is built at the foot of the sacred Cerro Blanco and incorporates some rocky outcrops into one of the patios suggests that this may also have been somewhere honouring *apus*, or mountain spirits.

Behind the *huaca* are some frescoed rooms, discovered by a grave robber in the early 1990s, displaying multicoloured murals (mostly reds and blues). The most famous of these paintings has been called *The Rebellion of the Artefacts* because, as is fairly common on Mochica ceramics, all sorts of objects are depicted attacking human beings, getting their revenge, or rebelling. All in all, some 6000 square metres of polychrome reliefs have been uncovered. Oddly enough, the excavation work here is being well financed by the company that now owns virtually all the country's beer labels.

The Chicama Valley

Chicama is the next valley north of the Río Moche, 35km from Trujillo. In the Mochica and Chimu eras the Río Chicama was connected to the fields of Chan Chan by a vast system of canals and aqueducts over 90km long, and the remains of this irrigation system, fortresses, and other evidence from over six thousand years of residence can still be seen around the valley.

Today, however, the region looks like a single enormous sugar-cane field, although in fact it's divided among a number of large sugar-producing co-operatives, originally family-owned **haciendas** that were redistributed during the military government's agrarian reforms in 1969. The sugar cane was first brought to Peru from India by the Spaniards and quickly took root as the region's main crop. Until early in the twentieth century, the haciendas were connected with Trujillo by a British-operated rail line, whose lumbering old wagons used to rumble down to Trujillo full of molasses and return loaded with crude oil; they were, incidentally, never washed between loads. Although the region still produces nearly half of Peru's sugar, it has diversified within the last thirty years or so to specialize in wheat, rice and mechanical engineering

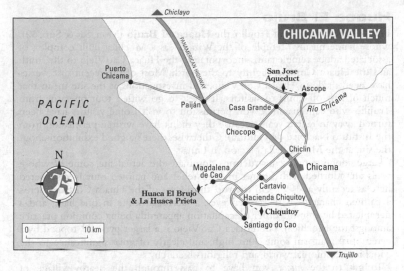

CHICAMA VALLEY

Chiclayo

PANAMERICAN HIGHWAY

Puerto Chicama

PACIFIC OCEAN

N

Paiján

San Jose Aqueduct

Ascope

Casa Grande

Río Chicama

Chocope

Chiclin

Magdalena de Cao

Chicama

Huaca El Brujo & La Huaca Prieta

Cartavio

Hacienda Chiquitoy

Chiquitoy

Santiago do Cao

0   10 km

Trujillo

as well. These days, Chicama is also well known for the fine Cascas semi-*seco* wine it produces. The haciendas are also renowned for the breeding of **caballos de paso** – horses reared to compete in dressage and trotting contests – a long-established sport that's still popular with Peruvian high society. For more laid-back recreation, the isolated seaside village of **Puerto Chicama**, 65km north of Trujillo, offers excellent surfing opportunities.

Like the Moche, the Chicama Valley is full of **huacas** and ancient sites – **Huaca El Brujo**, **La Huaca Prieta**, **Chiquitoy** and **Ascope** – and the locals have a long tradition as *huaqueros*, or grave robbers. Rumours abound about vile deaths from asphyxiation, a slow process sometimes lasting days, for anyone who ventures into a tomb: "*Le llamó la huaca*", they say – "the *huaca* called him".

Getting there

There are buses and colectivos to sites in the Chicama Valley, but it is a good day-trip from Trujillo and many people prefer to go on a **guided tour** from there (see p.375), or to hire a **taxi** with driver and guide for the day ($20–30). The whole valley is also well served by local colectivos, and although they have no fixed timetables, it's quite easy to get from one village or site to another. If you want to go by public transport from Trujillo, catch one of the **buses** marked "Puerto Chicama", "Paijan", "Chicama" or "Ascope", which leave every thirty minutes from opposite Casinelli's Museum, or earlier on the route from the Ovalo Larco (at the western end of Pizarro, which becomes Avenida Larco as it leaves the town centre) as well from the Mercado Mayorista (where most of the buses start). To get to El Brujo or Chiquitoy from Trujillo, take a bus to Chocope from the Chicago bus terminal on Avenida America Sur, then pick up a colectivo from Chocope. For Chiquitoy to Cartavio and for El Brujo to Magdalena de Cao, colectivos run every ten to fifteen minutes to Cartavio (50¢) and every thirty minutes to Magdalena (25¢) from Chocope. If you can't face the walk, you can usually find taxis in Chicama or Chocope who'll take you to the sites for a few dollars per person.

Huaca El Brujo

Fifty kilometres north of Trujillo, the **Huaca El Brujo** (Mon, Sat & Sun; $2), whose name means "Temple of the Wizard", is a Mochica-built complex of associated adobe temple ruins incorporating the Huaca Cao Viejo to the south and the Huaca Cortada, slightly to the north. Most of the recent discoveries have been made in Huaca Cao Viejo, and investigations at the site mean that much of it is off limits to visitors. It's best to go with a tour operator from Trujillo who can guarantee you permission to visit (some visitors have been turned away in recent years because they didn't have written permission from the Instituto Nacional de Cultura). Otherwise, there's a good exhibition about the site at the Museo de la Nación in Lima.

Large adobe temple constructions dominate the actual site, some of whose walls are adorned with figures in high relief and painted murals, discovered here as recently as 1990. On the top, third layer of the Huaca Cortada there's a painted character with startled eyes, a sacrificial knife in one hand and a decapitated head in the other (decapitation apparently being common practice amongst the Mochica). The Huaca Cao Viejo is a larger pyramid, topped by a ceremonial platform some 30m high, and clearly of great significance to the Mochica ceremonial world and religious hierarchy.

To get to the *huaca*, you have to pass through the nearby village of **Magdalena de Cao**, about 5km from the site and the nearest place that local colectivos actually pass through; Magdalena de Cao is the ideal place to sample *chicha del año*, an extra-strong form of maize beer brewed in the valley.

La Huaca Prieta

Quite literally a heap of rubbish, **La Huaca Prieta** sits right next to the Playa El Brujo at the edge of the ocean, ten minutes' walk west of the Huaca El Brujo. It may be a garbage dump but it is one that has been accumulating rubbish for some 6500 years, and is crowded with evidence and clues about the evolution of culture and human activity on this coast. This small, dark hill is about 12m high and owes its colouration to thousands of years of decomposing organic remains. On the top, there are signs of subterranean dwellings, long since excavated by archeologists Larco Hoyle and Junius Bird.

Chiquitoy

The well-preserved ruins of **Chiquitoy** (daily 8am–6pm) are rarely visited – stuck out as they are on an empty desert plain unconnected by any road – but are worth the walk it takes to get there. To reach the site from Hacienda Chiquitoy, take the right track which leads off into the desert (ask at the hacienda, if you're not sure about which track), follow this across the flat pampa for 5–6km (an hour's walk) and you can't miss the site. Chiquitoy's well-preseved **ruins** consist of a temple complex with a three-tiered pyramid – very Mayan-like – in front of a walled, rectangular sector. There is evidence of some dwellings and a large courtyard, too, though little is known about its history.

Ascope

Twelve kilometres northeast of Chicama, on a small road off to the right of the Panamerican Highway, the settlement of **ASCOPE** is principally of interest for its great earthen **aqueduct**, just a couple of kilometres outside town. Standing 15m high and still an impressive site even after 1400 years, it carried water across the mouth of this dry valley up until 1925, when the aqueduct was damaged by heavy rains. The San Jose, as the aqueduct is known, was one of a series of canal bridges traversing ravines along the La Cumbre irrigation system, which joined the Moche and Chicama valleys during the Mochica and Chimu periods.

Puerto Chicama

PUERTO CHICAMA, known also as **MALABRIGO**, 13km northwest of Paijan, is a small fishing village which used to serve as a port for the sugar haciendas, but is now a **surfers'** centre, with the best surfing waves on Peru's pacific coast. If you want a **place to stay**, try the *Hostal El Hombre* (❷), the traditional surfers' place, or *Hostal Chicama* (❷), both with a nice sea view. The place has a real lack of facilities and there's seldom any boards to hire locally – which won't affect serious surfers, who generally bring their own boards. But this isn't as good a place to learn how to surf as the gentler water of Máncora (see p.447). Here, according to surfers, you can find "the longest lefthand wave in the world". You can catch one of the **buses** from Trujillo marked "Puerto Chicama", "Paijan", "Chicama" or "Ascope", which leave every 30min from opposite Casinelli's Museum.

Cajamarca and the Northern Circuit

Whether or not you are planning to venture to the nearby sites or the rainforest, **Cajamarca** is worth a visit. A sierra town, it is second only to Cusco in the grace of its architecture, the drama of its mountain scenery, and, above all, the friendliness of its people. There are two main routes from Trujillo, each exciting and spectacular. The speediest way is to head up the coast via **Pacasmayo**, then turn inland along a relatively new paved road which follows the wide Río Jequetepeque valley, passing small settlements and terraced fields as well as the large dam *la represa Gallito Ciego*, an impressive structure at Km 35. Regular buses and colectivos from Trujillo do this route, completing the journey in about eight hours. A slower route (two days at least) is by bus along the old road, currently in a poor state of repair, from Trujillo through **Huamachuco** and **Cajabamba**. Adventurous travellers may choose to make a loop, known as the **Northern Circuit** (also known as the **Circuito Nororiental**, see p.417), going up by one route and returning by the other.

The proud and historic city of Cajamarca remains relatively unaffected by the tourist trade, despite its intrinsic appeal as the place where Pizarro captured and eventually killed the Inca emperor, Atahualpa. It also makes a very dramatic starting point for visiting the ruins of **Chachapoyas** and the jungle regions around **Tarapoto** and **Yurimaguas**, although most people choose the faster and more frequented route from Chiclayo via Olmos and Jaen to access this region.

Cajamarca

An attractive city that's almost Mediterranean in appearance, **CAJAMARCA**, at more than 2700m above sea level, squats below high mountains in a neat valley. Despite the altitude, the city's climate is surprisingly pleasant, with daytime temperatures ranging from 6–23°C; the rainy season is between the months of December and March. The city's stone-based architecture reflects the cold nights up here – charming as it all is, with elaborate stone filigree mansions, churches and old Baroque facades, most buildings are actually quite austere in appearance. Cajamarca is never overcrowded with tourists; in fact, it's unusual to see any foreign travellers outside of the main season, June to September. The narrow streets are, however, usually thronging with locals going to and from the market or busy at their daily toil. Things have changed, though, in recent years following the discovery of Peru's largest **gold mine** at nearby Yanacocha, in the hills to the west of the city. Giving a welcome boost in particular to the economy of the town, about 500kg of gold was being produced daily by the mine in 2002. The look and feel of the city has changed little, but many locals are concerned about problems with associated immigration, and river and subterranean watercourse pollution because of the chemicals involved in the extraction and refining process.

Some history

The fertile Cajamarca basin was domesticated long before cows arrived to graze its pastures, or fences were erected to parcel up the flat valley floor. As far back as 1000 BC it was occupied by well-organized tribal cultures, the earliest sign of the Chavín culture's influence on the northern mountains. The existing sites, scattered all about this region, are evidence of advanced civilizations capable of producing elaborate stone constructions without hard metal tools, and reveal permanent settlement from the **Chavín** era right through until the arrival of the conquering **Inca** army in the 1460s. Over the next seventy years, Cajamarca developed into an important provincial garrison town, evidently much favoured by Inca emperors as a stopover on their way along the Royal Highway between Cusco and Quito. With its hot springs, it proved a convenient spot for rest and recuperation after the frequent Inca battles with "barbarians" in the eastern forests. The city was endowed with sun temples and sumptuous palaces, and their presence must have been felt even when the supreme Inca was over 1000km away to the south in the capital of his empire.

Atahualpa, the last Inca lord, was in Cajamarca in late 1532, relaxing at the hot springs, when news came of **Pizarro** dragging his 62 horsemen and 106 foot soldiers high up into the mountains. Atahualpa's spies and runners kept him well informed of the Spaniards' movements, and he could quite easily have destroyed the small band of weary aliens in one of the rocky passes to the west of Cajamarca. Instead he waited patiently until Friday, November 15, when a dishevelled group entered the silent streets of the deserted Inca city. For the first time, Pizarro saw Atahualpa's camp, with its sea of cotton tents, and an army of men and long spears. Estimates varied, but there were between 30,000 and 80,000 Inca warriors, outnumbering the Spaniards by at least 200 to 1.

Pizarro was planning his coup along the same lines that had been so successful for Cortés in Mexico: he would capture Atahualpa and use him to control the realm. The plaza in Cajamarca was perfect for the following day's operation, as it was surrounded by long, low buildings on three sides, so Pizarro stationed his men there. The next morning, nothing happened and Pizarro became anxious. In the afternoon, however, Atahualpa's army began to move in a ceremonial procession, slowly making their way across the plain towards the city of Cajamarca. Tension mounted in the Spanish camp. As the Indians came closer they could be heard singing a graceful lament and their dazzlingly bright clothes could be made out.

Leaving most of his troops outside on the plain, Atahualpa entered with some five thousand men, unarmed except for small battleaxes, slings and pebble pouches. He was carried into the city by eighty noblemen in an ornate litter – its wooden poles covered in silver, the floor and walls with gold and brilliantly coloured parrot feathers. The emperor himself was poised on a small stool, richly dressed with a crown placed upon his head and a thick string of magnificent emeralds around his aristocratic neck. Understandably bewildered to see no bearded men and not one horse in sight, he shouted – "Where are they?"

A moment later, the Dominican friar, Vicente de Valverde, came out into the plaza; with the minimum of reverence to one he considered a heathen in league with the devil, he invited Atahualpa to dine at Pizarro's table. The Lord Inca declined the offer, saying that he wouldn't move until the Spanish returned all the objects they had already stolen from his people. The friar handed Atahualpa his Bible and began a Christian discourse which no one within earshot could understand. After examining this strange object Atahualpa threw it on the floor, visibly angered. Vicente de Valverde, horrified at such a sacrilege, hurried back to shelter screaming – "Come out! Come out, Christians! Come at these enemy dogs who reject the things of God."

Two cannons signalled the start of what quickly became a massacre. The Spanish horsemen flew at the five thousand Indians, hacking their way through flesh to overturn the litter and capture the emperor. Knocking down a two-metre-thick wall, many of the Inca troops fled onto the surrounding plain with the cavalry at their heels. The Spanish foot soldiers set about killing those left in the square with such speed and ferocity that in a short time most of them were dead. Not one Indian raised a weapon against the Spaniards.

To the Spanish, it was obvious why Atahualpa, an experienced battle leader, had led his men into such a transparent trap. He had underestimated his opponents, their crazy ambitions, and their technological superiority – steel swords, muskets, cannons, and horse power. Whatever the explanation, it surely was one of the world's most horrific massacres of indigenous people, and it represented a bloody beginning to Cajamarca's colonial history.

Arrival and information

Most people arrive in Cajamarca **by bus**, at one of the main bus company offices on the third block of Avenida Atahualpa (see Listings, p.398, for details), a major arterial route running almost directly east out of the city. If you **fly** into Cajamarca it'll probably be with the daily flight from Lima with ATSA ($60), or with Aero Condor on one of its connections with Trujillo and Chimbote; you'll arrive at the airport, 3km out of town along Avenida Arequipa. Buses leave from just outside the airport every twenty minutes or so for the market area, a couple of blocks below the Plaza de Armas in the city (40¢). Alternatively, a motorcycle taxi there costs less than $1, or a taxi will be around $1–1.50. A taxi to the Inca Baths costs $2–3.

Free maps and **tourist information** are available from the ITINCI office in the Belén Complex, on block 6 of Calle Belén (Mon–Fri 7.30am–1pm & 2.15–5.30pm; ☎044/822903). Alternatively, the University Museum, Arequipa

269 (Mon–Fri 7am–2.45pm), has some leaflets and maps, as do many of the tour companies listed on p.398, which can give advice and information; Sierra Verde Tours and Cumbe Mayo Tours on the plaza and the nearby Cajamarca Tours (see Listings p.398) are among the most helpful. Free tourist information is also available from the University office at Batán 289, next door to the museum.

Accommodation

Most of Cajamarca's **accommodation** is in the centre of the city, around the Plaza de Armas, although there are also some interesting options, such as the *Hostal Galvez* with its natural hot spring baths, a few kilometres away at Baños del Inca.

In Cajamarca

Hostal Los Balcones de la Recoleta Amalia Puga 1050 ☎/℗ 044/823003, ✉ hscajama@correo.dnet.com.pe. A beautifully restored late nineteenth-century building wrapped around a courtyard full of flowers. All rooms have private bath and some have period furniture. ❸–❹

Hostal Cajamarca 2 de Mayo 311 ☎044/821432. A lovely and very pleasant colonial building set around an attractive courtyard with an excellent restaurant, *Los Faroles*; comfortable and reasonable value. ❺

Hostal Colonial Inn Los Heroes 350 ☎/℗ 044/825300. Halfway between the town centre and the bus offices, in an old, brightly painted building. Rooms are without or with bath, plus it has a Chinese restaurant. ❷–❸

Hostal Los Jazmines Amazonas 775 ☎044/821812, ✉ assado@hotmail.com. A pleasant new hostel in a converted colonial house plus a courtyard with cafetería. Some rooms have private bath. ❷

Hostal La Merced Chanchamayo 140 ☎044/822171. A small, friendly hostel which offers good value; clean, with private bath and access to laundry facilities. You might have to ask for hot water; towels, soap and toilet paper not generally provided. ❷

Hostal Plaza Amalia Puga 669 ☎044/822058. Situated in a lovely old building on the Plaza de Armas, but a bit run-down. It's still good value, though, and rooms come with or without private bath. ❸

Hostal El Portada del Sol Pisagua 731. A charming colonial house, where all rooms have private bath. ❹

Hostal El Portal de Marques Comercio 644 ☎/℗ 044/828464, ⊛ www.portaldelmarques.com. An attractive colonial house with a nice courtyard out back, clean and tidy rooms, carpets, private bath and TV; pretty good value. ❹

Hostal Prado La Mar 580. Close to the market, this relatively new place offers private baths in some rooms, TV in all; very good value. ❸

Hostal San Francisco Belén 790 ☎044/823070. Not particularly pleasant or clean, but cheap – and some rooms have small balconies. ❷

Hostal Santa Apolonia Jr Amalia Puga 649, Plaza de Armas ☎044/827207, ℗828574. A pleasant enough if style-less place, it has a small lounge and clean rooms. ❺

Hotel Casa Blanca Jr Dos de Mayo 446 ☎044/822141. A fine old mansion tastefully modernized to produce a comfortable hotel with rickety wooden floors, hot water and private baths and TVs in every room. ❹

Hotel El Ingenio Av Via de Evitamiento 1611-1709 ☎044/827121, ✉ ingeniocai@terra.com.pe. A rather plush and very pleasant hotel located in a wonderful, converted old mansion; it has a fine bar and restaurant, aimed largely at mine workers. ❻–❼

Out of town

Albergue Baños del Inca located behind the thermal bath complex ☎044/838385 or 838563, ℗838249, ⊛ www.Cajamarca.net. This place has youth hostel-style dormitories as well as a number of chalets, all very comfortable and with their own built-in thermal bathrooms, TV, minibar, bedroom and living room; many also have views and direct access to the complex of atmospheric steaming baths. Highly recommended and excellent value. ❶–❹, suites ❼

Hacienda San Antonio at Km 5 on the Baños del Inca road, then 1 or 2km down its signposted driveway ☎044/830905, ✉ hsanantonio@terra.com.pe. An old hacienda with about 150 beds, its own chapel, dairy and very attractive gardens, close to the Río Chonta. There are open fireplaces and all rooms have private bath and are fully fitted. Breakfast and a ride on their *caballos de paso* horses are included. ❻

CAJAMARCA

▲ Baños del Inca & Celendín

▲ Bus co. offices & Cajabamba

► Trujillo

◄ Airport & Ventanillas de Otuzco

► Cumbemayo & Hacienda San Vicente

▼ Bambamarca

ACCOMMODATION

Hostal Los Balcones	11
Hostal Cajamarca	10
Hostal Colonial Inn	12
Hostal Los Jazmines	4
Hostal La Merced	1
Hostal Plaza	3
Hostal El Portada del Sol	6
Hostal El Portal de Marques	5
Hostal Prado	2
Hostal San Francisco	7
Hostal Santa Apalonia	3
Hostal Sucre	9
Hotel Casa Blanca	8

RESTAURANTS AND BARS

Amadeus Restaurant	L
Bairon Video Pub	G
El Batan	A
Casca Nueces	H
Discoteca Los Frailones	M
Los Jazmines	F
Peña Up & Down	C
Pizzeria Vaca Loca	J
Restaurant Los Cajamarques	I
Restaurant Los Faroles	K
Restaurant Salas	E
Restaurant El Zarco	D
Usha Usha	B

0 — 100 m

University & T.I. Museum

Central Market

Palacio de Los Condes de Uceda

Cathedral

PLAZA DE ARMAS

Iglesia & Convent San Francisco & La Dolorosa

Atahualpa's Ransom Room

Belén Complex

Archeology & Ethnography Museum

Cerro Santa Apolonia

Hospedaje Manco Capac Manco Capac 712. A very basic, inexpensive hostel run by the local parish, right in front of the entrance to the thermal baths, really aimed at poorer Peruvians who need access to the baths; bathroom is shared. ❶
Hostal Galvez Manco Capac 552 ☎044/820203. Right beside the Baños del Inca, some 6km from the city centre, this comfortable hotel has thermally heated water pumped straight to your room. ❺
Hotel Hacienda San Vicente 2km west of the city centre towards Cumbe Mayo ☎044/822644,

☎821423, ✉hacienda-san-vicente@yahoo.com. A luxuriously renovated hacienda with the full range of facilities. Room designs have been strongly influenced by Gaudí's works. ❼
Posada del Puruay 5km north of the city ☎044/827928, ✉postmast@p-puruay.com.pe. A country mansion converted into a luxury hotel-museum. All rooms have colonial furniture as well as full mod cons, but the place is especially notable for its ecological approach and has an organic garden. ❽

The City

The city is laid out in a grid system centred around the **Plaza de Armas**, which was built on the site of the original triangular courtyard where Pizarro captured the Inca leader Atahualpa in 1532. Today the plaza is distinguished by its lovely low trees, fine grass and a wealth of topiary: interestingly trimmed bushes adorn the square, most cut into the shapes of Peruvian animals, such as llamas. On the northwest side of the plaza is the late seventeenth-century **Cathedral** (daily 7am–7pm; free), its walls incorporating various pieces of Inca masonry, and its interior distinguished only by a splendid Churrigueresque altar created by Spanish craftsmen. On the other side of the plaza is the strange-looking **Iglesia San Francisco** (Mon–Fri noon–6pm; free), in whose sanctuary the bones of Atahualpa are thought to lie, though they were originally buried in the church's cemetery. Attached to the church, the **San Francisco convent** houses a **museum** (Mon–Sat 3–6pm; 50¢) devoted to religious art – not as good as the one in Cusco, but still giving an interesting insight into the colonial mind.

One of Cajamarca's unique features was that, until relatively recently, none of the churches had towers, in order to avoid the colonial tax rigidly imposed on "completed" religious buildings. The eighteenth-century chapel of **La Dolorosa** (Mon–Sat 10am–5pm; free), next to San Francisco, followed this pattern; it does, however, display some of Cajamarca's finest examples of stone filigree, both outside and in.

Around the Plaza de Armas

The most famous sight in town, the so-called **Atahualpa's Ransom Room** or El Cuarto del Rescate (Mon–Fri 9am–1pm & 3–5.50pm, Sat & Sun 9am–12.30pm; $5, which also includes entry to the Belén Complex (see below), at Amalia Puga 722, is the only Inca construction still standing in Cajamarca. Lying just off the Plaza de Armas, across the road from the Iglesia San Francisco, the Ransom Room can, however, be a little disappointing, especially if you've been waiting a long time, as it is simply a small rectangular room with Inca stonework in the back yard of a colonial building. It has long been claimed that this is the room which Atahualpa, as Pizarro's prisoner, promised to fill with gold in return for his freedom, but historians are still in disagreement

Cajamarca entrance tickets
One **ticket** allows entrance to three of Cajamarca's main attractions, **Atahualpa's Ransom Room**, the **Iglesia Belén**, and the **Archeology and Ethnography Museum** (all Mon–Fri 9am–1pm & 3–6pm). The ticket costs $1.50, and can be bought at any of the three sites.

△ Cabillito fishing boats

about whether this was just Atahualpa's prison cell, rather than the actual Ransom Room. There is, however, a line drawn on the wall at the height to which it was supposed to be filled with treasure, and you can also see the stone on which Atahualpa is thought to have been executed. The room's bare Inca masonry is notably poorer than that which you find around Cusco, and the trapezoidal doorway is a post-Conquest construction – probably Spanish rather than native. A far better example of colonial stone craft can be seen at the **Palacio de los Condes de Uceda** (9am–4pm; free), Apurimac 719, on the other side of the plaza, one block beyond the cathedral. This splendid colonial mansion has been taken over and conserved by the Banco de Credito, but you are free to wander in and have a look around.

A block north of the Plaza de Armas, in the streets around Apurimac, Amazonas, Arequipa and Leticia, you'll find Cajamarca's **Central Market** (daily 6am–5pm). Because Cajamarca is the regional centre for a vast area, its street market is one of the largest and most interesting in Peru – you can find almost anything here from slingshots, herbs and jungle medicines to exotic fruit and vegetables, as well as the usual cheap plastic imports. It is generally a busy, friendly place, but beware of pickpockets.

Slightly further north along Arequipa is the **University Museum**, at no. 269 (Mon–Fri 7am–2.45pm; 35¢). As well as having a good range of informative tourism leaflets and brochures, it has fascinating collections of ceramics, textiles and other objects spanning some three thousand years of culture in the Cajamarca basin; the museum also includes mummies, carved stones, drawings of the Cumbe Mayo petroglyphs and some erotic pots. Look out for the work of Andres Zevallos, whose representations of local people are reminiscent of Ribera and whose landscapes are in the style of Matisse.

The Belén Complex

The **Belén Complex** (Mon–Fri 9am–1pm & 3–5.50pm, Sat & Sun 9am–12.30pm; $5 for the whole complex plus El Cuarto del Rescate) of buildings, on Calle Belén just southeast of the plaza, houses a variety of institutions, including two hospitals (in the lower part, the Hospital de Hombres has an exceptionally attractive stone-faced patio with fountains), a small medical museum, part of the university administration, the National Institute of Culture, and the **Iglesia Belén**, whose lavish interior boasts a tall cupola replete with oversized angels.

However, the most interesting part of the complex is the **Archeology and Ethnography Museum**. Located in what used to be the Hospital de Mujeres, over the road from the main complex, the museum displays ceramics and weavings from the region, as well as one or two objects that have been brought here from the jungle tribes to the east. Look out for the elaborate stone carvings on the archway at the entrance to the museum, which depict a locally infamous woman with four breasts and symbolize female fertility, and which date from the time when the building was a women's hospital.

Eating and drinking

You can eat very well in Cajamarca. There are some sophisticated **restaurants** – like *El Cajamarques* - specializing in the local, meat-based cuisine. But there are also lots of smaller speciality shops worth visiting to try out their pastries or fresh fruit ice creams.

Amadeus Restaurant 2 de Mayo 930, just above the plaza ☎044/829815. A rather elegant restaurant serving pastas and pizzas as well as quality comida criolla and international dishes.

El Batán Jr del Batán 369. Set in a converted colonial building, there's an art gallery on the first floor and other paintings adorn the dining room walls. Good food, including local dishes that don't appear on the tourist menus, plus live music on Fridays and Saturdays.

El Cajamarques Amazonas 770 ☎044/822128. An upmarket, traditional Cajamarca cuisine restaurant decorated with colonial paintings, weapons and other artefacts. The cooking is excellent; portions emphasize quality rather than quantity.

Casca Nueces Amalia Puga 554. Very popular with locals for its delicious *humitas* (sweet maize-meal pasties) and large slices of cream cake.

Heladería Holanda Amalia Puga 657, on the plaza ☎074/830113. There's a real artisan at work here preparing some excellent ice cream using local milk and fresh fruit; try the unique coca ice cream: it might even be good for the altitude.

Los Jazmines Amazonas 775. Located in the hotel of the same name, it serves a good selection of snacks at the back of an attractive courtyard.

Panadería Campos Comercio 661. Serves great pastries and cakes, as well as local cheeses; you can't sit down here, as it's really a shop with food counters where you can try the excellent local fare. Also sells the best postcards in Cajamarca, mostly taken by Sr Campos himself.

Pizzería Vaca Loca San Martín 330. If you can stomach the name (Mad Cow), this busy place serves the town's best pizzas.

Restaurant Los Faroles *Hostal Cajamarca*, Jr Dos de Mayo 311. One of the best restaurants in town for criolla dishes, served in a quiet, plush atmosphere.

Restaurant Salas Jr Amalia Puga 637, Plaza de Armas ☎044/822876. A small restaurant with an old-fashioned atmosphere and good service. Similar to *El Zarco*, but slightly more upmarket and with better food, particularly the breakfasts, though the portions are smaller.

Restaurant El Zarco Jr del Batán 170 ☎044/823421. One of the few local cafés to stand out in Cajamarca, *El Zarco* is always packed with locals. It plays a wide range of mostly Latin music and offers an enormous variety of massive, tasty dishes (excellent trout). By no means upmarket, but its plethora of friendly red-coated waiters gives it a refined, 1920s atmosphere.

Nightlife and entertainment

Nightlife isn't really Cajamarca's strong point, but nevertheless it does possess at least one unique music venue – *Peña Usha Usha* (see below) – that no one should miss out on. A few others also play host to vibrant local music, often incorporating violins as well as the more usual Andean instruments and guitars. During fiesta times in particular, you should have no trouble finding traditional music and dancing. At weekends, many of the **peñas** host good live music, and the clubbier **video pub** or **disco** scene is at its liveliest.

Discos and peñas

Bairon Video Pub Amalia Puga 699, on the corner of the Plaza de Armas. Serves a good range of drinks to a background of ultraviolet lighting and a loud video screen blasting out pop and salsa hits. Upstairs is for couples only.

Discoteca Las Frailones corner of Peru with Cruz de la Piedra, 6 blocks up Santa Apolonia from the plaza. Probably the best disco in town, it plays all kinds of music and has fantastic views over the city from the dance floor.

Peña Up & Down Tarapaca 782. Something for everyone, but really aimed at the younger crowd; it has a *peña*, pub and disco on different floors, but

the rooms are small and it can get quite hectic when full.

Peña Usha Usha Amalia Puga 320. The best venue in town for criolla music, particularly at weekends but also frequently during the week when owner Jaime Valera inspires locals and tourists alike with his incredibly good and versatile guitar playing and singing. Often lit only by candle, this bar should appeal to everyone.

Video Club Casablanca Jr Dos de Mayo 448, on the Plaza de Armas, above the *Hotel Casa Blanca*. Spacious and upmarket video bar offering karaoke. Gets very lively at weekends.

Fiestas

The best time to visit Cajamarca is during May or June for the **Festival of Corpus Christi**. Until the early twentieth century this was the country's premier festival, which has been superseded by the Inti Raymi sun festival held at Sacsayhuaman in Cusco. This too coincided with the traditional Inca sun festival and was led by the elders of the Canachin family, who, in the Cajamarca area, were directly descended from local pre-Inca chieftains. The procession here still attracts Indians from all around, but increasing commercialism is eating away at its traditional roots. Nevertheless it's fun, and visited by relatively few non-Peruvian tourists, with plenty of parties, bullfights, *caballos de paso* meetings, and an interesting trade fair. The city's other main fiesta is **Cajamarca Day**, usually around February 11, which is celebrated with music, dancing, processions and fireworks.

Listings

Airlines Aero Continente, 2 de Mayo 574; Aero Condor, Jr Dos de Mayo 323 ☎044/825674. Cajamarca Tours (see Tour and travel agents below) is one of the better travel agencies in town for sorting out flights and buying air tickets.

Banks and exchange Banco Continental, Jr Tarapaca 725; Banco de Credito, C Comercio 679; Banco de la Nación, Jr Tarapaca 647; and Interbanc, Plaza de Armas. *Cambistas* hang out along Jr del Batán, between *Restaurant El Zarco* and the Plaza de Armas. There's a good casa de cambio at Jr Arequipa 724 (Mon–Fri 9am–1.45pm & 3.30–7pm) opposite the Banco de Credito.

Buses Cruz del Sur, Av Atahualpa 313 (☎044/822488); Empresa Arberia, Av Atahualpa 315 (☎044/826812); Expreso Cajamarca and Transportes Arberia, Atahualpa 290 (☎044/823337); Palacios, Independencia 350 (☎044/822600); El Cumbe, Independencia 270; Vulkano, Av Atahualpa 318 (☎044/821090); Transportes Atahualpa, Atahualpa 330; and Emtrafesa, Atahualpa 281 (☎044/208348), for Trujillo, Chiclayo or Lima.

Car rental Promotora Turística, Manco Capac 1098, Baños del Inca (☎044/823149); and Cajamarca Tours, Jr Dos de Mayo 323 (☎044/822813 or 822532).

DHL and Western Union Cajamarca Tours (see Tour and travel agents below)

Hospital Mario Urteaga 500 ☎044/822156.

Internet Cybernet, Jr del Comercio 924, on the plaza.

Photography Centro Plaza, Jr 2 de Mayo 484, has films, cameras and does developing; Video Plaza Filmaciones, Amalia Puga 681; or Foto Andina, Amalia Puga 663.

Police Plaza Amalia Puga 807 ☎044/822944.

Post office Amazonas 443. Mon–Sat 8am–7pm.

Shopping For leathercraft, ceramics, woollens, jewellery and local hats (*sombreros de paja*) famous throughout Peru for their quality, try the inexpensive artesania stalls lining the steps up to the sanctuary on Cerro Santa Apolonia and also in block 7 of Calle Belén; one of the best artesania shops in town is without doubt Quinde, Jr 2 de Mayo 264 (☎044/821031, ✉rochy-cid@yahoo .com), which shouldn't be missed; there's also the Casa Luna, Jr 2 de Mayo 334, which not only sells good artesania and exhibits and sells a range of local artwork and crafts, but also has a cafetería and sometimes does story telling for children.

Taxis Taxi Seguro, Av Independencia 373 (☎044/825103), are the best.

Telephone office Cabinas Publicas (daily 7am–11pm) can be found on the plaza at Jr 2 de Mayo 460, just below the *Hotel Casa Blanca*.

Tour and travel agents Aventura Cajamarca, Jr Dos de Mayo 444 (☎044/822141); Cajamarca Tours, Jr Dos de Mayo 323 (☎044/825674, ✉cajamarcatours@yahoo.com), are the best for air tickets; Cumbe Mayo Tours, Amalia Puga 635 (☎044/822938); Sierra Verde Tours, Jr 2 de Mayo 448 (☎074/830905, ✉sierraverde_2000 @yahoo.es), offer the complete range of local tours – to Cumbe Mayo ($7), Ventanillas de Otuzco ($5), City Tour ($8 including entrance tickets) Kuntur Huasi, ($35), horse-riding and even 5–6-day trips to Kuelap and other sites on way to and around Chachapoyas ($250–600 per person depending on how many days and size of group); Inca Bath Tours, Amalia Puga 807 (☎044/821828). Most tours cost about $7 for a long half-day to local sites or $25–35 for a full day.

Around Cajamarca

Within a short distance of Cajamarca, there are several attractions that can easily be visited on a day-trip from the city. The closest is the **Cerro Santa Apolonia**, with its pre-Inca carved rocks, though these are not nearly as spectacular as the impressive aqueduct at **Cumbe Mayo**, or the ancient temple at **Kuntur Huasi**. However, the most popular trip from Cajamarca is to the steaming-hot thermal baths of **Baños del Inca**, just 5km from the city centre. A four-kilometre walk from Cajamarca lies the small village of **Aylambo**, known for its ceramics workshops, where you can even try your hand at making your own pots.

Cerro Santa Apolonia

A short stroll southeast from Cajamarca's Plaza de Armas, two blocks along Jirón 2 de Mayo, brings you to a path up the **Cerro Santa Apolonia**, a hill that overlooks the city and offers great views across the valley. At the top of the hill are the sensitively landscaped and terraced gardens known as the **Parque Ecología** (daily 7am–6pm; 50¢), whose entrance is beside the Iglesia Santisima Virgen de Fatima, a small chapel at the top of the steps as you walk up from town. At the highest point in the park, you'll find what is thought to have been a sacrificial stone dating from around 1000 BC. It is popularly known as the Inca's Throne, and offers a great overview of the valley. Just 2km southwest of

AROUND CAJAMARCA

0   4 km

▼ *Trujillo & Chiclayo*

the hill, along the road to Cumbe Mayo, is a further group of ruins – prominent among them an old pyramid, known to the Spanish as a temple of the sun, but now called by the locals Agua Tapada, "covered water". Quite possibly, there is a subterranean well below the site – they're not uncommon around here and it might initially have been a temple related to some form of water cult.

Baños del Inca and the Ventanillas de Otuzco

Many of the ruins around Cajamarca are related to water, in a way that seems to both honour it in a religious sense and use it in a practical way. A prime example of this is the **Baños del Inca** (daily 5am–6.45pm; 80¢–$1.80, depending on the type and grade of bath – the quality ranges from the best, the Imperial, second best the Turistas, then the standard Pavilions A, B & C), just 5km east of the city. There is also an excellent new sauna (women only 8–10.45am & 2–4.45pm and mixed sessions 5–7.45am, 11am–1.45pm & 5–7.45pm; $2.80). The hot-water open pool is open 5am–6.45pm with sessions of up to 1hr 45min. It's a fifteen-minute bus ride from block 10 of Amazonas; local buses and colectivos leave when full, usually every ten minutes or so (20¢). As you approach you can see the steam rising from a low-lying set of buildings and hot pools. The baths, which date from pre-Inca times, have long been popular with locals, though the whole place could do with a bit of a face-lift. Having said that, wallowing in the thermal waters is a glorious way to spend an afternoon. There's a restored Inca bath within the complex, but the stonework, though very good, is not original. It was from here that the Inca army marched to their doom.

An enjoyable two-hour (one way) walk from the baths can be found by following the road to the pleasant pueblo of **Llacanora**; there are frequent **colectivos** to take you back to Cajamarca, but this service tends to fizzle out after 6pm. For those with more time, it's possible to walk from here (3–4hr one way), following the Río Chonta gently uphill to its source, to another important site, the **Ventanillas de Otuzco** ($1). The Ventanillas (Windows) are a huge pre-Inca necropolis where the dead chieftains of the Cajamarca culture were buried in niches, sometimes metres deep, cut by hand into the volcanic rock. If you don't fancy the walk, you can take one of the colectivos direct from Cajamarca to the Ventanillas (25¢), which leave every twenty minutes or so from Arequipa, just below the Central Market.

Aylambo

A four-kilometre walk along Avenida R. Castilla to the south of Cajamarca brings you to the small village of **Aylambo**, known for its ceramics workshops. You can buy a wide range of locally made earthenware products or even try your hand at making your own pottery. Special workshops are also laid on for children; ask at one of the tour agents in Cajamarca for details (see p.398). There are plenty of **buses** here from Avenida Independencia in Cajamarca (15min; 25¢), if you want to save your legs for the many trails that wind around the village through attractive, forested land.

Cumbe Mayo

Southwest of Cajamarca stands the ancient aqueduct and canal of **Cumbe Mayo**, stretching for over 1km in an isolated highland dale. Coming from

Cajamarca, just before you reach Cumbe Mayo, you'll see an odd natural rock formation, the Bosque de Piedras (Forest of Stones), where clumps of eroded limestone taper into thin, figure-like shapes – known locally as *los frailones* (the friars). A little further on, you'll see the well-preserved and skilfully constructed canal, built perhaps 1200 years before the Incas arrived here. Dotted along the canal there are some interesting petroglyphs attributed to the early Cajamarca culture. The amount of meticulous effort which must have gone into this, cut as it is from solid rock with perfect right angles and precise geometric lines, suggests that it served a more ritual or religious function rather than simply for irrigation purposes. In some places along the canal there are rocks cut into what look like tables, which were left by the quarrying of stones during the construction of the canal. Cumbe Mayo originally carried water from the Atlantic to the Pacific watershed (from the eastern to the western slopes of the Andes) via a complex system of canals and tunnels, many of which are still visible and in some cases operational. To the right-hand side of the aqueduct (with your back to Cajamarca) there is a large face-like rock on the hillside, with a man-made **cave** cut into it. This contains some 3000-year-old petroglyphs etched in typical Chavín style (you'll need a torch to see them) and dominated by the ever-present feline features. There's a small but interesting site **museum** with toilets at the entrance and, further on, past the first small hill, the guardian has a hut; if he doesn't catch visitors at the museum he usually finds them here ($1.50).

There are no buses from Cajamarca, and only infrequent combi colectivos. You can **walk** the 20km here in four or five hours, but the altitude here is 3600m, so it's not an easy stroll, starting from the back of the Cerro Santa Apolonia. Most people, though, take a **tour** (9am–2pm; $6–8 per person) with one of the companies listed on p.398, or, if you really want to do it independently, hire a **taxi** for $5–8. The *Parador Turístico* (no phone; ❷), by the museum in Cumbe Mayo, has basic, pleasant rooms, but is rarely open. Similarly, the small cafetería here is usually closed; so if you want to stay out here it's best to bring a tent, though you'll need to get permission first from the Instituto Nacional de Cultura, located in the Belén Complex by the tourist office.

Kuntur Huasi

From Cumbe Mayo it's possible to walk the 90km to a second ancient site – **Kuntur Huasi** – in the upper part of the Río Jequetepeque valley, to the east of the Cajamarca Basin. This, however, takes three or four days, so you'll need a tent and food. Hilary and George Bradt's *Backpacking and Trekking in Peru and Bolivia* has a detailed description and sketch map of the route: you'll need this, or at least a survey **map** of the area since the site is not marked. If you can't face the walk, you can get on the Trujillo **bus** from Avenida Atahualpa in Cajamarca to Chilete, a small mining town about 50km along the paved road to Pacasmayo. Here, you need to change to a local bus (leaving every hour or so) to the village of **San Pablo** (with two small, basic hotels), from where it's just a short downhill walk to the ruins. The journey can take from two to five hours by public transport, so most people choose the easiest option – an **organized tour** from Cajamarca for $15–25 per person (see p.398).

Largely destroyed by the ravages of time and weather, Kuntur Huasi was clearly once a magnificent temple. You can still make out a variation on Chavín designs carved onto its four stone monoliths. Apart from Chavín itself, this is the most important site in the northern Andes relating to the feline cult; golden ornaments and turquoise were found in graves here, but so far not enough work has been done to give a precise date to the site. The anthropomorphic carvings indicate differences in time, suggesting Kuntur Huasi was built during the late Chavín era, around 400 BC. Whatever its age, the pyramid is an imposing ruin amid quite exhilarating countryside.

South from Cajamarca: Huamachuco and Gran Pajaten

It's a long, rough, but rewarding journey south from Cajamarca to the small town of **Huamachuco**, jumping-off point for visiting the remote ruins of **Gran Pajaten**. The whole journey from Cajamarca to the ruins takes at least five days, and involves a combination of bus and hiking. To get to Huamachuco, take the Palacios **bus**, which leaves three times a week from Avenida Atahualpa in Cajamarca, for the five- or six-hour ride to Cajabamba, where you need to change for a more local bus for the three-hour journey on to Huamachuco. Virgen del Rosario buses from Atahualpa 315 in Cajamarca offer the fastest direct service to Cajabamba; Transportes Atahualpa are good too, but they're en route from Lima and can sometimes be delayed arriving in Cajamarca. Both leave in the early afternoon, along with Transportes Dias, who also offer an evening service, but if you can travel by day you'll be rewarded with spectacular views coming down from the green pastures of Cajamarca and across the almost tropical Condebamba valley before ascending to Cajabamba.

If you need to stay over in **CAJABAMBA**, just about the only reasonable **accommodation** can be found at the *Hostal Flores*, L.Pradon 137 (℡044/851086; ❶), on the plaza, where the simple rooms have private bath and are set around a pleasant courtyard. For **eating**, try the *Restaurant Cajabambino II*, at Grau 1193, next to the market, which serves up tasty plates of local trout and chicken dishes. The *Café Grau*, on Grau just before the plaza, offers excellent fruit salads and *alfajores* (shortbread busicuit type sandwich filled with *majar blanca* – a caramel-like sugar product). All the **bus companies** are located within a block of the market; those running between Cajabamba and Huamachuco include Transportes Anita (the fastest) and Transportes Gran Turismo. Both leave at 4am from in front of the market for the three-hour journey along a poor road.

Huamachuco

Infamous in Peru as the site of the Peruvian army's last-ditch stand against the Chilean conquerors back in 1879, **HUAMACHUCO**, at 3180m, is a fairly typical Andean market town, surrounded by partly forested hills and a patchwork of fields on steep slopes. The site of the battle is now largely covered by the small airport, while the large Plaza de Armas in the centre of town possesses an interesting colonial archway in one corner, which the Liberator Símon Bolivar once rode through. Now, however, it's flanked by the modern, rather ugly Cathedral.

From the plaza you can take a three-hour walk for about 6km to the dramatic circular pre-Inca fort of **Marca Huamachuco** (daily 6am–6pm; free), the main reason most travellers end up in this neck of the woods. Situated on top of one of several mountains dominating the town, it's hard to get a taxi to take you there, although Alosio Rebaza, at D. Nicolau 100 (℡044/441488) will transport people in his 4WD vehicle ($10 for up to 4, or $20 if you want him to wait for you). Some 3km long, the **ruins** date back to around 300 BC, when they probably began life as an important ceremonial centre, with additions dating from between 600 and 800 AD. The fort was possibly adopted as an administrative outpost during the Huari-Tiahuanaco era (600–1100 AD), although it evidently maintained its independence from the powerful Chachapoyas nation, who lived in the high forested regions to the north and east of here (see p.405). An impressive, commanding and easily defended position, Marca Huamachuco is also protected by a massive eight-metre-high wall surrounding its more vulnerable approaches. The *convento* complex, which consists of five circular buildings of varying sizes towards the northern end of the hill, is a later construction and was possibly home to a pre-Inca elite ruler and his selected concubines; the largest building has been partially reconstructed. A guardian controls entry to the *convento* buildings and should be offered a small tip ($1 per person). An information sheet providing a plan of the site and some brief details is available from the Municipalidad in Huamachuco.

Practicalities

Of the **bus** companies, Gran Turismo pull in at Balta 790; Anita at San Martín 700; Palacios at Castilla 167; Negreiros at Suarez 721 (off Balta); Agreda at block 7 of Balta; and Sanchez Lopez at Balta 1030 (though their booking office is on the plaza). Air Lider, at the airport, offer daily **flights** to Trujillo ($50 one way) in ten-seater planes.

For **accommodation**, try the *Hostal Huamachuco*, at Castilla 354 (℡044/441393; ❷), near the Plaza de Armas, for rooms with or without bath in their old building. There's also the *Noche Buena* (❸), on the plaza adjoining the Cathedral, which is modern, clean and has private bath and TV. Slightly cheaper but just as good is *Hotel San José*, on the plaza (℡044/441044; ❷), while the *Casa de Hospedaje Las Hortencias*, Castilla 130 (℡044/441049; ❷), has fairly basic rooms with bath in a friendly house and a nice courtyard where you can lounge around. All get full during festival times when you should try to book in advance.

The best bets for food are the **restaurants** *El Karibe*, on the Plaza de Armas, which serves guinea pig and goat, and the place in *Las Hortencias* hotel, which serves a delicious *caldo de gallina* (some of the finest hen stew you'll find anywhere) and a limited choice of other dishes. The *Café Venezia*, at San Martín 780, does great desserts and has excellent coffee made from beans fresh from the Marañón valley, while *Bar Michi Wasi*, at San Ramon 461 on the plaza, is small but trendy, with a nice atmosphere, and definitely the place to press locals for information about the local attractions. For **nightlife** there's *Cachimil*, Esquinas 5, two blocks from the plaza towards Trujillo, which also does good food and is a *peña* with dancing to traditional as well as Latino music. On the first weekend in August the **Fiesta de Waman Raymi** is held at nearby Wiracochapampa, bringing many people from the town and countryside to the Inti Raymi-style celebrations. Other festivals in the region include the **Fiesta de Huamachuco** (celebrating the founding of the city) on August 13–20, a week of festivities including a superb firework display on August 14 and aggressive male *turcos* dancers during the procession.

Money can be changed at the Caja Municipal or the Caja Rural, both on the plaza, or in several of the shops along the first few blocks of San Martín. The **market** is on block 9 of Balta.

The ruins of Gran Pajaten

Agreda **buses** connect Huamachuco twice weekly (Wed & Sat) with the village of **Chagual** (around 12 very bumpy hours) from where it's possible to hire mules and guides (from $5 a day per mule) for the four- or five-day trek via the settlements of Pataz (20km, a 6hr walk from Chagual) and Los Alisos (another 8km or 3hr walk) to the true trailhead for the extremely remote ruins of **Gran Pajaten** – a further three or four days' walk. Occasional mining vehicles also go from Chagual to Pataz. If you're interested in seeing these fantastic ruins of a sacred city, **permission** must first be obtained from the Instituto Nacional de Cultura (see p.406); and this is generally only given to those who can demonstrate a serious and specific interest and reason for visiting this special site. The South American Explorers' Club in Lima (see p.103) can also give advice. The main archeological site at Gran Pajaten is known as **Ruinas de la Playa**. Discovered in 1973, they cover some four hectares, with around 25 buildings, both round and square, built mainly of a slate-type stone. One of the round structures is thought to have been a temple, another living quarters. Many of the walls have geometric and anthropomorphic figures that have been created by the way in which these frequently thin stones are placed in the walls.

From Cajamarca to Chachapoyas

There are two routes up to Chachapoyas, the best, and by far the fastest, road leaving the coast from Chiclayo and Piura via Olmos, Jaen and Bagua; this road has fewer and lower passes. But a fascinating **alternative route to Chachapoyas**, though much more arduous (at least until the road is paved all the way), meandering and longer, goes direct from Cajamarca across the Andes, travelling via the pleasant town of Celendin, and stopping in Tingo, the entry point for the fabulous remains of the citadel of Kuelap, some way before Chachapoyas. The route winds through green mountain scenery, past dairy herds and small houses built in a variety of earthy colours, and crosses into the Marañón Valley beyond Leymebamba, reaching heights of almost 4000m before descending to the town of Chachapoyas. The whole trip takes at least twenty hours, and involves changing buses at **Celendin**.

The bus companies Inca Atahualpa (the better of the two) and Palacios both run daily services along the 112-kilometre route from Cajamarca to Celendin ($3–4, a 4–5hr trip), where you can get twice-weekly Transportes Virgen del Carmen and Empresa Jauro buses (Thurs & Sun) from Jr Caceres 108 (7 blocks from the Plaza de Armas) for the fourteen-hour ($6) journey to Chachapoyas. The seats are often sold out the day before, so buy tickets in advance if possible. If you have to break the journey overnight at Celendin, and need **accommodation**, try the *Hotel Loyers* (❷), on Jirón Galvez, *Hotel Amazonas*, Jr 2 de Mayo (❸), or the good value offered by the *Hostal Celendin,* Jr Unión 305 (☎044/855239, ℱ855041; ❷), set in a colonial-style building, and quite friendly, with private baths and its own restaurant. The *Restaurant Jalisco*, on the plaza, serves good breakfasts and other **food** (but watch out for overcharging). If you happen to be here on a Sunday, check out the great **market**, just a block north of the plaza, which has particularly good bargains in leather goods.

Chachapoyas, Kuelap and around

Though a pleasant enough town in its own right, **Chachapoyas** is unlikely to be your main destination if you're travelling in this stunning region. It's very rural, green and, as you'd expect, mountainous. The area is mostly cloud forest, especially as you travel west towards the fantastic **citadel of Kuelap** and, if you have the time, explore some of the other amazing archeological sites created by the unique pre-Inca **Chachapoyas culture** (see p.409). Highly civilized, they've left their mark in numerous tombs and impressively sophisticated fortifications. To a large extent the ancient culture lives on in some of the remote communities like **La Jalca,** whose seventeenth-century stone-built village **church** has the Chachapoyan zigzag built into its design. The houses in the village are lovely conical, thatched-roof constructions with walls of *tapial*-type mudwork.

Chachapoyas

CHACHAPOYAS, an unlikely capital, because it's really quite small, of the *departmento de Amazonas*, is poised on an exposed plateau between two river gorges, at 2234m above sea level. In Aymara, Chachapoyas means "the cloud people", perhaps a description of the fair-skinned tribes who used to dominate this region, living in one of at least seven major cities, each one located high up above the Utcubamba Valley on prominent, dramatic peaks and ridges. Many of the local inhabitants still have light-coloured hair and remarkably pale faces. The town today, although friendly and attractively surrounded by wooded hills, is of no particular interest to the traveller except as a base from which to explore the area's numerous archeological remains – above all the ruins of **Kuelap**. Even in the early twenty-first century, Chachapoyas remains well off the beaten track, though it has become a firm favourite for those who have made it to this remote and beautiful destination.

A small town by Peruvian standards, Chachapoyas was once a colonial possession rich with gold and silver mines as well as extremely fertile alluvial soil, before falling into decline during the Republican era. Recently, however, with the building of the Cajamarca road and the opening up of air travel, it has developed into a thriving little market town supporting a mostly Indian population of some seven thousand, with a reputation for being among the most friendly and hospitable people in Peru. The pleasant **Plaza de Armas** contains a colonial bronze fountain, a monument to Toribio Rodriguez de Mendoza, the cathedral and the municipal buildings. The town also possesses a couple of churches of some interest, notably the **Iglesia del Señor de Burgos**, known for its attractive colonial imagery, and the **Iglesia de Santa Ana**, the first of its kind built by the Spanish. There is very little tourism infrastructure in Chachapoyas or the surrounding region, but, if you are prepared to camp, you can explore a wealth of interesting sites in little-charted territory.

Arrival, information and getting around

The standard and fastest route to Chachapoyas is by bus from Chiclayo. The best company is Civa (℡074/778048), whose buses take around ten hours, arriving at their depot on block 3 of Ortiz Arrieta, just a block and a half from the Plaza de Armas in Chachapoyas. Trans Servis Kuelap, Bolognesi 536 (℡074/778128), has buses daily to Chiclayo. The other alternative is the longer, rougher route via Cajamarca (see opposite).

Nearly all **buses** arrive within a couple of blocks of the Plaza de Armas along blocks 3/4 of Jirón Ortiz Arrieta, or around the corner on Jirón Salamanca. **Chachapoyas airport** is 4km from the town (taxis cost $4–5), and has flights from Lima ($95–120) and Chiclayo ($75) a couple of times a week, and from Cajamarca ($50) up to three times a week; all flights should be booked as far in advance as possible, though regularity and reliability are a bit shaky. Calibri, on the Plaza de Armas, and Grupo Ocho (☎074/757391) and Transportes Aereas Andahuaylas, both based at the airport, are the main companies serving Chachapoyas. **Transport around town** tends to be by motorcycle rickshaws, which cost a flat rate of 30¢. For general **tourist information** ask at the Dirección Subregional de Industria y Turismo ITINCI, C Chincha Alta 445 (Mon–Fri; 9am–5.30pm; ☎074/757047), just a block from the plaza, but for advice on local archeological sites, try the **National Institute of Culture**, Jr Junin 817 (Mon–Fri 9am–6pm). The Banco de Credito, on the Plaza de Armas, will change dollars cash and travellers' cheques, and can sometimes give cash against Visa cards. The **post office** (Mon–Sat 8am–7pm) is at Dos de Mayo 438, though note that it's usually quicker to wait and post your letters from a coastal city. One well-known local **guide** is Martín Chumbe, Jr Piura 909 (☎074/757212), also contactable through the *Gran Vilaya Hotel* (see below), who speaks some English and charges around $25–30 a day for tours of sites in the region, including Kuelap. Other recommended guides include Julio Soto Valle, Jr Libertad 812 (☎074/757498) and Oscar Arce Caceres, *Hostal Estancia Chillo*, some 4 or 5km south of Tingo at the base of Kuelap ruins. **Telephone** calls should be made from the Telefónica office at Jr Triunfo 851.

Accommodation

Gran Vilaya Hotel Jr Ayacucho 755 ☎074/757664, 757100 or 757208. Located on the Plaza de Armas, this is a relatively comfortable and warm quality hotel, with its own restaurant; all rooms have private bath and hot water. ④–⑤

Hostal Danubio Plazuela Belén ☎074/757337. Very clean and peaceful, it has a restaurant and is popular with travellers. ②–③

Hostal Johumaji Jr Ayacucho 711 ☎074/757138. More basic but still reasonable value. ②

Hostal Kuelap Jr Amazonas 1057 ☎074/757136.

Clean and friendly, but most rooms have shared baths and no hot water. ②

Hotel Amazonas Jr Grau 565 ☎074/757199. A popular budget place on the Plaza de Armas, with an attractive traditional patio. Hot water and rooms with or without bath are available. ②–③

Hotel El Dorado Jr Ayacucho 1062 ☎074/757047. Comfortable, with hot water and some rooms have private bath. ②–③

Hotel Revash on the Plaza de Armas. This is comfortable and good value, with private bath and hot water. ②

Restaurants

Las Chozas de Marlissa Jr Ayacucho 1133. A friendly restaurant where typical local food combines tropical dishes with staple mountain meals based on rice and potatoes; at night it is also a good bar.

Cuyería, Pollería y Panadería Virgen Asunta Jr Puno 401. *The* place to go for roast guinea pig, though you have to order it a couple of hours in advance.

Mass Burger Jr Ortiz Arrieta 580. Centrally located and great for most of the usual snacks as well

as juices and other drinks; can offer vegetarian options.

Restaurant Chacha Jr Grau 565, next to the *Hotel Amazonas*. An excellent restaurant serving well-priced and well-prepared Peruvian fare.

Restaurant Kuelap Jr Ayacucho 820. Serves reasonably priced Peruvian dishes.

Restaurant Las Vegas Jr Amazonas 1091, corner with Chincha Alta. Good for basic hot meals, snacks and drinks.

Kuelap and Gran Vilaya

The main attraction for most travellers in the Chachapoyas region is the unrestored ruin of **Kuelap**, one of the most overwhelming pre-Inca sites in Peru.

Just 40km south of Chachapoyas (along the Cajamarca road), the ruins were discovered in 1843, above the tiny village of Tingo in the remote and verdant Utcubamba Valley. In 1993, Tingo was partly destroyed by flash floods, when more than a hundred homes were washed away, but it is still the main point of access for visiting the ruins. Also best reached from Tingo, but far less accessible – at least two days' walk – is the collection of ruins known as **Gran Vilaya**. If you intend to venture beyond Kuelap to Gran Vilaya, you must first obtain **permission** from the National Institute of Culture in Chachapoyas (see previous page). Among the other places possible to visit are the ruined city of **Purunllacta**, one of the likely capitals of the Chachapoyas people, and also **Carajía** and the **Pueblo de los Muertos**, two impressive cliff-face burial centres for the elite of this quite sophisticaed culture.

Getting there

If you're coming from Cajamarca and Celendin, the bus passes right through Tingo. It's possible to visit the ruins independently by taking a colectivo from the corner of Grau and Salamanca (6am or 7am) **from Chachapoyas to Tingo**. Alternatively, you can go on an organized day tour with a guide (from $20 per person; see opposite), or hire a horse at El Chillo ($5–10 per day), on the road to Tingo.

To get **from Tingo to Kuelap**, it's a hard but hugely rewarding 1500-metre climb (around 4hr up and about 2hr back down) from the west bank of the Río Utcubamba. Leave early to avoid the mid-morning sun, and remember to carry all the water you'll need with you. Mules or horses are usually available to hire from the hostel in Tingo ($5–10 per day). Alternatively, colectivos go from Tingo to the Kuelap car park (3hr).

Colectivos also go **from Tingo to Choctamal**, and it's then another five hours' or so walk **from Choctamal to Gran Vilaya**'s remote, largely unexplored and hard-to-find sites. The best way to reach them is with a decent guide and some mules – try Oscar Arce at

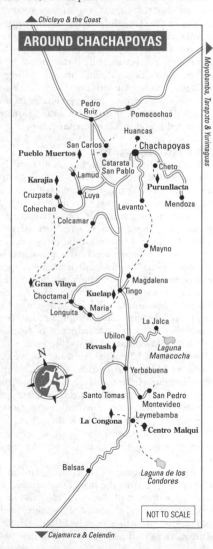

▲ Chiclayo & the Coast

AROUND CHACHAPOYAS

▶ Moyobamba, Tarapoto & Yurimaguas

Pedro Ruiz
Pomacochas
Huancas
San Carlos
Chachapoyas
Pueblo Muertos
Catarata San Pablo
Cheto
Karajia
Lamud
Cruzpata
Luya
Purunllacta
Cohechan
Levanto
Mendoza
Colcamar
Mayno
Gran Vilaya
Magdalena
Choctamal
Kuelap
Tingo
Longuita
Maria
La Jalca
Ubilon
Revash
Laguna Mamacocha
N
Yerbabuena
Santo Tomas
San Pedro Montevideo
La Congona
Leymebamba
Centro Malqui
Balsas
Laguna de los Condores

NOT TO SCALE

▼ Cajamarca & Celendin

Chillo (see *Estancia Chillo Hostal*, below). He can also take you to see the impressive ruins of **Santa Cruz**, **Machu Llaqta** and **Las Pilas**, all relatively easy one-day walks through stunning cloud forest. Note that once you get beyond Choctamal, it's often hard to use money, and it can prove handy to have some **trade goods** with you – pencils, fruit, chocolate, bread, canned fish or biscuits – and, of course, camping gear, unless you want to be completely dependent on the local hospitality.

Accommodation

Most people coming to see the ruins **camp** (you'll need a sleeping bag), but there are also a few **hostels** in the area. **Tingo** has a very basic, unnamed hostel (no phone; ❶), or, if you arrive too late to get in there, you can sometimes shelter in the village police station. Surprisingly, there's a small hostel with dormitory accommodation at the **Kuelap** site itself, the *Albergue de Kuelap* (no phone; ❶), run by the site guardian, who also sometimes provides food. Another equally basic place, the *Hostal El Bebedero* (❶), is situated about ten minutes' walk down the hill from the *Albergue*. A few kilometres beyond Tingo, in a place called **Chillo**, there's an eco-hostel, the *Estancia Chillo* (no phone; ❸), which has private baths, generates its own electricity, and whose owner is a reliable guide. For those continuing on to Gran Vilaya, there's also a small, unnamed hostel in **Choctamal** (no phone; ❷).

The Kuelap ruins

The ruined citadel of **Kuelap** (daily 8am–2pm; $4) is situated high on a ridge, about 3000m above sea level, commanding terrific views of the surrounding landscape, but it is the structure itself which immediately arrests your attention. Its enormous walls tower up to 20m high, and are constructed from gigantic limestone slabs arranged in geometric patterns, with some sections faced with rectangular granite blocks over forty layers high. Inside the ruins you come across hundreds of round stone houses decorated with a distinctive zigzag pattern (like the modern ceramics produced by the locals), small, carved animal heads, condor designs, and intricate serpent figures. There are also various enclosures and huge crumbling watchtowers partly covered in wild subtropical vegetation, shrubs, and even trees. One of these towers is an inverted, truncated cone containing a large, bottle-shaped cavity, possibly a place of torture, since archeologists have found human bones there, though these could date from after the original inhabitants of Kuelap had abandoned the citadel.

It has been calculated that some forty million cubic feet of building material was used at Kuelap, three times the volume needed to construct the Great Pyramid of Egypt. An estimated three thousand people would have lived here at its height, working mainly as farmers, builders and artisans and living in little round stone houses. It is the strongest, most easily defended of all Peruvian fortress cities and, occupied from about 600 AD by the Chachapoyas tribe, is thought to be the site which the rebel Inca Manco considered using for his last-ditch stand against the conquistadores in the late 1530s. He never made it here, ending up instead in the equally breathtaking Vilcabamba, northeast of Cusco.

The only resident today is the guardian from INC (Instituto Nacional de Cultura), who runs the hostel (see above), and sells soft drinks and sometimes beer near the top of the ruins. He can also give information about the other, smaller ruins in the immediate vicinity such as **Revash**, a thirteenth-century burial site consisting mainly of stone-built tombs near the village of Santo Tomas, and can direct you to the village of Choctamal, a five-hour walk.

The Gran Vilaya ruins

The name **Gran Vilaya** refers to a superb complex of almost entirely unexcavated ruins scattered over a wide area. Explorer Gene Savoy claimed to have "discovered" them in 1985, though travellers have been hiking into this area for years and there were several sketch maps of the ruins in existence years before he arrived. Despite Savoy's claim to have found thousands of buildings, a more conservative estimate puts the record at some 150 sites divided into three main political sections. About thirty of these sites are of note, and about fifteen of these are of real archeological importance.

Purunllacta

Among other charted ruins in the Utcubamba Valley are those of the archaic metropolis of **Purunllacta**. These can be reached fairly easily by taking the daily bus from Grau in Chachapoyas to Pipos on the Mendoza road. Get off here and walk to the village of **Cheto**, from where it's a short climb to the ruined city itself. The return trip is possible the same day, though it's more enjoyable to camp at the site.

Purunllacta was one of the seven major cities of the Chachapoyas culture – and probably the capital – before they were all conquered by the Inca Tupac Yupanqui in the 1470s. The **site** consists of numerous groups of buildings scattered around the hilltops, all interconnected by ancient roads and each one surrounded by elegant agricultural terraces. At the centre of the ruined city you can clearly make out rectangular stone buildings, plazas, stairways and platforms. The most striking are two storeys high, and made of carved limestone blocks. The explorer Gene Savoy estimated that the entire complex covered about 150 square kilometres – and even if the truth amounts to only a third of this calculation, it is an astonishing accomplishment.

Carajía

A characteristic of the Chachapoyas region is its **sarcophagi**, elaborately moulded, earthenware coffins, often stuck inaccessibly into horizontal crevices high up along cliff faces and painted in vivid colours. These were built by the Chachapoyas people in the twelfth and thirteenth centuries. A fine example – and a rewarding excursion from Chachapoyas – are the sarcophagi at **Carajía**. To get here, some 46km southwest of Chachapoyas, catch one of the early morning colectivos or pickups headed for **Luya** from Grau and Salamanca in Chachapoyas. At Luya ask for directions to **Shipata**, where the path to the sarcophagi begins. From Shipata, walk down one side of the valley, over a bridge and then up the other side for about five minutes before taking a less clearly marked path to your right. The entire, spectacular walk from Luya Vieja takes about four hours.

Pueblo de los Muertos

Another good example of sarcophagi is at the **Pueblo de los Muertos** (City of the Dead), some 30km to the north of Chachapoyas. Up to 2m high and carved with human faces, six were originally found here and three have been put back in their original sites to stare blankly across the valley from a natural fault in the rock face. Each one has been carefully moulded into an elongated egg-like shape from a mixture of mud and vegetable fibres, then painted purple and white with geometric zigzags and other superimposed designs. Savoy described them aptly as "standing like ten pins in a bowling alley", and most of them are still intact. If you get close, you can see that the casings are hollow, and some contain mummies wrapped in funerary shrouds; others are just filled with sun-bleached bones. Protected as they are from the weather by an overhang, these ancestors of the Chachapoyas race may well be watching over their land for another thousand years to come, though recent reports suggest that they have been looted and partially destroyed.

The Pueblo de los Muertos is easily reached by taking the daily Chiclayo **bus** from the market in Chachapoyas to Puente Tingobamba, at the settlement of Lamud. The sarcophagi are about three hours' walk from Puente; ask for directions there.

La Jalca

Almost three hours by road from Chachapoyas, the traditional village of **La Jalca** can be visited. There are a number of ruins within walking distance of here, but, as the folklore capital of this region, La Jalca has some amazing architecture in its own right. The most noticeable features are the stone walls around the village and the seventeenth-century stone-built **church,** which has the Chachapoyan zigzag built into its design. There's a good little hostel in town (no phone; ❷), locally owned and operated. The houses in the village, built in typical Chachapoyas fashion along the ridge, are lovely, conical thatched-roofed constructions with walls of *tapial*-type mudwork.

Leymebamba and Laguna de los Condores

About two-thirds of the way along the road from Chachapoyas to Cajamarca, in the section between Tingo and Celendin, you'll find the town of Leymebamba, some 80km (3–4hr) by road from Chachapoyas and another eight to ten hours from Cajamarca. This is the location for a superb museum – Museo de Leymebamba – which houses around 150 mummies from the Chachapoyas culture's mausoleum of the not-too-distant Laguna de los Condores. The museum itself is the product of local labour and skills, using traditional materials and construction techniques including stonework, timber and *tapial*. This is one of Peru's first new museums to have been lovingly constructed with local community participation, not only producing a fine, traditional-style building but also giving validation to traditional skills at the same time. As Leymebamba is a remote and insignificant market town, there are few services and often no electricity (particularly after 10 or 11pm on weekdays). There are only a couple of hostels, the best being the *Didogre*, 16 de Julio 320 (❷), which is nevertheless very basic. The only obvious reason for stopping off here is to visit the museum or to use it as a base for exploring further afield.

Into the jungle: Moyobamba to Iquitos

A very adventurous **journey by land and river** will take you on from Chachapoyas to the Peruvian jungle capital of Iquitos (see p.466) on the Amazon, not far from the Brazilian border. It's difficult to estimate the duration of this trip – there are always waits for connections and embarkations –but it's unlikely to take much less than a week's hard travelling, unless you take the easy way out, catching a scheduled internal flight from **Moyobamba** (though the airstrip is actually in nearby Rioja) or **Yurimaguas**. You can take one of Peru's best Amazon river trips – not as long as most, and reasonably straightforward – from Yurimaguas down the Río Huallaga by boat, further into the jungle, along the edge of one of Peru's best and least-visited protected lowland forests, the **Reserva Nacional de Pacaya Samiria** (see p.477 for details of this remote rainforest haven). To the south of this is the frontier town of **Tarapoto**, these days quite a centre for adventure trips mainly exploring the wildlife and flora of this region, and the gateway to Juanjui (see p.412) and the backroad along the edge of the rainforest to Tingo Maria – a route not presently recommended for travel because of its reputation for lawlessness and cocaine production.

Moyobamba

It takes about nine to ten hours in the dry season (and up to 15hr Dec–March) to reach **MOYOBAMBA**, 160km east of Chachapoyas. Situated just above the Río Mayo in a hot, humid, tropical forest environment, the town was founded in 1539 by Don Alonso de Alvarado on one of his earliest explorations into the Amazon jungle. Although a small town, it is the capital of the large, though sparsely populated *departmento* of San Martín. During the colonial period it was a camp for pioneers, missionaries and explorers, like **Pedro de Urzúa**, who used it as a base in his search for **cinnamon**. Having noticed Indians using dry buds that tasted of cinnamon in cooking, Urzúa kept his men busy looking for the potentially profitable spice. If he had been successful in finding cinnamon plantations in the jungles, where the Indians traded for it, then the Portuguese monopoly with the Spice Islands could have been challenged, Columbus's original aspirations fulfilled, and Moyobamba transformed into a rich city. As you can see today, however, Urzúa failed in his attempt, and Moyobamba is much the same as any other jungle town – hot, muddy and laid-back, with a cathedral and a few, but not many, decent hotels. The town was shaken up by a fairly heavy earthquake back in 1991, and signs of this are still visible, with some buildings still in disrepair.

An hour's walk (5km) south of the town are the hot thermal springs of **San Mateo** (daily 10am–6pm; 30¢); some 6km from town there are also the natural sulphur baths of **Oromina**, which are renowned for their medicinal properties. About 15km south of Moyobamba, you can see the spectacular waterfalls **Cataratas de Gera**. To get to the falls take a bus from Calle Miguel Grau some 21km to the village of Jepelacio ($1), then walk the 3km from here. Note that you need to obtain a free permit from Moyobamba's National Institute of Culture, block 3, Jirón Benavides, before visiting the falls.

Practicalities

The **tourist information** office is at the Dirección Regional de Industria y Turismo (☎094/562043, 🖷561431, 📧sanmartin@mitinci.gob.pe), Jr San

Martin 301. To get to Moyobamba from Chachapoyas, take a colectivo along the Mayo Valley to **Pedro Ruiz** ($3, a 2hr trip), then take another colectivo to **Rioja** ($10, a 7hr trip), where you need to change to yet another colectivo to Moyobamba ($1.50, a 1hr trip). Moyobamba is also served by the **airstrip** at nearby Rioja (see "Travel details", on p.450, for information about flights).

The cheapest **accommodation** in town is the *Quinta El Mayo*, Calle Canga (no phone; ❷); there's also the mid-range options like the clean *Hostal Inca* (❹), on Calle Alvarado; or the good-value, more comfortable *Puerto Mirador* (☎094/562594; ❺), on Calle Sucre, twenty minutes' walk or a $3 taxi ride from the town centre, with its own pool. The *Hostal Marcantonio* (☎094/562319; ❼) is by far the swishest place; it's very clean with good service and an excellent restaurant.

Tarapoto and around

Though much larger than Moyobamba, **TARAPOTO**, also known as the "City of Palms", has little to recommend it, except as a reasonable base in which to prepare for a jungle trip, or to do some **whitewater rafting** on the Río Mayo (ask at the tour company on the Plaza de Armas for details). The town, founded in 1772, lies just 420m above sea level and has an average daily temperature range of 29–37°C. The Río Huallaga flows on from here, via the Amazon, until it finally empties into the Atlantic Ocean many thousands of kilometres away. A strange sort of place, Tarapoto has a large **prison** and a big drug-smuggling problem, with people flying coca paste from here to Colombia, where it is processed into cocaine for the US market (see box, this page).

Practicalities

From the Plaza de Armas in Moyobamba there are several **colectivos** a day to Tarapoto ($6, a 4–5hr journey). Alternatively, you could catch the daily Chiclayo to Tarapoto **bus** ($14, a 20–22hr trip), which also stops at the Plaza de Armas; the Moyobamba to Tarapoto leg takes five hours and costs $7. Tarapoto has its own **airport**, too, 5km from the centre of town (see "Travel details", on p.450, for information about flights). The best **accommodation** in Tarapoto is at the comfortable *Hotel Río Shilcayo*, Pasaje Las Flores 224, Banda de Shilcayo (☎094/522225; ❺), with its own swimming pool. The *Hotel San Antonio*, less than a block southwest of the Plaza de Armas (❸), is better value for money, but only some rooms have private baths. The cheapest options are

---

South from Tarapoto: a traveller's warning

The route **south from Tarapoto** via Juanjui (150km) and Tingo Maria (a further 350km) through wild frontier jungle territory is not currently recommended for travellers. It passes through one of the most dangerous areas in Peru, dominated by the illegal **coca-growing industry**, as is most of the Huallaga Valley. This is inevitably associated with **drug smuggling**, which attracts big money to buy **arms** for terrorist groups, and the army have been present in the region for years. Now and again there are confrontations, Wild West-style shoot-outs involving all the interested parties, and the region remains more or less beyond the control of law and order. The situation suits some locals, and the illegal drug money and machine guns have a large influence on many people's lives. Ultimately, all current advice suggests that it's not worth the risk of travelling here at the moment.

the basic *Hostal Pasquelandia*, on Pimental (❶–❷), the *Hostal Melendez*, Calle Ursua (❶), and the *Hostal Central*, on Jirón San Martín (☎094/522234; ❶).

Eating out is surprisingly good, especially at the *Real*, Jr Moyobamba 331, which serves superb evening meals including a mix of standard Peruvian dishes augmented with jungle produce such as yucca, plantains or large fish steaks. The *Restaurant El Mesón*, on the Plaza de Armas, offers a good, cheap set-lunch menu, while *El Camarón*, on Jirón San Pablo de la Cruz, is renowned for its delicious Amazon river shrimp. Further afield – 45 minutes by colectivo – the pleasant restaurant *El Mono y El Gato* serves interesting local dishes, and is very close to the Cataratas de Ahuashiyacu, a popular local swimming spot. The **tourist information** office is at Oficina Zonal de Industria y Turismo (☎094/522567, ✉itatpto@viaexpresa.com.pe), Jr Angel Delgado, block 1.

Lamas

A pleasant day-trip from Tarapoto is to the nearby village of **LAMAS**, folklore capital of the *departmento* of San Martín, about 20km up into the forested hills and surrounded by large pineapple plantations. Colectivos to Lamas leave every hour or so from the Plaza de Armas in Tarapoto ($1; 30min). The inhabitants of this small, exotic, native settlement, and particularly the quarter known as Barrio Huayco, are reputed to be direct descendants of the Chanca tribe that escaped from the Andes to this region in the fifteenth century, fleeing from the conquering Inca army. The people keep very much to themselves, carrying on a highly distinctive lifestyle which displays an unusual combination of jungle and mountain Indian cultures – the women wear long blue skirts and colourfully embroidered blouses, and the men adorn themselves on ceremonial occasions with strings of brightly plumed, stuffed macaws. Everyone goes barefoot and speaks a curious dialect, a mixture of Quechua and Cahuapana (a forest Indian tongue), and the town is traditionally renowned for its *brujos* (wizards), who use the potent hallucinogen ayahuasca, for their nocturnal divinatory and healing sessions. The best month to visit is August when the village **festival** is in full swing. The days are spent dancing, and drinking, and most of the tribe's weddings occur at this time. There's no hotel here, but villagers may let you camp in their gardens; alternatively, you can easily make it here and back from Tarapoto in a day.

Yurimaguas

From Tarapoto it's another 140km north along pretty but rough jungle tracks to the frontier town of **YURIMAGUAS**. In the dry season you can do this journey by one of the frequent colectivos ($10) in about five or six hours, but from November to March it's more likely to take between eight and ten hours. Try and travel this route by day if possible, because there's less risk of being robbed or encountering trouble on the road. The bustling little market town of Yurimaguas has little to recommend it, other than its **three ports**, giving access to the Río Huallaga. The most important is the downriver port of **La Boca**, where all the larger boats leave from, including those to Iquitos. The port is located some fifteen to twenty minutes' walk from the town centre, or a $1 ride in a motorcycle rickshaw. The second, middle port, known as **Puerto Garcilaso**, is closer to the heart of Yurimaguas and mainly used by farmers bringing their produce into town from the nearby farms in smaller boats. The third, upper port, called **Puerto Malecón Shanuse**, is used primarily by fishermen.

Accommodation options in Yurimaguas include the *Hostal Cesar Gustavo* (❷), the most comfortable and friendly of the basic hostels, and the good-value *Hostal La Estrella* (❷). Slightly pricier, but better quality and with a good restaurant, is the *Hostal el Naranjo* (☎044/352650; ❸), while the *Hostal de Paz* (☎044/352123; ❸) is clean and friendly. For **food**, try the *Restaurant Copacabana*, which serves a range of Peruvian and standard international dishes, or the *Pollería Posada*, for chicken and chips. The *Café La Prosperidad* specializes in delicious fruit juices, and there's an excellent cevichería, *El Dorado*, by the Puerto Malecón Shanuse in Barrio La Loma.

Downriver to Iquitos

From Yurimaguas, you can travel all the way **to Iquitos** by river ($15–20 on deck or $20–30 for cabins, a 3–5-day trip). As soon as you arrive in Yurimaguas, head straight to La Boca port to look for boats, since they get booked up in advance. Boats leave regularly though not at any set times; it's simply a matter of finding a reliable captain (preferably the one with the biggest, newest or fastest-looking boat) and arranging details with him. The price isn't bad and includes food, but you should have your own hammock if you're sleeping on deck, and bring clean bottled water, as well as any extra treats, like canned fish, and a line and hooks (sold in the town's *ferreterías*) if you want to try fishing.

The scenery en route is electric: the river gets steadily wider and slower, and the vegetation on the riverbanks more and more dense. Remember, though, that during the day the sun beats down intensely and a sun-hat is essential to avoid **river fever** – cold sweats (and diarrhoea) caused by exposure to the constant strong light reflected off the water. On this journey the boats pass through many interesting settlements, including Santa Cruz and Lagunas, starting point for trips into the huge Pacaya-Samiria National Reserve (see Chapter Eight).

The Northern Desert

The **Northern Desert** remains one of the least-visited areas of Peru, mainly because of its distance from Lima and Cusco, the traditional hubs of Peru's tourist trail, but it is still an invaluable destination due to what the region offers in terms of landscape, wildlife, archeology and history. With a complex and strongly individualistic cultural identity that's quite distinct, its popular image is of a desolate zone of scattered rural communities – a myth that belies both the desert's past and its present. Before Pizarro arrived in this region during the sixteenth century, the Northern Desert was part of both the Inca and Chimu empires and hosted a number of local pre-Columbian cultures, so that in recent years the **Lambayeque Valley**, near Chiclayo, has become a focus of interest for archeologists. Various tombs and temples, full of gold, silver and precious stones such as emeralds, have been discovered, providing substantial information about life around here some thousand years ago. This means the region has really begun to rival southern Peru in what it offers the visitor in terms of excellent museums and breathtaking archeological remains, set against the beauty of the coastal desert environment, which contains some surprisingly vast and attractive *algarrobo* forests. Today, its main cities of **Chiclayo** and **Piura** are both important and lively commercial centres, serving not only the desert coast but large areas of the Andes as well.

The coastal resorts, such as the very trendy **Máncora** and **Punta Sal**, but also **Cabo Blanco** and, further south **La Pimentel**, are among the best reasons for stopping: though small, they usually have at least basic facilities for travellers, and, most importantly, the ocean is warmer here than anywhere else in the country. This real jewels of the region, however, are its archeological remains, particularly the **Valley of the Pyramids** at **Túcume**, the older pyramid complex of **Batán Grande**, two immense pre-Inca ceremonial centres within easy reach of **Chiclayo**. Equally alluring is the **Temple of Sipán**, where some of Peru's finest gold and silver grave goods were found within the last fifteen years. With the Andes rising over 6000m to the east, this northern coastal strip of Peru has always been slightly isolated, and even today access is restricted to just a few roads, including the main north–south Panamerican Highway, a new cross-desert road linking Chiclayo and Piura, and two minor routes straggling over the Andes.

If, like a lot of travellers, you decide to bus straight through from Trujillo to the Ecuadorian border beyond **Tumbes** (or vice versa) in a single journey, you'll be missing out on some unique attractions – and also the region's strong sense of **history**. It was at Tumbes that Pizarro's Andalucian sea pilot, Bartolomeo Ruiz, discovered the first evidence of civilization south of the equator – a large balsa sail raft – in 1527. And, five years on, it was off this northern coast that Pizarro and the conquistadores first dropped anchor, before coming ashore to change the course of Peru's history.

The Panamerican Highway from Trujillo to Chiclayo

The **Panamerican Highway**, mainstay of the north's transport system, offers the fastest route north from Trujillo, passing through an impressively stark and barren landscape with few towns of any significance – though the valleys here have yielded notable archeological finds dating from Peru's Early Formative period.

San Pedro de Lloc, the first settlement of any real size, stands out for miles around with its tall, whitewashed buildings and old town walls that contain the one mansion of note, the Casa de Raymondi (ask in the Biblioteca for the keyholder). There are a few reasonable restaurants here, including the *Bar-Recreo Los Espinos*, Jr 2 de Mayo 720. Some 3km from the town (ask for directions at the Biblioteca or one of the restaurants), at Cerro Chilco, it's still possible to visit the ruins of the ancient Indian settlement of Loc. Generally, though, San Pedro is a quiet little village with little to see, whose only claim to fame is its local culinary delicacy of stuffed lizards.

If these don't appeal, you may prefer to press on 10km north to the growing port town of **Pacasmayo**. Despite the town's grim initial appearance, the area around the old jetty, thought to be the largest and most attractive surviving pier on the coast of Peru, is not unattractive and possesses some dilapidated colonial mansions, and it's a good spot to get **buses** on to Cajamarca or along the coast to Chiclayo ($1.70; 2hr), Trujillo ($2; 2–3hr) and Lima ($10; 10–12hr).

7

Expresso Cajamarca, Roggero, Transportes Atahualpa, Linea and Vulkano all stop in the main street of Leoncio Prado; Emtrafesa's depot is at Av 28 de Julio 104, just around the corner; while Cruz del Sur are at Jr Espinar C-7/90. The seafront has one or two good seaside **hotels**, such as the *Hotel Pakatnamu*, Malecón Grau 103 (T044/521051; ❺), and *Hotel La Estacion*, Malecón Grau 69 (T044/521718, F521888, Eelhotel@terra.com.pe), which has rooms with TV and there's a weekend disco in the summer. *Hostal Cesar's Palace*, Leoncio Prado 1a (T044/521945; ❸), is also decent enough, with fairly comfortable rooms with TV. There' also the *Hotel Panamericana*, Leoncio Prado 18 (❶–❷), which is clean and offers rooms with or without baths. The seafront also has a good **restaurant**, *El Encuentro de Ignacio*, or try *Chifa Tip Top*, at Leoncio Prado C/18, which is cheap and very popular with locals. The **Banco de Credito** is on the small Plaza de Armas, near the seafront.

The one historical site along this stretch of road is a few kilometres north of Pacasmayo, just before the village of **Guadalupe**, where a track leads off left to the well-preserved ruins of **Pakatnamu** (The City of Sanctuaries), overlooking the mouth of the Río Jequetepeque. Being off the main road and far from any major towns, the ruins of this abandoned city have survived relatively untouched by treasure hunters or curious browsers. The remains were first excavated in 1938 and 1953 by archeologist Ubbelonde-Doering, who found a great complex of pyramids, palaces, storehouses and dwellings. Digging up the forecourts in front of the pyramids and some nearby graves, he discovered that the place was first occupied during the Gallinazo period (around 350 AD), then was subsequently conquered by the Mochica and Chimu cultures. You can get here by colectivo or bus from Pacasmayo, but you'll still have to walk the 6km from the main highway to the site. Note that it gets very hot around midday, and there's little shade and no food or drink available at the site, so bring your own.

Chiclayo and around

Some 770km north of Lima, and rapidly becoming one of Peru's larger cities, **Chiclayo** is an active commercial centre thanks more to its strategic position than to any industrial development. Originally it was just a small annex to the old colonial town of **Lambayeque**, 12km north, but things have swung the other way over the last century. Lambayeque is now a much smaller settlement but, unlike the city of Chiclayo, boasts two excellent museums. It's likely that before long Lambayeque will be subsumed as a suburb of Chiclayo, a city which itself has little of architectural or historical interest, but nevertheless makes a good base for visiting Lambayeque and the nearby archeological sites.

Apart from the historical interest, there are also a few attractive **beach** resorts and coastal towns to relax in and catch some sun, such as **La Pimentel** and **Santa Rosa**. Most places can be reached independently by taking a **colectivo** from the market area of Chiclayo, but you'll find it much easier to see all the archeological sites if you've got your own transport. You'll probably get the most out of these, however, by going with a knowledgeable local guide on an organized tour from Chiclayo. Taxi drivers can also be hired by the day or half-day (usually around $15–30).

Despite being the northern base of several successive ancient cultures, the Chiclayo region's most interesting period was during the first millennium AD in the Lambayeque Valley. First came the Mochica-dominated settlements, which produced such magnificent treasures as were recently encountered at the **Temple of Sipán**. Then followed the Sicán culture, equally rich in iconographic imagery and fine ritual objects and garments, and responsible for the enormous desert temple complex of **Batán Grande** and the city of pyramids at **Túcume**, which compare in importance with the Moche and Chimu complexes around Trujillo. More recent and far less inscrutable ruins are to be found in the colonial ghost town of **Zaña**.

The Chiclayo area and Lambayeque valley contains such a wealth of intriguing and appealing archeological sites that it's hard to know where to begin. Probably your best bet is to start off by learning a bit more about the history and culture of the region by taking in the four main museums. Two of these, the **Museo Brüning** (one of Peru's best ceramic museums) and the **Museo de las Tumbas Reales de Sipán** (Museum of the Royal Tombs of Sipán), are located in **Lambayeque** itself, just 12km or so from Chiclayo city. The other principal museums, **Museo del Sitio Túcume** and **Museo Sicán** (devoted to the Sicán culture originally based at Batán Grande), are further out, one in the Valley of the Pyramids itself, the other en route to Batán Grande in the town of Ferreñafe.

These museums are part of what Peruvian tourist authorities are trying to propagate as the **Circuito Nororiental**, in an attempt to boost travel in the north. The trail takes in Trujillo and the Moche Valley, all the sites around Chiclayo, beaches like Máncora and Punta Sal on the upper northern coastline, and the fantastic ancient citadel of Kuelap.

Chiclayo

Chiclayo is the commercial centre of northern Peru, and so is better famed for its banks than its heritage. Nevertheless it has its own attractions, even if most of the city is an urban sprawl modernizing and growing by the month. It's a hectic but friendly city and the heart of **CHICLAYO** is the central plaza, known as the **Parque Principal**, where there's a futuristic fountain that's elegantly lit at night. You'll also find the Neoclassical **cathedral** here, built in 1869 and with its main doorway supported by Doric columns, and the **Palacio Municipal**, a Republican edifice built in 1919. Along Calle San José, you'll find the **Convento Franciscano Santa Maria**, built in the early seventeenth century but destroyed, apart from the second cloister, by El Niño rains in 1961. But the main focus of activity is along **Avenida José Balta**, between the plaza and the town's fascinating **Central Market**. Packed daily with food vendors at the centre, and other stalls around the outside, this is one of the best markets in the north – and a revelation if you've just arrived in the country. The market boasts a whole section of live animals, including wild fox cubs, canaries, and even the occasional condor chick, and you can't miss the ray fish, known as *la guitarra*, hanging up to dry in the sun before being made into a local speciality – *pescado seco*. But the most compelling displays are the herbalists' shops, selling everything from herbs and charms to whale bones and hallucinogenic cacti.

Elsewhere in town there's the small, attractive chapel of **La Véronica** on Calle Torres Paz. Built at the end of the nineteenth century, its most notable feature is the altarpiece of silver- and gold-leaf. The **Plazuela Elías Aguirre**, just around the corner from here is a small shady square which has a statue in honour of the *comandante* of this name, who was a local hero serving the Republicans in the Battle of Angamos during the War of the Pacific.

At weekends, Chiclayo families crowd out to the **beaches** of **Santa Rosa** and **La Pimentel** – each well served by buses from the market area. Santa

Rosa is the main fishing village on the Chiclayo coast, from where scores of big, colourful boats go out early every morning, along with the occasional *caballito de tortora*, reed canoes that have been used here for almost two thousand years. On Sunday afternoons, *Chiclayanos* congregate for the **horse races** at the town's Santa Victoria Hipódromo, 2km south of the Plaza de Armas just off the Avenida Roosevelt.

Arrival, information and city transport

The José Abelado Quiñones González **airport** is 2km east of town, and easily reached by taxi for $3–5. **Buses** connecting Chiclayo with La Pimentel and Lambayeque use the Terminal Terrestre Oeste, on the first block of Angamos, just off block 1 of San José. Services for all the southern cities – Trujillo, Lima and so on – use the Terminal Terrestre La Victoria on Calle Mochica, where it meets the Panamericana Sur, which has a waiting area, a left-luggage deposit and a hostel. For **tourist information** there are kiosks in the Parque Principal and nearby just a block down Balta Sur. Better still, the main **Regional Tourist Office** is just a couple of blocks from the Parque Principal at Sáenz

Peña 839 (Mon–Fri 9am–5.30pm, Sat 9am–1pm; ☎074/233132 or 238112, Ⓕ238112). At Av Balta 506 you'll find the INDECOPI **Tourist Protection** office, but hopefully you won't need to visit them. Assistance, advice and sometimes maps are available from the Tourist Police (readily available at the office Mon–Sat 8am–6pm but also on call 24hr; ☎074/236700 ext311) at Sáenz Peña 830. You can also try the information desk at the *Hotel Garza* (see below). Alternatively, you can contact the tourist police (see Listings, overleaf). Although not essential, since tickets to most sites and museums can still be bought independently, it's possible to buy a general Lambayeque Tourist Ticket ($5), available from the Instituto Nacional de Cultura, Av Gonzalez 375 (☎074/237261), in Chiclayo and sometimes also available from the main local archeological museums; the ticket covers the main museums and sites in the region, including those at Túcume, Sipán, Lambayeque, Ferreñafe and Batán Grande.

The centre of town is fine to **walk** around, but if you need a **taxi** try Chiclayo Rent-a-Car, Av Grau 520, Santa Victoria (☎074/229390, Ⓕ237512), which also has offices at the *Gran Hotel Chiclayo* (see below) and the airport (☎074/244291).

Accommodation

Finding **a place to stay** is relatively simple in Chiclayo; but if you want peace and quiet, or to camp, you might prefer one of the out-of-town options like the beautiful *Hospedaje Los Horcones* (see p.429 for details), right near the Museo de Sitio at Túcume, a place in the Valley of the Pyramids and, with a car or taxi, a terrific base from which to explore all the other sites in the region. Most of the good, reasonably priced hotels in the city are around the Plaza de Armas. If you'd rather stay out at one of the beaches, you can **camp** at both Santa Rosa and La Pimentel, provided you ask local permission first, and there's a cheapish hotel at Santa Rosa.

Gran Hotel Chiclayo Av Federico Villareal 115 ☎074/234911, Ⓕ223961, Ⓦwww.business.com.pe/granhotel. The best, most luxurious hotel in town, with its own pool, though a little way from the centre. ❼

Hostal Sicán Av Izaga 356 ☎074/237618. Nicely decorated, central, friendly, and has TVs in rooms; price includes breakfast. ❹

Hotel Costa de Oro Av José Balta 399 ☎074/232869. This basic, comfortable place offers rooms with or without bath. ❹–❺

Hotel Europa on Elías Aguirre ☎074/237919. A very clean hotel with extremely friendly service. ❸

Hotel Garza Bolognesi 756 ☎074/228172. Very central and pretty comfortable, with a pool and sauna, good food and a staff that provides useful tourist information. They also rent out cars and jeeps. ❼

Hotel Las Musas Los Faiques 101, Urb Santa Victoria ☎074/239884, Ⓕ273450, Ⓦwww.lasmusashotel.com. Upmarket lodgings that are a little less expensive than you'd expect, with excellent service, nice rooms, a cool lobby and casino. ❼

Hotel Royal San José 787 ☎074/233421. A brilliant budget option offering large, quite elegant rooms at excellent prices, some overlooking the Parque Principal (watch out for the Sunday morning parades), with or without private bath. ❷

Restaurants and nightlife

The best of Chiclayo's **restaurants**, for top criolla cooking, is the excellent *Pueblo Viejo*, Izaga 900, though it's better still when there's live music on Fridays. If you can't get in here, try the *Restaurant Mi Tia*, Elías Aguirre 698, for snacks, pasta and goat dishes at very reasonable prices. Specializing in typical Chiclayano cooking, there's the good-value *Restaurant Romana*, Av Balta 512 (open all day; ☎074/223598); or, right on the Plaza de Armas, the *Restaurant Las Americas*, Elías Aguirre 824, which offers decent international dishes and good, basic criolla fare. Slightly more upmarket is *El Huaralino*, La Libertad 155, Urbino Santa Victoria, which does Chiclayano dishes, including *tortilla de raya*. For good set breakfasts, the *Snack Bar 775*, at Ugarte 775, offers the best value and is close to the *Hotel Europa*. The *Restaurant La Plazuela*, at San José 299 on the Plaza Elías Aguirre, is okay for inexpensive fare but better for just sitting outside watching the goings-on in the little plaza. The best vegetarian options are *Govinda*, at Balta 1029 (daily 8am–8pm), which has a wide variety of dishes including yogurts, fruits and omelettes, and *Super Yogurt*, at San José 575, for yogurts and health foods. Of the two good pizzerias on Balta Sur, just a few blocks down from the Parque Principal, *Pizzeria Nueva Venecia*, Av Balta 365 (℡074/233384), is best.

For a little **nightlife**, try the *Discotek Pub Las Leathers*, San José 604, lively and close to the main plaza; *Centro Turístico El Señorio*, Izaga 654, which has food and live criolla music on Friday and Saturday after 10.30pm. For more up-tempo music, try the trendy but friendly *Yomiuri*, Sáenz Peña 997, which serves drinks and Japanese food in the evenings but doesn't warm up until quite late. The **disco** *Excess*, on Virgilio D'Allors, is lively, while *La Gaviota*, another disco, at Alfonso Ugarte 401 in La Pimentel, can be fun at weekends.

Listings

Airlines Aero Andino, Los Cipreses 191, Los Parques, Chiclayo ℡074/233161, ℻224351, ✉aeroandino@llampayec.rcp.net.pe; Aero Continente, Los Cipreses 191, Urbino Los Parques ℡074/233161; LanPeru, Av Sáenz Peña 637 ℡074/236475; and Expreso Aereo, 7 de Enero 873 ℡074/241688.

Banks and exchange The main banks are concentrated around the Parque Principal. *Cambistas* can be found on the corners of the Parque Principal, particularly José Balta, or there's the casa de cambio Hugo Barandiaran at Av Balta 641A (Mon–Fri 9.30am–5pm) next to the Banco Continental. The best bank for changing travellers' cheques is the Banco de Credito, Balta Sur 888.

Buses Civa, Bolognesi 714 (℡074/223434), for Chachapoyas and Lima; Cruz del Sur, Bolognesi 888 (℡074/237965), for Lima; Empresa El Cumbe, Quiñones 425 (℡074/231454), for Cajamarca; Dias, Bolognesi 536, for Cajamarca and Cajabamba or Celendin; Empresa Huancabamba, Bolognesi 536, for Huancabamba; Ejetur, Bolognesi 536, for Rioja, Moyobamba, Tarapoto and Yurimaguas; El Cumbe, Bolognesi 536, for Cajamarca; Turismo Jaen, Bolognesi 536, for Bagua Chica and Moyobamba; Oltursur, Av Balta 598 (℡074/237789), for Trujillo and Tumbes; Emtrafesa, Av Balta 110 (℡074/234291), for Cajamarca, Tumbes, Piura, Trujillo and Lima; Linea, Bolognesi 638 (℡074/233497), for Piura, Trujillo, Cajamarca, Huaraz or Lima; Tepsa, Bolognesi 536 (℡074/236981), for Tumbes and Tacna; Transportes Arberia, Bolognesi 536 (℡074/234421), for Cajamarca; Trans Servis Kuelap, Bolognesi 536 (℡074/271318), for daily buses to Chachapoyas; and Vulkano, Bolognesi 638 (℡074/233497), for Trujillo and Cajamarca. The town's Terminal Terrestre has smaller, slower buses serving the locality and up and down the coast.

Courier service DHL, Elías Aguirre 576.

Internet Click-Click Cybercafé, close to the plaza at San José 604, upstairs; 512kb Internet, upstairs at San José block 473; Abaco Internet Cabins, Av Luis Gonzales 507; and Internet Cabins, San José 104.

Photography Casa I Fotografía at Av Balta 863 has films and developing.

Post office Elías Aguirre, 7 blocks west of the plaza (Mon–Sat 8am–7pm).

Telephones Telefónica del Peru, Balta 815; a Locutorio Publico at Balta 827 with another at Elías Aguirre 631 within a stone's throw of the plaza.

Taxi A very reliable local taxi driver who is available by the day or half-day is Carloman Perez Castro, Los Ceibos 147, Pasaje 9 de Octubre (℡074/97639).

Tour operators Tours around the area include trips to Túcume, Batán Grande and the Museo Brüning, plus occasional shamanic tours, last 4–8hr and cost $15–30. The best are offered by Sipán Tours, 7 de Enero (℡/℻074/229053, ✉Sipántours@terra.com.pe) and InkaNatura Travel, San Martin 120, Of 302 ℡074/209948, ✉omlamprt@chavin.rcp.net.pe, or in Lima ℡01/2718156). Other companies include: Imperio Tours, Jr Diego de Almagro 256, Of 204 in front of the Banco de la Nación (℡074/206371); Lizu Tours, Elías Aguirre 418, second floor

(℡074/228871, ✉lizu_tours@latinmail.com); Sobre Vuelos Turísticos offer flights over the main archeological sites and panoramas with Aero Andino.

Tourist Police (readily available at the office Mon–Sat 8am–6pm but also on call 24hr; ℡074/236700 ext311) at Sáenz Peña 830. **Western Union** Elías Aguirre 576.

Chiclayo's coast: La Pimentel, Santa Rosa, Monsefú and Etén

An attractive beach resort with a population of some 23,000 just 14km southwest of Chiclayo, **La Pimentel** is a pleasant settlement with an attractive colonial-style heart around the Plaza Diego Ferre. More importantly, though, it offers a decent, safe **beach** for swimming and **surfing** (competitions take place in Dec and Jan). It became a busy port under military rule in the 1970s, exporting agricultural products from the co-operative haciendas, but it's now better known for its small-scale fishing industry, much of it using the traditional *caballitos del mar* (made of tortora reeds). For a small fee (25¢) you can access the long pier that divides the seafront *malecón* in two, where you can watch the fishermen. There are plenty of seafood **restaurants** at the south end near to where the *caballitos del mar* are stacked.

More picturesque is the small fishing village of **La Caleta Santa Rosa**, about 5km south of La Pimentel. Here the beach is crowded with colourful boats and fishermen mending nets; the best and freshest ceviche in the Chiclayo area can be found in the **restaurants** on the seafront here (try the *Restaurant Puerto Magnolia*). The area known as El Faro (the lighthouse), slightly to the south of Santa Rosa, is the best location for **surfing**. Continuing from here along the road inland for about 5km, you come to the small town of **Monsefú**, known as the "city of flowers" because of the local cottage industry that supplies blooms to the area. It's also known for its fine straw hats, straw-rolled cigarettes and the quality of its cotton, all of which you can buy at the

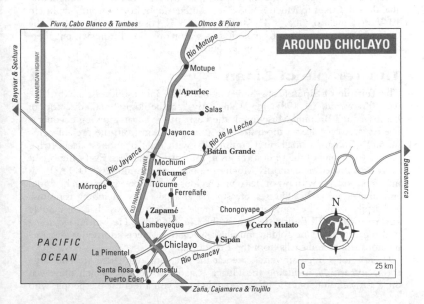

daily market. Another 4km south from here you come to the colonial village of **Etén** and its nearby ruined church, the Capilla del Milagro, built after of a vision of the Christ child in 1649. Southwest, towards the sea, lie the wide avenues of **Puerto Etén**, just another 4km away. The town has some well-tended plazas, but its most interesting feature is a derelict iron pier built in 1873 to receive and export goods by rail; nearby there are abandoned nineteenth-century train carriages.

La Pimentel is easily reached by **bus** every thirty minutes from block 5 of Vicente Vega in Chiclayo (30¢). Regular **colectivos** from Avenida Ugarte connect Chiclayo with La Pimentel, Santa Rosa, Monsefú and Puerto Etén (30¢). There's also relatively inexpensive and okay **accommodation** at the *Garnola Hostal*, Jr Quiñones 109 (☎074/452964; ❷), offering a selection of rooms, some with fine sea views, a laundry area on the roof and parking next door.

⑦ Zaña

The ruined colonial settlement of **Zaña** sits in the desert about 12km away from the modern town of Mocupe, itself 38km south of Chiclayo along the Panamerican Highway. Elaborate arches, columns and sections of old churches, such as the once elegant Convento de San Agustín, stand partly overgrown by shrubs, giving evidence of what was once an opulent city. Founded in 1553, it became a centre for meting out justice to thieves, witches and errant slaves, but its wealth actually originated from the nearby port of Cherrepe, from where it controlled the passage of vessels along the coast between Lima and Panama. Zaña rapidly grew rich, and its subsequent excesses were soon notorious, attracting the attention of pirates, including a band led by one Edward Davis, who sacked the place in 1668. The city subsequently lost much of its prestige and most of the important families moved out, the rest following a few years later when news arrived of another English pirate off the Peruvian coast – Francis Drake. The final blow came in 1720, when the waters of the Río Zaña swept through the streets, causing such damage that the settlement was abandoned. **Buses** to Mocupe and Zaña can be caught hourly from 7 de Enero 1349 in Chiclayo (50¢, a 45–60min trip). It is possible to get one of the Chiclayo tour companies to include this sector on a local itinerary, but there are none specifically arranged on a regular basis.

The Temple of Sipán

The **Temple of Sipán** (Tues–Sun 9am–6pm; $2), 33km southeast of Chiclayo, was discovered in 1987 by Walter Alva, archeologist and director of Lambayeque's Brüning Museum, in the heart of the sugar-growing co-operative Agraria Pomalca, in the district of Zaña, just 2km from the present community of Sipán, a small rural community with little of interest itself. It has proved to be one of the richest tombs in the entire Americas. Every important individual buried here, mostly Mochica nobles from around 200–600 AD, was interred prostrate with his or her own precious-metal grave goods, such as gold and silver goblets, headdresses, breastplates and jewellery including turquoise and lapis lazuli. The most important grave uncovered was that of a noble known today as **El Señor de Sipán**, the Lord of Sipán. He was buried along with a great many fine golden and silver decorative objects adorned with semi-precious stones and shells from the Ecuadorian coast.

There's not a huge amount to see at the site, although there are two large adobe **pyramids**, including the Huaca Rajada, in front of which there was once a royal tomb; but the place certainly gives you a feel for the people who lived here almost two thousand years ago, and it's one of the few sites in Peru whose treasures were not entirely plundered by either the conquistadores or more recent grave robbers. There's also a **site museum**, displaying photos and illustrations of the excavation work plus replicas of some of the discoveries.

To get here take one of the **combi colectivos** (80¢, a 45min trip) which leave Chiclayo every morning from Jr 7 de Enero 1552, or alternatively from Avenida Arica, six blocks east of the Mercado Modelo. If you want to stay overnight at the site, there are a couple of **rooms** available at the *Parador Turística* (❷), or you can **camp** ($1) in the grounds.

Pampagrande, Cerro Mulato and Chongoyape

Pampagrande is, amazingly, a rarely visited site even though it was one of the largest and most active Mochica ceremonial centres in the region. Located in the desert some 20km more or less west of the Temple of Sipán, it can be reached along dusty tracks, but you'll need a local driver to find it. Also worth a visit is the site of **Cerro Mulato**, near the hill town of **Chongoyape**, some 80km out of Chiclayo along the attractive Chancay Valley. From here, or directly from Chiclayo either via Sipán or Chongoyape, another dirt road traces an alternative route through the desert to Cerro Mulato; here you can see some impressive Chavín petroglyphs, and in the surrounding region, a number of Chavín graves dating from the fifth century BC. There's also a conservation area at Chaparri (turn left at the entrance to Chongoyape for the Cruz de Mira Costa). **Buses** to Chongoyape leave every hour or so from Pedro Ruiz in Chiclayo ($1.50, a 90min trip). But to see all these sites at the same time in one day you really need to hire a local man with a car, preferably but not essentially, a 4WD. Tour companies and taxi drivers in Chiclayo can help with this (see Listings, p.420).

Ferreñafe

FERREÑAFE, just 18km northeast of Chiclayo, founded in 1550 by Captain Alfonso de Osorio, was once known as the "land of two faiths" because of the local tradition of believing first in the power of spirits and second in the Catholic Church. These days the town is best known for the new and very good **Museo Nacional de Sicán** (Tues–Sun 9am–6pm; $2), which has an audio-visual introduction and a large collection of exhibits, mostly models depicting daily life and burials of the Sicán people. One central room is full of the genuine treasures, including the famous ceremonial headdresses and masks. Ferreñafe also boasts more Miss Peru winners than any other town; still, you'll probably only be visiting if you're en route to that same centre of Sicán culture.

Buses to Ferreñafe leave from the centre of Chiclayo every hour and, if you want to stay over, there are several restaurants and two basic **hostels**, including one run by the municipalidad, named, prosaically, the *Hotel Municipalidad* (❸). You can follow the new road, which leaves Ferreñafe from the northern end of town, to Batán Grande (see below). It's about a fifteen- to twenty-minute drive on this road.

Batán Grande

The site at **Batán Grande**, 57km northeast of Chiclayo, incorporates over twenty pre-Inca temple pyramids, and over ninety percent of Peru's ancient

The Sicán culture

Having first come to light in the early 1990s, the **Sicán culture** is associated with the Naymlap dynasty, based on a wide-reaching political confederacy emanating from the Lambayeque Valley between around 800 and 1100 AD. Legend has it that a leader called **Naymlap** arrived by sea with a fleet of balsa boats, his own royal retinue and a female green stone idol. Having been sent to establish a new civilization, Naymlap set about building temples and palaces near the sea in the Lambayeque Valley. On his death, Naymlap was entombed and his spirit was said to fly away to another dimension. The region was successfully governed by Naymlap's twelve grandsons, until one of them was tempted by a witch to move the green stone idol. Legend has it that this provoked a month of heavy rains and flash floods, rather like the effects of El Niño today, bringing great disease and death in its wake. Indeed, glacial ice cores analysed in the Andes above here have shown the likelihood of a powerful El Niño current around 1100 AD.

The Sicán civilization, like that of Mochica culture in the Moche Valley around Trujillo, depended on a high level of irrigation technology combined with a tight political coherence, not least concerning the difficult issues surrounding rights of access to water supplies in such a vast and dry desert region. The civilization also had its own copper money and sophisticated ceramics, many of which featured an image of the flying **Lord of Sicán**. The main thrust of the Lord of Sicán designs is a well-dressed man, possibly Naymlap himself, with small wings, a nose like a bird's beak and, sometimes, talons rather than feet. The Sicán culture showed a marked change in its burial practices from that of the Mochicas, almost certainly signifying a change in the prevalent beliefs about life after death. Whilst the Mochica people were buried in a lying position – like the Mochica warrior in his splendid tomb at Sipán (see p.422) – the new Sicán style was to inter its dead in a sitting position.

The Sicán monetary system, the flying Lord of Sicán image and much of the culture's religious and political infrastructures were all abandoned after the dramatic environmental disasters caused by the El Niño in 1100 AD. Batán Grande, the culture's largest and most impressive city, was partly washed away and a fabulous new centre, a massive city of over twenty adobe pyramids at Túcume (see Túcume see p.426), was constructed in the Leche Valley. This relatively short-lived culture was taken over by Chimu warriors from the south around 1370 AD, who absorbed the Lambayeque Valley, some of the Piura Valley area and about two-thirds of the Peruvian desert coast into their empire.

gold artefacts are estimated to have come from here – where, as you'll notice, there are over 100,000 holes, dug over the centuries by treasure hunters. Batán Grande is known to have developed its own copper-smelting works, which produced large quantities of flat copper plates between 5 and 10cm long. These artefacts, called *naipes*, are thought by archeologists to have been used and exported to Ecuador as a kind of monetary system.

The **Sicán culture** arose to fill the void left by the demise of the Mochica culture around 700 AD (see box, this page), and were the driving force in the region from 800 to 1100 AD, based here at Batán Grande. Known to archeologists as the Initial Lambayeque Period, judging by the beauty and extent of the pyramids here, this era was clearly a flourishing one. Nevertheless, Batán Grande was abandoned in the twelfth century and the Sicán moved across the valley to Túcume (see p.426), probably following a deluge of rains (El Niño) causing devastation, epidemics and a lack of faith in the power of the ruling elite. This fits neatly with the legend of the Sicán leader Naymlap's descendants, who evidently brought this on themselves by sacrilegious behaviour. Geological evidence suggests that there was indeed a very severe El Niño phenomenon around this time. There is also some evidence that the pyramids were deliberately burnt, supporting the latter theory.

The main part of the **site** that you visit today was mostly built between 750 and 1250 AD, comprising the Huaca del Oro, Huaca Rodillona, Huaca Corte and the Huaca Las Ventanas, where the famous **Tumi de Oro** was uncovered in 1936. The tomb of **El Señor de Sicán** (not to be confused with the tomb of El Señor de Sipán), on the north side of the Huaca El Loro, contained a noble with two women and two children and five golden crowns; these finds are exhibited in the excellent museum in Ferreñafe (see p.423). From the top of these pyramids you can just about make out the form of the ancient ceremonial plaza on the ground below.

The **interpretative centre here**, at the main entrance to what is known as the Sanctuario Nacional Bosque de Pomac, has a cafetería, hostel **accommodation** (no phone and rarely available; ❷), a **camping** area, and a small, interesting archeological museum with a scale model of the site. It also frequently offers **horse-riding** access to the main temple complex. To visit the site in just one day, it's best to take a **guided tour** or taxi from Chiclayo (see p.420) or Ferreñafe, though you could take public transport: **colectivos** to Batán Grande pueblo (10km beyond the site) leave each morning from block 16 of 7 de Enero in Chiclayo – go as early as possible and ask to be dropped at the interpretative centre ($1.50, a 2hr trip; check with the driver for return journey times). **Buses** for Batán Grande pueblo also pass the interpretative centre, leaving the Terminal Terrestre Norte in Chiclayo from 6.30am daily, with the last one leaving Batán Grande pueblo for Chiclayo at around 4.30pm. To speed things up, it's sometimes possible to hire a taxi in Batán Grande pueblo for half a day ($15–20).

Part of the beauty of this site comes from its siting at the heart of an ancient forest, dominated by *algarrobo* trees, spreading out over some 13,400 hectares, a veritable oasis in the middle of the desert landscape. This National Sanctuary of the Pomac Forest is the largest dry forest in western South America. A kilometre or so in from the interpretative centre you'll find the oldest *algarrobo* tree in the forest, the **árbol milenario**; over a thousand years old, its spreading, gnarled mass is still the site for pagan rituals, judging from the offerings hanging from its twisted boughs, but it's also the focus of the Fiesta de las Cruces on May 3. In the heart of the reserve is a section known as the Bosque de Poma, where over forty species of birds have been identified and most visitors see some iguanas and lizards scuttling into the undergrowth. Rarer, but still hanging around, are wild foxes, deer and anteaters. There's also a **mirador** (viewing platform) in the heart of the forest, from where it's possible to make out many of the larger *huacas*.

Another road in and out of the forest which is hard to trace but passes by the Huaca El Loro, comes from the nearby village of Illimo, the next settlement north of Túcume. You'll need a decent car, preferably but not essentially 4WD, and a local driver or good map. If you take this route you'll be rewarded by close contact with small, scattered desert communities, mainly goat herders and peasant farmers many of whose houses are still built out of adobe and lath.

Lambayeque

A short **colectivo** ride 12km north from Chiclayo market or with Brüning Expreso combis from Vicente de la Vega in Chiclayo, **LAMBAYEQUE** is an old colonial town that must have been a grand place in the seventeenth century but fell into decay in the twentieth. It's now, however, showing signs of recovery, not least because of its important museums and its vibrant Sunday **markets**. Of the town's buildings worth seeing, the early eighteenth-century church of **San Pedro**, parallel to the main square between the two principal streets of 2 de Mayo and 8 de Octubre, is still holding up and is the most impressive edifice in the town, with two attractive front towers and fourteen balconies. But the dusty streets of Lambayeque are better known for their handful of colonial *casonas*, such as **La Casa Cúneo**, 8 de Octubre 328, and a few doors down **La Casa Descalzi**, which has a fine *algarrobo* doorway in typical Lambayeque Baroque style. **La Casa de la Logia Masónica** (Masonic Lodge), at the corner of calles 2 de Mayo and San Martín, is also worth checking out for its superb balcony, which has lasted for about four hundred years and, at 67m, is thought to be the longest in Peru.

Lambayeque's main draw, however, is its two fantastic museums. The oldest, though quite new itself, is the modern **Museo Arqueológico Nacional Brüning** on block 7 of Avenida Huamachuco (daily 9am–6pm; $2). Named after its founder, an expert in the Mochica language and culture, the museum possesses superb collections of early ceramics, much of which has only recently resurfaced and been put on display. This museum has only just re-opened, bringing from its vaults some of the fine ceramics found over the last hundred years or so in the region, and having lost its most recent main collection to Lambayeque's new jewel, the **Museo de las Tumbas Reales de Sipán** (Museum of the Royal Tombs of Sipán; daily 9am–5pm; $2), which opened in 2002. This stunning new museum is an imposing concrete sculpture-like construction in the form of a semi-sunken or truncated pyramid, reflecting the form and style of the treasures it holds inside. This mix of modernity and indigenous pre-Columbian influence is a fantastic starting point for exploring the archeology of the valley. You'll need a good hour or two to see and experience all the exhibits, which include a large collection of gold, silver and copper objects from the tomb of **El Señor de Sipán** (see p.422), including his main emblem, a staff, known as El Cetro Cuchillo, found stuck to the bones of his right hand in his tomb. The tomb itself is also reproduced as one of the museum's centrepieces down on the bottom of the three floors. The top floor mainly exhibits ceramics and the second floor is dedicated to El Señor de Sipán's ornaments and treasures. Background music accompanies the visitor around the museum circuit using instruments and sounds associated with pre-Hispanic cultures of the region.

The Lambayeque Valley has long been renowned for turning up pre-Columbian metallurgy – particularly gold pieces from the neighbouring hill graveyard of **Zacamé** – and local treasure hunters have sometimes gone so far as to use bulldozers to dig them out, but it's the addition of the Sipán treasures that's given the biggest boost to Lambayeque's reputation, and the museum is now one of the finest in South America.

On a rather more prosaic note, Lambayeque is also known for its sweet pastry cakes – filled with *manjar blanca* and touted under the unlikely name of *King-Kongs*. In any of the town's streets, you'll be bombarded by street vendors pushing out piles of the cake, shouting "King-Kong! King-Kong!" For **accommodation**, the *Hostal Brüning*, Av S Bolivar 578 (☎074/283549; ❸), is fine. To exchange **money**, the Banco de Credito is opposite the main market, on Ramon Castillo at the corner with Atahualpa.

Túcume and around

The site of **Túcume** (daily 8am–4.30pm; $2, 80¢ for students; guides sometimes available from $2), also known as the **Valley of the Pyramids**, contains

26 adobe pyramids, many clustered around the hill of **El Purgatorio** (197m), also known as Cerro La Raya (after a ray fish that lives within it, according to legend), some 33km north from Chiclayo. Although the ticket office closes at 4.30pm and the museum shortly after this, the site is accessible after these hours and the main sectors of the site are clearly marked with good interpretive signs.

Covering more than 200 hectares, Túcume was occupied initially by the **Sicán** culture, which began building here around 1100 AD after abandoning Batán Grande. During this time, known as the Second Lambayeque Period, the focus of construction moved to Túcume where an elite controlled a complex administrative system and cleared large areas of *algarrobo* forest (as is still the case around the Valley of the Pyramids and Cerro El Purgatorio at Túcume).

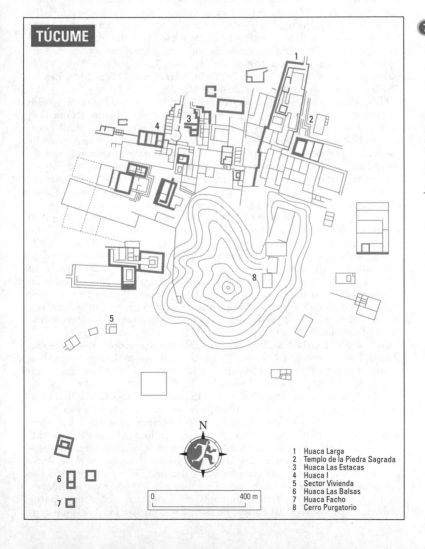

TÚCUME

N

0   400 m

1 Huaca Larga
2 Templo de la Piedra Sagrada
3 Huaca Las Estacas
4 Huaca I
5 Sector Vivienda
6 Huaca Las Balsas
7 Huaca Facho
8 Cerro Purgatorio

Seafaring vessels were also essential to the development of this new powerful elite. The Sicán people were clearly expert seamen and traded along the coast as far as Ecuador, Colombia and quite probably Central America. To the east, they also traded with the sierra and the jungle regions beyond. They were expert metallurgists working with gold, silver, copper and precious stones. Their elaborate funerary masks are astonishingly vivid and beautiful.

At Túcume's peak, in the thirteenth and early fourteenth centuries, it was probably a focus of annual pilgrimage for a large section of the coastal population, whose Sicán leaders were high priests with great agro-astrological understanding, adept administrators, a warrior elite, and expert artisans. It wasn't long, however, before things changed, and around 1375 AD the **Chimu** invaded from the south. Within another hundred years the **Incas** had arrived, though they took some twenty years to conquer the Chimu, during which time it appears that Túcume played an important role in the ensuing military, magical and diplomatic intrigues. Afterwards, the Incas transported many Chimu warriors to remote outposts in the Andes, in order to maximize the Incas' political control and minimize the chances of rebellion. By the time the **Spanish** arrived, just over half a century later, Túcume's time had already passed. When the Spanish chronicler, Pedro Cieza de Leon, passed by here in 1547, it was already in ruins and abandoned.

Today, Túcume remains an extensive site with the labyrinthine ruins of walls and courtyards still quite visible, if slightly rain-washed by the impact of recent heavy El Niño weather cycles, and you can easily spend two or three hours exploring. The site has two clearly defined sectors: North is characterized by the large monumental structures; while the South has predominantly simpler structures and common graveyards. The adobe bricks utilized were loaf-shaped, each with their maker's mark, indicating control and accounting for labour and tribute to the elite. Some of the pyramids have up to seven phases of construction, showing that building went on more or less continuously.

There's a **viewing point**, reached by a twisting path that leads up Cerro El Purgatorio hill, from where you can get a good view of the whole city. This hill, circular and cone-shaped, at the very centre of the occupied area, was and still is considered by locals to be a sacred mountain. Access to it was restricted originally, though there is evidence of later Inca constructions, for example an altar site. It is still visited these days by the local *curanderos*, healing wizards who utilize shamanic techniques and the psychoactive San Pedro cactus in their weekly rituals which researchers believe are similar to those of their ancestors, and which could be one possible explanation for the name El Purgatorio (the place of the purge).

The excellent, architecturally distinctive **Museo de Sitio** (daily, 9am–5pm though site is generally accessible 24hr) at the entrance to the site, has exhibits relating to the work of Thor Heyerdahl, who found in Túcume the inspiration for his *Kon Tiki* expedition in 1946 when he sailed a raft built in the style of ancient Peruvian boats from Callao, near Lima, right across the Pacific Ocean to Polynesia, as he tried to prove a link between civilizations on either side of the Pacific. The museum also covers the work of archeologist Wendell Bennet, who in the late 1930s was the first person to scientifically excavate at the site. More esoterically, Túcume has a local reputation for magical power, and a section of the museum has been devoted to a display of local *curanderismo*, Peru's ancient healing art, still performed around the site. There's also an attractive picnic area, and a ceramic workshop where they use 2500-year-old techniques. Beside the museum the local community have kitchens where they prepare and sell traditional regional **food**. The museum, completed in 1991, was constructed to reflect the style – known as *la ramada* - of colonial chapels in this region, built by local indigenous craftsmen centuries ago and using much the same materials.

Shamanic healing is a strong local tradition and one renowned healer, Don Victor Bravo who helped to design the shamanic section of the museum's exhibits, lives very close to the ruins of Túcume; anyone seriously interested in participating in one of his *mesa* ceremonies (see p.430) might try asking for an introduction through the *Hospedaje Rural Los Horcones* (see below).

Practicalities

To get to the site from Chiclayo, take a **colectivo** marked "Túcume" ($1.25, a 50min trip), which leaves every thirty minutes or so from block 6 of Manuel Pardo (they can be picked up as they pass through Lambayeque) or from the street beyond Bolivar on the way out of Chiclayo towards Lambayeque; sometimes colectivos can also be picked up from corner of Pedro Ruiz and Avenida Ugarte, close to the Mercado Modelo in Chiclayo. Get off at the small fork in the sandy road just a few kilometres beyond the town of Mochumi. In Túcume there's a well-signposted **tourist information** (daily 8am–5pm) centre on the main road, Avenida Federico Villareal, just before turn-off to the plaza; they have a 3D model of the pyramid site plus some books, maps and leaflets to give away.

The town of Túcume, based alongside the old Panamerican Highway (now re-routed in a straighter line across the desert, north to Piura) just a couple of kilometres west of the Valley of the Pyramids, doesn't have a lot to offer visitors, though the *Restaurant La Sabrosa*, block 3 of Calle Federico Villareal (3 blocks beyond the tourist office), serves reasonably tasty and cheap set menus at lunchtime. There's also a *Snack Bar Jugeria* on the north side of the plaza. There are two small **hospedajes** in town, the tricky to find *Hospedaje Acafala* (☎074/422029; ❷), located about one block before the tourist office on Federico Villareal as you come into town, and *Hostal Las Balsas* (no phone; ❷), Avenida Agosto Belguia, the street by Túcume's market. The only places to **change money** in town are the Banco de la Nación, half a block south of the plaza, and the Ferretería Don Jose, just before the police station and petrol garage at the northern end of town.

From Túcume's plaza follow the right-hand road to the pyramids and the Museo de Sitio, a dusty two-kilometre walk, or better, take a **mototaxi** or **combi colectivo** for less than $1. At the end of the fields, where the road divides (left to *Hospedaje Los Horcones* and right to the museum), the track is signposted to the right for the 30m or so to the ticket office.

Accommodation and camping is possible here too. Lodgings – plus camping sites, shower blocks and local home-cooked food – are available at the *Hospedaje Rural Los Horcones* (☎074/800052 or in Lima ☎01/4474534, 4453373 or 8025205, ⊛www.infoperu.org/Loshorcones; ❹), whose buildings and hotel have been constructed with traditional materials in a style reflecting that of the pyramid site next door. Nearby, right in front of the Museo de Sitio, the *Complejo Turistico Las Piramides* (☎074/995959 or in Trujillo ☎044/370178, ✉laspiramidestucume@terra.com) has a nice campsite ($6 including breakfast) with showers, campfire and *parillada* (grilling) facilities, as well as a restaurant which is fully open at holiday times and a refreshment kiosk almost always open during daylight hours; they also organize excursions to local sites and ruins as well as horse-riding tours.

Túcume Viejo

Less than 2km from the Túcume ruins is the village of **Túcume Viejo**, reached by turning left along the sand track at the fork in the road just before you get to the site museum. Although there are no tourist facilities as such, it makes for an interesting thirty-minute walk, checking out the crumbling colonial adobe walls and a once painted adobe brick gateway as well as the church, all of which have an elegant and rather grandiose feel, suggesting perhaps that the early colonists were trying to compete for attention with the Valley of the Pyramids. There's also the **Museo Santos Vera**, a local *curandero's* museum full of magical paraphernalia, less than a kilometre beyond the entrance to the village. En route to Túcume Viejo, some 500m beyond the *Hospedaje Rural Los Horcones*, a right-hand track takes you to the **Huaca Sagrada**, part of the pyramid complex which is difficult to find, located as it is on the northern side of the Huaca Larga and effectively closed off from the main site. There's not that much to see there at the moment since the remaining small temple is closed off and the stone can just be glimpsed through gaps in the wall; at present the archeologists' priority is to protect the *huaca* from the encroaching growth of the pueblo's current inhabitants.

Apurlec

Apurlec, some 60km north of Chiclayo, at Km 52/53 of the Panamerican Highway is another vast adobe settlement, 30km north of Túcume. First occupied in the eighth century BC, it was still flourishing five hundred years later under the great Chimu planners and architects. Scattered over a huge area, the adobe remains of pyramids, forts, palaces, temples, storehouses and long city streets have been eroded over the years by heavy rains but remain quite recognizable. To get here, stay on the Túcume colectivo (see above) for another fifteen minutes or so past the town (ask the driver where to get off and keep your eyes open for the big sign on the right-hand side of the road), and make sure you bring something to drink and a sun-hat, as Apurlec has no shade or refreshments. To get the lie of the land you really need to start by climbing the small, conical hill at the edge of the original site. The are absolutely no facilities here and the remote site has been more or less forgotten by everyone; only go here in groups.

Salas

About twenty minutes by car from Túcume, taking a back road for 17km off the old Panamerican Highway at Km 47 (27km north of Túcume) brings you to the **pueblo of Salas**, known locally as the capital of folklore medicine on the coast of Peru. Here the ancient traditions of *curanderismo* are so strong that it's the major source of income for the village. Most nights of the week, but especially Tuesdays and Fridays, there'll be healing sessions going on in one or other of the houses in the village, generally starting around 10pm and ending at roughly 4am. The sessions, or *mesas*, are based on the ingestion of the hallucinogenic San Pedro cactus and other natural plants or herbs; and they do cost money (anything up to $200 a night, though the amount is usually fixed and can be divided between as many as five to ten participants). Combining healing with divination, the *curanderos* utilize techniques and traditions handed down from generation to generation from the ancient Sicán culture. To contact a *curandero* about participating in a session the best bet is to ask a local tour operator, or a trustworthy taxi driver from Túcume, to take you to the village one afternoon to see what can be arranged.

North to Piura: through the Sechura Desert

Buses and colectivos between Chiclayo and Piura tend to use the Panamerican Highway, cutting across the **Sechura Desert** and bypassing the town of Olmos. Chiclayo bus companies (see p.420) do the journey in three hours ($3), while plenty of slightly faster colectivos ($6, a 3hr trip) leave daily from Pedro Ruiz and Luis Gonzalez.

A few colectivos take the old **coastal route** to Piura, via the oil refinery of **Bayovar** and the beach resort of **Sechura**, a journey of around six hours. These buses run towards the Bayovar turn-off, then switch up to the coast at a vast obelisk and roundabout right in the middle of one of the world's driest deserts. To the south, accessible only on foot with 4WD vehicles, are the **Sechura hills** – an isolated and unofficial wildlife reserve of wild goats, foxes, and the occasional condor. There is no **water** in the region, and it's a good three-day walk from the road to the beach; maps are available in Lima, however, if you're interested in a serious exploration. The beaches here, on the **Bahía de Nonura**, are really the last of Peru's remaining virgin coastline, and are teeming with wildlife, including dolphins, turtles, sea lions, sometimes penguins, and a host of different seabirds – but no people once you're away from the oil refinery, which is on the northern point of the Sechura Peninsula, and a few kilometres to the west of the main road, which continues north. This big beach area is also reputed to have Peru's best **surfing**, but note that a special entry permit is required from Petro Peru at their headquarters in Lima (Av Paseo de la República 3361 ℡01/4425000 or 4425033) to get to the best (and the only accessible) sections beyond the refinery. You can only camp here, and there are no facilities whatsoever.

North of the roundabout there is little more than a handful of hermit goatherders and two or three scattered groups of roadside restaurants, until just before Sechura, where you'll find a few tiny hamlets – basically clusters of huts on the beach – inhabited by the same fishing families since long before the Conquest. The last of these, **Parachique**, has recently developed into a substantial port with its own fish-meal factory; the others are all very simple, their inhabitants using sailing boats to fish, and often going out to sea for days at a time.

Sechura

The small town of **SECHURA**, 52km south of Piura, has a quaint seventeenth-century **church** on the main square, whose tall twin towers lend the town an air of civilization. Local legend has it that the church was built over an ancient temple, from where an underground tunnel containing hidden treasure led out to the ocean. To the south of the town – between the sea and road – a long line of white crescent **dunes**, or *lomas*, reaches into the distance. Local people claim that these were used by the Incas as landmarks across the desert.

If you want to **stay** overnight here you can **camp** virtually anywhere (including the beach), or stay in a **hostel**, such as the *Hospedaje de Dios* (❸). There are several **restaurants**, the best being *Don Gilberto's* on the main plaza. The town's **food market**, just off the main square, takes place on weekdays and is good for picnic supplies.

Piura and around

The city of **PIURA** feels very distinct from the rest of the country, cut off to the south by the formidable Sechura Desert, and to the east by the Huancabamba mountains. The people here see themselves primarily as Piurans rather than Peruvians, and the city has a strong oasis atmosphere, entirely dependent on the vagaries of the Río Piura – known colloquially since Pizarro's time as the Río Loco, or Crazy River. In spite of this precarious existence, Piura is the oldest colonial city in Peru. During the twentieth century – despite weathering at least two serious droughts and eight major floods (the last in 1998) – it grew into a *departmento* of well over 1.5 million people, around a quarter of whom actually live in the city. With temperatures of up to 38°C from January to March, the region is known for its particularly wide-brimmed straw sombreros, worn by everyone from the mayor to local goat-herders. You'll have plenty of opportunities to see these in **Piura Week** (first two weeks of Oct), when you'll find the town in high spirits, but beds are a little scarce so it's best to book in advance.

Francisco Pizarro spent ten days in Piura in 1532 en route to his fateful meeting with the Inca overlord, Atahualpa, at Cajamarca. By 1534 the city, then known as San Miguel de Piura, had well over two hundred Spanish inhabitants, including the first Spanish women to arrive in Peru. All were hungry for a slice of the action – and treasure – but although Pizarro kept over 57,000 pesos of his spoils looted from the native inhabitants, he only gave 15,000 to the Spanish Piurans, which was the cause of some considerable resentment, and possibly the origin of the town's isolationist attitude. Pizarro did, however, encourage the development here of an urban class, trained for trade rather than war. As early as the 1560s, there was a flourishing trade in the excellent indigenous Tanguis cotton, and Piura today still produces a third of the nation's cotton.

Arrival, city transport and information

El Dorado **buses** from Trujillo and Tumbes, Dorado Express buses from Tumbes, Sullana and Aguas Verdes, buses from Chiclayo, and EPPO buses from Talara and Máncora all arrive around blocks 11 and 12 of Avenida Sanchez Cerro. All other buses arrive at their companies' offices (see Listings, p.436 for addresses). **Colectivos**, mainly from Tumbes and Talara, also arrive and depart from the middle of the road at block 11 of Avenida Sanchez Cerro, ten minutes' stroll from the centre of town. If you arrive by one of the daily **planes** from Lima, Trujillo, Talara or Tumbes, you'll land at Piura airport (for flight information call ☎074/327733), 2km east of the city; a taxi into the centre costs $2–3. The quickest way of getting around the city is by the ubiquitous **motorcycle rickshaw**, which you can hail just about anywhere for 50¢. In-town **taxi** rides are set at $1.

The official **tourist office** in Piura offers friendly and useful advice from the Municipal building on the Plaza de Armas (Mon–Fri 9am–1pm & 4–8pm, Sat 9am–1pm), or you can also get information from the Ministry of Tourism, Jr Lima 775 (Mon–Fri 9am–1pm & 4–6pm; ☎074/327013). Failing these, your best bet is one of the helpful tour companies listed on p.436.

Accommodation

A wide range of **hotels** and **hostels** is spread throughout the town, with most of the cheaper ones on or around Avenida Loreto or within a few blocks of Avenida Grau and the Plaza de Armas.

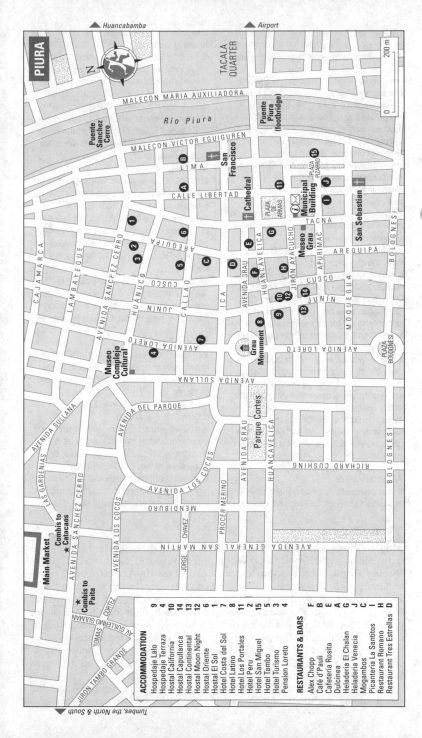

▲ *Huancabamba*   ▲ *Airport*

TACALA QUARTER

MALECON MARIA AUXILIADORA

Rio Piura

Puente
Sanchez
Cerro

Puente
Piura
(footbridge)

MALECON VICTOR EGUIGUREN

LIMA   San
Francisco

⑮
PLAZA
PIZARRO

Ⓑ

Cathedral   ⑪

Ⓐ

CALLE LIBERTAD

PLAZA
DE
ARMAS

Municipal
Building   Ⓘ

San Sebastian

①

Ⓒ   TACNA

②   AREQUIPA

Ⓖ   Museo
Grau

③   ④   Ⓒ   Ⓔ

⑤   Ⓓ   Ⓕ   Ⓗ   APURIMAC   AREQUIPA   BOLOGNES

⑥   HUANCAVELICA   JIRON AYACUCHO

HUANUCO   CUSCO   ⑩   ⑫   CUSCO

CALLAO   ⑨   ⑬   ⑭   JUNIN

JUNIN

ICA   ⑧

⑦   Grau
Monument

Museo
Complejo
Cultural

④

AVENIDA LORETO   AVENIDA GRAU

AVENIDA SULLANA

AVENIDA DEL PARQUE

Parque Cortes

AVENIDA GRAU

PLAZA
BOLOGNESI

AVENIDA LORETO

HUANCAVELICA   RICHARD CUSHING   BOLOGNESI

MENDIBURO   PROCER MERINO

AVENIDA LOS COCOS

AVENIDA GENERAL SAN MARTIN

JORGE   CHAVEZ

Main Market   Combis to
★ Catacaos

Combis to
★ Paita

CAJAMARCA   LAMBAYEQUE   AVENIDA SANCHEZ CERRO

AVENIDA SANCHEZ CERRO

LAS GARDENIAS   AVENIDA SULLANA

AV GUILLERMO GULMAN   TOMAS   CORTEZ   JIRON TAMBO GRANDE

200 m

N

ACCOMMODATION	
Hospedaje Lalo	9
Hospedaje Terraza	4
Hostal California	10
Hostal Capullana	14
Hostal Continental	13
Hostal Moon Night	12
Hostal Oriente	6
Hostal El Sol	1
Hotel Costa del Sol	7
Hotel Latino	8
Hotel Los Portales	11
Hotel Peru	2
Hotel San Miguel	15
Hotel Tambo	5
Hotel Turismo	3
Pension Loreto	4

RESTAURANTS & BARS	
Alex Chopp	F
Café d'Pauli	B
Cafeteria Rosita	E
Dulcinea	A
Heladeria El Chalan	G
Heladeria Venecia	J
Mogambos	C
Picanteria La Santitos	I
Restaurant Romano	H
Restaurant Tres Estrellas	D

Budget

Hospedaje California Junin 835 ☎074/328789. A family-run establishment, brightly painted and decorated with plastic flowers, giving it a somewhat kitschy feel. Good value and popular with backpackers, there are no private baths but rooms are usually equipped with fans. ❷

Hospedaje Lalo C Junin 838 ☎074/307178. Very basic but relatively safe hostel with only shared bathrooms; close to and opposite the much better *Hospedaje California*. ❷

Hospedaje Terraza Av Loreto 530. Cleaner and a much more pleasant option than some of the affordable lodgings in this area, but still pretty basic. ❶–❷

Hostal Capullana Junin 925. Cleanish, welcoming and all doubles have private bath, plus there are some cheaper singles. ❷

Hostal Continental Junin 924 ☎074/334531. Pretty friendly service, and rooms are somewhat basic, though some come with bath. ❷

Hostal Moon Night Junin 899 ☎074/336174. Offers more than average mod cons, private bath, TV, spacious rooms and is clean. Hotels with this kind of name in Peru are generally aiming for the lovers' market; but it's still comfortable and pretty central. ❷

Hostal Oriente Callao 446 ☎074/304011. This clean, friendly family-run hostel has a spacious lobby with TV and is well managed. Rooms are mostly small and some are a bit stuffy; available with or without bath. ❷

Hotel Turismo Huánuco 526 ☎074/309098. A clean, modern-looking hotel, with good service; rooms available with or without baths but there's no hot water. ❷

Moderate

Hostal Diplomatic Tacna 342 ☎074/325243, ☏332485. Quite plush for Piura, all the rooms have baths and hot water. ❹

Hostal El Sol Sanchez Cerro 411 ☎074/324461, ☏326307, ✉elsol@mail.udep.edu.pe. Clean and largely carpeted, with a small cafetería, this secure place has pleasant rooms (though the front ones can be noisy) with TV and air-conditioning. ❹

Hotel Latino Huancavelica 720 ☎074/335114, ✉hoslatino@hotmail.com. A large, fairly modern establishment aimed primarily at Peruvian business travellers, it is centrally located with all the usual facilities. ❹

Hotel Peru Arequipa 476 ☎074/333421, ☏331530. Good-value hotel with a spacious lobby and good restaurant/bar, its smart rooms have TV, telephone, fan and private bath. ❹

Hotel San Miguel corner of Lima with Apurimac on the Plaza Pizarro ☎074/305122. A decently priced, comfortable hotel with some rooms overlooking the plaza, and cable TV. There's also a cafetería. ❹

Hotel Tambo Callao 546 ☎074/326440 or 325379. A tidy, spacious hotel, where all rooms come with private bath and a fan. Could do with a lick of paint, but it is nevertheless good value. ❸

Expensive

Hotel Costa del Sol Loreto 649 ☎074/302864, ⓦwww.hotelcostadelsol.go.to. A luxurious hotel with pool, casino, Internet facilities, car park, and restaurant. ❼

Hotel Los Portales C Libertad 875 ☎074/321161, ☏325920, ✉hoteles@peru.itete.com.pe. A luxury hotel set in a lovely old building; the rooms are full of character and very clean, but slightly overpriced. ❽

Hotel Vicus Av Guardia Civil B-3, Urbino Miraflores ☎074/341186. Located beyond the city centre in a pleasant setting, this is a comfortable and quiet hotel with good service. ❻

The City

Modern **Piura** is divided by the river, with most of the action and all the main sights falling on the west bank. Within a few blocks of the main bridge, the **Puente Piura**, is the spacious and attractive **Plaza de Armas**, shaded by tall tamarind trees planted well over a hundred years ago. On the plaza you'll find a "Statue of Liberty", also known as La Pola (The Pole), and the **cathedral** (daily 7am–7pm: free), where the town's poorest folk tend to beg. Though not especially beautiful, the Cathedral boasts impressive bronze nails decorating its main doors, and inside, the spectacularly tasteless gilt altars and intricate wooden pulpit are worth a look. Surrounding the plaza, you'll see some pastel-coloured low colonial buildings that clash madly with the tall, modern glass and concrete office buildings nearby.

One block towards the river from the Plaza de Armas, along Jirón Ayacucho, you'll find a delightful elongated square, called **Plaza Pizarro**, which is also known as the Plaza de 3 Culturas. Every evening the Piurans promenade up and down here, chatting beside elegant modern fountains and beneath tall shady trees. One block east of here, you reach the Río Piura, usually little more than a trickle of water with a few piles of rubbish and some white egrets, gulls and terns searching for food. The riverbed is large, however, indicating that when Piura's rare rains arrive, the river rises dramatically; people who build their homes too close to the dry bed regularly have them washed away. The river is spanned by the old bridge, Puente Piura, which connects central Piura with the less aesthetic east-bank quarter of **Tacala**, renowned principally for the quality and strength of its fermented *chicha* beer.

A block south of the Plaza de Armas, along Tacna, you'll find the **Museo Casa Grau** (Mon–Sat 8am–1pm & 4–7pm; free), nineteenth-century home of Admiral Miguel Grau, one of the heroes of the War of the Pacific (1879–80), in which Chile took control of Peru's valuable nitrate fields in the south and cut Bolivia's access to the Pacific. The museum's exhibits include a model of the British-built ship, the *Huascar*, Peru's only successful blockade runner, as well as various military artefacts. A display of the region's archeological treasures, and in particular the ceramics from Cerro Vicus (see p.436), can be found at the **Museo Complejo Cultural** (Mon–Fri 9am–5.30pm, Sat 9am–1pm; $1) on Huánuco, one block west of Avenida Loreto.

The town's daily **market**, in the north of the city, is worth a visit for its well-made straw hats (invaluable in the desert), ceramics made in the village of Simbila, and a variety of leather crafts.

Eating, drinking and nightlife

Most of Piura's **restaurants** and **cafés** are centred around the Plaza de Armas area, with many of the cafés specializing in delicious ice cream. Piura's speciality is a very sweet toffee-like delicacy, called *natilla*, which can be bought at street stalls around the city. There are no specifically vegetarian restaurants in town, but the *Cafetería Rosita* can usually help out, and the health-food café *Canimedes* can be found at Lima 440, serving breakfasts, yogurt and fig breads. In the evenings, you'll find most Piurans strolling around the main streets, chatting in the plazas, and drinking in the cheap **bars** along the roads around Junin. For a spot of late-night **drinking and dancing**, there's *Blue Moon*, Ayacucho 552 (℡074/335013), popular with locals and starting around 10pm; *JL Disco Bar*, Av Grau 495, loud and hectic at weekends, upstairs; *La Nueva Calesa*, Jr Ayacucho 565; *Studio 1*, in the Centro Comercial; and *Tony's*, Avenida Guardia Civil de Castilla in the Urb. Miraflores on the other side of town. *Alex Chopp* (see below) is okay, though primarily a drinking venue.

Alex Chopp Huancavelica 538. A popular nightspot with a friendly atmosphere, serving good beers and fine seafood in the evenings.

Café d'Pauli Lima 541. This is a smart new café serving ice creams, lovely cakes, teas and good coffee; very smart; a bit pricey but worth it for the delicious fare.

Cafetería Rosita Av Grau 223. Serves delicious sandwiches and green tamales, as well as great breakfasts.

Dulcinea Libertad 597. A small bar and mini-supermarket, very central and well stocked with breads, pies, pasties and sweet pastries.

Heladeria El Chalan Plaza de Armas. Excellent service in a bright and busy atmosphere; serves sandwiches, juices, cakes and wonderful ice creams; they also have a smarter, newer place behind the Cathedral.

Heladeria Venecia C Libertad 1007. Choose your ice cream from a wide variety of flavours and enjoy it on the cool and elegant patio.

Picantería La Santitos La Libertad 1014. Only open for lunches, it serves a good choice of traditional criolla dishes such as *majado de yuca* (mashed *yuca* with pieces of pork) and *seco de chavelo* (mashed plantain with pieces of beef), in a renovated colonial house.

Restaurant Tres Estrellas Arequipa 702. The

best restaurant in town for serious criolla dishes; try the goat (*cabrito*) with rice and tamales.
Snack Bar Mogambo Av Arequipa 620. Good for juices, sandwiches, mariscos and relatively inex-

pensive set menus.
Snack Bar Romano Ayacucho 580. A popular and quite large local backstreet eating house serving a host of reasonably priced dishes.

Listings

Airlines Aero Continente, C Libertad 951 ℡074/325635; and TANS, Libertad 422.

Banks and exchange The Banco Continental is on the Plaza de Armas, at the corner of Ayacucho and Tacna. *Cambistas* are at block 7 of Av Arequipa, near the corner of Av Grau; but by far the safest and quickest casa de cambio is Piura Dolar by block 6 of Av Arequipa.

Buses CIAL, Bolognesi 817 (℡074/304250), for Huaraz, Lima and Tumbes; Cruz del Sur, Av Circunvalación 160 (℡074/305955 or 337094), for Lima and the coast; Coop de El Dorado, Av Sanchez Cerro 1119 (℡074/325875), for Trujillo, Chiclayo and north; Transporte Loja, Av Sanchez Cerro, for the alternative Ecuadorian crossing via Loja (10 hr, 3 daily); Emtrafesa, Los Naranjos 255, Urb. Club Grau (℡074/337093), for Chiclayo, Trujillo and Tumbes; Linea, Av Sanchez Cerro 1215 ℡074/327821), for Chiclayo and Tumbes; Transportes Chiclayo, Sanchez Cerro 1121 (℡074/322251), for Chiclayo; Tepsa, Av Loreto

1195 (℡074/323721), for Trujillo and Tumbes; Trans Piura, Loreto 1253 (℡074/329131), for Tumbes, Chiclayo, Trujillo and Lima; Trans/Vulcano, Sanchez Cerro 1215 (℡074/327821), for Trujillo and Chiclayo; and Trans-EPPO, Sanchez Cerro 1141 (℡074/331160), for Talara and Máncora.

Internet There's an Internet café at Sanchez Cerro 265, large and busy. Daily 9am–11pm.

Photography Foto Estudio Carrasco, Grau 401, is okay for both films and developing; Foto Color, Grau 364, sells films, develops and has a limited amount of camera equipment for sale.

Post office Plaza de Armas, on the corner of C Libertad and Ayacucho. Mon–Sat 9am–7pm.

Shopping There's a supermarket, good for general provisions, by the Grau monument; and for local sweets, nuts and fruit the shop at Sanchez Cerro 285 is hard to beat.

Tour operators Piura Tours, Ayacucho 585 (℡074/328873); and Tallan Tours, Tacna 258n (℡074/334647).

Catacaos

Just 12km south of Piura is the friendly, dusty little town of **CATACAOS**, worth a visit principally for its excellent, vast **market** (there's something here most days, but it's best weekends 10am–4pm). Just off the main plaza – which boasts a public TV given to the town by the mayor – the market sells everything from food to crafts, even filigree gold and silver work, with the colourful hammocks hanging about the square being a particularly good buy. The town is also renowned for its **picanterías** (spicy food restaurants), which serve all sorts of local delicacies, such as *tamalitos verdes* (little green-corn pancakes), fish-balls, *chifles* (fresh banana or sweet potato chips), goat (*seco de cabrito*) and the local *chicha* beer. One of the better restaurants is the friendly *La Chayo*, San Francisco 493 (℡074/370121), which serves huge portions and lets you sample the *chicha* before buying. While you're here you could also try the sweet medicinal drink *algarrobina*, made from the berries of a desert tree, and available from bars and street stalls. The **church** is worth a peep, too, having been recently repainted rather brightly. There is no accommodation to speak of.

From Piura, regular combi **colectivos** for Catacaos leave when full, usually every twenty minutes or so (25¢, a 20min trip), from the terminal in block 12 of Sanchez Cerro, or from the far side of Puente Piura.

Cerro Vicus

At **Cerro Vicus**, 27km east of Piura on the old Panamerican Highway to Chiclayo, you'll find an interesting pre-Inca site, just 500m to the left of the main road. There are no buildings still visible at the site, probably due to the occasional heavy rains which can destroy adobe ruins, but you can see a number of L-shaped tombs, some up to 15m deep. These graves contained ceramics and metal artefacts revealing several styles, early Mochica being the most predominant. The artefacts were superbly modelled in a variety of human, animal and architectural forms, and you can see good examples of them in the Museo Complejo Cultural in Piura (see p.435).

To reach Cerro Vicus, take any of the Olmos **buses** or **colectivos**, which leave every hour or so from Sanchez Cerro in Piura. Ask to be dropped off at Km 449 of the Panamerican Highway, then walk across the sand to the tombs on the hill. Most buses, and some trucks, will stop if you wave them down beside the road for the return trip to Piura.

Paita and Colán

Fifty kilometres northwest of Piura lies its port and closest major settlement, **PAITA**. Set on a small peninsula a little south of the mouth of the Río Chira, it is Peru's fifth largest port, but is best known to many Peruvians as the former home of **Manuela Saenz**, the tragic mistress of Simón Bolivar during the Wars of Liberation. After the 1828 skirmishes with Colombia (of which Bolivar was dictator), Manuela was ostracized by Peruvian society, dying here in poverty in 1856. Her house (it has a plaque on it) is in the old quarter of town, just up from the petrol station and across from the market, but it is not open to the public. A good **place to stay** is the *Hotel Las Brisas*, Aurora 201 (☎074/611023; ❷), on the seafront, while the *Chifa Hong Kong*, Junin 358, is well known amongst locals for its authentic **food**. For a beer with a view, try the *Club de la Libertad*, on the seafront; it's a crumbling old wooden building commanding a fine panorama across the bay and port from its terrace.

To the north of Paita, you'll find the once exclusive bay of **COLÁN**. This is still a good place to swim, though the old seaside residences that used to echo with the chatter of wealthy land-owning families are now pretty much destroyed, many washed away in 1983 by the swollen Río Chira amid the

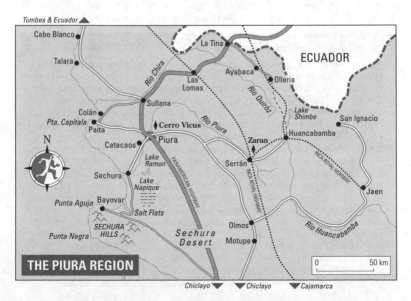

THE PIURA REGION

Chiclayo ▼   ▼ Chiclayo   ▼ Cajamarca

dramatic floods of that rainy season, with others currently looking ready to tumble into the sea. The **church** in Colán (ask for the key-holder in the village), however, is a state-protected building and has been recently renovated, due to its claim to be the oldest church in Peru and the first where mass was said in South America. From the tower there are fine views over the pueblo of **San Lucas de Colán**, the sandy spit on which the beach settlement sits, and the salt flats between the two, which incidentally is a great spot for bird-watching and sometimes floods, cutting off the two communities. There are a couple of expensive **lodges** here, the *Sol de Colán* (❻) and the *Colán Lodge* (❺), both offering a range of bungalows, pool, cafetería and games rooms. The only other place is the *Hospedaje Frente el Mar* (☏074/615465; ❸); it's small, basic, and perhaps slightly overpriced, but the sea comes right up to the terrace. There are a few decent small beaches nearby, including **Yacila** and **Cangrejos**.

Buses and **colectivos** to Paita (75¢, a 1hr trip) and Colán leave from Sanchez Cerro in Piura every hour or so, the latter generally when full. Your best bet is Transportes Dora, Sanchez Cerro 1387, which has a direct service from Piura to Paita (most of the others stop en route). For Colán from Paita, combi colectivos leave when full (usually every hour), from the top end of the market (50¢, a 20min journey).

East of Piura: to Huancabamba

One of the more adventurous routes around Piura takes you into the hills to the east and – after some 215km and fifteen hours by daily bus or truck from the market area in Piura – to the remote village of **Huancabamba**. The road goes via the town of **Serran**, where you can still see the ruins of the Inca settlement of Zaran, just a short walk from the modern settlement.

Up until the Spanish conquest, Huancabamba was an important crossroads on the Inca Royal Highway, which traversed the Andes, connecting the Inca Empire from present-day Santiago in Chile to Quito in Ecuador. At Huancabamba a side road went down to the coast, linking with the ancient

---

How Pizarro found Atahualpa

It was at Serran, then a small Inca administrative centre, that **Pizarro** waited in 1532 for the return of a small troop of soldiers that he had sent up the Inca Royal Highway on a discovery mission. It took the soldiers, led by Hernando de Soto, just two days and a night to reach the town of Cajas, now lost in the region around Huancabamba and Lake Shimbe. At Cajas, the Spaniards gained their first insight into the grandeur and power of the Inca Empire, although, under orders from Atahualpa, the 2000-warrior garrison had slunk away into the mountains. The Spaniards were not slow to discover the most impressive Inca buildings – a sacred convent of over five hundred virgins who had been chosen at an early age to dedicate their lives to the Inca religion. The soldiers raped at will, provoking the Inca diplomat who was accompanying De Soto to threaten the troops with death for such sacrilege, especially as they were only 300km from Atahualpa's camp at Cajamarca. This information about Atahualpa's whereabouts was exactly what De Soto had been seeking. After a brief visit to the adjacent, even more impressive, Inca town of Huancabamba – where a tollgate collected duties along the Royal Highway – he returned with the Inca diplomat to rejoin Pizarro. Realizing that he had provided the Spanish with vital information, the Inca diplomat agreed to take them to Atahualpa's camp – a disastrous decision resulting in the massacre at Cajamarca (see p.390).

desert thoroughfare at Zaran, while another branch headed east to Jaen along the forested Marañón watershed, a trading link with the fierce jungle head-hunters of the Aguaruna tribe. Even before the Incas arrived, the people of Huancabamba had an extremely active trade, ferrying goods such as feathers, animal skins, medicines and gold from the jungle Indians to the coastal cultures of the Mochica and, later, Chimu. In places, near the modern village of Huancabamba, the actual Inca town here has been lost, but you can still make out stretches of that thoroughfare in the ancient stone slabs, quite easy to spot alongside the modern road. Huancabamba means "valley of the stone spirit guardians", which is quite fitting, since you can still see the tall, pointed stones guarding fields in the sheltered valley.

Today, the village, which is apparently slipping down its hill on very watery foundations, is famous throughout Peru for its **curanderos** – healing wizards, who use herbal and hallucinogenic remedies in conjunction with ritual bathing in sacred lagoons such as Lake Shimbe, 2000m high and seven hours' mule ride above the town. The lake area above the town is inhospitable, with sparse, marshy vegetation. It is usually possible to hire mules and a guide from Huancabamba to take you up to **the lakes** – or even on the five-day trek, fol-lowing the route of the old Inca Highway, to **Ayabaca** and the nearby Inca fortress of **Ayapate**. These trips, though, are only for the really adventurous, and it's not a good idea to go alone or without a local guide.

North of Piura: Talara and Cabo Blanco

Leaving Piura, the Panamerican Highway heads directly north, passing through the large town of **SULLANA** after 40km. This major transport junction has little of interest to travellers, except perhaps as a rest before or after taking the inland route to Ecuador. If you do stop, take a quick look at the **Plaza de Armas**, which boasts fine views over the Río Chira, and is the location for the old church of La Santisima Trinidad. There are many **hotels** between Avenida Lama and the Plaza: try the *Hostal El Chorre*, Tarapaca 501 (☏074/507006; ❸), which is decent value and offers private bathrooms, TVs, laundry and a cafetería; the *Hostal Tarapaca*, Tarapaca 731 (☏074/503786; ❷), which also has private baths and is quiet and friendly, though slightly more basic; and the *Hospedaje San Miguel*, Farfan 204 (☏074/502789; ❶), the cheapest of the lot, which has rooms off a central passageway that share bathrooms, but is clean. For **eating**, one of the best places is *Bima Chopp*, in the plaza, which has good set menus and is popular with locals; for Chinese food, the best is the *Chifa Kam Loy*, at San Martín 925. Most **bus companies** have their offices on or just off Avenida Lama; EPPO and Emtrafesa are at the corner of Callao with Pierola, offering regular departures to Talara. EPPO also have buses twice daily to Máncora, while Emtrafesa serves Tumbes and Chiclayo. There are regular **combis** from Avenida Lama to Piura and Paita, each one hour away (75¢), while the faster **colectivos** cost slightly more. Combis for the inland border crossing with Ecuador at La Tina leave in the morning from Avenida Buenos Aires, close to the main market.

Talara

TALARA, some 70km further north, would be more attractive if it wasn't for the entrance to the city being strewn with rubbish, a depressing sight of plas-tic bags impaled on bushes for almost a kilometre. All roads into the town are in a poor state of repair. Until 1940, it was no more than a small fishing hamlet, though its deep-water harbour and tar pits had been used since Pizarro's time for caulking wooden ships – Pizarro had chosen the site for the first Spanish settlement in Peru, but it proved too unhealthy and he was forced to look elsewhere, eventually hitting on Piura. Talara takes its name and function from the country's most important coastal oilfield, and it was the town's **oil reserves** that were directly responsible for Peru's last military coup in 1968. President Belaunde, then in his first term of office, had given subsoil concessions to the multinational company IPC, declaring that "if this is foreign imperialism what we need is more, not less of it". A curious logic, it led to the accusation that he had signed an agreement "unacceptable to true Peruvians". Within two months of the affair, and as a direct consequence, he was deposed and exiled. One of the initial acts of the new revolutionary government was to nationalize IPC and declare the Act of Talara null and void. Today the town is highly industrialized, with several fertilizer plants as well as the oil business, although you can find an unpolluted **beach** at La Pena, 2km away.

If you really need to spend the night here, there are a few reasonable **hotels** in the commercial centre, such as the *Hotel Gran Pacifico*, on Avenida Aviación (℡074/385450; **❼**), which has a fantastic swimming pool, or the more modest *Hostal Talara*, Av Ejercito 217 (℡074/382186; **❸**), where there are rooms with or without bath. For buses, there's Transportes Chiclayo, at Parque 66/2 (℡074/382360), Cruz del Sur at Av F-5 (℡074/385434) and Tepsa at Av Martires Petroleros, Mza. D Lotes 5-6 (℡074/381572).

Cabo Blanco

Thirty kilometres or so north of Talara, there's a turning off the highway to the old fishing hot spot of **CABO BLANCO**. It is just off the cape here that the cold Humboldt current meets the warm, equatorial El Niño – a stroke of providence that creates an extraordinary abundance of marine life. Thomas Stokes, a British resident and fanatical fisherman, discovered the spot in 1935, and it was a very popular resort in the post-war years. Hemingway stayed for some months in 1951, while two years later the largest fish ever caught with a rod was landed here – a 710-kilo black marlin. Changes in the offshore currents have brought a decline in recent years, but international fishing competitions still take place, and the area is much reputed for swordfish. The fishing club where Hemingway is supposed to have written *The Old Man and the Sea* offers accommodation (**❻**), which includes access to a nice pool, an excellent seafood restaurant, and fishing and water-sports facilities. It also has one of the few free and official **campsites** in Peru.

From here to Tumbes the Panamerican Highway cuts across a further stretch of desert, for the most part keeping tightly to the Pacific coastline. It's a straight road, except for the occasional detour around bridges destroyed by the 1998 El Niño, but not a dull one, with immense views along the rolling surf and, if you're lucky, the occasional school of dolphins playing close to the shore. To the right of the road looms a long hill, the **Cerros de Amotape**, named after a local chief whom Pizarro had killed in 1532 as an example to potential rebels. Just to the north of this wooded hill is the ancient Inca Highway, though it can't be seen from this road.

Tumbes and the northern beaches

About 30km from the Ecuadorian border and 287km north of Piura, **TUMBES** is usually considered a mere pit stop for overland travellers. However, the city has a significant history and, unlike most border settlements, is a surprisingly warm and friendly place. On top of that, it's close to some of Peru's finest **beaches** and the country's only serious mangrove swamp, **Los Bosques de Manglares**. In the rural areas around the city, nearly half of Peru's tobacco leaf is produced.

Tumbes was the first town to be "conquered" by the Spanish and has maintained its importance ever since – originally as the gateway to the Inca Empire and more recently through its strategic position on the controversial **frontier with Ecuador**. Despite three regional wars – in 1859, 1941–42 and 1997–98 – the exact line of the border remains a source of controversy, although relations at the close of the millennium seemed to be at an all-time high, with huge numbers of Peruvians crossing the border to buy cheaper Ecuadorian products. Maps of the frontier vary depending on which country you buy them in, with the two countries claiming a disparity of up to 150km in some places along the border. The traditional enmity between Peru and Ecuador and the continuing dispute over the border mean that Tumbes has a strong Peruvian army presence and a consequent strict ban on photography anywhere near military or frontier installations. Most of the city's hundred thousand people are engaged in either transport or petty trading across the frontier, and are quite cut off from mainstream Peru, being much nearer to Quito than Lima, 1268km to the south.

Tumbes itself may not have much to offer the traveller beyond decent hotels, restaurants, some okay bars and better money-changing options than at the Ecuadorian frontier, but the region around it is rich in ocean and mangrove wildlife. In fact, the area may well be the most attractive for beach life in the whole of Peru. These days the beach resort of **Máncora** is where people come from as far away as Lima for holidays, making it a very busy place in December and January and some holiday weekends. But there are plenty of other beautiful beaches and, inevitably, plans for development in store – though these won't be reality for quite some time.

Some history

Pizarro didn't actually set foot in Tumbes when it was first discovered by the Spanish in 1527. He preferred to cast his eyes along the Inca city's adobe walls, its carefully irrigated fields, and its shining temple, from the comfort and safety of his ship. However, with the help of translators he set about learning as much as he could about Peru and the Incas during this initial contact. An Inca noble visited him aboard ship and even dined at his table. The noble was said to be especially pleased with his first taste of Spanish wine and the present of an iron hatchet.

The Spaniards who did go ashore – a Captain Alonso de Molina and his black servant – made reports of such grandeur that Pizarro at first refused to believe them, sending instead the more reliable Greek cavalier, Pedro de Candia. Molina's descriptions of the temple, lined with gold and silver sheets, were confirmed by Candia, who also gave the people of Tumbes their first taste of European technological might – firing his musket to smash a wooden board to pieces. With Candia's testimony, Pizarro had all the evidence he needed; after sailing another 500km down the coast, as far as the Santa Valley, he returned to

Panama and then back to Spain to obtain royal consent and support for his projected conquest.

The Tumbes people hadn't always been controlled by the Incas. The area was originally inhabited by the **Tallanes**, related to coastal tribes from Ecuador who are still known for their unusual lip and nose ornaments. In 1450 they were conquered for the first time – by the **Chimu**. Thirteen years later came the **Incas**, organized by Tupac Inca, who bulldozed the locals into religious, economic, and even architectural conformity in order to create their most northerly coastal terminus. A fortress, temple and sun convent were built, and the town was colonized with loyal subjects from other regions – a typical Inca ploy, which they called the *mitimaes* system. The valley had an efficient irrigation programme, allowing them to grow, among other things, bananas, corn and squash.

It didn't take Pizarro long to add his name to the list of Tumbes' conquerors. But after landing on the coast of Ecuador in 1532, with a royal warrant to conquer and convert the people of Peru to Christianity, his arrival at Tumbes was a strange affair. Despite the previous friendly contact, some of the Spanish were killed by Indians as they tried to beach, and when they reached the city it was completely deserted with many buildings destroyed, and, more painfully for Pizarro, no sign of gold. It seems likely that Tumbes' destruction prior to Pizarro's arrival was the result of inter-tribal warfare directly related to the **Inca Civil War**. This, a war of succession between Atahualpa and his half-brother, the legitimate heir, Huascar, was to make Pizarro's role as conqueror a great deal easier, and he took the town of Tumbes without a struggle.

Arrival, city transport and information

Most **buses** coming to Tumbes arrive at offices along Avenida Tumbes Norte (also known as Avenida Teniente Vasquez), or along Piura, although a new Terminal Terrestre is planned for the near future. Ormeño and Continental buses from Ecuador stop at Av Tumbes Norte 216. See Listings, p.444, for full details of bus company offices. Comite **colectivos** also pull in on Tumbes Norte, at no. 308 (T074/525977). If you're **flying** in from Lima, note that Tumbes airport is often very quiet, particularly at night, when there's no access to food or drink. A taxi into town should cost around $5, about a twenty-minute journey.

Tumbes is quite pleasant and easy to get around **on foot**, or you can hail one of the many **motorcycle rickshaws**, which will take you anywhere in the city for around 50¢. **Tourist information** is available from the first floor of the Centro Cívico, on the Plaza de Armas (8am–1pm & 2–6pm).

Accommodation

Central Tumbes is well endowed with places **to stay**. Some of the better budget options are strung out from the Plaza de Armas along Calle Grau, an attractive old-fashioned hodgepodge of a street, lined with wooden colonial buildings.

Hostal Chicho Av Tumbes Norte 327 T074/522282. New and good value; some rooms come with private bath and TV. Ones at the back are quieter. **3**

Hostal Cordova Jr Abad Pusil 777 T074/523981. Some rooms have private bath, and although comforts are minimal, it's reasonable value. **2**

Hostal Florian C Piura 414 T074/522464, F524725. A large hotel, slightly down-at-heel, but with comfortable beds at reasonable rates. Most rooms have private bath. **3**

Hostal Gandolfo Bolognesi 118 T074/522868. Small, budget rooms that are decent for the price. **1**

Hostal Italia C Grau 733 T074/526164. Slightly

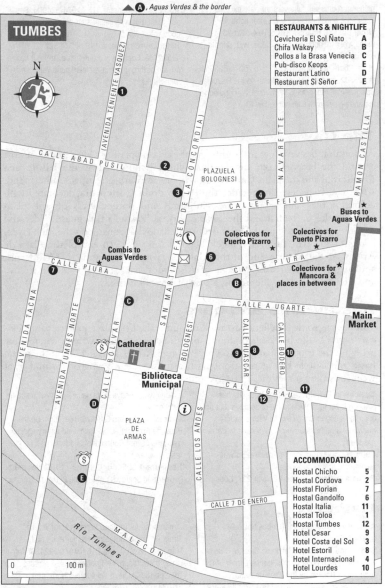

▲ A , Aguas Verdes & the border

TUMBES

N

RESTAURANTS & NIGHTLIFE

Cevichería El Sol Ñato	A
Chifa Wakay	B
Pollos a la Brasa Venecia	C
Pub-disco Keops	D
Restaurant Latino	D
Restaurant Si Señor	E

AVENIDA TENIENTE VASQUEZ

CALLE ABAD PUSIL

PASEO DE LA CONCORDIA

PLAZUELA BOLOGNESI

NAVARETTE

RAMON CASTILLA

CALLE F FEIJOU

★ Buses to Aguas Verdes

Colectivos for Puerto Pizarro ★

Colectivos for Puerto Pizarro ★

Combis to Aguas Verdes

SAN MARTIN

CALLE PIURA

CALLE PIURA

Colectivos for Mancora & places in between ★

CALLE A UGARTE

Main Market

AVENIDA TACNA

AVENIDA TUMBES NORTE

CALLE BOLIVAR

BOLOGNESI

CALLE HUASCAR

CALLE BODERO

Cathedral

Biblióteca Municipal

CALLE GRAU

PLAZA DE ARMAS

CALLE LOS ANDES

CALLE 7 DE ENERO

ACCOMMODATION

Hostal Chicho	5
Hostal Cordova	2
Hostal Florian	7
Hostal Gandolfo	6
Hostal Italia	11
Hostal Toloa	1
Hostal Tumbes	12
Hotel Cesar	9
Hotel Costa del Sol	3
Hotel Estoril	8
Hotel Internacional	4
Hotel Lourdes	10

Río Tumbes

MALECON

0   100 m

▼ Mancora, Piura & Southern Peru

run-down, but it's a characterful old building. Rooms are with or without bath. ❸

Hostal Sol del Costa Av San Martín 275 ☎074/523991, Ⓕ 525862, ⓦwww .costadelsolperu.com. It has a nice pool, very comfortable rooms with air-conditioning and private

baths, cable TV; close to the Plaza de Armas. ❻

Hostal Toloa Av Tumbes Norte 430 ☎074/523771. A reasonable choice, but the road outside is very noisy and it's opposite a large military establishment. ❷

Hostal Tumbes C Grau 614 ☎074/522203. Very

pleasant rooms with showers that are excellent value; the ones upstairs have better light. **②**
Hotel Cesar C Huascar 333 ⓣ074/522883. Small, very friendly and good value, with simple rooms. **③**
Hotel Costa del Sol San Martín 275 ⓣ074/523991, ⓕ525862. A smart revamped hotel on the Plazuela Bolognesi; all rooms have TV, minibar, air-conditioning and private bath with hot water. **⑧**

Hotel Estoril Huascar 317 ⓣ074/524906. Small and plain, but with genial staff and exceptionally good value. **②**
Hotel Lourdes Bodero 118 ⓣ074/522126, ⓕ522758. Located in a quiet side street, it has private bathrooms and is clean, good value and friendly. **③**

The City

Although it has very few real sights, Tumbes is a surprisingly elegant city, at least around the broad **Plaza de Armas**, which is bounded by the **Biblioteca Municipal** and the plain **Cathedral**, with an amphitheatre at its southern end. An attractive pedestrian precinct, the **Paseo de la Concordia**, decorated with colourful tiles and several large sculptures and statues, leads off the plaza between the Cathedral and the *biblioteca* to the Plazuela Bolognesi. Older and slightly grubby is the long **Malecón** promenade that runs along the high riverbanks of the Río Tumbes, a block beyond the southern end of the Plaza de Armas. At the western end of the Malecón, you can see a massive Modernist **sculpture**, *Tumbes Paraiso del Amor y el Eterno Verano* (Tumbes Paradise of Love and Eternal Summer), depicting a pair of lovers kissing.

Restaurants and bars

Tumbes has some excellent **restaurants** and is the best place in Peru to try *conchas negras* – the black clams found only in these coastal waters, where they grow on the roots of mangroves. The *Pub-disco Keops*, Bolivar 121, on the plaza, has a rustic-style **bar** at the front with a music scene going on behind it; at weekends they sometimes have live music.

Cevichería El Sol Ñato Bolivar 608. The best place in town for a wide range of seafood, but only open for lunches; try a ceviche with *conchas negras* or a huge steaming dish *of sudado de pescado*.
Chifa Wakay C Huascar 417. Dishes up well-priced, tasty Chinese food.
Pollos a la Brasa Venecia Bolivar 237. Does

exactly what it says in its name – a great place for chicken.
Restaurant Latino C Bolivar 163. Right on the Plaza de Armas, this old-fashioned eatery specializes in excellent Continental and American breakfasts.
Restaurant Si Señor C Bolivar 119. Serves mostly beer and seafood, right on the Plaza de Armas.

Listings

Airlines Aero Continente, Tumbes Norte 217 ⓣ074/522350.
Banks and exchange Banco de Credito, C Bolivar 227, and Banco de la Nación, on the corner of C Grau and C Bolivar, by the Plaza de Armas. *Cambistas* are at the corner of Bolivar with Piura.
Bus companies CIAL, Av Tumbes Norte 586, for Lima; Cruz del Sur, Av Tumbes Norte 319 (ⓣ074/522350), for Lima and the coast; El Dorado, Piura 454, for Máncora; Emtrafesa, Av Tumbes Norte 397 (ⓣ074/525850), for Chiclayo and Trujillo; Nor Pacífico, Av Tumbes Norte, for Piura, Chiclayo and Máncora; Ormeño and

Continental, Av Tumbes Norte 319, for Trujillo; Santa Rosa, Av Tumbes Norte, for Piura and Máncora; Tepsa, Tacna 216 (ⓣ074/522428), for Lima; Trans Olano, Av Tumbes Norte 324; and Transportes Chiclayo, Av Tumbes Norte 466 (ⓣ074/525260), for Chiclayo.
Photographic equipment Foto Estudio Gunes, Bolognesi 127.
Post office San Martín 240. Mon–Sat 7am–7pm.
Telephones The Telefónica del Peru office is on San Martín in the same block as the post office. Ravitel telephone and fax point is at Av Tumbes Norte 322.

Tour operators Tumbes Tours, Av Tumbes Norte 341 (☎074/522481), runs a number of tours including a 4-day/3-night trip exploring the nearby Puerto Pizarro mangrove swamp and beaches from $20 per person per day, depending on size of group. Manglares Tours, Av Tumbes Norte 313 (☎074/522887), can organize local tours with guides, though they specialize in air tickets. Preferencial Tours, Grau 427, are good for tourist information and are very friendly.

Around Tumbes

Along the coast around Tumbes you'll find some of the best **beaches** in the country, with a pleasantly warm sea for swimming. Among them are Caleta de la Cruz, 23km southwest (45min), reputed to be the bay where Pizarro first landed, **Punta Sal**, 50km southwest (1–2hr), Zorritos, 34km southwest (1hr) and **Máncora**, about 100km to the south (2hr). Buses to all four resorts leave daily from the main market in Tumbes, on Ramon Castillo, but return buses aren't that frequent, so check return times with the driver before you leave Tumbes. Nor Pacífico and Santa Rosa buses (see Listings, above) also go to Máncora from their offices in Tumbes.

The ruined Inca city of **San Pedro de las Incas** lies 5km south of the modern town in the village of Corrales, and although there's not a lot that you can make out these days it's still a pleasant walk, and both the temple and fortress are recognizable. It used to be on the Inca coastal highway to Cajamarca, which was vital in Pizarro's rapid advance towards the Inca Atahualpa. The ruins are 1km from the modern Panamerican Highway, and cows and goats from the nearby hamlet of San Pedro wander freely among the ancient adobe walls, devastated by centuries of intermittent flooding.

Puerto Pizarro

If you've never seen a mangrove swamp, **PUERTO PIZARRO** is perhaps worth a visit, 13km further on, though it has no specific link with the conquistador and the waterfront today is full of rubbish. This ancient fishing port was a commercial harbour until swamps grew out to sea, making it inaccessible for large boats and permanently disconnecting Tumbes from the Pacific. You can take short **boat trips** ($12 per person) out to the **Isla de Amor**, where there's a bathing beach and some **mangrove creeks** in which it's possible to see the *rhizopora* tree's dense root system and wildlife. Overlooking the port, the brightly painted bungalows of the **hotel** *Puerto Pizarro* (❸) occupy the only nice bit of waterfront; the hotel has a pool, private bathrooms, palm trees and a restaurant-café. **Combis** leave every thirty minutes or so from the corner of Calle Piura with Navarette in Tumbes (50¢, 20min), or you can take an organized tour with one of companies in Listings above.

Punta Sal

Located some 2km along a track from Km 1187 of the Panamerican Highway, also known in the north as the Panamericana Norte, **Punta Sal**, considered by many to be the best beach in Peru, has extensive sands and attractive rocky outcrops, swarming with crabs at low tide. It's a safe place to swim and a heavenly spot for diving in warm, clear waters. Several **hotels** here were destroyed by the 1998 El Niño, but the best place to stay is still the plush but friendly *Hotel Caballito del Mar* (☎074/540058 or from Lima 01/2414455, ☏4476562, ⓦ www.hotelcaballito.com.pe; ❺–❻), overlooking the sea at the southern end of the beach, with its own swimming pool by the exquisite beach (very peaceful in low season), a restaurant, sun terraces and very comfortable rooms. Less expensive is the *Hostal Hua* (☎074/608365, ☻ huapuntasal@yahoo.com; ❹),

The Tumbes protected areas

The Tumbes region is well endowed with natural resources, not least the three major **protected areas** of the Sanctuario Nacional Los Manglares de Tumbes, the Parque Nacional de Cerros de Amotape and the Zona Reservada de Tumbes. These, plus the El Angulo Hunting Reserve, encompass many habitats only found in this small corner of the country. If you're short of time it is just about possible to travel between these in just a day, but contact the local conservation organization – Pronaturaleza, Av Tarapaca 4-16, Urbino Fonavi (☎074/523412), on the outskirts of Tumbes – beforehand for impartial, expert advice. Permission from **INRENA**, opposite Pronaturaleza's office, is needed to enter all of these areas, though this is a formality for which no fees are payable.

The **Sanctuario Nacional Los Manglares de Tumbes** covers 3000 of the remaining 4750 hectares of **mangrove swamps** left in Peru, which are under serious threat from fishing and farming (shrimp farming in particular), to which an equal amount of land is already dedicated around Tumbes. The best way to visit the sanctuary is via the Pronaturaleza centre near Zarumilla, here called **CECODEM** (Centro de Conservación para el Desarrollo de los Manglares); combis run from Tumbes market to Zarumilla regularly (50¢, a 20min trip), from where it's only 7km down a track to CECODEM; a motorcycle taxi will cost $1.50, and you can arrange for the driver to return to pick you up. If arranged in advance with Pronaturaleza in Tumbes (at least one day before), CECODEM offer a walking **tour** (2–3hr) following a raised walkway through the mangroves and a canoe trip with a guide ($12 for up to 6 people). The centre also presents a lot of interpretative material about the mangroves, of which there are five species here. Red mangrove is the most common and this is where the *conchas negras* thrive, although the 1998 El Niño weather introduced large amounts of fresh water into the shell beds here, causing significant damage. The mangroves also contain over 200 bird species, including eight endemic species, such as the rather splendid mangrove eagle.

The **Zona Reservada de Tumbes**, which extends right up to the Ecuadorian border, covers 75,000 hectares of mainly tropical forest. The best route is inland, due south from Tumbes via Pampas de Hospital and El Caucho to El Narranjo and Figueroa on the border, but transport from Tumbes is only regular as far as Pampas de Hospital, and only occasional further on to El Caucho, which is where the best forest is. Potential sightings include monkeys, many bird species, small cats and snakes, while the Río Tumbes crocodile is a highly endangered species, found only at two sites along this river. There is some small hope for this unique creature in the form of a local breeding programme, but the whole area is under threat from gold-mining, mainly from across the border in Ecuador at the headwaters of the river. Pollution, too, from Tumbes is generating further disturbance.

The **Parque Nacional Cerros de Amotape** covers over 90,000 hectares, which contain seven distinct habitats, including the best-preserved region of dry forest anywhere along the Pacific coast of South America. Access is via Corrales, 5km south of Máncora, or via Chillo, just north of Sullana; you'll need permission from INRENA to visit (see above, or if coming via Chillo you can visit them en route at Encuentro de los Pilares). Animals that you just might see here include the black parrot, desert foxes, deer, white-backed squirrels, *tigrillos* (ocelots), puma and white-winged turkeys. Remember to take all your drinking and other water needs with you when entering this zone.

---

towards the middle of the beach, an older and more rustic wooden building, where some rooms have ocean views and the service is decent, plus there's a restaurant; **camping** is also permitted. There are no shops in Punta Sal, so you unless you want to be totally dependent on the hotels and restaurants, take some food and drink with you. In the low season you'll probably have a beautiful beach pretty much to yourself; in high season it's a good idea to book your accommodation in advance. There's also the *Punta Sal Club Hotel* (contact in Lima at Miguel Dasso 126, Of 210 ☎01/4425961 or 02/4425992, ⓦwww.puntasal.com.pe; ❼), with very comfortable beach cabin-style accommodation, swimming pool, laundry and great bar and restaurant facilities; it also offers fishing, horse-riding and snorkelling and is right on one of the best parts of the beach. Fishing trips, pretty well world-famous from here for the very high concentration of striped and black marlin, cost from around $230 for a half-day (you can take up to six people for this, double the price for a full day).

Máncora

Easily the trendiest beach in Peru these days, even attracting the young surf crowd from Ecuador, Máncora (ⓦwww.vivamancor.com) is also a highly welcome and very enjoyable stopover when travelling along the north coast. Well served by public transport and spread out along the Panamerican Highway, parallel to a beautiful sandy beach, it retains its charm and rivals some of the Brazilian beaches of the northeast. Swimming is safe and the surfing can be pretty good.

In fact Máncora is the north coast's current major **surfing** centre, rivalling Chicama near Trujillo at least in its popularity if not quite for its waves. You can hire gear from several places, including the Soledad Surf Company (☎01/9830425 in Lima), which sells and rents equipment as well as offering surf and Spanish lessons, or the from *Godwanaland* restaurant for around $1.50 per hour.

At the north end of the main drag, there's a plaza and just beyond this there's sometimes a street market, though only the usual clothing, shoes and food. Between here and the south end you'll find most of the town's hotels and restaurants, and a promenade with hippie artesania stalls, selling sea-inspired crafts and jewellery.

Practicalities

All the main **hotels** are located between the bridge at the south entrance to town and the plaza towards the north end, though there are several cheaper basic **hostels** strung out along the southern end of the Panamerican Highway. The *Hospedaje Crillon,* C Paita 168 (☎074/858131; ❷), has small basic rooms and shared bathrooms, but it's clean, friendly and located in the attractive, plant-laden pedestrianized little street parallel to Avenida Piura; the comfortable *Hostal Sausalito* (☎074/858058, ⓔjcvigoe@terra.com.pe; ❹) is pretty comfortable and has private bathrooms and TV, with quieter rooms to the back, and the price includes breakfast. The *Hostal Sol y Mar* (☎074/858106 and 858088 24hr, ⓔhsolymar@hotmail.com; ❷) is probably the best value and very popular with the surfing crowd; it is right on the beach, has a good swimming pool and games courts, plus a decent restaurant and bar, private baths, and its own little shop and Internet café. The *Hostal El Mar* (❺) overlooks the sea, has smart, cabin-like rooms, private baths, and hammocks, and meals are included; the *Hospedaje Grecia,* Av Piura 624 (☎074/858098; ❷–❸), is a small family-run pad, half-house/half-hostel, offering clean rooms with fans, TV and private baths; and the *Hostal Las Olas* (☎074/858109; ❸–❹) also overlooks the sea and includes either breakfast or full board. The *Hospedaje Don Carlos,* Av Piura 641 (☎074/858007; ❷–❸, TV optional), is not particularly stylish but the rooms are okay and Don Carlos himself is very friendly. The *Hotel Las Garzas,* Av Piura 262 (☎074/858110; ❸), has thirteen rooms, a restaurant and parking facilities plus a nice garden with hammocks; quite quiet and peaceful for this town. There's a **notice board** advertising rooms and bungalows for rent, as well as surfing lessons, in the Locutorio Publico **telephone** office and shop, on block 5 of Avenida Piura opposite the small church and close to the Banco de la Nación. Nearby you'll find the Cabinas Internet Máncora at Av Piura 605.

For eating, there's a surplus of **restaurants** in the centre of town, mainly along the Panamerican Highway. One of the best is the *Restaurant Arplan*, and opposite this are the *Espada*, at Av Piura 655 (℡074/858097), and the *San Pedro*, Av Piura 657 (℡074/858083), also among the best in town offering a range of fish dishes, including surprisingly affordable lobster; generally speaking, though, their prices are not that cheap. The *Restaurant Las Gemelitas* is the best and cheapest in town for seafood dishes; it's a little hard to find, though, up the side street by the street market (turn right at the mini-market shop Virgen de la Puerta, opposite the Panificadora Rico Pan) after the modern sliver of a little plaza, *Restaurant Jugeria Regina's*, in the centre, is good for fruit salads and breakfasts; and, opposite, the *Jugeria Mi Janet*, Carretera Panamericana, Av Piura 682, is also good. There's a hectic **nightlife** scene, especially during Peruvian holiday times, but the only club as such is *Las Terrazas*, on the main drag, backing onto the beach. Apart from this place, many of the cafés turn into nightspots when there's demand and the *Café Teyk Away* at the southern entrance, beachside, to Máncora is one of the better places to hang out in the evenings, serving cocktails, beer and pizza to the rhythms of Bob Marley.

The **bus companies** are all in the main street, Avenida Piura, where you can buy tickets for their selection of daily and nightly services up or down the coast, connecting Tumbes with Lima and the major cities in between. Transportes EPPO run five buses between here and Piura ($3, a 3hr journey) from their office just north of the plaza, towards the northern end of Máncora. Other bus companies, including the quality service of Cruz del Sur, Av Piur 656 (℡074/858107) almost as good Civa, Av Piura 656 (℡074/858026), and a close third, Ormeño, Av Piura 499 (℡074/858334), go daily to Piura and, Chiclayo and have connections for Cajamarca (and also have buses from Ecuador). El Dorado, Av Grau 111 (an extension of Piura), run south to Piura, Chiclayo and Trujillo daily and nightly. Nor Pacífico and Santa Rosa buses stop at the plaza en route between Tumbes and Piura. **Colectivos** depart from near the EPPO office for Los Oreganos (50¢, a 30min trip), from where there are other **combis** to Talara ($1, a 1hr trip). Colectivos and combis also patrol up and down the Panamerican Highway looking for passengers for Tumbes ($2, a 1.5–2hr trip).

Crossing the border at Aguas Verdes

Crossing the border is relatively simple in either direction. Two kilometres before the busy frontier settlement of **Aguas Verdes**, you'll find the **Peruvian immigration office** (daily 9am–noon & 2–5pm), where you get an exit or entry stamp and tourist card for your passport. Once past these buildings, it's a fifteen-minute walk or a short drive to Aguas Verdes. **Combis** for the border leave Tumbes from block 3 of Tumbes Norte, but ensure that it's going all the way to the border; some continue to Zarumilla or Aguas Verdes. A **taxi** from Tumbes costs $4–5. From Aguas Verdes, you just walk over the bridge into the Ecuadorian border town of **Huaquillas**, and the **Ecuadorian immigration office** (daily 8am–1pm & 2–6pm), where you'll get your entry or exit stamps and tourist card. If coming from Ecuador to Peru, Tumbes is the nicer place to stay close to the border; it has a greater choice of hotels and restaurants and it's much easier to make southerly connections from here. If going north, frequent buses depart to all the major destinations in Ecuador from Huaquillas. The best bet is to go on to Cuenca (5hr), an attractive, small Ecuadorian city and a major cultural centre, although Machala is nearer (75km) and has some accommodation and other facilities.

If you're coming into Peru from Ecuador, it's simply a reversal of the above procedure, though another option is to take a bus direct from the frontier to Sullana ($5, 2–3hr), from where there are buses and colectivos regularly to Piura (50¢, 45min).

In both directions the authorities occasionally require that you show an onward ticket out of their respective countries. Unless you intend to recross the border inside a week or two, it's not worth taking out any local currency: changing Peruvian nuevo soles in Ecuador or Ecuadorian sucres in Peru usually involves a substantial loss, and inflation is such that even two weeks can make quite a difference. The area of **no-man's-land** between the two countries' posts is basically a street market where everyone gets hassled to change money – grab a taxi to ease the passage. The best policy is to change as little money as possible (because of the poor exchange rates mentioned above) and, if you take a taxi, be firm on the price in advance.

The **Peruvian customs** point, a concrete complex in the middle of the desert between the villages of Cancas and Máncora and more than 50km south of the border, was inactive following the 1999 agreements between Ecuador and Peru. When it is operating, however, most buses are pulled over and passengers have to get out and often have to show documents to the customs police, while the bus and selected items of luggage are searched for contraband goods. This rarely takes more than twenty minutes, as they are quite efficient.

Crossing the border via La Tina and Loja

The alternative frontier crossing between **La Tina** and **Macará** is easiest approached by combi from Sullana, leaving from Avenida Buenos Aires, near the main market, in the mornings ($3, a 3hr trip). Hours for the **Peruvian immigration office** are the same as at Aguas Verdes (daily 9am–noon & 2–5pm), as are those for the **Ecuadorian immigration office** (daily 8am–1pm & 2–6pm).

There's nowhere to stay in La Tina, but a couple of basic **hostels** are to be found in Macará in Ecuador. Buses on to **Loja** (5hr) depart from Macará and it may be possible to connect on arrival and travel from Sullana to Macará in one day. Macará is 3km from the border; **motorcycle taxis** (50¢, a 10min trip) take people from the border into town. There are also buses direct to Loja from Piura (see p.436). The journey between the border and Macará is extremely hot – take and drink plenty of fluids. You can change **money** (dollars, sucres or soles) in Macará, and in La Tina or at the bank (Mon–Fri) on the Ecuadorian side of the international bridge. The main advantage of this route is basically the scenery en route to Loja.

Travel details

Buses and colectivos

Cajamarca to: Celendin (6 daily; 4–5hr); Chachapoyas (2 weekly via Celendin; 14hr); Chiclayo (10 daily; 7–9hr); Lima (several daily;

15hr); Cajabamba (6 daily; 5hr).
Chachapoyas to: Cajamarca (2 weekly via Celendin; 15hr); Chiclayo (several daily; 10–12hr); Rioja/Moyobamba (3 daily; 9–12hr).
Chiclayo to: Cajamarca (10 daily; 7–9hr);

Chachapoyas (1 daily; 10–12hr); Huancabamba (2 weekly; 15hr); Lima (6–8 daily; 14hr); Piura (12 daily; 4hr); Trujillo (12 daily; 3hr); Tumbes (6 daily; 10hr).

Piura to: Chiclayo (12 daily; 2–3hr); Huancabamba (2–3 daily; 12hr); Lima (10 daily; 13–15hr); La Tina and Loja (3 daily; 10–12hr); Tumbes (8 daily; 4–6hr).

Rioja/Moyobamba to: Chachapoyas (3 daily; 9–12hr); Tarapoto (5 daily; 4–5hr).

Trujillo to: Cajamarca (several daily; 8hr); Chiclayo (12 daily; 3hr); Lima (12 daily; 9hr); Piura, via Chiclayo (8 daily; 7hr); Yurimaguas (2–3 daily; 12–15hr).

Tumbes to Aguas Verdes (hourly; 20min); Chiclayo (8 daily; 10hr); Lima (8 daily; 23hr); Puerto Pizarro (hourly; 25min).

Flights

Cajamarca to: Chachapoyas (2 weekly; 1hr); Chimbote (3 weekly; 1hr 30min); Lima (1 daily; 2hr); Trujillo (3 weekly; 1hr).

Chachapoyas to: Cajamarca (2 weekly; 1hr);

Chiclayo (2 weekly; 1hr 30min); Lima (3 weekly; 2hr).

Chiclayo to: Cajamarca (1 daily; 40min); Chachapoyas (2 weekly; 1hr 30min); Iquitos (1 daily; 2hr); Lima (2 daily; 2hr); Piura (2 daily; 30min); Rioja/Moyobamba (2 weekly; 1hr); Talara (1 daily; 1hr); Tarapoto (2 weekly; 90min); Trujillo (1 daily; 45min); Tumbes (1 daily; 75min).

Piura to: Lima, via Chiclayo (2 daily; 2hr); Trujillo (1 daily; 1hr).

Rioja/Moyobamba to: Chiclayo (2 weekly; 1hr); Iquitos (3 weekly; 1hr 30min); Lima (6 weekly; 2hr); Tarapoto (2–4 weekly; 30min); Trujillo (1 weekly; 75min).

Tarapoto to: Iquitos (6 weekly; 1hr 30min); Lima (daily; 1hr 30min); Rioja/Moyobamba (2–4 weekly; 30min); Yurimaguas (1–2 weekly; 25min).

Trujillo to: Chiclayo (1 daily; 45min); Iquitos (4 weekly; 2hr); Lima (2 daily; 2hr 30min); Piura (1 daily; 1hr); Rioja/Moyobamba (1 weekly; 75min).

Tumbes to: Chiclayo (1 daily; 75min); Lima (2 daily; 2hr 30min).

Yurimaguas to: Iquitos (3 weekly; 90min); Lima (1 daily; 2hr 30min); Tarapoto (1–2 weekly; 25min).

8

The jungle

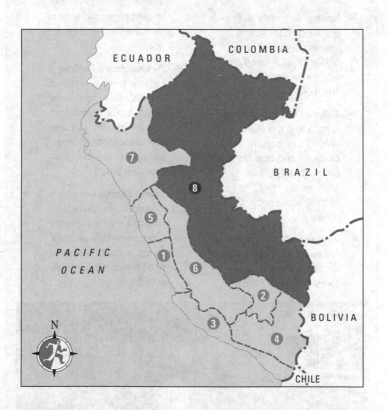

CHAPTER 8

Highlights

* **Tambopata-Candamo
  Reserve** You will be
  hard-pushed to find
  anywhere as rich in flora
  and fauna as this, the
  most biodiverse area of
  rainforest in the Amazon.
  See p.507

* **Iquitos** A fun city with a
  great nightclub scene,
  ridiculously hot by day
  and very *caliente* by the
  relative cool of the night.
  See p.466

* **Dolphin watching** Quite
  common in the rivers
  around Iquitos, pink river
  dolphins and blue dol-
  phins are a fantastic
  sight as they leap
  around your canoe. See
  p.480

* **Jungle walk** Few experiences are as memorable
  as a trek along a rain-
  forest trail with a local

  guide who vividly brings
  to life the various layers
  of the jungle eco-
  system. See p.480

* **Pacaya Samiria** Remote
  and stunningly beautiful,
  this reserve is one of the
  least-visited and yet the
  largest protected area of
  rainforest in Peru. See
  p.477

* **Ayahuascero healing** A
  hallucinatory experience,
  usually in a jungle settlement, as the shaman's
  ancient chants waft over
  the silver moonlit leafy
  canopy above the clear-
  ing. See p.483

* **Manu Biosphere
  Reserve** Another excellent place to experience
  a relatively pristine rainforest and also see plenty of jungle wildlife. See
  p.510

8

The jungle

T he Amazon, the rainforest, the selva, the jungle, the green hell (*el infierno verde*) – all attempt to name this huge, vibrant area of Peru. Whether you look at it up close, from the ground or a boat, or fly over it in a plane, the Peruvian **jungle** seems endless. In fact, it is disappearing at an alarming rate. However, while awareness of its importance as a unique eco-system and as a vital component of the global environment (not to mention the wealth of wildlife and sheer beauty of the vegetation) has brought it into the international spotlight, few people think of Peru in terms of jungle. In fact, well over half the country is covered by dense tropical rainforest, with its eastern regions offering unrivalled access to the world's largest and most famous jungle, the **Amazon.**

Of the Amazon's original area, around four million square kilometres (about 80 percent) remain intact, fifteen percent of which lie in Peru, where they receive over 2000mm of rainfall a year and experience average temperatures of 25–35°C. It's the most bio-diverse region on Earth, and much that lies beyond the main waterways remains relatively untouched and often unexplored. Jaguars, anteaters and tapirs roam the forests, huge anaconda snakes live in the swamps, toothy caimans (of the South American *Alligatoridae* family) sunbathe along riverbanks, and trees like the enormous shihuahuaco, strong enough to break an axe head, rise like giants from the forest floor. Furthermore, there are over fifty indigenous tribes scattered throughout the Peruvian section alone, many surviving primarily by hunting, fishing and gathering, as they have done for thousands of years.

At about six times the size of England, or equal to the size of California, it's not surprising that the Peruvian Amazon possesses a variety of ecotypes. Easier to access than many other South American jungle regions, increasing numbers of travellers are choosing to spend time here, and the tangled, sweltering and relatively accessible **Amazon Basin** never fails to capture the imagination of anyone who ventures beneath its dense canopy. In the **lowland areas**, away from the seasonally flooded riverbanks, the landscape is dominated by red, loamy soil, which can reach depths of 50m. Reaching upwards from this, the primary forest – mostly comprising a huge array of tropical palms, with scatterings of larger, emergent tree species – regularly achieves evergreen canopy heights of 50m. At ground level the vegetation is relatively open (mostly saplings, herbs and woody shrubs), since the trees tend to branch high up, restricting the amount of light available. At higher altitudes, the large belt of **cloud forest (ceja de selva)** that sweeps along the eastern edges of the Andes has been the focus of significant oil-prospecting during the last decade and has revealed some of the world's largest remaining fossil-fuel reserves.

The biggest river in the world, the **Río Amazonas** originally flowed east to west, but when the Andes began to rise along the Pacific edge of the continent around 100 million years ago, the waters became an inland sea. Another 40 million years of geological and climatic action later saw this "sea" break through into the Atlantic, which reversed the flow of water and gave birth to the mighty 6500-kilometre river. Starting in Peru as an insignificant glacial trickle on the Nevada Misma, northeast of the Colca Canyon, the waters swell as they move down through the Andes, passing Cusco before gaining the name **Río Tambo** and cascading down through the cloud forest, passing through the Toto,

Santiago, Apurimac, Ene and Tambo valleys until they reach the Ashaninka tribal territories in the Gran Pajonal. At this point, the Río Tambo meets the **Río Urubamba**, the major sacred river of the Incas that rushes past Machu Picchu down through rocky canyons. When these two already massive headwaters meet, in the rainforest more or less directly east of Lima in the heart of Peru, together they form the much larger **Río Ucayali**, which is already less than 200m above the level of the Atlantic Ocean, still many thousands of miles away. After their merge point, at the insignificant jungle town of **Atalaya**, the river and its tributaries – still the basis of jungle transport – are characterized by slow, wandering courses. Erosion and deposits continue to shift these courses, and oxbow lakes are constantly appearing and disappearing, adding enormous quantities of time and fuel to any river journey in the lowlands. In fact, as it languidly meanders past **Iquitos**, an isolated, land-locked, but passionate and vibrant city, on its way towards Brazil and eventually the Atlantic, it's still at least a two-week journey by boat to the mouth of a river which, at any one moment, carries around twenty percent of the world's fresh water.

Some history

Many archeologists think that the initial spark for the evolution of Peru's high cultures came from the jungle. Evidence from **Chavín**, **Chachapoyas** and **Tantamayo** cultures seems to back up such a theory – they certainly had continuous contact with the jungle areas – and the **Incas** were unable to dominate the tribes, their main contact being peaceful trade in treasured items such as plumes, gold, medicinal plants and the sacred coca leaf. At the time of the **Spanish conquest**, fairly permanent settlements seem to have existed along all the major jungle rivers, the people living in large groups to farm the rich alluvial soils, but the arrival of the Europeans appears to have begun the process of breaking these up into smaller and scattered groups (a process exacerbated by the nineteenth-century rubber boom – see overleaf).

Yet the Peruvian jungle still resisted major colonization. Although **Alonso de Alvarado** had led the first Spanish expedition, cutting a trail through from Chachapoyas to Moyobamba in 1537, most incursions ended in utter disaster, defeated by the ferocity of the tribes, the danger of the rivers, climate, and wild animals – and perhaps by the inherent alien character of the forest. Ultimately, apart from the white man's epidemics (which spread faster than the men themselves), the early conquistadores had relatively little impact on the populations of the Peruvian Amazon. Only **Orellana**, on his intrepid explorations along the Río Amazonas, managed to glimpse the reality of the rainforest, though even he seemed to misunderstand it when he was attacked by a tribe of blond women, one of whom managed to hit him in the eye with a blow-gun dart. These "women" are nowadays considered to be men of the Yagua tribe (from near Iquitos), who wear straw-coloured, grass-like skirts and headdresses.

By the early eighteenth century the **Catholic Church** had made serious but still vulnerable inroads into the region. Resistance to this culminated in 1742 with an indigenous uprising in the central forest region led by an enigmatic character from the Andes calling himself Juan Santos Atahualpa. Many missions were burnt, missionaries and colonists killed, and Spanish military expeditions defeated. The result was that the central rainforest remained under the control of the indigenous population for the next ninety years or so; in fact, as recently as 1919 the Ashaninka Indians were blockading rivers and ejecting missionaries and foreigners from their ancestral lands.

As "white-man's" technology advanced, so too did the possibilities of conquering Amazonia. The 1830s saw the beginning of a hundred years of massive and

Outside the few main towns, there are hardly any sizeable settlements, and the jungle population remains dominated by between 35 and 62 **indigenous tribes** – the exact number depends on how you classify tribal identity – each with its own distinct language, customs and dress. After centuries of external influence (missionaries, gold seekers, rubber barons, soldiers, oil companies, anthropologists, and now tourists), many jungle Indians speak Spanish and live pretty conventional, westernized lives, preferring jeans, football shirts and fizzy bottled drinks to their more traditional clothing and manioc beer (the tasty, filling and nutritious *masato*). But while many are being sucked into the money-based labour market, others, increasingly under threat, have been forced to struggle for their cultural identities and territorial rights, or to retreat as far as they are presently able beyond the new frontiers of so-called civilization. In 1996, for instance, oil workers encountered some previously uncontacted groups while clearing tracts of forest for seismic testing in the upper Río de las Piedras area of Madre de Dios, northwest of Puerto Maldonado. In this region it appears that some of the last few uncontacted tribal communities in the Amazon – Yaminahua, Mashco Piro and Amahuaca Indians – are keeping their distance from outside influences.

In 2002 these same remote groups came out of the forest en masse to prevent further intrusion by aggressive **illegal loggers** in their last remaining territory at the headwaters of the Río de las Piedras. In August of that year some four hundred naked Indians appeared on the riverbanks as a flotilla of illegal logging launches made its way upstream from Puerto Maldonado. Shaking and rattling their bows and arrows, the Indians raised long vines as a barrier across the river and then attacked the boats, badly injuring several loggers (for more on the story of these natives' fight for independence, see p.588).

For most of the traditional or semi-traditional tribes, the jungle offers a **semi-nomadic** existence, and in terms of material possessions, they have, need and want very little. Communities are scattered, with groups of between ten and two hundred people, and their sites shift every few years. For subsistence they depend on small, cultivated plots, fish from the rivers, and game from the forest, including wild pigs, deer, monkeys and a great range of edible birds. The main species of edible jungle fish are *sabalo* (a kind of oversized catfish), *carachama* (an armoured walking catfish), the feisty piranha (generally not quite as dangerous as Hollywood makes out), and the giant *zungaro* and *paiche* – the latter, at up to 200kg, being the world's largest freshwater fish. In fact, food is so abundant that jungle dwellers generally spend no more than three to four days a week engaged in subsistence activities.

painful exploitation of the forest and its population by **rubber barons**. Many of these wealthy men were European, eager to gain control of the raw material, desperately needed following the discovery of the vulcanization process, and during this era the jungle regions of Peru were better connected to Brazil, Bolivia, the Atlantic, and ultimately Europe, than they were to Lima or the Pacific coast. The peak of the boom, from the 1880s to just before World War I, had a prolonged effect. Treating the natives as little more than slaves, men like the notorious **Fitzcarrald** (see box, p.498) made overnight fortunes, and large sections of the forests were explored and subdued. In 1891, for example, the British-owned Peruvian Corporation was granted the 500,000-hectare "Perene Colony" in the central rainforest in payment of debts owed by the Peruvian state. That the granted land was indigenous territory was ignored – the Ashaninka who lived in the area were considered a captive labour force that was part of the concession. The process only fell into decline when the British explorer Markham took Peruvian rubber plants to Malaysia, where the plants grew equally well but were far easier to harvest.

Nineteenth-century colonialism also saw the progression of the **extractive frontier** along the navigable rivers, which involved short-term economic exploitation based on the extraction of other natural materials, such as timber and animal skins; coupled to this was the advance of the **agricultural frontier** down from the Andes. Both kinds of expansion assumed that Amazonia was a limitless source of natural reserves and an empty wilderness – misapprehensions that still exist today. The agricultural colonization tended to be by poor, landless peasants from the Andes and was concentrated in the Selva Alta, on the eastern slopes of that range. From the 1950s these *colonos* became a massive threat to the area's ecosystem when, supported by successive government land grants, credit and road building, subsistence farmers and cattle ranchers inflicted large-scale deforestation.

In the 1960s, President Belaunde saw the colonization of Amazonia as central to his political platform, believing it to be a verdant, limitless and "unpopulated" frontier that was ripe for development, offering land to the landless masses. New waves of *colonos* arrived and, once again, indigenous inhabitants were dispossessed and yet more rainforest cleared. Things quietened down between 1968 and 1980, during the military regime, but when Belaunde returned to power in 1980, peasant colonization continued, by and large along tenuous penetration roads built by the government, but also with further state sponsorship and funding by international banks. Between 1985 and 1995, new factors such as the rise of terrorism and the illegal cocaine industry began to threaten the cultures and environment of the Peruvian Amazon. Since the mid-1990s the immediate threats to this region have shifted more towards petroleum and gas exploration and exploitation, illegal lumber extraction and gold-mining.

The threat to the forest

Over the last few decades, the intrusion of **oil and timber companies** has seen repeated exploitation of the rainforest. Even worse, vast tracts of forest have disappeared as successive waves of *colonos* have cleared trees to grow cash crops (especially coca). Since the late 1980s, conservationists have shown that this large-scale, haphazard **slash-and-burn agriculture** is unsustainable. The rainforest's nutrients are held in the vegetative and animal life-forms that live, die and are consumed and transformed into new life, mainly by fungal and insect species; the soil itself contains less than twenty percent of the nutrients, so jungle quickly turns to desert when its plant life is destroyed. The decline in nutrient yields has been irreversible.

When the Peruvian economy began to suffer in the mid-1980s, foreign credit ended and those with substantial private capital fled, mainly to the US. The government, then led by the young Alan Garcia, was forced to abandon the jungle region, and both its colonist and indigenous inhabitants were left to survive by themselves. This effectively opened the doors for the **coca barons**, who had already established themselves during the 1970s in the Huallaga Valley, and they moved into the gap left by government aid in the other valleys of the *ceja de selva* – notably the Pichis-Palcazu and the Apurimac-Ene. During the next ten years, illicit coca production was responsible for some ten percent of the deforestation that occurred in the Peruvian Amazon during the entire twentieth century; furthermore, trade of this lucrative crop led to significant corruption and, more importantly, supported the rise of **terrorism**. Strategic alliances between coca-growers (the colonists), smugglers (Peruvians and Colombians) and the terrorists (mainly, but not exclusively, Sendero Luminoso) led to a large area of the Peruvian Amazon becoming utterly lawless. Each party to this alliance gained strength and resources whilst the indigenous peoples of the region suffered, stuck seemingly powerless in the middle.

Over the last ten years the Peruvian authorities have persecuted the *colonos* for the one crop that made them money, and their greatest successes in this area have come largely from among the indigenous groups themselves, like the Ashaninka tribe. Armed by the authorities, they were among the vanguard of resistance to the **narco-terrorists**, whose movement, once rooted in politics and agriculture, had become bloodthirsty, power-hungry and highly unpopular. In the aftermath of the civil war, which began to fizzle out with the capture of Sendero's leader in 1992, the international financial institutions, whose earlier loans had helped fund the disastrous colonization, started to at least partly determine development policy in the Peruvian Amazon so that those same loans could be repaid, and resources such as fossilfuels, lumber and land were privatized and sold to the highest bidder.

President Fujimori's neo-liberal agenda led to new investment in this legitimate exploitation, which was unfortunately mirrored by a huge increase in **illegal mining**. Hordes of landless peasants from the Cusco region also flocked into the Madre de Dios to make their fortune from **gold-mining**. In itself this was neither illegal nor an environmental threat, but the introduction of front-loader machines and trucks – which supplanted child labour in the mines in the early 1990s – increased the environmental damage and rate of territorial consumption by this unregulated industry. By 1999, a massive desert had appeared around Huaypetue, previously a small-time frontier mining town, and the neighbouring communities of Amarakeiri Indians (who have been panning for gold in a small-scale, sustainable fashion for some thirty years) are in serious danger of losing their land and natural resources.

As the danger from terrorism faded in the mid-1990s, **oil and gas exploration** by multinational companies began in earnest. Initially the Peruvian government appeared to be bending over backwards to assist them, and the reserves discovered – mainly in the Madre de Dios and the Camisea – were believed to be of world-shattering importance, with only the Amazonian indigenous organizations and environmental conservationists active in opposition. For the moment, the momentum seems to have slowed right down, as the decision to drill in the Río de las Piedras has been reversed and work has stopped in the Camisea. But the reserves are still there and the Camisea, at least, is likely to be eventually exploited, possibly by little-known companies that are difficult to control or lobby from the environmentalist's perspective. At macroeconomic and political levels this easing-off appears to be due more to an unforeseen extension of Fujimori's policies than genuine concern for environmental protection or the territorial and resource rights of the tribal groups. Ultimately, the Peruvian government was not prepared to offer the multinational oil companies as big a monopoly over the country's power supply industry as they desired.

In the late 1990s, the price of coca continued to drop in Peru as production shifted to Colombia, and many peasants and jungle Indians alike were seriously looking for **alternative cash crops**, such as the traditional chocolate and coffee products or newer options like *uña de gato* (a newly rediscovered medicinal herb) and *barbasco* (a natural pesticide).

Mining and petroleum and gas exploitation continues apace, but with improvements to the jungle road infrastructure and the attention of the global timber markets turning from Southeast Asia back to the Amazon in recent years, it seems that the illegal, and sometimes legal but unsustainable, loggers are the major threat to the remaining Indian cultures and their lush tropical rainforest environment. The way things are going it's hard to see how much longer the indigenous peoples can maintain their traditional territories; without the forest the present forest-dwellers' children will be without a means of surviving or earning a living. Action by the Peruvian authorities and international agencies is required immediately to hold any hope of halting this contemporary devastation and ethnocide.

Getting into the jungle

Given the breadth and quality of options, it's never easy to decide which bit of the jungle to head for. Your three main criteria will probably be budget, ease of access, and the depth and nature of jungle experience you're after. Flying to any of the main jungle towns is surprisingly cheap and can save an arduous few days' journey overland, and once you've arrived, a number of **excursions** can be made easily and cheaply, though the best experience comprises a few nights at one of the better **jungle lodges**. For a more intimate (but often necessarily tougher) experience, it's easy enough to arrange a **camping expedition** and a guide, travelling in canoes or speedboats into the deeper parts of the wilderness. A further, costlier option, mainly restricted to a few operators based in Iquitos, is to take a **river cruise** on a larger boat. This offers two significant advantages: firstly, the boats are comfortable, with good service and food; and secondly, the programmes take you to remote areas in style, and can then penetrate the deeper forest (such as the rarely visited Pacaya Samiria National Reserve) in wellequipped speedboats. Unlike lodge-based operations, both canoe expeditions and cruises aren't fixed to specific locations, so they can customize programmes and routes. Hotels and tours tend to work out cheaper while there is less demand due to the annual cycle of US and European holiday seasons, though growing trends in **ecological tourism** and, more recently, psychedelic or jungle **mystic experiences**, are bringing groups throughout the year.

Most easily accessed by air from Lima or by boat from Brazil, the **NORTHERN SELVA** can also be reached from the northern Peruvian coast via an increasingly popular but still very adventurous route that takes the Río Huallaga from Yurimaguas (see p.466), a four to five day boat journey that can be broken by a visit to the immense **Pacaya Samiria National Reserve** at the heart of the upper Amazon. Capital of the remote and massive frontier region of Loreto, **Iquitos** is one of Peru's most welcoming cities, despite the presence of oil wells, cocaine traffickers and the US Drug Enforcement Agency. It's also the most organized and established of the Peruvian Amazon's tourist destinations, and has many reputable companies offering a range of jungle visits, from luxury lodges and cruises (see p.679) to rugged survival expeditions. From Iquitos you can catch a ferry upstream to the growing town of **Requena**, similar to how Iquitos was around fifty years ago, and even further upriver to Pucallpa, where you'll find the first possible direct road link to Lima.

Pucallpa is the largest port and a rapidly growing industrialized jungle town in the **CENTRAL SELVA**, best reached by scheduled air flights or the largely paved road from Lima. Nearby is **Lago Yarinacocha**, an attractively developed lake resort that has declined in popularity as a major destination since the mid-1980s, mainly due to a combination of terrorist infiltration, over-industrialization and the improvement of facilities in other competing jungle regions. However, it remains a good introduction to the rainforest and is reached by a relatively easy overland trip from Lima. Another sector of this central jungle region – **Chanchamayo** – can be reached by road in eight to twelve hours from Lima. Winding fast but precariously down from the

Jungle hazards

Going even a little off the beaten track in the jungle involves arduous travelling, through an intense mesh of plant, insect and animal life. It's an environment that's not to be taken lightly: apart from the real chance of getting lost (see p.464), the popular image of poisonous snakes, jaguars and mosquitoes is based on fact, though these dangers don't actually come hunting for you. Always consult your doctor on how to prevent diseases before departing for Peru if you are planning to spend *any* time in the rainforest regions.

•**DENGUE FEVER** There is no inoculation against **dengue fever**, a mosquito-transmitted viral infection that occurs mainly in urban Amazonia, and the best prevention is by avoiding bites (see "Malaria" below, though note that the dengue mosquito is primarily diurnal). Symptoms include high fevers, headache, severe pains in muscles and joints, vomiting and a red skin rash after the first few days. The illness usually lasts around ten days and can be treated with paracetamol. If hemorrhaging occurs (in this, as well as in any other case, of course), see a doctor immediately. Recovery is usually complete within a few weeks.

•**JIGGERS** Small insects that live in cut grass, **jiggers** can also be a very irritating problem; they stick to and bury their heads in your ankles before slowly making their way up your legs to the groin, causing you to itch furiously. You can either pick them out one by one as the natives do, or apply sulphur cream (ask for the best ointment from a *farmacia* in any jungle town).

•**LEISHMANIASIS** Endemic to certain zones, **Leishmaniasis** (known in Peru as *uta*) is transmitted by sandfly bites and is rarely contracted by short-term visitors to the jungle. Symptoms start with skin sores that begin to ulcerate, followed by fever and swelling of the spleen. There is no prophylactic and if untreated it can lead to severe degeneration of skin and facial tissue, usually around the upper lip and lower nose areas. There is treatment in the form of heavy metal injections, but many untreated cases among relatively malnourished Peruvian peasants and Indians have resulted in permanent and quite horrific disfigurement.

•**MALARIA** The most significant disease in the Amazon, **malaria** has two common forms in South America: *Plasmodium vivax* and *Plasmodium falciparum*. The latter is the most common, but both are found in the Peruvian Amazon and thought to be fast adapting to modern medicines. Of the **prophylactics**, many have side-effects (some psychological, others physiological), so do some independent research as well as consulting your doctor. Mosquitoes are mainly, but not exclusively nocturnal, coming out at dusk and disappearing at sunrise; the best **protection** is to use roll-

---

Andean heights of Tarma, the Carretera Central is now paved all the way to **Satipo**, a jungle frontier town, relatively close to the **Río Ene**, the name given to the Amazon's major headwater after the Río Apurimac merges with a major tributary, the Río Mantaro, as it pours down from the Huancayo area of the sierra. En route to Satipo the road passes through the cloud forest via La Merced, from where there are bus connections to the fascinating and unique Tirolean settlement of **Pozuzo**.

The jungles of southeastern Peru are bursting with biodiversity and are now excellently supplied in terms of lodges, guides, boats and flights to enable budget travellers and those with more money and less time to get deep into the jungle for the full experience. Cusco is the best base for trips into the **SOUTHERN SELVA**, with road access to the frontier town of **Puerto Maldonado**, itself a good base for budget travellers. The nearby forests of **Madre de Dios** boast the **Tambopata–Candamo Reserved Zone** and the **Bahuaja–Sonene National Park**, an enormous tract of virgin rainforest close to the Bolivian border. Many naturalists argue that this region is the most bioon DEET (diethyltoluamide) repellents, to wear clothing that's treated with diluted DEET repellent and covers exposed skin, and to sleep under mosquito nets. Note that DEET harms plastics. Even with the best effort possible, you can't be sure of avoiding bites, especially when camping in the rainforest or on night walks, so always take what your GP prescribes. Malaria starts three or four weeks after contact, usually with a combination of severe nausea, high fevers, delirium and chills; get medical help as soon as possible if you have these symptoms – it's easier to treat in the early stages.

•**PARASITES** Parasites are quite common, so it's best to **boil drinking water** and use sterilizing tablets or crystals. Around human settlements, including the muddier parts of larger towns, you can pick up parasites through the soles of your feet; the best precaution is to wear shoes rather than flip-flops or sandals. Also, get a medical check-up at a centre that specializes in tropical diseases when you return home.

•**RIVER SICKNESS** The most likely hazard you'll encounter is **river sickness**, a general term for the effect of the sun's strong rays reflected off the water. After several hours on the river, particularly at midday and without a hat, you may get the first symptom – the runs – sometimes followed by nausea or shaking fever; in extreme cases these can last for a day or two. Anti-diarrhoea medicine should help (Lomotil, Imodium, or something similar); otherwise drink plenty of fluids and take rehydration salts dissolved in water.

•**SNAKES** It's unlikely that you will encounter any **snakes**. If you do, nearly all of them will disappear as quickly as they can – only the poisonous *shushupe* (a bushmaster) is fearless. The fer-de-lance, or *jergon*, is also quite common; it's smaller and packs less venom than the bushmaster, but can still be deadly. Most bites occur by stepping on a sleeping snake or picking it up with a handful of vegetation; be constantly aware of this possibility. If anyone does get bitten, the first thing to remember is to keep calm – most deaths result from shock, not venom. Try to kill the snake for identification, but, more importantly, apply a temporary tourniquet above the bite and find medical help *immediately*. Some natives have remedies even for a potentially deadly *shushupe* bite.

•**YELLOW FEVER** **Yellow fever** is simple to prevent by a shot that covers you for ten years. Consult your doctor to find the nearest inoculation centre, and remember to obtain a **certificate of inoculation**, which you are sometimes required to show on entry into many of Peru's jungle regions. If you can't, you run the risk of being subject to on-the-spot inoculation, wherever you may be.

diverse on Earth, and thus the best place to head for wildlife. An expedition into the **Manu Reserved Zone** (part of the larger **Manu National Biosphere Reserve**) will also bring you into one of the more exciting wildlife regions in South America. For a quicker and cheaper taste of the jungle, you can go by bus from Cusco via Ollantaytambo to **Quillabamba**, on the **Río Urubamba**, which flows north along the foot of the Andes, through the dangerous and unforgettable whitewater rapids of the **Pongo de Mainique**.

Getting around the jungle

The three most common forms of **river transport** are canoes (*canoas*), speedboats (*deslizadoras*), and larger riverboats (*lanchas*). Whichever you choose, it's a good idea to make sure you can get along with the boatman (*piloto*) or captain and that he really does know the rivers. **Canoes** can be anything from a small dugout with a paddle, useful for moving along small creeks and rivers, to a large eighteen-metre canoe with panelled sides and a *peque-peque* (on-board engine)

All visits
• certificate of inoculation against yellow fever (check with your embassy for prevailing health requirements).
• malaria pills (start course in advance as directed by prescribing doctor).
• roll-on insect repellent containing DEET.
• suitable clothing (wear socks, trousers and long sleeves in the evenings).
• toilet paper.
• waterproof poncho, cagoule (hooded nylon pack-away raincoat) or overclothes.

3–5 days at a lodge or basic facility
• anti-diarrhoea medicine (eg, Lomotil or Imodium).
• blanket or thick cotton sheet for sleeping.
• mosquito net for sleeping under.
• multipurpose knife (with can and bottle opener).
• plastic bags for packing and lining your bags with (a watertight box is best for camera equipment and other delicate valuables). Note that cardboard boxes dissolve on contact with an Amazon river or rain shower.
• sun-hat (especially for river travel).
• torch and spare batteries.
• waterproof matches and a back-up gas lighter.

5 days or more away from facilities
• candles.
• compass and a whistle (in case you get lost).
• cooking pots and stove (or the ability to cook over a fire and a supply of dry wood), plus eating utensils.
• filled water container (allow for a gallon a day).
• first-aid box or medical kit (including tweezers, needles, scissors, plasters, bandages, adhesive tape, sterile dressings, antiseptic cream, antibiotics and painkillers).
• fishing line and hooks (unsalted meat makes good bait).
• food supplies (mainly rice, beans, cans of fish, crackers, noodles and fruit; chocolate is impractical, as it melts).
• gifts for people you might encounter (batteries, knives, fish-hooks and line, camera film, and so on).
• a hammock or mat, plus a couple of blankets.
• insect-bite ointment (antihistamines, tiger balm, or *mentol china*; toothpaste as a last resort).
• a good knife and machete.
• quick-dry clothing.
• petrol for boats, useful for bargaining for rides.
• rope.
• running shoes, sandals (ideally plastic or rubber); rubber boots or strong walking boots if you're going hiking.
• water sterilizers (good tablets, crystals or a decent filter).

or a more powerful outboard motor. **Speedboats** tend to have lightweight metal hulls and are obviously faster and more manoeuvrable, but also more expensive. **Riverboats** come in a range of sizes and vary considerably in their river-worthiness, and you should always have a good look at the boat before buying a ticket or embarking on a journey – note that the smaller one- or two-deck riverboats are frequently in worse condition (and noisier) than larger ones. The best are the Iquitos-based tour boats, with cabins for up to thirty passengers, dining rooms, bars, sun lounges and even Jacuzzis on board. Next best are the larger vessels with up to three decks that can carry two hundred passengers, with hammock spaces and a few cabins (for which you pay two to three times as much); if you're over 1.8m tall, it's best to take a hammock as the bunks may be too small. Always try to get a berth as close as possible to the front of the boat, away from the noise of the motor. On the larger riverboats (especially between Pucallpa and Iquitos, or Tabatinga and Iquitos) you can save money on hotels by literally hanging around in your hammock, as most captains allow passengers to sling one up and sleep on board for a few days before departure. Riverboats travelling upstream tend to stay close to the bank, away from the fast central flow, and while this means longer journeys, they're much more visually interesting than travelling up the middle of the river, particularly on the larger ones where it can be hard to make out even huts on the banks.

Anyone who intends **hitching** along the river system should remember that the further you are away from a town, the harder it is to lay your hands on **fuel** (even if you should come across a multinational company drilling in the middle of the forest). You'll always be expected to contribute financially, but however much you offer, no one will take you upriver if they're short on fuel – and most people are most of the time. Taking your own supply (a 55-gallon container, for example) is a little difficult but isn't a bad idea if you're going somewhere remote. As a last resort it's possible to get hold of a **balsa raft** and paddle (downstream) from village to village, but this has obvious dangers and is certainly not an option if there are any rapids to negotiate (eg, certain death awaits anyone who would be foolish enough to attempt to go through the Pongo de Mainique on the Río Urubamba by raft). In addition to the obvious dangers of rapids, travelling alone by river places you in severe risk of getting lost, or simply stuck on an unpopulated riverbank for the night (or even a week or more in many remote areas) before finding a passing boat or local settlement. It certainly isn't advisable to travel these rivers without the help of someone who knows the river extremely well; this inevitably means a good tour company with professional guides, or reliable local Indian guides.

A basic rule of thumb is to always try to be with a reliable **local guide**. They don't need to have official status but they should be experienced in the region and willing to help out (remember that natives are often the best guides). There are several ways of enlisting this kind of help: by paying significant sums for a commercially operated jungle tour; by going to the port of a jungle town and hiring someone and his boat; or by hopping along the rivers from one village to the next with someone who is going that way anyway and who will be able

---

Jungle permits

To enter certain areas, such as the Pacaya Samiria National Reserve, or the Manu and Tambopata-Candamo reserved zones, you'll need to obtain permission first. This is often done for you if you're on an organized tour; otherwise, contact the **Instituto Nacional de Recursos Naturales (INRENA)**, C Diesisiete 355, Urbino El Palomar, Lima 27 (Mon–Fri 9am–5pm; ☏01/2243298, ✉inrenabibli@terra.com.pe), or C Ricardo Palma 113, fourth floor, Iquitos (☏094/232980, ✉rnps-zrg@meganet .com.pe). It's not usually difficult to get a permit unless there's a good reason, such as for specially restricted areas (eg, in Manu Biosphere Reserve – see p.510) or suspected hostility from indigenous locals (in 1980, for example, a German-led wildlife expedition was attacked by Indians – the first thing they knew about it was a sheet of arrows flying towards their canoe).

to introduce you to the villagers at the next stage. This last and most adventurous option will normally involve long waits in remote settlements, but the jungle is an essentially laid-back place, and if there's one thing certain to get a *selvatico* (jungle dweller) mad, it's a gringo with a loud voice and pushy manner. If you choose to travel this way, remember that you are imposing yourself on the hospitality of the locals and that you are dependent on them: be sensitive to their needs, their privacy and their possessions and take **goods and cash** to offer them in return for any help. Fishing hooks, nylon fishing line, tins of fish, trade cloth, clothes, fresh batteries and even shotgun cartridges are usually appreciated.

Getting lost is no fun and can happen very easily. Just by straying a hundred metres from camp, the river, or your guide, you can find yourself completely surrounded by a seemingly impenetrable canopy of plant life. It's almost impossible to walk in a straight line through the undergrowth, and one trail looks very much like the next to the unaccustomed eye. Your best bet, apart from shouting as loud as you can or banging the base of big buttress-root trees as Indians do when they get lost on hunting forages, is to find moving water and follow it downstream to the main river, where someone will eventually find you waiting on the bank. If you get caught out overnight, the three best places to sleep are beside a fire on the river bank, high up in a tree that isn't crawling with biting ants, or in a hammock.

The northern selva: Iquitos and Río Amazonas

At the "island" city of **Iquitos**, by far the largest, most fun and most exciting of Peru's jungle towns, there are few sights as magnificent as the **Río Amazonas**. Its tributaries start well up in the Andes, and when they join together several hours upstream from the town, the river is already several kilometres wide, though a mere 116m above sea level. The town's location, surrounded in all directions by brilliant green forest and hemmed in by the maze of rivers, streams, and lagoons, makes for a stunning entry to the northern jungle.

Most people visit Iquitos briefly with a view to moving on into the **rainforest** but, wisely, few travellers actually avoid the place entirely. It's a busy, cosmopolitan tourist town with a buzzing population of about 300,000, and connected to the rest of the world by river and air only. Iquitos is the kind of place that lives up to all your expectations of a jungle town, from its elegant reminders of the rubber-boom years to the atmospheric shantytown suburb of **Puerto Belén**, one of Werner Herzog's main locations for his film *Fitzcarraldo* (see p.472), and where you can buy almost anything, from fuel to ayahuasca.

Tourist facilities here have developed gradually over the last thirty years – the town has a friendly café- and club-scene, interesting museums and beautiful buildings, and the surrounding region has some great island and lagoon beaches, a range of easy excursions into the rainforest, and the possibility of continuing down the Amazon into Colombia or Brazil. The area has also become something of a **spiritual focus**, particularly for gringos seeking a visionary experience with one of the many local shamans who utilize the sacred and powerful hallucinogenic ayahuasca vine in their religious psycho-healing sessions (see p.483).

When to go

Unlike most of the Peruvian selva, the **climate** here is little affected by the Andean topography, so there is no rainy season as such; instead, the year is divided into "high water" (Dec–May) and "low water" (June–Nov) seasons. The upshot is that the weather is always hot and humid, with temperatures averaging 23–30°C and with an annual rainfall of about 2600mm. Most visitors come between May and August, but the high-water months are perhaps the best time for seeing **wildlife**, because the animals are crowded into smaller areas of dry land.

As for Iquitos itself, the carnival known as **Omagua** (local dialect for "low-land swamp") has grown in vigour over recent years and now involves not only townspeople, but hundreds of Indians as well, with plenty of chanting and dancing. The main thrust of activities (as always) is on the Friday, Saturday and Sunday before Ash Wednesday, and on the Monday the town celebrates with the traditional Umisha dance around a sacred tree selected for the purpose. It's similar to maypole dancing in Britain, though in Iquitos the dancers strike the tree with machetes; when it eventually falls, children dive in to grab their share of the many gifts previously suspended from it.

Perhaps the best time to visit Iquitos, however, is at the end of June (supposedly June 23–24, but actually spread over 3 or 4 days), when the main **Fiesta de San Juan** takes place. Focused around the small artesania market of San Juan (San Juan being the patron saint of Iquitos), some 4km from the city and quite close to the airport, it's the traditional time for partying and for eating *juanes*, delicious little balls of rice and chicken wrapped in jungle leaves; the best place for these is in San Juan itself. June is also the time for **Iquitos Week**, centred around the Fiesta de San Juan though tending to spread right across the month. In October the municipality's tourism directorate organizes an **international rafting competition**, which draws enthusiasts from every continent for a short five hour, nineteen-kilometre river race, plus a longer six-day race. Jetski racing is being planned, though the environmental issues might well outweigh the tourism benefits of this. At the end of the month there's the **Spirits of the Jungle** festival, which coincides with Halloween and All Souls. For more on this, contact the Iquitos tourist information office (p.467).

Iquitos

IQUITOS had its beginnings in 1739 when Jesuit José Bahamonde established settlements at Santa Barbara de Nanay and Santa Maria de Iquitos on the Río Mazán. It was a particularly daunting task, as the missionaries here faced the task of converting the fierce Iquito Indians, renowned as marksmen with their long poison-dart blowpipes. There are only one or two families of the Iquito tribe left, living on the upper Río Nanay, and these days the region is better known for the Yaguar, Bora and Witoto tribes, whose handicraft can be seen virtually everywhere you turn in the modern city.

The original town was founded in 1757 under the name of San Pablo de los Napeanos, but the present centre was established in 1864. By the end of the nineteenth century Iquitos was, along with Manaus in Brazil, one of *the* great rubber towns. From that era of grandeur a number of structures survive, but during the last century the town vacillated between prosperity – as far back as 1938, the area was explored for oil – and the depths of depression. However, its strategic position on the Amazon, which makes it accessible to large ocean-going ships from the distant Atlantic, has ensured its importance. At present, still buoyed by the export of timber, petroleum, tobacco and Brazil nuts, and dabbling heavily in the trade of wild animals, tropical fish and birds, as well as an insecticide called *barbasco*, long used by natives as a fish poison, Iquitos is in a period of quite wealthy expansion.

One interesting **environmental change** that seems to be happening at Iquitos is that the river has receded significantly from the main riverfront, which has necessitated moving the town's downriver port away from its centre. Some locals blame downstream canalization for this shift, others point to a drop in rainfall along the Amazon's headwaters in other parts; or it may be that increasing deforestation of the *ceja de selva* higher up means that, during the rainy season, rainwater simply runs off the surface, leaving none to gradually filter down during the dry season. Whatever the reason, the riverfront now stretches all the way from the old port and market of **Belén**, which the Amazon waters hardly reach any more, to the newer floating port of **Puerto Masusa**, 3km downriver.

Expeditions around Iquitos are the most developed in the Peruvian jungle, offering a wide and often surprising range of attractions. As usual, anything involving overnight stays is going cost a fair bit, though there are also cheap day-trips. With all organized visits to Indian villages in this area, expect the inhabitants to put on a quick show, with a few traditional dances and some singing, before they try to sell you their handicraft (occasionally over-enthusiastically). Prices range from $1 to $5 for necklaces, feathered items (mostly illegal to take out of the country), bark-cloth drawings, string bags (often excellent value) and blowguns; most people buy something, since the Indians don't actually charge for the visit. While the experience may leave you feeling somewhat ambivalent – the men, and particularly the women, only discard Western clothes for the performances – it's a preferable situation to the times when visits were imposed on communities by unscrupulous tour companies. Visitors are now these Indians' major source of income, and it seems that the Bora and Yaguar alike have found a niche they can easily exploit within the local tourist industry.

Arrival, information and getting around

If you've come by boat from Yurimaguas (5 days), Pucallpa (6–7 days), Leticia or Tabatinga (both 3 days), you'll arrive at **Puerto Masusa**, some eleven blocks northeast of the Plaza de Armas. Flights land at Iquitos **airport**, Aeropuerto Internacional de Francisco Secada Vignetta (℡094/260147), 5km southwest of town and connected by taxis ($3–4) and cheaper *motokars* ($2). Once you're off the plane, you're likely to be surrounded by a horde of desperate touts, all trying to persuade you to take their jungle tours or stay in their lodges; at this stage, the best thing to do is to avoid conversation with any of them, apart perhaps from saying you'll meet them in a couple of hours – which will give you time to get settled in and think about where you want to go and how much you are prepared to pay (see p.479 for advice on choosing guides and tours). **Buses** pull in on the Plaza de Armas and on calles Huallaga and La Condamine.

The local *consejo* run a helpful **tourist information** kiosk at the airport, though it's not always operational; the very helpful and friendly main tourist office is in the City Hall building on the Plaza de Armas at Napo 226 (Mon–Sat 9am–5.30pm, Sun 9am–noon; ℡094/235621, Ⓦwww.siturismo .org.pe), which also sells CDs of the region's music and videos of local attractions. They have brochures and maps, can advise on hotels, keep a list of registered tour operators and guides, and can help book accommodation. *Iquitos Review* newspaper produced in English and circulated in the Iquitos area, through hotels, tour offices and some shops; as well as being loaded with fascinating jungle tales, it is also a good source of information (published monthly from an office at Nanay 184 ℡094/243357). City tours of Iquitos itself are offered by many of the tour companies and some hotels (try the *Hostal La Pascana* for tickets); they take about three hours, usually leave daily at 9am and again at 2pm, costing around $9–10.

For **getting around** Iquitos you'll probably want to make use of the rattling **motokars**; alternatively, **motorbikes** can be rented – try the shop near the Ferretería Union (block 2 of Raymondi), or the one at Yavari 702. Expect to pay around $2 an hour or $10 for twelve hours (you'll need to show your passport and licence), and remember to check the brakes before leaving. For getting around town by **car**, try the office at Tute Pinglo 431 (℡094/235857). If you want to get onto the river itself, **canoes** can be rented very cheaply from the port at Bellavista (see p.475).

For **money change** it's best not to do it on the street with the *cambistas* who have a bit of a reputation (particularly at the corner of Prospero with Morona) for ripping tourists off, especially after around 8pm. Use one of the casas de cambio on Sargento Lores or the banks (see p.474). The street kids, too, have a growing reputation for picking pockets, but they're certainly not all bad and a new Transit House has been built for them in Iquitos, so things may improve.

Accommodation

Like every other jungle town, Iquitos is a little expensive, but the standard of its **hotels** is very good and the range allows for different budgets. Even a room in an average sort of place will include a shower and fan, and many others offer cable TV and minibars.

Budget

Hobo Hideout - The Great Amazon Safari and Trading Company Putumayo 437 ℡094/234099, Ⓦwww.safarisareus.net. A unique backpacker hostel in the heart of Iquitos, superb food as well (also functions as a restaurant for evening meals, but it's a good idea to book your meal – often

offering some sort of wild game – in the mornings); they offer a range of different rooms, some with own bathrooms. The owner, Jimmy Ford, also leads adventure jungle tours. ❷–❸

Hostal La Libertad Arica 361 ℡/℉094/235763. A fine backpackers' place; rooms have private bathrooms, hot water and cable TV, plus there's a

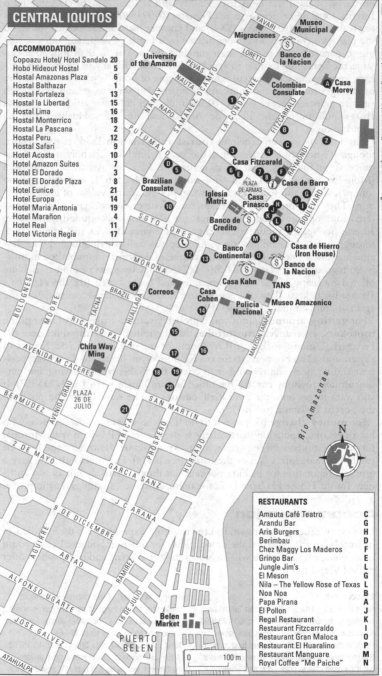

CENTRAL IQUITOS

Puerto Masusa (Brazil), Leticia (Colombia), Pucallpa & Yurimaguas ▶

▲ Airport & Quistacocha

ACCOMMODATION

Copoazu Hotel/ Hotel Sandalo	20
Hobo Hideout Hostal	5
Hostal Amazonas Plaza	6
Hostal Balthazar	1
Hostal Fortaleza	13
Hostal la Libertad	15
Hostal Lima	16
Hostal Monterrico	18
Hostal La Pascana	2
Hostal Peru	12
Hostal Safari	9
Hotel Acosta	10
Hotel Amazon Suites	7
Hotel El Dorado	3
Hotel El Dorado Plaza	8
Hotel Eunice	21
Hotel Europa	14
Hotel Maria Antonia	19
Hotel Marañon	4
Hotel Real	11
Hotel Victoria Regia	17

RESTAURANTS

Amauta Café Teatro	C
Arandu Bar	G
Aris Burgers	H
Berimbau	D
Chez Maggy Los Maderos	F
Gringo Bar	E
Jungle Jim's	L
El Meson	G
Nila – The Yellow Rose of Texas	L
Noa Noa	B
Papa Pirana	A
El Pollon	J
Regal Restaurant	K
Restaurant Fitzcarraldo	I
Restaurant Gran Maloca	O
Restaurant El Huaralino	P
Restaurant Manguare	M
Royal Coffee "Me Paiche"	N

Map labels

Museo Municipal
Yavari
Migraciones
Loretto
Banco de la Nacion
University of the Amazon
Pevas
Casa Morey
Colombian Consulate
Fitzcarrald
Casa Fitzcarald
Casa de Barro
Plaza de Armas
Casa Pinasco
Iglesia Matriz
Brazilian Consulate
Banco de Credito
El Boulevard
Banco Continental
Casa de Hierro (Iron House)
Banco de la Nacion
Casa Kahn
TANS
Correos
Casa Cohen
Policia Nacional
Museo Amazonico
Chifa Way Ming
Malecon Tarapaca
Río Amazonas
Plaza 26 de Julio
San Martin
Belen Market
Puerto Belen

Streets

Nanay, Napo, Putumayo, Samanez Ocampo, Nauta, La Condamine, Raimondi, Sgto Lores, Morona, Brazil, Tacna, Huallaga, Ricardo Palma, Avenida M Caceres, Bolognesi, Moore, Bermudez, Avenida Grau, Arica, Prospero, Hurtado, 2 de Mayo, Garcia Sanz, 9 de Diciembre, J C Arana, Aguirre, Abtao, Alfonso Ugarte, Jose Galvez, Atahualpa, Ramirez, 16 de Julio

N

0   100 m

restaurant. It's also home to a good tour company (see p.482). **②**–**③**

Hostal Lima Prospero 549 ℡ 094/235152. Rooms have private bath and fans; it doesn't look much from the outside but is surprisingly pleasant, possessing a certain jungle flavour, with parrots on the patio. Good value. **②**

Hostal Monterico Arica 633 ℡/℗ 094/235395. Dark rooms and somewhat basic, but it is clean, has a nice enough atmosphere and is safe. **③**

Hostal La Pascana Pevas 133 ℡094/231418, ℗233466, ℮hs_pascana@lima.business.com.pe. Appealing doubles based around a small courtyard close to the river, less than two blocks from the Plaza de Armas. Clean, friendly, with book exchange and travel service; popular with travellers, it offers a ventilated, quiet haven from Iquitos sometimes hectic street life. Best to book in advance. **③**

Hostal Peru Prospero 318 ℡ 094/234961. Good value, if rather down-at-heel, though still popular with locals and travellers alike, perhaps because of its old-fashioned architecture and fittings. It has shared bathrooms, fans in all rooms and for $2 extra you can have cable TV. **②**

Hotel Baltazar Contamine 256 ℡094/232240. Slightly run-down but safe and central, with friendly service. Rooms with air-conditioning and TV available, or you pay less for just a fan; has hot water. **②**–**④**

Hotel Sandalo Prospero 616 ℡094/234761, ℗243643, ℮comesa@iquitos.net. A good value, this place has pretty comfortable rooms and includes breakfast in the price; they will also arrange for airport transfers. Rooms have cable TV and minibars; the lobby has a nice jungle feel. **②**–**③**

Moderate

Copoazu Hotel Jr Prospero 644 ℡ 094/232373, ℮hcopoazu_iqtpe@manguare.com.pe. A modern hotel with comfortable rooms; fairly central location offering good value, airport transfer, 24hr room service, money change and a safe if required. **③**–**④**

Hostal Safari Napo 118 ℡094/233828. Less than a block from the plaza, with clean and comfortable rooms, though a little dark. It can be noisy on weekend evenings. **④**

Hotel Acosta Huallaga corner with Calvo ℡/℗094/231761. Clean and quite smart, though not all that friendly. Same owners as the plusher *Hotel Victoria Regia* (see below). **⑤**

Hotel Amazon Suites Napo 274, on the Plaza de Armas ℡094/243088. A rather odd place, aimed mostly at the business traveller, offering rooms and suites, a small pool and Jacuzzi. **⑤**–**⑦**

Hotel Eunice Arica 780 ℡ 094/233405, ℗243607. Some amazingly large rooms, some with stereos, TV and minibar. Very friendly and good value. **⑤**

Hotel Europa Prospero 494 ℡094/231123, ℗235483, ℮heuropa@telematic.com.pe. Central and pleasant, with a restaurant and bar. All rooms have cable TV and private bathrooms. **⑤**

Hotel Marañón Fitzcarrald with Nauta 285 ℡094/242673, ℗231737. A new, centrally located hotel with small pool, restaurant/bar, and cable TV plus minibars in all rooms; this is a good-value, mid-range choice; price includes breakfast. **⑤**

Hotel Maria Antonia Prospero 616 ℡094/234761, ℗234264. Friendly staff and a pleasant enough place, though nothing special. Cable TV and a laundry service are offered. **④**

Expensive

El Dorado Hotel Napo 362 ℡094/232574, ℗221985, ℮dorado@tvs.com.pe. A good hotel with a small pool, less than a block from the Plaza de Armas. **⑥**

Hostal Amazon Garden C Pantago 417, by the Parque Zonal, just off Yavari ℡094/236140, ℮amazonas@amazongardenhotel.com.pe; or contact through Amazon Tours and Cruises (see p.482). A new hotel with comfortable air-conditioned rooms, hot showers, probably the nicest outdoor pool in the city, efficient service, and a restaurant and bar. **⑥**

Hostal Amazonas Plaza de Armas, corner of Napo and Fitzcarrald ℡/℗094/242431. A smart, if uninspiring, modern place, with pleasant, plain rooms that have cable TV, minibars, and hot water. **⑥**

Hotel El Dorado Plaza Napo 258, Plaza de Armas ℡094/222555, ℗224304, ℗www.eldoradoplaza.com. A superb hotel, arguably the best in the Amazon, and the first-ever 5-star in Iquitos. There's the expected great service, a nice pool, a *maloca*-style bar, quality restaurant, and some fantastic rainforest-inspired paintings by the local artist Francisco Grippa (see p.470) scattered about. The vast, air-conditioned lobby features a glass lift rising to all six floors. **⑧**

Hotel Victoria Regia Ricardo Palma 252 ℡094/231983, ℗232499, ℮chasa@meganet.com.pe. A luxurious place with a small pool, good security and sterling service. **⑧**

Real Hotel Malecón Tarapaca ℡094/231011. The former *Gran Hotel Iquitos*, this really doesn't look so grand today, despite its location right between El Boulevard and the Malecón Tarapaca. Nevertheless it seems to do good conference trade, offering 76 rooms with commanding views towards the Amazon, and it's comfortable. **⑥**

The Town

Much of Iquitos' appeal is derived from being the starting point for excursions into the rainforest (see p.476), but the town is an interesting place in its own right. Like Manaus, Iquitos is world-famous for its architecture, mainly created during the rubber boom. Many of the late eighteenth- and early nineteenth-century buildings are decorated with Portuguese tiles (*azulejos*), some of which are brilliantly extravagant in their Moorish inspiration, and the **Casa Kahn**, on block 1 of Sargento Lores, is a particularly fine example.

On the southeast conrer of the **Plaza de Armas**, you'll find the unusual, majestic **Casa de Fierro** (Iron House), now home to a restaurant, but originally created by Eiffel for the 1889 Paris exhibition and shipped out to Iquitos in pieces by one of the rubber barons to be erected here in the 1890s.

Outside, the plaza is still weirdly dominated by the towering presence of a much more massive multi-storey hotel building, dilapidated and deserted, which was built in the boom of the early 1980s – initiated by the then President Belaunde's drive to open up the Amazon in economic terms – before the economy slumped and terrorism temporarily slowed tourism in the region right down. These days its sole function appears to be as a high foundation for antennas. The plaza's modern fountain is attractive when illuminated at night, though its sound is generally drowned out by the mototaxis and cars whizzing around the square. On the southwest side of the plaza is the **Iglesia Matriz**, the main Catholic church, whose interior paintings depicting biblical scenes are by the Loretano artists Americo Pinasco and Cesar Calvo de Araujo (Loreto is the *departmento* Iquitos is located in).

One block southeast of Plaza de Armas are the two best sections of the **old riverfront**, El Boulevard and Malecón Tarapaca, where there is some major restoration going on. **El Boulevard** is the busiest of the two areas, especially at night, full of bars and restaurants and with a small **amphitheatre** where some kind of entertainment occurs most nights, from mini-circuses to mime, comedy and music. The **Malecón Tarapaca** boasts some fine old mansions, one of which, at Tarapaca 262, with lovely nineteenth-century *azulejo* work, is presently one of the town's better bakeries. Also on Malecón Tarapaca is the municipal museum, **Museo Amazonico** (Mon–Fri 8am–1pm & 3–7pm, Sat 8–noon; $1, 60¢ for students), devoted to the region's natural history and tribal culture. Its collection includes some unusual life-sized human figures in traditional dress from different Amazon tribes; each fibreglass sculpture was made from a cast that had encapsulated the live subject for an hour or so. There's also a gallery devoted to previous *prefectos* of Loreto, some oil paintings, a few stuffed animals and a small military museum.

Amazon Art Gallery

In the Punchana sector of Iquitos, the **Amazon Art Gallery**, Trujillo 438 (call for an appointment ☎094/253120), exhibits the work of the Peruvian painter Francisco Grippa and a few other national and local artists. Grippa, who lives and works mainly in Pevas, arrived in the Amazon in the late 1970s after being educated in Europe and the US, and his work, described variously as figurative and expressionist, displays an obsession with light and colour, focusing on subjects such as Shipibo Indians, jungle birds and rainforest landscapes; you can see examples at ⓦwww.art-and-soul.com/grippa. There's more art to be found at **Galería Amauta**, Nauta 248, where there are exhibitions of oil paintings, caricatures and photographs, mostly by local artists.

△ Toco Toucan

Puerto Belén

The most memorable part of town, **Puerto Belén** looms out of the main town at a point where the Amazon, until recently, joined the Río Itaya inlet. Consisting almost entirely of wooden huts raised on stilts and, until a few years ago, also floating on rafts, the district has earned fame among travellers as the "Venice of the Peruvian Jungle". Actually more Far Eastern than Italian in appearance, it has changed little over its hundred or so years, remaining a poor shanty settlement trading in basics like bananas, manioc, fish, turtle and crocodile meat. Whilst filming *Fitzcarraldo* here, Herzog merely had to make sure that no motorized canoes appeared on screen: virtually everything else, including the style of the *barriada* dwellings, looks exactly like a slumtown from the nineteenth century. The annual flooding by the Río Amazonas here means that all the wooden buildings close to the river side of Belén are on wooden stilts or two or three storeys tall, allowing the occupants to retreat upstairs in the high-water season. Ask for directions to Pasaje Paquito, the busy herbalist alley in the heart of this frenetic Amazon river economic community, which synthesizes the very rich flavour of the place.

Eating and drinking

Food in Iquitos is exceptionally good for a jungle town, specializing in fish dishes but catering pretty well for any taste. Eating out is something of a popular pastime in the lively, even energetic evenings, which usually stretch out well into the early hours of the morning, particularly at weekends. We've given telephone numbers where reservations are advised. There are some good bars and pubs which serve excellent grub, such as the *Fitzcarraldo* and the *Arandu* bar on the Boulevard. The first block of Putumayo, very close to the plaza, is surprisingly becoming rapidly known as "Little England" for bars like *Jungle Jim's Pub*, *Regal Restaurant/Bar*, *Mad Mick's Trading Post* and, perhaps incongruously, *Nila – The Yellow Rose of Texas*. This is always a busy spot at night and arguably the best area for drinking.

Anita Bar Fitzcarrald 232. A cool and dark bar, with even cooler beer, close to the plaza.

Arandu Bar El Boulevard. A pleasant atmosphere and very popular for drinks early in the evening.

Aris Burgers Prospero 127 ☎094/231479. Actually serving more than burgers (though these are quite delicious), including plates with a variety of river fish and even *caiman* meat, plus the best French fries in town. It's the most popular meeting spot in Iquitos and a bit of a landmark for taxi and *motokar* drivers.

Chez Maggy Los Maderos Raymondi 218. Reasonable pasta and pizzas in quite a pleasant environment, but somehow pizzas and hot tropical weather don't seem to mix that well.

Gringo Bar Arica 108. A popular meeting point for drinks, though with little character, virtually in the lobby of the *Hotel Amazonas Plaza*.

Heladeria La Favorita Prospero 413. A roomy café specializing in juices and delicious jungle-fruit-flavoured ice creams.

El Jardin Loreto 453. This is the best vegetarian place in town, serving great combinations of jungle and regular produce; good juices too.

Jugeria Paladar Prospero 245. A small café serving excellent juices and local snacks.

Jungle Jim's Pub Putumayo 168 ☎094/235294. Very central, with tables inside and out on the street, this is the newest English pub in town. *Jungle Jim's* serves a superb range of drinks as well as great regional cuisine (an excellent place to eat alligator if that's what you feel like after a jungle trip). Will accept most major credit cards and stays open as late as customers want.

El Meson El Boulevard ☎094/231857. A popular restaurant serving a wide range of local dishes – try the *tacacho* (plantains and pork), or *pescado a la Loretano* (fish). It's not cheap, though a good meal can be had for well under $10, and the location is perfect, right at the heart of El Boulevard and with tables out front.

Nila - The Yellow Rose of Texas Putumayo 180 ☎094/241010. Very tasty local dishes and reasonably priced menu; good location near the plaza with tables outside on the street. Great coffee.

El Pollon Prospero 151. A spacious restaurant and café fronting the Plaza de Armas. Popular with locals, especially at lunchtime, it serves a wide

range of tasty meals, cool juices and ice creams.
Regal Restaurant Putumayo 282 ☎094/222732.
Upstairs in the Casa de Fierro, this is a busy place with a very pleasant, almost colonial ambience, run by the British Consul and his wife. The food, mainly traditional local dishes, is great, plus there are ceiling fans, fine views over the Plaza de Armas from Eiffel's iron balcony, and a large pool table inside. *Paiche* fish is a speciality.
Restaurant Fitzcarraldo Napo 100
☎094/243434. A great place, close to the nightly action and located on the corner of the Malecón in the old headquarters of the once very successful Orton Bolivian Rubber Company; it was bought from them by Fitzcarrald in 1897, just two months before he drowned on a trip into the jungle. It isn't cheap but serves some of the best salads in town plus good pastas, fish and comida criolla.
Restaurant Gran Maloca Sargento Lores 170
☎094/233126 ✉maloca@tvs.com.pe. One of Iquitos' finest restaurants, lavishly decorated, with jungle paintings adorning the walls and a high-

ceilinged, cool interior. Food is excellent, with nice jungle ice creams.
Restaurant El Huaralino Huallaga 490
☎094/223300. Some of the best comida criolla in town with great set-lunch menus; so popular with locals that it's often hard to get a table. Large and airy in a fairly central, ventilated location.
Restaurant Manguare Jr Prospero 251. Set-lunch menus here are very good value; the food is pretty good in this busy little environment, full of office workers in the early weekday afternoons.
Royal Coffee "Me Paiche" Putumayo 133
☎094/231304. Decent pizzas, pastas and sandwiches, plus a range of other meals, snacks and drinks. Reasonably priced and usually fairly quiet. If you phone in an order, they can also deliver to your hotel.
El Sitio Block 4 of Sargento Lores. A very creative snack bar-cum-restaurant, it's inexpensive and produces delicious *anticuchos*, tamales, *juanes* and fruit juices; best to get there before 9pm, or you'll miss out on the tastiest treats.

Nightlife

Whilst mainly an extension of eating out and meeting friends in the main streets, the **nightlife** in Iquitos is pretty good, and there are a number of highly charged discos, clubs and bars worth knowing about. They're quite easy to locate, especially if you are up and about after 11pm in the downtown areas, particularly around the Plaza de Armas and nearby Malecón Tarapaca.

Iquitos has an unusually active gay scene for a Peruvian jungle town, mainly due to many gays fleeing here during the terrorist years (the mid-1980s to the early 1990s), when they suffered persecution, and there are now four or five dedicated **gay clubs** here.

Agricobank Pablo Rosell 300 ☎094/236113. Live *chicha* and other Latino styles.
Amauta Café Teatro Nauta 250 ☎094/233109. Different music – from jazzy jungle creole to folk-lore and female singers performing romantic ballards – from day to day. It also serves drinks and snacks, and there are tables outside. Mon–Sat 10pm–2am.
Arfil Mañoso Sargento Lores S-2 ☎094/233413. A bit of a pickup joint with quite a few girls that you're expected to pay for, though it does play some reasonable music sometimes and has a fun atmosphere. It's also about 14 blocks northwest from the centre of town. Mon–Sat 10pm–late; $6 entrance.
Berimbau Putumayo 467. One of the newest and flashiest nightclubs in Iquitos; very central and pretty hectic. It plays good rock and Latin dance music most nights, serves cool drinks at several bars on different levels by different dance floors. Good air-conditioning, which is pretty important here.

Noa Noa Fitzcarrald 298 ☎094/242310. Easily identified after 11.30pm by the huge number of flashy motorbikes lined up outside, this is the liveliest Iquitos club, attracting young and old, gringo and Iquiteño alike. It has three bars and plays lots of Latino music, including the latest technocumbia. Mon–Sat 10pm–late; $6 entrance.
Papa Pirana Loreto 220 ☎094/242333. This club has the biggest dance floor and frequently presents live shows of music, dance and comedy; very popular with locals and tourists alike. One of the hottest scenes in town at weekends. Tues–Sun opens 10pm.

Gay clubs

Bar La 4.40 opposite the Hospital Regional, in Punchana. Good music and a reasonable bar.
Calipso on block 10 of Putumayo. Another fun gay bar, located in an old house and playing ambient and tropical music. Not exclusively gay. Thurs–Sat midnight–5am; 50¢.

Las Castañitas in front of the electricity power plant in the suburb of Punchana. Best to take a taxi to this glitzy little joint, because it's a little hard to find.

Discoteca 2003 on block 25 of Putumayo. Located a little way out of the centre of town, but a lively and pleasant spot which usually gets going after 11pm. Thurs–Sat.

Tragoteca La Jarra on Av Quinones, near the Pamachicha restaurant. Small but popular, this music bar kicks off from around 10pm Thurs–Sun evenings.

Listings

Airlines Aero Continente, Prospero 232 (℡094/235990), fly daily to Lima, with connections for Cusco and other main Peruvian destinations; TANS, for Pucallpa, Tarapoto and Lima, Sargento Lores 127 (℡094/234632); for very reasonably priced flights to Requena, Angamos, and Santa Rosa there's Grupo 42 whose office is at Prospero 215 (℡094/221071 or 221086).

Banks and exchange Banco de Credito, Putumayo 201; Banco Wiese, Prospero 282, for MasterCard; Banco de la Nación; Banco Continental, Prospero Block 3, with a 24hr ATM, and also on Sargento Lores, block 1; Interbanc, Prospero 336; Banco Latino, Prospero 332; and the Banco del Trabajo, block 1 of Prospero, has an ATM taking Visa. Casa de cambio, corner of Sargento Lores with Prospero. The only place said to be reasonably safe for changing with *cambistas* (especially okay with Genaro Sullo, Fernando Echegalier and Danilo Melendez) on the street is at the corner of Morona with Arica, by the post office.

Consulates Brazil, Morona 238 ℡094/232081; Colombia, corner of Nauta with Callao ℡094/231461; UK, Putumayo 182 ℡094/222732.

Courier services A DHL service is available at Prospero 648 (℡094/232131).

Instituto Nacional de Cultura Huallaga 274, ⓦwww.siturismo.org.pe.

Internet facilities *Snack Bar Internet*, Fitzcarrald 131, is a groovy bar with some 20 terminals, quite fast and less than half a block from the plaza; *Jungle Net*, Putumayo 382, a very good 24hr Internet café, with good rates and service, also offers national and international phone service; *Coconet*, Fitzcarrald 131, is a good Internet café; *La Real Internet*, Prospero 582, close to the *Hotel Europa*, reasonably fast; *Cabinas Internet*, Prospero 507, has a dark interior and isn't quite as fast as the others, but cheaper.

Jungle supplies Mad Mick's Trading Post, Putumayo 184b. Very centrally located, this shop has been specifically established to provide the basic essentials for a jungle trip, including rubber boots, rainproof ponchos, sun-hats, fishing tackle etc; run by an amenable, if eccentric, Englishman and his Peruvian wife. They will rent out rubber boots, $8 hire cost ($4 charge, $4 deposit), with deposit returned in exchange for boots after jungle trip.

Laundry LavaCenter, Prospero 459 ℡094/242136; Lavandería Imperial, Putumayo 150; Lavandería Popular, C Loreto 640.

Migraciones Block 4 of Nauta ℡094/235371. Mon–Fri 8am–1pm & 1.30–4.30pm.

Pacaya Samiria National Reserve Office Ricardo Palma 113, third floor ℡094/233980, ⓔrnps-zrg@aeci.org.pe. Good for maps, information on the National Reserve and permission to enter it.

Pharmacies Botica Amazonicas, Prospero 699 ℡094/231832; Botica Virgen de Chapi, Prospero 461.

Photography Foto Aspinar, Prospero 271; Foto Digital, Prospero 467; Tema Color, Prospero 283.

Police Tourist police, Sargento Lores 834 ℡094/242801.

Post office SERPOST, Arica 482. Mon–Sat 8am–7.30pm.

Shopping Artesanias La Jungla, Prospero 483 (baskets, mats, hammocks, gourds, postcards and souvenirs); Artesanias Sudamerica, Casa de Fierro, Plaza de Armas, Prospero 175 (hammocks and alpaca goods); Artesanias, Prospero 572 and Artesanias Todo Peru, Prospero 685 (hammocks, hats, jewellery, musical instruments and souvenirs); Bazar Daniela, 9 de Diciembre 234 (useful trade items for visiting local villages, such as cloth, beads and coloured threads); Comercial Cardinal, Prospero 300 (fishing tackle, compasses, knives); Taller de Arte, Prospero 593/595 (carved wooden sculptures and household artefacts).

Telephones Sargento Flores 321. Daily 7am–11pm.

Short trips and tours from Iquitos

The closest place you can get to without a guide or long river trip is **Padre Isla**, an island opposite town in the midst of the Amazon, over 14km long and with beautiful beaches during the dry season. It's easily reached by canoe from Belén or the main waterfront. Alternatively, some 4km northeast of the centre of Iquitos, just fifteen minutes by bus, is the suburb of **Bellavista** on the Río Nanay. Now the main access point for smaller boats to all the rivers, there's a rather small (and smelly) market selling jungle products, plus some bars and shops clustered around a port, where you can rent canoes for short trips at around $5 an hour. Like Iquitos, Bellavista has recently been experiencing its highest and lowest recorded water levels, with all of the associated flooding and drying up; the bars sit on their stilts high above dried mud during the dry season, and the boats are moored some forty metres further out than they used to be. From Bellavista you can set out by canoe ferry for **Playa Nanay**, the best beach around Iquitos, where bars and cafés are springing up to cater to the weekend crowds. Be aware that currents here are pretty strong, and although there are lifeguards, drownings have occurred.

About twenty minutes by boat from Bellavista, involving a fifteen minute walk from the beach village in the dry season, but accessible all the way when the river is high, is the fascinating **Pilpintuwasi Butterfly Farm** (Tues–Sun 9am–5pm; ☎094/232665, ✉pilpintuwasi@hotmil.com; $5, $3 for students); located near the village of Padre Cocha, it allows you to explore a fantastic array of butterflies in a natural environment, plus a number of jungle animals, all rescued from certain death (rather than being bought for display).

From the corner of Bermudez and Moore, behind the church on the Plaza 28 de Julio, microbuses go to the lagoon at **Quistococha** (a 20–30min journey; $1 entry). Taxis and mototaxis can be picked up anywhere in town, but from the Plaza de Armas should cost around $3 or $5, respectively; if you like, you can also try the hot, three-hour walk there (13.5km); head along the airport road, turning left at the last fork before the airport. One kilometre long, and up to 8m deep, the waters have been taken over by the Ministry of Fishing for the breeding of giant *paiche*, and there's an interesting **zoo** and a small site **museum** of jungle natural history, as well as a small lakeside beach, restaurant and bar and an aviary.

On the western edge of Iquitos, an affluent of the Nanay forms a long lake called **Moronacocha**, a popular resort for swimming and water-skiing; some 5km further out (just before the airport) another lake, **Rumococha**, has facilities on the Río Nanay for fishing and hunting. Beyond this, still on the Nanay, are the popular weekend beach and white sands of **Santa Clara**. The village of **Santo Tomas** is only 16km from here; a worthwhile trip and well connected by local buses, this agricultural and fishing village, located on the banks of the Río Nanay, is renowned for its jungle artesania, and has another beach, on the **Lago Mapacocha**, where you can swim and canoe. There's also one really good fish restaurant here, on the riverfront, run by the Chrichigno family (they also rent jet skis and water skis); it's better during the day, before the mosquitoes come out. If you get the chance, try to make your visit coincide with Santo Tomas' **fiesta** (Sept 23–25), a huge party with dancing and *chicha* music.

Short tours in the area include a boat trip that sets out from Bellavista and travels up the Río Momón to visit a community of Yaguar or Bora Indians at **San Andres**, just beyond *Amazon Camp* (see p.480), then goes downriver to **Serpentario Las Boas**, an anaconda farm near the mouth of the Momón. Here you can see and touch anacondas and more (boas, sloths and monkeys, to name a few), slithering around in what is essentially someone's backyard. The whole trip lasts around two hours and costs about $5–10 per person (including a $2 tip at Serpentario Las Boas), depending on the size of group. A longer tour, lasting around four hours and costing $10–20, includes the above but also takes you onto the Río Amazonas to visit an alligator farm at **Barrio Florida** and to watch dolphins playing in the river.

Moving on

From Puerto Masusa – the port area in northern Iquitos for downriver boats – **speedboats** go downstream to Santa Rosa, Tabatinga and Leticia (all on the three-way frontier, see p.483) several times a week, taking up to ten hours there and twelve hours back, for around $40. The main companies have their offices on Raymondi, just a few blocks from the Plaza de Armas: Expreso Loreto, Raymondi 384 (℡094/238021); Transporte Itaya, Loreto 141 (℡094/238690); Transtur, Raymondi 328 (℡094/242367); and Transportes Rapido, Raymondi 346. There is also Brastours, Jr Condamine 384 (℡094/223232), who specialize in boats and flights to Tabatinga, Brazil.

Larger **riverboats** go upstream from Puerto Masusa to Lagunas (3 days) Yurimaguas (5 days), Pucallpa (6–7 days), or downstream to Pevas (about 1 day), Leticia and Tabatinga (both 3 days). Check with the commercial river transporters for a rough idea of departure dates and times, and keep an eye out for the highly recommended *Juliana* (used by Herzog in his film) and the *Oro Negro*, which costs $40 to the border, including food but not drink. Take along a good book, plenty of extra food and drink, a hammock, a sweater and one or two blankets; it's usually possible to sling your hammock up and sleep free of charge on the larger boats in the days leading up to the unpredictable departure. It's also advisable to secure your baggage with a chain to a permanent fixture on the deck and also keep bags locked, as **theft** is quite common.

Around Iquitos

The massive river system around Iquitos offers some of the best access to Indian villages, lodges and primary rainforest in the entire Amazon. If you want to go it alone, colectivo boats run up and down the **Río Amazonas** more or less daily, and although you won't get deep into the forest without a guide or the facilities offered by the lodge and tour companies, you can visit some of the larger riverine settlements on your own.

One of the first major settlements on the banks of the Amazon is the small river town of **Tamshiyacu**, en route to Nauta upstream; a couple of hostels, including the *Hospedaje Mercedes* (❶), just beyond the plaza, and the *Hospedaje Dianita* (❶) a little beyond, accompanied by a few bars and stores, make it a useful stopping point, if you need one. A long day's ride (130km) further **upstream from Iquitos** lies **Nauta**, at the mouth of the Río Marañón. South from Nauta, **Bagazan** is another couple of hours (40km) further up the Río Ucayali, after which it's another 50km to **Requena** (see p.494), at the mouth of the Río Tapiche. A new road from Iquitos to Nauta has considerably shortened the journey and has begun to open up tourism to the west of Nauta on the ríos Marañón and Tigre and into the Pacaya Samiria National Reserve (see below), which is only a short boat ride from Nauta, though the best sectors of the reserve are arguably easier to get to from Lagunas. The upper Río Tigre is also excellent for its access to wildlife, but it's at least three days away by boat.

Lagunas

There are excellent organized tours to take from **LAGUNAS**, close to the Pacaya Samiria Reserve and some three days upstream from Nauta ($10–25 depending on whether you take hammock space or a shared cabin). The first day takes you to the "start" of the Río Amazonas, where the Ucayali and the Marañón rivers merge; the second day carries you along the Marañón towards Lagunas, where you arrive on the third day. It's also some twelve hours downstream from Yurimaguas and accessible from there by colectivo boat ($5). There are a couple of **hostels** in Lagunas: the *Hostal Montalban* (**②**), on the Plaza de Armas, is basic and small but suffices, as does the slightly cheaper *Hostal La Sombra* (**①**) at Jr Vasquez 1121.

Lagunas is the main starting point for trips into the huge **Pacaya Samiria National Reserve**, comprising around two million hectares of virgin rainforest (about 1.5 percent of the total landmass of Peru) leading up to the confluence between the Marañón and the Huallaga rivers, two of the largest Amazon headwaters and possessing between them the largest protected area of seasonally flooded jungle in the Peruvian Amazon. The reserve is a swampland during the rainy season (Dec–March), when the streams and rivers all rise, arguably comparable to the Tambopata-Candamo Reserved Zone in southeastern Peru or the Pantanal swamps of southwestern Brazil in the density of astonishingly visible wildlife. It's possible to arrange **guides** here (about $10 a day per person, less if you're in a group) and to spend as long as you like in the

reserve. This region is home to the Cocoma tribe whose main settlement is Tipishca, where the native community are now directly involved in eco-tourism. It's quite possible to take a public ferryboat or *lancha* up to Pacaya Samiria, but advisable not to give yourself too tight a schedule for the outing as a whole (partly because you may want to stay longer than you think but also partly due to unreliable public transport services). You should of course be well prepared with mosquito nets, hammocks, insect repellent and all the necessary food and medicines (see p.462). Officially you should obtain permission from the reserve office (see Listings p.463) to get into the reserve, but not everyone does. The reserve office also provides maps and information on the region, when available. It's good for visitors to this area to remember that around 90,000 people, mostly indigenous communities, still live in the reserve's forest. In recent years some of the communities have been collaborating on ecological conservation projects, such as sustainable management plans for the aquatic river turtles and certain fish species.

From Lagunas, it's possible to explore the Tibilo area, which is rich in birds and monkeys. In the dry season, the lower Pacaya river area is excellent for bird-spotting, around the temporary ponds and lakesides. This is one of the best jungle regions in South America, not least because of its massive extent and the seasonal flooding which significantly increases the wildlife safari options.

Pevas

Downstream from Iquitos lies **PEVAS**, some 190km to the east and reached in a day by colectivo riverboat or in a few hours by speedboat. The oldest town in the Peruvian Amazon, it's an attractive, largely palm-thatched town and still a frontier place. The economy here is based primarily on fishing (visit the *mercado*, where produce is brought in by boat every day), and dugout canoes are the main form of transport, propelled by characteristically ovoid-bladed and beautifully carved paddles, which are often sold as souvenirs, sometimes painted with designs. The Witoto and Bora Indians, largely concentrated around Pevas, actually arrived here in the 1930s after being relocated from the Colombian Amazon. They are now virtually in everyday contact with the riverine society of Pevas, producing quality artefacts for sale to passers-by and yet retaining much of their traditional knowledge of songs, dances, and legends, plus significant ethno-pharmacological practice in rainforest medicine. The nearby Bora village of Puca Urquillo is a good example, a large settlement based around a Baptist church and school, whose founders moved here from the Colombian side of the Río Putumayo during the hardships of the rubber era rather than be enslaved.

Artist Francisco Grippa also lives in Pevas, though his work is actually exhibited in Iquitos at the Amazon Art Gallery (see p.470), while the surrounding flood forest is home to hundreds of caimans and significant birdlife, including several types of parrots, eagles and kingfishers. The area is good for bird- and butterfly-watching, and November, in particular, is a great time to study orchids and bromeliads in bloom; it's also noted for its fishing – piranha being one of the easiest kinds to catch. A number of local Indian groups can be visited, including the Bora, the Witoto and the less-visited Ocainas. Costs are from $60 per person per day, with extra for speedboat transport from Iquitos.

For a good **place to stay**, try the *Casa de la Loma* (write to GreenTracks, PO Box 555, Iquitos; ☎/⒡094/221184, ⓦwww.greentracks.com; ❷), run by an American nurse, also contactable in the US (write to 10 Town Plaza 231, Suite

231, Durango, CO 81301; ☎1-800/9-Monkey, ℻970/247-8378). Avelardo is a recommended local guide who speaks good English and is very knowledgeable about the local culture, flora and wildlife. Set on a small hill close to Pevas, the lodge was set up by two nurses from Oregon who operate a free clinic here for the two thousand or so local inhabitants. They have five large bedrooms with shared bathrooms, and there's electricity, a refrigerator and a kitchen. Visits can be customized.

Lodges, cruises and guides

If you're planning on an expedition beyond the limited network of roads around Iquitos, you'll have to take an organized trip with a **lodge operator**, a **river cruise** or hire a **freelance guide**. The larger local entrepreneurs have quite a grip on the market, and even the few guides who remain more or less independent are hard to bargain with since so much of their work comes through the larger agents. That said, they mostly have well worked-out itineraries, though you should always deal with an established office – check out which companies are registered at the tourist office in Iquitos – and insist on a written contract and receipt. Be aware that there's no shortage of con artists among the many **touts** around town, some of whom brandish brochures that have nothing to do with them. Under no circumstances should you hand them any money.

Before approaching anyone it's a good idea to know more or less what you want in terms of time in the forest, total costs, personal needs and comforts, and things you expect to see. A general rule of thumb is that any expedition of fewer than five days is unlikely to offer more wildlife than a few birds, some monkeys, and maybe a crocodile if you're lucky; any serious attempt to visit virgin forest and see wildlife in its natural habitat requires a week or more. That said, if Iquitos is your main contact with the Amazon and you're unlikely to return here, you can rent a boat for an overnight trip from upwards of $40–50 per person. A group in low season may well be able to negotiate a three-day trip for as little as $25–30 per person per day, though there will be little guarantee of quality at this price. One or two of the smaller camps sometimes offer deals from as little as $25, but make sure they provide all the facilities you require. There's an almost infinite amount of jungle to be rewardingly explored in any direction from Iquitos. One of the less-visited but nevertheless interesting areas – at least in terms of being relatively accessible yet still quite untouched and wild – lies east between Iquitos and the Brazilian border. Pevas, for instance, is a good base (see opposite) for making river trips more or less independently, at least without going through an Iquitos tour company, though it's always a good idea to make use of local guides.

Lodges

Guided tours require some kind of camp set-up or tourist **lodge** facilities. There are two main types of jungle experience available from Iquitos – what

---

Tourist Protection Service

If your jungle trip really doesn't match what the agency led you to believe when selling you the tickets, it would help future visitors if you report this to the local tourist office and/or the 24-hour hotline of the **Tourist Protection Service** in Iquitos (☎094/233409, ℮postmaster@indecopi.gob.pe).

Peruvian tour operators describe as "conventional" (focusing on lodge stays) and what they describe as "adventure trips" (going deeper into the jungle). Prices given are per person.

Amazon Camp contact through Amazon Tours and Cruises (see p.482). A pleasant conventional lodge on the Río Momón between the Yaguar and Bora Indian villages. This place can be visited in a day-trip, though it's more fun and better value to stay longer. Around $100 per night.

Amazon Explorama CEIBA TOPS contact Explorama, Av La Marina 340, Iquitos (☎094/253301, ℻252533, ℮ceibatops@explorama.com, ❀www.explorama.com), or Box 445, Iquitos; toll-free in the US ☎1-800/707-5275. Explorama are the top operator in the region, with over 35 years' experience and over 500 beds across their various lodges and locations; they aren't cheap, but do offer great quality. Explorama also now have their own very well-equipped river ferryboat – the *Amazon Queen* (see opposite). Some 40km from Iquitos, this is the most luxurious lodge in the Peruvian Amazon, with a fantastic jungle swimming pool, bars and dining areas, surrounded by 40 hectares of primary forest and 160 hectares of *chacra* and secondary growth. Accommodation is in smart conventional bungalows with air-conditioning and flushing toilets, or in simpler bungalow-huts. There are 75 rooms. Can be visited in conjunction with other Explorama lodges; $100–400 per day, depending on size of group, length of trip and the number of lodges visited.

Amazon Explorama CTS Field Station (Amazon Conservatory for Tropical Studies) contact Explorama (see above). An hour's walk from the company's *ExplorNapo Lodge* (see below), this particular establishment owns some 750 hectares of primary forest and was designed for research though it's available for short visits and is quite comfortable, with separate rooms and good shared dining and bathroom facilities. There's an interpreted medicinal plant trail, but the really special feature is the well-maintained canopy walkway (the Amazon's longest), whose top-most platform is 35m high. Can be visited in conjunction with other Explorama lodges; $100–400 per day, depending on size of group, length of trip and the number of lodges visited.

Amazon Explorama Lodge contact Explorama (see above). In a 195-hectare reserve and 90km from Iquitos, this was Explorama's first lodge. Well equipped, it retains its rustic charm and acts as base camp for long-range programmes. Bora Indian talking drums (*manguare*) announce meal times in the dining room and guides often play Peruvian music in the bar during the evenings.

Bedrooms have no locks and are simple but attractive, with individual mosquito nets; toilets are latrine-style but well maintained, and showers are cold. A few animals – including a tapir, an otter and several macaws – come and go around the place, and you can swim with dolphins in the Amazon, plus there are night walks and visits to the nearby Yaguar Indians. Can be visited in conjunction with other Explorama lodges; $100–400 per day, depending on size of group, length of trip and the number of lodges visited.

Amazon Paradise Lodge Putumayo 132, Iquitos. A quite comfortable and conventional lodge, down-river from Iquitos and close to the town of Indiana. Around $35 for a day-trip, $50 for overnighting.

Amazon Rainforest Lodge Putumayo 159, Iquitos ☎094/233100 or 241628, ℻242231, ℮schneide@amauta.rcp.net.pe, ❀www.geocities.com/junglelodge or ❀www.amazon-lodge.com; in Lima ☎01/4455620, ℻4472651. Up the Río Momón (1–3hr, depending on water levels), the heart of this large lodge, run by an English resident, is a thatched native-style *maloca* dining room and bar. Accommodation is in bungalows with bathrooms and private toilets, with hammock spaces out front for relaxing. The pool is not always functioning. There are conventional trips to local Indians, fishing, jungle walks, bird-watching, plus ayahuasca sessions ($20) with local healers, one of whom has built a temple space at the back of the lodge. This isn't the best lodge for swish accommodation or for wildlife (though monkeys do often pass through), but you can walk to the Río Napo (8hr), or go further up the Momón to one of the two main headwaters, the Juano and Agua Planea creeks (both 3hr), the former noted for its marmosets. From $30 to $60 a day, the more expensive options including airport transfers, river travel, guides and food.

Cocoma Lodge Piura 1072 ☎094/251185. Operated by the Cocoma Indian community in the Pacaya Samiria Reserve, they offer adventure and shamanic trips as required; plenty of wildlife including dolphins, howler and black monkeys. Pretty good value from around $40 a day.

Cumaceba Lodge Putumayo 184 ☎/℻094/232229 or 610656, ℮cumaceba.lodge@mailcity.com. A highly recommended budget option on the Río Yanayacu, some 40km downriver from Iquitos (45min by speedboat), with accommodation in private rustic bungalows with individual bathrooms. They have the usual communal dining area and hammock lounge, while lighting is by kerosene lamps. They take visitors to the local Yaguar village and on jungle walks; bird- and dolphin-watching also form part of their programmes. Optional extras include trips to the Pacaya Samiria National Reserve, water-skiing (June–Nov) and ayahuasca sessions. They also run an explorer camp downriver. Around $120 for three days.

ExplorNapo Lodge contact Explorama (see above). Over ninety miles from Iquitos, on the Río Sucusari (Orejon Indian for "way in and out"). The palm-roofed buildings, hammock areas and dining room/bar are linked by thatch-covered walkways. The lodge controls 3000 hectares of surrounding forest, the ExplorNapo Reserve, and during full moons you can sometimes hear Tropical Screech Owls and the Common Potoos (related to owls). Further into the forest there is a jungle camp – *ExplorTambos* – where visitors can experience a night out in the middle of the forest away from any lodge, lights or people. Two hours' walk from *ExplorNapo Lodge* deep into primary forest, this is in many ways the ultimate jungle experience. A small collection of open-sided *tambo*-style huts, offering a night close to the earth, the elements and, of course, the animals. Can be visited in conjunction with other Explorama lodges; $100–400 per day, depending on size of group, length of trip, the level of quality and number of lodges visited.

The Great Amazon Safari and Trading Company Putumayo 437 ℡094/234099 ⓦwww.safarisareus.net. Run by the North American Jimmy Ford, this company has its own speedboat and offers customized jungle trips; from $25 a day for local trips or from $50 a day for longer expeditions. The 5-day trips or longer offer genuine jungle expedition options.

Heliconia Amazon River Lodge Prospero 574, Iquitos ℡094/235132, or contact via the *Hotel Victoria Regia* (see p.469); or Las Camelias 491, Oficina 503, San Isidro, Lima ℡01/4219195, ⓕ4424338, ⓔchasali@telematic.edu.pe. A pleasant lodge, 80km downriver from Iquitos, with accommodation in twin rooms with private bathrooms. They offer a basic 3-day programme at around $100 per day.

Loving Light Amazon Lodge Putumayo 128, Iquitos ℡094/243180, ⓦwww.junglelodge.com;

or 7016 248th Ave NE, Redmond, WA 98053, US (℡425/836-9431). A range of adventurous tours, from jungle walks and piranha fishing to wildlife observation and camping, plus ayahuasca sessions with local *curanderos* ($20). The lodge itself is about 120km upriver from Iquitos, and is only a few years old. From $50 a day if booking locally, up to $100 if booking through the US (though this includes help with transport in Peru, plus the support of a US-registered office).

Muyuna Putumayo 163 ℡094/242858, ⓦwww.muyana.com. The lodge is based 120km upriver from Iquitos, up a tributary called Yanayacu, fairly close to the Reserva Nacional de Pacaya Samiria. Attractive and very pleasant cabin accommodation, with private rooms and showers; they offer jungle walking, river safari trips in canoes and other traditional excursions like piranha fishing, searching out Vittoria regia (now named Vittoria amazonica) plants and alligator spotting. The Río Yanayacu is also pretty good for wildlife (see the photos in their ground-floor office). They use their own dedicated guides, many of whom have a university background. Their jungle tours and lodge work hard to distinguish themselves from competitors as protectors of wild animals' right to remain free rather than be kept in zoos or cages. Their role is to provide a service to enable people to see the animals, with respect, in the forest. This stance ensures their reputation as one of the greenest eco-tour companies in the region. They're reliable and all their tours are sold directly by them to their clients; well recommended, the standard charge is around $80 a day.

Refugio Altiplano Lodge Napo 145 ℡094/224020. Noted mainly for its ayahuasca ceremonies, this relatively new operator, run by a Scot, takes its groups to a lodge on the Río Tamshiyacu some 50km upriver from Iquitos.

Sinchicuy Lodge Pevas 246, Iquitos ℡094/231618. Reasonably priced, though a little too near a native village for there to be much wildlife in the immediate vicinity. From $35 per day.

Zungarococha Ricardo Palma 242, Iquitos ℡094/231959. The kind of comfortable rooms and bar associated with good middle-range conventional lodges, but only 14km from Iquitos by road. From $60 to $70 a day.

Riverboat and cruise operators

Amazon Explorama – Amazon Queen Ferryboat Av La Marina 340, Iquitos ℡094/252530 or 252526 or 253301, ⓕ252533, ⓦwww.explorama.com; or Box 445, Iquitos; toll-

free in the US ℡1-800/707-5275. A superbly converted ferryboat now operating with up to 180 passengers and 9 crew. Mainly connecting Iquitos with Exporama's busiest lodge, CEIBA TOPS, and sometimes travelling down the Amazon and up the Río Napo. With its 365-horsepower engine it makes CEIBA TOPS in about 90min. It has a large very comfortable lounge, card deck and carpeted bar on the second deck.

Amazon Tours and Cruises Requena 336, Iquitos ☎094/231611, ℱ231265, ⓦwww .amazontours.com; in the US 8700 W Flaglet St S/190, Miami, FL 33174 ℱ305/227-1880. Five luxury boats, running up the Río Amazonas to Requena, Pacaya Samiria National Reserve and down to Pevas, Leticia and Manaus, not quite as smart as those operated by Junglex, but better

value and still of a high standard. The company is planning to speed up access to the rainforest with flights to places such as Requena and Leticia.

Junglex Av Quinones 1980, Iquitos ☎094/261583; in the US ☎205/428-1700, ℱ428-1714, ⓔintlexp@aol.com.net. Five luxury boats of varying sizes, possibly the fanciest on the Amazon. A variety of expensive trips go to areas such as Requena, up the Río Ucayali and on to the Río Tapiche, and even up into the wilder reaches of the Río Yanayacu to visit Lago Umaral, a great area for wildlife. They also go to the Pacaya Samiria National Reserve.

Freelance guides

There are some good independent contacts who can help you find the right trip. The Iquitos tourist office (see p.467) has a list of registered **freelance guides**, and the following are all recommended. Juan Nicholas Maldonado (Pasaje Porvenir H-36, block 19 of Putumayo, Iquitos; ☎094/222350, ⓔamazonjuan2000@yahoo.com), also contactable through *Nila - The Yellow Rose of Texas* (see p.472), speaks excellent English and is one of the most reliable sources of general information in the whole Loreto *departmento*. He also runs day outings, river trips and guides longer expeditions, plus he can put you in touch with a couple of other people. Carlos Grandes, who speaks some English and runs very good trips, usually over 200km upriver from Iquitos using colectivo riverboats to keep costs down (from $25 per person per day), and his daughter Silvia Grandez, contactable through the *Hostal La Libertad* (see p.467, or silvia_grandez@origimail.com.ar), are both well recommended and offer expeditions, (her's charge from $30 per person) depending on the size of the group, which can last up to 25 days; although she doesn't speak English, some of her assistant guides do. They sometimes operate from a base camp at Veagali (250km from Iquitos) and around the bountiful wildlife area of Lago Curahuate. Walter Wacho Soplin via the *Hobo Hideout Hostel*, Putumayo 437 ☎094/234099 in Iquitos, or directly on ⓔwacho@lycos.com) is a freelance guide who frequently works for some of the larger lodges but has his own small lodge too, near Panguana village, some one to two hours from Iquitos; he speaks pretty good English and is a knowledgeable and capable jungle guide. Alex Weill Renfigo (☎094/940739, ⓦwww.jungletrips.4d2.net) runs a company called Ecological Jungle Trips, tailoring them to the client's needs from short three- or four-day trips to longer seven- to ten-day adventures (price varies according to whether you use the speedboat or local river bus; $30–70 a day).

Other recommendations include Richard Fowler (☎094/677645, ⓔaukoo@hotmail.com, or via Chinchilejo Expeditions at Napo 272 ☎094/674559 or 937325), based in Iquitos though from the US, a popular naturalist guide who offers customized survival and wilderness trips; and David Rios, who speaks English and runs trips down to Río Mazán and nearby lakes (though this area isn't brilliant for wildlife, being too close to Iquitos), and Pepe Lopez, who speaks limited English, is highly responsible and operates excellent tours, both contactable through the tourist office. Newer on the scene, but also offering adventurous trips upriver and deeper into the rainforest, sometimes as far as the Río Galvez, a tributary of the Río Aucayacu, relatively deep into the interior from the riverside town of Genaro Herrera, are Blue Morpho, run by Hamilton Souther and Moises Torres Monte Luis, whose office is located at

Psychedelic tourism and teacher plants

Ayahuasca sessions, or psychedelic tourism, have become a booming business in Iquitos. For background information on ayahuasca and other teacher plants, consult the Contexts section of this book (p.556). A new facility has opened near Iquitos, operated by an NGO – the Centro Medico ONG Shapinguito (Iquitos–Nauta road Km 45.5 ☎094/231566, with an Iquitos office at Tacna 327); open to all interested parties, this clinic offers healing and working with ayahuasca usually in association with the female shaman Norma Panduro Navarro. Costs start at as little as $300 a month, including room and board as well as ayahuasca ceremonies. A well-known local ayahuasca guide is Francisco Montes (Sachamama, 18km from Iquitos on the road to Nauta). Another popular shaman is Agustin Rivas, a famous sculptor who has dedicated over thirty years to working with ayahuasca; his sessions are run through *Yushintayta Lodge*, contactable via the *Hostal La Pascana,* Pevas 133 (☎094/231418); the lodge is located on the Río Tamshiyacu. In addition, many if not most of the jungle lodges around Iquitos regularly organize ayahuasca sessions for their clients. Similarly, many of the independent guides will organize sessions with shamans at their jungle camps. This sacred business is not regulated at all right now and, given the extremely sensitive states of mind achieved by ingesting ayahuasca (which can be much more powerful than LSD), it's important not only to feel comfortable with the scene and setting, but also with the person leading it. There are a number of websites worth checking out:

🌐www.shamanism.co.uk
🌐www.peruherbals.com
🌐www.wasai.com/Ayahuasca.htm
🌐www.bluemorphotours.com

Ramon Castilla 1012 (☎094/223678, ✉bluemorphotours@hotmail.com, or in US via 237 Plateau Ave, Santa Cruz, CA 95060 ☎831/425-7437). Operating a camp in a primary forest area, their trips offer mid-price-range ($50–80) adventure rather than luxury and really demand a minimum of five or six days' commitment; they can sometimes organize ayahuasca shamanic ceremonies. Jimmy Ford of the Great Amazon Safari and Trading Company (see p.481) offers equally adventurous safaris, but tends to cover a different territory, downriver towards the border with Brazil.

The three-way frontier

Leaving or entering Peru via the Amazon river inevitably means experiencing the **three-way frontier**. The cheapest and most common route is by river from Iquitos, some twelve hours in a *lancha rapida* or three to four days downriver in a standard *lancha* river boat (see p.476 for details of companies operating boats from Iquitos downriver). Some services go all the way to **Leticia (Colombia)** or **Tabatinga (Brazil)**, but many stop at one of the two small Peruvian frontier settlements of Santa Rosa or Islandia; at Chimbote, a few hours before you get to Santa Rosa and on the right as you head towards the frontier, is a small police post, the main **customs checkpoint** (*guarda costa*) for river traffic. The region is interesting in its own right as the home of the Tikuna Indians, once numerous but today down to a population of around 10,000. It's possible to arrange visits to some native communities from Leticia, and you can buy some of their excellent craftwork – mainly string bags and hammocks – from stores in that town.

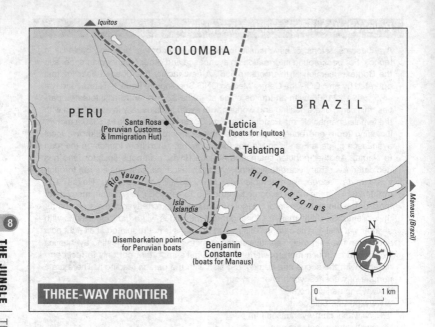

SANTA ROSA is your last chance to complete formalities with Migraciones if you haven't already done so at the Iquitos office (see p.474) – essentially obtaining an **exit stamp** from Peru, if you're leaving, or getting an **entry stamp and tourist card** if arriving, which can take up to an hour. On larger boats, you often don't have to disembark here, as the Migraciones official may board the vessel and do the paperwork there and then. There are several cafés and few **hostels**, but the small *La Brisa del Amazonas* (❸) is also a **restaurant** whose owner is a useful contact for local **information**. Ferryboats connect the town with Tabatinga and Leticia. **Islandia** is in the middle of the river, on the Peruvian side of the border, and has no hotels; from here you have to take the ferry to Tabatinga or Leticia across the river to enter Brazil or Colombia; most boats prefer to use Tabatinga, especially in low-water season – it's a long, muddy hike from the quay to the surfaced streets of Leticia, whereas at Tabatinga's two ports, the road goes right to the water's edge.

The only other way of crossing these three borders is by **flying** – a much less interesting approach, but not necessarily a more expensive one (though there's an airport departure tax of $2). Flights from Iquitos to Santa Rosa are operated by TANS, and both Varig and Rico fly to Manaus via Tabatinga at least three times a week. TANS tickets can be bought from Señor Teddy, who operates out of one of the restaurants in this tiny town – just ask anywhere for him. From Leticia, Avianca fly to a few major Colombian cities, including Bogotá, several times a week.

Into Colombia: Leticia

Having grown rich on tourism and contraband (mostly cocaine), **LETICIA** has more than a touch of the Wild West about it, but is still relatively safe. There's no physical border at the port or between Leticia and Tabatinga, though disembarking passengers sometimes have to go through a **customs check**, so carry your passport at all times. If you want to go on **into Colombia**, the cheapest way is to take a canoe to Puerto Asis, where you can latch on to the bus transport system, but to do this, or to stay overnight, you'll need to get a Colombian tourist card from the consulate at Iquitos (see p.474), or at Manaus if coming from Brazil. Alternatively, head straight for the DAS office (Departmento Administrativo de Seguridad, C 9, 9–62, ☎098/5927189 or 5924878; open 24hr) just a few blocks from the port.

If you do stay, be warned that it's a lively town, with *cumbia* and salsa music blasting out all over the place, and that by Peruvian (and even Colombian) standards, it's expensive. Best of the basic **hotels** are *Residencial Monserrate* (❸) and *Residencial Leticia* (❷), but much nicer are the *Colonial*, near the port square at Carrera 10 (☎098/0057919; ❻), and the swish *Anaconda* at Carrera 11 (☎098/5927891 or 5927119; ❽), which has a pool and an attractive *maloca*-style bar. The cheapest **place to eat**, and with the greatest variety of food, is at the riverside market, though the *Bucaneer* and *La Taguara* **cafés**, both at Carrera 10, are much better.

Into Brazil: Tabatinga

Smaller than Leticia, **TABATINGA** is hardly the most exciting place in South America, and many people stuck here waiting for a boat or plane to Manaus or Iquitos prefer to hop over the border to Leticia for the duration of their stay, even if they don't plan on going any further into Colombia. There are two docks here: at the smaller of the two, where lesser boats and canoes come and go with local produce and passengers, you'll encounter **customs checks**; Port Bras, the larger dock, is where you find the big *recreo* boats heading for Manaus. Brazilian **entry and exit formalities** are processed at the Policia Federal office (☎092/4122180; 10am–8pm, though 24hr for emergencies); if you're entering Brazil you'll usually be asked to show an exit ticket or prove that you have $500. There are a few **places to stay**. Try the *Hotel Paje*, Rue Pedro Teixeira (☎092/4122558; ❷), or the much nicer and friendlier *Hotel Te Contei*, Av da Amizade 1813 (☎092/4122377 or 4132566; ❹), which is entered via the rickety spiral stairway over a pizzeria of the same name. There are a handful of other **restaurants** dotted about, mainly by the smaller dock.

Continuing on downstream **into Brazil** on boats to Manaus, a four- to seven-day journey that is often very crowded, costs $40 to $80 depending on their size, condition and whether or not you require a cabin. They leave from both Tabatinga and **Benjamin Constante**, on the other side of the Amazon, usually starting from the former in the early afternoons (frequently on Wednesdays, but also less regularly on most other days of the week) and calling at the latter an hour or so later. If there are no boats in Tabatinga, however, it may be worth taking a speedboat ferry ($7; a 30min trip) to Benjamin Constante to see if there are any departing just from there. If you've arrived from Iquitos on a boat that's continuing all the way to Manaus, it's important to let the captain know whether or not you need to go into Tabatinga to quickly sort your visa business (use a taxi) and then meet the boat at Benjamin Constante. Bear in mind that it's virtually impossible to get from Islandia to the federal police in Tabatinga and then back to Benjamin Constante in less than an hour and a half.

Blue Moon Tour Agency, Rua General Sampaio 740 (☎092/4122227) in Tabatinga, specializes in cheap flights and boat trips from here to Peru.

The central selva

Although an interesting region, the **central selva** around **Pucallpa** doesn't have the strong appeal of the other jungle areas, and it's a tourist destination that suffered greatly during the political violence of the late 1980s and early 1990s. Recovery has been slow, yet Pucallpa is still one of Peru's fastest-growing cities, and its population of around 300,000 is well over ten times that of thirty years ago. With its relatively new status as the capital of the independent *departmento* of Ucayali, and its oil refineries and massive timber industry, the city represents the modern phase of the jungle's exploitation more than any other.

For travellers here, the big attraction is **Lago Yarinacocha** – a huge, beautiful, but by no means remote oxbow lake where you can swim and rest up, watch schools of dolphin and – at a cost – go on wildlife expeditions or visit some nearby native communities. The city is also a main point of departure for trips downstream to the more obvious destination of Iquitos, a 1000-kilometre, week-long journey. Pucallpa is well connected to Lima and elsewhere, and, like Iquitos, is more thoroughly developed than other jungle towns. Similarly, both cities' indigenous Indian life is becoming increasingly westernized, and as this happens, so tourism in these areas becomes increasingly packaged – or as they say in Peru, *convencional*. If you want to avoid the more conventional tours, it's really a matter of taking your chances travelling by river to a more remote area and looking for a local guide, or (the simpler and safer option) just going to Yarinacocha and talking to the boatmen by the lakeside port.

To the south, and reachable more or less directly overland from Pucallpa via a rugged bus route, is the **Chanchamayo** area of cloud forest – famous for its coffee. The main town here is **Satipo**, at the end of the road from Lima.

Chanchamayo and Satipo

Chanchamayo Valley marks the real beginning of the central selva directly east of Lima. Buses depart daily from the capital to the valley towns of **San Ramon** and **La Merced**. Separated by only 10km of road, some 2500m below Tarma, they are surrounded by exciting hiking country. Getting there from La Oroya, the road winds down in ridiculously precipitous curves, keeping tight to the sides of the **Río Palca Canyon**, at present used for generating hydro-electric power. Originally a forest zone inhabited only by Campa-Ashaninka Indians, the last century saw much of the best land cleared by invading missionaries, rubber and timber companies and, more recently, waves of settlers from the Jauja Valley. **Satipo**, a small frontier town, is a few hours deeper into the rainforest and, although there's really little tourism infrastructure here yet, it's a reasonable base from which to explore.

San Ramon and La Merced
The smaller of the twin settler towns, **SAN RAMON**, is probably the nicer place to break your journey, though La Merced is the communications hub and better for road connections deeper into the selva. One of the best **hostels** in San Ramon is the *Hotel Conquistador*, at Progreso 298 (☎064/331157, ℱ331771; ❸), or there's *Progreso* (❷), also on Calle Progreso, which is reasonably priced though pretty basic. *El Refugio Hotel*, Av El Ejercito 490

(☎064/331082; ❹), is a three-star hotel and, along with the *Hostal Golden Gate*, on the Carretera Marginal Km 102 at Puente Herrera (☎064/531483; ❸–❹), also pretty good. *Gat Gha Kum*, Carretera Central Km 96, in the Zona Salsipuedes (☎064/331538; ❸), is small and somewhat remote but arguably the most attractive hostel in the San Ramon area; except perhaps for the *Hospedaje El Rancho*, on Calle Tulumayo s/n Playa Hermosa (☎064/331076; ❸–❹). **Foodwise**, the *Restaurant Chanchamayo's*, Av San Ramon s/n, serves some of the best-quality regional and international food; or for okay Chinese meals try the *Chifa Siu*, Calle Progreso 440. The chicken from *Broaster Chanchamayo*, Calle Progreso 380, is delicious and worth stopping for.

The main reason for travellers to stop off here is for a taster of the *ceja de selva*, the cloud forest zone along the western edge of the Amazon. If you've got the money, you can head deeper into the lower Amazon basin by taking one of the daily **air taxis** to the jungle towns of Satipo, Atalaya or Pucallpa from the airstrip on the small plateau above town. The valley around San Ramon is rich in tropical fruit plantations and productive *chacras* (gardens), much of whose produce is transported over the Andes by road to Lima.

The market town of **LA MERCED**, some 10km further down the attractive valley, is larger and busier than San Ramon, with more than twelve thousand inhabitants, a thriving market, and several hectic restaurants and bars crowded around the Plaza de Armas. **Accommodation** is plentiful with offerings like the *Hotel Reyna*, Jr Palca 259 (☎064/531780 or 531780; ❷–❸), which has twenty clean bedrooms, some with private baths; *Hostal El Rosario*, Av Circunvalación 577 (☎064/531358; ❸), is smaller and less central. The best *hospedaje* in La Merced is *Gian's Hospedaje*, Pampa San Carlos s/n (☎064/531887; ❷–❸), closely followed by the *Complejo Turístico El Mirador Shelin's*, Av Zuchetti 113 (☎064/532040; ❷–❸) and the *Hostal El Eden*, Jr Ancash 347–351 (☎064/532340 or 531183; ❷). *Hostal Los Victor*, Jr Tarma 373 (☎064/531026; ❶), on the Plaza de Armas, has rooms with or without baths and is one of the better budget options. The *Hostal Residencial Rey*, Jr Junin 103 (☎064/531185 or 531185; ❹), is clean and friendly too. For **food**, the Restauarant *Shambari Campa*, Jr Tarma 389, serves some good local dishes. For chicken you'll find it hard locally to beat the *Broaster Chanchamayo*, Jr Junin 580; while for meat cuts in general, the *Restaurant El Gaucho*, Av Ancash s/n, is better. A reasonable Chinese can meal can be ordered at the *Chifa Siu*, Jr Junin 310. Also, the *Restaurant Ling*, in Jiron Junin by the plaza on the corner opposite the Banco de Credito, serves pretty good food and is much more popular with locals than the tourist-oriented restaurants in town. **Buses** leave more or less constantly from the **Terminal Terrestre** in La Merced, where it's just a matter of checking out which bus, combi or car is going where, and when.

Close to La Merced, the **Jardín Botánico El Perezoso**, 15km from town, is said to have some 10,000 species of plants; it requires about two hours for a thorough visit. Also nearby, about 5km from the town, the **Catarata El Tirol** waterfalls have a 35-metre drop into an attractive plunge pool. To get here it's ten minutes in a car to the Pueblo of Playa Hermosa, then a pleasant 45-minute (2km) walk along a dirt tack surrounded by orchids and lianas.

The newly paved road down from La Merced to Satipo passes through the rapidly growing settlement of **Pichanaki** where the *Hostal Santa Maria*, Av Micaela Bastidas 438 (no phone; ❷), and the *Hotel Loreto*, Av Santa Rosa 582 (☎064/347010; ❸), are both reasonably okay; also the *Hostal Oro Café*, Jr Micaela Bastidas 166 (☎064/347222; ❷–❸), which has the added attraction of its own little restaurant for breakfasts. Alternatives for grub here include the *Restaurante El Parralito*, Av Micaela Bastidas 544 (☎064/331078), serving up some decent snacks and full meals, as well as having inexpensive set menus at lunchtime.

Satipo

SATIPO, accessible by a three- to four-hour bus ride east from La Merced, is a real jungle frontier town, where the indigenous Ashaninka Indians come to buy supplies and trade. First developed around the rubber extraction industry some eighty years ago, it now serves as an economic and social centre for a widely scattered population of over forty thousand colonists, offering them tools, food supplies, medical facilities, banks and even a cinema. With the surfacing of the road all the way from Lima, a veritable flat carpet unfurling through the jungle valleys, many more colonists have moved into the region, but the rate of development is putting significant pressure on the last surviving groups of traditional forest dwellers, mainly the Ashaninka tribe, who have mostly taken up plots of land and begun to compete with colonist farmers or moved into one of the ever-shrinking zones out of permanent contact with the rest of Peru. You'll see the tribespeople in town, unmistakable in their reddish-brown or cream *cushma* robes. Satipo is the southernmost large town on the jungle-bound Carretera Marginal, but the road is continuing further and should soon reach Puerto Ocopa – a passable dirt track already does, and buses travel along it – from where it's possible to get river boats down the Río Tambo to Atalaya.

An ideal town in which to get kitted out for a jungle expedition, or merely to sample the delights of the selva for a day or two, Satipo possesses an interesting daily **market**, at its best at weekends, and an **airstrip**. The town sits in the middle of a beautiful landscape; a fascinating walk is to follow the path from the other side of the suspension bridge to one of the plantations beyond town. Further afield, local colectivos go to the end of the Carretera Marginal into relatively new settled areas such as that around **San Martin de Pangoa** – a frontier settlement that is frequently attacked by armed bandits or terrorists who live on coca plantations in the forest (hence the sandbags lined up outside the police stations).

Satipo's best **accommodation** is at the *Hotel Majestic*, Jr Colonos Fundadores 408 (℡064/545762 or 545762; ❸), has deliciously cool rooms but no hot water. The *Hostal San Jose*, Av Augusto B. Leguia 684 (℡064/545105; ❸), is quite large and the beds are clean; and there's also the *Hostal Palmero*, C Manuel Prado 228 (℡064/545020 or 545020; ❷), which has over forty beds and is bearable but noisy. Other basic accommodation is available around the market area and along the road to the airstrip. For **eating**, the *Café Yoly*, between the plaza and the market, is great for coffee, snacks and breakfasts, while the *Restaurant Turístico Oasis*, Jr Junin 628, has a wide range of jungle cuisine available in a large, ethnically decorated place where you can also buy local crafts, mainly of Ashaninka origin. One of the better restaurants around Satipo is the *Laguna Blanca*, Av Marginal via Río Negro.

Accessible from the town by car and foot are **petroglyphs** and **waterfalls** on the Río Mazamari (ask at the *Restaurant Oasis* for details), which is also a popular fishing spot.

Instead of retracing your steps via La Merced and San Ramon, you can follow a breathtaking direct road to **Huancayo** – Los Andes buses do the twelve-hour journey daily (May–Oct). For the adventurous, a flight to **Atalaya** (see p.516), deeper into the central selva, is an exciting excursion, though this is way off the tourist trail and any potential visitors should be warned that facilities are few and it's real jungle frontier stuff. Two commercial air-taxi companies fly most days, or on demand if you can pay the $400 per hour air-taxi rate, to both Sepahua and Atalaya.

Oxapampa and Pozuzo

Pretty well off the beaten track, some 78km by road north of La Merced, and nearly 400km east of Lima, lies the small settlement of **OXAPAMPA**, dependent for its survival on timber and coffee, living happily on the bank of the Río Chontabamba. Most of the forest immediately around the town has been cleared for cattle grazing, coffee plantations and timber, and the indigenous **Amuesha Indians**, disgruntled at being pushed out of the way, are battling hard on local, national and international levels for their land rights. Strongly influenced in architecture, blood and temperament by the nearby Tyrolean settlement of Pozuzo, this is actually quite a pleasant frontier town in its own way, with a surprisingly good **place to stay**, the *Hotel El Rey* (❸). Just 25km from Oxapampa lies the Parque Nacional Yanachoja Chemillen, a 12,000-hectare reserve dominated by dark mountains and vivid landscapes, where grasslands and cloud forest merge and separate. There are quantities of bromeliads, orchids, cedars and even the odd spectacled bear, some jaguar and around 427 bird species here. It's also home to around sixty Yanesha Indian communities. The town of **Vila Rica**, some 72km from Oxapampa, lying at 1480m in the *ceja de selva*, offers overland access to the Pichis and Palcazu valleys, the region's principal producers of coffee, pineapple and coca. Only 12km from town you'll find the Catarata El Encanto (The Spell or Enchantment Waterfalls) which has three sets of falls; frequently a rainbow appears and there are deep, dangerous plunge pools.

POZUZO, some 87km north (about 2–3hr) of Oxapampa and at only 820m above sea level, is a weird combination of European rusticism and native Peruvian culture. It represents the survivors of a unique eighteenth-century social experiment, a project to open up the Amazon using European peasants as settlers. Some 80km down the valley from Oxapampa, along a very rough road that crosses over two dozen rivers and streams, its wooded chalets with sloping Tyrolean roofs have endured ever since the first Austrian and German colonists arrived in the 1850s. As part of the grand plan to establish settlements deep in the jungle – brainchild of President Ramon Castilla's economic adviser, a German aristocrat – eighty families left Europe in 1857; seven emigrants died at sea and six more were killed by an avalanche, which caused another fifty to turn back only 35km from here. The local dance and music is still strongly influenced by the German colonial heritage. Many of this unusual town's present inhabitants still speak German, eat *schitellsuppe*, waltz very well and dance the polka. The *Hostal Tyrol* (❹) and *Hotel Maldonado* (❷) are the best **places to stay**. **Trucks** for Pozuzo leave every couple of days from opposite the *Hotel Bolivar* in Oxapampa. The church, nineteenth-century Capilla San José de Pozuzo, is a wooden rectangular structure containing wooden images of the Virgin brought from Germany. The hanging bridge over the Río Huancabamba was donated to the community by Emperor Wilhelm II of Prussia in 1914.

Visitors to the Oxapampa and Pozuzo areas are recommended to check in advance of going with their embassy or the South American Explorers' Club in Lima (see p.103) who should have the very latest on what's happening in this region and whether or not it's safe to travel here.

Pucallpa

Long an impenetrable refuge for Cashibo Indians, **PUCALLPA** was developed as a camp for rubber gatherers at the beginning of the twentieth century. In

1930 it was connected to Lima by road (850km of it), and since then its expansion has been intense and unstoppable. Sawmills – most of the parquet floors in Lima originated here – surround the city and spread up the main highway towards Tingo María and the mountains, and an impressive floating harbour has been constructed at the new port of **La Hoyada**. Until 1980 it was a province in the vast Loreto *departmento*, controlled from Iquitos, but months of industrial action eventually led to the creation of a separate *departmento* – Ucayali. The end of financial restrictions from Iquitos, which exports down the Amazon to the Atlantic, and the turn of traffic towards the Pacific were significant changes. The new floating dock can service cargo boats of up to 3000 tons, and in 1996, the selling off of contracts for oil exploitation to foreign companies by Fujimori's government gave Pucallpa a further burst of energy and finance (though this particular effect has eased off in recent years).

Although in many ways a lively and vibrant city, there is little here of great interest to travellers, most of whom get straight in a *motokar* or a local bus for **Lago Yarinacocha**. If you stay a while, though, it's difficult not to appreciate Pucallpa's relaxed feel – or the entrepreneurial optimism in a city whose red-mud-splattered streets are fast giving way to concrete and asphalt.

Arrival, information and city transport

From Lima, Pucallpa is served by several **bus companies**, all of which go via Huánuco (roughly the halfway point); the full journey is supposed to take approximately 24 hours but can take longer; note that it's often difficult to get seats on the buses if you pick them up outside of Lima. If you arrive with Tepsa, you'll get off outside their offices at Jr Raymondi 649; Ucayali Express offices are by the corner of 7 de Junio with San Martín; while if you travel with León de Huánuco, you disembark close to the Parque San Martín, at the corner of Jr 9 de Diciembre and Jirón Vargas. Boats arrive at the **floating port** of La Hoyada on the eastern side of town, about 2km from the Plaza de Armas ($1 by *motokar*, $2.50 by taxi). Pucallpa **airport** is only 5km west of town and is served by buses (20min; 35¢), *motokars* (15min; $1.50) and taxis (10min; $4–5). Aero Continente and Lan Peru operate flights between Pucallpa and Lima and Iquitos, and TANS fly here from Tarapoto, Lima and Iquitos once a week. There are also irregular services run by Air Taxis (℡064/575221), based at the airport, from Cruzeiro do Sul just over the Brazilian border.

Tourist information is available at the regional office on block 2 of Raimondi (℡/℗064/571506), or from Laser Viajes y Turismo, Av 7 de Junio 1043 (℡/℗064/573776). Exchange is at Banco de Credito, Calle Tarapaca, two blocks from the Plaza de Armas towards the main market by Parque San Martín, though for good rates on dollars cash try the *cambistas* on Calle Tarapaca, where it meets the Plaza de Armas. Payphones are available at Telefónica del Peru, Ucayali 357, or on Jirón Independencia; Internet services are offered by several places in Pucallpa, but the best is probably the ISTU, Av San Martín 383 ($2.50 per hour; itsu@pol.com.pe). For snail mail, the post office is at San Martín 418 (Mon–Fri 8am–8pm, Sat 8am–2pm). Artesanía shops can be found at: Jr Mariscal Cáceres cdra.5, Jr Ucayali cdra. 7, Jr 7 de Junio cdra. 1 & 10.

One of the best ways of **getting around** Pucallpa is as the locals do, by **motorbike**; these can be rented by the hour (about $2) from the workshop at Raymondi 654. Otherwise, colectivos leave from near the food market on Avenida 7 de Junio, while **motokars** and **taxis** can be picked up almost anywhere in town.

Accommodation

Pucallpa is full of **hotels**, old and new, and most of the better ones are grouped around the last few blocks of Jirón Tacna and Jirón Ucayali, near the Parque San Martín. At the top end, the *Hotel Sol del Oriente*, Jr San Martín 552 (℡064/575154, ℱ575510; ❹), is an attractive old building with a fine pool and excellent service; the *Hotel Inambu*, Federico Basadre 271 (℡064/576822; ❸), is almost as good, and has an excellent restaurant, although no pool. Still at the upper end of the scale for Pucallpa, the *Gran Hotel Mercedes*, Raymondi 610 (℡064/575120; ❸–❹), is pretty good value and has the added attractions of a popular bar and a fairly nice pool. The *Hostal Confort*, centrally located at Coronel Portillo 381 (℡064/576091; ❸), is a good, moderately priced alternative. Slightly cheaper, the *Hotel Amazonas*, Coronel Portillo 729 (℡064/576080; ❸), is quite comfortable, and has clean rooms with fans and private bathrooms. Considerably more basic, there's the *Hostal Mori* (❷), Jr Independencia 1114, which is reasonably comfortable and quite friendly and clean, though bathrooms are shared.

The Town and around

If you have an hour or so to while away in the town itself, both the downtown **food market** on Independencia and the older central **market** on 2 de Mayo are worth checking out; the latter in particular has interesting and varied stalls full of jungle produce. The port of **La Hoyada** and the older nearby **Puerto Italia** are also interesting places, bustling with activity by day. The only other attractions in town are the **Usko-Ayar Amazonia School of Painting**, at Jr Sanchez Cerro 467 (Mon–Fri 10am–5pm; free; ⓦwww.egallery.com/amazon.html, ⓦwww.tengai.co.uk/usko-ayar or ⓦwww.sensorium.com/usko/Pablo.html), the home of the school's founding father, the self-taught artist Pablo Amaringo. Once a *vegetalista-curandero*, Dom Amaringo used to use the hallucinogenic ayahuasca, as do most Peruvian jungle healers, as an aid to divination and curing; his students' works, many of which are displayed at his house, display the same ayahuasca-inspired visions of the forest wilderness as his own paintings do.

On Calle Inmaculada, the **Regional Natural History Museum** (Mon–Sat 9am–6pm; $1.50) exhibits dried and stuffed Amazon insects, fish and animals and has good displays of local crafts, including ceramics produced by the Shipibo Indians, plus other material objects such as clothing and jewellery from local Indian tribes. There are also works by the Pucallpa-born wood sculptor Augustin Rivas, who once ran an artists' haven at Lago Yarinacocha, but now runs ayahuasca sessions in the Iquitos region.

Some 6km out of town, along the highway towards Lima, there's a small lakeside settlement and zoological park at Barboncocha. Known as the **Parque Natural de Barboncocha** (daily 9am–5.30pm; $1), it consists of almost two hundred hectares of lakeside reserve with plenty of alligators, birds and boa constrictors, as well as caged monkeys and a black jaguar. Colectivos to Barboncocha (25min; 60¢) can be caught from near the food market on Avenida 7 de Junio; or hail a motorcycle taxi (20min; $3) from anywhere in town.

Eating

Restaurants are fairly plentiful and include the *Chifa Han Muy*, Jr Inmaculada 247, which does a wonderful blend of Peruvian Chinese and tropical jungle cuisine. For international cuisine, it's hard to beat the restaurant in the *Hostal*

Inambu, Federico Basadre 271. Slightly cheaper and very good for fish dishes, like the local speciality *patarashca* (fresh fish cooked in *bijao* leaves), or the delicious *sarapatera* (soup in a turtle shell), there's the *Restaurant El Golf*, at Jr Huascar 545, or the *Restaurant El Alamo*, on block 26 of Carretera Yarinacocha.

Lago Yarinacocha

Some 9km from Pucallpa, and easily reached by bus or colectivo (20min; 30–50¢) from the food market on the corner of Independencia and Ucayali, **Lago Yarinacocha** is without doubt a more attractive place to stay than the city itself. A contrast to the southern jungle lakes, its waters are excellent for swimming and there is considerable settlement around its banks. River channels lead off towards small villages of Shipibo Indians, luxury tourist lodges, and the slightly bizarre Summer Institute of Linguistics. This last place is the headquarters of an extremely well-equipped, US-funded missionary organization, their aim being to bring God to the natives by translating the New Testament into all Indian languages. At present they're working on over forty, "each as different from each other as Chinese is from Greek".

Puerto Callao and the lake

The lake's main centre, and the place where most travellers stay, is **PUERTO CALLAO**, a town known locally (and slightly ironically) as the "Shangri-la de la Selva", where the bars and wooden shacks are animated by an almost continuous blast of *chicha* music. The settlement boasts one of the best jungle

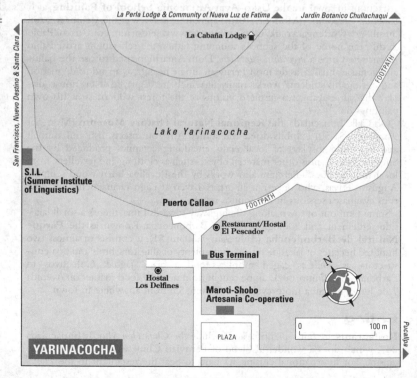

La Perla Lodge & Community of Nueva Luz de Fatima ▲   Jardin Botanico Chullachaqui ▲

La Cabaña Lodge

San Francisco, Nuevo Destino & Santa Clara ◄

Lake Yarinacocha

FOOTPATH

**S.I.L.
(Summer Institute
of Linguistics)**

Puerto Callao   FOOTPATH

⊙ **Restaurant/Hostal
El Pescador**

■ **Bus Terminal**

⊙ **Hostal
Los Delfines**

**Maroti-Shobo
Artesania Co-operative**

N

0   100 m

PLAZA

YARINACOCHA

Pucallpa ▲

Pucallpa

Indian craft workshops in the Amazon, the **Moroti-Shobo Crafts Co-operative** – a project originally organized by Oxfam but now operated by the local Shipibo and Conibo Indians. Located on the main plaza, it sells some beautifully moulded ceramics, carved wood and dyed textiles, most of them very reasonably priced.

Various **excursions** to see wildlife, visit Indian villages, or just to cross the lake, are all touted along the waterfront. The standard day-trip goes to the Shipibo village of **San Francisco** ($10 per person), sometimes continuing to the slightly remoter settlements of **Nuevo Destino** and **Santa Clara** (around $15 per person). San Francisco is now almost completely geared towards tourism, so for a more adventurous trip you'll do better to hire a *peque-peque* canoe and boatman on your own (from around $30 a day); these canoes can take up to six or seven people and you can share costs, though if you want to go further afield (say on a 3-day excursion) expect prices to rise to $150 a day.

There's also an interesting botanical garden, the **Jardín Botánico Chullachaqui** (daily 9am–5pm; free) on the far right-hand side of the lake. To reach it you have to take a *peque-peque* canoe, a 45-minute ride ($2) from Callao Puerto, then walk for almost half an hour down a clearly marked jungle trail. On arrival, you'll find a well-laid-out garden in a beautiful and very exotic location with over 2300 medicinal plants, mostly native to the region.

Towards the waterfront are most of the liveliest **bars** (try *El Grande Paraiso*); if you fancy something quieter, the lodges around the lake (see below) make a good spot for an evening drink; of the **restaurants**, the best is probably *El Cucharon*. As for **hotels**, *El Pescador* (no phone; ❷) offers good if basic accommodation, as does *Hostal Los Delphines* (☏064/571129; ❷–❸); and both offer off-season deals in the ❶ range. You can also **camp** anywhere along the lake, though bear in mind that you'll need to keep a lookout for thieves, but if you fancy something more luxurious, try the **tourist lodges** that surround the lake: they're far more expensive than a basic hotel, but are wonderfully positioned. The well-established *La Cabaña* (❺) – possibly the first jungle lodge built in Peru – is an excellent place to stay, though the management requests bookings in advance, not least so that they can send their boat to Puerto Callao to meet visitors; they have an office in Pucallpa at Jr 7 de Junio 1043 (☏064/616679, ℻579242). Another comfortable lodge, *La Perla* (no phone; ❹–❺), which has a highly recommended restaurant for patrons, is located more or less next door to *La Cabaña* but is slightly cheaper, with the price including full board; accommodation (in bungalows) is similar to that of *La Cabaña*, though it's a smaller place with a different, perhaps more intimate, atmosphere. Like *La Cabaña*, it can be reached only by boat.

Not a lodge at all, it is sometimes possible to stay in the Medical Centre (❶) at the village of **NUEVA LUZ DE FATIMA**, a small settlement a little further down the same bank of Yarinacocha, beyond *La Perla* lodge. Gilber Reategui, an English-speaking neighbour of the Medical Centre, can arrange for meals if required; he is also recommended as a jungle guide – he has a *peque-peque* called *Mi Normita*, which is usually beached at Puerto Callao on the lake when not touring. Write to Sr Gilber Reategui, c/o Ruperto Perez, Maynas 350, Yarinacocha, Pucallpa, Ucayali, Peru for advance bookings.

Downriver to Iquitos

Travelling **from Pucallpa to Iquitos** on a boat sounds more agreeable than it actually is. Very few Peruvians, except boatmen, would ever dream of it – over 1000km of water separates the two towns, with very little in between but the endless undulations of the river and verdant forest hemming you in on either side. However, if you are going that way, you may want to relax in a hammock for a few days and arrive in the style the rubber barons were accustomed to.

Large **riverboats** generally leave Pucallpa from La Hoyada port, 4km from the Plaza de Armas along Avenida Mariscal, while smaller **launches and canoes** tend to go from Puerto Italia, which is slightly nearer. The cheapest and most effective way of finding a boat is to go down to the ports and ask around. Try to fix a price and a departure date with a reputable-looking outfit; it should cost around $30 per person, including food, but if you want a cabin this can rise to about $50. Few boats on this stretch of water actually have cabins, though, and while they're useful for securing your gear in, you'll probably be more comfortable (and certainly cooler) sleeping in a hammock, strung under some mosquito netting. It's quite usual for passengers to string them up several days before departure – which can mean great savings on hotel costs and less risk of the boat leaving without you. If the captain asks for money upfront, don't give the whole bundle to him; you may never see him or his boat again. Additionally, even when everything looks ready for departure, don't be surprised if there is a delay of a day or two – boats leave frequently but unpredictably. Food on board can be very unappetizing, so it's worth taking some extra luxuries, like a few cans of fish, a packet or two of biscuits, and several bottles of water. Depending on how big the boat is and how many stops it makes, the journey to Iquitos normally takes five to seven days. Before you leave there's a certain amount of **paperwork** to go through, since this is a commercial port and one of the main illicit cocaine trails; you'll have to show your documents to the port police (PIP) and get permission from the naval office (your captain should help with all of this).

En route to Iquitos, boats often stop at the settlements of Contamana (10hr; $7) and Requena (a further 4–5 days; $20). In theory it's possible to use these as pitstops – hopping off one boat for a couple of days while waiting for another – but you may end up stuck here for longer than you bargained. There isn't much at **CONTAMANA**, on the right bank of the Ucayali, but it's okay to **camp**, and **food** can be bought without any problem. A better stopping point is the larger and more pleasant **REQUENA**, developed during the rubber boom on an isolated stretch of the Río Ucayali, a genuine jungle town that is in many ways like Iquitos was just fifty years ago. There are a couple of basic **hostels** here and one quite good one (contact the *Hostal Amazon Garden* in Iquitos; see p.469), or you can **camp** on the outskirts of town. For those going downstream, it's about a day's journey from Iquitos, with **boats** leaving regularly (around $15 a person). You can also access Pacaya Samiria National Reserve (see p.477) by boat from here, though most people reach it from Lagunas. A few hours to the north, just a few huge bends away, the Río Marañón merges with the Ucayali to form the mighty Amazon.

The southern selva: Madre de Dios and the Río Urubamba

A large, forested region, with a manic climate (usually searingly hot and humid, but with sudden cold spells – *friajes* – between June and August, due to icy winds coming down from the Andean glaciers), the **southern selva** regions of Peru have only been systematically explored since the 1950s and were largely unknown until the twentieth century, when rubber began to leave Peru through Bolivia and Brazil, eastwards along the rivers.

Named after the broad river that flows through the heart of the southern jungle, the still relatively wild *departmento* of **Madre de Dios**, like so many remote areas of Peru, is changing rapidly. Living in one of the last places affected by the rubber boom at the turn of the century, the natives here – many of whom struggle to maintain their traditional ways of life, despite the continuing efforts of *colonos* and some of the less enlightened Christian missionaries – were left pretty much alone until the push for oil in the 1960s and 1970s brought roads and planes, making this now the most accessible part of the Peruvian rainforest. As the oil companies moved out, so prospectors took their place, panning for gold dust along the river banks, while agribusiness moved in to clear mahogany trees or harvest the bountiful Brazil nuts. Today the main problems facing the Indians, here as elsewhere, are loss of territory, the merciless pollution of their rivers, devastating environmental destruction (caused mainly by large-scale gold-mining), and new waves of oil exploration by multinationals.

Madre de Dios is centred on the fast-growing river town of **Puerto Maldonado**, near the Bolivian border, supposedly founded by legendary explorer and rubber baron **Fitzcarrald**. The town, which extends a tenuous political and economic hold over the vast *departmento*, has a population of over 25,000, a city centre with one or two traffic policemen, and evening classes where row upon row of young locals train for the future in front of the glare of PC monitors. But while the *departmento's* scattered towns and villages are interesting for their Wild West energy and spirit, most visitors come for the wildlife, especially in the strictly protected **Manu Biosphere Reserve** – still essentially an expedition zone – and the cheaper, less well-known **Tambopata–Candamo Reserved Zone**, chiefly visited by groups staying at lodges; between these areas encompass some of the most exciting jungle and richest flora and fauna in the world.

The newest protected area is **Bahuaja–Sonene National Park**, created in 2000, surrounded largely by a massive rainforest area formed by Tambopata, and is intended to show the Peruvian government's support for this region as an ecological treasure. Taken together, these three zones comprise some 1.5 million hectares, almost the size of Manu (15,000 square kilometres), and if you add on the Maididi National Park – just across the border in Bolivia – the protected area in this corner of the Amazon exceeds 50,000 square kilometres. ·

As in all jungle regions, human activity here is closely linked to the river

system, and Manu and Tambopata are actually among the most easily reached parts of the Amazon: from Cusco, Manu is either a day's journey by bus then a couple days more by canoe, or a thirty-minute flight in a light aircraft; Tambopata, meanwhile, is a forty-minute scheduled flight (or 3- to 10-day truck journey), plus a few hours in a motorized canoe.

Slightly less accessible than the protected zones, but nevertheless rewarding for many budget travellers staying in Puerto Maldonado, are **Lago Sandoval** and the huge expanse of **Lago Valencia**, both great wildlife locales east along the Río Madre de Dios and close to the Bolivian border. At the least, you're likely to spot a few caimans and the strange hoatzin birds, and if you're lucky, larger mammals such as capybara, tapir, or, less likely, a jaguar – and at Valencia, you can fish for piranha. A little further southeast of here, less than a couple of hours in a decent motorized launch, lies **Las Pampas del Heath**, the only tropical grassland within Peru. It now lies within the Bahuaja-Sonene National Park, so special permission is needed from the INRENA office (see p.463) to visit it. The grasslands extend eastward across northern Bolivia to the Pantanal region of Brazil, itself one of the wildlife gems of the Americas.

The **Río Madre de Dios** itself is fed by two main tributaries, the **Río Manu** and the **Río Alto Madre de Dios**, which roll off the Paucartambo Ridge (just north of Cusco), which divides the tributaries from the **Río Urubamba** watershed and delineates Manu Biosphere Reserve. At Puerto Maldonado, the Madre de Dios meets with the **Río Tambopata** and the **Río de las Piedras**, then flows on to Puerto Heath, a day's boat ride away on the Bolivian frontier. From here it continues through the Bolivian forest into Brazil to join the great **Río Madeira**, which eventually meets the Amazon near Manaus.

West of Puerto Maldonado, on the other side of Cusco from the Río Madre de Dios, the **Río Urubamba** flows on past Machu Picchu and down to the jungle area around the town of **Quillabamba**, before gushing beyond the end of the road at the frontier settlement of **Kiteni** and then falling through the rapids at the **Pongo de Mainique** and into the lowland rainforest, where it continues north to Iquitos, then east to the Atlantic Ocean many thousands of kilometres away.

Madre de Dios indigenous groups

Off the main Madre de Dios waterways, within the system of smaller tributaries and streams, live a variety of different **indigenous groups**. All are depleted in numbers due to contact with the last century's Western influences and diseases, but while some have been completely wiped out over the last twenty years, several have maintained their isolation. Many tribes were acculturated as late as the 1950s and 1960s, and occasionally "uncontacted" groups turned up during the 1980s and 1990s. These are, however, usually segments of a larger tribe that split or dispersed with the arrival of the rubber barons, and they are fast being secured in controllable mission villages. Most of the native tribes that remain in, or have returned to, their traditional territories now find themselves forced to take on seasonal work for the *colonos* who have staked claims around the major rivers. In the dry season (May to Nov), this usually means panning for gold – the region's most lucrative commodity. In the rainy season, Brazil nut (or, rather, Peru nut) collection takes over. The timber industry, too, is well established, and most of the accessible large cedars are already gone.

If you go anywhere in the jungle, especially on an organized tour, you're likely to stop off at a **tribal village** for at least half an hour or so, and the more you know about the people, the more you'll get out of the visit. Downstream from Puerto Maldonado, the most populous indigenous group are the **Ese Eja** tribe (often wrongly, and derogatorily, called Huarayos by *colonos*). Originally semi-nomadic hunters and gatherers, the Ese Eja were well-known warriors who fought the Incas and, later on, the Spanish expedition of Alvarez Maldonado – eventually establishing fairly friendly and respectful relationships with both. Under Fitzcarrald's reign, they apparently suffered greatly. Today they live in fairly large communities and have more or less abandoned their original bark-cloth robes in favour of shorts and T-shirts.

Upstream from Puerto Maldonado live several native tribes, known collectively (again, wrongly and derogatorily) as the Mashcos but actually comprising at least five separate linguistic groups – the **Huachipaeri**, **Amarakaeri**, **Sapitoyeri**, **Arasayri** and **Toyeri**. All typically use long bows – over 1.5m – and lengthy arrows, and most settlements will also have a shotgun or two these days, since less time can be dedicated to hunting when they are panning for gold or working timber for *colonos*. Traditionally, they wore long bark-cloth robes and had long hair, and the men often stuck eight feathers into the skin around their lips, making them look distinctively fierce and cat-like. Having developed a terrifying hatred of white people during the rubber era, they were eventually conquered and settled by missionaries and the army about forty years ago. Many Huachipaeri and Amarakaeri groups are now gaining an insight into the realities of the outside world, and some of their young men and women have gone through university education and are returning to their villages.

Puerto Maldonado

A remote settlement even for Peru, **PUERTO MALDONADO** is a frontier colonist town with strong links to the Cusco region and a great fervour for bubbly jungle *chicha* music. With an economy based on gold-panning and Brazil-nut gathering from the rivers and forests of Madre de Dios, it has grown enormously over the last twenty years from a small, laid-back outpost of civilization to a busy market town. Today it's the thriving, safe (and fairly expensive) capital of a region that feels very much on the threshold of major upheavals, with a rapidly developing tourist industry.

It was rubber, however, that led to the settlement's establishment at the beginning of the twentieth century. During the 1920s came the game hunters, who dominated the economy of the region, and after them, mainly in the 1960s, came the exploiters of mahogany and cedar trees – leading to the construction of Boca Manu airstrip, just before the oil companies moved in during the 1970s. Most of the townspeople, riding coolly around on Honda motorbikes, are second-generation *colonos*, but there's a constant stream of new and hopeful arrivals – rich and poor boys from all parts of South America, and even the occasional gang from the US.

The lure, inevitably, is **gold**. Every rainy season the swollen rivers deposit a heavy layer of gold dust along their banks and those who have been quick enough to stake claims on the best stretches have made substantial fortunes. In such areas there are thousands of unregulated miners, using large front-loader earth-moving machines, destroying a large section of the forest, and doing so very quickly. Gold-lust is not a new phenomenon here – the gold-rich rivers have brought Andean Indians and occasional European explorers to the region for centuries. Even the Incas may well have utilized a little of the precious

The saga of Fitzcarrald

Fitzcarrald (often mistakenly called Fitzcarraldo) is associated with the founding of Puerto Maldonado, but he actually died some twelve years before the event, though his story is relevant to the development of this region. While working rubber on the Río Urubamba, Fitzcarrald evidently caught the gold bug after hearing rumours from local Ashaninka and Machiguenga Indians of an Inca fort protecting vast treasures, possibly around the Río Purus. Setting out along the Mishagua, a tributary of the Río Urubamba, he managed to reach its source, and from there walked over the ridge to a new watershed which he took to be the Purus, though it was in fact the Río Cashpajali, a tributary of the Río Manu. Leaving men to clear a path, he returned to Iquitos, and in 1884 came back to the region on a boat called *La Contamana*. He took the boat apart, and, with the aid of over a thousand Ashaninka and other Indians, carried it across to the "Purus". But, as he cruised down, attacked by tribes at several points, Fitzcarrald slowly began to realize that the river was not the Purus – a fact confirmed when he eventually bumped into a Bolivian rubber collector.

Though he'd ended up on the wrong river, Fitzcarrald had discovered a link connecting the two great Amazonian watersheds. In Europe, the discovery was heralded as a great step forward in the exploration of South America, but for Peru it meant more rubber, a quicker route for its export, and the beginning of the end for Madre de Dios' indigenous tribes. Puerto Maldonado was founded in 1902, and as exploitation of the region's rubber peaked, so too was there an increase in population of workers and merchants, with Madre de Dios ultimately becoming a *departmento* of Peru in 1912. German director Werner Herzog thought this historical episode a fitting subject for celluloid, and in 1982 directed the epic *Fitzcarraldo*.

stuff – the Inca emperor Tupac Yupanqui is known to have discovered the Río Madre de Dios, naming it the Amarymayo ("serpent river"). Perhaps, too, it's more than coincidental that one suggested location for the legendary city of "**El Dorado**"(known in southern Peru as **Paititi**), where the Incas hid their most valuable golden objects from the Spanish conquerors, is in the high forests close to the Río Alto Madre de Dios.

In town, the main street, **León de Velarde**, immediately establishes the town's stage-set feel, lined with bars, hardware shops, and a pool-room. At one end is the **Plaza de Armas**, with an attractive, if bizarre, Chinese pagoda-style clock tower at its centre, and along another side a modern **Municipalidad** – where, not much more than ten years ago, a TV was sometimes set up for the people to watch an all-important event like a soccer game. These days there are satellite TV dishes all over town and the youth of Puerto Maldonado are as familiar with computer software as they are with jungle mythology. The streets, mostly muddy but for a few concreted main drags, show few signs of wealth, despite the gold dust that lures peasants here from the Andes. If you're considering a river trip, or just feel like crossing to the other side for a walk, follow Jirón Billingshurst, or take the steep steps down from the Plaza de Armas to the **main port**, situated on the Río Madre de Dios – one of the town's most active corners.

There are two main routes out of Puerto Maldonado: Avenida Fitzcarraldo brings you out at the cattle ranches on the far side of the airstrip; while if you turn off on 28 de Julio, you can take the road as far as you like in the direction of Laberinto, Quincemil and Cusco. A regular bus and colectivo ($5) service now connects Puerto Maldonado with **Laberinto** (leaving from the *Hotel Wilson*, or from the main market on Ernesto Rivero), some ninety minutes away. Formerly a gold-mining frontier settlement, since the early 1990s it has been surpassed in importance by the settlement of **Masuko**, deeper into the forest, and is now important mainly for its role as an upriver port for Puerto Maldonado; most boats going upstream start here, though if you're planning to visit Manu Biosphere Reserve, you should set out from Cusco (for more details, see p.512).

Arrival, information and getting around

If you arrive by plane, the blast of hot, humid air you get the moment you step out onto the **airport**'s runway is an instant reminder that this is the Amazon Basin. Aero Continente operate daily jets from Lima via Cusco, while Aero Condor and Aero Santander offer cheaper, daily propeller planes from Cusco. Military Grupo Ocho planes also jet in from Cusco several times weekly, but you need to check their schedule at Cusco airport. There are also two or three flights weekly to other jungle destinations in Madre de Dios, such as Iberia; check with travel agents or the new airline companies on arrival in Peru. Unless you're being picked up as part of an organized tour, **airport transfer** is simplest and coolest by *motokar*, costing around $2.50 for the otherwise very hot eight-kilometre walk.

Most of the **trucks** from Cusco arrive after a tough 500-kilometre journey at Puerto Maldonado main market on Calle Ernesto Rivero, or block 19 of La Unión, also by the market. It's a laborious, three- to ten-day journey down from the glacial highlands, depending on how much it's raining; the worst period is generally between December and March. After passing into the *ceja de selva*, the muddy track winds its slippery way through dense tropical vegetation, via the small settlement at Quincemil.

The quickest way of **getting around town** and its immediate environs is to hail a *motokar* (75¢ in-town flat rate, but check before getting in) or passenger-carrying motorbikes (30¢, also a flat rate). If you fancy doing a bit of running about on your own, or have a lot of ground to cover in town, moped rental is a useful option; you'll find a reasonable place at Av Gonzalez Prada 321, by the *Hotel Wilson* ($1 for 1hr, $10 for 12hr; no deposit, but passports and driving licences required). Make sure there's ample petrol in the tank.

Puerto Maldonado has two main **river ports**, one on the Río Tambopata, at the southern end of León de Velarde, the main street, the other on the Río Madre de Dios, at the northern end of León de Velarde; from the former, there's a very cheap **ferry** service across the river to the newish road to Brazil. From either it's possible to hire a **boatman and canoe** for a river trip; prices usually start at $25 per person for a day journey, for a minimum of two people; this rises to $35 for trips of two to four days. Boats are equipped with a *peque-peque* or small outboard motor, and usually take up to twelve people (see also "Around Puerto Maldonado", p.503). If you're prepared to pay significantly more (from $100 a day per person, again for a minimum of two), you can find boatmen with speedboats and larger outboard motors.

However you get here, you have to go through a yellow fever **vaccination checkpoint** at Puerto Maldonado's small but clean, modern and air-

PUERTO MALDONADO

Río Madre de Dios

National Police & Immigration Office
❶

Viewing Platform
❷ over river

Port area
(Madre de Dios)

BILLINGHURST

LORETO

Ⓐ

CARRION

Ⓑ

Captain
of the Port

CUSCO

☎

Municipal
Building

PLAZA
DE
ARMAS

Cinema

Ⓒ

❸

2 DE MAYO

Banco
de la Nación

Ⓒ $$

Banco de Credito

G PRADA

Ⓓ ❹

Ⓔ

Explorer's Inn
Offices

Ⓕ

Aero Continente

Ⓖ

N

PIURA

ERNESTO RIVERO

J TRONCOSO

❺

Old
Market

La Mascota
(hammock shop)

LEON DE VELARDE

AREQUIPA

26 DE DICIEMBRE

Market

Ⓗ

MOQUEGUA

TACNA

$

Money
Change

0   200 m

ICA

ACCOMMODATION		RESTAURANTS	
Cabaña Quinta	3	La Casa Nostra	G
Hotel Wilson	5	Chifa Wa Seng	F
Moderno	1	Club Witite	A
Reyport	4	Pizzaria Chez Maggy	C
Wasai	2	Pollos a la Brasa La Estrella	D
		Restaurant Califa	B
		La Tiendacita Blanca	H
		Tu Dulce Espera	E

▼ Hotel Don Carlos & Port Area (Tambopata)

conditioned airport, where there's also a **tourist information** kiosk and arte-sania shops. For entry and exit stamps, the **immigration office** is at 26 de Diciembre 356, one block from the Plaza de Armas.

Accommodation

Puerto Maldonado has a reasonable range of **hotels**, most of them either on or within a couple of blocks of León de Velarde. All the better hotels offer pro-tection against mosquitoes and some sort of air-conditioning.

Cabaña Quinta Cusco 535 ☎084/571863 or 571045, ⓕ571890. This is very comfortable, with rooms surrounded by an attractive garden, plus there's an excellent bar-restaurant. ❹–❺

Don Carlos Velarde 1271 ☎084/571029, ⓕ571323. This overlooks the Río Tambopata and some rooms have TVs. Outside the heart of town. ❹

Hostal Amarumayo Libertad 433 ☎084/572661. This is a good deal, not least because it has a small pool and friendly staff. Some 6km northwest from the town centre, but only five minutes from the airport. ❸–❹

Hostal Reyport Velarde 457 ☎084/571177. Friendly but sometimes noisy. ❷–❸

Hotel Iñapari ☎084/572575, ⓕ572155. Run by a Spanish couple, Isabel and Javier. Accommodation is in bungalows next to the forest,

an atmospheric place to start a visit to the jungle (Javier organizes several trips), and the price includes excellent breakfasts and dinners. ❹

Hotel Wilson Av Gonzalez Prada 335 ☎084/572838. This rather basic hotel has private bathrooms but seems quite neglected. ❷

Moderno Billingshurst 357 ☎084/571063. A brightly painted and well-kept hotel, with some-thing of a frontier-town character. ❶

Wasai Billingshurst ☎/ⓕ084/571355, ⓔwasai@telematic.edu.pe, or in Cusco ⓘ084/572290. The best of the more expensive options, offering fine views over the Río Madre de Dios, and a swimming pool with a waterfall and bar set among trees, overlooking a canoe-builders' yard. All rooms are cabin-style with TV and show-er, and staff here also staff organize local tours and run the *Wasai Lodge* (see p.509). ❺

Eating, drinking and nightlife

You should have no problem finding a good **restaurant** in Puerto Maldonado. Delicious river fish are always available, even in ceviche form, and there's veni-son or wild pig fresh from the forest (try *estofado de venado*). One of the best (though also priciest) eateries is the one in the *Wasai* (see above), where you can enjoy an enormous plate of food while watching life pass by along the river. The restaurant at the *Cabaña Quinta* (see above) is hard to beat for its excellent three-course set lunches, often including fresh river fish and fried manioc, while just around the corner, on Piura, the *Restaurant Califa* serves great lunches and specializes in fish and jungle crops.

The cosy *Pizzeria Chez Maggy*, on the Plaza de Armas, is very popular with travellers and locals alike, and at weekends you may have to wait a while for a table; there are no exotic toppings, but it's hard to believe how they can pro-duce such good **pizzas** in this jungle environment. If you like grilled **chick-en**, you're spoiled for choices: try *Pollos a la Brasa La Estrella*, Velarde 474, for the tastiest. On 2 de Mayo, at no. 253, *Chifa Wa Seng* successfully combines tra-ditional **Chinese** meals with an abundance of jungle foodstuffs. For **vegetar-ian food** there's *Natur*, at Velarde 928, but their dishes are a little uninspiring.

Along León de Velarde are a number of **cafés and bars**, one or two of which have walls covered in typical *selvatico*-style paintings, developed to represent and romanticize the dreamlike features of the jungle – looming jaguars, brightly plumed macaws talking to each other in the treetops, and deer drinking water from a still lake. Locals are very keen on sweet and savoury **snacks**, and if you fancy trying some yourself pop into *Tu Dulce Espera*, *La Tiendacita Blanca* or *La Casa Nostra*, all on the fifth block of Velarde. The first sells typical sweets, while the latter two offer traditionally prepared, delicious tropical fruit **juices** (including mango, passionfruit, pineapple and carambola – a local favourite), for less than 50¢ a glass, as well as tamales, *papas rellenas* (stuffed potatoes) and a range of exotic-looking cakes. Also on León de Velarde, the old **market** (mornings only) has excellent juices, fresh fruit and vegetables, while the best place for Brazil nuts is the general store at Velarde 570. Delicious (but hard to eat) aguaje palm fruits are sold at several street corners along Velarde.

There's very little **nightlife** in this laid-back town, especially during the week – most people just stroll around, stopping occasionally to sit and chat in the Plaza de Armas or in bars along the main street. At weekends and fiesta times, however, it's possible to sample *chicha* music (one of the jungle's greatest delights for many people), salsa, which has infiltrated the jungle over the last ten years, and a more recent arrival, the Colombian rhythms of *cumbia* – the latest fads being *technocumbia* and *chichiperalta*. All are loud and easy to move to, and on Friday and Saturday nights, you can usually pinpoint a concert just by following the sound of an electric bass guitar. The best **club** in town is *Witite*, at Velarde 153 (Fri & Sat; 50¢ for men on Sat), which has a surprisingly advanced sound system that plays the whole range of Latino music – though spiders' webs frequently adorn the speakers at this cool spot. There are several other **music bars** (weekends only) clustered around the plaza.

Listings

Airlines Aero Continente, León de Velarde 506/508 ☎084/573702; TANS, León de Velarde 160; and Grupo Ocho, block 6 of 2 de Mayo (no phone).

Banks and exchange There are two banks on the plaza: Banco Credito, Arequipa 334; and Banco de la Nación, Jr Daniel Carrion 233 (both Mon–Fri 9am–1pm & 5–7pm). *Cambistas* usually hang out on the corner of Prada and Puno, near the *Hotel Wilson*. Your hotel might also change dollars.

Captain's office León de Velarde, between Av Gonzalez Prada and 2 de Mayo. For permits to travel by river into the jungle. Mon–Sat 8am–6pm.

INRENA Instituto Nacional de Recursos Naturales is where you have to go for permission to enter the National Parks of the region: Dirección Sub-regional Agraria Madre de Dios, Av 28 de Julio 482.

Post office León de Velarde 675, opposite the corner of Jr Jaime Troncoso. Mon–Sat 8am–8pm, Sun 8am–3pm.

Shopping Excellent-value hammocks are available from La Mascota, León de Velarde 599, on the corner of Gonzalez Prada.

Telephones The main offices of Telefónica del Peru are on block 7 of Puno (daily 7am–11pm). There are also public phones in most parts of town.

Tour agencies Turismo de los Angeles, Jr Puno 657 ☎084/571070.

Onward travel: into Brazil

The route into Brazil was first opened for use by trucks in the late 1980s and is still not commonly used by independent travellers. The dirt road was significantly improved in the late 1990s, though it still might take a while for vehicles during the rainy season, particularly the section between Iberia (close to the Brazilian frontier) and Iñapari (see opposite); generally speaking, you should reach **Iñapari** within a day or two. There is almost no forest along the road now, just secondary growth and *chacra* farms and gardens.

There are currently no regular flights to Brazil from Puerto Maldonado, but details about ad-hoc services can be obtained from Oeste Redes Aereo on Prada, opposite the *Hotel Wilson*; prices are about $40–80. A daily bus to Iberia departs at 8am ($3; a 5–6hr journey) from the quay opposite town over the Río Madre de Dios; several colectivos also make this trip ($7; a 4hr journey). Just outside Iberia is an interesting **Reserve and Information Centre** set up by the local Rubber Tappers Association.

From Iberia, regular, if infrequent, colectivos travel the remaining 70km to the border settlement of **IÑAPARI** ($3; a 90min trip), where there are a couple of basic hostels. Note that **exit stamps** are obtained in Iñapari, rather than Puerto Maldonado. In the dry season it's possible to walk across the Río Acre into **ASSIS**, in Brazil; otherwise you have to take the ferry. The **hostel** (❷) here, on the main plaza, is much nicer than those in Iñapari. Regular buses and colectivos travel from Assis to **Brasileia** (by no means to be confused with the capital) where Brazilian **entry stamps** can be obtained, then on to **Xapuri** and **Río Branco** (totalling another day or two at most).

Around Puerto Maldonado

Madre de Dios boasts spectacular virgin lowland rainforest and exceptional wildlife. Brazil-nut tree trails, a range of lodges, some excellent local guides and ecologists, plus indigenous and colonist cultures are all within a few hours of Puerto Maldonado. Serious jungle trips can be made here with relative ease and without too much expense, and this part of the Amazon offers easy and uniquely rewarding access to rainforest that is much less disturbed than that around Iquitos, or Manaus in the heart of the Brazilian Amazon, for example. There are two main ways to explore: firstly, by arranging your own boat and boatman; and secondly, though considerably more expensive, by taking an excursion up to one of the lodges.

Less than one hour downriver from Puerto Maldonado (90min on the return upriver) is **LAGO SANDOVAL**, a large lake where the Ministry of Agriculture have introduced the large *paiche* fish. At its best on weekday mornings (it gets quite crowded at other times), there are decent opportunities for spotting wildlife, in particular **birds** similar to those at Lago Valencia. You may even spot a **giant otter** (*Pteronura brasiliensis*); for more on these endangered creatures, see p.510. It's also possible to walk to the lake (about 1hr), and once here boatmen and canoes can usually be obtained by your guide for a couple of hours, as can food and drink. Incidentally, if you're travelling to the lake by river, most guides show you the ruined hulk of an old boat. If they claim it had anything to do with Fitzcarrald, don't believe them; it may be similar in style to Fitzcarrald's, but in fact it's smaller and is a far more recent arrival – it's a hospital boat that was in use until two or three decades ago.

It takes the best part of a day by canoe with a *peque-peque*, or around two hours in a *lancha* with an outboard, to reach the huge lake of **LAGO VALENCIA** from Puerto Maldonado. On the way you can stop off to watch some gold-panners on the Madre de Dios and visit a small settlement of Ese Eja Indians; about thirty minutes beyond, you turn off the main river into a narrow channel that connects with the lake. Easing onto the lake itself, the sounds of the canoe engine are totally silenced by the weight and expanse of water. Towards sunset it's quite common to see caimans basking on the muddy banks, an occasional puma, or the largest rodent in the world, a capybara, scuttling away into the forest. Up in the trees around the channel lie hundreds of hoatzin birds, or *gallos* as they are called locally – large, ungainly creatures with orange and brown plumage, long wings and distinctive spiky crests. The strangest feature of the hoatzin is the claws at the end of their wings, which they use to help them climb up into overhanging branches beside rivers and lakes. They have almost lost the power of flight.

There's a police control post on the right as you come out onto the lake, where you must register passports and show your port **captain's permit** (see opposite). Beyond, reached via a slippery path above a group of dugout canoes,

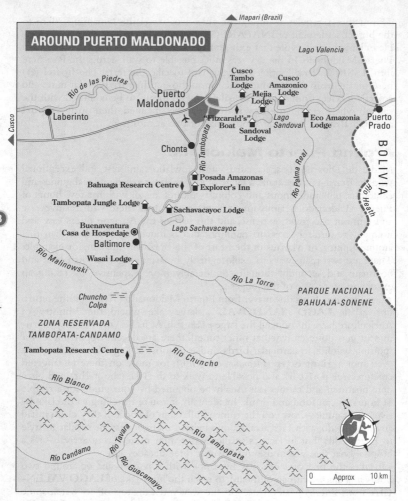

is the lake's one real settlement, a cluster of thatched huts around a slightly larger schoolhouse. Fewer than fifty people live here – a schoolteacher, a lay priest, the shop owner, and a few fishing families. Some tour groups stay in a small **camp** further down, a seasonal nut-collectors' *campamento*, comprising just one cooking hut with an adjacent sleeping platform. By day most people go for a **walk in the forest** – something that's both safer and more interesting with a guide, though whichever way you do it you'll immediately sense the energy and abundance of life. Quinine trees tower above all the trails, surpassed only by the Tahuari hardwoods, trees so tall and solid that jungle shamans describe themselves in terms of their power. Around their trunks you'll often see *pega-pega*, a parasitic ivy-like plant that the shamans mix with the hallucinogenic ayahuasca into an intense aphrodisiac. Perhaps more useful to know about are the liana vines; one thin species dangling above the paths can be used to take away the pain from a *shushupe* snake-bite. Another, the *maravilla* or *palo de agua*, issues a cool stream of fresh water if you chop a section, about half a metre long, and put it to your lips. You may come upon another vine, too – the sinister *matapalo* (or *renaco*), which sometimes extends over dozens of trees, sucking the sap from up to a square kilometre of jungle.

You can also take a **canoe up the lake** for a bit of fishing, passing beaches studded with groups of lazy-looking turtles sunning themselves in line along the top of fallen tree trunks – when they notice the canoe, each one topples off, slowly splashing into the water one after another. It takes a bit more to frighten the **white caimans** away; many can be seen soaking in the sun's strong rays along the margin of the lake. Sometimes over 2m in length, they're a daunting sight, although they won't bite unless you happen to step on one. At night, it's possible to glide along the water, keeping close to the bank, looking for the amber glint reflected from a pair of caiman eyes as the beam from your torch catches them. This is how the locals hunt them, fixing the crocs with a beam of light, then moving closer before blasting them with a shotgun; unless you're really hungry (the meat is something of a delicacy), it's best just to look into their gleaming eyes in the pitch darkness. The only sound on the lake will be the grunting of corvina fish vibrating up through the bottom of the canoe.

Both Lago Valencia and Lago Sandoval are superbly endowed with **birdlife**. In addition to the hoatzin there are kingfishers, cormorants, herons, egrets, pink flamingos, skimmers, macaws, toucans, parrots and gavilans. And behind the wall of trees along the banks hide deer, wild pigs and **tapir**. If you're lucky enough to catch a glimpse of a tapir you'll be seeing one of South America's weirdest creatures – almost the size of a cow, with an elongated rubbery nose and spiky mane. In fact, the tapir is known in the jungle as a *sachavaca* ("forest cow" – *sacha* is Quechua for "forest" and *vaca* is Spanish for "cow"). The easiest fish to catch are **piranha** – all you need is some line, a hook, and a chunk of unsalted meat; throw this into the lake and you've got yourself a piranha.

Another good trip, if you've got at least three days to spare (two nights minimum), is up to the **Río Heath**, a national rainforest sanctuary, though while the **Pampas del Heath** are excellent for macaws they don't have the primary forest necessary for a great variety of wildlife. A shorter trip – five hours up and about two hours down – is to **Tres Chimbales**, where there are a few houses belonging to the Infierno community on the Río Tambopata; it's possible to spend two or three days watching for wildlife, walking in the forest and fishing. From here you can visit **Infierno** village itself – spread out along the river, you can see glimpses of thatched and tin-roofed huts.

One other possibility, though something not commonly done by gringos, is to **travel into Bolivia** on one of the cargo boats that leave more or less every week from Puerto Maldonado. Before embarking on this, however, you'll have to clear your passport and visa with the Puerto Maldonado police and Migraciones offices (see p.501). Puerto Pardo is the last Peruvian frontier settlement (Bolivian formalities can usually be dealt with at the frontier post of Puerto Heath, from where you continue by river to Riberalta). Be aware that the journey from Puerto Maldonado to Riberalta is rough and usually takes ten to fourteen days; always make sure that the boat is going all the way or you might get stuck at the border, which, by all accounts, is not much fun, and you might have to wait days for another boat. From Riberalta there are land and air connections to the rest of Bolivia, as well as river or road access into Brazil via the Río Madeira or Guajara-Mirim.

Organized tours

Compared to independent travel, an **organized excursion** saves time and adds varying degrees of comfort. It also ensures that you go with someone who knows the area, probably speaks English, and, if you choose well, can introduce you to the flora, fauna and culture of the area. It's also worth noting that you are less likely to get ripped off with a registered company with a fixed office and contact details, especially if you should need redress afterwards.

Most people book a trip in Cusco before travelling to Puerto Maldonado, though it is possible to contact most of the operators in Puerto itself, either at the airport or through one of the offices (see below), or through the cafés on León de Velarde. Flying from Cusco is the quickest way to reach Puerto Maldonado, and most Cusco agencies will organize plane tickets ($40–50) for you if you take their tours. The cheapest option is a two-day and one-night tour of the Puerto area, but on these you can expect to spend most of your time travelling and sleeping. Frankly, the Amazon deserves a longer visit, and you're only looking at $25–50 more for an extra day.

Of the ever-increasing number of **lodges** and **tour operators** around Puerto Maldonado, mainly on the ríos Madre de Dios and Tambopata, all offer a good taste of the jungle, but the quality of the experience varies from area to area and lodge to lodge – all lodges tend to offer full board and include transfers, though always check the level of service and ask to see photos at the lodges' offices in Cusco or Lima. It's also worth checking out what costs will be once you're there; complaints are common about the price of drinks, although given the distance they've travelled, the mark-up is hardly surprising. Remember, too, that even the most luxurious place is far removed from normal conveniences, and conditions tend to be rustic and relatively open to the elements. Varying in capacity (the largest can accommodate up to a hundred, the smaller no more than a dozen or so), most lodges have huts, cabins or bungalows built from wood and palm fronds gathered from the forest. Toilets can be anything from standard WC closets covered in mosquito netting to earth privies, while sleeping arrangements can range from bunk rooms to pretty comfy twin doubles with doors and mosquito-net windows. Food is generally good, though you might want to take supplements or treats. Note that most lodges require guests to get up very early in the morning of the day of departure in order to arrive at Puerto Maldonado airport in good time – generally speaking, the nearer the lodge to the town, the longer you can sleep in.

Lodges and tour operators

There are endless **lodges** and **tour companies** to choose from these days, many of them offering a reasonable level of service and access to some of the most biodiverse rainforest regions in the world. It's a good idea to shop around before arriving: that way you can spend time getting a feel of what's available. Otherwise, you can just walk up Plateros, Saphi and Procuradores, or around the Plaza de Armas, in cusco and you'll find most of their offices. Many of the longer, more established companies have their offices out of the centre. One thing worth bearing in mind is that it's possible to buy a jungle package which does not include the airfare; this can work to your advantage, especially if you're able to secure one of the discounted air tickets (to as low as $29 from the standard $59 each way) from Cusco to Puerto Maldonado. It's worth checking what deals are on at the time with all of the airline companies (see Listings, p.502).

Bahuaja Research Centre ⊤/Ⓕ084/573348. A small lodge aimed at the less wealthy traveller. It's fairly basic – toilets and showers are shared – but has a pleasant setting. Visits go to Tres Chimbales and Lago Sachavacayoc, with guiding in English and Spanish, plus there are extensive trails in the surrounding forest. The research side of the operation is associated with the UK organization Greenforce. From $165 per person for 4 days and 3 nights.

Buenaventura Casa de Hospedaje
☏ 084/572590, ✉ jerko_herrera@exite.com.pe. Located in the community of Baltimore, 4hr upriver from Puerto Maldonado (6–7hr by *peque-peque*). Adjoining a family home and *chacra* gardens, this is a good but bare-bones place, with shared toilets and showers. The trail system is quite limited, but trips go to the nearby waterfall and Chuncho *colpa* (guides speak Spanish only). $20 per day per person full board, $15 without.

Casa Machiguenga contactable through Manu Expeditions (see p.517). Owned by the Machiguenga Indian communities of Tayakome and Yombebato, though run by a German NGO as the Machiguenga are still undergoing a capacity-building programme. It's pretty rustic, with accommodation in huts, though with mod cons such as hot water and showers available. $35–45 per night per person.

Cusco Amazonico Lodge Pasaje J. C. Tello C-13, Urbanización Santa Monica, Cusco ☏ 084/235314, ✉ koechlin@inkaterra.com.pe; in Lima ☏ 01/4226574, ℻ 4226574, ✉ reservas @inkaterra.com.pe. Set up by a French-Peruvian venture in 1975, comforts here include a cocktail bar and good food (often a buffet). The main excursion is to Lago Sandoval, some 20min upriv-

er, and guides speak several languages. The lodge owns 10,000 hectares of forest surrounding it and has recently established a monkey island. From $160 per person for 3 days and 2 nights ($25 supplement for a single).

Cusco Tambo Lodge Plateros 351, Cusco ☏ 084/222332 or 236159; or at the airport in Puerto Maldonado. A little rough for accommodation (wooden huts with bunks and mosquito nets) and not quite such a beautiful location as the others, this isn't for those seriously interested in wildlife. Although classified as a jungle trip, it's only about 11km from Puerto Maldonado and there's little forest in the area; instead, you get *chacra* fields and gardens. However, it's reliable and inexpensive, you don't have to invest heavily in food or equipment, plus it offers airport transfers. There are jungle walks, visits to Lago Sandoval and a gold-panning beach upstream, plus a viewing tower from which to see the distant forest. $30–35 per person per night.

Eco Amazonia Lodge Portal de Panes 109, Oficina 6, Cusco ☏ 084/236159, ℻ 225068, ✉ ecolodge@chasqui.unsaac.edu.pe; Av Larco 1083, Oficina 408, Miraflores, Lima ☏/℻ 01/2422708; ⓦ www.unsaac.edu.pe/CUSCO/TURISMO/Agencia /EcoAmazonia. Less than two hours downriver of Puerto Maldonado, this large establishment offers basic bungalows and dormitories. The area abounds in stunning oxbow lakes but can't claim

---

Tambopata-Candamo Reserved Zone

Arguably containing some of the world's finest and most biodiverse rainforest, the Tambopata-Candamo Reserved Zone is accessible from many of the lodges in the Puerto Maldonado region. Entrance to the area costs $2 per person for those staying at lodges, or up to $20 for anyone camping independently. Initially an area of less than 6000 hectares, it was transformed into a Reserved Zone, mainly due to the scientific work of the adjacent *Explorer's Inn* lodge. In 1990, after further studies had proved the value of the forest in terms of biodiversity conservation, the reserved sector was expanded to almost 1.5 million hectares. In 2000 the Bahuaja-Sonene National Park was enlarged, and incorporated almost 250,000 hectares of the original Tambopata-Candamo Reserved Zone. It's not possible to visit the National Park, except for licensed operators coming down from the Alto Tambopata on rafting expeditions or on tours to one of the major macaw **colpas** (salt-licks) in the region. Like most licks, they attract wild birds and animals because they offer the salts, minerals and clay required for nutrition and as a digestive aid by these creatures. Although reducing the Tambopata-Candamo Reserved Zone, the expansion of the National Park is something of a major success for conservation in Peru. For more details, contact: **TReeS** (c/o John Forrest, Tambopata Reserve Society, PO Box 33153, London NW3 4DR, UK), a UK organization with strong links with the Tambopata area; they should be able to offer you detailed and up-to-date information on the situation and the environmental work going on there. They can also advise you about many of the lodges.

the variety of flora and fauna of the Tambopata-Candamo Reserved Zone, though it is recommended for bird-watching, plus it has swamp-forest platforms and is the only lodge in the area with tree-canopy access. Packages usually include visits to Lago Sandoval, about 30min upriver, plus organized visits can be made to the Palma Real community, though this is often anticlimactic and of dubious value to both tribe and tourist. There's also a monkey island. From $40 to $60 per person per night according to length of stay.

Explorandes San Fernando 320, Miraflores, Lima ⓣ01/4450532, ⓕ4454686, ⓔPostmast@Exploran.com.pe. A veteran company operating whitewater rafting expeditions, including a 12-day trip starting out from Puno by road, then travelling down through cloud forest, and finally rafting through class III to V rapids along the Río Tambopata to Puerto Maldonado, where the last night is spent in a lodge. $1495 per person, for a minimum of four people.

Explorer's Inn Plateros 365, Cusco ⓣ084/235342; or in the Peruvian Safaris Lima office, Alcanfores 459, Miraflores ⓣ01/447888 or 4474761, ⓕ2418427, ⓦwww.peruviansafaris.com; office in Puerto Maldonado at Av Fitzcarrald 136 ⓣ084/572078. In the Tambopata-Candamo Reserved Zone, 58km (about 3hr) in a motorized *canoa* upriver from Puerto Maldonado, this is a large, well-organized lodge where research has contributed towards building a world-record list of species (580 birds and 1230 butterflies; apparently more than have been discovered in any other similarly-sized forest region). Spanish- or English-speaking guides are available (boots are provided for jungle walks), and there are excellent displays, mostly in English, about rainforest ecology, plus there are radio links to the outside world. Food is good, and accommodation is generally in twin rooms with private bath, and full board is included. The price includes airport transfers, with expeditions to a nearby macaw salt-lick (*colpa*) – generally requiring one night camping out – plus there's a superb network of well-marked jungle trails. From $180 per person for 3 days and nights; enquire about rates for special-interest visitors (eg ornithologists).

Iñapari Amazon Adventures c/o Solo Selva, Plateros 364, Cusco ⓣ084/228590, ⓕ247259, ⓦwww.soloselva.com. This outfit offer quite rough but well organized and adventurous safaris in the Río de las Piedras region, as well as other rivers on request. In the Piedras they frequently visit the Río Pariamanu, Lago Lucerna, a macaw clay-lick. They use native guides. Prices start at around $160 for 3 nights and $310 for 5.

Inotawa Expeditions Fonavi J9, Puerto Maldonado (daily 9–11am & 4–5pm) ⓣ084/572511; or Lima 01/4674560, ⓦwww.inotawaexpeditions.com. Located on the Río Tambopata quite close to the start of the Bahuaja-Sonene National Park, they have a nice lodge in a good location; they offer expeditions to Colpa Colorado, a macaw and animal salt-lick a further 8 hours into the forest from their lodge. Prices start at around $150 for 3 days/2 nights and $400 for five nights, but the minimum group required is 6.

Mejia Lodge ⓣ084/571428. On the shores of the popular Lago Sandoval, this rustic-style lodge is perfect for canoe exploration of the lake. It's rarely full, so it's fine to just turn up here by canoe from Puerto Maldonado without prior arrangement (get the boatman to drop you off on the trail). One of two lodges on the lake, this is an expanded family home with ten doubles and basic, shared toilet facilities. $15–$20 per person per day (dependent on season and open to negotiation), including food.

Posada Amazonas Lodge and Tambopata Research Centre contact through Rainforest Expeditions, Aramburu 166, 4B, Lima 18 ⓣ01/4218347 or 2214182, ⓕ4218183, ⓦwww.perunature.com. This is probably the region's best lodge for its relationship with locals – it's owned by the Ese Eja community of Infierno (though mainly non-native members work here) – and for its wildlife research. There's great bird diversity in seven distinct, easily accessible habitats, plus good populations of primates and large mammals. Resident researchers act as guides (different languages available), and most packages include a visit to Lago Tres Chimbadas; additional trips to the Tambopata macaw *colpa* (6–8hr upriver) can be arranged, involving a night at the remote Tambopata Research Centre (TRC); a minimum of 6 days is recommended for complete tours. The lodge itself features large, stylish doubles with shared bath, set in three native-style buildings, plus a central dining area-cum-bar and lecture room. From $90 per day per person.

Sachavacayaco Lodge contact through the *Cabaña Quinta* (see p.501). A small lodge offering a relatively rustic, more intimate and quiet experience than most, 3–4hr upriver from Puerto Maldonado. Visits usually go to Lago Sachavacayoc, with mostly Spanish-speaking guides. From $150 for 3 days/2 nights per person, minimum of 4 people.

Sandoval Lodge InkaNatura, Manuel Bañon 461, San Isidro, Lima ⓣ01/4402022, ⓦwww.inkanatura.com, or Av Sol 821, second floor, Cusco ⓣ084/226392, ⓔinkanatura@chavin.rcp.net.pe. On the shores of Lago Sandoval, and usually accessed by canoe, this is the only lodge offering regular trips to this zone. It's medium-sized and features one large communal building as a bar and dining room, plus it boasts electricity and hot water. Most groups spend time on the lake or explore the small, well-trodden surrounding trail system, and there's also a small platform on the Río Heath. Guides speak several languages, including English. From $60 to $80 per person per day, depending on size of group, nature of visit and length of stay.

Tambopata Jungle Lodge Av Pardo 705, Cusco ℗084/225701, ℉238911, ®www .tambopatalodge.com. Located in the Tambopata-Candamo Reserved Zone, 12km up the Río Tambopata from the *Explorer's Inn*, nearly 4hr from Puerto Maldonado. The lodge has comfortable, individual cabin-style accommodation and offers excellent tours of the forest, mainly in Spanish and English. It's located quite close to a community of *colonos*, some of whom farm while others pan for gold. Trips include a visit to Lago Condenado and sometimes Lago Sandoval, plus the Chuncho *colpa* by arrangement. From $160 per person for 3 days/2 nights.

Wasai Lodge owned by the *Wasai* hotel in Puerto Maldonado, C Arequipa 242; or in Cusco through Solo Selva, Plateros 364 ℗084/228590, ℉247259, ®www.soloselva.com. Four hours upriver from Puerto Maldonado is this relatively new and smallish lodge set in the forest, with a pleasant jungle bar and dining area. Spanish- and English-speaking guides are available, with 15km of trails in the vicinity plus trips to the Chuncho *colpa* on request. Usually from $340 per person for 4 days and 3 nights, but sometimes offered with promotional discounts at around $175; including a visit to Lago Sandoval plus the last night at the *Wasai* (avoiding the early morning start); $500 for 7 days/6 nights, including a visit to the *colpa*.

Independent travel

Travelling independently can be rewarding, though note that most of the major river trips (including Lago Valencia) require visitors to obtain **permission** from the Captain's Office in Puerto Maldonado (see Listings p.502) – though boatman and guides generally do this and also organize payment of entry fees for you at the **INRENA office** in Iquitos at Pevas 350–363 (℗084/231330 or 232980, ℉234861, ℮rnps-zrg@aeci.org.pe). Even if you do end up doing this yourself it's normally quite straightforward, though it can be a battle to be heard over the *chicha* music on the Captain's radio.

Fortunately, it's still possible to get your own expedition together without spending a fortune. For limited excursions all you need is a boat and boatman, permission from the Captain's Office and basic essentials (see box on p.462). One of the most important aspects of any boat trip is finding the right boatman: three **recommended guides** include the pretty reliable and well-organized Willy Wither, who has lived in the area for many years and goes to a wide range of places by canoe and on foot (he usually meets flights at Puerto Maldonado airport and speaks mainly Spanish); Javier Salazar, who owns the *Hotel Iñapari* (see p.501) and often takes groups up the Río de las Piedras and guides in English, Spanish or French; and Romel Nacimiento, a boat-owner and guide who specializes in day-trips to Lago Sandoval, and who can usually be found at the Madre de Dios river port (ask around to find out where he is). Alternatively, ask around town or go down to the port to speak to a few of the guys who have canoes and motors. If there are six or more of you, these do-it-yourself trips (*always* go with a guide) can cost under $25 a day per person, all-inclusive; expect to pay between $50 and $120 a day for a reasonable launch (big enough for eight), with a decent outboard motor, a guide-cum-boatman, and fuel. All guides should have a Ministerio de Turismo *carnet* (ID card).

Whichever way you organize it, if you have the opportunity to spend several days exploring the Río Tambopata, try and get up as far as the mouth of the Río Tavara, where the wildlife is still abundant. No *colonos* have ever settled this far upstream and the jungle is wild, though not totally virgin – when Colonel Fawcett (a British explorer who vanished in the Amazon in the early twentieth century on a quixotic search for an ancient city he had heard about from the Indians) came through here, rubber extraction was already going on and a mule track running from Puno down the Tavara valley had been established.

Manu Biosphere Reserve

Encompassing almost two million hectares of virgin cloud- and rainforest on the foothills of the eastern Andes, the Manu area was created in 1973 as a national park, and then elevated to the status of Biosphere Reserve by UNESCO in 1977. In 1987 it became a World Natural Heritage Site. About half the size of Switzerland, the **Manu Biosphere Reserve** covers a total of 1,881,200 hectares of relatively pristine rainforest, from crystalline cloud-forest streams and waterfalls down to slow-moving, chocolate-brown rivers in the dense lowland jungle – a uniquely varied environment. The only permanent residents within this vast area are the teeming forest wildlife, a few virtually uncontacted native groups who have split off from their major tribal units (Yaminahuas, Amahuacas and Machiguenga), the park guards, and the scientists at a biological research station situated just inside the park on the beautiful Lago Cocha Cashu, where flocks of macaws pass the time cracking open Brazil nuts with their powerful, highly adapted beaks.

For **flora and fauna**, the Manu is pretty much unbeatable in South America, home to 20,000 vascular plant types (one five-square-kilometre area was found to contain 1147 species of vascular plants, almost as many as in the whole of Great Britain), with over 5000 flowering plants, 1200 species of butterfly, 1000 types of bird, 200 kinds of mammal and an unknown quantity of reptiles and insects. Rich in macaw salt-licks, otter lagoons, prowling jaguars, there are thirteen species of monkey and seven species of macaw in Manu, and it still contains other species in serious danger of extinction, such as the giant otter and the black caiman (*Melanosuchus niger*).

The reserve is divided into three zones. **Zone A** is the core zone, the **National Park** (1,532,806 hectares), which is strictly preserved in its natural state. **Zone B** is a Buffer Zone (257,000 hectares, generally known as the **Reserved Zone** and set aside mainly for controlled research and tourism. **Zone C** is the Transitional or **Cultural Zone** (91,394 hectares), an area of human settlement for controlled traditional use. Accessible only by boat, any expedition to Manu is very much in the hands of the gods, thanks to the

The Otorongo otters

The **giant otters** of Lago Otorongo are one of the world's most endangered species, and contact with people has to be minimized for their safety and long-term conservation. They are also bio-indicators of the environment, since they only live where there is clean, healthy water and a wide choice of fish, so conservation of this rainforest environment is of primary importance. Only the oldest female of the group is mated with, so reproduction is very slow – the "queen" otters only have two or three cubs a year, usually around October, which can be expected to live for around thirty years. The top-ranking male otters are responsible for defending the group and do very little fishing, taking the catch from younger males instead.

Although they appear friendly as they play in their large family groups, they can be very aggressive, able to keep jaguars at bay and kill caimans who approach their lakeside nesting holes, which they mark by mixing male urine with clay at the entrance.

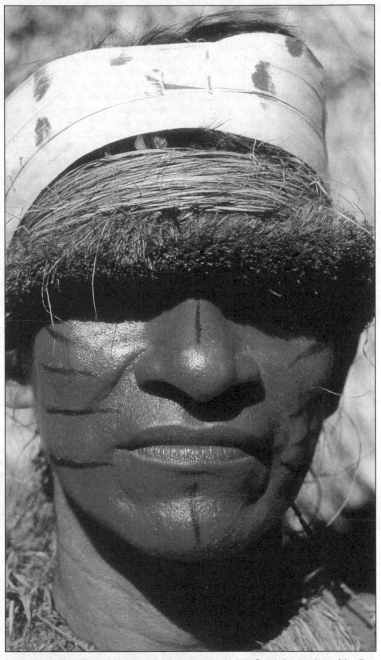

△ Bora Indian, headman of the village

temperamental jungle environment; the region experiences a rainy season from December to March, and is best visited between May and August when it's much drier, although at that time the temperatures often exceed 30°C.

The highlight of most organized visits to Manu is the trail network and lakes of **Cocha Salvador** (the largest of Manu's oxbows, at 3.5km long) and **Cocha Otorongo**, both bountiful jungle areas rich in animal, water and birdlife. The latter is best known for the family of **giant otters** (see box, p.510) which live here; because of this, canoeing is not permitted, but there is a floating platform which can be manoeuvred to observe the otters fishing and playing from a safe distance (though your guide has to book a time for this): 30–50m is good enough to observe and photograph them, though as this is Manu's most popular tourist area, you're likely to meet other groups and there can be severe competition for access to the platform. Other wildlife to look out for includes the plentiful **caimans**, including the two- to three-metre white alligators and the rarer three- to five-metre black ones, and you can usually see several species of **monkey** (including dusky titis, woolly monkeys, red howlers, brown capuchins and the larger spider monkeys – known locally as *maquisapas*). Sometimes big mammals such as **capybara** or **white-lipped peccaries** (called *sajinos* in Peru) also lurk in the undergrowth.

The flora of Manu is as outstanding as its fauna. Huge **cedar trees** can be seen along the trails, covered in hand-like vines climbing up their vast trunks (most of the cedars were taken out of here between 1930 and 1963, before it became a protected area). The giant **catahua trees**, many over 150 years old, are traditionally the preferred choice for making dugout canoes – and some are large enough to make three or four – though second choice is the **lagarto tree**.

Just east of Zone B, but often visited in combination with it or with Zone C, is the **Manu Wildlife Centre**, a comfortable lodge some ninety minutes downriver from Boca Manu by motorized dugout. Owned by Manu Expeditions (see p.517) and the non-profit Selva Sur Conservation Group, it's located on privately owned rainforest and is built of the same sustainable local materials that the native Machiguenga Indians use – bamboo, wood, and palm-frond roofing – and all rooms are screened with mosquito nets. It operates hides close to a superb salt-lick where small parrots and larger more colourful macaws can be seen. It claims to be strategically located in an area of forest that has the highest diversity of micro-habitats in the Manu, and *tierra-firme* (lowland forest that doesn't get flooded), transitional flood plain, varzea and bamboo forest are all found close by, and an astounding 530 bird species have been recorded in one year alone. The Blanquillo macaw and parrot salt-lick is only thirty minutes away by river, with floating blinds to access the wildlife attracted here. About an hour's walk through the forest there's also a large *colpa* where tapirs and Brocket deer regularly come. The centre also features mobile canopy towers, making it possible to see more birds and even monkeys; access to these is by rope and harness, but there's also a static canopy platform with a spiral stairway.

The only viable way of **visiting Manu** is by joining an organized tour through one of the main Cusco agents, which is safer and generally cheaper than doing it yourself; you share the work and responsibilities, you can look after each other if you get ill or something goes wrong, and there's security in numbers. However, you can travel independently as far as Boca Manu, but unless you've secured a highly elusive special permit (see box opposite), you then have to head away from the reserve on one of the canoes that go most weeks (cargo and river permitting) to Puerto Maldonado. For this you'll need to be well stocked and prepared for a rough voyage of several days – plus a few more if you have to hitch along the way. The only significant settlement en route is **Boca Colorado** at the confluence of the ríos Colorado and Madre de Dios, a small gold-miner's service town full of vermin, human and animal. Remember, this region is well off the beaten tourist trail and is relatively wild territory, populated by *colonos*, indigenous Indians, and even smugglers and terrorists.

Into the reserve

Manu Biosphere Reserve is better reached from Cusco than it is from Puerto Maldonado. Flying direct to Boca Manu (see p.516) will dramatically affect the price and the amount of time you get in the reserve (it's only a 30–45min flight but costs $300–400), and twin-engined planes can be chartered from the airport in Cusco. Most people, however, travel there on transport organized by their tour operators; otherwise, **buses** operated by Gallito de las Rocas (Av Manco Capac 105, Cusco; ☏084/277255) go to Pilcopata and usually beyond to Salvación at about 10am most Mondays and Fridays ($7; a 10–14hr journey depending on road conditions). **Trucks**, generally loaded to the brim with beer, fuel and passengers, leave Cusco from Avenida Huascar, and some from the Coliseo, every Monday, Wednesday, Friday and Sunday for Shintuya ($6; a 20–30hr journey in good conditions). All of the necessary **provisions and equipment** (see box on p.462) should be bought in Cusco, and this is one journey where you'll definitely need as much petrol as you can muster (a 55-gallon drum is probably enough). A sleeping mat is also a good idea even if only to sit on during the long journey to Shintuya; if the truck is carrying fuel, wear old clothes and cover your baggage properly. If you can afford one luxury, make it a sturdy pair of binoculars, preferably brought with you from home.

The first four- to six-hour stage is by road to the attractive town of **Paucartambo** (see p.183), over stupendous narrow roads with fine panoramas of the region's largest glaciated mountain of Ausungate, a major *apu* – or god – for the Incas and also the locals today. From Paucartambo onwards, the precipitous and gravelly nature of the road down through the cloud forest to the navigable sections of the Río Alto Madre de Dios means that access is supposedly limited to one direction per day, except Sunday, when it's a free-for-all. You can travel down on Monday, Wednesday and Friday, and back up on Tuesday, Thursday and Saturday.

It's another 30km to the turn-off to **Tres Cruces** (see p.184); from here the road winds down, at times along narrow stretches of quite bad track with drops

---

Manu permits

Permits to visit Manu are granted to groups only (mainly to established tour companies operating out of Cusco), and done so according to quotas, in order to limit the number of people in the reserve at any one time and throughout any particular year. It's virtually impossible to get permission by going it alone, and no settlers, hunters or missionaries are allowed in, while tourists are allowed into Zones B and C only as part of organized visits with guides, following the basic rules of non-interference with human, animal or vegetable life. Zone A is restricted to the occasional scientist (usually biologists or anthropologists) and indigenous groups, including the recently contacted Nahua people. However, if you're a naturalist, photographer, or can demonstrate a serious interest, then it is sometimes possible to gain a **special permit** for restricted areas; contact INRENA in Lima (see p.463).

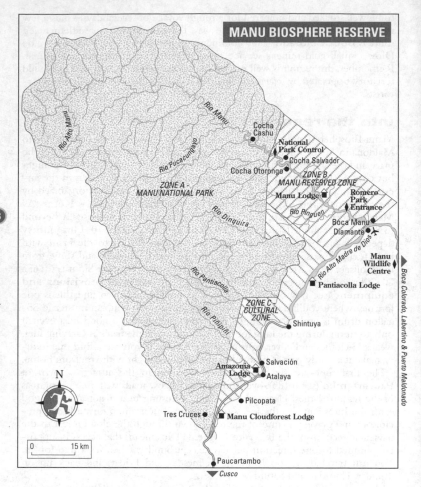

MANU BIOSPHERE RESERVE

Rio Alto Manu

Rio Manu

Cocha Cashu

National Park Control

Cocha Salvador

Cocha Otorongo

ZONE B - MANU RESERVED ZONE

Rio Pucacungayo

ZONE A - MANU NATIONAL PARK

Manu Lodge

Romero Park Entrance

Rio Pinguen

Boca Manu

Rio Dinquira

Diamante

Manu Wildlife Centre

Rio Alto Madre de Dios

Rio Pantiacolla

Pantiacolla Lodge

Rio Pinipini

ZONE C - CULTURAL ZONE

Shintuya

N

Amazónia Lodge

Salvación

Atalaya

Pilcopata

Tres Cruces

Manu Cloudforest Lodge

0   15 km

Paucartambo

Cusco

Boca Colorado, Laberinto & Puerto Maldonado

of well over 300m only a few feet away. Somehow the beauty overrides the scariness for most people, and a surprising amount of wildlife can usually be spotted as the track continues downhill – andean guans, mountain motmots, woodcreepers, oropendulas and the brilliant-red *gallo de las rocas* (the national bird of Peru) can all be seen. Of course, you're more likely to get a glimpse of these if you're travelling with a good guide who has a well-trained eye.

The first settlement you come to in the high jungle is **Chontachaca**, which is Quechua for "Chonta Bridge" (*chonta* being the common hardwood palm whose wood is used throughout the Peruvian Amazon for Indian bows and arrow points). Vehicles rarely stop here, and shortly beyond you pass through the slightly larger **Patria**, another frontier-type village, where coca is grown in some quantities. Turkeys, pigs and children play beside the road and the town's grassed-over, neglected concrete fountain says a lot about this place, which is more famous for its cock-fighting fiestas than anything else. Around here the jungle is being cleared for cash crops and, occasionally during the 1990s, so much vegetation was being burned that planes were occasionally unable to land in Cusco because of the rising smoke.

At the next town, **PILCOPATA**, the road crosses a river over a new steel bridge; to the right, a rickety old wooden one is left to decay in memory of a truck that destroyed it and fell into the water in the mid-1990s. Most buses and trucks stop here for the night, and there's a basic **hotel** (**❶**), a few small shops and a simple market here. The road then skirts the Río Alto Madre de Dios, which eventually merges with the Río Manu to form the great Río Madre de Dios. The forest around here hides some fascinating **petroglyphs**, etched onto boulders by Indians before the Spanish arrived. However, these are along the

The Diamante Piro (the Yine tribe)

The Diamante community of **Piro Indians**, known as the Yine, were brought to the region from the lower Urubamba river, way beyond the Manu area, by rubber barons over a hundred years ago. Some of the community are said to want to return to the Urubamba, but are scared to travel there overland because of possible retribution by other indigenous groups who live in the reserve and who still, generations later, hold grudges against them for the violence during the rubber era. In 1987, some Piro guides and the Peruvian president Belaunde were attacked by sheets of arrows as they travelled in the then national park. Since then, things have improved substantially and these days the Piro-Yine are actively engaged in a tourism project – the Yine Project.

This scheme is a co-production between a Cusco eco-tourism operator (Pantiacolla Tours along with an American partner, Ryan Burtoft, who organizes and runs the lodge), and the Yine from Diamante, near Boca Manu. Since the creation of Manu Biosphere Reserve, the Yine are no longer able to hunt on the north bank of the Río Alto Madre de Dios, but they have not gained any compensatory involvement in tourism. Just a few of them work as boat drivers, cook's assistants and such. There has never been a Yine guide in Manu. Currently the Yine generate much of their cash income by selling logging rights on their land (which is on the south side of the Río Alto Madre de Dios, between Boca Manu airstrip and Diamante), and the goal of the project is to replace this income by involving the Yine in tourism. Since visiting Manu is currently only an eco-tourism experience, with no cultural content, this is an attempt to broaden what is available for visitors to the region, as well as providing a new and sustainable source of income for the indigenous people of the area. The initial stage of the Yine Project, offers one- or two-day extensions to people visiting Manu Biosphere Reserve, so that they can experience something of the cultural side of the rainforest — ie meet the people who have lived there for millennia, and make contact with their traditions. They have built a very nice lodge (*Yine Lodge*) at the Boca Manu airstrip, which ten years from now will be owned and run by the Yine. The Pantiacolla people are training Yine to guide tourists in the rainforest, and the hope is that eventually there will be Yine guiding in Manu, as well as owning and running the lodge. You can take a walk through the forest with Ryan and two Yine guides, from Boca Manu airstrip to Diamante. The Yine have agreed to stop hunting in this part of their land, to save it for tourism. There is a secret mammal clay lick here (one of the keys to successful rainforest wildlife viewing), but this will not be opened up until they have developed a means to protect it from poachers. In Diamante (quite a pleasant native community) it's possible to have an excellent lunch of very good *juanes* and *masato*, and even get body-painted with *huito*, whose startling purple effects do not show up for a few hours, though they don't disappear entirely for almost a month. You can also paddle from here to the Boca Manu airstrip, where lessons are sometimes available in the arts of Yine archery, pottery-making and basketwork. Contact info: Pantiacolla Tours, Plateros 360, Cusco ☎084/238323, ⓕ252696, ⓦwww.pantiacolla.com.

Río Pishiyura, hidden in the restricted area of Manu and reported to be protected by a still largely unacculturated group of Mashco-Piro Indians, who shoot arrows at intruders. This is also one of the areas where the legendary Inca city of gold – **El Dorado**, or **Paititi** – is reputed to lie.

The following day takes you on to the small riverside settlement of **ATALAYA** (10–12hr from Cusco); some tours cross the river to spend the night at an old hacienda which has been converted into an attractive tourist lodge – *Amazonia Lodge* (❺, half board), 600m above sea level on the edge of the cloud forest. The food here is excellent and it's one of the few Peruvian jungle lodges to have solar-heated showers; the owners can be contacted in Cusco (Ramiro Yabar Calderon, C Matara 334 ☎084/231370, ✉amazonia@correo.dnet.com.pe). They offer full board and excursions in the region and frequently work with Manu Expeditions (see opposite). There are also a few **restaurants** in town.

Twenty minutes down the road from Atalaya, at the pueblo of **Salvación**, 28km before Shintuya, the Manu Biosphere Reserve has an office where your guide will usually be expected to show his permits. There are also a couple of rough **hostels** and one or two places to catch some **food** – a bowl of jungle soup or, if you're lucky, fish with manioc. Trucks, mostly carrying timber, go from here to Cusco every Tuesday, Thursday and Saturday. Two hours beyond Atalaya, at **SHINTUYA**, the road finishes. The **Dominican Mission** here has been in existence for forty years, though recently many of the indigenous members have left after making good money with their chainsaws – some of them now own trucks to facilitate the supply of timber out to Cusco and beyond. There's no hotel, but there's no problem about **camping** if you ask permission – the best spot is beside the small stream that enters the main river (the water is cleaner here). Keep a watchful eye on your baggage, as Shintuya also has a sizeable transient population, passing to and from the gold-mining areas downriver. If you're travelling independently, all that remains to do is to seek out a canoe and a reliable boatman/guide, and if you've brought some of your own fuel to bargain with, it should be relatively easy to find a decent deal at the mission; the Moscosa family (especially Cesar, Pepe and Darwin) are reliable guides. Boats from Shintuya cost from around $300 for a week (though it can be double this if it's a busy season); if it's big enough, and most are, the boat can be shared between as many as seven or eight, and the price of an extra week isn't that much more. Remember that things happen on a different timescale in the Peruvian jungle, so get the boat organized as soon as you arrive, and try to make an early start the next day. If it can be arranged, it's a good idea to take a surplus, small dugout canoe for entering smaller channels and lagoons. Alternatively, you might be able to catch one of the cargo boats prepared to take passengers direct to Boca Colorado (see p.518), for around $25.

Downriver, in a *lancha* with outboard motor, it's half a day down the Alto Madre de Dios to **BOCA MANU**, a mere 300m above sea level and little more than a small settlement of a few families living near the airstrip, though this is likely to change, as oil and gas exploration in the Madre de Dios region has restarted, and Boca Manu may well become utilized by helicopters and service planes, just as it was in the late 1970s when oil companies had a contract for exploration here. There's no hostel (people do **camp** on the other side of the river, but these are mostly visiting Indians or tour groups) and while there is a small shop here (prices double those in Cusco, with no guarantee of supply), the population mainly serves the gold-mining settlements downstream towards Puerto Maldonado. Close by is the native Piro community of **Diamante**, responsible for managing the **airstrip**, a major link to Cusco. In

1983, when it was controlled by cocaine smugglers, the airstrip was the scene of Hollywood-style drama when an unmarked Colombian plane was overloaded with cocaine. The plane crashed into the vegetation at the end of the airstrip, and the gang leader had his men torch the plane; its remains are still there in the undergrowth. The Peruvian army later regained control of the strip, but now the Piro make a little money from each flight that uses it and sell good, cheap, artesania at the small hut that serves as the airport terminal.

Organized tours

There are quite a few **organized tours** competing for travellers who want to visit Manu. Many are keen to keep the impact of tourism to a minimum, which means limiting the number of visits per year (it's already running well into the thousands). However, they do vary quite a bit in quality of guiding, level of comfort and price range. If you go with one of the companies listed below, you can generally be confident that they have a good reputation both for the way they treat their tourists and the delicate ecology of the rainforest itself.

Caiman Plateros 359, Cusco ☎084/254041, ℱ254042, ✉explorcaiman@terra.com.pe. A relatively new company, but with some experienced and professional guides, Caiman specialize in Manu, basically offering 4 days and 3 nights from around $300. Their 6- 9-day tours are better, since they do include exploring within the Manu reserve itself, including Lago Otorongo, with a chance of spotting the giant river otter family that lives there (more in the region of $500–600).

Ecological Adventures Manu Plateros 356, Cusco ☎084/261640, ℱ225562, ⓦwww .manuaventures.com. Jungle-trip specialists and one of the first operators running trips into Manu, with their own vehicles, boats and multilingual guides. Their camping-based tours are cheaper than most, with the 8-day option going in and out by bus, but they also offer shorter options which go in by bus and out by plane. Tour-only price for 5-night trip from $580.

Expediciones Vilca Plateros 363, Cusco ☎084/251872, ℱ244751, ⓦwww.cbc.org.pe/manuvilca; or at C Saphi 456 ☎084/681002. Manu specialists, they have a good reputation and their guides are well informed, taking eco-tourism seriously. Their 8-day tour includes camping in Zone B, plus a visit to the macaw lick at Blanquillo as well as 3 nights in *albergues*, from around $600–790, depending on whether you take a bus or plane in. They also offer 5- and 6-day trips, including flights to and/or from Boca Manu from around $720.

InkaNatura Travel Av Sol 821, second floor, Cusco ☎084/226392, ⓦwww.inkanatura.com; or in Lima via InkaNatura Travel, Manuel Bañon 461, San Isidro, Lima ☎01/4402022, ℱ4229225. InkaNatura offer customized travel, from 4 to 5 days, operating from the Manu Wildlife Centre,

where one of the nearby highlights is the world's largest tapir salt-lick. They also accommodate people at the *Cock of the Rock Lodge*, 6hr by road from Cusco, in one of the best cloud-forest locations for bird-watching. $1050–1150; discounts available to groups of 6 or more. The lodge is owned and operated principally by Selva Sur, a Cusco-based nonprofit conservation group. Bookings through its own in-house travel agency, InkaNatura Travel.

Manu Expeditions Av Pardo 895, PO Box 606, Cusco ☎084/226671, ℱ236706, ✉Adventure@ManuExpeditions.com. One of the best and the most responsible companies, run by a British ornithologist. They offer 3- to 9-day camping expeditions into Zone B and to the Manu Wildlife Centre (see p.512), with solar-powered radio communications and a video machine. Thoroughly recommended, the guides and service are top-quality, good English is spoken, they offer air and overland transfers to Boca Manu (they have their own overland transport), and food, beds (or riverside campsite) and bird-blinds are all included. $688–1595; discounts available to South American Explorers' Club members.

Manu Nature Tours Av Pardo 1046, Cusco ☎084/252721, ℱ234793, ⓦwww.manuperu.com; or Portal Comercio, 195 Plaza de Armas, Cusco ☎/ℱ084/252526. A highly professional company that operates *Manu Lodge*, one of only two within Zone B, where you can join their 4- to 8-day programmes. They also run 3-day trips to *Manu Cloud Forest Lodge* in their private reserve by the southeast boundary of Zone A, where torrent ducks, *gallos* and even woolly monkeys are often seen. $268–299 for *Manu Cloud Forest Lodge*, $1040–2065 for 4- to 8-day programmes; discounts available to South American Explorers' Club members.

Pantiacolla Tours Plateros 360, Cusco
ⓣ084/238323, ⓕ252696,
ⓦwww.pantiacolla.com. A company with a growing reputation for serious eco-adventure tours. Their cheapest option is also the longest, a 9-day tour that takes groups in and out by bus and boat, while the more expensive 5- to 7-day trips go in by road and out by plane from Boca Manu. They have an excellent lodge on the Río Alto Madre de Dios at Itahuania, and their tours into Zone B are based in tents at prepared campsites. $675–795; discounts available to South American Explorers' Club members.

Onward travel to Puerto Maldonado

It is possible, if adventurous, to follow an unregulated overland route with little infrastructure from Boca Manu to Puerto Maldonado. Although you're more likely to have already found a boat going downriver from Shintuya, many will also pick up at Boca Manu for the one-day journey downstream ($10) to the sleazy gold-mining frontier town of **BOCA COLORADO** (also known as **Banco Minero**), at the mouth of the Río Colorado. Boca Colorado has a number of very basic **hotels**, but all have rats running around – they can be heard scampering across wooden-planked floorboards when the town generator goes off and the settlement's televisions fade into silence at 11pm every night. There are also a few simple **restaurants** serving surprisingly tasty food. It's possible to **camp** but, again, don't let your gear out of your sight. From here it's at least one more day ($10–15 as a passenger in boats going in the same direction, depending on the speed of the boat) on to **LABERINTO** – see p.499 – from where it's a two-hour bus ride to Puerto Maldonado.

The Río Urubamba and around

Traditionally the home of the Matsiguenga and Piro Indians, the **Río Urubamba** rolls down from the Inca's Sacred Valley to the humid lower Andean slopes around the town of **Quillabamba**, little more than a pit stop, and at the end of the rail line from Cusco (though due to a landslide this is likely to be out of operation between Machu Picchu and Quillabamba for the forseeable future). For the next eighty or so unnavigable kilometres, the Urubamba is trailed by a dirt road to the small settlement of **Kiteni**, where it meets with the tributary Río Kosrentni, then continues to the smaller settlement of Monte Carmelo. From here on, the easily navigable Río Kiteni becomes the main means of transport, a smooth 3500km through the Amazon Basin to the Atlantic, interrupted only by the impressive **Pongo de Mainique** – whitewater rapids, less than a day downstream, which are generally too dangerous to pass in the months of November and December.

Unlike the Manu Biosphere Reserve, most of the Urubamba has been colonized as far as the Pongo, and much of it beyond has suffered more or less permanent exploitation of one sort or another for over a hundred years (rubber, cattle, oil and, more recently, gas). Consequently, this isn't really the river for experiencing pristine virgin forest, but it is nevertheless an exciting and remote challenge and a genuine example of what's going on in the Amazon today. Far fewer tour companies operate in the Río Urubamba region than do in Manu or Madre de Dios, but as the political situation continues to improve, and entrepreneurial optimism revives further around Cusco, it seems likely that more adventure tours will become available in the lower Urubamba and that the area will open up further to organized river-rafting and forest-trekking.

Quillabamba

A rapidly expanding market town, growing fat on profits from coffee, tropical fruits, chocolate and, to a certain extent perhaps, the proceeds of cocaine production, **QUILLABAMBA** is the only Peruvian jungle town that's easily accessible by road, and the main attraction here for tourists is a quick look at the selva. Coming from Cusco, the initial section of road is a narrow gravel track along precipitous cliffs, notoriously dangerous in the rainy season, but after a few hours, having travelled over the magical Abra Malaga – the main pass on this road – the slow descent towards Chaullay starts. From here on, you'll see jungle vegetation beginning to cover the valley sides; the weather gets steadily warmer and the plant life thickens as you gradually descend into the Urubamba Valley.

Your first sight of the town, which tops a high cliff, is of old tin roofs, adobe outskirts and coca leaves drying in the gardens. It's a pleasant enough place to relax, and you can get all the gear you need for going deeper into the jungle; the **market** sells all the necessities like machetes, fish-hooks, food and hats. Just ten minutes' walk from here, the **Plaza de Armas**, with its shady fountain statue of the town's little-known benefactor, Don Martín Pío Concha, is the other major landmark. Other than that, though about 4km away, the once attractive river beach at **Sambaray** is a bit of a dump these days; much nicer and quite a popular resort is the nearby waterfall area of **Siete Tinjas**.

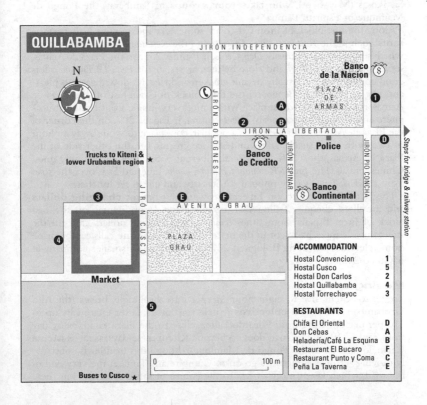

QUILLABAMBA

N

JIRÓN INDEPENDENCIA

Banco
de la Nación

PLAZA
DE
ARMAS

JIRÓN BOLOGNESI

JIRÓN LA LIBERTAD

JIRÓN ESPINAR

Police

JIRÓN PIO CONCHA

Steps for bridge & railway station

Trucks to Kiteni &
lower Urubamba region

Banco
de Credito

Banco
Continental

AVENIDA GRAU

JIRÓN CUSCO

PLAZA
GRAU

Market

Buses to Cusco

0   100 m

ACCOMMODATION

Hostal Convencion   1
Hostal Cusco   5
Hostal Don Carlos   2
Hostal Quillabamba   4
Hostal Torrechayoc   3

RESTAURANTS

Chifa El Oriental   D
Don Cebas   A
Heladería/Café La Esquina   B
Restaurant El Bucaro   F
Restaurant Punto y Coma   C
Peña La Taverna   E

Practicalities

The main town is a stiff climb from the river and the train station, over a bridge then up a series of steps, though the station is presently defunct due to a landslide. **Buses** from Calle Huascar in Cusco terminate by the market and Plaza Grau side of town; **colectivos** from Calle General Buendio, by the San Pedro railway station in Cusco, or the plaza in Ollantaytambo, terminate near the market in Quillabamba, as do trucks (best picked up from the plaza in Ollantaytambo).

For **accommodation**, the *Hotel Cusco*, Jr Cusco 233 (☎084/281161; ❷), near Plaza Grau and the market square, is somewhat run-down at present though it suffices, while the *Hostal Quillabamba*, Av Prolongación Miguel Grau 590 (☎084/281369; ❸), very close to the market, offers exceptionally good value, given that its modern rooms are comfortable and that it has a car park, swimming pool, hot water and a good restaurant. Just around the corner, the *Hostal Señor de Torrechayoc*, Av Grau 548 (☎084/281553; ❷), has modern, clean rooms with or without bath. The *Hotel Don Carlos*, Jr Libertad 546 (☎084/281371; ❺), is a relatively luxurious, newish hotel just up from the Plaza de Armas – cozy, friendly and popular with Peruvians. Rooms are smart and the place has a pleasant garden courtyard; it's also a good place to make connections for organized (though relatively costly) overland trips to Kiteni, and river trips onwards from there. The *Hostal Convención*, Pio Concha 212 (☎084/281093; ❶), is a basic but quaint place with a communal bathroom and no hot water; it's also the base for the Yoyato Club Tourism Adventure run by Sr. Rosas (May–Sept), who takes **tour groups** to Sambaray, the Pongo de Mainique or Espíritu Pampa.

Along the first block of Jirón Cusco are some very inexpensive little **restaurants**, such as the *Restaurant Los Amantes* and the *Restaurant La Estrella*, both of which serve decent set meals. *Don Cebas*, Jr Espinar 235, on the Plaza de Armas, serves snacks and drinks, and close by the bar-restaurant *Peña La Taverna* offers good cool drinks and usually decent chicken and rice; it's downbeat and pleasant. The *Restaurant El Bucaro*, on the third block of Grau, just off the Plaza de Armas, is a spit-and-sawdust place with a nice, very jungle frontier-like atmosphere and very cheap set meals. The *Heladeria*, Jr España 207, on the corner of the Plaza de Armas and Libertad, is a popular, cool place to while away an hour or two, with good snacks and wonderful ice creams. On the other side of the Plaza de Armas, the *Chifa El Oriental*, Libertad 375, serves surprisingly good Chinese meals. The *Snack-Restaurant Punto-y-coma*, Libertad 501, over the road from the *Heladeria*, is very popular for its tasty and cheap set lunches.

The Banco de Credito, on Libertad, is your best bet for **changing dollars** and travellers' cheques; failing that, try the Banco Continental, on the first block of Jirón España. Sometimes *cambistas* will change dollars cash on the street outside these banks, or in the better hotels. **Telephone** calls can be made from Telefónica del Peru, Bolognesi 237–249, or there's a smaller company at Jr Cusco 242.

Moving on

To get to Kiteni, five to eight hours deeper into the jungle, **buses** (the Alto Urubamba service) and **colectivos** (trucks start at $3; faster estate cars up to $10 per person) leave from Ricardo Palma, close to the Plaza Grau, every day from 8am to 10am. The road does go beyond Kiteni these days, as far as Monte Carmelo (almost to the Pongo de Mainique), though this frontier is constantly moving – trucks sometimes go on to Cumpire and Tinta at the very end of the road, which keeps more or less to the course of the Urubamba, but these little settlements offer nothing much for the independent traveller. Heading back to Cusco, the Hidalgo bus leaves Quillabamba from the market area several times a week, as do the bus companies Turismo Ampay and the less reliable Carhuamayo; trucks (from block 5 of San Martín) are more frequent, but slower, and there are currently no trains.

Kiteni and the Pongo de Mainique

By the time you reach **KITENI**, the Río Urubamba is quite wide and, with the forest all around, the valley is hotter, more exotic and much greener than before. Still a small *poblado*, until over 25 years ago Kiteni was a small Matsiguenga Indian village. With its ramshackle cluster of buildings, all wooden except for the schoolhouse and the clinic (where you can get yellow fever shots if you haven't already done so), it is still a one-street town, with more mules than cars.

On **arrival**, trucks and buses stop at a chain across the dirt track. Here you have to register with the *guardia* in their office on the right before walking into the town. About 100m straight down the road, at the other end of town is the basic dormitory-type **hostel**, the *Hotel Kiteni* (❶) – a friendly place, attractively situated beside the bubbling Río Kosrentni, and serving good set **meals**; there are no locks on doors so don't leave your valuables lying around. Next to the *Hotel Kiteni* there's an *oroya* (stand-up cable car) for people to pull themselves across the river; a ten-minute stroll on the far bank takes you to an *albergue* that has been officially closed for several years but still occasionally rents out a few rooms for trips organized in advance by agencies or groups from Cusco; it offers seclusion, spoken English, and excellent food for only a few dollars a night. The last transport (mostly combis) from Kiteni to Quillabamba generally leaves at 3–3.30pm daily (a 6hr trip).

The Pongo de Mainique

Kiteni's main draw – beyond its small jungle-settlement atmosphere – is as a jumping-off point for the awe-inspiring **Pongo de Mainique**, possibly the most dangerous 2km of (barely) navigable river in the entire Amazonian system, made famous by Michael Palin in his travel documentary. Just before you reach the *pongo* there's a community at **San Idriato**. The people here, known as the Israelites, founded their village around a biblical sect; the men leave their hair long and, like Rastas, they twist it up under expandable peaked caps. Not far from San Idriato there's a basic tourist lodge, again now out of general use, right at the mouth of the rapids – a wonderful spot. Across the Urubamba from San Idriato the small community of **Shinguriato**, upstream from the Río Yuyato mouth, is the official entrance to the *pongo* itself.

The rapids and beyond

You'll have heard a lot about the **Pongo de Mainique** before you get there – from the boatmen, the local Matsiguenga Indians, *colonos*, and the Israelites. They are dangerous at any time of year, and virtually impossible to pass during the rainy season (Nov–Jan). As you get nearer, you can see a forested mountain range directly in front of you; the river speeds up, and as you approach closer still it's possible to make out the great cut made through the range over the millennia by the powerful Urubamba. Then, before you realize, the craft is whisked into a long canyon with soaring rocky cliffs on either side: gigantic volcanic boulders look like wet monsters of molten steel; stone faces can be seen shimmering under cascades; and the danger of the *pongo* slips by almost

Tours down the Urubamba to the *pongo* can sometimes be arranged with one of the Cusco adventure tour operators detailed below. Other people may approach you in Quillabamba or Kiteni for a trip to the *pongo* and perhaps a little camping and fishing; the merits of these are entirely dependent upon the price you have to pay and the confidence you have in the guide. If there are enough of you, though, it might be more economical to **rent a canoe and boatman** (preferably with a powerful outboard motor) for a couple of days; this will cost from around $70 a day. To arrange any of these options you'll do best hanging around the port at Kiteni, on the beach behind the *guardia*'s huts, or asking in one of the few bars and cafés.

To go downriver without renting a boat or taking an organized trip is a matter of being at the dock early every morning and asking every boat that leaves if it's going to the *pongo*. Boats do take goods and people to the lower Urubamba communities, and are often more than willing to take extra passengers for a relatively small fee. Have all your baggage with you in case one is going, but check whether it's coming back up. This way a return trip shouldn't cost more than about $40; if you want to go all the way to Sepahua, expect to pay around $55 one way. You might have to wait a few days until there's one going all the way, but this is much easier than going hungry on a desolate beach somewhere below the *pongo*. Boats tend to arrive from downstream in the afternoon and it's often worth checking with them when they intend to go back. A boat with a powerful motor takes about five to six hours to reach the *pongo*; a *peque-peque* canoe will usually need around ten hours.

Apumayo C Garcilaso 265, Oficina 3, Cusco ☎084/246018, ✆apumayo@mail .cosapidata.com.pe. Offering rafting on the Urubamba and Apurimac rivers, they have great expertise and can organize programmes to suit any group's agenda. They usually work with groups pre-booked before arriving in Peru.

Eric Adventures Plateros 324, Cusco ☎084/232244, ✆239772. A relative newcomer to the business, these specialists have developed a pretty good reputation for whitewater rafting.

Explorandes Av Garcilaso 316A, Wanchaq, Cusco ☎084/238380, ✆233784, ⊛www.explorandes.com; or San Fernando 320, Miraflores, Lima ☎01/445-0532 or 4458683, ✆4454686. A long-established company who operate whitewater-rafting expeditions mainly on the Apurimac, but they can sometimes be persuaded to work in the Quillabamba or Kiteni *pongo* region.

Instinct Procuradores 50, Cusco ☎084/238366, ⊛www.rcp.net.pe/instinct. A well-organized river-rafting company who offer rugged trips to tackle some difficult grades and will take groups down the Urubamba.

Mayuc Portal Confiturias 211, Cusco ☎/✆084/232666, ⊛www.mayuc.com; PO Box 422, Cusco. A highly reliable and experienced company with the knowledge and flair to organize any tour or trek of your choice.

---

unnoticed, the walls of the canyon absorbing all your attention. The main hazard is actually a drop of about 2m, which is seen and then crossed in a split second. Now and then boats are overturned at this dangerous drop, usually those that try the run in the rainy season – although even then natives somehow manage to come upstream in small, non-motorized dugouts.

Beyond the *pongo* the river is much gentler, but on all major curves as far down as the Camisea tributary (about 2 days on a raft) there is **whitewater**. Settlements along this stretch are few and far between – mostly native villages, settlements of *colonos*, or missions. If your boat is going straight back through the *pongo* to Kiteni, you'll have to make a quick choice about whether to try your luck going downstream or return to the relative safety and luxury of town. If you decide to go further, the next significant settlement is

SEPAHUA; between here and the *pongo* there are just a few Machiguenga missions and a presently empty, massive oil- and gas-exploration camp near the village of Nuevo Mundo. Sepahua has a **hotel** (❷), a few shops and bars, and a **runway** with fairly regular flights to Satipo (for the road connection with Lima). However, the settlement is a good two or three days downstream by motorized canoe from the *pongo* (depending on the type and size of motor), or four to five days on a raft: to be dropped off in between could mean waiting a week on the riverbank for another boat or raft to hitch with. To be on the safe side, you'll need food for at least ten days if you're going to do this.

From Sepahua, it's another couple of days downstream to **ATALAYA**, where the Río Urubamba meets the Río Tambo to form the Ucayali. Run mainly by local Ashaninka Indian leaders (following successful development and land-titling projects), it's a small and relatively isolated jungle town with a reputation for lawlessness. For a **place to stay** here, try the *Hotel Denis* (❷) or the cheaper but less pleasant *Hostal d'Souza* (❶). For moving on, there are weekly **flights** to Satipo, Pucallpa, and, less frequently, to Lima; information on these can be obtained from the TANS office near the airport. By **boat**, it's another few days from here to Pucallpa, and at least five or six more to Iquitos. To get to Lima, you can catch a boat (generally daily) for a day's travel along the Río Tambo to Puerto Ocopa, after which it's a few hours along a dirt road to Satipo, then ten to twelve hours by a new, surfaced road to Lima, via La Merced and Tarma; several buses daily cover this route, plus there are colectivos between Satipo and La Merced.

Travel details

Buses and trucks

Cusco to: Puerto Maldonado (several weekly; 2–6 days); Shintuya (1–2 every Mon, Wed, Fri & Sat; 18–24hr); Quillabamba via Ollantaytambo (2–3 most days; 12hr), or via Calca Lares (2–3 weekly; 24hr).
Iquitos to: Nauta (daily; 3–5hr).
Lima to: Pucallpa (daily; 14hr, or 24hr via Huánuco); La Merced (several daily; 5–6hr).
La Merced to: Lima (several daily; 5–6hr); Pucallpa, via Puerto Bermudez (weekly, 24hr); Satipo (several daily; 4–6hr).
Puerto Maldonado to: Cusco (several weekly; 2–6 days); Iberia (very irregularly; 8–12hr).

Boats

Boca Manu to: Shintuya (irregular, 1 daily on average; 6hr); Puerto Maldonado (irregular; 2–4 days).

Iquitos to: Leticia and Tabatinga (several weekly; 9–12hr or 3–4 days, depending on boat); Pucallpa (several weekly; 5–7 days); Nauta (1 or 2 daily; 8–10hr).
Pucallpa to: Iquitos (several weekly; 5–7 days); Nauta (several weekly; 5–6 days).
Shintuya to: Boca Manu (irregular, 1 daily on average; 6hr); Puerto Maldonado (irregular; 2–4 days).

Flights

Iquitos to: Lima (several daily; 2hr); Pucallpa (daily; 1hr 30mins); Santa Rosa (weekly; 1hr 30mins); Tarapoto (several weekly; 1hr).
Pucallpa to: Lima (1 daily; 1hr 30min); Tarapoto (several weekly; 1hr).
Puerto Maldonado to: Cusco (several daily; 1hr); Iberia (2–3 weekly; 30min) Lima (daily; 2hr); Trujillo (daily; 2hr).

Contexts

Contexts

The historical framework

The first Peruvians were descendants of the nomadic tribes which had crossed into the Americas during the last Ice Age (40,000–15,000 BC), when a combination of ice packs and low sea levels exposed a neck of solid "land" that spanned what's now the Bering Strait. Following herds of game animals from Siberia into what must have been a relative paradise of fertile coast, wild forest, mountain and savannah, successive generations continued south through Central America. Some made their way down along the Andes, into the Amazon, and out onto the more fertile areas of the Peruvian and Ecuadorian coast, while others found their niches en route.

In a number of tribes there seem to be cultural memories of these long migrations, encapsulated in their traditional mythologies – though these aren't really transcribable into written histories. There is, however, archeological evidence of human occupation in Peru dating back to around 15,000–20,000 BC, concentrated in the **Ayacucho Valley**, where these early Peruvians lived in caves or out in the open. Around 12,000 BC, slightly to the north in the **Chillon Valley** (just above modern Lima), comes the first evidence of significant craft skills – stone blades and knives for hunting. At this time there were probably similar groups of hunter tribes in the mountains and jungle too, but the climatic conditions of these zones make it unlikely that any significant remains will ever be found.

The difficulties of traversing the rugged terrain between the highlands and coast evidently proved little problem for the early Peruvians. From 8000 to 2000 BC, **migratory bands** of hunters and gatherers alternated between camps in the lowlands during the harsh mountain winters and highland summer "resorts", their actual movements well synchronized with those of wild animal herds. One important mountain encampment from this **Incipient Era** has been discovered at **Lauricocha**, near Huánuco, at an altitude of over 4000m. Here the art of working stone – eventually producing very fine blades and arrow points – seems to have been sophisticated, while at the same time a growing cultural imagination found expression in cave paintings depicting animals, hunting scenes and even dances. Down on the coast at this time other groups were living on the greener *lomas* belts of the desert in places like **Chilca** to the south, and in the mangrove swamps around **Tumbes** to the north.

An awareness of the potential uses of plants began to emerge around **5000 BC** with the **cultivation** of seeds and tubers (the potato being one of the most important "discoveries" later taken to Europe), to be followed over the next two millennia by the introduction, presumably from the Amazon, of gourds, Lima beans, then squashes, peanuts, and eventually cotton. Towards the end of this period a climatic shift turned the coast into a much more arid belt and forced those living there to try their hand at **agriculture** in the fertile riverbeds, a process to some extent paralleled in the mountains.

With a stable agricultural base, permanent settlements sprang up all along the coast, notably at **Chicama**, **Asia** and **Paracas**, and in the sierra at **Kotosh**. The population began to mushroom, and with it came a new consciousness, perhaps influenced by cultural developments within the Amazon Basin to the east: **cultism** – the burial of the dead in mummy form, the capturing of trophy heads, and the building of grand religious structures – made its first appearance. At the same time there were also overwhelming technological advances in the spheres of weaving, tool-making and ornamental design.

The pyramids of Caral

Located in a relatively remote spot in the desert coast in a landscape which looks more lunar than agricultural, archeologists have recently uncovered one of the most important archeological finds in a hundred years or more. Thought to be the oldest city in the Americas, the archeological remains of Caral have overturned many assumptions made by archeologists in recent decades. Possibly the most important discovery since Machu Picchu was rediscovered in 1911, this site represents human achievements going on four thousand years earlier than the Incas. The stone-built ceremonial structures at Caral were flourishing a hundred years before the Great Pyramid at Giza was built. It is one of around a dozen sites in the Supe Valley 120km north of Lima, just 22km inland from the ocean. Radiocarbon dating proves that the site was fully functioning for around five hundred years, from around 2600 BC, complete with six stone platform mounds, with ceremonial plazas below and irrigation channels serving the surrounding fields. First discovered in 1905, Caral was then largely ignored by archeologists because, though large, no gold or even ceramics had ever been unearthed. It was, in fact, a pre-ceramic site whose importance resided in another technology, that of early domestication of plants including cotton, squashes, beans and guava.

Some of the best artefacts discovered here, in a ceremonial fire pit by the circular amphitheatre, include 32 flutes made from pelican and animal bones and engraved with the figures of birds and even monkeys, demonstrating a connection with the Amazon region even this long ago.

The six mounds, or pyramids, are arranged together around a large plaza. Archeologists believe that the pyramids were constructed in a maximum of two phases, which tends to suggest the need for particularly complex social structures for planning, decision-making and the mobilization of a large sector of the population to provide sufficient labour as and when it was required.

Around the pyramids there is evidence that there were many residential structures. Inside one of the houses, archeologists have discovered the remains of one body which was buried in the wall and appears to have been a natural death rather than the sign of a sacrifice.

Before the advent of urban living and stone ceremonial pyramids at Caral, the region was only populated by a few coastal villages, each with around a hundred inhabitants. Around 2700 BC it appears that a number of larger villages emerged, quite possibly based around the success of cultivation as well as revolutionary and ingenious practices, such as the creation of nets which could be used for fishing and carrying produce. The introduction of cotton fishing nets would have transformed the lives of coastal communities, giving them sufficient and relatively easy protein, more spare time to evolve social and religious practices and surplus food to trade with neighbouring communities. The emergence of barter- and tribute-based market centres, perhaps closely aligned with sacred centres of pilgrimage, would have begun to take on greater significance as the emerging society depended more and more on the fruit of farming and coastal communities. There would have been a strong interdependence between coastal fishing communities and agricultural communities irrigating the foothills just a half a day's walk inland from the ocean.

At its heyday it's thought that at least three thousand people were living in Caral. If the other seventeen yet-unexcavated sites in the area had held similar-sized populations, then the total population living, working and worshipping in the Supe Valley around 4600 years ago might have been as high as 20,000 or even more. It appears to have been abandoned quite rapidly after about five hundred years of booming inhabitance; theories as to why include the possibility of drought, which would have forced them to move to another valley in search of available water and even more fertile soils.

The Chavín Cult

From around 1200 BC to 200 AD – the **Formative Era** – agriculture and village life became established. Ceramics were invented, and a slow disintegration of regional isolation began. This last factor was due mainly to the widespread dispersal of a religious movement, the **Chavín Cult**. Remarkable in that it seems to have spread without the use of military force, the cult was based on worship of nature spirits, and an all-powerful feline creator god. This widespread feline image rapidly exerted its influence over the northern half of Peru and initiated a period of inter-relations between people in fertile basins in the Andes and some of the coastal valleys. How and where the cult originated is uncertain, though it seems probable that it began in the eastern jungles, possibly spreading to the Andes (and eventually the coast) along the upper Río Marañón. There may well have been a significant movement of people and trade goods between these areas and the rainforest regions, too, as evidenced by the many jungle-bird feathers incorporated into capes and headdresses found on the coast. More recent theories, however, suggest that the flow may have been in the opposite direction, starting on the coast. The stone and adobe temples, for instance, in the Sechín area, pre-date the Chavín era, yet seem to be culturally linked.

The Chavín Cult was responsible for excellent progress in **stone carving** and **metallurgy** (copper, gold and silver) and, significantly, for a ubiquity of temples and pyramids which grew up as religious and cultural centres. The most important known centre was the temple complex at **Chavín de Huantar** in Ancash, though a similar one was built at **Kotosh** near Huánuco; its influence seems to have spread over the northern highlands and coast from Chiclayo down as far as the Paracas Peninsula (where it had a particularly strong impact). There were immense local variations in the expressions of the Chavín Cult: elaborate metallurgy in the far north; adobe buildings on stone platforms in the river valleys; excellent ceramics from **Chicama**; and the extravagant stone engravings from Chavín itself. In the mountains life must have been very hard, based on subsistence agriculture and pilgrimages to the sacred shrines – most of which probably originated around ideas formulated by an emergent caste of powerful priest-chiefs. On the coast there was an extra resource – seafood – to augment the meagre agricultural yields.

Towards the **end of the Chavín phase**, an experimental period saw new centres attempting to establish themselves as independent powers with their own distinct cultures. This gave birth to **Gallinazo** settlements in the Viru Valley; the **Paracas culture** on the south coast (with its beautiful and highly advanced textile technology based around a cult of the dead); and the early years of **Tiahuanaco** development in the Lake Titicaca region. These three cultural upsurges laid the necessary foundations for the flourishing civilizations of the subsequent Classical Era.

The Classical Era

A diverse period – and one marked by intense development in almost every field – the **Classical Era** (200–1100 AD) saw the emergence of numerous distinct cultures, both on the coast and in the sierra. The best-documented, though not necessarily the most powerful, are the **Mochica** and **Nazca** cultures (both probably descendants of the coastal Paracas culture) and the **Tiahuanaco**, all forebears of the better-known Incas. In recent years, though, archeological discoveries in the Lambayeque Valley on the north coast have revealed important ceremonial centres – particularly the **Sicán** culture's massive sacred complex of truncated pyramids at **Batán Grande**. Contemporaneous with the Mochica, to the south, there is also strong evidence that the Sicán revered the same demonic spirit or god, named **Ai-Apaec** in the Mochica language, the "Winged Decapitator", who kept the world of human life and death in order. Ai-Apaec is also associated with the veritable treasure-trove found in the royal tombs at **Sipán**, just south of Lambayeque, and those of the Vicus culture, to the north, near Piura.

The **Mochica culture** has left the fullest evidence of its social and domestic life, all aspects of which, including its work and religion, are vividly represented in highly realistic pottery. The first real urban culture in Peru, its members maintained a firm hierarchy, an elite group combining both secular and sacred power. Ordinary people cultivated land around clusters of dwelling sites, dominated by sacred pyramids – man-made *huacas* dedicated to the gods. The key to the elite's position was probably their organization of large irrigation projects, essential to the survival of these relatively large population centres in the arid desert of the north coast. In the Mochica region, nature and the world of the ancestors seem the dominant cultural elements; occasional human sacrifices were offered and trophy heads were captured in battle. The peak of their influence came around 500 to 600 AD, when they had cultural and military control of the coast from Piura in the north to the Nepena Valley in the south.

More or less contemporaneous with the Mochica, the **Nazca culture** bloomed for several hundred years on the south coast. The Nazca are thought to be responsible for the astonishing lines and drawings etched into the Pampa de San José, though little is known for certain about their society or general way of life. The Nazca did, however, build an impressive temple complex in the desert at **Cahuachi**, and their burial sites have turned up thousands of beautiful ceramics whose abstract designs can be compared only to the quality and content of earlier Paracas textiles.

Named after its sacred centre on the shore of Lake Titicaca, the **Tiahuanaco culture** developed at much the same time as the Mochica – with which, initially at least, it peacefully coexisted. Tiahuanaco textiles and pottery spread along the desert, modifying both Mochica and Nazca styles and bending them into more sophisticated shapes and abstract patterns. The main emphasis in Tiahuanaco pottery and stonework was on symbolic elements featuring condors, pumas and snakes – more than likely the culture's main gods, representing their respective spheres of the sky, earth and underworld. In this there seem obvious echoes of the deified natural phenomena of the earlier Chavín cult.

Although initially peaceable, the Tiahuanaco influence is associated in its decadent phase with **militarism**. Originating either at Huari, in the sierra near Ayacucho, or on the central coast, this forceful tendency extended from 650 to 1100 AD and was dominated by what today is called the **Huari-Tiahuanaco**

culture. The ruins at Huari cover some eight square kilometres and include high-walled enclosures of field stones laid and plastered with mud, decorated only by a few stone statues along Tiahuanaco lines. Whether or not this was the actual inspirational centre, by around 1000 AD Huari-Tiahuanaco features were dominant in the art forms over virtually all of Peru.

In the north the Valley of the Pyramids, or **Túcume**, was another major ceremonial centre, covering more than two hundred hectares. Initially begun by the Sicán culture, who started building here around 1100 AD after abandoning their earlier centre at Batán Grande, it reached its peak in the thirteenth and early fourteenth centuries, during the power vacuum in the Mochica Valley, between the decline of the Mochica and the rise of the Chimu. Archeologists believe that this must have been a time of abundance and population growth for this desert region, with optimum weather conditions for agriculture, the improvement of irrigation techniques, and plentiful seafood.

An increasing prevalence of **intertribal warfare** characterized the era's later period, culminating in the erection of defensive forts, a multiplication of ceremonial sites (including over sixty large pyramids in the Lima area), and, eventually, the uprooting of Huari-Tiahuanaco influence on the coast by the emergence of three youthful mini-empires – the **Chimu**, the **Cuismancu** and the **Chincha**. In the mountains its influence mysteriously disappeared to pave the way for the separate growth of relatively large tribal units such as the **Colla** (around Titicaca), the **Inca** (around Cusco) and the **Chanca** (near Ayacucho).

Partly for defensive reasons, this period of isolated development sparked off a city-building urge which became almost compulsive by the Imperial Period in the thirteenth century. The most spectacular urban complex was **Chan Chan** (near modern Trujillo), built by the **Chimu** on the side of the river opposite to earlier Mochica temples but indicating a much greater sophistication in social control, the internal structure of the culture's clan-based society reflected in the complex's intricate layout. By now, with a working knowledge of bronze manufacture, the Chimu spread their domain from Chan Chan to Tumbes in the north and Paramonga in the south – dominating nearly half the Peruvian coastline. To the south they were bounded by the **Cuismancu**, less powerful, though capable of building similar citadels (such as Cajamarquilla near Lima) and of comparable attainment in craft industries. Further down the coastline, the **Chincha** – known also as the **Ica culture** – also produced fine monuments and administrative centres in the Chincha and Pisco valleys. The lower rainfall on the southern coast, however, didn't permit the Chincha state – or (to an extent) the Cuismancu – to create urban complexes anything near the size of Chan Chan.

The Incas

With the **Inca Empire** (1200–1532) came the culmination of the city-building phase and the beginnings of a kind of Peruvian unity, with the Incas, although originally a tribe of no more than around 40,000, gradually taking over each of the separate coastal empires. One of the last to go – almost bloodlessly, and just sixty years before the Spanish conquest – was the Chimu, who for much of this **Imperial Period** were a powerful rival.

Based in the valleys around Cusco, the Incas were for the first two centuries of their existence much like any other of the larger mountain tribes. Fiercely

The Inca emperors

Manco Capac (cultural hero ca. 1200)	Viracocha Inca
Sinchi Roca	Pachacuti (1438–71)
Lloque Yupanqui	Topac Yupanqui (1471–93)
Mayta Capac	Huayna Capac (1493–1525)
Capac Yupanqui	Huascar (1525–32)
Inca Roca	Atahualpa (1532–33)
Yahuar Huaca	

protective of their independence, they maintained a somewhat feudal society, tightly controlled by rigid religious tenets, though often disrupted by inter-tribal conflict. The founder of the dynasty – around 1200 – was **Manco Capac**, who passed into Inca mythology as a cultural hero. Historically, however, little definite is known about Inca developments or achievements until the accession in 1438 of Pachacuti, and the onset of their great era of expansion.

Pachacuti, most innovative of all the Inca emperors, was the first to expand their traditional tribal territory. The beginnings of this expansion were in fact not of his making but the response to a threatened invasion by the powerful, neighbouring Chanca Indians during the reign of his father, **Viracocha**. Viracocha, feeling the odds to be overwhelming, left Cusco in Pachacuti's control, withdrawing to the refuge of Calca along the Río Urubamba. Pachacuti, however, won a legendary victory – Inca chronicles record that the very stones of the battlefield rose up in his defence – and, having vanquished the most powerful force in the region, shortly took the Inca crown for himself.

Within three decades Pachacuti had consolidated his power over the entire sierra region from Cajamarca to Titicaca, defeating in the process all main imperial rivals except for the Chimu. At the same time the capital at **Cusco** was spectacularly developed, with the evacuation and destruction of all villages within a ten-kilometre radius, a massive programme of agricultural terracing (watched over by a skyline of agro-calendrical towers), and the construction of unrivalled palaces and temples. Shrewdly, Pachacuti turned his forcible evacuation of the Cusco villages into a positive plan, relocating the Incas in newly colonized areas. He also extended this practice towards his subjugated allies, conscripting them into the Inca armies while their chiefs remained as hostages and honoured guests at Cusco.

Inca territory expanded north into Ecuador, almost reaching Quito, under the next emperor – **Topac Yupanqui** – who also took his troops down the coast, overwhelming the Chimu and capturing the holy shrine of Pachacamac. Not surprisingly the coastal cultures influenced the Incas perhaps as much as the Incas influenced them, particularly in the sphere of craft industries. Even compared to Pachacuti, Topac Yupanqui was nevertheless an outstandingly imaginative and able ruler. During the 22 years of his reign (1471–93) he pushed Inca control southwards as far as the Río Maule in Chile; instigated the first proper census of the empire and set up the decimal-based administrative system; introduced the division of labour and land between the state, the gods and the local *allyus*; invented the concept of Chosen Women (Mamaconas); and inaugurated a new class of respected individuals (the Yanaconas). An empire had been unified not just physically but also administratively and ideologically.

At the end of the fifteenth century the Inca Empire was thriving, vital as any civilization before or since. Its politico-religious authority was finely tuned, extracting what it needed from its millions of subjects and giving what was necessary to maintain the status quo – be it brute force, protection or food. The only obvious problem inherent in the Inca system of unification and domination was one of over-extension. When **Huayna Capac** continued Topac Yupanqui's expansion to the north he created a new Inca city at **Quito**, one which he personally preferred to Cusco and which laid the seed for a division of loyalties within Inca society. At this point in history, the Inca Empire was probably the largest in the world even though it had neither horse nor wheel technology. The empire was over 5500km long, stretching from southern Colombia right down to northern Chile, with Inca highways covering distances of around 30,000km in all.

Almost as a natural progression from over-extending the empire in this way, the divisions in Inca society came to a head even before Huayna Capac's death. Ruling the empire from Quito, along with his favourite son **Atahualpa**, Huayna Capac installed another son, **Huascar**, at Cusco. In the last year of his life he tried to formalize the division – ensuring an inheritance at Quito for Atahualpa – but this was fiercely resisted by Huascar, legitimate heir to the title of Lord Inca and the empire, and by many of the influential Cusco priests and nobles. In 1527, when Huayna Capac died of the white man's disease, smallpox, which had swept down overland from Mexico in the previous seven years, killing over thirty percent of the indigenous population, civil war broke out. Atahualpa, backed by his father's army, was by far the stronger and immediately won a major victory at the Río Bamba – a battle that, it was said, left the plain littered with human bones for over a hundred years. A still bloodier battle, however, took place along the Río Apurimac at Cotabamba in 1532. This was the decisive victory for Atahualpa, and with his army he retired to relax at the hot baths near Cajamarca. Here, informed of a strange-looking, alien band, successors of the bearded adventurers whose presence had been noted during the reign of Huayna Capac, they waited.

The Spanish conquest

Francisco Pizarro, along with two dozen soldiers, stumbled upon and named the Pacific Ocean in 1513 while on an exploratory expedition in Panama. From that moment his determination, fired by native tales of a fabulously rich land to the south, was set. Within eleven years he had found himself financial sponsors and set sail down the Pacific coast with the priest Hernando de Luque and Diego Almagro.

With remarkable determination, having survived several disastrous attempts, the three explorers eventually landed at **Tumbes** in 1532. A few months later a small band of Spaniards, totalling less than 170 men, arrived at the Inca city of **Cajamarca** to meet the leader of what they were rapidly realizing was a mighty empire. En route to Cajamarca, Pizarro had learned of the Inca civil wars and of Atahualpa's recent victory over his brother Huascar. This rift within the empire provided the key to success that Pizarro was looking for.

The day after their arrival, in what at first appeared to be a lunatic endeavour, Pizarro and his men massacred thousands of Inca warriors and captured Atahualpa. Although ridiculously outnumbered, the Spaniards had the advantages of surprise, steel, cannons, and, above all, mounted cavalry. The **decisive battle** was over in a matter of hours: with Atahualpa prisoner, Pizarro was effectively in control of the Inca Empire. Atahualpa was promised his freedom if he could fill the famous ransom room at Cajamarca with gold. Caravans overladen with the precious metal arrived from all over the land and within six months the room was filled: a treasure worth over 1.5 million pesos, which was already enough to make each of the conquerors extremely wealthy. Pizarro, however, chose to keep the Inca leader as a hostage in case of Indian revolt, amid growing suspicions that Atahualpa was inciting his generals to attack the Spanish. Atahualpa almost certainly did send messages to his chiefs in Cusco, including orders to execute his brother Huascar who was already in captivity there. Under pressure from his worried captains, Pizarro brought Atahualpa to trial in July 1533, a mockery of justice in which he was given a free choice: to be burned alive as a pagan or strangled as a Christian. They baptized him and then killed him.

With nothing left to keep him in Cajamarca, Pizarro made his way through the Andes to Cusco where he crowned a puppet emperor, **Manco Inca**, of royal Indian blood. After all the practice that the Spaniards had had in imposing their culture on the Aztecs in Mexico, it took them only a few years to replace the Inca Empire with a working colonial mechanism. Now that the Inca civil wars were over, the natives seemed happy to retire quietly into the hills and get back to the land. However, more than wars, **disease** was responsible for the almost total lack of initial reaction to the new conquerors. The native population of Peru had dropped from some 32 million in 1520 to only five million by 1548 – a decline due mainly to new European ailments such as smallpox, measles, bubonic plague, whooping cough and influenza.

Colonial Peru

Queen Isabella of Spain indirectly laid the original foundations for the political administration of Peru in 1503 when she authorized the initiation of an **encomienda system**, which meant that successful Spanish conquerors could extract tribute for the Crown and personal service in return for converting the natives to Christianity. They were not, however, given title to the land itself. As governor of Peru, Pizarro used the *encomienda* system to grant large groups of Indians to his favourite soldier-companions. In this way the basic colonial land-tenure structure was created in everything but name. "Personal service" rapidly came to mean subservient serfdom for the native population, many of whom were now expected to raise animals introduced from the Old World (cattle, hens, etc) on behalf of their new overlords. Many Inca cities were rebuilt as Spanish towns, although some, like Cusco, retained native masonry for their foundations and even walls. Other Inca sites, like Huánuco Viejo, were abandoned in favour of cities in more hospitable lower altitudes. The Spanish were drawn to the coast for strategic as well as climatic reasons – above all to maintain constant oceanic links with the homeland via Panama.

The **foundation of Lima** in 1535 began a multilayered process of satellite dependency which continues even today. The fat of the land (originally mostly gold and other treasures) was sucked in from regions all over Peru, processed in Lima, and sent on from there to Spain. Lima survived on the backs of Peru's municipal capitals which, in turn, extracted tribute from the scattered *encomenderos*. The *encomenderos* depended on local chieftains (*curacas*) to rake in service and goods from even the most remote villages and hamlets. At the lowest level there was little difference between Inca imperial exploitation and the economic network of Spanish colonialism. Where they really varied was that under the Incas the surplus produce circulated among the elite within the country, while the Spaniards sent much of it to a monarch on the other side of the world.

In 1541 Pizarro was assassinated by a disgruntled faction among the conquistadores who looked to Diego Almagro as their leader, and for the next seven years the nascent colonial society was rent by civil war. In response, the first **viceroy** – Blasco Nuñez de Vela – was sent from Spain in 1544. His task was to act as royal commissioner and to secure the colony's loyalty to Spain; his fate was to be killed by Gonzalo Pizarro, brother of Francisco. But Royalist forces, now under Pedro de la Gasca, eventually prevailed – Gonzalo was captured and executed, and Crown control firmly re-established.

Colonial society

During this time, **Peruvian society** was being transformed by the growth of new generations: Creoles, descendants of Spaniards born in Peru, and *mestizos*, of mixed Spanish and native blood, created a new class structure. In the coastal valleys where populations had been decimated by European diseases, slaves were imported from Africa. There were over 1500 black slaves in Lima alone by 1554. At the same time, as a result of the civil wars and periodic Indian revolts, over a third of the original conquerors had lost their lives by 1550. Nevertheless effective power remained in the hands of the independent *encomenderos*.

In an attempt to dilute the influence of the *encomienda* system, the Royalists divided the existing twenty or so municipalities into **corregimentos**, smaller units headed by a *corregidor*, or royal administrator. They were given the power to control the activities of the *encomenderos* and exact tribute for the Crown – soon becoming the vital links in provincial government. The pattern of constant friction between *encomenderos* and *corregidores* was to continue for centuries, with only the priests to act as local mediators.

Despite the evangelistic zeal of the Spanish, **religion** changed little for the majority of the native population. Although Inca ceremonies, pilgrimages and public rituals were outlawed, their mystical and magical base endured. Each region quickly reverted to the pre-Inca cults deep-rooted in their culture and cosmology. Over the centuries the people learned to absorb symbolic elements of the Catholic faith into their beliefs and rituals – allowing them, once again, to worship relatively freely. Magic, herbalism and divination have continued strongly at the village level and have successfully pervaded modern Peruvian thought, language, and practice. (The Peruvian World Cup soccer squad in 1982 enlisted – in vain – the magical aid of a *curandero*.) At the elite level, the Spanish continued their fervent attempts to convert the entire population to their own ritualistic religion. They were, however, more successful with the rapidly growing *mestizo* population, who shared the same cultural aspirations.

Miraculous occurrences became a conspicuous feature in the popular Peruvian Catholic Church, the greatest example being Our Lord of Miracles, a cult which originated among the black population of colonial Lima. In the devastating earthquake of 1665, an anonymous mural of the Crucifixion on the wall of a chapel in the poorest quarter was supposedly the only structure left standing. The belief that this was a direct sign from God took hold among the local population, and Our Lord of Miracles remains the most revered image in Peru. Thousands of devotees process through the streets of Lima and other Peruvian towns every October, and even today many women dress in purple throughout the month to honour Our Lord of Miracles.

In return for the salvation of their souls the native population was expected to surrender their bodies to the Spanish. Some forms of service (*mita*) were simply continuations of Inca tradition – from keeping the streets clean to working in textile mills. But the most feared was a new introduction, the *mita de minas* – **forced work in the mines**. With the discovery of the "mountain of silver" at Potosi (now Bolivia) in 1545, and of mercury deposits at Huancavelica in 1563, it reached new heights. Forced off their smallholdings, few Indians who left to work in the mines ever returned. Indeed, the mercury mines at Huancavelica were so dangerous that the quality of their toxic ore could be measured by the number of weekly deaths. Those who were taken to Potosi had to be chained together to stop them from escaping: if they were injured, their bodies were cut from the shackles by sword to save precious time. Around three million Indians worked in Potosi and Huancavelica alone; some had to walk over 1000km from Cusco to Potosi for the privilege of working themselves to death.

In 1569, **Francisco Toledo** arrived in Peru to become viceroy. His aim was to reform the colonial system so as to increase royal revenue while at the same time improving the lot of the native population. Before he could get on with that, however, he had to quash a rapidly developing threat to the colony – the appearance of a **neo-Inca state**. After an unsuccessful uprising in 1536, Manco Inca, Pizarro's puppet emperor, had disappeared with a few thousand loyal subjects into the remote mountainous regions of **Vilcabamba**, northwest of Cusco. With the full regalia of high priests, virgins of the sun, and the golden idol of Punchau (the Sun God), he maintained a rebel Inca state and built himself impressive new palaces and fortresses between Vitcos and Espiritu Pampa – well beyond the reach of colonial power. Although not a substantial threat to the colony, Manco's forces repeatedly raided nearby settlements and robbed travellers on the roads between Cusco and Lima.

Manco himself died at the hands of a Spanish outlaw, a guest at Vilcabamba who hoped to win himself a pardon from the Crown. But the neo-Inca state continued under the leadership of Manco's son, Sairi Tupac, who assumed the imperial fringe at the age of 10. Tempted out of Vilcabamba in 1557, Sairi Tupac was offered a palace and a wealthy life by the Spanish in return for giving up his refuge and subversive aims. He died a young man, only three years after turning to Christianity and laying aside his father's cause. Meanwhile Titu Cusi, one of Manco's illegitimate sons, declared himself emperor and took control in Vilcabamba.

Eventually, Titu Cusi began to open his doors. First he allowed two Spanish friars to enter his camp, and then, in 1571, negotiations were opened for a return to Cusco when an emissary arrived from Viceroy Toledo. The talks broke down before the year was out and Toledo decided to send an army into Vilcabamba to rout the Incas. They arrived to find that Titu Cusi was already dead and his brother, **Tupac Amaru**, was the new emperor. After fierce fighting and a near-escape, Tupac Amaru was captured and brought to trial in Cusco. Accused of plotting to overthrow the Spanish and of inciting his followers to raid towns, Tupac Amaru was beheaded as soon as possible – an act by Toledo that was disavowed by the Spanish Crown and which caused much distress in Peru.

Toledo's next task was to firmly establish the viceregal position – something that outlasted him by some two centuries. He toured highland Peru seeking ways to improve Crown control, starting with an attempt to curb the excesses of the *encomenderos* and their tax-collecting *curacas* (hereditary native leaders) by implementing a programme of **reducciones** – the physical resettlement of

Indians in new towns and villages. Hundreds of thousands of peasants, perhaps millions, were forced to move from remote hamlets into large conglomerations, or *reducciones*, in convenient locations. Priests, or *corregidores*, were placed in charge of them, undercutting the power of the *encomenderos*. Toledo also established a new elected position – the local mayor (or *varayoc*) – in an attempt to displace the *curacas*. The *varayoc*, however, was not necessarily a good colonial tool in that, even more than the *curacas*, his interests were rooted firmly in the *allyu* and in his own neighbours, rather than in the wealth of some distant kingdom.

Rebellion

When the Hapsburg monarchy gave way to the Bourbon kings in Spain at the beginning of the eighteenth century, shivers of protest seemed to reverberate deep in the Peruvian hinterland. There were a number of serious **native rebellions** against colonial rule during the next hundred years. One of the most important, though least known, was that led by **Juan Santos Atahualpa**, a *mestizo* from Cusco. Juan Santos had travelled to Spain, Africa and, some say, to England as a young man in the service of a wealthy Jesuit priest. Returning to Peru in 1740 he was imbued with revolutionary fervour and moved into the high jungle region between Tarma and the Río Ucayali where he roused the forest Indians to rebellion. Throwing out the whites, he established a millenarian cult and, with an Indian army recruited from several tribes, successfully repelled all attacks by the authorities. Although never extending his powers beyond Tarma, he lived a free man until his death in 1756.

Twenty years later there were further violent native protests throughout the country against the enforcement of *repartimiento*. Under this new system the peasants were obliged to buy most of their essential goods from the *corregidor*, who, as monopoly supplier, sold poor-quality produce at grossly inflated prices.

In 1780, another *mestizo*, José Gabriel Condorcanqui, led a rebellion, calling himself **Tupac Amaru II**. Whipping up the already inflamed peasant opinion around Cusco into a revolutionary frenzy, he imprisoned a local *corregidor* before going on to massacre a troop of nearly six hundred Royalist soldiers. Within a year Tupac Amaru II had been captured and executed but his rebellion had demonstrated both a definite weakness in colonial control and a high degree of popular unrest. Over the next decade several administrative reforms were to alter the situation, at least superficially: the *repartimiento* and the *corregimento* systems were abolished. In 1784, Charles III appointed a French nobleman – Teodoro de Croix – as the new viceroy to Peru and divided the country into seven *intendencias* containing 52 provinces. This created tighter direct royal control, but also unwittingly provided the pattern for the Republican state of federated *departmentos*.

The end of the eighteenth century saw profound changes throughout the world. The North American colonies had gained their independence from Britain; France had been rocked by a people's revolution; and liberal ideas were spreading everywhere. Inflammatory newspapers and periodicals began to appear on the streets of Lima, and discontent was expressed at all levels of society. A strong sense of **Peruvian nationalism** emerged in the pages of *Mercurio Peruano* (first printed in the 1790s), a concept that was vital to the coming changes. Even the architecture of Lima had changed in the mid-eighteenth century, as if to welcome the new era. Wide avenues suddenly appeared, public parks were opened, and palatial salons became the focus for the discourse of gentlemen. The philosophy of the Enlightenment was slowly but surely pervading attitudes even in remote Peru.

When, in 1808, Napoleon took control of Spain, the authorities and elites in all the Spanish colonies found themselves in a new and unprecedented position. Was their loyalty to Spain or to its rightful king? And just who was the rightful king now?

Initially, there were a few unsuccessful, locally-based protests in response both to this ambiguous situation and to the age-old agrarian problem, but it was only with the intervention of outside forces that independence was to become a serious issue in Peru. The American War of Independence, the French Revolution, and Napoleon's invasion of Spain all pointed towards the opportunity of throwing off the shackles of colonialism, and by the time Ferdinand returned to the Spanish throne in 1814, Royalist troops were struggling to maintain order throughout South America. Venezuela and Argentina had already declared their independence, and in 1817 San Martín liberated Chile by force. It was only a matter of time before one of the great liberators – **San Martín** in the south or **Bolívar** in the north – reached Peru.

San Martín was the first to do so. Having already liberated Argentina and Chile, he contracted an English naval officer, Lord Cochrane, to attack Lima. By September 1819 the first rebel invaders had landed at Paracas. Ica, Huánuco and then the north of Peru soon opted for independence, and the Royalists, cut off in Lima, retreated into the mountains. Entering the capital without a struggle, San Martín proclaimed Peruvian **independence** on July 28, 1821.

The Republic

San Martín immediately assumed political control of the fledgeling nation. Under the title "Protector of Peru" he set about devising a workable **constitution** for the new nation – at one point even considering importing European royalty to establish a new monarchy. A libertarian as well as a liberator, San Martín declared freedom for slaves' children, abolished Indian service, and even outlawed the term "Indian". But in practice, with Royalist troops still controlling large sectors of the sierra, his approach did more to frighten the establishment than it did to help the slaves and peasants whose problems remain, even now, deeply rooted in their social and territorial inheritance.

The development of a relatively stable political system took virtually the rest of the nineteenth century, although Spanish resistance to independence was finally extinguished at the battles of Junin and Ayacucho in 1824. By this time, San Martín had given up the political power game, handing it over to **Simón Bolívar**, a man of enormous force with definite tendencies towards megalomania. Between them, Bolívar and his right-hand man, Sucre, divided Peru in half, with Sucre first president of the upper sector, renamed Bolivia. Bolívar himself remained dictator of a vast Andean Confederation – encompassing Colombia, Venezuela, Ecuador, Peru and Bolivia – until 1826. Within a year of his withdrawal, however, the Peruvians had torn up his controversial constitution and voted for the liberal **General La Mar** as president.

On La Mar's heels raced a generation of *caudillos*, military men, often *mestizos* of middle-class origins who had achieved recognition (on either side) in the battles for independence. The history of the early republic consists almost entirely of internal disputes between the Creole aristocracy and dictatorial *caudillos*. Peru plunged deep into a period of domestic and foreign plot and counterplot, while the economy and some of the nation's finest natural resources withered away.

Generals **Santa Cruz** and **Gamarra** stand out as two of the most ruthless players in this high-stakes power game: overthrowing La Mar in 1829, Santa Cruz became president of Bolivia and Gamarra of Peru. Four years later the liberal Creoles fought back with the election of General Orbegoso to the presidency. Gamarra, attempting to oust Orbegoso in a quiet palace coup, was overwhelmed and exiled. But the liberal constitution of 1834, despite its severe limitations on presidential power, still proved too much for the army – Orbegoso was overthrown within six months.

Unable to sit on the sidelines and watch the increasing pandemonium of Peruvian politics, Santa Cruz invaded Peru from Bolivia and installed himself as "Protector" in 1837. Very few South Americans were happy with this situation, least of all Gamarra, who joined with other exiles in Chile to plot revenge. After fierce fighting, Gamarra defeated Santa Cruz at Yungay, restored himself as president of Peru for two years, then died in 1841. During the next four years Peru had six more presidents, none of notable ability.

Ramon Castilla was the first president to bring any real strength to his office. On his assumption of power in 1845 the country began to develop more positively on the rising wave of a booming export in guano (birdshit) fertilizer. In 1856, a new moderate constitution was approved and Castilla began his second term of office in an atmosphere of growth and hope – there were rail lines to be built and the Amazon waterways to be opened up. Sugar and cotton became important exports from coastal plantations and the guano deposits alone yielded a revenue of $15 million in 1860. Castilla abolished Indian tribute and managed to emancipate slaves without social-economic disruption by buying them from their "owners"; guano income proved useful for this compensation.

His successors fared less happily. **President Balta** (1868–72) oversaw the construction of most of the rail lines, but overspent so freely on these and a variety of other public and engineering works that it left the country on the brink of economic collapse. In the 1872 elections an attempted military coup was spontaneously crushed by a civilian mob, and Peru's first civilian president – the laissez-faire capitalist **Manuel Pardo** – assumed power.

The War of the Pacific

By the late nineteenth century Peru's foreign debt, particularly to England, had grown enormously. Even though interest could be paid in guano, there simply wasn't enough. To make matters considerably worse, Peru went to war with Chile in 1879.

Lasting over four years, this "**War of the Pacific**" was basically a battle for the rich nitrate deposits located in Bolivian territory. Peru had pressured its ally Bolivia into imposing an export tax on nitrates mined by the Chilean-British Corporation. Chile's answer was to occupy the area and declare war on Peru and Bolivia. Victorious on land and at sea, Chilean forces had occupied Lima by the beginning of 1881 and the Peruvian president had fled to Europe. By

1883 Peru "lay helpless under the boots of its conquerors", and only a diplomatic rescue seemed possible. The **Treaty of Ancón**, possibly Peru's greatest national humiliation, brought the war to a close in October 1883.

Peru was forced to accept the cloistering of an independent Bolivia high up in the Andes, with no land link to the Pacific, and the even harder loss of the nitrate fields to Chile. The country seemed in ruins: the guano virtually exhausted and the nitrates lost to Chile, the nation's coffers were empty and a new generation of *caudillos* prepared to resume the power struggle all over again.

The twentieth century

Modern Peru is generally considered to have been born in 1895 with the forced resignation of General Caceres. However, the seeds of industrial development had been laid under his rule, albeit by foreigners. In 1890 an international plan was formulated to bail Peru out of its bankruptcy. The **Peruvian Corporation** was formed in London and assumed the $50 million national debt in return for "control of the national economy". Foreign companies took over the rail lines, navigation of Lake Titicaca, vast quantities of guano, and were given free use of seven Peruvian ports for 66 years as well as the opportunity to start exploiting the rubber resources of the Amazon Basin. Under Nicolás de Piérola (president 1879–81 and 1895–99), some sort of stability had begun to return by the end of the nineteenth century.

In the early years of the twentieth century, Peru was run by an oligarchical clan of big businessmen and great landowners. Fortunes were made in a wide range of exploitative enterprises, above all sugar along the coast, minerals from the mountains, and rubber from the jungle. Meanwhile, the lot of the ordinary peasant worsened dramatically.

One of the most powerful oligarchs, **Augusto Leguía** rose to power through his possession of franchises for the New York Insurance Company and the British Sugar Company. He became a prominent figure, representing the rising bourgeoisie in the early 1900s, and in 1908 he was the first of their kind to be elected president. Under his rule the influence of foreign investment increased rapidly, with North American money taking ascendancy over British. It was with this capital that Lima was modernized – parks, plazas, the Avenida Arequipa and the Presidential Palace all date from this period. But for the majority of Peruvians, Leguía did nothing. The lives of the mountain peasants became more difficult, and the jungle Indians lived like slaves on the rubber plantations. Not surprisingly, Leguía's time in power coincided with a large number of Indian rebellions, general discontent and the rise of the first labour movement in Peru. Elected for a second term, Leguía became still more dictatorial, changing the constitution so that he could be re-elected on another two occasions. A year after the beginning of his fourth term, in 1930, he was ousted by a military coup – more as a result of the stock market crash and Peru's close links with US finance than as a consequence of his other political failings.

During Leguía's long dictatorship, the **labour movement** began to flex its muscles. A general strike in 1919 had established an eight-hour day, and ten years later the unions formed the first National Labour Centre. The worldwide Depression of the early 1930s hit Peru particularly badly; demand for its main exports (oil, silver, sugar, cotton and coffee) fell off drastically. Finally, in 1932, the Trujillo middle class led a violent uprising against the sugar barons and the primitive working conditions on the plantations. Suppressed by the army, nearly five thousand lives are thought to have been lost in the uprising, many of the rebels being taken out in trucks and shot among the ruins of Chan Chan.

The rise of the **APRA** – the American Popular Revolutionary Alliance – which had instigated the Trujillo uprising, and the growing popularity of its leader, **Haya de la Torre**, kept the nation occupied during World War II. Allowed to participate for the first time in the 1945 elections, APRA chose a neutral candidate – **Dr Bustamante** – in place of Haya de la Torre, whose fervent radicalism was considered a vote loser. Bustamante won the elections, with APRA controlling 18 out of 29 seats in the Senate and 53 out of 84 in the Chamber of Deputies.

Post-war euphoria was short-lived, however. Inflation was totally out of hand and apparently unaffected by Bustamante's exchange controls; during the 1940s the cost of living in Peru rose by 262 percent. With anti-APRA feeling on the rise, the president leaned more and more heavily on support from the army, until General Odría led a coup d'état from Arequipa in 1948 and formed a military junta. By the time Odría left office, in 1956, a new political element threatened oligarchical control – the young **Fernando Belaunde** and his **National Youth Front** (later Acción Popular), demanding "radical" reform. Even with the support of APRA and the army, Manuel Prado barely defeated Belaunde in the next elections: the unholy alliance between the monied establishment and APRA has been known as the "marriage of convenience" ever since.

The economy remained in dire straits. Domestic prices continued to soar and in 1952 alone there were some two hundred strikes and several serious riots. Meanwhile much more radical feeling was aroused in the provinces by **Hugo Blanco**, a charismatic *mestizo* from Cusco who had joined a Trotskyist group – the Workers Revolutionary Party – which was later to merge with the FIR – the Revolutionary Left's Front. In La Convención, within the *departmento* of Cusco, Blanco and his followers created nearly 150 syndicates, whose peasant members began to work their own individual plots while refusing to work for the hacienda owners. Many landowners went bankrupt or opted to bribe workers back with offers of cash wages. The second phase of Blanco's "reform" was to take physical control of the haciendas, mostly in areas so isolated that the authorities were powerless to intervene. Blanco was finally arrested in 1963 but the effects of his peasant revolt outlived him: in future, Peruvian governments were to take agrarian reform far more seriously.

Back in Lima, the elections of 1962 had resulted in an interesting deadlock, with Haya de la Torre getting 33 percent of the votes, Belaunde 32 percent, and Odría 28.5 percent. Almost inevitably, the army took control, annulled the elections, and denied Haya de la Torre and Belaunde the opportunity of power for another year. By 1963, though, neither Acción Popular nor APRA was sufficiently radical to pose a serious threat to the establishment. Elected president for the first time, Belaunde quickly got to work on a severely diluted programme of agrarian reform, a compromise never forgiven by his left-wing supporters. More successfully, though, he began to draw in quantities of foreign capital. President de Gaulle of France visited Peru in 1964 and the first British foreign secretary ever to set foot in South America arrived in Lima two years later. Foreign investors were clamouring to get in on Belaunde's ambitious development plans and obtain a rake-off from Peru's oil fields. But by 1965 domestic inflation had so severely damaged the balance of payments that confidence was beginning to slip away from Belaunde's international stance.

Land reform and the military regime

By the mid-1960s, many intellectuals and government officials saw the agrarian situation as an urgent economic problem as well as a matter of social justice. Even the army believed that **land reform** was a prerequisite for the development of a larger market, without which any genuine industrial development would prove impossible. On October 3, 1968, tanks smashed through the gates into the courtyard of the Presidential Palace. General Velasco and the army seized power, deporting Belaunde and ensuring that Haya de la Torre could not even participate in the forthcoming elections.

The new government, revolutionary for a **military regime**, gave the land back to the workers in 1969. The great plantations were turned virtually overnight into co-operatives, in an attempt to create a genuinely self-determining peasant class. At the same time guerrilla leaders were brought to trial, political activity was banned in the universities, indigenous banks were controlled, foreign banks nationalized, and diplomatic relations established with East European countries. By the end of military rule, in 1980, the land reform programme had done much to abolish the large capitalist landholding system.

Even now, though, a shortage of good land in the sierra and the lack of decent irrigation on the coast mean that less than twenty percent of the landless workers have been integrated into the co-operative system – the majority remain in seasonal work and/or the small-farm sector. One of the major problems for the military regime, and one which still plagues the economy, was the **fishing crisis** in the 1970s. An overestimation of the fishing potential led to the build-up of a highly capital-intensive fish-canning and fish-meal industry, in its time one of the world's most modern. Unfortunately, the fish began to disappear because of a combination of ecological changes and over-fishing – leaving vast quantities of capital equipment inactive and thousands of people unemployed.

Although undeniably an important step forward, the 1968 military coup was always an essentially bourgeois revolution, imposed from above to speed up the transformation from a land-based oligarchy to a capitalist society. Paternalistic, even dictatorial, it did little to satisfy the demands of the more extreme peasant reformers, and the military leaders eventually handed back power voluntarily in democratic elections.

The 1970s and 1980s

After twelve years of military government the 1980 elections resulted in a centre-right alliance between Acción Popular and the Popular Christian Party. **Belaunde** resumed the presidency having become an established celebrity during his years of exile and having built up, too, an impressive array of international contacts. The policy of his government was to increase the pace of development still further, and in particular to emulate the Brazilian success in opening up the Amazon – building new roads and exploiting the untold wealth in oil, minerals, timber and agriculture. But inflation continued as an apparently insuperable problem, and Belaunde fared little better in coming to terms with either the parliamentary Marxists of the United Left or the escalating guerrilla movement led by Sendero Luminoso.

Sendero Luminoso (the Shining Path), founded in 1970, persistently discounted the possibility of change through the ballot box. In 1976 it adopted armed struggle as the only means to achieve its "anti-feudal, anti-imperial" revolution in Peru. Following the line of the Chinese Gang of Four, Sendero was led by **Abimael Guzman** (alias **Comrade Gonzalo**), whose ideas it claimed to be in the direct lineage of Marx, Lenin and Chairman Mao. Originally a brilliant philosophy lecturer from Ayacucho (specializing in the Kantian theory of space), before his capture by the authorities in the early 1990s Gonzalo lived mainly underground, rarely seen even by Senderistas themselves.

Sendero was very active during the late 1980s and early 1990s, when it had some 10,000–15,000 secret members. Rejecting Belaunde's style of technological development as imperialist and the United Left as "parliamentary cretins", they carried out attacks on business interests, local officials, police posts, and anything regarded as outside interference with the self-determination of the peasantry. On the whole, members were recruited from the poorest areas of the country and from the Quechua-speaking population, coming together only for their paramilitary operations and melting back afterwards into the obscurity of their communities.

Although strategic points in Lima were frequently attacked – police stations, petrochemical plants and power lines – Sendero's main centre of activity was in the sierra around **Ayacucho** and **Huanta**, more recently spreading into the remote regions around the central selva and a little further south in **Vilcabamba** – site of the last Inca resistance, a traditional hide-out for rebels, and the centre of Hugo Blanco's activities in the 1960s. By remaining small and unpredictable, Sendero managed to wage its war on the Peruvian establishment with the minimum of risk of major confrontations with government forces.

Belaunde's response was to tie up enormous amounts of manpower in counter-insurgency operations whose main effect seemed to be to increase popular sympathy for the guerrillas. In 1984 more than six thousand troops, marines and anti-terrorist police were deployed against Sendero, and at least three thousand people, mostly peasants, are said to have been killed. "Disappearances", especially around Ayacucho, still occur and most people blame the security forces for the bulk of them. In August 1984 even the chief of command of the counter-insurgency forces joined the criticism of the government's failure to provide promised development aid to Ayacucho. He was promptly dismissed for his claims that the problems were "the harvest of 160 years of neglect" and that the solution was "not a military one".

By 1985, new urban-based terrorist groups like the Movimiento Revolucionario Tupac Amaru (**MRTA**) began to make their presence felt in the shantytowns around Lima. Belaunde lost the **1985 elections**, with APRA taking power for the first time and the United Left also getting a large percentage of the votes.

Led by a young, highly popular new president, **Alan García**, the APRA government took office riding a massive wave of hope. Sendero Luminoso, however, continued to step up its tactics of anti-democratic terrorism, and the isolation of Lima and the coast from much of the sierra and jungle regions became a very real threat. With Sendero proclaiming their revolution by "teaching" and terrorizing peasant communities on the one hand, and the military evidently liquidating the inhabitants of villages suspected of "collaboration" on the other, these years were a sad and bloody time for a large number of Peruvians.

Sendero's usual tactics were for an armed group to arrive at a peasant community and call a meeting. During the meeting it was not uncommon for them publicly to execute an "appropriate" local functionary – like a Ministry of Agriculture official or, in some cases, foreign aid workers – as a statement of persuasive terror. In May 1989 a British traveller found himself caught in the middle of this conflict and was shot in the head after a mock trial by

Senderistas in the plaza of Olleros, a community near Huaraz in Ancash, which had offered him a bed for the night in its municipal building. Before leaving a village, Sendero always selected and left "intelligence officers", to liaise with the terrorists, and "production officers", to ensure that there was no trade between the village and the outside world – particularly with Lima and the international market economy.

Guzman's success had lain partly with his use of Inca millennial mythology and partly in the power vacuum left after the implementation of the agrarian reform and the resulting unrest and instability, and Sendero's power, and even its popular appeal, advanced throughout the 1980s. In terms of territorial influence, it had spread its wings over most of central Peru, much of the jungle and to a certain extent into many of the northern and southern provincial towns.

Much of Sendero's funding came from the **cocaine trade**. Vast quantities of coca leaves are grown and partially processed all along the margins of the Peruvian jungle. Much of this is flown clandestinely into Colombia where the processing is completed and the finished product exported to North America and Europe for consumption. The thousands of peasants who came down from the Andes to make a new life in the tropical forest throughout the 1980s found that coca was by far the most lucrative cash crop. The cocaine barons paid peasants more than they could earn elsewhere and at the same time bought protection from Sendero (some say at a rate of up to $10,000 per clandestine plane-load).

The 1980s, then, saw the growth of two major attacks on the political and moral backbone of the nation – one through terrorism, the other through cocaine. With these two forces working hand in hand the problems facing García proved insurmountable. To make things worse, a right-wing death squad – the **Rodrigo Franco Commando** – appeared on the scene in 1988, evidently made up of disaffected police officers, army personnel and even one or two Apristas (APRA members).

The appointment of **Agustin Mantilla** as Minister of the Interior in May 1989 suggested knowledge and approval of the RFC at the very highest level. Mantilla was widely condemned as the man behind the emergence of the death squads and their supply of arms. He was known to want to take back by force large areas of the central Andes simply by supplying anti-Senderista peasants with machine guns. Opposition to the arming of the peasantry was one topic on which the military and human rights organizations seemed to agree. Many of the arms would probably have gone straight to Sendero, and such action could easily have set in motion a spiral of bloody civil war beyond anyone's control.

The **MRTA** had less success than the Senderistas, losing several of their leaders to Lima's prison cells. Their military confidence and capacity were also devastated when a contingent of some 62 MRTA militants was caught in an army ambush in April 1988; only eight survived from among two truckloads.

Meanwhile, the once young and popular President Alan García got himself into a financial mess and went into exile, having been accused by the Peruvian judiciary of high-level corruption and stealing possibly millions of dollars from the people of Peru. His bad governance probably put an end to APRA's chances of ever getting political control of Peru again.

The 1990s

1990 proved to be a turning point for Peru. In the run-up to that year's elections, there were four main candidates: the popular and internationally renowned author Mario Vargas Llosa, with his new right-wing coalition, Fredemo; Luís Alvacastro, general secretary of APRA (and minister in charge of the economy under Garcia); Alfonso Barrantes in control of a new left-wing grouping, Acuerdo Socialista; and Henry Peace of the United Left.

Vargas Llosa was the easy favourite as the poll approached, although he had blotted his copybook somewhat during 1989, when he had briefly bowed out of the electoral process, accusing his fellow leaders within Fredemo (which is essentially an alliance between Acción Popular and the Popular Christian Party) of making it impossible for him to carry on as a candidate. Still, by the time of the election he was back, and firmly in charge. APRA, having had five pretty disastrous years in power, were given virtually no chance of getting Alvacastro elected, and the left were severely split. Barrantes was by far the most popular candidate on that side. However, in creating Acuerdo Socialista, and thereby taking away half of the United Left's vote, he effectively spoilt both their chances.

In the event, the real surprise came with lightning speed from a totally unexpected quarter in the guise of an entirely new party – Cambio 90 (Change 90), formed only months before the election – led by a young college professor of Japanese descent, **Alberto Fujimori**. Fujimori came a very close second to Vargas Llosa in the March election, with 31 percent of the total against Llosa's 35 percent. Since a successful candidate must gain half the votes to become president, a second round was scheduled for June.

Once the initial shock of the result had been absorbed, Fujimori rapidly became favourite to win the **second poll**, on the grounds that electors who had voted for left-wing parties would switch their allegiance to him. While Vargas Llosa offered a Thatcherite, monetarist economic shock for Peru, Fujimori recommended protecting all public industries of strategic importance – the oil industry being one of the most important. Llosa was for selling such companies off to the private sector and exposing them to the full power of world market forces. However, ordinary Peruvians were clearly worried that such policies would bring them the kind of hardships that had beset Brazilians or Argentinians, and Fujimori swept into power in the second round of voting, almost immediately adopting many of Vargas Llosa's policies – the price of many basics such as flour and fuel trebled overnight. Fujimori did, however, manage to turn the nation around and gain an international confidence in Peru, reflected in the country's stock exchange – one of the fastest-growing and most active in the Americas.

However, the real turning point, economically and politically, was the capture of Sendero's leader **Abimael Guzman** in September 1992. Captured at his Lima hide-out (a dance school) by General Vidal's secret anti-terrorist police, DINCOTE, even Fujimori had not known about the raid until it had been successfully completed. With Guzman in jail, and presented very publicly on TV as the defeated man, the political tide shifted. The international press no longer described Peru as a country where terrorists looked poised to take over, and Fujimori went from strength to strength, while Sendero's activities were reduced to little more than the occasional car bomb in Lima as they were hounded by the military in their remote hide-outs along the eastern edges of the Peruvian Andes. A massive boost to Fujimori's popularity, in the elections of 1995 he gained over sixty percent of the vote. Perhaps it was also a recognition that his strong policies had paid off as far as the economy was concerned – inflation dipped from a record rate of 2777 percent in 1989 to ten percent in 1996.

The mid-1990s was also the time when the **MRTA** terrorists battled with Fujimori and his government. Oddly, in 1995, a 26-year-old American woman,

Lori Helen Berenson Mejia, was arrested with an MRTA cell and given a life sentence. Then, on December 17, 1996, the MRTA really hit the headlines when they infiltrated the Japanese Ambassador's residence, which they held under siege for 126 days, with over three hundred hostages. Some of these were released after negotiation, but Fujimori refused to give in to MRTA demands for the freedom of hundreds of their jailed comrades. Peruvian forces stormed the building in March 1997 as the terrorists were playing football inside the residence, massacring them all, with only one hostage perishing in the skirmish. Fujimori's reputation as a hard man and a successful leader shot to new heights.

He continued to grow in popularity, despite Peru going to **war with Ecuador** briefly in January 1995, May 1997, and more seriously in 1998. The Ecuadorian army, which was accused of starting the fighting, imposed significant losses on the Peruvian forces. This dispute was inflamed by the presence of large oilfields in the region, currently on what the Peruvians claim is their side of the border, a claim the Ecuadorians bitterly dispute: Ecuadorian maps continue to show the border much further south than Peruvian maps. The two countries signed a formal peace treaty in 1998, although the dispute remains fresh in most people's minds.

In economic terms, Fujimori also seemed to be just about holding his own. Despite many aid organizations confirming widespread poverty and unemployment in Peru, and the nation being hit hard by the El Niño of 1998, the economy stayed buoyant. Politically, too, Fujimori gained substantially in July 1999, when he appeared on TV, live from Huancayo, to announce the imminent capture of **Oscar Ramirez Durand**, alias Comrade Feliciano, Guzman's number two and the leader of Sendero Luminoso. An army battalion had already been sent to the Huancayo region in 1997 to destroy Sendero's stronghold; it took them two years, but they managed to achieve a result just in time for the start of the 2000 electoral campaign. At the end of the twentieth century, Sendero were left with only a few scattered remnants in one or two parts of the sierra and *ceja de selva*, and just one active cell in the cocaine-producing region of the Huallaga valley.

The twenty-first century

The run-up to the **elections** of April 9, 2000, was marked by Fujimori's controversial decision to stand for a third term of office, despite the constitution only allowing for two continuous terms. His rationale was that since the constitution was introduced during his second term, he was entitled to stand for one more. Even with his firm control of the media (especially TV), the election campaign saw strong opposition in the person of Alejandro Toledo, a *serrano* Perú Posible candidate representing the interests of Andean cities and communities. Toledo had worked his way up from humble beginnings to UN and World Bank economist before standing for president; such was the worry over his popularity that a smear campaign surfaced a few weeks before the voting, accusing him of shunning an illegitimate daughter and organizing a disastrous financial pyramid scheme in the early 1990s.

Fujimori polled 49.87 percent of the vote, missing outright victory by just 14,000 votes; Toledo followed behind with just over 40 percent. There were unproven allegations of fraud and vote rigging, and Toledo eventually withdrew from the contest. However, Fujimori was forced to resign in November 2000 following revelations that his head of intelligence, Vladimiro Montesinos, had been videotaped bribing politicians before the last election and had also secreted away hundreds of millions of dollars (believed to be drug money) into Swiss and other bank accounts around the world. It quickly became clear that Montesinos had exerted almost complete control of the president, the army, the intelligence service and the cocaine mafia during the preceding few years. Soon after, Fujimori fled to Japan.

New elections were held in April 2001, which Toledo won easily, inheriting a cynical populace and a troubled domestic situation, with slow economic growth and deteriorating social conditions. His first few years have been rocky: in June 2002, riots broke out in Arequipa, over Toledo's government's attempts to privatize the city's electric utility, followed a month later by paralysing transportation strikes and then furious demonstrations in the northern *ceja de selva* region.

One good sign for Peru is that it seems to have so far withstood the economic downturns suffered by both Argentina and Brazil in recent years, aided significantly by its booming mining sector; indeed, the economic growth rate in 2002 was the highest for five years, despite more than half the population still living in poverty.

Cultural chronology of Peru

20,000–10,000 BC

First evidence of human settlement in Peru. Cave dwellings in the Ayacucho Valley; stone artefacts in the Chillon Valley.

8000–5000 BC

Nomadic tribes, and more permanent settlement in fertile coastal areas. Cave paintings and fine stone tools.

5000–2000 BC

Introduction of cultivation and stable settlements. Early agricultural sites include notably the pyramid-based culture of Caral, and also the older Huaca Prieta in the Chicama Valley, and Kotosh.

1200 BC–200 AD

Formative Era and emergence of the Chavín Cult, with great progress in ceramics and metallurgy. Temple complex at Chavín de Huantar, and important sites at Kotosh and Sechin.

300 AD

Technological advance marked above all in the Viru Valley – the Gallinazo culture – and at Paracas.

Sites in the Viru Valley, at Paracas, and the growth of Tiahuanaco culture around Lake Titicaca.

200–1100 AD

Classical cultures emergent throughout the land. Mochica culture and Temples of the Sun and Moon near Trujillo; further Tiahuanaco development; Nazca Lines and Cahuachi complex on the coast; Wilkawain temple; Huari complex; and Tantamayo ruins.

1200

The age of the great city-builders. Well-preserved adobe settlements survive at Chan Chan (near Trujillo) and Cajamarquilla (Lima).

1438–1532

Expansion of the Inca Empire from its bases around Cusco, north into Ecuador and south into Chile. Inca sites survive throughout Peru, but the greatest are still around Cusco – Sacsayhuaman and Machu Picchu above all. Inca Highway constructed from Colombia to Chile; parts still in existence.

1535

Foundation of Lima. Colonial architecture draws heavily on Spanish influences, though native craftsmen also leave their mark. Church building above all – at Arequipa (Santa Catalina Convent) and around Cusco. The Spanish city of Cusco incorporates much Inca stonework. Meanwhile, the rebel Incas build new cities around Vilcabamba. Throughout colonial rule building follows European fashions, especially Baroque, including churches, mansions and a few public buildings.

1870s

Construction of the high-altitude rail lines and other engineering projects. First exploitation of Amazonian rubber.

1890–1930

Much modernization in Lima (Presidential Palace, etc), grandiose public buildings elsewhere. Massive urban growth in Lima from the 1930s onwards.

1963

Organized shantytowns begin to grow around Lima.

1980s

Development of the jungle – timber trade, oil companies and settlers threaten traditional tribal life and ecology; construction of the "Marginal Highway" into central Amazon resumed; rise of the most serious terrorist threat ever posed in Peru, Sendero Luminoso, the Maoist revolutionary group which proved exceptionally bloodthirsty.

1990s

Road improvements under Fujimori; and a firm hand to deal with Sendero Luminoso and MRTA.

2000–2003

Fujimori flees to Japan, economic instability, protests over coca eradication programme and attempt to privatize utility in Arequipa.

C

CONTEXTS | The historical framework

Inca life and achievement

In less than a century, the Incas developed and knitted together a vast empire peopled by something like twenty million Indians. They established an imperial religion in some harmony with those of their subject tribes; erected monolithic fortresses, salubrious palaces and temples; and, astonishingly, evolved a viable economy – strong enough to maintain a top-heavy elite in almost godlike grandeur. To understand these achievements and get some idea of what they must have meant in Peru five or six hundred years ago, you really have to see for yourself their surviving heritage: the stones of Inca ruins and roads; the cultural objects in the museums of Lima and Cusco; and their living descendants who still work the soil and speak Quechua – the language used by the Incas to unify their empire. What follows is but the briefest of introductions to their history, society and achievements.

Inca society

The Inca Empire rapidly developed a **hierarchical structure**. At the highest level it was governed by the **Sapa Inca**, son of the sun and direct descendant of the god Viracocha. Under him were the priest-nobles – the royal **allyu** or kin-group which filled most of the important administrative and religious posts – and, working for them, regional *allyu* chiefs, **curacas** or *orejones*, responsible for controlling tribute from the peasant base. One third of the land belonged to the emperor and the state; another to the high priests, gods, and the sun; the last third was for the *allyu* themselves. Work on the land, then, was devoted to maintaining the empire rather than mere subsistence, though in times of famine storehouses were evidently opened to feed the commoners.

Life for **the elite** wasn't, perhaps, quite as easy as it may appear; their fringe benefits were matched by the strain and worry of governing an empire, sending armies everywhere, and keeping the gods happy. The Inca nobles were nevertheless fond of relaxing in thermal baths, of hunting holidays, and of conspicuous eating and drinking whenever the religious calendar permitted. *Allyu* chiefs were often unrelated to the royal Inca lineage, but their position was normally hereditary. As lesser nobles (*curacas*) they were allowed to wear earplugs and special ornate headbands; their task was to both protect and exploit the commoners, and they themselves were free of labour service.

The hierarchical network swept down the ranks from the important chiefs in a decimalized system. One of the *curacas* might be responsible for 10,000 men; under him two lower chiefs were each responsible for 5000, and so on until in the smallest hamlets there was one man responsible for ten others. Women weren't counted in the census. For the Incas, a household was represented by the man and only he was obliged to fulfil tribute duties on behalf of the *allyu*. Within the family the woman's role was dependent on her relationship with the dominant man – be he father, brother, husband, or eldest son.

In their conquests the Incas absorbed **craftsmen** from every corner of the empire. Goldsmiths, potters, carpenters, sculptors, masons and *quipumayocs* (accountants) were frequently removed from their homes to work directly for the emperor in Cusco. These skilled men lost no time in developing into a new and entirely separate class of citizens. The work of even the lowest servant in the palace was highly regulated by a rigid division of labour. If a man was employed to be a woodcutter he wouldn't be expected to gather wood from the forests; that was the task of another employee.

Throughout the empire young girls, usually about 9 or 10 years old, were constantly selected for their beauty and serene intelligence. Those deemed perfect enough were taken to an *acclahuasi* – a special sanctuary for the "**chosen women**" – where they were trained in specific tasks, including the spinning and weaving of fine cloth, and the higher culinary arts. Most chosen women were destined ultimately to become *mamaconas* (Virgins of the Sun) or the concubines of either nobles or the Sapa Inca himself. Occasionally some of them were sacrificed by strangulation in order to appease the gods.

For most Inca **women** the allotted role was simply that of peasant/domestic work and rearing children. After giving birth a mother would wash her baby in a nearby stream to cleanse and purify it and return virtually immediately to normal daily activities, carrying the child in a cradle tied on her back with a shawl. As they still are today, most babies were breast-fed for years before leaving their mothers to take their place in the domestic life-cycle. As adults their particular role in society was dependent first on sex, then on hierarchical status.

Special regulations affected both the **old** and **disabled**. Around the age of 50, a man was likely to pass into the category of "old". He was no longer capable of undertaking a normal workload, he wasn't expected to pay taxes, and he could always depend on support from the official storehouses. Nevertheless, the community still made small demands by using him to collect firewood and other such tasks; in much the same way the kids were expected to help out around the house and in the fields. In fact children and old people often worked together, the young learning directly from the old. Disabled people were obliged to work within their potential – the blind, for instance, might de-husk maize or clean cotton. Inca law also bound the deformed or disabled to marry people with similar disadvantages: dwarfs to dwarfs, blind to blind, legless to legless.

The **Inca diet** was essentially vegetarian, based on the staple potato but encompassing a range of other foods like *quinoa*, beans, squash, sweet potatoes, avocados, tomatoes and manioc. In the highlands emphasis was on root crops like potatoes, which have been known to survive in temperatures as low as 15°C at over 5000m. On the valley floors and lower slopes of the Andes maize cultivation predominated.

The importance of **maize** both as a food crop and for making *chicha* increased dramatically under the Incas; previously it had been grown for ceremony and ritual exchange, as a status rather than a staple crop. The use of **coca** was restricted to the priests and Inca elite. Coca is a mild narcotic stimulant which effectively dulls the body against cold, hunger and tiredness when the leaves are chewed in the mouth with a catalyst such as lime or calcium. The Incas believed its leaves possessed magical properties; they could be cast to divine future events, offered as a gift to the wind, the earth, or the mountain *apu*, and they could be used in witchcraft. Today it's difficult to envisage the Incas' success in restricting coca-growing and use; even with helicopters and machine guns the present-day authorities are unable to control its production.

Expansion and control

In Inca eyes the known world was their empire, and **expansion** therefore limitless. They divided their territories into four basic regions, or **suyos**, each radiating from the central plaza in Cusco: Chincha Suyo (northwest), Anti Suyo (northeast), Cunti Suyo (southwest) and Colla Suyo (southeast). Each *suyo* naturally had its own particular problems and characteristics but all were approached in the same way – initially being demoralized or forced into submission by the Inca army, later absorbed as allies for further conquests. In this way the Incas never seemed to overextend their lines to the fighting front.

The most impressive feature of an **Inca army** must in fact have been its sheer numbers – a relatively minor force would have included 5000 men. Their armour usually consisted of quilted cotton shirts and a small shield painted with designs or decorated with magnificent plumes. The common warriors – using slingshots, spears, axes and maces – were often supported by archers drafted from the "savages" living in the eastern forests. When the Spanish arrived on horseback the Incas were quick to invent new weapons: large two-handed hardwood swords and *bolas* (wooden balls connected by a string), good for tangling up the horses' legs. The only prisoners of war traditionally taken by a conquering Inca army were chieftains, who lived comfortably in Cusco as hostages against the good behaviour of their respective tribes. Along with the chiefs, the most important portable idols and *huacas* of conquered peoples were held in Cusco as sacred hostages. Often the children of the ruling chieftains were also taken to Cusco to be indoctrinated in Inca ways.

This pragmatic approach towards their subjects is exemplified again in the Inca policy of **forced resettlement**. Whole villages were sometimes sent into entirely new regions, ostensibly to increase the crop yield of plants like coca or corn and to vary their diet by importing manioc and chillis – though it was often criminals and rebellious citizens who ended up in the hottest, most humid regions. Large groups of people might also be sent from relatively suspect tribes into areas where mostly loyal subjects lived, or into the newly colonized outer fringes of the empire; many trustworthy subjects were also moved into zones where restlessness might have been expected. It seems likely that the whole colonization project was as much a political manoeuvre as a device to diversify the Inca economic or dietary base. As new regions came under imperial influence, the threat from rebellious elements was minimized by their geographical dispersion.

Economy, agriculture and building

The main **resources** available to the Inca Empire were agricultural land and labour, mines (producing precious and prestigious metals such as gold, silver or copper), and fresh water, abundant everywhere except along the desert coast. With careful manipulation of these resources, the Incas managed to keep things moving the way they wanted. Tribute in the form of **service** (*mita*) played a crucial role in maintaining the empire and pressurizing its subjects into ambitious building and irrigation projects. Some of these projects were so grand that they would have been impossible without the demanding whip of a totalitarian state.

Although a certain degree of local barter was allowed, the state regulated the distribution of every important product. The astonishing Inca **highways** were one key to this economic success. Some of the tracks were nearly 8m wide and at the time of the Spanish conquest the main Royal Highway ran some 5000km, from the Río Ancasmayo in Colombia down the backbone of the

Andes to the coast at a point south of the present-day Santiago in Chile. The Incas never used the wheel, but gigantic llama caravans were a common sight tramping along the roads, each animal carrying up to 50kg of cargo.

Every corner of the Inca domain was easily accessible via branch roads, all designed or taken over and unified with one intention – to dominate and administer an enormous empire. **Runners** were posted at *chasqui* stations and *tambo* rest-houses which punctuated the road at intervals of between 2km and 15km. Fresh fish was relayed on foot from the coast and messages were sent with runners from Quito to Cusco (2000km) in less than six days. The more difficult mountain canyons were crossed on bridges suspended from cables braided out of jungle lianas (creeping vines) and high passes were – and still are – frequently reached by incredible stairways cut into solid rock cliffs.

The primary sector in the economy was inevitably **agriculture** and in this the Incas made two major advances: large terracing projects created the opportunity for agricultural specialists to experiment with new crops and methods of cultivation, and the transportation system allowed a revolution in distribution. Massive agricultural **terracing projects** were going on continuously in Inca-dominated mountain regions. The best examples of these are in the Cusco area at Tipón, Moray, Ollantaytambo, Pisac and Cusichaca. Beyond the aesthetic beauty of Inca stone terraces, they have distinct practical advantages. Terraced hillsides minimize erosion from landslides, and using well-engineered stone channels gives complete control over irrigation. Natural springs emerging on the hillsides became the focus of an intricate network of canals and aqueducts extending over the surrounding slopes which had themselves been converted into elegant stone terraces. An extra incentive to the Inca mind must surely have been their reverence of water, one of the major earthly spirits. The Inca terraces are often so elaborately designed around springs that they seem to be worshipping water as much as utilizing it.

Today, however, it is Inca construction which forms their lasting heritage: vast **building projects** masterminded by high-ranking nobles and architects, and supervised by expert masons with an almost limitless pool of peasant labour. Without paper, the architects resorted to imposing their imagination onto clay or stone, making miniature models of the more important constructions – good examples of these can be seen in Cusco museums. More importantly, Inca masonry survives throughout Peru, most spectacularly at the fortress of Sacsayhuaman above Cusco, and on the coast in the Achirana aqueduct, which even today still brings water down to the Ica Valley from high up in the Andes. In the mountains, Inca stonework gave a permanence to edifices which would otherwise have needed constant renovation. The damp climate and mould quickly destroy anything but solid rock; Spanish and modern buildings have often collapsed around well-built Inca walls.

Arts and crafts

Surprisingly, Inca masonry was rarely carved or adorned in any way. Smaller stone items, however, were frequently ornate and beautiful. High technical standards were achieved, too, in **pottery**. Around Cusco especially, the art of creating and glazing ceramics was highly developed. They were not so advanced artistically, however; Inca designs generally lack imagination and variety, tending to have been mass-produced from models evolved by previous cultures. The most common pottery object was the *aryballus*, a large jar with a conical base and a wide neck, thought to have been used chiefly for storing *chicha*. Its decoration was usually geometric, often associated with the backbone of a fish: the central spine of the pattern was adorned with rows of spikes radiating from either side. Fine plates were made with anthropomorphic handles, and large numbers of cylindrically tapering goblets – *keros* – were manufactured, though these were often of cedar wood rather than pottery.

The refinements in **metallurgy**, like the ceramics industry, were mostly developed by craftsmen absorbed from different corners of the empire. The Chimu were particularly respected by the Incas for their superb metalwork. Within the empire, bronze and copper were used for axe-blades and tumi knives; gold and silver were restricted to ritual use and for nobles. The Incas smelted their metal ores in cylindrical terracotta and adobe furnaces, which made good use of prevailing breezes to fire large lumps of charcoal. Molten ores were pulled out from the base of the furnace. Although the majority of surviving metal artefacts – those you see in museums – have been made from beaten sheets, there were plenty of cast or cut solid gold and silver pieces, too. Most of these were melted down by the conquistadores, who weren't especially interested in precious objects for their artistic merit.

Religion

The Inca **religion** was easily capable of incorporating the religious features of most subjugated regions. The setting for beliefs, idols and oracles, more or less throughout the entire empire, had been preordained over the previous two thousand years: a general recognition of certain creator deities and a whole pantheon of nature-related spirits, minor deities and demons. The customary form of worship varied a little according to the locality, but everywhere they went the Incas (and later the Spanish) found the creator god among other animistic spirits and concepts of power related to lightning, thunder and rainbows. The Incas merely superimposed their variety of mystical, yet inherently practical, elements onto those that they came across.

The main religious novelty introduced with Inca domination was their demand to be recognized as direct descendants of the creator-god **Viracocha**. A claim to divine ancestry was, to the Incas, a valid excuse for military and cultural expansion. They felt no need to destroy the *huacas* and oracles of subjugated peoples; on the contrary, certain sacred sites were recognized as intrinsically holy, as powerful places for communication with the spirit world. When ancient shrines like Pachacamac, near Lima, were absorbed into the empire they were simply turned over to worship on imperial terms.

The sun is the most obvious symbol of Inca belief, a chief deity and the visible head of the state religion (Viracocha was a less direct, more ethereal, force). The sun's role was overt, as life-giver to an agriculturally-based empire, and its cycle was intricately related to agrarian practice and annual ritual patterns. To think of the Inca religion as essentially sun worship, though, would be far too simplistic. There were distinct layers in **Inca cosmology**: the level of creation, the astral level and the earthly dimension.

The first, highest level corresponds to Viracocha as the creator-god who brought life to the world and society to mankind. Below this, on the astral level, are the celestial gods: the sun itself, the moon and certain stars (particularly the

Pleiades, patrons of fertility). The earthly dimension, although that of man, was no less magical, endowed with important *huacas* and shrines which might take the form of unusual rocks or peaks, caves, tombs, mummies and natural springs.

The astral level and earthly dimension were widespread bases of worship in Peru before the Incas rose to power. The favour of the creator was the critical factor in their claims to divine right of imperial government, and the hierarchical structure of religious ranking also reflects the division of the religious spheres into those that were around before, during, and after the empire and those that only stayed as long as Inca domination lasted. At the very top of this **religio-social hierarchy** was the Villac Uma, the high priest of Cusco, usually a brother of the Sapa Inca himself. Under him were perhaps hundreds of high priests, all nobles of royal blood who were responsible for ceremony, temples, shrines, divination, curing and sacrifice within the realm, and below them were the ordinary priests and chosen women. At the base of the hierarchy, and probably the most numerous of all religious personalities, were the **curanderos**, local curers practising herbal medicine and magic, and making sacrifices to small regional *huacas*.

Most **religious festivals** were calendrically based and marked by processions, sacrifices and dances. The Incas were aware of lunar time and the solar year, although they generally used the blooming of a special cactus and the stars to gauge the correct time to begin planting. Sacrifices to the gods normally consisted of llamas, *cuys* or *chicha* – only occasionally were chosen women and other adults killed. Once every year, however, young children were apparently sacrificed in the most important sacred centres.

Divination was a vital role played by priests and *curanderos* at all levels of the religious hierarchy. Soothsayers were expected to talk with the spirits and often used a hallucinogenic snuff from the vilca plant to achieve a trance-like state and communion with the other world. Everything from a crackling fire to the glance of a lizard was seen as a potential omen, and treated as such by making a little offering of coca leaves, coca spittle, or *chicha*. There were specific problems which divination was considered particularly accurate in solving: retrieving lost things; predicting the outcome of certain events (the oracles were always consulted prior to important military escapades); receiving a vision of contemporaneous yet distant happenings; and the diagnosis of illness.

Ancient wizardry in modern Peru

Bearing in mind the country's poverty and the fact that almost half the population is still pure Amerindian, it isn't altogether surprising to discover that the ancient shamanic healing arts are still flourishing in Peru. Evidence for this type of magical health therapy stretches back over three thousand years on the Peruvian coast. Today, healing wizards, or *curanderos* (Spanish for "healers"), can be found in every large community, practising healing based on knowledge which has been passed down from master to apprentice over millennia. *Curanderos* offer an alternative to the expensive, sporadic and often unreliable service provided by scientific medics in a developing country like Peru. But as well as being a cheaper, more widely available option, *curanderismo* is also closer to the hearts and understanding of the average Peruvian.

With the resurgence of herbalism, aromatherapy, exotic healing massages and other aspects of New Age "holistic" health, it should be easier for us in the West to understand *curanderismo* than it might have been a decade or so ago. Combine "holistic" health with psychotherapy, and add an underlying cultural vision of spiritual and magical influences, and you are some way towards getting a clearer picture of how healing wizards operate.

There are two other important characteristics of modern-day Peruvian *curanderismo*. Firstly, the last four hundred years of Spanish domination have added a veneer of Catholic imagery and nomenclature to Peruvian beliefs. Nature spirits and denizens have become saints or demons, ancient mountain spirits and their associated annual festivals continue disguised as Christian ceremonies. Equally important for any real understanding of Peruvian shamanism is the fact that most, if not all, *curanderos* use hallucinogens. The tribal peoples in the Peruvian Amazon who have managed, to a large extent, to hang on to their culture in the face of the oncoming industrial civilization, have also maintained their spiritual traditions. In almost every Peruvian Amazon tribe these traditions include the regular use of hallucinogenic brews to give a visionary ecstatic experience. Sometimes just the shaman partakes, but more often the shaman and his patients, or entire communities, will indulge together, singing traditional spirit-songs which help control the visions. The hallucinogenic experience, like the world of dreams, is the Peruvian forest Indian's way of getting in touch with the **ancestral world** or the world of spirit matter.

The origins of shamanism

The history of healing wizards in Peru matches that of the ritual use of hallucinogens and appears to have emerged alongside the first major temple-building culture – **Chavín** (1200 BC–200 AD). Agriculture, ceramics and other technical processes, including some metallurgy, had already been developed by 1200 BC, but Chavín demonstrates the first unified and widespread cultural movement in terms of sacred architectural style, and the forms and symbolic imagery used in pottery throughout much of Andean and coastal Peru during this era. Chavín was a religious cult which seems to have spread from the central mountains, quite possibly from the large temple complex at Chavín de Huantar near Huaraz. Taking hold along the coast, the image of the central Chavín deity was woven, moulded, and carved onto the finest funerary cloths, ceramics and stones. Generally represented as a complex and demonic-looking feline deity, the Chavín god always has fangs and a stern face. Many of the idols also show serpents radiating from the deity's head.

As far as the central temple at Chavín de Huantar is concerned, it was almost certainly a centre of sacred pilgrimage, built up over a period of centuries into a large ceremonial complex used at appropriate calendrical intervals to focus the spiritual, political, and economic energies of a vast area (at least large enough to include a range of produce for local consumption from tropical forest, high Andean and desert coast regions). The magnificent stone temple kept growing in size until, by around 300 BC, it would have been one of the largest religious centres anywhere in the world, with some three thousand local attendants. Among the fascinating finds at Chavín there have been bone snuff-tubes, beads, pendants, needles, ceremonial spondylus shells (imported from Ecuador) and some **quartz crystals** associated with ritual sites. One quartz crystal, covered in red pigment, was found in a grave, placed after death in the mouth of the deceased. Contemporary anthropological evidence shows us that quartz crystals still play an important role in shamanic ceremonies in Peru, the Americas, Australia and Asia. The well-documented Desana Indians of Colombia still see crystals as a "means of communication between the visible and invisible worlds, a crystallization of solar energy, or the Sun Father's semen which can be used in esoteric undertakings".

In one stone relief on the main temple at Chavín the feline deity is depicted holding a large **San Pedro cactus** in his hand. A Chavín ceramic bottle has been discovered with a San Pedro cactus "growing" on it; and, on another pot, a feline sits surrounded by several San Pedros. Similar motifs and designs appear on the later Paracas and Mochica craft work, but there is no real evidence for the ritual use of hallucinogens prior to Chavín. One impressive ceramic from the Mochica culture (500 AD) depicts an owl-woman – still symbolic of the female shaman in contemporary Peru – with a slice of San Pedro cactus in her hand. Another ceramic from the later Chimu culture (around 1100 AD) shows a woman healer holding a San Pedro.

As well as coca, their "divine plant", the **Incas** had their own special hallucinogen: vilca (meaning "sacred" in Quechua). The vilca tree (probably *Anadenanthera colubrina*) grows in the cloud-forest zones on the eastern slopes of the Peruvian Andes. The Incas used a snuff made from the seeds, which was generally blown up the nostrils of the participant by a helper. Evidently the Inca priests used vilca to bring on visions and make contact with the gods and spirit world.

Shamanism today

Still commonly used by *curanderos* on the coast and in the mountains of Peru, the San Pedro cactus (*Trichocereus panchanoi*) is a potent hallucinogen based on active mescaline. The *curandero* administers the hallucinogenic brew to his or her clients to bring about a period of revelation when questions are asked of the intoxicated person, who might also be asked to choose some object from among a range of magical curios which all have different meanings to the

Psychedlic tourism

The best way of contacting the Amerindian plant medicine cosmos is through local guides or tourist lodges in and around Iquitos (see p.483). For a little over $1100 it's possible to get a two-week package deal including pickup from Lima, a flight to Iquitos, a boat to a jungle lodge, food, accommodation and at least two ayahuasca sessions with a local shaman. Shorter and cheaper sessions are available if you just want to suss out the situation once you arrive in Iquitos. More possibilities are available in and around Cusco (see p.150). If you want to do some research before coming out, which is definitely advised, take a look at: ⓦwww.ayahuasca-shamanism.co.uk.

healer. Sometimes a *curandero* might imbibe San Pedro (or one of the many other indigenous hallucinogens) to see into the future, retrieve lost souls, divine causes of illness, or discover the whereabouts of lost objects.

On **the coast**, healing wizards usually live near the sea on the fringes of a settlement. Most have their own San Pedro plant which is said to protect or guard their homes against unwanted intruders by letting out a high-pitched whistle if somebody approaches. The most famous *curandero* of all used to live just outside Trujillo on the north coast of Peru. Eduardo Calderon – better known in Peru as **El Tuno** – was a shaman and a healer. His work consisted of treating sick and worried people who came to him from hundreds of miles around by utilizing a combination of herbalism, magical divination and a kind of psychic shock therapy involving the use of San Pedro.

Many coastal wizards get their most potent magic and powerful plants from a small zone in the northern Andes. The mountain area around Las Huaringas and Huancabamba, to the north of Chiclayo and east of Piura, is where a large number of the "great masters" are believed to live and work. But it is in the Amazon Basin of Peru that shamanism continues in its least-changed form.

Even on the edges of most jungle towns there are *curanderos* healing local people by using a mixture of jungle Indian shamanism and the more Catholicized coastal form. These wizards generally use the most common tropical forest hallucinogen, **ayahuasca** (from the liana *Banisteriopsis caapi*). Away from the towns, among the more remote tribal people, ayahuasca is the key to understanding the native consciousness and perception of the world – which for them is the natural world of the elements and the forest plus their own social, economic and political setup within that dominant environment.

The Shipibo tribe from the central Peruvian Amazon are famous for their excellent ceramic and weaving designs: extremely complex geometric patterns usually in black on white or beige, though sometimes reds or yellows too. These designs were traditionally inspired by visions received while the shaman was under the influence of ayahuasca, whose effect is described as "the spirits coming down".

It is clearly hard to generalize with any accuracy across the spectrum of healing wizards still found in modern Peru, yet there are definite threads connecting them all. On a practical level even the most isolated jungle shaman may well have trading links with several coastal *curanderos* – there are many magical cures imported via a web of ongoing trans-Andean trading partners to be found on the *curanderos'* street market stalls in Lima, Trujillo, Arequipa and Chimbote. It has been argued by some of the most eminent Peruvianists that the initial ideas and spark for the Chavín culture came up the Marañón Valley from the Amazon. If this is so, then these ideas could well have brought with them – some three thousand years ago – the first shamanic teachings to the rest of ancient Peru, possibly even the use of power plants and other tropical forest hallucinogens, since these are so critical to understanding even modern-day Peruvian Amazon Indian religion. One thing which can certainly be said about ancient healing wizards in modern Peru is that they question the very foundations of our rational scientific perception of the world.

Peruvian music

Latin America's oldest musical traditions are those of the Amerindians of the Andes. Their music is best known outside these countries through the characteristic panpipes of poncho-clad folklore groups. However, there's a multitude of rhythms and popular musics found here that deserve a lot more recognition, including *huayno* and *chicha*, still relatively unknown abroad, as well as the distinct coastal tradition of Afro-Peruvian music, rooted in black slaves brought to work in the mines.

For most people outside Latin America the sound of the Andes is that of bamboo panpipes and *quena* flutes. What is most remarkable is that these instruments have been used to create music in various parts of this large area of mountains – which stretch 7200km from Venezuela down to southernmost Chile – since before the time of the Incas. Pre-Conquest Andean instruments – conch-shell trumpets, shakers which used nuts for rattles, ocarinas, wind instruments and drums – are ever-present in museum collections. And the influence of the Inca Empire means that the Andean region and its music spreads far beyond the mountains themselves. It can be defined partly through ethnicity, partly through language – **Quechua** (currently spoken by over six million people) and **Aymara**, both of which are spoken alongside Spanish and other Amerindian languages.

The dominant areas of Andean culture are **Peru**, Ecuador and Bolivia, the countries with the largest indigenous Amerindian populations in South America. Here, in rural areas, highly traditional Andean music, probably little different from pre-Inca times, still thrives today at every kind of celebration and ritual. But beyond this is a huge diversity of music, differing widely not only between countries but between individual communities. Andean people tend to identify themselves by the specific place they come from: in music, the villages have different ways of making and tuning instruments and composing tunes, in the same way as they have distinctive weaving designs, ways of dressing or wearing their hats. Use of different scales involving four, five, six and seven notes and different singing styles are also found from place to place, tied to specific ritual occasions and the music which goes with them.

Andean music can be divided roughly into three types: firstly, that which is of **indigenous origin**, found mostly amongst rural Amerindian peoples still living very much by the seasons with root Amerindian beliefs; secondly, music of **European origin**; and thirdly, **mestizo music**, which continues to fuse the indigenous with European in a whole host of ways. In general, Quechua people have more vocal music than the Aymara.

Traditional music

Panpipes, known by the Aymara as *siku*, by the Quechua as *antara* and by the Spanish as *zampoña*, are ancient instruments, and archeologists have unearthed panpipes tuned to a variety of scales. While modern panpipes – played in the city or in groups with other instruments – may offer a complete scale, allowing solo performance, traditional models are played in pairs, as described by sixteenth-century chroniclers. The pipes share the melody, each with alternate notes of a whole scale, so that two or more players are needed to pick out a single tune using a hocket technique. Usually one player leads and the other follows. While symbolically this demonstrates reciprocity within the community, practically it enables players to play for a long time without getting too "high" from dizziness caused by over-breathing.

Played by blowing (or breathing out hard) across the top of a tube, panpipes come in various sizes, those with a deep bass having very long tubes. Several tubes made of bamboo reed of different length are bound together to produce a sound that can be jaunty, but also has a melancholic edge depending on tune and playing style. Many tunes have a minor, descending shape to them. Playing is often described as "breathy" as over-blowing is popular to produce harmonics. In general those who play panpipes love dense overlapping textures and often syncopated rhythms.

Simple **notched-end flutes**, or **quenas**, are another independent innovation of the Andean highlands found in both rural and urban areas. The most important pre-Hispanic instrument, they were traditionally made of fragile bamboo (though often these days from plumbers' PVC water pipes) and played in the dry season, with **tarkas** (vertical flutes – like a shrill recorder) taking over in the wet. *Quenas* are played solo or in ritual groups and remain tremendously popular today, with many virtuoso techniques.

Large **marching bands of drums and panpipes**, playing in the co-operative "back and forth" leader/follower style that captivated the Spanish in the 1500s, can still be seen and heard today. The drums are deep-sounding, double-headed instruments known as *bombos* or *wankaras*. These bands exist for parades at life-cycle fiestas, weddings and dances in the regions surrounding the Peruvian–Bolivian frontier and around Lake Titicaca. Apart from their use at fiestas, panpipes are played mainly in the dry season, from April to October.

There is something quite amazing about the sound of a fifty-man panpipe band approaching, especially after they've been playing for a few hours and have had a few well-earned drinks. It is perfectly normal for a whole village to come together to play as an orchestra for important events and fiestas. Andean villages are usually composed of *ayllus* (extended families) whose land is often divided up so that everyone gets a share of various pastures, but with everyone working together at key times such as harvest and when caring for communal areas. Music is an integral part of all communal celebrations and symbolically represents that sharing and interdependence: drinks are drunk from communal glasses which everyone will empty in turn. The organization and values of each community are reflected in the very instrument an individual plays, down to the position of players within circles and groups.

Folk music festivals to attract and entertain the tourist trade are a quite different experience to music in the village context. While positively disseminating the music, they have introduced the notion of judging and the concept of "best" musicianship – ideas totally at odds with rural community values of diversity in musical repertoire, style and dress.

Charangos and mermaids

The **charango** is another key Andean instrument whose bright, zingy sounds are familiar worldwide. This small guitar – with five pairs of strings – was created in imitation of early guitars and lutes brought by the Spanish colonizers, which Amerindian musicians were taught to play in the churches. Its small size is due to its traditional manufacture from armadillo shells, while its sound quality comes from the indigenous aesthetic which has favoured high pitches from the pre-Columbian period through to the present.

In rural areas in southern Peru, particularly in the Titicaca region and province of Canas, the *charango* is the key instrument – used by young, single men to woo and court the female of their choice. In this area the tradition often involves the figure of a **mermaid**, *la sirena*, who offers supernatural aid to the young men embarking on a musical pursuit of their chosen one. The ethnomusicologist Tom Turino records that most towns and villages around Titicaca claim a *sirena* lives in a nearby spring, river, lake or waterfall, and notes that new *charangos* are often left overnight in such places – wrapped in a piece of woven cloth, along with gifts – to be tuned and played overnight by the *sirena*. Some villagers construct the sound box in the shape of a mermaid, including her head and fish tail, to invest their *charango* with supernatural power.

When young men go courting at the weekly markets in larger villages they will not only dress in their finest clothes, but get up their *charangos* in elaborate coloured ribbons. These represent the number of women their *charango* has supposedly conquered, thus demonstrating their manliness and the power of their instrument. At times a group of young people will get together for the ancient **circle dance** called the *Punchay Kashwa,* where the men form a half-circle playing their *charangos*, facing a half-circle of young women. Both groups dance and sing in bantering "song duelling" fashion, participants using a set syllabic and rhyming pattern so that they can quickly improvise. "Let's go walking" one might call, with a riposte such as "A devil like you makes me suspicious", or an insult like "In the back of your house there are three rotten eggs".

In Peru, the *charango* was regarded until the 1960s as an "Indian" instrument of the rural, lower classes. Brought to towns and cities by rural migrants, it crossed over when Spanish-speaking middle-class musicians – who until then had only played European instruments such as guitars and mandolins – began to play it, and also as a result of the cultural evaluation following the 1969 Revolution. The Peruvian ideological movement known as **Indigenismo**, active between 1910 and 1940, was also influential in the *charango's* reappraisal. *Indigenismo* was a regionalist and nationalistic movement that lauded indigenous culture as the true Peruvian culture, rejecting criolla and Hispanic values. The movement was particularly strong in Cusco, where *charango* performance by *mestizos* became part of its identity.

Charango styles

Charangos were originally made from the shell of an armadillo but as the animal has become rare and protected, today's instruments are made of wood. There are many sizes and varieties: from those capable of deeper, richer, bass sounds, with large round backs, to flat-backed instruments with more strident metal strings.

Tunings vary from place to place and from musician to musician, with some preferring metal strings, others nylon, to suit a variety of strumming and plucking techniques. Nylon strings are often thought to produce "deeper", "clearer", "sweeter" sounds. In certain areas of Peru, for instance at the time of potato planting, a *charango* may play potato-planting songs and dances strictly in strumming style with a single-line melody vibrating amongst open sounding strings. In contrast **mestizo styles** – used when playing Creole musical forms such as *waynos, marineras, yaravís* and *vals criollo* – may favour plucked melodic playing styles which can be very complex.

Song and brass

Most **singing** in the Andes is done by women, and the preferred style is very high-pitched – almost falsetto to European ears. There are songs for potato-growing, reaping barley, threshing wheat, marking cattle, sheep and goats, for building houses, for traditional dances and funerals and many other ceremonies.

The astonishing diversity of music, ensembles and occasions can be heard clearly on the superb *Smithsonian Folkways Traditional Music of Peru* series, documented and compiled by music ethnologist Raúl Romero. These recordings are mainly from the Mantaro Valley, an area known for its saxophone and clarinet ensembles, and include women singing accompanied by the ancient *tinya* drum and violin, and also the harp as well as clarinets and brass bands. There are so many festivities with music that the music profession is considered profitable, and there are a great number of **brass bands** (first introduced in the 1920s as part of mandatory military service) as well as **orchestras** (*típicas*) composed of saxophones, clarinets, violins and diatonic harp.

Romero notes that urbanization, modernization and migration, rather than undermining the need for traditional music, has led to its successful adaptation of new forms, and revival. He also notes the importance of *mestizo* and bilingual Spanish-Quechua culture in this process.

The context of the musical performance is still the determining factor in its style. Music which continues pre-Hispanic models is to be found within the context of closed community and ritual. Music which is *mestizo*, recreating regional traditions, is dynamically driven by the fiesta system. New musical styles have evolved through migration to the capital Lima, with radio, vinyl and CD as their main vehicles of communication.

Music in Cusco

Music explodes from every direction in the once Inca lands, but nowhere more so than in **Cusco**, a good first base for getting to grips with Andean music. Stay a week or two and you will hear just about every variety of Andean folk music that is still performed.

The streets are the best place to start. Most street musicians are highly talented performers and will play for hours on end. Around noon, you might see **Leandro Apaza** making his way down the great hill of Avenida Tullumayo. Carrying an Andean harp on his shoulder, he is led down the street by a small boy because, like many accomplished regional musicians, he is blind. He will turn right onto Hatun Rumiyoq, the narrow alley that every visitor to Cusco visits at some time to see the large stone perfectly fitted into place in the side wall of Inca Roca's palace. Leandro sets up his harp directly across from the great stone. **Benjamin Clara**, who sometimes accompanies him on mandolin, may already be there waiting. Benjamin cannot always meet Leandro downtown as he is lame as well as sightless and needs to be carried (see Discography, *Blind Street Musicians of Cusco*, p.568).

The two are there to earn their living by playing the traditional music of the Quechua people. Their repertoire includes a host of styles, the most recognizable being the *huayno*, an unmistakable dance rhythm reminiscent of a hopped-up waltz, which once heard is not easily forgotten. It is musically cheerful, though the lyrics can be sorrowful, and sometimes full of double meaning, occasionally sexually explicit – a fact often not realized by those who cannot understand Quechua.

Blind musician **Don Antonio Sulca**, of Ayacucho, is one of the great masters of the Andean harp – one of the mountains' most characteristic instruments. This huge harp has a sound box built like a boat and a mermaid's head decoration (like many *charangos*). Its form is thought to have evolved from the harp brought from Spain in the sixteenth century and the Celtic harp brought by the Jesuits to the missions. It has 36 strings spanning five octaves and including resonant bass notes. In processions in the Andes, harpists often sling their instruments upside down across their shoulders, plucking with a remarkable backhanded technique.

Sulca plays solo or, more often, with his group **Ayllu Sulca**, composed of members of his *ayllu* (his extended family), on fiddles and mandolins. Their songs are mostly *huaynos* sung in Quechua. The most familiar of them, *Huerfano pajarillo* (*Little Orphan Bird*), about a bird that has strayed too far from home, is an allegory of the plight of the Amerindians forced to migrate to earn a living. His stately style of playing *yaravís* – slow sad tunes – is unmatched. A pre-Hispanic form, they probably acquired their doleful, introspective character during the early colonial period, when at least eighty percent of the Amerindian population perished. The *yaraví* composed at the death of the last member of the Inca royal family, Tupac Amaru, in 1781, became the best-known of all Peruvian tunes – **El Condor Pasa (Flight of the Condor)**.

Don Antonio Sulca also plays **dance music** from the early twentieth century, when forms like the foxtrot, waltz and tango were given the Inca touch to produce hybrid forms like the sublime waltz **incaico** *Nube Gris* (*Grey Cloud*). His version of his city's unofficial hymn, *Adiós pueblo Ayacucho* (*Farewell, People of Ayacucho*), celebrates emotional ties to the place where the Amerindians beat back the Spanish at the time of the Conquest.

Very few such musicians achieve any kind of media fame. If they do, it usually means the chance to perform in small clubs or restaurants for a meagre guaranteed wage plus whatever they receive in tips. One such individual is **Gabriel Aragón**. Another blind musician, he is a huge man, obviously *mestizo*, and possessed of a gentle voice and a soft touch on his harp. His fame means that he will often travel for an engagement, which may be a club date, a wedding or a traditional festival. At his restaurant gigs, he serves up some of the finest traditional folk melodies, ballads and dance tunes – a nostalgic repertoire greatly appreciated by older members of the community.

Conjuntos and concerts

Cusco's tavern scene, like that of any urban region, also plays host to young *cholo* and *mestizo* groups. They are constantly on the move throughout the evening, playing one set in each of the available venues in town during the tourist season. You can pick the club with your favourite ambience and settle in – most of the groups will pass through in the course of an evening, so you are almost bound to hear each of them at some point as the entertainment goes on all night long.

This kind of "one-night tour" is limited only by the size of a city. In Lima, for example, a group of this type might confine itself to a specific area of town. The smaller mountain villages, by contrast, might have only one nightspot – and if they are lucky a local band. In regions of heavy tourism, such as Cusco or Ollantaytambo, there is usually a proliferation of groups. If you end up at one of these mini-fiestas, you may be egged on to dance, especially if you are a woman, and definitely be forced to join in a drink. Go along with it, do your best, and don't mind being the butt of the odd joke. It will be worth it.

The ensembles typically consist of five to seven members. Their **instrumentation** includes one or two guitars, a *charango*, *quenas*, other flutes, panpipes and simple percussion. Harps, considered something of a dying art due to their size, weight, fragility and cost, are rarer these days. Most of the musicians are adept at more than one instrument and are likely to switch roles during their set. Their performing is a social event, and their tour a rolling party as they are usually accompanied on their rounds by friends (you are welcome to join them).

As these musicians grow older many of them end up in the backup band of a veteran professional, rather than in a group of traditional musicians. This type of **conjunto** is most likely to be made up of urban middle-class musicians, usually serious students of music since early in life. They often have some type of classical training, may be able to compose and arrange, and, although emotionally tied to ancestral heritage, the bulk of their repertoire is newly composed using traditional idioms played on both modern and traditional instruments. They will also be able to play a variety of standards – classic pieces of traditional highland folk. These ensembles are usually quite well paid and do not normally move about throughout the evening. They play at the more elite nightclubs, hotel lounges and arts centres and sometimes if lucky tour abroad.

Although by the very nature of their own background and that of their audience, these bands are not staunch traditionalists, they are promoted as such by those in charge of international cultural exchange. On tour abroad, they usually play well-known traditional pieces, and often accompany **folkloric dance groups**, while another part of their repertoire may be what is marketed as **Andean New Age** music, a blend of traditionalism with modern sounds. The vocal presentation of these groups is generally more accessible to foreign ears than the piercing falsetto tones of a traditional vocalist.

Huaynos and orquestas típicas

Europeans may know the Andes through the sound of bamboo panpipes and *quenas*, but visit the Peruvian central sierra and you find a music as lively and energetic as the busy market towns it comes from – a music largely unknown outside the country. These songs and dances are **huaynos**, one of the few musical forms that reaches back to pre-Conquest times, although the **orquestas típicas** that play them, from sierra towns like Huancayo, Ayacucho and Pucará, include saxophones, clarinets and trumpets alongside traditional instruments like violins, *charangos* and the large Amerindian harp.

The music is spirited and infectious, the focus gradually shifting from Inca past and a pan-Andean image to the contemporary cultures of regional departments. Because of the larger size of the *provinciano* colonies from Ancash, Junin and Ayacucho in Lima, the urban-country style primarily grew up around performers from these departments, including Pastorita Huancarina (Ancash), Hermanos Zevallos (Junin), Flor de Huancayo (Junin), Princesita de Yungay (Ancash) and Paisanita Ancashina (Ancash). Names such as Paisanita Ancashina (Little Fellow Countrywoman from Ancash) clearly evoke nostalgia of place and *paisano* loyalty, helping to ensure commercial success and bolster regional group unity and pride.

While some voices maintain the high-pitched dense quality of Andean singing, many major stars incorporate Western vibrato (absent in traditional Andean singing) and a clear – from the diaphragm – vocal style. As musicians have become more professional, specializing in certain styles, technical performance on instruments has become cleaner and instrumental breaks hotter. Arrangements too have become tighter and follow other urban popular forms with vocal verses and instrumental solos.

The names of the singers express the passion of the people for the flora and fauna of their homeland – **Flor Pucarina** (The Flower of Pucará) and **Picaflor de los Andes** (Hummingbird of the Andes) are two of those singing in the 1960s represented on GlobeStyle's *huayno* compilation. Another CD of this music, on the Arhoolie label, features the most celebrated *huayno* singer of all time – **El Jilguero de Huascarán**. When he died in 1988, thousands of people packed the streets of Lima to attend his funeral, and recordings he made over thirty years ago are still sold on the streets today.

The buoyant, swinging rhythms of *huayno* songs are deceptive, for the lyrics fuse joy and sorrow. The musical style is regionally marked with typical *mestizo* instrumental ensembles of the region represented and musical features, such as specific guitar runs, identifying musicians with, for example, Ayacucho or Ancash. Sung in a mixture of Spanish and Quechua, they tell of unhappy love and betrayal, celebrate passion, and often deliver homespun philosophy. As Picaflor sings in *Un pasajero en tu camino*: "On the road of romance, I'm only a passenger without a destination". At the same time, texts often allude to region of origin or specific towns, important hooks for local audiences.

As well as in their sierra home, *huaynos* can be heard in Lima and other coastal towns, where they were brought by Andean migrants in the 1950s. Before then the music of the coastal towns and cities was **música criolla**, heavily influenced by music from other parts of Latin America, Spain and Europe – a bourgeois music including everything from foxtrot to tango, which filtered down to the working class, often as hybrids called, for example, Inca-Fox. In the 1950s and 1960s, migrants who often found themselves living in desperate poverty in the shantytowns, scraping a living as maids, labourers or streettraders, would meet up at a Lima *coliseo* (a form of stadium) on a Sunday to dance to their music and assert identity and pride.

Between 1946 and 1949 there were thirty such centres for *espectaculos folkloricos* in Lima, but only two remained by the mid-1970s and there are none left today. A blend of resources from the two worlds, this music served as an aid to *provincianos* in the process of forging a new identity for themselves. But the *coliseos* began to lose their public as people began to demand more traditional performances of highland music and dance. In the 1960s and 1970s regionalmigrant clubs began to take control over the commercial entrepreneurs who had failed to reward the musicians well. Sunday performances switched to these new clubs which gave a share of the fee to the musicians and featured traditions specifically from their home regions.

Urban *huaynos* are performed and recorded by **orquestas típicas** and enjoy enormous popularity. In the rural areas the style is more rustic. Andean highland settlements are isolated by deep river valleys, making communication difficult in the past. Because of this, students of Quechua are tormented by the extreme variation in language sometimes found between two relatively close villages. One would expect a similar variation between song styles; this is sometimes the case, but the *huayno* beat is pan-Andean. Each district does add its own peculiar flavour, but as the saying goes, a *huayno* is a *huayno*, at least until you listen closely. During daylight hours, some forty Lima radio stations broadcast nothing but *huaynos*. Shortwave-radio fans, or visitors to Peru, can tune in for a quick education.

Afro-Peruvian music

Afro-Peruvian music has its roots in the communities of black slaves brought to work in the mines along the Peruvian coast. As such, it's a fair way from the Andes, culturally and geographically. However, as it developed,

Susana Baca

The singer who looks like bringing the Afro-Peruvian scene to international acclaim beyond Latin America is **Susana Baca**, who grew up in the black coastal neighbourhood of Chorrillos outside Lima. Interviewed at WOMAD 1998, she recalled family traditions of getting together for a Sunday meal, and then making music, with her father playing guitar, her mother, aunts, uncles and friends singing and dancing. By the time she was a teenager and first heard the recordings of Nicomedes Santa Cruz, she realized she had absorbed quite a repertoire of the traditional songs black people had carried with them to Peru as slaves.

Susana Baca runs her own Instituto Negrocontinuo, with her husband Ricardo Pereira; its aim is to promote and increase the diffusion of Afro-Peruvian music, and to link together old and young musicians through a series of workshops on all aspects of the music and its culture. Her passion for this project first emerged at school and has increased steadily over the years. "We studied the culture of the Spanish and of the Incas which made the Andean girls proud, but we black girls didn't find our people in the history of Peru at all", recalls Baca. "Blacks came to Peru as servants of Spanish and Portuguese, as slaves to be bought and sold. As a child I was aware that we had our way of cooking, our music, dances, even our own traditional medicines – but it was only in the 1960s that this was first really asserted in public. A lot of people until then had been silenced, some ashamed of the whole history of slavery, of the sufferings of their great grandparents, rejecting their past. But then it began to take on a positive hue and people began to understand what it meant to be black."

One of the essential instruments of Afro-Peruvian music is the *cajón* – a box which the percussionist sits astride, leaning down to play. This is the same *cajón* that eventually made its way into Spanish flamenco – through Paco de Lucía who, according to an apocryphal story, played in Lima in 1978 and first heard the *cajón* played at a party. Susana remembers, "It's true, I was there, I even sang and there was a great group of Peruvian musicians playing and of *cajoneros*, and Paco de Lucía liked it all so much they gave him a *cajón*. The instrument is so important because it carries the rhythm and the voice sings within that dialogue between guitar and *cajón*. My mother always said that it was the box of the people who carried fruit and worked in the ports. When they had a free moment they used them to play and sing and dance. Later they had a more special construction, different woods with a hole in one side that gives a more sophisticated sound, more reverberation. Cuba and Brazil also have similar traditions which also emerged amongst black musicians in ports."

Baca's own performing style is intimate and rooted in close contact with her band "Nothing is written down, the musicians improvise and invent, so we need to be able to see each other's eyes to make a good performance, to share and enjoy and release the power of the music. You can hear it in *La Canción para el Señor de los Milagros* (*The Song for the Lord of Miracles*). It's a song of adoration for a Christ who is celebrated for two days in October in Lima. It's now one of the most important popular festivals – people follow the Christ figure in such numbers through the streets the city comes to a halt. It's wonderful. They asked me to sing that sacred song and I do."

particularly in the twentieth century, it drew on Andean and Spanish, as well as African, traditions, while its modern exponents also have affinities with Andean *nueva canción*. The music was little known even in Peru until the 1950s, when it was popularized by the seminal performer Nicomedes Santa Cruz, whose body of work was taken a step further in the 1970s by the group Peru Negro. Internationally, it has had a recent airing through David Byrne's Luaka Bop label, issuing the compilation, *Peru-Negro*, and a solo album by Susana Baca.

Nicomedes Santa Cruz is the towering figure in the development of Afro-Peruvian music. A poet, musician and journalist, he was the first true musicologist to assert an Afro-Peruvian cultural identity through black music and dance, producing books and recordings of contemporary black music and culture in Peru. In 1959, with his group **Conjunto Cumanana**, he recorded the album *Kumanana*, followed in 1960 by *Ingá* and *Décimas y poemas Afroperuanos*. In 1964 he recorded a four-album set *Cumanana*, now regarded as the bible of Afro-Peruvian music. Santa Cruz himself followed in the footsteps of **Porfirio Vasquez**, who came to Lima in 1920 and was an early pioneer of the movement to regain the lost cultural identity of Afro-Peruvians. A composer of *décimas*, singer, guitarist, *cajonero* (box player) and *zapateador* (dancer), he founded the Academia Folklórica in Lima in 1949. Through Santa Cruz's work and that of the group **Peru Negro** and the singer and composer **Chabuca Granda**, Latin America came to know Afro-Peruvian dances, the names of which were given to their songs such as *Toro Mata*, *Samba-malató*, *El Alcatraz* and *Festejo*.

Chicha

Chicha, the fermented maize beer, has given its name to a new and hugely popular brew of Andean tropical music – a fusion of urban *cumbia* (local versions of the original Colombian dance), traditional highland *huayno*, and rock. The music's origins lie in the massive migration of Amerindians from the inner mountain areas to the shantytowns around cities such as Arequipa and Lima. *Chicha* emerged in Lima in the early 1960s and by the mid-1980s had become the most widespread urban music in Peru. Most bands have lead and rhythm guitars, electric bass, electric organ, a *timbales* and conga player, one or more vocalists (who may play percussion) and, if they can, a synthesizer.

The first *chicha* hit, and the song from which the movement has taken its name, was *La Chichera* (*The Chicha Seller*) by **Los Demonios de Mantaro** (The Devils of Mantaro), who hailed from the central highlands of Junin. Another famous band are **Los Shapis**, another provincial group established by their 1981 hit *El Aguajal* (*The Swamp*), a version of a traditional *huayno*. **Pastorita Huaracina** is one of the more well-known female singers. Another good band – and the first to get a Western CD release – are **Belem**, based in Lima.

While most lyrics are about love in all its aspects, nearly all songs actually reveal an aspect of the harshness of the Amerindian experience – displacement, hardship, loneliness and exploitation. Many songs relate to the great majority of people who have to make a living selling their labour and goods in the unofficial "informal economy", ever threatened by the police. Los Shapis' *El Ambulante* (*The Street Seller*) opens with a reference to the rainbow colours of the Inca flag and the colour of the ponchos the people use to keep warm and transport their wares. "My flag is of the colours and the stamp of the

Compilations

Afro-Peruvian Classics: The Soul of Black Peru (Luaka Bop, US). Music of the black slaves brought to work in the mines of the coastal areas, which began to gain recognition in Peru in the 1940s. Popularized in the last 25 years, first by seminal musicologist and performer, Nicomedes Santa Cruz, then by Peru Negro, the group who got the music going in the 1970s, and by the great Chabuca Granda; later Susana Baca and Cecilia Barraza continued the style. A unique blend of Spanish, Andean and African traditions, this is different than Caribbean and other Latin black cultures. This compilation includes the definitive dance song *Toro Mata*, the first Afro-Peruvian success outside Peru, covered by the Queen of Salsa, Celia Cruz. A fine collection intended to introduce the music to a wider audience outside Peru, it does a great job.

The Blind Street Musicians of Cusco: Peruvian Harp and Mandolin (Music of the World, US). Stirringly played *marineras*, *huaynos*, traditional tunes and instrumental solos exactly as heard on the streets of Cusco in 1984–85 from Leandro Apaza on a 33-stringed harp; Benjamin Clara Quispé and Carmen Apaza Roca on armadillo-shelled mandolins (not *charangos*); Fidel Villacorte Tejada on *quena*. Excellent ambience recorded in musicians' homes and *chichería* bars.

Flutes and Strings of the Andes (Music of the World, US). The superbly atmospheric recordings of amateur musicians from Peru – harpists, *charanguistas*, fiddlers, flautists and percussionists, recorded in 1983–84 on the streets and at festivals – bring you as close to being there as you can get without strapping on your pack and striding uphill.

From the Mountains to the Sea: Music of Peru, The 1960s (Arhoolie, US). Brilliant window into the mix of indigenous, *criolla*, *mestizo*, Latin, tropical and European styles to be found in the capital, including Peruvian rock, *cumbias*, *valses*, *boleros*, *sanjuanitos*, *huaynos*, tangos. Captures the spirit of many different groups, combinations of instruments and atmospheres.

Huayno Music of Peru Vols 1 and 2 (Arhoolie, US). These excellent collections of *huayno* music from the 1950s to the 1980s focus on a slightly more local style than the GlobeStyle disc. Vol 1 includes songs from the master, Jilguero del Huascarán, while Vol 2 is drawn from the recordings of Discos Smith, a small label that released *huayno* and *criolla* music in the late 1950s and 1960s.

Huaynos and Huaylas: The Real Music of Peru (GlobeStyle, UK). A tremendous selection of urban *orquestas típicas*, who replace traditional instruments with saxophones, clarinets and violins, this is a real eye- and ear-opener. The performers include the late Picaflor de los Andes, and Flor Pucarina, with a host of songs expressing loss and love rooted in the Peruvian countryside.

Kingdom of the Sun (Nonesuch Explorer, US). An atmospheric mix of Peru's Inca heritage and religious festivals recorded in Ayacucho, Chuschi and Paucartambo.

Mountain Music of Peru (Smithsonian Folkways, US). John Cohen's selection, including a song that went up in the *Voyager* spacecraft, brings together music from remote corners of the mountains where music is integral to daily life, and urban songs telling of tragedies at football matches. Good sleeve notes, too.

Peru and Bolivia. The Sounds of Evolving Traditions. Central Andean Music and Festivals (Multicultural Media, US). Lively, accessible introduction to today's sounds from both Peru and Bolivia, from Japanese aficionado Norio Yamamoto's brilliant and diverse selection of recordings. Each piece in its natural context from people's homes to clubs to fiestas to streets with live local audiences. Harps, violins, drums, panpipes, and much more. Moving from Cusco to Ayacucho, La Paz to Lima, Lake Titicaca and back to Marcapata village near Cusco. Good notes.

The Rough Guide to Music of the Andes (World Music Network). A vigorous and broad range of Andean music from contemporary urban-based groups – including key 1960s musicians Los Kjarkas and Ernesto Cavou, and their 1980s European travelling brethren Awatinas and Rumillajta; soloists Emma Junaro, Jenny Cardenas and Susana Baca; seminal Chilean group Inti Illimani and new song singer Victor Jara. Plus saxes and clarinets from Picaflor de los Andes.

Traditional Music of Peru: Vol 1 Festivals of Cusco; Vol 2 The Mantaro Valley; Vol 3 Cajamarca and the Colca Valley; Vol 4 Lambayeque (Smithsonian Folkways, US). A definitive series of field recordings from the 1980s and 1990s of music from specific areas. Includes the whole spectrum of music to be heard if you travelled around the whole of Peru. Excellent CD booklets, too.

Artists and albums

Ayllu Sulca

Blind harpist Don Antonio Sulca encapsulates everything that is *mestizo* music – the emergence of a hybrid blend between Amerindian and Spanish cultures. A virtuoso since early childhood, he plays as a soloist but mostly as part of his band – his *ayllu* – which includes three of his sons.

Music of the Incas (Lyrichord, US). Accompanied by violin, mandolin and *quenas*, Sulca plays ancient Inca melodies and more recent waltzes with pace and swing, including rustic versions of salon music.

Susana Baca

One of the few Afro-Peruvian artists touring worldwide, Susana Baca grew up in the coastal barrio of Chorrillos and learned traditional Afro-Peruvian songs from her family (see box, p.566). Dedicated to recuperating and strengthening this past and making it relevant to the present, she runs the Instituto Negrocontinuo (Black Continuum) in Lima and is as involved with the integral dance and other aspects of Afro-Peruvian culture as the music.

Susana Baca (Luaka Bop/Warner Bros). Taking up the mantle of Chabuca Granda and Nicomedes Santa Cruz, these are fine versions of Afro-Peruvian and criolla classics sung with conscious emotion and passion.

Belem

Belem are one of the bands which have made *chicha* a force to be reckoned with in urban Peru.

Chicha (Tumi, UK). A pioneering release of Peru's hot fusion music. Belem's mix of *huayno*, salsa, *cumbia*, and a touch of rock, deserves a listening. Andean pipe music, it ain't.

Arturo "Zambo" Cavero and Oscar Aviles

Arturo "Zambo" Cavero is one of the great male voices of black Peruvian music, as well as being an accomplished *cajón* player. During the 1980s he teamed up with Oscar Aviles to become a celebrated partnership, their music seen as reflecting the suffering, patriotism and passion of the black people of Peru. As a key member of the group Los Morochucos, Oscar Aviles gained the reputation of being "*La Primera Guitarra del Peru*" – Peru's leading Creole guitarist.

Y siguen festejando juntos (IEMPSA, Peru). Classic Afro-Peruvian music with the most representative voice and guitar musicians on the scene.

continued over

On the Wings of the Condor (Tumi, UK). One of the most popular Andean albums ever, but none the worse for that: the engaging sound of the panpipes and *charangos*, smoothly and beautifully arranged.

Hermanos Santa Cruz

Hermanos Santa Cruz are family members of Nicomedes Santa Cruz.

Afro Peru (Discos Hispanos, Peru). Carrying on the tradition and heritage laid down by their forefathers, the Santa Cruz brothers present a 1990s version of Afro-Peruvian traditions.

Nicomedes Santa Cruz

The first true musicologist to assert Afro-Peruvian cultural identity through black music and dance.

Kumanana (Philips, Peru), *Socabon* (Virrey, Peru). Two albums showcasing Santa Cruz's majestic musicological studies of Afro-Peruvian music and culture.

rainbow/For Peru and America/Watch out or the police will take your bundle off you!/Ay, ay, ay, how sad it is to live/How sad it is to dream/I'm a street seller, I'm a proletarian/Selling shoes, selling food, selling jackets/I support my home".

Chicha has effectively become a youth movement, an expression of social frustration for the mass of people suffering racial discrimination in Peruvian society.

Peru's performers

Many performers have achieved mass appeal and recording contracts in Peru and can support themselves solely by their work as musicians. Nationally celebrated performers include **Florcita de Pisaq** (a *huayno* vocalist), **Pastorita Huaracina** (a singer of both *cholo* and *mestizo* varieties) and **Jaime Guardía** (a virtuoso of the *charango*).

These performers take pride in being bearers of tradition, play at most traditional festivals and hire themselves out to wealthier villages to provide music for those festive events that require it. Although they may hold little attraction for the wealthy urban population (who tend to deny their roots), they often appear at large venues in major urban areas. They appeal to the displaced *campesinos* and city migrants who live in the *pueblos jóvenes*, or squatter settlements, which have sprung up on the outskirts of the large coastal cities.

Recordings of these artists are generally only available locally, but they can sometimes be found in shops catering for Latin American immigrants. Occasionally, an artist of this type will end up on an album collection.

Front rooms and festivals

There is a large contingent of non-professional musicians, and, in Peruvian cities, the middle class often perform in impromptu ensembles **at home** in their living rooms. They tend to play *huaynos* or *chicha*, styles accompanied by falsetto singing in Spanish or Quechua, and often a mixture of both.

The only way to hear a performance in someone's living room is, of course, to get yourself invited. Fortunately, this isn't difficult to do in the Andes, where only a committed sociopath could avoid making friends. To speed the process, bring alcohol with you, accept every drink offered, be sure to encourage others to drink from your bottle, eat everything served to you, and ask to learn the words and sing along. You'll quickly pick up the dance steps.

For the less gregarious, **festivals** are an equally rewarding source of traditional music. One of the best takes place in January on the **Isla Amantaní** in Lake Titicaca, its exact date, as is often the case in the Andean highlands, determined by astronomical events. This particular festival occurs during a period often called the "time of protection", when the rainy season has finally begun. It is related to the cleansing of the pasturage and water sources; stone fences are repaired, walking paths repaved, and the stone effigies and crosses that guard the planting fields replaced or repaired. A single-file "parade" of individuals covers the entire island, stopping to appease the deities and provide necessary maintenance at each site. At the front are local non-professional musicians, all male, playing drums and flutes of various types.

There are, too, festivals that are celebrated on a larger scale. On the day of the June solstice (midwinter in the Andes) the Inca would ceremonially tie the sun to a stone and coax it to return south, bringing warmer weather and the new planting season. **Inti Raymi**, the Festival of the Sun, is still observed in every nook and cranny in the Andean republics, from the capital city to the most isolated hamlet. The celebration, following a solemn ritual that may include a llama sacrifice, is more of a carnival than anything else. Parades of musicians, both professional bands and thrown-together collages of amateurs, fill the streets. You will be expected to drink and dance until you drop, or hide in your room. This kind of party can run for several days, so be prepared. Anyone spending more than two weeks in the Andes is almost bound to witness a festival of some sort.

Written by Jan Fairley, with thanks to Thomas Turino and Raúl Romero, Gilka Wara Céspedes, Martin Morales and Margaret Bullen. Adapted from the *Rough Guide to World Music, Vol 2.*

C

CONTEXTS | Peruvian music

Wildlife and ecology

Peru boasts what is probably the most diverse array of wildlife of any country on earth; its varied ecological niches span an incredible range of climate and terrain. And although mankind has occupied the area for perhaps twenty thousand years, there has been less disturbance there, until relatively recently, than in most other parts of our planet. For the sake of organization this piece follows the country's usual regional divisions – coastal desert, Andes mountains and tropical jungle – though a more accurate picture would be that of a continuous intergradation, encompassing literally dozens of unique habitats. From desert the land climbs rapidly to the tundra of mountain peaks, then down again into tropical rainforest, moving gradually through a whole series of environments in which many of the species detailed below overlap.

The coast

The coastal desert is characterized by an abundant sea life and by the contrasting scarcity of terrestrial plants and animals. The Humboldt current runs virtually the length of Peru, bringing cold water up from the depths of the Pacific Ocean and causing any moisture to condense out over the sea, depriving the mainland coastal strip and lower western mountain slopes of rainfall. Along with this cold water, large quantities of nutrients are carried up to the surface, helping to sustain a rich planktonic community able to support vast numbers of fish, preyed upon in their turn by a variety of coastal birds: gulls, terns, pelicans, boobies, cormorants and wading birds are always present along the beaches. One beautiful specimen, the Inca tern, although usually well camouflaged as it sits high up on inaccessible sea cliffs, is nevertheless very common in the Lima area. The Humboldt penguin, with grey rather than black features, is a rarer sight – shyer than its more southerly cousins, it is normally found in isolated rocky coves or on offshore islands. Competing with the birds for fish are schools of dolphins, sea lion colonies and the occasional coastal otter. Dolphins and sea lions are often spotted off even the most crowded of beaches or scavenging around the fishermen's jetty at Chorrillos, near Lima.

One of the most fascinating features of Peruvian birdlife is the vast, high-density colonies: although the number of species is quite small, their total population is enormous. Many thousands of birds can be seen nesting on islands like the Ballestas, off the **Paracas Peninsula**, or simply covering the ocean with a flapping, diving carpet of energetic feathers. This huge bird population, and the **Guanay cormorant** in particular, is responsible for depositing mountains of guano (bird droppings), which form a traditional and potent source of natural fertilizer.

In contrast to the rich coastal waters the **desert** lies stark and barren. Here you find only a few trees and shrubs; you'll need endless patience to find wild animals other than birds. The most common animals are feral **goats**, once domesticated but now living wild, and **burros** (or donkeys) introduced by the Spanish. A more exciting sight is the attractively coloured **coral snake** – shy but deadly and covered with black and orange hoops. Most animals are more active after sunset; when out in the desert you can hear the eerily plaintive call of the *huerequeque* (or **Peruvian thick-knee** bird), and the barking of the little **desert fox** – alarmingly similar to the sound of car tyres screeching to a halt. By day you might see several species of small birds, a favourite being the vermilion-headed **Peruvian fly-catcher**. Near water – rivers, estuaries, and lagoons – desert wildlife is at its most populous. In addition to residents such as **flamingos**, **herons** and **egrets**, many migrant birds pause in these havens between October and March on their journeys south and then back north.

In order to understand the coastal desert you have to bear in mind the phenomenon of **El Niño**, a periodic climatic shift caused by the displacement of the cold Humboldt current by warmer equatorial waters; it last occurred in 1998. This causes the plankton and fish communities either to disperse to other locations or to collapse entirely. At such a period the shore rapidly becomes littered with carrion since many of the sea mammals and birds are unable to survive in the much tighter environment. Scavenging condors and vultures, on the other hand, thrive, as does the desert where rain falls in deluges along the coast, with a consequent bloom of vegetation and rapid growth in animal populations. When the Humboldt current returns, the desert dries up, its animal populations decline to normal sizes (another temporary feast for the scavengers), and at least ten years usually pass before the cycle is repeated. Generally considered a freak phenomenon, El Niño is probably better understood as an integral part of coastal ecology; without it the desert would be a far more barren and static environment, virtually incapable of supporting life.

The mountains

In the **Peruvian Andes** there is an incredible variety of habitats. That this is a mountain area of true extremes becomes immediately obvious if you fly across, or along, the Andes towards Lima – the land below shifting from high *puna* to cloud forest to riparian valleys and eucalyptus tracts (introduced from Australia in the 1880s). The complexity of the whole makes it incredibly difficult to formulate any overall description that isn't essentially misleading: climate and vegetation vary according to altitude, latitude and local characteristics.

The Andes divides vertically into three main regions, identified by the Incas from top to bottom as the Puna, the Qeswa and the Yunka. The **Puna,** roughly 3800–4300m above sea level, has an average temperature of 3–6°C, and annual rainfall of 500–1000mm. Typical animals here include the main Peruvian cameloids – llamas, alpacas, guanacos and *vicuñas* – while crops that grow well here include the potato and *quinoa* grain. At 2500–3500m, the **Qeswa** has average temperatures of around 13°C, and a similar level of rainfall at 500–1200mm. The traditional forest here, including Andean pines, is not abundant and has been largely displaced by the imported Australian eucalyptus trees; the main cultivated crops include maize, potatoes and the nutritious *kiwicha* grain. The *ceja de selva* (cloud forest) to high forest on the eastern side of the Andes in the relatively low-lying **Yunka**, at 1200–2500m, has at least twice as much rain as the other two regions and abundant wildlife, including Peru's national bird, the red-crested *gallito de las rocas* (cock-of-the-rocks). Plant life, too, is prolific, not least the orchids. On the western side of the Andes there is much less rainfall and it's not technically known as the Yunka, but it does share some characteristics: both sides have wild river canes (*caña brava*), and both are suitable for cultivating bananas, pineapples, *yuca* and coca.

Much of the Andes has been settled for over two thousand years – and hunter tribes go back another eight thousand years before this – so larger predators are rare, though still present in small numbers in the more remote regions. Among the most exciting you might actually see are the **mountain cats**, especially the **puma**, which lives at most altitudes and in a surprising number of habitats. Other more remote predators include the shaggy-looking **maned wolf** and the likeable **spectacled bear**, which inhabits the moister forested areas of the Andes and actually prefers eating vegetation to people.

The most visible animals in the mountains, besides sheep and cattle, are the cameloids – the wild **vicuña** and **guanaco**, and the domesticated **llama** and **alpaca**. Although these species are clearly related, zoologists disagree on whether or not the alpaca and llama are domesticated forms of their wild relatives. Domesticated they are, however, and have been so for thousands of years; studies reveal that cameloids appeared in North America some forty to fifty million years ago, crossing the Bering Straits long before any humans did. From these early forms the present species have evolved in Peru, Bolivia, Chile, Argentina and Ecuador, and there are now over three million llamas – 33 percent in Peru and a further 63 percent over the border in Bolivia. The alpaca population is just under four million, with 87 percent in Peru and only 11 percent in Bolivia.

Of the two wild cameloids, the *vicuña* is the smaller and rarer, living only at the highest altitudes (up to 4500m) and with a population of just over 100,000, although it is stronger in numbers in Peru than the guanaco, of which there are around 4000 here (there are over 500,000 in Argentina alone).

Andean deer are quite common in the higher valley and with luck you might even come across the rare **mountain tapir**. Smaller animals tend to be confined to particular habitats – rabbit-like **viscachas**, for example, to rocky outcrops; **squirrels** to wooded valleys; and **chinchillas** (Peruvian chipmunks) to higher altitudes.

Most birds also tend to restrict themselves to specific habitats. The **Andean goose** and **duck** are quite common in marshy areas, along with many species of waders and migratory waterfowl. A particular favourite is the elegant, very pink, **Andean flamingo**, which can usually be spotted from the road between Arequipa and Puno where they turn Lake Salinas into one great red mass. In addition, many species of passarines can be found alongside small streams. Perhaps the most striking of them is the **dipper**, which hunts underwater for larval insects along the stream bed, popping up to a rock every so often for air and a rest. At lower elevations, especially in and around cultivated areas, the **ovenbird** (or horneo) constructs its nest from mud and grasses in the shape of an old-fashioned oven; while in open spaces many birds of prey can be spotted, the comical **caracaras, buzzard-eagles** and the magical **red-backed hawks** among them. The **Andean condor** (see "Birds", p.580) is actually quite difficult to see up close as, although not especially rare, they tend to soar at tremendous heights for most of the day, landing only on high, inaccessible cliffs, or at carcasses after making sure that no one is around to disturb them. A glimpse of this magnificent bird soaring overhead will come only through frequent searching with binoculars, perhaps in relatively unpopulated areas, or at one of the better-known sites such as the Cruz del Condor viewing platform in the Colca Canyon (see p.265).

Tropical rainforest

Descending the eastern edge of the Andes, you pass through the distinct habitats of the Puna, Qeswa and Yunka before reaching the lowland jungle or rainforest. In spite of its rich and luxuriant appearance, the **rainforest** is in fact extremely fragile. Almost all the nutrients are recycled by rapid decomposition, with the aid of the damp climate and a prodigious supply of insect labour, back into the vegetation – thereby creating a nutrient-poor soil that is highly susceptible to large-scale disturbance. When the forest is cleared, for example, usually in an attempt to colonize the area and turn it into viable farmland, there is not only heavy soil erosion to contend with but also a limited amount of nutrients in the earth, only enough for five years of good harvests and twenty years' poorer farming at the most. Natives of the rainforest have evolved cultural mechanisms by which, on the whole, these problems are avoided: they tend to live in small, dispersed groups, move their gardens every few years and obey sophisticated social controls to limit the chances of overhunting any one zone or any particular species.

Around eighty percent of the Amazon rainforest was still intact at the start of the twenty-first century, but for every hardwood logged in this forest, an average of 120 other trees are destroyed and left unused or simply burnt. Over an acre per second of this magnificent forest is burned or bulldozed, equating to an area the size of Great Britain, every year, even though this doesn't make economic sense. According to the late rainforest specialist Dr Alwyn Gentry, just one hectare of primary rainforest could yield up to $9000 a year from sustainable harvesting of wild fruits, saps, resins and timber – yet the average income per hecatre from ranching or plantations in the Amazon is a meagre $30 a year.

Amazon flora and fauna

The most distinctive attribute of the Amazon Basin is its overwhelming abundance of plant and animal species. Over six thousand species of plant have been reported from one small 250-acre tract of forest, and there are at least a thousand species of birds and dozens of types of monkeys and bats spread about the Peruvian Amazon. There are several reasons for this marvellous natural diversity of flora and fauna. Most obviously, it is warm, there is abundant sunlight, and large quantities of mineral nutrients are washed down from the Andes – all of which help to produce the ideal conditions for forest growth. Secondly, the rainforest has enormous structural diversity, with layers of vegetation from the forest floor to the canopy 30m above providing a vast number of niches to fill. Thirdly, since there is such a variety of habitat as you descend the Andes, the changes in altitude mean a great diversity of localized ecosystems.

The great diversity of flora has assisted the evolution of equally varied fauna in the Amazon. With the rainforest being stable over longer periods of time than temperate areas (there was no Ice Age here, nor any prolonged period of drought), the fauna has had freedom to evolve, and to adapt to often very specialized local conditions. But if the Amazon Basin is where most of the plant and animal species are in Peru, it is not easy to see them. Movement through the vegetation is limited to narrow trails and along the rivers in a boat. The river banks and flood plains are richly diverse areas: here you are likely to see

caimans, macaws, toucans, oropendulas, terns, horned screamers and the primitive **hoatzins** – birds whose young are born with claws at the wrist to enable them to climb up from the water into the branches of overhanging trees. You should catch sight, too, of one of a variety of **hawks** and at least two or three species of **monkeys** (perhaps the **spider monkey**, the **howler**, or the **capuchin**). And with a lot of luck and more determined observation you may spot a rare **giant river otter**, **river dolphin**, **capybara**, or maybe even one of the **jungle cats**.

In the jungle proper you're more likely to find mammals such as the **pecary** (wild pig), **tapir**, **tamandua tree sloth** and the second largest cat in the world, the incredibly powerful **spotted jaguar**. Characteristic of the deeper forest zones, too, are many species of birds, including **hummingbirds** (more common in the forested Andean foothills), **manakins** and **trogons**, though the effects of widespread hunting make it difficult to see these around any of the larger settlements. Logging is proving to be another major problem for the forest fauna since with the valuable trees dispersed among vast areas of other species in the rainforest, a very large area must be disturbed to yield a relatively small amount of timber. Deeper into the forest, however, and the further you are from human habitation, a glimpse of any of these animals is quite possible. Most of the bird activity occurs in the canopy, 30–40m above the ground, but with such platforms as the ACEER Canopy Walkway ☏094/252530, Ⓦwww.explorama.com, things are a little easier.

Amazon flora

Aguaje palm (*Mauritia flexuosa*) A tropical swamp plant, commonly growing up to 15m tall, with fan-shaped leaves that can be be over 2m long, and barrel-shaped fruit (6–7cm long) with a purple, plastic-like skin. The thin layer of yellow pulp beneath the skin is consumed raw, made into a drink, or used to flavour ice cream. The leaves can be used for roof-thatch or, more commonly, floor-matting. Younger leaves are utilized to make ropes, hammocks, net bags and sometimes baskets.

Ayahuasca (*Banisteriopsis caapi*) Interpreted from Quechna as "Vine of the Soul" or "Vine of the Dead", this is found exclusively in northwest Amazonia and is also called *yage* and *caap*. These names also refer to the hallucinogenic brew, in which ayahuasca is the main ingredient, used widely in the Peruvian Amazon and by *curanderos*.

Brazil nut tree (*Bertholletia excelsa*) Up to 30m tall, these take over ten years to reach nut-bearing maturity, when a single specimen can produce over 450kg every year during the rainy season.

Breadfruit (*Artocarpus altilis*) The tree known locally as *pan del arbol*, related to the rubber tree, is cut open and dried so that the large brown beans can be taken and boiled for eating. Only in Central America are the whole fruits eaten and even in Peru, people only bother with these when they are out of bananas and *yuca* (manioc). The sap is a good medicine for hernias.

Caimetillo Some spots in the primary forest are devoid of ground growth apart from this one species of small tree. Many Indians see these glades as *supay chacras* ("demons' gardens") and they keep away from them at night. The scientific explanation is that the azteca ant that lives on them has such acidic faeces that nothing else can grow where they live.

Capirona Related to the eucalyptus, this tree protects itself from insects by shedding its bark every two to three months. A fast grower, achieving 12m in just five years, it burns long and well and is consequently sold as firewood. Its sap can be applied to the throat for laryngitis, or mixed with lime and used as a gargle.

Catahua (*Eurocrypitan*) A large, hardwood emergent tree reaching nearly 50m, this tree depends on the Saki monkey for reproduction and seed dispersal. Its fruits are poisonous to most other animals.

Charapilla A gigantic tree, characterized by its six-metre base and a trunk over 1m in diameter. One of the hardest trees in the Iquitos region, it is rarely cut for timber because of its light yellowy colour. Young Conibo warriors were once tested for their strength and ability by how long they took to cut through the wood of ones that had already fallen. The fruit is eaten roasted, although the Achual of the Río Tigre prefer to eat them raw. The leaves are small and used for birth control by the Conibo.

Coca Cocaine is just one of the alkaloids in coca leaves, which are traditionally sacred to Andeans. A vital aid in coping with the altitude, climate and rigours of the region, they help withstand low temperatures and act as a hunger depressant. Research also shows that they have a nutritional value, containing more calcium than any other edible plant, which is important in the Andes, an area with few dairy foods.

Epiphytes Often shrub-like plants, epiphytes live in the crowns or branching elbows of trees but are functionally independent of them. In the higher jungle areas, they are extremely common and diverse, encompassing various species of orchids, cacti, bromeliads and aroids. There are over five-hundred varieties of orchids recorded in the Amazon, many of them to be found in the *ceja de selva*.

Genipap (*Genipa americana*) Also called *huito*, this is related to coffee but is quite different. Growing up to 20m, it has small creamy flowers and fruit that's eaten ripe or used to make an alcoholic drink that alleviates arthritic pains and bronchial ailments. Unripe juice is taken for stomach ulcers. The sap turns from transparent to blue-black after exposure to the air and is used as a dye, or body and face paint.

Inga (*Inga edulis*) Belonging to the mimosa family and growing to over 35m, there are over 350 species in the *Inga* genus. Its most distinctive feature is its long bean pods containing sweet white pulp and large seeds, which some Indian groups use to treat dysentry.

Manioc The most important of cultivated plants in the Peruvian Amazon, and known in Peru as *yuca*, its most useful parts are the large, phallic-shaped tuber roots, the brunt of many indigenous jokes. High in carbohydrates and enzymes, which assist digestion of other foods, it is roasted (to get rid of the cyanide it contains) or brewed to make *masato* beer. It is also the basis of tapioca. As far as its medicinal functions go, the juice from the tubers is applied as a head wash for scabies or can be mixed with water to ease diarrhoea.

Monkey-ladder vine (*Leguminosae casalpinioideae*) Also known as the turtle-ladder vine, this unusual-looking vine spirals high up to blossom in the canopy of primary forests.

Peach palm Also known as the *pihuayao*, and common in most areas of the Peruvian rainforest, its new shoots are the source for the Yaguar and Witoto Indians' "grass" skirts and headdresses. The bark of the stems is used for interior wall partitions in native houses. The cork-like insides of the stems are made into sleeping mats, a particularly important symbol of marriage among the Achual tribe along the Río Tigre. From its fallen trunks, the larvae of beetles are gathered as a delicacy by many indigenous groups.

Quinilla This yellow flowering tree is easy to spot, not so much by its tall, straight forty-metre trunk, but by the sweetly scented carpet of flowers beneath it, or the yellow, cauliform patterns of its canopy, seen when flying over the forest.

Rubber tree (*Hevea brasiliensis*) Known as *jebe* in Peru and *seringuera* closer to the Brazilian border, as a valuable export these trees were the key to the Amazon's initial exploitation.

Sabre pentana (*Lupuna*) A softwood tree, mainly used as ply and now in danger of extinction, this is still one of the most impressive plants in the Peruvian Amazon, at nearly 50m tall and home to harpy eagles, which nest in the same tree for life (if the tree is felled, the bird dies with it by refusing to eat again). The trees are scattered across the forest and are sometimes used by Indians as landmarks when travelling along the rivers.

Stilt palm (*Socratea exorrhiza*) Also abundant in the Amazon, reaching heights of up to 15m, with a thin trunk and very thorny stilt roots that grow like a tepee above the ground. Its long thin leaves are used by some indigenous groups as a treatment for hepatitis. The most utilized part is the hard bark, which can be taken off in one piece for use as flooring or wall slats.

Thatch palm (*Lepidocaryum tenue*) A relatively thin plant growing to around 4m and with a noticeably ringed trunk. Its leaves are used as roof-thatch throughout the Peruvian Amazon.

Ungurahui palm (*Oenocarpus bataua*) The rotting trunks of this palm are home to the suri larvae of the rhinoceros beetle, a favoured food of local Indians. Its green fruits can also be squeezed for their oil, which is used to treat vomiting, diarrhoea and even malaria. The trunk and leaves are often used in house construction.

Walking palm (*Socratea exercisia*) The wood is often used for parquet flooring. Tradition has it that it developed spikes to protect itself against the now extinct giant sloth, which used to push it over.

Wild mango (*Grias neuberthii*) The wild mango tree is frequently seen as an ornamental plant around rainforest lodges. A member of the Brazil nut family, it's actually unrelated to the true mango (*Mangifera indica*), but can grow up to 20m, with thin, spindly trunks and branches. Their delicate yellow flowers are odorous, but the fruit can be eaten raw, boiled or roasted and has a medicinal function as a purgative; the seed is grated to treat venereal tumours and associated fevers, as well as being used as an enema to cure dysentery. The bark can be used to induce vomiting.

Amazon fauna

Anteaters There are four main types of anteater in Peru; all have powerful curved front claws but no teeth, using instead their long tongues to catch insects in holes and rotting vegetation, and share long, tube-like snouts. They have only one baby at a time, which clings to the mother's back when they move through the forest. Giant anteaters (*Myrmecophaga tridactyla*), which can be 2m long with hairy non-prehensile tails, are black, orange-brown and whiteish, with a a diagonal black and white shoulder stripe. Solitary creatures, they can be seen day or night, and, while normally passive, can defend themselves easily with their powerful front legs. Collared anteaters, or southern tamandua (*Tamandua tetradactlya*), are smaller, at less than 1m long. Arboreal and terrestrial, they too are nocturnal and diurnal, though they move slowly as they have poor eyesight. Northern tamandua (*Tamandua mexicana*) are restricted to the northern jungles in Peru. The silky or pygmy anteater (*Cyclopes didactylus*) is quite small, rarely exceeding 25cm in length. It's a smoky grey to golden colour on the upper parts, sometimes with dark brown stripes from its shoulders to its rear. It's also distinguished by the soft whistling noise it makes.

Armadillos Of the giant armadillos and nine-banded long-nosed armadillos, the former are up to 1m long, the latter usually half this. Both are covered in bony armour and have small heads with wide-set ears and grey to yellow colouring. Mostly nocturnal, they tend to feed on ants and termites, some fruit and even small prey. Giant armadillos are good diggers and live in burrows.

Bats Bat species comprise almost forty percent of all mammals in the Amazon, and all North, Central and South American bats belong to the suborder *Microchiroptera*. Vampire bats, which feed on the blood of mammals, are known to transmit rabies and are commonest in cattle-ranching areas rather than remote forest zones.

Brazilian tapir (*Tapirus terrestris*) Known as *sachavaca* ("forest cow" in Quechua) in Peru, this is the largest forest land mammal at around 2m long, brown to dark grey in colour and with a large upper lip. Their tails are stumpy, their feet three-toed and their backs noticeably convex. Largely nocturnal, they browse swampy forests for fruit and grasses.

Capybara (*Hydrochaeris hydrochaeris*) The world's largest (but friendly) rodent, the tan or grey capybara can be over 1m and will give warning yelps to its family when scared. They eat aquatic vegetation and grasses, but are also known to fish and eat lizards when they come across them.

Dolphins The pink river dolphin (*Inia geoffrensis*) is about 2m long and has a noticeable dorsal fin. They feed exclusively on fish and will swim with or within a few metres of people. The smaller grey dolphin or tucuxi (*Sotalia fluviatilis*) achieves a maximum length of 1.5m and has a more prominent dorsal fin, and usually jumps further and is more acrobatic than the pink dolphin.

Giant otter (*Pteronura brasiliensis*) Just over 1m long, ending in a thickish tail with a flattened tip. Their alarm call is a snort and they are very aggressive when in danger. They eat fish and move in extended family groups, with the males doing the least fishing but the most eating.

Manatee (*Trichechus inunguis*) Almost 3m in length, with a large tubular body, a flat tail, short front flippers and a whiskery face, this aquatic mammal is relatively common in the Iquitos area. They feed on water hyacinths and other aquatic vegetation, taking advantage of the high-water season to graze on the flooded riverside floor.

Paca (*Agouti paca*) Chestnut-brown and white-striped, this large, fat rat- and pig-like creature has plenty of flesh but a tiny tail, hardly visible beneath the rump hair. It's primarily nocturnal and feeds on roots and fallen fruit.

Peccaries (*Tayassuidae*) Peccaries, or wild boar, are stocky with relatively spindly legs and biggish heads. The white-lipped peccary (*Tayassu pecari*) is up to 1m long and moves quickly in dangerous herds of fifty to a few hundred. Their diet is fruit and palm nuts, which they scour vast tracts of forest to find. The collared peccary (*Tayassu tajacu*) is smaller and moves in groups of five to twenty.

Red brocket deer (*Mazama americana*) Rarely much over 1m in length, these are mostly brown to grey, with large eyes, and the males have unbranched antlers which slope back. They are found in the forest or at waterholes, feeding on fruit and fungi.

Sloths. The most common sloth in Peru is the brown-throated three-toed sloth (*Bradypus variegatus*). Up to 1m in length, they have small, round heads and whitish or brown faces with a short tail and long limbs. Their claws help them cling to branches, where they spend most of their time sleeping, but their slow movement makes them hard to spot (though you may see them around jungle lodges, where they are often kept as pets).

Cats

Large cats in Peru include the black, elongated **Jaguarundi** (*Felis yagouaroundi*) and the slender, spotty **Margay** (*Felis wieldii*). But better known are the **Ocelots** (*Felis pardalis*), smallish with black spots and thin stripes on their torso, with short tails and long slender legs. Operating by day and night, they hunt rodents, lizards and birds, mostly in the rainforest.

Jaguar (*Pantera onca*) Powerfully built, jaguars are almost 2m long, with black spots on silvery to tan fur; they hunt large mammals, though they fish too. Mainly rainforest dwellers, they are most frequently spotted sunning themselves on fallen trees. If you meet one, the best way to react is to make lots of noise.

Puma (*Felis concolor*) Brown to tan in colour, pumas hunt by day and night, preferring large mammals, but stooping to snakes, lizards and rats. They're most likely to be encountered in the Andes, and although wary of humans, can be dangerous. Guides advise waving one's arms around and shouting in these situations.

Primates

All South American primates are monkeys, which form a group of their own – **Platyrrhini** – subdividing into three main families: marmosets and tamarins (*Callitrichidae*); monkeys (*Cebidae*); and the Goeldi's monkey (*Callimiconidae*). Each of these has many types within it.

Capuchin monkey (*Cebus apella*) Reddish-brown, with a black cap and paler shoulders, this noisy creature moves in groups of up to twenty while searching for fruit, palm nuts, birds' eggs and small lizards.

Dusky titi monkey (*Callicebus moloch*) The necks of these reddish-brown creatures are hidden by thick fur, giving them a stocky appearance belied by their hairless faces. Eating leaves and fruit, they are found in dense forest near swamps, or bamboo thickets beside rivers.

Pygmy marmoset (*Cebuella pygmaea*) These rarely achieve more than 15cm in length, and are distinguished by their tawny to golden-grey head and forequarters and mane of hair, plus slender tails. Found in the lower understorey of the trees in flood forests, they feed on tree sap, insects and fruit.

Saddle-backed tamarin (*Saguinus fuscicollis*) The most widespread species of tamarin in the forests of Manu and around Iquitos, though there are a further thirteen subspecies of these. Black to reddish-brown, they are diurnal and arboreal, living under the tree canopy and eating nectar, fruit and insects.

Spider monkey (*Ateles paniscus*) These are entirely black, with a small head and long arms, legs and tail, and can be seen swinging through the primary forest in groups of up to twenty. Highly sociable, intelligent and noisy, they feed on fruit, flowers and leaves.

Woolly monkey (*Lagothrix lagothricha*) Mostly brown, they have a strong tail, which helps them travel through the upper and middle storeys of the forest in groups of up to sixty. They eat fruit, palm nuts, seeds and leaves and are found in primary forest, including wooded flood plains.

Birds

Andean condor (*Vultur gryphus*) Up to 1.3m long, with a wingspan of 3.5m and mostly black with a white neck ruff and white wing feathers, these are rarely seen in groups of more than two or three. Their habitat is mainly at 2000–5000m, but they are also seen on the coast of Peru, feeding off carrion.

Black-headed cotingas (*Cotingidae*) Related to flycatchers, they have a symbiotic relationship with a number of fruiting trees. The scaled fruiteater (*Ampelioden tschudii*) is frequently seen in the upper canopy, usually alone but sometimes in pairs or, less frequently, in large mixed flocks.

Curassow (*Crax mitu*) Their well-developed crests are mainly black, with a shiny blue mantle; both the bill and legs are red. Their booming song can be heard as they move in small flocks of two to five birds.

Fasciated tiger-heron (*Tigrisoma fasciatum*) Graceful river birds with short, dusky bills and a black crown, named for the stripy appearance of their rufous and white underparts.

Hawk (*Buteo magnirostris*) Grey to brown in colour, these are not great flyers or hunters, depending mainly on insects, vertebrates and small birds.

Hoatzin (*Opisthocomus hoazin*) Their most distinctive features are long mohican crests and the hooks which the young have on their shoulders. Also, they haven't evolved full stomachs and their chromosomes are close to those of chickens. Usually spotted in sizeable and gregarious gangs, they are poor flyers and hide in swampy areas. Indians use hoatzins' feathers for arrow flights.

Hummingbirds (*Trochilidae*) Distinguished by the fastest metabolisms and wing beats of any bird (up to 80 per second) and the ability to rotate their wings through 180 degrees, some varieties are the smallest birds in the world. Many tribes have a special place for hummingbirds in their religious beliefs.

Macaws (*Psittacidae*) Noisy, gregarious creatures with strong bills, macaws mate for life (which can be as long as 100 years), and pairs fly among larger flocks. Common macaws in Peru include the blue and yellow macaw (*Ara ararauna*) which grows to almost 1m and has a very long pointed tail, the scarlet macaw (*Ara macao*), and the red and green macaw (*Ara cloroptera*).

Nunbirds With slender red bills and mostly black plumage, black-fronted nunbirds (*Monasa nigrifrons*) are found in ones or twos at all levels of the rainforest and are noted for their noisy performance in the early evenings. White-fronted nunbirds (*Monasa morphoeus*) are slightly smaller and with a white forehead but are similar in behaviour.

Oropendulas (*Icteridae*) Related to the blackbird family, these like living near human habitations, their vibrant croaking making them unmistakable. One of the commonest varieties is the large black oropendula (*Gymnostinaps guatimoziuus*), which has with a long brilliant lemon-yellow tail, with two black central tail feathers.

Swainson's thrush (*Catharus ustulatus*) Small in stature but magnificent in voice, this timid, solitary bird lives mainly in lower primary forest. The Lawrence thrush is able to imitate other bird calls (over 100 have been noted from one bird alone).

Tinamous (*Tinamidae*) Rather like chickens with long beaks, the many varieties include the rare black tinamou (*Tinamus osgoodi*), the great tinamou (*Tinamus major*), noted for its tremulous whistling noises, and the grey tinamou (*Tinamus tao*), similar in behaviour to the great tinamou.

Toucans (*Ramphastidae*) Unmistakable for their colourful plumage and large bill, there are many varieties. One of the more common is the white-throated toucan (*Ramphastos tucanus*), also one of the largest, mainly black but with bursts of orange and red and a white throat and chest. Rarer and smaller is the yellow-ridged toucan (*Ramphastos culminatus*), with a distinctive yellow ridge across the top and a yellow and blue band close to the eyes.

Trumpeters (*Psophiidae*) Common, largely terrestrial birds that eat vegetation, small lizards and shiny objects (gold, silver and sometimes diamonds), they are often kept as pets in Indian and colonist settlements. The grey-winged trumpeter (*Psophia crepitans*) tends to be recognized by its nocturnal guttural sounds, which sound like the loud purring of a cat. Grey in the wild, its wings turn white in captivity.

Vultures (*Cathartidae*) Carrion-eaters, this family includes the Andean condor (see p.580) and the stunning king vulture (*Sarcoramphus papa*), which has mainly white plumage with black rump, tail and flight feathers. It's mostly spotted in solitary flight and sometimes in pairs. Other vultures include the turkey vulture (*Cathartes aura*), the greater yellow-headed vulture (*Cathartes melambrotus*), the lesser yellow-headed vulture (*Cathartes burrovianus*), and the black vulture (*Coragyps atratus*) seen around every rubbish dump throughout Peru.

Reptiles and amphibians

Amphibians Frogs grow to surprising sizes in Peru. Most are nocturnal and their chorus is heard along every Amazonian river after sunset. The most commonly spotted is the cane toad (*Bufo marinus*), which secretes toxins that protects it. More common still is the leaf-litter dweller (*Bufo typhonius*), but it's harder to spot as it imitates the colours and forms of dead leaves.

Caimans (*Alligatoridae*) There are four types of caiman in Peru. The black caiman (*Melanosuchus niger*) is increasingly rare due to hunting, while the spectacled caiman (*Caiman crocodilus*) is usually sunbathing along river beaches. The smaller musky caiman and smooth-fronted caiman are found in small tributaries and lakes.

Iguanas Often reaching up to a metre long and marked by a spiky crest along their backs, these are wholly vegetarian leaf-eaters which can be seen sleeping on high branches soaking up the sun. Less often they can be seen swimming in rivers, mainly to get away from predators, such as hawks.

Snakes Peru has the world's widest variety of snakes, but it's rare to meet these anacondas, rainbow boas (*Epicrates cenchria*), fer-de-lances (*Bothrops atrox*) or bushmasters (*Lachesis muta*) in the Amazon. Anacondas kill mainly by twisting their tails around tree roots in lakes or riverbanks, then floating out from this before attacking. They also stun fish by violently expelling air from their coiled bodies. Smaller snakes tend to be scared of people and you're more likely to see them in retreat than heading for you.

Yellow-footed tortoise (*Geochelone denticulata*) The only land tortoise in the Amazon, it can grow up to around 1m long but is generally half this size. In prehistoric times, however, they reached the proportions of a Volkswagen Beetle.

Preparation

As **preparation** for all this, **Lima Zoo**, in the Parque de las Leyerdas, is well worth a visit. It contains a good collection of most of the animals mentioned above, particularly the predators, and since there are few inexpensive or particularly handy field guides, this is the best way to familiarize yourself with what you might see during the rest of your journey. Be prepared, however, to see animals kept in appalling conditions. You might also check out the Natural History Museum in Lima and the Ministry of Agriculture's "Vida Silvestre" section for publications and offprints on Peruvian flora and fauna. Relevant books are listed in the "Books" section (p.597).

Indigenous rights and the destruction of the rainforest

Within the next generation Peru's jungle tribes may cease to exist as independent cultural and racial entities in the face of persistent and increasing pressure from external colonization. The indigenous people of the Peruvian jungles are being pushed off their land by an endless combination of slash-and-burn colonization, big oil companies, gold-miners, timber extractors and coca-growing farmers organized by drug-trafficking barons and, at times, "revolutionary" political groups.

All along the main rivers and jungle roads, settlers are flooding into the area. In their wake, forcing land-title agreements to which they have no right, are the main timber companies and multinational oil corporations. In large tracts of the jungle the fragile selva ecology has already been destroyed; in others the tribes have been more subtly disrupted by becoming dependent on outside consumer goods and trade or by the imposition of evangelical proselytizing groups, and the Indian way of life is being destroyed.

The first **Law of Native Communities**, introduced in 1974, recognized the legal right of indigenous peoples to own lands that were held collectively and registered as such with the Ministry of Agriculture. Despite this recognition, however, the military government of the time wasn't trying to stop colonization. Such land titling as did occur was a two-edged sword – whilst it guaranteed a secure land base to some communities, it implied that land not so titled was unavailable to them, effectively making it available for colonization.

However, as the most significant legal tool they had in the 1970s, land rights legislation was adopted by the indigenous communities to help protect their territory, even if the creation of native communities as legal entities represented the imposition of a non-indigenous socio-political structure. New self-determination groups sprang up throughout the 1970s and 1980s, such as the Inter-ethnic Association for the Development of the Peruvian Amazon (AIDESEP) and the Coalition of Indigenous Nationalities of the Peruvian Amazon (CONAP). Since then more regional political structures have been established, usually based on natural geographical boundaries such as rivers. These function as intermediaries between the community and the national levels of Amazonian political organization.

In 1999, a new law was drafted claiming conservation, sustainable development and respect for indigenous communities as its objectives. Received with dismay by all the major organizations working in these fields, there were

Ashaninka projects

There are a number of **projects** working with the Ashaninka to rebuild their communities and strengthen their territorial and economic position. Contact the Rainforest Foundation in London (Suite A5, City Cloisters, 196 Old St, London EC1V 9FR; ⓦ www.rainforestfoundationuk.org) or the ACPC in Lima (ⓔ acpc@correo.dnet .com.pe) for more information. There is also an **Ashaninka website** at ⓦ www .rcp.net.pe/ashaninka.

An Amarakaeri Indian of Madre de Dios speaks for himself

Below is an account by a local Amarakaeri Indian from the southeast province of Madre de Dios, a witness to the way of life that colonists and corporations are destroying. Originally given as testimony to a human rights movement in Lima, it is reprinted by permission of Survival International.

"We Indians were born, work, live, and die in the basin of the Madre de Dios River of Peru. It's our land – the only thing we have, with its plants, animals, and small farms: an environment we understand and use well. We are not like those from outside who want to clear everything away, destroying the richness and leaving the forest ruined forever. We respect the forest; we make it produce for us.

Many people ask why we want so much land. They think we do not work all of it. But we work it differently from them, conserving it so that it will continue to produce for our children and grandchildren. Although some people want to take it from us, they then destroy and abandon it, moving on elsewhere. But we can't do that; we were born in our woodlands. Without them we will die.

In contrast to other parts of the Peruvian jungle, Madre de Dios is still relatively sparsely populated. The woodlands are extensive, the soil's poor, so we work differently from those in other areas with greater population, less woodland, and more fertile soils. Our systems do not work without large expanses of land. The people who come from outside do not know how to make the best of natural resources here. Instead they devote themselves to taking away what nature gives and leave little or nothing behind. They take wood, nuts, and above all gold.

The man from the highlands works all day doing the same thing whether it is washing gold, cutting down trees, or something else. Bored, he chews his coca, eats badly, then gets ill and leaves. The engineers just drink their coffee and watch others working.

We also work these things but so as to allow the woodland to replenish itself. We cultivate our farms, hunt, fish and gather woodland fruits, so we do not have to bring in supplies from outside. We also make houses, canoes, educate our children, and enjoy ourselves. In short we satisfy almost all our needs with our own work, and without destroying the environment.

In the upper Madre de Dios River wood is more important than gold, and the sawmill of Shintuya is one of the most productive in the region. Wood is also worked in other areas to make canoes and boats to sell, and for building houses for the outsiders. In the lower region of the river we gather nuts – another important part of our economy. Much is said about Madre de Dios being the forgotten Department of Peru. Yet we are not forgotten by people from outside nor by some national and foreign companies who try to seize our land and resources. Because of this we have formed the Federation of Indian Peoples of Madre de Dios to fight for the defence of our lands and resources.

C

immediate strikes and protests throughout the Amazon region. However, it actually seemed to sidestep these basic issues and appeared to encourage investment in large-scale developments without regard for environmental issues, introducing tax breaks for private investors while failing to give the same benefits to locals. There appeared to have been no consultation with the regions involved, let alone with conservation organizations or the political organs of the indigenous population.

Poisonous gold and black gold

At least as serious a threat to the indigenous peoples of the Peruvian rainforest are **oil exploration** and **gold-mining**, which are an enormous potential threat to the rainforest in Peru.

As the danger from terrorism faded in the mid-1990s, Fujimori's politico-economic agenda opened the way for **oil and gas exploration**. Initially, the government appeared to be bending over backwards to assist multinationals exploit the reserves discovered, mainly in the Madre de Dios and Camisea areas. The Amazonian indigenous organizations and environmental conservationists were in opposition, and the momentum of fossil-fuel exploitation in the Peruvian Amazon has slowed right down for the moment, although this is more likely to be an unforeseen extension of Fujimori's policies than genuine concern, as the government was not prepared to offer the companies as big a monopoly over the Peruvian power-supply industry as they desired. Consequently, the multinationals pulled out of the Camisea project in mid-1998 after investing many millions, and substantially reduced their plans for the Madre de Dios region. The threat is still there, however – in 1999, the Peruvian Energy Minister claimed that there were over sixty companies expressing an interest in the Camisea gas reserves.

Illegal gold-mining is at its worst in the south-eastern jungles of Madre de Dios, home to the Amarakaeri Indians, where monster-sized machinery is transforming one of the Amazon's most biodiverse regions into a huge muddy scar. A number of gold-miners have already moved into the unique Tambopata Reserved Zone, a protected jungle area where giant otters, howler monkeys, king vultures, anacondas and jaguars are regularly spotted.

All plant life around each mine is turned into gravel, known in Peru as *cancha*, for just a few ounces of gold a day. Front-loading machines move up to about 30m depth of soil, which is then washed on a wooden sluice where high-pressure hoses separate the silt and gold from mud and gravel. Mercury, added at this stage to facilitate gold extraction, is later burnt off, causing river and air pollution. The mines are totally unregulated, and the richer, more established mining families tend to run the show, having the money to import large machines upriver from Brazil or by air from Chile.

The indigenous tribes are losing control of their territory to an ever-increasing stream of these miners and settlers coming down from the high Andes. As the mercury pollution and suspended mud from the mines upstream kill the life-giving rivers, they have to go deeper and deeper into the forest for fish, traditionally their main source of protein. Beatings and death threats from the miners and police are not uncommon.

There is a hope that **improved gold-mining technology** can stem the tide of destruction in these areas. Mercury levels in Amazon rivers and their associated food chains are rising at an alarming rate. However, with raw mercury available for only $13 a kilo there is little obvious economic incentive to find ways of using less hazardous materials. Cleaner gold-mining techniques have, however, been developed in Brazil. Astonishingly simple, the new method utilizes a wooden sluice with a gentler slope (instead of a steeper, ridged slope) to extract the gold from the washed river sediment and gravel. Trials have shown that this increases gold yields by up to forty percent, and the addition of a simple sluice box at the base of the slope has also led to the recovery of some 95 percent of the mercury used in the process. The same project has also developed a procedure of test boring to estimate quantities of gold in potential gravel deposits, which minimizes unnecessary and uneconomic earth-moving in search for gold. If taken on board by gold-miners in the Amazon and elsewhere, these techniques should reduce environmental damage. However, the fact remains that pressure by **international environmental groups**, and the publicity that they generate, continues to make a difference.

Biopiracy

Patents protecting corporations' intellectual property rights are being taken out on traditional Andean and Amazon plants. This "biopiracy" reduces options for developing countries to reap any benefits that their wealth of plant resource and ethnobotanical knowledge might generate. South America has been called the "biopiracy capital of the world". Any "equitable sharing of the benefits" as required by the Biodiversity Convention is a difficult goal if the bioprospector can slash intellectual property rights over whatever he/she finds.

Bioprospecting is argued to be an important tool for sustainable development and the conservation of resources through sustainable and fair sharing of benefits. Some argue that it is legalized "biopiracy". It is also quite a boom industry as well as being seen as a "green" investment.

Theoretically, corporations and research institutions gain from exploitation of genetic gems, while communities providing raw materials and knowledge share in the profits. At the same time, biodiversity conservation is promoted. But many communities and NGOs working with them claim that the "biopirates" have not lived up to their promises. Furthermore, they say that money is not enough; they also demand scientific and intellectual credit.

Over the past three years, two US companies have also taken out patents on maca, another traditional Andean crop used for centuries as a sexual stimulant. Examples of maca germplasm are held in trust by the International Potato Centre (CIP) in Peru. In this case, though, the companies have steered clear of patenting any particular variety. Instead, they have identified and patented the active ingredients present in the roots.

Although maca exports to these companies have risen rapidly in the past few years, its price has fallen as production has increased, so reducing the returns to the Peruvian farmers who feel they have lost "control" of their crop.

Indigenous peoples' and farmers' organizations from the Andes and the Amazon are calling on two US companies to abandon patents related to maca, and they are asking the Peruvian government and the World Intellectual Property Organization (WIPO) to investigate and condemn monopoly claims related to maca that appropriate traditional knowledge of farming communities. Geneva-based, WIPO promotes intellectual property as a means of protecting traditional knowledge.

Again, their claims have a basis in international law. In April 2003, the Biodiversity Convention was ratified, giving countries the ability to make money from genes, drugs and other products developed from their native plants and other wildlife. In an ideal world, therefore, companies developing products such as yellow beans or "natural Viagra" from traditional crop varieties should be paying royalties to the originators of the product – the farmers of the Andes and other regions of the world whose "prior art" is currently being exploited and "pirated"

The coalition is also asking the Lima-based International Potato Centre to take action to prohibit intellectual property claims – not just on seeds and genetic material, but also on the traditional knowledge of indigenous communities. The coalition is asking them to declare a moratorium on the patenting of all Andean crop germplasm and its genetic components as well as indigenous knowledge related to these genetic materials.

For further information check out the Erosion, Technology and Concentration Action Group website: Ⓦ www.etcgroup.org.

Indian resistance

Since the early 1970s, the indigenous rainforest nations, in particular the **Campa Ashaninka** from the much threatened central jungle area, and more recently the uncontacted Mashco-Piro, who came out to defend their land with bows and arrows against illegal loggers in 2002, have been co-ordinating opposition to these external threats.

Indians confront illegal loggers

Four hundred naked jungle Indians tried to protect their ancestral forests in the Peruvian Amazon in July 2002 by running vines across the murky, slow-moving Río de las Piedras in what is arguably the remotest corner of our planet. The vines were used successfully to stop several motorized canoes full of chainsaw-equipped loggers who were heading upriver in search of mahogany trees for the lucrative international markets. Once they had them trapped, the Indians fired five-foot-long arrows made from river cane, with feather flights and hardwood tips, at the terrified loggers who were attempting to steal trees illegally from what is an established Indian reserve for uncontacted native groups.

The biggest jungle Indian attack on the outside world in Peru for over thirty years, the incident has brought to public attention one of the last significant groups of uncontacted rainforest Indians and, further, the fact that they are prepared to act together to defend their forests. The four hundred are believed to represent a total population of around 1500 semi-nomadic uncontacted peoples who have been systematically retreating from the frontier of Western civilization for at least 130 years, ever since the peak of the rubber boom in the late nineteenth century. This area of forest represents their last-ditch stand – from here there is nowhere for them to go. The situation remains very tense in the area and Victor Pesha, president of the region's Federation of Native Peoples fears that genocide might follow if the illegal loggers are allowed to return upriver to the headwaters of the Río de las Piedras and take the trees they want by force. These uncontacted Amazon Indians, believed to be of the Mashco-Piro group, represent probably the last uncontacted tribal peoples on the planet. According to Victor Pesha, around twenty people were killed in clashes between natives and loggers in the region during the first few months of 2002.

Illegal logging is now the major threat to the rainforest in this corner of the Peruvian Amazon, which contains the largest remaining store of virgin mahogany trees in Peru. However, not only do the loggers destroy many hectares of forest to take out just one highly valuable mahogany tree, but they also bring with them flu and other viruses which are frequently deadly to previously uncontacted peoples, in much the same way that many millions of Peruvian Indians, over a third of the total population, are believed to have died of influenza and measles as it spread from Central America before Pizarro ever set foot in Peru.

In 2003 the authorities were considering the use of force, if necessary, to remove illegal loggers, but the operation is clearly complicated by the fact that the president-elect of this newly created political region is also evidently head of the local illegal logging mafia. Following the incident in July 2002, pressure from environmentalists and NGOs supporting the rights of indigenous people has moved the Ministry of Agriculture and an inter-ministerial commission to plan an operation to use the army and police to remove the illegal loggers.

While the problem of illegal logging is not restricted to this corner of the Amazon, it is particularly bad here for a number of reasons. The forest is pristine, very rich in timber and biodiversity, and it is one of the most remote areas of rainforest left on Earth, a wilderness hidden away in a large green splot beside a dotted line on the map, vainly representing both Brazil and Peru's remotest frontiers. In October 2002, in a neighbouring watershed of this corner of the Amazon Basin, some illegal Peruvian loggers were caught by Ashaninka Indians – they had been stealing trees on land just over the border in Brazil. The Ashaninka took the loggers hostage, releasing them later to the Brazilian Federal Police.

The Ashaninka situation

More worldly-wise than the uncontacted Mashco-Piro, Ashaninka tribal representatives, sometimes working in conjunction with indigenous political umbrella organizations, have gone increasingly regularly to Lima to get publicity and assert their claims to land. For the Ashaninka, this territorial struggle has been and continues to be for titles on the **Ene** and **Tambo**, the only regions left to them after four centuries of "civilizing" influence. In publicity terms they have met with some success. The exploitation of the forests has become a political issue, fuelled in the early 1980s within Peru (and outside) by the bizarre events surrounding Werner Herzog's filming of *Fitzcarraldo*, a film *about* exploitation of Indians, yet whose director so angered local communities that at one stage they burned down a whole production camp.

With the rise of Sendero Luminoso things got much worse for some indigenous Peruvian Amazon groups. Again, the Ashaninka suffered greatly because of their close proximity to the Sendero heartlands. Sendero are now virtually extinct, due in part to the fierce stand taken by the Ashaninka themselves, and in the last few years, the Ashaninka have regained control of much of the territory they had lost to the terrorists. The biggest problem they face now is one of organized land invasions by settlers, who frequently have the support of regional authorities. In many cases, the political revolutionary fervour of the late 1980s and early 1990s has been replaced by a spreading religious evangelicalism.

While the Indians have certainly undergone a radical growth in political awareness, in real terms they have made little progress. Former President Belaunde, whose promises of human rights in the late 1970s led to many thousands of Ashaninka making their way down to polling stations by raft to vote for him, has merely speeded up the process of colonization, and in the Ene region alone, the Indians face multinational claims to millions of acres of their territory. To make matters worse, President Fujimori changed the law in 1995 to allow colonization of Indian lands if they had been "unoccupied" for two years or more. Obviously, with many of the traditional rainforest Indians

Survival for Tribal Peoples

Survival for Tribal Peoples is a worldwide organization supporting tribal peoples, standing for their right to decide their own future and helping them protect their lives, lands and rights. Survival have been active in campaigning against the threats to tribal land and way of life posed by oil exploration and exploitation in Peru and have assisted the Ashaninka tribe over the years in their cause. For more information contact them at Survival, 6 Charterhouse Buildings, London EC1M 7ET, UK ☎ 020 7687 8700, ⓕ 7687 8701, ⓦ www.survival-international.org.

having a semi-nomadic existence, depending on hunting and gathering for survival, colonists can take over an area of forest claiming it as uninhabited, even though it's part of traditional territory. This law change particularly affected the Ashaninka, who had already been forced to leave their usual scattered settlements for self-protection against the terrorists. At the close of the twentieth century, they had largely moved back into their original settlements and territories, though closely followed by more waves of colonists. The civil war against Sendero, in which the Ashaninka played a significant role, did much to unite the traditionally scattered Ashaninka nation, but whether or not it has prepared them sufficiently well to hold things together remains to be seen.

C

CONTEXTS | Indigenous rights and the destruction of the rainforest

Peru's white gold

In recent decades, not only have poverty and the promise of a better life led thousands of Peruvian peasants down the road of guerrilla warfare and bloody terror, but also many of them, sometimes the same individuals, have transformed the most sacred plant of the Incas into one of the world's most commercial cash crops. Seen by many peasants as a road to fortune and freedom, for others cocaine is a scourge, bringing violence, the mobsters and deforestation in its wake.

The only people who make decent money engage in "cooking" **cocaine**. Illegal "kitchens", makeshift coke refineries, have become the main means of livelihood for many ordinary peasant families, as the equipment is simple – oil drums, a few chemicals, paraffin and a fire. Bushels of coca leaves are dissolved in paraffin and hydrochloric acid, heated, and stirred, eventually producing the pasta, which is then washed in ether or acetone to yield powdery white cocaine.

Peru's coca industry netted an estimated $3 billion in 1984 – twenty percent of the country's gross national product. By the end of the 1980s this figure was much higher and the problem had become an issue of global dimensions. However, a combination of market saturation and political pressure from the US, backed up by anti-cocaine money and hardware like police helicopters, seems to have changed the situation substantially. In 1996 the Peruvian price of cocaine had dropped by over fifty percent on the street, down to almost $4 a gram. Colombian drug cartels were buying less from Peru, having been hit hardest by US anti-cocaine policies, and the protection once afforded by Sendero Luminoso terrorists had turned into more of a liability than anything else. By the end of the twentieth century there was also increasing US intervention, including aerial patrols over the northern jungle border between Peru and Colombia firing on unmarked planes that refuse to identify themselves. Production of cocaine in Peru has dropped further while it has started to rise in Colombia, and these lower levels of supply have brought Peru's internal price for cocaine back up to a street level of $10 a gram. It seems unlikely that cocaine production will be reduced much further, since there are always new export opportunities and a steady home market; but the basic crop – coca plants – no longer offers quite the relatively stable, safe and so much more remunerative option to small-time cash-croppers that it did just a couple of years ago.

Coca, the plant from which cocaine is derived, has travelled a long way since the Incas distributed this "divine plant" across fourteenth-century Andean Peru. Presented as a gift from the gods, coca was used to exploit slave labour under the Spanish rule: without it the Indians would never have worked in the gruelling conditions of colonial mines such as Potosi.

The isolation of the active ingredient in coca, **cocaine**, in 1859, began an era of intense medical experimentation. Its numbing effects have been appreciated by dental patients around the world, and even Pope Leo XIII enjoyed a bottle of the coca wine produced by an Italian physician, who amassed a great fortune from its sale in the nineteenth century. The literary world, too, was soon stimulated by this white powder: in 1885 Robert Louis Stevenson wrote *Dr Jekyll and Mr Hyde* during six speedy days and nights while taking this "wonder drug" as a remedy for his tuberculosis, and Sir Arthur Conan Doyle, writing in the 1890s, used the character of Sherlock Holmes to defend the use of cocaine. On a more popular level, coca was one of the essential ingredients in

Coca-Cola until 1906. Today, cocaine is the most fashionable – and expensive – of drugs.

From its humble origins cocaine has become very big business. Unofficially, it may well be the biggest export for countries like Peru and Bolivia, where coca grows best in the Andes and along the edge of the jungle. While most mountain peasants always cultivated a little for personal use, many have now become dependent on it for obvious economic reasons: coca is still the most profitable cash crop and is readily bought by middlemen operating for extremely wealthy cocaine barons. A constant flow of semi-refined coca – pasta, the basic paste – leaves Peru aboard Amazon riverboats or unmarked light aircraft heading for the big-time laboratories in Colombia. From here the pure stuff is shipped or flown out, mostly to the US via Miami or Los Angeles. Much of the rest is refined in Peruvian cocaine "kitchens" in the *ceja de selva* or Lima, before finding its way into the nostrils of wealthy Limeños, or going over the border into Brazil and further afield.

Few people care to look beyond the wall of illicit intrigue that surrounds this highly saleable contraband. In the same vein as coffee or chocolate, the demand for this product has become another means through which the privileged world controls the lives of those in the developing world, at the same time endangering the delicate environmental balance of the western edge of Amazonia. As Peruvian Indians follow world market trends by turning their hands to the growing and "cooking" of coca, more staple crops like cereals, tubers and beans are cultivated less and less.

It's a change brought about partly by circumstance. Agricultural prices are state-controlled, but manufactured goods and transport costs rise almost weekly, preventing the peasants from earning a decent living from their crops. Moreover, the soil is poor and crops grow unwillingly. Coca, on the other hand, grows readily and needs little attention.

Peruvian recipes

Peruvian cooking – even in small restaurants well away from the big cities – is appealing stuff. The nine recipes below are among the classics, fairly simple to prepare and (with a couple of coastal exceptions) found throughout the country. If you're travelling and camping you'll find all the ingredients listed readily available in local markets; we've suggested alternatives if you want to try them when you get home. All quantities given are sufficient for four people.

Ceviche

A cool, spicy dish, eaten on the Peruvian coast for at least the past thousand years.

1kg soft white fish (lemon sole and halibut are good, or you can mix half fish, half shellfish)
2 large onions, sliced
1 or 2 chillis, chopped
6 limes (or lemons, but these aren't so good)
1 tbsp olive oil
1 tbsp fresh coriander or cilantro leaves
salt and pepper to taste

Wash and cut the fish into bite-sized pieces. Place in a dish with the sliced onions. Add the chopped chilli and coriander. Make a marinade using the lime juice, olive oil, salt and pepper. Pour over the fish and place in a cool spot until the fish is "soft cooked" (from 10 to 60min). Serve with boiled potatoes (preferably sweet) and corn on the cob.

Papas a la Huancaina

An excellent and ubiquitous snack – cold potatoes covered in a mildly *picante* cheese sauce.

1 kg potatoes, boiled
1 or 2 chillis, chopped
2 cloves of garlic, chopped
200g soft goat's cheese (feta is ideal, or cottage cheese will do)
6 saltines or crackers
1 hardboiled egg
1 small can of evaporated milk

Chop very finely or liquidize all the above ingredients except for the potatoes. The mixture should be fairly thin but not too runny. Pour sauce over the thickly sliced potatoes. Arrange on a dish and serve garnished with lettuce and black olives. Best served chilled.

Palta Rellena

Stuffed avocados – another very popular snack.

2 avocados, soft but not ripe
1 onion, chopped

2 tomatoes, chopped
2 hardboiled eggs, chopped
200g cooked chicken or tuna fish, cold and flaked
2 tbsp mayonnaise

Cut the avocados in half and remove the stones. Scoop out a little of the flesh around the hole. Gently combine all other the ingredients before piling into the centre of each avocado half.

Causa
About the easiest Peruvian dish to reproduce outside the country, though there are no real substitutes for Peruvian tuna and creamy Andean potatoes.

1kg potatoes
200g tuna fish
2 avocados, the riper the better
4 tomatoes
salt and black pepper
1 lemon

Boil the potatoes and mash to a firm, smooth consistency. Flake the tuna fish and add a little lemon juice. Mash the avocados to a pulp, add the rest of the lemon juice, some salt and black pepper. Slice the tomatoes. Press one quarter of the tuna fish over this, then a quarter of the avocado mixture on top. Add a layer of sliced tomato. Continue the same layering process until you have four layers of each. Cut into rough slices. Serve (ideally chilled) with salad, or on its own as a starter.

Locro de Zapallo
A vegetarian standard found on most set menus in the cheaper, working-class restaurants.

1kg pumpkin
1 large potato
2 cloves of garlic
1 tbsp oregano
1 cup of milk
2 corn on the cobs
1 onion
1 chilli, chopped
salt and pepper
200g cheese (mozarella works well)

Fry the onion, chilli, garlic and oregano. Add half a cup of water. Mix in the pumpkin as large cut lumps, slices of corn on the cob, and finely chopped potato. Add the milk and cheese. Simmer until a soft, smooth consistency, and add a little more water if necessary. Serve with rice or over fish.

Pescado a la Chorillana
Probably the most popular way of cooking fish on the coast.

4 pieces of fish (cod or any other white fish will do)
2 large onions, chopped
4 large tomatoes, chopped

1 or 2 chillis, chopped into fairly large pieces
1 tbsp oil
half a cup of water

Grill or fry each portion of fish until done. Keep hot. Fry separately the onions, tomatoes, and chilli. Add the water to form a sauce. Pile the hot sauce over each portion of fish and serve with rice.

Asado
A roast. An expensive meal for Peruvians, though a big favourite for family gatherings. Only available in fancier restaurants.

1kg or less of lean beef
2 cloves of garlic
200g butter
1 tin of tomato purée
salt and pepper
1 tbsp soy sauce
2 tomatoes
1 chilli, chopped

Cover the beef with the premixed garlic and butter. Mix the tomato purée with salt, pepper and soy sauce. Liquidize the tomatoes with the chopped chilli. Spread both mixtures on the beef and cook slowly in a covered casserole dish for four or five hours. Traditionally the *asado* is served with *pure de papas*, which is simply a runny form of mashed potatoes whipped up with some butter and a lot of garlic. A very tasty combination.

Quinoa Vegetable Soup
Quinoa – known as "mother grain" in the Andes – is "a natural whole grain with remarkable nutritional properties", quite possibly a "supergrain" of the future. It's simple and tasty to add to any soups or stews.

4 cups of water
quarter of a cup of *quinoa*
half a cup of diced carrots
quarter of a cup of diced celery
2 tbsp finely chopped onions
quarter of a green pepper
2 mashed cloves of garlic
1 tbsp vegetable oil
half a cup of chopped tomatoes
half a cup of finely chopped cabbage
1 tbsp salt
some chopped parsley

Gently fry the *quinoa* and all the vegetables (except the cabbage and tomatoes) in oil and garlic until browned. Then add the water, cabbage and tomatoes before bringing to the boil. Season with salt and garnish with parsley.

Aji de Gallina
Literally translated as "Chillied Chicken", this is not as spicy as it sounds, but utilizes a delicious cheesy yellow sauce.

1 chicken breast
1 cup of breadcrumbs
2 soupspoons of powdered yellow chilli
50g of parmesan cheese
50g of ground nuts
1 cup of evaporated milk (more if the sauce seems too dry)
1 sliced onion (red or white)

Boil the chicken breast, then strain and fry it for a bit. Mix the hot chicken water with the breadcrumbs. Meanwhile, in a pot, heat two tablespoons full of olive oil and brown the onions. Mix in the yellow chilli powder. Mix in the breadcrumbs as liquidized as possible. After a few minutes still on the heat, add in the parmesan cheese, the chicken, salt to taste and finally the ground nuts. Boil for another ten minutes. Add the evaporated milk just before serving and stir in well. Decorate the plate with boiled potatoes, preferably of the Peruvian yellow variety (if not white will do), cut into cross-sectional slices about a centimetre or so thick. Add a sliced egg and black olives on top.

Thanks to Señora Delia Arvi Tarazona for this recipe.

Books

There are few books published exclusively about Peru and very few Peruvian writers ever make it into English. Many of the classic works on Peruvian and Inca history are now out of date, though frequently one comes across them in libraries around the world or bookshops in Lima and Cusco. Travel books, coffee-table editions and country guides are also generally available in Lima bookshops. Others can be obtained through the South American Explorers' Club, Avenida Portugal 146, Breña, between avenidas Bolivia and España (Mon–Sat 9.30am–5pm; ☎01/4250142, ⓦwww.samexplo.org), or from their main US office at 126 Indian Creek Rd, Ithaca, NY 14850 (☎607/277-0488, Ⓕ277-6122).

Inca and ancient history

Anthony Aveni *Nasca: Eighth Wonder of the World* (British Museum Press). One of the more recent works on the amazing Nazca Lines and sites, by a leading scholar who has spent twenty years excavating here. Contains much on the history of the Nazca people and explores the complex relationships between water, worship, social order and the environment.

Kathleen Berrin *The Spirit of Ancient Peru: Treasures from the Museo Arqueológico Rafael Larco Herrera* (o/p). Essentially a detailed exhibition catalogue with essays by reputable Andeanists and plenty of quality illustrations and photographs representing one of Peru's finest collections of mainly pre-Inca artefacts.

Hiram Bingham *Lost City of the Incas* (Greenwood Publishing, US). The classic introduction to Machu Picchu: the exploration accounts are interesting but many of the theories should be taken with a pinch of salt. Widely available in Peru.

Peter T. Bradley *The Lure of Peru: Maritime Intrusion into the South Sea 1598–1701* (o/p). A historical account of how the worldwide fame of the country's Inca treasures attracted Dutch, French and English would-be settlers, explorers, merchants and even pirates to the seas and shores of Peru. It includes descriptions of naval blockades of Lima and various waves of buccaneers and their adventures in search of Peru.

Richard Burger *Chavín and the Origins of Andean Civilisation* (Thames and Hudson). A collection of erudite essays, essential reading for anyone seriously interested in Peruvian prehistory.

Geoffrey Hext Sutherland Bushnell *Peru* (o/p). A classic, concise introduction to the main social and technological developments in Peru from 2500 BC to 1500 AD; well illustrated, if dated in some aspects.

Pedro De Cieza De Leon *The Discovery and Conquest of Peru (Latin America in Transition)* (Duke University Press). A new paperback version of the classic post-Conquest chronicler account.

Evan Hadingham *Lines to the Mountain Gods: Nazca and the Mysteries of Peru* (University of Oklahoma, US). One of the more down-to-earth books on the Nazca Lines, including maps and illustrations – also available through the South American Explorers' Club in Lima.

John Hemming *The Conquest of the Incas* (Papermac). The authoritative narrative tale of the Spanish conquest, very readably brought to life from a mass of original sources.

Thor Heyerdahl, Daniel Sandweiss and Alfredo Navárez *Pyramids of Túcume*. A recently published description of the archeological site at Túcume plus the life and society of the civilization which created this important ceremonial and political centre around 1000 years ago. Widely available in Peruvian bookshops.

Richard Keatinge (ed) *Peruvian Prehistory* (Cambridge University Press). One of the most up-to-date and reputable books on the ancient civilizations of Peru – a collection of serious academic essays on various cultures and cultural concepts through the millennia prior to the Inca era.

Ann Kendall *Everyday Life of the Incas* (o/p). Accessible, very general description of Peru under Inca domination.

Alfred L. Kroeber and Donald Collier *The Archeology and Pottery of Nazca, Peru: Alfred Kroeber's 1926 Expedition* (Altamira, 1998). A historical perspective on the archeology of Peru.

J. Alden Mason *Ancient Civilisations of Peru* (Penguin). Reprinted in 1991, an excellent summary of the country's history from the Stone Age through to the Inca Empire.

Michael E. Moseley *The Incas and their Ancestors* (Thames and Hudson). A fine overview of Peru before the Spanish conquest, which makes full use of good maps, diagrams, sketches, motifs and photos.

William Hickling Prescott *History of the Conquest of Peru* (Random

House). Hemming's main predecessor – a nineteenth-century classic that remains a good read, if you can find a copy.

Johan Reinhard *Nazca Lines: A New Perspective on their Origin and Meaning* (Los Pinos, Lima). Original theories about the Lines and ancient mountain gods – available through the South American Explorers' Club and the better bookshops in Lima. The same author also wrote *The Sacred Centre: Machu Picchu* (Nuevas Imagenes, Lima), a fascinating book, drawing on anthropology, archeology, geography and astronomy to reach highly probable conclusions about the sacred geology and topograpy of the Cusco region, and how this appears to have been related to Inca architecture, in particular Machu Picchu.

Gene Savoy *Antisuyo: The Search for the Lost Cities of the Amazon* (o/p). Exciting account of Savoy's important explorations, plus loads of historical detail.

Garcilasco de la Vega *The Royal Commentaries of the Incas* (2 vols, o/p). Many good libraries have a copy of this, the most readable and fascinating of contemporary historical sources. Written shortly after the Conquest, by a "Spaniard" of essentially Inca blood, this work is the best eyewitness account of life and beliefs among the Incas.

Oscar Medina Zevallos *The Enigma of Machu Picchu* available from (Ⓦ www.cuscobooks.com). Written by a Peruvian explorer and historical writer, this book tries to answer some of the difficult questions posed by Machu Picchu.

Modern history and society

Americas Watch *Peru under Fire: Human Rights since the Return to Democracy* (Human Rights Watch). A good summary of Peruvian politics

of the 1980s.

Susan E. Benner and Kathy S. Leonard *Fire from the Andes: Short Fiction by Women from Bolivia, Ecuador,* and Peru (University of New Mexico Press, 2001). A fascinating read of unique and passionate writing.

Eduardo Calderon *Eduardo El Curandero: The Words of a Peruvian Healer* (North Atlantic Books). Peru's most famous shaman – El Tuno – outlines his teachings and beliefs in his own words.

Carlos Cumes and Romulo Lizarraga Valencia *Pachamamas Children: Mother Earth and her Children of the Andes in Peru* (Llewellyn Publications, US). A New Age look at the culture, roots and shamanistic aspects of modern Peru.

F. Bruce Lamb and Manuel Cordova-Rios *The Wizard of the Upper Amazon* (Atlantic Books). Masterful reconstruction of the true story of Manuel Cordoba Rios – "Ino Moxo" – a famous herbal healer and *ayahuascero* from Iquitos who was kidnapped and brought up by Indians in the early twentieth century. Offers significant insight into indigenous psychedelic healing traditions.

Holligan de Diaz-Limaco *Peru in Focus* (Latin American Bureau, London, 1998). A good (if small) general reader on Peru's history, politics, culture and environment.

Sewell H. Menzel *Fire in the Andes: U.S. Foreign Policy and Cocaine Politics in Bolivia and Peru* (University Press of America). A good summary of US anti-cocaine activities in these two countries, written by credible academics.

Keith Muscutt *Warriors of the Clouds: A Lost Civilization in the Upper Amazon of Peru* (University of New Mexico Press). Some superb photos of the ruins and environment left behind by the amazing Chachapoyas culture of northern Peru.

Nicole Maxwell *Witch-Doctor's Apprentice* (o/p). A very personal and detailed account of the author's research into the healing plants used by Amazonian Peruvian tribes; a highly informative book on plant lore.

E. Luis Martin *The Kingdom of the Sun: A Short History of Peru* (o/p). The best general history, concentrating on the post-Conquest period and bringing events up to the 1980s.

David Scott Palmer (ed) *Shining Path of Peru* (C. Hurst & Co, UK; St Martin's Press, US). A modern history compilation of meticulously detailed essays and articles by Latin American academics and journalists on the early and middle phases of Sendero Luminoso's civil war in Peru.

Michael Reid *Peru: Paths to Poverty* (o/p). A succinct analysis tracing Peru's economic and security crisis of the early 1980s back to the military government of General Velasco.

Orin Starn, Carlos Degregori and Robin Kirk (eds), *The Peru Reader: History, Culture, Politics* (Latin American Bureau, UK; Duke University Press, US). One of the best overviews yet of Peruvian history and politics, with writing by characters as diverse as Mario Vargas Llosa and Abimael Guzman (imprisoned ex-leader of Sendero Luminoso).

Flora and fauna

Allen Altman and B. Swift *Checklist of the Birds of Peru* (Buteo Books). A useful summary with photos of different habitats.

J.L. Castner, S.L. Timme and J.A. Duke *A Field Guide to Medicinal and Useful Plants of the Upper Amazon* (Feline Press). A guide to the most common and useful plants of the Upper Amazon, of interest to enthusiasts and scientists alike. Contains handy colour plates.

L.H. Emmons *Neotropical Rainforest Mammals: A Field Guide* (University of Chicago Press). An excellent paperback with over 250 pages of authoritative text, 29 colour plates, and other illustrations covering 260 species.

V. de Feo *Medicinal and Magical Plants in the Northern Peruvian Andes* (Fitoterapia 63: 417-440). A key book for students of ethnobotany or anyone interested in learning the finer details of plant magic in Peru.

Steven L. Hilty and William L. Brown *A Guide to the Birds of Colombia* (Princeton University Press, US; OUP, UK). One of the few classic ornithology guides covering the fascinating and rich birdlife of Peru and its surrounding countries. It contains 69 colour and black and white plates, is 836 pages long and has a useful index.

M. Koepke *The Birds of the Department of Lima* (Harrowood Books). A small but classic guide, for many years the only one available that covered many of Peru's species, and still good for its excellent illustrations.

Richard E. Schultes and Robert F. Raffauf *The Healing Forest* (Dioscorides Press). An excellent and erudite large-format paperback on many of the Amazon's most interesting plants. It's well illustrated with exquisite photographs and is a relatively easy read.

Richard E. Schultes and Robert F. Raffauf *Vine of the Soul* (Synergetic Press). One of the best large-format books about the indigenous use and chemical basis of the hallucinogenic plant *ayahuasca*, so commonly used by tribal peoples in Peruvian Amazonia.

Walter Wust *Manu: el ultimo refugio* (Nuevas Imagenes, Lima). This is an excellent coffee-table book on the wildlife and flora of Manu National Park by one of Peru's foremost wildlife photographers. Available in most good bookshops in Lima and Cusco.

Travel

Timothy E. Albright and Jeff Tenlow *Dancing Bears and the Pilgrims Progress in the Andes: Transformation on the Road to Quolloriti* (University of Texas). A slightly dry report on the Snow Star annual festival of Quolloriti, which is attended by tens of thousands of Andean peasants at the start of every dry season.

Patrick Leigh Fermor *Three Letters from the Andes* (Penguin). Three long letters written from Peru in 1971 describing the experiences of a rather uppercrust mountaineering expedition.

Christopher Isherwood *The Condor and the Cows* (o/p). A diary of Isherwood's South American trip after World War II, most of which took place in Peru. Like Theroux, Isherwood eventually arrives in Buenos Aires, to meet Jorge Luis Borges.

Dervla Murphy *Eight Feet in the Andes* (Flamingo). An enjoyable account of a rather adventurous journey Dervla Murphy made across the Andes with her young daughter and a mule. It can't compare with her Indian books, though.

Matthew Paris *Inca Kola, A Travellers Tale of Peru* (Phoenix). Very amusing description of travelling in Peru, with a perspicacious look at Peruvian culture, past and present.

Tom Pow *In the Palace of Serpents: An Experience of Peru* (Canongate Press). A well-written insight into travelling in Peru, spoilt only by the fact that Tom Pow was ripped off in Cusco and lost his original notes. Consequently he didn't have as wonderful a time as he might have and seemed to miss the beauty of the Peruvian landscapes and the wealth of its history and culture.

Paul Theroux *The Old Patagonian Express* (Penguin). Theroux didn't much like Peru, nor Peruvians, but for all the self-obsessed pique and disgust for most of humanity, at his best – being sick in trains – he is highly entertaining.

Hugh Thomson *The White Rock* (Phoenix, 2002). One of the best travelogue books on Peru for some time, focusing mainly on the archeological explorations and theories of an English Peruvianist.

George Woodcock *Incas and Other Men* (o/p). An enjoyable, light-hearted tour, mixing modern and ancient history and travel anecdotes, that is still a good introduction to Peru over fifty years after the event.

Ronald Wright *Cut Stones and Crossroads: A Journey in the Two Worlds of Peru* (Penguin). An enlightened travel book and probably the best general travelogue writing on Peru over the last few decades, largely due to the author's depth of knowledge of his subject.

Peruvian writers

Martín Adán *The Cardboard House* (Graywolf Press). A poetic novel based in Lima and written by one of South America's best living poets.

Ciro Alegría *Broad and Alien is the World* (Merlin Press). Another good book to travel with, this is a distinguished 1970s novel offering persuasive insight into life in the Peruvian highlands.

Jose Maria Arguedas *Deep Rivers* (Pergamon Press, Spanish-language edition only), *Yawar Fiesta* (Quartet Books). Arguedas is an *indigenista* – writing for and about the native peoples. *Yawar Fiesta* focuses on one of the most impressive Andean peasant ceremonial cycles involving the annual rite of pitching a live condor against a bull, the condor representing the indigenous Indians and the bull the Spanish conquistadores.

Mario Vargas Llosa *Death in the Andes* (Faber & Faber), *A Fish in the Water* (Farrar, Straus and Giroux), *Aunt Julia and the Scriptwriter* (Picador), *The Time of the Hero* (Picador), *Captain Pantoja and the Special Service* (Faber), *The Green House* (Picador), *The Real Life of Alejandro Mayta* (Faber), *The War of the End of the World* (Faber), *Who Killed Palomino Molero?* (Faber). The best-known and the most brilliant of

contemporary Peruvian writers, Vargas Llosa is essentially a novelist but has also written on Peruvian society, run his own TV current affairs programme in Lima, and even made a (rather average) feature film. *Death in the Andes* deals with Sendero Luminoso and Peruvian politics in a style which goes quite a long way towards illuminating popular Peruvian thinking in the late 1980s and early 1990s. His ebullient memoir, *A Fish in the Water*, describes, among other things, Vargas Llosa's experience in his unsuccessful running for the Peruvian presidency. *Aunt Julia*, the best-known of his novels to be translated into English, is a fabulous book, a grand and comic novel spiralling out from the stories and exploits of a Bolivian scriptwriter who arrives in Lima to work on Peruvian radio soap operas. In part, too, it is autobiographical, full of insights and goings-on in Miraflores society. Essential reading – and perfect for long Peruvian journeys.

Cesar Vallejo *Collected Poems of Cesar Vallejo* (Penguin). Peru's one internationally renowned poet – and deservedly so. Romantic but highly innovative in style, it translates beautifully.

Novels set in Peru

Peter Mathiessen *At Play in the Fields of the Lord* (Collins Harvill). A celebrated American novel, which catches the energy and magic of the Peruvian selva.

James Redfield *The Celestine Prophecy* (Bantam). A best-selling novel that uses Peru as a backdrop. Despite not having much to say about Peru, it's a popular topic of conversation among travellers these days; some were actually inspired to visit Peru from having read this intriguing book, which expresses with some clarity many New Age concepts and beliefs. Unfortunately the book's descriptions of the Peruvian people, landscapes, forests and culture bear so little relationship to the Peruvian reality that it feels like the author has never been anywhere near Peru.

Specialist guides

John Biggar *The High Andes: A Guide for Climbers* (Andes, 93 Queen St, Castle Douglas, Kirkcudbrightshire Scotland DG7 1EH). The first comprehensive climbing guide to the main peaks of the Andes, with a main focus on Peru but also covering Bolivia, Ecuador, Chile, Argentina, Colombia and Venezuela.

Ben Box *Cusco and the Inca Train* (Footprints). A good general guide to Peru's most popular destination.

Hilary and George Bradt *Backpacking and Trekking in Peru and Bolivia* (Bradt). Detailed and excellent coverage of some of Peru's most rewarding hikes – worth taking if you're remotely interested in the idea, and good anyway for background on wildlife and flora.

Charles Brod *Apus and Incas: A Cultural Walking and Trekking Guide to Cusco* (Bradt). An interesting selection of walks in the Cusco area. Available locally.

Richard Danbury *The Inca Trail: Cuzco and Machu Picchu.* Good, highly informative and smoothly written guide to this trekking destination, with fine contextual pieces. Also includes practical information for Lima.

Peter Frost *Exploring Cusco* (Nuevas Imagenes, Lima). A very practical and stimulating site-by-site guide to the whole Cusco area (where it is widely available in bookstores). Unreservedly recommended if you're spending more than a few days in the region, and also for armchair archeologists back home.

Peter Frost and Jim Bartle *Machu Picchu Historic Sanctuary* (Nuevas Imagenes). A well-written and beautifully photographed coffee-table book on South America's most alluring archeological site.

Latin Works *Machu Picchu Guide* (Latin Works, The Netherlands). A small booklet with accurate detail on the various compounds within the archeological site.

Copeland Marks *Exotic Kitchens of Peru* (M. Evans and Co, Inc). Released in 2001, this is the latest book on Peruvian food, cooking and the culture and variety of the country's types of kitchens.

David Mazel *Pure and Perpetual Snow: Two Climbs in the Andes.* Climbing reports on Ausungate and Alpamayo peaks. Available locally or from the South American Explorers' Club.

Lynn Meisch *A Traveller's Guide to El Dorado and the Incan Empire* (Penguin). Huge paperback full of fascinating detail – well worth reading before visiting Peru.

Language

Language

Language

Although Peru is officially a Spanish-speaking nation, a large proportion of its population, possibly more than half, regard Spanish as their second language. When the conquistadores arrived, Quechua, the official language of the Inca Empire, was widely spoken everywhere but the jungle. Originally known as Runasimi (from *runa*, "person", and *simis*, "mouth"), it was given the name *Quechua* – which means "high Andean valleys" – by the Spanish.

Quechua was not, however, the only pre-Columbian tongue. There were, and still are, well over **thirty Indian languages** within the jungle area and, up until the late nineteenth century, **Mochica** had been widely spoken on the north coast for at least 1500 years.

With such a rich linguistic history it is not surprising to find non-European words intruding constantly into any Peruvian conversation. **Cancha**, for instance, the Inca word for courtyard, is still commonly used to refer to most sporting areas – *la cancha de basketball*, for example. Other linguistic survivors have even reached the English language: **llama, condor, puma** and **pampa** among them. Perhaps more interesting is the great wealth of traditional **Creole slang** – utilized with equal vigour at all levels of society. This complex speech, much like Cockney rhyming slang, is difficult to catch without almost complete fluency in Spanish, though one phrase you may find useful for directing a taxi driver is *de fresa alfonso* – literally translatable as "of strawberry, Alfonso" but actually meaning "straight on" (*de frente al fondo*).

Once you get into it, **Spanish** is the easiest language there is – and in Peru people are eager to understand even the most faltering attempt. You'll be further helped by the fact that South Americans speak relatively slowly (at least compared to Spaniards in Spain) and that there's no need to get your tongue round the lisping pronunciation.

Among **dictionaries,** you could try the *Dictionary of Latin American Spanish* (University of Chicago Press).

Pronunciation

The rules of **pronunciation** are pretty straightforward and, once you get to know them, strictly observed. Unless there's an accent, words ending in d, l, r, and z are **stressed** on the last syllable, all others on the second last. All **vowels** are pure and short.

A somewhere between the "A" sound of back and that of father

E as in get

I as in police

O as in hot

U as in rule

C is soft before E and I, hard otherwise: **cerca** is pronounced "serka".

G works the same way, a guttural "H" sound (like the ch in loch) before E or I, a hard G elsewhere – **gigante** becomes "higante".

H is always silent

J is the same sound as a guttural G: **jamón** is pronounced "hamon".

LL sounds like an English Y: **tortilla** is pronounced "torteeya".

N is as in English unless it has a tilde (accent) over it, when it becomes NY: **mañana** sounds like "manyana".

QU is pronounced like an English K.

V sounds more like B, **vino** becoming "beano".

X is slightly softer than in English – sometimes almost SH – except between vowels in place names where it has an "H"

sound – for example México (Meh-Hee-Ko) or Oaxaca.

Z is the same as a soft C, so **cerveza** becomes "servesa".

Below is a list of a few essential words and phrases, though if you're travelling for any length of time a dictionary or phrase book is obviously a worthwhile investment – some specifically Latin American ones are available (see above). If you're using a **dictionary**, bear in mind that in Spanish CH, LL, and Ñ count as separate letters and are listed after the Cs, Ls, and Ns respectively.

Words and phrases

Basics

Yes, No	Sí, No	Open, Closed	Abierto/a, Cerrado/a
Please, Thank you	Por favor, Gracias	With, Without	Con, Sin
Where, When	Dónde, Cuando	Good, Bad	Buen(o)/a, Mal(o)/a
What, How much	Qué, Cuanto	Big, Small	Gran(de), Pequeño/a
Here, There	Aquí, Allí	More, Less	Más, Menos
This, That	Este, Eso	Today, Tomorrow	Hoy, Mañana
Now, Later	Ahora, Más tarde	Yesterday	Ayer

Greetings and responses

Hello, Goodbye	Hola, Adiós	I don't speak Spanish	(No) Hablo español
Good morning	Buenos días	My name is . . .	Me llamo . . .
Good afternoon/night	Buenas tardes/noches	What's your name?	¿Como se llama usted?
See you later	Hasta luego		
Sorry	Lo siento/disculpeme	I am English	Soy inglés(a)
Excuse me	Con permiso/perdón	. . . American	americano/a
How are you?	¿Como está (usted)?	. . . Australian	australiano/a
I (don't) understand	(No) Entiendo	. . . Canadian	canadiense
Not at all/	De nada	. . . Irish	irlandés(a)
You're welcome		. . . New Zealander	neozelandés(a)
Do you speak	¿Habla (usted) inglés?	. . . Scottish	escosés(a)
English?		. . . Welsh	galés(a)

Hotel and transport needs

I want	Quiero	Give me. . .	Deme. . .
I'd like	Querría	(one like that)	(uno así)
Do you know. . .?	¿Sabe. . .?	Do you have. . .?	Tiene . . .?
I don't know	No sé	. . .the time	. . .la hora
There is (is there)?	(¿)Hay(?)	. . .a room	. . .un cuarto

. . .with two beds/ double bed . . .	. . .con dos camas/ cama matrimonial	. . .the bus station	. . .la estación de autobuses
It's for one person (two people)	es para una persona (dos personas)	. . .the train station	. . .la estación de ferrocarriles
. . .for one night (one week)	. . .para una noche (una semana)	. . .the nearest bank	. . .el banco más cercano
It's fine, how much is it?	¿Está bien, cuánto es?	. . .the post office	. . .el correo
It's too expensive	Es demasiado caro	. . .the toilet	. . .el baño/sanitario
Don't you have anything cheaper?	¿No tiene algo más barato?	Where does the bus to. . . leave from?	¿De dónde sale el camión para. . .?
Can one. . . ?	¿Se puede. . .?	Is this the train for Lima?	¿Es éste el tren para Lima?
. . .camp (near) here?	¿. . .acampar aquí (cerca)?	I'd like a (return) ticket to. . .	Querría un boleto (de ida y vuelta) para. . .
Is there a hotel nearby?	¿Hay un hotel aquí cerca?	What time does it leave (arrive in. . .)?	¿A qué hora sale (llega en. . .)?
How do I get to. . .?	Por dónde se va a. . .?	What is there to eat?	¿Qué hay para comer?
Left, right, straight on	Izquierda, derecha, derecho	What's that?	¿Qué es eso?
Where is. . .?	¿Dónde está. . .?	What's this called in Spanish?	¿Como se llama este en Castillano?

Some useful accommodation terms

Ventilador	Desk fan or ceiling fan	Cama matrimonial	Double bed
		Sencillo	Single bed
Aire-acondicionado	Air-conditioned	Cuarto simple	Single room
Baño colectivo /compartido	Shared bath	Impuestos	Taxes
Agua caliente	Hot water	Hora de salida	Check-out time (usually between 12.30 and 2pm)
Agua fría	Cold water		

Eating and drinking

Basics

Arroz	Rice	revueltos	scrambled
Avena	Oats (porridge)	Mermelada	Jam
Galletas	Biscuits	Miel	Honey
Harina	Flour	Mostaza	Mustard
Huevos	Eggs	Pan (integral)	Bread (brown)
fritos	fried	Picante de. . .	spicy dish of . . .
duros	hard-boiled	Queso	Cheese
pasados	lightly boiled		

Soup (sopas) and starters

Caldo	Broth	Huevos a la rusa	Egg salad
Caldo de gallina	Chicken broth	Palta	Avocado
Causa	Mashed potatoes and shrimp	Palta rellena	Stuffed avocado
		Papa rellena	Stuffed fried potato
Conchas a la parmesana	Scallops with Parmesan	Sopa a la criolla	Noodles, vegetables and meat

Seafood (mariscos) and fish (pescado)

Calamares	Squid	Langosta	Lobster
Camarones	Shrimp	Langostino a lo macho	Crayfish in spicy shellfish sauce
Cangrejo	Crab		
Ceviche	Marinated seafood	Lenguado	Sole
Chaufa de mariscos	Chinese rice with seafood	Paiche	Large jungle river fish
Cojinova		Tiradito	Ceviche without onion or sweet potato
Corvina	Sea bass		
Erizo	Sea urchin	Tollo	Small shark
Jalea	Large dish of fish with onion	Zungarro	Large jungle fish

Meat (carnes)

Adobo	Meat/fish in mild chilli sauce	Estofado	Stewed meat (usually served with rice)
Aji de galina	Chicken in chilli sauce	Higado	Liver
Anticuchos	Skewered heart (usually lamb)	Jamón	Ham
		Lechón	Pork
Bifstek (bistek)	Steak	Lomo asado	Roast beef
Cabrito	Goat	Lomo saltado	Sautéed beef
Carapulcra	Pork, chicken and potato casserole	Mollejitos	Gizzard
Carne a lo pobre	Steak, fries, egg and banana	Pachamanca	Meat and vegetables, cooked over hot buried stones
Carne de res	Beef	Parillada	Grilled meat
Chicharrones	Deep-fried pork skins	Pato	Duck
Conejo	Rabbit	Pavo	Turkey
Cordero	Lamb	Pollo (a la brasa)	Chicken (spit-roasted)
Cuy	Guinea pig (a traditional dish)	Tocino	Bacon
		Venado	Venison

Vegetables (legumbres) and side dishes

Aji	Chilli	Choclo	Corn on the cob
Camote	Sweet potato	Fideos	Noodles
Cebolla	Onion	Frijoles	Beans

Hongos	Mushrooms	Tallarines	Spaghetti noodles
Lechuga	Lettuce	Tomates	Tomatoes
Papa rellena	Fried potato balls, stuffed with olives, egg and mincemeat	Yuca a la Huancaina	Manioc (like a yam) in spicy cheese sauce

Fruit

Chirimoya	Custard apple (green and fleshy outside, tastes like strawberries and cream)	Maracuya	Passion fruit
		Palta	Avocado
		Piña	Pineapple
Lucuma	Small nutty fruit (used in ice creams and cakes)	Tuna	Pear-like cactus fruit (refreshing but full of hard little seeds)

Sweets (dulces)

Barquillo	Ice cream cone	Mazamorra morada	Fruit/maize jelly
Flan	Crème caramel	Panqueques	Pancakes
Helado	Ice cream	Picarones	Doughnuts with syrup
Keke	Cake		
Manjar blanco	Sweetened condensed milk		

Snacks (bocadillos)

Castañas	Brazil nuts	Sandwich de lechón	Pork salad sandwich
Chifles	Fried banana slices	Tamale	Maize-flour roll stuffed with olives, egg, meat and vegetables
Empanada	Meat or cheese pie		
Hamburguesa	Hamburger		
Salchipapas	Potatoes, sliced frankfurter sausage and condiments	Tortilla	Omelette-cum-pancake
Sandwich de butifara	Ham and onion sandwich	Tostados	Toast

Fruit juices (jugos)

Especial	Fruit, milk, sometimes beer	Papaya	Papaya
Fresa	Strawberry	Piña	Pineapple
Higo	Fig	Platano	Banana
Manzana	Apple	Surtido	Mixed
Melón	Melon	Toronja	Grapefruit
Naranja	Orange	Zanahoria	Carrot

Beverages (bebidas)

Agua	Water	Limonada	Real lemonade
Agua mineral	Mineral water	Masato	Fermented manioc beer
Algarrobina	Algarroba-fruit drink		
Cafe	Coffee	Pisco	White-grape brandy
Cerveza	Beer	Ponche	Punch
Chicha de jora	Fermented maize beer	Ron	Rum
Chicha morada	Maize soft drink	Te	Tea
Chilcano de pisco	Pisco with lemonade	....con leche	....with milk
Chopp	Draught beer	....de anis	....aniseed tea
Cuba libre	Rum and coke	....de limón	....lemon tea
Gaseosa	Soft carbonated drink	....hierba luisa	....lemon-grass tea
Leche	Milk	....manzanilla	....camomile tea

❶ Numbers and days

1	un/uno, una	70	setenta
2	dos	80	ochenta
3	tres	90	noventa
4	cuatro	100	cien(to)
5	cinco	101	ciento uno
6	seis	200	doscientos
7	siete	201	doscientos uno
8	ocho	500	quinientos
9	nueve	1000	mil
10	diez	2000	dos mil
11	once	first	primero/a
12	doce	second	segundo/a
13	trece	third	tercero/a
14	catorce		
15	quince	Monday	lunes
16	dieciséis	Tuesday	martes
20	veinte	Wednesday	miércoles
21	veintiuno	Thursday	jueves
30	treinta	Friday	viernes
40	cuarenta	Saturday	sábado
50	cincuenta	Sunday	domingo
60	sesenta		

Glossary of Peruvian terms

Allyu Kinship group, or clan

Apu Mountain god

Arriero Muleteer

Barrio Suburb, or sometimes shantytown

Burro Donkey

Cacique Headman

Callejón Corridor, or narrow street

Campesino Peasant, country dweller, someone who works in the fields

Ceja de la selva Edge of the jungle

Chacra Cultivated garden or plot

Chaquiras Pre-Columbian stone or coral beads

Chicha Maize beer, or a form of Peruvian music

Colectivo Collective taxi

Cordillera Mountain range

Curaca Chief

Curandero Healer

Empresa Company

Encomienda Colonial grant of land and native labour

Extranjero Foreigner

Farmacia Chemist

Flacoa Skinny (common nickname)

Gordoa Fat (common nickname)

Gringo A European or North American

Hacienda Estate

Huaca Sacred spot or object

Huaco Pre-Columbian artefact

Huaquero Someone who digs or looks for huacos

Jirón Road

Lomas Place where vegetation grows with moisture from the air rather than from rainfall or irrigation

Mamcona Inca Sun Virgin

Peña Nightclub with live music

Plata Silver; slang for "cash"

Poblado Settlement

Pueblos Jóvenes Shantytowns

Puna Barren Andean heights

Quebrada Stream

Selva Jungle

Selvatico Jungle dweller

Serrano Mountain dweller

Sierra Mountains

Soroche Altitude sickness

Tambo Inca Highway rest-house

Tienda Shop

Tramites Red tape, bureaucracy

Unsu Throne, or platform

Index

and small print

Index

Map entries are in colour

I

INDEX

615

Twenty Years of Rough Guides

In the summer of 1981, Mark Ellingham, Rough Guides' founder, knocked out the first guide on a typewriter, with a group of friends. Mark had been travelling in Greece after university, and couldn't find a guidebook that really answered his needs.There were heavyweight cultural guides on the one hand – good on museums and classical sites but not on beaches and tavernas – and on the other hand student manuals that were so caught up with how to save money that they lost sight of the country's significance beyond its role as a place for a cool vacation. None of the guides began to address Greece as a country, with its natural and human environment, its politics and its contemporary life.

Having no urgent reason to return home, Mark decided to write his own guide. It was a guide to Greece that tried to combine some erudition and insight with a thoroughly practical approach to travellers' needs. Scrupulously researched listings of places to stay, eat and drink were matched by careful attention to detail on everything from Homer to Greek music, from classical sites to national parks and from nude beaches to monasteries. Back in London, Mark and his friends got their Rough Guide accepted by a farsighted commissioning editor at the publisher Routledge and it came out in 1982.

The Rough Guide to Greece was a student scheme that became a publishing phenomenon. The immediate success of the book – shortlisted for the Thomas Cook award – spawned a series that rapidly covered dozens of countries. The Rough Guides found a ready market among backpackers and budget travellers, but soon acquired a much broader readership that included older and less impecunious visitors. Readers relished the guides' wit and inquisitiveness as much as the enthusiastic, critical approach that acknowledges everyone wants value for money – but not at any price.

Rough Guides soon began supplementing the "rougher" information – the hostel and low-budget listings – with the kind of detail that independent-minded travellers on any budget might expect. These days, the guides – distributed worldwide by the Penguin group – include recommendations spanning the range from shoestring to luxury, and cover more than 200 destinations around the globe. Our growing team of authors, many of whom come to Rough Guides initially as outstandingly good letter-writers telling us about their travels, are spread all over the world, particularly in Europe, the USA and Australia. As well as the travel guides, Rough Guides publishes a series of dictionary phrasebooks covering two dozen major languages, an acclaimed series of music guides running the gamut from Classical to World Music, a series of music CDs in association with World Music Network, and a range of reference books on topics as diverse as the Internet, Pregnancy and Unexplained Phenomena. Visit **www.roughguides.com** to see what's cooking.

SMALL PRINT

Rough Guide credits

Text editor: Chris Barsanti
Managing Director: Kevin Fitzgerald
Series editor: Mark Ellingham
Editorial: Martin Dunford, Jonathan Buckley, Kate Berens, Ann-Marie Shaw, Helena Smith, Olivia Swift, Ruth Blackmore, Geoff Howard, Claire Saunders, Gavin Thomas, Alexander Mark Rogers, Polly Thomas, Joe Staines, Richard Lim, Duncan Clark, Peter Buckley, Lucy Ratcliffe, Clifton Wilkinson, Alison Murchie, Matthew Teller, Andrew Dickson, Fran Sandham, Sally Schafer, Matthew Milton, Karoline Densley (UK); Andrew Rosenberg, Yuki Takagaki, Richard Koss, Hunter Slaton (US)
Design & Layout: Link Hall, Helen Prior, Julia Bovis, Katie Pringle, Rachel Holmes, Andy Turner, Dan May, Tanya Hall, John McKay, Sophie Hewat (UK); Madhulita Mohapatra,

Umesh Aggarwal, Sunil Sharma (India)
Cartography: Maxine Repath, Ed Wright, Katie Lloyd-Jones (UK); Manish Chandra, Rajesh Chhibber, Jai Prakesh Mishra (India)
Cover art direction: Louise Boulton
Picture research: Sharon Martins, Mark Thomas
Online: Anja Mutic-Blessing, Jennifer Gold, Suzanne Welles, Cree Lawson (US); Manik Chauhan, Amarjyoti Dutta, Narender Kumar (India)
Finance: Gary Singh
Marketing & Publicity: Richard Trillo, Niki Smith, David Wearn, Chloë Roberts, Demelza Dallow, Claire Southern (UK); Geoff Colquitt, David Wechsler, Megan Kennedy (US)
Administration: Julie Sanderson
RG India: Punita Singh

Publishing information

This fifth edition published September 2003 by **Rough Guides Ltd**,
80 Strand, London WC2R 0RL.
345 Hudson St, 4th Floor,
New York, NY 10014, USA.
Distributed by the Penguin Group
Penguin Books Ltd,
80 Strand, London WC2R 0RL
Penguin Putnam, Inc.
375 Hudson Street, NY 10014, USA
Penguin Books Australia Ltd,
487 Maroondah Highway, PO Box 257,
Ringwood, Victoria 3134, Australia
Penguin Books Canada Ltd,
10 Alcorn Avenue, Toronto, Ontario,
Canada M4V 1E4
Penguin Books (NZ) Ltd,
182–190 Wairau Road, Auckland 10,
New Zealand
Typeset in Bembo and Helvetica to an original design by Henry Iles.
Printed in Italy by LegoPrint S.p.A

664pp includes index
A catalogue record for this book is available from the British Library

ISBN 1-84353-074-0

The publishers and authors have done their best to ensure the accuracy and currency of all the information in **The Rough Guide to Peru**, however, they can accept no responsibility for any loss, injury, or inconvenience sustained by any traveller as a result of information or advice contained in the guide.

Help us update

We've gone to a lot of effort to ensure that the fifth edition of **The Rough Guide to Peru** is accurate and up to date. However, things change – places get "discovered", opening hours are notoriously fickle, restaurants and rooms raise prices or lower standards. If you feel we've got it wrong or left something out, we'd like to know, and if you can remember the address, the price, the time, the phone number, so much the better.

We'll credit all contributions, and send a copy of the next edition (or any other Rough Guide if you prefer) for the best letters. Everyone who writes to us and isn't already a subscriber will receive a copy of our full-colour thrice-yearly newsletter. Please mark letters: **"Rough Guide Peru Update"** and send to: Rough Guides, 80 Strand, London WC2R 0RL, or Rough Guides, 4th Floor, 345 Hudson St, New York, NY 10014. Or send an email to **mail@roughguides.com**

Have your questions answered and tell others about your trip at
www.roughguides.atinfopop.com

Acknowledgements

Dilwyn Jenkins would like to thank the following for their additional accounts, research and other vital support: Carlos Montenegro; Chris Barsanti; Aiden, Tess & Bethan; Dora Lucio Meza Ortiz; Antonio and Jorge Montenegro; Rosana Correa Alamo; Susie & Martin Cannon; Carloman from Chiclayo; Coco – Jorge Victor Gonzales Cusirramos; Pablo Rey de Castro; Mirko Fontana Piskulich; Alberto Cafferata (Pony Expeditions); Rafael Belmonte (Peru Expeditions); Baltazar Saenz Sousa; Carmelo Blanco Rodriguez; Pablo Portillo Benavides & Fernando Palao Herrera; Peter Jenson & Jaime Acevedo (Explorama); Henry Aguilar; Don Javier Arevalo (and Alicia); Peter and Leo Frost; John Forrest; Graham Preston; Howard and Maxwell Davis ; Katia Fabiola Cerna Rivera; and last but obviously most importantly, the family members left behind - Claire, Max and Teilo.

Readers' letters

Thanks to all the readers who took the trouble to write in with their comments and suggestions (and apologies to anyone whose name we've misspelt or omitted):

A big thank you to the many readers who took the time to make suggestions for this guide: Andres Alcazar, Ange Barlow, Edith Bowman, Jennifer Brooks, Mimi Butler, Andrew Caird, Milagros Alvarez Calderon, Ann Christian, Lisbet and Benoit Diers, Paul Dungey, Gonzalo Durant, Julie Frost, Mandy Fry, Jeanette Gerritsma, Dan Goldberg, Diane Goodpasture, David Horton, Stephen Howard, Samir Hussain, David Jordan, Isabelle Lindenmayer, Ian Mace, Alan Michell, Jessica Nussey, Noelia Olázabal, Anne Scholz, Claudia Senecal, Jane Simon, Joe Stern, William Taygan, Alan Thornhill, Kiloran Townsend, Matt Walker, Michael White, Børre Wickstrøm, Karen Wood, Allison Wright and the many folks who contacted us by email but preferred to remain anonymous.

15. San Blas Cathedral, Plaza de Armas © Peter Wilson
16. Trekking near Lake Llanganuco © Kathy Jarvis/South American Pictures
17. Carved stone head inside the tunnels of Chavín de Huantar © Jamie Marshall
18. Caballito *totora* boat © Tony Morrison/South American Pictures Cotahuasi Canyon © Heinz Plenge/Foto Natur
19. Ashaninka Indian family © David Ramsdale/South American Pictures
20. Colonial-era houses, Plaza de Armas, Trujillo © Tony Morrison/South American Pictures
21. Cotahuasi Canyon © Heinz Plenge/Foto Natur
22. Huaca Pucllana © Peter Wilson
23. Tambopata, local man in canoe © Chris Coe/Axiom
24. Spanish-style dishes © Tony Morrison/South American Pictures
25. Nazca Lines, Andean spur © Tony Morrison/South American Pictures
26. Dolphin watching © Heinz Plenge/Foto Natur
27. Floating Islands, Lake Titicaca © Peter Wilson
28. River Mantaro near Jauja © Tony Morrison/South American Pictures
29. The arch of San Francisco, Ayacuno © Heinz Plenge/Foto Natur
30. Floating suburb of Puerto Belén © Kathy Jarvis/South American Pictures

Black and whites

Miraflores apartments, Lima © Tony Morrison/South American Pictures

Lima Barranco suburb, Municipal Plaza © Tony Morrison/South American Pictures

Train at Aguas Calientes © Kathy Jarvis/South American Pictures

Inca ruins, Ollantaytambo © Jamie Marshall

Inca stonework, Machu Picchu © Chris Coe/Axiom

Brown pelicans © Tony Morrison/South American Pictures

Paracas peninsular and bay © Dilwyn Jenkins

Monkey figure, Nazca lines © Tony Morrison/South American Pictures

Terraces of the Colca canyon © Peter Wilson

Street scene, Achoma © Peter Wilson

Porters, Callejón de Huaylas © Kathy Jarvis/South American Pictures

Peak of Huascarán viewed from Lago Llanganuco © Jamie Marshall

Interior of church, Ayacucho © Heinz Plenge/Foto Natur

Shepherd leading cattle in the highlands near Tarma © Ric Ergenbright/Corbis

Intricate adobe walls at the Chan Chan complex © Jamie Marshall

Caballito *totora boat* © Tony Morrison/South American Pictures

Floating suburb of Belén © Kathy Jarvis/South American Pictures

Toco toucan © Tony Morrison/South American Pictures

Bora Indian, headman of the village © J Sparshatt/Axiom

SMALL PRINT

Rough Guides music & reference

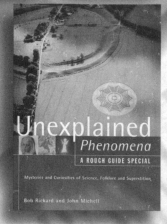

Music Reference Guides

CD Guides

Mini Guides

"The Rough Guides are near-perfect
reference works"
Philadelphia Inquirer

www.roughguides.com

Rough Guide Music Guides

NOTES

NOTES

NOTES

NOTES

NOTES

Policy and Practice in Bilingual Education

BILINGUAL EDUCATION AND BILINGUALISM

Series Editor
Professor Colin Baker, University of Wales, Bangor

Other Books in the Series

Building Bridges: Multilingual Resources for Children
    MULTILINGUAL RESOURCES FOR CHILDREN PROJECT
A Parents' and Teachers' Guide to Bilingualism
    COLIN BAKER
Teaching Science to Language Minority Students
    JUDITH W. ROSENTHAL
Working with Bilingual Children
    M.K. VERMA, K.P. CORRIGAN and S. FIRTH (eds)

Other Books of Interest

Coping with Two Cultures
    PAUL A. S. GHUMAN
European Models of Bilingual Education
    HUGO BAETENS BEARDSMORE (ed.)
Foundations of Bilingual Education and Bilingualism
    COLIN BAKER
Immigrant Languages in Europe
    GUUS EXTRA and LUDO VERHOEVEN (eds)
Language Diversity Surveys as Agents of Change
    JOE NICHOLAS
Making Multicultural Education Work
    STEPHEN MAY
Opportunity and Constraints of Community Language Teaching
    SJAAK KROON
Sociolinguistic Perspectives on Bilingual Education
    CHRISTINA BRATT PAULSTON
The World in a Classroom
    V. EDWARDS and A. REDFERN

Please contact us for the latest book information:
Multilingual Matters Ltd, Frankfurt Lodge, Clevedon Hall,
Victoria Road, Clevedon, Avon BS21 7SJ, England